MARKETING

Concepts and Strategies

EUROPEAN EDITION

SALLY DIBB
University of Warwick

LYNDON SIMKIN
University of Warwick

WILLIAM M. PRIDE
Texas A & M University

O. C. FERRELL
Memphis State University

HOUGHTON MIFFLIN COMPANY

BOSTON   LONDON

D0490839

PART OPENING IMAGES: Part I, Guido Alberto Rossi/The Image Bank; Part II, Dawson Jones/Stock, Boston; Part III, Wayne Eastep Inc.; Part IV, photo courtesy of Media General; Part V, Guido Alberto Rossi/The Image Bank; Part VI, Hing/Norton; Part VII, Brett Froomer/The Image Bank.

Copyright © 1991 by Houghton Mifflin Company. All rights reserved.

No part of this work may be reproduced or transmitted in any form or by any means, electronic or mechanical, including photocopying and recording, or by any information storage or retrieval system without the prior written permission of Houghton Mifflin Company unless such copying is expressly permitted by copyright law. Address inquiries to College Permissions, Houghton Mifflin Company, One Beacon Street, Boston, MA 02108.

ISBN: 0–395–54352–5

CDEFGHIJ–D–95432

BRIEF CONTENTS

CONTENTS

PART III   DISTRIBUTION DECISIONS   267

PART VI   MARKETING MANAGEMENT

PREFACE

In the 1980s, few expected the Berlin Wall to come tumbling down, resulting eventually in the unification of Germany. Few could have predicted that 1991 would commence with a major war in the Persian Gulf involving many Western powers. There is no question that we live in an increasingly complex and changing world. Recent political and economic upheavals have shaken established systems to their foundations; ease of communication and commercial exchange has transformed us into a global society; and for many people, environmental concerns have become a number one priority. To provide insights into marketing in such a changing environment, *Marketing: Concepts and Strategies* presents a comprehensive framework, integrating traditional marketing concepts with the realities of the 1990s.

The study of marketing has always been relevant because it is a key element in the functioning of today's society. Our economy, our lifestyles, and our physical well-being are directly or indirectly influenced by marketing activities. *Marketing: Concepts and Strategies* has been widely used because it provides comprehensive coverage of the subject of marketing while stimulating student interest through its readable, accessible style and extensive use of up-to-date, topical examples.

For many years, *Marketing: Concepts and Strategies* has led the market in America. However, many European business schools and colleges also realised the text had significant merits, ranging from its comprehensive coverage of key marketing concepts and strategic issues; to its integrated use of product and market examples, background statistics, and explanation of current trends and practices; to its lively, colourful presentation. It seemed a natural progression, then, to further enhance the basic features of the text for the European market by publishing a version geared specifically for that audience. Thus, with numerous suggestions from colleagues and students, we have focused on facts and issues particular to Europe in the 1990s—especially those relating to the market research industry, the advertising and promotion industry, and the marketing environment in general. Many of the examples, cases, and updates included in this version involve products, brands, and markets well known to European consumers, industrial markets, and marketers.

CHANGES IN THIS EDITION

Marketing: Concepts and Strategies has always focused on the concepts most relevant to the development and implementation of marketing strategies. To keep pace with new developments in the teaching and practice of marketing, this edition provides more comprehensive coverage of the key topics of market segmentation, targeting, and positioning (clearly explaining the link between these tasks); a thorough review of the evolution of modern retailing in the U.K. and Europe; and the most comprehensive and up-to-date coverage of international marketing and of marketing ethics and social responsibility—an increasingly important area of concern to consumers and marketers alike. With the much vaunted 1992 deregulatory changes in the European Community (EC), a great emphasis has been placed on elements of the marketing environment which do, and increasingly will, impact upon the activities of marketing organisations within Europe.

- The marketing environment, of great concern to all marketers, impacts on consumers, suppliers, and marketers. With changing boundaries and political philosophies in Europe and deregulation within the European Community, the marketing environment is likely to impact even more on marketing activities within Europe. Changing consumer attitudes towards environmental issues and the increasing importance of the "Green" movement, also will have major influences on the way consumers perceive products, what companies will have to provide, and the way marketing will function.

- Market segmentation has for many years been recognised as key prerequisite to the development of successful marketing strategy. A rewritten chapter focuses on the rationale behind market segmentation, its effective use, and methods for segmenting markets. The chapter continues to look at the necessity for targeting segments and then the need and process for positioning products and brands successfully into targeted segments against competitors' products.

- The retailing chapter, rewritten, examines in detail the types of retail organisations, their chosen locations and the strategic implications of these, the role of marketing to the modern retail company, and current strategic issues in retailing.

- In including a new chapter entitled Marketing Ethics and Social Responsibility, we have provided a new approach to one of the most important yet misunderstood topics in marketing. We offer a framework for understanding ethical decision-making and delineate ethical issues that students will confront in the real world of marketing. We also emphasise the need for social responsibility in organisations and provide approaches for making socially responsible decisions that are effective and successful in the business community.

- The chapter relating to strategic market planning has been updated to include a greater focus on creating the differential advantage and examining strategies for competing effectively.

- The international chapter has been completely revised to include a section on regional trade alliances and markets. Topics include Europe 1992 and the impact of increasing integration of eastern Europe within continental Europe, Pacific Rim nations, and the U.S. and Canada Free Trade Agreement.

The overall design and basic features of the text were carefully reviewed and revised, following discussions with lecturers and students, to make the material as fresh and appealing as possible.

- We have created a new attractive visual presentation of the content to stimulate readers' interest. In addition, we have made the writing more lively, readable, and concise.

- We have also included many new examples of challenges facing real organisations as they market products and attempt to take advantage of unexpected opportunities in this changing world.
- Marketing Updates integrate fundamental marketing issues and concepts with the real-world practice of marketing. These inserts are generally about well-known companies and focus on issues that students will be able to relate to easily.
- Each chapter continues to include two cases, most of which are completely new and the rest updated for the 1990s.

In addition, text coverage has been completely revised and updated to include major changes and additions such as the following:

- A greater emphasis on environmental issues and the protection of our environment, plus EC changing regulatory influence (see especially Chapters 2 and 20).
- New coverage on VALS lifestyles and segmentation bases, plus recent research findings in the area of segmentation (see Chapter 3).
- The latest research and new developments in our understanding of consumer buying behaviour (see Chapter 4).
- Material on recent developments, issues, and the nature of the market research industry (see Chapter 6).
- More in-depth discussion of environmentally safe packaging (see Chapter 7).
- Expanded coverage of the merger trend among wholesalers (see Chapter 10).
- A new section on retail positioning and expanded coverage on retail locations and types of retailers (see Chapter 11).
- An updated section on recent findings related to information processing and communication in marketing, plus a discussion of the aims of promotion in modern marketing (see Chapter 13).
- A more concise and strategic approach to understanding the nature and impact of advertising and publicity, taking account of the recent growth of the public relations industry (see Chapter 14).
- A completely revised and updated section on sales promotion (see Chapter 15).
- A total reorganisation of the chapter on strategic market planning, including more concise coverage of portfolio analysis and a new section outlining the marketing plan (see Chapter 18).
- A new section on internal marketing (see Chapter 19).
- Updated and increased depth of coverage on industrial marketing (see Chapter 21).
- More in-depth coverage of services marketing incorporating the latest research in this area and increased emphasis of non-business marketing as a subset of services marketing (see Chapter 22).

Despite these changes, we believe that users of earlier editions will find the European edition to have the same strengths that have made previous editions so popular. This edition, like its predecessors, explores the depth and breadth of the field, combining detailed real examples with comprehensive coverage of marketing concepts and strategies used widely throughout the business world. By focusing on the universal concerns of marketing decision makers, we demonstrate that marketing is a vital and challenging field of study—and a part of our world that influences almost everything we do.

FEATURES OF THE EUROPEAN EDITION

Our goal has been to provide a comprehensive and practical introduction to marketing, easy both to teach and to read. The entire book is structured to excite students about marketing and to make learning comprehensive and efficient.

- *Learning objectives* open each chapter, providing students an overview of new concepts.
- A *vignette* introduces each chapter's marketing issues using product or market examples.
- *Examples* of familiar products and organisations make concrete and specific the generalisations of marketing theory.
- At least two *Marketing Updates* in each chapter, focusing on recognisable firms and products, extend the discussion of marketing topics and decisions.
- Numerous *figures, tables,* and *photographs* augment the text and increase comprehension. Where appropriate, current trade and industry statistics are presented to add perspective.
- A complete chapter *summary* reviews the major topics discussed.
- A *list of important terms* (highlighted in the text) provides a study aid, helping students expand their marketing vocabulary.
- *Discussion and review questions* encourage further study and exploration of chapter material.
- Two concise, stimulating *cases* provoke discussion at the end of each chapter.
- A *diagram of the text's organisation* at the beginning of each part shows students how material in the upcoming part relates to the rest of the book.
- *Appendices* discuss career opportunities in marketing and provide additional insights into financial analysis in marketing.
- A *glossary* at the end of the text defines close to 700 important marketing terms.
- A *name index* and a *subject index* enable students to find topics of interest quickly.

TEXT ORGANISATION

We have organised the seven parts of *Marketing: Concepts and Strategies* to give students a theoretical and practical understanding of marketing decision making. Part I presents an overview of marketing, discusses general marketing concepts, and considers the marketing environment, types of markets, target market analysis, buyer behaviour, and marketing research. Part II focuses on the conceptualisation, development, and management of products. Part III examines marketing channels, institutions, and physical distribution. Part IV covers promotion decisions and methods, including advertising, personal selling, sales promotion, and publicity. Part V is devoted to pricing decisions and Part VI to marketing management and discussions of ethics and social responsibility in marketing strategic market planning, organisation, implementation, and control. Part VII explores strategic decisions in industrial, service, non-business, and international marketing.

STUDENT SUPPLEMENTS

In addition to numerous instructor support materials (discussed in the front of the Instructor's Manual), the package for this text includes aids to both teaching and learning:

- A Study Guide helps students to review and integrate chapter content.
- *Marketing Cases*, Fourth Edition, supplements the cases in the text with 42 others that demonstrate how marketing decisions are made.
- *Marketing: A Simulation*, Second Edition, gives student teams working on microcomputers valuable experience in making marketing decisions.
- *Microstudy Plus*, a self-instructional program for microcomputers, reinforces learning of key concepts.
- *Micromarket: Computer Applications*, a Lotus-based disk, includes exercises that provide hands-on experience in making marketing decisions.

Through the years, lecturers and students have sent us many helpful suggestions for improving the text and ancillary components. We invite your comments, questions, or criticisms. We want to do our best to provide materials that enhance the teaching and learning of marketing concepts and strategies. Your suggestions will be sincerely appreciated.

Sally Dibb
Lyndon Simkin
William M. Pride
O. C. Ferrell

ACKNOWLEDGMENTS

This text would not have happened without the support and encouragement of the American authors, William Pride and O. C. Ferrell, plus the comments and enthusiasm from fellow marketing lecturers at Warwick and, above all, from our students past and present. Specific thanks must go to:

- Robin Wensley, Professor of Marketing and Strategic Management and Chairman of Warwick Business School, for sustained encouragement and motivation
- Sue Foxon, long suffering Marketing Group secretary for her tolerance, understanding, and painstaking manuscript preparation
- Derek Williams, for text on-line searches and acting as statistical librarian
- The editor and staff of *Marketing* magazine, for keeping us all abreast of current practices and trends

A number of individuals have made many helpful comments and recommendations in their reviews of this or earlier editions. We appreciate the generous help of these reviewers.

Jens Maier
London Business School

Pierre McDonagh
University of Wales

David Marshall
University of Edinburgh

William L. Cron
Southern Methodist University

Gwen Fontenot
University of Northern Colorado

Joe F. Alexander
Abilene Christian University

Bernard LaLonde
Ohio State University

Kent B. Monroe
Virginia Polytechnic Institute

Linda K. Anglin
Mankato State University

Charles Gross
University of New Hampshire

George Avellano
Central State University

Emin Babakus
Memphis State University

Dean C. Siewers
Rochester Institute of Technology

Guy Banville
Creighton University

Richard C. Becherer
Wayne State University

Harrison Grathwohl
California State University—Chico

Salah S. Hassan
George Washington University

Steven Shipley
Governor's State University

Tinus Van Drunen
Universiteit Twente (Netherlands)

Robert Solomon
Stephen F. Austin State University

Thomas E. Barry
Southern Methodist University

W. R. Berdine
California State Polytechnic Institute

Philip Kemp
DePaul University

Virginia Larson
San Jose State University

Lee R. Duffus
University of Tennessee

Ron Lennon
Barry University

Roger Blackwell
Ohio State University

Mark I. Alpert
University of Texas at Austin

Larry Chonko
Baylor University

William Brown
University of Nebraska at Omaha

John Buckley
Orange County Community College

Karen Burger
Pace University

Pat J. Calabro
University of Texas at Arlington

Terry M. Chambers
Appalachian State University

William G. Browne
Oregon State University

Robert Copley
University of Louisville

Russell Belk
University of Utah

Siva Balasabramanian
University of Iowa

Blaine S. Greenfield
Bucks County Community College

Joseph Hair
Louisiana State University

Charles L. Hilton
Eastern Kentucky University

Joseph Cangelosi
East Tennessee State University

Ken Jensen
Bradley University

Peter Bloch
Louisiana State University

Douglas Kornemann
Milwaukee Area Technical College

Ernest F. Cooke
Memphis State University

Jay D. Lindquist
Western Michigan University

John I. Coppett
University of Houston—Clear Lake

Jackie Brown
University of San Diego

Norman E. Daniel
Arizona State University

Lloyd M. DeBoer
George Mason University

Charles A Bearchell
California State University—Northridge

David J. Fritzsche
University of Portland

Robert F. Dwyer
University of Cincinnati

Bodo Schlegelmilch
University of Edinburgh

Thomas Falcone
Indiana University of Pennsylvania

David H. Lindsay
University of Maryland

Richard A. Lancioni
Temple University

Shanna Greenwalt
Southern Illinois University

Linda Calderone
*State University of New York
College of Technology at Farmingdale*

Joseph Ballinger
Stephen F. Austin State University

Wanda Blockhus
San Jose State University

Thomas V. Greer
University of Maryland

Paul N. Bloom
University of North Carolina

Charles Vitaska
Metropolitan State College

James C. Carroll
University of Southwestern Louisiana

James F. Wenthe
University of Georgia

William Prescutti
Duquesne University

Joseph Guiltinan
University of Notre Dame

Timothy Hartman
Ohio University

Barbara Coe
North Texas State University

Stanley Scott
Boise State University

Benjamin J. Cutler
Bronx Community College

Merlin Henry
Rancho Santiago College

Thomas Ponzurick
West Virginia University

Charles L. Lapp
University of Dallas

Ronald Schill
Brigham Young University

John Lavin
Waukesha County Technical Institute

Jack McNiff
*State University of New York
College of Technology at Farmingdale*

Hugh E. Law
East Tennessee University

Kenneth L. Rowe
Arizona State University

Richard J. Semenik
University of Utah

Sue Ellen Neeley
University of Houston—Clear Lake

Winston Ring
University of Wisconsin—Milwaukee

Beheruz N. Sethna
Clarkson College

Stewart W. Bither
Pennsylvania State University

Terence A. Shimp
University of South Carolina

Dale Varble
Indiana State University

James Brock
Montana State University

Paul Londrigan
Mott Community College

Don Scotton
Cleveland State University

Anthony Lucas
Community College of Allegheny County

Carlos W. Moore
Baylor University

William Lundstrom
Old Dominion University

Ken Wright
*West Australia College of Advanced
Education—Churchland Campus*

John McFall
San Diego State University

Michael Peters
Boston College

Stan Madden
Baylor University

Steven J. Shaw
University of South Carolina

Gerald L. Manning
Des Moines Area Community College

Hal Teer
James Madison University

Dillard Tinsley
Stephen F. Austin State University

Sumner M. White
Massachusetts Bay Community College

Arthur Prell
Lindenwood College

Brian Meyer
Mankato State University

David R. Rink
Northern Illinois University

Lee Meadow
Bentley College

Robert A. Robicheaux
University of Alabama

John R. Brooks, Jr.
Houston Baptist University

Harold S. Sekiguchi
University of Nevada—Reno

Stephen J. Miller
Oklahoma State University

Bruce Stern
Portland State University

Keith Murray
Northeastern University

Roy R. Grundy
College of DuPage

Irene Lange
California State University—Fullerton

Gail Marco
Robert Morris College

Jack M. Starling
University of North Texas

Carol Morris-Calder
Loyola Marymount University

Terrence V. O'Brien
Northern Illinois University

Allan Palmer
*University of North Carolina at
Charlotte*

J. Paul Peter
University of Wisconsin—Madison

Alan R. Wiman
Rider College

Kathy Pullins
Columbus State Community College

Victor Quinones
University of Puerto Rico

George Wynn
James Madison University

Ralph DiPietro
Montclair State College

Melvin R. Crask
University of Georgia

Jim L. Grimm
Illinois State University

Del I. Hawkins
University of Oregon

James D. Reed
Louisiana State University—Shreveport

Barbara Unger
Western Washington University

William Rhey
University of Tampa

Ed Riordan
Wayne State University

Michael L. Rothschild
University of Wisconsin—Madison

Sheldon Somerstein
City University of New York

Claire F. Sullivan
Metropolitan State University

Robert D. Hisrich
University of Tulsa

Jerome Katrichis
Temple University

William Staples
*University of Houston—
Clear Lake*

George C. Hozier
University of New Mexico

Glen Riecken
East Tennessee State University

Rosann L. Spiro
Indiana University

John R. Huser
Illinois Central College

Donald L. James
Fort Lewis College

Yvonne Karsten
Mankato State University

James McAlexander
Iowa State University

William M. Kincaid, Jr.
Oklahoma State University

Alan A. Greco
University of N. Carolina—Charlotte

Hale Tongren
George Mason University

Priscilla LaBarbara
New York University

Roy Klages
State University of New York at Albany

Patricia Laidler
Massasoit Community College

Bert Rosenbloom
Drexel University

James Underwood
University of S.W. Louisiana

Phil Flood
*College of Marketing & Design,
Dublin*

Poondi Varadarajan
Texas A & M University

David M. Landrum
Central State University

Paul J. Solomon
Univeristy of South Florida

Elaine O'Brien
University of Strathclyde

Robert Grafton-Small
St. Andrews University

AN ANALYSIS OF
MARKETING OPPORTUNITIES

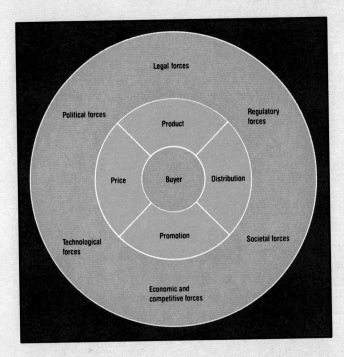

In Part I we introduce the field of marketing and provide a broad perspective from which to explore and analyse various components of the marketing discipline. In the first chapter we define marketing and discuss why an understanding of it is useful in many aspects of everyday life, including one's career. We provide an overview of general strategic marketing issues such as market opportunity analysis, target markets, and marketing mix development. Marketers should understand how environmental forces can affect customers and their responses to marketing strategies. In Chapter 2 we discuss political, legal, regulatory, societal, economic and competitive, and technological forces in the environment. Chapter 3 focuses on one of the major steps in the development of a marketing strategy: selecting and analysing target markets. Understanding elements that affect buying decisions enables marketers to better analyse customers' needs and evaluate how specific marketing strategies can satisfy those needs. In Chapter 4 we examine consumer buying decision processes and factors that influence buying decisions. We stress organisational markets, organisational buyers, the buying centre, and the organisational buying decision process in Chapter 5. Chapter 6 includes a discussion of the role of a marketing information system and the basic steps in the marketing research process. ◆

1 AN OVERVIEW OF STRATEGIC MARKETING

Objectives

To understand the definition of marketing

To understand why a person should study marketing

To gain insight into the basic elements of the marketing concept and its implementation

To understand the major components of a marketing strategy

To gain a sense of general strategic marketing issues, such as market opportunity analysis, target market selection, and marketing mix development

J ust when established video game companies were suffering from severe, worldwide sales decline, Nintendo of Japan introduced its Nintendo Entertainment System to take the devastated video game industry by storm. Nintendo believed the depressed market to be due to frustrated, rather than fickle, customers.

Nintendo officials recognised that overproduction and poor product quality caused the industry's crash. Nintendo's strategy was to offer the consumer more sophisticated, arcade-quality games while keeping a strict watch over product quality and availability. Nintendo now has £1.6 billion in sales of the £2 billion video game market and in the U.K. is looking to increase its share of the £48 million market.

In the U.S.A., the company's video game success generated a variety of other ventures: a Saturday morning cartoon programme, a cereal, a magazine with a total of more than one million paid subscriptions, and an assortment of T-shirts, lunch-boxes, posters, and school supplies. Meanwhile, in the U.K., Serif Games and the Virgin Group, who distribute Nintendo games, are spending a substantial amount on advertising. The aim is to make video games the top-selling U.K. toy. Nintendo marketers are eager to make their company name synonymous with this success.

The primary goal of Nintendo's marketing effort is to maintain high product quality. Nintendo strictly controls the supply and number of licensed game titles. It provides each game licensee with a shrink-wrapped package bearing the official Nintendo Seal of Approval. It also carefully monitors the total volume of systems and cartridges shipped to retailers, irritating some retailers, as they are unable to meet customer demands. ◆

Based on information from James Cox, "Nintendo Keeps the Frenzy High," *USA Today,* 21 Nov. 1989, pp. 1B–2B; Joe Mandese, "Power Plays," *Marketing & Media Decisions,* March 1989, pp. 101–103, 106; Stewart Wolpin, "How Nintendo Revived a Dying Industry," *Marketing Communications,* May 1989, pp. 36–38, 40; "Toys and Games: The International Market," *Euromonitor,* 1987; Bill Britt, "Nintendo Sparks Boom," *Marketing,* 26 July 1990, p. 5; Robert Preston, "Easy Answers Are Wrong Answers," *The Independent on Sunday,* 23 December 1990, p. 2.

Why is Nintendo successful in an industry that some analysts view as declining? The company is using effective marketing efforts. Nintendo has determined what customers want: high-quality, arcade-like video games. Its marketing effectiveness is reflected in the fact that it has achieved a large share of the video game market in just a few years.

This first chapter is an overview of the concepts and decisions covered in the text. In this chapter we first develop a definition of marketing and explain each element of the definition. Then we look at some of the reasons why people should study marketing. We introduce the marketing concept and consider several issues associated with implementing it. Next we define and discuss the major tasks associated with marketing strategy: market opportunity analysis, target market selection, marketing mix development, and management of marketing activities. We conclude by discussing the organisation of this text.

MARKETING DEFINED

If you ask several people what *marketing* is, they will respond with a variety of descriptions.[1] Marketing encompasses many more activities than most people realise. Since it is practised and studied for many different reasons, it has been, and continues to be, defined in many ways, for academic, research, or applied business purposes. According to the U.K. Chartered Institute of Marketing,

> Marketing is the management process responsible for identifying, anticipating and satisfying consumers' requirements profitably.

A rather different definition has been developed by the American Marketing Association (AMA):

> Marketing is the process of planning and executing the conception, pricing, promotion, and distribution of ideas, goods, and services to create exchanges that satisfy individual and organizational goals.[2]

This definition is widely accepted by academics and marketing managers.[3] It emphasises that marketing focuses on planning and executing activities to satisfy customers' demands. Whereas earlier definitions restricted marketing as a business activity, this definition is broad enough to indicate that marketing can occur in non-business organisations.

Although both of the above definitions are acceptable, we believe that marketing should be defined still more broadly. A definition of marketing should indicate that marketing consists of activities performed by individuals and organisations. In addi-

1. M. Baker, "One More Time—What is Marketing?" in *The Marketing Book,* M. Baker, Ed., (London: Heinemann/Chartered Institute of Marketing, 1987).

2. Peter D. Bennett, ed., *The Dictionary of Marketing Terms* (Chicago, Ill.: American Marketing Association, 1988), p. 115. Reprinted by permission.

3. O. C. Ferrell and George Lucas, "An Evaluation of Progress in the Development of a Definition of Marketing," *Journal of the Academy of Marketing Science,* Fall 1987, p. 17.

TABLE 1.1 *Possible decisions and activities associated with marketing mix variables*

MARKETING MIX VARIABLES	POSSIBLE DECISIONS AND ACTIVITIES
PRODUCT	Develop and test-market new products; modify existing products; eliminate products that do not satisfy customers' desires; formulate brand names and branding policies; create product guarantees and establish procedures for fulfilling guarantees; plan packages, including materials, sizes, shapes, colours, and designs
DISTRIBUTION	Analyse various types of distribution channel; design appropriate distribution channels; design an effective programme for dealer relations; establish distribution centres; formulate and implement procedures for efficient product handling; set up inventory controls; analyse transportation methods; minimise total distribution costs; analyse possible locations for plants and wholesale or retail outlets
PROMOTION	Set promotional objectives; determine major types of promotion to be used; select and schedule advertising media; develop advertising messages; measure the effectiveness of advertisements; recruit and train salespersons; formulate payment programmes for sales personnel; establish sales territories; plan and implement sales promotion efforts such as free samples, coupons, displays, sweepstakes, sales contests, and co-operative advertising programmes; prepare and disseminate publicity releases
PRICE	Analyse competitors' prices; formulate pricing policies; determine method or methods used to set prices; set prices; determine discounts for various types of buyer; establish conditions and terms of sales

tion, it should acknowledge that marketing activities occur in a dynamic environment. Thus we define marketing as follows:

> **Marketing** consists of individual and organisational activities that facilitate and expedite satisfying exchange relationships in a dynamic environment through the creation, distribution, promotion, and pricing of goods, services, and ideas.

In this definition, an **exchange** is the provision or transfer of goods, services, and ideas in return for something of value. Any product may be involved in a marketing exchange. We assume only that individuals and organisations expect to gain a reward in excess of the costs incurred. So that our definition may be fully understood, we now examine each component more closely.

■ **Marketing Consists of Activities**

Marketing products effectively requires many activities. Some are performed by producers; some are accomplished by intermediaries, who buy products from producers or from other intermediaries and resell them; and some are even performed by purchasers. Marketing does not include all human and organisational activities, but only those aimed at facilitating and expediting exchanges. Table 1.1 lists several major categories and examples of marketing activities. Note that this list is not all-inclusive. Each activity could be subdivided into more specific activities.

FIGURE 1.1
Exchange between buyer and seller

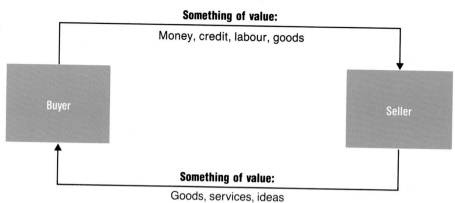

Something of value:
Money, credit, labour, goods

Buyer

Seller

Something of value:
Goods, services, ideas

■ **Marketing Is Performed by Individuals and Organisations**

All organisations perform marketing activities to facilitate exchanges. Businesses as well as non-business organisations, such as colleges and universities, charitable organisations, community theatres, and hospitals, perform marketing activities. For example, colleges and universities and their students engage in exchanges. To receive instruction, knowledge, entertainment, a degree, the use of facilities, and sometimes room and board, students give up time, money, and perhaps services in the form of labour; they may also give up opportunities to do other things. Likewise, many religious institutions engage in marketing activities to satisfy their "customers". For example, in the U.S.A., Willow Creek Community Church in South Barrington, Illinois conducted a survey to determine why some of the residents did not attend any local church. The church used the survey results to develop programmes to satisfy the religious needs of these residents.[4] Even the sole owner of and worker in a small corner shop decides which products will sell, arranges deliveries to the shop, prices and displays products, advertises, and serves customers.

■ **Marketing Facilitates Satisfying Exchange Relationships**

For an exchange to take place, four conditions must exist. First, two or more individuals, groups, or organisations must participate. Second, each party must possess something of value that the other party desires. Third, each party must be willing to give up its "something of value" to receive the "something of value" held by the other party. The objective of a marketing exchange is to receive something that is desired more than what is given up to get it, that is, a reward in excess of costs. Fourth, the parties to the exchange must be able to communicate with each other to make their somethings of value available.[5]

Figure 1.1 illustrates the process of exchange. The arrows indicate that the parties communicate that each has something of value available to exchange. Note, though, that an exchange will not necessarily take place just because these four conditions exist. Nevertheless, even if there is no exchange, marketing activities still have occurred. The somethings of value held by the two parties are most often products

4. Thomas A. Stewart, "Turning Around the Lord's Business," *Fortune,* 25 Sept. 1989, pp. 116–28.

5. Philip Kotler, *Marketing Management: Analysis, Planning, Implementation, and Control,* 6th ed. (Englewood Cliffs, N.J.: Prentice-Hall, 1988), p. 6.

FIGURE 1.2 *Customer satisfaction.*
Mail order company John Moores tries to build strong customer relationships through a guarantee of satisfaction.

SOURCE: Courtesy of The Littlewoods Organisation.

and/or financial resources, such as money or credit. When an exchange occurs, products are traded for other products or for financial resources.

An exchange should be *satisfying* to both the buyer and the seller. In fact, in a study of marketing managers, 32 percent indicated that creating customer satisfaction was the most important concept in a definition of marketing.[6] Marketing activities, then, should be orientated towards creating and maintaining satisfying exchange relationships. Marketing Update 1.1 focuses on how companies build strong relationships with customers. To maintain an exchange relationship, the buyer must be satisfied with the good, service, or idea obtained in the exchange; the seller must be satisfied with the financial reward or something else of value received in the exchange. For instance, to encourage satisfying exchange relationships with its customers, Littlewoods Group, which markets clothing through catalogues (see Figure 1.2), does not sell anything that its employees would not be comfortable wearing

6. Ferrell and Lucas, p. 20.

COMPANIES THAT CUSTOMERS LOVE

There are some companies that customers just seem to love; for whatever reason, these relatively few firms have the advantage of a devoted clientele. Usually, clients are attracted to certain businesses because of product or service quality, or both. Since competitors of these popular companies are eager to capture the customers who consistently return to their favourites, the beloved firms must keep striving to maintain their reputations as superior businesses.

According to a customer-service consulting firm, to keep a customer a business typically spends one-fifth of the amount that it spends on acquiring a new one. It makes sound financial sense for business owners to invest in training employees to focus on customers' desires and listen attentively to customers' complaints and suggestions. A handful of disgruntled customers each telling numerous relatives and friends about even minor dissatisfactions might significantly harm the reputation of a business.

Practices as minor as ensuring that the bonnet of a car is free from black fingerprints after an oil change or that there are plenty of paper napkins to accompany a home-delivered piping-hot pizza can sometimes make the difference when a customer is deciding which firm to call on. Companies with large and loyal followings tend to pay close attention to details, realising that the details are what normally differentiates firms.

Seattle-based Nordstrom Inc., a department store chain, has built its sparkling reputation on customer service and attention to detail. Customers obviously love Nordstrom: it is number one in sales per square foot among all the department stores in the United States. As customers walk through the doors of a Nordstrom store, their coats are courteously accepted in a cloakroom. Live piano music creates a distinct atmosphere. Nordstrom even provides parents of infants with tables for changing nappies. The 90-year-old company recently expanded to the East Coast after years of exclusively serving the western United States. The primary concern of Nordstrom executives is that their new stores live up to the status and service quality of their established locations. In Europe, Marks & Spencer and Sainsbury's have a similar customer orientation.

Victor Alhadeff, founder of Egghead Software, took what he learned as an employee of Nordstrom and applied it to the computer software industry. Alhadeff allows his customers to try out software before they purchase it—a practice almost unheard of among software sellers. He offers a wide selection of merchandise and has a very liberal goods-return policy. Judging by Alhadeff's success, his commitment to pleasing customers will make Egghead Software a strong competitor and another of the small number of companies that customers love.

SOURCES: Ripley Hotch, "Treat Customers with Respect," *Nation's Business,* Nov. 1988, p. 30; Tom Peters, "Know How to Profit in Your Own Time? Service Pays," *Houston Chronicle,* 4 Jan. 1988, p. IV-2; and Francine Schwadel, "Courting Shoppers," *Wall Street Journal,* 1 Aug. 1989, pp. A1, A9.

FIGURE 1.3
Building satisfying customer relationships. In this advertisement, Toyota is promoting the idea that it desires to build long-term customer relationships by providing high-quality service.

SOURCE: Courtesy of Toyota Motor Sales

themselves. Furthermore, the telephonists who answer the firm's freephone order number are knowledgeable about the company's goods and can make suggestions about styles, sizes, and colours. These and other activities ensure that Littlewoods' customers are not only satisfied with the exchange, but that they keep calling back to order more clothing. Ensuring customer satisfaction has maintained Littlewoods Group's market in the face of stiff competition.

Maintaining a positive relationship with buyers is an important goal for a seller, regardless of whether the seller is marketing cereal, financial services, or an electric generating plant. Through buyer-seller interaction, the buyer develops expectations about the seller's future behaviour. To fulfil these expectations, the seller must deliver on promises made. Over time, a healthy buyer-seller relationship results in interdependencies between the two parties. The buyer depends on the seller to furnish information, parts, and service; to be available; and to provide satisfying products in the future. For example, car buyers depend on Toyota and other car makers to provide quality vehicles, as well as service, guarantees, information about various car models, fair prices, and convenient dealer locations. The Toyota advertisement in Figure 1.3 emphasises the firm's commitment to high-quality service. The seller depends on the buyer to continue purchasing from the seller. Toyota depends on buyers to purchase its cars to supply it with the funds needed to meet its organisational objectives.

■ Marketing Occurs in a Dynamic Environment

The marketing environment consists of many changing forces: laws, regulations, political activities, societal pressures, changing economic conditions, and technological advances. Each of these dynamic forces has an impact on how effectively marketing activities can facilitate and expedite exchanges. For example, the development and acceptance of facsimile (fax) machines has given businesses another vehicle through which to promote their products. Some office suppliers and restaurants send advertisements about their goods and services to businesses and individuals through their fax machines.

■ Marketing Involves Products, Distribution, Promotion, and Pricing

Marketing means more than simply advertising or selling a product; it involves developing and managing a product that will satisfy certain needs. It focuses on making the product available at the right place, at the right time, and at a price that is acceptable to customers. It also requires transmitting the kind of information that will help customers determine whether the product will in fact be able to satisfy their needs.

■ Marketing Focuses on Goods, Services, and Ideas

We already have used the word *product* a number of times in this chapter. For purposes of discussion in this text, a *product* is viewed as being a good, a service, or an idea. A *good* is a physical entity one can touch. A Ford Escort, a compact disc player, Kellogg's Frosties, a bar of soap, and a kitten in a pet shop are examples of goods. A *service* is the application of human and mechanical efforts to people or objects in order to provide intangible benefits to customers. Services such as air travel, dry cleaning, hairdressing, banking, medical care, and child care are just as real as goods, but an individual cannot actually touch them. *Ideas* include concepts, philosophies, images, and issues. For instance, a marriage counsellor gives couples ideas and advice to help improve their relationships. Other marketers of ideas include political parties, churches, and schools.

WHY STUDY MARKETING?

After considering the definition of marketing, one can understand some of the obvious reasons why the study of marketing is relevant. In this section we discuss several perhaps less obvious reasons why one should study marketing.

■ Marketing Activities Are Used in Many Organisations

In Europe and the United States between 25 and 33 percent of all civilian workers perform marketing activities. The marketing field offers a variety of interesting and challenging career opportunities, such as personal selling, advertising, packaging, transport, storage, marketing research, product development, wholesaling, and retailing. In addition, many individuals who work for non-business organisations engage in marketing activities. Marketing skills are used to promote political, cultural, church, civic, and charitable activities. The advertisement in Figure 1.4 encourages support of the World Wildlife Fund, a non-profit organisation. Whether a person earns a living through marketing activities or performs them without compensation in non-business settings, marketing knowledge and skills are valuable assets.

FIGURE 1.4
Promotion of a non-profit organisation.
The World Wildlife Fund uses marketing efforts to obtain contributions.

Will this become the only way to save the rain forests?

Fifty-four irreplaceable acres of tropical rain forest are wiped out every minute. Yet we need every acre desperately.

Rain forests house more than half the world's animals and plants. And they're crucial to maintain the earth's fresh water supply. Without rain forests, we could be living in a burning, barren desert.

That's why World Wildlife Fund needs your help to save the rain forests and thousands of species that call them home. We're fighting for their survival and, ultimately, our own.

So send for information now. Help us save life on earth. Otherwise, better save this picture.

World Wildlife Fund
Dept. A, 1250 24th St. NW, Washington, D.C. 20037
Prepared as a public service by Ogilvy & Mather
WWF

SOURCE: World Wildlife Fund/The Conservation Fund

■ **Marketing Activities Are Important to Businesses and the Economy**

A business organisation must sell products to survive and to grow. Directly or indirectly, marketing activities help sell an organisation's products. By doing so, they generate financial resources that can be used to develop innovative products. New products allow a firm to better satisfy customers' changing needs, which in turn enables the firm to generate more profits. For example, each year *Fortune* magazine publishes a list of what its staff considers the top products. Recently, among these products of the year were the Sony Video Walkman, NEC Ultralite Laptop computer, Ricoh Mirai camera, Max Factor's No Colour Mascara, and Wilson Profile tennis racket.[7] All these products produced considerable profit for the firms that introduced them.

Our highly complex economy depends heavily on marketing activities. They help produce the profits that are essential not only to the survival of individual businesses, but also to the health and ultimate survival of the economy as a whole. Profits are essential to economic growth because without them businesses find it

7. Edward C. Baig, "Products of the Year," *Fortune*, 5 Dec. 1988, pp. 89–98.

TABLE 1.2 *National survey results regarding marketing myths*

MYTHS	STRONGLY AGREE	SOMEWHAT AGREE	NEITHER AGREE NOR DISAGREE	SOMEWHAT DISAGREE	STRONGLY DISAGREE
Marketing and selling are about the same thing	12.1% (245)	31.8% (645)	23.4% (476)	21.2% (431)	11.5% (234)
A grocery store owner takes home at least $3 for every $10 bag of groceries sold	19.5% (400)	23.9% (486)	30.4% (619)	15.0% (305)	11.1% (226)
Products that are advertised a great deal cost more	30.7% (625)	36.4% (741)	13.9% (282)	13.3% (270)	5.7% (117)
Wholesalers make high profits that significantly increase prices consumers pay	35.6% (725)	37.9% (771)	16.0% (326)	8.1% (164)	2.4% (49)
Marketing is the same thing as advertising	13.1% (265)	36.2% (734)	22.9% (465)	20.0% (406)	7.7% (157)

SOURCE: William M. Pride and O. C. Ferrell; a national survey of U.S. households, 1985. Reprinted by permission of the authors.

difficult, if not impossible, to buy more raw materials, hire more employees, attract more capital, and create the additional products that in turn make more profits.

■ **Marketing Knowledge Enhances Consumer Awareness**

Besides contributing to a nation's well-being, marketing activities permeate our lives. In fact, they help us improve the quality of our lives. Studying marketing activities allows us to weigh costs, benefits, and flaws more effectively. We can see where they need to be improved and how to accomplish that goal. For example, if you have had an unsatisfactory experience with a guarantee, you may have wished that laws were enforced more strictly to make sellers fulfil their promises. Similarly, you may have wished that you had more information about a product—or more accurate information—before you purchased it. Understanding marketing enables us to evaluate the corrective measures (such as laws, regulations, and industry guidelines) that may be required to stop unfair, misleading, or unethical marketing practices. The results of a U.S. survey presented in Table 1.2 indicate that there is a considerable lack of knowledge about marketing activities, as reflected by the sizeable proportion of respondents who agree with the myths in the table.

■ **Marketing Costs Consume a Sizeable Portion of Buyers' Income**

The study of marketing will make you aware that many marketing activities are necessary to provide people with satisfying goods and services. Obviously, these marketing activities cost money. In fact, about one-half of a buyer's income goes for marketing costs. A family with a monthly income of £1,000, of which £250 goes on taxes and savings, spends about £600 on goods and services. Of this amount, £250 (25 percent of total income) goes for marketing activities. Clearly, if marketing expenses consume that much of your income, you should know how this money is used.

THE MARKETING CONCEPT

Some organisations have tried to be successful by buying land, building a factory, equipping it with people and machines, and then making a product that they believe consumers need. However, these organisations frequently fail to attract buyers with what they have to offer because they defined their business as "making a product" rather than as "helping potential customers satisfy their needs and wants". Such organisations have failed to implement the marketing concept.

According to the **marketing concept**, an organisation should try to provide products that satisfy customers' needs through a co-ordinated set of activities that also allows the organisation to achieve its goals. Customer satisfaction is the major aim of the marketing concept. First an organisation must find out what will satisfy customers. With this information, it then attempts to create satisfying products. But the process does not end there. The organisation must continue to alter, adapt, and develop products to keep pace with customers' changing desires and preferences. For example, as indicated in the advertisement in Figure 1.5, Reader's Digest tries to learn what customers want and to provide products that satisfy those desires. The marketing concept stresses the importance of customers and emphasises that marketing activities begin and end with them.

In attempting to satisfy customers, businesses must consider not only short-run, immediate needs but also broad, long-term desires. Trying to satisfy customers' current needs by sacrificing their long-term desires will only create future dissatisfaction. For instance, people want efficient, low-cost energy to power their homes and cars, yet they react adversely to energy producers who pollute the air and water, kill wildlife, or cause disease or birth defects. To meet these short- and long-run needs and desires, a firm must co-ordinate all its activities. Production, finance, accounting, personnel, and marketing departments must work together.

The marketing concept is not a second definition of marketing. It is a way of thinking—a management philosophy guiding an organisation's overall activities. This philosophy affects all the efforts of the organisation, not just marketing activities. However, the marketing concept is by no means a philanthropic philosophy aimed at helping customers at the expense of the organisation. A firm that adopts the marketing concept must not only satisfy its customers' objectives but also achieve its own goals, or it will not stay in business long. The overall goals of a business might be directed towards increasing profits, share of the market, sales, or a combination of all three. The marketing concept stresses that an organisation can best achieve its goals by providing customer satisfaction. Thus, implementing the marketing concept should benefit the organisation as well as its customers.

■ **Evolution of the Marketing Concept**

The marketing concept may seem like an obvious and sensible approach to running a business. However, businesspeople have not always believed that the best way to make sales and profits is to satisfy customers. A famous example is Henry Ford's marketing philosophy for cars in the early 1900s: "The customers can have any colour car they want as long as it is black." The philosophy of the marketing concept emerged in the third major era in the history of business, preceded by the production and the sales eras. Surprisingly, nearly forty years after the marketing era began, many businesses still have not adopted the marketing concept.

FIGURE 1.5
Using the marketing concept.
Reader's Digest is sending a clear message that its people are making a difference by finding out what customers want and then fulfilling those customers' desires.

Reader's Digest is known as the company that makes a difference—and these are some of the people who help us meet that challenge.

They're part of our global team of 7,000 men and women dedicated to producing and delivering products and services that meet the needs of our customers all over the world.

From magazines that enrich and inspire to books that provide page after page of helpful advice. From music albums that offer hours of listening pleasure to videos that are both informative and entertaining.

We make a difference because our people make *the* difference. By taking the time to learn what our customers want and then fulfilling the promise to deliver.

Reader's Digest. We're a leading force in providing knowledge and entertainment to the world through magazine and book publishing, music and video products, travel and financial services. We also provide significant support for programs for youth, education, the arts and humanities, both directly and through Reader's Digest Foundation.

Reader's Digest

Making the difference.

We make a difference in 100 million lives worldwide.

SOURCE: Reprinted with permission from the Reader's Digest Association, Inc., 1990.

The Production Era.   During the second half of the nineteenth century, the Industrial Revolution was in full swing in Europe and the United States. Electricity, railways, the division of labour, the assembly line, and mass production made it possible to manufacture products more efficiently. With new technology and new ways of using labour, products poured into the market-place, where consumer demand for manufactured goods was strong. This production orientation continued into the early part of this century, encouraged by the scientific management movement that championed rigidly structured jobs and pay based on output.

The Sales Era.   In the 1920s, the strong consumer demand for products subsided. Businesses realised that products, which by this time could be made quite efficiently, would have to be "sold" to consumers. From the mid-1920s to the early 1950s, businesses viewed sales as the major means of increasing profits. As a result, this period came to have a sales orientation. Businesspeople believed that the most important marketing activities were personal selling and advertising.

The Marketing Era.   By the early 1950s, some businesspeople began to recognise that efficient production and extensive promotion of products did not guarantee that customers would buy them. These businesses, and many others since then, found that they must first determine what customers want and then produce it, rather than simply make products first and then try to change customers' needs to correspond with what is being produced. As more organisations have realised the importance of knowing customers' needs, businesses have entered into the marketing era—the era of customer orientation.

■ Implementing the Marketing Concept

A philosophy may sound reasonable and look good on paper, but that does not mean it can be put into practice easily. The marketing concept is a case in point. To implement it, an organisation must focus on some general conditions and recognise several problems. Because of these conditions and problems, the marketing concept has yet to be fully accepted by many businesses.

Because the marketing concept affects all types of business activities, and not just marketing activities, the top management of an organisation must adopt it whole-heartedly. High-level executives must incorporate the marketing concept into their philosophies of business management so completely that it becomes the basis for all the goals and decisions that they set for their firms. They must also convince other members of the organisation to accept the changes in policies and operations that flow from their acceptance of the marketing concept.

As the first step, management must establish an information system that enables it to discover customers' real needs and to use the information to create satisfying products. Because such a system is usually expensive, management must be willing to commit money and time for development and maintenance. Without an adequate information system, an organisation cannot be customer orientated.

Management's second major task is to restructure the organisation. We pointed out that if a company is to satisfy customers' objectives as well as its own, it must co-ordinate all its activities. To achieve this, the internal operations and the overall objectives of one or more departments may need restructuring. If the head of the marketing unit is not a member of the organisation's top-level management, he or she should be. Some departments may have to be abolished and new ones created. Implementing the marketing concept demands the support not only of top management, but also of managers and staff at all levels within the organisation.

Even when the basic conditions of establishing an information system and reorganising the company are met, the firm's new marketing approach may not work perfectly. First, there is a limit to a firm's ability to satisfy customers' needs for a particular product. In a mass production economy, most business organisations cannot tailor products to fit the exact needs of each customer. Second, although a company may attempt to learn what customers want, it may be unable to do so, and when the organisation does correctly identify customers' needs, it often has a difficult time developing a product that satisfies those needs. Many companies spend considerable time and money to research customers' needs and yet still create some products that do not sell well. Third, by striving to satisfy one particular segment of society, a firm sometimes dissatisfies other segments. Certainly, government and non-business organisations also experience this problem. Fourth, a business organisation may have difficulty maintaining employee morale during any restructuring needed to co-ordinate the activities of various departments. Management must clearly explain the reasons for the various changes and communicate its own enthusiasm for the marketing concept.

FIGURE 1.6
Components of the marketing mix and marketing environment

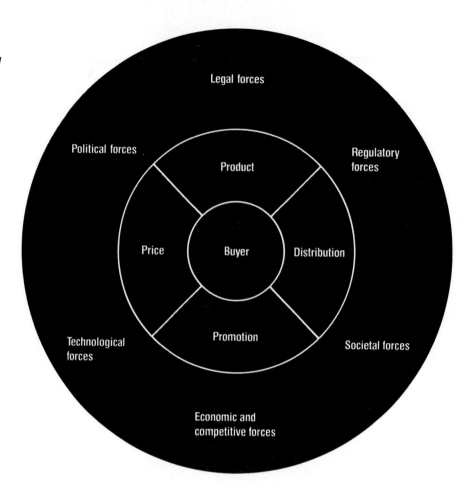

MARKETING STRATEGY

To achieve the broad goal of expediting desirable exchanges, an organisation's marketing managers are responsible for developing and managing marketing strategies. Specifically, a **marketing strategy** encompasses selecting and analysing a target market (the group of people whom the organisation wants to reach) and creating and maintaining an appropriate **marketing mix** (product, distribution, promotion, and price) that will satisfy those people. A marketing strategy articulates a plan for the best use of the organisation's resources and tactics to meet its objectives.

When marketing managers attempt to develop and manage marketing activities, they must deal with two broad sets of variables: those relating to the marketing mix and those that make up the marketing environment. The marketing mix decision variables—product, distribution, promotion, and price—are factors over which an organisation has control. As Figure 1.6 shows, these variables are constructed around the buyer. The marketing environment variables are political, legal, regulatory, societal, economic and competitive, and technological forces. These factors are subject to less control by an organisation, but they affect buyers' needs as well as marketing managers' decisions regarding marketing mix variables.

FIGURE 1.7
Marketing strategy tasks

Generic marketing management tasks

Marketing opportunity analysis and target market selection

- The marketing environment (Chapter 2)
- Target market evaluation (Chapter 3)
- Consumer markets and buying behaviour (Chapter 4)
- Organisational markets and buying behaviour (Chapter 5)
- Marketing research and information systems (Chapter 6)

Marketing mix development

- Product decisions (Chapters 7 and 8)
- Distribution decisions (Chapters 9, 10, 11, and 12)
- Promotion decisions (Chapters 13, 14, and 15)
- Price decisions (Chapters 16 and 17)

Marketing management

- Strategic market planning (Chapter 18)
- Implementing strategies and measuring performance (Chapter 19)
- Marketing ethics and social responsibility (Chapter 20)

To develop and manage marketing strategies, marketers must focus on several marketing tasks: marketing opportunity analysis, target market selection, marketing mix development, and effective marketing management. Figure 1.7 lists these tasks, along with the chapters of this book in which they are discussed.

■ **Marketing Opportunity Analysis**

A *marketing opportunity* exists when circumstances allow an organisation to take action towards reaching a particular group of customers. An opportunity provides a favourable chance or opening for the firm to generate sales from identifiable markets. For example, during a heat wave, marketers of electric fans have a marketing opportunity—an opportunity to reach customers who need electric fans.

Marketers should be capable of recognising and analysing marketing opportunities. An organisation's long-term survival depends on developing products that satisfy its customers. Few organisations can assume that products popular today will interest buyers ten years from now. A marketing organisation can choose among several alternatives for continued product development through which it can achieve its objectives and satisfy buyers. It can modify existing products (for example, by removing preservatives from jams and sauces to address increasing health consciousness among customers), introduce new products (such as PG Tips instant tea granules or Batchelors Micro Chef), and delete some that customers no longer want (such as disc cameras). A company may also try to market its products to a greater number of customers, convince current customers to use more of a product, or perhaps expand marketing activities into additional countries. Diversification into new product offerings through internal efforts or through acquisitions of other organisations may be viable options for a firm. For example, BSN Groupe, a French consumer goods marketer of pasta, bakery goods, and other products, bought RJR Nabisco's European consumer goods division, gaining the rights to market a number of highly successful Nabisco products in Europe. An organisation's ability to pursue any of these alternatives successfully depends on its internal characteristics and the forces within the marketing environment.

Internal Organisational Factors. The primary factors inside an organisation that should be considered when analysing marketing opportunities are organisational objectives, financial resources, managerial skills, organisational strengths and weaknesses, and cost structures. Most organisations have overall organisational objectives. Some marketing opportunities may be consistent with these objectives; others are not, and to pursue them is hazardous. Frequently, the pursuit of such opportunities ends in failure or forces the company to alter its long-term objectives.

Obviously, a firm's financial resources constrain the type of marketing opportunities it can pursue. Typically, an organisation does not develop projects that can bring economic catastrophe. In some situations, however, a firm must invest in a high-risk opportunity, because the costs of not pursuing the project are so high. Thus a computer manufacturer, such as IBM, must conduct product research and development and produce computers featuring cutting-edge technology, such as the IBM PS/2 95, if it wants to remain competitive with other computer makers.

The skills and experience of its management also limit the types of opportunities that an organisation can pursue. A company must be particularly cautious when exploring the possibility of entering unfamiliar markets with new products. If it lacks appropriate managerial skills and experience, the firm can sometimes acquire them by hiring additional managerial personnel.

Like people, most organisations have strengths and weaknesses. Because of the types of operation in which a firm is engaged, it normally has employees with specialised skills and technological information. Such characteristics are a strength when launching marketing strategies that require them. However, they may be a weakness if the company tries to compete in new, unrelated product areas.

An organisation's cost structure may be an advantage if the company pursues certain marketing opportunities and a disadvantage if it pursues others. Such factors as geographic location, employee skills, access to raw materials, and type of equipment and facilities all can affect the cost structure.

Marketing Environment Forces. The *marketing environment*, which consists of political, legal, regulatory, societal, economic and competitive, and technological forces, surrounds the buyer and the marketing mix (see Figure 1.6). We explore each major environmental force in considerable depth in Chapter 2. Marketers know that they cannot predict changes in the marketing environment with certainty. Even so, over the years, marketers have become more systematic in taking these forces into account when planning their competitive actions.[8]

Marketing environment forces affect a marketer's ability to facilitate and expedite exchanges in three general ways. First, they influence customers by affecting their

8. Gene R. Laczniak and Robert F. Lusch, "Environment and Strategy in 1995: A Survey of High-Level Executives," *Journal of Consumer Marketing,* Spring 1986, p. 28.

lifestyles, standards of living, and preferences and needs for products. Because a marketing manager tries to develop and adjust the marketing mix to satisfy consumers, the effects of environmental forces on customers also have an indirect impact on the marketing mix components. Second, marketing environment forces help determine whether and how a marketing manager can perform certain marketing activities. Third, the environmental forces may affect a marketing manager's decisions and actions by influencing buyers' reactions to the firm's marketing mix.

Although forces in the marketing environment are sometimes viewed as "uncontrollables", a marketing manager may be able to influence one or more of them. However, marketing environment forces fluctuate quickly and dramatically, which is one reason why marketing is so interesting and challenging. Because these forces are highly interrelated, a change in one may cause others to change. For example, after four major oil spills in the U.S.A. within three months in 1989 (in Alaska, Delaware, Rhode Island, and Texas), people's feelings towards the shipping of petroleum products and towards oil companies in general became less positive. As outrage over the damage increased, the federal government took legal action against the companies and individuals responsible for the accidents. The U.S. Congress considered legislation to regulate the shipping of petroleum products and to halt exploration for oil in some particularly sensitive areas. The oil companies then began to seek new technology to prevent spills and to clean them up quickly and safely. In addition, the world's major oil companies formed the Petroleum Industry Response Organization (PIRO) and established a £150 million fund for research and activities designed to quicken the response to accidents and make transporting petroleum safer.[9]

Even though changes in the marketing environment produce uncertainty for marketers and, at times, hurt marketing efforts, they can also create opportunities. After the 1989 oil spills, for example, more companies began developing and marketing products designed to contain or dissipate spilled oil. Thus a marketer must be aware of changes in environmental forces not only to adjust to and influence them but to capitalise on the opportunities they provide.

■ **Marketing Strategy: Target Market Selection**

A **target market** is a group of persons for whom a firm creates and maintains a marketing mix that specifically fits the needs and preferences of that group. When choosing a target market, marketing managers try to evaluate possible markets to see how entering them would affect the company's sales, costs, and profits. Marketers also attempt to determine whether the organisation has the resources to produce a marketing mix that meets the needs of a particular target market and whether satisfying those needs is consistent with the firm's overall objectives. The size and number of competitors already marketing products in possible target markets are also of concern.

Marketing managers may define a target market as a vast number of people or as a relatively small group. For example, Ford produces cars suitable for the bulk of the population (although specific models are quite narrowly targeted: the family runaround Fiesta or the executive Scorpio). Porsche focuses its marketing effort on a small proportion of the population. Porsche believes that it can compete more effectively by concentrating on an affluent target market. Although a business may

9. Ken Wells, "Credibility Gap: Oil Industry's Inability to Contain Spills at Sea Poses Political Trouble," *Wall Street Journal,* 26 June 1989, pp. A1, A4.

658.
S003/327

concentrate its efforts on one target market through a single marketing mix, businesses often focus on several target markets by developing and employing multiple marketing mixes. Reebok, for example, markets different types of shoes to meet the specific needs of joggers, walkers, aerobics enthusiasts, and other groups.

Target market selection is crucial to generating productive marketing efforts. At times, products and organisations fail because marketers do not identify the appropriate customer groups at which to aim their efforts. Organisations that try to be all things to all people typically end up not satisfying the needs of any customer group very well. It is important for an organisation's management to designate which customer groups the firm is trying to serve and to have adequate information about these customers. The identification and analysis of a target market provide a foundation on which a marketing mix can be developed.

■ **Marketing Strategy: Marketing Mix Development**

As mentioned earlier, the marketing mix consists of four major components: product, distribution, promotion, and price. These components are called marketing mix decision variables because a marketing manager decides what type of each component to use and in what amounts. A primary goal of a marketing manager is to create and maintain a marketing mix that satisfies consumers' needs for a general product type. Notice in Figure 1.6 that the marketing mix is built around the buyer (as is stressed by the marketing concept). Bear in mind, too, that the forces of the marketing environment affect the marketing mix variables in many ways.

Marketing mix variables often are viewed as controllable variables because they can be changed. However, there are limits to how much these variables can be altered. For example, because of economic conditions or government regulations, a manager may not be free to adjust prices daily. Changes in sizes, colours, shapes, and designs of most tangible goods are expensive; therefore, such product features cannot be altered very often. In addition, promotional campaigns and the methods used to distribute products ordinarily cannot be changed overnight.

Marketing managers must develop a marketing mix that precisely matches the needs of the people in the target market. Before they can do so, they have to collect in-depth, up-to-date information about those needs. The information might include data about the age, income, ethnic origin, sex, and educational level of people in the target market; their preferences for product features; their attitudes towards competitors' products; and the frequency and intensity with which they use the product. Armed with these kinds of data, marketing managers are better able to develop a product, distribution system, promotion programme, and price that satisfy the people in the target market.

Let us look more closely at the decisions and activities related to each marketing mix variable (product, distribution, promotion, and price). Table 1.1 is a partial list of the decisions and activities associated with each marketing mix variable.

The Product Variable.   As noted earlier, a product can be a good, a service, or an idea. The **product variable** is the aspect of the marketing mix that deals with researching consumers' product wants and designing a product with the desired characteristics. It also involves the creation or alteration of packages and brand names and may include decisions about guarantees and repair services. The actual production of products is not a marketing activity.

Product variable decisions and related activities are important because they directly involve creating products and services that satisfy consumers' needs and wants.

Marketing Update 1.2 focuses on Trusthouse Forte's revised marketing strategy. To maintain a satisfying set of products that will help an organisation achieve its goals, a marketer must be able to develop new products, modify existing ones, and eliminate those that no longer satisfy buyers or yield acceptable profits. For example, after realising that competitors were capturing large shares of the low-calorie market, Heinz introduced new product items under its Weight Watchers name.

The Distribution Variable.   To satisfy consumers, products must be available at the right time and in a convenient location. In dealing with the **distribution variable**, a marketing manager seeks to make products available in the quantities desired to as many customers as possible and to keep the total inventory, transport, and storage costs as low as possible. A marketing manager may become involved in selecting and motivating intermediaries (wholesalers and retailers), establishing and maintaining inventory control procedures, and developing and managing transport and storage systems.

The Promotion Variable.   The **promotion variable** relates to activities used to inform one or more groups of people about an organisation and its products. Promotion can be aimed at increasing public awareness of an organisation and of new or existing products. In addition, promotion can serve to educate consumers about product features or to urge people to take a particular stance on a political or social issue. It may also be used to keep interest strong in an established product that has been available for decades. The advertisement in Figure 1.8 is an example.

The Price Variable.   The **price variable** relates to activities associated with establishing pricing policies and determining product prices. Price is a critical component of the marketing mix because consumers are concerned about the value obtained in an exchange. Price often is used as a competitive tool; in fact, extremely intense price competition sometimes leads to price wars. For example, airlines like Pan Am, British Airways, and Virgin are engaged in ruthless price-cutting in the battle for transatlantic routes. Price can also help to establish a product's image. For instance, if the makers of Calvin Klein's Obsession tried to sell that perfume in a two-litre bottle for £3, consumers probably would not buy it because the low price would destroy the prestigious image of Obsession.

Developing and maintaining an effective marketing mix is a major requirement for a strong marketing strategy. Thus, as indicated in Figure 1.7, a large portion of this text (Chapters 7 through 17) focuses on the concepts, decisions, and activities associated with the components of the marketing mix.

■ **Marketing Management**

Marketing management is a process of planning, organising, implementing, and controlling marketing activities to facilitate and expedite exchanges effectively and efficiently. Effectiveness and efficiency are important dimensions of this definition. *Effectiveness* is the degree to which an exchange helps achieve an organisation's objectives. *Efficiency* is the minimisation of resources an organisation must spend to achieve a specific level of desired exchanges. Thus the overall goal of marketing management is to facilitate highly desirable exchanges and to minimise as much as possible the costs of doing so.

Planning is a systematic process of assessing opportunities and resources, determining marketing objectives, developing a marketing strategy, and developing plans

FIGURE 1.8
Promotion of an established brand.
Levi's reminds parents that though children like Levi's jeans because they are fashionable, the jeans are sturdy and sensible as well.

SOURCE: Levi Strauss and Co.

for implementation and control. Planning determines when and how marketing activities will be performed and who is to perform them. It forces marketing managers to think ahead, to establish objectives, and to consider future marketing activities. Effective planning also reduces or eliminates daily crises.

Organising marketing activities refers to developing the internal structure of the marketing unit. The structure is the key to directing marketing activities. The marketing unit can be organised by function, product, region, type of customer, or a combination of all four.

Proper implementation of marketing plans hinges on co-ordination of marketing activities, motivation of marketing personnel, and effective communication within the unit. Marketing managers must motivate marketing personnel, co-ordinate their activities, and integrate their activities both with those in other areas of the company and with the marketing efforts of personnel in external organisations, such as advertising agencies and market research firms. An organisation's communication system must allow the marketing manager to stay in contact with high-level management, with managers of other functional areas within the firm, and with personnel involved in marketing activities both inside and outside the organisation.

TRUSTHOUSE FORTE HOTELS

Research has shown there to be five key groups or segments in the London hotel market:

International business travellers
International leisure travellers
U.K. business travellers
U.K. tourists/leisure travellers
Banqueting and functions

Clearly, each group requires different hotel facilities, locations, price points, and service levels; associated hotel promotion needs to be related to the target customers' perceptions and desires.

Trusthouse Forte (THF), the largest European hotel operator, has nearly twenty hotels in London. A few of these were purpose-built but most have been converted from large, impressive historic buildings. The portfolio includes hotels such as the Grosvenor House (recently voted the best deluxe hotel in Europe), functional four-star hotels such as the Cumberland, and the no-frills, budget-orientated, two-star properties with no en-suite bathrooms, such as the Regent Palace Hotel.

Until recently, all THF hotels have been branded under the THF name, whether they were good, moderate, or indifferent; internationally or locally focused; small hotels in market towns or large operations adjacent to airports. In London, all THF hotels were marketed together in one brochure, portraying a uniform image. The company has now realised that Grosvenor House customers would not want the Regent Palace level of accommodation, service, image, or price, and vice versa. Marketing the hotels together ignores the benefits of targeting specific hotels at the type of customers to whom the individual hotels appeal.

Hotels with similar target customers, amenities and price points are now being grouped and each group is being marketed separately to its respective target customers. Customer needs should be better met, promotional activity more precisely targeted, and hotel amenities and service levels developed in line with exact customer expectations.

SOURCES: *The London Hotel Market,* Warwick University, 1989; English Tourist Board; *MEAL; Sunday Telegraph,* 27 August 1989; "THF to Rename?" *Caterer and Hotelkeeper* 10–16 January 1991, p. 12.

The marketing control process consists of establishing performance standards, evaluating actual performance by comparing it with established standards, and reducing the difference between desired and actual performance. An effective control process has four requirements. It should ensure a rate of information flow that allows the marketing manager to quickly detect differences between actual and planned levels of performance. It must accurately monitor different kinds of activities and be flexible enough to accommodate changes. The control process must be economical so that its costs are low relative to the costs that would arise if there were no controls. Finally, the control process should be designed so that both managers and subordinates can understand it. To maintain effective marketing control, an organisation needs to develop a comprehensive control process that evaluates marketing operations at regular intervals. In Chapters 19 and 20 we examine the planning, organising, implementing, and controlling of marketing activities in greater detail.

The Organisation of This Book

Figure 1.6 is a map of the overall organisation of this book. Chapter 2 discusses the marketing environment variables listed in the outer portion of Figure 1.6. Then we move to the centre of the figure, analysing markets, buyers, and marketing research in Chapters 3, 4, 5, and 6. Chapters 7 through 17 explore the marketing mix variables, starting with the product variable and moving clockwise around Figure 1.6. Chapters 18 and 19 discuss strategic market planning, organisation, implementation, and control. Chapter 20 explores marketing ethics and social responsibility. Chapters 21, 22, and 23 scrutinise decisions and activities that are unique to industrial marketing, international marketing, and services marketing. If, as you study, you wonder where the text is leading, look again at Figure 1.6.

Summary

Marketing consists of individual and organisational activities that facilitate and expedite satisfying exchange relationships in a dynamic environment through the creation, distribution, promotion, and pricing of goods, services, and ideas. An exchange is the provision or transfer of goods, services, and ideas in return for something of value. Four conditions must exist for an exchange to occur: (1) two or more individuals, groups, or organisations must participate; (2) each party must have something of value desired by the other; (3) each party must be willing to give up what it has in order to receive the value held by the other; and (4) the parties to the exchange must be able to communicate with each other to make their somethings of value available. In an exchange, products are traded either for other products or for financial resources, such as cash or credit. Products can be goods, services, or ideas.

It is important to study marketing because it permeates our lives. Marketing activities are performed in both business and non-business organisations. Moreover, marketing activities help business organisations generate profits, the life-blood of a capitalist economy. The study of marketing enhances consumer awareness. Finally, marketing costs absorb about half of what the consumer spends.

The marketing concept is a management philosophy which prompts a business organisation to try to satisfy customers' needs through a co-ordinated set of activities that also allows the organisation to achieve its goals. Customer satisfaction is the major objective of the marketing concept. The philosophy of the marketing concept emerged during the 1950s, after the production and the sales eras. To make the marketing concept work, top management must accept it as an overall management philosophy. Implementing the marketing concept requires an efficient information system and sometimes the restructuring of the organisation.

Marketing strategy involves selecting and analysing a target market (the group of people whom the organisation wants to reach) and creating and maintaining an appropriate marketing mix (product, distribution, promotion, and price) to satisfy this market. Marketing strategy requires that managers focus on four tasks to achieve set objectives: (1) marketing opportunity analysis, (2) target market selection, (3) marketing mix development, and (4) marketing management.

Marketers should be able to recognise and analyse marketing opportunities, which are circumstances that allow an organisation to take action towards reaching a particular group of customers. Marketing opportunity analysis involves reviewing both internal factors (organisational objectives, financial resources, managerial skills, organisational strengths, organisational weaknesses, and cost structures) and external ones (the political, legal, regulatory, societal, economic and competitive, and technological forces of the marketing environment).

A target market is a group of persons for whom a firm creates and maintains a marketing mix that specifically fits the needs and preferences of that group. It is important for an organisation's management to designate which customer groups the firm is trying to serve and to have some information about these customers. The identification and analysis of a target market provide a foundation on which a marketing mix can be developed.

The four variables that make up the marketing mix are product, price, promotion, and distribution. The product variable is the aspect of the marketing mix that deals with researching consumers' wants and designing a product with the desired characteristics. A marketing manager tries to make products available in the quantities desired to as many customers as possible and to keep the total inventory, transport, and storage costs as low as possible—the distribution variable. The promotion variable relates to activities used to inform one or more groups of people about an organisation and its products. The price variable refers to establishing pricing policies and determining product prices.

Marketing management is a process of planning, organising, implementing, and controlling marketing activities to facilitate and expedite exchanges effectively and efficiently. Planning is a systematic process of assessing opportunities and resources, determining marketing objectives, developing a marketing strategy, and developing plans for implementation and control. Organising marketing activities refers to developing the internal structure of the marketing unit. Properly implementing marketing plans depends on co-ordinating marketing activities, motivating marketing personnel, and effectively communicating within the unit. The marketing control process consists of establishing performance standards, evaluating actual performance by comparing it with established standards, and reducing the difference between desired and actual performance.

Important Terms

Marketing
Exchange
Marketing concept
Marketing strategy
Marketing mix
Target market

Product variable
Distribution variable
Promotion variable
Price variable
Marketing management

Discussion and Review Questions

1. What is marketing? How did you define marketing before you read this chapter?
2. Why should someone study marketing?
3. Discuss the basic elements of the marketing concept. Which businesses in your area use this concept? In your opinion, have these businesses adopted the marketing concept? Explain.
4. Identify several business organisations in your area that obviously have not adopted the marketing concept. What characteristics of these organisations indicate non-acceptance of the marketing concept?
5. Describe the major components of a marketing strategy. How are the components related?
6. Identify the tasks involved in developing a marketing strategy.
7. What are the primary issues that marketing managers consider when conducting a market opportunity analysis?
8. What are the variables in the marketing environment? How much control does a marketing manager have over environmental variables?
9. Why is the selection of a target market such an important issue?
10. Why are the elements of the marketing mix known as variables?
11. What types of management activities are involved in the marketing management process?

Cases

1.1   Harris Queensway: Furniture and Carpets

In 1957 Phillip Harris's family had three carpet shops in London. By 1987 there were 440 carpet shops throughout the U.K. with sales of £109.2 million and operating profits of £12.36 million. Carpets were sold by Harris Queensway from 128 vast edge-of-town discount warehouses (or sheds), branded as Carpetland or General George. In towns there were Harris Carpets shops and Vogue concessionary departments in Debenhams department stores. Allied Carpets, the major competitor, had sales of £125 million in 1987.

The company diversified into retailing furniture with the acquisition of Queensway Discount Warehouses Ltd. By 1987, the furniture division had 410 stores and a total of 4.6 million square feet of retailing space, 60 percent of which was in edge-of-town sheds (Queensway), the remainder being Times Furnishings town-centre shops. In 1986, the group further diversified with the addition of Ultimate electrical stores and Harvey's soft furnishings. In 1987, the group's pre-tax profits peaked at £42.1 million.

In 1988, the bubble burst. For three years running, profits crashed. The founder, Sir Phil Harris, left the company, electricals and soft furnishings were sold off and there were major property disposals. The renamed Lowndes Queensway (carpets and furniture) has just been put into receivership. High interest rates and reduced U.K. consumer spending contributed to the company's problems: furniture and carpets are infrequent, major items of consumer spending, purchases which are postponed when times are hard.

The company's problems, however, were much more deeply rooted. Harris was a discounter—"pile it high, sell it cheap"—with low-cost retail outlets. The U.K. furniture industry was the only sector of consumer spending which had seen no real growth. Low product and design innovation did not inspire frequent changes of furniture by consumers. The company's philosophy was sales-led—the antithesis of modern marketing. Any available, low-cost product was poorly displayed in hanger-like sheds or in cramped, poorly laid-out town-centre shops. The consumer was not consulted.

Research showed that consumers did not perceive a need to change carpets or furniture unless they moved to a new house. No company had ever attempted to persuade them otherwise. Consumers were used to the innovative electrical goods retailers and fashion clothing companies which throughout the 1980s provided stylish merchandise and stores with an appealing ambience. Quite simply, the product-led discounting tactics of the Queensway group were deterring many customers rather than providing the right product in suitably designed stores with professional assistance, price points, and merchandise to appeal to the growth segments in the market. The company ignored the principles of marketing: it did not consult customers and differentiated itself purely on price; there was no formal market research undertaken and no marketing department.

SOURCES: *EIU Retail Business Quarterly,* March 1989; *Retail's* supplement on Harris Queensway, Winter 1987; "Consumer Buying Behaviour in the Furniture Market", *Search Ad,* June 1987.

Questions for Discussion

1. Evaluate Harris Queensway's discounting approach.
2. What environmental problems are faced by such a non-marketing and non-market-research-led company?

1.2   RJR Nabisco Focuses on Strategic Marketing

Most of us are familiar with the red triangle trademark on packages of Nabisco biscuits and crackers. This instant recognition is due to RJR Nabisco's understanding of the marketing concept. The company realises that it must carefully coordinate its activities both to satisfy customer needs and to achieve its own objectives. Marketing was the key to success for the many different companies that made up R.J. Reynolds Industries and Nabisco Brands, Inc., before they were united under the name RJR Nabisco in 1985. Strategic marketing planning is crucial to the success of this huge company, which has annual sales of more than $17 billion.

R.J. Reynolds bought Nabisco to take advantage of Nabisco's strengths and to minimise its own organisational weaknesses. After purchasing Nabisco, officials at R.J. Reynolds developed numerous marketing strategies to accommodate an assortment of many different brands. Now the marketing department must devote itself to such disparate products as Winston, Salem, and Camel cigarettes; Oreo cookies; Planters peanuts; Ritz crackers; and Del Monte pineapples, all of which are sold throughout the world.

The directors of RJR Nabisco restructured and streamlined the organisation, trying to increase productivity and reduce waste. For example, they moved the Planters (peanuts) and Life Savers (confectionery) units into the tobacco division. The action led to more efficient distribution of these products because they are frequently sold in the same outlets. Company executives sold the Heublein Inc. liquor division and Kentucky Fried Chicken.

Tobacco is still the primary moneymaker for RJR Nabisco, accounting for 60 percent of the corporation's earnings. The company's profit margin on tobacco products is 29 percent. It costs the company a mere 17 cents to produce a pack of cigarettes, which it then sells to distributors for about 80 cents. RJR Nabisco's share of the tobacco market is about 32.5 percent; however, there has been an overall decline in the U.S. consumption of tobacco products. To meet the goal of being the low-cost cigarette producer, RJR Nabisco built Tobaccoville, a $1 billion supermodern production facility in North Carolina. Tobaccoville allowed the company to cut its tobacco work force by nearly 20 percent, saving the company at least $60 million per year. Now operating at full capacity, the plant manufactures 110 billion cigarettes per year, one-fifth of the entire industry's production.

RJR Nabisco is a leader in many of the U.S.A.'s food markets as well. Oreo biscuits have been the number-one seller in the market for more than seventy years. The company's crackers are still on top after several decades, and its nutritious cereals are rapidly gaining market share as consumers become more health conscious. RJR Nabisco officials plan to continue restructuring in this area, trimming operations and selling those units that do not fit in.

RJR Nabisco management constantly analyses and adjusts its marketing mix to maintain and increase its profit margin. The corporate leadership is strongly committed to research and development and is creating new products and improving older ones.

Distribution and promotion are also important to RJR Nabisco. The company tries to make its products available to distributors at low prices in order to pass on the savings to consumers. New facilities have opened so that adequate supplies of products may be readily obtainable. RJR Nabisco vigorously promotes its products and plans to increase promotional expenditure. In the past, Nabisco promotions have been some of the most innovative and memorable within the industry. RJR Nabisco faces the challenge of targeting many diverse products at equally diverse target markets.

Obviously, marketing is very important to RJR Nabisco and its continuing success. The company's officials recognise the significance of the marketing concept and employ strategic market planning both to accomplish company goals and to meet consumer needs. With effective marketing, RJR Nabisco is able to make its products available to consumers, to make consumers aware of new products, and to establish a reasonable pricing policy. Perhaps marketing is as essential to RJR Nabisco as the cream filling is to an Oreo.

SOURCES: Melvin J. Grayson, *27 Million Daily: The Story of Nabisco Brands* (Parsippany, N.J.: Nabisco Brands, 1984); Kevin Maney, "Move Shows It's Not Giving up Tobacco," *USA Today,* 22 June 1987, pp. 1, 2B; Bob Messenger, "The Leading 50 Prepared Food and Beverage Processors," *Prepared Foods,* July 1986, pp. 40–46; *The RJR Nabisco 1986 Annual Report;* and Bill Saporito, "The Tough Cookie at RJR Nabisco," *Fortune,* 18 July 1988, pp. 32–46.

Questions for Discussion

1. What is the purpose or role of the marketing strategies used by RJR Nabisco?
2. Does RJR Nabisco attempt to follow the marketing concept? Explain.
3. What types of environmental forces are most likely to influence the marketing of RJR Nabisco's tobacco brands?

2 THE MARKETING ENVIRONMENT

Objectives

To understand the concept of the marketing environment and the importance of environmental scanning and analysis

To identify the types of political forces in the marketing environment

To understand how laws and their interpretation influence marketing practices

To determine how government regulations and self-regulatory agencies affect marketing activities

To identify societal issues that marketers must deal with as they make decisions

To understand how economic and competitive factors affect organisations' ability to compete and customers' willingness and ability to buy products

To explore the effects of new technology on society and on marketing activities

S ince 1961 the Cold War had been symbolised by the Berlin Wall. West Berlin was effectively sealed off, creating a separate city, with its own political and transport infrastructure, central business area and museums, television stations and airport—an enclave of flourishing capitalism within Communist East Germany, inaccessible to the residents of the other "half" of the city. In the 1980s, under the leadership of President Gorbachev, the U.S.S.R. saw major social and political changes. To the surprise of most western observers, in 1989 the Berlin Wall was first opened—by the East German authorities on instructions from Moscow—and then demolished. Families and communities in East and West Berlin were reunited. In 1990 the two Germanies became a single country once again.

Throughout the whole Eastern Bloc, barriers to the West came down. Few, if any, western countries had anticipated such upheaval and the resultant marketing opportunities. McDonald's has opened a branch in Moscow; Unilever and Procter & Gamble are launching cosmetics and detergents in the Eastern Bloc; Volvo is driving into the U.S.S.R. A joint venture company, Logovaz, owned by Volvo and the giant Vaz Soviet car maker, is to greatly increase the number of Volvo cars on Russian streets. Previously there were 5,000 Volvo diplomatic cars. Showrooms are planned in Moscow, Leningrad, and Tbilisi. Opportunities in all fields have emerged which few marketers could have predicted at the start of 1989. ◆

Based on information from "Advertisers Move in on New Germany," *Marketing*, 10 January 1991, p. 15; Paul Gosling, "Marketing Makes Its Mark on East Europe," *The Independent on Sunday*, 6 January 1991, p. 21; "P&G Gambles on Eastern Europe Move," *Marketing*, 10 January 1991, p. 15; Ken Read, "Volvo Drives into Russia," *Coventry Evening Telegraph*, 12 February 1991, p. 21.

As you can see from this example, various forces can have a tremendous impact on the decisions and activities of marketers. This chapter explores the political, legal, regulatory, societal, economic and competitive, and technological forces that make up the marketing environment. First we define the marketing environment and consider why it is critical to scan and analyse it. Then we discuss the political forces that generate government actions affecting marketing activities. We examine the effects of laws and regulatory agencies on these activities and describe the desires and expectations of society. Next we consider the effects of general economic conditions: prosperity, recession, depression, and recovery. We also examine several types of economic forces that influence companies' ability to compete and consumers' willingness and ability to buy. Finally, we analyse the major dimensions of the technological forces in the environment.

EXAMINING AND RESPONDING TO THE MARKETING ENVIRONMENT

The **marketing environment** consists of external forces that directly or indirectly influence an organisation's acquisition of inputs and generation of outputs. Inputs might include personnel, financial resources, raw materials, and information. Outputs could be information (such as advertisements), packages, goods, services, or ideas. As indicated in Chapter 1 and as shown in Figure 1.6, we view the marketing environment as consisting of six categories of forces: political, legal, regulatory, societal, economic and competitive, and technological. Although there are numerous environmental factors, most fall into one of these six categories.

Whether they fluctuate rapidly or slowly, environmental forces are always dynamic. Changes in the marketing environment create uncertainty, threats, and opportunities for marketers. Although the future is not very predictable, marketers can estimate what will happen. We can say with certainty that marketers will continue to modify their marketing strategies in response to the dynamic environment. Marketing managers who fail to recognise changes in environmental forces leave their firms unprepared to capitalise on marketing opportunities or to cope with threats created by changes in the environment. If an organisation cannot deal with an unfavourable environment, it may go under. On Merseyside and Tyneside during the OPEC-led recession of the mid-1970s many manufacturers cut back on their work-forces, causing unemployment rates of over 40 percent in many suburbs. Many local retailers and small shopkeepers, restaurants and take-aways, and garages had not anticipated the extent of the unemployment or its effect on their businesses. Dozens of small, local businesses closed down. The 1990 Gulf crisis caused huge rises in the price of petrol. The U.K. car-buying public became even more concerned about miles per gallon, with a resultant decline in the sales of high-horsepower sports cars and executive saloons. Thus monitoring the environment is crucial to an organisation's survival and to the long-term achievement of its goals.

■ **Environmental Scanning and Analysis**

To monitor changes in the marketing environment effectively, marketers must engage in environmental scanning and analysis. **Environmental scanning** is the process of collecting information about the forces in the marketing environment. Scanning involves observation; perusal of secondary sources, such as business, trade, government, and general-interest publications; and market research. However, managers must be careful not to gather so much information that sheer volume makes analysis impossible.

Environmental analysis is the process of assessing and interpreting the information gathered through environmental scanning. A manager evaluates the information for accuracy, tries to resolve inconsistencies in the data, and, if warranted, assigns significance to the findings. Through analysis, a marketing manager seeks to describe current environmental changes and to predict future changes. By evaluating these changes, the manager should be able to determine possible threats and opportunities linked to environmental fluctuations. Understanding the current state of the marketing environment and recognising the threats and opportunities arising from changes within it help marketing managers assess the performance of current marketing efforts and develop marketing strategies for the future.

■ Responding to Environmental Forces

In responding to environmental forces, marketing managers can take two general approaches: to accept environmental forces as uncontrollable or to confront and mould them. If environmental forces are viewed as uncontrollable, the organisation remains passive and reactive towards the environment. Instead of trying to influence forces in the environment, its marketing managers tend to adjust current marketing strategies to environmental changes. They approach market opportunities discovered through environmental scanning and analysis with caution. On the other hand, marketing managers who believe that environmental forces can be shaped adopt a proactive approach. For example, if a market is blocked by traditional environmental constraints, they may apply economic, psychological, political, and promotional skills to gain access to it or operate within it. Once they identify what blocks a market opportunity, marketers can assess the power of the various parties involved and develop strategies to try to overcome environmental forces.[1]

In trying to influence environmental forces, marketing management may seek to create market opportunities or to extract greater benefits relative to costs from existing market opportunities. For instance, a firm losing sales to competitors with lower-priced products may strive to develop technology that would make its production processes more efficient; greater efficiency would allow it to lower the prices of its own products. Political action is another way of affecting environmental forces. Thus in America, the Daylight-Saving Time Coalition—a group of candy, sporting goods, and barbecue products manufacturers; convenience stores; fast-food chains; and greenhouses—successfully lobbied Congress to switch the date for the start of daylight-saving time from the last Sunday to the first Sunday in April. The coalition argued that the extra daylight would boost its members' sales by millions of dollars. Similarly, U.K. retailers are lobbying government to permit full Sunday trading and legal opening of retail outlets. A proactive approach, then, can be constructive and bring desired results. However, managers must recognise that there are limits on how much an environmental force can be shaped and that these limits vary across environmental forces. Although an organisation may be able to influence the enactment of laws through lobbying, it is unlikely that a single organisation can significantly increase the national birthrate or move the economy from recession to prosperity.

We cannot generalise and say that either of these approaches to environmental response is better than the other. For some organisations, the passive, reactive

1. Philip Kotler, "Megamarketing," *Harvard Business Review,* March-April 1986, pp. 117–24.

approach is most appropriate, but for other firms, the aggressive approach leads to better performance. The selection of a particular approach depends on an organisation's managerial philosophies, objectives, financial resources, customers, and human skills and on the composition of the set of environmental forces within which the organisation operates.

The rest of this chapter explores in detail each of the six environmental forces—political, legal, regulatory, societal, economic and competitive, and technological.

POLITICAL FORCES

The political, legal, and regulatory forces of the marketing environment are closely interrelated. Legislation is enacted, legal decisions are interpreted by the courts, and regulatory agencies are created and operated, for the most part, by persons elected or appointed to political offices or by civil servants. Legislation and regulations (or the lack of them) reflect the current political outlook. Consequently, the political force of the marketing environment has the potential to influence marketing decisions and strategies.

Marketing organisations need to maintain good relations with elected political officials for several reasons. When political officials are well disposed towards particular firms or industries, they are less likely to create or enforce laws and regulations unfavourable to these companies. For example, political officials who believe that oil companies are making honest efforts to control pollution are unlikely to create and enforce highly restrictive pollution control laws. In addition, governments are big buyers, and political officials can influence how much a government agency purchases and from whom. Finally, political officials can play key roles in helping organisations secure foreign markets.

Many marketers view political forces as beyond their control; they simply try to adjust to conditions that arise from those forces. Some firms, however, seek to influence political events by helping to elect to political office individuals who regard them positively. Much of this help is in the form of contributions to political parties. A sizeable contribution to a campaign fund may carry with it an implicit understanding that the party, if elected, will perform political favours for the contributing firm. There are, though, strict laws governing donations and lobbying in most countries.

LEGAL FORCES

A number of laws influence marketing decisions and activities. Our discussion will focus on procompetitive and consumer protection laws and their interpretation.

■ **Procompetitive Legislation**

Procompetitive legislation is enacted to preserve competition and to end various practices deemed unacceptable by society. We describe the most important of these in greater detail next.

Monopolies and Mergers.   In the U.K. the Secretary of State for Trade and Industry and the **Director General of Fair Trading** can refer monopolies for investigation by the **Monopolies and Mergers Commission**, an independent body whose members are drawn from a variety of backgrounds, including lawyers, economists, industrialists and trade unionists. The legislation defines a monopoly as a situation where at least a quarter of a particular kind of good or service is supplied by a single person or a group of connected companies, or by two or more people acting in a way which prevents, restricts, or distorts competition. Local monopolies can also be referred to the commission.

If the commission finds that a monopoly operates against the public interest, the Secretary of State for Trade and Industry has power to take action to remedy or prevent the harm which the commission considers may exist. Alternatively, the Director General may be asked to negotiate undertakings to remedy the adverse effects identified by the commission. The government believes that the market is a better judge than itself of the advantages and disadvantages of mergers, so most takeovers and proposed mergers are allowed to be decided by the companies' shareholders. However, when too much power would be placed in the hands of one organisation, company, or person, the government will insist on a Monopolies and Mergers Commission appraisal. If the commission believes it is against the public interest for a takeover or merger to proceed, then it will prohibit any agreement between the companies or organisations involved.

Financial Services Act 1986.   The Director General of Fair Trading is required to consider the implications for competition of rules, regulations, guidance, and other arrangements and practices of the regulatory bodies, investment exchanges, and clearing houses. The Director General must report to the Secretary of State for Trade and Industry whenever a significant or potentially significant effect on competition has been identified. This legislation is for the protection of investors, and the Secretary of State may refuse or revoke recognition of the organisation or require it to make alterations to its activities.

Anticompetitive Practices.   The Director General of Fair Trading can investigate any business practice, whether in the public or private sector, which may restrict, distort, or prevent competition in the production, supply, or acquisition of goods or services in Britain. The Secretary of State has power to take remedial action.

Restrictive Trade Practices Act 1976.   If two or more people who are party to the supply of goods or services in Britain accept some limitation on their freedom to make their own decisions about matters such as prices or conditions of sale, the Director General of Fair Trading must be notified and such an agreement must be registered. Once an agreement has been registered, the Director General is under a general duty to refer it to the Restrictive Practices Court, and the court must declare the restrictions in it contrary to the public interest unless the parties can satisfy the court that the public interest is not an issue. The vast majority of agreements never reach the court because parties elect to give up the restrictions rather than go through such a procedure.

European Community.   The objective of the European Community's competition policy is to ensure that there is free and fair competition in trade between member states, and that the government trade barriers which the **Treaty of Rome** seeks to dismantle are not replaced by private barriers which fragment the Common Market.

The European Commission has powers to investigate and terminate alleged infringements and impose fines. The Treaty of Rome prohibits agreements or concertive practices which may affect trade between member states and aims to prevent restriction or distortion of competition within the Common Market.[2]

Most countries have similar legislation. For example, in America the Sherman Antitrust Act prevents monopolistic situations; the Clayton Act specifically prohibits price discrimination; and the Federal Trade Commission Act broadly prohibits unfair methods of competition and empowers the Federal Trade Commission to work with the Department of Justice to enforce the provisions of the Clayton Act. The Wheeler-Lea Act essentially makes unfair and deceptive acts or practices unlawful, regardless of whether they injure competition. The Robinson-Patman Act deals with discriminatory price differentials.[3]

■ Consumer Protection Legislation

The second category of regulatory laws, *consumer protection legislation,* is not a recent development. However, consumer protection laws mushroomed in the mid-1960s and early 1970s. A number of them deal with consumer safety, while others relate to the sale of various hazardous products such as flammable fabrics and toys that might injure children. The Fair Trading Act (1973) provides a machinery—headed by the Director General of Fair Trading—for continuous review of consumer affairs, for actions dealing with trading practices which unfairly affect consumers' interests, for action against persistent offenders under existing law, and for the negotiation of self-regulatory codes of practice to raise trading standards.

Consumers' interests with regard to the purity of food, the description and performance of goods and services, and pricing information are safeguarded by the Food Act (1984), the Medicines Act (1968), the Misrepresentations Act (1967), the Trade Descriptions Act (1968), the Prices Act (1974), the Unfair Contract Terms Act (1977), the Sale of Goods Act (1979), the Supply of Goods and Services Act (1982), and the Consumer Protection Act (1987). The marking and accuracy of quantities are regulated by the Weights and Measures Act (1985). The Consumer Credit Act of 1974 provides comprehensive protection for consumers who enter into credit or hire transactions. The Consumer Protection Act of 1987 implements a harmonised European Community code of civil law covering product liability, creates a general criminal offence of supplying unsafe consumer goods, makes it an offence to give any misleading price indication, and consolidates the powers provided under safety-related acts. The Financial Services Act (1986) offers greater protection to investors by establishing a new regulatory framework for the industry.

In addition, consumer advice and information are provided to the general public at the local level by the Citizens' Advice Bureaux and the Trading Standards or Consumer Protection departments of local authorities, and in some areas by specialist Consumer Advice Centres. The independent, non-statutory National Consumer Council, which receives government finance, ensures that consumers' views are made known to those in government and industry. Nationalised industries have consumer councils whose members investigate questions of concern to the consumer, and many trade associations in industry and commerce have established codes of practice. In addition, several private organisations work to further con-

2. *Britain 1990: An Official Handbook* (London: Central Office of Information, 1990).

3. Joseph Plummer, "The Concept of Application of Life Style Segmentation," *Journal of Marketing,* January 1974, p. 34.

sumer interests, the largest of which is the **Consumers' Association**, funded by the subscriptions of its membership of over one million people. The Association conducts an extensive programme of comparative testing of goods and investigation of services; its views and test reports are published in its monthly magazines and other publications.

■ **Interpreting Laws**

Laws certainly have the potential to influence marketing activities, but the actual effects of the laws are determined by how marketers and the courts interpret them. Laws seem to be quite specific because they contain many complex clauses and subclauses. In reality, however, many laws and regulations are stated in vague terms that force marketers to rely on legal advice rather than their own understanding and common sense. Because of this vagueness, some organisations attempt to gauge the limits of certain laws by operating in a legally questionable way to see how far they can go with certain practices before being prosecuted. Other marketers, however, interpret regulations and statutes very conservatively and strictly to avoid violating a vague law.

Although court rulings directly affect businesses accused of specific violations, they also have a broader, less direct impact on other businesses. When marketers try to interpret laws in relation to specific marketing practices, they often analyse recent court decisions, both to understand better what the law is intended to do and to gain a clearer sense of how the courts are likely to interpret it in the future.

REGULATORY FORCES

Interpretation alone does not determine the effectiveness of laws and regulations; the level of enforcement by regulatory agencies is also significant. Some regulatory agencies are created and administered by government units; others are sponsored by non-governmental sources.

■ **U.K. Government**

Ministry of Agriculture, Fisheries and Food.   This ministry develops and controls policies for agriculture, horticulture, fisheries and food, and has responsibilities for environmental and rural issues and food policies.

Department of Employment.   The department controls the Employment Service, employment policy and legislation; training policy and legislation; health and safety at work; industrial relations; wages councils; equal opportunities; small firms and tourism; statistics on labour and industrial matters for the U.K.; the Careers Service; and international representation on employment matters.

Department of Energy.   This department controls policies for all forms of energy, including its efficient use and the development of new sources, as well as the government's relations with the energy industries.

Department of the Environment.   The DoE controls policies for planning and regional development, local government, new towns, housing, construction, inner city matters, environmental protection, water, the countryside, sports and recreation, conservation, historic buildings and ancient monuments, and the Property Services Agency.

Export Credit Guarantee Department. The department is responsible for the provision of insurance for exporters against the risk of not being paid for goods and services, access to bank finance for exports, and insurance cover for new investment overseas.

Central Statistical Office. The Office prepares and interprets statistics needed for central economic and social policies and management; it co-ordinates the statistical work of other departments.

Department of Trade and Industry. The DTI controls industrial and commercial policy, promotion of enterprise and competition in the U.K. and abroad, investor and consumer protection. Specific responsibilities include industrial innovation policy; regional industrial policy; business development, management development, business/education links; international trade policy; commercial relations and export promotions; competition policy; company law; insolvency; consumer protection and safety; radio regulations; and intellectual property.

Department of Transport. This department is responsible for land, sea, and air transport; sponsorship of the nationalised transport authorities and British Rail; domestic and international civil aviation; international transport agreements; shipping and ports industries; navigation issues, HM Coastguard, and marine pollution; motorways and trunk roads; road safety; and oversight of local authority transport.

■ **Local Authorities**

The functions of the U.K. local authorities are far-reaching; some are primary duties whereas others are purely discretionary. Broadly speaking, functions are divided between county and district councils on the basis that the county council is responsible for matters requiring planning and administration over wide areas or requiring the support of substantial resources, while district councils on the whole administer functions of a more local significance. English county councils are generally responsible for strategic planning, transport planning, highways, traffic regulations, local education, consumer protection, refuse disposal, police, the fire service, libraries and the personal social services. District councils are responsible for environmental health, housing decisions, and most planning applications, and refuse collection. They may also provide some museums, art galleries and parks. At both county and district council level, arrangements depend on local agreements.

Most countries in Europe have a similar structure: resource-hungry issues with wide-ranging social and political consequences are controlled centrally. Planning and service provision within the community are viewed as being better controlled at the local level by the communities which themselves will experience the advantages or problems resulting from such decision-making. The European Community aims to establish commonly accepted parameters for planning, service provision and regulation, and a framework to assist in inter- and intra-country disputes.

■ **Non-governmental Regulatory Forces**

In the absence of governmental regulatory forces and in an attempt to prevent government intervention, some businesses try to regulate themselves. For example, many newspapers have voluntarily banned advertisements for telephone chat services which were being used for undesirable activities, not technically illegal. Trade associations in a number of industries have developed self-regulatory programmes. Even though these programmes are not a direct outgrowth of laws, many were established to stop or stall the development of laws and governmental regulatory groups that would regulate the associations' marketing practices. Sometimes trade associations establish codes of ethics by which their members must abide or risk censure by other members, or even exclusion from the programme. For example, many cigarette manufacturers have agreed, through a code of ethics, not to advertise their products to children and teenagers. The IBA Code of Advertising Standards and Practice aimed to keep broadcast advertising "legal, decent, honest and truthful".[4]

Self-regulatory programmes have several advantages over governmental laws and regulatory agencies. They are usually less expensive to establish and implement, and their guidelines are generally more realistic and operational. In addition, effective industry self-regulatory programmes reduce the need to expand government bureaucracy. However, these programmes also have several limitations. When a trade association creates a set of industry guidelines for its members, non-member firms do not have to abide by them. In addition, many self-regulatory programmes lack the tools or the authority to enforce guidelines. Finally, guidelines in self-regulatory programmes are often less strict than those established by government agencies.

■ **Deregulation**

Governments can drastically alter the environment for companies. In the U.K. the privatisation of the public utilities created new terms and conditions for their suppliers and subcontractors. The sales of Jaguar and Rover in the car industry and of British Airways created commercially lean companies which suddenly had new impetus to be major competitors in their industries. The expected deregulation in the European Community by 1992 has created opportunities across borders and also new threats. Car manufacturers were previously able to restrict certain models to specific countries. They placed rigorous controls on their dealers (forbidding them to retail cars produced by rival manufacturers in the same showroom or on the same site), many of which will now be swept aside.

SOCIETAL FORCES

Societal forces comprise the structure and dynamics of individuals and groups and the issues that engage them. Society becomes concerned about marketers' activities when those activities have questionable or negative consequences. For example, in recent times well-publicised incidents of unethical behaviour by marketers and others have perturbed and even angered consumers. Chapter 20 therefore takes a detailed look at marketing ethics and social responsibility. When marketers do a good job of satisfying society, praise or positive evaluation rarely follows. Society expects marketers to provide a high standard of living and to protect the general quality of life. In this section we examine some of society's expectations, the vehicles used to express those expectations, and the problems and opportunities that marketers experience as they try to deal with society's often contradictory wishes.

■ **Living Standards and Quality of Life**

In our society, most people want more than just the bare necessities; they want to achieve the highest standard of living possible. For example, we want our homes to offer not only protection from the elements, but also comfort and a satisfactory

4. *The IBA Code of Advertising Standards and Practice* (London: Independent Broadcasting Authority, December 1977), p. 3.

FIGURE 2.1

Environmentally concerned.
National Power expresses its concern for the environment by sponsoring the Green Awards for Marketing and the Environment.

SOURCE: Marketor's Livery Company

lifestyle. We want food that is safe and readily available, in many varieties and in easily prepared forms. We use our clothing to protect our bodies, but most of us want a variety of clothing for adornment and to project an "image" to others. We want vehicles that provide rapid, safe, and efficient travel. We desire communication systems that give us information from around the globe—a desire apparent in the popularity of products such as facsimile machines and the twenty-four-hour news coverage provided by the cable and satellite television networks. In addition, we want sophisticated medical services that prolong our life and improve our physical appearance. We also expect our education to equip us both to acquire and to enjoy a higher standard of living.

Our society's high material standard of living is not enough. We also desire a high degree of quality in our lives. Since we do not want to spend all our waking hours working, we seek leisure time for hobbies, voluntary work, recreation, and relaxation. The quality of life is enhanced by leisure time, clean air and water, an unlittered earth, conservation of wildlife and natural resources, and security from radiation and poisonous substances. A number of companies are expressing concerns about the quality of life. National Power, for example, sends a clear message in Figure 2.1 that it is committed to environmental excellence.

Because of these desires, consumers have become increasingly concerned about environmental issues such as pollution, waste disposal, and the so-called greenhouse effect. Society's concerns have created both threats and opportunities for marketers. For example, one of society's biggest environmental problems is lack of space for refuse disposal, especially of plastic materials such as disposable nappies and Styrofoam packaging, which are not biodegradable. In the United States, several cities have passed laws banning the use of all plastic packaging in stores and restaurants, and governments around the world are considering similar legislation. This trend has created problems for McDonald's and other fast food restaurants, which will have to develop packaging alternatives. Other firms, however, see such environmental problems as opportunities. Procter & Gamble, for example, markets cleaners in bottles made of recycled plastic.[5] Environmentally responsible, or "green", marketing is increasingly extensive. For example, the German companies Audi, Volkswagen, and BMW are manufacturing "cleaner" cars, which do not pollute the atmosphere as much as traditional ones. Italian chemical companies are investing billions to reduce toxic wastes from their plants, and British industry is investing equally large sums to scrub acid emissions from power stations and to treat sewage more effectively.[6] Marketing Update 2.1 provides additional details on how Tesco and other firms are using "green" marketing to satisfy customers' concerns about the environment.

As these examples illustrate, changes in the forces of the marketing environment require careful monitoring and often demand a clear and effective response. Since marketing activities are a vital part of the total business structure, marketers have a responsibility to help provide what members of society want and to minimise what they do not want.

■ **Consumer Movement Forces**

The **consumer movement** is a diverse collection of independent individuals, groups, and organisations who seek to protect the rights of consumers. The main issues pursued by the consumer movement fall into three categories: environmental protection, product performance and safety, and information disclosure. The movement's major forces are individual consumer advocates, consumer organisations and other interest groups, consumer education, and consumer laws.

Consumer advocates, such as David Tench, take it upon themselves to protect the rights of consumers. They band together into consumer organisations, either voluntarily or under government sponsorship. Some organisations, such as the Consumers' Association, operate nationally, whereas others are active at local levels. They inform and organise other consumers, raise issues, help businesses develop consumer-orientated programmes, and pressure legislators to enact consumer protection laws. Some consumer advocates and organisations encourage consumers to boycott products and businesses to which they have objections.

Educating consumers to make wiser purchasing decisions is perhaps one of the most far-reaching aspects of the consumer movement. Increasingly, consumer education is becoming a part of school curricula and adult education courses. These courses cover many topics—for instance, what major factors should be considered when buying specific products, such as insurance, housing, cars, appliances and furniture, clothes, and food. The courses also cover the provisions of certain consumer protection laws and provide the sources of information that can help individuals become knowledgeable consumers.

5. Brian Bremner, "A New Sales Pitch: The Environment," *Business Week*, 24 July 1989, p. 50.

6. Robin Knight, with Eleni Dimmler, "The Greening of Europe's Industries," *U.S. News & World Report*, 5 June 1989, pp. 45–46.

GROCERY RETAILERS FOCUS ON "GREEN" MARKETING

With a new ecological awareness, consumers today want their environment protected from pollutants, toxins, and exploitation. Environmental, or "green", marketing is a way for marketers to appeal to consumers' environmental concerns. "Green" products are safer for the environment and include items such as biodegradable bin liners and nappies, tissues made from recycled paper, and detergent that is free of phosphates. By effectively marketing such products, a company can improve its bottom line as well as the biosphere.

The media have bombarded the public with information on the desperate state of European beaches, acid rain levels, oil spillages in the Mersey or the damage done to Alaskan waters by the eleven million gallons of oil spilled by the *Exxon Valdez*. Taking note of the crises and disasters, consumers have shown an interest in products that do not endanger the environment in any way.

Tesco was among the first businesses to embrace the notion of green marketing. Tesco is an influential leader in the retail industry and wants to offer shoppers the option of purchasing environmentally safe products instead of ones that contribute to pollution and landfill problems. The company's executives want to stock merchandise with packaging that is better for the environment in three respects—manufacturing, use, and disposal.

Through advertisements, Tesco announced that it was seeking "safe" products to sell in its stores.

A survey found that many people were willing to pay extra for a product packaged with recyclable or biodegradable materials. More than 53 percent stated that they had not bought a particular product in the last year because they were worried about that product's effect on the environment. As Tesco executives see it, environmental concerns may loom so large for consumers that they will affect everyday decisions. The company has, however, been accused by environmental groups of being one of many companies which have "jumped on the green band-wagon" in order to charge higher prices for products central to consumers' grocery purchasing. Safeway has adopted a lower profile. It has been retailing environmentally friendly products for over a decade but has not used publicity to promote its caring approach in the manner recently adopted by Tesco and other retailers. Irrespective of the approach adopted, both Safeway and Tesco—along with their suppliers— have responded to the "greening" of society.

SOURCES: Christy Fisher and Judith Graham, "Wal-Mart Throws 'Green' Gauntlet," *Advertising Age,* 21 Aug. 1989, pp. 1, 66; Jeremy Main, "Here Comes the Big New Cleanup," *Fortune,* 21 Nov. 1988, pp. 102–103, 106, 110, 112, 114, 118; Kevin Maney, "Companies Make Products Nicer to Nature," *USA Today,* 23 Aug. 1989, pp. 1B–2B; Bill Britt, "Safeway Dons Green Mantle," *Marketing,* 26 April 1990, p. 2; and Safeway management.

ECONOMIC AND COMPETITIVE FORCES

The economic and competitive forces in the marketing environment influence both marketers' and customers' decisions and activities. In this section, we first examine the effects of general economic conditions. We also focus on buying power, willingness to spend, spending patterns, and competition. Then we look at competitive forces, including types of competitive structures, competitive tools, and methods for monitoring competitive behaviour.

■ General Economic Conditions

The overall state of the economy fluctuates in all countries. These changes in general economic conditions affect (and are affected by) the forces of supply and demand, buying power, willingness to spend, consumer expenditure levels, and the intensity of competitive behaviour. Therefore, current economic conditions and changes in the economy have a broad impact on the success of organisations' marketing strategies. Fluctuations in the economy follow a general pattern often referred to as the business cycle. In the traditional view, the business cycle consists of four stages: prosperity, recession, depression, and recovery.

During **prosperity**, unemployment is low and total income is relatively high. Assuming a low inflation rate, this combination causes buying power to be high. To the extent that the economic outlook remains prosperous, consumers generally are willing to buy. In the prosperity stage, marketers often expand their product mixes (product, distribution, promotion, and price) to take advantage of the increased buying power. They sometimes capture a larger market share by intensifying distribution and promotion efforts.

Because unemployment rises during a **recession**, total buying power declines. The pessimism that accompanies a recession often stifles both consumer and business spending. As buying power decreases, many consumers become more price- and value-conscious; they look for products that are basic and functional. For instance, people ordinarily reduce their consumption of more expensive convenience foods and strive to save money by growing and preparing more of their own food. Individuals buy fewer durable goods and more repair and do-it-yourself products. During a recession, some firms make the mistake of drastically reducing their marketing efforts and thus damage their ability to survive. Obviously, marketers should consider some revision of their marketing activities during a recessionary period. Because consumers are more concerned about the functional value of products, a company must focus its marketing research on determining precisely what product functions buyers want and then make sure that these functions become part of its products. Promotional efforts should emphasise value and utility.

A **depression** is a period in which unemployment is extremely high, wages are very low, total disposable income is at a minimum, and consumers lack confidence in the economy. Governments have used both monetary and fiscal policies to offset the effects of recession and depression. Monetary policies are employed to control the money supply, which in turn affects spending, saving, and investment by both individuals and businesses. Through the establishment of fiscal policies, the government is able to influence the amount of savings and expenditures by adjusting the tax structure and by changing the levels of government spending. Some economic experts believe that the effective use of monetary and fiscal policies can completely eliminate depressions from the business cycle.

Recovery is the stage of the business cycle in which the economy moves from depression or recession to prosperity. During this period, the high unemployment rate begins to decline, total disposable income increases, and the economic gloom that lessened consumers' willingness to buy subsides. Both the ability and the willingness to buy rise. Marketers face some problems during recovery—for example, the difficulty of ascertaining how quickly prosperity will return and of forecasting the level of prosperity that will be attained. In this stage, marketers should maintain as much flexibility in their marketing strategies as possible to be able to make the needed adjustments as the economy moves from recession to prosperity.

■ Consumer Demand and Spending Behaviour

Marketers must understand the factors that determine whether, what, where, and when people buy. In Chapters 4 and 5 we look at behavioural factors underlying these choices, but here we focus on the economic components: buying power, willingness to purchase, and spending patterns.

Buying Power. The strength of a person's **buying power** depends on the size of the resources that enable the individual to purchase and on the state of the economy. The resources that make up buying power are goods, services, and financial holdings. Fluctuations of the business cycle affect buying power because they influence price levels and interest rates. For example, during inflationary periods, when prices are rising, buying power decreases because more pounds or ECUs are required to buy products. Tables 2.1 and 2.2 compare 1980 and 1990 prices for selected products.

The major financial sources of buying power are income, credit, and wealth. From an individual's viewpoint, **income** is the amount of money received through wages, rents, investments, pensions, and subsidy payments for a given period, such as a month or a year. Normally, this money is allocated among taxes, spending for goods and services, and savings. The average annual family income in the United States is approximately $25,986; in the United Kingdom it is £15,118.[7] However, because of the differences in people's educational levels, abilities, occupations, and wealth, income is not equally distributed in any country.

Marketers are most interested in the amount of money that is left after payment of taxes. After-tax income is called **disposable income** and is used for spending or saving. Because disposable income is a ready source of buying power, the total amount available in a nation is important to marketers. Several factors affect the size of total disposable income. One, of course, is the total amount of income. Total national income is affected by wage levels, rate of unemployment, interest rates, and dividend rates. These factors in turn affect the size of disposable income. Because disposable income is the income left after taxes are paid, the number of taxes and their amount directly affect the size of total disposable income. When taxes rise, disposable income declines; when taxes fall, disposable income increases.

Disposable income that is available for spending and saving after an individual has purchased the basic necessities of food, clothing, and shelter is called **discretionary income**. People use discretionary income to purchase entertainment, holidays, cars, education, pets and pet supplies, furniture, appliances, and so on. Changes in total

7. Judith Waldrop, "Inside America's Households," *American Demographics*, Mar. 1989, pp. 22–23; *National Income and Expenditure Survey* (London: Central Statistical Office, 1990).

TABLE 2.1   *A comparison of 1980 and 1990 prices for selected grocery products*

PRODUCT	AVERAGE[a] PRICE (PENCE)		PRODUCT	AVERAGE[a] PRICE (PENCE)	
	1990	1980		1990	1980
Beef: home-killed			**Butter**		
Best beef mince	159	92	Home produced, per 250 g	61	43
Brisket (without bone)	192	111	New Zealand, per 250 g	58	42
Rump steak[b]	376	235	Danish, per 250 g	71	46
Stewing steak	181	113	**Lard, per 250 g**	17	15
Lamb: home-killed			**Cheese**		
Loin (with bone)	274	152	Cheddar type	150	94
Shoulder (with bone)	132	98	**Eggs**		
Leg (with bone)	222	145	Size 2 (65–70 g), per dozen	124	71
Lamb: imported (frozen)			Size 4 (55–60 g), per dozen	106	65
Loin (with bone)	192	111	**Milk**		
Shoulder (with bone)	92	76	Pasteurised, per pint	30	17
Leg (with bone)	177	117	**Coffee**		
Pork: home-killed			Pure, instant, per 100 g	131	102
Leg (foot off)	142	92	**Sugar**		
Belly[b]	108	67	Granulated, per kg	59	35
Loin (with bone)	176	111	**Fresh vegetables**		
Shoulder (with bone)	152	138	Potatoes, old loose		
Bacon			White	19	7
Streaky[b]	134	82	Red	19	8
Gammon[b]	211	126	Potatoes, new loose	30	13
Back, not vacuum packed	205	117	Tomatoes	69	52
Ham (not shoulder), per 4 oz	74	163	Cabbage, greens	35	13
Sausages			Cabbage, hearted	26	12
Pork	101	61	Cauliflower, each	60	21
Beef	97	54	Carrots	40	13
Pork luncheon meat, 12 oz can	53	38	Onions	34	16
Corned beef, 12 oz can	91	84	Mushrooms, per 4 oz	32	16
Chicken: roasting, oven ready			**Fresh fruit**		
Fresh or chilled 3 lb	98	52	Apples, cooking	44	22
Fresh and smoked fish			Apples, dessert	46	24
Cod fillets	249	107	Pears, dessert	58	28
Haddock fillets	277	116	Oranges, each	20	22
Bread			Bananas	53	27
White loaf, sliced, 800 g	50	34			
White loaf, unwrapped, 800 g	64	37			
White loaf, unsliced, 400 g	42	24			
Brown loaf, sliced, small	43	25			

[a] Per lb unless otherwise stated.
[b] Or Scottish equivalent.

SOURCE: *Employment Gazette,* Central Statistical Office, June 1980 and July 1990. Reprinted by permission of the Controller of Her Majesty's Stationery Office.

TABLE 2.2 *U.K. retail prices: Detailed figures for various groups, sub-groups and sections for 15 May 1990*

	INDEX (JAN. 1987 = 100)	PERCENTAGE CHANGE OVER (MONTHS) 1	PERCENTAGE CHANGE OVER (MONTHS) 12		INDEX (JAN. 1987 = 100)	PERCENTAGE CHANGE OVER (MONTHS) 1	PERCENTAGE CHANGE OVER (MONTHS) 12
ALL ITEMS	126.2	0.9	9.7	FOOD (CONTINUED)			
Food and catering	121.2	1.1	8.7	Coffee and other hot drinks	90.7		–6
Alcohol and tobacco	120.9	1.9	10.0	Soft drinks	136.6		11
Housing and household				Sugar and preserves	123.6		6
expenditure	139.8	0.9	15.2	Sweets and chocolates	108.3		4
Personal expenditure	117.6	0.5	5.4	Potatoes	126.5		15
Travel and leisure	118.6	0.5	4.7	of which, unprocessed			
All items excluding seasonal				potatoes	135.9		19
food	126.3	1.0	9.7	Vegetables	122.3		11
All items excluding food	127.4	0.9	9.9	of which, other fresh			
Seasonal food	123.6	0.2	12.5	vegetables	121.5		13
Food excluding seasonal	119.4	1.2	8.2	Fruit	121.6		11
All items excluding housing	118.8	1.0	6.7	of which, fresh fruit	124.2		11
All items excluding mortgage				Other foods	119.0		8
interest	122.1	0.8	8.1	CATERING	125.0	0.9	8.1
Consumer durables	111.6	0.5	3.8	Restaurant meals	125.9		8
FOOD	120.1	1.1	8.9	Canteen meals	124.7		9
Bread	119.8		6	Take-aways and snacks	123.7		8
Cereals	123.6		7	ALCOHOLIC DRINK	123.8	1.9	10.6
Biscuits and cakes	119.9		8	Beer	125.9		11
Beef	125.6		4	on sales	126.7		11
Lamb	119.4		3	off sales	120.0		8
of which, home-killed lamb	122.7		2	Wines and spirits	120.8		10
Pork	125.4		14	on sales	124.5		11
Bacon	127.0		19	off sales	118.2		9
Poultry	114.8		13	TOBACCO	114.8	2.1	8.5
Other meat	116.4		12	Cigarettes	115.1		8
Fish	116.3		10	Tobacco	112.9		9
of which, fresh fish	126.1		18	HOUSING	166.7	0.8	23.8
Butter	119.4		3	Rent	136.9		12
Oil and fats	116.0		9	Mortgage interest payments	211.5		33
Cheese	120.0		8	Rates and community			
Eggs	117.7		12	charges	171.7		34
Milk, fresh	121.4		8	Water and other payments	148.4		13
Milk products	124.3		7	Repairs and maintenance			
Tea	130.1		19	charges	122.7		8

discretionary income affect the sales of these products—especially cars, furniture, large appliances, and other costly durable goods.

Credit enables people to spend future income now or in the near future. However, credit increases current buying power at the expense of future buying power. Several factors determine whether consumers use or forego credit. First, credit

TABLE 2.2 *continued*

	INDEX (JAN. 1987 = 100)	PERCENTAGE CHANGE OVER (MONTHS)			INDEX (JAN. 1987 = 100)	PERCENTAGE CHANGE OVER (MONTHS)	
		1	12			1	12
HOUSING (continued)				**MOTORING EXPENDITURE**	119.4	0.5	3.6
Do-it-yourself materials	120.9		8	Purchase of motor vehicles	116.8		1
Dwelling insurance and ground rent	173.5		6	Maintenance of motor vehicles	126.8		10
FUEL AND LIGHT	**114.3**	**2.3**	**7.4**	Petrol and oil	116.3		5
Coal and solid fuels	100.2		2	Vehicles tax and insurance	126.3		3
Electricity	121.1		8	**FARES AND OTHER TRAVEL COSTS**	**122.4**	**0.5**	**6.8**
Gas	111.5		8	Rail fares	128.2		9
Oil and other fuels	104.3		11	Bus and coach fares	125.8		5
HOUSEHOLD GOODS	**115.1**	**0.5**	**4.7**	Other travel costs	115.3		6
Furniture	116.3		5	**LEISURE GOODS**	**112.2**	**0.6**	**4.7**
Furnishings	116.6		4	Audio-visual equipment	89.9		–1
Electrical appliances	106.2		1	Records and tapes	100.0		2
Other household equipment	119.0		7	Toys, photographic and sports goods	113.8		5
Household consumables	123.3		6	Books and newspapers	130.3		8
Pet care	108.8		5	Gardening products	123.2		7
HOUSEHOLD SERVICES	**117.9**	**0.7**	**5.5**	**LEISURE SERVICES**	**123.4**	**0.5**	**8.0**
Postage	112.6		6	Television licences and rentals	110.1		6
Telephones, telemessages, etc.	106.1		5	Entertainment and other recreation	132.5		9
Domestic services	127.0		9				
Fees and subscriptions	125.7		4				
CLOTHING AND FOOTWEAR	**115.6**	**0.5**	**4.6**				
Men's outerwear	116.7		6				
Women's outerwear	111.4		3				
Children's outerwear	117.6		2				
Other clothing	118.8		6				
Footwear	116.5		6				
PERSONAL GOODS AND SERVICES	**121.7**	**0.5**	**7.0**				
Personal articles	107.2		3				
Chemists goods	124.7		9				
Personal services	132.8		9				

NOTES: 1 Indices are given to one decimal place to provide as much information as is available, but precision is greater at higher levels of aggregation, that is at sub-group and group levels.
2 The structure of the published components of the index was recast in February 1987.

SOURCE: *Employment Gazette,* Central Statistical Office, July 1990. Reprinted by permission of Her Britannia Majesty's Stationery Office.

must be available to them. Interest rates, too, affect consumers' decisions to use credit, especially for expensive purchases such as homes, appliances, and cars. When credit charges are high, consumers are more likely to delay buying expensive items. Use of credit is also affected by credit terms, such as the size of the down payment and the amount and number of monthly payments.

A person can have a high income and very little wealth. It is also possible, but not likely, for a person to have great wealth but not much income. **Wealth** is the accumulation of past income, natural resources, and financial resources. It may exist in many forms, including cash, securities, savings accounts, jewellery, antiques, and property. Like income, wealth is unevenly distributed. The significance of wealth to marketers is that as people become wealthier they gain buying power in three ways: they can use their wealth to make current purchases, to generate income, and to acquire large amounts of credit.

Buying power information is available from government sources, trade associations, and research agencies. One of the most current and comprehensive sources of buying power data is the Central Statistical Office's *National Income and Expenditure Survey*. Table 2.3 shows this survey's findings on effective buying income data and buying power data.

Income, wealth, and credit equip consumers to purchase goods and services. Marketing managers should be aware of current levels and expected changes in buying power in their own markets because buying power directly affects the types and quantities of goods and services that consumers purchase, as we see later in our discussion of spending patterns. Just because consumers have buying power, however, does not mean that they will buy. Consumers must also be willing to use their buying power.

Consumers' Willingness to Spend. People's **willingness to spend** is, to some degree, related to their ability to buy. That is, people are sometimes more willing to buy if they have the buying power. However, a number of other elements also influence willingness to spend. Some elements affect specific products; others influence spending in general. A product's absolute price and its price relative to the price of substitute products influence almost all of us. The amount of satisfaction currently received or expected in the future from a product already owned may also influence consumers' desire to buy other products. Satisfaction depends not only on the quality of the functional performance of the currently owned product, but also on numerous psychological and social forces.

Factors that affect consumers' general willingness to spend are expectations about future employment, income levels, prices, family size, and general economic conditions. If people are unsure whether or how long they will be employed, willingness to buy ordinarily declines. Willingness to spend may increase if people are reasonably certain of higher incomes in the future. Expectations of rising prices in the near future may also increase the willingness to spend in the present. For a given level of buying power, the larger the family, the greater the willingness to buy. One of the reasons for this relationship is that as the size of a family increases, a larger amount of money must be spent to provide the basic necessities of life to sustain the family members. Finally, perceptions of future economic conditions influence willingness to buy. For example, in the late 1980s, rising short-term interest rates cooled consumers' willingness to spend.

Consumer Spending Patterns. Marketers must be aware of the factors that influence consumers' ability and willingness to spend, but they should also analyse how consumers actually spend their disposable incomes. Marketers obtain this information by studying consumer spending patterns. **Consumer spending patterns** indicate the relative proportions of annual family expenditures or the actual amount of money spent on certain kinds of goods and services. Families are usually categorised by one of several characteristics, including family income, age of the household head, geographic area, and family life cycle. There are two types of spending patterns: comprehensive and product-specific.

The percentages of family income allotted to annual expenditures for general classes of goods and services constitute **comprehensive spending patterns**. Comprehensive spending patterns or the data to develop them are available in government publications and in reports produced by the major market research companies and by trade associations. In Table 2.3, comprehensive spending patterns are classified by the life cycle of the family.

Product-specific spending patterns indicate the annual monetary amounts families spend for specific products within a general product class. Information sources used to construct product-specific spending patterns include government publications, trade publications, and consumer surveys.

A marketer uses spending patterns to analyse general trends in the ways that families spend their incomes for various kinds of products. Analyses of spending patterns yield information that a marketer can use to gain perspective and background for decision-making. However, spending patterns reflect only general trends and thus should not be used as the sole basis for making specific decisions.

■ Assessment of Competitive Forces

Few firms, if any, operate free of competition. Broadly speaking, all firms compete with each other for consumers' money. From a more practical viewpoint, however, a business generally defines **competition** as those firms that market products that are similar to, or can be substituted for, its products in the same geographic area. For example, a local Tesco supermarket manager views all grocery stores in town as competitors but almost never thinks of other types of local or out-of-town stores (DIY or electrical, for example) as competitors. In this section, we consider the types of competitive structure and the importance of monitoring competitors.

Types of Competitive Structure. The number of firms that control the supply of a product may affect the strength of competition. When only one or a few firms control supply, competitive factors will exert a different sort of influence on marketing activities than when there are many competitors. Table 2.4 presents four general types of competitive structure: monopoly, oligopoly, monopolistic competition, and perfect competition.

A **monopoly** exists when a firm turns out a product that has no close substitutes. Because the organisation has no competitors, it completely controls the supply of the product and, as a single seller, can erect barriers to potential competitors. In reality, the monopolies that survive today are some utilities, such as telephone, electricity, and cable companies, which are heavily regulated. These monopolies are tolerated because of the tremendous financial resources needed to develop and operate them; few organisations can obtain the resources to mount any competition against a local electricity producer, for example.

An **oligopoly** exists when a few sellers control the supply of a large proportion of a product. In this case, each seller must consider the reactions of other sellers to changes in marketing activities. Products facing oligopolistic competition may be homogeneous, such as aluminium, or differentiated, such as cigarettes and cars. Usually, barriers of some sort make it difficult to enter the market and compete with

TABLE 2.3 *Pattern of U.K. expenditure per household analysed by level of income*

	GROSS NORMAL WEEKLY INCOME OF HOUSEHOLD					
	Lowest 20%	2nd quintile group	3rd quintile group	4th quintile group	Highest 20%	All households
Total number of households	1,453	1,453	1,453	1,453	1,453	7,265
Total number of persons	2,181	3,131	3,908	4,352	4,708	18,280
Total number of adults	1,775	2,493	2,764	3,089	3,519	13,640
AVERAGE NUMBER OF PERSONS PER HOUSEHOLD						
All persons	1.501	2.155	2.690	2.995	3.240	2.516
Males	0.585	1.014	1.374	1.502	1.668	1.229
Females	0.916	1.140	1.316	1.493	1.573	1.288
Adults	1.222	1.716	1.902	2.126	2.422	1.877
Persons under 65	0.571	1.032	1.628	1.989	2.299	1.504
Persons 65 and over	0.651	0.684	0.275	0.137	0.123	0.374
Children	0.279	0.439	0.787	0.869	0.818	0.639
Children under 2	0.054	0.061	0.099	0.083	0.067	0.073
Children 2 and under 5	0.075	0.075	0.161	0.142	0.103	0.111
Children 5 and under 18	0.151	0.303	0.527	0.644	0.648	0.455
Persons working	0.120	0.538	1.272	1.765	2.145	1.168
Persons not working	1.381	1.617	1.418	1.231	1.096	1.348
Men 65 and over	0.712	0.743	0.312	0.149	0.117	0.406
Others	0.668	0.875	1.106	1.082	0.979	0.942
Average age of head of household	61	57	47	44	45	51
	NUMBER OF HOUSEHOLDS					
HOUSING BY TYPE OF TENURE						
Rented unfurnished	1,039	573	318	194	77	2,201
Local authority	853	469	269	155	60	1,806
Housing association	79	37	12	11	6	145
Other	107	67	37	28	11	250
Rented furnished	63	45	48	24	27	207
Rent-free	22	41	32	18	14	127
Owner-occupied	329	794	1,055	1,217	1,335	4,730
In process of purchase	45	235	667	958	1,094	2,999
Owned outright	284	559	388	259	241	1,731

[a] This information is available on a regional basis.
[b] Percentage standard error.

oligopolies. For example, because of the enormous financial outlay required, few companies or individuals could afford to enter the oil-refining or steel-producing industries. Moreover, some industries demand special technical or marketing skills that block the entry of many potential competitors.

Monopolistic competition exists when a firm with many potential competitors attempts to develop a differential marketing strategy to establish its own market

TABLE 2.3 *continued*

COMMODITY OR SERVICE GROUP TOTALS[a]	AVERAGE WEEKLY HOUSEHOLD EXPENDITURE (£)					
	Lowest 20%	2nd quintile group	3rd quintile group	4th quintile group	Highest 20%	All households
Housing:						
Gross	25.12 (1.3)[b]	31.37 (1.5)[b]	36.48 (2.0)[b]	40.59 (1.7)[b]	61.94 (3.7)[b]	39.10 (1.4)[b]
Net	12.87 (2.7)	28.13 (1.8)	35.82 (2.1)	40.39 (1.7)	61.84 (3.7)	35.81 (1.5)
Fuel	8.15 (1.7)	9.41 (1.8)	10.66 (2.2)	10.86 (1.6)	13.29 (1.4)	10.48 (0.8)
Food	17.92 (1.4)	27.89 (1.3)	37.96 (1.3)	46.13 (1.2)	61.49 (1.2)	38.28 (0.7)
Alcoholic drink	2.25 (6.1)	5.33 (4.3)	9.15 (3.4)	11.92 (3.3)	17.29 (3.8)	9.19 (2.0)
Tobacco	2.73 (4.3)	4.08 (4.1)	5.01 (3.8)	5.37 (3.9)	5.06 (4.5)	4.45 (1.9)
Clothing and footwear	3.89 (6.6)	7.32 (4.7)	14.01 (4.4)	17.88 (3.2)	29.49 (3.2)	14.52 (2.0)
Household goods	5.72 (16.1)	7.75 (5.5)	14.01 (6.1)	19.39 (6.6)	28.16 (5.0)	15.01 (3.1)
Household services	3.11 (3.0)	5.23 (4.0)	7.72 (4.3)	10.27 (4.5)	22.67 (8.9)	9.80 (4.4)
Personal goods and services	2.57 (6.9)	4.61 (4.4)	6.69 (3.7)	8.88 (3.1)	17.91 (7.0)	8.13 (3.4)
Motoring expenditure	3.06 (12.1)	11.51 (8.0)	24.75 (5.5)	37.62 (4.6)	49.6 (4.0)	25.31 (2.6)
Fares and other travel costs	1.59 (5.8)	2.62 (5.8)	4.46 (13.8)	5.96 (14.3)	9.76 (6.0)	4.88 (5.0)
Leisure goods	2.78 (6.7)	5.50 (5.8)	9.16 (4.6)	11.83 (4.5)	18.97 (4.3)	9.65 (2.4)
Leisure services	3.79 (9.5)	7.25 (6.8)	12.11 (9.1)	20.19 (6.9)	47.33 (9.7)	18.13 (5.6)
Miscellaneous	0.29 (35.9)	0.31 (13.9)	0.64 (9.4)	0.99 (8.0)	1.67 (11.1)	0.78 (6.2)
All expenditure groups	70.72	126.95	192.14	247.69	384.54	204.41
Percentage standard error	2.3	1.5	1.5	1.3	1.9	1.1
	AVERAGE WEEKLY EXPENDITURE PER PERSON (£)					
All expenditure groups	47.11	58.92	71.44	82.70	118.68	81.24

SOURCE: "Family Expenditure Survey," Central Statistical Office, 1988. Reprinted by permission of the Controller of Her Majesty's Stationery Office.

share. For example, Levi's has established a differential advantage for its blue jeans through a well-known trade mark, design, advertising, and a quality image. Although many competing brands of blue jeans are available, this firm has carved out its market share through use of a differential marketing strategy.

Perfect competition, if it existed at all, would entail a large number of sellers, not one of which could significantly influence price or supply. Products would be

TABLE 2.4 *Selected characteristics of competitive structures*

TYPE OF STRUCTURE	NUMBER OF COMPETITORS	EASE OF ENTRY INTO MARKET	PRODUCT	KNOWLEDGE OF MARKET	EXAMPLES
Monopoly	One	Many barriers	Almost no substitutes	Perfect	Railways (British Rail), many government departments
Oligopoly	Few	Some barriers	Homogeneous or differentiated (real or perceived differences) products	Imperfect	Airlines, petroleum retailers, some utility providers
Monopolistic competition	Many	Few barriers	Product differentiation with many substitutes	More knowledge than oligopoly; less than monopoly	Jeans, fast food, audio-visual
Perfect competition	Unlimited	No barriers	Homogeneous products	Perfect	The London Commodity Markets, vegetable farms

homogeneous, and there would be full knowledge of the market and easy entry into it. The closest thing to an example of perfect competition would be an unregulated agricultural market.

Few, if any, marketers operate in a structure of perfect competition. Perfect competition is an ideal at one end of the continuum, with monopoly at the other end. Most marketers function in a competitive environment that falls somewhere between these two extremes.

Competitive Tools.   Another set of factors that influences the level of competition is the number and types of competitive tools used by competitors. To survive, a firm uses one or several available competitive tools to deal with competitive economic forces. Once a company has analysed its particular competitive environment and decided which factors in that environment it can or must adapt to or influence, it can choose among the variables that it can control to strengthen its competitive position in the overall market-place.

Probably the first competitive tool that most organisations grasp is price. Bic, for example, markets disposable pens and lighters that are similar to competing products but less expensive. However, there is one major problem with using price as a competitive tool: competitors will often match or beat the price. This threat is one of the primary reasons for employing non-price competitive tools that are based on the differentiation of market segments, product offering, promotion, distribution, or enterprise.[8]

By focusing on a specific market segment, a marketer sometimes gains a competitive advantage. For instance, Apple Computers and International Business Machines (IBM) have each tried to gain a competitive edge by incorporating product features that make their brands distinctive to some extent. Firms use distinguishing promotional methods to compete, such as advertising and personal selling. Competing producers sometimes use different distribution channels to prevail over each other. Merchants may compete by placing their outlets in locations that are convenient for a large number of shoppers.

Monitoring Competition. Marketers in an organisation need to be aware of the actions of major competitors. They should monitor what competitors are currently doing and assess the changes occurring in the competitive environment. Monitoring allows firms to determine what specific strategies competitors are following and how those strategies affect their own. It can also guide marketers as they try to develop competitive advantages and aid them in adjusting current marketing strategies, as well as in planning new ones. Information may come from direct observation or from sources such as salespeople, customers, trade publications, syndicated marketing research services, distributors, and marketing studies.

An organisation needs information about competitors that will allow its marketing managers to assess the performance of its own marketing efforts. Comparing their company's performance with that of competitors helps marketing managers recognise strengths and weaknesses in their own marketing strategies. Data about market shares, product movement, sales volume, and expenditure levels can be useful. However, accurate information on these matters is often difficult to obtain.

TECHNOLOGICAL FORCES

The word *technology* brings to mind creations of progress such as computers, superconductors, lasers, and heart transplants. Even though such items are outgrowths of technology, none of them is technology. **Technology** has been defined as the knowledge of how to accomplish tasks and goals.[9] Often this knowledge comes from scientific research. The effects of technology are broad in scope and today exert a tremendous influence on our lives.

Technology grows out of research performed by businesses, universities, and non-profit organisations. Much of this research is paid for by governments, which support investigations in a variety of areas, including health, defence, agriculture, energy, and pollution. Because much centrally funded research requires the use of specialised machinery, personnel, and facilities, a sizeable proportion of this research is conducted by large business organisations or research institutions that already possess the necessary specialised equipment and people.

8. Wroe Alderson, *Dynamic Marketing Behavior* (Homewood, Ill.: Irwin, 1965), pp. 195–97.

9. Reprinted by permission from Herbert Simon, "Technology and Environment," *Management Science*, Volume 19, Number 10, June 1973. Copyright 1973, The Institute of Management Sciences.

The rapid technological growth of the last several decades is expected to continue through the 1990s. Areas that hold great technological promise include digital electronics, artificial intelligence, superconductors, materials research, and biotechnology. Current research is investigating new forms of memory chips and computers that are a hundred times faster and smaller than current models. Because these and other technological developments will clearly have an impact on buyers' and marketers' decisions, we now turn, in our discussion, to the effects of technology on society and marketers. We then consider several factors that influence the adoption and use of technology.

■ The Impact of Technology

Marketers must be aware of new developments in technology and their possible effects because technology can and does affect marketing activities in many different ways. Consumers' technological knowledge influences their desires for goods and services. To provide marketing mixes that satisfy consumers, marketers must be aware of these influences.

The various ways in which technology affects marketing activities fall into two broad categories. It affects consumers and society in general, and it influences what, how, when, and where products are marketed.

Effects of Technology on Society.   Technology determines how we, as members of society, satisfy our physiological needs. In various ways and to varying degrees, eating and drinking habits, sleeping patterns, sexual activities, and health care are all influenced by both existing technology and changes in technology. Technological developments have improved our standard of living, thus giving us more leisure time; they have also enhanced information, entertainment, and education. As indicated in Figure 2.2, General Dynamics supports a programme in which robotics are used to stimulate students and enhance their education.

Nevertheless, technology can detract from the quality of life through undesirable side effects, such as unemployment, polluted air and water, and other health hazards. Marketing Update 2.2 describes Avis's introduction of catalytic converters across its fleet to curtail air pollution.Some people believe that further applications of technology can soften or eliminate these undesirable side effects. Others argue, however, that the best way to improve the quality of our lives is to decrease the use of technology.

Effects of Technology on Marketing.   Technology also affects the types of products that marketers can offer. The introduction and general acceptance of cassette tapes and compact discs drove manufacturers of vinyl long-playing (LP) albums out of business or forced them to invest in new technology. Yet this technology provided new marketing opportunities for recording artists and producers, record companies, retailers, and those in related industries. The following items are only a few of the many thousands of existing products that were not available to consumers twenty years ago: disposable 35mm cameras, cellular telephones, ultralight laptop computers, and high-resolution television.

Computer technology helps make warehouse storage and keeping track of stored products more efficient and, therefore, less expensive. Often these savings can be passed on to consumers in the form of lower prices. Because of technological changes in communications, marketers now can reach large masses of people through a variety of media more efficiently. The development and widespread use of

FIGURE 2.2
Technology advances education.
General Dynamics helps to support a programme in which robotics are used to improve educational opportunities.

The new teacher has 137 microchips, an infrared sensor, and little rubber wheels.

When he gets the chance to teach science, he comes alive. And so do his students.

He is Tharogem I, robot star of Project RobotACTS.™ It's a new education project developed by the Thames Science Center in New London, Connecticut, and now supported by the National Science Foundation.

Tharogem gets kids excited about the principles of physics. And about programming. And about building simple robots of their own.

He gets us excited, too. We're concerned that so few American students are inspired by physical sciences. That's why we at General Dynamics helped start this program. So far, more than 6,000 Eastern Connecticut students have seen Tharogem demonstrate principles of light, sound, electricity, magnetism, and math.

In return, the students are demonstrating something, too. Enthusiasm for learning.

GENERAL DYNAMICS
A Strong Company For A Strong Country

SOURCE: Courtesy of General Dynamics

facsimile machines and services, for example, allows marketers to send their advertisements or sales specifications directly to selected groups of customers who want their products.

Technological advances in transport enable consumers to travel further and more often to shop at a larger number of stores. Changes in transport also have affected producers' ability to get products to retailers and wholesalers. The ability of present-day manufacturers of relatively lightweight products to reach any of their dealers within twenty-four hours (via overnight express delivery services, such as TNT and Federal Express) would astound their counterparts of fifty years ago.

■ **Adoption and Use of Technology**

Through a procedure known as **technology assessment**, some managers try to foresee the effects of new products and processes on their firm's operation, on other business organisations, and on society in general. With the information gained through a technology assessment, management tries to estimate whether the benefits of using a specific kind of technology outweigh the costs to the firm and to society at large. The degree to which a business is technologically based will also influence how its management responds to technology. Firms whose products and product changes grow out of recent technology strive to gather and use technological information.

AVIS GOES GREENER

Avis UK has decided to introduce catalytic converters across its 20,000-strong fleet to boost the car rental firm's "green" image. Rover 800s are the first to be fitted with catalytic converters. Avis and market leader Hertz both claim to be ahead in the race to have the "cleanest" fleet, and both claim to have been the first to convert their entire fleet to run on unleaded petrol.

"A clean fleet is what customers have come to expect of the leading company," stated Hertz PR director Naomi Graham. Cynics believe the car rental companies are cultivating a caring image so as to protect themselves against draconian taxes which may lie ahead for the rental sector. Hertz has allied with the Tidy Britain Group—all Hertz cars carry a Tidy Bag to discourage drivers from littering roadsides. Hertz is also working with the Environmental Transport Association to encourage customers to make part of their journey by train when possible. Whatever the motives—commercial or with an environmental conscience—Avis and Hertz have responded to changing consumer attitudes and social responsibilities.

SOURCE: "Green Battle Accelerates with Avis Move," *Marketing,* 30 August 1990, p. 4; "Business Travel Survey," *Financial Times,* 23 March 1988; *The Hertz Report,* Hertz, 1986 and 1989.

Although available technology could radically improve their products (or other parts of the marketing mix), some companies may put off applying this technology as long as their competitors do not try to use it. The extent to which a firm can protect inventions stemming from research also influences its use of technology. How secure a product is from imitation depends on how easily it can be copied by others without violating its patent. If new products and processes cannot be protected through patents, a company is less likely to market them and make the benefits of its research available to competitors.

How a company uses (or does not use) technology is important for its long-run survival. A firm that makes the wrong decisions may well lose out to the competition. Poor decisions may also affect its profits by requiring expensive corrective actions. Poor decisions about technological forces may even drive a firm out of business.

SUMMARY

The marketing environment consists of external forces that directly or indirectly influence an organisation's acquisition of inputs (personnel, financial resources, raw materials, information) and generation of outputs (information, packages, goods, services, ideas). The marketing environment includes political, legal, regulatory, societal, economic and competitive, and technological forces.

To monitor changes in these forces, marketers should practise environmental scanning and analysis. Environmental scanning is the process of collecting information about the forces in the marketing environment; environmental analysis is the process of assessing and interpreting the information obtained in scanning. This information helps marketing managers predict opportunities and threats associated with environmental fluctuation. Marketing management may assume either a passive, reactive approach or an active, aggressive approach in responding to these environmental fluctuations. The choice depends on an organisation's structure and needs and on the composition of the environmental forces that affect it.

The political, legal, and regulatory forces of the marketing environment are closely interrelated. The current political outlook is reflected in legislation and regulations or the lack of them. The political environment may determine what laws and regulations affecting specific marketers are enacted and how much the government purchases and from which suppliers; it can also be important in helping organisations secure foreign markets.

Legislation affecting marketing activities can be divided into procompetitive legislation—laws designed to preserve and encourage competition—and consumer protection laws. The Restrictive Trade Practices Act and the Competition Act sought to prevent monopolies and activities that limit competition; legislation such as the Financial Services Act, the Sale of Goods Act, and the Consumer Credit Act were directed towards more specific practices. Consumer protection laws generally relate to product safety and information disclosure. The actual effects of legislation are determined by how marketers and the courts interpret the laws.

Regulatory agencies influence most marketing activities. Regulatory units, such as the Monopolies and Mergers Commission and the Director General of Fair Trading, usually have the power to enforce specific laws and some discretion in establishing operating rules and drawing up regulations to guide certain types of industry practices. Self-regulation by industry represents another regulatory force; marketers view this type of regulation more favourably than government action because they have more opportunity to take part in creating the guidelines. Self-regulation may be less expensive than government regulation, and its guidelines are generally more realistic. However, such regulation generally cannot assure compliance as effectively as government agencies.

Societal forces refer to the structure and dynamics of individuals and groups and the issues that concern them. Many members of our society want a high standard of living and a high quality of life, and they expect business to help them achieve these goals. The consumer movement is a diverse collection of independent individuals, groups, and organisations that attempt to protect the rights of consumers. The major issues taken up by the consumer movement fall into three categories: environmental protection, product performance and safety, and information disclosure. Consumer rights organisations inform and organise other consumers, raise issues, help businesses develop consumer-orientated programmes, and pressure legislators to enact consumer protection laws.

The economic factors that can strongly influence marketing decisions and activities are general economic conditions, buying power, willingness to spend, spending patterns, and competitive forces. The overall state of the economy fluctuates in a general pattern known as a business cycle. The stages of the business cycle are prosperity, recession, depression, and recovery.

Consumers' goods, services, and financial holdings make up their buying power— that is, their ability to purchase. The financial sources of buying power are income, credit, and wealth. After-tax income used for spending or saving is called disposable income. Disposable income left after an individual has purchased the basic necessities of food, clothing, and shelter is called discretionary income. Two measures of buying power are effective buying income (which includes salaries, wages, dividends, interest, profits, and rents, less taxes) and the buying power index (a weighted index consisting of population, effective buying income, and retail sales data). The factors that affect consumers' willingness to spend are product price, the level of satisfaction obtained from currently used products, family size, and expectations about future employment, income, prices, and general economic conditions. Consumer spending patterns indicate the relative proportions of annual family expenditures or the actual amount of money spent on certain kinds of goods and services. Comprehensive spending patterns specify the percentages of family income allotted to annual expenditures for general classes of goods and services. Product-specific spending patterns indicate the annual amounts families spend for specific products within a general product class.

Although all businesses compete for consumers' spending, a company's direct competitors are usually the businesses in its geographic area that market products that resemble its own or can be substituted for them. The number of firms that control the supply of a product may affect the strength of competition. There are four general types of competitive structure: monopoly, oligopoly, monopolistic competition, and perfect competition. Marketers should monitor what competitors are currently doing and assess the changes occurring in the competitive environment.

Technology is the knowledge of how to accomplish tasks and goals. Product development, packaging, promotion, prices, and distribution systems are all influenced directly by technology. Several factors determine how much and in what way a particular business will make use of technology; these factors include the firm's ability to use technology, consumers' ability and willingness to buy technologically improved products, the firm's perception of the long-run effects of applying technology, the extent to which the firm is technologically based, the degree to which technology is used as a competitive tool, and the extent to which the business can protect technological applications through patents.

IMPORTANT TERMS

Marketing environment
Environmental scanning
Environmental analysis
Procompetitive legislation
Director General of Fair Trading
Monopolies and Mergers
   Commission
Treaty of Rome
Consumers' Association
Societal forces
Consumer movement
Prosperity
Recession
Depression
Recovery
Buying power

Income
Disposable income
Discretionary income
Wealth
Willingness to spend
Consumer spending patterns
Comprehensive spending patterns
Product-specific spending patterns
Competition
Monopoly
Oligopoly
Monopolistic competition
Perfect competition
Technology
Technology assessment

DISCUSSION AND REVIEW QUESTIONS

1. Why are environmental scanning and analysis so important?
2. How are political forces related to legal and governmental regulatory forces?
3. Describe marketers' attempts to influence political forces.
4. What types of procompetitive legislation directly affect marketing practices?
5. What is the major objective of most procompetitive laws? Do the laws generally accomplish this objective? Why or why not?
6. What types of problems do marketers experience as they interpret legislation?
7. What are the goals of the Monopolies and Mergers Commission? How does it affect marketing activities?
8. Name several non-governmental regulatory forces. Do you believe that self-regulation is more or less effective than governmental regulatory agencies? Why?
9. Describe the consumer movement. Analyse some active consumer forces in your area.
10. In what ways can each of the business cycle stages affect consumers' reactions to marketing strategies?
11. What business cycle stage are we experiencing currently? How is this stage affecting business firms in your area?

12. Define income, disposable income, and discretionary income. How does each type of income affect consumer buying power?
13. How is consumer buying power affected by wealth and consumer credit?
14. How is buying power measured? Why should it be evaluated?
15. What factors influence a consumer's willingness to spend?
16. What does the term *technology* mean to you?
17. How does technology affect you as a member of society? Do the benefits of technology outweigh its costs and dangers?
18. Discuss the impact of technology on marketing activities.
19. What factors determine whether a business organisation adopts and uses technology?

■ CASES

2.1   Suzuki Samurai Copes with Safety Controversy

Officials of the Japanese Suzuki Motor Corp. and its American subsidiary, Suzuki of America Automotive Corp., were extremely pleased with the sales figures of the Suzuki Samurai after it was introduced in the United States in late 1985. The Samurai, a four-wheel-drive sport/utility vehicle, appealed to a wide range of consumers. College students, off-road enthusiasts, and urban professionals all seemed to love the sporty look and fun image of the Samurai. Its low price tag also helped sales immensely. The popularity of the Samurai might have turned it into a target, though, as more and more attention was focused on it. Today, Suzuki Samurai sales are at a low point as dealers try to cope with questions about its safety. Throughout Europe dealerships have seen a similar pattern.

Suzuki's troubles with the Samurai began when NBC in America reported on the Samurai's tendency to roll over. Soon afterwards, Consumer Union, publishers of *Consumer Reports*, gave the Samurai a "not acceptable" rating in its magazine, the first such rating the magazine had handed out in ten years. Researchers for *Consumer Reports* claim that during common evasive manoeuvres—for example, if a driver were to swerve back and forth on the road to avoid an accident—the Samurai is likely to roll over. Consumer Union was so concerned about the safety of the Samurai that it demanded that Suzuki recall the 150,000 Samurais then on the road, refund owners' purchase price, and remove the vehicle from the market. In the U.K., consumer programmes and the BBC's "Top Gear" widely reported the situation in America.

One of several lawsuits has been filed against Suzuki by a Pennsylvania physician on behalf of all Samurai owners. The doctor believes that Suzuki purposely attempted to conceal knowledge of the Samurai's instability. Another lawsuit charges that Suzuki promoted the safety of the Samurai even though the company knew the vehicle was unsafe. The suit maintains that Suzuki and the firm that handles its public relations and advertising continuously committed mail and wire fraud and conspiracy to screen the Samurai's design flaws. The lawsuit refers to the National Traffic Highway Safety Administration's figures that show forty-four Samurai rollover incidents resulting in at least twenty-five deaths and more than sixty injuries.

Suzuki officials maintain that the Samurai is as safe as any other four-wheel-drive vehicle. A high-ranking Suzuki executive called *Consumer Reports'* rollover accounts "defamatory". Suzuki executives charge that *Consumer Reports'* researchers changed their roll-over test methodology when they were testing the Samurai. Furthermore, regarding the twenty-five deaths linked to Samurai roll-overs, Suzuki directors assert that more than 50 percent of the accidents in which these deaths occurred can be attributed to drunk drivers.

Unlike German Audi AG officials, who initially did not respond to consumer complaints of sudden acceleration in their Audi 5000, Suzuki executives are aggressively battling the allegations against the Samurai. Suzuki officials have increased their advertising budget to publicly address safety issues. Suzuki has placed more than $1.5 million into its television media schedule to respond to the *Consumer Reports* indictment. A few months after the *Consumer Reports* article became public, Suzuki began an extensive buyer and dealer incentive programme, and sales of Samurais rocketed. Suzuki managers saw this as a sign of declining public concern over the roll-over issue. Suzuki was mistaken, however. Once it removed the generous incentives, Samurai sales began to sink again.

Suzuki officials are determined to fight their way out of this controversy, even though the fight is very expensive. Suzuki stands to lose public credibility if it cannot successfully prove the Samurai's roadworthiness. Many Suzuki officials are worried that the controversy surrounding the Samurai will spread to other Suzuki products and that sales figures of its other cars and even motorcycles will be adversely affected.

Meanwhile, Suzuki continues to sell Samurais, even though the figures are not as high as anticipated before the controversy. Suzuki managers were pleased when the Center for Auto Safety's petition to the federal government for the recall of Samurais was refused. Suzuki will have to work hard to restore the reputation of its Samurai. The Japanese automobile company may have a difficult time keeping the sporty little four-wheel-drive on the road.

SOURCES: Cleveland Horton and Raymond Serafin, "Wounded by Samurai?" *Advertising Age,* 20 June 1988, p. 101; " 'Samurai Rollover Rap Is Bum,' Suzuki Says," *Ward's AutoWorld,* July 1988, p. 34; "Samurai Sales Hit Record," *Chicago Sun Times,* 6 Sept. 1988; Janice Steinberg, "Suzuki Acts to Right Slipping Samurai Sales," *Advertising Age,* 25 July 1988, p. S-10; "Suit Charges Safety Fraud by Suzuki," *Star-Ledger* (Newark, N.J.), 15 June 1988; "Suzuki Calls Consumer Group's Safety Tests on Samurai 'Flawed,' " *Los Angeles Times,* 10 June 1988; "Suzuki Revamps Ads to Combat Safety Charges," *Detroit News,* 4 Mar. 1988; "Ten Products That Made News in 1988," *Advertising Age,* 2 Jan. 1989, p. 12.; and "Top Gear," BBC, 1989.

Questions for Discussion

1. What kinds of environmental forces is Suzuki facing regarding the safety issue?
2. Evaluate Suzuki's way of dealing with the safety controversy.
3. What improvements could be made in Suzuki's approach to coping with the safety issue?

2.2   The *Wall Street Journal* Faces a Challenging Environment

For more than a hundred years the writers, editors, and reporters of the *Wall Street Journal* have provided readers with important information on the business environment of the United States and the world. The paper started when Charles H. Dow, Edward D. Jones, and their silent partner, Charles M. Bergstresser, began printing a four-page afternoon business newspaper that sold for 2 cents a copy. In 1902, the publisher C. W. Barron purchased the paper and turned over its control to his wife. Today Barron's descendants still own a controlling interest in the paper.

Published by Dow Jones & Co., the *Wall Street Journal* is among the country's most prestigious papers. Its experienced staff and ultramodern printing facilities make the *Wall Street Journal* a lofty model for other newspapers. Businesspeople in many parts of the world read it almost religiously. Its reliability and relatively traditional format make the *Journal* a comfortable cornerstone of American business, and its nearly two million subscribers are clear evidence of the paper's success. However, recent developments have made many at the *Journal* uneasy about the future.

They worry that today's extremely busy businessperson simply does not have the forty minutes to an hour needed to peruse the paper every morning. Present-day businesspeople, especially high-ranking company executives, must make decisions quickly and so want a more immediate, up-to-the-minute medium of information. Electronic information systems, with their instantaneous data retrieval capabilities, may soon make the *Wall Street Journal* obsolete.

Moreover, the *Journal*'s subscription list is shrinking and advertising sales are down. Largely because of the bull market in the 1980s, business news has become very popular. Daily newspapers across the United States have extended their coverage of business, investments, and the economy; business programmes on network and cable television now draw large audiences; and more people than ever are reading business magazines. As readers seek business information from these media, they are less likely to rely on the *Wall Street Journal*. Advertisers have diverted their funds as well, to cover the extended business press. The *Wall Street Journal* now has ten localised editions that its directors hope will lure new advertisers.

The *Journal*'s staff attributes its problems to three major events: (1) the October 1987 stock market crash that reduced the number of investors; (2) the large number of layoffs that occurred because of mergers and streamlining efforts in corporate America; and (3) new competition, especially from electronic information transmittal. However, the paper's management expects it to survive all challenges.

Ironically, another part of the Dow Jones & Co. family poses perhaps the greatest competitive threat to the *Wall Street Journal*. The Dow Jones Information Services Group is growing rapidly. Its new DowVision information system is on the cutting edge of electronic business information. By using Dow Jones News/Retrieval, subscribers can call up *Journal* stories on their personal computers early on publication day and also receive up-to-the-minute accounts of financial developments in London and Tokyo. One investment banker has indicated that the *Journal*'s circulation problems during the last five years can be traced to Information Services.

Management at the *Journal* hopes that busy executives will continue to take time to read their newspaper. But as time becomes more valuable and crucial to businesspeople and investors, many may opt to get their business news directly from their personal computers. The staff at the *Wall Street Journal* believes that accurate, timely, important, and fair news coverage will be enough to hold their readers' attention and loyalty, whether it appears on a printed page or on a computer screen.

SOURCES: Dennis Farney, "One Newspaper's Century: The Inside Story," *Wall Street Journal*, 23 June 1989, pp. C1, C3–C4, C12; Patrick Reilly, "Expanding Its Horizons," *Advertising Age*, 19 June 1989, pp. 43–44; and Alex Taylor III, "A Tale Dow Jones Won't Tell," *Fortune*, 3 July 1989, pp. 100–102, 106, 108–109.

Questions for Discussion

1. Which environmental forces are influencing the performance of the *Wall Street Journal* the most? Explain.
2. Could some of the environmental forces that are adversely affecting the *Journal* be treated as opportunities instead of threats?
3. Has the *Wall Street Journal's* management employed a passive approach or an active approach in dealing with environmental forces? Explain.

3 SEGMENTING MARKETS, TARGETING, POSITIONING, AND EVALUATION

Objectives

To understand the definition of a market

To recognise the types of markets

To learn how firms segment markets

To understand targeting decisions

To learn about strategies for positioning

To gain an understanding of sales potential

To become familiar with sales forecasting methods

London is a leading provider of business and tourist hotel accommodation, with four main groups of customers: international and British business-people seeking extensive bedroom, business and leisure amenities; international leisure travellers who want central locations but few hotel amenities as they explore the city; U.K. weekend "bargain-breakers" looking for low-cost central accommodation close to the sights; and business and social groups for banquets and functions. Rank and Thistle Hotels (the Athenian, Royal Lancaster, Royal Westminster, Tower Thistle) both market several upper-middle-ranking hotels with standardised service levels and amenities and uniform brandings. Mount Charlotte Hotels, the second largest operator in the U.K., has many three-star and several two- and four-star establishments, offering value for money to the budget-orientated business traveller and bargain-break leisure customer, with no uniform brand. Trusthouse Forte (THF), in addition to its recently acquired Crest Hotels, has seventeen hotels in London, ranging from the de luxe Grosvenor House and the functional business-based Cumberland to the no-frills Regent Palace Hotel.

London—like any capital city—is a viable, competitive and sizeable market for hotel accommodation, conferences, and banqueting. There are clearly perceived market segments, with most hotel operators—high or low profile—targeting specific hotel users and pitching their offers accordingly. This is achieved either through distinct brand image (Rank and Thistle), by product, service levels, pricing, and promotion (Mount Charlotte), or by convoluted sub-brands (THF Exclusive, Posthouse, Forte Hotels, individual hotel brands). ◆

Based on information in Ellen Freilich, "Salomon Sees Opportunity in European Hotel Chains," Reuters 1990; "Room at the Inn—The Outlook for Britain's Hotel Industry over the Next Years," *Management Today*, December 1989, pp. 99–108; Gareth David, "The Hotel Market Strategies of John Jarvis and Peter Tyne," *Sunday Times*, 22 July 1990.

otel companies like Trusthouse Forte, Rank, and Mount Charlotte understand that not all hotel customers want the same things. To satisfy these different needs it is necessary for companies to single out groups of customers and aim some or all of their marketing activities at these groups. The key is then to develop and maintain a marketing mix which satisfies the particular requirements of customers in these groups.

This chapter considers the nature of markets, first defining the term and describing the different types. It then reviews the concepts of segmentation, targeting, and positioning by considering strategies often used to select target markets. Next, it considers the variables used to segment markets and approaches to product positioning. Finally, it discusses market measurement and primary sales forecasting techniques.

WHAT ARE MARKETS?

The term "market" has a number of meanings. It used to refer primarily to the place where goods were bought and sold. It can also refer to a large geographic area. In some cases the word refers to the relationship between the demand and supply of a specific product. For instance, "What is the state of the market for gold?" Sometimes, "market" is used to mean the act of selling something.

For the purposes of this text, a **market** is an aggregate of people who, as individuals or in organisations, have needs for products in a product class and who have the ability, willingness, and authority to purchase such products. In general use, the term *market* sometimes refers to the total population—or mass market—that buys products. However, our definition is more specific: it refers to persons seeking products in a specific product category. For example, students are part of the market for textbooks, as well as markets for calculators, pens and pencils, paper, food, music, and other products. Obviously, there are many different markets in any economy. In this section, the requirements for markets are considered in conjunction with these different types.

■ **Requirements for a Market**

For a group of people to be a market, it must meet the following four requirements.

1. The people must need or want a particular product. If they do not, then that group is not a market.
2. The people in the group must have the ability to purchase the product. Ability to purchase is a function of their buying power, which consists of resources such as money, goods, and services that can be traded in an exchange situation.
3. The people in the group must be willing to use their buying power.
4. The people in the group must have the authority to buy the specific products.

Individuals can have the desire, the buying power, and the willingness to purchase certain products but may not be authorised to do so. For example, school students may have the desire, the money, and the willingness to buy alcoholic beverages, but a brewer does not consider them a market because until they are 18 years old, they are prohibited by law from buying alcohol. An aggregate of people that lacks any one of the four requirements thus does not constitute a market.

Types of Markets

Markets can be divided into two categories: consumer markets and organisational or industrial markets. These categories are based on the characteristics of the individuals and groups that make up a specific market and the purposes for which they buy products. A **consumer market** consists of purchasers and/or individuals in their households who intend to consume or benefit from the purchased products and who do not buy products for the main purpose of making a profit. Each of us belongs to numerous consumer markets for such products as housing, food, clothing, vehicles, personal services, appliances, furniture, and recreational equipment. Consumer markets are discussed in more detail in Chapter 4.

An **organisational**, or **industrial**, **market** consists of individuals or groups that purchase a specific kind of product for one of three purposes: resale, direct use in producing other products, or use in general daily operations. The four categories of organisational, or industrial, markets—producer, reseller, government, and institutional—are discussed in Chapter 5.

SELECTING TARGET MARKETS

In Chapter 1 we say that a marketing strategy has two components: (1) the selection of the organisation's target market and (2) the creation and maintenance of a marketing mix that satisfies that market's needs for a specific product. Regardless of the general types of markets on which a firm focuses, marketing management must select the firm's target markets. The next section examines two general approaches to identifying target markets: the total market approach and market segmentation.

Total Market Approach or Market Segmentation?

In some situations marketers define the total market for a particular product or service as their target market. Companies which develop a single marketing mix aimed at all potential customers in a market are said to be adopting an **undifferentiated** or mass-market approach. The assumption is that all customers in that market have similar needs and wants and can, therefore, be satisfied with a single marketing mix—a standard product or service, similar price levels, one method of distribution, and a promotional mix aimed at everyone.

Increasingly, marketers in both consumer and industrial markets are facing the fact that no two customers are ever exactly the same. Different individuals and organisations have varying characteristics, needs, wants, and interests. The result? Few markets where a single product or service is satisfactory for all. The extensive array of goods on supermarket shelves reflects basic differences in customers' requirements. The trend, it seems, is away from a mass-marketing approach. Even markets which were traditionally undifferentiated are undergoing change, with an ever-increasing number of products on offer. For instance, the market for food seasoning used to be dominated by salt. Now, low-sodium substitutes are being offered as alternatives for the increasingly health-conscious consumer.

The mass-market approach is, it seems, appropriate only under two conditions. The first occurs when there is little variation in the needs of customers for a specific product. This is increasingly rare. The market for clothing, for example, is one which would never fall into this category because of the wide variation of customer preference in this area. The second condition is that the organisation must develop and sustain one marketing mix which satisfies everyone. If the number of customers is large, the commitment in terms of company resources and managerial expertise can be considerable when a sizeable portion of a market is targeted.

FIGURE 3.1
Market segmentation approach

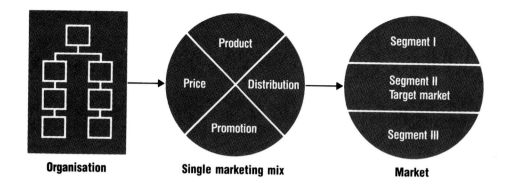

In circumstances where an undifferentiated approach is inappropriate or impractical, marketers use market segmentation to try to improve customer satisfaction. This technique involves identifying groups of customers in markets who share similar buying needs and characteristics. By identifying and understanding such groups, marketers are better able to develop product or service benefits which are appropriate for these groups (see Figure 3.1). They do this by creating new product and branding concepts which are backed up with promotional campaigns to appeal to the particular target segment. Decisions about pricing and distribution strategies are also made with the specific customer segment in mind. For example, clothing sold through Victoria's Secret is manufactured for youthful female consumers. This is reflected in both the product styling and promotional campaign (see Figure 3.2).

APPLYING MARKET SEGMENTATION

Markets in which all consumers have different requirements are termed **heterogeneous markets.** For example, the market for watches is quite diverse. Timex (see Figure 3.3) provides watches for consumers seeking a fashionable but practical, lower-priced watch whereas the Rolex market seeks a more upscale, exclusive watch. In completely heterogeneous markets the only way to satisfy everyone is by offering tailor-made or bespoke products. This rather rare situation tends to be more prevalent in organisational markets, where, for example, plant machinery is designed for a specific task and situation. This, of course, is an extreme case. In the vast majority of markets the aggregation of customers into groups with similar product needs and wants is perfectly feasible. **Market segmentation** is the process by which customers in markets with some heterogeneity can be grouped into smaller, more similar or homogenous segments. In so doing, a balance is sought between obtaining reasonably substantial groups and ensuring sufficient similarity to allow individuals to be offered a standard marketing mix.

Having identified market segments, marketers must decide which, if any, they intend to enter. A marketing programme which covers all elements of the marketing mix can then be designed to suit the particular requirements of those segments targeted. Sears-owned British Shoe Corporation dominates the U.K. footwear retailing sector, mainly through medium- and budget-priced chains such as Dolcis, Saxone, and Freeman Hardy Willis. The company realised it was not catering for the upper end of the market, which had lower volumes but higher unit margins. Cable & Co. was duly launched to cater for this segment of the market.

FIGURE 3.2

Appealing to a particular market segment. Victoria's Secret clothing is targeted toward a certain type of consumer.

Whoever she is, we have exactly what she wants.

A full range of exquisitely detailed lingerie. In delicious satins. Gossamer silks. The finest cottons.

You'll find the most personal gifts in the world at Victoria's Secret. And if the gift is for yourself? So much the better. You deserve it.

Call 1-800-HER-GIFT for the location of the Victoria's Secret nearest you, or a complimentary copy of our catalogue.

What do women really want? That's

VICTORIA'S SECRET
No. 10 Margaret Street, London W1

SOURCE: Victoria's Secret Stores, 10 Margaret St., London, Division of The Limited, Inc.

Companies which have turned to market segmentation have done so with good reason. Amex, Burtons, and TSB have all demonstrated that success can follow the effective implementation of market segmentation strategies. In the U.K. market for tea (see Marketing Update 3.1), segmentation has been essential in order to satisfy the diverse customer needs.

It seems that careful segmentation can make it easier for firms to identify different market opportunities. Furthermore, having a better understanding of different customer groups makes it simpler to exploit opportunities which arise. For example, it can help minor players in the market to achieve a foothold in a particular niche, perhaps by identifying an opportunity not directly exploited by market leaders. There are basically four types of product and market opportunities which can be pursued:

1. *Market Penetration*   Increasing the percentage of sales in present markets by taking sales from the competition. The makers of Alberto Balsam and Timotei shampoos engage in advertising programmes which compete for each other's market share.

FIGURE 3.3

Supplying a heteroge-
neous market.
The watch market is het-
erogeneous, as indicated
by the need for inexpen-
sive, functional watches
such as Timex and more
costly and prestigious
watches such as Rolex.

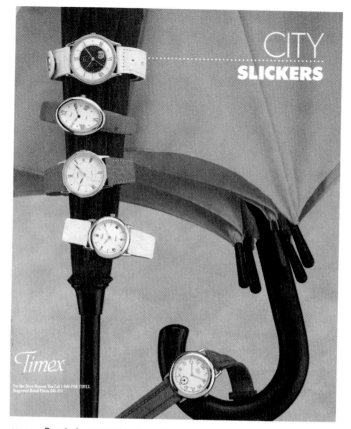

SOURCE: Permission granted by Timex Corporation.

2. *Product Development*   Offering new or improved products to current markets by expanding the range of products on offer. The U.K. washing powder market has undergone much change over recent years with, for example, the introduction of new liquid products such as Persil and Ariel Liquids.

3. *Market Development*   Developing existing products in new markets by finding new applications and/or customer groups. Evian, one of the major players in the market for mineral water, now offers its product in a mist spray. The Evian Brumisateur atomiser (see Figure 3.4) is being marketed as a new concept in skin care, to be used before a moisturiser.

4. *Diversification*   Moving into different markets by offering new products. For example, Bic followed its success in the ballpoint pen market by moving into disposable razors and perfumes.

THE ADVANTAGES OF MARKET SEGMENTATION

Segmentation has a number of advantages associated with it which make it easier for companies to develop and capitalise on such opportunities. These advantages can be considered at the customer level, in relation to the competition, or in terms of the effectiveness of resource allocation and strategic planning.

THE CASE OF TEA

Tea, central to the British way of life, with 200 million cups drunk each day, is a market in transition. The recent proliferation of product offerings apparently relates to differences in the drink's preparation and use. Customers with varying needs are having different product types and forms targeted at them. Perhaps the most critical factor is the way the user prepares the drink.

In terms of product use, there are obvious, distinctive customer groups for manufacturers to target. Not everyone, though, is looking for the same benefits when they buy. For some, the level of convenience is important; for others, flavour and quality are the key. Improving tea-bag and instant tea technology has largely satisfied the need for convenience and has made the drink a real alternative to instant coffee, particularly in the work environment. Manufacturers have responded to varying flavour and quality requirements with a host of different quality blends and types of tea, such as Earl Grey, Ceylon, and China. There are also less obvious aspects which are entwined with British culture. Tradition tells us that the tea pot must be warmed, only freshly boiled water used, and the drink left to brew. For many customers the act of preparing and in some cases sharing the drink is essential to the enjoyment. To these customers, tea-bags and especially instant tea mixes are often regarded as unacceptable forms of the product.

	FORM OF PRODUCT	BRAND
TEA POT	Loose Leaf Standard Tea Bags	Twinings Sainsbury's Kenya Blend

CUP OR MUG	One-cup Tea Bags
	  Tag Bags
	  Round Tea Bags
	Instant
		Typhoo One Cup
		Tetley
		PG Instant

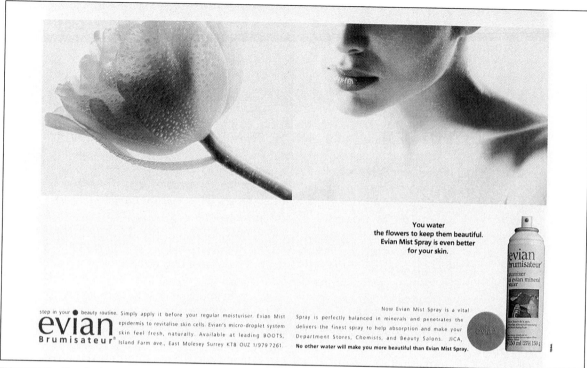

FIGURE 3.4 *Developing existing products in new markets.*
Evian, one of the major players in the market for mineral water, now offers its product as a mist spray for skin care.

SOURCE: Courtesy of PBWA Advertising, Inc. for Laboratoire d'Hygiène Dermatologique d'Evian.

■ **Customer Analysis**

By segmenting markets it is possible to achieve a better understanding not only of customers' needs and wants but also of their other characteristics. The sharper focus which segmentation offers allows consideration of the personal, situational, and behavioural factors which characterise customers in a particular segment. In short, questions about how, why and what customers buy can be addressed. If they are closely in touch with segments, marketers can be responsive to even slight changes in what target customers want. An appropriate response can then follow much more quickly.

■ **Competitor Analysis**

Most markets are characterised by intense competition. Within this environment, companies need to understand the nature of the competition they face. Who are the main competitors? At which segments are they targeting their products? Answering these and other similar questions allows marketers to make decisions about which are the most appropriate segments to target and what kind of competitive advantage should be sought. Companies that do not understand how the market divides up risk competing head-on with larger, better-resourced entities.

■ **Effective Resource Allocation**

All companies have limited resources. To target the whole of the market is usually unrealistic. The IBM case discussed below shows how Apple and NCR were able to compete by ploughing their resources into certain target segments. The effectiveness of personnel and material resources can be greatly improved when they are more narrowly focused at a particular segment of customers.

Despite some recent difficulties, IBM is still regarded as something of a legend in the computer industry. During the 1960s, the company recognised that there was a need for certain industry standards. IBM argued that, when customers' needs changed, it would not be feasible to dispose of existing equipment and expertise and begin again. There was a need to upgrade to equipment which spoke similar languages and had similar physiology. Through this insight, IBM became that standard. The company was able to offer a complete package of service, training, consultancy, maintenance, and software support. Its corporate image was built to an extent where the "in" industry "joke" suggested that the data processing manager who bought non-IBM equipment which failed would be rapidly moving jobs. For IBM's competitors this powerful competitive advantage presented a dilemma. How could they compete successfully against such odds? Curiously, for some companies the best solution was not to compete at all. These organisations chose to work around IBM, to specialise and focus on certain segments or niches in the market. For example, NCR concentrated on the retailing and banking markets, Apple on the education market. Some of the software companies (e.g., Microsoft) adopted a similar strategy.

■ **Strategic Marketing Planning**

Companies which operate in a number of segments are unlikely to follow the same strategic plans in all of them. Dividing markets up allows marketers to develop plans that give special consideration to the particular needs and requirements of customers in different segments. The time-scale covered by the strategic plan can also be structured accordingly. This is because in some markets change occurs more rapidly in certain segments than in others. The market for records is a typical example. While the appeal of classical music remains fairly steady, tastes for pop change very rapidly. Companies like EMI clearly need to consider this when developing corporate plans.

SEGMENTING, TARGETING AND POSITIONING

The process by which segmentation takes place consists of three main elements: segmentation, targeting, and positioning. Figure 3.5 gives an overview of these elements.

■ **Segmenting the Market**

There are many ways in which customers can be grouped and markets segmented. In separate markets, different variables are appropriate. The key is to understand which are the most suitable for distinguishing between different product requirements. Understanding as much as possible about what the customers in segments are really like is also important. Marketers who "know" their targets are more likely to design an appropriate marketing mix for them. For example, of all sectors of U.K. retailing, only the furniture retailers experienced no real growth during the buoyant 1980s. Consumer research revealed that product design and quality were viewed as uninspiring, giving little reason to make replacement purchases. Surprising for most furniture retailers was the finding that consumers were often forced to decide between buying a new lounge or dining-room suite and going abroad for a first or second holiday each year. Companies had to gear their promotion accordingly—attempting to make their products appear more exciting while taking into account the various budgeting considerations of a typical household.

FIGURE 3.5
Basic elements of segmentation

Segmentation
- Consider variables for segmenting market.
- Look at profile of emerging segments.
- Validate segments emerging.

Targeting
- Decide on targeting strategy.
- Which and how many segments should be targeted?

Positioning
- Understand consumer perceptions.
- Position products in the mind of the consumer.
- Design appropriate marketing mix.

■ Targeting Strategy

Once segments have been identified, decisions about how many and which customer groups to target can be made. The options, which will be explored in more detail later in the chapter, include:

- concentrating on a single segment with one product
- offering one product to a number of segments
- targeting a different product at each of a number of segments

The choices which companies make must take into consideration the resource implications of following a particular strategy. The actions of Apple and NCR described above illustrate that careful focusing of resources is essential.

■ Positioning the Product

Companies must decide precisely how and where in targeted segments to aim a product or products, brand or brands. The needs and wants of targeted customers must be translated into a tangible mix of product, price, promotion, and distribution. The consumers' view of the product and where it is positioned relative to the competition is particularly critical. After all, the paying public does not always perceive a product or brand in the way the manufacturer would like. Yugo and Lada cars are, to the chagrin of management, widely perceived with ridicule by the car-buying public.

SELECTING SEGMENTATION VARIABLES

Segmentation variables or **bases** are the dimensions or characteristics of individuals, groups, or organisations that are used for dividing a total market into segments. There is no single or best way to segment a market. Companies must choose from an array of different options.[1,2] In consumer markets, background customer charac-

1. R. Frank and Y. Wind, *Market Segmentation* (Englewood Cliffs, N.J.: Prentice-Hall, 1972).

2. Yoram Wind, "Issues and Advances in Segmentation Research," *Journal of Marketing Research*, August 1978, pp. 317–337.

teristics like age, sex, and occupation—which are relatively easy to obtain, and measure through observation and questioning—are very widely used. In organisational markets, customer size, location, and product use are often the focus.

Several factors are considered in selecting segmentation variables. The variables chosen should relate to customers' needs for, uses of, or behaviour towards the product. Indeed, there is no "magic" associated with segmentation. Clifford and Cavanagh succinctly put the technique into perspective:

> High growth companies succeed by identifying and meeting the needs of certain kinds of customer, not all customers, for special kinds of products and service, not all products or all services. Business academics call this market segmentation. Entrepreneurs call it common sense.[3]

Stereo equipment marketers might segment the stereo market on the basis of income and age—but not on the basis of religion, because one person's music equipment needs do not differ much from those of persons of other religions. Furthermore, if individuals or organisations in a total market are to be classified accurately, the segmentation variable must be measurable. For example, segmenting a market on the basis of intelligence or moral standards would be quite difficult because these attributes are hard to measure accurately.

■ **Variables for Segmenting Consumer Markets**

Companies developing their strategy for segmentation can choose one or several variables or bases from a wide range of choices. Table 3.1 comprehensively illustrates the options available for the marketer of consumer goods. These divide into variables like demographics and socio-economics that relate to basic customer characteristics and product-related behavioural factors, such as purchase and usage behaviour.

■ **Basic Customer Characteristics**

Demographic Variables.   The ease with which demographic variables can be measured has largely contributed to their widespread usage in segmenting markets. The characteristics most often used include age, sex, family, race, and religion. Because these factors can be closely related to customers' product needs and purchasing behaviour, understanding them often helps marketers target their efforts more effectively. Companies which manufacture toiletries, such as Elida Gibbs, for example, make a range of different sizes to satisfy the requirements of buyers ranging from singles to large families.

Age is widely used for segmentation purposes. The marketing of ready-to-eat breakfast cereals is typical of this. For example, Kellogg's targets children with fun products designed to appeal to younger tastes—Frosties and Coco Pops. Meanwhile, the more nutrition- and fitness-conscious adult market is served with high-fibre and low-sugar products such as Nutri Grain and Fruit 'n Fibre. In the service sector too there is no longer a standard offering for all. For example, in banking, efforts are increasingly focused on age-related segments. The very young customer, university undergraduates, and the over-50s are all offered packages tailored to their particular needs (see Figure 3.6).

Population statistics help marketers to understand and keep track of changing age profiles. The population of Europe, which is increasing at a rate of 0.6 percent a year, expects to see a 25 percent fall in the 15- to 25-year-old age band between 1985 and 1995, with the biggest drop in West Germany and Denmark (see Table 1

3. Donald K. Clifford, Jr., and Richard E. Cavanagh, *The Winning Performance: How America's High-Growth Companies Succeed* (New York: Bantam Books, 1985), p. 53.

TABLE 3.1 *Variables for segmenting consumer markets*

BASIC CUSTOMER CHARACTERISTICS

Because of the ease with which information concerning basic customer characteristics can be obtained and measured, the use of these variables is widespread.

DEMOGRAPHICS

Age
Sex
Family
Race
Religion

The family life-cycle concept is an imaginative way of combining demographic variables.

SOCIO-ECONOMICS

Income
Occupation
Education
Social class

Different income groups have different aspirations in terms of cars, housing, education, etc.

GEOGRAPHIC LOCATION

Country
Region
Type of urban area (conurbation/village)
Type of housing (affluent suburbs/inner city)

PERSONALITY, MOTIVES AND LIFESTYLE

Holiday companies often use lifestyle to segment the market. Club Med, for example, concentrates on young singles while other tour operators cater especially for senior citizens or young families.

PRODUCT-RELATED BEHAVIOURAL CHARACTERISTICS

PURCHASE BEHAVIOUR

Customers for tinned foods, like baked beans, may be highly brand loyal to Heinz or HP or may shop purely on the basis of price.

PURCHASE OCCASION

A motorist making an emergency purchase of a replacement tyre, while on a trip far from home, is less likely to haggle about price than the customer who has a chance to "shop around".

BENEFITS SOUGHT

When customers buy toothpaste they seek different benefits. For some, fresh breath and taste are essential while for others fluoride protection is the key. Macleans Sensitive caters for a minority group which requires treatment for sensitive teeth.

CONSUMPTION BEHAVIOUR AND USER STATUS

Examining consumption patterns can indicate where companies should be concentrating their efforts. Light or non-users are often neglected. The important question to ask is why consumption in these groups is low.

ATTITUDE TO PRODUCT

Different customers have different perceptions and preferences of products offered. Car manufacturers from Skoda to Porsche are in the business of designing cars to match customer preferences, changing perceptions as necessary.

3.2). Over the same time period, however, the number of 25- to 45-year-olds is expected to rise. Given the relative affluence of this particular group, a wide range of companies (for example, the leisure and service industries) might expect to reap the benefits of this increase by the turn of the century. Interestingly, though the advertisement in Figure 3.7 is promoting a newspaper for children aged 8 to 12, it is also targeted toward these children's parents, who are most likely to be in the 25- to 45-year old group.

In some markets, including clothes, cosmetics, alcoholic drinks, books, magazines, and even cigarettes, gender has long been a key demographic variable. In other markets, its use is more recent. European Community statistics show that while women and girls represent 51.4 percent of the population, men and boys account for

FIGURE 3.6

Segmentation according to demographic variables.

Barclays Bank offers packages tailored to age-related consumer needs.

SOURCE: Courtesy of Barclays Bank.

48.6 percent. The confectionery market is one which traditionally did not segment on the basis of sex. Chocolate manufacturer Cadburys changed this by developing assortments aimed primarily at men. Tribute, with packaging and promotion designed specifically for men, was one of these.

Marketers have also turned to ethnicity as a means of segmenting markets for goods such as food, music, and clothing and for services such as banking and insurance. The U.S. Hispanic population illustrates the importance of ethnicity as a segmentation variable. Made up of people of Mexican, Cuban, Puerto Rican, and Central and South American heritage, this ethnic group is growing five times faster than the general population. Consequently, more and more companies that market consumer packaged goods—including Campbell Soup Co. and Procter & Gamble—have been targeting U.S. Hispanic consumers. They view the Hispanic segment as attractive because of the market size and its growth potential. However, targeting Hispanic customers is not an easy task. For example, although marketers have long believed that Hispanic consumers are exceptionally brand loyal and prefer Spanish-language broadcast media, recent research has failed to support this notion. Not only do advertisers disagree about the merits of Spanish-language media; they also question whether it is suitable to advertise to Mexicans, Puerto Ricans, and

TABLE 3.2 *European population statistics and projections (000's)*

	POPULATION AT LAST CENSUS				PREDICTION FOR 1995		
	Year	0–14	15–64	65+	0–14	15–64	65+
BELGIUM	1981	1,972	6,422	1,415	1,766	6,404	1,559
DENMARK	1981	968	3,151	1,005	849	3,455	804
FRANCE	1982	n/a	n/a	n/a	11,194	37,338	7,807
WEST GERMANY	1970	14,071	38,574	8,006	9,502	41,004	9,477
GREECE	1981	n/a	n/a	n/a	2,347	6,434	1,387
IRELAND	1981	1,044	2,030	369	1,161	2,533	389
ITALY	1981	12,128	36,944	7,485	9,307	39,071	9,128
LUXEMBOURG	1981	67	248	50	71	253	49
NETHERLANDS	1971	n/a	n/a	n/a	2,653	10,325	2,050
PORTUGAL	1981	n/a	n/a	n/a	2,129	7,263	1,427
SPAIN	1981	9,686	20,189	7,871	7,647	26,745	5,630
UNITED KINGDOM	1981	11,455	35,465	8,169	11,593	37,385	9,166

SOURCES: UN Population and Vital Statistics Report; National Statistical Offices; UN World Population Prospects, European Marketing Data and Statistics, 1990.

Cubans using a common Spanish language.[4] Each culture has its own unique language—thus, to lump Hispanic groups together does not allow the message to effectively reach each segment. These findings suggest that marketers should carefully research the Hispanic market segment before developing marketing mixes for it.

Product needs also vary according to marital status and the number and age of children. Figure 3.8 illustrates patterns of expenditure on a full range of products for different household types. These factors are collectively taken into consideration by the *family life-cycle* concept. Some of the more obvious markets where the impact of different life-cycles is seen are tourism, housing, and financial services. The family life-cycle has been broken down in several different ways. Table 3.3 illustrates a fairly comprehensive scheme which, in practice, is often simplified.

The scheme is based on the assumption that individuals in different life-cycle stages have varying product needs. Marketers can respond to this by targeting such groups with marketing mixes designed to capitalise on the differences. For example, parents whose children have grown up and left home tend to have more disposable income than those with young children. Relative spend on electronics, holidays, and cars therefore tends to be higher. Critics of the life-cycle concept point out that it can be difficult to decide to which categories families belong. In some cases households do not appear to fit at all. Single-parent families and couples without children are examples of this.

Obviously, this discussion of demographic variables is not exhaustive. However, the variables described above probably represent the most widely used demographics. Other examples of the use of demographics include segmenting the cosmetic and hair-care markets on the basis of race and directing certain types of foods and clothing towards people of specific religious sects.

4. Joseph G. Albonetti and Luis V. Dominguez, "Major Influences on Consumer-Goods Marketers' Decision to Target U.S. Hispanics," *Journal of Advertising Research,* February-March 1989, pp. 9–11.

FIGURE 3.7

Combining segmentation variables.

In this advertisement, *The Daily Telegraph* is promoting its new newspaper for children, while targeting its message to both older and younger readers.

SOURCE: Courtesy of *The Daily Telegraph*.

Socio-Economic Variables. This group of variables includes income, occupation, education and social class. Some marketing academics and practitioners include certain of these variables under the demographics label.

Income is often used to divide markets because it strongly influences people's product needs. It affects their ability to buy (discussed in Chapter 2) and their aspirations for a certain style of living. Examples include housing, furniture, clothing, cars, food and certain kinds of sporting goods. For example, the jewellery shown in Figure 3.9 is clearly aimed at very high earners.

The occupation of the household head is known to have an impact on the types of products and services which are purchased. The type of housing which individuals and families own or rent is strongly linked to this variable (see Table 3.4). It is obvious, for example, that sales of products for refurbishment and decoration, such as paints and wallpapers, will be dominated by those professions which have owner-occupier status.

Other socio-economic variables which may be used to segment markets include education level and social class, which in the U.K. are often thought to be two of the most appropriate ways of aggregating readers of daily newspapers.

Geographic Variables. Consumers in different geographic locations are subject to varying conditions in terms of climate, terrain, natural resources and population density. Markets may be divided into regions because one or more geographic

FIGURE 3.8
Pattern of expenditure for different household types

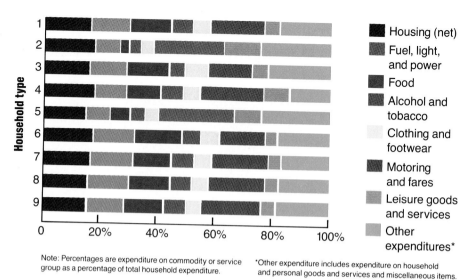

Note: Percentages are expenditure on commodity or service group as a percentage of total household expenditure.

*Other expenditure includes expenditure on household and personal goods and services and miscellaneous items.

Household type	Composition	No. of cases	Average weekly household expenditure (all items) £
1	All households	7,265	204.41
2	1 adult retired, mainly dependent on state pension	613	55.52
3	1 adult nonretired	826	131.62
4	1 adult with 1 or more children	308	120.56
5	1 man, 1 woman retired, mainly dependent on state pensions	305	97.77
6	1 man, 1 woman nonretired	1,423	244.32
7	1 man, 1 woman, 1 child	578	237.76
8	1 man, 1 woman, 2 children	897	262.57
9	1 man, 1 woman, 3 children	258	277.99

SOURCE: "Family Expenditure Survey," Central Statistical Office, 1988. Reprinted by permission of the Controller of Her Majesty's Stationery Office.

variables cause customers to differ from one region to another. A company that sells products throughout the European Community will, for example, need to reflect the different languages spoken in the labelling of its goods.

City size can be an important segmentation variable. Some marketers want to focus their efforts on cities of a certain size. For example, one franchised restaurant organisation will not locate in cities of less than 100,000 people. It has concluded that a smaller population base could make the operation unprofitable. Other firms, however, seek out opportunities in smaller towns. The major petroleum retailers, such as Esso and Shell, have traffic-density thresholds, below which they perceive a local market as unviable. It is, therefore, quite common—particularly in villages and small towns in rural areas—to have petroleum retailing dominated by independent garage owners and the smaller petroleum companies.

Market density refers to the number of potential customers within a unit of land area, such as a square kilometre. Although market density is related generally to population density, the correlation is not exact. For example, in two different geographic markets of approximately equal size and population, the market density for

TABLE 3.3
*Wells and Gubar
life-cycle stages*

Bachelor stage (young single people not living with parents)
Newly married couples without children
Full nest I (youngest child under 6)
Full nest II (youngest child 6 or over)
Full nest III (older married couple with dependent children)
Empty nest I (no children living at home, family head in work)
Empty nest II (family head retired)
Solitary survivor (in work)
Solitary survivor (retired)

SOURCE: From *Consumer Market Research Handbook,* Third Edition, R. Worcester and J. Downham, eds. (ESOMAR) (England: McGraw-Hill Book Company (UK) Limited, 1986), p. 394. Courtesy of the European Society for Opinion and Marketing Research, Amsterdam.

office supplies might be much higher in one area than in the other if it contains a significantly greater proportion of business customers. Market density may be a useful segmentation variable because low-density markets often require different sales, advertising, and distribution activities from high-density markets.

The U.S.A. is just one country where climate is commonly used as a geographic segmentation variable because it has such a broad impact on people's behaviour and product needs. The many product markets affected by climate include air conditioning and heating equipment, clothing, gardening equipment, recreational products, and building materials.

Locality: ACORN. ACORN (A Classification of Residential Neighbourhoods) develops geographic location as a segmentation base one stage further. Information taken from U.K. census data allows people to be grouped according to a number of factors including geography, socio-economics, and culture. In total, 40 different variables are considered including household size, number of cars, type of occupation, family size, and characteristics.

The underlying concept is that customers living in different residential neighbourhoods have different profiles in respect of these variables. Their product needs in terms of styling and features therefore also vary. Consumers can be classified under ACORN on the basis of the postcode of their home. They can then be allocated to one of the groups in Table 3.5.

These categories further subdivide to give a total of 38 neighbourhoods. For example, the older terraced housing (D) group (see Figure 3.10) splits into:

- unmodernised terraces, older people
- older terraces, lower-income families
- tenement flats lacking amenities

Marketing Update 3.2 discusses the use of ACORN to target prospective British Coal customers.

Personality, Motives, and Lifestyle. Marketers sometimes use variables such as personality characteristics, motives, and lifestyle to segment markets. The variables can be used by themselves to segment a market or in combination with other types.

Personality characteristics are useful when a product is similar to many competing products and consumers' needs are not significantly affected by other segmentation

FIGURE 3.9

Segmentation according to socio-economic variables.
This ad is clearly aimed at consumers who are high earners.

SOURCE: Ad for Dahne and Weinstein by Oscar Heyman and Sons, N.Y.

variables. However, attempting to segment a market according to personality characteristics has caused problems. Although marketing practitioners have long believed that consumer choice and product use should vary with personality and lifestyle, marketing research has shown only weak relationships. However, the weakness of such relationships may not be the result of lack of association between consumer choice and personality traits. Personality traits are difficult to measure accurately because most existing personality tests were developed for clinical use, not for segmentation purposes. As the reliability of more recent measurement instruments increases, a greater association between personality and consumer behaviour has been demonstrated.[5] It is certainly the case that personality sometimes influences the clothes, make-up and hair styles which individuals adopt. Links with other purchase behaviour therefore also seem likely.

When a market is segmented according to a motive, it is divided on the basis of consumers' reasons for making a purchase. Product durability, economy, convenience, and status are all motives that affect the types of product purchased and the choice of stores in which they are bought. For example, one motive for the purchase

5. John L. Lastovicka and Erich A. Joachimsthaler, "Improving the Detection of Personality-Behavior Relationships in Consumer Research," *Journal of Consumer Research*, March 1988, pp. 583–587.

TABLE 3.4 *Expenditure of households by occupation of head of household (000's)*

	OCCUPATION OF HEAD OF HOUSEHOLD							
	Profes-sional	Employers and managers	Inter-mediate non-manual	Junior non-manual	Skilled manual	Semi-skilled manual	Unskilled manual	All house-holds with employee heads
TOTAL NUMBER OF HOUSEHOLDS	312	781	502	395	1,032	528	154	3,725
TOTAL NUMBER OF PERSONS	878	2,316	1,265	981	3,329	1,524	415	10,768
TOTAL NUMBER OF ADULTS	626	1,610	925	722	2,250	1,051	298	7,523
HOUSING BY TYPE OF TENURE								
Rented unfurnished	8	43	58	62	257	183	78	693
Local authority	3	32	42	36	223	156	74	566
Housing association	2	2	4	5	12	14	3	42
Other	3	9	12	21	22	13	1	85
Rented furnished	15	18	24	13	19	18	7	120
Rent-free	10	14	1	13	7	22	1	68
Owner-occupied	279	706	419	307	749	305	68	2,844
In process of purchase	251	613	350	243	636	232	44	2,379
Owned outright	28	93	69	64	113	73	24	465

SOURCE: "Family Expenditure Survey," Central Statistical Office, 1988. Reprinted by permission of the Controller of Her Majesty's Stationery Office.

of soft drinks in two-litre bottles or six-packs is economy. At the other extreme, certain brands of champagne are marketed in terms of status to consumers who place particular importance on self-image.

Lifestyle segmentation groups individuals according to how they spend their time, the importance of items in their surroundings (their homes or their jobs, for example), their beliefs about themselves and broad issues, and some socio-economic characteristics such as income and education.[6] Lifestyle analysis provides a broad view of buyers because it encompasses numerous characteristics related to people's activities, interests, and opinions (see Table 3.6). It can be thought of as going beyond a simple understanding of personality.

Psychographics is the main technique used to measure lifestyle. However, its use has been, and probably will continue to be, limited for several reasons. First, psychographic variables are more difficult than other types of segmentation variables to measure accurately. Second, the relationships among psychographic variables and consumers' needs are sometimes obscure and unproven. Third, segments that result from psychographic segmentation may not be reachable.[7] For example, a marketer may determine that highly compulsive individuals want a certain type of clothing. However, no specific stores or specific media vehicles—such as television or radio programmes, newspapers, or magazines—appeal precisely to this group and this group alone. Psychographic variables can sometimes offer a useful way of better understanding segments which have been defined using other base variables.

6. Joseph T. Plummer, "The Concept and Application of Life Style Segmentation," *Journal of Marketing*, January 1974, p. 33.

7. James F. Engel, Roger D. Blackwell and Paul W. Miniard, *Consumer Behavior* (Orlando, Fla.: Dryden Press, 1990), pp. 348–349.

TABLE 3.5
ACORN groups

A	Agricultural areas
B	Modern family housing, higher incomes
C	Older housing of intermediate status
D	Older terraced housing
E	Council estates—Category I
F	Council estates—Category II
G	Council estates—Category III
H	Mixed inner metropolitan areas
I	High status non-family areas
J	Affluent suburban housing
K	Better-off retirement areas

SOURCE: CACI, Limited, London.

■ **Product-Related Behavioural Characteristics**

Marketers can also segment markets on the basis of an aspect of consumers' behaviour towards the product. This might relate to the way the particular product is used or purchased, for example, or perhaps to the benefits which consumers require from it.

Purchase behaviour can be a useful way of distinguishing between groups of customers, giving marketers insight into the most appropriate marketing mix. For example, brand-loyal customers may require a different kind of treatment from those who switch between brands. On-pack sales promotions are often geared towards the latter group.

It is often possible to distinguish between customers in terms of the occasion on which they buy a particular product. In different sets of circumstances the customer can be seen to apply different product selection criteria. Inevitably this will impact on the choice which is made. For instance, a customer who buys an airline ticket in haste to visit a sick relative will probably be less concerned about airline and price than one who is booking a holiday four months hence.

Benefit segmentation is the division of a market according to the benefits that consumers want from the product.[8] Although most types of market segmentation are based on the assumption that there is a relationship between the variable and customers' needs, benefit segmentation is different in that the benefits the customers seek *are* their product needs. Thus individuals are segmented directly according to their needs. By determining the benefits desired, marketers may be able to divide people into groups that are seeking certain sets of benefits.

The effectiveness of benefit segmentation depends on several conditions. First, the benefits people seek must be identifiable. Second, using these benefits, marketers must be able to divide people into recognisable segments. Finally, one or more of the resulting segments must be accessible to the firm's marketing efforts.

Individuals can be divided into users and non-users of a particular product. Users can then be classified further as heavy, moderate, or light. To satisfy a specific user group, marketers sometimes create a distinctive product, set special prices, or initiate special promotion and distribution activities. Thus airlines such as Cathay Pacific

---

8. Russell I. Haley, "Benefit Segmentation: A Decision-Oriented Research Tool", *Journal of Marketing*, July 1968, pp. 30–35.

FIGURE 3.10 *ACORN Group D: Older terraced housing.*
These areas are characterised by housing in pre-1914 terraced streets and tenements accommodating a high proportion of households living on very low incomes. Some of the housing still has no bath or inside WC and suffers from inadequate ventilation, heating and cooking facilities. There is a lack of suitable areas where children can play.

In larger towns, these areas often house many young families who cannot afford or are unable to find other accommodation. In small towns, where traditional industries are often in decline, the areas contain a more settled, elderly population. There are few modern retail outlets here as such areas, characterised by declining population figures and low incomes, are not commercially attractive.

SOURCE: CACI, Limited, London.

or Delta offer frequent flier programmes, which reward customers who regularly fly on their planes with free trips and discounts on rental cars and lodging. Light or non-users of products often receive little attention from manufacturers. There is a tendency sometimes to dismiss these groups when developing a marketing programme. For example, research in the holiday industry tends to focus on feedback from current customers, often forgetting to question why non-users failed to buy.

How customers use or apply the product may also determine segmentation. To satisfy customers who use a product in a certain way, some feature—say, packaging, size, texture, or colour—may have to be designed with special care to make the product easier to use, safer, or more convenient. For instance, Crest, Colgate, and other brands of toothpaste are now packaged with pump dispensers because consumers wanted easier-to-use packaging. In addition, special distribution, promotion, or pricing activities may have to be created.

The varying attitude of customers towards products is another set of variables which can be used to segment markets. Clothing retailers like River Island and Zy

BRITISH COAL TAKES ACORN ADVICE . . .

ACORN is continuing to offer companies essential help in targeting direct mail to very specific markets.

This has been clearly demonstrated when direct marketing agency RCF commissioned CACI to provide a clearer picture of the Solid Fuel Advisory Service (SFAS) customer base.

CACI took a sample of the SFAS's present customers—both in gas areas and non-gas areas. By analysing where customers were coming from, in both ACORN and geographical tests, it became clear that they were very strongly segmented. Certain groups of people were far more likely to become customers than others.

This information was then used to target direct mail to a finely tuned audience.

RCF carried out an initial 70,000 test mailing on behalf of the SFAS; this significantly exceeded targets in generating new leads. As a result of this success an additional mailing of 750,000 has been sent to two groups of customers, promoting central heating systems to consumers in 'non-gas' areas, and open fire heating to those in gas-connected areas.

The full results of this mailing are not known as yet.

SOURCE: Reprinted by permission of CACI Limited, London.

TABLE 3.6
Characteristics re-
lated to activities,
interests and opin-
ions

ACTIVITIES	INTERESTS	OPINIONS
Work	Family	Themselves
Hobbies	Home	Social issues
Social events	Job	Politics
Vacation	Community	Business
Entertainment	Recreation	Economics
Club membership	Fashion	Education
Community	Food	Products
Shopping	Media	Future
Sports	Achievements	Culture

SOURCE: Reprinted, adapted, from Joseph Plummer, "The Concept and Application of Life Style Segmentation," *Journal of Marketing*, January 1974, p. 34. Reprinted by permission of the American Marketing Association.

are particularly conscious of this. While one customer seeks outfits which are practical and comfortable, another is concerned only with achieving a highly fashionable image.

As this brief discussion shows, consumer markets can be divided according to numerous characteristics. Some of these variables, however, are not particularly helpful for segmenting industrial or organisational markets.

■ **Variables for Segmenting Organisational Markets**

Like consumer markets, industrial or organisational markets are sometimes segmented, but the marketers' aim is to satisfy the needs of organisations for products. Marketers may segment organisational markets according to geographic location, type of organisation, customer size, and product use.

Geographic Location. We noted that the demand for some consumer products can vary considerably among geographic areas because of differences in climate, terrain, customer preferences, or similar factors. Demand for organisational products also varies according to geographic location. For example, the producers of certain types of timber divide their markets geographically because their customers' needs vary regionally. Geographic segmentation may be especially appropriate for reaching industries that are concentrated in certain locations. For example, textiles are concentrated in West Yorkshire, cutlery in Sheffield, brewing in Burton, and lace in Nottingham. Examples in other countries include heavy industry concentrated around Lille or in the Ruhr Valley and banking in Zurich.

Type of Organisation. A company sometimes segments a market by the types of organisations within that market. Different types of organisations often require different product features, distribution systems, price structures, and selling strategies. Given these variations, a firm may either concentrate on a single segment with one marketing mix (concentration strategy) or focus on several groups with multiple mixes (multisegment strategy). A carpet producer could segment potential customers into several groups, such as car makers, carpet contractors (firms that carpet large commercial buildings), housing developers, carpet wholesalers, and large retail carpet outlets.

FIGURE 3.11
*Single-variable
segmentation*

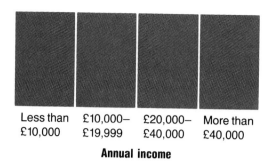

Less than £10,000	£10,000– £19,999	£20,000– £40,000	More than £40,000

Annual income

Customer Size. An organisation's size may affect its purchasing procedures and the types and quantities of products it wants. Size can thus be an effective variable for segmenting an organisational market. To reach a segment of a particular size, marketers may have to adjust one or more marketing mix components. For example, customers who buy in extremely large quantities are sometimes offered discounts. In addition, marketers often have to expand personal selling efforts to serve larger organisational buyers properly. Because the needs of larger and smaller buyers tend to be quite distinct, marketers frequently use different marketing practices to reach various customer groups.

Use of Product. Certain products, especially basic raw materials such as steel, petroleum, plastics, and timber, are used in numerous ways. How a company uses products affects the types and amounts of the products purchased, as well as the method of making the purchase. For example, computers are used for engineering purposes, basic scientific research, and business operations, such as word processing, bookkeeping, and telephone service. A computer producer may segment the computer market by types of use because organisations' needs for computer hardware and software depend on the purpose for which the products are purchased.

■ Single-Variable or Multivariable Segmentation

Selecting the appropriate variable for market segmentation is an important marketing management decision because the variable is the primary factor in defining the target market. So far, we have discussed segmentation by one variable. In fact, more than one variable can be used, and marketers must decide the number of variables to include.

Single-variable segmentation is achieved by using only one variable. The segmentation shown in Figure 3.11 is based on income alone. (Although the areas on the graph are the same size, this does not mean that the segments are the same size or equal in sales potential.) Single-variable segmentation, the simplest form of segmentation, is the easiest to perform. However, a single characteristic gives marketers only moderate precision in designing a marketing mix to satisfy individuals in a specific segment.

To achieve **multivariable segmentation**, more than one characteristic is used to divide a total market (see Figure 3.12). Notice in the figure that the market is segmented by three variables: income, population density, and volume usage. The people in the highlighted segment earn more than £25,000, are urban dwellers, and are heavy users. Multivariable segmentation provides more information about the individuals in each segment than does single-variable segmentation. More is known about the people in each segment of Figure 3.12 than about those in the segments

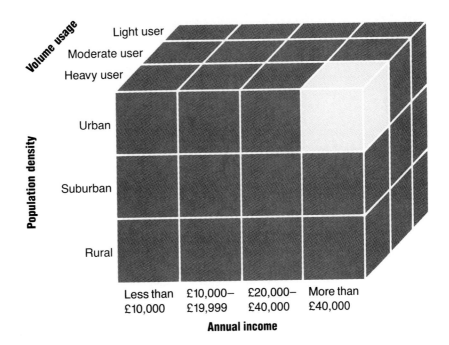

FIGURE 3.12
Multivariable segmentation

of Figure 3.11. This additional information may allow a company to develop a marketing mix that will satisfy customers in a given segment more precisely.

The major disadvantage of multivariable segmentation is that the larger the number of variables used, the greater the number of resulting segments. This proliferation reduces the sales potential of many of the segments. Compare, for example, the number and size of the segments in Figure 3.11 with the number and size of those in Figure 3.12.

The use of additional variables can help create and maintain a more exact and satisfying marketing mix. However, when deciding on single-variable or multivariable segmentation, a marketing manager must consider whether additional variables will actually help improve the firm's marketing mix. If using a second or third variable does not provide information that ensures greater precision, there is little reason to spend more money to gain information about the extra variables.

ENSURING THE EFFECTIVENESS OF SEGMENTATION

Whatever base variables are used, haphazard implementation can lead to ineffective market segmentation. The result can be measured in missed opportunities and inappropriate investment. Satisfying the following criteria can help to avoid problems of this type. The first assumption is that there are real differences in the needs of consumers for the product or service. There is no value in attempting to segment a homogeneous market. In addition to this, segments revealed must be:

measurable: easy to identify and measure. Some basis must be found for effectively separating individuals into groups or segments with relatively homogenous product or service needs.

substantial: large enough to be sufficiently profitable to justify developing and maintaining a specific marketing mix.

accessible: easy to reach with the marketing mix developed. For example, the promotional effort should target the relevant consumers.

stable: the question of segment stability over time is not often addressed. If companies are to make strategic decisions on the basis of revealed segments, they need to be reasonably certain that those segments will be around long enough for action to be taken.

UNDERSTANDING THE PROFILE OF MARKET SEGMENTS

Whatever the variable, or combination of variables, used to group customers, it is inevitable that a more comprehensive understanding of what those individuals are like will be needed. For example, a company which segments the market for shoes on the basis of age, focusing on customers in their late teens, would do well to understand as much as possible about its particular target group in other respects. What reference groups influence them? Where do they live? Where and when do they shop? What social background are they from? What motivates them? The list is almost endless. The more comprehensive the image developed, the better the opportunity to develop an effective marketing mix with maximum appeal.

Building up a fuller picture of target segments is sometimes called profiling and the variables used in the description are termed **descriptors**. The types of descriptors available to marketers are the same as the variables used to segment markets in the first place, that is, demographics, socio-economics, and so on. This is sometimes a cause of confusion for students who struggle to remember whether they are dealing with base or descriptor variables. The simplest explanation is that while base variables should discriminate between customer needs, descriptors are simply used to enrich the picture, to help summarise what else can be gleaned about the customers in a particular segment. This gives added inspiration to the creative team developing the product and promotional material and helps to fine tune decisions on price and distribution. Overall, the aim is to maximise the impact of the marketing mix on the customer, relative to the competition.

TARGETING STRATEGIES

Decisions about targeting centre on two major segmentation strategies: the concentration strategy and the multisegment strategy. Whether a company chooses to adopt one or the other, the decisions which are made should be based on a clear understanding of company capabilities and resources, the nature of the competition, and the characteristics of the product markets in question.

■ **Concentration Strategy**

When an organisation directs its marketing efforts towards a single market segment by creating and maintaining one marketing mix, it is employing a **concentration strategy**. Lamborghini, for example, focuses on the luxury sports car segment and directs all its marketing efforts towards high-income individuals who want to own high-performance luxury cars. The chief advantage of the concentration strategy is that it allows a firm to specialise. The firm can analyse the characteristics and needs of a distinct customer group and then focus all its energies on satisfying that group's needs. A firm can generate a large sales volume by reaching a single segment. In addition, concentrating on a single segment permits a firm with limited resources to

FIGURE 3.13
Multisegment strategy

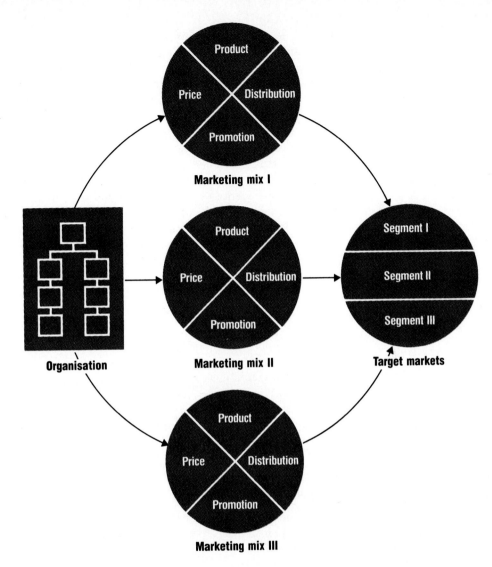

compete with much larger organisations, which may have overlooked some smaller segments.

Specialisation, however, means that a company puts all its eggs in one basket—clearly a disadvantage. If a company's sales depend on a single segment and the segment's demand for the product declines, the company's financial strength also declines. Moreover, when a firm penetrates one segment and becomes well entrenched, its popularity may keep it from moving into other segments. For example, Ferrari would have trouble moving into the economy car segment, whereas Hyundai would find it difficult to enter the luxury car segment.

■ **Multisegment Strategy**

With a **multisegment strategy** (see Figure 3.13), an organisation directs its marketing efforts at two or more segments by developing a marketing mix for each selected segment. After a firm uses a concentration strategy successfully in one market segment, it sometimes expands its efforts to additional segments. For example, Jockey underwear has traditionally been aimed at one segment: men. However, the company now markets underwear for women and children as well. The marketing mixes used for a multisegment strategy may vary as to product differences, distribution methods, promotion methods, and prices.

A business can usually increase its sales in the aggregate market through a multi-segment strategy because the firm's mixes are being aimed at more people. A company with excess production capacity may find a multisegment strategy advantageous because the sale of products to additional segments may absorb this excess capacity. On the other hand, a multisegment strategy often demands a greater number of production processes, materials, and people; thus production costs may be higher than with a concentration strategy. Keep in mind also that a firm using a multisegment strategy ordinarily experiences higher marketing costs. Because this strategy usually requires more research and several different promotion plans and distribution methods, the costs of planning, organising, implementing, and controlling marketing activities increase. Figure 3.14 highlights the factors which affect the choice of target market segments and which require consideration prior to entering a particular segment or segments.

POSITIONING

Figure 3.5 illustrated the link between market segmentation, targeting, and positioning. Having identified the segments in a market and decided on which segment (or segments) to target, a company must position its product, service or idea. According to Wind, "a product's positioning is the place a product occupies in a given market, as perceived by the relevant group of customers; that group of customers is known as the target segment of the market".[9] Harrison states that the position of a product is

> the sum of those attributes normally ascribed to it by the consumers—its standing, its quality, the type of people who use it, its strengths, its weaknesses, any other unusual or memorable characteristics it may possess, its price and the value it represents.[10]

Positioning starts with a product—a piece of merchandise, a service, a company, an institution, or even a person. **Positioning** is not what is done to the product, it is what is created in the minds of the target customers; the product is positioned in the minds of these customers and is given an image.[11] There may be a few cosmetic changes to the product—to its name, price, packaging, styling, or channel of distribution—but these are to facilitate the successful promotion of the image desired by the target customers. The product must be perceived by the selected target customers to have a distinct image and position vis-à-vis its competitors. Product differentiation is widely viewed as the key to successful marketing; the product must stand out and have a clearly defined position.

■ **Determining a Position**

Positions are described by variables and within parameters which are important to the customers and which essentially are selected by them. Price may be the key in grocery shopping, service level in selecting an hotel, quality and reliability when purchasing an electrical appliance such as a washing machine, value for money when choosing which theme park to visit. In-depth market research (often focus group

9. Y. Wind, "Going to Market: New Twist for Some Old Tricks," *Wharton Magazine*, **4**, 1980.

10. T. Harrison, *A Handbook of Advertising Techniques* (London: Kogan Page, 1987), p. 7.

11. A. Ries and J. Trout, *Positioning: The Battle for Your Mind* (New York: McGraw-Hill, 1981).

FIGURE 3.14

*Factors affecting choice
of target market strategy*

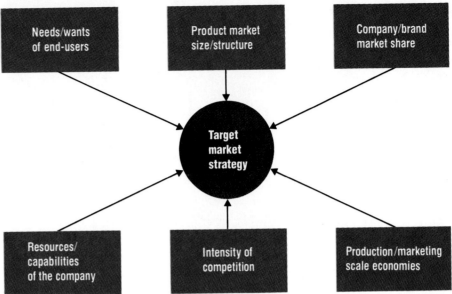

SOURCE: Data from D. Cravens, *Strategic Marketing* (Homewood, Ill.: Irwin, 1982).

discussions) is required to understand adequately customer motivations and expectations in a particular market. Management's intuition is not always sufficient. For example, research revealed that C1, C2, D and E social group consumers often have to decide between replacement lounge or dining-room furniture and a family package holiday abroad. Managers at most leading furniture retailers perceived other furniture retailers to be their competitors, when in reality they were additionally competing for consumers' disposable income against other diverse product areas. In this budget-conscious sector of the furniture-buying market, retailers believed only price to be important. In-depth research proved that value for money was perceived to be the main purchase consideration, which included product quality and durability in addition to price.

Consumers generally assign positions to a company or a product which is the market leader—and which probably has the highest profile—and the limited number of competitors they can recollect are orientated to this market leader. Occasionally the market leader in the mind of the consumer may not be the genuine market leader in terms of market share, but it is the one most visible at that time, possibly because of heavy promotional exposure. Customers respond to the attributes of a product and to its promotional imagery, but the product's position as perceived by its target customers is affected by the reputation and image of the company, coupled with its other products, and by the activities of its competitors. Marketing Update 3.3 discusses the importance of clear positioning for long-standing brand leaders.

In-depth market research leads to an understanding of how consumers perceive products, which marketing variables they believe to be most important and by what magnitude. Such research examines consumer perceptions of various brands or companies which operate in the market under scrutiny. **Perceptual mapping** is a tool commonly adopted by marketers and market researchers to visually depict such consumer perceptions and prioritising of brands and their perceived attributes. Figure 3.15 illustrates a hypothetical example where consumers thought product-range width and price were the key characteristics of the market. A cross marks the

FIGURE 3.15
*Positioning map of hypo-
thetical consumer pref-
erences*

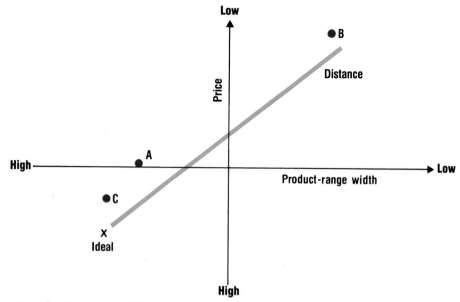

SOURCE: From D. Knee and D. Walters, *Strategy in Retailing* (Herts, England: Philip Allan, 1985), p. 27. Reproduced by permission of Philip Allan, a division of Prentice-Hall International.

ideal position, with high product-range width and above-average price (typical of high-quality shopping goods such as cameras or hi-fi systems). Brands (or companies) *A* and *C* are perceived as being relatively close to the ideal—their pricing policy does not fully match the image required—but brand (or company) *B* is viewed as being too cheap, with inadequate product-range width. Figure 3.16 illustrates how consumers of children's wear in the U.K. realised that the positioning of Adams (see Case 11.1) had shifted to reflect improvements in the quality of its merchandise, stores and personnel. Adams had successfully repositioned its brand to move away from being perceived as a budget-orientated retailer.

■ **Steps in Determining a Positioning Plan**

There should be no mystique associated with positioning a product. Common sense and a step-by-step approach lead to a product's clear positioning:

1. Define the segments in a particular market.
2. Decide which segment (or segments) to target.
3. Understand what the target consumers expect and believe to be most important when deciding on the purchase.
4. Develop a product (or products) which caters specifically for these needs and expectations.
5. Evaluate the positioning and images, as perceived by the target customers, of competing products in the selected market segment (or segments).
6. Select an image which sets your product (or products) apart from the competing products, thus ensuring the chosen image matches the aspirations of the target customers. (The selected positioning and imagery must be credible: consumers would not believe Lada or Skoda if they promoted their cars in the same manner as Porsche or Lotus.)
7. Tell your target consumers about the product (promotion) as well as making it readily available at the right price: this is the development of the full marketing mix.

PERSUADERS IN THE SUPERMARKET

The 1980s witnessed great social and political change worldwide. Nielsen, however, has identified that not everything changes: of the top ten grocery brands in the U.K., most first appeared on average 43 years ago. The most popular brand, Unilever's Persil with annual sales of over £200 million, has been in production for 80 years; Coca-Cola, in sixth position, is over a century old. The youngest brand in the top ten, Unilever's Flora margarine, hit the shelves in 1964.

The entrenchment and dominance of the leading grocery brands, coupled with their huge marketing budgets, make it difficult for new entrants to survive. Increasingly, the value of such well-established brands is recognised in corporate takeovers.

But why are consumers so wedded to the old brands? In blind product tests most consumers did not distinguish between PG Tips, Typhoo, and retailers' own-label tea. Nielsen research shows that of the top fifty brands, consumers can only identify three in blind tests: KitKat, Twix, and Lucozade.

Positioning and hefty promotional support have led to this entrenchment. Advertising and promotional activities have protected these brands, created financial barriers to entry, and encouraged consumers to be loyal. Consumers are reassured by the familiar positioning of their favourite brands and by the costly financial support the manufacturers give to promoting and emphasising their brands' positioning.

SOURCES: Information from Clive Wolman, "Golden Oldies Are Still Top of the Shops," *The Mail on Sunday,* 3 December 1989, used by permission of Solo Syndication & Literary Agency Ltd., London; and information from Nielsen Marketing Research, 1989, courtesy of NCH Promotional Services.

FIGURE 3.16
U.K. children's wear:
 positioning of major re-
tailers, featuring the repositioning of Adams

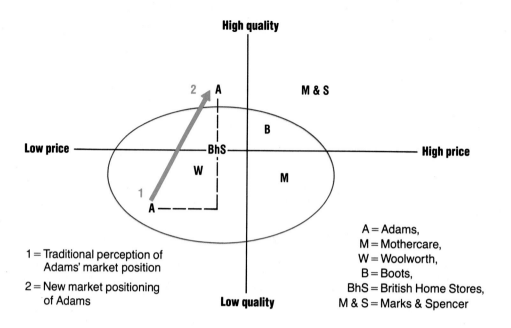

1 = Traditional perception of
    Adams' market position
2 = New market positioning
    of Adams

A = Adams,
M = Mothercare,
W = Woolworth,
B = Boots,
BhS = British Home Stores,
M & S = Marks & Spencer

EVALUATING MARKETS AND FORECASTING SALES

Whether taking a total market approach or opting for segmentation, a marketer must be able to measure the sales potential of the chosen target market or markets. Moreover, a marketing manager must determine the portion or share of the selected market that the firm can capture relative to its objectives, resources, and managerial skills, as well as to those of its competitors. Developing and maintaining a marketing mix consume a considerable amount of a company's resources. Thus the target market or markets selected must have enough sales potential to justify the cost of developing and maintaining one or more marketing mixes.

The potential for sales can be measured along several dimensions, including product, geographic area, time, and level of competition.[12] With respect to product, potential sales can be estimated for a specific product item (for example, diet Coke) or an entire product line (for example, Coca-Cola, Coca-Cola classic, diet Coke, diet caffeine-free Coke, and cherry Coca-Cola are one product line). A manager must also determine the geographic area to be included in the estimate. In relation to time, sales potential estimates can be short range (one year or less), medium range (one to five years), or long range (longer than five years). The competitive level specifies whether sales are being estimated for a single firm or for an entire industry. Thus marketers measure sales potential for both the entire market and for their own firms and then develop a sales forecast (Figure 3.17).

**■ Market and
Sales Potentials**

Market potential is the total amount of a product that customers will purchase within a specified period at a specific level of industrywide marketing activity. Market potential can be stated in terms of monetary value or units and can refer to a total market or to a market segment. As shown in Figure 3.17, market potential depends on economic, social, and other marketing environment factors. When ana-

12. Philip Kotler, *Marketing Management: Analysis, Planning, and Control*, 6th ed. (Englewood Cliffs, N.J.: Prentice-Hall, 1988), p. 257.

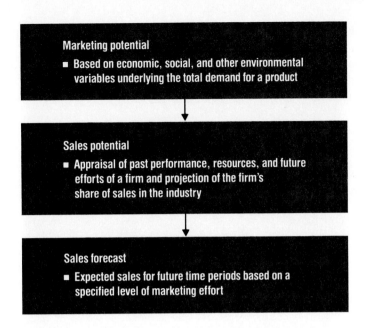

Marketing potential
- Based on economic, social, and other environmental variables underlying the total demand for a product

Sales potential
- Appraisal of past performance, resources, and future efforts of a firm and projection of the firm's share of sales in the industry

Sales forecast
- Expected sales for future time periods based on a specified level of marketing effort

lysing market potential, it is important to specify a time frame and to indicate the relevant level of industry marketing activities. Pan Am determined that in one year 3,300,000 customers travelled to Europe on its planes—more customers than any other airline had (see Figure 3.18). Based on these findings, Pan Am marketers were able to estimate the market potential for European travel in the following year, taking into account other environmental factors.

Note that marketers have to assume a certain general level of marketing effort in the industry when they estimate market potential. The specific level of marketing effort certainly varies from one firm to another, but the sum of all firms' marketing activities equals industry marketing efforts. A marketing manager must also consider whether and to what extent industry marketing efforts will change. For instance, in estimating the market potential for the spreadsheet software industry, Microsoft must consider changes in marketing efforts by Lotus and other software producers. If marketing managers at Microsoft know that Lotus is planning to introduce a new version of the Lotus 1-2-3 Spreadsheet product with a new advertising campaign, this fact will contribute to Microsoft's estimate of the market potential for computer software.

Sales potential is the maximum percentage of market potential that an individual firm within an industry can expect to obtain for a specific product. Several general factors influence a company's sales potential. First, the market potential places absolute limits on the size of the company's sales potential. Second, the magnitude of industrywide marketing activities has an indirect but definite impact on the company's sales potential. Those activities have a direct bearing on the size of the market potential. When Pizza Hut advertises home-delivered pizza, for example, it indirectly promotes pizza in general; its commercials may, in fact, help sell competitors' home-delivered pizza. Third, the intensity and effectiveness of a company's marketing activities relative to those of its competitors affect the size of the company's sales potential. If a company is spending twice as much as any of its competitors on marketing efforts and if every pound spent is more effective in generating sales, the firm's sales potential will be quite high compared with that of its competitors.

FIGURE 3.18

Determining market potential.

Pan Am determined that 3,300,000 people used its airline to travel to Europe in one year—more customers than any other airline. Based on these statistics, and accounting for any changes in environmental factors, Pan Am marketers can estimate market potential for the next year.

SOURCE: Courtesy of Pan American World Airways, Inc.

There are two general approaches to measuring sales potential: breakdown and buildup. In the **breakdown approach**, the marketing manager first develops a general economic forecast for a specific time period. Next, market potential is estimated on the basis of this economic forecast. The company's sales potential is then derived from the general economic forecast and the estimate of market potential.

In the **buildup approach**, an analyst begins by estimating how much of a product a potential buyer in a specific geographic area, such as a sales territory, will purchase in a given period. Then the analyst multiplies that amount by the total number of potential buyers in that area. The analyst performs the same calculation for each geographic area in which the firm sells products and then adds the totals for each area to calculate the market potential. To determine the sales potential, the analyst must estimate, by specific levels of marketing activities, the proportion of the total market potential that the company can obtain.

For example, the marketing manager of a regional paper company with three competitors might estimate the company's sales potential for bulk gift-wrapping paper using the buildup approach. The manager might determine that each of the sixty-six paper buyers in a single sales territory purchases an average of 10 rolls

TABLE 3.7

TABLE 3.7
The sales potential calculations for bulk wrapping paper (Market potential: 18,255 rolls)

TERRITORY	NUMBER OF POTENTIAL CUSTOMERS	ESTIMATED PURCHASES	TOTAL
1	66	10 rolls	660 rolls
2	62	10	620
3	55	5	275
4	28	25	700
5	119	5	595
6	50	20	1,000
7	46	10	460
8	34	15	510
9	63	10	630
10	55	10	550
		Total company sales potential	6,000 rolls

annually. For that sales territory, then, the market potential is 660 rolls annually. The analyst follows the same procedure in each of the firm's other nine sales territories and then totals the sales potential for each sales territory (see Table 3.7). Assume that this total market potential is 18,255 rolls of paper (the quantity expected to be sold by all four paper companies). Then the marketing manager would estimate the company's sales potential by ascertaining that it could sell about 33 percent of the estimated 18,255 rolls at a certain level of marketing effort. The marketing manager might develop several sales potentials, based on several levels of marketing effort.

Whether marketers use the breakdown or the buildup approach, they depend heavily on sales estimates. To get a clearer idea of how these estimates are derived, we turn to sales forecasting.

Developing Sales Forecasts

A **sales forecast** is the amount of a product that the company actually expects to sell during a specific period at a specified level of marketing activities. The sales forecast differs from the sales potential: it concentrates on what the actual sales will be at a certain level of marketing effort, whereas the sales potential assesses what sales are possible at various levels of marketing activities, assuming that certain environmental conditions will exist. Businesses use the sales forecast for planning, organising, implementing, and controlling their activities. The success of numerous activities depends on the accuracy of this forecast.

A sales forecast must be time specific. Sales projections can be short (one year or less), medium (one to five years), or long (longer than five years). The length of time chosen for the sales forecast depends on the purpose and uses of the forecast, the stability of the market, and the firm's objectives and resources.

To forecast sales, a marketer can choose from a number of forecasting methods. Some of them are arbitrary; others are more scientific, complex, and time-consuming. A firm's choice of method or methods depends on the costs involved, the type of product, the characteristics of the market, the time span of the forecast, the purposes of the forecast, the stability of the historical sales data, the availability of required information, and the forecasters' expertise and experience.[13] The common forecasting techniques fall into five categories: executive judgement, surveys, time series analysis, correlation methods, and market tests.

Executive Judgement.   At times, a company forecasts sales chiefly on the basis of **executive judgement**, which is the intuition of one or more executives. This approach is highly unscientific but expedient and inexpensive. Executive judgement may work reasonably well when product demand is relatively stable and the forecaster has years of market-related experience. However, because intuition is swayed most heavily by recent experience, the forecast may be overly optimistic or overly pessimistic. Another drawback to intuition is that the forecaster has only past experience as a guide for deciding where to go in the future.

Surveys.   A second way to forecast sales is to question customers, sales personnel, or experts regarding their expectations about future purchases.

Through a **customer forecasting survey**, marketers can ask customers what types and quantities of products they intend to buy during a specific period. This approach may be useful to a business that has relatively few customers. For example, a computer chip producer that markets to less than a hundred computer manufacturers could conduct a customer survey. PepsiCo, though, has millions of customers and cannot feasibly use a customer survey to forecast future sales, unless its sampling is known to reflect the entire market, which is hard to verify.

Customer surveys have several drawbacks. Customers must be able and willing to make accurate estimates of future product requirements. Although industrial buyers can sometimes estimate their anticipated purchases accurately from historical buying data and their own sales forecasts, many cannot make such estimates. In addition, for a variety of reasons, customers may not want to take part in a survey. Occasionally, a few respondents give answers that they know are incorrect, making survey results inaccurate. Moreover, customer surveys reflect buying intentions, not actual purchases. Customers' intentions may not be well formulated, and even when potential purchasers have definite buying intentions, they do not necessarily follow through with them. Finally, customer surveys consume much time and money.

In a **sales-force forecasting survey**, members of the firm's sales force are asked to estimate the anticipated sales in their territories for a specified period of time. The forecaster combines these territorial estimates to arrive at a tentative forecast.

A marketer may survey the sales staff for several reasons. The most important one is that the sales staff is closer to customers on a daily basis than other company personnel; therefore it should know more about customers' future product needs. Moreover, when sales representatives assist in developing the forecast, they are more likely to work toward its achievement. Another advantage of this method is that forecasts can be prepared for single territories, for divisions consisting of several territories, for regions made up of multiple divisions, and then for the total geographic market. Thus the method readily provides sales forecasts from the smallest geographic sales unit to the largest.

Despite these benefits, a sales-force survey has certain limitations. Salespeople can be too optimistic or pessimistic because of recent experiences. In addition,

13. David Hurwood, Elliot S. Grossman, and Earl Bailey, *Sales Forecasting* (New York: Conference Board, 1978), p. 2.

salespeople tend to underestimate the sales potential in their territories when they believe that their sales goals will be determined by their forecasts. They also dislike paperwork because it takes up the time that could be spent selling. If the preparation of a territorial sales forecast is time-consuming, the sales staff may not do the job adequately.

None the less, sales-force surveys can be effective under certain conditions. If, for instance, the salespeople as a group are accurate—or at least consistent—estimators, the overestimates and underestimates should balance each other out. If the aggregate forecast is consistently over or under actual sales, then the marketer who develops the final forecast can make the necessary adjustments. Assuming that the survey is well administered, the sales force can have the satisfaction of helping to establish reasonable sales goals. It can also be assured that its forecasts are not being used to set sales quotas.

When a company wants an **expert forecasting survey**, it hires experts to help prepare the sales forecast. These experts are usually economists, management consultants, advertising executives, academics, or other persons outside the firm who have solid experience in a specific market. Drawing on this experience and their analyses of available information about the company and the market, the experts prepare and present their forecasts or answer questions regarding a forecast. Using experts is expedient and relatively inexpensive. However, because they work outside the firm, experts may not be as motivated as company personnel to do an effective job.

Time Series Analysis.   The technique by which the forecaster, using the firm's historical sales data, tries to discover a pattern or patterns in the firm's sales over time is called **time series analysis**. If a pattern is found, it can be used to forecast sales. This forecasting method assumes that the past sales pattern will continue in the future. The accuracy, and thus the usefulness, of time series analysis hinges on the validity of this assumption.

In a time series analysis, a forecaster usually performs four types of analysis: trend, cycle, seasonal, and random factor.[14] **Trend analysis** focuses on aggregate sales data, such as a company's annual sales figures, from a period of many years to determine whether annual sales are generally rising, falling, or staying about the same. Through **cycle analysis**, a forecaster analyses sales figures (often monthly sales data) over a period of three to five years to ascertain whether sales fluctuate in a consistent, periodic manner. When performing **seasonal analysis**, the analyst studies daily, weekly, or monthly sales figures to evaluate the degree to which seasonal factors, such as climate and holiday activities, influence the firm's sales. **Random factor analysis** is an attempt to attribute erratic sales variations to random, non-recurrent events, such as a regional power failure, a natural disaster, or political unrest in a foreign market. After performing each of these analyses, the forecaster combines the results to develop the sales forecast.

Time series analysis is an effective forecasting method for products with reasonably stable demand, but it is not useful for products with highly erratic demand. Joseph E. Seagram & Sons, a U.S. importer and producer of spirits and wines, uses several types of time series analysis for forecasting and has found them quite accu-

14. Kenneth E. Marino, *Forecasting Sales and Planning Profits* (Chicago: Probus Publishing, 1986), p. 155.

rate. For example, Seagram's forecasts of industry sales volume have proved correct within ±1.5 percent, and the firm's sales forecasts have been accurate within ±2 percent.[15] Time series analysis is not always so dependable.

Correlation Methods.   Like time series analysis, correlation methods are based on historical sales data. When using **correlation methods**, the forecaster attempts to find a relationship between past sales and one or more variables such as population, per capita income, or gross national product. To determine whether a correlation exists, the forecaster analyses the statistical relationships among changes in past sales and changes in one or more variables—a technique known as regression analysis. The object of regression analysis is a mathematical formula that accurately describes a relationship between the firm's sales and one or more variables; however, the formula indicates only an association, not a causal relationship. Once an accurate formula has been established, the analyst plugs the necessary information into the formula to derive the sales forecast.

Correlation methods are useful when a precise relationship can be established. However, a forecaster seldom finds a perfect correlation. Furthermore, this method can be used only when the available historical sales data are extensive. Ordinarily, then, correlation techniques are futile for forecasting the sales of new products.

Market Tests.   Conducting a **market test** involves making a product available to buyers in one or more test areas and measuring purchases and consumer responses to distribution, promotion, and price. Even though test areas are often cities with populations of 200,000 to 500,000, test sites can be larger metropolitan areas or towns with populations of 50,000 to 200,000, or ITV regions. A market test provides information about consumers' actual purchases rather than about their intended purchases. In addition, purchase volume can be evaluated in relation to the intensity of other marketing activities—advertising, in-store promotions, pricing, packaging, distribution, and the like. On the basis of customer response in test areas, forecasters can estimate product sales for larger geographic units. For example, Cadbury's Wispa first appeared in the Tyne Tees area of northeast England. Sales showed management that the company had to build more production capacity to cope with a national roll-out of the brand and full launch.

Because it does not require historical sales data, a market test is an effective tool for forecasting the sales of new products or the sales of existing products in new geographic areas. The test gives the forecaster information about customers' real actions rather than intended or estimated behaviour. A market test also gives a marketer an opportunity to test various elements of the marketing mix. But these tests are often time-consuming and expensive. In addition, a marketer cannot be certain that the consumer response during a market test represents the total market response or that such a response will continue in the future.

■ **Using Multiple Forecasting Methods**   Although some businesses depend on a single sales-forecasting method, most firms use several techniques. A company is sometimes forced to use several methods when it markets diverse product lines, but even for a single product line several forecasts may be needed, especially when the product is sold in different market segments. Thus a producer of car tyres may rely on one technique to forecast tyre sales for new cars and on another to forecast the sales of replacement tyres. Varia-

15. Hurwood, Grossman, and Bailey, p. 61.

tion in the length of the needed forecasts may call for several forecast methods. A firm that employs one method for a short-range forecast may find it inappropriate for long-range forecasting. Sometimes a marketer verifies the results of one method by using one or several other methods and comparing results.

SUMMARY

A market is an aggregate of people who, as individuals or as organisations, have needs for products in a product class and who have the ability, willingness, and authority to purchase such products. A consumer market consists of purchasers and/or individuals in their households who intend to consume or benefit from the purchased products and who do not buy products for the main purpose of making a profit. An organisational or industrial market consists of persons and groups who purchase a specific kind of product for resale, direct use in producing other products, or use in day-to-day operations. Profit is not always necessarily a motive. Because products are classified according to use, the same product may be classified as both a consumer product and an organisational product.

Marketers use two general approaches to identify their target markets: the total market and the market segmentation approaches. A firm using a total market approach designs a single marketing mix and directs it at an entire market for a particular product. The total market approach can be effective when a large proportion of individuals in the total market have similar needs for the product and the organisation can develop and maintain a single marketing mix to satisfy those needs.

Markets made up of individuals with diverse product needs are called heterogeneous markets. The market segmentation approach divides the total market into groups consisting of people who have similar product needs. Profiling segments identified in terms of other variables can help build up a fuller picture. This can help in the design of a marketing mix (or mixes) that more precisely matches the needs of persons in a selected segment (or segments). A market segment is a group of individuals, groups, or organisations sharing one or more similar characteristics that cause them to have relatively similar product needs. There are two major types of targeting strategy. In the concentration strategy, the organisation directs its marketing efforts towards a single market segment through one marketing mix. In the multisegment strategy, the organisation develops different marketing mixes for two or more segments. The decisions which are made about the appropriate segment or segments to enter are linked to (amongst others) considerations about company resources, expertise, and the nature of customers and competitors.

Certain conditions must exist for market segmentation to be effective. First, consumers' needs for the product should be heterogeneous. Second, the segments of the market should be measurable so that the segments can be compared with respect to estimated sales potential, costs, and profits. Third, at least one segment must be substantial enough to have enough profit potential to justify developing and maintaining a special marketing mix for that segment. Fourth, the firm must be able to access the chosen segment with a particular marketing mix. Fifth, the segment should be reasonably stable over time.

Segmentation variables are the dimensions or characteristics of individuals, groups, or organisations that are used for dividing a total market into segments. The segmentation variable should be related to customers' needs for, uses of, or behaviour towards the product. Segmentation variables for consumer markets can be grouped into two broad categories which relate either to customer characteristics— demographics (age, sex, family, race, religion), socio-economics (income, occupation, education, social class), geography (country, region, urban area, housing), personality, motives, and lifestyle—or to product-related behaviour—purchase behaviour and occasion, benefits sought, consumption behaviour and user status, and attitude to product. Segmentation variables for organisational markets include geographic factors, type of organisation, customer size, and product use. Besides selecting the appropriate segmentation variable, a marketer must also decide how many variables to use. Single-variable segmentation involves only one variable, but in multivariable segmentation, more than one characteristic is used to divide a total market. Having decided which segment or segments to target, the marketer must position the product: it must have a clearly defined image in the minds of its target consumers. The product's positioning must be perceived by its consumers to be different from the positions of competing products. Perceptual maps assist marketers in graphically depicting the relative positions of the products in a particular market. Although a product's attributes and styling, along with its pricing, service levels and channel of distribution, contribute to how consumers perceive the product, a marketer uses mainly promotion to establish a product's positioning.

Whether using a total market or a market segmentation approach, a marketer must be able to measure the sales potential of the target market or markets. Market potential is the total amount of a product that customers will purchase within a specified period at a specific level of industrywide marketing activity. Sales potential is the maximum percentage of market potential that an individual firm within an industry can expect to obtain for a specific product. There are two general approaches to measuring sales potential: breakdown and buildup. A sales forecast is the amount of a product that the company actually expects to sell during a specific period of time and at a specified level of marketing activities. Several methods are used to forecast sales: executive judgement, surveys (customer, sales force, and executive surveys), time series analysis (trend analysis, cycle analysis, seasonal analysis, random factor analysis), correlation methods, and market tests. Although some businesses may rely on a single sales forecasting method, most organisations employ several different techniques.

Important Terms

Market
Consumer market
Organisational, or industrial, market
Total market (or undifferentiated) approach
Heterogeneous markets
Market segmentation
Segmentation variables (bases)
Market density
Benefit segmentation
Single-variable segmentation

Multivariable segmentation
Descriptors
Concentration strategy
Multisegment strategy
Positioning
Perceptual mapping
Market potential
Sales potential
Breakdown approach
Buildup approach
Sales forecast

Executive judgement
Customer forecasting survey
Sales-force forecasting survey
Expert forecasting survey
Time series analysis
Trend analysis

Cycle analysis
Seasonal analysis
Random factor analysis
Correlation methods
Market test

DISCUSSION AND REVIEW QUESTIONS

1. What is a market? What are the requirements for a market?
2. In your local area, is there a group of people with unsatisfied product needs who represent a market? Could this market be reached by a business organisation? Why or why not?
3. Identify and describe the two major types of market. Give examples of each.
4. What is the total market approach? Under what conditions is it most useful? Describe a present market situation in which a company is using a total market approach. Is the business successful? Why or why not?
5. What is the market segmentation approach? Describe the basic conditions required for effective segmentation. Identify several firms that use the segmentation approach.
6. List the differences between the concentration and the multisegment strategies. Describe the advantages and disadvantages of each strategy.
7. Identify and describe four major categories of variables that can be used to segment consumer markets. Give examples of product markets that are segmented by variables in each category.
8. What dimensions are used to segment industrial or organisational markets?
9. How do marketers decide whether to use single-variable or multivariable segmentation? Give examples of product markets that are divided through multivariable segmentation.
10. Why is a marketer concerned about sales potential when trying to find a target market?
11. What is a sales forecast and why is it important?
12. Under what conditions are market tests useful for sales forecasting? Discuss the advantages and disadvantages of market tests.

CASES

3.1   Changing Trends in Holiday Marketing

In 1990 the package holiday was forty years old. Initially responsible for a boom in the holiday industry, the appeal of the low-priced, mass-produced package is now diminishing. Destinations like Benidorm and Torremolinos are losing out while capacity on long-haul destinations, such as America and the Far East, continues to rise.

The aspirations of holiday-makers, and with them the face of the travel industry, are changing. Demands for more exotic destinations and a larger range of activity-based holidays are coupled with a refusal to tolerate the poor quality often associated with the cheap and cheerful package. Increasingly the customer is demanding personal attention, with holidays designed specifically. The result? An increasing range of specialised offerings—from wine-tasting trips, scuba-diving adventures and pony-trekking breaks through to painting holidays in France—targeting smaller segments.

Thomas Cook's response, in the shape of its new Travel by Appointment bureaux, demonstrates how seriously the industry is taking the change. This follows the company's decision in 1987 to pull out of short-haul holidays altogether, focusing instead on the long-haul sector. Travel by Appointment centres, which cater for customers seeking unusual holiday experiences, aim to develop the high-margin, luxury end of the market. The emphasis is on personal service, provided by company "specialists" who tailor the trip to suit the customer, and no queues! A spokesperson for Thomas Cook commented, "It did not seem right that someone wanting a £6,000 round-the-world trip should have to queue behind someone buying a return flight to Paris."

Financially the changes seem to make sense. By 1988 almost 12 million Britons were holidaying overseas. Competition for their business was intense, with price wars forcing profit margins down, in some cases to less than one pound per holiday. The future, it seems, lies in selling a smaller number of better-quality and high-margin holidays, targeted at narrower customer groups.

SOURCES: Franny Moyle, "Picking Quality and Packing More Choice," *Marketing Week*, 12 January 1990; Martin Wroe, "Tourists Set off in Search of a World of Their Own," *Independent on Sunday*, 10 June 1990; M. Labrou, "Ten Marketing Case Studies," University of Warwick MBA Dissertation, 1989.

Questions for Discussion

1. How should Thomas Cook position its Travel by Appointment bureaux?
2. At whom should the bureaux be targeted?
3. How has Thomas Cook responded to changes in the marketing environment?

3.2   The U.K. Market for Hosiery

The U.K. market for hosiery has undergone significant development in recent years with a change in consumer attitudes towards the four basic product categories: tights, stockings, knee tights (pop socks), and support hose. Women's hosiery, it seems, is no longer viewed as just another everyday necessity. Instead, stockings and tights have become highly personal fashion accessories with the potential to demand higher prices than before. The increasing percentage of women at work has helped to establish a demand for wider choice with consumers seeking different types of hosiery for different occasions.

Major manufacturers have exploited the product development opportunities which have arisen by introducing a variety of new ranges and styles: different colours, patterns, prints and textures have all competed for consumers' attention. The result has been a significant increase in total retail sales value. Table 3.8 illustrates the value of U.K. sales of women's hosiery for the period 1983 to 1988.

The market for hosiery in the U.K. is dominated by major players Pretty Polly and Courtaulds, followed by Charnos and the Nottingham Manufacturing Company. Merchandise is available through a range of outlets including grocers, drapers, department stores, chain and variety stores, and chemists.

TABLE 3.8
U.K. sales of women's hosiery, 1983–1988

YEAR	PAIRS (MILLIONS)	TOTAL RETAIL SALES (£M) (CURRENT PRICES)	AVERAGE PRICE PER PAIR (£)
1983	550	275	0.50
1984	542	290	0.51
1985	550	320	0.52
1986	546	375	0.60
1987	554	390	0.59
1988°	551	413	—
1989°°	548	442	—

* estimated
** projected

Traditionally a fibre and textile manufacturer, U.K.–based Courtaulds has, during the last few years, diversified into other related areas. Out of a total turnover of £2.6 billion in 1988/1989, the clothing sector of its textile business was £395 million. Up until the end of 1988, Courtaulds' hosiery was marketed under two brand names: Kayser and Aristoc. While Kayser was aimed mainly at grocers' outlets, appearing alongside retailers' own brands, the Aristoc range had a more upmarket image.

Following an earlier announcement that the company planned to revitalise its Aristoc brand with a £1 million advertising campaign, in September 1988, Courtaulds decided to drop the Kayser brand altogether. All efforts were to be focussed on Aristoc. At the same time, a broadening of the outlets through which Aristoc was available took place. In addition to selling through its traditional outlets of department stores and independent ladies' wear outlets, Aristoc replaced Kayser on the food and grocery retailers' shelves. The logic was clear: with a high average purchase frequency of 22 pairs of hosiery per woman each year, Courtaulds expected a significant increase in the volume sold through grocers. As a Courtaulds' spokesperson informed the press, "We are offering grocers our best stock while strengthening the brand in our traditional market-place."

SOURCES: "Stockings and Tights," Mintel: *Marketing Intelligence Report*, February 1989; "Stockings and Tights," Mintel: *Marketing Intelligence Report*, May 1987; *Drapers' Record*, 22 February 1986, p. 24; *Drapers' Record*, 1 May 1988, p. 22; *Grocer*, 4 October 1986, p. 51; *Grocer*, 22 October 1988, p. 44; *Courtaulds Annual Report*, 1988/89; Michael Labrou, "Ten Marketing Case Studies," University of Warwick MBA Dissertation, 1989.

Questions for Discussion

1. What variables might be appropriate for segmenting the hosiery market?
2. Why did Courtaulds decide to drop the Kayser brand in favour of Aristoc?
3. How should Courtaulds have gone about positioning the Aristoc brand following the replacement of Kayser on the grocery retailers' shelves?

4 CONSUMER BUYING BEHAVIOUR

Objectives

To understand the types of consumer buying behaviour and stages in the consumer buying decision process

To recognise the stages of the consumer buying decision process

To explore how personal factors may affect the consumer buying decision process

To learn about the psychological factors that may affect the consumer buying decision process

To examine the social factors that influence the consumer buying decision process

To understand why it is important that marketers attempt to understand consumer buying behaviour

T-shirts illustrate some of the factors that influence consumers' purchasing decisions. At times, people want to express their membership in a particular group and T-shirts provide a vehicle for this expression. For example, a fan may purchase a rock group T-shirt. Likewise, supporters of environmental causes may declare themselves allied to a particular group or association by the T-shirts they wear.

People buy T-shirts that communicate something about their personality. A T-shirt that says "I Am A UFO" may express a sense of humour whereas one that says "All this and brains too!" may express a sense of confidence (or conceit). An owner (or would-be owner) of a BMW may express personal status from product ownership by displaying the car's logo on a T-shirt.

T-shirts can also be used as ritual artefacts to commemorate alcohol consumption, rock music concerts, or even a specific athletic contest. For some young people, identifying with these events may commemorate or symbolise adolescent initiation into adulthood.

Consumers' desires to express their personality in a comic way led to the development of Lin-Tex Marketing. Lin-Tex began putting comic strip characters, like those from "Bloom County" and "Mother Goose and Grimm," on T-shirts. In the U.S., the company now has 15 nationally known comic strips under exclusive license, and 1990 sales were estimated at $7 million. The success of Lin-Tex Marketing is evidence that a good understanding of the forces that shape consumer behaviour is helpful in reaching profitable market segments. ◆

Based on information from T. Bettina Cornwell, "T-Shirts as Wearable Diary: An Examination of Artifact Consumption and Garnering Related to Life Events," *Advances in Consumer Research*, Vol. 17, 1990; Al Ebbers, "Shirt Tales," *Nation's Business*, Jan. 1990, p. 17.

A symbolic communication is expressed through the clothes that consumers buy and wear. T-shirts are a good example of this symbolic communication. **Buying behaviour** consists of the decision processes and acts of people involved in buying and using products.[1] **Consumer buying behaviour** refers to the buying behaviour of ultimate consumers, those who purchase products for personal or household use, not for business purposes. Marketers should analyse consumer buying behaviour for several reasons. First, buyers' reactions to a firm's marketing strategy have a great impact on the firm's success. Second, as indicated in Chapter 1, the marketing concept stresses that a firm should create a marketing mix that satisfies customers. To find out what satisfies customers, marketers must examine the main influences on what, where, when, and how consumers buy. Third, by gaining a better understanding of the factors that affect buying behaviour, marketers can better predict how consumers will respond to marketing strategies.

Although marketers may try to understand and influence consumer buying behaviour, they cannot control it. Some critics credit them with the ability to manipulate buyers, but marketers have neither the power nor the knowledge to do so. Their knowledge of behaviour comes from what psychologists, social psychologists, and sociologists know about human behaviour in general. Even if marketers wanted to manipulate buyers, the lack of laws and principles in the behavioural sciences would prevent them from doing so.

In this chapter we begin by examining the types of decision-making that consumers engage in. Then we analyse the major stages of the consumer buying decision process and consider the personal, psychological, and social factors that influence it. We conclude by assessing the importance of understanding consumer buying behaviour.

TYPES OF CONSUMER BUYING BEHAVIOUR

Consumers usually want to create and maintain a collection of products that satisfy their needs and wants in both the present and future. To achieve this objective, consumers make many purchasing decisions. For example, people must make several decisions daily regarding food, clothing, shelter, medical care, education, recreation, or transport. As they make these decisions, they engage in different decision-making behaviours. The amount of effort, both mental and physical, that buyers expend in decision-making varies considerably from situation to situation. Consumer decisions can thus be classified into one of three broad categories: routine response behaviour, limited decision-making, and extensive decision-making.[2]

A consumer practises **routine response behaviour** when buying frequently purchased, low-cost items that need very little search and decision effort. When buying such items, a consumer may prefer a particular brand, but he or she is familiar with several brands in the product class and views more than one as being

1. James F. Engel, Roger D. Blackwell, and Paul W. Miniard, *Consumer Behavior,* 5th ed. (Hinsdale, Ill.: Dryden Press, 1986), p. 5.

2. John A. Howard and Jagdish N. Sheth, *The Theory of Buyer Behavior* (New York: Wiley, 1969), pp. 27–28.

acceptable. The products that are bought through routine response behaviour are purchased almost automatically. Most buyers, for example, do not spend much time or mental effort selecting a soft drink or a snack food. If the nearest soft-drink machine does not offer Sprite, they will quite likely choose a 7-Up or Lilt instead.

Buyers engage in **limited decision-making** when they buy products occasionally and when they need to obtain information about an unfamiliar brand in a familiar product category. This type of decision-making requires a moderate amount of time for information-gathering and deliberation. For example, if Procter & Gamble introduces an improved Tide washing powder, buyers will seek additional information about the new product, perhaps by asking a friend who has used the product or watching a commercial, before they make a trial purchase.

The most complex decision-making behaviour, **extensive decision-making**, comes into play when a purchase involves unfamiliar, expensive, or infrequently bought products—for instance, cars, homes, or private education. The buyer uses many criteria to evaluate alternative brands or choices and spends much time seeking information and deciding on the purchase.

By contrast, **impulse buying** involves no conscious planning but rather a powerful, persistent urge to buy something immediately. For some individuals, impulse buying may be the dominant buying behaviour. Impulse buying, however, often provokes emotional conflicts. For example, a man may want to have the new golf bag he just saw right away and so purchases it on the spot, but he also feels guilty because he knows his finances are limited that month.

The purchase of a particular product does not always elicit the same type of decision-making behaviour.[3] In some instances, we engage in extensive decision-making the first time we buy a certain kind of product but find that limited decision-making suffices when we buy the product again. If a routinely purchased, formerly satisfying brand no longer pleases us, we may use limited or extensive decision processes to switch to a new brand. For example, if we notice that the petrol we normally buy is making our car's engine knock, we may seek out a higher octane brand through limited or extensive decision-making.

THE CONSUMER BUYING DECISION PROCESS

As defined earlier, a major part of buying behaviour is the decision process used in making purchases. The **consumer buying decision process**, shown in Figure 4.1, includes five stages: (1) problem recognition, (2) information search, (3) evaluation of alternatives, (4) purchase, and (5) post-purchase evaluation. Before we examine each stage, consider these important points. First, the actual act of purchasing is only one stage in the process; the process is begun several stages before the actual purchase. Second, even though, for discussion purposes, we indicate that a purchase occurs, not all decision processes lead to a purchase; the individual may end the process at any stage. Finally, not all consumer decisions always include all five stages. Persons engaged in extensive decision-making usually go through all stages of this decision process, whereas those engaged in limited decision-making and routine response behaviour may omit some stages.

3. G. Foxall, "Consumer Behaviour," in *The Marketing Book*, M. Baker, Ed. (London: Heinemann/Chartered Institute of Marketing, 1987).

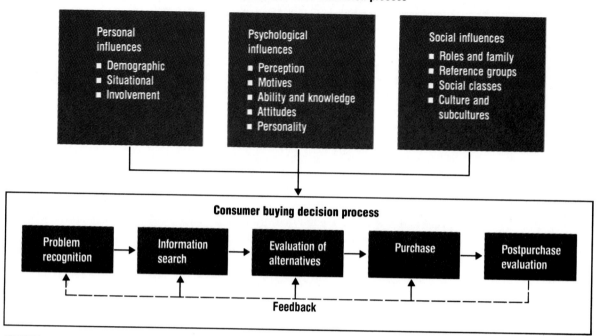

Possible influences on the decision process

Personal influences	Psychological influences	Social influences
■ Demographic ■ Situational ■ Involvement	■ Perception ■ Motives ■ Ability and knowledge ■ Attitudes ■ Personality	■ Roles and family ■ Reference groups ■ Social classes ■ Culture and subcultures

Consumer buying decision process

Problem recognition → Information search → Evaluation of alternatives → Purchase → Postpurchase evaluation

Feedback

FIGURE 4.1 *Consumer buying decision process and possible influences on the process*

■ Problem Recognition

Problem recognition occurs when a buyer becomes aware that there is a difference between a desired state and an actual condition. For example, consider a marketing student who wants a reliable, advanced calculator for use in a finance course. When her old calculator stops working, she recognises that a difference exists between the desired state—a reliable calculator—and the actual condition—a non-working calculator. She therefore decides to buy a new calculator.

Sometimes a person has a problem or need but is unaware of it. As shown in Figure 4.2, some consumers might not be aware of the advantages of using a bath gel. Marketers use sales personnel, advertising, and packaging to help trigger recognition of such needs or problems. For example, a university bookshop may advertise business and scientific calculators in the university newspaper at the beginning of the term. Students who see the advertisement may recognise that they need calculators for their course work. The speed of consumer problem recognition can be rather slow or quite rapid.

■ Information Search

After recognising the problem or need, the buyer (if continuing the decision process) searches for information about products that will help resolve the problem or satisfy the need. For example, the above-mentioned student, after recognising the need for a calculator, may search for information about different types and brands of calculators. Information is acquired over time from the consumer's surroundings. However, we must remember that the impact of the information depends on how the consumer interprets it.

There are two aspects to an information search. In the **internal search**, buyers first search their memory for information about products that might solve the problem. If they cannot retrieve enough information from their memory for a

FIGURE 4.2
Problem recognition.
Neutrogena makes consumers aware of the advantages of its product.

Good morning!

Neutrogena®
rainbath®
shower
and
bath gel

SOURCE: Neutrogena Corporation, Los Angeles, CA.

decision, they seek additional information in an **external search**. The external search may focus on communication with friends or relatives, comparison of available brands and prices, marketer-dominated sources, and/or public sources. An individual's personal contacts—friends, relatives, associates—often are credible sources of information because the consumer trusts and respects them. Utilising marketer-dominated sources of information, which include salespersons, advertising, package labelling, and in-store demonstrations and displays, typically does not require much effort on the consumer's part. Buyers can also obtain information from public sources—for instance, government reports, news stories, consumer publications, and reports from product-testing organisations. Consumers frequently view information from public sources as highly credible because of its factual and unbiased nature.

Consumer groups are increasingly demanding access to all relevant product information. However, the greater the quantity of information available, the more the buyer may be overloaded with information. Research indicates that consumers make poorer choices when faced with large amounts of information.[4] Improving the quality of information and stressing features important to buyers in the decision process may help buyers make better purchase decisions.

4. Kevin L. Keller and Richard Staelin, "Effects of Quality and Quantity of Information on Decision Effectiveness," *Journal of Consumer Research*, September 1987, pp. 200–213.

How consumers use and process the information obtained in their search depends on features of the information itself, namely, availability, quantity, quality, repetition, and format. If all the necessary information for a decision is available in the store, consumers may have no need to conduct an internal information search. Having all information externally available makes the consumer's decision process easier,[5] increases utilisation of the information, and may thus facilitate a purchase.

Repetition, a technique well known to advertisers, increases consumer learning of information. When seeing or hearing an advertising message for the first time, the recipient may not grasp all its important details but learns more details as the message is repeated. Nevertheless, even when commercials are initially effective, repetition eventually causes the phenomenon of "wear-out": consumers pay less attention to the commercial and respond to it less favourably than they did at first.[6]

The format in which information is transmitted to the buyer may also determine its use. Information can be presented verbally, numerically, or visually. For many consumer tasks, pictures are remembered better than words, and the combination of pictures and words further enhances learning.[7] Consequently, marketers pay great attention to the visual components of their advertising materials.

A successful information search yields a group of brands that a buyer views as possible alternatives. This group of products is sometimes called the buyer's *evoked set*. For example, an evoked set of calculators might include those made by Texas Instruments, Hewlett-Packard, Tandy, Sharp, and Casio.

■ Evaluation of Alternatives

To evaluate the products in the evoked set, a buyer establishes criteria for comparing the products. These criteria are the characteristics or features that the buyer wants (or does not want). For example, one calculator buyer may want a solar-powered calculator with a large display and large buttons, whereas another may have no preference as to the size of features but happens to dislike solar-powered calculators. The buyer also assigns a certain level of importance to each criterion; some features and characteristics carry more weight than others. Using the criteria, a buyer rates and eventually ranks the brands in the evoked set. The evaluation stage may yield no brand that the buyer is willing to purchase; in that case, a further information search may be necessary.

Marketers can influence consumers' evaluation by *framing* the alternatives—that is, by the manner in which the marketer describes the alternative and its attributes. Framing can make a characteristic seem more important to a consumer and can facilitate its recall from memory. For example, by stressing a car's superior petrol consumption over that of a competitor's, a car manufacturer can direct consumers' attention towards this point of superiority. Framing affects the decision processes of inexperienced buyers more than those of experienced ones.[8] If the evaluation of alternatives yields one or more brands that the consumer is willing to buy, the consumer is ready to move on to the next stage of the decision process—the purchase.

5. Gabriel Biehal and Dipankar Chakravarti, "Consumers' Use of Memory and External Information in Choice: Macro and Micro Perspectives," *Journal of Consumer Research,* March 1986, pp. 382–405.

6. Bobby J. Calder and Brian Sternthal, "Television Commercial Wearout: An Information Processing View," *Journal of Marketing Research,* May 1980, pp. 173–186.

7. Michael J. Houston, Terry L. Childers, and Susan E. Heckler, "Picture-Word Consistency and the Elaborative Processing of Advertisements," *Journal of Marketing Research,* November 1987, pp. 359–369.

8. James R. Bettman and Mita Sujan, "Effects of Framing on Evaluation of Comparable and Noncomparable Alternatives by Expert and Novice Consumers," *Journal of Consumer Research,* September 1987, pp. 141–154.

■ Purchase

In the purchase stage, the consumer chooses the product or brand to be bought. The selection is based on the outcome of the previous evaluation stage and on other dimensions. Product availability may influence which brand is purchased. For example, if the brand ranked the highest in evaluation is not available, the buyer may purchase the brand that is ranked second.

During this stage, the buyer also picks the seller from whom he or she will buy the product. The choice of the seller may affect the final product selection—and so may the terms of sale, which, if negotiable, are determined during the purchase decision stage. Other issues such as price, delivery, guarantees, maintenance agreements, installation, and credit arrangements are discussed and settled. Finally, the actual purchase takes place during this stage, unless, of course, the consumer terminates the buying decision process before reaching that point.

■ Post-purchase Evaluation

After the purchase, the buyer begins evaluating the product to ascertain if its actual performance meets expected levels. Many of the criteria used in evaluating alternatives are applied again during the post-purchase evaluation. The outcome of this stage is either satisfaction or dissatisfaction. These feelings strongly influence consumers' motivation and information-processing. Consumers' satisfaction or dissatisfaction determines whether they make a complaint, communicate with other possible buyers, and purchase the product again.[9] The impact of the post-purchase evaluation is illustrated by the feed-back loop in Figure 4.1.

Shortly after a purchase of an expensive product, the post-purchase evaluation may result in **cognitive dissonance**—doubts that occur because the buyer questions whether the right decision was made in purchasing the product. For example, after buying an expensive calculator, the marketing student may feel guilty about the purchase or have doubts about whether she purchased the right brand and quality. A buyer who experiences cognitive dissonance may attempt to return the product or may seek positive information about it to justify that choice.

As shown in Figure 4.1, there are three major categories of influences that are believed to affect the consumer buying decision process: personal, psychological, and social factors. The remainder of this chapter focuses on these factors. Although we discuss each major factor separately, keep in mind that their effects on the consumer decision process are interrelated.

PERSONAL FACTORS INFLUENCING THE BUYING DECISION PROCESS

A **personal factor** is one that is unique to a particular person. Numerous personal factors can influence purchasing decisions. In this section we consider three categories of them: demographic factors, situational factors, and level of involvement.

■ Demographic Factors

Demographic factors are individual characteristics such as age, sex, race, ethnic origin, income, family life-cycle, and occupation. (These and other characteristics were discussed in Chapter 3 as possible variables for segmentation purposes.) Demographic factors have a bearing on who is involved in family decision-making. For example, it is estimated that by the mid-1990s the U.K. will have the largest market

9. Robert A. Westbrook, "Product/Consumption-Based Affective Responses and Postpurchase Processes," *Journal of Marketing Research,* August 1987, pp. 258–270.

TABLE 4.1 *Projected demographic population by age and sex, 1995 official forecasts (in thousands)*

	TOTAL	MALE	FEMALE	0–14	15–64	65 +	NOTES
EEC MEMBERS							
Belgium	9,729	4,747	4,982	1,766	6,404	1,559	
Denmark	5,108	2,507	2,601	849	3,455	804	
France	56,338	27,756	28,582	11,194	37,338	7,807	a
West Germany	59,983	29,118	30,864	9,502	41,004	9,477	a
Greece	10,168	5,053	5,115	2,347	6,434	1,387	
Ireland	4,083	2,051	2,032	1,161	2,533	389	a
Italy	57,506	27,960	29,546	9,307	39,071	9,128	
Luxembourg	373	182	191	71	253	49	
Netherlands	15,028	7,413	7,615	2,653	10,325	2,050	
Portugal	10,819	5,273	5,547	2,129	7,263	1,427	
Spain	40,022	19,706	20,316	7,647	26,745	5,630	
United Kingdom	58,144	28,483	29,661	11,593	37,385	9,166	
EEC TOTAL	327,301	160,249	167,052	60,219	218,210	48,873	

a UN estimates (medium variant)

SOURCE: National Statistical Offices/UN World Population Prospects; "European Marketing Data & Statistics," *Euromonitor,* 1989, p. 135. Reprinted by permission.

for children's toys and clothes in the EEC, with the highest proportion of children in the population. Table 4.1 shows the EEC official population projections by age and sex for the year 1995.

Children aged 6 to 17 are known to have more influence in the buying decision process for breakfast cereals, ice-cream, soft drinks, and even the family car than ever before.[10] Demographic factors may also partially govern behaviour during a specific stage of the decision process. During the information stage, for example, a person's age and income may affect the number and types of information sources used and the amount of time devoted to seeking information.

Demographic factors also affect the extent to which a person uses products in a specific product category. Consumers in the 15 to 24 age group often purchase furniture, appliances, and other household basics as they establish their own households. On the other hand, those in the 45 to 54 age group spend more money on luxury and leisure products after their children have left home.[11] Brand preferences, store choice, and timing of purchases are other areas on which demographic factors have some impact. Consider, for example, how differences in occupation result in variations in product needs. A schoolteacher may earn roughly the same annually as a plumber. Yet the teacher and the plumber spend their incomes differently because the product needs that arise from these two occupations vary considerably. Although both occupations require the purchase of work clothes, the teacher buys suits and the plumber buys jeans and work shirts. The vehicles they drive also vary to some extent. Where and what they eat for lunch are likely to be different. Finally, the "tools" that they purchase and use in their work are not the same. Thus occupation clearly affects consumer buying behaviour.

10. Patricia Sellers, "The ABC's of Marketing to Kids," *Fortune,* 8 May 1989, p. 115.

11. Judith Waldrop, "Inside America's Households," *American Demographics,* March 1989, pp. 20–27.

■ Situational Factors

Situational factors are the external circumstances or conditions that exist when a consumer is making a purchase decision. Sometimes a consumer engages in buying decision-making as a result of an unexpected situation. For example, a person may hurriedly buy a plane ticket to spend the last few days with a dying relative. Yet in other circumstances the same individual might spend many weeks shopping around for a discounted package holiday. Or a situation may arise that causes a person to lengthen or terminate the buying decision process. For instance, a consumer who is considering the purchase of a personal computer and is laid off from work during the stage of evaluating alternatives may decide to reject the purchase entirely.

Situational factors can influence a consumer's actions during any stage of the buying decision process, and in a variety of ways. Uncertainty about future marital status may sway a consumer against making a purchase. On the other hand, a conviction that the supply of necessary products is sharply limited may impel people to buy them. For example, consumers have purchased and hoarded petrol and various food products when these products were believed to be in short supply. Even the weather may affect buying behaviour. A hurricane warning usually sends U.S. coastal residents rushing to stock up on bottled water, batteries, and emergency food supplies in just the same way as U.K. citizens hurry to buy candles at times of threatened electricity power cuts. These and other situational factors can change rapidly; their influence on purchase decisions can be sudden and can also subside quickly.

The time available to make a decision is a situational factor that strongly influences consumer buying decisions. If there is little time for selecting and purchasing a product, a person may make a quick choice and purchase a readily available brand. The amount of available time also affects the way consumers process the information contained in advertisements[12] and the length of the stages within the decision process. For example, if a family is planning to buy a washing machine for a new house, its members may gather and consider a great deal of information. They may read consumer magazines, talk to friends and salespersons, look at a number of advertisements, and spend a good deal of time on comparative shopping in a number of stores. However, if the family's 20-year-old Hotpoint washing machine suddenly breaks down and cannot be repaired, the extent of the information search, the number of alternatives considered, and the amount of comparative shopping may be much more restricted. Indeed, given the limited-time factor, if these family members were reasonably satisfied with the performance of the old machine, they may buy another Hotpoint because they know the brand.

■ Level of Involvement

Many aspects of consumer buying decisions are affected by the individual's **level of involvement**—the importance and intensity of interest in a product in a particular situation. A buyer's level of involvement determines why he or she is motivated to seek information about certain products and brands but virtually ignores others. The extensiveness of the buying decision process varies greatly with the consumer's level of involvement. The sequence of the steps in this process may also be altered. Low-involvement buyers may form an attitude about a product and evaluate its features after purchasing it rather than before.[13] Conversely, high-involvement buyers spend much time and effort researching their purchase beforehand. In Figure 4.3, IBM provides an 0800 number which buyers may use to gain additional infor-

12. Houston, Childers, and Heckler, pp. 359–369.

13. Thomas S. Robertson and Hubert Gatignon, "Competitive Effects on Technology Diffusion," *Journal of Marketing*, July 1986, pp. 1–12.

FIGURE 4.3

Reaching consumers who have a high level of involvement.
IBM provides a strong service policy supporting its computer equipment. An 0800 number is also provided for high-involvement buyers who may want additional information.

SOURCE: Courtesy of International Business Machines Corporation.

mation about its office equipment. Computers are products that undergo a great deal of investigation before they are chosen.

A consumer's level of involvement depends on a number of factors. Consumers tend to be more involved in the purchase of high-priced goods and of products that are visible to others, such as clothing, furniture, or cars. As levels of perceived risk increase, involvement levels are likely to rise. Furthermore, individuals may experience enduring involvement with a product class. *Enduring involvement* is an ongoing interest in a product class because of personal relevance. For example, people often have enduring involvement with products associated with their leisure activities. Their search and information-gathering processes for these products occur over extensive periods of time. Photography enthusiasts enjoy reading about and examining new types of cameras and films; skiers frequent sports shops even during the summer months.

Buyers may also experience *situational involvement* resulting from the particular circumstance or environment in which they find themselves. This type of involvement is temporary because the conditions that triggered the high degree of involvement may change.[14] If a person is searching for a silver tray as a wedding present, for example, he or she may experience a high level of involvement in the purchase decision. The person's information search and evaluation of alternatives may be extensive. However, once the selection has been made, he or she no longer sees a silver tray as being personally relevant.

Many purchase decisions do not generate great involvement on the consumer's part. When the involvement level is low, as with routine response purchases, the buying is almost automatic, and the information search and evaluation of alternatives are extremely limited. For example, food shopping represents low-involvement purchase decisions for many consumers; products are chosen out of habit and with minimal effort. Marketing Update 4.1 discusses Benckiser's expansion into the soap powder market with its new "mix-your-own" laundry detergent— a product that will necessarily increase consumers' level of involvement. It will be interesting to see whether the company is ultimately successful in this venture. Major competitors are holding back to witness the outcome.

PSYCHOLOGICAL FACTORS INFLUENCING THE BUYING DECISION PROCESS

Psychological factors operating within individuals partly determine people's general behaviour and thus influence their behaviour as consumers. The primary psychological influences on consumer behaviour are (1) perception, (2) motives, (3) ability and knowledge, (4) attitudes, and (5) personality. Even though these psychological factors operate internally, later in this chapter we will see that they are very much affected by social forces outside the individual.

■ **Perception**

Are the horsemen in Figure 4.4 riding to the left or to the right? It could be either way depending on how you perceive the riders. Different people perceive the same thing at the same time in different ways. Similarly, the same individual at different times may perceive the same item in a number of ways. **Perception** is the process of selecting, organising, and interpreting information inputs to produce meaning. **Information inputs** are the sensations received through sight, taste, hearing, smell, and touch. When we hear an advertisement, see a friend, smell polluted air or water, or touch a product, we receive information inputs.

As the definition indicates, perception is a three-step process. Although we receive numerous pieces of information at once, only a few of them reach awareness. We select certain inputs and ignore many others because we do not have the ability to be conscious of every input at the same time. This phenomenon is sometimes called **selective exposure** because we select inputs that are to be exposed to our awareness. If you are concentrating on this paragraph, you probably are not aware that cars are outside making noise, that the light is on, or that you are touching this book. Even though you are receiving these inputs, you ignore them until they are mentioned.

There are several reasons why some types of information reach awareness while others do not. An input is more likely to reach awareness if it relates to an antici-

14. Ibid.

MIX-YOUR-OWN DETERGENTS

The German cleaning products company Benckiser is moving into the soap powders market with the launch of a novel mix-your-own laundry detergent, Storch. This launch puts Benckiser into head-on competition with Henkel, Procter & Gamble and Unilever, which dominate a DM 35 billion laundry detergent market, twice the size of the market in the U.K. Storch and its Unilever owned rival, Skip, consist of separately packaged units of detergent, stain remover, and water softener. Consumers can tailor the mix to their own needs and reduce waste water pollution by opting not to include bleach. The launches, both set for the end of 1990, initially did not spur Procter & Gamble or Henkel to retaliate. Procter & Gamble preferred to push its compact Dash Ultra 3, "because it is the superior concept and is easier to handle by consumers." Meanwhile, marketers at the German based Henkel turned their attention to the launch of Persil Supra, and the first relaunch of an East German brand, Spee, a joint venture with Genthin, an East German manufacturer.

Globally, however, Henkel is experimenting with the new "mix-your-own" approach. Henkel Austria and Henkel Italy are testing their markets with a Skip/Storch type product under the brand name of Atlas. While the compact detergents tell consumers they need only one product to do all their laundering jobs, the splitting up of the functions and dosages leaves the decision to the consumer. Both Unilever and Benckiser acknowledge that consumers will need to be re-educated about product usages, and that there will be hefty promotional spend with TV, press, and radio campaigns to support the launch of these brands.

SOURCE: Joachim Schypek, "New Player in German Soap Powders Market," *Marketing,* 4 October 1990, p. 17; "Benckiser Pushes Ahead with Storch," *Marketing,* 31 January 1991, p. 13; "Benckiser's Finish," New Products 1990, *Harvest,* May 1990; "Detergents and Laundry Aids," London: *Mintel,* March 1989; Karen Hoggan, "Finish Dishes Up Green Detergent," *Marketing,* 17 May 1990, p. 2.

FIGURE 4.4
Are the horsemen riding to the left or to the right?

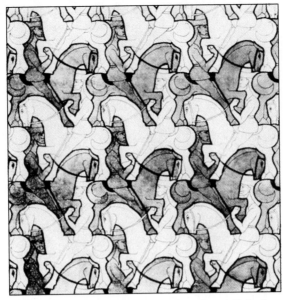

SOURCE: © 1988 M.C. Escher c/o Cordon Art—Baarn—Holland.

pated event. For example, a person hoping to attend a forthcoming concert is likely to listen to a radio advertisement containing ticket information for the concert. An input is likely to reach awareness if the information helps satisfy current needs. Thus you are more likely to notice a commercial for Kentucky Fried Chicken if you are hungry. Finally, if the intensity of an input changes significantly, the input is more likely to reach awareness. When a store manager reduces a price slightly, we may not notice because the change is not significant, but if the manager cuts the price in half, we are much more likely to recognise the reduction.

The selective nature of perception leads to two other conditions: selective distortion and selective retention. **Selective distortion** is changing or twisting currently received information. This condition can occur when a person receives information that is inconsistent with personal feelings or beliefs. For example, on seeing an advertisement promoting a brand that he or she dislikes, a person may distort the information to make it more consistent with previous views. This distortion substantially lessens the effect of the advertisement on the individual. In the **selective retention** phenomenon, a person remembers information inputs that support personal feelings and beliefs and forgets inputs that do not. After hearing a sales presentation and leaving the shop, a customer may forget many of the selling points if they contradict pre-existing beliefs.

The information inputs that do reach awareness are not received in an organised form. To produce meaning, an individual must enter the second step of the perceptual process—organise and integrate the new information with that already stored in memory. Ordinarily, this organising is done rapidly.

Interpretation—the third step in the perceptual process—is the assignment of meaning to what has been organised. A person bases interpretation on what is familiar, on knowledge already stored in memory. For this reason, a manufacturer that changes a package design faces a major problem. Since people look for the product in the old, familiar package, they may not recognise it in the new one.

Unless a package change is accompanied by a promotional programme that makes people aware of the change, a firm may lose sales.

Although marketers cannot control people's perceptions, they often try to influence them. Several problems may arise from such attempts, however. First, a consumer's perceptual process may operate in such a way that a seller's information never reaches that person. For example, a buyer may block out a shop assistant's sales presentation. Second, a buyer may receive a seller's information but perceive it differently from what was intended. For example, when a toothpaste producer advertises that "35 percent of the people who use this toothpaste have less decay," a customer could infer that 65 percent of the people who use the product have more tooth decay. Third, a buyer who perceives information inputs that are inconsistent with prior beliefs is likely to forget the information quickly. Thus if a salesperson tells a prospective car buyer that a particular model is highly reliable and requires few repairs but the customer does not believe this, the customer probably will not retain the information very long.

In addition to perceptions of packages, products, brands, and organisations, individuals also have self-perceptions. That perception is called the person's **self-concept** or self-image. It is reasonable to believe that a person's self-concept affects purchase decisions and consumption behaviour. The results of some studies suggest that buyers purchase products that reflect and enhance their self-concepts. For instance, a person might purchase Levi's jeans and rugby shirts to project a casual, relaxed self-concept.

■ Motives

A **motive** is an internal energising force that directs a person's activities towards satisfying a need or achieving a goal. Motivation is the set of mechanisms for controlling movement towards goals.[15] A buyer's actions at any time are affected by a set of motives rather than by just one. At a single point in time, some motives in the set have priority, but the priorities of motives vary from one time to another. For example, a person's motives for having a cup of coffee are much stronger right after waking up than just before going to bed. Motivation also affects the direction and intensity of behaviour. Individuals must choose which goals to pursue at a particular time.

Motives that influence where a person purchases products on a regular basis are called **patronage motives**. A buyer may use a particular shop because of such patronage motives as price, service, location, honesty, product variety, or friendliness of salespeople. For example, Tianguis, a southern California grocery chain, stocks a wide variety of Hispanic products, such as empanadas and tortilla mixes, with Spanish labels and has Spanish speakers on the check-outs, as well as mariachi bands, to encourage the area's large Hispanic population to frequent its stores.[16] To capitalise on patronage motives, a marketer should try to determine why regular customers patronise a store and then emphasise these characteristics in the store's marketing mix.

Marketers conduct motivation research to analyse the major motives that influence consumers to buy or not buy their products. In Figure 4.5, Wrigley's clearly is marketing its chewing gum to those concerned with physical health and well-being. Motives, which often operate at a subconscious level, are difficult to measure.

15. James R. Bettman, *An Information Processing Theory of Consumer Choice* (Reading, Mass.: Addison-Wesley, 1979), pp. 18–24.

16. Alfredo Corchado, "Hispanic Supermarkets Are Blossoming," *Wall Street Journal*, 23 Jan. 1989, p. B1.

FIGURE 4.5
Identifying consumer motives.
Wrigley's identifies physical well-being as a motive to purchase its product.

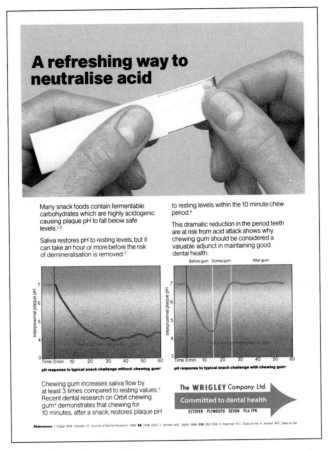

SOURCE: Wrigley Company, Ltd.

Because people ordinarily do not know what motivates them, marketers cannot simply ask them about their motives. Most motivation research relies on interviews or projective techniques.

When researchers study motives through interviews, they may use in-depth interviews, focus groups, or a combination of the two. In an **in-depth interview**, the researcher tries to get the subject to talk freely about anything at all in order to create an informal atmosphere. The researcher may ask general, non-directed questions and then probe the subject's answers by asking for clarification. An in-depth interview may last for several hours. In a **focus group**, the interviewer—through leadership that is not highly structured—tries to generate discussion about one or several topics in a group of six to twelve people. Through what is said in the discussion, the interviewer attempts to discover people's motives relating to some issue such as the use of a product. The researcher usually cannot probe as far in a focus group as in an in-depth interview. To determine the subconscious motives reflected in the interviews, motivation researchers must be extremely well trained in clinical psychology. Their skill in uncovering subconscious motives from what is said in an interview determines the effectiveness of their research. Both in-depth and focus group techniques can yield a variety of information. For example, they might help marketers discover why customers continue to buy high-calorie fried foods even though most say they are trying to reduce their intake of cholesterol and calories.

Projective techniques are tests in which subjects are asked to perform specific tasks for particular purposes while in fact they are being evaluated for other purposes. Such tests are based on the assumption that subjects will unconsciously "project" their motives as they perform the required tasks. However, subjects should always be informed that the test is an unstructured evaluation. Researchers trained in projective techniques can analyse the materials a subject produces and make predictions about the subject's subconscious motives. Some common types of projective techniques are word-association tests and sentence-completion tests.

Motivation research techniques can be reasonably effective but are far from perfect. Marketers who want to research people's motives should obtain the services of professional psychologists skilled in the methods of motivation research.

■ Ability and Knowledge

Individuals vary in their **ability**—their competence and efficiency in performing tasks. One ability of interest to marketers is an individual's capacity to learn. **Learning** refers to changes in a person's behaviour caused by information and experience. The consequences of behaviour strongly influence the learning process. Behaviour that results in satisfying consequences tends to be repeated. For example, when a consumer buys a Snickers chocolate bar and likes it, he or she is more likely to buy a Snickers the next time. In fact, the individual will probably continue to purchase that brand until it no longer provides satisfaction. But when the effects of the behaviour are no longer satisfying, the person will switch to a different brand, perhaps, or stop eating chocolate bars altogether.

When making purchasing decisions, buyers have to process information. Individuals have differing abilities in this regard. For example, when purchasing a home computer, a well-educated potential buyer who has experience with computer systems may be able to read, comprehend, and synthesise the considerable quantities of information found in the technical brochures for various competing brands. On the other hand, another buyer with more limited abilities may be incapable of performing this task and will have to rely on information obtained from advertisements or from a sales representative of a particular brand.

Another aspect of an individual's ability is knowledge. **Knowledge** is made up of two components: familiarity with the product and expertise, which is the individual's ability to apply the product.[17] The duration and intensity of the buying decision process depends on the buyer's familiarity with or prior experience in purchasing and using the product. For example, in Figure 4.6, Nike, a well-known manufacturer of trainers for adults and children, builds awareness that its product is also available in infant sizes. The individual's knowledge influences his or her search for, recall, and use of information.[18]

When making purchase decisions, inexperienced buyers may use different types of information from more experienced shoppers who are familiar with the product and purchase situation. Inexperienced buyers use price as an indicator of quality more frequently than buyers who have some knowledge of a particular product category.[19] Thus two potential purchasers of an antique desk may use quite different

17. Joseph W. Alba and J. Wesley Hutchinson, "Dimensions of Consumer Expertise," *Journal of Consumer Research,* March 1987, pp. 411–454.

18. Akshay R. Rao and Kent B. Monroe, "The Moderating Effect of Prior Knowledge on Cue Utilization in Product Evaluations," *Journal of Consumer Research,* September 1988, pp. 253–264.

19. Ibid.

FIGURE 4.6
Building consumer awareness.
Nike intensifies awareness of its product by expanding consumers' knowledge about its full line of trainers for infants.

SOURCE: Nike Inc.

types of information in making their purchase decision. The inexperienced buyer is likely to judge the desk's value by the price, whereas the more experienced buyer may seek information about the craftsman, period, and place of origin to judge the desk's quality and value.

Consumers who lack expertise may seek the advice of others when making a purchase or take along a friend. More experienced buyers have greater confidence; they also have more knowledge about the product or service and can tell which features are reliable indicators of product quality. For example, consider two young bank-clerks who want reliable cars for travel back and forth to work. One has no expertise with regard to cars and is unsure about what features to use to judge one. He finds the information given in the brochures confusing and feels intimidated by the salesperson. Therefore he goes for advice to his father, who has purchased many cars, and takes him along to the showroom when making the purchase. The other bank-clerk has been interested in cars all her life. Even though this is her first car purchase, she is an expert on cars and knows what features are important. She is confident and knowledgeable and makes her purchase decision unassisted.

Marketers sometimes help customers to learn about their products and to gain experience with them. Free samples encourage trial and reduce purchase risk.

In-store demonstrations aid consumers in acquiring knowledge of product uses. Test drives give new car purchasers some experience with a car's features. Consumers also learn when they experience products indirectly, by way of information from salespersons, advertisements, friends, and relatives. Through sales personnel and advertisements, marketers offer information before (and sometimes after) purchases to influence what consumers learn and to create a more favourable attitude towards the products.

Although marketers seek to influence what a consumer learns, their attempts are seldom fully successful. Marketers encounter problems in attracting and holding consumers' attention, providing consumers with the kinds of information that are important for making purchase decisions, and convincing them to try the product.

■ Attitude

Attitude refers to knowledge and positive or negative feelings about an object or activity. The objects or acts towards which we have attitudes may be tangible or intangible, living or non-living. For example, we have attitudes towards sex, religion, politics, and music, just as we do towards cars, football, and pizza.

An individual learns attitudes through experience and interaction with other people. Just as attitudes are learned, they can also be changed. Nevertheless, an individual's attitudes remain generally stable and do not change from moment to moment. Likewise, at any one time, a person's attitudes do not all have equal impact; some are stronger than others.

Consumer attitudes towards a firm and its products greatly influence the success or failure of the firm's marketing strategy. When consumers have strong negative attitudes towards one or more aspects of a firm's marketing practices, they may not only stop using the firm's product but also urge their relatives and friends to do likewise. For example, following concern about apartheid in South Africa, many consumers in Europe chose to boycott South African products. Likewise, when an oil spill from the supertanker *Exxon Valdez* fouled beaches and killed wildlife in Alaska's Prince William Sound, the public judged Exxon's response to cleaning up the spill as inadequate and cosmetic. As a result, many consumers boycotted Exxon products. Nearly twenty thousand Exxon credit card holders cut up their cards and sent them back to Exxon, exhorting their friends to do the same.

Since attitudes can play such an important part in determining consumer behaviour, marketers should measure consumer attitudes towards prices, package designs, brand names, advertisements, salespeople, repair services, store locations, features of existing or proposed products, and social responsibility activities. Several methods can help marketers gauge these attitudes. One of the simplest ways is to question people directly. An attitude researcher for Keytronics, a computer-keyboard manufacturer, for example, might ask respondents what they think about the style and design of Keytronics' newest keyboard. Projective techniques used in motivation research can also be employed to measure attitudes. Sometimes marketers evaluate attitudes through attitude scales. An **attitude scale** usually consists of a series of adjectives, phrases, or sentences about an object. Subjects are asked to indicate the intensity of their feelings towards the object by reacting to the adjectives, phrases, or sentences in a certain way. For example, if a marketer were measuring people's attitudes towards oil companies, respondents might be asked to state the degree to which they agree or disagree with a number of statements, such as "Oil companies engage in environmentally sound drilling and exploration activities."

When marketers determine that a significant number of consumers have strong negative attitudes towards an aspect of a marketing mix, they may try to change consumer attitudes to make them more favourable. This task is generally long, expensive, and difficult and may require extensive promotional efforts. For example, in the U.K., the Milk Marketing Board has used advertising to focus consumers' attention on the nutritional and energy value of milk. This contradicts some of the health concerns about cholesterol in dairy products. Similarly, both business and non-business organisations try to change people's attitudes about many things, from health and safety to product prices and features.

■ **Personality**

Personality includes all the internal traits and behaviours that make a person unique. Each person's unique personality arises from both heredity and personal experiences. Personalities are typically described as having one or more characteristics, such as compulsiveness, ambitiousness, gregariousness, dogmatism, authoritarianism, introversion, extroversion, aggressiveness, competitiveness. Marketing researchers attempt to find relationships among such characteristics and buying behaviour. Even though a few links between several personality characteristics and buyer behaviour have been determined, the results of many studies have been inconclusive. Some researchers see the apparently weak association between personality and buying behaviour as due to unreliable measures rather than a lack of relationship.[20] A number of marketers are convinced that a consumer's personality does influence the types and brands of products purchased. For example, the type of clothing, jewellery, or car that a person buys may reflect one or more personality characteristics.

At times, marketers aim advertising campaigns at general types of personalities. In doing so, they use positively valued personality characteristics, such as gregariousness, independence, or competitiveness. Products promoted this way include drinks, cars, cigarettes, and clothing.

Social Factors Influencing the Buying Decision Process

The forces that other people exert on buying behaviour are called **social factors**. As shown in Figure 4.1, they can be grouped into four major areas: (1) roles and family influences, (2) reference groups, (3) social classes, and (4) culture and subcultures.

■ **Roles and Family Influences**

All of us occupy positions within groups, organisations, and institutions. Associated with each position is a **role**—a set of actions and activities that a person in a particular position is supposed to perform, based on the expectations of both the individual and surrounding persons. Because people occupy numerous positions, they also have many roles. For example, a man may perform the roles of son, husband, father, employee or employer, church member, civic organisation member, and student in an evening class. Thus there are several sets of expectations placed on each person's behaviour.

20. John L. Lastovika and Erich A. Joachimsthaler, "Improving the Detection of Personality-Behavior Relationships in Consumer Research," *Journal of Consumer Research,* March 1988, pp. 583–587.

An individual's roles influence both general behaviour and buying behaviour. The demands of a person's many roles may be inconsistent and confusing. To illustrate, assume that the man mentioned above is thinking about buying a boat. While he wants a boat for fishing, his children want one suitable for water-skiing. His wife wants him to delay the boat purchase until next year. A colleague at work insists that he should buy a particular brand, known for high performance. Thus an individual's buying behaviour is partially affected by the input and opinions of family and friends.

Family roles relate directly to purchase decisions. The male head of household is likely to be involved heavily in the purchase of products such as alcohol and tobacco. Although female roles have changed, women still make buying decisions related to many household items, including health-care products, washing products, household cleansers, and food. Husbands and wives participate jointly in the purchase of a variety of products, especially durable goods. Some students aged 16 to 24 may be rebellious; their brand loyalty can be quite changeable. Marketers frequently promote their products during school and college holidays to catch this hard-to-reach group at a time when they are more receptive to a promotional message.[21] Children are making many purchase decisions and influencing numerous household purchase decisions that traditionally were made only by husbands and wives. When two or more family members participate in a purchase, their roles may dictate that each is responsible for performing certain tasks: initiating the idea, gathering information, deciding whether to buy the product, or selecting the specific brand. The particular tasks performed depend on the types of products being considered.

Marketers need to be aware of how roles affect buying behaviour. To develop a marketing mix that precisely meets the needs of the target market, marketers must know not only who does the actual buying, but also what other roles influence the purchase. Because sex roles are changing so rapidly, marketers must ensure that their information is current and accurate.

■ **Reference Groups**   A group becomes a **reference group** when an individual identifies with it so much that he or she takes on many of the values, attitudes, or behaviour of group members. The person who views a group as a reference group may or may not know the actual size of the group. Most people have several reference groups, such as families, friends, religious, civic, and professional organisations.

A group can be a negative reference group for an individual. Someone may have been a part of a specific group at one time but later rejected its values and members. One can also specifically take action to avoid a particular group.[22] However, in this discussion we refer to reference groups as those that the individual involved views positively.

A reference group may serve as a point of comparison and a source of information for an individual. A customer's behaviour may change to be more in line with the actions and beliefs of group members. For example, a person might stop buying one brand of audio cassette and switch to another on the advice of members of the reference group. Generally, the more conspicuous a product, the more likely it is that the brand decision will be influenced by reference groups. An individual may

21. Martha T. Moore, "Spring Break: Brand Names Chase Sales," *USA Today,* 17 Mar. 1989, p. B1.

22. Henry Assael, *Consumer Behavior and Marketing Action* (Boston: Kent Publishing, 1987), p. 369.

also seek information from the reference group about other factors regarding a prospective purchase, such as where to buy a certain product. The degree to which a reference group will affect a purchase decision depends on an individual's susceptibility to its influence and the strength of his or her involvement with the group.

A marketer sometimes tries to use reference-group influence in advertisements by suggesting that people in a specific group buy a product and are highly satisfied with it. In this type of appeal, the advertiser hopes that many people will accept the suggested group as a reference group and buy (or react more favourably to) the product. Whether this kind of advertising succeeds depends on three factors: how effectively the advertisement communicates the message, the type of product, and the individual's susceptibility to reference-group influence.

■ Social Classes

Within all societies, people rank others into higher or lower positions of respect. This ranking results in social classes. A **social class** is an open group of individuals who have similar social rank. A class is referred to as "open" because people can move into and out of it. The criteria for grouping people into classes vary from one society to another. In the United Kingdom, as in other western countries, many factors are taken into account, including occupation, education, income, wealth, race, ethnic group, and possessions. In the Soviet Union, wealth and income are less important than education and occupation in determining social class: although Russian doctors and scientists do not make a great deal of money, they are highly valued in Russian society. A person who is ranking someone does not necessarily apply all of a society's criteria. The number and the importance of the factors chosen depend on the characteristics of the individual being ranked and the values of the person who is doing the ranking.

To some degree, persons within social classes develop and assume common patterns of behaviour. They may have similar attitudes, values, language patterns, and possessions. Social class influences many aspects of our lives. For example, it affects our chances of having children and their chances of surviving infancy. It influences our childhood training, choice of religion, selection of occupation, and how we spend our time. Because social class has a bearing on so many aspects of a person's life, it also affects buying decisions. For example, upper-class Europeans seem to prefer luxury automobiles such as the BMW and Mercedes-Benz, which symbolise their status, income, and financial comfort.

Social class determines to some extent the type, quality, and quantity of products that a person buys and uses. Social class also affects an individual's shopping patterns and the types of stores patronised. Advertisements are sometimes based on an appeal to a specific social class. See Table 4.2 for an analysis of the categories of social class in the U.K.

■ Culture and Subculture

Culture is everything in our surroundings that is made by human beings. It consists of tangible items, such as food, furniture, buildings, clothing, and tools, and intangible concepts, such as education, welfare, and laws. Culture also includes the values and wide range of behaviours that are acceptable within a specific society. The concepts, values, and behaviours that make up a culture are learned and passed on from one generation to the next.

Culture influences buying behaviour because it permeates our daily lives. Our culture determines what we wear and eat, where we live and travel. Certainly,

TABLE 4.2 *Socio-economic classification (JICNARS)*

SOCIAL GRADE	SOCIAL STATUS	HEAD OF HOUSEHOLD'S OCCUPATION	APPROXIMATE PERCENTAGE OF FAMILIES
A	Upper middle class	Higher managerial, administrative or professional	3
B	Middle class	Intermediate managerial, administrative or professional	10
C1	Lower middle class	Supervisory or clerical and junior managerial, administrative or professional	24
C2	Skilled working class	Skilled manual workers	30
D	Working class	Semi and unskilled manual workers	25
E	Those at lowest levels of subsistence	State pensioners or widows (no other earner), casual or lowest-grade workers	8

A—Upper middle class: The head of the household is a successful business or professional man, senior civil servant, or has considerable private means. A young man in some of these occupations who has not fully established himself may still be found in Grade B, though he should eventually reach grade A. In country or suburban areas, A-grade households usually live in large detached houses or in expensive flats. In towns, they may live in expensive flats or town houses in the better parts of town.

B—Middle class: In general, the heads of B-grade households will be quite senior people but not at the very top of their profession or business. They are quite well off, but their style of life is generally respectable rather than rich or luxurious . . . non-earners will be living on private pensions or on fairly modest private means.

C1—Lower middle class: In general it is made up of the families of small tradespeople and non-manual workers who carry out less important administrative, supervisory and clerical jobs, i.e., what are sometimes called "white-collar" workers.

C2—Skilled working class: Consists in the main of skilled manual workers and their families: the serving of an apprenticeship may be a guide to membership of this class.

D—Semi-skilled and unskilled working class: Consists entirely of manual workers, generally semi-skilled or unskilled.

E—Those at lowest levels of subsistence: Consists of old age pensioners, widows and their families, casual workers and those who, through sickness or unemployment, are dependent on social security schemes, or have very small private means . . .

SOURCE: From Peter M. Chisnall, *Marketing: A Behavioural Analysis* (Berkshire, England: McGraw-Hill Publishing Co. Ltd.,1976), pp. 114–115. Reprinted by permission.

society's interest in the healthiness of food has affected companies' approaches to developing and promoting their products. It also influences how we buy and use products and the satisfaction gained from them. In Figure 4.7, Sunpat promotes its product as a nutritious, high-fibre, and low-sugar item. In many western cultures, shortage of time is a growing problem because of the rise in the number of women who work and the current emphasis we place on physical and mental self-

FIGURE 4.7

Appealing to cultural standards.
Sunpat takes advantage of strong cultural acceptance of healthy foods by promoting key attributes of its peanut butter.

SOURCE: The Nestlé Company Ltd.

development. Many people do time-saving shopping and buy convenience and labour-saving products to cope with this problem.[23]

Because culture, to some degree, determines how products are purchased and used, it in turn affects the development, promotion, distribution, and pricing of products. Food marketers, for example, have had to make a multitude of changes in their marketing efforts. Thirty years ago most families ate at least two meals a day together, and the mother devoted four to six hours a day to preparing those meals. Now more than 60 percent of women in the 25 to 54 age group are employed outside the home, and average family incomes have risen considerably. These shifts, along with the problem of time scarcity, have resulted in dramatic changes in per capita consumption of certain foods such as shelf-stable foods like Pot Rice and Pot Noodles, frozen meals, and take-away foods.[24] Marketing Update 4.2 discusses Heinz's launch of its frozen Chinese ready meals.

When marketers sell products overseas, they often see the tremendous impact that culture has on the purchase and use of products. International marketers find

23. Leonard L. Berry, "The Time-Sharing Consumer," *Journal of Retailing,* Winter 1979, p. 69.

24. Mona Doyle, "The Metamorphosis of the Consumer," *Marketing Communications,* April 1989, pp. 18–22.

HEINZ LAUNCHES ITS NEW FROZEN READY MEALS

Heinz has teamed up with TV chef Ken Lo in launching its first line of frozen ready meals outside of its Weight Watchers banner. The ten premium Oriental products will feature in a range called, "Ken Lo—Memories of China," and include starters, main meals, and various types of rice, bought separately so that consumers can "mix and match."

Consumption of frozen specialty ready meals soared by 188 percent between 1985–1989, compared with a growth of 82 percent for the whole frozen ready meals market. The attraction of Chinese ready meals to Heinz is clear. While in the U.K. Indian frozen ready meals are worth about £24 million and growing, Chinese ready meals are worth only £13 million. Stir fry, popularised by United Biscuit's Ross Young brand, accounts for about half of the market. Heinz's products are more expensive than competitors' and will retail at around £2.39, consistent with their premium positioning.

Heinz believes that this is an undeveloped market, which combined with the predicted fall in people eating out as disposable income is reduced by the recession, has encouraged Heinz to invest heavily in the Chinese frozen ready meal sector. Heinz has diversified steadily away from its staid "57 Varieties"—its core baked beans and soups—for several years. It launched microwaveable snacks under the Lunch Bowl brand in 1989, and in the U.S., Weight Watchers is now a £170 million brand.

Heinz believes there has been a move by consumers to expect higher quality and greater variety in ready-to-eat frozen food. The increased ownership of microwave ovens has increased the potential of such products, and Heinz aims to establish itself as a leader in this sector.

SOURCE: Karen Hoggan, "Heinz Gives Eastern Promise," *Marketing,* 4 October 1990, p. 4; "Record Year for Frozen Foods," *Supermarketing,* 15 September 1989; Tom Lester, "The Unique Problems of Heinzight," *Marketing,* 1 November 1990, pp. 26–27.

that people in other regions of the world have different attitudes, values, and needs, which in turn call for different methods of doing business, as well as different types of marketing mixes. Some international marketers fail because they do not or cannot adjust to cultural differences. The effect of culture on international marketing programmes is discussed in greater detail in Chapter 23.

A culture can be divided into **subcultures** according to geographic regions or human characteristics, such as age or ethnic background. In any country, there are a number of different subcultures. Within these, there are even greater similarities in people's attitudes, values, and actions than within the broader culture. Relative to other subcultures, individuals in a certain subculture may have stronger preferences for specific types of clothing, furniture, or foods. For example, consumption of haggis tends to be confined to Scotland rather than England or Wales. Meanwhile, European teenagers seek out the latest trends in fashion from retailers like Benetton.

Marketers must recognise that even though their operations are confined to one country, state, or city, subcultural differences may dictate considerable variations in what products people buy. There will also be differences in how people make purchases—and variations in when they make them as well. To deal effectively with these differences, marketers may have to alter their product, promotion, distribution systems, or price to satisfy members of particular subcultures.

UNDERSTANDING CONSUMER BEHAVIOUR

Marketers try to understand consumer buying behaviour so that they can offer consumers greater satisfaction. Yet a certain amount of customer dissatisfaction remains. Some marketers have not adopted the marketing concept and so are not consumer orientated and do not regard customer satisfaction as a primary objective. Moreover, because the tools for analysing consumer behaviour are imprecise, marketers may not be able to determine accurately what is highly satisfying to buyers. Finally, even if marketers know what increases consumer satisfaction, they may not be able to provide it.

Understanding consumer behaviour is an important task for marketers. Even though research on consumer buying behaviour has not supplied all the knowledge that marketers need, progress has been made during the last twenty years and is likely to continue in the next twenty. Not only will refinements in research methods yield more information about consumer behaviour, but the pressures of an increasingly competitive business environment will make such information much more urgent for marketers.

SUMMARY

Buying behaviour is the decision processes and acts of people involved in buying and using products. Consumer buying behaviour refers to the buying behaviour of ultimate consumers, those who purchase products for personal or household use, not for business purposes. Analysing consumer buying behaviour is important to marketers; if they are able to determine what satisfies customers, they can implement the marketing concept and better predict how consumers will respond to different marketing strategies.

Consumer decisions can be classified into three categories: routine response behaviour, limited decision-making, and extensive decision-making. A consumer uses routine response behaviour when buying frequently purchased, low-cost items that require very little search and decision effort. Limited decision-making is used for products that are purchased occasionally and when a buyer needs to acquire information about an unfamiliar brand in a familiar product category. Extensive decision-making is used when purchasing an unfamiliar, expensive, or infrequently bought product. Impulse buying is not a consciously planned buying behaviour but involves a powerful, persistent urge to buy something immediately. The purchase of a certain product does not always elicit the same type of decision-making behaviour.

The consumer buying decision process includes five stages: problem recognition, information search, evaluation of alternatives, purchase, and post-purchase evaluation. Decision processes do not always culminate in a purchase, and not all consumer decisions include all five stages. Problem recognition occurs when a buyer becomes aware that there is a difference between a desired state and an actual condition. After recognising the problem or need, the buyer searches for information about products that will help resolve the problem or satisfy the need. In the internal search, buyers search their memories for information about products that might solve the problem. If they are unable to retrieve from memory sufficient information to make a decision, they seek additional information through an external search. A successful search will yield a group of brands, called an evoked set, that a buyer views as possible alternatives. To evaluate the products in the evoked set, a buyer establishes certain criteria by which to compare, rate, and rank the different products. Marketers can influence consumers' evaluation by framing the alternatives.

In the purchase stage, the consumer selects the product or brand on the basis of results from the evaluation stage and on other dimensions. The buyer also chooses the seller from whom he or she will buy the product. After the purchase, the buyer evaluates the product to determine if its actual performance meets expected levels. Shortly after the purchase of an expensive product, for example, the post-purchase evaluation may provoke cognitive dissonance, which is dissatisfaction brought on by the consumer's doubts as to whether he or she should have bought the product in the first place or would have been better off buying another brand that had also ranked high in the evaluation.

Three major categories of influences are believed to affect the consumer buying decision process: personal, psychological, and social factors. A personal factor is one that is unique to a particular person. Personal factors include demographic factors, situational factors, and level of involvement. Demographic factors are individual characteristics such as age, sex, race, ethnic origin, income, family life cycle, and occupation. Situational factors are the external circumstances or conditions that exist when a consumer is making a purchase decision. The time available to make a decision is a situational factor that strongly influences consumer buying decisions. An individual's level of involvement—the importance and intensity of interest in a product in a particular situation—also affects the buying decision process. Enduring involvement is an ongoing interest in a product class because of personal relevance. Situational involvement is a temporary interest resulting from the particular circumstance or environment in which buyers find themselves.

Psychological factors operating within individuals partly determine people's general behaviour and thus influence their behaviour as consumers. The primary psychological influences on consumer behaviour are perception, motives, ability and knowledge, attitudes, and personality. Perception is the process of selecting, organising, and interpreting information inputs (the sensations received through sight, taste, hearing, smell, and touch) to produce meaning. Selective exposure is the phenomenon of people selecting the inputs that are to be exposed to their awareness; selective distortion is changing or twisting currently received information. When a person remembers information inputs that support personal feelings and beliefs and forgets inputs that do not, the phenomenon is called selective retention. The second step of the perceptual process requires organising and integrating the new information with that already stored in memory. Interpretation—the third step in the perceptual process—is the assignment of meaning to what has been organised. In addition to perceptions of packages, products, brands, and organisations, individuals also have a self-concept, or self-image.

A motive is an internal energising force that directs a person's activities towards satisfying a need or achieving a goal. Patronage motives influence where a person purchases products on a regular basis. To analyse the major motives that influence consumers to buy or not buy their products, marketers conduct motivation research, using in-depth interviews, focus groups, or projective techniques.

Individuals vary in their ability—their competence and efficiency in performing tasks. Ability includes both learning and knowledge. Learning refers to changes in a person's behaviour caused by information and experience. Knowledge is made up of two components: familiarity with the product and expertise—the individual's ability to apply the product.

Attitude refers to knowledge and positive or negative feelings about an object or activity. Consumer attitudes towards a firm and its products greatly influence the success or failure of the firm's marketing strategy. Marketers measure consumers' attitudes with projective techniques and attitude scales.

Personality comprises all the internal traits and behaviours that make a person unique. Some marketers believe that a person's personality does influence the types and brands of products purchased.

The forces that other people exert on buying behaviour are called social factors. Social factors include the influence of roles and family, reference groups, social classes, and culture and subcultures. All of us occupy positions within groups, organisations, and institutions, and each position has a role—a set of actions and activities that a person in a particular position is supposed to perform, based on the expectations of both the individual and surrounding persons. A group is a reference group when an individual identifies with the group so much that he or she takes on many of the values, attitudes, or behaviours of group members. A social class is an open group of individuals who have similar social rank. Culture is everything in our surroundings that is made by human beings. A culture can be divided into subcultures on the basis of geographic regions or human characteristics, such as age or ethnic background.

Marketers try to understand consumer buying behaviour so that they can offer consumers greater satisfaction. Refinements in research methods will yield more information about consumer behaviour, and the pressure of an increasingly competitive business environment will spur marketers to seek fuller understanding of consumer decision processes.

IMPORTANT TERMS

Buying behaviour
Consumer buying behaviour
Routine response behaviour
Limited decision-making
Extensive decision-making
Impulse buying
Consumer buying
    decision process
Internal search
External search
Cognitive dissonance
Personal factors
Demographic factors
Situational factors
Level of involvement
Psychological factors
Perception
Information inputs
Selective exposure
Selective distortion

Selective retention
Self-concept
Motive
Patronage motives
In-depth interview
Focus group
Projective techniques
Ability
Learning
Knowledge
Attitude
Attitude scale
Personality
Social factors
Role
Reference group
Social class
Culture
Subcultures

DISCUSSION AND REVIEW QUESTIONS

1. Name the types of buying behaviour consumers use. List some products that you have bought using each type of behaviour. Have you ever bought a product on impulse?
2. What are the major stages in the consumer buying decision process? Are all these stages used in all consumer purchase decisions?
3. What are the personal factors that affect the consumer buying decision process? How do they affect the process?
4. How does a consumer's level of involvement affect his or her purchase behaviour?
5. What is the function of time in a consumer's purchasing decision process?
6. What is selective exposure? Why do humans engage in it?
7. How do marketers attempt to shape consumers' learning?
8. Why are marketers concerned about consumer attitudes?
9. How do roles affect a person's buying behaviour?
10. Describe reference groups. How do they influence buying behaviour? Name some of your own reference groups.
11. In what ways does social class affect a person's purchase decisions?
12. What is culture? How does it affect a person's buying behaviour?
13. Describe the subcultures to which you belong. Identify buying behaviour that is unique to your subculture.

4.1 Burger King Revamps Its Image

After years of declining market share, unsuccessful advertising campaigns, management upheaval, and finally a takeover by British-owned Grand Metropolitan, plc, Burger King Corp. wanted to change consumers' perceptions of the company and their attitudes towards it. Under a new chief executive officer, Barry Gibbons, Burger King altered its marketing mix to stem its declining market share (17 percent of the $60 billion fast-food market) and to change its image by relating the Burger King experience to consumers' self-concepts. In a break from fast-food marketers' traditional focus on price and treatment of their products as "commodities", Burger King developed a new advertising campaign, designed to set it apart from competitors and its own troubled past.

A random survey showed that the consumers who already used Burger King restaurants were overwhelmingly positive about the chain. Such satisfied patrons help boost sales by positive word-of-mouth advertising. But to push up sales and lure away competitors' customers, Burger King had to develop a new promotional campaign—one that would enhance consumers' perceptions of the second-largest hamburger chain. Using "attitude advertising", Burger King is now trying to establish a positive relationship with consumers and create a different image with its daring "sometimes you've gotta break the rules" advertising campaign. The campaign itself breaks a few of the fast-food industry's advertising rules.

The $150 million campaign focuses on getting both consumers and Burger King management to think differently about the company. The resulting advertisements play down traditional product shots and jingles and focus instead on entertainment, humour, and a spirit of independence. Although most fast-food advertisements have mouth-watering shots of food, the Burger King ads include only occasional glimpses of Burger King signs or products and avoid the traditional Burger King flame-broiling action shot. They attempt instead to provide an image of a Burger King experience that is fun and entertaining.

The campaign includes six "hip" television advertisements showing people "breaking the rules" to get Burger King food. In one, an aircraft-carrier's crew awaiting its "orders" receives Burger King food by helicopter. In another, a teenage boy uses his father's Mercedes to deliver a salad to a pretty girl. The intent is to position Burger King in the hearts of potential customers rather than trying to show the superiority of a specific product.

The radio advertising campaign also breaks the rules. Officials say that during two weeks of unprecedented saturation two-thirds of America will have heard ten Burger King radio commercials. The series of radio spots feature original Burger King songs from a variety of stars, including Mel Torme, John Lee Hooker, the Fabulous Thunderbirds, and Tone-Loc.

In an unusual (and appropriately rule-breaking) collaboration, Burger King hired two advertising agencies to handle the new advertising campaign. Rather than dividing responsibilities, the two agencies developed a team concept, with the idea that both would have equal creative input opportunities.

CEO Gibbons has changed more than just Burger King's promotion. To support the advertising and to contribute to the new Burger King image, he also made changes in product and price. Now there are daily 99 cent specials and Burger King doubles—double-decker burgers with different toppings.

Other changes affect the operation of individual franchisees' operations. By laying off 550 employees in the headquarters and company field offices, Burger King pared down its management hierarchy. Gibbons has insisted that all Burger King restaurants focus on uniformity, cleanliness, and teamwork. He has also sent out the message that Burger King will purge franchisees with sloppy, unprofitable restaurants by closing them or, if necessary, buying them. In addition, Burger King is remodelling many company-owned outlets and lowering the rent for new franchisees who lease their buildings from the company. Franchisees have been told to prepare for new menu boards and to clear space for more in-store displays.

All these actions have been taken to support the theme of entertainment, humour, and a fun experience. The changes in Burger King's marketing mix should help alter consumers' views of the company and make the Burger King image more consistent with consumer self-concepts, leading to a more positive attitude towards the firm.

SOURCES: Based on information from James Cox, "Bold Campaign Aims to Beef Up Market Share," *USA Today*, 28 Sept. 1989, pp. 1B, 2B; Bob Garfield, "Burger King Breaks from Indecisive Past," *Advertising Age*, 2 Oct. 1989, pp. 1, 68; Scott Hume, "A New 'Personality'," *Advertising Age*, 2 Oct. 1989, pp. 1, 66; Scott Hume, "Burger King Ads Will Count," *Advertising Age*, 2 Oct. 1989, p. 66; and Jane Weaver, "Getting Attitude: Creatives Scrutinize Ads Without Products," *Adweek*, 23 Oct. 1989, p. 27.

Questions for Discussion

1. How difficult will it be to change consumer perceptions about Burger King?
2. Burger King claims to use "attitude advertising". Based on the text discussion on attitudes, what should this advertising accomplish?
3. If the Burger King image is more consistent with the consumer's self-concept, what will be the result?

4.2 Mattessons Repositions Its Products

During 1989 and 1990 there were numerous food scares within the European Community. In the U.K., fears about salmonella and listeria reaped havoc in many key food areas. For months, egg sales plummeted as a result of salmonella infection; and beef sales have yet to recover following the discovery of Mad Cow disease and its possible mobility through the food chain to reach human consumers. The rapidly growing sector of ready-to-eat chilled foods also was put into recession by the discovery of listeria on many supermarket shelves. Pâté, too, suffered following a listeria scare.

Unilever subsidiary Mattessons Wall's has emerged from the battering of the recent food safety scares with a radical repositioning and massive cash boost for its pâté to sliced meat brand Mattessons. A £3.5 million television and press campaign will bury the brand's familiar mnemonic catch lines—such as "try saying Mattessons without saying mmm"—in an attempt to move up market with more adult-orientated lifestyle advertising.

The move sees the reintroduction of Mattessons' pâtés after the listeria scare forced them off supermarket shelves in July 1990. Unilever claims, though, that the brand repositioning is not connected with the crisis and has in fact been planned for eighteen months. Mattessons has jettisoned its former strategy and is aiming to satisfy the needs of an increasingly better educated and discerning consumer.

Mattessons claims 42 percent of the £14 million branded pâté market and 65 percent of the £130 million sliced meat sales, but admits that sales of pâté fell by 30 percent during the listeria scare. Unilever switched its Belgium supplier of pâté and revamped its production process. Now pâté is cooked in the tubs which are sold to the consumer, lowering the risk of infection caused by the transfer of food from factory moulds to retail packs.

Despite the scare, the relaunch, repositioning, and promotional campaigns do not stress the safety issue. Unilever believes that consumers remember the listeria scare but do not associate it with the Mattessons brand. Instead, the company is pushing the quality and taste of its repositioned pâté products.

SOURCES: Mike Johnson and Alan Mitchell, "Crisis in Food," *Marketing*, 26 October 1990, pp. 24–29; Mike Johnson, "Mattessons' Move Up Market Puts Pâté Back on Shelves," *Marketing*, 5 April 1990, p. 4; Karen Hoggan, "Meat Industry Banks on Recipe Data to Beef Up Sales," *Marketing* 27 September 1990, p. 5.

Questions for Discussion

1. An attitude refers to knowledge and positive or negative feelings about an object or activity. How have attitudes towards fresh foods changed during the last few years?
2. How might the U.K. meat industry change attitudes towards its products?
3. How can culture and subculture explain the consumption of beef or pâté? How might an industry body or manufacturer use this information in developing a marketing strategy for the consumption of its products?

5 ORGANISATIONAL MARKETS AND BUYING BEHAVIOUR

Objectives

To become familiar with the various types of organisational markets

To identify the major characteristics of organisational buyers and transactions

To understand several attributes of organisational demand

To become familiar with the major components of a buying centre

To understand the stages of the organisational buying decision process and the factors that affect this process

Orders for commercial aeroplanes are booming as loudly as the jumbo jets themselves. The Seattle-based Boeing Company has recently been besieged with requests from airlines for its 737s, 747s, 757s, and 767s. As an organisational marketer, Boeing has been immensely successful. Today Boeing holds 55 percent of the orders for commercial jet airliners in the world.

After convincing Northwest, KLM, United, Lufthansa, Cathay Pacific, and other airlines to buy its jets, Boeing now faces harsh criticism from these customers for falling several months behind the delivery schedule. These airlines, which had to adjust their flight schedules to compensate for a shortage of aircraft, have requested that Boeing give them cash discounts, complimentary spare parts, and other concessions because it did not fulfil its delivery promises.

Boeing has responded to the rush of orders by increasing its work-force to more than 155,000 employees, up 83 percent since 1983. Boeing is also enrolling workers in special training and quality control programmes. The company's executives are trying to force its suppliers to speed up delivery of aeroplane components, but many of Boeing's 1,500 suppliers require long product lead times. For example, landing gears for individual planes need to be ordered at least two years in advance.

With the public's growing concern for aeroplane safety and the high cost of hiring and training new workers, many analysts predict that Boeing will face tough times in the future, in spite of the current expansion of the market due to replacement of old fleets. As Boeing speeds up its production, declining quality may become a major problem. Already two of Boeing's major customers, Japan Air Lines and British Airways, have complained about poor quality.

To maintain its impressive market share, Boeing needs to carefully modernise and expand its plants, as well as use marketing to better serve present customers and attract new ones. ◆

Based on information from Doug Carroll, "But Boon in Orders Proves to Be a Bane," *USA Today,* 25 May 1989, pp. B1–B2; Maria Shao, "Trying Times at Boeing," *Business Week,* 13 Mar. 1989, pp. 34–36; and "Taking the Strain," *The Economist,* 28 Jan. 1989, p. 68.

Although Boeing is struggling with a problem—too many orders—its effective marketing efforts, as well as other factors, led to the problem. Boeing must now employ marketing efforts to keep customers contented while the problem is being resolved. Boeing's customers come from organisational markets; it does not serve ultimate customers directly. We defined an organisational or industrial market in Chapter 3 as consisting of individuals or groups that purchase a specific type of product for resale, for use in making other products, or for use in daily operations.

In this chapter we look more closely at organisational markets and organisational buying decision processes. We first discuss the various kinds of organisational markets and the types of buyers that make up these markets. Next we explore several dimensions of organisational buying, such as the characteristics of the transactions, the attributes and concerns of the buyers, the methods of buying, and the distinctive features of the demand for products sold to organisational purchasers. Finally, we examine organisational buying decisions by considering how they are arrived at and who makes the purchases.

TYPES OF ORGANISATIONAL MARKETS

In Chapter 3 we identify four kinds of organisational, or industrial, markets: producer, reseller, government, and institutional. The following section describes the characteristics of the customers that make up these markets. Table 5.1 shows the total turnover for U.K. businesses across these four types.

■ **Producer Markets**

Individuals and business organisations that purchase products for the purpose of making a profit by using them to produce other products or by using them in their operations are classified as **producer markets**. Producer markets include buyers of raw materials, as well as purchasers of semi-finished and finished items used to produce other products. For example, a manufacturer buys raw materials and component parts to use directly in the production of products. Grocers and supermarkets are part of the producer markets for numerous support products, such as paper and plastic bags, counters, scanners, and floor-care products. Farmers are part of the producer markets for farm machinery, fertiliser, seed, and livestock. A broad array of industries make up producer markets; they range from agriculture, forestry, fisheries, and mining to construction, transport, communications, and public utilities. The number of business units in European producer markets is enormous.

Manufacturers tend to be geographically concentrated. In Europe too this concentration occurs, with heavy industry centred around the Ruhr Valley in Germany and the Midlands and North-West in the U.K. This sometimes enables an industrial marketer to serve customers more efficiently. Within certain areas, production in just a few industries may account for a sizeable proportion of total industrial output.

■ **Reseller Markets**

Reseller markets consist of intermediaries, such as wholesalers and retailers, who buy finished goods and resell them to make a profit. (Wholesalers and retailers are discussed in Chapters 10 and 11.) Other than making minor alterations, resellers do

TABLE 5.1
*Number of legal
units in the United
Kingdom in 1989*

	TURNOVER SIZE (£ thousand)
Agriculture, forestry and fishing	116,826
Production	148,413
Mining and quarrying and public utilities	*1,469*
Manufacturing	*146,944*
Construction	217,727
Transport industries	66,239
Road transport and transport services	*63,728*
Other transport	*2,511*
Postal services and telecommunications	1,042
Wholesaling and dealing	117,072
Retailing	252,175
Finance, property and professional services	118,290
Catering	125,380
Motor trades	74,711
Business services and central offices	95,682
All other services	108,165
Total	**1,441,722**

SOURCE: *Business Monitor,* Central Statistical Office, 1989. Reprinted by permission of the Controller of Her Majesty's Stationery Office.

not change the physical characteristics of the products they handle. With the exception of items that producers sell directly to consumers, all products sold to consumer markets are first sold to reseller markets.

Wholesalers purchase products for resale to retailers, to other wholesalers, and to producers, governments, and institutions. Although some highly technical products are sold directly to end users, many products are sold through wholesalers who, in turn, sell products to other firms in the distribution system. Thus wholesalers are very important in helping to get a producer's product to customers. Wholesalers often carry many products, perhaps as many as 250,000 items. When inventories are vast, the reordering of products is normally automated and the wholesaler's initial purchase decisions are made by professional buyers and buying committees.

Retailers purchase products and resell them to final consumers. Some retailers carry a large number of items. Chemists, for example, may stock up to 12,000 items, and some supermarkets may handle as many as 20,000 different products. In small, family-owned retail stores, the owner frequently makes purchasing decisions. Large department stores have one or more employees in each department who are responsible for buying products for that department. As for chain stores, a buyer or buying committee in the central office frequently decides whether a product will be made available for selection by store managers. For most products, however, local store management makes the actual buying decisions for a particular store.

When making purchase decisions, resellers consider several factors. They evaluate the level of demand for a product to determine in what quantity and at what

FIGURE 5.1
Focusing on reseller markets.
Nabisco's message to resellers emphasises the profitability of stocking these brands.

SOURCE: Nabisco Biscuit Company

prices it can be resold. They assess the amount of space required to handle a product relative to its potential profit. In Figure 5.1, Nabisco's message to resellers, specifically grocers, deals with the profitability of the six featured brands. Retailers, for example, sometimes evaluate products on the basis of sales per square foot of selling area. Since customers often depend on a reseller to have a product when they need it, a reseller typically evaluates a supplier's ability to provide adequate quantities when and where wanted. Resellers also take into account the ease of placing orders and the availability of technical assistance and training programmes from the producer. More broadly, when resellers consider buying a product not previously carried, they try to determine whether the product competes with or complements products the firm is currently handling. These types of concerns distinguish reseller markets from other markets. Marketers dealing with reseller markets must recognise these needs and be able to serve them.

■ **Government Markets**

National and local governments make up **government markets**. They spend billions of pounds annually for a variety of goods and services to support their internal operations and to provide the public with education, water, energy, national defence, road systems, and health care.

TABLE 5.2 *U.K. central government: Current account (£ million)*

	1978	1979	1980	1981	1982	1983	1984	1985	1986	1987	1988
EXPENDITURE											
Final consumption:											
Current expenditure on goods and services:											
General public services	1,589	1,878	2,318	2,433	2,701	2,791	2,758	2,924	3,191	3,222	3,482
Defence	7,501	8,849	11,318	12,523	14,274	15,584	16,839	17,855	18,593	18,660	19,261
Public order and safety	618	713	964	1,127	1,259	1,402	1,577	1,599	1,946	2,164	2,431
Education	403	479	618	702	797	851	879	975	1,081	1,077	1,128
Health	7,343	8,488	10,971	12,631	13,199	14,994	15,741	16,763	17,938	19,759	21,802
Social security	716	809	1,031	1,273	1,461	1,505	1,560	1,670	1,580	2,050	2,366
Housing and community amenity	13	18	23	34	44	37	52	38	43	125	135
Recreational and cultural affairs	91	105	150	151	155	223	213	200	237	294	385
Fuel and energy	97	134	183	163	153	206	243	264	304	281	168
Agriculture, forestry and fishing	244	256	345	375	378	373	308	382	400	504	483
Mining and mineral resources, manufacturing and construction	192	126	124	319	324	299	335	388	353	360	420
Transport and communications	206	237	311	350	433	424	371	430	455	561	489
Other economic affairs and services	667	757	944	1,025	1,011	1,121	1,370	1,408	1,604	1,825	1,906
Total current expenditure on goods and services[1]	19,680	22,849	29,300	33,106	36,189	39,810	42,246	44,896	47,725	50,882	54,456
Non-trading capital consumption	466	552	689	773	811	844	896	983	1,081	1,177	1,265
Total final consumption	20,146	23,401	29,989	33,879	37,000	40,654	43,142	45,879	48,806	52,059	55,721

1. Net of the following income from fees and charges, etc (£ million):

1978	1979	1980	1981	1982	1983	1984	1985	1986	1987	1988
1,475	1,499	1,835	2,290	2,616	2,901	2,741	2,287	1,970	2,027	2,265

SOURCE: United Kingdom National Accounts, Central Statistical Office, 1989. Reprinted by permission of the Controller of Her Majesty's Stationery Office.

The amount spent by local government is increasing rapidly both because the services it provides have increased and because the costs of providing these services have increased. Table 5.2 shows U.K. government expenditure on goods and services from 1978 to 1988.

The types and quantities of products bought by government markets reflect social demands on various government agencies. As the public's needs for government services change, so does the demand for products by government markets. Because government agencies spend public funds to buy the products needed to provide services, they are accountable to the public. This accountability explains their relatively complex set of buying procedures. Some firms do not even try to sell to government buyers because they do not want to deal with so much red tape. However, many marketers have learned to deal efficiently with government procedures and do not find them to be a stumbling block. For certain products, such as defence-related items, the government may be the only customer.

The government makes its purchases through bids or negotiated contracts. To make a sale under the bid system, a firm must apply and be approved in order to be placed on a list of qualified bidders. When a government unit wants to buy, it sends out a detailed description of the products to qualified bidders. Businesses that wish to sell such products submit bids. The government unit is usually required to accept the lowest bid. When buying non-standard or highly complex products, a government unit often uses a negotiated contract. Under this procedure, the government unit selects only a few firms and then negotiates specifications and terms; it eventually awards the contract to one of the negotiating firms. In the U.K. most large defence-related contracts held by such companies as GEC, Ferranti and Plessey are made through negotiated contracts.

Although government markets can have complicated requirements, they can also be very lucrative. When the Post Office or government departments modernise obsolete computer systems, successful bidders can gain a billion pounds during the life of a contract, which is usually five years or more. Some firms have established separate departments to facilitate marketing to government units.

■ **Institutional Markets**

Organisations that seek to achieve charitable, educational, community, or other non-business goals constitute **institutional markets**. Members of institutional markets include churches, some hospitals, libraries, museums, universities, and charitable organisations. Institutions purchase millions of pounds' worth of products annually to provide goods, services, and ideas to congregations, students, patients, club members, and others. Because institutions often have different goals and fewer resources than other types of organisations, marketers may use special marketing activities to serve these markets.

DIMENSIONS OF ORGANISATIONAL BUYING

Having gained an understanding of the different types of organisational customer, we now need to consider the dimensions of organisational buying. First we examine several characteristics of organisational transactions. Then we discuss several attributes of organisational buyers and some of their primary concerns when making purchase decisions. Next we consider methods of organisational buying and the major types of purchases made by organisations. We conclude the section with a discussion of how the demand for industrial products differs from the demand for consumer products.

■ **Characteristics of Organisational Transactions**

Organisational (or industrial) transactions differ from consumer sales in several ways. Orders by organisational buyers tend to be much larger than individual consumer sales. Suppliers must often sell their products in large quantities to make profits; consequently, they prefer not to sell to customers who place small orders.

Generally, organisational purchases are negotiated less frequently than consumer sales. Some purchases involve expensive items, such as machinery, that are used for a number of years. Even the purchase of office equipment may involve careful consideration of its capabilities (see Figure 5.2). Other products, such as raw materials and component items, are used continuously in production and may have to be supplied frequently. However, the contract regarding the terms of sale of these items is likely to be a long-term agreement, requiring negotiations, for example, every third year.

Although negotiations in organisational sales are less frequent than in consumer sales, they may take much longer. Purchasing decisions are often made by a committee; orders are frequently large and expensive; and products may be custom-built. There is a good chance that several people or departments in the purchasing organisation will be involved. One department might express a need for a product; a second department might develop its specifications; a third might stipulate the maximum amount to be spent; and a fourth might actually place the order.

One practice unique to organisational sales is **reciprocity**, an arrangement in which two organisations agree to buy from each other. Reciprocal agreements that threaten competition are illegal. In the U.S.A., the Federal Trade Commission and the Justice Department take action to stop anticompetitive reciprocal practices. In Europe, too, such practices are often subject to regulation. None the less, it is reasonable to believe that a certain amount of reciprocal dealing occurs among small businesses and, to a lesser extent, among larger companies as well. Because reciprocity influences purchasing agents to deal only with certain suppliers, it can lower morale among agents and lead to less-than-optimal purchases.

■ Attributes of Organisational Buyers

We usually think of organisational buyers as being different from consumer buyers in their purchasing behaviour because they are better informed about the products they purchase. To make purchasing decisions that fulfill an organisation's needs, organisational buyers demand detailed information about products' functional features and technical specifications.

Organisational buyers, however, also have personal goals that may influence their buying behaviour. Most organisational purchasing agents seek the psychological satisfaction that comes with organisational advancement and financial rewards. Agents who consistently exhibit rational organisational buying behaviour are likely to achieve these personal goals because they are performing their jobs in ways that help their firms achieve organisational objectives. Suppose, though, that an organisational buyer develops a close friendship with a certain supplier. If the buyer values friendship more than organisational promotion or financial rewards, he or she may behave irrationally from the firm's point of view. Dealing exclusively with that supplier regardless of better prices, product qualities, or services from competitors may indicate an unhealthy or unethical alliance between the buyer and seller.

■ Primary Concerns of Organisational Buyers

When they make purchasing decisions, organisational customers take into account a variety of factors. Among their chief considerations are quality, delivery, service, and price.[1]

1. P. Green, P. Robinson, and Y. Wind, "The Determinant of Vendor Selection. The Evaluation Function Approach," *Journal of Purchasing*, August 1968.

FIGURE 5.2

One type of organisational purchase.
Fujitsu indicates that it sells satisfaction through an extensive mix of product features.

SOURCE: Fujitsu Europe Ltd.

Most organisational customers try to achieve and maintain a specific level of quality in the products they offer to their target markets. To accomplish this goal, they often buy their products on the basis of a set of expressed characteristics, commonly called *specifications*. Thus an organisational buyer evaluates the quality of the products being considered to determine whether or not they meet the necessary specifications.

Meeting specifications is extremely important to organisational customers. If a product fails to meet specifications and malfunctions for the ultimate consumer, the organisational customer may drop that product's supplier and switch to a different one. On the other hand, organisational customers are ordinarily cautious about buying products that exceed specifications because such products often cost more and thus increase an organisation's production costs.

Organisational buyers also value service. The services offered by suppliers influence directly and indirectly organisational customers' costs, sales, and profits. When tangible goods are the same or quite similar—as is true in the case of most raw materials—the goods may be sold at the same price in the same kind of containers and may have the same specifications. Under such conditions, the mix of services provided to customers is likely to be the major way that an organisational marketer gains a competitive advantage.

Specific services vary in importance. Among those commonly desired are market information, inventory maintenance, on-time delivery, repair services, and credit. Organisational buyers are likely to need technical product information, data regarding demand, information about general economic conditions, or supply and delivery information. Maintaining an adequate inventory is critical because it helps make products accessible when an organisational buyer needs them and reduces the buyer's inventory requirements and costs. Since organisational buyers are usually responsible for ensuring that the products are on hand and ready for use when needed, on-time delivery is crucial. Furthermore, reliable, on-time delivery saves the organisational customers money, enabling them to carry less inventory. Organisational purchasers of machinery are especially concerned about obtaining repair services and replacement parts quickly because equipment that cannot be used is costly. Caterpillar Inc., a manufacturer of earth-moving, construction, and materials-handling machinery, has built an international reputation, as well as high profits, by providing prompt service and replacement parts for its products around the world.

Suppliers can also give extra value to organisational buyers by offering credit. Credit helps improve an organisational customer's cash flow and reduce the peaks and valleys of capital requirements, thus lowering the firm's cost of capital. Although a single supplier cannot provide every possible service to its organisational customers, a marketing-orientated supplier creates a service mix that satisfies the target market.

Providing service has become even more critical for organisational marketers because customer expectations about service have broadened. Now, for instance, communication channels that allow customers to ask questions, complain, submit orders, and trace shipments are indispensable aspects of service. Organisational marketers also need to strive for uniformity of service, simplicity, truthfulness, and accuracy; develop customer service objectives; and monitor or audit their customer service programmes. Firms can monitor their service by formally surveying customers or informally calling on customers and asking questions about the service they have received. Marketers with a strong customer service programme reap a reward: their customers keep coming back long after the first sale.[2] To succeed with their programme, however, they must conduct research to determine customers' expectations in regard to product quality and service.[3] See Marketing Update 5.1 for a description of recent changes in the car parts market.

Price matters greatly to an organisational customer because it influences operating costs and costs of goods sold, and these costs affect the customer's selling price and profit margin. When purchasing major equipment, an industrial buyer views the price as the amount of investment necessary to obtain a certain level of return or savings. Thus an organisational purchaser is likely to compare the price of a machine with the value of the benefits that the machine will yield. Caterpillar lost market share to foreign competitors because its prices were too high. An organisational buyer does not compare alternative products strictly by price; other factors, such as product quality and supplier services, are also major elements in the purchase decision. For example, one study found that in the buying decision process for

2. John I. Coppett, "Auditing Your Customer Service Activities," *Industrial Marketing Management*, November 1988, pp. 277–284.

3. Thomas L. Powers, "Identify and Fulfill Customer Service Expectations," *Industrial Marketing Management*, November 1988, pp. 273–276.

CHANGES IN THE SUPPLY OF CAR PARTS

Companies supplying automotive parts to garages involved in car servicing and repairs are having to respond to significant market change. In the U.K. and Benelux countries, the balance of different outlet types is already shifting away from the traditional independent and car manufacturer-franchised garages towards the specialist and "fast-fit" operations. The fast-fit outlet (such as Kwik Fit), offering rapid service at competitive prices for replacement tyres, batteries, and exhausts, is also expected to become popular in other European countries.

Suppliers like Lucas and Bosch are having to gear their selling efforts to a changing customer base. It is essential that they are able to satisfy the particular needs of the new types of outlet.

One possible response is a change in supplier relationships with distributors, retailers, and garages. More co-operation between players with jointly agreed product ranges and methods of installation is a likely outcome of this. The underlying aim, it seems, is to shorten the length of distribution channels from manufacturer to the installing garage. The logic is that shorter channels can be more responsive to the changing characteristics and needs of the customer base. Although this is partly a reaction to changing customer needs, clearly this shortening of the distribution channel cuts out stages and people in the organisational buying process.

SOURCES: John Wormald and Erik Arnold, "Change and Opportunities in the Automotive Aftermarket," Booz Allen & Hamilton International (UK) Ltd, *EIU,* European Motor Business, November 1989, pp. 125–151; "Garages/Car Servicing," *Mintel,* Marketing Intelligence Report, May 1988, pp. 101–117; *Lucas Annual Report* 1989.

mainframe computer software operating systems, buyers indicated that intangible attributes, such as the seller's credibility and understanding of the buyer's needs, were very important in the decision process.[4]

■ **Methods of Organisational Buying**

Although no two organisational buyers go about their jobs in the same way, most use one or more of the following purchase methods: *description, inspection, sampling, or negotiation.* When the products being purchased are commonly standardised according to certain characteristics (such as size, shape, weight, and colour) and are normally graded using such standards, an organisational buyer may be able to purchase simply by describing or specifying quantity, grade, and other attributes. Agricultural produce often falls into this category. In some cases, a buyer may specify a particular brand or its equivalent when describing the desired product. Purchases on the basis of description are especially common between a buyer and seller who have established an ongoing relationship built on trust.

Certain products, such as large industrial equipment, used vehicles, and buildings, have unique characteristics and may vary regarding their condition. For example, a particular second-hand van might have a faulty transmission. Consequently, organisational buyers of such products must base their purchase decisions on inspection.

In buying based on sampling, a sample of the product is taken from the lot and evaluated. It is assumed that the characteristics of this sample represent the entire lot. This method is appropriate when the product is homogeneous—for instance, grain—and examination of the entire lot is not physically or economically feasible.

Some industrial purchasing relies on negotiated contracts. In certain instances, an organisational buyer describes exactly what is needed and then asks sellers to submit bids. The buyer may take the most attractive bids and negotiate with those suppliers. In other cases, the buyer may not be able to identify specifically what is to be purchased but can provide only a general description—as might be the case for a special piece of custom-made equipment. A buyer and seller might negotiate a contract that specifies a base price and contains provisions for the payment of additional costs and fees. These contracts are most likely to be used for one-time projects, such as buildings and capital equipment.

■ **Types of Organisational Purchases**

Most organisational purchases are one of three types: new-task purchase, modified re-buy purchase, or straight re-buy purchase. In a **new-task purchase**, an organisation makes an initial purchase of an item to be used to perform a new job or to solve a new problem. A new-task purchase may require the development of product specifications, vendor specifications, and procedures for future purchases of that product. To make the initial purchase, the organisational buyer usually needs a good deal of information. A new-task purchase is important to a supplier, for if the organisational buyer is satisfied with the product, the supplier may be able to sell the buyer large quantities of the product for a period of years.

In a **modified re-buy purchase**, a new-task purchase is changed the second or third time it is ordered or the requirements associated with a straight re-buy purchase are modified. For example, an organisational buyer might seek faster delivery, lower prices, or a different quality level of product specifications. A modified re-buy

4. Jim Shaw, Joe Giglierano, and Jeff Kallis, "Marketing Complex Technical Products: The Importance of Intangible Attributes," *Industrial Marketing Management,* 18 (1989), pp. 45–53.

situation may cause regular suppliers to become more competitive to keep the account. Competing suppliers may have the opportunity to obtain the business.

A **straight re-buy purchase** occurs when a buyer purchases the same products routinely under approximately the same terms of sale. Buyers require little information for these routine purchase decisions. The buyer tends to use familiar suppliers that have provided satisfactory service and products in the past. These suppliers try to set up automatic reordering systems to make reordering easy and convenient for organisational buyers. A supplier may even monitor the organisational buyer's inventory and indicate to the buyer what needs to be ordered.

■ Demand for Industrial Products

Products sold to organisational customers are called industrial products and, consequently, the demand for these products is called industrial demand. Unlike consumer demand, industrial demand is (1) derived, (2) inelastic, (3) joint, and (4) more fluctuating. As we discuss each of these characteristics, remember that the demand for different types of industrial products varies.

Derived Demand. Because organisational customers, especially producers, buy products to be used directly or indirectly in the production of goods and services to satisfy consumers' needs, the demand for industrial products derives from the demand for consumer products; therefore it is called **derived demand**. For example, the demand for certain types of computer chips derives from consumers' demands for faster and smaller personal computers. In the long run, no industrial demand is totally unrelated to the demand for consumer goods.

The derived nature of industrial demand is usually multilevel. Industrial sellers at different levels are affected by a change in consumer demand for a particular product. For instance, consumers today are more concerned with health and good nutrition than ever before, and as a result are purchasing products with less cholesterol and salt. When consumers stopped buying high-cholesterol cooking fats and margarine, the demand for equipment used in manufacturing these products also dropped. Thus factors influencing consumer buying of various food products affected food processors, equipment manufacturers, suppliers of raw materials, and even fast-food restaurants, which have had to switch to vegetable oils for frying. Changes in derived demand result from a chain reaction. When consumer demand for a product changes, a wave is set in motion that affects demand for all firms involved in the production of that consumer product.

Inelastic Demand. The demand for many industrial products at the industry level is inelastic, which simply means that a price increase or decrease will not significantly alter demand for the item. (The concept of price elasticity of demand is discussed further in Chapter 17.) Because many industrial products contain a number of parts, price increases that affect only one or two parts of the product may yield only a slightly higher per-unit production cost. Of course, when a sizeable price increase for a component represents a large proportion of the product's cost, then demand may become more elastic because the price increase in the component causes the price at the consumer level to rise sharply. For example, if manufacturers of aircraft engines substantially increase the price of these engines, forcing Boeing to raise the prices of the aircraft it manufactures, the demand for airliners may become more elastic as airlines reconsider whether they can afford to buy new aircraft. An increase in the price of windscreens, however, is unlikely to greatly affect the price of the airliners or the demand for them.

The characteristic of inelasticity applies only to industry demand for the industrial product, not to the demand curve faced by an individual firm. For example, suppose that a spark-plug producer increases the price of spark-plugs sold to manufacturers of small engines while its competitors continue to maintain their lower prices. The spark-plug manufacturer would probably experience reduced unit sales because most small-engine producers would switch to the lower-priced brands. A specific organisation is vulnerable to elastic demand, even though industry demand for a particular product is inelastic.

Joint Demand. The demand for certain industrial products, especially raw materials and components, is subject to joint demand. **Joint demand** occurs when two or more items are used in combination to produce a product. For example, a firm that manufactures axes needs the same number of axe handles as it does axe blades; these two products are demanded jointly. If there is a shortage of axe handles, then the producer will buy fewer axe blades.

Understanding the effects of joint demand is particularly important for a marketer selling multiple jointly demanded items. Such a marketer must realise that when a customer begins purchasing one of the jointly demanded items, a good opportunity exists for selling related products. Similarly, when customers purchase a number of jointly demanded products, the producer must exercise extreme caution to avoid shortages of any one of them because such shortages jeopardise the marketer's sales of all the jointly demanded products.

Demand Fluctuations. As already mentioned, the demand for industrial products may fluctuate enormously because it is derived from consumer demand. In general, when particular consumer products are in high demand, their producers buy large quantities of raw materials and components to ensure that they can meet long-run production requirements. In addition, these producers may expand their production capacity, which entails the acquisition of new equipment and machinery, more workers, and more raw materials and component parts.

Conversely, a decline in the demand for certain consumer goods significantly reduces the demand for industrial products used to produce those goods. In fact, under such conditions, a marketer's sales of certain products may come to a temporary standstill. When consumer demand is low, industrial customers cut their purchases of raw materials and components and stop buying equipment and machinery, even for replacement purposes.

A marketer of industrial products may notice changes in demand when its customers change their inventory policies, perhaps because of expectations about future demand. For example, if several dishwasher manufacturers who buy timers from one producer increase their inventory of timers from a two-week to a one-month supply, the timer producer will have a significant immediate increase in demand.

Sometimes price changes can lead to surprising temporary changes in demand. A price increase for an industrial item may initially cause organisational customers to buy more of the item because they expect the price to rise further. Similarly, demand for an industrial product may be significantly lower following a price cut because buyers are waiting for further price reductions. Fluctuations in demand can be significant in industries in which price changes occur frequently.

ORGANISATIONAL BUYING DECISIONS

Organisational (or **industrial**) **buying behaviour** refers to the purchase behaviour of producers, resellers, government units, and institutions. Although several of the same factors that affect consumer buying behaviour (discussed in Chapter 4) also influence organisational buying behaviour, a number of factors are unique to the latter. In this section we first analyse the buying centre to learn who participates in making organisational purchase decisions. Then we focus on the stages of the buying decision process and the factors that affect it.

■ **The Buying Centre**

Relatively few organisational purchase decisions are made by just one person; mostly, they are made through a buying centre. The **buying centre** refers to the group of people within an organisation who are involved in making organisational purchase decisions. These individuals include users, influencers, buyers, deciders, and gatekeepers.[5] One person may perform several of these roles. These participants share some goals and risks associated with their decisions.

Users are the organisation members who actually use the product being acquired. They frequently initiate the purchase process and/or generate the specifications for the purchase. After the purchase, they also evaluate the product's performance relative to the specifications. Influencers are often technical personnel, such as engineers, who help develop the specifications and evaluate alternative products. Technical personnel are especially important influencers when the products being considered involve new, advanced technology.

Buyers are responsible for selecting suppliers and actually negotiating the terms of purchase. They may also become involved in developing specifications. Buyers are sometimes called purchasing agents or purchasing managers. Their choices of suppliers and products, especially for new-task purchases, are heavily influenced by persons occupying other roles in the buying centre. For straight re-buy purchases, the buyer plays a major role in the selection of suppliers and in negotiations with them. Deciders actually choose the products and suppliers. Although buyers may be the deciders, it is not unusual for different people to occupy these roles. For routinely purchased items, buyers are commonly the deciders. However, a buyer may not be authorised to make purchases that exceed a certain monetary value, in which case higher-level management personnel are the deciders. Gatekeepers, such as secretaries and technical personnel, control the flow of information to and among the persons who occupy the other roles in the buying centre. Buyers who deal directly with suppliers may also be gatekeepers because they can control the flow of information. The flow of information from supplier sales representatives to users and influencers often is controlled by personnel in the purchasing department.

5. Frederick E. Webster, Jr., and Yoram Wind, *Organizational Buying Behavior* (Englewood Cliffs, N.J.: Prentice-Hall, 1972), pp. 78–80.

The number and structure of an organisation's buying centres are affected by the organisation's size and market position, by the volume and types of products being purchased, and by the firm's overall managerial philosophy regarding exactly who should be involved in purchase decisions. A marketer attempting to sell to an organisational customer should determine who is in the buying centre, the types of decisions each individual makes, and which individuals are the most influential in the decision process. Because in some instances many people make up the buying centre, marketers cannot contact all participants; instead, they must be certain to contact a few of the most influential.

■ **Stages of the Organisational Buying Decision Process**

Like consumers, organisations follow a buying decision process. It is summarised on the right-hand side of Figure 5.3. In the first stage, one or more individuals recognise that a problem or need exists. Problem recognition may arise under a variety of circumstances, for instance, when a machine malfunctions or a firm is modifying an existing product or introducing a new one. Individuals in the buying centre, such as users, influencers, or buyers, may be involved in problem recognition, but it may be stimulated by external sources, such as sales representatives.

The second stage of the process—development of product specifications—requires organisational participants to assess the problem or need and determine what will be necessary to resolve or satisfy it. During this stage, users and influencers, such as technical personnel and engineers, often provide information and advice for developing product specifications. By assessing and describing needs, the organisation should be able to establish product specifications.

Searching for possible products to solve the problem and locating suppliers is the third stage in the decision process. Search activities may involve looking in company files and trade directories, contacting suppliers for information, soliciting proposals from known suppliers, and examining catalogues and trade publications. The industrial advertisement in Figure 5.4 is an example of information available in trade publications. Some suppliers may not be viewed as acceptable because they are not large enough to supply the needed quantities, and others may have poor records of delivery and service. In some instances the product is not available from any existing supplier and the buyer must find a company that can design and build the product. Innovative companies, like 3M (see Marketing Update 5.2), are sought.

If all goes well, the search stage will result in a list of several alternative products and suppliers. The fourth stage is evaluating the products on the list to determine which ones (if any) meet the product specifications developed in the second stage. The advertisement in Figure 5.5 stresses the product performance characteristics of DRG Envelopes and helps potential customers determine if the product meets their specifications. At this point, too, various suppliers are evaluated according to multiple criteria, such as price, service, and ability to deliver.

The results of the deliberations and assessments in the fourth stage are used during the fifth stage to select the product to be purchased and the supplier from whom to buy it. In some cases, the buyer may decide to choose several suppliers. In others, only one supplier is selected—a situation known as sole sourcing. Sole sourcing has traditionally been discouraged except when a product is available from only one company; firms that have contracts with national governments are often required to have several sources for an item. Sole sourcing is becoming more popular today, partly because such an arrangement means better communications

FIGURE 5.3
Organisational buying decision process and factors that may influence it

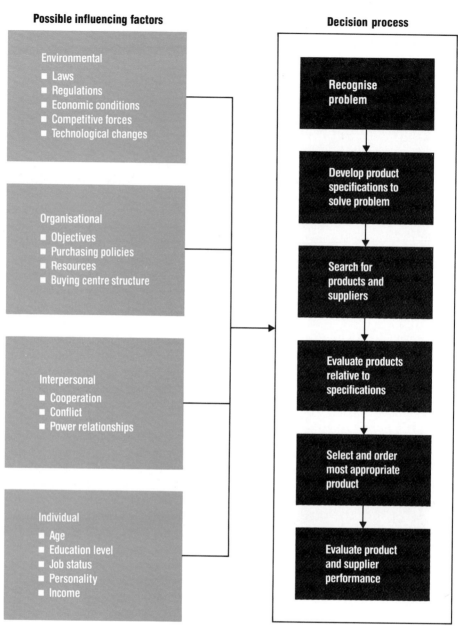

Possible influencing factors

Environmental
- Laws
- Regulations
- Economic conditions
- Competitive forces
- Technological changes

Organisational
- Objectives
- Purchasing policies
- Resources
- Buying centre structure

Interpersonal
- Cooperation
- Conflict
- Power relationships

Individual
- Age
- Education level
- Job status
- Personality
- Income

Decision process

Recognise problem

Develop product specifications to solve problem

Search for products and suppliers

Evaluate products relative to specifications

Select and order most appropriate product

Evaluate product and supplier performance

SOURCE: Adapted from Frederick E. Webster, Jr., and Yoram Wind, *Organizational Buying Behavior,* © 1972, pp. 33–37. Adapted by permission of Prentice-Hall, Englewood Cliffs, N.J.

between buyer and supplier, stability and higher profits for the supplier, and often lower prices for the buyer. However, most organisations still prefer to purchase goods and services from several suppliers because this approach lessens the possibility of disruption caused by strikes, shortages, or bankruptcy. The actual product is ordered in this fifth stage and specific details regarding terms, credit arrangements, delivery dates and methods, and technical assistance are worked out.

FIGURE 5.4

Trade publication information.
Texaco Chemical Company uses industrial advertisements to inform potential customers about its carbonates.

SOURCE: Courtesy of Texaco Chemical Company

During the sixth stage, the product's performance is evaluated by comparing it with specifications. Sometimes, even though the product meets the specifications, its performance does not adequately solve the problem or satisfy the need recognised in the first stage. In that case, the product specifications must be adjusted. The supplier's performance is also evaluated during this stage, and if it is found wanting, the organisational purchaser seeks corrective action from the supplier or searches for a new supplier. The results of the evaluation become feedback for the other stages and influence future organisational purchase decisions.

This organisational buying decision process is used in its entirety primarily for new-task purchases. Several of the stages, but not necessarily all, are used for modified re-buy and straight re-buy situations.

■ **Influences on Organisational Buying**

Figure 5.3 also lists the four major categories of factors that influence organisational buying decisions: environmental, organisational, interpersonal, and individual.

You may remember from Chapter 2 that environmental factors are uncontrollable forces such as politics, laws, regulations and regulatory agencies, activities of interest groups, changes in the economy, competitors' actions, and technological changes.

3M COMPANY: AN INNOVATIVE SOURCE

Since its early days, Minnesota Mining & Manufacturing, the St. Paul, Minnesota–based 3M Company, has had a reputation for innovation and creativity. Having developed over 60,000 products ranging from the popular Post-it note and familiar Scotch tape to a synthetic ligament for injured knees and translucent dental braces, 3M is a virtual new-product machine.

3M encourages employees to develop new products. Employees are allowed to spend 15 percent of their time at work on their own projects. They can apply for special 3M Genesis grants that provide researchers with up to $50,000 for individual projects. They can actually manage the new product if it proves to be successful. And management is as tolerant of experimental failures as it is supportive of potential blockbusters. 3M even ties employee promotions and bonuses to new product development.

Employees at 3M use their entrepreneurial spirit to pursue organisational markets as well. One 3M chemist created a special filter to clean lubricants in metal-working shops. The market for such a filter, even though it worked extremely well, was worth only one million dollars. Management was so impressed, however, that it allowed the employee to continue to tinker with the filter. Eventually, the worker entered into a joint venture with a 3M customer, PPG Industries Inc., which sells paint-primer systems to car manufacturers. Apparently, the filters PPG employees were using to strain out impurities were not very effective, and the 3M chemist's filters turned out to work much better. It was later discovered that the filters were also efficient strainers for machine oil, paint, edible oils, water, and beer. Now, the filters serve a $20 million market.

Employees at 3M are constantly trying to discover products that will fill industrial and organisational niches. The creative spirit at 3M gives employees the flexibility and encouragement they need to keep producing technological breakthroughs. It is no wonder that some business analysts consider 3M to be the most innovative company in the world.

SOURCES: Russell Mitchell, "Masters of Innovation," *Business Week,* 10 April 1989, pp. 58–63; Margaret Nelson, "Top Priority at 3M Is Communications," *Purchasing,* 10 March 1988, pp. 104–105, 109; and Thomas Osborn, "How 3M Manages for Innovation," *Marketing Communications,* November/ December 1988, pp. 17–22.

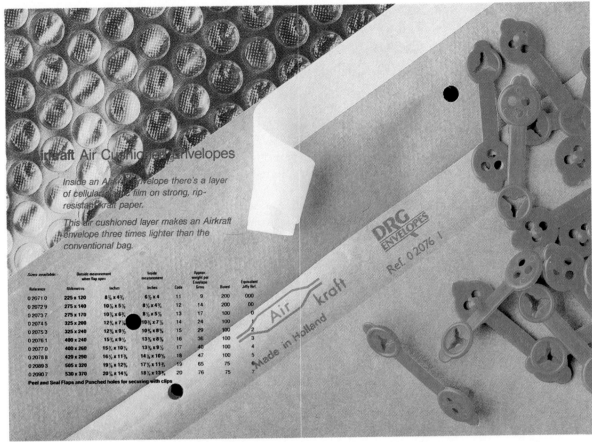

FIGURE 5.5 *Does the product meet specifications?*
The maker of DRG Envelopes emphasises product performance characteristics to assure customers that the product meets or exceeds their specifications.

SOURCE: John Dickinson Stationery

These forces generate a considerable amount of uncertainty for an organisation, and the uncertainty can make individuals in the buying centre apprehensive about certain types of purchase. Changes in one or more environmental forces can create new purchasing opportunities and make yesterday's purchase decisions look terrible. For example, rapid developments in computer and communications technology sometimes render newly purchased computer or telephone systems obsolete, or at least less desirable, in only a few years. For this reason, organisations approach the buying decision process for such products with special caution.

Organisational factors influencing the organisational buying decision process include the buyer's objectives, purchasing policies, and resources, as well as the size and composition of its buying centre. An organisation may have certain buying policies to which buying centre participants must conform. For instance, a firm's policies may mandate long-term contracts, perhaps longer than most sellers desire. The nature of an organisation's financial resources may require special credit arrangements. Any of these conditions could affect purchase decision processes.

The interpersonal factors are the relationships among the people in the buying centre. The use of power and the level of conflict among buying centre participants influence organisational buying decisions. Certain persons in the buying centre may be better communicators than others and may be more convincing. Often these interpersonal dynamics are hidden, making them difficult for marketers to assess.

Individual factors are the personal characteristics of individuals in the buying centre, such as age, education, personality, and position in the organisation. For example, a 55-year-old manager who has been in the organisation for twenty-five years may affect the decisions made by the buying centre differently from a 30-year-old person who has been employed for only two years. How influential these factors will be depends on the buying situation, the type of product being purchased, and whether the purchase is new-task, modified re-buy, or straight re-buy. The negotiating styles of people will undoubtedly vary within an organisation and from one organisation to another. To be effective, a marketer needs to know customers well enough to be aware of these individual factors and the effects they may have on purchase decisions.

SUMMARY

Organisational markets consist of individuals and groups that purchase a specific kind of product for resale, for direct use in producing other products, or for use in day-to-day operations. Producer markets include those individuals and business organisations that purchase products for the purpose of making a profit by using them to produce other products or by using them in their operations. Intermediaries who buy finished products and resell them for the purpose of making a profit are classified as reseller markets. Government markets consist of national and local governments, which spend billions of pounds annually for goods and services to support their internal operations and provide citizens with needed services. Organisations that seek to achieve charity, education, community, or other not-for-profit goals constitute institutional markets.

Organisational transactions differ from consumer transactions in several ways. The transactions tend to be larger, and negotiations occur less frequently, though they are often lengthy. Organisational transactions sometimes involve more than one person or one department in the purchasing organisation. They may also involve reciprocity, an arrangement in which two organisations agree to buy from each other. Organisational customers are usually viewed as more rational than ultimate consumers and as more likely to seek information about a product's features and technical specifications.

When purchasing products, organisational customers must be particularly concerned about quality, service, and price. Quality is important because it directly affects the quality of products the buyer's organisation ultimately produces. To achieve an exact level of quality, organisations often buy their products on the basis of a set of expressed characteristics, called specifications. Because services can have such a direct influence on a firm's costs, sales, and profits, such matters as market information, on-time delivery, and availability of parts can be crucial to an organisational buyer. Although an organisational customer does not depend solely on price to decide which products to purchase, price is of prime concern because it directly influences a firm's profitability.

Organisational buyers use several purchasing methods, including description, inspection, sampling, and negotiation. Most organisational purchases are new task, modified re-buy, or straight re-buy. In a new-task purchase, an organisation makes an initial purchase of an item to be used to perform a new job or to solve a problem. In a modified re-buy purchase, a new-task purchase is changed the second or third time it is ordered or the requirements associated with a straight re-buy purchase are modified. A straight re-buy purchase occurs when a buyer purchases the same products routinely under approximately the same terms of sale.

Industrial demand differs from consumer demand along several dimensions. Industrial demand derives from the demand for consumer products. At the industry level, industrial demand is inelastic. If the price of an industrial item changes, demand for the product will not change as much proportionally. Some industrial products are subject to joint demand, which occurs when two or more items are used in combination to make a product. Finally, because industrial demand derives from consumer demand, the demand for industrial products can fluctuate widely.

Organisational, or industrial, buying behaviour refers to the purchase behaviour of producers, resellers, government units, and institutions. Organisational purchase decisions are made through a buying centre—the group of people who are involved in making organisational purchase decisions. Users are those in the organisation who actually use the product. Influencers help develop the specifications and evaluate alternative products for possible use. Buyers are responsible for selecting the suppliers and negotiating the terms of the purchases. Deciders choose the products and suppliers. Gatekeepers control the flow of information to and among persons who occupy the other roles in the buying centre.

The stages of the organisational buying decision process are problem recognition, the development of product specifications to solve the problem, the search for products and suppliers, evaluation of products relative to specifications, selection and ordering of the most appropriate product, and evaluation of the product's and the supplier's performance.

Four categories of factors influence organisational buying decisions: environmental, organisational, interpersonal, and individual. The environmental factors include laws and regulations, economic conditions, competitive forces, and technological changes. Organisational factors influencing the organisational buying decision process include the buyer's objectives, purchasing policies, and resources, as well as the size and composition of its buying centre. The interpersonal factors are the relationships among the people in the buying centre. Individual factors are the personal characteristics of individuals in the buying centre, such as age, education, personality, position in the organisation, and income.

IMPORTANT TERMS

Producer markets
Reseller markets
Government markets
Institutional markets
Reciprocity
New-task purchase
Modified re-buy purchase

Straight re-buy purchase
Derived demand
Joint demand
Organisational (or industrial) buying
   behaviour
Buying centre

Discussion and Review Questions

1. Identify, describe, and give examples of four major types of organisational markets.
2. Regarding purchasing behaviour, why are organisational buyers generally considered more rational than ultimate consumers?
3. What are the primary concerns of organisational buyers?
4. List several characteristics that differentiate organisational transactions from consumer ones.
5. What are the commonly used methods of organisational buying?
6. Why do buyers involved in a straight re-buy purchase require less information than those making a new-task purchase?
7. How does industrial demand differ from consumer demand?
8. What are the major components of a buying centre?
9. Identify the stages of the organisational buying decision process. How is this decision process used when making straight re-buys?
10. How do environmental, organisational, interpersonal, and individual factors affect organisational purchases?

■ Cases

5.1 Faber-Castell Markets Low-Tech Products to Organisational Markets

When Faber-Castell Corp. finalised its acquisition of Eberhard Faber Inc., the rejoining of two major writing instrument companies was complete. Both firms trace their ancestry to Kaspar Faber, the inventor of pencil lead as we know it. In the late nineteenth century, the Faber pencil business split into three separate companies: German-based A.W. Faber-Castell Corp., Faber-Castell Corp., and Eberhard Faber.

Eberhard Faber, the originator of the familiar yellow pencil, had been producing wood-cased pencils since 1849, maintaining a 10 percent share of the $100 million pencil market. The company's sales of pencils, pens, erasers, and rubber bands had been increasing in Third World countries, but recent U.S. sales had been essentially static. As a result, Eberhard Faber's U.S. pencil sales accounted for less than 20 percent of its worldwide sales, and earnings had declined during recent years.

When the pencil market became particularly competitive in the early 1980s, Eberhard Faber's top management concluded that the key to greater U.S. profitability was marketing. At first the firm made some mistakes. For example, after producing yellow pencils for nearly a century, the company decided to introduce a natural-looking pencil: bare cedar wood covered with a coat of clear lacquer. Eberhard Faber projected a 15 percent market share for the new product, thinking that the current trend toward naturalness would carry over into the pencil market. But stationers avoided the new product, preferring to stick with a proven seller.

Another strategic miscalculation involved the company's redoubled efforts in art supplies, a market that yields greater profit margins than the highly competitive office supplies market. Because Eberhard Faber's Design markers were already successful, the company acquired several art supply firms, such as NSM, maker of leather portfolios. At the same time, however, the company began to neglect the commercial office supplies field that accounted for two-thirds of its total sales. In this market, which includes sales to corporations under private labels as well as the Eberhard Faber name, the firm found itself gaining a reputation for non-competitive pricing and sluggish new-product development, despite the consistently good quality and service it offered.

New executives tried to revamp every aspect of the company's ineffective marketing operation. To build sales among wholesale office suppliers, they increased the advertising budget, created new promotional programmes, and redesigned the company's catalogues and order sheets. They developed new products, such as five-sided erasers in stylish colours. With commodity products such as rubber bands, they marketed quality and price. Nearly every product package was updated. Office supplies distributors say such moves definitely improved the company's image.

Continuing to struggle despite its efforts, Eberhard Faber began seeking a buyer. Faber-Castell, seeing an opportunity to increase market share and protect the Faber trade name, bought Eberhard Faber. Now, there seems to be one clear pencil giant. Industry analysts are not quite sure about the direction and the strategies that Faber-Castell will adopt, but, despite all the high-tech developments of the recent years, there will probably always be a place for the familiar yellow pencil.

SOURCES: James Braham, "Ho-Hum: How Do You Peddle a Low-Tech Product?" *Industry Week,* 9 June 1986, pp. 53–56; "Faber-Castell Acquires Eberhard Faber," *Office Systems,* February 1988, p. 12; Alix M. Freedman, "The Next Thing You Know, They'll Change the Coke Formula," *Wall Street Journal,* 27 June 1985, p. E33; Martha E. Mangelsdorf, "I'm My Own Grandpa," *Inc.,* May 1988, p. 13; and Al Urbanski, "Eberhard Faber," *Sales & Marketing Management,* November 1986, pp. 44–47.

Questions for Discussion

1. What types of organisational markets (as classified in this chapter) purchase the products Faber-Castell makes?
2. Most purchases of Faber-Castell's office products would be of what type: new task, modified re-buy, or straight re-buy? Why?
3. Why were the "natural-looking" pencils less than successful?
4. Evaluate the changes made in this firm's marketing efforts.

5.2 Institutional Buying

Institutional buying can be extremely complex or very straightforward and simple. Warwick Business School, in common with many university departments, "purchases" certain items from the university's central stores and departments, as well as dealing directly with manufacturers and service providers. Some of these activities are routine re-buys, while many are specialist one-off purchases. However, even where items are bought on a relatively regular basis for similar needs and from regular suppliers, because of budgetary and internal political requirements there is often a protracted decision-making process with many influencers involved in determining the purchasing timescale, suppliers, and product specifications.

For example, photocopying paper is a frequent, routine re-buy, with Xerox paper being bought on a regular basis. Similarly, most stationery requirements are frequent repeat purchases from an on-going supplier base. At the other extreme, the school's new teaching and conference complex and extensions to its existing office facilities involved lengthy discussions within the school regarding teaching, research, and administrative needs as related to the image that the school wants to portray to its various publics and employees. The final decision was not taken by the Business School alone. The university, as provider of land and much of the funding, as well as offering support facilities, has to be actively involved in the process throughout. Because of the large sums of money involved, tenders have to be sought for the building and capital work, requiring detailed specifications to be determined.

Typical, though, of the school's buying behaviour is the purchase of computer hardware and software for individual research groups or members of faculty. Each teaching group has its own budget requirements, the school has overall budget constraints and needs, with the parent university having some influence on how money and resources are allocated. Each individual faculty member makes a bid for equipment (detailing requirements) to his or her teaching group, which in turn—if the bid is accepted—passes it on to a Technical Support Committee. In the light of the school's overall resource structure and current needs, taking into account university guidelines, the committee will either approve, defer, or reject the bid. Very often, even though the process seems complex, this decision-making can be relatively quick. However, depending on the university calendar and people's availability, there are occasions when decisions seem to be extremely protracted.

For a seller attempting to gain a foothold in such a market, clearly there are many customers and influencers that the promotional material and sales representative must target, with differing messages. The user of such computer equipment needs to know of its capabilities and reliability, plus user-friendliness. The budget holders need to take into consideration cost versus reliability and product specification, plus how the individual purchase fits into related purchases being made by the school for other members of staff and within the university as a whole.

This situation is typical for many corporations, organisations, and service businesses. It is difficult to generalise purchasing decisions within such institutions as there are many different types of buying, decision-makers, and influencers, with varying timescales, emotional and economic requirements, and political considerations.

SOURCES: Michael Hutt and Thomas Speh, *Business Marketing Management* (Chicago: The Dryden Press, 1989); E. Jerome McCarthy and William D. Perreault, *Basic Marketing* (Homewood, Ill.: Irwin, 1990); J. Paul Peter and Gerry C. Olson, *Consumer Behaviour: Marketing Strategy Perspectives* (Homewood, Ill.: Irwin, 1987); Donald Cowell, *The Marketing of Services* (London: Heinemann, 1984).

Questions for Discussion

1. Within large corporations and institutions, is it typical for committee decision-making and buying to take place?
2. How difficult is it to centralise buying practices in organisational markets?
3. How could a supplier of computer hardware (e.g. personal computers) identify customers, influencers, and decision-makers in such an organisation?

6 MARKETING RESEARCH AND INFORMATION SYSTEMS

Objectives

To understand the importance of and relationship between research and information systems in marketing decision-making

To distinguish between research and intuition in solving marketing problems

To learn the five basic steps for conducting a marketing research project

To understand the fundamental methods of gathering data for marketing research

N ot long ago, the role of the male in family purchases was well defined. Because males were the major income provider, they usually made the final decisions about important household purchases. In the 1990s, however, men are becoming more involved in purchasing decisions for a wider variety of products. In today's market, male roles and buying behaviours are more diverse and fragmented. As a result, marketing researchers today have a more difficult task in defining male target markets and designing ways to reach them.

One role that more men have taken on is food shopping. A mid-1980s report by the Campbell Soup Company and *People* magazine indicated that male shoppers accounted for 40 percent of all food purchases. About 37 percent of the men surveyed said they shopped for food more often than they did a few years ago. A 1989 study conducted for *Men's Health* also indicated that the number of men performing a larger share of the household shopping had increased to about 43 percent.

Marketing research has pinpointed several factors behind evolving male purchasing patterns: higher divorce rates, delayed marriages, changing sex roles within the family, and increasing numbers of working women. Men have often been stereotyped as inexperienced, impulsive, and disorganised shoppers. Although research has found that men are less likely than women to use lists, coupons, or to comparison shop, their buying habits appear to be linked more to age and marital status than to gender.

Because marketing research has identified these changes in men's purchasing patterns, astute food marketers are now targeting food and food-related items to both men and women. To attract more male shoppers, supermarkets are using product demonstrations during evening hours, purchasing guides, and newspaper ads that emphasise shopping ease and convenience. ◆

Based on information in Eileen B. Brill, "Super Marketers Pursue the New Consumers," *Advertising Age*, 13 Oct. 1986, p. S4; Scott Donaton, "Study Boosts Men's Buying Role," *Advertising Age*, 4 Dec. 1989, p. 48; Priscilla Donegan, "The Myth of the Male Shopper," *Progressive Grocer*, May 1986, pp. 36–38; Ronald D. Michman, "The Male Queue at the Checkout Counter," *Business Horizons*, May-June 1986, pp. 51–55; Eileen Prescott, "New Men," *American Demographics*, Aug. 1983, p. 16.

T̲o implement the marketing concept, marketers require information about the characteristics, needs and wants of their target markets. Given the intense competition in today's market-place, it is unwise to develop a product and then look for a market where it can be profitably sold. (The Sinclair C5 electric car is a prime example.) Marketing research and information systems that provide practical, unbiased information help firms avoid the assumptions and misunderstandings that could result in poor marketing performance.

In this chapter we focus on the ways of gathering information needed to make marketing decisions. We first distinguish between managing information within an organisation (a marketing information system) and conducting marketing research. Then we discuss the role of marketing research in decision-making and problem-solving, compare it with intuition, and examine the individual steps of the marketing research process. We also take a close look at experimentation and various methods of collecting data. In the final section, we consider the importance of marketing research and marketing information systems.

DEFINING MARKETING RESEARCH AND MARKETING INFORMATION SYSTEMS

Marketing research is the systematic design, collection, interpretation, and reporting of information to help marketers solve specific marketing problems or take advantage of marketing opportunities. It is a process for gathering information not currently available to decision-makers. Marketing research is conducted on a special-project basis, with the research methods adapted to the problems being studied and to changes in the environment. Table 6.1 lists the main problem categories for which European marketers use market research. Table 6.2 identifies the major market research agencies worldwide and in Europe. The Market Research Society defines research as:

> the collection and analysis of data from a sample of individuals or organisations relating to their characteristics, behaviour, attitudes, opinions or possessions. It includes all forms of marketing and social research such as consumer and industrial surveys, psychological investigations, observational and panel studies.[1]

A **marketing information system (MIS)** is the framework for the day-to-day management and structuring of information gathered regularly from sources both inside and outside an organisation. As such, an MIS provides a continuous flow of information about prices, advertising expenditure, sales, competition, and distribution expenses. When information systems are strategically created and then institutionalised throughout an organisation, their value is enhanced.[2] Figure 6.1 illustrates the chief components of an MIS.

The inputs into a marketing information system include the information sources inside and outside the firm assumed to be useful for future decision-making. Pro-

---

1. "Research" is accredited by The Market Research Society (Great Britain). Reprinted by permission.

2. Andrea Dunham, "Information Systems Are the Key to Managing Future Business Needs," *Marketing News,* 23 May 1986, p. 11.

TABLE 6.1
Future needs of market research in the European Community

FORECAST DIRECTION OF MARKET RESEARCH SPEND BY TYPE OVER NEXT 5 YEARS

	Top 6 Spend Currently	*More* Will Be Spent	*Less* Will Be Spent	Difference (More-Less)
Total number interviewed	184	184	184	
Percentage of users saying:	100	100	100	100
Usership & Attitude	59	37	2	35
Product Testing	56	34	6	28
Advertising Evaluation	49	28	6	22
Retail Audits	48	20	11	9
Consumer/Customer Panels	45	15	13	2
Corporate Image	41	21	8	13
Advertising Development	39	20	5	15
Campaign Tracking	38	21	5	16
Customer Satisfaction	38	21	3	18
Concept Evaluation	37	24	3	21
Distribution/Price Checks	14	9	1	8
Media (readership/viewing)	13	4	3	1
Post Launch Studies	13	8	1	7
Opinion/Social/Employee	13	8	3	5
Total Mix Testing	9	6	–	6
Sales Prediction (final mix)	9	6	2	4
Pack Testing	9	4	1	3
Price Testing/Modelling	5	2	2	–
Market Modelling	5	4	1	3
Sales Prediction (unfinished mix)	5	4	1	3
'Other Research'	9	5	1	4

SOURCE: "ESOMAR Annual Market Study," European Society for Opinion and Marketing Research, July 1989.

cessing information involves classifying it and developing categories for meaningful storage and retrieval. Marketing decision-makers then determine which information—the output—is useful for making decisions. Finally, feedback enables those who are responsible for gathering internal and external data to adjust the information inputs systematically.

Regular reports of sales by product or market categories, data on inventory levels, and records of salespersons' activities are all examples of information that is useful in making decisions. In the MIS, the means of gathering data receive less attention than do the procedures for expediting the flow of information. The main focus of the marketing information system is on data storage and retrieval, as well as on computer capabilities and management's information requirements. RJR Nabisco, for example, handles hundreds of thousands of consumer contacts each year, usually

TABLE 6.2 *The world's and Europe's major market research organisations*

WORLD TOP 10 MARKET RESEARCH COMPANIES, 1988

Research Company	Research Revenues ECU (m) (excluding associates)	US$ (m) (excluding associates)	Countries With Office	Head Office	Ownership
1. A.C. Nielsen	748	880	28	USA	Dun & Bradstreet, USA
2. IMS International	306	360	42	UK	Dun & Bradstreet, USA
3. Arbitron/SAMI/Burke	272	320	2	USA	Control Data Corp, USA
4. Pergamon AGB	173	203	21	UK	Maxwell Foundation°, UK
5. IRI	110	129	4	USA	Public Company, USA
6. GfK	98	115	15	D	Public Association, D
7. Research International	88	103	20	UK	WPP Group[†], UK
8. Video Research	68	80	1	J	Public Company, J
9. MRB Group	64	75	7	USA	WPP Group, UK
10. Infratest Burke Group	61	72	7	D	Private Company, D

TOP 10 MARKET RESEARCH ORGANISATIONS IN EC RECENT CHANGES OF OWNERSHIP/MERGERS

Rank Order	Research Company	EC Market Research Turnover (est. million ECU, 1988)	Acquired by/ Merged with		Year
1. A.C. Nielsen		240	Dun & Bradstreet	USA	1984
2. IMS International		127	Dun & Bradstreet	USA	1988
3. Pergamon AGB		100	Maxwell Foundation (acquired AGB Research)	UK	1988
4. GfK Group		88	No change (Public Association)	Germany	–
5. Research International		60	The Ogilvy Group	USA	1987
			WPP Group (acquired TOG)	UK	1989
6. Infratest/Burke		56	Infratest acquired Burke in Europe (Infratest is Private Corporation)	Germany	1980
			Proposed merger with Inter/View (NL) abandoned		1988
7. CECODIS		42	No change—closely held corporation	France	–
8. MRB Group		25	WPP Group (as part of JWT— previously US owned— acquisition)	UK	1987
9. Taylor Nelson/MaS Group		25	Addison Consultancy	UK	1986
10. NOP Group		20	MAI	UK	1989

° registered in Liechtenstein
[†] acquired The Ogilvy Group, the previous owners, mid-1989

SOURCE: "ESOMAR Annual Market Study", European Society for Opinion and Marketing Research, July 1989.

FIGURE 6.1

An organisation's marketing information system

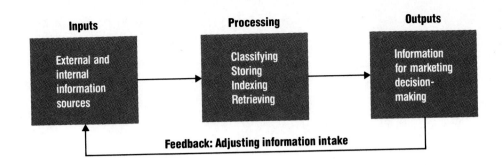

Figure 6.1 An organisation's marketing information system

Inputs	Processing	Outputs
External and internal information sources	Classifying Storing Indexing Retrieving	Information for marketing decision-making

Feedback: Adjusting information intake

enquiries about product usage, nutrition, and ingredients. This consumer feedback is computerised and made available on demand throughout the company's operating divisions. Marketing Update 6.1 describes how more and more companies are using Freephone 0800 telephone services to gather important data for their marketing information systems and marketing research.

The main difference between marketing research and marketing information systems is that marketing research is an information-gathering process for specific situations, whereas an MIS provides continuous data input for an organisation. Non-recurring decisions that deal with the dynamics of the marketing environment often call for a data search structured according to the problem and decision. Marketing research is usually characterised by in-depth analyses of major problems or issues. Often the information needed is available only from sources outside an organisation's formal channels of information. For instance, an organisation may want to know something about its competitors or to gain an unbiased understanding of its own customers. Such information needs may require an independent investigation by a marketing research firm.

Data brought into the organisation through marketing research become part of its **marketing databank**, a file of data collected through both the MIS and marketing research projects. The marketing databank allows researchers to retrieve information that is useful for addressing problems quite different from those that prompted the original data collection. Often a research study developed for one purpose proves valuable for developing a research method or indicating problems in researching a particular topic. For instance, data obtained from a study by Ford Motors on the buying behaviour of purchasers of its models may be used in planning future models. Consequently, marketers should classify and store in the databank all data from marketing research and the MIS to facilitate use of the information in future marketing decisions.

Databanks vary widely from one organisation to another. In a small organisation, the databank may simply be a large notebook, but many organisations employ a computer storage and retrieval system to handle the large volume of data. Figure 6.2 illustrates how marketing decision-makers combine research findings with data from an MIS to develop a databank. Although many organisations do not use the term *databank,* they still have some system for storing information. Smaller organisations may not use the terms *MIS* and *marketing research,* but they normally do perform these marketing activities.

After a marketing information system—of whatever size and complexity—has been established, information should be related to marketing planning. The following section discusses how marketers use marketing information, intuition, and judgement in making decisions.

FREEPHONE 0800 NUMBERS: NOT JUST FOR COMPLAINTS ANYMORE

Many companies have made Freephone 0800 numbers an integral part of their ongoing customer service programmes. Originally, these numbers were used as a way to satisfy consumer complaints. Persistent complaints often provide an early glimpse at changing consumer tastes, allowing a company to alter its marketing strategy accordingly. However, though hearing consumer complaints remains the top priority of 0800 phone lines, other uses for the service are on the rise.

Companies today are increasingly using 0800 numbers to solicit consumer opinions on a variety of matters, such as package colours, product taste, and advertising. Freephone numbers also help in spotting new fads and fashions, test-marketing new products, and finding and solving consumer problems before they get out of hand. In many cases, callers are asked to take part in focus groups or to test a new product. Information obtained in this manner can be added to a firm's marketing information system for later use.

Consumer attitudes towards 0800 numbers are also changing. When the numbers were first introduced, consumers saw them as a privilege given to them by business. Today consumers are starting to regard 0800 numbers as a right, and they react negatively to companies that do not provide Freephone numbers. As a result, the use of Freephone numbers by consumers is rising. In America, AT&T reported that the total number of calls on its Freephone lines in 1989 was roughly seven billion, up from about two billion in 1984. By 1992, the Freephone market is expected to grow to $6.8 billion, and consumer use of 0800 lines is expected to keep increasing well into the next century.

Although 0800 numbers provide many benefits to both consumers and companies, they are not cheap. It is estimated that starting an 0800 programme in a medium-sized firm would cost at least $250,000. Yearly staffing and maintenance costs raise this figure substantially. General Electric's GE Answer Center, considered the largest and the best of all 0800 programmes, costs the company about $10 million per year. Still, companies that provide 0800 numbers find them to be well worth the investment.

SOURCES: Brent Bowers, "Companies Draw More on 800 Lines," *Wall Street Journal,* 6 Nov. 1989, pp. B1, B8; Daniel Briere, "Toll-Free Services Market Set for Explosive Growth," *Network World,* 3 July 1989, pp. 1, 20–37; Carol Dixon, "Eight Tips for 800 Success," *Marketing Communications,* March 1989, pp. 50–51; "How to Use 800 Numbers Effectively," *Agency Sales Magazine,* May 1988, pp. 12–14; Ruth Podems, "What's in Store for the 1990's?" *Target Marketing,* Oct. 1988, pp. 22–23; Bristol Voss, "Telemarketing: A 10-Letter Word for 800 Numbers?" *Sales & Marketing Management,* Sept. 1988, pp. 97–98.

FIGURE 6.2

Combining marketing research and the marketing information system

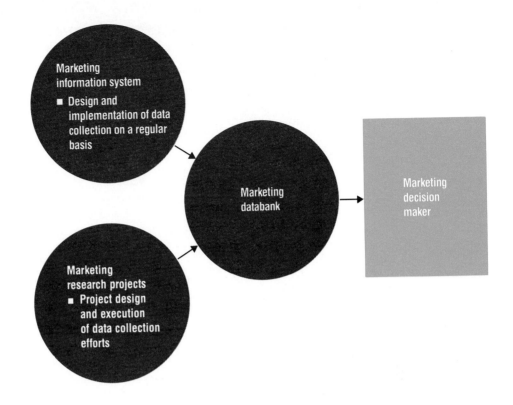

INFORMATION NEEDS AND DECISION-MAKING

The real value of marketing research and marketing information systems is measured by improvements in a marketer's ability to make decisions. Marketers should treat information in the same manner as other resources utilised by the firm, and they must weigh the costs of obtaining information against the benefits derived. Information is worthwhile if it results in marketing mixes that better satisfy the needs of the firm's target markets, leads to increased sales and profits, or helps the firm achieve some other goal.

Marketing research and marketing information systems provide the organisation with customer feedback, without which a marketer cannot understand the dynamics of the market-place. As managers recognise its benefits, they assign marketing research a much larger role in decision-making. For example, Japanese managers, who put much more faith in information they get directly from wholesalers and retailers, are beginning to grasp the importance of consumer surveys and scientific methods of marketing research as they seek ways to diversify their companies.[3]

The increase in marketing research activities represents a transition from intuitive to scientific problem-solving. In relying on *intuition*, marketing managers base decisions on personal knowledge and past experience. However, in *scientific decision-making*, managers take an orderly and logical approach to gathering information. They seek facts on a systematic basis, and they apply methods other than trial and error or generalisation from experience.

3. Johny K. Johansson and Ikujiro Nonaha, "Market Research the Japanese Way," *Harvard Business Review*, May-June 1987, pp. 16–22.

	RESEARCH	INTUITION
NATURE	Formal planning, predicting based on scientific approach	Preference based on personal feelings
METHODS	Logic, systematic methods, statistical inference	Experience and demonstration
CONTRIBUTIONS	General hypotheses for making predictions, classifying relevant variables, carrying out systematic description and classification	Minor problems solved quickly through consideration of experience, practical consequences

Despite the obvious value of formal research, marketing decisions are often made without it. Certainly, minor problems that must be dealt with at once can and should be handled on the basis of personal judgement and common sense. If good decisions can be made with the help of currently available information, then costly formal research may be superfluous. However, as the financial, social, or ethical risks increase or the possible courses of action multiply, full-scale research as a prerequisite for marketing decision-making becomes both desirable and rewarding.

We are not suggesting here that intuition has no value in marketing decision-making. Successful decisions blend both research and intuition. Statistics, mathematics, and logic are powerful tools in problem-solving, and the information they provide can reduce the uncertainty of predictions based on limited experience. But these tools do not necessarily bring out the right answers. Consider an extreme example. A marketing research study conducted for Xerox Corporation in the late 1950s indicated a very limited market for an automatic photocopier. Xerox management judged that the researchers had drawn the wrong conclusions from the study and decided to launch the product anyway. That product, the Xerox 914 copier, was an instant success. An immediate backlog of orders developed, and the rest is history. Though the Xerox example is an extreme one, by and large a proper blend of research and intuition offers the best formula for a correct decision. Table 6.3 distinguishes between the roles of research and intuition in decision-making.

THE MARKETING RESEARCH PROCESS

To maintain the control needed for obtaining accurate information, marketers approach marketing research in logical steps. The difference between good and bad research depends on the quality of the input, which includes effective control over the entire marketing research process. Figure 6.3 illustrates the five steps of the marketing research process: (1) defining and locating problems, (2) developing

FIGURE 6.3 *The five steps of the marketing research process*

hypotheses, (3) collecting data, (4) interpreting research findings, and (5) reporting research findings. These five steps should be viewed as an overall approach to conducting research rather than as a rigid set of rules to be followed in each project. In planning research projects, marketers must think about each of the steps and how they can best be adjusted for each particular problem.

Defining and Locating Problems

Problem definition, the first step towards finding a solution or launching a research study, focuses on uncovering the nature and boundaries of a negative, or positive, situation or question. The first sign of a problem is usually a departure from some normal function, such as conflicts between or failures in attaining objectives. If a corporation's objective is a 12 percent return on investment and the current return is 6 percent, this discrepancy should be a warning flag. It is a symptom that something inside or outside the organisation has blocked the attainment of the desired goal or that the goal is unrealistic. Decreasing sales, increasing expenses, or decreasing profits also signal problems. Conversely, when an organisation experiences a dramatic rise in sales, or some other positive event, it may conduct marketing research to discover the reasons and maximise the opportunities stemming from them. In Figure 6.4, Nielsen promotes its ability to identify and solve problems through sales analysis.

To pin down the specific causes of the problem through research, marketers must define the problem and its scope in a way that requires probing beneath the superficial symptoms. The interaction between the marketing manager and the marketing researcher should yield a clear definition of the problem. Depending on their abilities, the manager and the researcher can apply various methods to shape this definition. Traditionally, problem formulation has been viewed as a subjective, creative process. Today, however, more objective and systematic approaches are utilised. For example, the Delphi method for problem definition consists of a series of interviews with a panel of experts. With repeated interviews, the range of responses converges towards a "correct" definition of the problem.[4] This method introduces structure as well as objectivity into the process of problem definition. Researchers and decision-makers should remain in the problem definition stage until they have determined precisely what they want from the research and how they will use it.

The research objective specifies what information is needed to solve the problem. Deciding how to refine a broad, indefinite problem into a clearly defined and researchable statement is a prerequisite for the next step in planning the research: developing the type of hypothesis that best fits the problem.

4. Raymond E. Taylor, "Using the Delphi Method to Define Marketing Problems," *Business,* October–December 1984, p. 17.

FIGURE 6.4
Defining and locating problems.
Nielsen's marketing research division promotes its ability to isolate and identify problems.

When the numbers are down, you've got problems to solve.

A quick look at your sales figures can tell you when things aren't going according to the formula.
But it's not enough to know that the numbers are falling. You need to know why.
That's where Nielsen fits into the equation. We can analyze your scanning and causal data, transforming piles of facts into the power of information.
So you can quickly identify what your problems are and what you can do to solve them. Before the competition becomes a factor.
For more information, write to the information people at Nielsen Marketing Research, Nielsen Plaza, Northbrook, IL 60062, or call 312/498-7611.
We won't just give you the numbers. We'll show you how to make them add up.

Nielsen Marketing Research

Nielsen

SOURCE: Courtesy Nielsen Marketing Research

DEVELOPING HYPOTHESES

The objective statement of a marketing research project should include hypotheses drawn from both previous research and expected research findings. A **hypothesis** is an informed guess or assumption about a certain problem or set of circumstances. It is based on all the insight and knowledge available about the problem from previous research studies and other sources. As information is gathered, a researcher can test the hypothesis. For example, a food manufacturer such as H. J. Heinz might propose the hypothesis that children today have more influence on their families' buying decisions for ketchup and other grocery products. A marketing researcher would then gather data, perhaps through surveys of children and their parents, and draw conclusions as to whether the hypothesis was correct. Sometimes several hypotheses are developed during the actual study; the hypotheses that are accepted or rejected become the study's chief conclusions.

TABLE 6.4
Comparison of data-gathering approaches

PROJECT COMPONENT	EXPLORATORY STUDIES	DESCRIPTIVE OR CAUSAL STUDIES
PURPOSE	Provide general insights	Confirm insights / Verify hypotheses
DATA SOURCES	Ill defined	Well defined
COLLECTION FORM	Open-end	Structured
SAMPLE	Small	Large
COLLECTION PROCEDURE	Flexible	Rigid
DATA ANALYSIS	Informal	Formal
RECOMMENDATIONS	Tentative	Conclusive

SOURCE: Adapted from A. Parasuraman, *Marketing Research*, 1st ed., © 1986 by Addison-Wesley Publishing Co., Inc., Reading, Massachusetts, p. 122. Reprinted by permission of the publisher.

COLLECTING DATA

The kind of hypothesis being tested determines which approach will be used for gathering general data: exploratory, descriptive, or causal. When marketers need more information about a problem or want to make a tentative hypothesis more specific, they may conduct **exploratory studies**. For instance, they may review the information in the firm's databank or examine publicly available data. Questioning knowledgeable people inside and outside the organisation may also yield new insights into the problem. An advantage of the exploratory approach is that it permits marketers to conduct mini-studies with a very restricted database.

If marketers need to understand the characteristics of certain phenomena to solve a particular problem, **descriptive studies** can aid them. Such studies may range from general surveys of consumers' education, occupation, or age to specifics on how many consumers purchased Ice Cream Mars last month or how many adults between the ages of 18 and 30 eat some form of high-fibre cereal at least three times a week. Some descriptive studies require statistical analysis and predictive tools. For example, a researcher trying to find out how many people will vote for a certain political candidate may have to survey registered voters to predict the results. Descriptive studies generally demand much prior knowledge and assume that the problem is clearly defined. The marketers' major task is to choose adequate methods of collecting and measuring data.

Hypotheses about causal relationships call for a more complex approach than a descriptive study. In **causal studies**, it is assumed that a particular variable X causes a variable Y. Marketers must plan the research so that the data collected prove or disprove that X causes Y. To do so, marketers must try to hold constant all variables except X and Y. For example, to find out whether new carpeting, curtains, and ceiling fans increase the number of rentals in an apartment complex, marketers need to keep all variables constant except the new furnishings and the rental rate. Table 6.4 compares the features of these types of research studies.

Marketing researchers have two types of data at their disposal. **Primary data** are observed and recorded or collected directly from respondents. This type of data

FIGURE 6.5
Approaches to collecting data

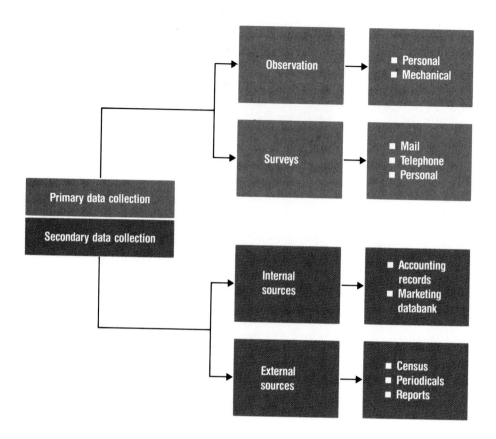

must be gathered by observing phenomena or surveying respondents. **Secondary data** are compiled inside or outside the organisation for some purpose other than the current investigation. Secondary data include general reports supplied to an enterprise by various data services. Such reports might concern market share, retail inventory levels, and consumers' buying behaviour. Figure 6.5 illustrates how primary and secondary sources differ. Commonly, secondary data are already available in private or public reports or have been collected and stored by the organisation itself. In Figure 6.6, AT&T focuses on the use of its database management services to improve companies' direct marketing programmes. In the next section, we discuss the methods of gathering both secondary and primary data.

■ **Secondary Data Collection**

Marketers often begin the marketing research process by gathering secondary data. They may use available reports and other information from both internal and external sources to study a marketing problem.

Internal sources of secondary data can contribute tremendously to research. An organisation's marketing databank may contain information about past marketing activities, such as sales records and research reports, which can be used to test hypotheses and pinpoint problems. An organisation's accounting records are also an excellent source of data but, strangely enough, are often overlooked. The large volume of data that an accounting department collects does not automatically flow to the marketing area. As a result, detailed information about costs, sales, customer

FIGURE 6.6
Collecting data.
AT&T promotes its database management services that use secondary and primary data sources to successfully identify and reach customers.

SOURCE: AT&T American Transtech

accounts, or profits by product category may not be part of the MIS. This situation occurs particularly in organisations that do not store marketing information on a systematic basis.

Secondary data can also be gleaned from periodicals, government publications, and unpublished sources. Periodicals such as *Investors' Chronicle, Business, Marketing, Campaign, Marketing Week, Euromonitor, Business Monitor, The Wall Street Journal,* and *Fortune* print general information that is helpful for defining problems and developing hypotheses. *Business Monitor* contains sales data for major industries. Table 6.5 summarises the major external sources of secondary data, excluding syndicated services.

Syndicated data services periodically collect general information, which they sell to clients. BARB, for example, supplies television stations and media buyers with estimates of the number of viewers at specific times. SAMI furnishes monthly information that describes market shares for specific types of manufacturers. Nielsen and AGB provide data about products primarily sold through retailers. This information includes total sales in a product category, sales of clients' own brands, and sales of important competing brands. In the U.S.A. the Market Research Corporation of America (MRCA) collects data through a national panel of consumers to

TABLE 6.5
*Guide to external sources
of secondary data*

TRADE JOURNALS	Virtually every industry or type of business has a trade journal. These journals give a feel for the industry—its size, degree of competition, range of companies involved, and problems. To find trade journals in the field of interest, check *The Source Book*, a reference book that lists periodicals by subject.
TRADE ASSOCIATIONS	Almost every industry, product category, and profession has its own association. Depending on the strength of each group, they often conduct research, publish journals, conduct training sessions, and hold conferences. A telephone call or a letter to the association may yield information not available in published sources.
INTERNATIONAL SOURCES	Periodical indexes, such as *Anbar*, are particularly useful for overseas product or company information. More general sources include the *United Nations Statistical Yearbook* and the *International Labour Organization's Yearbook of Labour Statistics*.
GOVERNMENT	The government, through its various departments and agencies, collects, analyses, and publishes statistics on practically everything. Government documents also have their own set of indexes. A useful index for government-generated information is the government's weekly *British Business*.
BOOKS IN PRINT (BIP)	BIP is a two-volume reference book found in most libraries. All books issued by publishers and currently in print are listed by subject, title, and author.
PERIODICAL INDEXES	Library reference sections contain indexes on virtually every discipline. The *ABI Inform*, for example, indexes each article in all major periodicals.
COMPUTERIZED LITERATURE-RETRIEVAL DATABASES	Literature-retrieval databases are periodical indexes stored in a computer. Books and dissertations are also included. Key words (such as the name of a subject) are used to search a database and generate references. Examples include Textline and Harvest.

provide information about purchases. MRCA maintains data on brands classified by age, race, sex, education, occupation, and family size.

Another type of secondary data, which is available for a fee, is demographic analysis. Companies, such as CACI or CNN, that specialise in demographic databanks have special knowledge and sophisticated computer systems to work with the very complex census databanks. As a result, they are able to respond to specialised

FIGURE 6.7
Relationship between independent and dependent variables

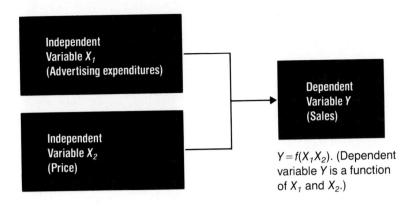

$Y = f(X_1, X_2)$. (Dependent variable Y is a function of X_1 and X_2.)

requests. Such information may be valuable in tracking demographic changes that have implications for consumer behaviour and the targeting of products.[5]

■ **Primary Data Collection**

The collection of primary data is a more lengthy and complex process than the collection of secondary data. The acquisition of primary data often requires an experimental approach to determine which variable or variables caused an event to occur.

Experimentation. **Experimentation** involves maintaining certain variables constant so that the effects of the experimental variables can be measured. For instance, when the WordPerfect Corp. tests a change in its WordPerfect word processing computer program, all variables should be held constant except the change in the program. **Marketing experimentation** is a set of rules and procedures by which data-gathering is organised to expedite analysis and interpretation.

In experimentation, an **independent variable** (a variable not influenced by or dependent on other variables) is manipulated and the resulting changes are measured in a **dependent variable** (a variable contingent on, or restricted to, one value or a set of values assumed by the independent variable). Figure 6.7 illustrates the relationship between these variables. For example, when Houghton Mifflin Company introduces a new edition of its *American Heritage Dictionary*, it may want to estimate the number of dictionaries that could be sold at various levels of advertising expenditure and prices. The dependent variable would be sales, and the independent variables would be advertising expenditures and price. Researchers would design the experiment so that other independent variables that might influence sales—such as distribution and variations of the product—would be controlled.

In designing experiments, marketing researchers must ensure that their research techniques are both reliable and valid. A research technique has **reliability** if it produces almost identical results in successive repeated trials. But a reliable technique is not necessarily valid. To have **validity**, the method must measure what it is supposed to measure, not something else. A valid research method provides data that can be used to test the hypothesis being investigated. For example, recent experiments on cold fusion by scientists at the University of Utah, Texas A & M University, and other institutions lack both reliability and validity because the re-

5. Ronald L. Vaughn, "Demographic Data Banks: A New Management Resource," *Business Horizons*, November-December 1984, pp. 38–42.

sults of the experiments have not been repeated in successive trials and the scientists are not sure whether their experiments are measuring energy produced as a result of fusion or some other process.

In America, one marketing research company, Information Resources, Inc., has brought a new dimension to experimental research by combining cable television, supermarket scanners, and computers. The company has placed its BehaviorScan microcomputers on televisions in thousands of households in major cities. The company can then track every commercial its panelists watch and every purchase they make in a supermarket or chemist's. The information provided by Information Resources helps marketers assess the effectiveness of their advertising by determining whether a viewer saw a particular advertisement and whether the advertisement led the viewer to buy the product.[6] (See Case 6.1, AGB's Superpanel, on the application of scanning and consumer panels in Europe.)

Experiments may be conducted in the laboratory or in the field; each research setting has advantages and disadvantages. In *laboratory settings,* participants or respondents are invited to a central location to react or respond to experimental stimuli. In such an isolated setting it is possible to control independent variables that might influence the outcome of an experiment. The features of laboratory settings might include a taste kitchen, video equipment, slide projectors, tape recorders, one-way mirrors, central telephone banks, and interview rooms. In an experiment to determine the influence of price (independent variable) on sales of a new canned soup (dependent variable), respondents would be invited to a laboratory—a room with table, chairs, and sample soups—before the soup was available in stores. The soup would be placed on a table with competitors' soups. Analysts would then question respondents about their reactions to the soup at various prices.

One problem with a laboratory setting is its isolation from the real world. It is simply not possible to duplicate all the conditions that affect choices in the marketplace. On the other hand, by controlling variables that cannot be controlled in the real world, laboratory experiments can focus on variables that marketers think may be significant for the success of a marketing strategy. Test market laboratories are being used more frequently today.[7]

The experimental approach can also be used in *field settings.* A taste test of Stork SB margarine conducted in a supermarket is one example of an experiment in a field setting. Field settings give the marketer an opportunity to obtain a more direct test of marketing decisions than laboratory settings do.

There are, however, several limitations to field experiments. Field experiments can be influenced or biased by unexpected events, such as the weather or major economic news. Carry-over effects of field experiments are impossible to avoid. What respondents have been asked to do in one time period will influence what they do in the next. For example, evaluations of competing advertisements may influence attempts to obtain objective evaluations of a firm's proposed advertising. The fact that previous advertising has been viewed influences respondents' evaluation of future advertising. Respondent co-operation may be difficult because respondents do not understand their role in the experiment. Finally, only a small number of variables can be controlled in field experiments. It is impossible, for example, to control competitors' advertising or their attempts to influence the

6. Gary Levin, "IRI Says Data Can Now Link Ads to Sales," *Advertising Age,* Jan. 26, 1987, pp. 3, 74.

7. Based on a survey conducted by Market Facts, Inc., Apr. 28, 1983.

outcome of the experiment. Tactics that competitors can use to thwart field efforts include couponing, reducing prices temporarily, and increasing advertising frequency.

Experimentation is used in marketing research to improve hypothesis testing. However, whether experiments are conducted in the laboratory or in the field, many assumptions must be made to limit the number of factors and isolate causes. Marketing decision-makers must recognise that assumptions may diminish the reliability of the research findings. For example, viewing proposed advertisements on a video-cassette recorder in a laboratory is different from watching the advertisements on television at home.

The gathering of primary data through experimentation may involve the use of sampling, survey methods, observation, or some combination of these techniques.

Sampling.   By systematically choosing a limited number of units, or a **sample**, to represent the characteristics of a total population, marketers can project the reactions of a total market or market segment. The objective of **sampling** in marketing research, therefore, is to select representative units from a total population. Sampling procedures are used in studying the likelihood of events based on assumptions about the future.

Since the time and the resources available for research are limited, it would be almost impossible to investigate all the members of a population. A **population**, or "universe", comprises all elements, units, or individuals that are of interest to researchers for a specific study. For example, if a Gallup poll is designed to predict the results of an election, all the registered voters in the country would constitute the population. A representative national sample of several thousand registered voters would be selected in the Gallup poll to project the probable voting outcome. The projection would be based on the assumption that no major political events would occur before the election.

Sampling techniques allow marketers to predict buying behaviour fairly accurately on the basis of the responses from a representative portion of the population of interest. Figure 6.8 illustrates how one company provides sampling facilities in many metropolitan markets in the United States. Sampling methods include random sampling, stratified sampling, area sampling, and quota sampling.

When marketers employ **random sampling**, all the units in a population have an equal chance of appearing in the sample. Random sampling is basic probability sampling. The various events that can occur have an equal or known chance of taking place. For example, a specific card in a pack should have a 1/52 probability of being drawn at any one time. Similarly, if every student at a university or college has a unique identification number and these numbers are mixed up in a large basket, each student's number would have a known probability of being selected. Sample units are ordinarily chosen by selecting from a table of random numbers statistically generated so that each digit, zero through nine, will have an equal probability of occurring in each position in the sequence. The sequentially numbered elements of a population are sampled randomly by selecting the units whose numbers appear in the table of random numbers.

In **stratified sampling**, the population of interest is divided into groups according to a common characteristic or attribute, and then a probability sample is conducted within each group. The stratified sample may reduce some of the error that could occur in a simple random sample. By ensuring that each major group or segment of the population receives its proportionate share of sample units, investi-

FIGURE 6.8

Sampling U.S. metropolitan markets. Quality Controlled Services provides marketing research services in 21 metropolitan locations.

SOURCE: Quality Controlled Services (U.S.A.)

gators avoid including too many or too few sample units from each stratum. Usually, samples are stratified when researchers believe that there may be variations among different types of respondents. For example, many political opinion surveys are stratified by sex, race, and age.

Area sampling involves two stages: (1) selecting a probability sample of geographic areas, such as blocks, census tracts, or census enumeration districts, and (2) selecting units or individuals within the selected geographic areas for the sample. This approach is a variation of stratified sampling, with the geographic areas serving as the segments, or primary units, used in sampling. To select the units or individuals within the geographic areas, researchers may choose every *n*th house or unit, or random selection procedures may be used to pick out a given number of units or individuals from a total listing within the selected geographic areas. Area sampling may be used when a complete list of the population is not available.

Quota sampling differs from other forms of sampling in that it is judgemental; that is, the final choice of respondents is left to the interviewers. A study of consumers who wear glasses, for example, may be conducted by interviewing any person who wears glasses. In quota sampling, there are some controls—usually limited to two or three variables such as age, sex, and education—over the selection of respondents. The controls attempt to ensure that representative categories of respondents are interviewed.

Quota samples are unique because they are not probability samples; not everyone has an equal chance of being selected. Therefore, sampling error cannot be measured statistically. Quota samples are used most often in exploratory studies, when hypotheses are being developed. Often a small quota sample will not be projected to the total population, although the findings may provide valuable insights into a problem. Quota samples are useful when people with some unusual characteristic are found and questioned about the topic of interest. A probability sample used to study people allergic to cats would be highly inefficient.

Survey Methods.   **Survey methods** include interviews by mail or telephone and personal interviews. Selection of a survey method depends on the nature of the problem, the data needed to test the hypothesis, and the resources, such as funding and personnel, that are available to the researcher. Table 6.6 summarises and compares the advantages of the various methods. Researchers must know exactly what type of information is needed to test the hypothesis and what type of information can be obtained through interviewing. Table 6.7 lists the most frequently used consumer survey techniques. The data are based on a survey of large American consumer goods and services companies. Table 6.8 summarises market research issues and techniques in the U.K.

Gathering information through surveys is becoming more difficult because respondent rates are declining. There is also an indication that people with higher incomes and education are most likely to respond. Problems include difficulty in hiring qualified interviewers and respondents' reluctance to take part in surveys because of over-long questionnaires, dull topics, and time pressures.[8] Moreover, fear of crime makes respondents unwilling to trust interviewers. The use of "sugging"—sales techniques disguised as market surveys—has also contributed to decreased respondent co-operation.

In *mail surveys*, questionnaires are sent to respondents, who are encouraged to complete and return them. Mail surveys are used most often when the individuals chosen for questioning are spread over a wide area and funds for the survey are limited. A mail survey is the least expensive survey method as long as the response rate is high enough to produce reliable results. The main disadvantages of this method are the possibility of a low response rate or of misleading results, if respondents are significantly different from the population being sampled.

Researchers can boost mail survey response rates by offering respondents some incentive to return the questionnaire. When using mail survey techniques, incentives and follow-ups have been found to consistently increase response rates. But promises of anonymity, special appeals for co-operation, and questionnaire length have no apparent impact on the response rate. Other techniques for increasing the response rate, such as advance notification, personalisation of survey materials, type of postage, corporate or university sponsorship, or foot-in-the-door techniques have had mixed results, varying according to the population surveyed.[9] Although such techniques may help increase the response rates, they can introduce sample-composition bias, or non-response bias, which results when those responding to a survey differ in some important respect from those not responding to the survey. In other words,

8. Martha Farnsworth Riche, "Who Says Yes?" *American Demographics,* February 1987, p. 8; George Gallup, Jr., "Survey Research: Current Problems and Future Opportunities," *Journal of Consumer Marketing,* Winter 1988, pp. 27–29.

9. Jeffrey S. Conant, Denise T. Smart, and Bruce J. Walker, "Mail-Survey Facilitation Techniques: An Assessment and Proposal Regarding Reporting Practices" (working paper, Texas A&M University, 1990).

TABLE 6.6 *Comparison of the three basic survey methods*

	MAIL SURVEYS	TELEPHONE SURVEYS	PERSONAL INTERVIEW SURVEYS
ECONOMY	Potentially the lowest cost per interview if there is an adequate return rate; increased postage rates are raising costs	Avoids interviewers' travel expenses; less expensive than in-home interviews; most common survey method	In-home interviewing is the most expensive interviewing method; shopping mall, focus-group interviewing may lower costs
FLEXIBILITY	Inflexible; questionnaire must be short, easy for respondents to complete; no probing questions; may take more time to implement than other survey methods	Flexible because interviewers can ask probing questions, encourage respondents to answer questions; rapport may be gained, but observations are impossible	Most flexible method; respondents can react to visual materials, help fill out questionnaire; because observation is possible, demographic data are more accurate; in-depth probes are possible
INTERVIEWER BIAS	Interviewer bias eliminated; questionnaires can be returned anonymously	Some anonymity; may be hard to develop trust among respondents	Refusals may be decreased by interviewers' rapport-building efforts; interviewers' personal attributes may bias respondents
SAMPLING AND RESPONDENTS' CO-OPERATION	Obtaining a complete mailing list is difficult; non-response is a major disadvantage	Sample must be limited to respondents with telephones and listed numbers; engaged signals, no answers, and non-response—including refusals—are problems	Not-at-homes are more difficult to deal with; focus-groups, shopping mall interviewing may overcome these problems

SOURCE: Miton M. Pressley, "Try These Tips to Get 50% to 70% Response Rate from Mail Surveys of Commercial Populations," *Marketing News,* Jan. 21, 1983, p. 16. Reprinted by permission of American Marketing Association.

response-enhancing techniques may alienate some people in the sample and appeal to others, making the results non-representative of the population of interest. Perhaps because of these problems and the others discussed earlier, the firms surveyed in Table 6.7 spent less than 5 percent of their research funds for direct mail surveys.[10]

Premiums or incentives encouraging respondents to return questionnaires have been effective in developing panels of respondents who are regularly interviewed by mail. Mail panels, which are selected to represent a market or market segment, are especially useful for evaluating new products, providing general information about

10. *Practices, Trends and Expectations for the Market Research Industry 1987,* Market Facts, Inc., 29 April 1987.

TABLE 6.7

Changes in the frequency of use of survey research techniques

	1978	1983	1987	1987 vs. 1983
Long-distance telephone	90%	91%	98%	+7
Shopping mall intercepts	89%	90%	86%	−4
Focus groups	87%	90%	98%	+8
Mail panel	53%	57%	67%	10
Custom mail	46%	33%	43%	+10
Purchase diary	46%	48%	37%	−11
Door-to-door	61%	47%	39%	−8
Trade surveys	33%	39%	40%	+1
Local telephone	67%	61%	°	°
Scanner panel	°	°	39%	°
Average number named	5.7	5.6	5.5	

° Not measured.

SOURCE: *Practices, Trends and Expectations for the Market Research Industry 1987,* Market Facts, Inc., 29 Apr. 1987, p. 23. Reprinted by permission.

consumers, and providing records of consumers' purchases. As Table 6.7 indicates, 67 percent of the companies surveyed used consumer mail panels, but these panels represented a major budget share for less than 15 percent of the companies.[11] It is interesting that 37 percent of the sample used consumer purchase diaries. (These surveys are similar to mail panels, but consumers keep track of purchases only.) Consumer mail panels and consumer purchase diaries are much more widely used than custom mail surveys, but they do have shortcomings. Research indicates that the people who take the time to fill out a consumer diary have a higher income and are more educated than the general population. If researchers include less educated consumers in the panel, they must risk poorer response rates.[12]

In *telephone surveys,* respondents' answers to a questionnaire are recorded by interviewers on the phone. A telephone survey has some advantages over a mail survey. The rate of response is higher because it takes less effort to answer the telephone and talk than to fill out a questionnaire and return it. If there are enough interviewers, telephone surveys can be conducted very quickly. Thus they can be used by political candidates or organisations seeking an immediate reaction to an event. In addition, this survey technique permits interviewers to gain rapport with respondents and ask probing questions. According to a survey by the Council of American Survey Research Organizations (CASRO), telephone interviewing is the preferred survey method in more than 40 percent of the projects conducted by commercial survey research firms.[13] The data in Table 6.7 show that virtually all the surveyed firms used telephone interviewing.

Telephone interviews do have drawbacks. They are limited to oral communication; visual aids or observation cannot be included. Interpreters of results must make adjustments for subjects who are not at home or who do not have telephones.

11. Ibid.

12. Riche, p. 8.

13. Diane K. Bowers, "Telephone Legislation," *Marketing Research,* March 1989, p. 47.

TABLE 6.8
The nature of the U.K. market research industry in 1989

TYPE OF RESEARCH

Consumer research on:	£ millions	%
Market measurement and structure	68	29
Research into products and services	53	22
Advertising and promotion	39	17
Media audience research	16	7
Omnibus surveys	8	3
Social surveys	7	3
Opinion research	3	1
Other consumer research	2	1
Non-consumer research	39	17
Total	235	100

NATURE OF FIELDWORK: PERCENTAGE OF RESEARCH TURNOVER ACCOUNTED FOR BY DIFFERENT INTERVIEW METHODS

	%
Personal interview	54
Telephone interview	15
Hall test	9
Group discussion	11
Self-completion survey	11

SOURCE OF REVENUE

Types of client company:	£ millions	Change %
Food/soft drinks manufacturers	38.0	+17
Media	22.2	+10
Alcoholic drinks	17.2	+32
Public services and utilities	16.5	+30
Health & beauty aids	16.1	+ 9
Business & industrial	14.1	+64
Vehicle manufacturers	13.3	+30
Financial services	13.3	+13
Advertising agencies	13.1	+ 7
Pharmaceutical companies	12.8	+10
Government and public bodies	9.3	+13
Travel/tourism	7.0	+19
Retailers	6.9	− 8
Household durables/hardware	6.3	+ 2
Household products manufacturers	5.3	+13
Tobacco	3.8	0
Oil	3.2	− 3
Other	16.6	+ 3

TABLE 6.8
continued

TURNOVER OF ASSOCIATION OF MARKET SURVEY ORGANISATIONS MEMBER COMPANIES 1989

Rank order by turnover (UK only)	1989 turnover £000's	Change in turnover %
1 AGB	44,906	+22.6
2 Nielsen Marketing Research	30,580	+16.8
3 Taylor Nelson/MāS Group	17,031	+ 3.6
4 Millward Brown	16,728	+25.6
5 Research International UK	16,156	− 5.1
6 MRB Group	15,676	+33.0
7 MIL Research Group	15,200	+21.6
8 NOP Group	14,809	+10.2
9 MORI	8,523	+58.4
10 The Research Business Group	8,452	+20.4
11 Research Services	7,619	+ 2.3
12 The Harris Research Centre	5,740	+20.7
13 The MBL Group	5,301	+11.9
14 Social Surveys (Gallup Poll)	4,251	+26.5
15 Gordon Simmons Research Group	4,111	+ 1.2
16 Burke Marketing	3,649	+16.2
17 Martin Hamblin Research	3,549	+21.3
18 FDS Market Research Group	3,475	+45.1
19 Public Attitude Surveys (PAS)	3,228	+ 7.5
20 Research & Auditing Services	3,043	+15.6
21 Communication Research Ltd	1,852	−18.4
22 Independent Research Bureau	1,710	+15.9
23 IFF Research	1,500	− 9.1
24 Cooper Research & Marketing (CRAM)	1,493	− 0.0
Total	238,582	+16.3

SOURCE: Association of Market Survey Organisations, 1989. Reprinted by permission of Millward Brown Market Research Limited, Warwick, England.

Telephone surveys, like mail and personal interview surveys, are sometimes used to develop panels of respondents who can be interviewed repeatedly to measure changes in attitudes or behaviour. Reliance on such panels is increasing.

Computer-assisted telephone interviewing integrates questionnaire, data collection, and tabulations and provides data to aid decision-makers in the shortest time possible. In computer-assisted telephone interviewing, the paper questionnaire is replaced by a computer monitor or video screen. Responses are entered on a terminal keyboard, or the interviewer can use a light pen (a pen-shaped torch) to record a response on a light-sensitive screen. On the most advanced devices, the interviewer merely points to the appropriate response on a touch-sensitive screen with his or her finger. Open-ended responses can be typed on the keyboard or recorded with paper and pencil.

Computer-assisted telephone interviewing saves time and facilitates monitoring the progress of interviews. Entry functions are largely eliminated; the computer determines which question to display on the screen, skipping irrelevant questions. Because data are available as soon as they are entered into the system, cumbersome hand computations are avoided and interim results can be quickly retrieved. With some systems, a microcomputer may be taken to off-site locations for use in data analysis. Some researchers say that computer-assisted telephone interviewing—including hardware, software, and operation costs—is less expensive than conventional paper and pencil methods.[14]

Marketing researchers have traditionally favoured the *personal interview survey,* chiefly because of its flexibility. Various audio-visual aids—pictures, products, diagrams, or pre-recorded advertising copy—can be incorporated into a personal interview. Rapport gained through direct interaction usually permits more in-depth interviewing, including probes, follow-up questions, or psychological tests. In addition, because personal interviews can be longer, they can yield more information. Finally, respondents can be selected more carefully, and reasons for non-response can be explored.

The nature of personal interviews has changed. In the past, most personal interviews, which were based on random sampling or pre-arranged appointments, were conducted in the respondent's home. Today, most personal interviews are conducted in shopping centres or malls. *Shopping mall intercept interviews* involve interviewing a percentage of persons who pass by certain "intercept" points in a centre. Although there are many variations of this technique, Table 6.7 indicates that shopping mall intercept interviewing is the third most popular survey technique, after telephone and focus-group interviewing. By 1987, not only did 86 percent of the major consumer goods and services companies use this technique, but almost half reported that shopping mall intercept interviewing was their major expenditure on survey research.[15]

Like any face-to-face interviewing method, shopping centre intercept interviewing has many advantages. The interviewer is in a position to recognise and react to respondents' non-verbal indications of confusion. Respondents can be shown product prototypes, videotapes of commercials, and the like, and reactions can be sought. The environment lets the researcher deal with complex situations. For example, in taste tests, researchers know that all the respondents are reacting to the same product, which can be prepared and monitored from the mall test kitchen or some other facility. In addition, lower cost, greater control, and the ability to conduct tests requiring bulky equipment make shopping mall intercept interviews popular.

Research indicates that given a comparable sample of respondents, shopping mall intercept interviewing is a suitable substitute for telephone interviewing.[16] In addition, there seem to be no significant differences in the completeness of consumer

14. Stephen M. Billig, "Go Slow, Be Wary When Considering Switch to Computer-Assisted Interviewing System," *Marketing News,* 26 Nov. 1982, sec. 2, p. 2.

15. *Practices, Trends and Expectations for the Market Research Industry 1987,* Market Facts, Inc., 29 April 1987.

16. Alan J. Bush and A. Parasuraman, "Mall Intercept Versus Telephone-Interviewing Environment," *Journal of Advertising Research,* April-May 1985, p. 42.

responses between telephone interviewing and shopping mall intercept interviewing. In fact, for questions dealing with socially desirable behaviour, shopping mall intercept respondents appear to be more honest about their past behaviour.[17]

On-site computer interviewing, a variation of the mall intercept interview, consists of respondents completing a self-administered questionnaire displayed on a computer monitor. In America, MAX (Machine Answered eXamination), a microcomputer-based software package developed by POPULUS Inc., a Greenwich, Connecticut, research firm, conducts such interviews in shopping malls. After a brief lesson on how to operate MAX, respondents can proceed through the survey at their own pace. According to its developers, MAX provides not only faster and more accurate information, but also consistency, for each respondent is asked questions in the same way. MAX is flexible because it can ask different sets of relevant questions depending on the respondent's previous answers. In addition, respondents' answers are entered directly onto a computer disc and can be analysed without someone having to code and key in the responses later, reducing the potential of information being incorrectly encoded. Its developers assert that "MAX is the interviewer we would all like to be. MAX is patient, nonjudgmental, remembering all that he is taught, and he keeps track of every answer."[18]

The object of a *focus-group interview* is to observe group interaction when members are exposed to an idea or concept. Often these interviews are conducted informally, without a structured questionnaire. Consumer attitudes, behaviour, lifestyles, needs, and desires can be explored in a flexible and creative manner through focus-group interviews. Table 6.7 indicates that 98 percent of the firms surveyed used focus-group interviewing in 1987. Questions are open-ended and stimulate consumers to answer in their own words. Researchers can ask probing questions to clarify something they do not fully understand or something unexpected and interesting that may help to explain consumer behaviour. Cadbury used information obtained from focus groups to change its advertising and test product concepts. The new advertisements and product launches pushed up Cadbury sales.[19] Marketing Update 6.2 describes the future of this marketing research technique.

Another research technique is the *in-home (door-to-door) interview.* As Table 6.7 indicates, 39 percent of the largest consumer companies use this technique. Because it may be desirable to eliminate group influence, the in-home interview offers a clear advantage when thoroughness of self-disclosure is important. In an in-depth interview of forty-five to ninety minutes, respondents can be probed to reveal their real motivations, feelings, behaviours, and aspirations. In-depth interviews permit the discovery of emotional "hot buttons" that provide psychological insights.[20]

Questionnaire Construction.   A carefully constructed questionnaire is essential to the success of any survey. Questions must be designed to elicit information that meets the study's data requirements. These questions must be clear, easy to understand, and directed towards a specific objective. Researchers need to define the objective before trying to develop a questionnaire because the objective determines

17. Alan J. Bush and Joseph F. Hair, Jr., "An Assessment of the Mall Intercept as a Data Collecting Method," *Journal of Marketing Research,* May 1985, p. 162.

18. Jeff Wiss, "Meet MAX: Computerized Survey Taker," *Marketing News,* 22 May 1989, p. 16.

19. Yorkshire Television's "The Marketing Mix" Series.

20. Hal Sokolow, "In-Depth Interviews Increasing in Importance," *Marketing News,* 13 Sept. 1985, p. 26.

FOCUS-GROUP INTERVIEWING IN THE 1990s

Focus-group interviews, which are generally informal group discussions about marketing ideas or concepts conducted by a marketer or marketing research firm, are used by most major organisations in developing marketing or business plans. In the 1980s, focus-group interviewing became one of the most widely practised types of marketing research, expanding from the packaged goods industry into financial services, hard goods, and industrial applications.

However, the function of focus-group interviewing is expected to change in the 1990s. Traditionally, companies have relied on focus-group interviews to define the input going into quantitative studies, but the new trend is to conduct focus-group interviews after tabulating research results, to provide insight into why the results were achieved. The trend is also towards higher costs (the average today is £800 to £1,500 for an extended, video-recorded group).

Other changes pertain to moderator guides and their reports. The moderator guides will be expected to involve clients in the development process. Their reports will concentrate on providing conclusions that interpret the findings and on making recommendations for action by the client. The reports will also contain fewer actual quotations from individual focus-group participants. The post–focus-group debriefing techniques are also being altered. The shift is towards disciplined debriefing that asks participants their reactions to the group session. Such debriefing can provide the link between concept development and application and serve as a rough check on validity and reliability.

Another new development in focus-group interviewing is the use of electronics to offer three-way capabilities. Computerised decision-making software can supplement research findings and consolidate opinions from three different audiences. For example, in health care research in a hospital setting, the three audiences would be former patients, physicians, and employees. The advantages of using electronics include easier scheduling of participating groups and more interaction among the three audiences.

SOURCES: Lynne Cunningham, "Electronic Focus Groups Offer 3-Way Capability," *Marketing News,* 8 Jan. 1990, pp. 22, 39; Thomas L. Greenbaum, "Focus Group Spurt Predicted for the '90s," *Marketing News,* 8 Jan. 1990, pp. 21, 22; and Nino DeNicola, "Debriefing Sessions: The Missing Link in Focus Groups," *Marketing News,* 8 Jan. 1990, pp. 20, 22.

the substance of the questions and the amount of detail. A common mistake in constructing questionnaires is to ask questions that interest the researchers but do not yield information useful in deciding whether to accept or reject a hypothesis. Finally, the most important rule in composing questions is to maintain impartiality.

The questions are usually of three kinds: open-ended, dichotomous, and multiple choice.

OPEN-ENDED QUESTION
What is your general opinion of the American Express Optima Card?

_____

_____

_____

DICHOTOMOUS QUESTION
Do you presently have an American Express Optima Card?

Yes _____
No   _____

MULTIPLE-CHOICE QUESTION
What age group are you in?

Under 20   _____
20–29   _____
30–39   _____
40–49   _____
50–59   _____
60 and over   _____

Researchers must be very careful about questions that a respondent might consider too personal or that might require him or her to admit activities that other people are likely to condemn. Questions of this type should be worded in such a way as to make them less offensive.

For testing special markets, where individuals (for instance, executives, scientists, and engineers) are likely to own or have access to a personal computer, questionnaires may be programmed on a computer disc and the discs delivered through the mail. This technique may cost less than a telephone interview and eliminate bias by simplifying flow patterns in answering questions. Respondents see less clutter on the screen than on a printed questionnaire; the novelty of the approach may also spark their interest and compel their attention.

Observation Methods.   When using **observation methods**, researchers record respondents' overt behaviour, taking note of physical conditions and events. Direct contact with respondents is avoided; instead, their actions are examined and noted systematically. For example, researchers might use observation methods to answer the question, "How long does the average McDonald's restaurant customer have to wait in line before being served?"

Observation may also be combined with interviews. For example, during personal interviews, the condition of a respondent's home or other possessions may be observed and recorded, and demographic information such as ethnic origin, approximate age, and sex can be confirmed by direct observation.

Data gathered through observation can sometimes be biased if the respondent is aware of the observation process. An observer can be placed in a natural market environment, such as a grocery store, without biasing or influencing shoppers' actions. However, if the presence of a human observer is likely to bias the outcome or if human sensory abilities are inadequate, mechanical means may be used to record behaviour. **Mechanical observation devices** include cameras, recorders, counting machines, and equipment to record physiological changes in individuals. For instance, a special camera can be used to record the eye movements of respondents looking at an advertisement; the sequence of reading and the parts of the advertisement that receive greatest attention can be detected. Electric scanners in supermarkets are mechanical observation devices that offer an exciting opportunity for marketing research. Scanner technology can provide accurate data on sales and consumers' purchase patterns, and marketing researchers may buy such data from the supermarket.

Observation is straightforward and avoids a central problem of survey methods: motivating respondents to state their true feelings or opinions. However, observation tends to be descriptive. When it is the only method of data collection, it may not provide insights into causal relationships. Another drawback is that analyses based on observation are subject to the biases of the observer or the limitations of the mechanical device.

INTERPRETING RESEARCH FINDINGS

After collecting data to test their hypotheses, marketers interpret the research findings. Interpretation is easier if marketers carefully plan their data-analysis methods early in the research process. They should also allow for continual evaluation of the data during the entire collection period. They can then gain valuable insight into areas that ought to be probed during the formal interpretation.

The first step in drawing conclusions from most research is displaying the data in table format. If marketers intend to apply the results to individual categories of the things or people being studied, cross-tabulation may be quite useful, especially in tabulating joint occurrences. For example, using the two variables, gender and purchase rates of car tyres, a cross-tabulation could show how men and women differ in purchasing car tyres.

After the data are tabulated, they must be analysed. **Statistical interpretation** focuses on what is typical or what deviates from the average. It indicates how widely responses vary and how they are distributed in relation to the variable being measured. This interpretation is another facet of marketing research that relies on marketers' judgement or intuition. Moreover, when they interpret statistics, marketers must take into account estimates of expected error or deviation from the true values of the population. The analysis of data may lead researchers to accept or reject the hypothesis being studied. As shown in Figure 6.9, SPSS, a noted statistical analysis package producer for marketing research, provides data analysis and presentation graphics.

Data require careful interpretation by the marketer. If the results of a study are valid, the decision-maker should take action; however, if it is discovered that a

FIGURE 6.9
Promoting data analysis software.
SPSS provides software for the statistical analysis of market research data.

SOURCE: SPSS Inc.

question has been incorrectly worded, the results should be ignored. For example, if a study by an electricity company reveals that 50 percent of its customers believe that meter-readers are "friendly", is that finding good, bad, or indifferent? Two important bench-marks help interpret the result: how the 50 percent figure compares with that for competitors and how it compares with a previous time period. The point is that managers must understand the research results and relate the results to a context that permits effective decision-making.[21]

REPORTING RESEARCH FINDINGS

The final step in the marketing research process is reporting the research findings. Before preparing the report, the marketer must take a clear, objective look at the findings to see how well the gathered facts answer the research question or support or negate the hypotheses posed in the beginning. In most cases, it is extremely doubtful that the study can provide everything needed to answer the research

21. Michael J. Olivette, "Marketing Research in the Electric Utility Industry," *Marketing News*, 2 Jan. 1987, p. 13.

question. Thus in the report the researcher must point out the deficiencies and the reasons for them.

The report presenting the results is usually a formal, written one. Researchers must allow time for the writing task when they plan and schedule the project. Since the report is a means of communicating with the decision-makers who will use the research findings, researchers need to determine beforehand how much detail and supporting data to include. They should keep in mind that corporate executives prefer reports that are short, clear, and simply expressed. Often researchers will give their summary and recommendations first, especially if decision-makers do not have time to study how the results were obtained. A technical report allows its users to analyse data and interpret recommendations because it describes the research methods and procedures and the most important data gathered. Thus, researchers must recognise the needs and expectations of the report user and adapt to them.

When marketing decision-makers have a firm grasp of research methods and procedures, they are better able to integrate reported findings and personal experience. If marketers can spot limitations in research from reading the report, then personal experience assumes additional importance in the decision-making process. Marketers who cannot understand basic statistical assumptions and data-gathering procedures may misuse research findings. Consequently, report writers should be aware of the backgrounds and research abilities of those who will rely on the report in making decisions. Clear explanations presented in plain language make it easier for decision-makers to apply the findings and diminish the chances of a report being misused or ignored. Talking with potential research users before writing a report can help researchers supply information that will indeed improve decision-making.

The Importance of Ethical Marketing Research

Marketing research and systematic information-gathering make successful marketing more likely. In fact, many companies, and even entire industries, have failed because of a lack of marketing research. The conventional wisdom about the evaluation and use of marketing research by marketing managers suggests that in future managers will rely on marketing research to reduce uncertainty and to make better decisions than they could without such information.[22]

Clearly, marketing research and information systems are vital to marketing decision-making. Because of this, it is essential that ethical standards be established and followed. Attempts to stamp out shoddy practices and establish generally acceptable procedures for conducting research are issues of great concern to marketing researchers. Other issues in marketing research relate to researcher honesty, manipulation of research techniques, data manipulation, invasion of privacy, and failure to disclose the purpose or sponsorship of a study in some situations. Too often respondents are unfairly manipulated and research clients are not told about flaws in data.

One common practice that hurts the image of marketing research is "sugging" ("selling under the guise of marketing research"). A leading marketing research

22. Hanjoon Lee, Frank Acits, and Ralph L. Day, "Evaluation and Use of Marketing Research by Decision Makers: A Behavioral Simulation," *Journal of Marketing Research,* May 1987, p. 187.

association (ESOMAR) is attempting to get research companies and marketing research firms worldwide to adopt codes and policies prohibiting this practice.[23] In the U.K., the Market Research Society lays down strict guidelines.

Because so many parties are involved in the marketing research process, developing shared ethical concern is difficult. The relationships among respondents who co-operate and share information, interviewing companies, marketing research agencies that manage projects, and organisations that use the data are interdependent and complex. Ethical conflict typically occurs because the parties involved in the marketing research process have different objectives. For example, the organisation that uses data tends to be result-orientated, and success is often based on performance rather than a set of standards. On the other hand, a data-gathering subcontractor is evaluated on the ability to follow a specific set of standards or rules. The relationships among all participants in marketing research must be understood so that decision-making becomes ethical. Without clear understanding and agreement, including mutual adoption of standards, ethical conflict will lead to mistrust and questionable research results.[24]

Marketing research is essential in planning and developing marketing strategies. Information about target markets provides vital input in planning the marketing mix and controlling marketing activities. It is no secret that companies can use information technology as a key to gaining an advantage over the competition.[25] In short, the marketing concept—the marketing philosophy of customer orientation—can be implemented better when adequate information about customers is available.

SUMMARY

To implement the marketing concept, marketers need information about the characteristics, needs, and wants of their target markets. Marketing research and information systems that furnish practical, unbiased information help firms avoid the assumptions and misunderstandings that could lead to poor marketing performance.

Marketing research is the systematic design, collection, interpretation, and reporting of information to help marketers solve specific marketing problems or take advantage of marketing opportunities. Marketing research is conducted on a special-project basis, with the research methods adapted to the problems being studied and to changes in the environment.

The marketing information system (MIS) is a framework for the day-to-day managing and structuring of information regularly gathered from sources both inside and outside an organisation. The inputs into a marketing information system include the information sources inside and outside the firm considered useful for future decision-making. Processing information involves classifying it and developing categories for meaningful storage and retrieval. Marketing decision-makers then deter-

23. Lynn Colemar, "It's Selling Disguised as Research," *Marketing News*, 4 Jan. 1988, p. 1.

24. O. C. Ferrell and Steven J. Skinner, "Ethical Behavior and Bureaucratic Structure in Marketing Research Organizations," *Journal of Marketing Research*, Feb. 1988, pp. 103–104.

25. Brandt Allen, "Make Information Services Pay Its Way," *Harvard Business Review*, January-February 1987, p. 57.

mine which information—the output—is useful for making decisions. Feedback enables those who are responsible for gathering internal and external data to adjust the information inputs systematically. Data brought into the organisation through marketing research become part of its marketing databank, a file of data collected through both the MIS and marketing research projects.

The increase in marketing research activities represents a transition from intuitive to scientific problem-solving. Intuitive decisions are made on the basis of personal knowledge and past experience. Scientific decision-making is an orderly, logical, and systematic approach. Minor, non-recurring problems can be handled successfully by intuition. As the number of risks and alternative solutions increases, the use of research becomes more desirable and rewarding.

The five basic steps of planning marketing research are (1) defining and locating problems, (2) developing hypotheses, (3) collecting data, (4) interpreting research findings, and (5) reporting the findings.

Defining and locating the problem—the first step towards finding a solution or launching a research study—means uncovering the nature and boundaries of a negative, or positive, situation or question. A problem must be clearly defined for marketers to develop a hypothesis—an informed guess or assumption about that problem or set of circumstances—which is the second step in the research process.

To test the accuracy of hypotheses, researchers collect data—the third step in the research process. Researchers may use exploratory, descriptive, or causal studies. Secondary data are compiled inside or outside the organisation for some purpose other than the current investigation. Secondary data may be collected from an organisation's databank and other internal sources; from periodicals, government publications, and unpublished sources; and from syndicated data services, which collect general information and sell it to clients.

Primary data are observed and recorded or collected directly from respondents. Experimentation involves maintaining as constants those factors that are related to or may affect the variables under investigation so that the effects of the experimental variables can be measured. Marketing experimentation is a set of rules and procedures under which the task of data-gathering is organised to expedite analysis and interpretation. In experimentation, an independent variable is manipulated and the resulting changes are measured in a dependent variable. Research techniques are reliable if they produce almost identical results in successive repeated trials; they are valid if they measure what they are supposed to measure and not something else. Experiments may take place in laboratory settings, which provide maximum control over influential factors, or in field settings, which are preferred when marketers want experimentation to take place in natural surroundings.

Other methods of collecting primary data include sampling, surveys, and observation. Sampling involves selecting representative units from a total population. In random sampling, all the units in a population have an equal chance of appearing in the sample. In stratified sampling, the population of interest is divided into groups according to a common characteristic or attribute, and then a probability sample is conducted within each group. Area sampling involves selecting a probability sample of geographic areas such as blocks, census tracts, or census enumeration districts and selecting units or individuals within the selected geographic areas for the sample. Quota sampling differs from other forms of sampling in that it is judgemental.

There are numerous survey methods, ranging from mail surveys, telephone surveys, computer-assisted telephone interviews, personal interview surveys, and shopping mall intercept interviews to on-site computer interviews, focus-group interviews, and in-home interviews. Questionnaires are instruments used to obtain information from respondents and to record observations; they should be unbiased and objective. Observation methods involve researchers recording respondents' overt behaviour and taking note of physical conditions and events. Observation may be facilitated by mechanical observation devices.

To apply research findings to decision-making, marketers must interpret and report their findings properly. Statistical interpretation is analysis that focuses on what is typical or what deviates from the average. After interpreting the research findings, the researchers must prepare a report of the findings that the decision-makers can use and understand.

Marketing research and systematic information-gathering increase the probability of successful marketing. In fact, marketing research is essential in planning and developing marketing strategies. Because of this, attempts to eliminate unethical marketing research practices and establish generally acceptable procedures for conducting research are important goals. However, because so many parties are involved in the marketing research process, shared ethical concern is difficult.

Important Terms

Marketing research
Marketing information system (MIS)
Marketing databank
Problem definition
Hypothesis
Exploratory studies
Descriptive studies
Causal studies
Primary data
Secondary data
Syndicated data services
Experimentation
Marketing experimentation
Independent variable

Dependent variable
Reliability
Validity
Sample
Sampling
Population
Random sampling
Stratified sampling
Area sampling
Quota sampling
Survey methods
Observation methods
Mechanical observation devices
Statistical interpretation

Discussion and Review Questions

1. What is the MIS likely to include in a small organisation? Do all organisations have a marketing databank?
2. What is the difference between marketing research and marketing information systems? In what ways do marketing research and the MIS overlap?

3. How do the benefits of decisions guided by marketing research compare with those of intuitive decision-making? How do marketing decision-makers know when it will be worthwhile to conduct research?
4. Give specific examples of situations in which intuitive decision-making would probably be more appropriate than marketing research.
5. What is the difference between defining a research problem and developing a hypothesis?
6. What are the major limitations of using secondary data to solve marketing problems?
7. List some of the problems of conducting a laboratory experiment on respondents' reactions to the taste of different brands of beer. How would these problems differ from those of a field study of beer taste preferences?
8. In what situation would it be best to use random sampling? Quota sampling? Stratified or area sampling?
9. *Non-response* is the inability or refusal of some respondents to co-operate in a survey. What are some ways to decrease non-response in personal door-to-door surveys?
10. Make some suggestions for ways to encourage respondents to co-operate in mail surveys.
11. If a survey of all homes with listed telephone numbers is conducted, what sampling design should be used?
12. Give some examples of marketing problems that could be solved through information gained from observation.

■ CASES

6.1 AGB's "Superpanel"

Christmas, 1990, AGB launched the largest on-line consumer panel in Europe. This "Superpanel" comprises 8,500 households dotted around Britain, each with a bar code scanner which captures information of every household's purchases. The scanner identifies which member of the family bought which product, when and from which retail/service outlet. According to market research group AGB, the panel's 28,000 individual members provide the most accurate reviews so far of the country's shopping patterns.

According to AGB's director Bill Blyth, 12 million market research interviews take place each year—70 percent of which are pen and paper exercises for small scale surveys. However, with the increase of bar coding on many products, the U.K. has been able to move closer to the U.S. where 70 percent of sales are recorded electronically at the point of sale. So far, AGB has invested £12 million into the "Superpanel" bar code scanner project. Ironically, one of the biggest problems the company had to overcome was the adverse reaction many U.K. consumers had to the technology and equipment involved.

Individuals in the Superpanel's households record purchases in the kitchen by simply wiping their AGB marketmeter wand over product bar codes. This records the product, size, weight, colour, price, special offer price, and country of origin.

Through AGB's in-home directory, even non-bar-coded goods are noted. The data are stored instantaneously in a telephone link. AGB's analysis also checks for errors and inconsistencies, such as abnormally high or low prices or own-label products that appear to have been purchased from a rival company. The analysis can compare store to store, brand to brand, brand to store, price to store, and any other permutations. Clients know key purchase days, mix of purchases, and who buys. There is a 72-hour turnaround on-line of results, or in print form every four weeks.

AGB claims that extrapolations of the panel figures, which lead to estimations of sales for various products, are some of the most accurate ever produced by the market research industry. "Superpanel's" customers include Lever Brothers, Central Television, and Bird's Eye Walls. Unilever's Lever Brothers used the information for the recent launch of Persil washing up liquid, in which sales were monitored on a daily basis and pricing, advertising, and sales strategies were adapted accordingly depending on regional performance. AGB now plans to tie in the "Superpanel" with its existing television viewing panels to allow various scenarios to be estimated in the development of forthcoming advertising campaigns and marketing strategies.

SOURCES: AGB Limited, London; Bill Blyth of AGB; Phil Dourado, "Board Makes Way for the Bar Code," *The Independent Sunday*, 13 January 1991, p. 21; AGB promotional material, 1991.

Questions for Discussion

1. Discuss how technology plays an increasing role in the gathering of marketing information and data.
2. To a marketer, how important is the capture of information pertaining to a household's entire spending pattern?
3. How could such data assist Lever's launch of Persil washing up liquid?

6.2 Nielsen's People Meter

Traditionally, the survey methods used to collect data for marketing research have been mail, telephone, or personal interviews. However, A. C. Nielsen Company pioneered the use of a microwave computerised rating system—called a *people meter*—to measure national television audiences in the U.S.A. Nielsen hopes to spread its use internationally.

People meters transmit demographic information overnight on what television shows people are watching, the number of households that are watching the shows, and which family members are watching. The data are recorded automatically when household members press buttons on the meter. The people meters replace the old National Audience Composition (NAC) diaries used for the past thirty years to determine the viewing habits of consumers.

People meters were initially placed in two thousand homes in 1987. The device enables Nielsen monitors to record second-by-second viewing choices of up to eight household members, with the viewers using remote control keyboards to record their programme selection. The people meter is the state of the art in electronic measuring equipment and underwent extensive testing and analysis before its introduction. According to Nielsen officials, the people meter determines national audience composition far more accurately than the old National Audience Composition

(NAC) diary: it is also a much faster means of giving advertisers information about the television shows that their target market is watching, enabling them to reach that target market with their commercials. A study published by Roland Soong in a 1988 issue of the *Journal of Advertising Research* concludes that "the people meter sample is considerably more reliable than a diary sample with the same total number of households". The accuracy is increased because a computer records at the time what show a person is viewing. Consequently, the system does not depend on an individual's memory, as the diary did.

Despite its speed and accuracy in measuring audience composition, the people meter was initially criticised by the U.S. networks because its data showed a smaller number of network television viewers than did the NAC diary. The three major networks questioned the accuracy of the people meters. Indeed, in 1987, both ABC and CBS asked Nielsen to continue to use the NAC diary rather than the people meter for that year. During that period, the two networks also based their sales and programming decisions solely on the NAC. But ABC became so dissatisfied with "declining standards" that it cancelled its contract with Nielsen early in the year. According to the network, the diary sample results were not as accurate because Nielsen had tied up most of its resources in the people meter. CBS also cancelled its contract with Nielsen, and both CBS and ABC refused to buy the people meter data. CBS signed a contract with AGB, Nielsen's major competitor, to use its people meter instead. NBC agreed to use the Nielsen device but also questioned the meter's reliability.

Nielsen's and AGB's people meters have registered consistently lower ratings than the old diary system, leading to confusion and controversy throughout the industry. The networks were unhappy. After all, the higher the rating for a programme, the more they could charge for commercial time during that programme, whereas lower ratings meant significant losses of revenue. To protect themselves against such losses, stemming from people meter ratings, the networks raised prices for commercial time by 15 to 25 percent in 1987. Advertisers get "make-good" time, or free-advertisement time, from a network when the ratings for a show it sponsors fall below the guidelines for the original purchase contract. The result of this make-good time is higher price tags for advertisers.

However, after three years of meter use, the attitude of the networks has changed. The meter data enable the networks to spot viewing trends more quickly and respond with changes in programming schedules. People meters have made it easier and faster to show ratings and demographic shifts. They may force a change in the demographic groupings currently used for negotiations and guarantees. People meters have also improved audience definition; by simply pushing a designated button, users furnish personal information, such as age, sex, income, education and ethnic background. This information gives the networks more opportunity to market their product, as opposed to selling it. In the view of most advertising and network executives, the people meter has had limited impact so far. But as one network marketing vice president noted, the real advantages of the available data remain to be seen.

SOURCES: Brian Donlon, "TV Rating Rivals Tune in New Device," *USA Today,* 16 Sept. 1987, pp. 1B, 2B; Verne Gay, "Networks Zap Debut of Meters," *Advertising Age,* 7 Sept. 1987, pp. 1, 56; "People Meters to Be Sole Tool for '87 Nielson TV Ratings," *Marketing News,* 30 Jan. 1987, p. 1; Roland Soong, "The Statistical Reliability of People Meter Ratings," *Journal of Advertising Research,* Feb.-March 1988, p. 56; and Wayne Walley, "Meters Set New TV Ground Rules," *Advertising Age,* 30 Oct. 1989, p.12.

Questions for Discussion

1. What are the advantages and disadvantages of Nielsen's people meter compared with its old diary method?
2. Why do you think that Nielsen switched from the NAC diary to the people meter?
3. Does the people meter collect primary or secondary data? Why?

II PRODUCT DECISIONS

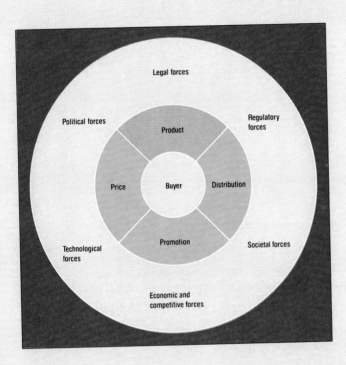

We are now prepared to analyse the decisions and activities associated with developing and maintaining effective marketing mixes. In Parts II through V we focus on the major components of the marketing mix: product, distribution, promotion, and price. Specifically, in Part II we explore the product ingredient of the marketing mix. Chapter 7 introduces basic concepts and relationships that must be understood if one is to make effective product decisions. Branding, packaging, and labelling are also discussed in this chapter. In Chapter 8 we analyse a variety of dimensions regarding product management, such as the ways that a firm can be organised to manage products, the development and positioning of products, product modification, and phasing out products. ◆

7 PRODUCT CONCEPTS

Objectives

To learn how marketers define products

To understand how to classify products

To become familiar with the concepts of product item, product line, and product mix and understand how they are connected

To understand the concept of product life cycle

To grasp the basic product identification concepts as they relate to branding, packaging, and labelling

U sing aggressive marketing and low prices, Carnival Cruise Lines has become the market leader in the cruise industry. Founded in 1972 by Ted Arison and currently headed by his son Micky, Carnival has no problem in keeping its eight ocean liners filled with passengers. The $5-billion-a-year cruise industry is likely to keep growing at a fast pace: in America alone, only 4 or 5 percent of those who could afford to take a cruise have actually done so.

To get Carnival where it is today, Arison changed the whole marketing strategy behind cruises. He made the ship itself the most important element of the cruise. Carnival therefore promotes its liners as "Fun Ships". Guests can enjoy three-, four-, or seven-day cruises; exotic ports of call; and all the food they can eat for about $395 to $2,395 (including airfare), some 20 percent less than on Carnival's competitors. Carnival ships offer casinos, gymnasiums, cocktail lounges, bingo, clay-pigeon shooting, shuffleboard, and Las Vegas–type shows.

Carnival also showers its passengers with service—the ratio of passengers to crew is two to one. Stewards are ready to bring drink refills, turn down bed sheets, or lay out clothing. The ship's waiters work long hours and receive short vacations but seem to be content; they remain with Carnival for an average of eight years. Carnival also shortened the duration of its cruises. Because of these activities, Carnival Cruise Lines began attracting younger and first-time customers.

Carnival works closely with travel agents, supplying them with a reservation system that allows cruises to be booked within minutes. It also sponsors a travel-agency-of-the-year competition and an incentive programme that gives agents recommending Carnival cruises the chance of a $1,000 reward. ◆

Based on information from "Carnival Shows Cruise Lines How to Hit High Seas," *U.S. News & World Report,* 29 Aug. 1988, p. 87; Eva Pomice, "Cruising to a Fortune Touting 'Love Boats' for the Masses," *U.S. News & World Report,* 1 Aug. 1988, pp. 43–44; Faye Rice, "How Carnival Stacks the Decks," *Fortune,* 16 Jan. 1989, pp. 108–110, 114, 116; and Paula Schnorbus, "Ain't We Got Fun!" *Marketing & Media Decisions,* March 1988, pp. 101–102, 104, 106.

T he product is an important variable in the marketing mix. Products such as the holiday cruises offered by Carnival Cruise Lines are among a firm's most crucial and visible contacts with buyers. If a company's products do not meet its customers' desires and needs, the company will fail unless it makes adjustments. Developing a successful product, as Carnival has done, requires knowledge of fundamental marketing and product concepts.

In this chapter we first introduce and define the concepts that help clarify what a product is and how buyers view products. Next we examine the concepts of product mix and product line to help us understand product planning. Then we explore the stages of the product life cycle. Each life-cycle stage generally requires a specific marketing strategy, operates within a certain competitive environment, and has its own sales and profit pattern. We conclude with a discussion of branding, packaging, labelling, and other characteristics that are a product's vital components.

What Is a Product?

A **product** is everything, both favourable and unfavourable, that one receives in an exchange. It is a complexity of tangible and intangible attributes, including functional, social, and psychological utilities or benefits.[1] A product can be an idea, a service, a good, or any combination of these three. This definition also covers supporting services that go with goods, such as installation, guarantees, product information, and promises of repair or maintenance. A **good** is a tangible physical entity, such as a box of Kellogg's Frosties or a Bic pen. A **service**, by contrast, is intangible; it is the result of the application of human and mechanical efforts to people or objects. Examples of services include Federal Express overnight delivery, medical examinations, and child care. (Chapter 22 provides a detailed discussion of services marketing.) **Ideas** are concepts, philosophies, images, or issues. They provide the psychological stimulus to solve problems or adjust to the environment. For example, the World Wildlife Fund promotes endangered-species issues.

When buyers purchase a product, they are really buying the benefits and satisfaction they think the product will provide. A Mazda MX5 sports car, for example, is purchased for excitement and fun, not just for transport. Services, in particular, are bought on the basis of promises of satisfaction. Promises, with the images and appearances of symbols, help consumers make judgements about tangible and intangible products.[2] Often, symbols and cues are used to make intangible products more tangible or real to the consumer. MasterCard, for example, uses globes to symbolise the firm's financial power and worldwide coverage.

1. Part of this definition is adapted from James D. Scott, Martin R. Warshaw, and James R. Taylor, *Introduction to Marketing Management,* 5th ed. (Homewood, Ill.: Irwin, 1985), p. 215.

2. Theodore Levitt, "Marketing Intangible Products and Product Intangibles," *Harvard Business Review,* May-June 1981, pp. 94–102.

CLASSIFYING PRODUCTS

Products fall into one of two general categories. Products purchased to satisfy personal and family needs are **consumer products**. Those bought for use in a firm's operations or to make other products are **industrial products**. Consumers buy products to satisfy their personal wants, whereas industrial buyers seek to satisfy the goals of their organisations.

The same item can be both a consumer product and an industrial product. For example, when consumers purchase light bulbs for their homes, light bulbs are classified as consumer products. However, when a large corporation purchases light bulbs to provide lighting in a factory or office, the light bulbs are considered industrial products because they are used in the daily operations of the firm. Thus the buyer's intent—or the ultimate use of the product—determines whether an item is classified as a consumer or an industrial product.

Why do we need to know about product classifications? The main reason is that classes of products are aimed at particular target markets, and this affects distribution, promotion, and pricing decisions. Furthermore, the types of marketing activities and efforts needed differ among the classes of consumer or industrial products. In short, the entire marketing mix can be affected by how a product is classified. In this section we examine the characteristics of consumer and industrial products and explore the marketing activities associated with some of them.

■ **Consumer Products**

The most widely accepted approach to classifying consumer products relies on the common characteristics of consumer buying behaviour. It divides products into four categories: convenience, shopping, specialty, and unsought products. However, not all buyers behave in the same way when purchasing a specific type of product. Thus a single product can fit into all four categories. To minimise this problem, marketers think in terms of how buyers *generally* behave when purchasing a specific item. In addition, they recognise that the "correct" classification can be determined only by considering a particular firm's intended target market. With these thoughts in mind, let us examine the four traditional categories of consumer products.

Convenience Products. **Convenience products** are relatively inexpensive, frequently purchased items on which buyers exert only minimal purchasing effort. They range from bread, soft drinks, and chewing gum to petrol and newspapers. The buyer spends little time planning the purchase or comparing available brands or sellers. Even a buyer who prefers a specific brand will readily choose a substitute if the preferred brand is not conveniently available.

Classifying a product as a convenience product has several implications for a firm's marketing strategy. A convenience product is normally marketed through many retail outlets. Because sellers experience high inventory turnover, per-unit gross margins can be relatively low. Producers of convenience products such as Smith's crisps and Crest toothpaste expect little promotional effort at the retail level and thus must provide it themselves in the form of advertising and sales promotion. Packaging is also an important element of the marketing mix for convenience products. The package may have to sell the product because many convenience items are available only on a self-service basis at the retail level.

FIGURE 7.1 *Shopping product.*
Olympus cameras, as well as most other brands of camera, are shopping products.

SOURCE: Reproduced courtesy of Olympus Cameras

Shopping Products.   **Shopping products** are items on which buyers are willing to expend considerable effort in planning and making the purchase. Buyers allocate time for comparing stores and brands with respect to prices, product features, qualities, services, and perhaps guarantees. Appliances, furniture, bicycles, stereos, and cameras (as shown in Figure 7.1) are examples of shopping products. These products are expected to last a fairly long time and thus are purchased less frequently than convenience items. Even though shopping products are more expensive than convenience products, few buyers of shopping products are particularly brand loyal. If they were, they would be unwilling to shop and compare among brands.

To market a shopping product effectively, a marketer considers several key issues. Shopping products require fewer retail outlets than convenience products. Because they are purchased less frequently, inventory turnover is lower, and middlemen expect to receive higher gross margins. Although large sums of money may be required to advertise shopping products, an even larger percentage of resources is likely to be used for personal selling. Usually, the producer and the middlemen expect some co-operation from one another with respect to providing parts and repair services and performing promotional activities.

Specialty Products.   **Specialty products** possess one or more unique characteristics, and a significant group of buyers is willing to expend considerable effort to obtain them. Buyers actually plan the purchase of a specialty product; they know exactly what they want and will not accept a substitute. An example of a specialty product is a Jaguar car or a painting by Andy Warhol. When searching for specialty products, buyers do not compare alternatives; they are concerned primarily with finding an outlet that has a pre-selected product available.

The fact that an item is a specialty product can affect a firm's marketing efforts in several ways. Specialty products are often distributed through a limited number of retail outlets. Like shopping goods, they are purchased infrequently, causing lower inventory turnover and thus requiring relatively high gross margins.

Unsought Products.   **Unsought products** are purchased when a sudden problem must be solved or when aggressive selling is used to obtain a sale that otherwise would not take place. In general, the consumer does not think of buying these products regularly. Emergency car repairs and cemetery plots are examples of unsought products. Life insurance and encyclopaedias, in contrast, are examples of products that need aggressive personal selling. The salesperson tries to make consumers aware of the benefits that can be derived from buying such products.

■ **Industrial Products**

Industrial products are usually purchased on the basis of an organisation's goals and objectives. Generally, the functional aspects of the product are more important than the psychological rewards sometimes associated with consumer products. Industrial products can be classified into seven categories according to their characteristics and intended uses: raw materials, major equipment, accessory equipment, component parts, process materials, consumable supplies, and industrial services.[3]

Raw Materials.   **Raw materials** are the basic materials that actually become part of a physical product. They include minerals, chemicals, agricultural products, and materials from forests and oceans. They are usually bought and sold according to grades and specifications, and in relatively large quantities.

Major Equipment.   **Major equipment** includes large tools and machines used for production purposes, such as cranes and stamping machines. Normally, major equipment is expensive and intended to be used in a production process for a considerable length of time. Some major equipment is custom-made to perform specific functions for a particular organisation, but other items are standardised and perform similar tasks for many types of firms. Because major equipment is so expensive, purchase decisions are often made by high-level management. Marketers of major equipment frequently must provide a variety of services, including installation, training, repair and maintenance assistance, and even help in financing the purchase.

Accessory Equipment.   **Accessory equipment** does not become a part of the final physical product but is used in production or office activities. Examples include typewriters, fractional-horsepower motors, calculators, and tools. Compared with major equipment, accessory items are usually much cheaper; purchased routinely,

3. Robert W. Haas, *Industrial Marketing Management*, 3rd ed. (Boston: Kent Publishing, 1986), pp. 15–25.

Current data shows 25% of all computer print ribbon is made with ICI fibre. How's that for world trade figures?

ICI manufactures in 40 countries and sells to over 150.

ICI *World Class*

FIGURE 7.2 *An example of a process material.*
ICI fibre is a process material used in the manufacture of computer print ribbon.

SOURCE: Courtesy of ICI, UK. Created by Saatchi & Saatchi.

with less negotiation; and treated as expenditure items rather than capital items because they are not expected to last as long. Accessory products are standardised items that can be used in several aspects of a firm's operations. More outlets are required for distributing accessory equipment than for major equipment, but sellers do not have to provide the multitude of services expected of major equipment marketers.

Component Parts.   **Component parts** become a part of the physical product and are either finished items ready for assembly or products that need little processing before assembly. Although they become part of a larger product, component parts can often be easily identified and distinguished. Spark-plugs, tyres, clocks, and switches are all component parts of the car. Buyers purchase such items according to their own specifications or industry standards. They expect the parts to be of specified quality and delivered on time so that production is not slowed or stopped. Producers that are primarily assemblers, such as most lawn-mower or computer manufacturers, depend heavily on the suppliers of component parts.

Process Materials.   **Process materials** are used directly in the production of other products. Unlike component parts, however, process materials are not readily identifiable. For example, Reichhold Chemicals markets a treated fibre product: a phenolic-resin, sheet-moulding compound, which is used in the production of flight deck instrument panels and cabin interiors for aircraft. Although the material is not identifiable in the finished aircraft, it retards burning, smoke, and formation of toxic gas if moulded components are subjected to fire or high temperatures. In Figure 7.2, ICI promotes the fact that 25 percent of all computer print ribbon is made with ICI fibre. As with component parts, process materials are purchased according to industry standards or the purchaser's specifications.

Consumable Supplies.   **Consumable supplies** facilitate production and operations but do not become part of the finished product. Paper, pencils, oils, cleaning agents, and paints are in this category. Because such supplies are standardised items used in a variety of situations, they are purchased by many different types of organisation. Consumable supplies are commonly sold through numerous outlets and are purchased routinely. To ensure that supplies are available when needed, buyers often deal with more than one seller. Because these supplies can be divided into three subcategories—maintenance, repair, and operating (or overhaul) supplies —they are sometimes called **MRO items**.

Industrial Services.   **Industrial services** are the intangible products that many organisations use in their operations. They include financial, legal, marketing research, computer programming and operation, and caretaking services. Printing services for business fall into the industrial services category. Purchasers must decide whether to provide their own services internally or obtain them outside the organisation. This decision depends greatly on the costs associated with each alternative and how frequently the services are needed.

Product Line and Product Mix

Marketers must understand the relationships among all the products of their organisation if they are to co-ordinate the marketing of the total group of products. The following concepts help describe the relationships among an organisation's products. A **product item** is a specific version of a product that can be designated as a distinct offering among an organisation's products, for example, Heinz' tomato soup. A **product line** includes a group of closely related product items that are considered a unit because of marketing, technical, or end-use considerations. All the tinned soups manufactured by Heinz constitute one of its product lines. To come up with the optimum product line, marketers must understand buyers' goals. Figure 7.3 depicts Century Furniture's line of dining chairs. Specific items in a product line reflect the desires of different target markets or the different needs of consumers.

A **product mix** is the composite, or total, group of products that an organisation makes available to customers. For example, all the personal care products, fabric washing products, and other products that Procter & Gamble manufactures constitute its product mix. The **depth** of a product mix is measured by the number of different products offered in each product line. Marketing Update 7.1 describes Kellogg's efforts to add depth to its cereal product line. The **width** of the product mix is measured by the number of product lines a company offers. Figure 7.4 illustrates these concepts by showing the width of the product mix and the depth of each product line for selected Procter & Gamble products in the U.K. Procter &

FIGURE 7.3

A product line.
This collection of products represents Century Furniture's line of dining chairs.

Look what we made for dinner.

If you'd like Queen Anne, Duncan Phyfe
or Jay Spectre at your table, they're available from Century Furniture.
Altogether, in fact, we offer 160 different styles of dining chairs and 65 impeccable finishes.
Including several faithful reproductions
from the collections of the Smithsonian Institution and British National Trust.
So why not call 1-800-852-5552 for more information,
or for the name of a store near you selling Century Furniture.
After all, nothing contributes more to a good dinner than the right company.

Century Furniture

SOURCE: Courtesy of Century Furniture

Gamble is known for using distinctive branding, packaging, and consumer advertising to promote individual items in its detergent product line. Dreft, Tide, Bold, Ariel, and Daz—all Procter & Gamble detergents—share the same distribution channels and similar manufacturing facilities. Yet each is promoted as distinctive, and this claimed uniqueness adds depth to the product line.

PRODUCT LIFE CYCLES

Just as biological cycles progress through growth and decline, so do product life cycles. A new product is introduced into the market-place; it grows; and when it loses appeal, it is terminated.[4] Recall that our definition of a product focuses on tangible and intangible attributes. The total product might be not just a good, but also the ideas and services attached to it. Packaging, branding, and labelling techniques alter or help create products, so marketers can modify product life cycles. (Marketing strategies for different life-cycle stages are discussed in Chapter 8.)

As Figure 7.5 shows, a **product life cycle** has four major stages: (1) introduction, (2) growth, (3) maturity, and (4) decline. As a product moves through its cycle, the

4. M. J. Thomas, "Product Development Management," in *The Marketing Book*, M. Baker, ed. (London: Heinemann/The Chartered Institute of Marketing, 1987).

Fabric Washing Products	Oral Hygiene Products	Toilet Soaps	Teenage Skin Care Products	Hair Care Products	Household Cleaners
Dreft 1937	Crest 1975	Camay 1958	Clearasil 1960	Head & Shoulders 1973	Flash 1958
Tide 1950	Denclen Liquid Denture Cleaner 1981	Fairy Toilet Soap 1966	Biactol 1978	Vidal Sassoon 1983	Flash Liquid 1986
Daz 1953		Zest 1982	Ultra Clearasil 1988	Pantene Vitamin Hair Tonic 1983	Flash Cream 1988
Fairy Snow 1957					Flash Spray 1989
Ariel 1969					
Bold 1972					
Daz Automatic 1979					
Ariel Automatic 1981					
Dreft Automatic 1984					
Ariel Automatic Liquid 1986					
Ariel Rapide 1988					
Daz Automatic Liquid 1988					
Fairy Automatic 1989					
Fairy Automatic Liquid 1989					
Bold Liquid 1989					
Ariel Ultra 1989					
Daz Ultra 1990					
Bold Ultra 1990					
Fairy Ultra 1990					

Product line depth (vertical axis)

Product mix width (horizontal axis)

FIGURE 7.4 *The concepts of width of product mix and product depth applied to selected Procter & Gamble products*

SOURCE: Information provided and reprinted by permission of The Procter & Gamble Company, Public Affairs Division, 1 Procter & Gamble Plaza, Cincinnati, OH 45202–3315.

strategies relating to competition, promotion, distribution, pricing, and market information must be periodically evaluated and possibly changed. Astute marketing managers use the life-cycle concept to make sure that the introduction, alteration, and termination of a product are timed and executed properly. By understanding the typical life-cycle pattern, marketers are better able to maintain profitable products and drop unprofitable ones.

■ **Introduction**

The **introduction stage** of the life-cycle begins at a product's first appearance in the market-place, when sales are zero and profits are negative. Profits are below zero because initial revenues are low and at the same time the company generally must incur large expenses for promotion and distribution. Notice in Figure 7.5 how sales should move upwards from zero, and profits also should move upwards from a position in which they are negative due to high expenses.

Because of cost, very few product introductions represent major inventions. Developing and introducing a new product can mean an outlay of many millons. The failure rate for new products is quite high, ranging from 60 to 90 percent, depending on the industry and how product failure is defined. For example, in the food and drinks industry, 80 percent of all new products fail.[5] More typically, product intro-

5. "New Product Failure: A Self-Fulfilling Prophecy?" *Marketing Communications,* April 1989, p. 27.

KELLOGG CO. ADDS DEPTH TO ITS CEREAL LINE

Kellogg Co., the 100-year-old cereal company based in Battle Creek, Michigan, was widely criticised when it did not diversify into markets other than cereals, while its major competitors, General Mills and Quaker Oats, ventured into other product categories. No one is questioning Kellogg's decision now. The company dominates the U.S. cereal market, having captured 41 percent of the dry cereal market. Kellogg's goal is a 50 percent market share.

To achieve its dominance of the cereal industry, Kellogg introduced a number of successful new cereals, such as Mueslix (a European-style muesli mixture), Nutrific (a healthy combination of raisins, bran, barley, and almonds), and Pro Grain (a multigrain cereal coated with honey). Kellogg has also strongly supported its established brands: its world-famous Corn Flakes, Frosted Flakes, Rice Krispies, Fruit Loops, and Special K. None of these brands has lost a single market-share point in more than six years. Kellogg has had success with line extensions as well.

Kellogg also benefited from a trend among adults for healthy, tasty breakfast foods as opposed to the standard high-fat, high-cholesterol breakfasts of the past. Spotting this trend early, the company introduced more nutritious cereals—Mueslix, Nutrific, and Pro Grain—and even added fruit and nuts to some of its older brands, gaining a huge advantage over the competition. Cereal companies are now trying to position their products against Kellogg brands that have been going strong for years.

Moreover, Kellogg has increased its research and development spending to about $40 million a year. The company uses extensive marketing research, including psychographic research, to find out why consumers buy a specific brand of cereal. Kellogg executives also increased advertising budgets, doubling them in the last few years. A marketer at Kellogg boasted confidently, "We know more about the ready-to-eat-cereal market than anybody else." The stable management at Kellogg seems to know how to put that cereal knowledge to use. For example, Kellogg cereal packages are either white or honey-coloured to evoke an image of health and purity.

SOURCES: Julie Liesse Erickson, "Cereal Makers Roll More Oats," *Advertising Age,* 6 Mar. 1989, p. 34; Rebecca Fannin, "Crunching the Competition," *Marketing & Media Decisions,* March 1988, pp. 70–75; and Wendy Zellner, "Kellogg Rides the Health Craze," *Business Week,* 14 Apr. 1989, pp. 28–31.

FIGURE 7.5
The four stages of the product life-cycle

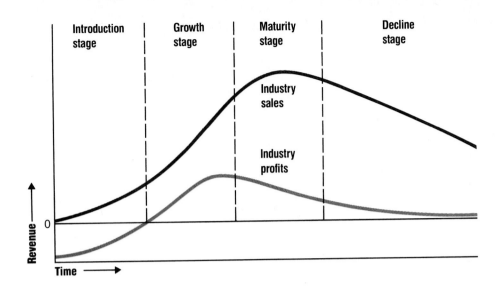

ductions involve a new packaged convenience food, a new car model, or a new fashion in clothing rather than a major product innovation.

Potential buyers must be made aware of the new product's features, uses, and advantages. Two difficulties may arise at this point. Only a few sellers may have the resources, technological knowledge, and marketing know-how to launch the product successfully; and the initial product price may have to be high, to recoup expensive marketing research or development costs. Given these difficulties, it is not surprising that many products never get beyond the introduction stage.

■ **Growth**

During the **growth stage**, sales rise rapidly and profits reach a peak and then start to decline (see Figure 7.5). The growth stage is critical to a product's survival because competitive reactions to its success during this period will affect the product's life expectancy. For example, California Cooler successfully marketed the first "wine cooler" but today competes against approximately fifty other brands. Mars faces a similar situation with its Ice Cream Mars product. Profits decline late in the growth stage as more competitors enter the market, driving prices down and creating the need for heavy promotional expenses. At this point a typical marketing strategy encourages strong brand loyalty and competes with aggressive emulators of the product. During the growth stage, an organisation tries to strengthen its market share and develop a competitive niche by emphasising the product's benefits.

Aggressive promotional pricing, including price cuts, is typical during the growth stage. The cellular telephone industry in the United States is currently in the growth stage. Many competitors have entered the market. By adjusting their prices competitively, cellular telephone manufacturers such as Motorola and service providers such as McCaw Cellular Communications are able to maintain their market lead during the growth stage. Consequently, they extend the life expectancy of their product far beyond that of marginal competitors. In the U.K., the battle between Cellnet and Vodaphone is much more tightly fought.

■ **Maturity**

During the **maturity stage**, the sales curve peaks and starts to decline and profits continue to decline (see Figure 7.5). This stage is characterised by severe competition, as many brands are in the market. Competitors emphasise improvements and differences in their versions of the product. As a result, during the maturity stage weaker competitors are squeezed out or lose interest in the product. For example, some brands of video-recorders will perish as the VCR moves through the maturity stage.

During the maturity phase, the producers who remain in the market must make fresh promotional and distribution efforts; advertising and dealer-orientated promotions are typical during this stage of the product life-cycle. The promoters must also take into account the fact that, as the product reaches maturity, buyers' knowledge of it attains a high level. Consumers of the product are no longer inexperienced generalists but instead are experienced specialists.

■ **Decline**

During the **decline stage**, sales fall rapidly (see Figure 7.5). New technology or a new social trend may cause product sales to take a sharp turn downwards. When this happens, the marketer considers pruning items from the product line to eliminate those not earning a profit. At this time, too, the marketer may cut promotion efforts, eliminate marginal distributors, and, finally, plan to phase out the product.

Because most businesses have a product mix consisting of multiple products, a firm's destiny is rarely tied to one product. A composite of life-cycle patterns is formed when various products in the mix are at different cycle stages. As one product is declining, other products are in the introduction, growth, or maturity stage. Marketers must deal with the dual problem of prolonging the life of existing products and introducing new products to meet organisational sales goals. For example, Kodak has prolonged the product life-cycle of its 110mm cameras by adding built-in flashes, waterproof bodies, and other features. But Kodak has also continued to introduce new products, including the disposable 35mm Kodak Fling; Breeze, a new line of 35mm cameras; and Ektar, a new line of colour films specifically for 35mm single-lens reflex cameras. In the next chapter you will learn more about the development of new products and how they can be managed in their various life-cycle stages.

BRANDING

In addition to making decisions about actual products, marketers must make many decisions associated with branding, such as brands, brand names, brand marks, trade marks, and trade names. A **brand** is a name, term, design, symbol, or any other feature that identifies one seller's good or service as distinct from those of other sellers. A brand may identify one item, a family of items, or all items of that seller.[6] A **brand name** is that part of a brand which can be spoken—including letters, words, and numbers—such as 7-Up. A brand name is often a product's only distinguishing characteristic. Without the brand name, a firm could not identify its products. To consumers, brand names are as fundamental as the product itself. Brand names simplify shopping, guarantee quality, and allow self-expression.[7]

The element of a brand that is not made up of words, but is often a symbol or design, is called a **brand mark**. One example is the symbol of a baby on Procter &

6. Peter D. Bennett, ed., *Dictionary of Marketing Terms* (Chicago: American Marketing Association, 1988), p. 18. Reprinted by permission.

7. James U. McNeal and Linda Zeren, "Brand Name Selection for Consumer Products," *MSU Business Topics*, Spring 1981, p. 35.

Gamble's Fairy Liquid. A **trade mark** is a legal designation indicating that the owner has exclusive use of a brand or a part of a brand and that others are prohibited by law from using it. To protect a brand name or brand mark, a company must register it as a trade mark with the appropriate patenting body. Finally, a **trade name** is the full and legal name of an organisation, such as Ford Motor Company or Safeway Stores, Inc., rather than the name of a specific product.

■ Benefits of Branding

Branding provides benefits for both buyers and sellers. Brands help buyers identify specific products that they do and do not like, which in turn facilitates the purchase of items that satisfy their needs and reduces the time required to purchase the product. Without brands, product selection would be quite random because buyers could have no assurance that they were purchasing what they preferred. A brand also helps buyers evaluate the quality of products, especially when they are unable to judge a product's characteristics. That is, a brand may symbolise a certain quality level to a purchaser, and in turn the person lets that perception of quality represent the quality of the item. A brand helps to reduce a buyer's perceived risk of purchase. In addition, a brand may offer a psychological reward that comes from owning a brand that symbolises status. Certain brands of watches (Rolex) and cars (Mercedes-Benz), for example, fall into this category.

Sellers benefit from branding because each company's brands identify its products, which makes repeat purchasing easier for consumers. Branding helps a firm introduce a new product that carries the name of one or more of its existing products because buyers are already familiar with the firm's existing brands. Branding also facilitates promotional efforts because the promotion of each branded product indirectly promotes all other products that are similarly branded. Marketing Update 7.2 illustrates the value of creating brands.

Branding also helps sellers by fostering brand loyalty. To the extent that buyers become loyal to a specific brand, the company's market share for that product achieves a certain level of stability, allowing the firm to use its resources more efficiently. When a firm develops some degree of customer loyalty to a brand, it can charge a premium price for the product. For example, brand-loyal buyers of Anadin aspirin are willing to pay two or three times more for Anadin than for a store brand of aspirin even though both have the same amount of pain-relieving agent. However, brand loyalty is declining, partly because of marketers' increased reliance on sales, coupons, and other short-term promotions, and partly because of the sometimes overwhelming array of similar new products from which consumers can choose. In the U.S., a *Wall Street Journal* survey found that 12 percent of consumers are not loyal to any brand, whereas 47 percent are brand loyal for one to five product types. Only 2 percent of the respondents were brand loyal for more than sixteen product types (see Figure 7.6). To stimulate loyalty to their brands, some marketers are stressing image advertising, mailing personalised catalogues and magazines to regular users, and creating membership clubs for brand users.[8]

■ Types of Brands

The two categories of brands are manufacturer and own-label brands. **Manufacturer brands** are initiated by producers and ensure that producers are identified with their products at the point of purchase, for example, Green Giant, Walls ice-cream, and Apple Computer. A manufacturer brand usually requires a producer

---

8. Ronald Alsop, "Brand Loyalty Is Rarely Blind Loyalty; Rise in Coupons, Choices Blames for '80s Erosion," *Wall Street Journal*, 19 Oct. 1989, pp. B1, B6.

"PRODUCERS URGED TO SET UP BRAND NAMES"

A major seminar at the Hong Kong Convention Centre in 1990 urged manufacturers to establish brand names in order to expand their share of world markets. Hong Kong manufacturers that produce the same quality products as those being sold under popular brand names could, the seminar claimed, make better profits with their own brands. Products move faster and commodity producers are elevated to quality producers with brands, stated Lam Soon managing director Raymond Ch'ien.

Video Technology Group chairman Allan Wong added that manufacturers could not be just original equipment manufacturers as they would be limited by the financial conditions of an importer. Wong pointed to the many difficulties when testing a new brand name and the need to have product uniqueness and a lack of head-on rivals. The Trade Development Council is encouraging the territory to design, manufacture and market its own brand-name products to expand its share of world markets. The seminar displayed 2,000 brand-name products developed by more than 200 local manufacturers.

SOURCE: *South China Morning Post* (Business Post), 7 September 1990; Hong Kong Watchmakers on Brink of Export Spurt," *Financial Times,* 4 July 1990, p. 7a.

to become involved in distribution, promotion, and, to some extent, pricing decisions. Brand loyalty is created by promotion, quality control, and guarantees; it is a valuable asset to a manufacturer. The producer tries to stimulate demand for the product, which tends to encourage middlemen to make the product available.

Own-label brands (also called **private brands**, **store brands**, or **dealer brands**) are initiated and owned by resellers—wholesalers or retailers. The major characteristic of private brands is that the manufacturers are not identified on the products. Retailers and wholesalers use own-label brands to develop more efficient promotion, to generate higher gross margins, and to improve store images. Own-label brands give retailers freedom to purchase products of a specified quality at the lowest cost without disclosing the identity of the manufacturer. Familiar retailer brand names include St Michael (Marks and Spencer) and Yessica (C & A) (see Figure 7.7). Many successful private brands are distributed nationally. Sometimes retailers with successful own-label brands start manufacturing their own products to gain more control over product costs, quality, and design with the hope of increasing profits.

Competition between manufacturer brands and own-label brands (sometimes called "the battle of the brands") is intensifying in several major product categories, particularly cheese, orange juice, sugar, and soft drinks. Own-label brands now account for approximately 13 percent of all supermarket sales.[9] For manufacturers, developing multiple manufacturer brands and distribution systems has been an effective means of combating the increased competition from own-label brands. By developing a new brand name, a producer can adjust various elements of a marketing mix to appeal to a different target market. For example, Scott Paper has developed lower-priced brands of paper towels; it has tailored its new products to a target market that tends to buy own-label brands.

Manufacturers find it hard to ignore the marketing opportunities that come from producing own-label brands for resellers. If a manufacturer refuses to produce an own-label brand for a reseller, a competing manufacturer will. Moreover, the production of own-label brands allows the manufacturer to use excess capacity during periods when its own brands are at non-peak production. The ultimate decision whether to produce an own-label or a manufacturer brand depends on a company's resources, production capabilities, and goals.

■ **Selecting and Protecting a Brand**

Marketers should consider a number of factors when they select a brand name. The name should be easy for customers (including foreign buyers, if the firm intends to market its products in other countries) to say, spell, and recall. Short, one-syllable names such as Tide often satisfy this requirement. If possible, the brand name should suggest in a positive way the product's uses and special characteristics; negative or offensive references should be avoided. For example, a deodorant should be branded with a name that connotes freshness, dryness, or long-lasting protection, as do Sure and Right Guard. The name should indicate the product's major benefits. If a marketer intends to use a brand for a product line, it must be compatible with all the products in the line. Finally, a brand should be designed so that it can be used and recognised in all the various types of media. Finding the right brand name has become a challenging task because many obvious product names have already been used. Figure 7.8 shows trade mark registrations in the U.K. between 1980 and 1989.

9. Judann Dagnoli, "New Study Blasts Private Labels," *Advertising Age,* 19 June 1989, p. 34.

FIGURE 7.6

Percentage of users of selected products who are loyal to one brand

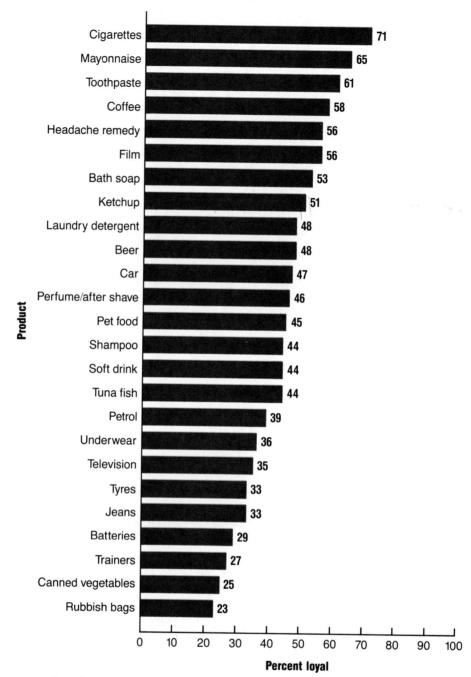

Product	Percent loyal
Cigarettes	71
Mayonnaise	65
Toothpaste	61
Coffee	58
Headache remedy	56
Film	56
Bath soap	53
Ketchup	51
Laundry detergent	48
Beer	48
Car	47
Perfume/after shave	46
Pet food	45
Shampoo	44
Soft drink	44
Tuna fish	44
Petrol	39
Underwear	36
Television	35
Tyres	33
Jeans	33
Batteries	29
Trainers	27
Canned vegetables	25
Rubbish bags	23

SOURCE: Data taken from the Centennial Survey, *The Wall Street Journal,* 19 Oct. 1989, p. B1.

FIGURE 7.7
A familiar retailer brand.
Yessica is a retailer
brand found exclusively
at C & A.

SOURCE: Courtesy of Yessica C & A

A marketer should also design a brand that can be protected easily through registration. Because of their designs, some brands can be legally infringed upon more easily than others. To protect its exclusive rights to a brand, the company must make certain that the selected brand is not likely to be considered an infringement of any existing brand already registered with the relevant patent office. This task may be complex because infringement is determined by the courts, which base their decisions on whether a brand causes consumers to be confused, mistaken, or deceived about the source of the product.[10] McDonald's is one company that aggressively protects its trade marks against infringement; it has brought charges against a number of companies with "Mc" names because it fears that the use of the "Mc" will give consumers the impression that these companies are associated with or owned by McDonald's.[11]

If possible, a marketer must guard against allowing a brand name to become a generic term used to refer to a general product category. Generic terms cannot be

10. George Miaoulis and Nancy D'Amato, "Consumer Confusion and Trademark Infringement," *Journal of Marketing,* April 1978, pp. 48–49.

11. Diane Schneidman, "Use of 'Mc' in Front of Travel Firms' Names Leads to Lawsuits," *Marketing News,* 20 Nov. 1987, p. 17.

FIGURE 7.8
U.K. trade marks registered 1980–1989.

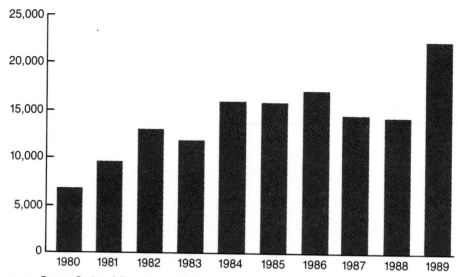

SOURCE: *Patents, Designs & Trade Marks 1989* (London: Her Majesty's Stationery Office, 1989).

protected as exclusive brand names. For example, names such as aspirin, escalator, and shredded wheat—all brand names at one time—were eventually declared generic terms that refer to product classes; thus they no longer could be protected. To keep a brand name from becoming a generic term, the firm should spell the name with a capital letter and use it as an adjective to modify the name of the general product class, as in Kellogg's Rice Krispies. An organisation can deal with this problem directly by advertising that its brand is a trade mark and should not be used generically. The firm can also indicate that the brand is trade-marked with the symbol ®.

Firms that try to protect a brand in a foreign country frequently encounter problems. In many foreign countries, brand registration is not possible; the first firm to use a brand in such a country has the rights to it. In some instances, a company actually has had to buy its own brand rights from a firm in a foreign country because the foreign firm was the first user in that country.

Marketers trying to protect their brands must also contend with brand counterfeiting. In many countries, for instance, one can purchase fake General Motors parts, Cartier watches, Yves St Laurent perfume, Walt Disney character dolls, and a host of other products that are illegally marketed by manufacturers that do not own the brands. Many counterfeit products are manufactured overseas—in South Korea or Taiwan, for example—but some are counterfeited in the countries in which they are sold. The International Anti-Counterfeiting Coalition estimates that roughly $60 billion in annual world trade involves counterfeit merchandise. The sale of this merchandise, obviously, reduces the brand owners' revenues from marketing their own legitimate products.

Brand counterfeiting is particularly harmful because the usually inferior counterfeit product undermines consumers' confidence in the brand and their loyalty to it. After unknowingly purchasing a counterfeit product, the buyer may blame the legitimate manufacturer if the product is of low quality or—even worse—if its use results in damage or injury. Since the counterfeiting problem has grown so serious, many firms are taking legal action against counterfeiters. Others have adopted such measures as modifying the product or the packaging to make counterfeit items easier to detect, conducting public awareness campaigns, and monitoring distributors to ensure that they stock only legitimate brands.[12]

■ **Branding Policies**

Before it establishes branding policies, a firm must first decide whether to brand its products at all. If a company's product is homogeneous and similar to competitors' products, it may be difficult to brand. Raw materials, such as coal, sand, and farm produce, are hard to brand because of the homogeneity of such products and their physical characteristics.

Some marketers of traditionally branded products have embarked on a policy of not branding, often called generic branding. A **generic brand** indicates only the product category (such as aluminium foil) and displays legally required labelling but does not include the company name or other identifying terms. Supermarkets that sell generic brands often price them lower than their comparable own-label items. Purchasers of generic-brand grocery items tend to be concentrated in middle-income, large households that are price conscious and predisposed to select regularly low-priced alternatives, as opposed to temporarily lower-priced products.[13] Although at one time generic brands, e.g. Tesco's Yellow Pack, may have represented as much as 5 percent of all grocery sales, today they account for less than 1 percent.

If a firm chooses to brand its products, it may opt for one or more of the following branding policies: individual, overall family, line family, and brand-extension branding. **Individual branding** is a policy of naming each product differently. As mentioned earlier, Procter & Gamble relies on an individual branding policy for its line of detergents, which includes Tide, Bold, Dash, Cheer, and Oxydol. A major advantage of individual branding is that if an organisation introduces a poor product, the negative images associated with it do not contaminate the company's other products. An individual branding policy may also facilitate market segmentation when a firm wishes to enter many segments of the same market. Separate, unrelated names can be used, and each brand can be aimed at a specific segment.

In **overall family branding**, all of a firm's products are branded with the same name or at least part of the name, such as Kraft and Heinz. Unlike individual branding, overall family branding means that the promotion of one item with the family brand promotes the firm's other products.

Sometimes an organisation uses family branding only for products within a single line. This policy is called **line family branding**. Colgate-Palmolive, for example, produces a line of cleaning products that includes a cleanser, a powdered detergent, and a liquid cleaner, all under the name Ajax. Colgate also produces several brands of toothpaste, none of which carries the Ajax brand.

Brand-extension branding occurs when a firm uses one of its existing brand names as part of a brand for an improved or new product that is usually in the same

12. Ronald F. Bush, Peter H. Bloch, and Scott Dawson, "Remedies for Product Counterfeiting," *Business Horizons,* January-February 1989, pp. 59–65; Pete Engardio, with Todd Vogel and Dinah Lee, "Companies Are Knocking off the Knockoff Outfits," *Business Week,* 26 Sept. 1988, pp. 86–88; and Michael Harvey, "A New Way to Combat Product Counterfeiting," *Business Horizons,* July-August 1988, pp. 19–28.

13. Martha R. McEnally and Jon M. Hawes, "The Market for Generic Brand Grocery Products: A Review and Extension," *Journal of Marketing,* Winter 1984, pp. 75–83.

product category as the existing brand. The makers of Arrid deodorant eventually extended the name Arrid to Arrid Extra-Dry and Arrid Double-X. In the U.K., Lever Brothers has launched a full range of household cleaners under its Domestos bleach brand name. There is one major difference between line family branding and brand-extension branding. With line family branding, all products in the line carry the same name, but with brand-extension branding, this is not the case. The producer of Arrid deodorant, for example, also makes other brands of deodorants. Line family branding and brand-extension branding are both popular.

An organisation is not limited to a single branding policy. Instead, branding policy is influenced by the number of products and product lines the company produces, the characteristics of its target markets, the number and types of competing products available, and the size of its resources. Anheuser-Busch, for example, uses both individual and brand-extension branding. Most of its brands are individual brands; however, the Michelob Light brand is an extension of the Michelob brand.

■ Brand Licensing

A recent trend in branding strategies involves the licensing of trademarks. By means of a licensing agreement, a company may permit approved manufacturers to use its trademark on other products for a licensing fee. Royalties may be as low as 2 percent of wholesale revenues or better than 10 percent. The licensee is responsible for all manufacturing, selling, and advertising functions and bears the costs if the licensed product fails. Not long ago, only a few firms licensed their corporate trademarks but today licensing is a multibillion-dollar business, and it is growing. Harley-Davidson, for example, has authorised the use of its name on non-motorcycle products such as cologne, wine coolers, gold rings, and shirts. McDonald's has licensed a line of children's sportswear, called McKids, to Sears in the U.S.A.

The advantages of licensing range from extra revenues and low cost to free publicity, new images, and trade mark protection. For example, Coca-Cola has licensed its trade mark for use on glassware, radios, trucks, and clothing in the hope of protecting its trade mark. Similarly, Jaguar has licensed a range of leisurewear. However, brand licensing is not without drawbacks. The major ones are a lack of manufacturing control, which could hurt the company's name, and bombarding consumers with too many unrelated products bearing the same name. Licensing arrangements can also fail because of poor timing, inappropriate distribution channels, or mismatching of product and name.

PACKAGING

Packaging involves the development of a container and a graphic design for a product. A package can be a vital part of a product, making it more versatile, safer, or easier to use. Like a brand name, a package can influence customers' attitudes towards a product and so affect their purchase decisions. For example, several producers of sauces and ketchups have packaged their products in squeezable containers to make use and storage more convenient. Package characteristics help shape buyers' impressions of a product at the time of purchase or during use. In this section we examine the main functions of packaging and consider several major packaging decisions. We also analyse the role of the package in a marketing strategy.

■ Packaging Functions

Effective packaging means more than simply putting products in containers and covering them with wrappers. First of all, packaging materials serve the basic purpose of protecting the product and maintaining its functional form. Fluids such as milk, orange juice, and hair spray need packages that preserve and protect them; the packaging should prevent damage that could affect the product's usefulness and increase costs. Since product tampering has become a problem for marketers of many types of goods, several packaging techniques have been developed to counter this danger. Some packages are also designed to foil shoplifting.

Another function of packaging is to offer convenience for consumers. For example, small sealed packages—individual-sized boxes or plastic bags that contain liquids and do not require refrigeration—strongly appeal to children and young adults with active lifestyles. The size or shape of a package may relate to the product's storage, convenience of use, or replacement rate. Small, single-serving cans of vegetables, for instance, may prevent waste and make storage easier. A third function of packaging is to promote a product by communicating its features, uses, benefits, and image. At times, a re-usable package is developed to make the product more desirable. For example, ice-cream containers can be re-used for food storage.

■ Major Packaging Considerations

As they develop packages, marketers must take many factors into account. Obviously, one major consideration is cost. Although a variety of packaging materials, processes, and designs are available, some are rather expensive. In recent years, buyers have shown a willingness to pay more for improved packaging, but there are limits. Marketers should try to determine, through research, just how much customers are willing to pay for packages.

As already mentioned, developing tamper-resistant packaging is very important. Although no package is "tamper-proof", marketers can develop packages that are difficult to tamper with and which also make any tampering evident to resellers and consumers. Because new, safer packaging technologies are being explored, marketers should be aware of changes in packaging technology and legislation and be prepared to make modifications that will ensure consumer safety. One packaging innovation includes an inner pouch that displays the word "open" when air has entered the pouch after opening. Marketers also have an obligation to inform the public of the possibilities and risks of product tampering by educating consumers on how to recognise possible tampering and by placing warnings on packaging.[14] For example, baby food manufacturers such as Cow and Gate and Heinz use a special metal jar top with a pop-up disc which shows when the jar has been opened. Consumers are expressly warned to watch out for this. Although effective tamper-resistant packaging may be expensive to develop, when balanced against the costs of lost sales, loss of consumer confidence and company reputation, and potentially expensive product liability lawsuits, the costs of ensuring consumer safety are minimal.[15]

Marketers must also decide whether to package the product singly or in multiple units. Multiple packaging is likely to increase demand because it increases the amount of the product available at the point of consumption (in one's home, for

14. Fred W. Morgan, "Tampered Goods: Legal Developments and Marketing Guidelines," *Journal of Marketing*, April 1988, pp. 86–96.

15. Ibid.

example). However, multiple packaging does not work for infrequently used products because buyers do not like to tie up their disposable income in an excess supply or store these products for a long time. Multiple packaging can, however, make products easier to handle and store (as in the case of six-packs used for soft drinks); it can also facilitate special price offers, such as a two-for-one sale. In addition, multiple packaging may increase consumer acceptance of a product by encouraging the buyer to try it several times. On the other hand, because they must buy several units, customers may hesitate to try the product at all.

Marketers should consider how much consistency is desirable among an organisation's package designs. No consistency may be the best policy, especially if a firm's products are unrelated or aimed at vastly different target markets. To promote an overall company image, a firm may decide that all packages are to be similar or include one major element of the design. This approach is called **family packaging**. Sometimes it is used only for lines of products, as with Campbell soups, Weight Watchers' foods, and Planters nuts.

A package's promotional role is an important consideration. Through verbal and non-verbal symbols, the package can inform potential buyers about the product's content, features, uses, advantages, and hazards. A firm can create desirable images and associations by its choice of colour, design, shape, and texture. Many cosmetics manufacturers, for example, design their packages to create impressions of richness, luxury, and exclusiveness. A package performs a promotional function when it is designed to be safer or more convenient to use, if such characteristics help stimulate demand.

To develop a package that has a definite promotional value, a designer must consider size, shape, texture, colour, and graphics. Beyond the obvious limitation that the package must be large enough to hold the product, a package can be designed to appear taller or shorter. For instance, thin vertical lines make a package look taller; wide horizontal stripes make it look shorter. A marketer may want a package to appear taller because many people perceive something that is taller as being larger.

Colours on packages are often chosen to attract attention. People associate specific colours with certain feelings and experiences. Red, for example, is linked with fire, blood, danger, and anger; yellow suggests sunlight, caution, warmth, and vitality; blue can imply coldness, sky, water, and sadness.[16] When selecting packaging colours, marketers must decide whether a particular colour will evoke positive or negative feelings when it is linked to a specific product. Recent interest in protecting the environment has increased the popularity of green packaging, for example. Marketers must also decide whether a specific target market will respond favourably or unfavourably to a particular colour. Cosmetics for women are more likely to be sold in pastel packaging than are personal-care products for men. Packages designed to appeal to children often use primary colours and bold designs.

Packaging must also meet the needs of middlemen. Wholesalers and retailers consider whether a package facilitates transportation, storage, and handling. Resellers may refuse to carry certain products if their packages are cumbersome.

A final consideration is whether to develop packages that are environmentally responsible. In the U.S.A., a Cable News Network report on the growing waste disposal problem stated that nearly 50 percent of all refuse consists of discarded

---

16. James U. McNeal, *Consumer Behavior: An Integrative Approach* (Boston: Little, Brown, 1982), pp. 221–222.

plastic packaging, such as Styrofoam containers, plastic soft-drink bottles, carrier bags, and other packaging.[17] Plastic packaging material does not biodegrade, and paper requires the destruction of valuable forest lands. Consequently, a number of companies are exploring packaging alternatives; they are also recycling more materials. McDonald's is recycling its foam sandwich containers; H. J. Heinz is looking for alternatives to its plastic ketchup squeeze bottles; Procter & Gamble markets Downy fabric softener in concentrated form, which requires less packaging than the ready-to-use version. However, sales of concentrated Downy have been poor, and customers do not like Wendy's new paper plates and coffee cups; they prefer the old non-degradable foam ones. Other companies searching for alternatives to environmentally harmful packaging have experienced similar problems.[18] Thus marketers must carefully balance society's desires to preserve the environment against consumers' desires for convenience.

■ **Packaging and Marketing Strategy**

Packaging can be a major component of a marketing strategy. A unique cap or closure, a better box or wrapper, or a more convenient container may give a firm a competitive edge. As shown in Figure 7.9, Del Monte's Yogurt Cup, packaged in an airtight, pop-top, single-serving container, needs no refrigeration. Since it is targeted at children, the package has been designed to go wherever they go. Manufacturers of beer, detergents, and most packaged foods spend a great deal of money to research consumers' reactions to packages. In the case of established brands, marketers must evaluate and change package designs to keep them looking stylish and up-to-date. For example, Procter & Gamble re-packaged its dominant Fairy Liquid dishwashing detergent with a drip-free cap and stressed its biodegradable ingredients.

As package designs improve, it becomes harder for any one product to dominate because of packaging. However, marketers still attempt to gain a competitive edge through packaging. Skilled artists and package designers, who have experience in marketing research, test packaging to see what sells well, not just what is aesthetically appealing. Since the typical large store stocks fifteen thousand items or more, products that stand out are more likely to be bought.

LABELLING

Labelling too is an important dimension relating to packaging, for both promotional and informational reasons and for legal reasons. The food and drug administrations and consumer protection agencies in different countries have varying requirements in terms of warnings, instructions, certifications, and manufacturer's identifications. Increasingly, however, the EC is demanding similar standards in all member countries. Despite the fact that consumers have responded favourably to the inclusion of this type of information on labels, evidence as to whether they actually use it has been mixed. Several studies indicate that consumers do not use nutritional information, whereas other studies indicate that the information is useful. Labels can also promote a manufacturer's other products or encourage proper use of products and therefore greater satisfaction with them.

17. "Not in My Backyard," CNN Special Report, Cable News Network, 19 Dec. 1988.

18. Alecia Swasy, "Ecology and Buyer Wants Don't Jibe," *Wall Street Journal*, 23 Aug. 1989, p. B1.

FIGURE 7.9

Strategic packaging.
Del Monte uses a single-serving, airtight, pop-top package that needs no refrigeration for its Yogurt Cup product.

SOURCE: Reprinted with permission of Del Monte Corporation

Colour and eye-catching graphics on labels overcome the jumble of words—known to designers as "mouse print"—that have been added to satisfy government regulations. Because so many similar products are available, an attention-getting device, or "silent salesperson", is needed to attract interest. As one of the most visible parts of a product, the label is an important element in the marketing mix.

OTHER PRODUCT-RELATED CHARACTERISTICS

When developing products, marketers make many decisions. Some of these decisions involve the physical characteristics of the product; others focus on less tangible support services that are very much a part of the total product.

■ Physical Characteristics of the Product

A crucial question that arises during product development is how much quality to build into the product. A major dimension of quality is durability. Higher quality often demands better materials and more expensive processing, which increase production costs and, ultimately, the product's price. In determining the specific level of quality, a marketer must ascertain approximately what price the target market views as acceptable. In addition, a marketer usually tries to set a level for a specific product that is consistent with the firm's other products that carry a similar brand. Obviously, the quality of competing brands is another consideration.

A product's physical features require careful consideration by marketers and by those in research and development. Product development personnel at Gillette spent considerable resources dealing with the Sensor Razor's physical features (see Marketing Update 7.3). The prime basis for decisions about the physical features should be the needs and wants of the target market. If marketers do not know what physical features people in the target market want in a product, it is highly unlikely that the product will be satisfactory. Even a firm whose existing products have been designed to satisfy target market desires should continue to assess these desires periodically to determine whether they have changed enough to require alterations in the product.

■ **Supportive Product-Related Services**

All products, whether they are goods or not, possess intangible qualities. "When prospective customers can't experience the product in advance, they are asked to buy what are essentially promises—promises of satisfaction. Even tangible, testable, feelable, smellable products are, before they're bought, largely just promises."[19] Here we briefly discuss three product-related services: guarantees, repairs and replacements, and credit. There are of course many other product-related services and product intangibles.

The type of guarantee a firm provides can be a critical issue for buyers, especially when expensive, technically complex goods such as appliances are involved. A **guarantee** specifies what the producer will do if the product malfunctions. For example, Draperite home furnishings offers a money-back guarantee (as shown in Figure 7.10). In recent years, government actions have required a guarantor to state more simply and specifically the terms and conditions under which the firm will take action. Because guarantees must be more precise today, marketers are using them more vigorously as tools to give their brands a competitive advantage. Washing machine manufacturers, like Hoover, for example, are increasingly using guarantees as a competitive tool by providing longer periods of guarantee protection.

Although it is more difficult to provide guarantees for services than for goods, some service marketers do guarantee customer satisfaction. An effective service guarantee should be unconditional, easy to understand and communicate, meaningful, easy to invoke, and easy and quick to collect on. The retailer John Lewis Partnership guarantees 100 percent satisfaction in every way. The customer can return a product and get a replacement, a refund, or a credit for the returned good. Photographic processors such as SupaSnaps offer free processing on prints not ready within 24 hours. Such guarantees of satisfying the customer are beneficial because they force the service provider to focus on customers' definitions of good service. They also provide clear performance standards, generate feedback from customers on the quality of the service, and help build customer loyalty and sales.[20]

19. Theodore Levitt, "Marketing Intangible Products and Product Intangibles," *Harvard Business Review,* May-June 1981, p. 96.

20. Christopher W. L. Hart, "The Power of Unconditional Service Guarantees," *Harvard Business Review,* July-August 1988, pp. 54–62.

FIGURE 7.10
A guarantee.
Draperite offers a
money-back guarantee
of satisfaction with its
product.

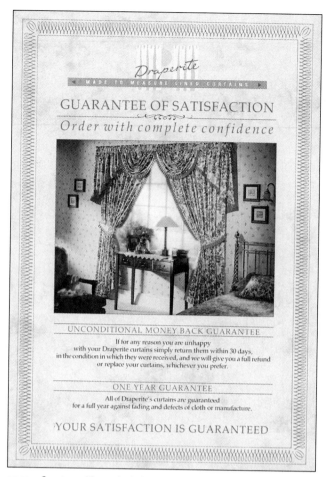

SOURCE: Courtesy of Draperite Ltd.

A marketer must also be concerned with establishing a system to provide replacement parts and repair services. This support service is especially important for expensive, complex industrial products that buyers expect to last a long time. Although the producer may furnish these services directly to buyers, it is more common for the producer to provide such services through regional service centres or middlemen. Regardless of how services are provided, it is important to customers that they be performed quickly and correctly.

Finally, a firm must sometimes provide credit services to customers. Even though credit services place a financial burden on an organisation, they can yield several benefits. One of them is that a firm may acquire and maintain a stable market share. Many major oil companies, for example, have competed effectively against petrol discounters by providing credit services. For marketers of relatively expensive items, offering credit services enables a larger number of people to buy the product, thus enlarging the market for the item. Another reason for offering credit services is to earn interest income from customers. The types of credit services offered depend on the characteristics of target market members, the firm's financial resources, the type of products sold, and the types of credit services that competitors offer.

DEVELOPMENT OF GILLETTE'S SENSOR RAZOR

If early sales figures are any indication, Gillette Company's high-tech razor, the Sensor, is a shaving sensation. Gillette has already invested 13 years, an estimated $200 million in research and development, and another $110 million on first-year television and print advertisement campaigns to launch the new product. Clearly, it's important that the $3.75 razor (a five-pack of cartridges costs about $3.79), or "shaving system", performs well to justify these high costs. Although some Gillette executives had been hesitant about making such a large investment (because its existing razors were already so profitable), so far Gillette's gamble seems justified. After the Sensor's initial advertising blitz, Gillette's production wasn't even able to keep pace with retailers' demands as Sensors quickly disappeared off shop shelves.

The Sensor is thought to be the most important product Gillette has ever introduced, as the company tries to regain the market share lost to disposable razors manufactured by Bic Corp. and other competitors. Gillette, which makes disposables as well, is the current market leader in North America and Europe, with about 67 percent of the entire shaver market. But because the gross profit on shaving systems is much higher than it is on disposable razors, Gillette is eager to build an increased interest in the Sensor and establish market dominance for itself.

In 1977, a Gillette design engineer came up with the concept of a shaving cartridge housing blades that would float on springs and thus follow the contours of a man's face, giving an extremely comfortable and close shave. Years later, Gillette assembled a nine-member Sensor task force that worked on the razor seven days a week for 15 months.

The resulting product is an engineering and manufacturing marvel. The Sensor's cartridge contains two ultra-thin blades that are fused to a supporting space bar by micro-lasers. The blades "float" on springs made out of a resin called Noryl, a strong material that keeps its bounce over time. The design's complexity makes it difficult for competitors to copy the cartridge.

SOURCES: Alison Fahey, "Gillette Readies Sensor," *Advertising Age,* 18 Sept. 1989, pp. 1, 81; Alison Fahey, "Sensor Sensation," *Advertising Age,* 5 Feb. 1990, pp. 4, 49; Keith Hammonds, "Do High-Tech Razors Have the Edge?" *Business Week,* 22 Jan. 1990, p. 83; and Keith Hammonds, "How a $4 Razor Ends Up Costing $300 Million," *Business Week,* 29 Jan. 1990, pp. 62–63.

SUMMARY

A product is everything, both favourable and unfavourable, that one receives in an exchange. It is a complex set of tangible and intangible attributes, including functional, social, and psychological utilities or benefits. A product can be an idea, a service, a good, or any combination of these three. When consumers purchase a product, they are buying the benefits and satisfaction that they think the product will provide.

Products can be classified on the basis of the buyer's intentions. Thus consumer products are those purchased to satisfy personal and family needs. Industrial products, on the other hand, are purchased for use in a firm's operations or to make other products. Consumer products can be subdivided into convenience, shopping, specialty, and unsought products. Industrial products can be divided into raw materials, major equipment, accessory equipment, component parts, process materials, consumable supplies, and industrial services.

A product item is a specific version of a product that can be designated as a distinct offering among an organisation's products. A product line is a group of closely related product items that are considered a unit because of marketing, technical, or end-use considerations. The composite, or total, group of products that an organisation makes available to customers is called the product mix. The depth of a product mix is measured by the number of different products offered in each product line. The width of the product mix is measured by the number of product lines a company offers.

The product life-cycle describes how product items in an industry move through (1) introduction, (2) growth, (3) maturity, and (4) decline. The life-cycle concept is used to make sure that the introduction, alteration, and termination of a product are timed and executed properly. The sales curve is at zero at introduction, rises at an increasing rate during growth, peaks at maturity, and then declines. Profits peak towards the end of the growth stage of the product life-cycle. The life expectancy of a product is based on buyers' wants, the availability of competing products, and other environmental conditions. Most businesses have a composite of life-cycle patterns for various products. It is important to manage existing products and develop new ones to keep the overall sales performance at a desired level.

A brand is a name, term, design, symbol, or any other feature that identifies one seller's good or service as distinct from those of other sellers. A brand name is that part of a brand which can be spoken; the element that cannot be spoken is called a brand mark. A trade mark is a legal designation indicating that the owner has exclusive use of a brand or a part of a brand and that others are prohibited by law from using it. A trade name is the legal name of an organisation. Branding can benefit both marketers and customers. A manufacturer brand is initiated by a producer and makes it possible for producers to be identified with their products at the point of purchase. An own-label brand is initiated and owned by a reseller. When selecting a brand, a marketer should choose one that is easy to say, spell, and recall and that alludes to the product's uses, benefits, or special characteristics. A generic brand indicates only the product category and does not include the company name or other identifying terms. Major branding policies are individual branding, overall family branding, line family branding, and brand-extension branding.

Packaging offers protection, economy, convenience, and promotion. When developing a package, marketers must consider packaging costs relative to the needs of target market members. There are other considerations as well: how to make packages tamper-resistant; whether to use multiple packaging and family packaging; how to design the package as an effective promotional tool; how best to accommodate middlemen; and whether to develop biodegradable packaging.

Labelling is an important aspect of packaging, for promotional, informational, and legal reasons. Various regulations and regulatory agencies can require that products be labelled or marked with warnings, instructions, certifications, and manufacturer's identifications.

When creating products, marketers must take into account other product-related considerations, such as physical characteristics and less tangible support services. Specific physical product characteristics that require attention are the level of quality, product features, textures, colours, and sizes. Support services that may be viewed as part of the total product include guarantees, repairs and replacements, and credit services.

IMPORTANT TERMS

Product	Width (of product mix)
Good	Product life-cycle
Service	Introduction stage
Ideas	Growth stage
Consumer products	Maturity stage
Industrial products	Decline stage
Convenience products	Brand
Shopping products	Brand name
Specialty products	Brand mark
Unsought products	Trade mark
Raw materials	Trade name
Major equipment	Manufacturer brands
Accessory equipment	Own-label brands
Component parts	Generic brand
Process materials	Individual branding
Consumable supplies	Overall family branding
MRO items	Line family branding
Industrial services	Brand-extension branding
Product item	Family packaging
Product line	Labelling
Product mix	Guarantee
Depth (of product mix)	

DISCUSSION AND REVIEW QUESTIONS

1. List the tangible and intangible attributes of a spiral notebook. Compare the benefits of the spiral notebook with those of an intangible product, such as life insurance.
2. A product has been referred to as a "psychological bundle of satisfaction". Is this a good definition of a product? Why or why not?

3. Is a roll of carpet in a shop a consumer product or an industrial product? Defend your answer.
4. How do convenience products and shopping products differ? What are the distinguishing characteristics of each type of product?
5. Would a stereo system that sells for £400 be a convenience, shopping, or specialty product?
6. In the category of industrial products, how do component parts differ from process materials?
7. How does an organisation's product mix relate to its development of a product line? When should an enterprise add depth to its product lines rather than width to its product mix?
8. How do industry profits change as a product moves through the four stages of its life-cycle?
9. What is the relationship between the concepts of product mix and product life-cycle?
10. What is the difference between a brand and a brand name? Compare and contrast the terms *brand mark* and *trade mark*.
11. How does branding benefit an organisation?
12. What are the distinguishing characteristics of own-label brands?
13. Given the competition between own-label brands and manufacturer brands, should manufacturers be concerned about the popularity of own-label brands? How should manufacturers fight back in the brand battle?
14. The brand name Xerox is sometimes used generically to refer to photocopying machines. How can Xerox Corporation protect this brand name?
15. Identify and explain the four major branding policies and give examples of each. Can a firm use more than one policy at a time? Explain your answer.
16. Describe the functions that a package can perform. Which function is most important? Why?
17. Why is the determination of a product's quality level an important decision? What major factors affect this decision?

■ CASES

7.1   Kodak's Disposable Cameras

Eastman Kodak, one of the world's leading photographic companies, makes innovation part of its everyday company strategy. Recently, Kodak introduced a line of single-use, or disposable, cameras. These cameras are very simple to operate: all one needs to do is aim and push a button. There are no adjustments for light level, exposure time, or focusing. After shooting all the exposures, the customer hands in the entire camera to the film processor. Depending on the model, these cameras retail from $8.35 for the Fling, to around $14 for the more specialised models. One model is a modified wide-angle camera; another can take pictures up to twelve feet underwater. They all use 35mm colour film.

Very inexpensive to produce, these cameras are basically just a roll of film in an encasement of plastic that has an elementary lens on the front and a minimum of internal parts. Kodak executives hope that the disposable cameras (Kodak prefers the name "single-use" cameras) will become highly profitable.

The idea for the waterproof disposable camera emerged from a Kodak engineer's rafting trip that exposed his camera equipment to water damage. In this model, Weekend 35, the ultrasonically sealed plastic outer body protects the camera's internal parts and film from sand and dirt, as well as from water, snow, and rain. Since Kodak engineers originally designed the disposable prototype on a three-dimensional computer-aided system, they found it fairly easy to devise a waterproof disposable and perfect their new design on a computer terminal. They even contrived a special viewfinder suitable for use with a scuba mask.

The Stretch, Kodak's disposable panoramic camera, came into existence because of a consumer's frustration in attempting to photograph the Grand Canyon. Already having a lens that was capable of producing extra-wide photos, Kodak engineers built a camera around it.

Kodak management targets the cameras at several different groups. The first segment consists of children who are just learning about photography. The company views the disposables as ideal "starter" cameras: they are easy to use and the photographer is almost guaranteed an acceptable print. Youngsters might not be able to afford more expensive cameras, and their parents are spared the agony of thinking what a $300 model will look like after an enthusiastic child gets through with it.

Another target is the impulse buyer, who might spot the camera on the way out of a supermarket. The impulse buyer might want the disposable camera because it could be ready for special occasions, such as a spontaneous picnic or sporting event. According to Kodak marketers, serious or professional photographers might also be interested in owning a low-cost camera when a particular assignment might put expensive equipment in jeopardy. Smaller disposable cameras are also easy to carry around. Still others who might opt for one of the disposable models are tourists or travellers who simply forget their cameras. However, forgetful individuals should beware: a disposable camera can cost twice as much as a roll of film.

SOURCES: "Kodak Develops Cameras for the Young and Forgetful," *Machine Design*, 7 Apr. 1988, p. 18; Leslie Helm, "Playing Leapfrog in Disposable Cameras," *Business Week*, 1 May 1989, p. 34; Francesca Lunzer Kritz, "Cameras for Forgetful Snapshooters," *U.S. News & World Report*, 10 July 1989, pp. 58–59; "New Products from Kodak," *New York Times*, 19 Apr. 1989, p. D4; Dan Richards, "Kodak's Wild Disposables are Wide and Wet; Fuji's is a Tele!" *Popular Photography*, July 1989, pp. 26, 85, 95.

Questions for Discussion

1. Does the addition of disposable cameras to Kodak's product mix add depth, width, or both of these dimensions to this product mix?
2. If Kodak's executives decided to use a common brand name for all three of its disposable cameras, what brand name would you propose? Explain.
3. To what degree, if any, does the sale of disposable cameras reduce or cut into the sales of Kodak's other cameras?

7.2 Disney Expands Its Product Mix

After the death of its founder, Walt Disney, in 1966, the Walt Disney Company seemed to lose its creative edge. As other studios diversified into television and video, Disney seemed content with its library of feature films and animated classics. The company was producing only three or four new movies a year, most of which failed at the box office. Disney also pulled out of television after twenty-nine years of network programming. By the mid-1980s, Disney was dependent on theme parks and real estate development for about 75 percent of its revenues.

Today, however, Disney executives are intent on recapturing—and building on—the old Disney magic. Company executives say the Disney name, culture, movies, and library are the company's biggest resources, and Disney's plan is to simultaneously rejuvenate old assets and develop new ones. While continuing its traditional appeal to the family segment of the movie market, Disney, through its Touchstone Pictures division, is turning out films for adult audiences as well. The company is releasing both old and new programmes for television syndication and testing new promotional and licensing projects. In addition, the Disney theme park has been exported. The Tokyo Disneyland is attracting millions of people a year, and a $2 billion Euro Disneyland is scheduled to open near Paris in 1992. Disney's overall strategy is to channel the company's revived creativity into improved theme parks, to use the parks to generate interest in Disney films, and to promote both parks and merchandise through Disney television shows.

Disney received its new lease on life a few years ago when threats of a corporate takeover prompted the company to replace its top executives. The new management moved quickly to tap the resources of the Disney television and film library. About two hundred Disney films and cartoon packages are now available on videocassette, and other classic films, such as *Snow White*, will now be released every five years instead of every seven. The studio plans to release one new animated movie for children every eighteen months and about a dozen adult films a year.

Disney is back on network television as well, with the return of the Disney Sunday Movie. The company also produces the comedy show "The Golden Girls", along with two top-rated Saturday morning cartoon shows. Following the lead of other studios, Disney has moved into television syndication by marketing packages of feature films, old cartoons, and "Wonderful World of Disney" programmes. The company is syndicating "The Disney Afternoon", a block of children's cartoons that will run from 3 to 5 P.M. New shows are also being produced for syndication. They include the popular game show "Win, Lose or Draw", a business news programme, and film reviews by Gene Siskel and Roger Ebert. In an otherwise flat cable television market, the number of subscribers to the family-orientated Disney Channel has jumped dramatically—to four million. The channel now offers twenty-four-hour features and more original programming than any other pay service. Disney has even signed an agreement with the Chinese government to broadcast a weekly television series starring Mickey Mouse and Donald Duck. The company may license the Chinese to produce Disney merchandise as well.

In the United States, too, marketing of Disney characters is receiving considerable emphasis. Recently, Mickey, Donald, and others visited hospital wards and marched in parades in a 120-city tour. Snow White and all seven dwarfs made a special appearance on the floor of the New York Stock Exchange to promote the celebration of Snow White's fiftieth birthday. Minnie Mouse now has a trendy new look and appears on clothing and watches and in a fashion doll line. Disney is also working with toy companies to develop new characters, such as Fluppy Dogs and Wuzzles, both of which will be sold in stores and featured in television shows. In addition, the company has opened non-tourist retail outlets. Located primarily in shopping malls, Disney stores carry both licensed products and exclusive theme park merchandise.

Disney's revitalised market presence has been credited with increasing attendance at the Disney theme parks to more than fifty million people. In Florida,

Disney has recently completed new hotels and a movie studio/tour attraction. Moreover, Disney is constructing a fifty-acre water park and adding $1.4 billion worth of new attractions to Walt Disney World. The company is also considering regional centres that would combine restaurants and shopping with evening entertainment.

Disney intends eventually to reduce the company's financial dependence on parks and hotels. The strategy is to triple the proportion of company profits from movies and television and to acquire such distribution outlets as movie theatres, television stations, and record companies. Recent business deals with Procter & Gamble Co., McDonald's Corp., Coca-Cola Co., Time Inc., M&M/Mars, and Sears, Roebuck and Co. will help increase Disney's profits and market presence still further.

SOURCES: Dudley Clendinen, "Disney's Mouse of Marketing," *New York Times,* 22 Nov. 1986, p. 41-L; Pamela Ellis-Simon, "Hi Ho, Hi Ho," *Marketing & Media Decisions,* September 1986, pp. 52–54; Andrea Gabor and Steve L. Hawkins, "Of Mice and Money in the Magic Kingdom," *U.S. News & World Report,* 22 Dec. 1986, pp. 44–46; Ronald Grover, "Disney's Magic," *Business Week,* 9 Mar. 1987, pp. 62–65; Scott Hume, "Sears Gains Exclusivity with Disney Contract," *Advertising Age,* 23 Nov. 1987, p. 63; Stephen Koepp, "Do You Believe in Magic?" *Time,* 25 Apr. 1988, pp. 66–76; Marcy Magiera, "Disney Tries Retailing," *Advertising Age,* 1 June 1987, p. 80; Myron Magnet, "Putting Magic Back in the Kingdom," *Fortune,* 5 Jan. 1987, p. 65; Raymond Roel, "Disney's Marketing Touch," *Direct Marketing,* January 1987, pp. 50–53; Stephen J. Sansweet, "Disney Co. Cartoons Are Going to China in Commercial Foray," *Wall Street Journal,* 23 Oct. 1986, p. 19; Susan Spillman, "Animation Draws on Its Storied Past," *USA Today,* 15 Nov. 1989, pp. 1B–2B; Wayne Walley, "Disney Enlists Time Inc., Mars to Honor Mickey," *Advertising Age,* 6 June 1988, pp. 3, 110; Wayne Walley, "P & G, Disney Link Videos, Products," *Advertising Age,* 18 Jan. 1988, p. 1; and Wayne Walley, "Roger Rabbit Makes Splash," *Advertising Age,* 27 June 1988, pp. 3, 110.

Questions for Discussion

1. Disney's product mix consists of many products. Does Disney have product lines? If so, what are they?
2. Disney labels many of its new films for adults as Touchstone Productions. With a famous name like Disney, why does the firm not use the Disney name?
3. Do the products in the Disney product mix have product life-cycles? Explain.

8 DEVELOPING AND MANAGING PRODUCTS

Objectives

To become aware of organisational alternatives for managing products

To understand the importance and role of product development in the marketing mix

To become aware of how existing products can be modified

To learn how product deletion can be used to improve product mixes

To gain insight into how businesses develop a product idea into a commercial product

To acquire knowledge about product positioning and the management of products during the various stages of the products' life cycles

T oy companies have introduced hundreds of dolls over the years, but there is only one Barbie. Ninety percent of all American girls between the ages of 3 and 11 own at least one and usually more. In the U.K., Barbie, the number one best-selling toy for Christmas 1990, or Sindy have a place in most girls' bedrooms. Other Mattel products have come and gone, but Barbie sales remain strong. In the toy industry, short-lived fads and complete failures are the norm. Thus, Mattel's successful management of Barbie, now over 30 years old, is a remarkable achievement.

Mattel has allowed Barbie to evolve along with the times—a difficult feat considering the amount of social change occurring since the doll's introduction in 1959. Barbie has become a model, a surgeon, an astronaut, and an aerobics instructor. However, Mattel has purposely not defined Barbie's personality, so that she can be anyone a child wants her to be. She drives a Corvette and a Ferrari and manages to adorn herself with the latest styles.

Mattel employs nine fashion designers and a staff of hair stylists to keep Barbie in vogue. Mattel fashion experts patrol malls and amusement parks to spot the latest fashion trends. Mattel designs all of Barbie's clothes and electronically transfers the designs to factories in Malaysia. Largely because of Barbie and her glamorous tastes, Mattel is the fourth biggest producer of women's garments in the United States.

To keep consumer interest high, Mattel has introduced numerous non-clothing accessories, including Barbie houses, furniture, cars, luggage, wigs, and appliances. Mattel has even provided Barbie with a social setting consisting of friend Midge and boyfriend Ken. Mattel's objective is to maintain high demand for Barbie by keeping her contemporary and by continuing to introduce Barbie-related products. ◆

Based on information in Patrick E. Cole, "Mattel Is Putting Its Dollhouse in Order," *Business Week*, 28 Aug. 1989, pp. 66–67; Barbara Kantrowitz, "Hot Date: Barbie and G.I. Joe," *Newsweek*, 20 Feb. 1989, p. 59; and Doug Stewart, "In the Cutthroat World of Toy Sales, Child's Play Is Serious Business," *Smithsonian*, December 1989, pp. 73–76, 78, 80–83; Delwyn Swingewood, "Fashion Dolls Locked in Fight for Sales," *The Independent on Sunday*, 23 December 1990, p. 15.

T o compete effectively and achieve its goals, an organisation such as Mattel must be able to adjust its product mix in response to changes in buyers' preferences. A firm often has to modify existing products, introduce new products, or eliminate products that were successful perhaps only a few years ago. These adjustments and the way a firm is organised to make them are facets of product management.

This chapter first examines how businesses are organised to develop and manage products. Then we look at several ways to improve a product mix, including modifying the quality, function, or style of products; deleting weak products; and developing new products. The process of developing a new product from idea generation to commercialisation is described in detail. We also examine product positioning—how marketers decide where a product should fit into the field of competing products and which benefits to emphasise. Finally, we consider issues and decisions associated with managing a product through the growth, maturity, and declining stages of its life cycle.

ORGANISING TO MANAGE PRODUCTS

A company must often manage a complex set of products, markets, or both. Often, too, it finds that the traditional functional form of organisation—in which managers specialise in business functions such as advertising, sales, and distribution—does not fit its needs. Consequently, management must find an organisational approach that accomplishes the tasks necessary to develop and manage products. Alternatives to functional organisation include the product manager approach, the market manager approach, and the venture team approach.

A **product manager** is responsible for a product, a product line, or several distinct products that make up an interrelated group within a multi-product organisation. A **brand manager**, on the other hand, is responsible for a single brand, for example, Maxwell House coffee or Persil washing powder. A product or brand manager operates cross-functionally to co-ordinate the activities, information, and strategies involved in marketing an assigned product. Product managers and brand managers plan marketing activities to achieve objectives by co-ordinating a mix of distribution, promotion (especially sales promotion and advertising), and price. They must consider packaging and branding decisions and work closely with personnel in research and development, engineering, and production. Marketing research helps product managers to understand consumers and find target markets. The product or brand manager approach to organisation is used by many large, multiple-product companies in the consumer package goods business.

A **marketing manager** is responsible for managing the marketing activities that serve a particular group or class of customers. This organisational approach is particularly effective when a firm engages in different types of marketing activities to provide products to diverse customer groups. A company might have one market manager for industrial markets and another for consumer markets. These broad market categories might be broken down into more limited market responsibilities.

A **venture** or **project team** is designed to create entirely new products that may be aimed at new markets. Unlike a product or marketing manager, a venture team is responsible for all aspects of a product's development: research and development, production and engineering, finance and accounting, and marketing. Venture teams work outside established divisions to create inventive approaches to new products and markets. As a result of this flexibility, new products can be developed to take advantage of opportunities in highly segmented markets.

The members of a venture team come from different functional areas of an organisation. When the commercial potential of a new product has been demonstrated, the members may return to their functional areas, or they may join a new or existing division to manage the product. The new product may be turned over to an existing division, a marketing manager, or a product manager. Innovative organisational forms such as venture teams are necessary for many companies, especially well-established firms operating primarily in mature markets. These companies must take a dual approach to marketing organisation. They must accommodate the management of mature products and also encourage the development of new ones.[1]

MANAGING THE PRODUCT MIX

To provide products that satisfy target markets and achieve the organisation's objectives, a marketer must develop, alter, and maintain an effective product mix (although seldom can the same product mix be effective for long). An organisation's product mix may need several types of adjustments. Because customers' attitudes and product preferences change, their desire for a product may wane. People's fashion preferences obviously change quite often, but their attitudes to and preferences for most products also change over time.

In some cases a company needs to alter its product mix for competitive reasons. A marketer may have to delete a product from the mix because a competitor dominates the market for that product. Similarly, a firm may have to introduce a new product or modify an existing one to compete more effectively. A marketer may expand a firm's product mix to take advantage of excess marketing and production capacity.

Regardless of the reasons for altering a product mix, the product mix must be managed. In strategic market planning, many marketers rely on the portfolio approach for managing the product mix. The **product portfolio approach** tries to create specific marketing strategies to achieve a balanced mix of products that will bring maximum profits in the long run. The most time-consuming task in a portfolio analysis is collecting data about the products and their performance along selected dimensions. This requires hard data from the company's marketing information system (MIS)—for instance, on sales, profitability, market share, and industry growth. We examine product portfolio models in Chapter 18 in the discussion of strategic market planning. Here we consider three major ways to improve a product mix: modifying an existing product, deleting a product, and developing a new product.

■ Modifying Existing Products

Product modification means changing one or more characteristics of a firm's product. It is most likely to be used in the maturity stage of the product life cycle, to give a firm's existing brand a competitive advantage. Altering a product mix this way entails less risk than developing a new product.

1. Roger C. Bennet and Robert G. Cooper, "The Product Life Cycle Trap," *Business Horizons*, September-October 1984, pp. 7–16.

Under certain conditions, product modification can indeed improve a firm's product mix. First, the product must be modifiable. Second, existing customers must be able to perceive that a modification has been made (assuming that the modified item is still aimed at them). Third, the modification should make the product more consistent with customers' desires so that it provides greater satisfaction. There are three major ways to modify products: quality modifications, functional modifications, and style modifications.

Quality Modifications.   **Quality modifications** are changes that relate to a product's dependability and durability. Usually, they are executed by altering the materials or the production process. Reducing a product's quality may allow an organisation to lower its price and direct the item at a larger target market.

By contrast, increasing the quality of a product may give a firm an advantage over competing brands. In fact, quality improvement has become a major tool for successfully competing with foreign marketers. Higher quality may enable a company to charge a higher price by creating customer loyalty and by lowering customer sensitivity to price. However, higher quality may require the use of more expensive components, less standardised production processes, and other manufacturing and management techniques that force a firm to charge higher prices.[2] Some firms, such as Rover, Volvo, and Caterpillar, are finding ways to both increase quality and reduce costs.

Functional Modifications.   Changes that affect a product's versatility, effectiveness, convenience, or safety are called **functional modifications**; they usually require that the product be redesigned. Typical product categories which have undergone considerable functional modifications include office and farm equipment, appliances and cleaning products. Procter & Gamble, as shown in Figure 8.1, modified Pampers and improved their effectiveness. Functional modifications can make a product useful to more people, which enlarges its market. This type of change can place a product in a favourable competitive position by providing benefits competing items do not offer. Functional modifications can also help an organisation achieve and maintain a progressive image. At times, too, functional modifications are made to reduce the possibility of product liability claims.

Style Modifications.   **Style modifications** change the sensory appeal of a product by altering its taste, texture, sound, smell, or visual characteristics. In making a purchase decision a buyer is swayed by how a product looks, smells, tastes, feels, or sounds. Thus a style modification may strongly affect purchases. For years car makers have relied on style modifications.

Through style modifications, a firm can differentiate its product from competing brands and thus gain a sizeable market share. The major drawback in using style modifications is that their value is determined subjectively. Although a firm may strive to improve the product's style, customers may actually find the modified product less appealing.

■ **Deleting Products**

Generally, a product cannot satisfy target market customers and contribute to the achievement of an organisation's overall goals indefinitely. **Product deletion** is the process of eliminating a product that no longer satisfies a sufficient number of cus-

2. Lynn W. Phillips, Dae R. Chang, and Robert D. Buzzell, "Product Quality, Cost Position and Business Performance: A Test of Some Key Hypotheses," *Journal of Marketing*, Spring 1983, pp. 26–43.

FIGURE 8.1
Functional modification. Procter & Gamble employs functional improvement by making its nappies more absorbent.

E̲ver since Adam and Eve, boys and girls have been wet in different places.

High time for Pampers Boy and Girl.

Pampers Boy has a narrower design with more absorbency in front, where boys wet more.

Pampers Girl has a wider design with more absorbency in the middle, where girls wet more.

Of course, each has Pampers special lockaway core which helps keep wetness away from baby's skin, but now with more help where each needs it most.

The driest boy and girl is a Pampers Boy and Girl.

SOURCE: Procter & Gamble Ltd.

tomers. A declining product reduces an organisation's profitability and drains resources that could be used instead to modify other products or develop new ones. A marginal product may require shorter production runs, which can increase per-unit production costs. Finally, when a dying product completely loses favour with customers, the negative feelings may transfer to some of the company's other products.

Most organisations find it difficult to delete a product. It was probably a hard decision for Austin Rover to drop the TR7 sports car and admit that it was a failure. A decision to drop a product may be opposed by management and other employees who feel the product is necessary in the product mix. Salespeople who still have some loyal customers are especially upset when a product is dropped. Considerable resources and effort are sometimes spent trying to change the product's marketing mix to improve its sales and thus avoid having to delete it.

Some organisations delete products only after they have become heavy financial burdens. Robert Maxwell's newspaper, the London *Daily News*, closed after only a few weeks, having cost him £25 million in losses. A better approach is some form of systematic review in which each product is evaluated periodically to determine its impact on the overall effectiveness of the firm's product mix. Such a review should analyse a product's contribution to the firm's sales for a given period and include estimates of future sales, costs, and profits associated with the product. It should

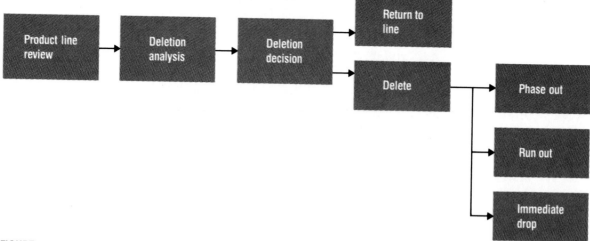

FIGURE 8.2 *Product deletion process*

SOURCE: Martin L. Bell, *Marketing: Concepts and Strategy,* 3rd ed., p. 267; copyright © 1979, Houghton Mifflin Company. Reproduced by permission of Mrs. Martin L. Bell.

also gauge the value of making changes in the marketing strategy to improve the product's performance. A systematic review allows an organisation to improve product performance and to ascertain when to delete products. Although many companies do systematically review their product mixes, a research study found that few companies have formal, written policies on the process of deleting products. The study also found that most companies based their decisions to delete weak products on poor sales and profit potential, low compatibility with the firms' business strategies, unfavourable market outlook, and historical declines in profitability.[3]

Basically, there are three ways of deleting a product: to phase it out, run it out, or drop it immediately (see Figure 8.2). A phase-out approach lets the product decline without a change in the marketing strategy. No attempt is made to give the product new life. A run-out policy exploits any strengths left in the product. Intensifying marketing efforts in core markets or eliminating some marketing expenditures, such as advertising, may cause a sudden spurt of profits. This approach is commonly taken for technologically obsolete products, such as older models of computers and calculators. Often the price is reduced to get a sales spurt. The third alternative, dropping an unprofitable product immediately, is the best strategy when losses are too great to prolong the product's life.

■ **Developing New Products**

Developing and introducing new products is frequently expensive and risky. Thousands of new consumer products are introduced annually, and, as indicated in Chapter 7, anywhere from 60 to 90 percent of them fail. Lack of research is a leading cause of new-product failure. Other often-cited causes are technical problems in design or production and errors in timing the product's introduction. Although new-product development is risky, so is failure to introduce new products. For example, the makers of Timex watches gained a large share of the watch market through effective marketing strategies during the 1960s and early 1970s. By 1983, Timex's market share had slipped considerably, in part because the company had

3. Douglas M. Lambert and Jay U. Sterling, "Identifying and Eliminating Weak Products," *Business,* July-September 1988, pp. 3–10.

FIGURE 8.3
A new product.
The Invergordon is an
example of a new
product.

SOURCE: Courtesy of The Invergordon Distillers Limited

failed to introduce new products. In recent times, however, Timex has introduced a number of new products and regained market share.

The term *new product* can have more than one meaning. A genuinely new product—as the video-recorder once was—offers innovative benefits. But products that are different and distinctly better are often viewed as new. The following items (listed in no particular order) are product innovations of the last thirty years: Post-It note-pads, disposable lighters, birth-control pills, personal computers, felt-tip pens, seat belts, disposable razors, compact disc players, quartz watches, and soft contact lenses. Thus, a new product can be an innovative variation on an existing product, such as The Invergordon shown in Figure 8.3. It can also be a product that a given firm has not marketed previously, although similar products may be available from other companies. The first company to introduce a video player, for example, clearly was launching a new product. However, if Boeing introduced a video player brand, this would also be viewed as a new product for Boeing because that organisation has not previously marketed video players.

Before a product is introduced, it goes through the six phases of **new-product development** shown in Figure 8.4: (1) idea generation, (2) screening, (3) business analysis, (4) product development, (5) test marketing, and (6) commercialisation. A product may be dropped, and many are, at any stage of development. In this section, we will look at the process through which products are developed, from the inception of an idea to a product offered for sale.

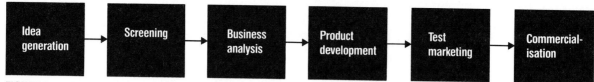

FIGURE 8.4 *Phases of new-product development*

Idea Generation.   Businesses and other organisations seek product ideas that will help them achieve their objectives. This activity is **idea generation**. The fact that only a few ideas are good enough to be commercially successful underscores the difficulty of the task. Although some organisations get their ideas almost by chance, firms that are trying to effectively manage their product mixes usually develop systematic approaches for generating new product ideas. At the heart of innovation is a purposeful, focused effort to identify new ways to serve a market. Unexpected occurrences, incongruities, new needs, industry and market changes, and demographic changes all may indicate new opportunities.[4]

New product ideas can come from several sources. They may come from internal sources—marketing managers, researchers, sales personnel, engineers, or other organisational personnel. Brainstorming and incentives or rewards for good ideas are typical intrafirm devices for stimulating the development of ideas. For example, the idea for 3M Post-It adhesive-backed yellow notes came from an employee. As a church choir member, he used slips of paper for marking songs in his hymn-book. Because the pieces of paper fell out, he suggested developing an adhesive-backed note.[5] Hewlett-Packard keeps its labs open to engineers twenty-four hours a day to help generate ideas; it also encourages its researchers to devote 10 percent of company time to exploring their own ideas for new products.[6]

New product ideas may also arise from sources outside the firm—customers, competitors, advertising agencies, management consultants, and private research organisations. Johnson & Johnson, for example, acquired the technology for its new clear orthodontic braces through a joint venture with Saphikon, the developer of the technology behind the braces.[7] Sometimes, potential buyers of a product are questioned in depth to discover what attributes would appeal to them. Asking weekend fishermen what they wanted in a sonar fish finder led Techsonic to develop its LCR (liquid crystal recorder) fish finder. In the U.S.A., annual sales of the LCR reached $31 million within one year. The practice of asking customers what they want from its products has helped Techsonic maintain its leadership in the industry.[8]

Screening Ideas.   In the process of **screening ideas**, those with the greatest potential are selected for further review. During screening, product ideas are analysed to determine whether they match the organisation's objectives and resources.

4. Peter F. Drucker, "The Discipline of Innovation," *Harvard Business Review,* May-June 1985, pp. 67–68.

5. Lawrence Ingrassia, "By Improving Scotch Paper, 3M Gets New Product Winner," *Wall Street Journal,* 31 Mar. 1983, p. 27.

6. Jonathan B. Levine, "Keeping New Ideas Kicking Around," *Business Week,* Innovation 1989 issue, p. 128.

7. Joseph Weber, "Going over the Lab Wall in Search of New Ideas," *Business Week,* Innovation 1989 issue, p. 132.

8. Joshua Hyatt, "Ask and You Shall Receive," *Inc.,* September 1989, pp. 90–101.

The company's overall ability to produce and market the product is also analysed. Other aspects of an idea that should be weighed are the nature and wants of buyers and possible environmental changes. Compared with other phases, the largest number of new product ideas are rejected during the idea-screening phase.

At times a checklist of new-product requirements is used when making screening decisions. It encourages evaluators to be systematic and so reduces the chances of their overlooking some fact. If a critical factor on the checklist remains unclear, the type of formal research described in Chapter 6 may be needed. To screen ideas properly, it may be necessary to test product concepts: a product concept and its benefits can be described or shown to consumers. Several product concepts may be tested to discover which might appeal most to a particular target market.

Business Analysis. During the **business analysis** stage, the product idea is evaluated to determine its potential contribution to the firm's sales, costs, and profits. In the course of a business analysis, evaluators ask a variety of questions: Does the product fit in with the organisation's existing product mix? Is demand strong enough to justify entering the market and will the demand endure? What types of environmental and competitive changes can be expected, and how will these changes affect the product's future sales, costs, and profits? Are the organisation's research, development, engineering, and production capabilities adequate? If new facilities must be constructed, how quickly can they be built and how much will they cost? Is the necessary financing for development and commercialisation on hand or obtainable at terms consistent with a favourable return on investment?

In the business analysis stage, firms seek market information. The results of consumer polls, along with secondary data, supply the specifics needed for estimating potential sales, costs, and profits. At this point, a research budget should explore the financial objectives and related considerations for the new product.

Product Development. **Product development** is the phase in which the organisation finds out if it is technically feasible to produce the product and if it can be produced at costs low enough to make the final price reasonable. To test its acceptability, the idea or concept is converted into a prototype, or working model. The prototype should reveal tangible and intangible attributes associated with the product in consumers' minds. The product's design, mechanical features, and intangible aspects must be linked to wants in the market-place. Failure to determine how consumers feel about the product and how they would use it may lead to the product's failure. For example, the Sinclair C5 electric buggy was developed as a serious on-road single-seater car, intended for city or country use. In reality, drivers felt too low to the ground and that they would be safer in heavy traffic on a bicycle. Campus students ended up using the remaining stocks as on-pavement runabouts. Testing to determine how consumers view the product idea is therefore very important in the product development stage. As indicated in Marketing Update 8.1, Fisher-Price spends considerable time and money on research and development associated with its new products.

The development phase of a new product is frequently lengthy and expensive; thus a relatively small number of product ideas are put into development. If the product appears sufficiently successful during this stage to merit test-marketing, then during the latter part of the development stage marketers begin to make decisions regarding branding, packaging, labelling, pricing, and promotion for use in the test-marketing stage.

FISHER-PRICE'S PRODUCT RESEARCH AND DEVELOPMENT

Fisher-Price, a division of Quaker Oats Co., takes toys very seriously: it runs a play laboratory to try to determine which new toys—its own and the competition's—will be the most popular with children. The play laboratory is part of an entire child research department at Fisher-Price where adults closely watch children at play. One-way mirrors hide researchers from the children, who frolic in a room filled with a large selection of toys. For Fisher-Price, the knowledge gained through this observation plays a major role in deciding which toys to place on the market.

The research and development personnel at Fisher-Price carefully examine how a child interacts with a toy, looking for a quality they term "play value". They see play value as the most important attribute of a new toy, as well as the most difficult to assess accurately.

Toy researchers make sure that toys can withstand rough handling. They analyse toys for potential hazards, such as hinges that might hurt small fingers or tiny parts that might pose a danger to very young children. Sometimes adult researchers are even called upon to chew toys to see if any parts come loose. New toys face strenuous and extensive safety testing. Every piece of a new toy, in addition to the finished product, is scientifically abused to ensure that it will be safe in the hands of a child.

Executives at Fisher-Price know that it is the toys themselves that will ultimately spell success or failure for the company. Consequently, Fisher-Price dedicates a large part of its budget to research and development and a large chunk of its time to watching children play.

SOURCES: Doug Stewart, "In the Cutthroat World of Toy Sales, Child's Play Is Serious Business," *Smithsonian,* December 1989, pp. 73–76, 78, 80–83; Mary Lynne Vellinga, "Fisher-Price," Rochester, New York, *Democrat and Chronicle,* 4 Apr. 1988; and David J. Wallace, "Fisher-Price Toys with TV," *Advertising Age,* 13 Feb. 1989, p. S-8.

Test-Marketing. A limited introduction of a product in geographic areas chosen to represent the intended market is called **test-marketing**. Its aim is to determine the reactions of probable buyers. For example, after McDonald's developed fried chicken products for its fast-food menu, it test-marketed the idea in certain McDonald's restaurants to find out how those customers felt about eating chicken at McDonald's.[9] (Marketing Update 8.2 details how McDonald's is test-marketing pizza.) Test-marketing is *not* an extension of the development stage; it is a sample launching of the entire marketing mix. Test-marketing should be conducted only after the product has gone through development and after initial plans regarding the other marketing mix variables have been made.

Companies of all sizes use test-marketing to lessen the risk of product failure. The dangers of introducing an untested product include undercutting already profitable products and, should the new product fail, loss of credibility with distributors and customers. Lever Brothers launched Wisk—previously only a washing powder—in liquid form in 1986. However, Lever had misjudged consumer usage. Many blocked machines later, P&G's liquid Ariel came with Arielettes, containers to be placed inside the machines together with the clothes. Reformulations have now overcome the problems with Wisk and its competitors.

Test-marketing provides several benefits. It lets marketers expose a product in a natural marketing environment to gauge its sales performance. While the product is being marketed in a limited area, the company can seek to identify weaknesses in the product or in other parts of the marketing mix. A product weakness discovered after a nationwide introduction can be expensive to correct. Moreover, if consumers' early reactions are negative, marketers may not be able to persuade consumers to try the product again. Thus making adjustments after test-marketing can be crucial to the success of a new product. Test-marketing also allows marketers to experiment with variations in advertising, price, and packaging in different test areas and to measure the extent of brand awareness, brand switching, and repeat purchases that result from alterations in the marketing mix.

The accuracy of test-marketing results often hinges on where the tests are conducted. Selection of appropriate test areas is very important. The validity of test-market results depends heavily on selecting test sites that provide accurate representation of the intended target market. The criteria used for choosing test cities or television regions depend on the product's characteristics, the target market's characteristics, and the firm's objectives and resources. Even though the selection criteria will vary from one company to another, the kind of questions that Table 8.1 presents can be helpful in assessing a potential test market.

Test-marketing is not without risks, however. Not only is it expensive, but also a firm's competitors may try to interfere. A competitor may attempt to "jam" the test programme by increasing advertising or promotions, lowering prices, and offering special incentives—all to combat the recognition and purchase of a new brand. Any such devices can invalidate test results. Sometimes, too, competitors copy the product in the testing stage and rush to introduce a similar product. It is therefore desirable to move quickly and commercialise as soon as possible after testing.

Because of these risks, many companies are using alternative methods to gauge consumer preferences. One such method is simulated test-marketing. Typically, consumers at shopping centres are asked to view an advertisement for a new product and given a free sample to take home. These consumers are subsequently

9. "Winging It at McDonald's," *USA Today,* 5 Sept. 1989, p. 1B.

TABLE 8.1

Questions to consider when choosing test markets

1. Is the area typical of planned distribution outlets?
2. Is the city relatively isolated from other cities?
3. What local media are available, and are they co-operative?
4. Does the area have a dominant television station? Does it have multiple newspapers, magazines, and radio stations?
5. Does the city contain a diversified cross-section of ages, religions, and cultural/societal preferences?
6. Are the purchasing habits atypical?
7. Is the city's per capita income typical?
8. Does the city have a good record as a test city?
9. Would testing efforts be easily "jammed" by competitors?
10. Does the city have stable year-round sales?
11. Are retailers who will co-operate available?
12. Are research and audit services available?
13. Is the area free from unusual influences, such as one industry's dominance or heavy tourist traffic?

SOURCE: Adapted from "A Checklist for Selecting Test Markets," copyright 1982 *Sales & Marketing Management.* Reprinted by permission of Sales & Marketing Management.

interviewed over the phone and asked to rate the product. The major advantages of simulated test-marketing are lower costs and tighter security, which reduces the flow of information to competitors and eliminates jamming. Scanner-based test-marketing is another, more sophisticated version of the traditional test-marketing method.[10] Some marketing research firms, such as A. C. Nielsen Company, offer test-marketing services to help provide independent assessment of products.

Commercialisation. During the **commercialisation** phase, plans for full-scale manufacturing and marketing must be refined and settled, and budgets for the project must be prepared. Early in the commercialisation phase, marketing management analyses the results of test-marketing to find out what changes in the marketing mix are needed before the product is introduced. For example, the results of test-marketing may tell the marketers to change one or more of the product's physical attributes, modify the distribution plans to include more retail outlets, alter promotional efforts, or change the product's price. However, as more and more changes are made based on test-marketing findings, the test-marketing projections may become less valid.

During this phase, the organisation also has to gear up for production. Consequently, it may face sizeable capital expenditures for plant and equipment and may need to hire additional personnel.

The product enters the market during the commercialisation phase. When introducing a product, marketers often spend enormous sums of money for advertising, personal selling, and other types of promotion. These expenses, together with capital outlays, can make commercialisation extremely costly; such expenditures may not be recovered for several years. For example, when Guinness introduced Kaliber

10. Eleanor Johnson Tracy, "Testing Time for Test Marketing," *Fortune,* 29 Oct. 1984, pp. 75–76.

TEST MARKETING MCDONALD'S PIZZA

Eager to take a bigger bite out of the dinner market, McDonald's is trying to offer other items besides its traditional burgers, French fries, and Chicken McNuggets. Executives of the franchise giant, which is based in Oak Brook, Illinois, think that pizza might bring in more afternoon and early evening traffic —the slowest sales period for McDonald's—as well as more revenue. Pizza is a $20-billion-a-year industry that keeps growing.

Several years ago, McDonald's experimented with mini pizzas designed for individual meals but decided to terminate the "McPizzas" after they did not perform well in test marketing. The new pizzas, called McDonald's Pizzas, are full-sized, fourteen-inch pizzas. Sold only after 4 P.M., they come in four varieties, with prices ranging from $6 to $10. Customers in test-market cities may choose from among cheese, sausage, pepperoni, or "deluxe" types. McDonald's will not sell pizza by the slice. The company is test marketing the pizzas in and around Evansville, Indiana, and in some cities in Kentucky. Around Evansville, owners of local pizza parlours are concerned about the new competition.

Unlike the McPizzas, McDonald's new pizzas are made from fresh ingredients and baked to order. They can also be baked and served very fast. Since McDonald's customers get their Big Macs almost instantaneously, the company's management worried about the reaction to a long wait for a pizza. This problem was solved by developing a special superfast oven that bakes a pizza in five and a half minutes. A McDonald's spokesperson pointed out that the company wants to maintain its reputation for quick service and that a five- or six-minute wait is still extremely fast service for a pizza.

Test marketing results for the new product have been favourable. However, McDonald's, true to its character of being very cautious when introducing new products, has no current plans to offer pizza in every one of its eight thousand outlets across the United States or in Europe. It is taking a wait-and-see approach. Thus consumers outside the test area may not taste McDonald's pizza for a very long time—if ever. After all, McDonald's test marketed its now popular salads for twelve years.

SOURCES: Stuart Elliott, "McDonald's Hopes McPizza Will Deliver," *USA Today,* 25 Aug. 1989, p. 1B; Richard Gibson, "McDonald's Fires Fast Pitch at Pizza Buffs," *Wall Street Journal,* 28 Aug. 1989, p. B4; and John Schwartz, "You Deserve a Pizza Today," *Newsweek,* 11 Sept. 1989, p. 46.

non-alcoholic lager, the company spent millions of pounds on advertising to communicate the new product's attributes.

Commercialisation is easier when customers accept the product rapidly. There is a better chance of this occurring if marketers can make them aware of a product's benefits. The following stages of the **product adoption process** are generally recognised as those that buyers go through in accepting a product:

1. *Awareness.* The buyer becomes aware of the product.
2. *Interest.* The buyer seeks information and is receptive to learning about the product.
3. *Evaluation.* The buyer considers the product's benefits and determines whether to try it.
4. *Trial.* The buyer examines, tests, or tries the product to determine its usefulness, relative to his or her needs.
5. *Adoption.* The buyer purchases the product and can be expected to use it when the need for this general type of product arises again.[11]

This adoption model has several implications for the commercialisation phase. First, the company must promote the product to create widespread awareness of its existence and its benefits. Samples or simulated trials should be arranged to help buyers make initial purchase decisions. At the same time, marketers should emphasise quality control and provide solid guarantees to reinforce buyer opinion during the evaluation stage. Finally, production and physical distribution must be linked to patterns of adoption and repeat purchases. (The product adoption process is also discussed in Chapter 13.)

Products are not usually launched nationwide overnight but are introduced through a process called a roll-out. In a roll-out, a product is introduced in stages, starting in a set of geographic areas and gradually expanding into adjacent areas. Thus, Cadbury's Wispa bar appeared initially in the north-east of England. It may take several years to market the product nationally. Sometimes the test cities are used as initial marketing areas, and the introduction becomes a natural extension of test-marketing.

Gradual product introduction is popular for several reasons. It reduces the risks of introducing a new product. If the product fails, the firm will experience smaller losses if the item has been introduced in only a few geographic areas than if it has been marketed nationally. Furthermore, a company cannot introduce a product nationwide overnight because the system of wholesalers and retailers, necessary to distribute a product, cannot be established that quickly. The development of a distribution network may take considerable time. Keep in mind also that the number of units needed to satisfy the national demand for a successful product can be enormous, and a firm usually cannot produce the required quantities in a short time (see Case 8.1).

Despite the good reasons for introducing a product gradually, marketers realise that this approach creates some competitive problems. A gradual introduction allows competitors to observe what a firm is doing and to monitor results, just as the firm's own marketers are doing. If competitors see that the newly introduced product is successful, they may enter the same target market quickly with similar products. In addition, as a product is introduced region by region, competitors may expand their marketing efforts to offset promotion of the new product.

11. Adapted from Everett M. Rogers, *Diffusion of Innovations* (New York: Macmillan, 1962), pp. 81–86.

FIGURE 8.5
Product positioning.
When a customer
chooses one product
over another, it is usually
because the product has
been firmly established
as having attributes par-
ticularly suited to the
customer's needs and
wants.

SOURCE: Robert Fried/Stock, Boston

PRODUCT POSITIONING

The term **product positioning** refers to the decisions and activities intended to create and maintain a certain concept of the firm's product (relative to competitive brands) in customers' minds (see Figure 8.5). When marketers introduce a product, they attempt to position it so that it seems to possess the characteristics the target market most desires. This projected image is crucial. *Product position* is the customers' concept of the product's attributes relative to their concept of competitive brands. Crest has been positioned as a fluoride toothpaste that fights dental decay and Close-Up as a whitening toothpaste that enhances sex appeal.

Product positioning is part of a natural progression when market segmentation is used. Segmentation lets the firm aim a given brand at a portion of the total market. Effective product positioning helps serve a specific market segment by creating an appropriate concept in the minds of customers in that market segment. For example, Lucozade traditionally had the image of a "pick-me-up" to be drunk during illness. Advertisements featuring sick and ailing children were less appropriate than when the brand was first introduced. Beecham Foods repositioned the product by switching the focus of promotion to healthy adults (the Daley Thompson commercials), so that the "pick-me-up" concept was not lost.

RADION REVENGE

"Persil washes whiter" is a slogan few could have missed since the 1950s. From the summer of 1990 there was a new proposition: Persil also washes dishes. For decades Persil had been the leader in the market for washing powders and liquids for clothes. Persil washing-up liquid was launched with an £8 million promotional campaign to compete with the previously undisputed champion of the kitchen sink, Fairy Liquid.

In 1989, Fairy challenged Persil on its home ground by launching an automatic washing powder and liquid; now Persil is striking back. This is the latest clash between the two giants of household detergents, Lever Brothers (Unilever) and Procter & Gamble (P&G). Fairy (P&G) accounted for half the £120 million Britain spends annually on washing-up liquid. Lever's Persil had sales of £192 million in the washing powder/liquid market.

P&G is unlikely to ignore Persil's brand extension; the company—widely viewed as one of the world's most ruthless marketing organisations—has always reacted aggressively to competitor activity. When the company discovered Lever's intention to launch a new detergent, Radion, with the promise that it would remove "stale odours", it had its own advertisements on television before Radion commercials hit the screen. P&G's advertising asked a housewife if her clothes smelled. "Don't be daft," she replied. "I use Ariel"—a P&G product!

The Persil washing-up liquid development is the latest example of the practice of brand extension: a brand name being given to a product which shares similar values with previously branded products (Persil washing powder and liquid in this case).

SOURCE: "Persil Dishes Dirt in Suds War," *The Independent on Sunday,* 19 August 1990, p. 21; Barry Pritchard, "Soaps Slip Ahead with Ariel in the Lead," *Marketing,* 16 August 1990, p. 7; Mat Toor, "Why Lever's Radion Just Loves to be Hated," *Marketing,* 5 July 1990, p. 9; "Detergent Liquid Shares," *Harvest* 1990; "Liquid Detergents Take the Milk Carton Route," *The Grocer,* 7 April 1990.

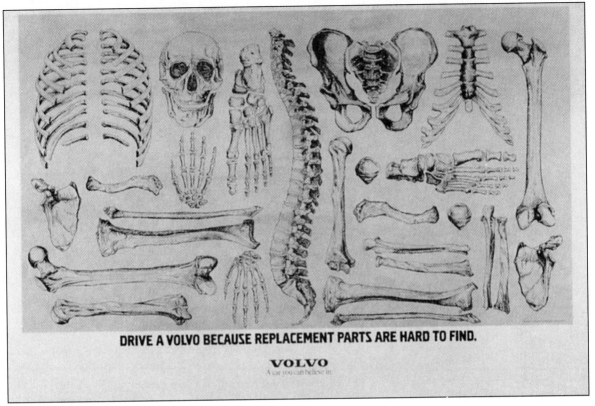

DRIVE A VOLVO BECAUSE REPLACEMENT PARTS ARE HARD TO FIND.

VOLVO
A car you can believe in.

FIGURE 8.6 *Product positioning.*
Volvo has positioned itself to avoid competition by accenting its cars' safety characteristics for many years.

SOURCE: Courtesy of Volvo

A firm can position a product to compete head-on with another brand, as Pepsi has done against Coca-Cola, or to avoid competition, as 7-Up has done relative to other soft-drink producers. Head-to-head competition may be a marketer's positioning objective if the product's performance characteristics are at least equal to competitive brands and if the product is priced lower (Marketing Update 8.3 describes the competition between Lever Brothers and Procter & Gamble in the washing powder/liquid market.) Head-to-head positioning may be appropriate even when the price is higher if the product's performance characteristics are superior. Conversely, positioning to avoid competition may be best when the product's performance characteristics are not significantly different from competing brands. Moreover, positioning a brand to avoid competition may be appropriate when that brand has unique characteristics that are important to some buyers. Volvo, for example, has for years positioned itself away from competitors by focusing on the safety characteristics of its cars (see Figure 8.6). Competitors sometimes mention safety issues in their advertisements only temporarily.

Avoiding competition is critical when a firm introduces a brand into a market in which it already has one or more brands. Marketers usually want to avoid cannibalising sales of their existing brands, unless the new brand generates substantially larger profits. When Coca-Cola reintroduced Tab, it attempted to position the cola so as to minimise the adverse effects on Diet Coke sales. Tab was positioned as the diet drink containing calcium—catering specifically to a female target market.

If a product has been planned properly, its attributes and brand image will give it the distinctive appeal needed. Style, shape, construction, quality of work, and colour help create the image and the appeal. If they can easily identify the benefits, then of course buyers are more likely to purchase the product. When the new product does not offer some preferred attributes, there is room for another new product or for repositioning an existing product.

MANAGING PRODUCTS AFTER COMMERCIALISATION

Most new products start off slowly and seldom generate enough sales to produce profits immediately. As buyers learn about the new product, marketers should be alert for product weaknesses and make corrections quickly, to prevent its early demise. Marketing strategy should be designed to attract the segment that is most interested and has the fewest objections. If any of these factors need adjustment, this action, too, must be taken quickly to sustain demand. As the sales curve moves upwards and the break-even point is reached, the growth stage begins.

■ **Marketing Strategy in the Growth Stage**

As sales increase, management must support the momentum by adjusting the marketing strategy. The goal is to establish the product's position and to fortify it by encouraging brand loyalty. As profits increase, the organisation must brace itself for the entrance of aggressive competitors, who may make specialised appeals to selected market segments.

During the growth stage, product offerings may have to be expanded. To achieve greater penetration of an overall market, segmentation may have to be used more intensely. That would require developing product variations to satisfy the needs of people in several different market segments. Marketers should analyse the product position regarding competing products and correct weak or omitted attributes. Quality, functional, or style modifications may be required.

Gaps in the marketing channels should be filled during the growth period. Once a product has won acceptance, new distribution outlets may be easier to obtain. Sometimes marketers tend to move from an **exclusive** or **selective** exposure to a more **intensive** network of dealers to achieve greater market penetration. Marketers must also make sure that the physical distribution system is running efficiently and delivering supplies to distributors before their inventories are exhausted. Because competition increases during the growth period, service adjustments and prompt credit for defective products are important marketing tools.

Advertising expenditure may be lowered slightly from the high level of the introductory stage but is still quite substantial. As sales increase, promotion costs should drop as a percentage of total sales. A falling ratio between promotion expenditure and sales should contribute significantly to increased profits. The advertising messages should stress brand benefits. Coupons and samples may be used to increase market share.

After recovering development costs, a business may be able to lower prices. As sales volume increases, efficiencies in production can result in lower costs. These savings may be passed on to buyers. If demand remains strong and there are few competitive threats, prices tend to remain stable. If price cuts are feasible, they can improve price competition and discourage new competitors from entering the market. For example, when compact disc players were introduced in the early 1980s, they carried an £800 price tag. Primarily because of the price, the product was positioned as a "toy for audiophiles"—a very small market segment. To generate mass market demand, compact disc player manufacturers dropped their prices to around £150, and the cost of discs also dropped. The price is now at a point where the margin is low but the turnover is high. Although less than 25 percent of homes have a compact disc player, compact discs now account for one-third of music purchases.

■ **Marketing Strategy for Mature Products**

Because many products are in the maturity stage of their life cycles, marketers must deal with these products and be prepared to improve the marketing mix constantly. During maturity, the competitive situation stabilises and some of the weaker competitors drop out. It has been suggested that as a product matures, its customers become more experienced and specialised (especially for industrial products). As these customers gain knowledge, the benefits they seek may change as well. Thus new marketing strategies may be called for.[12]

Marketers may need to alter the product's quality or otherwise modify it. A product may be rejuvenated through different packaging, new models, or style changes. Sales and market share may be maintained or strengthened by developing new uses for the product. In Figure 8.7, Heinz is suggesting new uses for its salad cream.

During the maturity stage of the cycle, marketers actively encourage dealers to support the product. Dealers may be offered promotional assistance in lowering their inventory costs. In general, marketers go to great lengths to serve dealers and provide incentives for selling the manufacturer's brand, partly because own-label or retailer brands are a threat at this time. As we discuss in Chapter 7, own-label brands are both an opportunity and a threat to manufacturers, who may be able to sell their products through recognised own-label or retailer brand names as well as their own. However, own-label or retailer brands frequently undermine manufacturers' brands. Yet if manufacturers refuse to sell to own-label dealers, competitors may take advantage of this opportunity.

To maintain market share during the maturity stage requires moderate and sometimes heavy advertising expenditure. Advertising messages focus on differentiating a brand from numerous competitors, and sales promotion efforts are aimed at both consumers and resellers.

A greater mixture of pricing strategies is used during the maturity stage. In some cases, strong price competition occurs and price wars may break out. On the other hand, firms may compete in other ways than through price. Marketers develop price flexibility to differentiate offerings in product lines. Markdowns and price incentives are more common, but prices may rise if distribution and production costs increase.

■ **Marketing Strategy for Declining Products**

As a product's sales curve turns downwards, industry profits continue to fall. A business can justify maintaining a product as long as it contributes to profits or enhances the overall effectiveness of a product mix. In this stage, marketers must determine whether to eliminate the product or seek to reposition it in an attempt to extend its life. Usually, a declining product has lost its distinctiveness because

12. F. Stewart DeBruicker and Gregory L. Summe, "Make Sure Your Customers Keep Coming Back," *Harvard Business Review*, January-February 1985, pp. 92–98.

FIGURE 8.7

Promoting new product uses.

Heinz is promoting new uses for its Salad Cream by suggesting different ways to serve it.

SOURCE: HJ Heinz Company

similar competing products have been introduced. Competition engenders increased substitution and brand switching as buyers become insensitive to minor product differences. For these reasons, marketers do little to change a product's style, design, or other attributes during its decline. New technology, product substitutes, or environmental considerations may also indicate that the time has come to delete a product.

During a product's decline, outlets with strong sales volumes are maintained and unprofitable outlets are weeded out. An entire marketing channel may be eliminated if it does not contribute adequately to profits. Sometimes a new marketing channel, such as a factory outlet, will be used to liquidate remaining inventory of an obsolete product. As sales decline, the product becomes more obscure, but loyal buyers seek out dealers who carry it.

Advertising expenditure is at a minimum. Advertising of special offers may slow the rate of decline. Sales promotions, such as coupons and premiums, may temporarily regain buyers' attention. As the product continues to decline, the sales staff shifts its emphasis to more profitable products.

To have a product return a profit may be more important to a firm than to maintain a certain market share through repricing. To squeeze out all possible remaining profits, marketers may maintain the price despite declining sales and competitive pressures. Prices may even be increased as costs rise if a loyal core market still wants the product. In other situations, the price may be cut to reduce existing inventory so that the product can be deleted. Severe price reductions may be required if a new product is making an existing product obsolete.

SUMMARY

Developing and managing products is critical to an organisation's survival and growth. The various approaches available for organising product management share common activities, functions, and decisions necessary to guide a product through its life cycle. A product manager is responsible for a product, a product line, or several distinct products that make up an interrelated group within a multi-product organisation. A brand manager is a product manager who is responsible for a single brand. Marketing managers are responsible for managing the marketing activities that serve a particular group or class of customers. A venture or project team is sometimes used to create entirely new products that may be aimed at new markets.

The product portfolio approach attempts to create specific marketing strategies to achieve a balanced product mix that will produce maximum long-run profits. To maximise the effectiveness of a product mix, an organisation usually has to alter its mix through modification of existing products, deletion of a product, or new-product development. Product modification is changing one or more characteristics of a firm's product. This approach to altering a product mix can be effective when the product is modifiable, when customers can perceive the change, and when customers want the modification. Quality modifications are changes that relate to a product's dependability and durability. Changes that affect a product's versatility, effectiveness, convenience, or safety are called functional modifications. Style modifications change the sensory appeal of a product.

Product deletion is the process of eliminating a product that no longer satisfies a sufficient number of customers. Although a firm's personnel may oppose product deletion, weak products are unprofitable, consume too much time and effort, may require shorter production runs, and can create an unfavourable impression of the firm's other products. A product mix should be systematically reviewed to determine when to delete products. Products to be deleted can be phased out, run out, or dropped immediately.

A new product may be an innovation that has never been sold by any organisation, or it can be a product that a given firm has not marketed previously, although similar products have been available from other organisations. Before a product is introduced, it goes through the six phases of new-product development. In the idea generation phase, new product ideas may come from internal or external sources. In the process of screening ideas, those with the greatest potential are selected for further review. During the business analysis stage, the product idea is evaluated to determine its potential contribution to the firm's sales, costs, and profits. Product development is the stage in which the organisation finds out if it is technically feasible to produce the product and if it can be produced at costs low enough for the final price to be reasonable. Test-marketing is a limited introduction of a product in areas chosen to represent the intended market. The decision to enter the commercialisation phase means that full-scale production of the product begins and a complete marketing strategy is developed. The process that buyers go through in accepting a product includes awareness, interest, evaluation, trial, and adoption.

Product positioning comprises the decisions and activities intended to create and maintain a certain concept of the firm's product (relative to competitive brands) in customers' minds. Product positioning is part of a natural progression when market segmentation is used. A firm can position a product to compete head-on with another brand or to avoid competition.

As a product moves through its life cycle, marketing strategies may require continual adaptation. In the growth stage, it is important to develop brand loyalty and a market position. In the maturity stage, a product may be modified or new market segments may be developed to rejuvenate its sales. A product that is declining may be maintained as long as it makes a contribution to profits or enhances the product mix. Marketers must determine whether to eliminate the declining product or try to reposition it to extend its life.

IMPORTANT TERMS

Product manager	New-product development
Brand manager	Idea generation
Marketing manager	Screening ideas
Venture or project team	Business analysis
Product portfolio approach	Product development
Product modification	Test-marketing
Quality modifications	Commercialisation
Functional modifications	Product adoption process
Style modifications	Product positioning
Product deletion	

DISCUSSION AND REVIEW QUESTIONS

1. What organisational alternatives are available to a firm with two product lines having four product items in each line?
2. When is it more appropriate to use a product manager than a marketing manager? When might an alternative or combined approach be used?
3. What type of organisation might use a venture team to develop new products? What are the advantages and disadvantages of such a team?
4. Do small companies that manufacture one or two products need to be concerned about developing and managing products? Why or why not?
5. Why is product development a cross-functional activity within an organisation? That is, why must finance, engineering, manufacturing, and other functional areas be involved?
6. Develop information sources for new product ideas for the car industry.
7. Some firms believe that they can omit test-marketing. What are some of the advantages and disadvantages of test-marketing?

8. Under what conditions is product modification appropriate for changing a product mix? How does a quality modification differ from a functional modification? Can an organisation make one modification without making the other?

9. Give several reasons why an organisation might be unable to eliminate an unprofitable product.

■ CASES

8.1 Cadbury's Wispa

Cadbury and Rowntree dominate the U.K. confectionery market and are, with Nestlé and Suchard, the key European manufacturers. Whereas other companies produce sweets and chocolate products, only chocolate-based products are made by Cadbury. It is, therefore, crucial for Cadbury to maintain its dominance in this sector of the market. The company is always looking for product development opportunities to bring new chocolate-based goods onto the market, most recently, milk drinks, ice-cream products, and cream liquors.

In the early 1980s the market was moving away from the traditional chocolate bar to the self-eat countline bar: single products eaten by individuals. This was the fastest-growing sector of the market. Originally created for ease of packaging for manufacturers, countline bars matched a behavioural opportunity—fast food purchases from the majority of retail outlets (even forecourts) by people on the move. For the consumer, they were also an innovative reshaping and repackaging of their "beloved" chocolate into new products. In a market where 70 percent of purchase decisions are made on impulse, point-of-sale displays are essential, packaging must be dramatic and distinctive, and promotional material must reinforce the desire to buy.

After problems in determining a product name which was not previously registered, and which qualitative research showed consumers identified as having the right "feel" to match the product's attributes, Cadbury created Wispa. Full test-marketing was conducted in the Tyne Tees television region of north-east England. Wispa was launched in October 1981. Ten weeks later the product was withdrawn. Demand was so great that initial production capacity and stock levels could not cope with the test market, let alone with any proposed full commercialisation and national roll-out. The company spent £12 million on new plant in Bournville.

Cadbury had identified a new sector in the market, a fresh consumer need. In the period while production was being geared up, however, Rowntree reacted. Seeing the opportunity, Rowntree remodelled its Aero bar into a chunky, countline form with tremendous success. Undaunted, Cadbury relaunched Wispa, achieving 9.5 million sales in its first week. Wispa is now the leader in this sizeable and highly competitive sector of the chocolate confectionery market.

SOURCES: Yorkshire Television, "The Marketing Mix," 1986; Cadbury and Rowntree *Annual Reports;* Cadbury Ltd., "Confectionery Market Review," 1987, 1988, 1989, 1990; "Focus on Confectionery," *The Grocer,* 31 March 1990; "The Sweet Facts of 1989," Rowntree Macintosh, 1990.

Questions for Discussion

1. Why did Cadbury diversify into the countline market?
2. Was Rowntree's reaction with Aero well planned? Is such a reaction typical in consumer markets?
3. Could Cadbury's supply problems have been forecast?

8.2 Harley-Davidson's Product Management

Harley-Davidson Motor Co., with its headquarters in Milwaukee, has come roaring back to profitability after a decade of troubles. Strong competition from Japanese motorcycle manufacturers—Honda, Suzuki, Yamaha, and Kawasaki—caused Harley's market share for superheavyweight motorcycles (motorcycles with engine displacements greater than 850 cubic centimeters) to drop from 99.7 percent in 1972 to 23 percent in 1983. Harley simply could not compete with Japan's high-tech machines, low prices, and attractive designs. Harley executives were forced to re-evaluate their entire organisation. Today Harley once again is the U.S. market-share leader for superheavyweight motorcycles, largely because of its commitment to new-product development and improved product quality.

Realising the importance of product quality, Harley product managers understood that they had to turn to their customers for help. They began surveying customers to determine what was wanted in or on a motorcycle. Harley learned that bikers are very vocal about their likes and dislikes: motorcycle enthusiasts were eager to share their views on Harley products and how they could be improved.

Because of huge growth in the early 1970s, Harley was more interested in increasing production than in developing new products or improving product quality. The resulting motorcycles were inferior and outdated when compared with Japanese vehicles. When Harley sales figures plummeted, its executives knew that they had to undertake drastic modifications to ensure the company's survival. They increased the annual research and development budget from $2 million to $14 million.

Willie G. Davidson, Harley's vice-president for styling and the grandson of one of the founders, began to attend biker rallies to gather ideas for potential product innovations. Seeing that many bikers liked to customise their motorcycles, he noted the most promising customer "developments" and suggested that Harley mimic these in the factory. In 1980, Harley engineers created a completely redesigned chassis and a new line of engines ranging from 883 to 1340 cc displacement. Davidson invented a new model, the Super Glide. Then Davidson introduced the Low Rider, the Wide Glide, and other successful models.

A senior vice-president at Harley-Davidson views Davidson as an artistic genius. According to this executive, Davidson performed virtual miracles by simply manipulating transfers and paint in the years before Harley-Davidson was able to bring new engines on-stream. Harley's survival may be due to the new models Davidson was able to create by cosmetically changing existing models. The Japanese motorcycle makers started copying Harley designs.

Customer complaints caused the company to introduce its quality-audit programme. A few days before a new model, the Cafe Racer, was scheduled to come off the production line, an employee shocked a Harley executive with news of severe defects in the model. Deciding to make the Cafe Racer a new symbol of Harley-Davidson product quality, the CEO dispatched a team of engineers, service supervisors, and manufacturing managers to correct the problems. It cost the company about $100,000 to mend only a hundred of the Cafe Racers, but management believed that the investment in quality was worth it.

Harley improved the quality of its products by implementing three integrated programmes: just-in-time manufacturing (called "materials-as-needed", or "MAN", at Harley), statistical operator control (SOC), and heavy reliance on employee involvement. The MAN system freed Harley from a bulky inventory and increased plant productivity. SOC gives assembly-line workers responsibility for the quality of individual parts. By consulting with line workers, Harley managers and engineers have been able to improve manufacturing processes and, consequently, improve motorcycles. None of these successful programmes required large capital investment—Harley improved product quality by enhancing procedures.

Harley's product development strategies still continue to evolve as the company grows stronger. The company has even called its new power train the Evolution Engine. Clearly, Harley executives are determined to keep their customers happy and the product innovations rolling.

SOURCES: Vaughn Beals, "Harley-Davidson: An American Success Story," *Journal for Quality and Participation,* June 1988, pp. A19–A23; Vaughn Beals, "Operation Recovery," *Success,* February 1989, p. 16; "How Harley Beat Back the Japanese," *Fortune,* 25 Sept. 1989, pp. 155, 157, 162, 164; Tani Mayer, "Harley-Davidson Rides High," *Financial World,* 18 Oct. 1988, pp. 16, 18; Gary Miller, "Harley's Teerlink Thrives as Rank-and-File Kind of Guy," *Business Journal,* Milwaukee, Wisconsin, 17 July 1989, TRN 39:E9.

Questions for Discussion

1. Why did Harley's share of the superheavyweight motorcycle market drop so drastically between 1972 and 1983?
2. What sources did Harley use to generate new product ideas?
3. What steps has Harley taken to regain its competitiveness?

PART III DISTRIBUTION DECISIONS

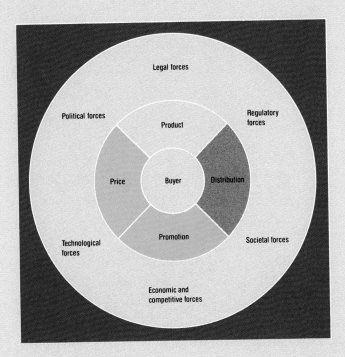

Providing customers with satisfying products is important but not enough for successful marketing strategies. These products must also be available in adequate quantities in accessible locations at the times when customers desire them. The chapters in Part III deal with the distribution of products and the marketing channels and institutions that provide the structure for making products available. In Chapter 9 we discuss the structure and functions of marketing channels and present an overview of institutions that make up these channels. In Chapter 10 we analyse the types of wholesalers and their functions. In Chapter 11 we focus on retailing and retailers. Specifically, we examine the types of retailers and their roles and functions in marketing channels. Finally, in Chapter 12 we analyse the decisions and activities associated with the physical distribution of products, such as order processing, materials handling, warehousing, inventory management, and transport. ◆

9 MARKETING CHANNELS

Objectives

To understand the marketing channel concept and the types of marketing intermediaries in the channel

To discuss the justification of channel members

To examine the structure and function of the channel system

To explore the power dimensions of channels, especially the concepts of co-operation, conflict, and leadership

*I*n the U.K., as in most European countries, most people have a current account at a bank into which salaries, pensions, or grant cheques are paid and from which cash is drawn, bills are paid and cheques are written. The U.K. banking scene is dominated by National Westminster, Barclays, Midland, Lloyds and TSB. Each of these companies is similar, with like-for-like products, services, personnel, branches and locations. Differentiation has been difficult, generally centring on promotional imagery or minor tactical changes to, for example, opening hours or service charges. For most bank account holders, however, the branch with its restricted opening hours, formal ambience and town centre location—irrespective of which company operates it—is the only point of contact for most transactions.

In 1989 Midland Bank, with massive promotional support (£6 million), broke the mould. "Firstdirect" bypassed the traditional marketing channel by being based on telephone transactions. A purpose-built administrative centre was created in Leeds, guaranteeing immediate response to calls, 24 hours a day. All transactions can be completed over the telephone, even the payment of bills. Initial reactions were positive, with many non-Midland account holders switching over to Firstdirect. The services available were not new but the chosen marketing channel was totally innovative: one very convenient for customers not able to reach a branch in its town centre location with its restricted openings. ◆

Based on information in "Midland Fails to Bank on a Third Successive Win," *Marketing*, 19 July 1990, p. 7; Mat Toor, "Taxis Fare Well with Firstdirect," *Marketing*, 19 April 1990, p. 1; Clare Sambrook, "TV Teaser Questions Firstdirect's Chances," *Marketing*, 5 October 1989, p. 2; and *Marketing*, September, October, November 1989.

Distribution refers to activities that make products available to customers when and where they want to purchase them. Choosing which channels of distribution to use is a major decision in the development of marketing strategies.

This chapter focuses on the description and analysis of channels of distribution, or marketing channels. We first discuss the main types of channels and their structures and then explain the need for intermediaries, as well as analysing the functions they perform. Next we outline several forms of channel integration. We explore how marketers determine the appropriate intensity of market coverage for a product and how they consider a number of factors when selecting suitable channels of distribution. Finally, after examining behavioural patterns within marketing channels, we look at several legal issues that affect channel management.

THE STRUCTURES AND TYPES OF MARKETING CHANNELS

A **channel of distribution** (sometimes called a **marketing channel**) is a group of individuals and organisations that direct the flow of products from producers to customers. Providing customer benefits should be the driving force behind all marketing channel activities. Buyers' needs and behaviour are therefore important concerns of channel members.

Making products available benefits customers. Channels of distribution make products available at the right time, in the right place, and in the right quantity by providing such product-enhancing functions as transport and storage. Although consumers do not see the distribution of a product, they value the product availability that channels of distribution make possible.

Most, but not all, channels of distribution have marketing intermediaries. A **marketing intermediary**, or middleman, links producers to other middlemen or to ultimate users of the products. Marketing intermediaries perform the activities described in Table 9.1. There are two major types of intermediaries: merchants and functional middlemen (agents and brokers). **Merchants** take title to products and resell them, whereas **functional middlemen** do not take title.

Both retailers and wholesalers are intermediaries. Retailers purchase products for the purpose of reselling them to ultimate consumers. Merchant wholesalers resell products to other wholesalers and to retailers. Functional wholesalers, such as agents and brokers, expedite exchanges among producers and resellers and are compensated by fees or commissions. For purposes of discussion in this chapter, all wholesalers are considered merchant middlemen unless otherwise specified.

Channel members share certain significant characteristics. Each member has different responsibilities within the overall structure of the distribution system, but mutual profit and success can be attained only if channel members co-operate in delivering products to the market.

Although distribution decisions need not precede other marketing decisions, they do exercise a powerful influence on the rest of the marketing mix. Channel decisions are critical because they determine a product's market presence and buyers' accessibility to the product. The strategic significance of these decisions is further heightened by the fact that they entail long-term commitments. For example, it is

TABLE 9.1
Marketing channel activities that intermediaries perform

CATEGORY OF MARKETING ACTIVITIES	POSSIBLE ACTIVITIES REQUIRED
Marketing information	Analyse information such as sales data; perform or commission market research studies
Marketing management	Establish objectives; plan activities; manage and co-ordinate financing, personnel, and risk-taking; evaluate and control channel activities
Facilitating exchange	Choose product assortments that match the needs of buyers
Promotion	Set promotional objectives, co-ordinate advertising, personal selling, sales promotion, publicity, and packaging
Price	Establish pricing policies and terms of sales
Physical distribution	Manage transport, warehousing, materials handling, inventory control, and communication

much easier for an organisation to change prices or packaging than to change distribution systems already in place.

Because the marketing channel most appropriate for one product may be less suitable for another, many different distribution paths have been developed in most countries. The links in any channel, however, are the merchants (including producers) and agents who oversee the movement of products through that channel. Although there are many various marketing channels, they can be classified generally as channels for consumer products or channels for industrial products.

Channels for Consumer Products

Figure 9.1 illustrates several channels used in the distribution of consumer products. Besides the channels listed, a manufacturer may use sales branches or sales offices (discussed in Chapter 10).

Channel A describes the direct movement of goods from producer to consumers. Customers who pick their own fruit from commercial orchards or buy double glazing from door-to-door salespeople are acquiring products through a direct channel. A producer that sells its goods directly from its factory to end users and ultimate consumers is using a direct marketing channel. Although this channel is the simplest, it is not necessarily the cheapest or the most efficient method of distribution.

Channel B, which moves goods from producer to retailers and then to consumers, is the frequent choice of large retailers, for they can buy in quantity from a manufacturer. Such retailers as Marks and Spencer, Tesco and Sainsbury, for example, sell clothing, food, and many other items that they have purchased directly from the producers. Cars are also commonly sold through this type of marketing channel.

A long-standing distribution channel, especially for consumer products, channel C takes goods from producer to wholesalers, then to retailers, and finally to consumers. It is a very practical option for a producer that sells to hundreds of thousands of consumers through thousands of retailers. A single producer finds it hard to do business directly with thousands of retailers. For example, consider the number of retailers that market Wrigley's chewing-gum. It would be extremely difficult, if not impossible, for Wrigley's to deal directly with all the retailers that sell its brand of

FIGURE 9.1
Typical marketing channels for consumer products

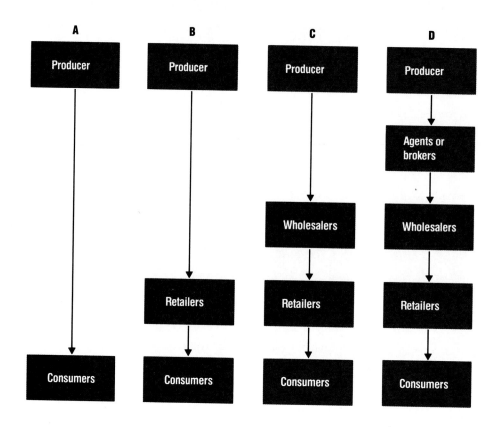

gum. Manufacturers of tobacco products, some home appliances, hardware, and many convenience goods sell their products to wholesalers, who then sell to retailers, who in turn do business with individual consumers.

Channel D—through which goods pass from producer to agents to wholesalers to retailers and only then to consumers—is frequently used for products intended for mass distribution, such as processed food. For example, to place its biscuit line in specific retail outlets, a food processor may hire an agent (or a food broker) to sell the biscuits to wholesalers. The wholesalers then sell the biscuits to supermarkets, vending machine operators, and other retail outlets.

Contrary to popular opinion, a long channel may be the most efficient distribution channel for consumer goods. When several channel intermediaries are available to perform specialised functions, costs may be lower than if one channel member is responsible for all the functions.

■ **Channels for Industrial Products**

Figure 9.2 shows four of the most common channels for industrial products. As with consumer products, manufacturers of industrial products sometimes work with more than one level of wholesalers.

Channel E illustrates the direct channel for industrial products. In contrast to consumer goods, many industrial products—especially expensive equipment, such as steam generators, aircraft, and computers—are sold directly to the buyers. For example, Mitsubishi Aircraft International Corporation, a subsidiary of Mitsubishi Heavy Industries Ltd., sells its Diamond I jets directly to corporate buyers. The direct channel is most feasible for many manufacturers of industrial goods because

FIGURE 9.2
Typical marketing channels for industrial products

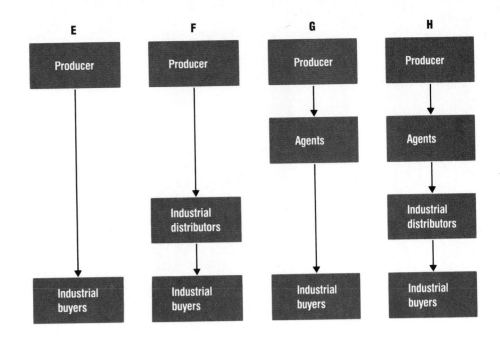

they have fewer customers, and those customers are often clustered geographically. Buyers of complex industrial products also can receive technical assistance from the manufacturer more easily in a direct channel.

If a particular line of industrial products is aimed at a large number of customers, the manufacturer may use a marketing channel that includes industrial distributors, merchants who take title to products (channel F). Mitsubishi fork-lifts and other construction products, for example, are sold through industrial distributors. Building materials, operating supplies, and air-conditioning equipment are frequently channelled through industrial distributors.

Channel G—producer to agents to industrial buyers—is often the choice when a manufacturer without a marketing department needs market information, when a company is too small to field its own sales force, or when a firm wants to introduce a new product or enter a new market without using its own salespeople. Thus a large soybean producer might sell its product to animal-food processors through an agent.

Channel H is a variation of channel G: goods move from producer to agents to industrial distributors and then to industrial buyers. A manufacturer without a sales force may rely on this channel if its industrial customers purchase products in small quantities or if they must be resupplied frequently and therefore need access to decentralised inventories. Japanese manufacturers of electronic components, for example, work through export agents that sell to industrial distributors serving small producers or dealers overseas. Chapter 21 presents more information about marketing channels for industrial products.

■ Multiple Marketing Channels

To reach diverse target markets, a manufacturer may use several marketing channels simultaneously, with each channel involving a different group of intermediaries. For example, a manufacturer turns to multiple channels when the same product is directed to both consumers and industrial customers. When Twinings sells tea-bags for household use, the tea-bags are sold to supermarkets through grocery whole-

FIGURE 9.3
Dual distribution.
Kellogg's reaches ulti-
mate consumers by sell-
ing direct to large retail
chains and by working
with food wholesalers
who sell to smaller re-
tailers.

...for a healthy business.

SOURCE: Used by permission of Kellogg Company

salers or, in some cases, directly to the retailers, whereas the tea-bags going to restaurants or institutions follow a different distribution channel. In some instances, a producer may prefer **dual distribution**: the use of two or more marketing channels for distributing the same products to the same target market. Kellogg's sells its cereals (see Figure 9.3) direct to large retail grocery chains and to food wholesalers that, in turn, sell them to retailers. Dual distribution can cause dissatisfaction among wholesalers and smaller retailers.

JUSTIFICATIONS FOR INTERMEDIARIES

Even if producers and buyers are located in the same city, there are costs associated with exchanges. As Figure 9.4 shows, if five buyers purchase the products of five producers, twenty-five transactions are required. If one intermediary serves both producers and buyers, the number of transactions can be reduced to ten. Intermediaries become specialists in facilitating exchanges. They provide valuable assistance because of their access to, and control over, important resources for the proper functioning of the marketing channel.

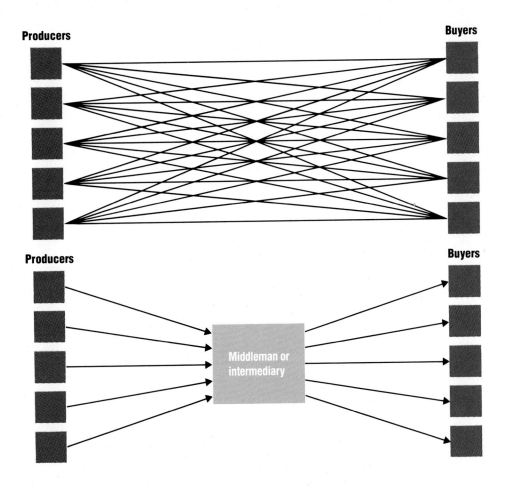

FIGURE 9.4
Efficiency in exchanges provided by an intermediary

Producers

Buyers

Producers

Buyers

Middleman or intermediary

Nevertheless, the press, consumers, public officials, and other marketers freely criticise intermediaries, especially wholesalers. Table 9.2 indicates that in a recent U.S. survey of the general public 74 percent believed that "wholesalers frequently make high profits, which significantly increase prices that consumers pay." The critics accuse wholesalers of being inefficient and parasitic, and consumers often wish to make the distribution channel as short as possible. Consumers assume that the fewer the intermediaries, the lower the prices of goods sold to them. It is obvious that, because threats to eliminate them come from both ends of the marketing channel, wholesalers must be careful to perform only those marketing activities that are truly desired. To survive, they must be more efficient and more service orientated than alternative marketing institutions.

Critics who suggest that eliminating wholesalers would lower prices for consumers do not recognise that this would not eliminate the need for the services wholesalers provide. Other institutions would have to perform those services, and consumers would still have to fund them. In addition, all producers would have to deal directly with retailers or consumers, meaning that every producer would have to keep voluminous records and hire enough personnel to deal with every customer. Even in a direct channel, consumers might finish paying a great deal more for products because prices would reflect the costs of inefficient producers' operations.

TABLE 9.2 *Consumer misunderstanding about wholesalers*

Statement: *Wholesalers frequently make high profits, which significantly increase prices that consumers pay.*

	TOTAL %	MALE %	FEMALE %
Strongly agree	35.5	33	38
Somewhat agree	38	40	36
Neither agree nor disagree	16	14	18
Somewhat disagree	8	9	7
Strongly disagree	2.5	4	1

SOURCE: O.C. Ferrell and William M. Pride, National multistage area probability sample of 2,045 households, 1985. Reprinted by permission of the authors.

To illustrate the efficient service that wholesalers provide, assume that all wholesalers were eliminated. Because there are millions of retail stores in Europe, a widely purchased consumer product—say confectionery—would require an extraordinary number of sales contacts, possibly more than a million, to maintain the current level of product exposure. For example, Mars would have to deliver its confectionery, purchase and service thousands of vending machines, establish warehouses all over Europe, and maintain fleets of delivery vans. Selling and distribution costs for confectionery would sky-rocket. Instead of a few contacts with food brokers, large retail organisations, and various merchant wholesalers, confectionery manufacturers would face hundreds of thousands of expensive contacts with and shipments to smaller retailers. Such an operation would be highly inefficient, and its costs would necessarily be passed on to consumers. Chocolate bars would cost more, and they would be much harder to find. Ultimately it is clear that wholesalers provide a far more efficient and less expensive service not only for manufacturers but for consumers as well.

FUNCTIONS OF INTERMEDIARIES

Before we examine the functions of intermediaries in some detail, we should note that a distribution network helps overcome two major distribution problems. Consider a firm that manufactures jeans. The company specialises in the goods it can produce most efficiently, denim clothing. To make jeans the most economical way possible, the producer turns out a hundred thousand pairs of jeans each day. Few persons, however, want to buy a hundred thousand pairs of jeans. Thus the quantity of jeans that the company can produce efficiently is more than the average customer wants. We call this a *discrepancy in quantity*.

An **assortment** is a combination of products put together to provide benefits. A consumer creates and holds an assortment. The set of products made available to customers is an organisation's assortment. Most consumers want a broad assortment of products. In addition to jeans, a consumer wants to buy shoes, food, a car, a stereo, soft drinks, and many other products. Yet our jeans manufacturer has a

FIGURE 9.5
Sorting activities conducted by intermediaries

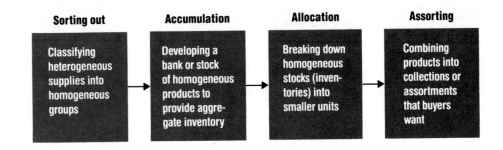

Sorting out	Accumulation	Allocation	Assorting
Classifying heterogeneous supplies into homogeneous groups	Developing a bank or stock of homogeneous products to provide aggregate inventory	Breaking down homogeneous stocks (inventories) into smaller units	Combining products into collections or assortments that buyers want

narrow assortment because it makes only jeans (and perhaps a few other denim clothes). There is a *discrepancy in assortment* because a consumer wants a broad assortment, but an individual manufacturer produces a narrow assortment.

Quantity and assortment discrepancies are resolved through the sorting activities of intermediaries in a marketing channel. **Sorting activities** are functions that allow channel members to divide roles and separate tasks. Sorting activities, as Figure 9.5 shows, may be grouped into four main tasks: sorting out, accumulation, allocation, and assorting of products.[1]

■ **Sorting Out**

Sorting out, the first step in developing an assortment, is the separating of conglomerates of heterogeneous products into relatively uniform, homogeneous groups based on product characteristics such as size, shape, weight, or colour. Sorting out is especially common in the marketing of agricultural products and other raw materials, which vary widely in size, grade, and quality and would be largely unusable in an undifferentiated mass. A tomato crop, for example, must be sorted into tomatoes suitable for canning, those suitable for making tomato juice, and those for sale in retail food stores.

Sorting out for specific products follows a set of predetermined standards. The sorter must know how many classifications to use and the criteria for each classification and must usually provide for a group of miscellaneous leftovers as well. Certain product characteristics can be categorised more easily than others; appearance and size of agricultural products are more readily apparent than flavour or nutritional content, for instance. Because the overall quality of a crop or supply of raw material is likely to vary from year to year or from region to region, classifications must be somewhat flexible.

Changing consumer needs and new manufacturing techniques influence the sorting-out process. If sorting out results in manufactured goods with minor defects, these damaged or irregular products are often marketed at lower prices through factory outlet stores, which are growing in consumer popularity. Improved processing also permits the use of materials that might have been culled previously, such as the paper and aluminium now being recycled. In some industries, producers have stopped using natural materials because the manufacturing process demands the greater uniformity possible only with synthetic materials. Sorting out thus helps alleviate discrepancies in assortment by making relatively homogeneous products available for the next step, accumulation.

1. Wroe Alderson, *Marketing Behavior and Executive Action* (Homewood, Ill.: Irwin, 1957), pp. 201–211.

■ Accumulation

Accumulation is the development of a bank or inventory of homogeneous products that have similar production or demand requirements. Farmers who grow relatively small quantities of tomatoes, for example, transport their sorted tomatoes to central collection points, where they are accumulated in large lots for movement into the next level of the channel.

Combining many small groups of similar products into larger groups serves several purposes. Products move through subsequent marketing channels more economically in large quantities because transport rates are lower for bulk loads. In addition, accumulation gives buyers a steady supply of products in large volumes. If Del Monte had to frequently purchase small amounts of tomatoes from individual farmers, the company's tomato products would be produced much less efficiently. Instead, Del Monte buys bulk loads of tomatoes through brokers, thus maintaining a continuous supply of uniform-quality materials for processing. Accumulation lets producers continuously use up stocks and replenish them, thus minimising losses from interruptions in the supply of materials.

For both buyer and seller, accumulation also alleviates some of the problems associated with price fluctuations and highly seasonal materials. Buyers may obtain large-volume purchases at lower prices because sellers are anxious to dispose of perishable goods; purchasing agents may accumulate stocks of materials in anticipation of price rises. In other cases, sellers may receive higher prices because they enter into long-term supply contracts with producers or they agree to store accumulated materials until the producer is ready for them. Accumulation thus relieves discrepancies in quantity. It enables intermediaries to build up specialised inventories and allocate products according to customers' needs.

■ Allocation

Allocation is the breaking down of large homogeneous inventories into smaller lots. This process, which addresses discrepancies in quantity, enables wholesalers to buy efficiently in lorry or container loads and then apportion products by cases to other channel members. A food wholesaler, for instance, serves as a depot, allocating products according to market demand. The wholesaler may divide a single lorryload of Del Monte canned tomatoes among several retail food stores.

Because supply and demand are seldom in perfect balance, allocation is influenced by several factors (and can sometimes resemble rationing). At times price is the overriding consideration. The highest bidder, or perhaps the buyer placing the largest order, is allocated most of the stock. At other times an intermediary gives preference to customers whose loyalty has been established or to those whose businesses show the most growth potential. In still other cases, products are allocated through compromise and negotiation.

Depending on the product, allocation may begin with the manufacturer and continue through several levels of intermediaries, including retailers. Allocation ends when the ultimate user selects the desired quantity of a particular product from the assortment of products available.

■ Assorting

Assorting is the process of combining products into collections or assortments that buyers want to have available in one place. Assorting eliminates discrepancies in assortment by grouping products in ways that satisfy buyers. The same food wholesaler that supplies supermarkets with Del Monte tomato products may also buy canned goods from competing food processors so that grocery stores can choose from a wide assortment of canned fruits and vegetables.

Buyers want an assortment of products at one location because of some task they want to perform or some problem they want solved. A buyer looking for a variety of products, all serving different purposes, requires a broad assortment from which to choose; a buyer with more precise needs or interests will seek out a narrower, and deeper, product assortment.

Assorting is especially important to retailers, and they strive to create assortments that match the demands of consumers who patronise their stores. Although no single customer is likely to buy one of everything in the store, a retailer must anticipate the probability of purchase and provide a satisfactory range of product choices. The risk involved is greater for some retailers than for others. For example, supermarkets purchase staple foods repeatedly, and these items can be stocked with little risk. But clothing retailers who misjudge consumer demand for "hot" fashion items can lose money if their assortments contain too few (or too many) of these products. Discrepancies in assortment reappear, in fact, when retailers fail to keep pace with shifts in consumer attitudes. New specialists—such as retail outlets for computer products—may even enter the market to provide assortments existing retailers do not offer.

CHANNEL INTEGRATION

Channel functions may be transferred among intermediaries and to producers and even customers. This section examines how channel members can either combine and control most activities or pass them on to another channel member. Remember, though, that the channel member cannot eliminate functions; unless buyers themselves perform the functions, they must pay for the labour and resources needed for the functions to be performed. The statement that "you can eliminate middlemen but you can't eliminate their functions" is an accepted principle of marketing.

Many marketing channels are determined by consensus. Producers and intermediaries co-ordinate their efforts for mutual benefit. Some marketing channels, however, are organised and controlled by a single leader, which can be a producer, a wholesaler, or a retailer, depending on the industry. The channel leader may establish channel policies and co-ordinate the development of the marketing mix. Sears, for example, is a channel leader for several of the many products it sells.

The various links or stages of the channel may be combined under the management of a channel leader either horizontally or vertically. Integration may stabilise supply, reduce costs, and increase co-ordination of channel members.

■ **Vertical Channel Integration**

Combining two or more stages of the channel under one management is **vertical channel integration**. One member of a marketing channel may purchase the operations of another member or simply perform the functions of the other member, eliminating the need for that intermediary as a separate entity. Total vertical integration encompasses all functions from production to ultimate buyer; it is exemplified by oil companies that own oil wells, pipelines, refineries, terminals, and service stations.

Whereas members of conventional channel systems work independently and seldom co-operate, participants in vertical channel integration co-ordinate their efforts to reach a desired target market. This more progressive approach to distribution

FIGURE 9.6

Corporate vertical marketing system (VMS). By opening and operating its own production facilities and service stations, Esso has created a corporate VMS.

SOURCE: Reproduced with kind permission of Esso Petroleum UK Ltd.

enables channel members to regard other members as extensions of their own operations. At one end of an integrated channel, for example, a manufacturer might provide advertising and training assistance, and the retailer at the other end would buy the manufacturer's products in quantity and actively promote them.

In the past, integration has been successfully institutionalised in marketing channels called vertical marketing systems. A **vertical marketing system** (**VMS**) is a marketing channel in which a single channel member co-ordinates or manages channel activities to achieve efficient, low-cost distribution aimed at satisfying target market customers. Because the efforts of individual channel members are combined in a VMS, marketing activities can be co-ordinated for maximum effectiveness and economy, without duplication of services. Vertical marketing systems are also competitive, accounting for a growing share of retail sales in consumer goods.

Most vertical marketing systems today take one of three forms: corporate, administered, or contractual. The *corporate* VMS combines all stages of the marketing channel, from producers to consumers, under a single ownership. For example, Esso (see Figure 9.6) established a corporate VMS operating corporate-owned production facilities and service stations. Supermarket chains that own food-processing

FIGURE 9.7

*Comparison of a
conventional marketing
channel and a vertical
marketing system*

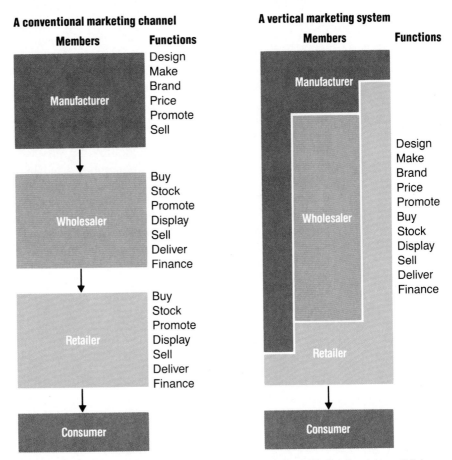

A conventional marketing channel

Members	Functions
Manufacturer	Design Make Brand Price Promote Sell
Wholesaler	Buy Stock Promote Display Sell Deliver Finance
Retailer	Buy Stock Promote Display Sell Deliver Finance
Consumer	

A vertical marketing system

Members	Functions
Manufacturer Wholesaler Retailer	Design Make Brand Price Promote Buy Stock Display Sell Deliver Finance
Consumer	

SOURCE: Adapted from *Strategic Marketing*, by David J. Kollat, Roger D. Blackwell, and James F. Robeson. Copyright © 1972 by Holt, Rinehart and Winston, Inc. Reprinted by permission of the publisher.

plants and large retailers that purchase wholesaling and production facilities are other examples of corporate VMSs. Figure 9.7 contrasts a conventional marketing channel with a VMS, which consolidates marketing functions and institutions.

In an *administered* VMS, channel members are independent, but a high level of inter-organisational management is achieved by informal co-ordination. Members of an administered VMS may agree, for example, to adopt uniform accounting and ordering procedures and to co-operate in promotional activities. Although individual channel members maintain their autonomy, as in conventional marketing channels, one channel member (such as the producer or a large retailer) dominates the administered VMS, so that distribution decisions take into account the system as a whole. Because of its size and power as a retailer, Marks and Spencer exercises a strong influence over the independent manufacturers in its marketing channels, as do Kellogg's (cereal) and Sony (television and other electronic products).

Under a *contractual* VMS, the most popular type of vertical marketing system, inter-organisational relationships are formalised through contracts. Channel members are linked by legal agreements that spell out each member's rights and obligations. For instance, franchise organisations such as McDonald's and Kentucky Fried

Chicken are contractual VMSs. Other contractual VMSs include wholesaler-sponsored groups such as Mace or IGA (Independent Grocers' Alliance) stores, in which independent retailers band together under the contractual leadership of a wholesaler. Retailer-sponsored co-operatives, which own and operate their own wholesalers, are a third type of contractual VMS.

■ Horizontal Channel Integration

Combining institutions at the same level of operation under one management constitutes **horizontal channel integration**. An organisation may integrate horizontally by merging with other organisations at the same level in a marketing channel level. For example, the owner of a dry-cleaning firm might buy and combine several other existing dry-cleaning establishments. Horizontal integration may enable a firm to generate sufficient sales revenue to integrate vertically as well.

Although horizontal integration permits efficiencies and economies of scale in purchasing, market research, advertising, and specialised personnel, it is not always the most effective method of improving distribution. Problems of "bigness" often follow, resulting in decreased flexibility, difficulties in co-ordination, and the need for additional marketing research and large-scale planning. Unless distribution functions for the various units can be performed more efficiently under unified management than under the previously separate managements, horizontal integration will not reduce costs or improve the competitive position of the integrating firm.

INTENSITY OF MARKET COVERAGE

Characteristics of the product and the target market determine the kind of coverage a product should get, that is, the number and kinds of outlets in which it is sold. To achieve the desired intensity of market coverage, distribution must correspond to the behaviour patterns of buyers. Chapter 7 divides consumer products into three categories—convenience products, shopping products, and specialty products—according to how consumers make purchases. In considering products for purchase, consumers take into account the replacement rate, product adjustment (services), duration of consumption, time required to find the product, and similar factors.[2] These variables directly affect the intensity of market coverage. Three major levels of market coverage are intensive, selective, and exclusive distribution.

■ Intensive Distribution

In **intensive distribution**, all available outlets are used for distributing a product. Intensive distribution is appropriate for convenience products such as bread, chewing-gum, beer, and newspapers. To consumers, availability means a store located nearby and minimum time necessary to search for the product at the store. Sales may have a direct relationship to availability. The successful sale of bread and milk at service stations or of petrol at convenience grocery stores has shown that the availability of these products is more important than the nature of the outlet. Convenience products have a high replacement rate and require almost no service. To meet these demands, intensive distribution is necessary, and multiple channels may be used to sell through all possible outlets.

2. Leo Aspinwall, "The Marketing Characteristics of Goods," in *Four Marketing Theories* (Boulder: University of Colorado Press, 1961), pp. 27–32.

Producers of consumer packaged items rely on intensive distribution. In fact, intensive distribution is one of Procter & Gamble's key strengths. It is fairly easy for this company to formulate marketing strategies for many of its products (soaps, detergents, food and juice products, and personal-care products) because consumers want availability provided quickly and intensively.

■ **Selective Distribution**

In **selective distribution**, only some available outlets in an area are chosen to distribute a product. Selective distribution is appropriate for shopping products. Durable goods such as typewriters and stereos usually fall into this category. Such products are more expensive than convenience goods. Consumers are willing to spend more searching time visiting several retail outlets to compare prices, designs, styles, and other features.

Selective distribution is desirable when a special effort—such as customer service from a channel member—is important. Shopping products require differentiation at the point of purchase. To motivate retailers to provide adequate pre-sale service, selective distribution and company-owned stores are often used. Many industrial products are sold on a selective basis to maintain a certain degree of control over the distribution process. For example, agricultural herbicides are distributed on a selective basis because dealers must offer services to buyers, such as instructions about how to apply the herbicides safely or the option of having the dealer apply the herbicide.

■ **Exclusive Distribution**

In **exclusive distribution**, only one outlet is used in a relatively large geographic area. Exclusive distribution is suitable for products that are purchased rather infrequently, consumed over a long period of time, or require service or information to fit them to buyers' needs. Exclusive distribution is not appropriate for convenience products and many shopping products. It is used often as an incentive to sellers when only a limited market is available for products. For example, cars such as the Aston Martin (shown in Figure 9.8) are sold on an exclusive basis. A producer that uses exclusive distribution generally expects a dealer to be very co-operative with respect to carrying a complete inventory, sending personnel for sales and service training, participating in promotional programmes, and providing excellent customer service.

SELECTION OF DISTRIBUTION CHANNELS

The process of selecting appropriate distribution channels for a product is often complex for a variety of reasons. Producers must choose specific intermediaries carefully, evaluating their sales and profit levels, performance records, other products carried, clientele, availability, and so forth. But producers must also examine other factors that influence distribution channel selection, including organisational objectives and resources, market characteristics, buyer behaviour, product attributes, and environmental forces.

■ **Organisational Objectives and Resources**

A producer must consider what it is trying to accomplish in the market-place and what resources can be brought to bear on the task. A company's objectives may be broad, such as higher profits, increased market share, and greater responsiveness to customers, or narrow, such as replacing an intermediary that has left the channel.

FIGURE 9.8

Using exclusive distribution.

The Aston Martin is a car sold under exclusive distribution.

SOURCE: Courtesy of Aston Martin Lagonda Limited

The organisation may possess sufficient financial and marketing clout to control its distribution channels—for example, by engaging in direct marketing or by operating its own fleet of lorries. On the other hand, an organisation may have no interest in performing distribution services or may be forced by lack of resources and experience to depend on middlemen.

The company must also evaluate the effectiveness of past distribution relationships and methods in light of its current goals. One firm might decide to maintain its basic channel structure but add members for increased coverage in new territories. Another company might alter its distribution channel so as to provide same-day delivery on all orders. When selecting distribution channels, organisational factors and objectives are important considerations.

■ **Market Characteristics**

Beyond the basic division between consumer markets and industrial markets, several market variables influence the design of distribution channels. Geography is one factor; in most cases, the greater the distance between the producer and its markets, the less expensive is distribution through intermediaries rather than through direct sales. A related consideration is market density. If customers tend to be clustered in several locations, the producer may be able to eliminate middlemen.

Transport, storage, communication, and negotiation are specific functions performed more efficiently in high-density markets. Market size—measured by the number of potential customers in a consumer or industrial market—is yet another variable. Direct sales may be effective if a producer has relatively few buyers for a product, but for larger markets the services of middlemen may be required.[3]

■ Buyer Behaviour

Buyer behaviour is a crucial consideration in selecting distribution channels. To be able to match intermediaries with customers, the producer must have specific, current information about customers who are buying the product and when and where they are buying it.[4] How customers buy is important as well. A manufacturer might find direct selling economically feasible for large-volume sales but inappropriate for small orders.

The producer must also understand how buyer specifications vary according to whether buyers perceive products as convenience, shopping, or specialty items (see Chapter 7). Customers for chewing-gum, for example, are likely to buy the product frequently (even impulsively) from a variety of outlets. Buyers of home computers, however, carefully evaluate product features, dealers, prices, and after-sale services. Buying patterns influence the selection of channels.

Buyers may be reached most effectively when producers are creative in opening up new distribution channels. In the U.K., effective distribution, the essential tool in the highly competitive soft drinks sector, is forcing brand leader Coca-Cola and Schweppes Beverages (CCSB) to find creative ways of extending distribution. CCSB is launching "Vendleader," a company to increase penetration of sales through vending machines.

■ Product Attributes

Another variable in the selection of distribution channels is the product itself. Because producers of complex industrial products must often provide technical services to buyers both before and after the sale, these products are usually shipped directly to buyers. Perishable or highly fashionable consumer products with short shelf-lives are also marketed through short channels. In other cases, distribution patterns are influenced by the product's value; the lower the price per unit, the longer the distribution chain. Additional factors to consider are the weight, bulkiness, and relative ease of handling the products. Producers may find wholesalers and retailers reluctant to carry items that create storage or display problems.[5]

■ Environmental Forces

Finally, producers making decisions about distribution channels must consider forces in the total marketing environment—that is, such issues as competition, ecology, economic conditions, technology, society, and law. Technology, for example, has made possible electronic scanners, computerised inventory systems such as EPOS (electronic point of sale), and electronic shopping devices, all of which are altering present distribution systems and making it harder for technologically unsophisticated firms to remain competitive. Changing family patterns and the emergence of important minority consumer groups are driving producers to seek new distribution meth-

3. Bert Rosenbloom, *Marketing Channels: A Management View* (Hinsdale, Ill.: Dryden, 1987), p. 160.

4. Ibid., p. 161.

5. Ibid., pp. 254–255.

ods for reaching market segments, and sometimes this search results in non-traditional approaches that increase competitive pressures. Interest rates, inflation, and other economic variables affect members of distribution channels at every level. Environmental forces are numerous and complex and must be taken into account if distribution efforts are to be appropriate, efficient, and effective.

BEHAVIOUR OF CHANNEL MEMBERS

The marketing channel is a social system with its own conventions and behaviour patterns. Each channel member performs a different role in the system and agrees (implicitly or explicitly) to accept certain rights, responsibilities, rewards, and sanctions for non-conformity. Moreover, each channel member expects certain things of every other channel member. Retailers, for instance, expect wholesalers to maintain adequate inventories and deliver goods on time. For their part, wholesalers expect retailers to honour payment agreements and keep them informed of inventory needs. In this section we discuss several issues related to channel member behaviour, including co-operation, conflict, and leadership. Marketers need to understand these behavioural issues to make effective channel decisions.

■ Channel Co-operation

Channel co-operation is vital if each member is to gain something from other members.[6] Without co-operation, neither overall channel goals nor member goals can be realised. Policies must be developed that support all essential channel members; otherwise, failure of one link in the chain could destroy the channel.

There are several ways to improve channel co-operation. A marketing channel should consider itself a unified system, competing with other systems. This way, individual members will be less likely to take actions that would create disadvantages for other members. Similarly, channel members should agree to direct their efforts towards a common target market so that channel roles can be structured for maximum marketing effectiveness, which in turn can help members achieve their individual objectives. It is crucial to define precisely the tasks that each member of the channel is to perform. This provides a basis for reviewing the intermediaries' performance and helps reduce conflicts because each channel member knows exactly what is expected of it.

■ Channel Conflict

Although all channel members work toward the same general goal—distributing products profitably and efficiently—members may sometimes disagree about the best methods for attaining this goal. Each channel member wants to maximise its own profits while maintaining as much autonomy as possible. However, if this self-interest creates misunderstanding about role expectations, the end result is frustration and conflict for the whole channel. For individual organisations to function together in a single social system, each channel member must clearly communicate and understand role expectations.

Because channel integration and co-ordination are achieved through role behaviour, channel conflict often stems from perceived or real unmet role expectations.

6. Wroe Alderson, *Dynamic Marketing Behavior* (Homewood, Ill.: Irwin, 1965), p. 239.

That is, members of the channel expect a given channel member to conduct itself in a certain way and to make a particular contribution to the total system. Wholesalers expect producers to monitor quality control and production scheduling, and they expect retailers to market products effectively. Producers and retailers expect wholesalers to provide co-ordination, functional services, and communication. But if members do not fulfil their roles—for example, if wholesalers or producers fail to deliver products on time or the producers' pricing policies cut into the margins of downstream channel members—conflict may ensue. Marketing Update 9.1 tells how IBM deals with potential channel conflict.

Channel conflicts also arise when dealers over-emphasise competing products or diversify into product lines traditionally handled by other, more specialised intermediaries. In some cases, conflict develops because producers strive to increase efficiency by circumventing intermediaries, as is happening in marketing channels for microcomputer software. Many software-only stores are establishing direct relationships with software producers, by-passing wholesale distributors altogether. Some dishonest retailers are also pirating software or making unauthorised copies, thus cheating other channel members out of their due compensation. Consequently, suspicion and mistrust are heightening tensions in software marketing channels.[7]

A manufacturer embroiled in channel conflict may ship late (or not at all), withdraw financing, use promotion to build consumer brand loyalty, and operate or franchise its own retail outlet. To retaliate, a retailer may develop store brands, refuse to stock certain items, focus its buying power on one supplier or group of suppliers, and seek to strengthen its position in the marketing channel. Although there is no single method for resolving conflict, an atmosphere of co-operation can be re-established if two conditions are met. First, the role of each channel member must be specified. To minimise misunderstanding, all members must be able to expect unambiguous, agreed-on levels of performance from each other. Second, channel members must institute certain measures of channel co-ordination, which requires leadership and the benevolent exercise of control.[8] To prevent channel conflict, producers, or other channel members, may provide competing resellers with different brands, allocate markets among resellers, define direct sales policies to clarify potential conflict over large accounts, negotiate territorial issues between regional distributors, and provide recognition to certain resellers for the importance of their role in distributing to others. Hallmark, for example, distributes its Ambassador greetings-card line in discount stores and its name brand Hallmark line in up-market department stores, thus limiting the amount of competition among retailers carrying its products.[9]

■ Channel Leadership

The effectiveness of marketing channels hinges on channel leadership. Producers, retailers, or wholesalers may assume this leadership. To become a leader, a channel member must want to influence and direct overall channel performance. Further-

7. Lanny J. Ryan, Gaye C. Dawson, and Thomas Galek, "New Distribution Channels for Microcomputer Software," *Business*, October-December 1985, pp. 21–22.

8. Adel I. El-Ansary, "Perspectives on Channel System Performance," in *Contemporary Issues in Marketing Channels*, ed. Robert F. Lusch and Paul H. Zinszer (Norman: University of Oklahoma Press, 1979), p. 50.

9. Kenneth G. Hardy and Allan J. Magrath, "Ten Ways for Manufacturers to Improve Distribution Management," *Business Horizons*, November-December 1988, p. 68.

CO-OPERATION IN IBM'S MARKETING CHANNELS

IBM, the world's fifth largest industrial corporation, is trying to recover from a period of slow growth. As part of the recovery process, IBM executives have restructured the company's complex distribution system. In the past, IBM has had problems when members of its direct sales force came into conflict with IBM independent distributors. To resolve these conflicts, IBM executives have instituted new policies that have brought about co-operation between these two groups.

Concerning the new policies, one IBM independent distributor has said that IBM "has never been more aggressive about working with, instead of working against, the third party channel". IBM's marketing officials have reshaped its "value-added channel"—distributors that receive preferential contractual terms and conditions in return for meeting a set of rigorous standards. IBM now manages the value-added distributors on an individual basis, offering different arrangements to each. The company's marketers determine individual distributor policy according to each distributor's market, the distributor's ability to sell products, and IBM salespeople's coverage in the distributor's territory. IBM marketers also award more favourable contracts to distributors whose software solutions to customer problems are compatible with IBM's computer hardware.

To encourage channel co-operation between distributors and direct salespeople, IBM has adopted a policy that requires direct-sales branch offices to pass on prospect leads to distributors. Moreover, IBM executives have installed a new accounts bonus programme to reward ambitious distributors and have allowed distributors access to IBM computer demonstration centres.

Formerly, IBM used the titles "value-added reseller" to refer to distributors that sold mainly minicomputers and "value-added dealers" to refer to those that sold primarily microcomputers. Now the company calls these distributors "authorised industry re-marketers". Under a new programme, authorised industry re-marketers receive special protection against price changes, an improved equipment-return policy, and a better warranty system. IBM marketers are encouraging authorised industry re-marketers and direct salespeople to call jointly on potential customers.

SOURCES: "Computers and Office Equipment," *Sales & Marketing Management,* June 1989, pp. 43–44; Joel Dreyfuss, "Reinventing IBM," *Fortune,* 14 Aug. 1989, pp. 31–35, 38; and Robert F. McCarthy, "IBM Muscles the Distribution Channel—Again," *Business Marketing,* August 1988, pp. 49–50, 52, 54, 56–57.

FIGURE 9.9
Determinants of channel leadership

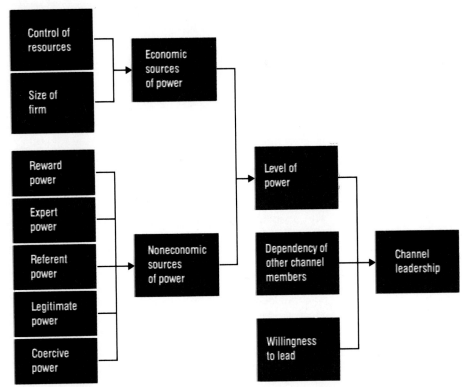

SOURCE: R.D. Michman and S.D. Sibley, *Marketing Channels and Strategies,* 2nd ed. (Worthington, Oh.: Publishing Horizons, Inc., 1980), p. 413. Reproduced by permission.

more, to attain desired objectives, the leader must possess **channel power**, which is the ability to influence another channel member's goal achievement. As Figure 9.9 shows, the channel leader derives power from seven sources, two of them economic and five non-economic.

The five non-economic powers—reward, expert, referent, legitimate, and coercive—are crucial for establishing leadership. A channel leader gains reward power by providing financial benefits. Expert power exists when other channel members believe that the leader provides special expertise required for the channel to function properly. Referent power emerges when other members strongly identify with and emulate the leader. Legitimate power is based on a superior-subordinate relationship. Coercive power is a function of the leader's ability to punish other channel members.[10]

In many countries, producers assume the leadership role in marketing channels. A manufacturer—whose large-scale production efficiency demands increasing sales volume—may exercise power by giving channel members financing, business advice, ordering assistance, advertising, and support materials. For example, BMW and Mercedes control their dealers totally, specifying showroom design and layout, discount levels, and quotas of models. Coercion causes dealer dissatisfaction that is

10. Ronald D. Michman and Stanley D. Sibley, *Marketing Channels and Strategies* (Columbus, Ohio: Grid Publishing, 1980), pp. 412–417.

stronger than any impact from rewards, so the use of coercive power can be a major cause of channel conflict.[11]

Retailers can also function as channel leaders, and with the domination of national chains and own-label merchandise they are increasingly doing so. Small retailers, too, may share in the leadership role when they command particular consumer respect and patronage in local or regional markets. Among large retailers, Boots, John Lewis, and Sainsbury base their channel leadership on wide public exposure to their products. These retailers control many brands and sometimes replace uncooperative producers. Marks & Spencer exercises power by dictating manufacturing techniques, lead-times, quality levels, and product specifications.

Wholesalers assume channel leadership roles as well, although they were more powerful decades ago, when most manufacturers and retailers were small, underfinanced, and widely scattered. Today wholesaler leaders may form voluntary chains with several retailers, which they supply with bulk buying or management services or which market their own brands. In return, the retailers shift most of their purchasing to the wholesaler leader. The Independent Grocers' Alliance (IGA) is one of the best-known wholesaler leaders in the United States. IGA's power is based on the expert advertising, pricing, and purchasing knowledge it makes available to independent business owners. Other wholesaler leaders such as Intersport or Mace might also help retailers with store layouts, accounting, and inventory control.

Legal Issues in Channel Management

The multitude of laws governing channel management are based on the general principle that the public is best served when competition and free trade are protected. Under the authority of such legislation as the Monopolies and Mergers Commission Fair Trading Act, Prices Act, Trade Description Act, and Consumer Protection Act, the courts and regulatory agencies determine under what circumstances channel management practices violate this underlying principle and must be restricted and when these practices may be permitted. Although channel managers are not expected to be legal experts, they should be aware that attempts to control distribution functions may have legal repercussions. The following practices are among those frequently subject to legal restraint.

Restricted Sales Territories

To tighten its control over the distribution of its products, a manufacturer may try to prohibit intermediaries from selling its products outside designated sales territories. The intermediaries themselves often favour this practice because it lets them avoid competition for the producer's brands within their own territories. Many companies have long followed the policy of restricting sales in this fashion. In recent years, the courts have adopted conflicting positions in regard to restricted sales territories. Although they have deemed restricted sales territories a restraint of trade among intermediaries handling the same brands (except for small or newly established companies), the courts have also held that exclusive territories can actually promote competition among dealers handling different brands. At present, the producer's

---

11. John F. Gaski and John R. Nevin, "The Differential Effects of Exercised and Unexercised Power Sources in a Marketing Channel," *Journal of Marketing Research*, July 1985, p. 139.

intent in establishing restricted territories and the overall effect of doing so on the market must be evaluated for each case individually.

■ **Tying Contracts**

When a supplier (usually a manufacturer or franchiser) furnishes a product to a channel member with the stipulation that the channel member must purchase other products as well, a *tying contract* exists.[12] Suppliers, for instance, may institute tying arrangements to move weaker products along with more popular items. To use another example, a franchiser may tie the purchase of equipment and supplies to the sale of franchises, justifying the policy as necessary for quality control and protection of the franchiser's reputation.

A related practice is full-line forcing. In this situation, a supplier requires that channel members purchase the supplier's entire line to obtain any of the products. Manufacturers sometimes use full-line forcing to ensure that intermediaries accept new products and that a suitable range of products is available to customers.

The courts accept tying contracts when the supplier alone can provide products of a certain quality, when the intermediary is free to carry competing products as well, and when a company has just entered the market. Most other tying contracts are considered illegal.

■ **Exclusive Dealing**

When a manufacturer forbids an intermediary to carry products of competing manufacturers, the arrangement is called *exclusive dealing*. A manufacturer receives considerable market protection in an exclusive dealing arrangement and may cut off shipments to an intermediary who violates such an agreement. Marketing Update 9.2 focuses on car manufacturers' control of their dealers.

An exclusive dealing contract is generally legally permitted if dealers and customers in a given market have access to similar products or if the exclusive dealing contract strengthens an otherwise weak competitor.

■ **Refusal to Deal**

Producers have the right to choose the channel members with whom they will do business (and the right not to choose others). Within existing distribution channels, however, suppliers may not refuse to deal with wholesalers or dealers just because these wholesalers or dealers have resisted policies that are anticompetitive or in restraint of trade. Suppliers are further prohibited from organising some channel members in refusal-to-deal actions against other members who choose not to comply with illegal policies.[13]

SUMMARY

Distribution refers to activities that make products available to customers when and where they want to purchase them. A channel of distribution, or marketing channel, is a group of individuals and organisations that direct the flow of products from producers to customers. In most channels of distribution, producers and customers are linked by marketing intermediaries or middlemen, called merchants if they take

12. Bert Rosenbloom, *Marketing Channels: A Management View* (Hinsdale, Ill.: Dryden Press, 1987), p. 98.
13. Ibid., pp. 96–97.

CAR DISTRIBUTION UNDER EC DEREGULATION

Most car manufacturers throughout Europe have their own dealer networks—a particular car showroom will be contractually obliged to retail one manufacturer's vehicles only. A few showrooms are owned by manufacturers but most are independently owned companies which have the Saab or Rover franchise, for example.

Manufacturers exert a great deal of control over their dealers, specifying corporate identity and showroom design, service levels, and selling techniques. Some, such as BMW or Mercedes, issue quotas of vehicles to individual dealers and specify every minute detail down to signage and showroom displays. Most manufacturers have used their power to force showrooms to stock only their own products, never cars of a rival manufacturer. Dealers generally have to be on solus sites, with no other franchise on their site.

European Community deregulation in 1992 changes the situation. Not only will consumers be able to buy a particular model from anywhere in the Community, with relaxed import/export restrictions, but dealers will be able to hold several rival manufacturers' franchises in the same showroom, or they will be able to locate on car showroom "retail parks." Legally, the balance of control will move away from the manufacturers. In practice, it remains to be seen how tightly they will continue to exert control and put pressure on dealers.

SOURCES: Willem Molle, "The Economics of European Integration," (Aldershot: Dartmouth, 1990); Guy de Jonquieres and David Buchan, "Japanese Car Import Agreement Threatened by EC Disarray," *Financial Times,* 25 September 1990, p. 1c; Paolo Cecchini, "The European Challenge 1992," Wildwood House, 1988; and Tony Cutler, Colin Haslam, John Williams, Karel Williams, *1992—The Struggle for Europe* (New York: BERG, 1989).

title to products and functional middlemen if they do not take title. Channel structure reflects the division of responsibilities among members.

Channels of distribution are broadly classified as channels for consumer products or channels for industrial products. Within these two broad categories, different marketing channels are used for different products. Although some consumer goods move directly from producer to consumers, consumer product channels that include wholesalers and retailers are usually more economical and efficient. Industrial goods move directly from producer to end users more frequently than do consumer goods. Channels for industrial products may also include agents, industrial distributors, or both. Most producers have dual or multiple channels so that the distribution system can be adjusted for various target markets.

Although intermediaries can be eliminated, their functions are vital and cannot be dropped; these activities must be performed by someone in the marketing channel or passed on to customers. Because intermediaries serve both producers and buyers, they reduce the total number of transactions that would otherwise be needed to move products from producer to ultimate users. Intermediaries' specialised functions also help keep down costs.

An assortment is a combination of products assembled to provide benefits. Intermediaries perform sorting activities essential to the development of product assortments. Sorting activities allow channel members to divide roles and separate tasks. Through the basic tasks of sorting out, accumulating, allocating, and assorting products for buyers, intermediaries resolve discrepancies in quantity and assortment. The number and characteristics of intermediaries are determined by the assortments and by the expertise needed to perform distribution activities.

Integration of marketing channels brings various activities under the management of one channel member. Vertical integration combines two or more stages of the channel under one management. The vertical marketing system is managed centrally for the mutual benefit of all channel members. Vertical marketing systems may be corporate, administered, or contractual. Horizontal integration combines institutions at the same level of channel operation under a single management.

A marketing channel is managed so that products receive appropriate market coverage. In choosing intensive distribution, producers strive to make a product available to all possible dealers. In selective distribution, dealers are screened to choose those most qualified for exposing a product properly. Exclusive distribution usually gives one dealer exclusive rights to sell a product in a large geographic area.

When selecting distribution channels for products, manufacturers evaluate potential channel members carefully. Producers also consider the organisation's objectives and available resources; the location, density, and size of a market; buyers' behaviour in the target market; characteristics of the product; and outside forces in the marketing environment.

A marketing channel is a social system in which individuals and organisations are linked by a common goal: the profitable and efficient distribution of goods and services. The positions or roles of channel members are associated with rights, responsibilities, and rewards, as well as sanctions for non-conformity. Channels function most efficiently when members co-operate, but when they deviate from their roles, channel conflict can arise. Effective marketing channels are usually a result of channel leadership.

Channel leaders can facilitate or hinder the attainment of other members' goals, and they derive this power from authority, coercion, rewards, referents, or expertise.

Producers are in an excellent position to structure channel policy and to use technical expertise and consumer acceptance to influence other channel members. Retailers gain channel control through consumer confidence, wide product mixes, and intimate knowledge of consumers. Wholesalers become channel leaders when they have expertise that other channel members value and when they can co-ordinate functions to match supply with demand.

IMPORTANT TERMS

Distribution
Channel of distribution
Marketing intermediary
Merchants
Functional middlemen
Dual distribution
Assortment
Sorting activities
Sorting out
Accumulation

Allocation
Assorting
Vertical channel integration
Vertical marketing system (VMS)
Horizontal channel integration
Intensive distribution
Selective distribution
Exclusive distribution
Channel power

DISCUSSION AND REVIEW QUESTIONS

1. Compare and contrast the four major types of marketing channels for consumer products. Through which type of channel is each of the following products most likely to be distributed: (a) new cars, (b) cheese biscuits, (c) cut-your-own Christmas trees, (d) new textbooks, (e) sofas, (f) soft drinks?
2. "Shorter channels are usually a more direct means of distribution and therefore are more efficient." Comment on this statement.
3. Describe an industrial distributor. What types of products are marketed through industrial distributors?
4. Under what conditions is a producer most likely to use more than one marketing channel?
5. Why do consumers often blame intermediaries for distribution inefficiencies? List several of the reasons.
6. How do the major functions that intermediaries perform help resolve the discrepancies in assortment and quantity?
7. How does the number of intermediaries in the channel relate to the assortments retailers need?
8. Can one channel member perform all channel functions?
9. Identify and explain the major factors that influence decision-makers' selection of marketing channels.
10. Name and describe firms that use (a) vertical integration and (b) horizontal integration in their marketing channels.
11. Explain the major characteristics of each of the three types of vertical marketing systems (VMSs).
12. Explain the differences among intensive, selective, and exclusive methods of distribution.

13. "Channel co-operation requires that members support the overall channel goals to achieve individual goals." Comment on this statement.
14. How do power bases within the channel influence the selection of the channel leader?

■ CASES

9.1 Marketing Channels for California Cooler

When California Cooler was introduced commercially in the early 1980s, the low-alcohol mixture of white wine and fruit juice was in a category by itself. Since then, as many as 150 cooler brands, both wine- and malt-based, have been jostling for a share of the cooler market, but California Cooler remains near the top, behind only Joseph E. Seagram and Sons' Seagram's Wine Coolers and E&J Gallo Winery's Bartles & Jaymes. Recently, California Cooler accounted for about 13.1 percent of the $1.6 billion cooler market; total sales (U.S.) of its citrus, orange, tropical fruit, and peach flavours were estimated at 9.1 million cases.

For the past several years, California Cooler has been owned by Brown-Forman Beverage Company, producer of such brands as Jack Daniel's Tennessee Whiskey and Southern Comfort. The product originated in the 1970s on a California beach, when Michael Crete mixed chablis and citrus juice in plastic tubs as an alternative to cold beer for his volleyball-playing friends. The cooler was the hit of the party, and during the next few years Crete kept experimenting with the formula, taking note of rising consumer interest in non-alcoholic and low-alcohol beverages. Convinced that his cooler had market potential, Crete—then working as a beer and wine distributor—began to give his wine customers bottled samples. The customers asked for more, and by 1981 Crete decided to go into cooler production full-time.

Crete and a friend from high school, Stuart Bewley, each put up $5,000 to start the business. Operating first out of an abandoned migrant farm workers' camp and later from a vacant wine warehouse in Lodi, California, the two did everything themselves: mixing, bottling, capping, and labelling. Initially, they also handled distribution, supplying their accounts from the back of Bewley's 1953 pickup.

After five months, with the wine cooler sales totaling 700 cases, demand was beginning to exceed the fledgling company's modest production rate. Crete and Bewley hired one employee, paying him in stock, and decided to broaden their distribution network. Despite California Cooler's wine content, Crete and Bewley found beer wholesalers more receptive to the new product than wine distributors. For one thing, from the outset Crete and Bewley followed standard beer marketing practice by using foil-wrapped 12.7-ounce bottles (which resembled imported beers), 4-pack cartons, and 24-bottle cases. In addition, the cooler—clearly intended as a leisure-time beverage, not as a drink to be sipped with meals—was directed primarily at beer and soft-drink consumers, not at wine drinkers. Furthermore, the cooler sold better when chilled, and most wine distributors declined to work in the refrigerated cases ("cold boxes"), where beer wholesalers predominated.

Eventually, several Adolph Coors distributors agreed to carry California Cooler, and in 1982 sales zoomed to 80,000 cases. Distributors liked California Cooler because it could be warehoused and handled alongside beer and required only some rearranging of products in the cold boxes. Moreover, the new beverage, priced at less than $1 a bottle and seldom discounted, offered distributors healthy profits.

Whereas most beer lines earned California distributors margins of 20 to 22 percent, California Cooler yielded returns closer to the 33 percent typical of wine products. California Cooler sold briskly and soon developed a following, even though at that point the product had been advertised only through in-store displays and by word of mouth.

The use of outside distribution enabled Crete and Bewley to move their wine cooler into mass markets that otherwise would have been out of reach. The California distributors who handled the cooler serviced various establishments, from family-owned off-licences to giant chain stores. After one year in outside distribution, California Cooler reached $1.4 million (180,000 gallons) in sales, and it was available throughout the state. The next year, after the company began distribution in Texas and Arizona, sales were up to $26 million wholesale. Within two more years, California Cooler was being handled by a network of 500 beer wholesalers and being distributed in 49 states.

The success of California Cooler was noticed by the wine industry, where sales had become flat and no new product had been introduced for years. Competing wine coolers quickly appeared on the market, including Bartles & Jaymes, Sun Country (Canandaigua Wine Co.), and Seagram's Coolers. (Sales volume of all coolers jumped 1,900 percent within the first two years after the product was introduced.) Retailers finally accepted coolers as a permanent category, allocating the products more shelf space. At the same time, however, retailers became more selective about the brands they carried, sometimes limiting their stock to the top five or six coolers, plus one or two regional brands. The ensuing struggle for market share led producers to cut prices and to engage in heavy promotional spending.

After a time, certain weaknesses in California Cooler's wholesale network became evident, particularly in comparison with Gallo's powerful and aggressive distribution system. For example, although the beer distributors that carried California Cooler visited retailers frequently, their territories were smaller than those of wine distributors and often overlapped. A retailer might be contacted by a single Gallo distributor with one price, but by several beer wholesalers, each quoting different prices. In addition, California Cooler's competitors could field larger, more experienced sales forces. California Cooler's sales volume continued to increase, but the product's market share began to decline.

Today, although acknowledging the marketing strength of its competitors, Brown-Forman (which paid Crete and Bewley more than $55 million, plus a percentage of future sales, for the ownership of California Cooler) insists that it has distribution muscle of its own. Brown-Forman recently reorganised and consolidated its sales territories for greater efficiency and strength in the distribution of its products, including California Cooler. Predicting continued growth in the cooler market, Brown-Forman executives plan to position California Cooler as a year-round beverage and will try to broaden the age segment targeted for the cooler. The company notes further that coolers now account for 25 percent of all wine products consumed in the United States and have entered foreign markets which are becoming increasingly important to the beverage business.

The number-one position in the wine cooler industry has changed three times in three years. With a new $30 million advertising and promotion campaign, a reformulation of the cooler ingredients, a redesigned package, and a new cherry-flavoured product, Brown-Forman officials hope to regain and maintain the leading spot.

SOURCES: "Brown-Forman Aims to Bolster Presence in Wine Cooler Market," *Wall Street Journal*, 11 June 1987, p. 8B; Brown-Forman Inc., *1987 Annual Report*, pp. 8–10; "The Concoction That's Raising Spirits in the Wine Industry," *Business Week*, 8 Oct. 1984, p. 182; Harvey M. Lederman, "Cooler Success Freezes out Most Competitors," *Advertising Age*, 6 Oct. 1986, p. S-1; Marcy Magiera, "A Cool Operator: California Cooler Gets Stylish As It Seeks to Ace Competitors," *Advertising Age*, 16 May 1988, pp. 3, 8; Paula Schnorbus, "Cool(ers) and the Gang," *Marketing & Media Decisions*, May 1987, pp. 127–128; Richard Street, "How They Became Kings of Coolers," *Nation's Business*, October 1985, p. 68; and Patricia Winters, "No Cooler on Beach," *Advertising Age*, 21 Mar. 1988, p. 80A.

Questions for Discussion

1. When establishing marketing channels for a product such as California Cooler, what important factors must be considered?
2. Why did Crete and Bewley select beer distributors to be part of the marketing channel for California Cooler?
3. Is California Cooler being distributed through intensive, selective, or exclusive distribution?

9.2 Channel Selection for Cincinnati Microwave's Escort and Passport Radar Detectors

For years motorists with a penchant for exceeding speed limits have been beating a mail-order path to the door of Cincinnati Microwave, maker of the Escort radar detector, a device that alerts speeding drivers to police radar signals. Though in recent years their sales have declined when compared with the exponential sales figures of their early years, the executives at Cincinnati Microwave think they can regain their old momentum.

The Escort came into being when electrical engineers James Jaeger and Michael Valentine analysed the workings of a radar detector Jaeger had just purchased and saw how the model could be improved. The two first offered their idea to Electrolert Inc., maker of the Fuzzbuster, the best-selling detector at that time. When Electrolert showed no interest, Valentine and Jaeger formed a partnership to build their own detectors. Working out of Jaeger's basement on money Valentine's father had lent them, the two entrepreneurs used sophisticated heterodyne technology to produce a detector with a microwave system to amplify and filter incoming signals, thereby increasing the detector's range and reducing false alarms.

To attract an up-market clientele, Jaeger and Valentine introduced the Escort at $245, a price almost twice that of competing models. They also decided to sell the product exclusively by mail. The fledgling company could not afford retail distribution, and direct marketing would minimise risk because the detectors could be manufactured as orders arrived and would not need to be shipped until customers' cheques or credit card payments had been cleared. In addition, mail-order distribution would enable Jaeger and Valentine to expand the company without tying up borrowed capital in extensive inventory.

Jaeger and Valentine published a toll-free telephone number in *Road & Track* and *Motor Trend* and took turns answering the phone. At first orders trickled in at a rate of 250 or so per month. By the end of the first year, Cincinnati Microwave had sold about 1,800 units. Then *Car & Driver* published the results of comparison tests on radar detectors, calling the Escort the most reliable and sensitive model on the market. The magazine also exposed the fraudulent claims of a competing firm, whose entry was merely an Escort with a different exterior. Escort sales took off. Within six months Cincinnati Microwave was swamped with more than 1,400 orders every month; at one point the company was thirty-three weeks behind in filling orders.

After a year of rapid growth, Cincinnati Microwave regained control of operations by expanding production, computerising many functions, and hiring more personnel. (During one period the company was adding ten to twenty new employees per week.) Four years after its founding, Cincinnati Microwave's revenues had risen from $2.1 million to $57.1 million. During the start-up period, Jaeger was in charge of production and Valentine handled marketing. After disagreements over strategy, however, Jaeger bought out Valentine and his father, floated the company, and began to delegate management functions to other executives.

Cincinnati Microwave expected the demand for radar detectors to level off after a few years, and increased competition from low-priced radar detectors, including some Japanese models, has hurt the company's sales immensely. Industry analysts think that Cincinnati Microwave made a huge mistake in not meeting competitors' prices on comparable radar detectors. Cincinnati Microwave's sales have also been hampered by the actions taken by some states to restrict the use of detectors.

Cincinnati Microwave's efforts to diversify into other product areas have not been successful. The company has discontinued its ventures into satellite television receivers and luggage. Cincinnati Microwave executives had great expectations from a product they named the Guardian Interlock. This device, an auto ignition interlock system designed to keep intoxicated drivers from starting their cars, never met anticipated sales predictions.

Currently, Cincinnati Microwave is entering the cellular telephone market in a joint marketing agreement with the telecommunications giant GTE. GTE Mobilnet will provide customers with cellular phone products and services, while Cincinnati Microwave will exclusively direct the advertising, selling, and distribution of the products. Executives from both companies think that cellular phones will appeal to the same customers who purchase high-performance radar detectors—a group that Cincinnati Microwave is intimately familiar with. GTE Mobilnet will also furnish service support to cellular phones sold under the Cincinnati Microwave name (these phones will be manufactured by Motorola Inc. under a separate agreement).

Cincinnati Microwave's major strengths are its reputation for excellent customer service and a mailing list of two million names. By expanding its product mix, the company hopes to regain the success it once had. However, Cincinnati Microwave does not intend to abandon the radar detector industry. It has increased its investment in electronics research and development and plans to continue offering premium performance items while becoming more competitive in price.

SOURCES: Warren Brown, "Radar Detector Maker Thrives Despite Attacks," *Washington Post,* 1 June 1986, p. F1; "Is Microwave's Future Calling with GTE Deal?" *Business Record* (Cincinnati, Ohio), 6 Mar. 1989; "Microwave Learning from Its Mistakes," *Cincinnati Enquirer,* 10 Aug. 1987, p. D6; "Microwave to Transfer Subsidiary's Product," *Cincinnati Business Courier,* 8 Mar. 1987, p. 9; Michele Morris, "Dollar Signs on a Radar Screen," *Financial World,* 22 Aug.-4 Sept. 1984, pp. 80–81; "New Market Detected," *Cincinnati Enquirer,* 6 July 1989; "Radar's Foe," *Barron's,* 23 Dec. 1985, pp. 35–36; Michael Rogers, "Speed Bumps Ahead for Cincinnati Microwave," *Fortune,* 28 Apr. 1986, p. 84; "Sales Drop Signals Problems for Cincinnati Microwave," *Cincinnati Enquirer,* 10 Aug. 1987, p. D1; Jolie B. Solomon, "Learning to Manage," *Wall Street Journal,* 20 May 1985, pp. 38C–40C; and Barry Stavro, "A License to Speed," *Forbes,* 10 Sept. 1984, p. 94.

Questions for Discussion

1. Why did Cincinnati Microwave initially select a direct distribution channel for its radar detectors?
2. What are the advantages and disadvantages of using a direct channel of distribution for products such as radar detectors?
3. If Cincinnati Microwave were to use a second marketing channel in addition to the direct channel, what channel would you recommend?

10 WHOLESALING

Objectives

To understand the nature of wholesaling in the marketing channel

To learn about wholesalers' activities

To understand how wholesalers are classified

To examine organisations that facilitate wholesaling

To explore changing patterns in wholesaling

McKesson Corporation is the leading wholesale distributor of health care products in the United States. Though it also distributes beauty aids, general merchandise, specialty foods, bottled water, and office supplies, its primary line of business is drug wholesaling. Throughout its existence, McKesson has revolutionised the health care industry by providing retailers with distribution innovations, new avenues of customer support, and electronic information systems.

Decades ago, McKesson executives realised that because their firm offered the same physical products as its competitors, it needed to differentiate itself from other drug wholesalers by offering retailers more services and benefits. McKesson's Economost electronic order-entry system assisted retailers in cutting costs. Giving retailers the capability to automatically order products using hand-held order-entry devices, McKesson reduced retailers' labour costs, product costs, and inventory holdings.

McKesson set out to assist in particular smaller retail chemists that were competing with the larger health care chains. It organised these stores into purchasing co-operatives, which could then receive volume discounts comparable to the ones given to giant chain operations. Using research gathered by its sales force, McKesson learned that the smaller stores wanted help with marketing research, shelf-management planning, centralised warehousing and storage, and co-operative advertising and joint marketing. McKesson assisted them in all these areas, thus establishing a loyal base of customers. Because of McKesson's efforts, the smaller chemists were able to offer consumers reduced prices and better services—making them more profitable and stable enterprises. ◆

Based on information in Eric Clemons and Michael Row, "A Strategic Information System: McKesson Drug Company's Economost," *Planning Review,* September-October 1988, pp. 14–19; Meghan O'Leary, "Getting the Most Out of Buying at Cost," *CIO,* August 1989, pp. 86–88; and William L. Trombetta, "Channel Systems: An Idea Whose Time Has Come in Health Care Marketing," *Journal of Health Care Marketing,* September 1989, pp. 26–35.

I n this chapter we focus on wholesaling activities (such as those provided by McKesson) within a marketing channel. We view wholesaling as all exchanges among organisations and individuals in marketing channels, except transactions with ultimate consumers. First we examine the importance of wholesalers and their functions, noting the services they render to producers and retailers alike. Then we classify various types of wholesalers and facilitating organisations. Finally, we explore changing patterns in wholesaling.

THE NATURE AND IMPORTANCE OF WHOLESALING

Wholesaling comprises all transactions in which the purchaser intends to use the product for resale, for making other products, or for general business operations. It does not include exchanges with ultimate consumers. Wholesaling establishments are engaged primarily in selling products directly to industrial, reseller, government, and institutional users.

A **wholesaler** is an individual or organisation engaged in facilitating and expediting exchanges that are primarily wholesale transactions. Only occasionally does a wholesaler engage in retail transactions, which are sales to ultimate consumers. There are more than 337,943 wholesaling establishments in the United States.[1]

THE ACTIVITIES OF WHOLESALERS

In America and in Europe more than 50 percent of all products are exchanged, or their exchange is negotiated, through wholesaling institutions. Owing to the strength of large, national retailers, in the U.K. wholesaling is not as important in consumer markets. There are also far fewer wholesalers. For example, just 27 wholesale companies and buying groups account for 85 percent of the grocery wholesale market. Of course, it is important to remember that the distribution of all goods requires wholesaling activities, whether or not a wholesaling institution is involved. Table 10.1 lists the major activities wholesalers perform. The activities are not mutually exclusive; individual wholesalers may perform more or fewer activities than Table 10.1 shows. Wholesalers provide marketing activities for organisations above and below them in the marketing channel.

■ **Services for Producers**

Producers, above wholesalers in the marketing channel, have a distinct advantage when they use wholesalers. Wholesalers perform specialised accumulation and allocation functions for a number of products, thus allowing producers to concentrate on developing and manufacturing products that match consumers' wants.

Wholesalers provide other services to producers as well. By selling a manufacturer's products to retailers and other customers and by initiating sales contacts with the manufacturer, wholesalers serve as an extension of the producer's sales force. Wholesalers also provide four forms of financial assistance. They often pay the costs of transporting goods; they reduce a producer's warehousing expenses and inventory

1. *Statistical Abstract of the United States,* 1989, p. 761.

TABLE 10.1
Major wholesaling activities

ACTIVITY	DESCRIPTION
Wholesale management	Planning, organising, staffing, and controlling wholesaling operations
Negotiating with suppliers	Serving as the purchasing agent for customers by negotiating supplies
Promotion	Providing a sales force, advertising, sales promotion, and publicity
Warehousing and product handling	Receiving, storing and stock keeping, order processing, packaging, shipping outgoing orders, and materials handling
Transport	Arranging and making local and long-distance shipments
Inventory control and data processing	Controlling physical inventory, book keeping, recording transactions, keeping records for financial analysis
Security	Safeguarding merchandise
Pricing	Developing prices and providing price quotations
Financing and budgeting	Extending credit, borrowing, making capital investments, and forecasting cash flow
Management and marketing assistance to clients	Supplying information about markets and products and providing advisory services to assist customers in their sales efforts

investment by holding goods in inventory; they extend credit and assume the losses from buyers who turn out to be poor credit risks; and when they buy a producer's entire output and pay promptly or in cash, they are a source of working capital. In addition, wholesalers are conduits for information within the marketing channel, keeping manufacturers up-to-date on market developments and passing along the manufacturers' promotional plans to other middlemen in the channel.

Ideally, many producers would like more direct interaction with retailers. Wholesalers, however, usually have closer contact with retailers because of their strategic position in the marketing channel. Besides, even though a producer's own sales force is probably more effective in its selling efforts, the costs of maintaining a sales force and performing the activities normally done by wholesalers are usually higher than the benefits received from better selling. Wholesalers can also spread their costs over many more products than most producers, resulting in lower costs per product unit. For these reasons, many producers have chosen to control promotion and influence the pricing of products and have shifted transport, warehousing, and financing functions to wholesalers.

■ **Services for Retailers**

Wholesalers help their retailer customers select inventory. In industries where obtaining supplies is important, skilled buying is essential. A wholesaler who buys is a specialist in understanding market conditions and an expert at negotiating final purchases. For example, based on its understanding of local customer needs and market conditions, a building-supply wholesaler purchases inventory ahead of season so that it can provide its retail customers with the building supplies they want when they want them.[2] A retailer's buyer can thus avoid the responsibility of looking for and co-ordinating supply sources. Moreover, if the wholesaler makes purchases for several different buyers, expenses can be shared by all customers. Another advantage is that a manufacturer's salespersons can offer retailers only a few products at a time, but independent wholesalers have a wide range of products available.

By buying in large quantities and delivering to customers in smaller lots, a wholesaler can perform physical distribution activities—such as transport, materials handling, inventory planning, communication, and warehousing—more efficiently and can provide more service than a producer or retailer would be able to do with its own physical distribution system. Furthermore, wholesalers can provide quick and frequent delivery even when demand fluctuates. They are experienced in providing fast delivery at low cost, which lets the producer and the wholesalers' customers avoid risks associated with holding large product inventories.

Because they carry products for many customers, wholesalers can maintain a wide product line at a relatively low cost. Often wholesalers can perform storage and warehousing activities more efficiently, permitting retailers to concentrate on other marketing activities. When wholesalers provide storage and warehousing, they generally take on the ownership function as well, an arrangement that frees retailers' and producers' capital for other purposes. Marketing Update 10.1 deals with the variety of services that Super Valu provides to retailers in America.

CLASSIFYING WHOLESALERS

Many types of wholesalers meet the different needs of producers and retailers. In addition, new institutions and establishments develop in response to producers and retail organisations that want to take over wholesaling functions. Wholesalers adjust their activities as the contours of the marketing environment change.

Wholesalers are classified along several dimensions. Whether a wholesaler is owned by the producer influences how it is classified. Wholesalers are also grouped as to whether they take title to (actually own) the products they handle. The range of services provided is another criterion used for classification. Finally, wholesalers are classified according to the breadth and depth of their product lines. Using these dimensions, we discuss three general categories, or types, of wholesaling establishments: (1) merchant wholesalers, (2) agents and brokers, and (3) manufacturers' sales branches and offices.

■ **Merchant Wholesalers**

Merchant wholesalers are wholesalers that take title to goods and assume the risks associated with ownership. These independently owned businesses, which make up about two-thirds of all wholesale establishments, generally buy and resell products to industrial or retail customers. A producer is likely to use merchant wholesalers when selling directly to customers would be economically unfeasible. From the producer's point of view, merchant wholesalers are also valuable for providing market coverage, making sales contacts, storing inventory, handling orders, collecting

2. Clarence Casson, "1988 Wholesaler Giants; Making All the Right Moves," *Building Supply Home Centers,* September 1988, p. 56.

SUPER VALU PROVIDES MANY SERVICES TO RETAILERS

Based in Elden Prairie, Minnesota, Super Valu Stores Inc. is the number two food wholesaling business in the United States (behind Fleming). Super Valu supplies grocery stores throughout the nation with food and non-food items from 18 distribution centres. In addition, Super Valu provides marketing assistance and design-planning services to the stores it serves. The wholesaler monitors stores' performances and makes subsequent operating suggestions on how the stores might improve. Super Valu executives encourage retailers to modernise their facilities and may even make arrangement recommendations.

Super Valu spends about 50 percent, or over $243 million, of its total budget on its wholesale operations. Top Super Valu executives are firmly committed to reinvesting in their business. Much of Super Valu's wholesale budget is currently devoted to the expansion and modernisation of warehouse facilities.

A computer innovation also has allowed Super Valu to monitor store orders and inventories more effectively—its electronic data interchange (EDI) system. EDI is a communications operation that uses electronic versions of such common business documents as purchase orders and invoices. By electronically communicating with retailers, Super Valu has cut down on ordering errors and provides much quicker service. In addition, the inventories of Super Valu's retailers have been reduced because they no longer have to overbuy to preserve sufficient stock levels. Super Valu executives are trying to convince their own suppliers to adopt EDI systems. They are pleased with the system's results and are eager to extend its applications.

As the general trend of consolidation in the grocery wholesale industry continues, it is likely that Super Valu will grow even larger. With its constant expansion and continued profitability, many Wall Street analysts consider Super Valu to be the best-managed company in its industry.

SOURCES: Torrey Byles, "Grocery Chain Says Invoices Key to Managing Inventory," *Journal of Commerce,* 26 Jan. 1989, p. F9; Harlan S. Byrne, "Super Valu Stores Inc.," *Barron's,* 24 Apr. 1989, pp. 49–50; "Super Valu Stores Inc.," *City Business/Twin Cities* (Minneapolis, Minnesota), 8 Feb. 1988, p. G7; "Super Valu Stores Inc.," *Corporate Report* (Minneapolis, Minnesota), 1 May 1989, p. C4; and "Super Valu to Increase Capital Spending 25%," *Supermarket News,* 27 Feb. 1989, pp. 1, 40.

FIGURE 10.1

Types of merchant wholesalers

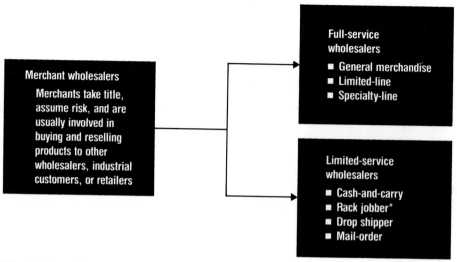

Merchant wholesalers

Merchants take title, assume risk, and are usually involved in buying and reselling products to other wholesalers, industrial customers, or retailers

Full-service wholesalers
■ General merchandise
■ Limited-line
■ Specialty-line

Limited-service wholesalers
■ Cash-and-carry
■ Rack jobber*
■ Drop shipper
■ Mail-order

*Rack jobbers, in many cases, provide such a large number of services that they can be classified as full-service, specialty-line wholesalers.

market information, and furnishing customer support.[3] Some merchant wholesalers are even involved in packaging and developing own-label brands to help their retailer customers be competitive.

During the past thirty years, merchant wholesalers have expanded their share of the wholesale market, despite competition from other types of intermediaries. Now, they account for more than half (58 percent) of all wholesale revenues.[4] As a rule, merchant wholesalers for industrial products are better established and earn higher profits than consumer-goods merchant wholesalers; the latter normally deal in products of lower unit value and face more competition from other middlemen. Industrial-products wholesalers are also more likely to have selective distribution arrangements with manufacturers because of the technical nature of many industrial products.

Merchant wholesalers go by various names, including wholesaler, jobber, distributor, assembler, exporter, and importer.[5] They fall into one of two broad categories: full-service and limited-service. Figure 10.1 illustrates the different types of merchant wholesalers.

Full-Service Merchant Wholesalers. **Full-service wholesalers** are middlemen who offer the widest possible range of wholesaling functions. Their customers rely on them for product availability, suitable assortments, bulk-breaking (breaking large quantities into smaller ones), financial assistance, and technical advice and service.[6] Full-service wholesalers provide numerous marketing services to interested customers. Many large grocery wholesalers, for example, help retailers with store design,

3. Bert Rosenbloom, *Marketing Channels: A Management View* (Hinsdale, Ill.: Dryden Press, 1987), p. 63.

4. *U.S. Census of Wholesale Trade*, May 1985, p. 207.

5. Rosenbloom, p. 34.

6. Ibid., p. 63.

site selection, personnel training, financing, merchandising, advertising, coupon redemption, and scanning. Although full-service wholesalers often earn higher gross margins than other wholesalers, their operating expenses are also higher because they perform a wider range of functions. Full-service merchant wholesalers may handle either consumer products or industrial products and are categorised as general merchandise, limited-line, or specialty-line wholesalers.

General Merchandise Wholesalers. **General merchandise wholesalers** are middlemen who carry a wide product mix but offer limited depth within the product lines. They deal in such products as medicines, hardware, non-perishable foods, cosmetics, detergents, and tobacco. General merchandise wholesalers develop strong, mutually beneficial relationships with local grocery stores, hardware and appliance shops, and local department stores, which are their typical customers. The small retailers often obtain everything they need from these wholesalers. General merchandise wholesalers for industrial customers provide supplies and accessories and are sometimes called *industrial distributors* or *mill supply houses.*

Limited-Line Wholesalers. **Limited-line wholesalers** are wholesalers who carry only a few product lines, such as groceries, lighting fixtures, or oil-well drilling equipment, but offer an extensive assortment of products within those lines. They provide a range of services similar to those of full-service merchandise wholesalers. Limited-line wholesalers for industrial goods serve relatively large geographic areas and provide technical expertise; in consumer goods, they supply single- or limited-line retailers. Computerworld, for example, is a limited-line wholesaler of single- and multi-user computer systems, dealing in six manufacturers' hardware but a limited number of product lines.

Specialty-Line Wholesalers. Of all the wholesalers, **specialty-line wholesalers** are the middlemen who carry the narrowest range of products, usually a single product line or a few items within a product line. For example, wholesalers that carry shellfish, fruit, or other food delicacies are specialty-line wholesalers. Marketing Update 10.2 discusses a successful specialty coffee wholesaler. Specialty-line wholesalers understand the particular requirements of the ultimate buyers and offer customers detailed product knowledge and depth of choice. To provide sales assistance to retailers, specialty wholesalers may set up displays and arrange merchandise. In industrial markets, specialty wholesalers often are better able than manufacturers to give customers technical advice and service.

Rack jobbers are specialty-line wholesalers who own and maintain their own display racks in supermarkets and drugstores. They specialise in non-food items—particularly branded, widely advertised products sold on a self-serve basis—that the retailers themselves prefer not to order and stock because of risk or inconvenience. Health and beauty aids, toys, books, magazines, hardware, housewares, and stationery are typical products rack jobbers handle. The rack jobbers send out delivery persons to set up displays, mark merchandise, stock shelves, and keep billing and inventory records; retailers need only furnish the space. Most rack jobbers operate on consignment and take back unsold products.

Limited-Service Merchant Wholesalers. **Limited-service wholesalers** provide only some marketing services and specialise in a few functions. Producers perform

SPECIALIST GROCERY WHOLESALING—CARWARDINES

Established in 1903, Carwardines retails quality coffees via high street shops and cafés. It is a small business, with a turnover of only a few hundred thousand pounds. Since 1988, the company has concentrated on the wholesale of quality coffees with a delivery and machinery service to the retail trade. Carwardines aims to provide absolutely fresh quality coffee blends, roasted, ground and packed to clients' specifications; filter machinery for those who need it; and speedy, reliable delivery service to its customers. For a wholesaler, Carwardines is a particularly customer-orientated business.

Concentrating on companies in London, Carwardines has three key target groups of customers.

- Predominantly up-market food and drink retailers such as cafés, sandwich shops and hotels, which themselves attract a discerning clientele

- Businesses such as solicitors and estate agents within London wishing to provide their guests and employees with premium quality coffee

- A discerning set of customers who are willing to pay a premium price for top quality taste and branded coffee

For such a specialist wholesaler/supplier dealing only in one product area, Carwardines has limited resources but must maintain high levels of customer service and product quality. There is little advertising undertaken, but much effort is put into personal selling and sales promotion (price discounts with bulk buying, machinery on loan, gifts to major customers). The company very much depends on reputation in a very competitive market, with a relatively small customer base. From being a product-orientated company, Carwardines has increasingly realised the need to develop a proactive marketing strategy and in particular to place more emphasis on promotional activity, so as to both maintain existing business and grow geographically and in terms of volume of customers.

SOURCES: Carwardines promotional literature; "Carwardines of London: Promotional Strategy," Dirk Sickmuller, University of Warwick, 1991; and J. Nicholson, Director, Carwardines.

TABLE 10.2 *Various services that limited-service merchant wholesalers provide*

	CASH-AND-CARRY	DROP SHIPPER[a]	MAIL ORDER
Physical possession of merchandise	Yes	No	Yes
Personal sales calls on customers	No	No	No
Information about market conditions	No	Yes	Yes
Advice to customers	No	Yes	No
Stocking and maintenance of merchandise in customers' stores	No	No	No
Credit to customers	No	Yes	Some
Delivery of merchandise to customers	No	No	No

[a] Also called *desk jobber.*

the remaining functions, or the functions are passed on to customers or other middlemen. Limited-service wholesalers take title to merchandise, but in many cases, they do not deliver merchandise, grant credit, provide marketing information, store inventory, or plan ahead for customers' future needs. Because they offer only restricted services, limited-service wholesalers are compensated with lower rates and thus earn smaller profit margins than full-service wholesalers.

Although certain types of limited-service wholesalers are few in number, they are important in the distribution of such products as specialty foods, perishable items, construction materials, and coal. In this section we discuss the specific functions of three typical limited-service wholesalers: cash-and-carry wholesalers, drop shippers, and mail-order wholesalers. (Table 10.2 is a summary of the services these wholesalers provide.)

Cash-and-Carry Wholesalers.   **Cash-and-carry wholesalers** are middlemen whose customers—usually small retailers and small industrial firms—will pay cash and furnish transport. In some cases, full-service wholesalers set up cash-and-carry departments because they cannot otherwise supply small retailers profitably. Cash-and-carry middlemen usually handle a limited line of products with a high turnover rate—for instance, groceries, building materials, electrical supplies, or office supplies.

Booker Cash and Carry has a national network in the U.K. of retail warehouses stocking fresh and frozen foods, cigarettes, wines and spirits, meat and provisions. Selling to the trade only, Booker offers bulk discounts to hotels, restaurants, the catering industry, and small, local shops.

Cash-and-carry wholesaling developed after 1920, when independent retailers began experiencing competitive pressure from large chain stores. Today cash-and-carry wholesaling offers advantages to wholesalers and customers alike. The wholesaler has no expenditures for outside salespersons, marketing, research, promotion, credit, or delivery, and the customer benefits from lower prices and immediate access to products. Many small retailers whose accounts were refused by other wholesalers have survived because of cash-and-carry wholesalers.

Drop Shippers. **Drop shippers**, also known as desk jobbers, are intermediaries who take title to goods and negotiate sales but never take actual possession of products. They forward orders from retailers, industrial buyers, or other wholesalers to manufacturers and then arrange for large shipments of items to be delivered directly from producers to customers. The drop shipper assumes responsibility for the products during the entire transaction, including the costs of any unsold goods.

Drop shippers are most commonly used in large-volume purchases of bulky goods, such as coal, coke, oil, chemicals, lumber, and building materials. Normally sold in wagonloads, these products are expensive to handle and ship relative to their unit value; extra loading and unloading is an added (and unnecessary) expense. One trend in this form of wholesaling is the use of more drop shipping from manufacturers to supermarkets. A drop shipment eliminates warehousing and deferred deliveries to the stores, and large supermarkets can sell entire lorryloads of products rapidly enough to make drop shipping profitable.[7]

Because drop shippers incur no inventory costs and provide only minimal promotional assistance, they have low operating costs and can pass along some of the savings to their customers. In some cases, drop shippers do offer planning services, credit, and personal selling.

Mail-Order Wholesalers. **Mail-order wholesalers** use catalogues instead of sales forces to sell products to retail, industrial, and institutional buyers. This is a convenient and effective method of selling small items to customers in remote areas. Mail order enables buyers to choose particular catalogue items and then send in their orders and receive shipments through the postal service or other carriers. Wholesalers can thus generate sales in locations that otherwise would be unprofitable to service.

Wholesale mail-order houses generally feature cosmetics, specialty foods, hardware, sporting goods, business and office supplies, and car parts. They usually require payment in cash or by credit card, and they give discounts for large orders. Mail-order wholesalers hold goods in inventory and offer some planning services but seldom provide assistance with promotional efforts.

■ **Agents
and Brokers**

Agents and brokers (see Figure 10.2) negotiate purchases and expedite sales but do not take title to products. They are **functional middlemen**, intermediaries who perform a limited number of marketing activities in exchange for a commission, which is generally based on the product's selling price. **Agents** are middlemen who represent buyers or sellers on a permanent basis. **Brokers** are usually middlemen whom either buyers or sellers employ temporarily. Together, agents and brokers account for 11.6 percent of the total sales volume of all U.S. wholesalers.[8]

Although agents and brokers perform even fewer functions than limited-service wholesalers, they are usually specialists in particular products or types of customer and can provide valuable sales expertise. They know their markets well and often form long-lasting associations with customers. Agents and brokers enable manufacturers to expand sales when resources are limited, to benefit from the services of a trained sales force, and to hold personal selling costs down. However, despite the

7. "Drop-Shipping Grows to Save Depot Costs," *Supermarket News,* 1 Apr. 1985, pp. 1, 17.

8. *U.S. Census of Wholesale Trade,* May 1985, p. 207.

FIGURE 10.2
*Types of agents
and brokers*

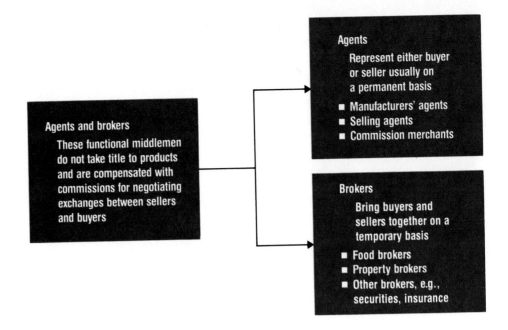

advantages they offer, agents and brokers face increased competition from merchant wholesalers, manufacturers' sales branches and offices, and direct sales efforts.

Here we look at three types of agents: manufacturers' agents, selling agents, and commission merchants. We also examine the brokers' role in bringing about exchanges between buyers and sellers. Table 10.3 summarises these services.

Manufacturers' Agents.   **Manufacturers' agents**—who account for over half of all agent wholesalers—are independent middlemen who represent two or more sellers and usually offer customers complete product lines. They sell and take orders year-round, much as a manufacturer's sales office does. Restricted to a particular territory, a manufacturers' agent handles non-competing and complementary products. The relationship between the agent and each manufacturer is governed by written agreements explicitly outlining territories, selling price, order handling, and terms of sale relating to delivery, service, and warranties. Manufacturers' agents are commonly used in the sale of clothing and accessories, machinery and equipment, iron, steel, furniture, automotive products, electrical goods, and certain food items.

Although most manufacturers' agents run small enterprises, their employees are professional, highly skilled salespersons. The agents' major advantages, in fact, are their wide range of contacts and strong customer relationships. These intermediaries help large producers minimise the costs of developing new sales territories and adjust sales strategies for different products in different locations. Agents are also useful to small producers that cannot afford outside sales forces of their own because the producers incur no costs until the agents have actually sold something. By concentrating on a limited number of products, agents can mount an aggressive sales effort that would be impossible with any other distribution method except producer-owned sales branches and offices. In addition, agents are able to spread operating expenses among non-competing products and thus can offer each manufacturer lower prices for services rendered.

TABLE 10.3 *Various services agents and brokers provide*

	BROKERS	MANUFACTURERS' AGENTS	SELLING AGENTS	COMMISSION MERCHANTS
Physical possession of merchandise	No	Some	No	Yes
Long-term relationship with buyers or sellers	No	Yes	Yes	Yes
Representation of competing product lines	Yes	No	No	Yes
Limited geographic territory	No	Yes	No	No
Credit to customers	No	No	Yes	Some
Delivery of merchandise to customers	No	Some	Yes	Yes

The chief disadvantage of using agents is the higher commission rate (usually 10 to 15 percent) they charge for new-product sales. When sales of a new product begin to build, total selling costs go up, and producers sometimes transfer the selling function to in-house sales representatives. For this reason, agents try to avoid depending on a single product line; most work for more than one manufacturer.

Manufacturers' agents have little or no control over producers' pricing and marketing policies. They do not extend credit, and they may not be able to provide technical advice. They do occasionally store and transport products, assist with planning, and provide promotional support. Some agents help retailers advertise and maintain a service organisation. The more services offered, the higher the agent's commission.

Selling Agents. **Selling agents** market either all of a specified product line or a manufacturer's entire output. They perform every wholesaling activity except taking title to products. Selling agents usually assume the sales function for several producers at a time and are often used in place of a marketing department. In contrast to other agent wholesalers, selling agents generally have no territorial limits and have complete authority over prices, promotion, and distribution. They play a key role in the advertising, marketing research, and credit policies of the sellers they represent, at times even advising on product development and packaging.

Selling agents, who account for about 1 percent of the wholesale trade, are used most often by small producers or by manufacturers who find it difficult to maintain a marketing department because of seasonal production or other factors. A producer having financial problems may also engage a selling agent. By so doing, the producer relinquishes some control of the business but may gain working capital by avoiding immediate marketing costs.

To avoid conflicts of interest, selling agents represent non-competing product lines. The agents play an important part in the distribution of coal and textiles, and they also sometimes handle canned foods, household furnishings, clothing, lumber, and metal products. In these industries, competitive pressures increase the importance of marketing relative to production, and the selling agent is a source of essential marketing and financial expertise.

Commission Merchants.   **Commission merchants** are agents who receive goods on consignment from local sellers and negotiate sales in large central markets. Most often found in agricultural marketing, commission merchants take possession of lorryload quantities of commodities, arrange for any necessary grading or storage, and transport the commodities to auction or markets where they are sold. When sales have been completed, an agent deducts a commission, plus the expense of making the sale, and then turns over the profits to the producer.

Sometimes called factor merchants, these agents may have broad powers regarding prices and terms of sale, and they specialise in obtaining the best price possible under market conditions. Commission merchants offer planning assistance and sometimes extend credit, but they do not usually provide promotional support. Because commission merchants deal in large volumes, their per unit costs are usually low. Their services are most useful to small producers who must get products to buyers but choose not to field a sales force or accompany the goods to market themselves. In addition to farm products, commission merchants may handle textiles, art, furniture, or seafood products.

Businesses—including farms—that use commission merchants have little control over pricing, although the seller can specify a minimum price. Generally, the seller is able to supervise the agent's actions through a check of the commodity prices published regularly in newspapers. Large producers, however, need to maintain closer contact with the market and so have limited need for commission merchants.

Brokers.   Brokers seek out buyers or sellers and help negotiate exchanges. In other words, brokers' primary purpose is to bring buyers and sellers together. Thus brokers perform fewer functions than other intermediaries. They are not involved in financing or physical possession, have no authority to set prices, and assume almost no risks. Instead, they offer their customers specialised knowledge of a particular commodity and a network of established contacts.

Brokers are especially useful to sellers of certain types of products who market those products only occasionally. Sellers of used machinery, seasonal food products, financial securities, and real estate may not know of potential buyers. A broker can furnish this information. The party who engages the broker's services—usually the seller—pays the broker's commission when the transaction is completed.

Food brokers—the most common type of broker—are intermediaries who sell food and general merchandise items to retailer-owned and merchant wholesalers, grocery chains, industrial buyers, and food processors. Food brokers enable buyers and sellers to adjust to fluctuating market conditions; they also aid in grading, negotiating, and inspecting foods (in some cases they store and deliver products). Because of the seasonal nature of food production, the association between broker and producer is temporary—though many mutually beneficial broker-producer relationships are resumed year after year. Because food brokers provide a range of services on a somewhat permanent basis and operate in specific geographic territories, they can more accurately be described as manufacturers' agents.

■ **Manufacturers'
Sales Branches
and Offices**

Sometimes called manufacturers' wholesalers, manufacturers' sales branches and offices resemble merchant wholesalers' operations. These producer-owned middlemen account for about 9 percent of wholesale establishments and generate approximately one-third (31 percent) of all wholesale sales.[9]

9. *U.S. Census of Wholesale Trade,* May 1985, p. 207.

Sales branches are manufacturer-owned middlemen selling products and providing support services to the manufacturer's sales force, especially in locations where large customers are concentrated and demand is high. They offer credit, deliver goods, give promotional assistance, and furnish other services. In many cases, they carry inventory (although this practice often duplicates the functions of other channel members and is now declining). Customers include retailers, industrial buyers, and other wholesalers. Branch operations are common in the electrical supplies, plumbing, lumber, and car parts industries.

Sales offices are manufacturer-owned operations that provide services normally associated with agents. Like sales branches, they are located away from manufacturing plants, but unlike branches, they carry no inventory. A manufacturer's sales offices or branches may sell products that enhance the manufacturer's own product line. For example, Hiram Walker, a distiller, imports wine from Spain to increase the number of products that its sales offices can offer wholesalers. United States Tobacco Company imports Borkum Riff smoking tobacco from Sweden to add variety to its chewing tobacco and snuff lines.

Manufacturers may set up sales branches or sales offices so they can reach customers more effectively by performing wholesaling functions themselves. A manufacturer may also set up these branches or offices when needed specialised wholesaling services are not available through existing middlemen. In some situations, however, a manufacturer may by-pass its wholesaling organisation entirely—for example, if the producer decides to serve large retailer customers directly. One major distiller bottles own-label spirits for a U.K. grocery chain and separates this operation completely from the company's sales office, which serves other retailers.

FACILITATING AGENCIES

The total marketing channel is more than a chain linking the producer, intermediary, and buyer. **Facilitating agencies**—transport companies, insurance companies, advertising agencies, market research agencies, and financial institutions—may perform activities that enhance channel functions. Note, however, that any of the functions these facilitating agencies perform may be taken over by the regular marketing intermediaries in the marketing channel.

The basic difference between channel members and facilitating agencies is that channel members perform the negotiating functions (buying, selling, and transferring title), whereas facilitating agencies do not.[10] In other words, facilitating agencies assist in the operation of the channel but do not sell products. The channel manager may view the facilitating agency as a sub-contractor to which various distribution tasks can be farmed out according to the principle of specialisation and division of labour.[11] Channel members (producers, wholesalers, or retailers) may rely on facilitating agencies because they believe that these independent businesses will perform various activities more efficiently and more effectively than they themselves could. Facilitating agencies are functional specialists who perform special tasks for channel members without getting involved in directing or controlling channel decisions. The

10. Rosenbloom, p. 61.

11. Ibid.

following sections describe the ways in which facilitating agencies provide assistance in expediting the flow of products through marketing channels.

■ Public Warehouses

Public warehouses are storage facilities available for a fee. Producers, wholesalers, and retailers may rent space in a warehouse instead of constructing their own facilities or using a merchant wholesaler's storage services. Many warehouses also order, deliver, collect accounts, and maintain display rooms where potential buyers can inspect products.

To use goods as collateral for a loan, a channel member may place products in a bonded warehouse. If it is too impractical or expensive to physically transfer goods, the channel member may arrange for a public warehouser to verify that goods are in the member's own facilities and then issue receipts for lenders.[12] Under this arrangement, the channel member retains possession of the products but the warehouser has control. Many field public warehousers know where their clients can borrow working capital and are sometimes able to arrange low-cost loans.

■ Finance Companies

Wholesalers and retailers may be able to obtain financing by transferring ownership of products to a sales finance company or bank, while retaining physical possession of the goods. Often called "floor planning", this form of financing enables wholesalers and retailers—especially car and appliance dealers—to offer a greater selection of products for customers and thus increase sales. Loans may be due immediately upon sale; so products financed this way are usually well known, sell relatively easily, and present little risk.

Other financing functions are performed by factors—organisations that provide clients with working capital by buying their accounts receivable or by lending money, using the accounts receivable as collateral. Most factors minimise their own risks by specialising in particular industries, the better to evaluate individual channel members within those industries. Factors usually lend money for a longer time than banks. They may help clients improve their credit and collection policies and may also provide management expertise.

■ Transport Companies

Rail, road, air, and other carriers are facilitating organisations that help manufacturers and retailers transport products. Each form of transport has its own advantages. Railways ship large volumes of bulky goods at low cost; in fact, a "unit train" is the cheapest form of overland transport for ore, grain, or other commodities. Air transport is relatively expensive but is often preferred for shipping high-value or perishable goods. Trucks, which usually carry short-haul, high-value goods, now carry more and more products because factories are moving closer to their markets. As a result of technological advances, pipelines now transport powdered solids and fluidised solid materials, as well as petroleum and natural gas.

Transport companies sometimes take over the functions of other middlemen. Because of the ease and speed of using air transport for certain types of products, parcel express companies, such as those mentioned in Figure 10.3, can eliminate the need to maintain large inventories and branch warehouses. In other cases, freight forwarders perform accumulation functions by combining less-than-full shipments into full loads and passing on the savings to customers—perhaps charging a wagon rate rather than a less-than-wagon rate.

12. Ibid, p. 62.

FIGURE 10.3
Facilitating agencies.
Parcel express companies such as DHL, Federal Express, and UPS facilitate and sometimes perform functions of marketing channel members.

SOURCE: Courtesy of DHL

■ Trade Shows and Trade Markets

Trade shows and trade markets enable manufacturers or wholesalers to exhibit products to potential buyers and thus help the selling and buying functions. **Trade shows** are industry exhibitions that offer both selling and non-selling benefits.[13] On the selling side, trade shows let vendors identify prospects; gain access to key decision-makers; disseminate facts about their products, services, and personnel; and actually sell products and service current accounts through contacts at the show.[14] Trade shows also allow a firm to reach potential buyers who have not been approached through regular selling efforts. In fact, research indicates that most trade show visitors have not been contacted by a sales representative of any company within the past year, and many are therefore willing to travel several hundred miles to attend trade shows to learn about new goods and services.[15] The non-selling benefits include opportunities to maintain the company image with competitors, customers, and the industry; gather information about competitors' products and

13. Thomas V. Bonoma, "Get More Out of Your Trade Shows," *Harvard Business Review,* January-February 1983, pp. 75–83.

14. Rosenbloom, p. 185.

15. "Trade Shows—Part 1; A Major Sales and Marketing Tool," *Small Business Report,* June 1988, pp. 34–39.

prices; and identify potential channel members.[16] Trade shows have a positive influence on other important marketing variables, including maintaining or enhancing company morale, product testing, and product evaluation.

Trade shows can permit direct buyer-seller interaction and may eliminate the need for agents. Companies exhibit at trade shows because of the high concentration of prospective buyers for their products. Studies show that it takes, on the average, 5.1 sales calls to close an industrial sale but less than 1 sales call (0.8) to close a trade show lead. The explanation for the latter figure is that more than half of the customers who purchase a product based on information gained at a trade show order the product by mail or by phone after the show. When customers use these more impersonal methods to gather information, the need for major sales calls to provide such information is eliminated.[17]

Trade markets are relatively permanent facilities that firms can rent to exhibit products year-round. At these markets, such products as furniture, home decorating supplies, toys, clothing, and gift items are sold to wholesalers and retailers. In the United States, trade markets are located in several major cities, including New York, Chicago, Dallas, High Point (North Carolina), Atlanta, and Los Angeles. The Dallas Market Center, which includes the Dallas Trade Mart, the Home-furnishing Mart, the World Trade Center, the Decorative Center, Market Hall, InfoMart, and the Apparel Mart, is housed in six buildings designed specifically for the convenience of professional buyers.

CHANGING PATTERNS IN WHOLESALING

The nature of the wholesaling industry is changing. The distinction between wholesaling activities that any business can perform and the traditional wholesaling establishment is becoming blurred. Changes in the nature of the marketing environment itself have transformed various aspects of the industry. For instance, they have brought about an increasing reliance on computer technology to expedite the ordering, delivery, and handling of goods. The trend towards globalisation of world markets has resulted in other changes, and astute wholesalers are responding to them. The two predominant shifts in wholesaling today are the consolidation of the wholesaling industry and the development of new types of retailers.

■ **Wholesalers Consolidate Power**

Like most major industries, the wholesale industry is experiencing a great number of mergers. Wholesaling firms are acquiring or merging with other firms primarily to achieve more efficiency in the face of declining profit margins. Consolidation also gives larger wholesalers more pricing power over producers. Some analysts have expressed concern that wholesalers' increased price clout will increase the number of single-source supply deals, which may reduce competition among wholesalers, as well as retailers and producers. Nevertheless, the trend towards consolidation of wholesaling firms appears to be continuing.[18]

16. Rosenbloom, p. 185.

17. Richard K. Swandby and Jonathan M. Cox, "Trade Show Trends: Exhibiting Growth Paces Economic Strengths," *Business Marketing,* May 1985, p. 50.

18. Joseph Weber, "Mom and Pop Move Out of Wholesaling," *Business Week,* 9 Jan. 1989, p. 91.

One of the results of the current wave of consolidation in the wholesale industry is that more wholesalers are specialising. For example, McKesson Corporation once distributed chemicals, wines, and spirits but now focuses only on medicines. The new larger wholesalers can also afford to purchase and make use of more modern technology to physically manage inventories, provide computerised ordering services, and even help manage their retail customers' operations.[19]

■ New Types of Wholesaler

The trend towards larger retailers—superstores and the like (discussed in Chapter 11)—will offer opportunities to, as well as threaten, wholesaling establishments. Opportunities will develop from the expanded product lines of these mass merchandisers. A merchant wholesaler of groceries, for instance, may want to add other low-cost, high-volume products that are sold in superstores. On the other hand, some limited-function merchant wholesalers may no longer have a role to play. For example, the volume of sales may eliminate the need for rack jobbers, who usually handle slow-moving products that are purchased in limited quantities. The future of independent wholesalers, agents, and brokers depends on their ability to delineate markets and furnish desired services.

SUMMARY

Wholesaling includes all transactions in which the purchaser intends to use the product for resale, for making other products, or for general business operations. It does *not* include exchanges with the ultimate consumers. Wholesalers are individuals or organisations that facilitate and expedite primarily wholesale transactions.

Except in the U.K. consumer markets, where the large multiple retailers dominate, more than half of all goods are exchanged through wholesalers, although the distribution of any product requires that someone must perform wholesaling activities, whether or not a wholesaling institution is involved. For producers, wholesalers perform specialised accumulation and allocation functions for a number of products, letting the producers concentrate on manufacturing the products. For retailers, wholesalers provide buying expertise, wide product lines, efficient distribution, and warehousing and storage services.

Various types of wholesalers serve different market segments. How a wholesaler is classified depends on whether the wholesaler is owned by a producer, whether it takes title to products, the range of services it provides, and the breadth and depth of its product lines. The three general categories of wholesalers are merchant wholesalers, agents and brokers, and manufacturers' sales branches and offices.

Merchant wholesalers are independently owned businesses that take title to goods and assume risk; they make up about two-thirds of all wholesale firms in the United States. They are either full-service wholesalers, offering the widest possible range of wholesaling functions, or limited-service wholesalers, providing only some marketing services and specialising in a few functions. Full-service merchant wholesalers include general-merchandise wholesalers, which offer a wide but relatively

19. Ibid.

shallow product mix; limited-line wholesalers, which offer extensive assortments in a few product lines; and specialty-line wholesalers, which offer great depth in a single product line or in a few items within a line. Rack jobbers are specialty-line wholesalers that own and service display racks in supermarkets and chemists. There are three types of limited-service merchant wholesalers. Cash-and-carry wholesalers sell to small businesses, require payment in cash, and do not deliver. Drop shippers own goods and negotiate sales but never take possession of products. Mail-order wholesalers sell to retail, industrial, and institutional buyers through direct-mail catalogues.

Agents and brokers, sometimes called functional middlemen, negotiate purchases and expedite sales but do not take title to products. They are usually specialists and provide valuable sales expertise. Agents represent buyers or sellers on a permanent basis. Manufacturers' agents offer customers the complete product lines of two or more sellers; selling agents market a complete product line or a producer's entire output and perform every wholesaling function except taking title to products; commission merchants receive goods on consignment from local sellers and negotiate sales in large central markets. Brokers, such as food brokers, negotiate exchanges between buyers and sellers on a temporary basis.

Manufacturers' sales branches and offices are vertically integrated units owned by manufacturers. Branches sell products and provide support services for the manufacturer's sales force in a given location. Sales offices carry no inventory and function much as agents do.

Facilitating agencies do not buy, sell, or take title but perform certain wholesaling functions. They include public warehouses, finance companies, transport companies, and trade shows and trade markets. In some instances, these organisations eliminate the need for a wholesaling establishment.

The nature of the wholesaling industry is changing in response to changes in the marketing environment. The predominant changes are the increasing consolidation of the wholesaling industry and the growth of new types of wholesalers.

IMPORTANT TERMS

Wholesaling
Wholesaler
Merchant wholesalers
Full-service wholesalers
General merchandise wholesalers
Limited-line wholesalers
Specialty-line wholesalers
Rack jobbers
Limited-service wholesalers
Cash-and-carry wholesalers
Drop shippers
Mail-order wholesalers
Functional middlemen

Agents
Brokers
Manufacturers' agents
Selling agents
Commission merchants
Food brokers
Sales branches
Sales offices
Facilitating agencies
Public warehouses
Trade shows
Trade markets

DISCUSSION AND REVIEW QUESTIONS

1. Is there a distinction between wholesalers and wholesaling? If so, what is it?
2. Would it be appropriate for a wholesaler to stock both interior wall paint and office supplies? Under what circumstances would this product mix be logical?
3. What services do wholesalers provide to producers and retailers?
4. Drop shippers take title to products but do not accept physical possession. Commission merchants take physical possession of products but do not accept title. Defend the logic of classifying drop shippers as wholesale merchants and commission merchants as agents.
5. What are the advantages of using agents to replace merchant wholesalers? What are the disadvantages?
6. What, if any, are the differences in the marketing functions that manufacturers' agents and selling agents perform?
7. Why are manufacturers' sales offices and branches classified as wholesalers? Which independent wholesalers are replaced by manufacturers' sales branches? Which independent wholesalers are replaced by manufacturers' sales offices?
8. "Public warehouses are really wholesale establishments." Please comment.
9. Discuss the role of facilitating organisations. Identify three facilitating organisations and explain how each type performs this role.

■ CASES

10.1   Anheuser-Busch and Its Wholesalers

St Louis–based Anheuser-Busch, Inc., is the world's largest brewing company, with a market share that is increasing steadily. It currently produces one out of every three beers sold in the United States. Anheuser-Busch's brewery sales have recently neared $6.5 billion. Its products include Budweiser, Michelob, Michelob Light, Bud Light, Bud Dry, and Michelob Classic Dark.

In the United States and in Caribbean countries, Anheuser-Busch distributes beer through a network of about 1,000 independently owned wholesalers and 10 company-owned wholesale operations—a distribution system considered the strongest in the brewing industry. Anheuser-Busch's independent wholesalers employ about 30,000 people, more than 18,000 of whom work in direct beer marketing positions. (One Anheuser-Busch distributor is Frank Sinatra, who owns Somerset Distributing in California.) Company-owned distributorships employ about 1,600 people. Wholesalers handle volumes ranging from 870 barrels to 1.1 million barrels annually.

Anheuser-Busch's effective distribution system is bolstered by a variety of co-operative arrangements with wholesalers. For example, the company tries to ensure that its beers are sold to wholesalers FOB (free on board) from the "least cost" brewery. That is, the wholesaler must supply or pay for transport from the brewery that can provide the product at the lowest shipping cost. But if a product must be shipped at a higher cost—perhaps because the nearest brewery does not produce a specific package—Anheuser-Busch compensates the wholesaler for the difference in cost. The company's traffic department also helps wholesalers arrange transport. Some twenty years ago, Anheuser-Busch introduced its wholesaler equity programme, and recently expanded it to give distributors exclusive territories where permitted by law. A wholesaler advisory panel, a cross-section of wholesalers and top company managers, meets regularly to discuss and act on industry issues.

In addition, the ten distributorships in the company's wholesale operations division serve as a testing ground for programmes that are made available to independent wholesalers. In one case, the company developed computer software to help wholesalers maximise retail shelf space. Anheuser-Busch wholesalers receive group discounts on computers, trucks, and insurance and can take company courses ranging from draught beer basics to dynamics of business readings. To build morale among wholesalers, Anheuser-Busch puts top executives in charge of its biggest-volume states (the company's president, August Busch III, handles California himself). Furthermore, every three years, the company throws a Las Vegas–style wholesalers' convention, with appearances by such celebrities as Bob Hope and Paul Newman.

Anheuser-Busch's most evident support for its distributors is its backing of special promotions: sporting events, college parties, rodeos, and festivals. The company may pay as much as half the cost of these events, in co-operation with local wholesalers. To improve sales of Michelob Light, for example, a local New York distributor decided to hold a Michelob Light Concentration Day. On that day, only Michelob Light was delivered to retailers. Tuxedo-clad representatives from the St Louis headquarters rode on delivery vans, accompanied by two Playboy Playmates. The distributorship sold 21,000 cases of Michelob Light in one day (it normally takes twenty days to sell that amount), and Anheuser-Busch is now staging Concentration Days in other cities.

The company has helped support everything from Chicago's Lithuanian festival to the Iron Man Triathlon in Hawaii. Just before Coors moved into the New York–New Jersey market, Anheuser-Busch supplied its wholesalers with a three-hundred-page "Coors Defense Plan", along with funding for promotional events that might have attracted Coors sponsorship. Coors was unable to reach an agreement with any major beer wholesalers and had to distribute through a soft-drink bottler instead.

For distributors, however, the price of such generous corporate support is unquestioned loyalty. Anheuser-Busch asks more of its wholesalers than any other brewer. Each year all distributors are requested to contribute ideas for local promotions—one for every brand. Furthermore, although the distributors are independent business owners, technically free to sell whatever they choose, Anheuser-Busch takes a dim view of wholesalers who decide to carry a competing product. When a Florida distributorship added Heineken and Amstel Light to its line, twenty-two Anheuser-Busch field managers swarmed in and rode on the company's vans for a week, and the distributor and his general manager were summoned to St Louis for a meeting with top management.

Anheuser-Busch defends its policies, maintaining that the company will not allow "greedy" wholesalers to jeopardise market share. Although Anheuser-Busch has a lead over all other brewers, the company is taking no chances. It has enthusiastically entered and is actively pursuing its foreign markets, especially in Britain, where it is trying to establish an equally effective distribution system. Anheuser-Busch has launched several non-beer beverages in recent years, including L.A. (a low-alcohol beer), Dewey Stevens (a low-calorie wine cooler aimed at women), and Zeltzer Seltzer (a flavoured sparkling water). So far these products have not been marketed aggressively, and they may never be highly profitable. But with rival brewers entering these new markets, Anheuser-Busch wants to be able to supply its distributors with competing products. Along with its share of the market, say Anheuser-Busch executives, the company intends to maintain its share of wholesalers.

SOURCES: Anheuser-Busch Cos., Inc., *Annual Report, 1986;* Paul Hemp, "'King of Beers' in a Bitter Battle in Britain," *Wall Street Journal,* 9 June 1988, p. 26; Michael Oneal, "Anheuser-Busch: The Scandal May Be Small Beer After All," *Business Week,* 11 May 1987, pp. 72–73; and Patricia Sellers, "How Busch Wins in a Doggy Market," *Fortune,* 22 June 1987, pp. 99–100.

Questions for Discussion

1. Are Anheuser-Busch's wholesalers merchant wholesalers? Explain your answer. Are they full-service or limited-service wholesalers? Why?
2. Why does Anheuser-Busch give its wholesale distributors so much support?
3. Why has Anheuser-Busch introduced non-beer products? Evaluate this practice.

10.2   Fleming Companies, Inc. Strives to Be Competitive

Fleming Companies, Inc., a food wholesaler based in Oklahoma City, services more than 5,200 food retailers in 37 states. It is now the U.S. industry leader in sales and is eager to retain this position. Fleming's annual $10.5 billion in sales makes it the largest food wholesaler in the United States, ahead of such staunch competitors as Minneapolis-based Super Valu Stores and Wetterau, located in Hazelwood, Missouri. As the wholesaling industry continues to consolidate and retailers demand more services from wholesalers, food wholesalers such as Fleming are forced to keep pace with these shifts.

Much of Fleming's growth in the past several years stems from its acquisition of other wholesale firms, a policy that has boosted its buying power, provided economies of scale, and allowed the company to spread fixed costs. With fewer than three hundred food wholesalers now remaining, Fleming is pursuing additional growth strategies to prepare for the day when acquisitions inevitably cease. Recently, Fleming acquired Malone & Hyde, a Memphis-based food wholesaler known for its innovative food distribution system. Fleming's CEO says that the firm will continue to acquire companies when there are mutual benefits for both Fleming and the company being bought.

Another of Fleming's growth strategies is to increase market share by offering a high degree of customer service. Fleming has long assisted its retail buyers with store planning and development, financial and insurance services, consumer services, printing, advertising, and other services—over one hundred services in all. Fleming was also one of the first wholesalers to electronically track the direct product profit of selected grocery items. Such information ultimately helps retailers determine which products are handled most economically. For years, too, Fleming has provided an extensive line of own labels, including IGA, Thriftway, and Piggly Wiggly, to give retailers a competitive tool against national brands. In addition, Fleming has established a Sales Training Institute to equip its sales and service representatives to meet retailers' needs more effectively. The institute covers such topics as electronic retail systems and retail counselling.

Fleming has always been a technological leader in the food wholesale industry. Soon, the company will introduce its computerised shelf tags in grocery stores. These tags provide the consumer with the price, size, and other information about a product and can be controlled by the retailer from a single control point, resulting in instantaneous price changes rather than the time-consuming manual method. Fleming is also experimenting with automatic ordering techniques that transfer inventory information directly from the check-out stand to a distribution centre.

Through mechanisation and computerisation, Fleming plans to continue to improve its transport, distribution, and warehouse systems. According to its top management, the company and the retailers already have unique market share positions in many of the leading cities throughout the United States. Fleming is striving to improve those market shares even more.

SOURCES: "Current Corporate Reports," *Barron's,* 13 Feb. 1989, p. 108; "Fleming Profit Declines 32%," *Supermarket News,* 13 Feb. 1989, p. 48; "Fleming Companies, Inc." *Wall Street Transcript,* 17 Apr. 1989, pp. 93,352–93,353, 93,359; and "Wholesaling," *Supermarket News,* 13 Mar. 1989, pp. 13–14, 16, 18, 20, 22–23.

Questions for Discussion

1. How would you classify Fleming as to the type of wholesaler?
2. In what ways is Fleming trying to gain an edge over its competitors?
3. What services is Fleming likely to be providing to producers?

11 RETAILING

Objectives

To understand the purpose and function of retailers in the marketing channel

To describe and distinguish major types of retailers and locations

To understand non-store retailing and franchising

To learn about strategic issues in retailing

During the 1960s an explosion in the number of supermarkets in the U.K. led to a revolution in grocery retailing. The traditional, independently owned corner shop was squeezed by the expanding national chains: Sainsbury, Tesco, Fine Fare, and the Co-op. These national grocery groups operated 6,000- to 12,000-square-foot self-service supermarkets located in town centres or on major suburban shopping parades. Tesco, with its "pile 'em high, sell it cheap" approach, led the way with over twenty openings each year, leading to 800 stores. In the 1970s, retailers such as Sainsbury, Marks & Spencer, and C&A were bringing greater sophistication to retailing. Consumers came to expect a pleasant store ambience, quality brands, and customer services. Tesco began to slip behind its arch-rival Sainsbury and the fast-emerging Asda, both of which were developing single-storey out-of-town superstores with free parking, extensive ranges, and improved customer service.

New management, led by Sir Ian MacLaurin, has totally revitalised Tesco. Concentrating on grocery and, in some stores, limited clothing ranges, the company has shed its former down-market discount image. Although there are still a number of older, 15,000- to 20,000-square-foot town-centre supermarkets, the company has invested heavily in customised one-floor, out-of-town superstores. In blind product consumer tests, the company's own-label products regularly out-perform manufacturer brands—which it also sells—and own-label products from its two rivals Sainsbury and Marks & Spencer. With computer-controlled inventory management, bar scanning, and EPOS systems, Tesco is at the forefront of retail technology. The company has a clearly positioned brand image and, with 375 stores (growing by 20 p.a.), 8,500,000 square feet of floorspace, 54,000 employees, turnover of over £5.4 billion and profits of £362 million, Tesco has remodelled its operations and its customer image and is one of the U.K.'s top retail groups. ◆

Based on information from Tesco management; *Tesco Annual Report*, 1990; and *EIU (Economic Intelligence Unit) Retail Business Quarterly*, December 1989.

B y using effective marketing, Tesco is now successful again—repositioning itself as a more stylish grocery retailer. Marketing methods that satisfy consumers serve well as the guiding philosophy of retailing. Retailers are an important link in the marketing channel because they are both marketers and customers for producers and wholesalers. They perform many marketing activities, such as buying, selling, grading, risk-taking, and developing information about consumers' wants. Of all marketers, retailers are the most visible to ultimate consumers. They are in a strategic position to gain feedback from consumers and to relay ideas to producers and intermediaries in the marketing channel. Retailing is an extraordinarily dynamic area of marketing.

In this chapter we examine the nature of retailing and its importance in supplying consumers with goods and services. We discuss the major retail locations and types of retail stores and describe several forms of non-store retailing, such as in-home retailing, telemarketing, automatic vending, and mail-order retailing. We also look at franchising, a retailing form that continues to grow in popularity. Finally, we present several strategic issues in retailing: location, product assortment, retail positioning, atmospherics, store image, scrambled merchandising, the wheel of retailing, the balance of retailing, retail technology, and the impact of the 1992 deregulation of the European Community.

THE NATURE OF RETAILING

Retailing includes all transactions in which the buyer intends to consume the product through personal, family, or household use. The buyers in retail transactions are ultimate consumers. A **retailer**, then, is an organisation that purchases products for the purpose of reselling them to ultimate consumers. Although most retailers' sales are to consumers, non-retail transactions occasionally occur when retailers sell products to other businesses. Retailing activities usually take place in a store or in a service establishment, but exchanges through telephone selling, vending machines, and mail-order retailing occur outside stores.

It is common knowledge that retailing is important to the national economy, being a large employer and major service sector component. Table 11.1 shows the volume and value of retail sales in the U.K. between 1985 and 1989. As the table shows, sales volume has increased more than fourfold over this time period. Also, most personal income is spent in retail stores.

By providing assortments of products that match consumers' wants, retailers create place, time, and possession utilities. *Place utility* is moving products from wholesalers or producers to a location where consumers want to buy them. *Time utility* involves the maintaining of specific business hours so that products are available when consumers want them. *Possession utility* means facilitating the transfer of ownership or use of a product to consumers.

In the case of services such as hairdressing, dry-cleaning, restaurants, and car repairs, retailers themselves develop most of the product utilities. The services of such retailers provide aspects of form utility associated with the production process.

TABLE 11.1
*Volume/value of U.K.
retail sales, 1985–1989*

VOLUME OF RETAIL SALES
(index: 1985 = 100; % change on previous year)

	1985	**1986**	**1987**	**1988**	**1989**
Index	100.0	105.3	111.5	119.2	121.8
% change	4.7	5.3	5.9	6.9	2.2

VALUE OF RETAIL SALES
(£ million; index: 1985 = 100; % change on previous year)

	1985	**1986**	**1987**	**1988**	**1989**
Total	87,920	95,657	104,009	114,736	122,736
Index	100.0	108.8	118.3	130.5	139.6
% change	9.1	8.8	8.7	10.3	7.0

SOURCE: From *Retail Business Quarterly Trade Review,* June 1990. Reprinted by permission of The Economist Intelligence Unit and from *Business Monitor,* July 1990, published by HMSO.

Retailers of services usually have more direct contact with consumers and more opportunity to alter the product in the marketing mix.

RETAIL LOCATIONS

■ **Central Business District**

The traditional hub of most cities and towns is the **central business district (CBD)**, the focus for shopping, banking, and commerce and hence the busiest part of the whole area for traffic, public transport, and pedestrians. Examples are London's Oxford and Regent Streets, the Champs Elysées in Paris or Berlin's Kufurstendamm.[1] The CBD is subdivided into zones: generally retailers are clustered together in a zone; banking and insurance companies locate together; legal offices occupy neighbouring premises; municipal offices and amenities are built on adjoining plots (town hall, library, law courts, art galleries).

Within the shopping zone certain streets at the centre of the zone will have the highest levels of pedestrian foot-fall and the main shops. In this area, known as the prime pitch, the key traders or magnets (Marks & Spencer, Boots or major department stores) will occupy prominent sites, so generating much of the foot-fall. Other retailers vie to be located close to these key traders so as to benefit from the customer traffic they generate. The highest rents are therefore paid for such sites. The CBD shopping centre—the city or town centre—generally offers shopping goods and some convenience items. Clothing, footwear, jewellery, cosmetics and financial services dominate the CBD. For the most part, grocers have moved out of town.

Property developers build shopping malls or centres in and around the CBD. Each development has one or more magnets both to attract shoppers and to encourage other retailers to locate within the development. Most city centres now have one

1. H. Carter, *The Study of Urban Geography* (London: Edward Arnold, 1972), pp. 205–247.

FIGURE 11.1
The composition of a typical central business district (CBD)

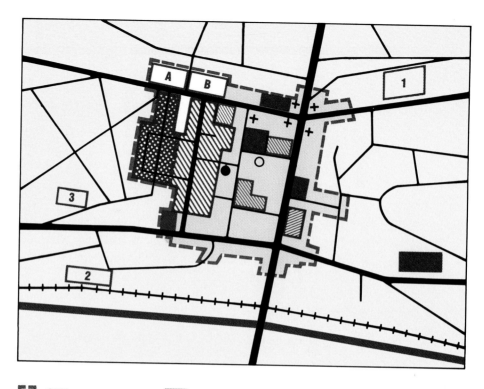

CBD

1 Bus station

2 Railway station

3 Coach station

━━ Main road

── Minor road

┿┿ Railway

▬▬ Canal

Banks, building societies, insurance companies

Solicitors/legal

Central shopping area

Head Post Office

Department stores

Market hall

A Law courts

B Town hall, art gallery, library

Covered shopping centres/malls

O Peak land value intersection (retail)

Zone in transition*

● Peak overall land value (CBD)

Sports stadium

+ Cinema/theatre

*The zone in transition is the land use between the CBD and suburban housing areas: light manufacturing, transport termini, wholesaling, garages, medical, multi-family residences.

SOURCE: Lyndon Simkin and Sally Dibb

or more covered shopping-centre developments (e.g., Eldon Square in Newcastle or Manchester's Arndale Centre).[2] On streets adjacent to this area of prime pitch, rents are lower but so is foot-fall. These secondary sites are suitable for specialty retailers or discounters, which have either lower margins or lower customer thresholds (the number of customers required to make a profit). Figure 11.1 shows the composition of a typical central business district (CBD).

2. J.A. Dawson, *Shopping Centre Development* (Harlow: Longman, 1983), Chapter 2.

Suburban Centres

Historically, as urban areas expanded during the early part of the twentieth century they joined and subsequently swallowed up neighbouring towns and villages. The shopping centres of these settlements survived to become **suburban centres** of the now larger city or town. Where the expansion of the town was planned, suburban centres were created at major road junctions to cater for local shopping needs and reduce demands and congestion in the CBD.[3] Suburban centres tend to offer convenience goods (frequently demanded, cheaper items such as groceries, drugs) and some shopping goods (clothing and footwear). Apart from a supermarket or limited range variety store (such as Woolworths), the shops tend to be 1,500- to 2,500-square foot small store outlets; many privately owned and, unlike those in the CBD, not part of national chains.

Edge of Town

During the 1970s, as rents in the CBD rose and sites sufficient for large, open-plan stores became harder to obtain, retailers looked to the green fields adjacent to outer-ring roads for expansion. The superstore era had dawned as the major grocery, carpets and furniture, electrical and DIY retailers opened free-standing "sheds." Needing more space to display stock and sell their goods than they could afford or obtain in the CBD or even suburban centre, but still requiring high traffic levels, they sought sites adjacent to major arteries into the CBD. Initially, planning authorities protected green-belt and undeveloped land so the retailers occupied disused warehouses and factory units in once thriving industrial and commercial areas.

The planners then began to realise that stylish retail outlets could brighten up areas, create employment, attract traffic and rejuvenate decaying zones. Major retail chains such as the grocery retailers with their frequently purchased convenience goods attracted large volumes of traffic. Relocating these stores to non-retail areas of the city, and particularly to **edge of town** sites, helped redistribute traffic volumes and make use of the latest infrastructure. Retailers no longer had to occupy run-down warehouses; they could acquire undeveloped land and provide purpose-built stores, parking facilities, and amenities for their customers.[4]

Retail Parks

The progression of the out-of-town concept and relaxation of planning regulations by local authorities have led to the mid-1980s initiation of the **retail park**. Free-standing superstores, each over 25,000 square feet, are grouped together to form retail villages or parks. Located close to major roads, they offer extensive free car parking. Most of the stores offer one-floor shopping with wide ranges. Grocery superstores locate so as to be easily accessible to their consumers, as do the retailers of large expensive shopping goods: carpets, furniture, electrical goods, toys. The extensive ranges and displays of DIY retailers make such locations viable.

Increasingly, planners are for the first time allowing clothing and footwear retailers to locate out-of-town. They initially feared the demise of the CBD, but forecasts now show that both CBD and out-of-town centres can survive serving the same town or city. Most retail parks provide only superstores, e.g. West Thurrock on the M25 London orbital motorway, but some have shopping malls of specialty and chain

3. Ibid.

4. Russell Schiller, "Out of Town Exodus," in *The Changing Face of British Retailing* (London: Newman Books, 1987), pp. 64–73.

FIGURE 11.2

The out-of-town shopping mall has reached Europe.
Gateshead's Metro Centre offers the major retail chains plus extensive leisure amenities and catering facilities.

SOURCE: Courtesy of The Metro Centre

stores, e.g. Birmingham's Merry Hill or Gateshead's Metro Centre. Leisure facilities are frequently incorporated to cater for a family day out: ice-skating rinks, cinemas, children's play areas, restaurants, fast-food outlets, and food courts (see Figure 11.2).

MAJOR STORE TYPES

■ Department and Variety Stores

Department stores are physically large—around 250,000 square feet—and occupy prominent positions in the traditional heart of the town or city, the central shopping centre. Most towns have at least one such store; larger towns and cities have the population size to support several. The smaller town's department store is generally independently owned, whereas the larger store groups such as Debenhams, House of Fraser, John Lewis, or Allders have stores in many cities. Within a department store, related product lines are organised into separate departments such as cosmet-

FIGURE 11.3
A shop-within-a-shop. Brides occupies a prominent position in this Debenhams store.

SOURCE: Courtesy of Bridal Fashions Ltd.

ics, men's and women's fashions and accessories, housewares, home furnishings, haberdashery, and toys. Each department functions as a self-contained business unit and the buyers for individual departments are fairly autonomous. Financial services, hairdressing, and restaurants or coffee shops act as additional pulls to attract customers into the store.

Quite often concessionaires operate shops-within-shops. Brides is the largest retailer of wedding apparel in the U.K. The company has its own bridal shops and agencies in secondary locations but also operates the bridal departments in most Debenhams and House of Fraser department stores (see Figure 11.3). Brides either pays a fixed rental per square foot of space occupied in the host department store or pays a percentage commission on its volume of business. In department stores, concessions or shops-within-shops are typical for fashion clothing, cosmetics, and housewares.

Throughout the 1970s and 1980s, with the growth of shopping malls and covered centres, the explosion in the number of specialty shops, and the move to out-of-town shopping, the demise of department stores was predicted. Yet they are still at the heart of many CBD shopping centres. With new management teams and investment, most departmental store groups are once again thriving and expanding, building new stores in towns where they were not previously represented and in out-of-town retail parks, as well as refurbishing existing outlets.

Variety stores tend to be slightly smaller and often are more specialised, offering a reduced range of merchandise. They tend to be middle-market in their appeal, price points are more critical, and the selection of additional services is limited, tending to be just coffee shops. C&A focuses on men's, women's, and children's clothing; Marks & Spencer on clothing and food; BhS and Littlewoods on clothing and housewares; Woolworths on housewares, records and tapes, children's clothes, and confectionery. Variety stores are characterised by low-cost facilities, self-service shopping, central payment points, and multiple purchases; they appeal to large heterogeneous target markets, especially price-conscious customers.

■ Grocery Supermarkets, Superstores, and Hypermarkets

In the 1960s, led by Sainsbury, Tesco and Fine Fare, grocery retailers expanded into 10,000-square-foot supermarkets either in the city centre or within suburban centres. As product ranges grew, self-service requirements called for more space; and as city centre rents rose, the age of the superstore arrived. Size requirements grew further still and there was an exodus from the city centre. In the 1980s the average grocery superstore grew from 25,000 square feet to 55,000 square feet, moving away from the suburban centre to either free-standing superstore sites or edge-of-town retail parks.

Supermarkets and grocery **superstores** are large, self-service stores which carry a complete line of food products as well as other convenience items—cosmetics, non-prescription drugs, and kitchenwares. Some, such as Asda or Tesco, sell clothing and small electrical appliances. Grocery superstores are laid out in departments for maximum efficiency in stocking and handling products but have central check-out facilities by the exits to the ample, free car parking. Prices are considerably lower than in the independently owned, suburban shopping centre–based supermarkets or neighbourhood grocery shops. Price-conscious consumers demanding greater choice, improved packaging and refrigeration, and widespread car ownership spurred the huge growth of the major grocery superstore retailers: Sainsbury, Tesco, Asda, Gateway, and Safeway.

Of the top retailers in the U.K. and in Europe (see Figure 11.4, Table 11.2 and Table 11.3), many are superstore-trading grocery companies. They are at the forefront of retail technology—bar-scanning **EPOS** (electronic point of sale) tills, shelf-allocation modelling, robotised warehouse stacking—and of monitoring changes in customer attitudes and expectations. Increasingly, to gain an edge over the competition, they are launching more own-label products with attributes equal to, if not better than, manufacturers' brands, which are also on sale. Marketing Update 11.1 describes the problems one pioneering small-store grocery chain experienced in trying to compete against the superstore.

Hypermarkets take the benefits of the superstore even further, using their greater size (over 100,000 square feet) to give the customer a wider range and depth of products. They are common in the U.S.A., France and Germany, but there are few genuine hypermarkets in the U.K. Savacentre and Carrefour are the largest superstore/hypermarket outlets.

Asda, based in Leeds, began as a discount retailer of grocery products in the northern industrial regions of the U.K. Needing large premises but unable to gain

BIG IDEAS, SMALL STORES

Designed as a high-tech fresh-food chain and originally planned for 30 sites over the next four years, The Food Store was in the hands of the receivers less than three months after its first store opened. The former managing director of Tie Rack, Neil Fairley, a founder of The Food Store, departed while receivers Spicer and Oppenheim searched for a buyer for the company.

The Food Store opened its only outlet in May 1990 in Putney, a well-off area of southwest London. It expected to combine the service of the traditional independent grocer with the technology of modern supermarkets, and thus offer cheaper prices. The company found difficulty in beating supermarket prices without the volume sales of the major grocery retailers. The Food Store offered a unique service—if customers desired, they could order goods over the telephone and collect them ready-packed from a cool storage room at their convenience, at no extra charge. The store layout also departed from traditional supermarket aisles, offering a food hall with individual fresh-food departments. Ironically, shopping-centre developers and the national grocery chains have picked up the idea and incorporated it within new store openings and refurbishments.

SOURCE: Suzanne Bidlake, "Pioneering Food Store Nipped in the Bud," *Marketing,* 16 August 1990, p. 5. Reprinted by permission.

FIGURE 11.4
*Sales of top ten retailers
in the U.K.*

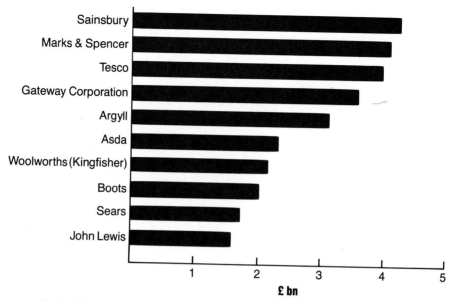

Sainsbury
Marks & Spencer
Tesco
Gateway Corporation
Argyll
Asda
Woolworths (Kingfisher)
Boots
Sears
John Lewis

1   2   3   4   5
£ bn

SOURCE: The Retail Rankings 1989. Reprinted by permission of Corporate Intelligence Research Publications Limited/*Marketing,* 30 March 1990.

TABLE 11.2

*The U.K.'s major retail-
ers (Top 100 retailers in
the U.K. by sub-sector
[December 1988])*

SUB-SECTOR	NUMBER OF RETAILERS IN THE TOP 100	SALES (£bn)	PERCENTAGE OF TOTAL SALES OF TOP 100
Grocers	12	20,740.9	35
Other food specialists	10	2,029.7	3.4
CTNs (news agents)	4	525	0.9
Off-licences	5	1,056	1.8
Clothing	7	2,523	4.3
Footwear	3	385	0.6
Furniture/carpets/household goods	6	1,451.9	2.5
Electrical and music goods	2	1,933	3.3
DIY and hardware	3	594	1.0
TV rental	2	1,470.5	2.5

SOURCE: Reprinted by permission of Corporate Intelligence Research Publications Limited/*Marketing,* 30 March 1990.

planning permission to build on green-field sites, the company operated initially from redundant cinemas and converted industrial warehouses. As the superstore era blossomed, Asda was a guiding force. Today the company is the market leader in superstore grocery retailing, with over one hundred purpose-built free-standing superstores offering manufacturer- and Asda-branded goods. The stores have over 50,000 square feet of one-floor retail space, pleasing ambience and additional amenities such as cafés, crêche facilities, and ample free parking. The company has a new

TABLE 11.3 *Europe's Main Retail Groups, 1987–1990*

SPAIN	Pta. million	**NETHERLANDS**	Gld. million
El Corte Ingles	370,000	Vendez	16,800
Hipermercados Pryca	170,255	Ahold	13,400
Saudisa-Continente	114,117	KKB	6,200
Alcampo	103,000	Samen Sterk	—
Galerias Preciados	90,000	Markant	—
Mercadona	54,000	Inkoopcombinatie	—
ITALY	Lr. billion	**WEST GERMANY***	DM million
Rinascente	2,715	Rewe, Cologne	24,550
Standa	2,623	Edeka, Hamburg	20,800
Despar	2,300	Metro, Dusseldorf	19,600
Benetton	1,275	Kaufhof, Cologne	8,898
Coin	745	C&C/Meister Primus, Nurnberg	8,146
Unico-op Firenze	710	BLV, Munich	1,450
FRANCE	Fr. million	Hurler, Munich	1,123
Leclerc	64,900	Aldi, Essen & Mulheim	19,500
Carrefour	56,500	Selex & Tania, Offenburg	17,000
Promodes	34,703	RHG Leibbrand, Bad Homburg	13,500
Docks de France	22,248	**DENMARK**	DKr. million
Euromarche	19,644	Co-ops	24,000
Genty Cathiard	18,243	Dansk Supermarked	11,000
Printemps	16,000	Dagrofa	7,000
		Hoki	4,000
		Oceka/NH	3,000
		Wessel & Vett	2,050

* Figures for the unified Germany are not yet available.

Authors; Warwick University Business Information Service; *Euromonitor*; DTI

distribution network, fully computerised and centralised, with on-line EPOS systems monitoring the exact stock requirements of each store.

■ **Discount Sheds and Superstores**

The move away from the city or town centre was not confined to multiple grocery retailers. Furniture, carpets, and electrical appliances require large display areas, ranges with strength in depth and, if possible, one-floor shopping. The concentration of retailers in the city centre led to limited store-opening opportunities (large enough sites were hard to find) and to high rents. When the electrical retailer Comet and furniture retailers Queensway and MFI sought out-of-town sites, they too were initially forced by the planning authorities to occupy disused warehouses and industrial units along arteries into the city centre. As the planners reviewed their regulations, these firms, along with the major DIY and toy retailers, developed purpose-built discount "sheds" or retail warehouses. Originally free-standing, these 20,000- to 35,000-square-foot stores are increasingly found in edge-of-town retail parks. See Marketing Update 11.2 for a description of one DIY merger.

The **discount sheds** are cheaply constructed, one-storey retail stores with no window displays and few add-on amenities. Orientated towards car-borne shoppers, they have large, free car parks and large stock facilities to enable shoppers to take delivery of their purchases immediately. Check-out points and customer services are kept to a minimum. As major retail groups have seen the cost benefits of location out-of-town, more companies have opened out-of-town free-standing or retail park

DIY* MERGER

Following its acquisition of Ward White, Boots became the owner of Payless DIY. W.H. Smith had created the Do-It-All DIY operation. Both chains were second-league players with 4 percent market share each and no hope of catching up and challenging Kingfisher's market leader, B&Q, with its 13 percent market share. Over a glass of wine at a City social event the marriage between Boots' and W.H. Smith's DIY chains was conceived. Together, Payless and Do-It-All will have nearly 9 percent of the market and a critical mass of over 230 stores around the country. The two groups had a good geographical fit, with very little store overlap. The new, enlarged company—trading under the name Do-It-All—will have lower costs, reduced management overheads and advertising spend, better margins resulting from increased buying power, greater sales volumes, and centralised distribution.

Because neither DIY operation was particularly successful, both Boots and W.H. Smith had reviewed the businesses. Payless profits were £20 million on turnover of £273 million, reduced to £8.7 million profits after interest payments. The 121 Do-It-All stores made a pre-tax profit of £7.7 million on turnover of £238 million. The merger is the result of Boots and W.H. Smith creating a joint venture company with each owning 50 percent. Boots received a net differential of £50 million to reflect the difference between the relative earnings and asset contributions of the two operations. The new Do-It-All is run autonomously by management brought in from the two parent companies.

* DIY: Do-it-yourself home maintenance/improvement products.

SOURCES: Verdict Research; Nerys Avery, "Banging Together a Bigger DIY Shed," *Investors Chronicle,* 8/14 June 1990, pp. 34–35; Suzanne Bidlake, "DIY Merger Bids to Build Up Sales," *Marketing,* 7 June 1990, p. 1; "Cogent to Sharpen Up Do-It-All," *Campaign,* 2 November 1990, p. 1.

superstores. Many customers would not tolerate the minimalist approach to ambience and service levels. Construction is still basic but more resources are devoted to shop-fitting expertise and customer service. Most retail groups selling electrical goods, carpets, furniture, toys, groceries, or DIY goods now operate superstores, not just the discounters. Increasingly, major variety store companies, departmental store groups, and clothing and footwear retailers are developing superstores: Marks & Spencer, Debenhams, and Sears are among them.

■ **Specialty Shops**

Most shopping centres and towns have a major department store. At the other end of the spectrum is the traditional corner shop. Few small shops these days retail a variety of product groups. In suburban areas such shops tend to specialise in retailing one convenience product category—newsagents with cigarettes and newspapers, greengrocers, chemists, hair salons, etc. In the town centre (CBD) few retailers of convenience goods, with their low margins, can afford the rents and business tax. Instead, the small store (2,500 square feet and under) retailers in the town centre specialise in shopping or comparison items: clothing, footwear, records and tapes, cosmetics, jewellery. Ownership of such retail outlets is increasingly concentrated in the hands of a few major retail groups (see Table 11.4), some of which also have retail brands which operate as department stores or out-of-town superstores. **Specialty shops** offer self-service but a greater level of assistance from store personnel. A typical 3,000-square-foot footwear or clothing retail store will have window displays to entice passing pedestrians, one or two check-out points, and three or four assistants. Such stores depend on the town centre's general parking facilities and on being in the proximity of a key trader, such as Boots or Marks & Spencer, which will generate pedestrian traffic.

■ **Convenience Stores**

As the number of neighbourhood grocery stores declined in the 1960s and 1970s with the expansion of the superstore-based national grocery chains, a niche emerged in the market to be filled by **convenience stores**. These shops sell essential groceries, alcoholic drinks, drugs, and newspapers outside the traditional 9.00 a.m. to 6.00 p.m. shopping hours. The major superstores extended their opening hours to 8.00 p.m. to facilitate after-work shopping, but no major retailers catered for "emergency" or top-up shopping. There was a resurgence of the traditional corner shop located in suburban housing estates, offering limited ranges but extended opening hours. Consumers pay a slight price premium but receive convenience in terms of location and opening hours. In the 1970s and 1980s, the voluntary groups (Spar, Mace, VG) and national retail groups such as Circle K and 7/Eleven repositioned their brands into the "open-all-hours" top-up or emergency shopping niche.

■ **Markets and Cash-and-Carry**

In most towns there are wholesale **markets** selling meat, greengrocery, fruit, flowers, and fish from which specialty retailers make their inventory purchases. Traditional, too, is the general retail market either in recently refurbished Victorian market halls or in council-provided modern halls adjacent to the town centre shopping malls. Such market halls sell fresh foods, clothing, and housewares; and they cater for budget-conscious shoppers who are typically of a middle- and down-market social profile.

The **cash-and-carry** warehouse, such as Booker, retails extensive ranges of groceries, tobacco, alcohol, beverages and confectionery to newsagents, small super-

TABLE 11.4
Large retail groups

Boots (chemists, car accessories, DIY)	Boots, Halfords, Do-It-All (with W.H. Smith), A. G. Stanley
Burton Group (fashion clothing shops and department stores)	Burton, Top Man, Principles/Principles for Men, Collier, Top Shop, Evans, Dorothy Perkins, Champion Sport, Secrets, Radius, Alias; Harvey Nichols and Debenhams
Dixons (electricals)	Dixons, Currys
Kingfisher (variety stores, chemists, electricals, DIY)	Woolworths, Superdrug, Comet, B&Q
Ratners (jewellery)	Ratners, H. Samuel, James Walker, Terry's, Watches of Switzerland
Sears (footwear, fashion clothing, jewellery, sportswear, children's wear, mail-order, department stores)	British Shoe Corporation (Freeman Hardy Willis, Trueform, Dolcis, Bertie, Cable & Co., Lilley & Skinner, Saxone, Manfield, Roland Cartier, Curtess, Shoe City); Fosters, Hornes, Zy, Bradleys, Your Price, Dormie; Miss Selfridge, Wallis, Warehouse; Milletts Leisure, Olympus Sports; Adams Childrenswear; Selfridges; Freemans
W.H. Smith (newsagency, books, records/tapes, DIY)	W. H. Smith, Waterstones, Paperchase, Our Price, Wee Three Records (USA), Do-It-All (with Boots)
Storehouse (furniture, fashion clothing, children's wear, variety stores)	Habitat, Richard Shops, Blazer, Mothercare, BhS

markets and convenience stores and the catering trade (hotels, guest houses, restaurants, and cafés). By purchasing from manufacturers in bulk, cash-and-carry companies can offer substantial price savings to their customers, who in turn can add a retail margin without alienating their customers.

■ Catalogue Showrooms

In a **catalogue showroom** one item of each product class is on display and the remaining inventory is stored out of the buyer's reach. Using catalogues which have been mailed to their homes or are on counters in the store, customers order the goods at their leisure. Shop assistants usually complete the order form and then collect the merchandise from the adjoining warehouse. Catalogue showrooms, such as Argos, regularly sell goods below list prices and often provide goods immediately. Higher product turnover, fewer losses through damage or shoplifting, and lower labour costs lead to their reduced retail prices. Jewellery, luggage, photographic equipment, toys, small appliances, housewares, sporting goods, garden furniture and power tools are the most commonly available items, listed by category and brand in the company's catalogue.

■ Categories

Table 11.5 summarises the major categories of retailing as defined in official DTI statistics. It is worth noting that the categories with the most stores do not necessarily top the league for highest turnover or profitability. The superstore and department store retailers have relatively fewer outlets but they account for large floor areas and include many of the U.K.'s main retail groups. European, and U.K. in particular, retail statistics are notoriously poor, being based on infrequent estimates rather than regular censuses. Agencies such as AGB, Euromonitor, Jordans, Mintel, and Verdict produce regular reports on retail sectors and consumer expectations based on commissioned market research surveys. These are available on subscription or occasionally, for the newest versions, through business libraries. These agencies tend to use categories similar to those discussed by the retail trade itself rather than the stilted, amalgamated official classification:

Food /grocery • CTN (confectionery, tobacco, news) • Off-licence/beverages
Men's/women's wear • Children's wear • Footwear/leather goods
Furniture/carpets/soft-furnishings
Electrical (small appliances, brown and white goods)
Hardware • DIY
Chemist/druggist
Books/greetings cards
Jewellers
Toys
Mixed retail businesses
Mail order
Restaurants/cafés/catering • Hotels
Banking/financial services

NON-STORE RETAILING AND HOME RETAILING

Non-store retailing is the selling of goods or services outside the confines of a retail facility. This form of retailing accounts for an increasing percentage of sales and includes personal sales methods, such as in-home retailing and telemarketing, and non-personal sales methods, such as automatic vending and mail-order retailing (which includes catalogue retailing).

Certain non-store retailing methods are in the category of **direct marketing**: the use of non-personal media or telesales to introduce products to consumers, who then purchase the products by mail or telephone. In the case of telephone orders, salespersons may be required to complete the sales. Telemarketing, mail-order, and catalogue retailing are all examples of direct marketing, as are sales generated by coupons, direct mail, and Freephone 0800 numbers.

■ In-Home Retailing

In-home retailing is selling via personal contacts with consumers in their own homes. Organisations such as Avon, Amway, and Betterware send representatives to the homes of pre-selected prospects. Traditionally, in-home retailing relied on a random door-to-door approach. Some companies now use a more efficient approach. They first identify prospects by reaching them by phone or mail or intercepting them in shopping malls or at consumer trade fairs. These initial contacts are limited to a brief introduction and the setting of appointments.

TABLE 11.5 *U.K. retail trade by sectors (standardised sectors)*

	FOOD RETAILERS		DRINK, CONFECTIONERY, & TOBACCO RETAILERS		CLOTHING, FOOTWEAR & LEATHER GOODS RETAILERS		HOUSEHOLD GOODS SHOPS		OTHER NON-FOOD RETAILERS		MIXED RETAIL BUSINESSES		HIRE & REPAIR BUSINESSES	
	1987	1986	1987	1986	1987	1986	1987	1986	1987	1986	1987	1986	1987	1986
BUSINESSES (NUMBER)	73,681	77,301	47,296	44,379	31,162	32,711	42,760	42,785	38,973	39,395	4,937	4,853	2,045	2,861
OUTLETS (NUMBER)	98,016	100,171	59,810	56,858	58,380	58,874	60,406	60,839	52,473	51,357	11,363	10,077	5,020	5,783
TURNOVER (£ MILLION)	35,880	34,761	10,363	9,969	10,077	9,199	17,001	14,719	8,812	8,234	18,354	18,224	1,288	1,319
AVERAGE SALES PER OUTLET (£ '000)	366	347	173	175	173	156	281	242	168	160	2,084	1,808	257	228
SHARE OF SALES (%)	35.2	36.0	10.2	10.3	9.9	9.5	16.7	15.3	8.7	8.5	18.0	18.9	1.3	1.5
GROSS MARGIN (%)	21.9	21.4	17.8	16.1	41.4	41.6	32.0	32.4	33.2	31.3	34.7	33.6	72.5	82.6

SOURCE: From *Retail Business Quarterly Trade Review*, June 1990. Reprinted by permission of The Economist Intelligence Unit.

Some in-home selling, however, is still undertaken without information about sales prospects. Door-to-door selling without a pre-arranged appointment is a tiny proportion of total retail sales, less than 1 percent. Because it has so often been associated with unscrupulous and fraudulent techniques, it is illegal in some communities. Generally, this method is regarded unfavourably because so many door-to-door salespersons are undertrained and poorly supervised. A big disadvantage of door-to-door selling is the large expenditure, effort, and time it demands. Sales commissions are usually 25 to 50 percent (or more) of the retail price; as a result, consumers often pay more than a product is worth. Door-to-door selling is used most often when a product is unsought—for instance, encyclopaedias, which most consumers would not be likely to purchase in a store.

A variation of in-home retailing is the home demonstration or party plan, which such companies as Tupperware, Ann Summers, and Mary Kay Cosmetics use successfully. One consumer acts as host and invites a number of friends to view merchandise at his or her home, where a salesperson is on hand to demonstrate the products. The home demonstration is more efficient for the sales representative than contacting each prospect door-to-door, and the congenial atmosphere partly overcomes consumers' suspicions and encourages them to buy. Home demonstrations also meet the buyers' needs for convenience and personal service. Commissions and selling costs make this form of retailing expensive, however. Additionally, successful party-plan selling requires both a network of friends and neighbours who have the time to attend such social gatherings and a large number of effective salespersons. With so many household members now holding full-time jobs, both prospects and sales representatives are harder to recruit. The growth of interactive telephone-computer home shopping may also cut into party-plan sales.

■ **Telemarketing**

More and more organisations—IBM, Merrill Lynch, Avis, Ford, Quaker Oats, Time, and American Express, to name a few—are using the telephone to strengthen the effectiveness of traditional marketing methods. **Telemarketing** is direct selling of goods and services by telephone based on either a cold canvass of the telephone directory or a pre-screened list of prospective clients. (In some areas, certain telephone numbers are listed with an asterisk to indicate the people who consider sales solicitations a nuisance and do not want to be bothered.) Telemarketing can generate sales leads, improve customer service, speed up collection of past-due accounts, raise funds for non-profit groups, and gather market data.[5]

In some cases, telemarketing uses advertising that encourages consumers to initiate a call or to request information about placing an order. This type of retailing is only a small part of total retail sales, but its use is growing. According to AT&T, U.S. companies spent $13.6 billion in one year on telemarketing phone calls and equipment (phones, lines, and computers). Telephone Marketing Resources, a U.S. telemarketing firm, estimates telephone sales of goods and services at $75 billion annually (the figure includes business-to-consumer sales and business-to-business sales).[6] Experts believe that similar growth will be seen in Europe in the next few years. Research indicates that telemarketing is most successful when combined with other marketing strategies, such as direct mail or advertising in newspapers, radio, and television.

5. Kenneth C. Schneider, "Telemarketing as a Promotional Tool—Its Effects and Side Effects," *Journal of Consumer Marketing*, Winter 1985, pp. 29–39.

6. Joel Dreyfuss, "Reach Out and Sell Something," *Fortune*, 26 November 1984, pp. 127–128.

Automatic Vending

Automatic vending makes use of machines and accounts for less than 1 percent of all retail sales. In the U.K. there are approximately 650,000 vending machines. Locations and the percentage of sales each generates are as follows:[7]

Plants and factories	38%
Public locations (e.g., stores)	26%
Offices	16%
Colleges and universities	6%
Government facilities	3%
Hospitals and nursing homes	3%
Primary and secondary schools	2%
Others	6%

Video game machines provide an entertainment service, and many banks now offer machines that dispense cash or offer other services, but these uses of vending machines are not reported in total vending sales volume.

Automatic vending is one of the most impersonal forms of retailing. Small, standardised, routinely purchased products (chewing gum, sweets, newspapers, cigarettes, soft drinks, coffee) can be sold in machines because consumers usually buy them at the nearest available location. Machines in areas of heavy traffic provide efficient and continuous services to consumers. The elimination of sales personnel and the small amount of space necessary for vending machines give this retailing method some advantages over stores. The advantages are partly offset by the expense of the frequent servicing and repair needed.

Mail-Order Retailing

Mail-order retailing involves selling by description because buyers usually do not see the actual product until it arrives in the mail. Sellers contact buyers through direct mail, catalogues, television, radio, magazines, and newspapers. A wide assortment of products such as compact discs, books, and clothing is sold to consumers through the mail. Placing mail orders by telephone is increasingly common. The advantages of mail-order selling include efficiency and convenience. Mail-order houses, such as Kays or Grattan, can be located in remote, low-cost areas and avoid the expenses of store fixtures. Eliminating personal selling efforts and store operations may result in tremendous savings that can be passed along to consumers in the form of lower prices. On the other hand, mail-order retailing is inflexible, provides limited service, and is more appropriate for specialty products than for convenience products.

When **catalogue retailing** (a specific type of mail-order retailing) is used, customers receive their orders by mail (see Figure 11.5), or they may pick them up if the catalogue retailer has stores, as does Littlewoods. Although in-store visits result in some catalogue orders, most are placed by mail or telephone. In the United States, General Foods created Thomas Garroway Ltd., a mail-order service supplying gourmet pasta, cheese, coffee, and similar items. Other packaged-goods manufacturers involved in catalogue retailing include Hanes, Nestlé, Thomas J. Lipton, Sunkist, and Whitman Chocolates.[8] These catalogue retailers are able to reach many two-income families who have more money and less time for special shopping. In

---

7. "V/T Census of the Industry Issue—1988," *Vending Times*, 1988, p. 49. Reprinted by permission.

8. Ronald Alsop, "Food Giants Take to Mails to Push Fancy Product Lines," *Wall Street Journal*, 28 Feb. 1985, p. 85.

FIGURE 11.5
Catalogue retailing. Freemans, one of the oldest and largest catalogue retailers, provides an extensive product mix to its customers.

Two great fashion names in one great catalogue *Freemans*

YES! Please rush me my *FREE* Autumn/Winter catalogue

Miss/Ms/Mrs/Mr _____
(Delete As Applicable)   (I am over 18)

Address _____

_____

Postcode _____ Tel. No. _____ S75

Our International Catalogue is available for overseas/
Eire customers. Please send £5 for your copy.

Post to: Freemans, FREEPOST, London SW99 0YX (no stamp needed)

Freemans

DIAL A CATALOGUE 0800 900 200 Quote Ref. S75

The right to refuse any application is reserved.

SOURCE: FREEMANS, 139 Clapham Rd., London SW99 OHR. 0800 900 200.

the U.K. manufacturers and store-focused retail groups tend not to be involved with catalogue or home shopping. The specialist mail-order companies such as GUS and Freemans dominate this sector. The U.K. mail-order market is worth over £5.4 billion, having grown by 113 percent since 1982.[9]

FRANCHISING

Franchising is an arrangement whereby a supplier, or franchisor, grants a dealer, or franchisee, the right to sell products in exchange for some type of consideration. For example, the franchisor may receive some percentage of total sales in exchange for furnishing equipment, buildings, management know-how, marketing assistance, and branding to the franchisee. The franchisee supplies labour and capital, operates the franchised business, and agrees to abide by the provisions of the franchise agreement. In the next section we look at the major types of retail franchises, the advantages and disadvantages of franchising, and trends in franchising.

9. Keynote Publications, 1989.

■ Major Types of Retail Franchises

Retail franchise arrangements can generally be classified as one of three general types. In the first arrangement, a manufacturer authorises a number of retail stores to sell a certain brand-name item. This franchise arrangement, one of the oldest, is common in the sales of cars and trucks, farm equipment, earth-moving equipment, and petroleum. The majority of all petrol is sold through franchised independent retail service stations, and franchised dealers handle virtually all sales of new cars and trucks. The second type of retail franchise occurs when a producer licenses distributors to sell a given product to retailers. This franchising arrangement is common in the soft-drinks industry. Most national manufacturers of soft-drink syrups—Coca-Cola, Pepsi-Cola—franchise independent bottlers, which then serve retailers. In the third type of retail franchise, a franchisor supplies brand names, techniques, or other services, instead of a complete product. The franchisor may provide certain production and distribution services, but its primary role in the arrangement is the careful development and control of marketing strategies. This approach to franchising, which is the most typical today, is used by many organisations, including Holiday Inn, McDonald's, Avis, Hertz, Kentucky Fried Chicken, Body Shop, Holland & Barrett, Pronuptia, and Benetton.

■ Advantages and Disadvantages of Franchising

Franchising offers several advantages to both the franchisee and the franchisor. It enables a franchisee to start a business with limited capital and to make use of the business experience of others. Moreover, an outlet with a nationally advertised name, such as Body Shop or Burger King, is often assured of customers as soon as it opens. If business problems arise, the franchisee can obtain guidance and advice from the franchisor at little or no cost. Franchised outlets are generally more successful than independently owned businesses: only 5 to 8 percent of franchised retail businesses fail during the first two years of operation, whereas approximately 54 percent of independent retail businesses fail during that period.[10] The franchisee also receives materials to use in local advertising and can take part in national promotional campaigns sponsored by the franchisor.

The franchisor gains fast and selective distribution of its products through franchise arrangements without incurring the high cost of constructing and operating its own outlets. The franchisor therefore has more capital available to expand production and to use for advertising. At the same time, it can ensure, through the franchise agreement, that outlets are maintained and operated to its own standards. The franchisor also benefits from the fact that the franchisee, being a sole proprietor in most cases, is likely to be very highly motivated to succeed. The success of the franchise means more sales, which translate into higher royalties for the franchisor.

Despite their numerous advantages, franchise arrangements also have several drawbacks. The franchisor can dictate many aspects of the business: decor, the design of employees' uniforms, types of signs, and numerous details of business operations. In addition, franchisees must pay to use the franchisor's name, products, and assistance. Usually, there is a one-time franchise fee and continuing royalty and advertising fees, collected as a percentage of sales. In addition, franchisees often must work very hard, putting in ten- and twelve-hour days, six days a week. In some cases, franchise agreements are not uniform: one franchisee may pay more than another for the same services. The franchisor also gives up a certain amount of control when entering into a franchise agreement. Consequently, individual establishments may not be operated exactly how the franchisor would operate them.

10. Al Urbanski, "The Franchise Option," *Sales & Marketing Management*, February 1988, pp. 28–33.

■ Trends in Franchising

Franchising has been used since the early 1900s, primarily for service stations and car dealerships. However, it has grown enormously since the mid-1960s. This growth has generally paralleled the expansion of the fast-food industry—the industry in which franchising is widely used. Of course, franchising is not limited to fast foods. Franchise arrangements for health clubs, pest control, hair salons, and travel agencies are widespread. The estate agency industry has also experienced a rapid increase in franchising. The largest U.S. franchising sectors, ranked by sales, are car and truck dealers (52.4 percent), service stations (14.4 percent), restaurants (9.9 percent), and non-food retailing (4.5 percent)—a pattern replicated in Europe.[11]

Strategic Issues in Retailing

Consumers often have vague reasons for making a retail purchase. Whereas most industrial purchases are based on economic planning and necessity, consumer purchases often result from social influences and psychological factors. Because consumers shop for a variety of reasons—to search for specific items, to escape boredom, or to learn about something new—retailers must do more than simply fill space with merchandise; they must make desired products available, create stimulating environments for shopping, and develop marketing strategies that increase store patronage. In this section we discuss how store location, property ownership, product assortment, retail positioning, atmospherics/design, store image, scrambled merchandising, central/regional management, technology, distribution, the wheel of retailing and 1992 EC deregulation affect these retailing objectives.

■ Location

Location, the least flexible of the strategic retailing issues, is one of the most important because location dictates the limited geographic trading area from which a store must draw its customers. Thus retailers consider a variety of factors when evaluating potential locations, including the location of the firm's target customers within the trading area, the kinds of products being sold, the availability of public transport, customer characteristics, and competitors' locations.[12] The relative ease of movement to and from the site is important, including pedestrian and vehicular traffic, parking, and transport. Most retailers prefer sites with high pedestrian traffic, although preliminary site investigations often include a pedestrian count to determine how many of the passers-by are truly prospective customers. Similarly, the nature of the area's vehicular traffic is analysed. Certain retailers, such as service stations and convenience stores, depend on large numbers of car-borne customers but try to avoid overly congested locations. In addition, parking space must be adequate for projected demand, and transport networks (major thoroughfares and public transport) must be able to accommodate customers and delivery vehicles.

Retailers also evaluate the characteristics of the site itself: the other stores in the area, particularly the proximity of key traders or magnets; the size, shape, and visibility of the plot or building under consideration; and the rental, leasing, or ownership terms under which the building may be occupied. Retailers also look for compatibility with nearby retailers because stores that complement each other draw more customers for everyone. This is particularly true for clothing, footwear, and

---

11. *Statistical Abstract of the U.S., 1989*, p. 760.

12. R.L. Davies and D. S. Rogers, *Store Location and Store Assessment Research* (Chichester: Wiley, 1984).

jewellery retailers.[13] When making site location decisions, retailers must select from among several general types of location: free-standing structures, traditional business districts, neighbourhood/suburban shopping centres, out-of-town superstores, and retail parks. In recent years retailers have been moving away from the traditional store assessment procedure of pedestrian counts and "eye-balling" the immediate site's location. Various agencies—notably CACI and SAMI—have detailed databases examining each shopping centre. Computer modelling has become more widespread, bringing a basis of objectivity to what was previously an intuitive decision-making process, based on few hard facts.[14]

■ **Property Ownership**

Property ownership is perpetually an issue in retailing. Some companies, such as Marks & Spencer, own the majority of their property portfolio. This gives security of tenure, saves on rents and lease negotiations, and adds to the book value of the company. To realise operating funds, companies often engage in "sale and leaseback" deals. Property companies buy the freehold to add to their assets but give a favourable lease immediately to the retailer. In recent years companies which once held the freehold for most of their stores have sold off property to make available operating funds for new computer systems, store refurbishment, or new store openings. Companies such as the Burton Group or Next argue that they are primarily retailers and funds should not be tied up in property ownership. Retailers that locate mainly in covered shopping centres and on retail parks generally have to accept lease agreements as the centre's developer maintains ownership of the property.

■ **Product Assortment**

The **product assortments** that retailers develop vary considerably in breadth and depth. As discussed earlier, retail stores are often classified according to their product assortments. Conversely, a store's type affects the breadth and depth of its product offerings, as shown in Figure 11.6. Thus a specialty store has a single product line but considerable depth in that line. Tie Rack stores and Fannie May Candy Shops, for example, carry only one line of products but many items within that line. In contrast, discount stores may have a wide product mix (such as housewares, automotive services, apparel, and food). Department stores may have a wide product mix with different product line depths. Nevertheless, it is usually difficult to maintain both a wide and a deep product mix because of the inventories required. In addition, some producers prefer to distribute through retailers that offer less variety so that their products get more exposure and are less affected by the presence of competing brands.

Issues of product assortment are often a matter of what and how much to carry. When retailers decide what should be included in their product assortments, they consider the assortment's purpose, status, and completeness.[15] *Purpose* relates to how well an assortment satisfies consumers and at the same time furthers the retailer's goals. *Status* identifies by rank the relative importance of each product in an assortment: for example, motor oil might have low status in a store that sells convenience foods. *Completeness* means that an assortment includes the products necessary to satisfy a store's customers; the assortment is incomplete when some

13. R.L. Davies, *Marketing Geography* (London: Methuen, 1976).

14. L. Simkin, "SLAM: Store Location Assessment Model—Theory and Practice," *OMEGA*, 17 (1) (1989), pp. 53–58.

15. C. Glenn Walters and Blaise J. Bergiel, *Marketing Channels*, 2nd ed. (Glenview, Ill.: Scott, Foresman, 1982), p. 205.

FIGURE 11.6

Relationships between merchandise breadth and depth for a typical discount store, department store, and specialty store

Discount store

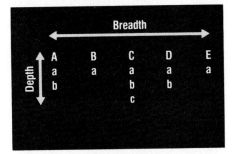

Department store

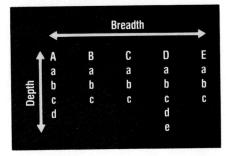

Specialty store

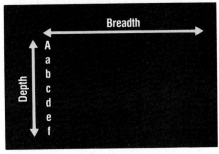

The capital letters represent the number of product lines, and the small letters depict the choices in any one product line. Thus it can be seen that discount stores are wide and shallow in merchandise assortment. Specialty stores, at the other extreme, have few product lines, but much more depth in the few they carry. The typical department store falls in between, having a broad assortment with many merchandise lines and medium depth in each line.

SOURCE: Robert F. Hartley, *Retailing: Challenge and Opportunity,* 3rd ed., p. 118. Copyright © 1984 by Houghton Mifflin Company. Used by permission.

products are missing. An assortment of convenience foods must include milk to be complete because most consumers expect to be able to buy milk when purchasing other food products. New products are added to (and declining products are deleted from) an assortment when they meet (or fail to meet) the retailer's standards of purpose, status, and completeness.

The retailer also considers the quality of the products to be offered. The store may limit its assortments to expensive, high-quality goods for upper-income market segments; it may stock cheap, low-quality products for low-income buyers; or it may try to attract several market segments by offering a range of quality within its total product assortment.

How much to include in an assortment depends on the needs of the retailer's target market. A discount store's customers expect a wide and shallow product mix, whereas specialty-store shoppers prefer narrow and deep assortments. If a retailer can increase sales by increasing product variety, the assortment may be enlarged. If a broader product mix ties up too much floor space or creates storage problems, however, the retailer may stock only the products that generate the greatest sales. Other factors that affect product assortment decisions are the personnel, store image, inventory control methods, and the financial risks involved.

■ **Retail Positioning**

Because of the emergence of new types of store (discount warehouses, superstores, hypermarkets) and the expansion of product offerings by traditional stores, competition among retailers is intense. Thus it is important for management to consider the retail organisation's market positioning. **Retail positioning** involves identifying an unserved or under-served market niche, or segment, and serving it through a strategy that distinguishes the retailer from others in the minds of people in that segment.[16]

There are several ways in which retailers position themselves.[17] A retailer may position itself as a seller of high-quality, premium-priced products that provides many services. A store such as Selfridges, which specialises in expensive high-fashion clothing and jewellery, sophisticated electronics, and exclusive home furnishings, might be expected to provide wrapping and delivery services, personal shopping consultants, and restaurant facilities. Fortnum & Mason, for example, emphasises superlative service, and even hires pianists to play in the entrance of its store.[18] Dixons, the electrical retailer, is often referred to as "the grown man's toy shop". Another type of retail organisation, such as Tesco, may be positioned as a marketer of reasonable quality products at everyday low prices. As indicated at the beginning of this chapter, Tesco has repositioned itself as one of the U.K.'s leading grocery retailers. However, while major U.K. grocery retailers position themselves as middle-to-up-market, Aldi, profiled in Marketing Update 11.3, is attempting to become successful as a discount grocery retailer.

■ Atmospherics

Atmospherics are often used to help position a retailer. **Atmospherics** are the physical elements in a store's design that appeal to consumers' emotions and encourage them to buy. Exterior and interior characteristics, layout, and displays all contribute to a store's atmosphere. Department stores, restaurants, hotels, service stations, and shops combine these elements in different ways to create specific atmospheres that may be perceived as warm, fresh, functional, or exciting.

Exterior atmospheric elements include the appearance of the storefront, the window displays, store entrances, and degree of traffic congestion. Exterior atmospherics are particularly important to new customers, who tend to judge an unfamiliar store by its outside appearance and may not enter the store if they feel intimidated by the building or inconvenienced by the car park. Because consumers form general impressions of shopping centres and business districts, the businesses and neighbourhoods surrounding a store will affect how buyers perceive the atmosphere of a store.

Interior atmospheric elements include aesthetic considerations such as lighting, wall and floor coverings, changing rooms, and store fixtures. Interior sensory elements also contribute to atmosphere. Colour, for example, can attract shoppers to a retail display. Many fast-food restaurants use bright colours such as red and yellow because these have been shown to make customers feel hungrier and eat faster, which increases turnover. Sound is another important sensory component of atmosphere and may consist of silence, soft music, or even noisiness. Scent may be relevant as well; within a store, the odour of perfume suggests an image different from that suggested by the smell of prepared food. A store's layout—arrangement of departments, width of aisles, grouping of products, and location of cashiers—is yet another determinant of atmosphere. Closely related to store layout is the element of crowding. A crowded store may restrict exploratory shopping, impede mobility, and decrease shopping efficiency.

16. George H. Lucas, Jr., and Larry G. Gresham, "How to Position for Retail Success," *Business,* April-June 1988, pp. 3–13.

17. G. J. Davies and J. M. Brooks, *Positioning Strategy in Retailing* (London: Paul Chapman, 1989).

18. Leslie Wayne, "Rewriting the Rules of Retailing," *New York TImes,* 15 Oct. 1989, p. F6.

ALDI EXPANDS

While the major U.K. grocery retailers recently positioned themselves as middle- to up-market, providing extensive ranges, own-label goods, improved customer service, and large stores with carefully conceived facilities and atmospherics, the budget-conscious sector of the market was left in the hands of Kwik Save.

With only 2,500 lines and concentrating on manufacturer brands, no-frills service, and small supermarkets in town centres or in the suburbs, Kwik Save has become one of the U.K.'s most successful companies.

DIFFERENT VIEWS OF SUCCESSFUL UK FOOD RETAILERS, SELECTED RATIOS AND RANKING

Company	Turnover (£m)	Operating profit (£m)	Market value (£m)	% return on net assets	% return on equity	Sales growth	PE ratio	Added value[1]
Sainsbury	5,659(1)[2]	369(1)	3,365(1)	21(4)	21(3)	11(2)	13.5(2)	12.3(3)
Tesco	4,717(2)	274(2)	2,350(2)	23(3)	18(4)	7(3)	12.6(4)	12.5(2)
Gateway	4,516(3)	205(3)	1,703(4)	21(5)	17(6)	–19(6)	10.8(6)	6.6(5)
Argyll	3,500(4)	156(4)	1,661(5)	25(2)	24(2)	1(4)	13.3(3)	10.1(4)
Asda	2,708(5)	156(5)	1,913(3)	18(6)	18(5)	1(5)	11.5(5)	1.2(6)
Kwik Save	1,181(6)	58(6)	848(6)	41(1)	27(1)	18(1)	17.6(1)	26.8(1)

[1] As percentage of input costs
[2] All rankings in brackets

John Kay, "Different Views of Successful U.K. Food Retailers, Selected Ratios and Ranking," *Accountancy.* Reprinted by permission.

Now, however, the market is changing. Aldi, the German discounter, has opened its first branches in the Midlands. Already one of Europe's largest grocery retailers, Aldi offers no luxuries, no customer services, on secondary sites with no expense devoted to store design and fitting out. Aldi concentrates on many of its own-label products but they—along with manufacturer brands—are displayed in their shipping containers (in boxes). A limited range of essentials for C2/DE shoppers, for whom price is the key, is the Aldi approach.

Discount grocery retailing has not been successful in the U.K. Tesco is still shaking off its former discount image; Supasave went into liquidation in 1982; Pricerite was carved up by Shoppers Paradise and Argyll; Shoppers Paradise itself was devoured and rebranded by Gateway in 1986. The only success story has been Kwik Save. For Aldi, however, U.K. grocery margins of 5 to 7 percent are perceived as high, enticing the company into the U.K. It remains to be seen whether Aldi can create a network of branches large enough to give it the necessary scale economies to trade on price. U.K. consumers have yet to accept its discount, limited-range positioning in a market led by such high-profile retailers as Sainsbury, Tesco, Gateway, Argyll (Safeway), Asda, and Marks & Spencer.

SOURCES: "King of the Discounts Invades the South," *Marketing,* 13 September 1990, pp. 38–39; "Aldi Arrives," *Marketing,* 9 May 1990, p. 3; and Nigel Cope, "Aldi Cuts the Cackle," *Business,* June 1990, pp. 78–80.

Once the exterior and interior characteristics and store layout have been determined, displays are added. Displays enhance the store's atmosphere and give customers information about products. When displays carry out a store-wide theme, during the Christmas season, for instance, they attract customers' attention and generate sales. So do displays that present several related products in a group, or ensemble. Interior displays of products stacked or hanging neatly on racks create one kind of atmosphere; marked-down items grouped together on a bargain table produce a different kind.

Retailers must determine the atmosphere the target market seeks and then adjust atmospheric variables to encourage the desired awareness and action in consumers. High-fashion boutiques generally strive for an atmosphere of luxury and novelty; discount department stores must not seem too exclusive and expensive. To appeal to multiple market segments, a retailer may create different atmospheres for different operations within the store; for example, the discount basement, the sports department, and the women's shoe department may each have a unique atmosphere.

■ **Store Image**

To attract customers, a retail store must project an image—a functional and psychological picture in the consumer's mind—that is acceptable to its target market. Although heavily dependent on atmospherics and design, a store's image is also shaped by its reputation for integrity, the number of services offered, location, merchandise assortments, pricing policies, promotional activities, community involvement, and the retail brand's positioning.[19]

Characteristics of the target market—social class, lifestyle, income level, and past buying behaviour—help form store image as well. How consumers perceive the store can be a major determinant of store patronage. Consumers from lower socio-economic groups tend to patronise small, high-margin, high-service food stores and prefer small, friendly building societies/loan companies over large, impersonal banks, even though these companies charge high interest. Affluent consumers look for exclusive, high-quality establishments that offer prestige products and labels.

Retailers should be aware of the multiple factors that contribute to store image and recognise that perceptions of image vary. For example, one study found that in America consumers perceived Wal-Mart and K mart differently although the two sold almost the same products in stores that looked quite similar, offered the same prices, and even had similar names. Researchers discovered that Wal-Mart shoppers spent more money at Wal-Mart and were more satisfied with the store than K mart shoppers were with K mart, in part because of differences in the retailers' images. For example, Wal-Mart employees wore waistcoats; K mart employees did not. Wal-Mart purchases were packed in paper bags while K mart used plastic bags. Wal-Mart had wider aisles, recessed lighting, and carpeting in some departments. Even the retailers' logos affected consumers' perceptions: Wal-Mart's simple white and brown logo appeared friendly and "less blatantly commercial," while K mart's red and turquoise blue logo conveyed the impression that the stores had not changed much since the 1960s. These atmospheric elements gave consumers the impression that Wal-Mart was more "up-market", warmer, and friendlier than K mart.[20]

19. Terence Conran, "The Retail Image," in *The Retail Report* (London: Healey & Baker, 1985).

20. Francine Schwadel, "Little Touches Spur Wal-Mart's Rise; Shoppers React to Logo, Decor, Employee Vests," *Wall Street Journal,* 22 Sept. 1989, p. B1.

Scrambled Merchandising

When retailers add unrelated products and product lines, particularly fast-moving items that can be sold in volume, to an existing product mix, they are practising **scrambled merchandising**. For example, a convenience store might start selling lawn fertiliser. Retailers adopting this strategy hope to accomplish one or more of the following: (1) to convert their stores into one-stop shopping centres, (2) to generate more traffic, (3) to realise higher profit margins, (4) to increase impulse purchases.

In scrambling merchandise, retailers must deal with diverse marketing channels and thus may reduce their own buying, selling, and servicing expertise. The practice can also blur a store's image in consumers' minds, making it more difficult for a retailer to succeed in today's highly competitive, saturated markets. Finally, scrambled merchandising intensifies competition among traditionally distinct types of stores and forces suppliers to adjust distribution systems so that new channel members can be accommodated. Asda is predominantly a grocery retailer. However, in most stores it has the "George" clothing ranges. In some stores it retails small electrical appliances, DIY goods, car accessories, but not in other stores. During the summer months, gardening supplies and equipment are sold. In the months leading up to Christmas, such floorspace is given over to children's toys and gifts.

The Wheel of Retailing

As new types of retail businesses come into being, they strive to fill niches in the dynamic environment of retailing. One hypothesis regarding the evolution and development of new types of retail stores is the **wheel of retailing**. According to this theory, new retailers often enter the market-place with low prices, margins, and status. The new competitors' low prices are usually the result of innovative cost-cutting procedures, and they soon attract imitators. Gradually, as these businesses attempt to broaden their customer base and increase sales, their operations and facilities become more elaborate and more expensive. They may move to more desirable locations, begin to carry higher-quality merchandise, or add customer services. Eventually, they emerge at the high end of the price/cost/service scales, competing with newer discount retailers who are following the same evolutionary process.[21]

For example, supermarkets have undergone many changes since their introduction in the 1920s. Initially, they provided limited services in exchange for lower food prices. However, over time they developed a variety of new services, including free coffee, gourmet food sections, and children's play areas. Now supermarkets are being challenged by superstores and hypermarkets, which offer more product choices than the original supermarkets and have undercut supermarket prices.

Figure 11.7 illustrates the wheel of retailing for department stores and discounters. Department stores such as Debenhams started out as high-volume, low-cost merchants competing with general stores and other small retailers; discount houses developed later, in response to the rising expenses of services in department stores. Many discounters now appear to be following the wheel of retailing by offering more services, better locations, high-quality inventories, and, therefore, higher prices. Some discount houses are almost indistinguishable from department stores.

Like most hypotheses, the wheel of retailing may not fit every case. For example, it does not adequately explain the development of convenience stores, specialty

---

21. Stanley C. Hollander, "The Wheel of Retailing," *Journal of Marketing,* July 1960, p. 37.

FIGURE 11.7

The wheel of retailing, which explains the origin and evolution of new types of retail stores

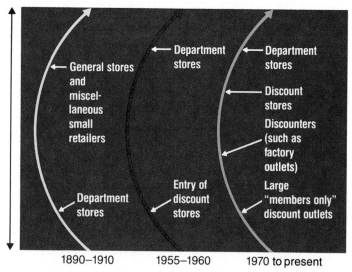

High prices and markups, many services, expensive surroundings

Low prices and markups, few services, austere surroundings

1890–1910   1955–1960   1970 to present

If the "wheel" is considered to be turning slowly in the direction of the arrow, then the department stores around 1900 and the discounters later can be viewed as coming on the scene at the low end of the wheel. As it turns slowly, they move with it, becoming higher-price operations, and at the same time leaving room for lower-price firms to gain entry at the low end of the wheel.

SOURCE: Adapted from Robert F. Hartley, *Retailing: Challenge and Opportunity,* 3rd ed., p. 42. Copyright 1984 by Houghton Mifflin Company. Used by permission.

stores, department store branches, and vending machine operations. Another major weakness of the theory is that it does not predict what retailing innovations will develop, or when. Still, the hypothesis works reasonably well in industrialised, expanding economies.

■ **Current Trends**

In addition to the strategic issues highlighted above, mention must also be made of some current trends with strategic implications. The **balance of retailing** is a well-documented subject: the balance of negotiating and buying power between retailers and their suppliers.[22] As more retailers devote shelf space to their own-label branded goods, the major manufacturers find themselves squeezed out. In the clothing market nearly all retailers now give precedence to their own-label goods. Marks & Spencer takes the situation to the extreme: only St Michael (Marks & Spencer's own-label) goods are on sale. The company dictates quality levels, lead times, packaging and delivery conditions and often the price it will pay to its suppliers![23] Two years ago Sainsbury threatened to de-stock Kellogg's cereals totally and Kellogg's refused to supply Sainsbury. Two giant brands were locked in a power struggle. Increasingly compromise and negotiation are leading to deals beneficial to

22. W.S. Howe, "UK Retailer Vertical Power, Market Competition and Consumer Welfare," *International Journal of Retail and Distribution Management,* 18(2), 1990, pp. 16–25.

23. K.K. Tse, "Marks & Spencer: A Manufacturer Without Factories," *International Trends in Retailing,* 6(2), 1989, pp. 23–36.

TABLE 11.6   *Current levels of electronic systems penetration in U.K. retailing*

	STORES ON-LINE (%)	SALES ON-LINE (%)	DPP SYSTEMS	AUTOMATIC STOCK RE-ORDERING	REGIONAL/ EXPERIMENTAL/ PRICING	EDI
Boots (BTC)	29	65	X	X	X	X
Burton	20	17				
Dixons—Currys	100	100		°		X
—Dixons	100	100		°		X
Empire	N/A	100	X			
Etam	0	0				
GUS	N/A	100	X	°		°
Kingfisher—F.W. Woolworth	Part	10		°		°
—Comet	100	100		°		°
—B&Q	75	85	X	X		X
—Superdrug	0	0				
Lowndes Queensway	65	46	°	X		°
Marks & Spencer	90	95		°		X
Next	85	90		X		X
Ratners	95	98		X		
Sears	35	45	°	°		°
W.H. Smith—Do-It-All	100	100	X	X	X	X
—Our Price	0	0		X		X
—UK/Retail/Books	70	85	X	X	°	°
Storehouse—Habitat	0	0				
—Mothercare	100	100		X		X
—BhS	100	100		X		X
Wickes—Wickes	100	100	X	X		X
—Malden	100	100	°			

° used to some extent.
DPP = Direct Product Profitability; EDI = Electronic Data Interface

SOURCE: Morgan Stanley/*International Journal of Retail & Distribution Management* (West Yorkshire, England: MCB University Press, 1990), Vol. 18, No. 2, p. 44. Reprinted by permission.

both sides of the equation: retailers receive preferential treatment and buying terms while manufacturers receive contracts to supply major retail chains exclusively with their own-label needs, often alongside their own manufacturer brands.[24]

Technology.   Retailers are turning to **retail technology** for improved productivity and often to create a competitive edge. Table 11.6 shows the current levels of electronic systems penetration in U.K. retailing. Bar-scanning and electronic point of sale (EPOS) systems enable companies to monitor exact consumer spending patterns on a store-by-store basis, to prevent stock-outs and to have detailed sales data to add weight to negotiations with suppliers. EFTPOS (electronic funds trans-

24. R.M. Grant, "Manufacturer–Retailer Relations: The Shifting Balance of Power," in *Business Strategy and Retailing* by Gerry Johnson (Chichester: Wiley, 1987), pp. 43–58.

fer at point of sale) equipment facilitates speedy payment for goods, thereby reducing check-out queues; the rapid debiting of customer accounts is to the benefit of the retailer's bank account and cash flow. Video screens and video walls bring a new medium for the promotion of goods and services, as well as for the transfer of information. The spread of computer systems has enabled consultants to develop computer graphic tools for the modelling of store location choice, customer demographics, and shelf-space allocation.[25]

Retail technology is not cheap—£60,000 to bring a typical shoe shop on-line with an EPOS system—but it often allows decision-makers to be fully aware of sales trends and customer needs. When linked to the warehouse network, the EPOS process brings increased speed and efficiency to the physical distribution process. Most national retail groups are centralising their distribution.[26] The grocery companies, for instance, have one or two huge, centrally located warehouses close to the heart of the motorway network. Through EPOS data, each store's exact requirements are dispatched from the central warehouse to match actual daily or weekly sales patterns. Often the warehouse is automated, with robotised handling. This reduces stock holdings in the store itself and centrally, and minimises safety stocks (the "extra" stock held to cater for surges in demand or supplier delays).

Dixons and Currys have two major warehouses which receive most of their deliveries from manufacturers. Small appliances are despatched to individual stores—to match each store's sales patterns—but white goods (too large to occupy branch space productively) are held at regional warehouses, each of which serves 30 or 40 branches and delivers direct to customers rather than to the shops. Prior to the introduction of EPOS and the move to warehouse centralisation, such fine-tuning would not have been possible.

Europe 1992.   Deregulation of the European Community in 1992 will have various implications for European retailers. Market leaders in the U.K., for example, once perceived as unassailable, are on a European scale relatively small. A grocery retailer with 8 percent of the U.K. market may have 1.5 percent of the European market. Large U.K. groups which previously bought out smaller regional U.K. retailers now find themselves being targeted for takeover by French and German retail groups. More non-U.K.–based companies are establishing footholds in the U.K. market, which was previously relatively free from Continental European competition (see Marketing Update 11.3). For many years, particularly in the more affluent south-east of England, retailers have found it difficult to attract high-calibre sales assistants and managers in competition for employment with other industrial sectors. Current research is anticipating an exaggeration of the problem as many U.K. residents move across the Channel to find employment.

SUMMARY

Retailing includes all transactions in which the buyer intends to consume the product through personal, family, or household use. Retailers, which are organisations that sell products primarily to ultimate consumers, are important links in the mar-

25. Lynd Morley, "Mapping the Future," *Retail Technology,* 2(7), 1988, pp. 40–42.

26. Tony Rudd, "Trends in Physical Distribution," in *The Changing Face of British Retailing* (London: Newman Books, 1987), pp. 84–93.

keting channel because they are customers for wholesalers and producers. Most retailing takes place inside stores or service establishments, but retail exchanges may also occur outside stores through telemarketing, vending machines, and mail-order catalogues. Retail institutions provide place, time, and possession utilities. In the case of services, retailers develop most of the product's form utility as well.

Retail stores are often classified according to width of product mix and depth of product lines. The major types of retail stores are department stores, variety stores, hypermarkets, superstores and supermarkets, discount sheds, specialty shops, convenience stores, markets, cash and carry, and catalogue showrooms. Department stores are large retail employers and characterised by wide product mixes in considerable depth for most product lines. Their product lines are organised into separate departments that function much as self-contained businesses do.

Specialty retailers offer substantial assortments in a few product lines. They include traditional specialty retailers, which carry narrow product mixes with deep product lines. Retail stores locate in the central business district—the traditional centre of the town—in suburban centres, in edge-of-town, free-standing superstores, or in retail parks. The national chains occupy the prime-pitch sites in the CBD and the edge-of-town sheds. Locally based independent retailers tend to dominate in the suburbs and focus on convenience and some comparison goods.

Non-store retailing is the selling of goods or services outside the confines of a retail facility. Direct marketing is the use of non-personal media or telesales to introduce products to consumers, who then purchase the products by mail or telephone. Forms of non-store retailing include in-home retailing (selling via personal contacts with consumers in their own homes), telemarketing (direct selling of goods and services by telephone based either on a cold canvass of the telephone directory or on a prescreened list of prospective clients), automatic vending (selling through machines), and mail-order retailing (selling by description because buyers usually do not see the actual product until it arrives in the mail).

Franchising is an arrangement whereby a supplier grants a dealer the right to sell products in exchange for some type of consideration. Retail franchises are of three general types: a manufacturer may authorise a number of retail stores to sell a certain brand-name item; a producer may license distributors to sell a given product to retailers; or a franchisor may supply brand names, techniques, or other services instead of a complete product. Franchise arrangements have a number of advantages and disadvantages over traditional business forms, and their use is increasing.

To increase sales and store patronage, retailers must consider several strategic issues. Location determines the trading area from which a store must draw its customers and should be evaluated carefully. When evaluating potential sites, retailers take into account a variety of factors, including the location of the firm's target market within the trading area, the kinds of products being sold, the availability of public transport, customer characteristics, and competitors' locations. The retailer must decide whether to invest heavily in owning freeholds or to negotiate leases. Retailers can choose among several types of locations: free-standing structures, traditional business districts, neighbourhood/suburban shopping centres, regional shopping centres, or retail parks. The width, depth, and quality of the product assortment should be of the kind that can satisfy the retailer's target market customers.

Retail positioning involves identifying an unserved or under-served market niche, or segment, and serving the segment through a strategy that distinguishes the retailer from others in people's minds. Atmospherics and design comprise the physical elements of a store's design that can be adjusted to appeal to consumers' emotions and thus induce them to buy. Store image, which various consumers perceive differently, derives not only from atmosphere, but also from location, products offered, customer services, prices, promotion, and the store's overall reputation. Scrambled merchandising adds unrelated product lines to an existing product mix and is being used by a growing number of stores to generate sales.

The wheel of retailing hypothesis holds that new retail institutions start as low-status, low-margin, and low-price operators. As they develop, they increase service and prices and eventually become vulnerable to newer institutions, which enter the market and repeat the cycle. However, the wheel of retailing hypothesis may not apply in every case. There is an ever-changing balance of power between retailers and their suppliers, emphasised with the growth of retailers' own-label brands, which compete with manufacturers' brands. EPOS and other systems have revolutionised retailing and—when coupled with new, often centralised, warehouse networks—have reduced stock-holdings, improved productivity, and minimised the risk of stock-outs. The reduction of European Community border controls and regulations is making the retailing environment much more fluid and dynamic: it holds new opportunities for expansion or strategic alliances in other countries, but also carries the risk of takeovers and increased competition in domestic markets.

Important Terms

Retailing	Catalogue showroom
Retailer	Non-store retailing
Central business district (CBD)	Direct marketing
Suburban centres	In-home retailing
Edge of town	Telemarketing
Retail park	Automatic vending
Department stores	Mail-order retailing
Variety stores	Catalogue retailing
Supermarkets	Franchising
Superstores	Location
EPOS	Product assortment
Hypermarkets	Retail positioning
Discount sheds	Atmospherics
Specialty shops	Scrambled merchandising
Convenience stores	Wheel of retailing
Markets	Balance of retailing
Cash-and-carry	Retail technology

Discussion and Review Questions

1. What are the major differences between specialty shops and department stores?
2. How does a superstore differ from a supermarket?
3. Evaluate the following statement: "Direct marketing and non-store retailing are roughly the same thing."
4. Why is door-to-door selling a form of retailing? Some consumers feel that direct mail-orders skip the retailer. Is this true?

5. If you were to open a retail business, would you prefer to open an independent store or to own a store under a franchise arrangement? Explain your preference.
6. What major issues should be considered when determining a retail site location?
7. Describe the major types of shopping centre. Give examples of each type in your area.
8. How does atmosphere add value to products sold in a store? How important are atmospherics for convenience stores?
9. How should one determine the best retail store atmosphere?
10. Discuss the major factors that help determine a retail store's image.
11. Is it possible for a single retail store to have an overall image that appeals to sophisticated shoppers, extravagant ones, and bargain hunters? Why or why not?
12. In what ways does the use of scrambled merchandising affect a store's image?
13. How has technology improved retail productivity?
14. What are the likely effects on U.K. retailing of the 1992 EC deregulation?

■ CASES

11.1 Adams

Mission statement: "Our mission is simple. . . . To become the No. 1 specialist children's wear retailer in the United Kingdom through the achievement of excellence throughout our business." Adams was an independently owned private family company. Now it is the children's wear division of the mighty Sears. From being a loss-making "me too" in a market dominated by Conran's Mothercare, Woolworth, and Boots, Adams has emerged as not only market leader in its sector but also as one of the few retailers in the U.K. to be improving on its financial performance during the current retailing recession. In 1987–88 net sales were £18 million. Now they are approaching a four-fold increase and by 1991–92 year end sales are projected to be £180 million. In 1987–88 there were 126 stores, still concentrated around the company's base in the Midlands. By 1990 the company traded from over 200 outlets and by the end of 1991–92 the projection is for 285 stores, making the company truly national. The company is currently evaluating the viability of franchising its brand and expanding overseas. Sears is confident that chairman Michael Adams and managing director David Carter-Johnson can maintain the recent growth and push sales per square foot over the £300 mark. Sears has committed capital investment of over £50 million until the end of 1992 for store openings and refurbishment.

What has led to the success and turnaround of Adams? Clear thinking and the development of a marketing strategy have enabled the management to take advantage of range omissions in Marks & Spencer and BhS and of the managerial and financial troubles in Mothercare. Adams researched its market, evaluating each competitor and determining the positioning of the major players. This analysis was in the light of extensive market research designed to understand the needs and expectations of targeted consumers: children up to the age of eight and their parents and grandparents.

Traditionally Adams' differential advantage had been price, but the company knew that "price alone will not be a sufficient differential advantage to take Adams forward to market leadership." Adams opted to focus upon design (of stores and merchandise), quality, value, and convenience. Consumer research revealed that product quality and durability dominated buyers' decision-making: the company's in-house quality control department is well resourced and increasingly sets industry standards. Young mothers often lack time and mobility, so that convenience of location and store layout is a key choice determinant. They are often relatively inexperienced shoppers of children's wear so the company has emphasised customer service and has extensive training facilities and programmes for all personnel.

The company has invested heavily in systems and programmes to facilitate its expansion. All stores are linked to the Nuneaton headquarters with EPOS. Warehousing is centralised and fully automated, and suppliers have to meet rigorous packaging and delivery requirements. The company has computer packages to assist with store-location assessment, layout and shelf-space allocation, merchandise planning and replenishment, stock control and distribution, and credit control.

SOURCES: *Adams 1987–1992*, by Adams Childrenswear Ltd.; Adams' management, 1989; John Thornhill, "Why Eight Is a Lucky Number," *Financial Times*, 13 December 1990; "Sears—Adams Childrenswear," *Harvest*, 1990.

Questions for Discussion

1. How can Adams sustain its stated differential advantage?
2. Discuss how systems must be integrated to assist management rather than control managers' time and thinking.
3. How can Adams monitor on an on-going basis its target customers' needs and the strength of competition from national children's wear retailers and one-off independents?

11.2 Co-op Calls Off Merger Scheme

The Co-operative movement, founded during the nineteenth century, was one of the U.K.'s first "national" retail brands. Today, the movement comprises a plethora of regional societies, some large, others small, many progressive, but with a large residue averse to change. Directors are "elected" by each society's members—the customers, many of whom are traditional neighbourhood shoppers who see no need to adopt modern store opening and building plans, layout, and customer service innovations. The result is that many analysts belive the movement has lost its way. Despite the number of stores within the Co-op fold and the density of geographic coverage, Sainsbury, Tesco and the other major grocery retailers have caught, overtaken, and left behind most societies.

Plans had been drawn up to consolidate—through a merger—two of the major arms of the Co-op empire, Co-operative Retail Services (CRS) and the Co-operative Wholesale Society (CWS), to create a £4 billion turnover supergroup within the Co-op movement. The merger would have strengthened the Co-op's position against the major grocery retailers, substantially bolstered the £750 million Co-op own-label brand and guaranteed it significant distribution (societies are not obliged to stock it), facilitated more joint promotions and advertising, and provided the merged supergroup with more negotiating power with suppliers (individual societies often buy unilaterally, with few bulk-buying economies).

CRS, the largest co-operative retail society in Europe, operates over 800 stores in the U.K. and provides services varying from dairies, funerals, and catering to holiday agencies. The CWS runs 450 stores and owns the Co-op brand label. This own label accounts for just 30 percent of products sold through the 80 independent retail societies. Although sizeable—the CRS has turnover of £1.3 billion—margins lag well behind those of the Co-op's rivals: Sainsbury with 7.6 percent and Tesco with 6.2 percent have significant leads, with few Co-op societies achieving margins over 4 percent. The Co-op movement seldom co-operates with itself: each society trades as an autonomous unit.

SOURCES: Verdict Research; Co-operative Movement managers; Suzanne Bidlake, "Co-op Calls off Merger Scheme," *Marketing,* 16 August 1990, p. 1; Susan Bidlake, "Co-op Lays Down the Law," *Marketing,* 31 May 1990, p. 1.

Questions for Discussion

1. What are the advantages for the Co-op of giving each society control of its own regional market?
2. What advantages do companies such as Sainsbury, Tesco, and Asda have over the Co-op? Why?
3. Can the benefits of centralised ownership and control be successfully merged with local or regional marketing autonomy?

12 PHYSICAL DISTRIBUTION

Objectives

To understand how physical distribution activities are integrated into marketing channels and overall marketing strategies

To examine three important physical distribution objectives: customer service, total distribution costs, and cost trade-offs

To learn how efficient order processing facilitates product flow

To illustrate how materials handling is a part of physical distribution activities

To learn how warehousing facilitates the storage and movement functions in physical distribution

To understand how inventory management is conducted to develop and maintain adequate assortments of products for target markets

To gain insight into how transport modes, which bridge the producer-customer gap, are selected and co-ordinated

How important can eight people be to a multinational clothing manufacturer and retailer? To Benetton, the Italian casual clothing company, the eight people who run the warehouse that handles the distribution of 50 million pieces of clothing a year are extremely important. These eight are responsible for processing 230,000 articles of clothing a day to serve 4,500 stores, of which 1,500 are located in Italy, 700 in the U.S.A. and 350 in the U.K. Though sales in the garment industry have sagged recently, Benetton is still selling tremendous amounts of knitted and cotton clothing. After their small clothing business expanded into an international fashion sensation, executives at Benetton realised that highly efficient physical distribution methods were a must.

Benetton has linked its sales agents, its factory, and its warehouse in an electronic loop. Suppose a student in London wants to buy a sweater identical to his older brother's Benetton sweater. He goes to a Benetton store and searches for it. He is disappointed when he finds that the sweater is not there. The salesperson assures him that the sweater will arrive in a month. The salesperson calls a Benetton sales agent, who places the sweater order on a personal computer. The information travels electronically to Italy, where a computer searches inventory data and finds that there are no more sweaters like the one requested. An order then automatically travels to a machine that selects the yarn and immediately starts to knit the sweater. Workers put the finished sweater in a box with a bar-coded label and send it to the warehouse. In the warehouse, a computer commands a robot to retrieve the sweater and any other merchandise that needs to be transported to the same store. ◆

Based on information in Brian Dumaine, "How Managers Can Succeed Through Speed," *Fortune*, 13 Feb. 1989, p. 59; Martha Groves, "Retailer Benetton Hopes to Crack Soviet Market," *Los Angeles Times*, 7 Jan. 1989, sec. IV, pp. 2, 4; and Lena H. Sun, "Too Much, Too Fast? Benetton Sportswear Rethinks Strategy of Rapid Store Expansion," *Washington Post*, 11 Oct. 1988, pp. E1, E4.

Benetton's use of well-managed physical distribution activities, facilitated through the latest technologically advanced equipment, has helped it become a very large and highly successful retail leader. Physical distribution deals with the movement and handling of goods and the processing of orders, activities necessary to provide a level of service that will satisfy customers. Even though physical distribution is costly, it creates time and place utility, which maximises the value of products by delivering them when and where they are wanted.

This chapter describes how marketing decisions are related to physical distribution. After considering basic physical distribution concepts, we outline the major objectives of physical distribution. We then examine each major distribution function: order processing, materials handling, warehousing, inventory management, and transport. We close the chapter with a discussion of marketing strategy considerations in physical distribution. While reading this chapter, keep in mind how important customer service is to physical distribution and how physical distribution is related to marketing channels.

The Importance of Physical Distribution

Physical distribution is a set of activities—consisting of order processing, materials handling, warehousing, inventory management, and transport—used in the movement of products from producers to consumers and end users. Planning an effective physical distribution system can be a significant decision in developing a marketing strategy. A company that has the right goods in the right place, at the right time, in the right quantity, and with the right support services is able to sell more than competitors who fail to accomplish these goals. Physical distribution is an important variable in a marketing strategy because it can decrease costs and increase customer satisfaction. In fact, speed of delivery, along with services and dependability, is often as important to buyers as cost.

Physical distribution deals with physical movement and inventory holding (storing and tracking inventory until it is needed) both within and among marketing channel members. Often one channel member will arrange the movement of goods for all channel members involved in exchanges. For example, a packing company ships fresh California cherries and strawberries (often by air) to remote markets on a routine basis. Frequently, buyers are found while the fruit is in transit.

The physical distribution system is often adjusted to meet the needs of a channel member. For example, a construction equipment dealer who keeps a low inventory of replacement parts requires the fastest and most dependable service when parts not in stock are needed. In this case, the distribution cost may be a minor consideration when compared with service, dependability, and promptness.

Physical Distribution Objectives

For most companies, the main objective of physical distribution is to decrease costs while increasing service. In the real world, however, few distribution systems manage to achieve these goals in equal measure. The large inventories and rapid transport essential to high levels of customer service drive up costs. On the other hand, reduced inventories and slower, cheaper shipping methods cause customer dissatisfaction. Physical distribution managers strive for a reasonable balance among service, costs, and resources. They determine what level of customer service is acceptable, yet realistic, develop a "system" outlook of calculating total distribution costs, and trade higher costs at one stage of distribution for savings in another. In this section we examine these three performance objectives more closely.

■ Customer Service

In varying degrees, all organisations attempt to satisfy customer needs and wants through a set of activities known collectively as customer service. Many companies claim that service to the customer is their top priority. Clearly, without customers, there would be no profit. Service may be as important in attracting customers and building sales as the cost or quality of the organisation's products.

Customers require a variety of services. At the most basic level, they need fair prices, acceptable product quality, and dependable deliveries.[1] In the physical distribution area, availability, promptness, and quality are the most important dimensions of customer service. These are the main factors that determine how satisfied customers are likely to be with a supplier's physical distribution activities.[2] Customers seeking a higher level of customer service may also want sizeable inventories, efficient order processing, availability of emergency shipments, progress reports, post-sale services, prompt replacement of defective items, and warranties. Customers' inventory requirements influence the level of physical distribution service they expect. For example, customers who want to minimise inventory storage and shipping costs may require that suppliers assume the cost of maintaining inventory in the marketing channel, or the cost of premium transport.[3] Because service needs vary from customer to customer, companies must analyse—and adapt to—customer preferences. Attention to customer needs and preferences is crucial to increasing sales and obtaining repeat sales. A company's failure to provide the desired level of service may mean the loss of customers.

Companies must also examine the service levels competitors offer and match those standards, at least when the costs of providing the services can be balanced by the sales generated. For example, companies may step up their efforts to identify the causes of customer complaints or institute corrective measures for billing and shipping errors. In extremely competitive businesses, such as the packaged food industry, firms may concentrate on product availability. To compete effectively, food processors may strive for inventory levels and order-processing speeds that are deemed unnecessary and too costly in other industries.[4]

Services are provided most effectively when service standards are developed and stated in terms that are specific, measurable, and appropriate for the product: for example, "98 percent of all orders filled within forty-eight hours". Standards should be communicated clearly to both customers and employees and rigorously enforced.

1. Carl M. Guelzo, *Introduction to Logistics Management* (Englewood Cliffs, N.J.: Prentice-Hall, 1986), p. 32.

2. John T. Mentzer, Roger Gomes, and Robert E. Krapfel, Jr., "Physical Distribution Service: A Fundamental Marketing Concept?" *Journal of the Academy of Marketing Science*, Winter 1989, p. 59.

3. Lloyd M. Rinehart, M. Bixby Cooper, and George D. Wagenheim, "Furthering the Integration of Marketing and Logistics Through Customer Service in the Channel," *Journal of the Academy of Marketing Science*, Winter 1989, p. 67.

4. Charles A. Taff, *Management of Physical Distribution and Transportation* (Homewood, Ill.: Irwin, 1984), p. 250.

In many cases, it is necessary to maintain a policy of minimum order size to ensure that transactions are profitable; that is, special service charges are added to orders smaller than a specified quantity. Many service policies also spell out delivery times and provisions for back-ordering, returning goods, and obtaining emergency shipments. The overall objective of any service policy should be to improve customer service just to the point beyond which increased sales would be negated by increased distribution costs.

■ Total Distribution Costs

Although physical distribution managers try to minimise the costs of each element in the system—order processing, materials handling, inventory, warehousing, and transport—decreasing costs in one area often raises them in another. By using a total-cost approach to physical distribution, managers can view the distribution system as a whole, not as a collection of unrelated activities. The emphasis shifts from lowering the separate costs of individual functions to minimising the total cost of the entire distribution system.

The total-cost approach calls for analysing the costs of all possible distribution alternatives, even those considered too impractical or expensive. Total-cost analyses weigh inventory levels against warehousing expenses, materials handling costs against various modes of transport, and all distribution costs against customer service standards. The costs of potential sales losses from lower performance levels are also considered. In many cases, accounting procedures and statistical methods can be used to figure total costs. Where hundreds of combinations of distribution variables are possible, computer simulations may be helpful. In no case is a distribution system's lowest total cost the result of using a combination of the cheapest functions; instead, it is the lowest overall cost compatible with the company's stated service objectives.

■ Cost Trade-offs

A distribution system that attempts to provide a specific level of customer service for the lowest possible total cost must use cost trade-offs to resolve conflicts about resource allocations. That is, higher costs in one area of the distribution system must be offset by lower costs in another area if the total system is to remain cost-effective.

Trade-offs are strategic decisions to combine (and re-combine) resources for greatest cost-effectiveness. When distribution managers regard the system as a network of interlocking functions, trade-offs become useful tools in a unified distribution strategy. Trade-offs are apparent in the distribution strategy of Swedish furniture retailer IKEA, which sells stylish, ready-to-assemble furniture in many countries (see Case 12.1). To ensure that each store carries enough inventory to satisfy customers in the area, IKEA groups its retail outlets into regions, each served by a separate distribution centre. In addition, each IKEA store carries a five-week back stock of inventory. Thus IKEA has chosen to trade higher inventory warehousing costs for improved customer service.[5]

Now that we have discussed several of the physical distribution objectives that marketers may pursue, we are ready to take a closer look at specific physical distribution activities. For the remainder of the chapter, we focus on order processing, materials handling, warehousing, inventory management, and transport.

5. Judith Graham, "IKEA Furnishing Its U.S. Identity," *Advertising Age*, 14 Sept. 1989, p. 79; and Jonathan Reynolds, "IKEA: A Competitive Company with Style," *Retail & Distribution Management (UK)*, May/June 1988, pp. 32–34.

ORDER PROCESSING

Order processing—the first stage in a physical distribution system—is the receipt and transmission of sales order information. Although management sometimes overlooks the importance of these activities, efficient order processing facilitates product flow. Computerised order processing, used by many firms, speeds the flow of information from customer to seller.[6] When carried out quickly and accurately, order processing contributes to customer satisfaction, repeat orders, and increased profits.

Generally, there are three main tasks in order processing: order entry, order handling, and order delivery.[7] Order entry begins when customers or salespersons place purchase orders by mail, telephone, or computer. In some companies, sales service representatives receive and enter orders personally and also handle complaints, prepare progress reports, and forward sales order information.[8]

The next task, order handling, involves several activities. Once an order has been entered, it is transmitted to the warehouse, where the availability of the product is verified, and to the credit department, where prices, terms, and the customer's credit rating are checked. If the credit department approves the purchase, the warehouse begins to fill the order. If the requested product is not in stock, a production order is sent to the factory or the customer is offered a substitute item.

When the order has been filled and packed for shipment, the warehouse schedules pick-up with an appropriate carrier. If the customer is willing to pay for rush service, priority transport is used. The customer is sent an invoice, inventory records are adjusted, and the order is delivered.

Order processing can be manual or electronic, depending on which method provides the greatest speed and accuracy within cost limits. Manual processing suffices for a small volume of orders and is more flexible in special situations; electronic processing is more practical for a large volume of orders and lets a company integrate order processing, production planning, inventory, accounting, and transport planning into a total information system.[9] In America, Wal-Mart and several hundred of its suppliers use electronic order-processing networks. Instead of sending paper purchase orders—which take five to ten days to reach their destination and then must be keyed into a supplier's system—Wal-Mart transmits purchase orders directly from its main data-processing centre to a participating vendor's computer.

MATERIALS HANDLING

Materials handling, or physical handling of products, is important for efficient warehouse operations, as well as in transport from points of production to points of consumption. The characteristics of the product itself often determine how it will be handled. For example, bulk liquids and gases have unique characteristics that determine how they can be moved and stored.

6. Rinehart, Cooper, and Wagenheim, p. 67.

7. Guelzo, pp. 35–36.

8. Taff, p. 240.

9. Ibid., p. 244.

FIGURE 12.1
Materials handling.
Hardware Wholesalers
automates its receiving
procedures for its stores.

SOURCE: Hardware Wholesalers

Materials handling procedures and techniques should increase the usable capacity of a warehouse, reduce the number of times a good is handled, and improve service to customers and increase their satisfaction with the product. Packaging, loading, movement, and labelling systems must be co-ordinated to maximise cost reduction and customer satisfaction (see Figure 12.1).

In Chapter 7 we note that the protective functions of packaging are important considerations in product development. Appropriate decisions about packaging materials and methods allow for the most efficient physical handling; most companies employ packaging consultants or specialists to accomplish this important task. Materials handling equipment is used in the design of handling systems. **Unit loading** is grouping one or more boxes on a pallet or skid; it permits movement of efficient loads by mechanical means, such as fork-lifts, trucks, or conveyor systems. **Containerisation** is the practice of consolidating many items into a single large container that is sealed at its point of origin and opened at its destination. The containers are usually eight feet wide, eight feet high, and ten, twenty, twenty-five, or forty feet long. They can be conveniently stacked and sorted as units at the point of loading; because individual items are not handled in transit, containerisation greatly increases efficiency and security in shipping.

WAREHOUSING

Warehousing, the design and operation of facilities for storing and moving goods, is an important physical distribution function. Warehousing provides time utility by enabling firms to compensate for dissimilar production and consumption rates. That is, when mass production creates a greater stock of goods than can be sold immediately, companies may warehouse the surplus goods until customers are ready to buy. Warehousing also helps stabilise the prices and availability of seasonal items. Here we describe the basic functions of warehouses and the different types of warehouses available. We also examine the distribution centre concept, a special warehouse operation designed so that goods can be moved rapidly.

■ **Warehousing Functions**

Warehousing is not limited simply to storage of goods. When warehouses receive goods by wagonloads or lorryloads, they break down the shipments into smaller quantities for individual customers; when goods arrive in small lots, the warehouses assemble the lots into bulk loads that can be shipped out more economically.[10] Warehouses perform these basic distribution functions:

1. *Receiving goods.* The merchandise is accepted, and the warehouse assumes responsibility for it.
2. *Identifying goods.* The appropriate stock keeping units are recorded, along with the quantity of each item received. The item may be marked with a physical code, tag, or other label, or it may be identified by an item code (a code on the carrier or container) or by physical properties.
3. *Sorting goods.* The merchandise is sorted for storage in appropriate areas.
4. *Dispatching goods to storage.* The merchandise is put away for later retrieval when necessary.
5. *Holding goods.* The merchandise is kept in storage and properly protected until needed.
6. *Recalling and picking goods.* Items customers have ordered are efficiently retrieved from storage and prepared for the next step.
7. *Marshalling the shipment.* The items making up a single shipment are brought together and checked for completeness or explainable omissions. Order records are prepared or modified as necessary.
8. *Dispatching the shipment.* The consolidated order is packaged suitably and directed to the right transport vehicle. Necessary shipping and accounting documents are prepared.[11]

■ **Types of Warehouses**

A company's choice of warehouse facilities is an important strategic consideration. By using the right warehouse, a company may be able to reduce transport and inventory costs or improve its service to customers; the wrong warehouse may drain company resources. Besides deciding how many facilities to operate and where to locate them, a company must determine which type of warehouse will be most appropriate. Warehouses fall into two general categories, private and public. In many cases, a combination of private and public facilities provides the most flexible approach to warehousing.

Private Warehouses. A **private warehouse** is operated by a company for shipping and storing its own products. Private warehouses are usually leased or purchased when a firm believes that its warehouse needs in given geographic markets are so substantial and so stable that it can make a long-term commitment to fixed facilities. They are also appropriate for firms that require special handling and

10. Guelzo, p. 102.

11. Adapted from *Physical Distribution Systems* by John F. Magee. Copyright 1967 McGraw-Hill, Inc. Reprinted by permission of the author.

storage features and want to control the design and operation of the warehouse. See Marketing Update 12.1 for a description of British Tubes Stockholding's warehousing and distribution functions.

Some of the largest users of private warehouses are retail chain stores.[12] Retailers such as Tesco, Marks & Spencer, MFI, or Carrefour find it economical to integrate the warehousing function with purchasing for and distribution to their retail outlets. When sales volumes are fairly stable, ownership and control of a private warehouse may provide benefits, such as property appreciation. Private warehouses, however, face fixed costs, such as insurance, taxes, maintenance, and debt expense. They also allow little flexibility when firms wish to move inventories to more strategic locations. Before tying up capital in a private warehouse or entering into a long-term lease, a company should consider its resources, the level of its expertise in warehouse management, and the role of the warehouse in its overall marketing strategy.

Public Warehouses.   **Public warehouses** rent storage space and related physical distribution facilities to other companies and sometimes provide distribution services such as receiving and unloading products, inspecting, reshipping, filling orders, financing, displaying products, and co-ordinating shipments. They are especially useful to firms with seasonal production or low-volume storage needs, companies with inventories that must be maintained in many locations, firms that are testing or entering new markets, and business operations that own private warehouses but occasionally require additional storage space. Public warehouses can also serve as collection points during product-recall programmes. Whereas private warehouses have fixed costs, public warehouses' costs are variable (and often lower) because users rent space and purchase warehousing services only as needed.

In addition, many public warehouses furnish security for products that are being used as collateral for loans, a service that can be provided at either the warehouse or the site of the owner's inventory. A **field public warehouse** is a warehouse established by a public warehouse at the owner's inventory location. The warehouser becomes the custodian of the products and issues a receipt that can be used as collateral for a loan. Public warehouses can also provide **bonded storage**, a warehousing arrangement under which imported or taxable products are not released until the owners of the products have paid customs duties, taxes, or other fees. Bonded warehouses enable firms to defer tax payments on such items until the products are delivered to customers.

The Distribution Centre.   A **distribution centre** is a large, centralised warehouse that receives goods from factories and suppliers, regroups them into orders, and ships them to customers quickly, with the focus being on active movement of goods rather than passive storage.[13] Distribution centres are specially designed for the rapid flow of products. They are usually one-storey buildings (to eliminate lifts) and have access to transport networks, such as motorways or railway lines. Many distribution centres are highly automated, with computer-directed robots, fork-lifts, and hoists collecting and moving products to loading docks. Although some public warehouses offer such specialised services, most distribution centres are privately owned.

12. James C. Johnson and Donald F. Wood, *Contemporary Physical Distribution & Logistics*, 2nd ed. (Tulsa, Okla.: PenWell Publishing Company, 1982), p. 356.

13. Guelzo, p. 102.

BRITISH TUBES STOCKHOLDING—AD HOC DISTRIBUTION

Steel stockholding in Europe is dominated by the nationalised industries' stockholding subsidiaries; in the U.K. the recently privatised British Steel subsidiaries have nearly half of the market. British Tubes Stockholding (BTS), for example, accounts for a quarter of the market and has seven warehouses throughout the U.K. plus two central distribution centres. BTS customers range from small general engineers to major oil companies. Market sectors include general engineering, ship-building, pipework fabricators, power generation contractors, management contractors, off-shore fabricators, oil companies, petrochemical and gas industries. BTS provides an international service for direct shipment to worldwide destinations.

BTS, like the other major stockholders, Brown and Tawse and Walkers, has grown by acquiring smaller, often locally orientated independents. Its distribution network is, therefore, rather ad hoc: two new, purpose-built warehouses that can handle the whole product range; some warehouses capable of stocking only a limited range; some outdated premises built many years ago with limited vehicle access and poor handling facilities; non-uniform coverage areas—some deal nationally, others locally, many intrude on neighbouring sales/delivery territories. In one case, the area sales force is capable of generating 40 percent more business volume than its warehouse can supply.

A new network of warehouses is now being developed. Large, infrequently demanded, bulky items are to be stocked centrally, still with under 24-hour delivery—better than the market requires—and all regional warehouses will have a product range in line with their customer requirements. New locations close to motorways will enable easy delivery from factories and importers while allowing easy collection or delivery to customers in each region. A computer monitors all stockholding, orders, and deliveries.

SOURCES: BTS management, 1988–1990; BTS promotional material, "Buying from Your Local Winning Team," 1988; "British Steel's Solid Strength," *Investors Chronicle*, 16–22 February 1990, p. 50; "British Steel: Manufacturer and Distributor," *Investors Chronicle*, 15–21 June 1990, p. 52.

They serve customers in regional markets and in some cases function as consolidation points for a company's branch warehouses.

Distribution centres offer several benefits. Foremost among them is improved customer service. Distribution centres ensure product availability by maintaining full product lines. The speed of their operations cuts delivery time to a minimum. In addition, they reduce costs. Instead of having to make many smaller shipments to scattered warehouses and customers, factories can ship large quantities of goods directly to distribution centres at bulk-load rates, which lowers transport costs; furthermore, rapid turnover of inventory lessens the need for warehouses and cuts storage costs. Some distribution centres also facilitate production by receiving and consolidating raw materials and providing final assembly for some products.

INVENTORY MANAGEMENT

Inventory management involves developing and maintaining adequate assortments of products to meet customers' needs. Because a firm's investment in inventory usually represents 30 to 50 percent of its total assets, inventory decisions have a significant impact on physical distribution costs and the level of customer service provided. When too few products are carried in inventory, the result is **stockouts**, or shortages of products, which cause brand switching, lower sales, and loss of customers. But when too many products (or too many slow-moving products) are carried, costs increase, as do the risks of product obsolescence, pilferage, and damage. The objective of inventory management, therefore, is to minimise inventory costs while maintaining an adequate supply of goods. Marketing Update 12.2 details how K mart is improving its inventory-handling methods.

There are three types of inventory costs. *Carrying costs* are holding costs; they include expenditures for storage space and materials handling, financing, insurance, taxes, and losses from spoilage of goods. *Replenishment costs* are related to the purchase of merchandise. The price of goods, handling charges, and expenses for order processing contribute to replenishment costs. *Stockout costs* include sales lost when demand for goods exceeds supply on hand and the clerical and processing expenses of back-ordering. All the costs of obtaining and maintaining inventory must be controlled if profit goals are to be achieved.

Inventory managers deal with two issues of particular importance. They must know when to reorder and how much merchandise to order. The **reorder point** is the inventory level that signals that more inventory should be ordered. Three factors determine the reorder point: the anticipated time between the date an order is placed and the date the goods are received and made ready for resale to customers; the rate at which a product is sold or used up; and the quantity of **safety stock** on hand, or inventory needed to prevent stockouts. The optimum level of safety stock depends on the general demand and the standard of customer service to be provided. If a firm is to avoid shortages without tying up too much capital in inventory, some systematic method for determining reorder points is essential.

The inventory manager faces several trade-offs when reordering merchandise. Large safety stocks ensure product availability and thus improve the level of customer service; they also lower order-processing costs because orders are placed less

K MART STREAMLINES INVENTORY PROCESSING

It is estimated that 75 percent of all adult Americans shop at K mart at least once every three months. Since discount general merchandise retailers are very successful (with total sales of more than $21 billion), it follows that they need extremely efficient physical distribution methods to meet their requirements. K mart has one of the largest distribution networks in the United States. Its new automated distribution system allows distribution centres to move products to the 2,300 K mart locations faster and less expensively than before.

When redesigning their distribution system, K mart executives decided to reduce inventory at the stores and at the various regional distribution centres. The company experimented with a system called "automatic replenishment" for its small appliances. Automatic replenishment is a "sell one, send one" system. When a store sells a blender, a regional distribution centre immediately ships another one to that store. The automatic replenishment system has worked so well for small appliances that K mart plans to set up the same system for large appliances, electronics, jewellery, and cameras. One K mart official remarked that automatic replenishment provides improved sales, gross margin, and inventory turnover.

Besides the automatic replenishment system, K mart has also installed a computer-assisted picking (CAP) system in its warehouses. The CAP system greatly speeds up the distribution process and reduces loader errors. K mart also saves money on labour as the CAP system has made many warehouse jobs obsolete.

K mart's distribution centres deliver information as well as products. A Kodak KAR-4000 computerised information system handles accounts payable and all correspondence to other K mart installations, as well as to outside vendors. K mart has also designed computerised packing and shipping systems that are used directly by employees on the warehouse floor. So far all of K mart's restructuring of its distribution system has saved the company money and speeded up the entire distribution process. K mart plans to automate its warehouses still further.

SOURCES: Steve Jacober, "K mart's New Directions for Hardgoods," *Discount Merchandising,* July 1988, pp. 18, 22, 24; Jay L. Johnson, "K mart's Automation Strategy," *Discount Merchandise,* June 1988, pp. 18, 20–21, 24; and "K mart Applies Automation to Information and Product Distribution," *IMC Journal,* January/February 1988, pp. 43–44.

FIGURE 12.2

Effects of order size on an inventory system

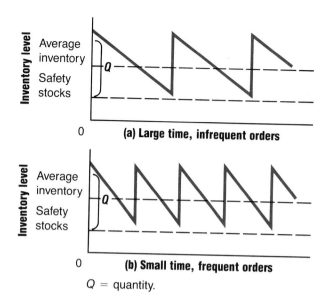

(a) Large time, infrequent orders

(b) Small time, frequent orders

Q = quantity.

frequently. Small safety stocks, on the other hand, cause frequent reorders and higher order-processing costs but reduce the overall cost of carrying inventory. (Figure 12.2 illustrates two order systems involving different order quantities but the same level of safety stocks. Figure 12.2(a) shows inventory levels for a given demand of infrequent orders; Figure 12.2(b) illustrates the levels needed to fill frequent orders at the same demand.)

To quantify this trade-off between carrying costs and order-processing costs, a model for an **economic order quantity (EOQ)** has been developed (see Figure 12.3); it specifies the order size that minimises the total cost of ordering and carrying inventory.[14] The fundamental relationships underlying the widely accepted EOQ model are the basis of many inventory control systems. Keep in mind, however, that the objective of minimum total inventory cost must be balanced against the customer service level necessary for maximum profits. Therefore, because increased costs of carrying inventory are usually associated with a higher level of customer service, the order quantity will often lie to the right of the optimal point in the figure, leading to a higher total cost for ordering and larger carrying inventory.

When management miscalculates reorder points or order quantities, inventory problems develop. Warning signs include an inventory that grows at a faster rate than sales, surplus or obsolete inventory, customer deliveries that are consistently late or lead times that are too long, inventory that represents a growing percentage of assets, and large inventory adjustments or write-offs.[15] However, there are several tools for improving inventory control. From a technical standpoint, an inventory system can be planned so that the number of products sold and the number of

14. The EOQ formula for the optimal order quantity is EOQ = 2DR/I, where EOQ = optimum average order size, D = total demand, R = cost of processing an order, and I = cost of maintaining one unit of inventory per year. For a more complete description of EOQ methods and terminology, see Frank S. McLaughlin and Robert C. Pickardt, *Quantitative Techniques for Management Decisions* (Boston: Houghton Mifflin, 1978), pp. 104–119.

15. "Watch for These Red Flags," *Traffic Management,* January 1983, p. 8.

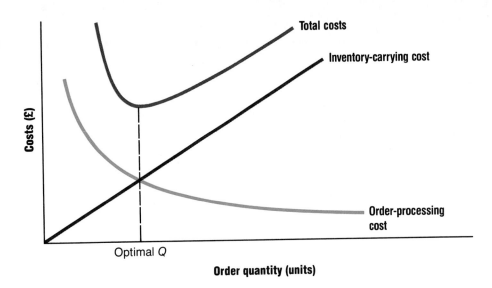

FIGURE 12.3
Economic order quantity (EOQ) model

Total costs

Inventory-carrying cost

Costs (£)

Order-processing cost

Optimal *Q*

Order quantity (units)

products in stock are determined at certain checkpoints. The control may be as simple as tearing off a code number from each product sold so that the correct sizes, colours, and models can be tabulated and reordered. A sizeable amount of technologically advanced electronic equipment is available to assist with inventory management. In many larger stores, such as Tesco and Toys "R" Us stores, check-out terminals connected to central computer systems instantaneously update inventory and sales records. For continuous, automatic updating of inventory records, some firms use pressure-sensitive circuits installed under ordinary industrial shelving to weigh inventory, convert the weight to units, and display any inventory changes on a video screen or computer printout.

Various techniques have also been used successfully to improve inventory management. The just-in-time concept, widely used in Japan, calls for companies to maintain low inventory levels and purchase products and materials in small quantities, just at the moment they are needed for production. Ford Motor Company, for example, sometimes receives supply deliveries as often as every two hours.[16] Just-in-time inventory management depends on a high level of co-ordination between producers and suppliers, but the technique enables companies to eliminate waste and reduce inventory costs significantly. When Polaroid implemented just-in-time techniques as part of its zero base pricing programme to reduce the overall cost of purchased materials, equipment, and services, it experienced cost reductions and savings averaging $20 million per year.[17]

Another inventory management technique, the 80/20 rule, holds that fast-moving products should generate a higher level of customer service than slow-moving products, on the theory that 20 percent of the items account for 80 percent of the sales. Thus an inventory manager attempts to keep an adequate supply of fast-selling items and a minimal supply of the slower-moving products.

16. David N. Burt, "Managing Suppliers Up to Speed," *Harvard Business Review,* July-August 1989, p. 128.

17. Ibid., p. 129.

TABLE 12.1 *Typical transport modes for various products*

RAILWAYS	MOTOR VEHICLES	WATERWAYS	PIPELINES	AIRWAYS
Coal	Clothing	Petroleum	Oil	Flowers
Grain	Paper goods	Chemicals	Processed coal	Perishable food
Chemicals	Computers	Iron ore	Natural gas	Instruments
Timber	Books	Bauxite	Water	Emergency parts
Cars	Fresh fruit	Grain		Overnight mail
Iron	Livestock			

TRANSPORT

Transport adds time and place utility to a product by moving it from where it is made to where it is purchased and used.[18] Because product availability and timely deliveries are so dependent on transport functions, a firm's choice of transport directly affects customer service. A firm may even build its distribution and marketing strategy around a unique transport system if the on-time deliveries, which that system ensures, will give the firm a competitive edge. In this section we consider the principal modes of transport, the criteria companies use to select one mode over another, and several methods of co-ordinating transport services. Table 12.1 illustrates typical transport modes for various products.

■ **Transport Modes**

There are five major **transport modes**, or methods of moving goods: railways, motor vehicles, inland waterways, airways, and pipelines. Each mode offers unique advantages; many companies have adopted physical handling procedures that facilitate the use of two or more modes in combination (see Table 12.2).

Motor Vehicles.   Motor vehicles provide the most flexible schedules and routes of all major transport modes because they can go almost anywhere. Trucks have a unique ability to move goods directly from factory or warehouse to customer, so they are often used in conjunction with other forms of transport that cannot provide door-to-door deliveries.

Although motor vehicles usually travel much faster than trains, they are somewhat more vulnerable to bad weather, and their services are more expensive. Trucks are also subject to the size and weight restrictions of the products they carry. In addition, carriers are sometimes criticised for high levels of loss and damage to freight and for delays due to rehandling of small shipments. In response, the road haulage industry is turning to computerised tracking of shipments and developing new equipment to speed loading and unloading.[19] In Europe, particularly the U.K., road

18. Peter D. Bennett, ed., *Dictionary of Marketing Terms* (Chicago: American Marketing Association, 1988), p. 204.

19. Guelzo, pp. 50–52.

TABLE 12.2
U.K. trade by transport modes

MODE	IMPORTS (000 TONNES)	EXPORTS (000 TONNES)
Railways	540	481
Road	6,281	4,513
Ship	53,344	82,920

haulage dominates in the distribution of most consumer and industrial products. Quick, flexible and relatively cost-efficient, it has overtaken rail, and motorway improvements will further strengthen its position.

Railways.   Railways carry heavy, bulky freight that must be shipped overland for long distances. Railways commonly carry minerals, sand, timber, pulp, chemicals, and farm products, as well as low-value manufactured goods and an increasing number of cars. They are especially efficient for transporting full carloads, which require less handling—and can therefore be shipped at lower rates—than smaller quantities. Some companies locate their factories or warehouses near major rail lines or on spur lines for convenient loading and unloading.

Although railways haul intercity freight, their share of the transport market has declined in recent years. High fixed costs, shortages of rail wagons during peak periods, poor maintenance of tracks and equipment, and increased competition from other carriers, mainly road hauliers, have plagued European rail operators. The Channel Tunnel will be rail orientated. Already British Rail and its French counterpart are building freight depots at numerous strategic locations in anticipation of increased rail freight.

Inland Waterways.   Water transport is the cheapest method of shipping heavy, low-value, non-perishable goods such as ore, coal, grain, sand, and petroleum products. Water carriers offer considerable capacity. Barges that travel along inland rivers, canals, and navigation systems can haul many times the weight of one rail wagon.

However, many markets are accessible to water only with supplementary rail or road transport. Furthermore, water transport is extremely slow and sometimes comes to a standstill during freezing weather. Companies that depend on water may ship their entire inventory during the summer and then store it for winter use. Droughts and floods also create difficulties for users of inland waterway transport. Because water transport is extremely fuel efficient, its volume is expected to double by the year 2000, but will still be only a very small percentage of total shipping.[20]

Airways.   Air transport is the fastest and most expensive form of shipping. It is used most often for perishable goods, for high-value, low-bulk items, and for prod-

20. Donald F. Wood and James C. Johnson, *Contemporary Transportation* (Tulsa, Okla.: Petroleum Publishing, 1980), p. 289.

ucts that must be delivered quickly over long distances, such as emergency shipments. The capacity of air transport is limited only by the capacity of individual aircraft. Medium-range jets can carry about 40,000 pounds of freight, and some new jet cargo planes equipped to carry containers can accommodate more than 200,000 pounds. Most air carriers transport a combination of passengers, freight, and mail.[21]

Although air transport accounts for less than 1 percent of total tonne-miles carried, its importance as a mode of transport is growing. Despite its expense, air transit can reduce warehousing and packaging costs and also losses from theft and damage, thus helping to lower total costs. However, the truck transport needed for pick-up and final delivery adds to cost and transit time.

Pipelines. Pipelines, the most automated transport mode, usually belong to the shipper and carry the shipper's products. Most pipelines carry petroleum products or chemicals. For example, the Trans-Alaska Pipeline, owned and operated by a consortium of oil companies that includes Exxon, Mobil, and British Petroleum, transports crude oil for its owners from remote oil-drilling sites in central Alaska to shipping terminals on the coast. Slurry pipelines have been developed to carry pulverised coal, grain, or wood chips suspended in water.

Pipelines move products slowly but continuously and at relatively low cost. They are a reliable mode of transport and ensure low product damage and theft. However, their contents are subject to as much as 1 percent shrinkage, usually from evaporation, and products must be shipped in minimum quantities of 25,000 barrels for efficient pipeline operation.[22] British and Scandinavian North Sea oil and natural gas depend on pipelines for transport and distribution. They have also been a source of concern to environmentalists, who fear that installation and leaks could harm plants and animals.

■ Criteria
for Selecting
Transport

Marketers select a transport mode on the basis of costs, transit time (speed), reliability, capability, accessibility, security, and traceability.[23] Table 12.3 summarises various cost and performance considerations that help determine the selection of transport modes. It is important to remember that these relationships are approximations and that the choice of a transport mode involves many trade-offs.

Costs. Marketers compare alternative means of transport to determine whether the benefits from a more expensive mode are worth the higher costs. Air freight carriers provide many benefits, such as high speed, reliability, security, and traceability, but at higher costs relative to other transport modes. When speed is less important, marketers prefer lower costs.

Recently, marketers have been able to cut expenses and increase efficiency. Railways, airlines, road hauliers, barges, and pipeline companies have all become more competitive and more responsive to customers' needs. Surveys reveal that in recent years transport costs per tonne and as a percentage of sales have declined, now

21. Taff, p. 126.

22. Guelzo, p. 53.

23. John J. Coyle, Edward Bardi, and C. John Langley, Jr., *The Management of Business Logistics* (St. Paul, Minn.: West, 1988), pp. 327–329.

TABLE 12.3 *Ranking of transport modes by selection criteria, highest to lowest*

	COST	TRANSIT TIME	RELIABILITY	CAPABILITY	ACCESSIBILITY	SECURITY	TRACEABILITY
MOST	Air	Water	Pipeline	Water	Road	Pipeline	Air
	Pipeline	Rail	Rail	Road	Rail	Water	Road
	Rail	Pipeline	Road	Rail	Air	Rail	Rail
	Road	Road	Air	Air	Water	Air	Water
LEAST	Water	Air	Water	Pipeline	Pipeline	Road	Pipeline

SOURCE: Selected information adapted from J. L. Heskett, Robert Ivie, and J. Nicholas Glaskowsky, *Business Logistics* (New York: Ronald Press, 1973). Reprinted by permission of John Wiley & Sons, Inc.

averaging 7.5 percent of sales. This figure varies by industry, of course: electrical machinery, textiles, and instruments have transport costs of only 3 or 4 percent of sales, whereas timber products, chemicals, and food have transport costs close to 15 percent of sales.

Transit Time. Transit time is the total time a carrier has possession of goods, including the time required for pick-up and delivery, handling, and movement between the points of origin and destination. Closely related to transit time is frequency, or number of shipments per day. Transit time obviously affects a marketer's ability to provide service, but there are some less obvious implications as well. A shipper can take advantage of transit time to process orders for goods en route, a capability especially important for agricultural and raw materials shippers. Some railways also let shipments already in transit be redirected, for maximum flexibility in selecting markets. For example, a load of peaches may be shipped to a closer destination if the fruit is in danger of ripening too quickly.

Reliability. The total reliability of a transport mode is determined by the consistency of service provided. Marketers must be able to count on their carriers to deliver goods on time and in an acceptable condition. Along with transit time, reliability affects a marketer's inventory costs, including sales lost when merchandise is not available. Unreliable transport necessitates higher inventory levels so that stockouts can be avoided. Reliable delivery service, on the other hand, enables customers to carry smaller inventories, at lower cost.

Capability. Capability is the ability of a transport mode to provide the appropriate equipment and conditions for moving specific kinds of goods. For example, many products must be shipped under controlled temperature and humidity. Other products, such as liquids or gases, require special equipment or facilities for their shipment.

Accessibility. A carrier's ability to move goods over a specific route or network (rail lines, waterways, or roads) is its accessibility.

Security. A transport mode's security is measured by the physical condition of goods upon delivery. A business organisation does not incur costs directly when goods are lost or damaged because the carrier is usually held liable in these cases. Nevertheless, poor service and lack of security will indirectly lead to increased costs and lower profits for the firm because damaged or lost goods are not available for immediate sale or use.

Traceability. Traceability is the relative ease with which a shipment can be located and transferred (or found if it is lost). Quick traceability is a convenience that some firms value highly. Shippers have learned that the tracing of shipments, along with prompt invoicing and processing of claims, increases customer loyalty and improves a firm's image in the market-place.[24]

■ **Co-ordinating Transport Services**

To take advantage of the benefits various types of carriers offer, and to compensate for their deficiencies, marketers often must combine and co-ordinate two or more modes of transport. In recent years, **intermodal transport**, as this integrated approach is sometimes called, has become easier because of new developments within the transport industry.

Several kinds of intermodal shipping are available, all combining the flexibility of road haulage with the low cost or speed of other forms of transport. Containerisation, discussed earlier, facilitates intermodal transport by consolidating shipments into sealed containers for transport by piggyback (shipping that combines truck trailers and railway flatcars), fishyback (truck trailers and water carriers), and birdyback (truck trailers and air carriers). As transport costs increase, intermodal services gain popularity. Intermodal services have been estimated to cost 25 to 40 percent less than all-road transport and account for about 12 to 16 percent of total U.S. freight transport business.[25]

Specialised agencies, **freight forwarders**, provide other forms of transport co-ordination. These firms combine shipments from several organisations into efficient lot sizes. Small loads (less than five hundred pounds) are much more expensive to ship than full truckloads and frequently must be consolidated. The freight forwarder takes small loads from various shippers, buys transport space from carriers, and arranges for the goods to be delivered to their respective buyers. The freight forwarder's profits come from the margin between the higher, less-than-carload rates charged to each shipper and the lower carload rates the agency pays. Because large shipments require less handling, the use of a freight forwarder can speed transit time. Freight forwarders can also determine the most efficient carriers and routes and are useful for shipping goods to foreign markets.

One other transport innovation is the development of **megacarriers**, which are freight companies that provide several methods of shipment, such as rail, road, and air service. Air carriers have increased their ground transport services. As they have expanded the range of transport alternatives, carriers have also put greater stress on customer service.

24. Thomas A. Foster and Joseph V. Barks, "Here Comes the Best," *Distribution*, September 1984, p. 25.

25. Allen R. Wastler, "Intermodal Leaders Ponder Riddle of Winning More Freight," *Traffic World*, 19 June 1989, pp. 14–15.

STRATEGIC ISSUES IN PHYSICAL DISTRIBUTION

The physical distribution functions discussed in this chapter—order processing, materials handling, warehousing, inventory management, and transport—account for about one-third of all marketing costs. Moreover, these functions have a significant impact on customer service and satisfaction, which are of prime importance to marketers. Effective marketers accept considerable responsibility for the design and control of the physical distribution system. They work to ensure that the organisation's overall marketing strategy is enhanced by physical distribution, with its dual objectives of decreasing costs while increasing customer service.

The strategic importance of physical distribution is evident in all elements of the marketing mix. Product design and packaging must allow for efficient stacking, storage, and transport; decisions to differentiate products by size, colour, and style must take into account the additional demands that will be placed on warehousing and shipping facilities. Competitive pricing may depend on a firm's ability to provide reliable delivery or emergency shipments of replacement parts; a firm trying to lower its inventory costs may offer quantity discounts to encourage large purchases. Promotional campaigns must be co-ordinated with distribution functions so that advertised products are available to buyers; order-processing departments must be able to handle additional sales order information efficiently. Distribution planners must consider warehousing and transport costs, which may influence—for example—the firm's policy on stockouts or its choice to centralise (or decentralise) its inventory.

No single distribution system is ideal for all situations, and any system must be evaluated continually and adapted as necessary. For instance, pressures to adjust service levels or reduce costs may lead to totally restructuring the marketing channel relationships; changes in transport, warehousing, materials handling, and inventory may affect speed of delivery, reliability, and economy of service. Marketing strategists must consider customers' changing needs and preferences and recognise that changes in any one of the major distribution functions will necessarily affect all other functions. Consumer-orientated marketers will analyse the various characteristics of their target markets and then design distribution systems to provide products at acceptable costs.

SUMMARY

Physical distribution is a set of activities that moves products from producers to consumers, or end users. These activities include order processing, materials handling, warehousing, inventory management, and transport. An effective physical distribution system can be an important component of an overall marketing strategy because it can decrease costs and increase customer satisfaction. Physical distribution activities should be integrated with marketing channel decisions and should be adjusted to meet the unique needs of a channel member. For most firms, physical distribution accounts for about one-fifth of a product's retail price.

The main objective of physical distribution is to decrease costs while increasing customer service. To this end, physical distribution managers strive to balance service, distribution costs, and resources. Companies must adapt to customers' needs and preferences, offer service comparable to or better than that of their competitors, and develop and communicate desirable customer service policies. The costs of providing service are minimised most effectively through the total-cost approach, which evaluates the costs of the system as a whole rather than as a collection of separate activities. Cost trade-offs must often be used to offset higher costs in one area of distribution with lower costs in another area.

Order processing, the first stage in a physical distribution system, is the receipt and transmission of sales order information. Order processing consists of three main tasks. Order entry is placing purchase orders from customers or salespersons by mail, telephone, or computer. Order handling involves checking customer credit, verifying product availability, and preparing products for shipping. Order delivery is provided by the carrier most suitable for a desired level of customer service. Order processing may be done manually or electronically, depending on which method gives the greatest speed and accuracy within cost limits.

Materials handling, or the physical handling of products, is an important element of physical distribution. Packaging, loading, and movement systems must be co-ordinated to take into account both cost reduction and customer requirements. Basic handling systems include unit loading on pallets or skids, movement by mechanical devices, and containerisation.

Warehousing involves the design and operation of facilities for storing and moving goods. Private warehouses are owned and operated by a company for the purpose of distributing its own products. Public warehouses are business organisations that rent storage space and related physical distribution facilities to other firms. Public warehouses may furnish security for products that are being used as collateral for loans by establishing field warehouses. They may also provide bonded storage for companies wishing to defer tax payments on imported or taxable products. Distribution centres are large, centralised warehouses specially designed for the rapid movement of goods to customers. In many cases, a combination of private and public facilities is the most flexible approach to warehousing.

The objective of inventory management is to minimise inventory costs while maintaining a supply of goods adequate for customers' needs. All inventory costs—carrying, replenishment, and stockout costs—must be controlled if profit goals are to be met. To avoid stockouts without tying up too much capital in inventory, a firm must have a systematic method for determining a reorder point, the inventory level at which more inventory is ordered. The trade-offs between the costs of carrying larger average safety stocks and the costs of frequent orders can be quantified in the economic order quantity (EOQ) model. Inventory problems may take the form of surplus inventory, late deliveries, write-offs, and inventory that is too large in proportion to sales or assets. Methods for improving inventory management include systems for determining the number of products sold and in stock and management techniques such as just-in-time and the 80/20 rule.

Transport adds time and place utility to a product by moving it from where it is made to where it is purchased and used. The five major modes of transporting goods are motor vehicles, railways, inland waterways, airways, and pipelines. Marketers evaluate transport modes with respect to costs, transit time (speed), reliability, capability, accessibility, security, and traceability; final selection of a transport mode involves many trade-offs. Intermodal transport allows marketers to combine the advantages of two or more modes of transport; it is facilitated by containerisation, by freight forwarders, who co-ordinate transport by combining small shipments from several organisations into efficient lot sizes, and by megacarriers, freight companies that offer several methods of shipment.

Physical distribution affects every element of the marketing mix: product, price, promotion, and distribution. To give customers products at acceptable prices, marketers consider consumers' changing needs and any shifts within the major distribution functions. Then they adapt existing physical distribution systems for greater effectiveness. Physical distribution functions account for about one-third of all marketing costs and have a significant impact on customer satisfaction. Therefore, effective marketers are actively involved in the design and control of physical distribution systems.

IMPORTANT TERMS

Physical distribution
Order processing
Materials handling
Unit loading
Containerisation
Warehousing
Private warehouse
Public warehouses
Field public warehouse
Bonded storage

Distribution centre
Stockouts
Reorder point
Safety stock
Economic order quantity (EOQ)
Transport
Transport modes
Intermodal transport
Freight forwarders
Megacarriers

DISCUSSION AND REVIEW QUESTIONS

1. Discuss the cost and service trade-offs in developing a physical distribution system.
2. What factors must physical distribution managers consider when developing a customer service mix?
3. Why should physical distribution managers develop service standards?
4. What is the advantage of using a total distribution cost approach?
5. What are the main tasks involved in order processing?
6. Discuss the advantages of using an electronic order-processing system. Which types of organisation are most likely to utilise electronic order processing?
7. How does a product's package affect materials handling procedures and techniques?
8. What is containerisation? Discuss the major benefits of containerisation.
9. Explain the major differences between private and public warehouses. What is a field public warehouse?
10. In what circumstances should a firm use a private warehouse instead of a public one?

11. The focus of distribution centres is on active movement of goods. Discuss how distribution centres are designed for the rapid flow of products.
12. Describe the costs associated with inventory management.
13. Explain the trade-offs inventory managers face when reordering merchandise.
14. How can managers improve inventory control? Give specific examples of techniques.
15. Compare the five major transport modes in terms of costs, transit time, reliability, capability, accessibility, security, and traceability.
16. What is transit time, and how does it affect physical distribution decisions?
17. Discuss the ways marketers can combine or co-ordinate two or more modes of transport. What is the advantage of doing this?
18. Identify the types of containerised shipping available to physical distribution managers.
19. Discuss how the four elements of the marketing mix affect physical distribution strategy.

■ CASES

12.1   IKEA Uses High-Tech Physical Distribution

IKEA, one of Europe's largest furniture retailers, has invaded the U.S. market. A few years ago, the Swedish firm made its debut with a two-storey, six-acre store just outside Philadelphia. A year later, a second store opened near Washington, D.C., bringing IKEA's worldwide total to 85 stores in 19 countries. Now IKEA has stores in the Baltimore, Pittsburgh, New York City, and Los Angeles metropolitan areas.

The attractive Scandinavian design and bright colours of IKEA's ready-to-assemble furniture and decorating accessories were an immediate success with American shoppers. Do-it-yourself furniture, however, is nothing new. U.K.-based Conran introduced European design to American mass markets several years before IKEA arrived, and other firms selling Scandinavian furniture, both assembled and knocked down, have been located within the United States since the 1960s. What sets IKEA apart, besides its low prices, is its trans-national distribution system. Both benefits are possible partly because of IKEA's innovative flat-pack technology.

About 95 percent of IKEA's fourteen thousand product offerings are sold knocked down in flat boxes, which lowers prices by saving storage space and cutting shipping costs. IKEA's central warehouse in Amhult, Sweden, is staffed by just three people using computer-controlled fork-lifts and thirteen robots. After a command from the keyboard operator, a fork-lift glides down the aisles of the 200-yard-long building to locate the designated pallets and bring them to the robots. The robots then follow magnetic strips on the floor to deliver the pallets to the shipping dock. Once the products reach an IKEA store, they are held (still boxed) in a self-service warehouse adjoining the store's showrooms. After shoppers browse through the showrooms and examine IKEA's glossy catalogue, they push supermarket-style trolleys into the self-service area, pull their boxed selections from bins and shelves, and proceed to the check-out. The customers themselves transport most purchases home, although delivery service for such heavy items as sofas and cabinets is available for a fee.

IKEA is continually experimenting with ways to flat-pack more product per box. Whereas fully assembled bentwood chairs, for example, are usually shipped six to a pallet, IKEA engineers have figured out how to pack in twenty-eight chairs un-assembled. By farming out its in-house designs to the most efficient manufacturers and suppliers it can find, IKEA cuts costs even further. IKEA's "creative sourcing" might mean that a carpenter supplies wooden parts for tables; a shirt manufacturer, seat covers; and a third supplier, screws and bolts. On the average, IKEA's retail prices are up to 50 percent lower than those of its competitors.

Philadelphia shoppers took to the IKEA system quickly—so quickly in fact that at first the Pennsylvania store was almost overwhelmed. During the four-day grand opening, 130,000 shoppers made their way through the store's stylish room settings. Sales for the first three months totalled $8 million, up $2 million from initial projections. Since then, crowds have levelled off at about 30,000 people a week; the Virginia store draws about 15,000 people on a typical weekend. The 1989 U.K. openings saw a similar pattern.

But success has not been without problems. First, the U.S. stores are too small. Inadequate warehouse space and loading platforms have necessitated a night shift just to replenish the stock. Second, demand has routinely exceeded supply in some product categories. At one point, the Philadelphia store had a backlog of 15,000 requests for out-of-stock items. IKEA maintains two distribution centres in Canada to service its stores there, but most of the stock for the U.S. stores comes from the main warehouse in Sweden, spending six to eight weeks in transit before arriving at one of the company's huge distribution centres. The stockouts are troublesome, because many of IKEA's product designs are modular: if one piece is unavailable, sales of the other pieces are delayed. IKEA is also concerned about first-time shoppers who find an item out of stock and never return for a second visit. IKEA has responded by increasing its warehouse stock.

IKEA managers have alleviated many supply problems by building a multi-million-dollar distribution centre in the Philadelphia area. The company also intends to use a greater number of U.S. suppliers. At present Canadian manufacturers provide some of the products for the U.S. stores (as well as about 20 percent of the items in Canadian stores), and some of IKEA's sofas are now made in Knoxville, Tennessee. Another possibility for avoiding distribution delays is the purchase of a private shipping line. Although IKEA offers mail-order service in Europe (and, in fact, started out as a mail-order furniture company), the company has no current plans to establish a mail-order business in the United States, despite a deluge of requests from customers.

Instead, IKEA's long-range U.S. strategy calls for several new stores over the next few years, supported by five regional distribution and marketing systems. For now, IKEA is concentrating on setting up new stores on both coasts.

SOURCES: Janet Bamford, "Why Competitors Shop for Ideas at IKEA," *Business Week,* 9 Oct. 1989, p. 88; Eugene Carlson, "How a Major Swedish Retailer Chose a Beachhead in the U.S.," *Wall Street Journal,* 7 Apr. 1987, p. 37; Kimberley Carpenter, "Help Yourself," *Working Woman,* Aug. 1986, p. 56; Pat Corwin, "The Vikings Are Back—With Furniture," *Discount Merchandising,* April 1987, p. 52; Peter Fuhrman, "The Workers' Friend," *Forbes,* 21 Mar. 1988, pp. 124, 128; Judith Graham, "IKEA Furnishing Its U.S. Identity," *Advertising Age,* 18 Sept. 1989, p. 79; Bill Kelley, "The New Wave from Europe," *Sales & Marketing Management,* Nov. 1987, pp. 45–51; Mary Krienke, "IKEA = Simple Good Taste," *Stores,* April 1986, p. 60; Kevin Maney, "Customers Flood USA IKEA Outlets," *USA Today,* 4 Nov. 1986, sec. B, p. 1; and Carolyn Pfaff, "IKEA: The Supermarket of Furniture Stores," *Adweek,* 3 May 1986, p. 26.

Questions for Discussion

1. What actions has IKEA taken to reduce its physical distribution problems?
2. Explain how IKEA's physical distribution system influences other parts of this organisation's marketing strategies.
3. In the future, what types of physical distribution problems must IKEA resolve with respect to its U.S. stores?

12.2 EC Transport Deregulation

In 1982, the U.K. government privatised the National Freight Company (NFC). Forty percent of the shareholding is owned by the 25,000 employees. The company now has a turnover of close of £1,500 million, up from £461 million in 1982, covering transport, distribution, parcels, travel agency and property development under the BRS, Lynx Express, Pickfords, SPD, and Hoults brands.

Excel Logistics, as NFC's distribution division was renamed in 1989, is operating in an increasingly competitive market. There has been significant fall-out, with the larger operators gaining dominance over the smaller, independent companies.

Excel, as with all European hauliers, is trading in a dynamic environment. The harmonisation of Europe in 1992—when the European Community removes much inter-country legislation and bureaucracy—has significant implications for all physical distribution in the Community, particularly for road hauliers.

When the national borders and transport regulations are removed, it is predicted that cross-Europe routes will improve, there will be standardisation across countries of technical, legal, and taxation requirements, and fewer delays at customs posts (which currently can equal a day for a journey from the U.K. to Italy). Transport costs will be reduced with the end of "cabotage," whereby U.K. operators, for example, often have to return with empty trucks as they are not allowed to pick up loads in other EC countries. With minimal borders and few regulations, interstate trade is set to increase but so will the ability of hauliers to operate and seek business in more countries, leading to more competition and further shake-out.

Hauliers are increasing their share of road transport. Only the major retailers which are investing heavily in creating company-owned distribution networks and infrastructure are seeing an increase in own-account haulage.

U.K. FREIGHT TRANSPORT BY ROAD (BILLION TONNE-KILOMETRES)

	1984	1985	1986	1987
Public haulage	62.3	66.6	68.7	77.1
Own-account haulage	34.2	32.5	32.4	31.5

Throughout the EC, companies that are relatively strong but already facing stiff competition, such as Excel/NFC in the U.K., will face new competitors, a dramatically altered trading environment, and new marketing challenges.

SOURCES: Office for Official Publications of the European Community (Brussels), *The European Community Transport Policy*, 1984; London: Keynote, *The Road Haulage Industry*, 1989; London: Jordans, *Britain's Top 300 Road Haulage Companies*, 1988; and M. Labrou, "Ten Marketing Cases," University of Warwick, MBA Dissertation, 1989.

Questions for Discussion

1. Can NFC continue to focus on being a U.K. operator?
2. How dependent are transport and distribution on external factors for growth or decline?
3. How real are the benefits to transport of EC deregulation?

PART **IV** PROMOTION DECISIONS

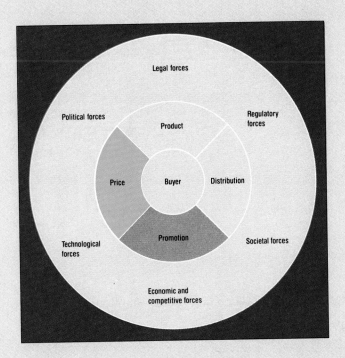

Part IV focuses on communication with target market members. A specific marketing mix cannot satisfy people in a particular target market unless they are aware of the product and where to find it. Some promotion decisions and activities relate to a specific marketing mix, whereas others, broader in scope, are geared to promoting the whole organisation. Chapter 13 presents an overview of promotion. We describe the communication process and the major promotion methods that can be included in promotional mixes. In Chapter 14, we analyse the major steps required to develop an advertising campaign, and we explain what public relations and publicity are and how they can be used. Chapter 15 deals with the management of personal selling and the role it can play in a firm's promotional mix. This chapter also explores the general characteristics of sales promotion and sales promotion techniques. ◆

13

PROMOTION: AN OVERVIEW

Objectives

To understand the role of promotion in the marketing mix

To examine the process of communication

To understand the product adoption process and its implications for promotional efforts

To understand the aims of promotion

To explore the elements of the promotional mix

To acquire an overview of the major methods of promotion

To explore factors that affect the choice of promotional methods

Richard Branson's Virgin Atlantic emerged in the mid-1980s to take on the world's most powerful airlines, initially across the Atlantic. Virgin Atlantic (VA) has quickly established itself as a major player on the routes it flies and in 1989 reported profits of £10 million on turnover of £75 million—the third most profitable international airline. VA initially competed on price, targeting the younger consumers of Virgin Records and Tapes—aspirers with still relatively tight budgets. In recent years, VA has targeted the lucrative business sector, improving its facilities and service levels.

Virgin Atlantic's advertising budget is small in comparison with its rivals', but it targets the magazines and newspapers read by businesspeople to great effect. Sales promotion is a powerful tool: a complimentary economy class ticket free with each upper class ticket; a scheme offering free ballooning in Egypt, a photo-safari in Kenya, etc.; cheap flights to America to take advantage of a weak dollar; live entertainment on flights.

The main promotional tactic has been publicity, largely on the back of Richard Branson's carefully engineered personality. Branson crossed the Atlantic in the Virgin Atlantic *Challenger*, nearly capturing the Blue Riband for the fastest sea crossing by a passenger ship; he supported the UK2000 campaign, flew a hot-air balloon across the Atlantic, created an AIDS charity foundation financed by the Mates condom, and sponsored FA Cup finalists Crystal Palace. At relatively low cost, Branson has successfully promoted Virgin Atlantic and created a major brand. ◆

Based on information in Mick Brown, "Richard Branson—The Inside Story," 1989; and the Virgin Atlantic Public Relations department; "This Week," *Marketing*, 17 May 1990, p. 9; "Virgin Atlantic Airways," *Harvest*, 1990.

O rganisations use various promotional approaches to communicate with target markets, as the preceding example illustrates. This chapter looks at the general dimensions of promotion. First we define and examine its role. Next, to understand how promotion works, we analyse the meaning and process of communication, as well as the product adoption process. The remainder of the chapter discusses the major types of promotional methods and the factors that influence an organisation's decision to use specific methods of promotion.

THE ROLE OF PROMOTION

People's attitudes towards promotion vary. Some hold that promotional activities, particularly advertising and personal selling, paint a distorted picture of reality because they provide the customer with only selected information. According to this view, the repetition of similar themes in promotion has brought about changes in social values, such as increased materialism.[1] It is held that promotional activities are unnecessary and wasteful and that promotion costs (especially advertising) are high—sometimes excessively so—resulting in higher prices. Still others take a positive view: that advertising messages often project wholesome values, such as affection, generosity, or patriotism,[2] or that advertising, as a powerful economic force, can free countries from poverty by communicating information.[3] Some observe that advertising of consumer products was a factor in the decline of communism and the move towards a free enterprise system in eastern Europe. However, none of these impressions is completely accurate.

The role of **promotion** is to communicate with individuals, groups, or organisations so as to directly or indirectly facilitate exchanges by informing and persuading one or more of the audiences to accept an organisation's products.[4] L. A. Gear, for example, recruited pop star Michael Jackson to communicate the benefits of its line of trainers.[5] Rock Against Drugs (RAD), a non-profit organisation, employs popular rock musicians, such as Lou Reed, to communicate its anti-drug messages to teenagers and young adults. Like L. A. Gear and RAD, marketers try to communicate with selected audiences about their company and its goods, services, and ideas in order to facilitate exchanges. Marketing Update 13.1 describes how The Coca-Cola Company used and continues to use promotion to gain a new position for its "new" Coke product.

Marketers indirectly facilitate exchanges by focusing information about company activities and products on interest groups (such as environmental and consumer

1. Richard W. Pollay, "On the Value of Reflections on the Values in 'The Distorted Mirror'," *Journal of Marketing*, July 1987, pp. 104–109.

2. Morris B. Holbrook, "Mirror, Mirror, on the Wall, What's Unfair in the Reflections on Advertising," *Journal of Marketing*, July 1987, pp. 95–103.

3. Richard N. Farmer, "Would You Want Your Granddaughter to Marry a Taiwanese Marketing Man?" *Journal of Marketing*, October 1987, pp. 111–116.

4. Colin Coulson-Thomas, *Marketing Communications* (London: Heinemann, 1986).

5. David Landis, "Michael Jackson Joins Sneakers Sales Pitch," *USA Today*, 14 Sept. 1989, p. 1B.

FIGURE 13.1
Information flows
into and out of an
organisation.

groups), current and potential investors, regulatory agencies, and society in general. Some marketers use *cause-related marketing,* which links the purchase of their products to philanthropic efforts for a particular cause. Cause-related marketing often helps a marketer boost sales and generate good will through contributions to causes that members of its target markets want to support. For example, American Express used cause-related marketing to encourage its credit card holders to use their cards more often and thus help to rebuild the Statue of Liberty. American Express pledged to donate a percentage of the value of all purchases charged on its card to rebuilding the statue.[6] Similarly, Procter & Gamble has tied promotional efforts for some of its products with contributions to the Special Olympics. Oxfam promotes use of the Visa card.

Viewed from this wider perspective, promotion can play a comprehensive communication role. Some promotional activities, such as publicity and public relations, can be directed towards helping a company justify its existence and maintain positive, healthy relationships between itself and various groups in the marketing environment. Record companies, television stations, media and personalities gave their services free to facilitate the global Live Aid fund-raising activities.

Although a company can direct a single type of communication—such as an advertisement—towards numerous audiences, marketers often design a communication precisely for a specific target market. A firm frequently communicates several different messages concurrently, each to a different group. For example, McDonald's may direct one communication towards customers for its Big Mac, a second message towards investors about the firm's stable growth, and a third communication towards society in general regarding the company's social awareness in supporting Ronald McDonald Houses in America, which provide support to families of children suffering from cancer.

To gain maximum benefit from promotional efforts, marketers must make every effort to properly plan, implement, co-ordinate, and control communications. Effective promotional activities are based on information from the marketing environment, often obtained from an organisation's marketing information system (see Figure 13.1). How effectively marketers can use promotion to maintain positive relationships depends largely on the quantity and quality of information an organisation takes in. For example, scares in the U.K. about the contamination of baby food led to manufacturers informing customers about specially developed safety tops. The problem was that the customers could see when a tinned food had been tampered with, but this was more difficult for food sold in glass jars. The manufacturers therefore stressed the safety "button" on jar lids, which popped up when the seal had been broken. Because the basic role of promotion is to communicate, we should analyse what communication is and how the communication process works.

6. P. "Rajan" Varadarajan and Anil Menon, "Cause-related Marketing: A Coalignment of Marketing Strategy and Corporate Philanthropy," *Journal of Marketing,* July 1988, pp. 58–74.

COCA-COLA REVAMPS COCA-COLA A SECOND TIME

In the face of declining market share, the Coca-Cola Company decided in 1985 to reformulate its flagship Coca-Cola brand to compete more directly with Pepsi, its sweeter arch-rival in the long-standing U.S. cola wars. The company had tested the new formula for years and was convinced that it was superior to the original formula as well as to other cola competitors. Consumers, however, rejected the reformulated Coca-Cola and demanded the return of their original favourite. Thus, three months after the launch of Coke, the company reintroduced the original formula under the name Coca-Cola Classic; the reformulated version remained on the market under the name Coca-Cola, or "new" Coke.

After five years on the market, "new" Coke had still failed to overtake Pepsi. In fact, at the end of the 1980s, "new" Coke fell off the top-ten soft-drink list and was called the "Edsel of the Eighties." (In the late 1950s, Ford launched its Edsel and lost $350 million with the model.) The product reached its peak in 1985 with roughly 7.5 percent of the soft-drink market. Market share eroded steadily from that point, down to about 1 percent of the market in the late 1980s. By contrast, Coca-Cola Classic and Pepsi each held 15.8 percent of the soft-drink market.

After reviewing the lacklustre performance of the sweeter "new" Coke, the company decided in 1990 to reposition it under the name Coke II to compete head-on with Pepsi in the U.S. The company hopes that with a new name, new look, and new promotion, Coke II can get past its rough start as an unwanted replacement for an American classic. The traditional red and white can was redesigned with splashes of blue—a Pepsi colour. Although the formula of the product was not altered, advertising for Coke II will focus on "real cola taste".

Coca-Cola promises to heat up the cola wars with a very strong promotional campaign for Coke II. Traditional promotional vehicles—television and radio advertising, taste tests, and coupons—will probably be used to convince sceptical consumers that Coke II tastes better than Pepsi. The success of Coke II's promotion campaign will probably determine whether consumers accept Coke II as a sweeter alternative to Coca-Cola Classic or view it as a Pepsi copy-cat with no clear brand identity.

SOURCES: Kate Fitzgerald, "Diet Coke Hits Recall Chart for First Time," *Advertising Age,* 2 Feb. 1990, p. 28; Michael J. McCarthy, "New Coke Gets New Name, New Can, New Chance," *Wall Street Journal,* 7 March 1990, pp. B1, B6; Thomas More, "He Put the Kick Back in Coke," *Fortune,* 26 Oct. 1987, pp. 46–56; and Cable News Network (TV), 7 March 1990.

PROMOTION AND THE COMMUNICATION PROCESS

Communication can be viewed as the transmission of information.[7] For communication to take place, however, both the sender and the receiver of the information must share some common ground. They must share an understanding of the symbols used to transmit information, usually pictures or words. For instance, an individual transmitting the following message may believe he or she is communicating with you:

在工厂吾人製造化粧品，在商店吾人銷售希望。

However, communication has not taken place because few of you understand the intended message.[8] Thus we define **communication** as a sharing of meaning.[9] Implicit in this definition is the notion of transmission of information because sharing necessitates transmission.

As Figure 13.2 shows, communication begins with a source. A **source** is a person, group, or organisation that has a meaning it intends and attempts to share with an audience. For example, a source could be a salesperson who wishes to communicate a sales message or an organisation that wants to send a message to thousands of consumers through an advertisement. A **receiver** or audience is the individual, group, or organisation that decodes a coded message. An audience is two or more receivers who decode a message. The intended receivers or audience of an advertisement for Cellnet cellular telephones, for example, might be businesspeople who must frequently travel by car.

To transmit meaning, a source must convert the meaning into a series of signs that represent ideas or concepts. This is called the **coding process**, or *encoding*. When coding meaning into a message, a source must take into account certain characteristics of the receiver or audience. First, to share meaning, the source should use signs that are familiar to the receiver or audience. Marketers who understand this fact realise how important it is to know their target market and to make sure that an advertisement, for example, is written in language that the target market can understand. Thus when Du Pont advertised its Stainmaster carpeting, it did not mention the name of the chemical used to make the carpet resistant to stains because it would have had little meaning to consumers seeing the advertisement. There have been some notable problems in translating English advertisements into Spanish for the U.S. Hispanic market segment. A beer advertisement with the tag line "Sueltate" was supposed to mean "Let go!" but actually invited Hispanics to "Get diarrhoea!" And an airline advertisement intended to entice Hispanics to fly first class on leather seats invited them instead to fly naked.[10] Thus it is important that people understand the language used in promotion.

7. John Rossiter and Larry Percy, *Advertising and Promotion Management* (New York: McGraw-Hill, 1987).

8. In case you do not read Chinese, this says, "In the factory we make cosmetics, and in the store we sell hope." Prepared by Chih Kang Wang.

9. Terence A. Shimp and M. Wayne Delozier, *Promotion Management and Marketing Communication* (Hinsdale, Ill.: Dryden Press, 1986), pp. 25–26.

10. Carlos E. Garcia, "Hispanic Market Is Accessible If Research Is Designed Correctly," *Marketing News*, 4 Jan. 1988, p. 46.

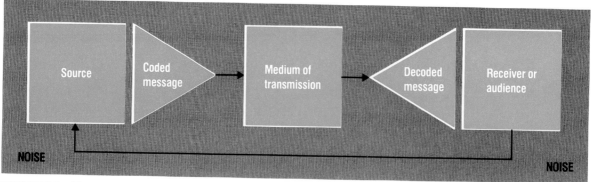

FIGURE 13.2 *The communication process*

Second, when coding a meaning, a source should try to use signs that the receiver or audience uses for referring to the concepts the source intends. Marketers should generally avoid signs that can have several meanings for an audience. For example, a national advertiser of soft drinks should avoid using the word *soda* as a general term for soft drinks. Although in some places soda is taken to mean *soft drink,* in others it may connote bicarbonate of soda, an ice-cream drink, or something that one mixes with Scotch whisky.

To share a coded meaning with the receiver or audience, a source must select and use a medium of transmission. A **medium of transmission** carries the coded message from the source to the receiver or audience. Transmission media include ink on paper, vibrations of air waves produced by vocal cords, chalk marks on a chalkboard, and electronically produced vibrations of air waves—in radio and television signals, for example.

When a source chooses an inappropriate medium of transmission, several problems may arise. A coded message may reach some receivers, but not the right ones. For example, suppose a local theatre group spends most of its advertising budget on radio advertisements. If theatregoers depend mainly on newspapers for information about local drama, then the theatre will not reach its intended target audience. Coded messages may also reach intended receivers in an incomplete form because the intensity of the transmission is weak. For example, radio signals can be received effectively only over a limited range that may vary depending on climatic conditions. Members of the target audience who live on the fringe of the broadcasting area may receive a weak signal; others well within the broadcasting area may also receive an incomplete message if they listen to their radios while driving or studying.

In the **decoding process**, signs are converted into concepts and ideas. Seldom does a receiver decode exactly the same meaning that a source coded. When the result of decoding is different from what was coded, **noise** exists. Noise has many sources and may affect any or all parts of the communication process. When a source selects a medium of transmission through which an audience does not expect to receive a message, noise is likely to occur. Noise sometimes arises within the medium of transmission itself. Radio static, faulty printing processes, and laryngitis are sources of noise. Interference on viewers' television sets during a commercial is noise and lessens the impact of the message. Noise also occurs when a source uses a sign that is unfamiliar to the receiver or that has a different meaning from the one the source intended. Noise also may originate in the receiver. As Chapter 4 dis-

FIGURE 13.3

Getting feedback.
With every complimentary tin of biscuits shipped, the Radisson Hotel receives feedback that its message was understood.

SOURCE: Ad courtesy of Radisson Hotels International, Minneapolis, MN

cusses, a receiver may be unaware of a coded message because his or her perceptual processes block it out or because the coded message is too obscure.

The receiver's response to a message is **feedback** to the source. The source usually expects and normally receives feedback, although it may not be immediate. During feedback, the receiver or audience is the source of a message that is directed towards the original source, which then becomes a receiver. Feedback is coded, sent through a medium of transmission, and is decoded by the receiver, the source of the original communication. It is logical, then, to think of communication as a circular process.

During face-to-face communication, such as a personal selling situation or product sampling, both verbal and non-verbal feedback can be immediate. Instant feedback lets communicators adjust their messages quickly to improve the effectiveness of their communication. For example, when a salesperson realises through feedback that a customer does not understand a sales presentation, he or she adapts the presentation to make it more meaningful to the customer. In interpersonal communication, feedback occurs through talking, touching, smiling, nodding, eye movements, and other body movements and postures.

When mass communication such as advertising is used, feedback is often slow and difficult to recognise. If Alton Towers increased its advertising in order to increase the number of visitors, it might be six to eighteen months before the theme park could recognise the effects of the expanded advertising. Although it is harder to recognise, feedback does exist for mass communication. Figure 13.3 illustrates a unique programme developed by the Radisson Hotel in America to obtain feedback on whether its message was received by its target market. Advertisers, for example, obtain feedback in the form of changes in sales volume or in consumers' attitudes and awareness levels.

Each communication channel has a limit on the volume of information it can handle effectively. This limit, called **channel capacity**, is determined by the least efficient component of the communication process. To illustrate this, think about communications that depend on vocal speech. An individual source can talk only so fast, and there is a limit to how much an individual receiver can take in aurally. Beyond that point, additional messages cannot be decoded; thus meaning cannot be shared. Although a radio announcer can read several hundred words a minute, a one-minute advertising message should not exceed 150 words because most announcers cannot articulate the words into understandable messages at a rate beyond 150 words per minute. This figure is the limit for both source and receiver, and marketers should keep this in mind when developing radio commercials. At times, a firm creates a television advertisement that contains several types of visual material and several forms of audio messages, all transmitted to viewers at the same time. Such communication may not be totally effective because receivers cannot decode all the messages simultaneously.

Now that we have explored the basic communication process, we consider more specifically how promotion is used to influence individuals, groups, or organisations to accept or adopt a firm's products. Although we briefly touch upon the product adoption process in Chapter 8, we discuss it more fully in the following section to gain a better understanding of the conditions under which promotion occurs.

PROMOTION AND THE PRODUCT ADOPTION PROCESS

Marketers do not promote simply to inform, educate, and entertain; they communicate to facilitate satisfying exchanges. One long-run purpose of promotion is to influence and encourage buyers to accept or adopt goods, services, and ideas. At times, an advertisement may be informative or entertaining, yet it may fail to get the audience to purchase the product. For example, some ads for business computers seem to be weak in communicating benefits—they focus instead on getting customers to feel good about the product. The ultimate effectiveness of promotion is determined by the degree to which it affects product adoption among potential buyers or increases the frequency of current buyers' purchases.

To establish realistic expectations about what promotion can do, one should not view product adoption as a one-step process. Rarely can a single promotional activity cause an individual to buy a previously unfamiliar product. The acceptance of a product involves many steps. Although there are several ways to look at the **product adoption process**, one common approach is to view it as consisting of five stages: awareness, interest, evaluation, trial, and adoption.[11]

In the awareness stage, individuals become aware that the product exists, but they have little information about it and are not concerned about getting more. When Peugeot launched its 405 model, for example, it used provocative teaser advertisements, which showed burning fields but not the car. As Figure 13.4 shows, later adverts did show the 405. Consumers enter the interest stage when they are moti-

11. Adapted from Everett M. Rogers, *Diffusion of Innovations* (New York: Free Press, 1962), pp. 81–86, 98–102.

FIGURE 13.4 *Building awareness.*
Following teaser advertisements, Peugeot aired commercials designed to interest people in learning more about the 405.

SOURCE: Peugeot Talbot

vated to get information about the product's features, uses, advantages, disadvantages, price, or location. During the evaluation stage, individuals consider whether the product will satisfy certain criteria that are crucial for meeting their specific needs. In the trial stage, they use or experience the product for the first time, possibly by purchasing a small quantity, by taking advantage of a free sample or demonstration, or by borrowing the product from someone. Supermarkets, for example, frequently offer special promotions to encourage consumers to taste products such as cheese, cooked meats, snacks, or pizza. During this stage, potential adopters determine the usefulness of the product under the specific conditions for which they need it.

Individuals move into the adoption stage by choosing the specific product when they need a product of that general type. Do not assume, however, that because a person enters the adoption process she or he will eventually adopt the new product. Rejection may occur at any stage, including adoption. Both product adoption and product rejection can be temporary or permanent.

For the most part, people respond to different information sources at different stages of the adoption process. Figure 13.5 illustrates the most effective sources for each stage. Mass communication sources, such as television advertising, are often effective for moving large numbers of people into the awareness stage. Producers of consumer goods commonly use massive advertising campaigns when introducing new products. They do so to create product awareness as quickly as possible within a large portion of the target market.

FIGURE 13.5
Effective promotion tools for reaching consumers in various stages of the product adoption process

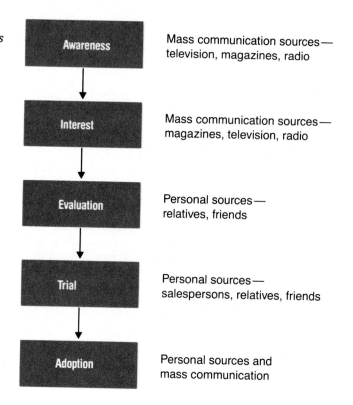

Awareness — Mass communication sources— television, magazines, radio

Interest — Mass communication sources— magazines, television, radio

Evaluation — Personal sources— relatives, friends

Trial — Personal sources— salespersons, relatives, friends

Adoption — Personal sources and mass communication

Mass communications may also be effective for people in the interest stage who want to learn more about a product. During the evaluation stage, individuals often seek information, opinions, and reinforcement from personal sources—relatives, friends, and associates. In the trial stage, individuals depend on salespersons for information about how to use the product properly to get the most out of it. Marketers must use advertising carefully when consumers are in the trial stage. If advertisements greatly exaggerate the benefits of a product, the consumer may be disappointed when the product does not meet expectations.[12] It is best to avoid creating expectations that cannot be satisfied because rejection at this stage will prevent adoption. Friends and peers may also be important sources during the trial stage. By the time the adoption stage has been reached, both personal communication from sales personnel and mass communication through advertisements may be required. Even though the particular stage of the adoption process may influence the types of information sources consumers use, marketers must remember that other factors, such as the product's characteristics, price, uses, and the characteristics of customers, also affect the types of information sources that buyers desire and believe.

Because people in different stages of the adoption process often require different types of information, marketers designing a promotional campaign must determine what stage of the adoption process a particular target audience is in before they can develop the message. Potential adopters in the interest stage will need different information from people who have already reached the trial stage.

12. Lawrence J. Marks and Michael A. Kamins, "Product Sampling and Advertising Sequence, Belief Strength, Confidence and Attitudes," *Journal of Marketing Research,* August 1988, pp. 266–281.

FIGURE 13.6
Distribution of product adopter categories

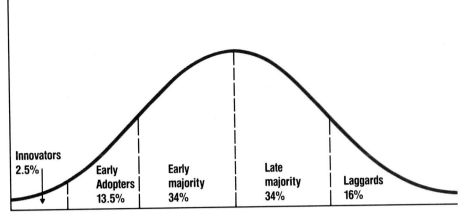

SOURCE: Reprinted with permission of The Free Press, a Division of Macmillan Inc., from *Diffusion of Innovations*, 3rd ed., by Everett H. Rogers. Copyright © 1962, 1971, 1983 by The Free Press.

When an organisation introduces a new product, people do not all begin the adoption process at the same time, and they do not move through the process at the same speed. Of those people who eventually adopt the product, some enter the adoption process rather quickly, whereas others start considerably later. For most products, too, there is a group of non-adopters who never begin the process.

■ **Product Adopter Categories**

Depending on the length of time it takes them to adopt a new product, people can be divided into five major adopter categories: innovators, early adopters, early majority, late majority, and laggards.[13] Figure 13.6 illustrates each adopter category and the percentage of total adopters that it typically represents. **Innovators** are the first to adopt a new product. They enjoy trying new products and tend to be venturesome. **Early adopters** choose new products carefully and are viewed as "the people to check with" by those in the remaining adopter categories. People in the **early majority** adopt just prior to the average person; they are deliberate and cautious in trying new products. **Late majority** people, who are quite sceptical about new products, eventually adopt them because of economic necessity or social pressure. **Laggards**, the last to adopt a new product, are orientated towards the past. They are suspicious of new products, and when they finally adopt the innovation, it may already have been replaced by a newer product. When developing promotional efforts, a marketer should bear in mind that people in different adopter categories often need different forms of communication and different types of information.

■ **Aims of Promotion Communication**

Product adoption is a major focus for any promotional activity. There are, though, five basic communications effects, which are defined as follows.[14]

Category Need. The consumer must realize he or she wants a particular product—particularly for innovative new-category product launches—and must perceive a **category need** in order to be motivated even to consider a product. When CD

13. Rogers, pp. 247–250.

14. John Rossiter and Larry Percy, *Advertising and Promotion Management* (New York: McGraw-Hill, 1987).

players were launched, many consumers had perfectly adequate album- and/or cassette-based hi-fi systems and did not see any need to purchase a CD player.

Brand Awareness.   The consumer must be able to identify (recognise or recall) a manufacturer's brand within the category in sufficient detail to make a purchase. The manufacturer must make its brand stand out, initially through product attributes supported by distinctive promotional activity. Sony wants consumers to be aware of *its* CD players rather than Aiwa or Amstrad players.

Brand Attitude.   Emotions and logic or cognitive beliefs combine to give the consumer a particular impression of a product. This **brand attitude** directs consumer choice towards a particular brand. Companies need customers to have a positive view of their brands.

Brand Purchase Intention.   Once a category need and brand awareness are established, if the consumer's brand attitude is favourable, he or she will decide to purchase the particular product and take the associated steps to make the purchase, showing **brand purchase intention.**

Purchase Facilitation.   Having decided to buy, the consumer requires the product to be readily available at a convenient location, at a suitable price, and from a familiar retailer. The manufacturer must ensure that other marketing factors (product, distribution, price, and promotion) do not hinder the purchase. Sony customers expect wide distribution from reputable retailers, with no budget pricing. Sony produces high-quality goods, but there are several well-respected competitors to Sony and the company must ensure product availability to avoid brand switching.

To gain a better understanding of how promotion can move people closer to the acceptance of goods, services, and ideas, we turn to the major promotional methods available to an organisation—the promotional mix.

THE PROMOTIONAL MIX

Several types of promotional methods can be used to communicate with individuals, groups, and organisations. When an organisation combines specific ingredients to promote a particular product, that combination constitutes the promotional mix for that product. The four possible ingredients of a **promotional mix** are advertising, personal selling, public relations, and sales promotion (see Figure 13.7). For some products, firms use all four ingredients; for other products, two or three will suffice. In this section we analyse the major ingredients of a promotional mix and the chief factors that influence an organisation to include specific ingredients in the promotional mix for a specific product. In Chapters 14 and 15 we analyse the promotional mix in greater detail.

■ **Promotional Mix Ingredients**   At this point we consider some general characteristics of advertising, personal selling, public relations, and sales promotion.

Advertising.   Advertising is a paid form of non-personal communication about an organisation and its products that is transmitted to a target audience through a mass

FIGURE 13.7
*Possible ingredients
of an organisation's
promotional mix*

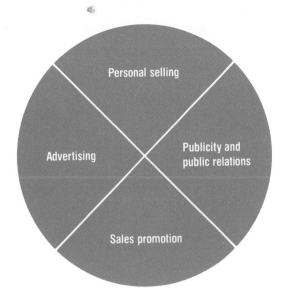

medium such as television, radio, newspapers, magazines, direct mail, public transport, outdoor displays, or catalogues. Individuals and organisations use advertising to promote goods, services, ideas, issues, and people. Because it is highly flexible, advertising offers the options of reaching an extremely large target audience or focusing on a small, precisely defined segment of the population. For instance, McDonald's advertising focuses on a large audience of potential fast-food consumers, ranging from children to adults, whereas advertising for DeBeers' diamonds focuses on a much smaller and specialised target market. Marketing Update 13.2 discusses the practice of "ambush" advertising during televised sporting events as rivals compete for the same audience.

Advertising offers several benefits. It can be an extremely cost-efficient promotional method because it reaches a vast number of people at a low cost per person. For example, the cost of a four-colour, one-page advertisement in the *Sunday Telegraph* magazine is £7,000. Because the magazine reaches 700,000 readers, the cost of reaching 1,000 subscribers is only £10. Advertising also lets the user repeat the message a number of times. Unilever advertises many of its products (cleaning products, foods, cosmetics) on television, in magazines, and through outdoor advertising. In addition, advertising a product in a certain way can add to its value. For example, Geo, which is sold and serviced by Chevrolet, is advertised as having more dealers in the U.S.A. than Honda, Toyota, and other Japanese companies combined. The visibility that an organisation gains from advertising enhances the firm's public image.

Advertising also has several disadvantages. Even though the cost per person reached may be low, the absolute monetary outlay can be extremely high, especially for commercials shown during popular television programmes. These high costs can limit, and sometimes prevent, the use of advertising in a promotional mix. Moreover, advertising rarely provides rapid feedback. Measuring its effect on sales is difficult, and it ordinarily has less persuasive impact on customers than personal selling.

"AMBUSH" ADVERTISING TO INCREASE

Sports Marketing Services (SMS) monitors television and press exposure of 3,500 sponsors across Europe. Pan-European distribution of sports programming is growing quickly, making advertisers more anxious to track the exposure of their brands through televised sponsored events in different TV markets. They are also keen to negotiate and enforce deals with broadcasters which exclude rivals from buying advertising spots around their sponsored programmes. This form of "ambush" advertising by a sponsor's rivals is highly developed in America.

With the U.K. Independent Television networks now permitting limited sponsorship of TV programmes, the tactic is likely to appear in the U.K. as well as in Europe. Sponsors increasingly want to know who will be advertising around or during their programme. If Volvo sponsors a golf event, Volvo executives have a vested interest in ensuring that Saab or Mercedes do not gain high exposure when Volvo's programme is broadcast. Spoiling tactics, for example, by Volvo's rivals give them an incentive to advertise around Volvo's programme.

SOURCES: Sports Marketing Surveys; *Marketing,* 9 August 1990, p. 11; Michael Kavanagh, "Sponsorship: View to a Killing," *Marketing,* 7 June 1990, pp. 26–27; "BBC Slams Sponsorship but Boosts Own," *Marketing,* 17 May 1990, p. 11; "This Week," *Marketing,* 31 May 1990, p. 11; Louella Miles, "Sponsorship Round-up," *Marketing,* 15 March 1990, p. 38; Joan Plachta, "A Survival Guide to Sponsorship," *Marketing,* 27 September 1990, pp. 31–34; "TV Sponsorship—The Creative Possibilities of the New Code," *Admap Campaign Seminar,* 29 January 1991.

Personal Selling. Personal selling involves informing customers and persuading them to purchase products through personal communication in an exchange situation. The phrase *to purchase products* should be interpreted broadly to encompass the acceptance of ideas and issues. Telemarketing, which Chapter 11 describes as direct selling over the telephone, relies heavily on personal selling.

Personal selling has both advantages and limitations when compared with advertising. Advertising is general communication aimed at a relatively large target audience, whereas personal selling involves more specific communication aimed at one or several persons. Reaching one person through personal selling costs considerably more than it does through advertising, but personal selling efforts often have a greater impact on customers. Personal selling also provides immediate feedback, which allows marketers to adjust their message to improve communication. It helps them determine and respond to customers' needs for information.

When a salesperson and customer meet face to face, they use several types of interpersonal communication. Obviously, the predominating communication form is language—both speech and writing. In addition, a salesperson and customer frequently use **kinesic communication**, or body language, by moving their heads, eyes, arms, hands, legs, or torsos. Winking, head nodding, hand gestures, and arm motions are forms of kinesic communication. A good salesperson can often evaluate a prospect's interest in a product or presentation by watching for eye contact and head nodding. **Proxemic communication**, a less obvious form of communication used in personal selling situations, occurs when either person varies the physical distance that separates the two people. When a customer backs away from a salesperson, for example, that individual may be saying that he or she is not interested in the product or may be expressing dislike for the salesperson. Touching, or **tactile communication**, can also be a form of communication; shaking hands is a common form of tactile communication in many countries.

Publicity and Public Relations. Publicity refers to non-personal communication in news story form about an organisation or its products, or both, that is transmitted through a mass medium at no charge. Examples of publicity include magazine, newspaper, radio, and television news stories about new retail stores, new products, or personnel changes in an organisation. Although both advertising and publicity are transmitted through mass communication, the sponsor does not pay the media costs for publicity and is not identified. Nevertheless, publicity should never be viewed as free communication. There are clear costs associated with preparing news releases and encouraging media personnel to broadcast or print them. A firm that uses publicity regularly must have employees to perform these activities or obtain the services of a public relations firm or an advertising agency. Either way, the firm bears the costs of the activities.

Publicity must be planned and implemented so that it is compatible with, and supportive of, other elements in the promotional mix. However, publicity cannot always be controlled to the extent that other elements of the promotional mix can be. For example, just as Perrier's contamination problems appeared to be easing, a BBC television programme showed that the "bottled at source" packaging was misleading because the bubbles were added during the bottling process. Sainsbury, the U.K.'s major grocery retailer, refused for many months to re-stock Perrier until the wording on the packaging was altered, creating much poor publicity for the French company. The public relations mechanism manages and controls the use of effective publicity (see Chapter 14).

FIGURE 13.8 *Example of a sales promotion.*
This coupon appearing in *Ideal Home* promotes the purchase of a special product at an attractive price.

SOURCE: Reproduced with the kind permission of *Ideal Home* Magazine

Sales Promotion.   Sales promotion is an activity or material that acts as a direct inducement, offering added value, or incentive for the product, to resellers, salespersons, or consumers.[15] Examples of sales promotion include coupons (see Figure 13.8), bonuses, and contests used to enhance the sales of a product. The term *sales promotion* should not be confused with *promotion;* sales promotion is but a part of the more comprehensive area of promotion, encompassing efforts other than personal selling, advertising, and publicity. Currently, marketers spend about half as much on sales promotion as they do on advertising. Sales promotion appears to be growing in use more than advertising.

Marketers frequently rely on sales promotion to improve the effectiveness of other promotional mix ingredients, especially advertising and personal selling. For example, some firms allocate 25 percent of their annual promotional budget to trade shows in order to introduce new products, meet key industrial personnel, and identify likely prospects.[16]

Marketers design sales promotion to produce immediate, short-run sales increases. For example, the major brewers such as Allied, Grand Metropolitan, and Whitbread use a continuous programme of a variety of sales promotion techniques to boost sales in the highly competitive beer and lager market: free drinks and prize competitions, scratch cards and trade incentives.

Generally, if a company employs advertising or personal selling, it either depends on them continuously or turns to them cyclically. However, a marketer's use of sales promotion tends to be irregular. Many products are seasonal. For example, Thomas Cook and Lunn Poly promote summer package holidays predominantly in the win-

15. This definition is adapted from John F. Luick and William L. Ziegler, *Sales Promotion and Modern Merchandising* (New York: McGraw-Hill, 1968), p. 4.

16. Roger A. Kerin and William L. Cron, "Assessing Trade Show Functions and Performance: An Exploratory Study," *Journal of Marketing,* July 1987, pp. 87–94.

ter and spring months. Qualcast pushes its lawn mowers and other gardening equipment from Easter onwards.

Now that we have discussed the basic components of an organisation's promotional mix, we need to consider how that mix is created. We must examine what factors and conditions affect the selection of the promotional methods that a specific organisation uses in its promotional mix for a particular product.

■ **Selecting Promotional Mix Ingredients**

Marketers vary the composition of promotional mixes for many reasons. Although all four ingredients can be included in a promotional mix, frequently a marketer selects fewer than four. In addition, many firms that market multiple product lines use several promotional mixes simultaneously.

An organisation's promotional mix (or mixes) is not an unchanging part of the marketing mix. Marketers can and do change the composition of their promotional mixes. The specific promotional mix ingredients employed and the intensity with which they are used depend on a variety of factors, including the organisation's promotional resources, objectives, and policies; characteristics of the target market; characteristics of the product; and cost and availability of promotional methods.

Promotional Resources, Objectives, and Policies. The quality of an organisation's promotional resources affects the number and relative intensity of promotional methods that can be included in a promotional mix. If a company's promotional budget is extremely limited, the firm is likely to rely on personal selling because it is easier to measure a salesperson's contribution to sales than to measure the effect of advertising. A business must have a sizeable promotional budget if it is to use regional or national advertising and sales promotion activities. Organisations with extensive promotional resources usually can include more ingredients in their promotional mixes. However, having larger promotional budgets does not imply that they necessarily will use a greater number of promotional methods.

An organisation's promotional objectives and policies also influence the types of promotion used. If a company's objective is to create mass awareness of a new convenience good, its promotional mix is likely to lean heavily towards advertising, sales promotion, and possibly publicity. If a company hopes to educate consumers about the features of durable goods, such as home appliances, its promotional mix may combine a moderate amount of advertising, possibly some sales promotion efforts designed to attract customers to retail stores, and a great deal of personal selling because this method is an excellent way to inform customers about these types of products. If a firm's objective is to produce immediate sales of consumer non-durables, such as paper products and many grocery goods, the promotional mix will probably stress advertising and sales promotion efforts.

Characteristics of the Target Market. The size, geographic distribution, and socio-economic characteristics of an organisation's target market also help dictate the ingredients to be included in a product's promotional mix. To some degree, market size determines the composition of the mix. If the size is quite limited, the promotional mix will probably emphasise personal selling, which can be quite effective for reaching small numbers of people. Organisations that sell to industrial markets and firms that market their products through only a few wholesalers frequently make personal selling the major component of their promotional mixes. When markets for a product consist of millions of customers, organisations use advertising and sales promotion because these methods can reach masses of people at a low cost per person. The Coca-Cola Company attempted to reach consumers through a non-traditional vehicle when it placed a commercial for diet Coke in the introduction of the home video version of the 1989 blockbuster, *Batman.* Warner Home Video, the distributor of *Batman,* believed that it would sell more than ten million copies of the videocassette, exposing millions of consumers to the diet Coke message at a low cost per person.[17]

The geographic distribution of a firm's customers can affect the combination of promotional methods used. Personal selling is more feasible if a company's customers are concentrated in a small area than if they are dispersed across a vast region. When the company's customers are numerous and dispersed, advertising may be more practical.

The distribution of a target market's socio-economic characteristics, such as age, income, or education, may dictate the types of promotional techniques that a marketer selects. For example, personal selling may be much more successful than print advertisements for communicating with less-educated people, where meaning or product attributes can be explained face to face.

Characteristics of the Product.   Generally, promotional mixes for industrial products concentrate on personal selling. In promoting consumer goods, on the other hand, advertising plays a major role. Treat this generalisation cautiously, however. Industrial goods producers do use some advertising to promote their goods, particularly in the trade press. Advertisements for computers, road-building equipment, and aircraft are not altogether uncommon, and some sales promotion is used to promote industrial goods. Personal selling is used extensively for services and consumer durables, such as home appliances, cars, and houses, and consumer convenience items are promoted mainly through advertising and sales promotion. Publicity appears in promotional mixes for industrial goods, consumer goods, and for services.

Marketers of highly seasonal products are often forced to emphasise advertising, and possibly sales promotion, because off-season sales will not support an extensive year-round sales force. Although many toy producers have sales forces to sell to resellers, a number of these companies depend to a large extent on advertising to promote their products.

The price of a product also influences the composition of the promotional mix. High-priced products call for more personal selling because consumers associate greater risk with the purchase of such products and usually want the advice of a salesperson. Few of us, for example, would be willing to purchase a refrigerator or personal computer from a self-service establishment. For low-priced convenience items, marketers use advertising rather than personal selling at the retail level. The profit margins on many of these items are too low to justify the use of salespersons, and most customers do not need advice from sales personnel when buying such products.

A further consideration in creating an effective promotional mix is the stage of the product life-cycle. During the introduction stage, a good deal of advertising may be necessary for both industrial and consumer products to make potential users aware of a new product. For many products, personal selling and sales promotion are helpful as well at this stage. In the case of consumer non-durables, the growth and

17. Marcy Magiera, "Holy Batvideo! Christmas Already?" *Advertising Age,* 11 Sept. 1989, p. 6.

maturity stages call for a heavy emphasis on advertising. Industrial products, on the other hand, often require a concentration of personal selling and some sales promotion efforts during these stages. In the decline stage, marketers usually decrease their promotional activities, especially advertising. Promotional efforts in the decline stage often centre on personal selling and sales promotion efforts.

The intensity of market coverage is still another factor affecting the composition of the promotional mix. When a product is marketed through intensive distribution, the firm depends strongly on advertising and sales promotion. A number of convenience products, such as lotions, cereals, and coffee, are promoted through samples, coupons, and cash refunds. Where marketers have opted for selective distribution, marketing mixes vary considerably as to type and amount of promotional methods. Items handled through exclusive distribution frequently demand more personal selling and less advertising. Expensive watches, furs, and high-quality furniture are typical products promoted heavily through personal selling.

A product's use also affects the combination of promotional methods. Manufacturers of highly personal products, such as non-prescription contraceptives, feminine hygiene products, and haemorrhoid treatments, count on advertising for promotion because many users do not like to talk with salespersons about such products.

Cost and Availability of Promotional Methods.   The cost of promotional methods is a major factor to analyse when developing a promotional mix. National advertising and sales promotion efforts require large expenditures. For example, in the U.K., television transmission charges for advertising in 1989 were £1,990 million and production costs were £296 million.[18] However, if the efforts are effective in reaching extremely large numbers of people, the cost per individual reached may be quite small, possibly a few pennies per person. Moreover, not all forms of advertising are expensive. Many small, local businesses advertise their products through local newspapers, magazines, radio stations, outdoor signs, and public transport.

Another consideration that marketers must explore when formulating a promotional mix is the availability of promotional techniques. Despite the tremendous number of media vehicles, a firm may find that no available advertising medium effectively reaches a certain market. For example, a personal healthcare product may be banned from being advertised on television, as are cigarettes in many countries. A stockbroker may find no suitable advertising medium for investors in Tottenham Hotspur Football Club: should he use financial publications, sports or general media? The problem of media availability becomes even more pronounced when marketers try to advertise in other countries. Some media, such as television, simply may not be available. Advertising is minimal in Scandinavia. In the U.K. only seven minutes of advertising are permitted per hour of television. The media that are available may not be open to certain types of advertisements. For example, in West Germany, advertisers were forbidden to make brand comparisons on television commercials. Other promotional methods have limitations as well. An organisation may wish to increase the size of its sales force but may be unable to find qualified personnel. In America, some state laws prohibit the use of certain types of sales promotion activities, such as contests. Such prohibited techniques are thus "unavailable" in those locales.

18. *Advertising Statistics Yearbook* (London: The Advertising Association, 1990), p. 68.

FIGURE 13.9
Comparison of push
and pull promotional
strategies

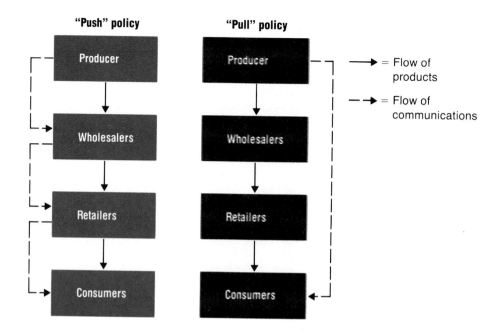

"Push" policy   **"Pull" policy**

→ = Flow of products

--→ = Flow of communications

■ Push Policy Versus Pull Policy

Another element that marketers should consider when they plan a promotional mix is whether to use a push policy or a pull policy. With a **push policy**, the producer promotes the product only to the next institution down the marketing channel. For instance, in a marketing channel with wholesalers and retailers, the producer promotes to the wholesaler because in this case the wholesaler is the channel member just below the producer (see Figure 13.9). Each channel member in turn promotes to the next channel member. A push policy normally stresses personal selling. Sometimes sales promotion and advertising are used in conjunction with personal selling to push the products down through the channel.

As Figure 13.9 shows, a firm using a **pull policy** promotes directly to consumers with the intention of developing a strong consumer demand for the products. It does so through advertising, sales promotion, and packaging that helps manufacturers build and maintain market share.[19] Because consumers are persuaded to seek the products in retail stores, retailers will in turn go to wholesalers or the producer to buy the products. The policy is thus intended to "pull" the goods down through the channel by creating demand at the consumer level.

SUMMARY

The primary role of promotion is to communicate with individuals, groups, or organisations in the environment to directly or indirectly facilitate exchanges.

Communication is a sharing of meaning. The communication process involves several steps. First, the source translates the meaning into code, a process known as

19. Alvin A. Achenbaum and F. Kent Mitchel, "Pulling Away from Push Marketing," *Harvard Business Review,* May-June 1987, p. 38.

coding or encoding. The source should employ signs familiar to the receiver or audience and choose signs that the receiver or audience uses for referring to the concepts or ideas being promoted. The coded message is sent through a medium of transmission to the receiver or audience. The receiver or audience then decodes the message and usually supplies feedback to the source. When the decoded message differs from the encoded one, a condition called noise exists.

The long-run purpose of promotion is to influence and encourage customers to accept or adopt goods, services, and ideas. The product adoption process consists of five stages. In the awareness stage, individuals become aware of the product. People move into the interest stage when they seek more information about the product. In the evaluation stage, individuals decide whether the product will meet certain criteria that are crucial for satisfying their needs. During the trial stage, the consumer actually tries the product. In the adoption stage, the consumer decides to use the product on a regular basis. Rejection of the product may occur at any stage. The adopters can be divided into five major categories—innovators, early adopters, early majority, late majority, and laggards—according to the length of time it takes them to start using a new product.

A manufacturer or retailer must establish a category need for a product. Consumers must be aware of a company's brands and have a favourable brand attitude towards the products. If the consumer decides to make a purchase, the company's overall marketing policy must guarantee distribution, suitable product quality and attributes, and set the relevant price points. These are all areas of successful promotional activity.

The promotional mix for a product may include four major promotional methods: advertising, personal selling, publicity, and sales promotion. Advertising is a paid form of non-personal communication about an organisation and its products that is transmitted to a target audience through a mass medium. Personal selling is a process of informing customers and persuading them to purchase products through personal communication in an exchange situation. Publicity is non-personal communication in news story form, regarding an organisation, its products, or both, that is transmitted through a mass medium at no charge, controlled by the public relations mechanism. Sales promotion is an activity or material that acts as a direct inducement, offering added value to or incentive for the product, to resellers, salespersons, or consumers.

There are several major determinants of what promotional methods to include in a promotional mix for a product: the organisation's promotional resources, objectives, and policies; the characteristics of the target market; the characteristics of the product; and the cost and availability of promotional methods. Marketers must also consider whether to use a push policy or a pull policy, or a combination of the two. With a push policy, the producer promotes the product only to the next institution down the marketing channel. Normally, a push policy stresses personal selling. A firm that uses a pull policy promotes directly to consumers with the intention of developing a strong consumer demand for the products. Once consumers are persuaded to seek the products in retail stores, retailers in turn go to wholesalers or the producer to buy the products.

Important Terms

Promotion
Communication
Source
Receiver
Coding process
Medium of transmission
Decoding process
Noise
Feedback
Channel capacity
Product adoption process
Innovators
Early adopters
Early majority

Late majority
Laggards
Category need
Brand awareness
Brand attitude
Brand purchase intention
Purchase facilitation
Promotional mix
Kinesic communication
Proxemic communication
Tactile communication
Push policy
Pull policy

Discussion and Review Questions

1. What is the major task of promotion? Do firms ever use promotion to accomplish this task and fail? If so, give several examples.
2. What is communication? Describe the communication process. Is it possible to communicate without using all the elements in the communication process? If so, which ones can be omitted?
3. Identify several causes of noise. How can a source reduce noise?
4. Describe the product adoption process. Under certain circumstances, is it possible for a person to omit one or more of the stages in adopting a new product? Explain your answer.
5. Describe a product that many people are in the process of adopting. Have you begun the adoption process for this product? If so, what stage have you reached?
6. What is category need? Illustrate your answer with examples.
7. Identify and briefly describe the four major promotional methods that can be included in an organisation's promotional mix. How does publicity differ from advertising?
8. What forms of interpersonal communication besides language can be used in personal selling?
9. How do market characteristics determine which promotional methods to include in a promotional mix? Assume that a company is planning to promote a cereal to both adults and children. Along what major dimensions would these two promotional efforts have to be different?
10. How can a product's characteristics affect the composition of its promotional mix?
11. Evaluate the following statement: "Appropriate advertising media are always available if a company can afford them."
12. Explain the difference between a pull policy and a push policy. Under what conditions should each policy be used?

13.1 Varta's "Green" Battery

In 1988 the U.K. market for batteries was worth £250 million and was dominated by Ever Ready and Duracell.

	Value (%)	Volume (%)
Ever Ready	49	50
Duracell	32	22
Vidor	5	7
Varta	2	3
Own-label	8	10
Others	5	8

The own-label sector (Tesco, Asda, Boots, etc.) was growing quickly, with batteries produced by Ever Ready, Duracell, and Vidor.

Environmentalists are concerned about disposed-of batteries which contain heavy, hazardous metals: zinc and mercury in zinc carbon batteries and cadmium in ni-cad rechargeable batteries. The Swiss government requires warning labels on batteries and restricts their mercury content; in 1989 the Swedish government banned all alkaline batteries; the European Community has reduced the permitted levels of heavy metal content and is to require all batteries to be sold with instructions on their safe disposal.

Varta AG is the largest battery producer in Europe, with a DM1.962 billion turnover in 1988. Varta produces all types of batteries but sales of consumer batteries outside Germany were DM726 million in 1988. German environmental groups have been powerful for many years, and Varta responded by developing technology which reduced the heavy metal content of its batteries. When these were launched in Europe in 1988, the U.K. was excluded as a market not ready to support a "green" battery.

The rapid "greening" of the U.K. government and consumers forced Varta executives to reconsider in 1989. Advertising began in the *Today* newspaper—"Like Today We Care about Tomorrow". A direct-mail campaign sent a green box containing a copy of the paperback *Green Consumers' Guide* and a packet of Varta "green mercury-free batteries that don't cost the Earth" to five hundred political, business and entertainment personalities, and key retailers.

On St David's Day a cadmium-free battery was launched. Packages containing the new product, together with two fresh leeks (the Welsh emblem), were distributed by courier. The direct mail was expanded, with packets of seeds and recycled card. Subsequent advertising targeted women, who buy the majority of household batteries. These advertisements featured a wistful baby and suggested the mother had a responsibility for making the world safe for her children. Varta's share of battery sales through grocery outlets rose to 14 percent from 9 percent as the major retailers pushed Varta's "green" batteries ahead of their own-label products. The Varta PR mechanism was quick to publicise each product improvement and promotional tactic.

SOURCES: Keynote, "Dry Batteries," 1988; *Management Today*, February 1989, pp. 56–60; *Marketing Week*, 12 May 1989, p. 55; and *Marketing*, 27 March 1989, p. 26.

Questions for Discussion

1. What were the reasons for Varta's success?
2. Why did large grocery retailers stock Varta batteries?
3. How important was promotion to Varta's success?

13.2   Branemark Dental Implants

Nobelpharma UK is a subsidiary of the Swedish ordnance and chemicals group Nobel Industries. Nobelpharma makes and supplies a range of titanium implants used for dental reconstruction. It is a world leader; all competitors' products are based on technology and clinical techniques pioneered by Nobelpharma.

In the U.K. there are ten dental schools which train a total of 600 dentists a year. Most of the 17,000 U.K. dentists work as general dental practitioners carrying out routine restorative work on teeth in dental surgeries. In addition there are 500 oral surgeons working in hospital units. The dental schools and trade press act as opinion leaders.

In 1987 Nobelpharma had a problem. Its product, the Branemark System, was superior but was not widely used. It was not compatible with traditional dentistry and its significant benefits were only apparent from inspection of a person already treated, and few such patients existed. Nobelpharma decided to provide local teams of oral surgeons with the treatment facilities and to encourage the general public to ask for the treatment from their dentists.

Media PR was the main weapon to stimulate interest among the public and general practitioners. Extensive reports appeared in all of the national press, major regional newspapers, the trade press, consumer magazines, general medical press, and on local and national television and radio. The first training course was held at Sheffield University; sales promotion—direct mail and incentives—was used to entice target dentists. A bilingual Swedish dentist toured the country, meeting general practitioners and oral surgeons in their surgeries, at seminars and exhibitions. Opinion leaders at dental schools were also "sold" the treatment. Advertising was used only to promote the training courses.

By 1988 the media PR campaign had initiated significant demand from potential customers, but few dental practices and hospital units had the necessary facilities. The company had not appreciated that its promotion would stimulate customer need rather than an immediate, favourable brand attitude in the profession. Competitors were not slow to pick up on the customer reaction; within a year 30 companies were in this market.

Nobelpharma launched a new promotional campaign to persuade dentists that its product was versatile, cost-effective, reliable and produced aesthetically pleasing results. National PR was discontinued and was replaced by a focused third-party endorsement recommendation campaign aimed at dentists. A series of information seminars under the British Dental Health Foundation targeted key opinion leaders, supported by training courses for interested general practitioners. Personal selling concentrated on the general practitioners, using two trained dentists as representatives.

Nobelpharma had still missed the oral surgeons—critical for the use of the Branemark System. Straumann UK, a major competitor, did not. By 1990, Nobelpharma was market leader by value but not by volume of implants. Its current promotion aims to increase the number of teams using Branemark, emphasising its quality and reliability. Third-party endorsement PR is still used; the sales force has been expanded and advertising is being used for the first time. The advertising stresses Nobelpharma's brand leadership and mainstream position, and includes an 0800 telephone information line on implants.

SOURCES: Nobelpharma Company Reports, 1987–1990; Branemark System promotional literature; and Chris Hunt, Warwick MBA, 1989.

Questions for Discussion

1. Is is possible to stimulate a new market without opening up opportunities for your competitors?
2. Should Nobelpharma have used advertising earlier in its promotional strategy?
3. Had Nobelpharma correctly prioritised its key target audiences?

14 ADVERTISING AND PUBLICITY

Objectives

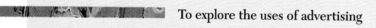

To explore the uses of advertising

To become aware of the major steps involved in developing an advertising campaign

To find out who is responsible for developing advertising campaigns

To gain an understanding of publicity

To analyse how publicity can be used

*T*wenty-five years ago Asda appeared in the Leeds area of the U.K., trading from disused cinemas and warehouses. In the late 1970s and 1980s this grocery retailer led the growth of out-of-town superstore retailing and is now the third largest food retailer in the country. To mark its twenty-fifth birthday celebrations the company launched a £1 million advertising campaign supported by publicity and sales promotion activities.

The eight-week television, radio, and press campaign created by agency Publicis had the pay-off "It 'Asda be worth celebrating" linking to the ongoing "It 'Asda be Asda" slogan initiated in 1989. The television commercial featured a Metro car, a trolley full of money, and a birthday cake—all features of the associated sales promotion. Asda gave away twenty-five Metro cars and £25,000 each week, as well as running in-store promotions with 25 percent markdowns on selected items.

In the company's north of England heartland, where Asda is well known, the campaign said "Thank you for shopping with us for 25 years." In the south of the country, the message was "We have a pedigree of 25 years." The advertising continued Asda's theme of quality and freshness but included tactical price-driven messages. ◆

Based on information in "It 'Asda Be a Celebration," Asda press release, 2 May 1990; ASDA press release, 12 September 1990; Karen Hogan, "£1m Ad Push for Asda Silver Jubilee Splash," *Marketing,* 31 May 1990, p. 9; and "Question Marks for Asda and Isosecles," *Harvest,* 1990.

T his chapter explores the many dimensions of advertising and publicity. Initially, we focus on how advertising is used. Then we examine the major steps by which an advertising campaign is developed and describe who is responsible for developing such campaigns. As we analyse publicity, we compare its characteristics with those of advertising and explore the different forms it may take. Then we consider how publicity is used and what is required for an effective public relations programme. Finally, we discuss negative publicity and some problems associated with the use of publicity.

THE NATURE OF ADVERTISING

Advertising permeates our daily lives. At times people view it positively; at other times they avoid it by taping television programmes and then zapping over the commercials with the fast-forward button of their videocassette recorders.[1] Some advertising informs, persuades, or entertains us; some of it bores, even insults, us. For example, consumer groups around the United States have been whitewashing billboards advertising tobacco products because they believe such advertisements encourage children to smoke.[2]

As mentioned in Chapter 13, **advertising** is a paid form of non-personal communication that is transmitted through mass media such as television, radio, newspapers, magazines, direct mail, public transport vehicles, and outdoor displays. An organisation can use advertising to reach a variety of audiences, ranging from small, precise groups, such as the stamp collectors of the Highlands, to extremely large audiences, such as all the buyers of trainers in the U.K.

When people are asked to name major advertisers, most immediately mention business organisations. (See Table 14.1 for a listing of the top ten advertisers by country in Europe for 1989–1990.) However, many types of organisations—including governments, churches, universities, civic groups, and charitable organisations—take advantage of advertising. For example, the U.K. government is one of the largest advertisers: "Heroin Screws You Up", Employment Training, the DTI Enterprise Initiative, etc. So even though we analyse advertising here in the context of business organisations, remember that much of what we say applies to all types of organisations.

Marketers sometimes give advertising more credit than it deserves. This attitude causes them to use advertising when they should not. For example, manufacturers of basic products such as sugar, flour, and salt often try to differentiate their products with minimal success. However, over the years, Saxa has tried to position its salt as different from the competition with the advertising slogan "Saxa Table Salt—lets the flavour flow".

Under certain conditions, advertising can work effectively for an organisation. The questions in Table 14.2 raise some general points that a marketer should consider when assessing the potential value of advertising as an ingredient in a product's promotional mix. The list is not all-inclusive. Numerous factors have a bearing on whether advertising should be used at all, and if so, to what extent.

1. *Students' Briefs* (London: The Advertising Association, 1988).

2. "CBS This Morning," CBS (TV), 11 April 1990.

TABLE 14.1 *Top ten advertisers by country in Europe, 1989–1990*

FRANCE

Renault
PSA Peugeot
Procter & Gamble
Henkel
PSA Citroën
SOPAD (Nestlé)
Volkswagen-VW
Fiat
Colgate-Palmolive
France Loto

BELGIUM

GB-Inno-BM
Opel (GM)
Ford
Toyota
Nissan
Renault
Volkswagen
Gervay-Danone
Philip Morris
Citroën

SPAIN

Renault
Government Depts.
El Corte Ingles (dept. store)
Citroën
Peugeot
ONCE (society for the blind)
Repsol (oil company)
Banco Bilbao Vizcaya
Pascual (drinks)
Onlae (national lottery)

NORWAY

Norske Meierier
Toyota
VAG
General Motors
SAS
Statens Info. Tjeneste
Denofa Lilleborg
Volvo
Ford
Hjemmet

GERMANY

Post, Bonn (Telecoms)
C&A Brenninkmeyer
Procter & Gamble
Henkel
Springer-Verlag
Opel (GM)
Ferrero
Daimler-Benz
Jacobs-Suchard
Effem

NETHERLANDS

Bergh & Jurgens
Rijksvoorlichtingsdienst
Philips
Procter & Gamble
Postbank
Douwe Egberts
Albert Heyn
PTT
Henkel
Nederlands Zuivel Bureau

FINLAND

SP Bank
Valio
Kesko
Aro-Yhtyma Cars
Korpivaara Cars
Veho Cars
OP Bank
Philips
OP-Kiinteistokeskus
Haka Autos

ITALY

Procter & Gamble
Fiat
Ferrero
Sagit
Barilla
Alfa-Lancia
Perfetti
Lever
Standa
Renault

DENMARK

FDB Co-op
Magasin Dept. Store
Dansk Supermarket
Aller Publisher
Lever
Illums Dept. Store
SAS
MD Foods
Kellogg's
Carlsberg

U.K.

Procter & Gamble
Lever Brothers
Kellogg's
British Telecom
Ford
Nestlé
Mars
Rover Group
Kraft General Foods
Gallaher Tobacco

SWEDEN

Kooperativa Fonbund
ICA
Ahlens
Hennes & Mauritz
Televerket
Volvo
Samhallsinformation
Philipsons Bil
B&W Stormarknader
VAG

SOURCE: "The Campaign Report," *Campaign,* 30 November 1990, pp. 1–24.

TABLE 14.2   *Some issues to consider when deciding whether to use advertising*

1. **Does the product possess unique, important features?**

   Although homogeneous products such as cigarettes, petrol, and beer have been advertised successfully, they usually require considerably more effort and expense than other products. On the other hand, products that are differentiated on physical rather than psychological dimensions are much easier to advertise. Even so, "being different" is rarely enough. The advertisability of product features is enhanced when buyers believe that those unique features are important and useful.

2. **Are "hidden qualities" important to buyers?**

   If by viewing, feeling, tasting, or smelling the product buyers can learn all there is to know about the product and its benefits, advertising will have less chance of increasing demand. Conversely, if not all product benefits are apparent to consumers on inspection and use of the product, advertising has more of a story to tell, and the probability that it can be profitably used increases. The "hidden quality" of vitamin C in oranges once helped explain why Sunkist oranges could be advertised effectively, whereas the advertising of lettuce has been a failure.

3. **Is the general demand trend for the product favourable?**

   If the generic product category is experiencing a long-term decline, it is less likely that advertising can be used successfully for a particular brand within the category.

4. **Is the market potential for the product adequate?**

   Advertising can be effective only when there are sufficient actual or prospective users of the brand in the target market.

5. **Is the competitive environment favourable?**

   The size and marketing strength of competitors and their brand shares and loyalty will greatly affect the possible success of an advertising campaign. For example, a marketing effort to compete successfully against Kodak film, Heinz baked beans, or Campbell soups would demand much more than simply advertising.

6. **Are general economic conditions favourable for marketing the product?**

   The effects of an advertising programme and the sale of all products are influenced by the overall state of the economy and by specific business conditions. For example, it is much easier to advertise and sell luxury leisure products (stereos, sailing boats, video cameras) when disposable income is high.

7. **Is the organisation able and willing to spend the money required to launch an advertising campaign?**

   As a general rule, if the organisation is unable or unwilling to undertake an advertising expenditure that as a percentage of the total amount spent in the product category is at least equal to the market share it desires, advertising is less likely to be effective.

8. **Does the firm possess sufficient marketing expertise to market the product?**

   The successful marketing of any product involves a complex mixture of product and consumer research, product development, packaging, pricing, financial management, promotion, and distribution. Weakness in any area of marketing is an obstacle to the successful use of advertising.

SOURCE: Adapted from Charles H. Patti, "Evaluating the Role of Advertising, " *Journal of Advertising,* Fall 1977, pp. 32–33. Reprinted by permission of the Journal of Advertising.

THE USES OF ADVERTISING

Advertising can serve a variety of purposes. Individuals and organisations use it to promote products and organisations, to stimulate demand, to offset competitors' advertising, to make salespersons more effective, to increase the uses of a product, to remind and reinforce customers, and to reduce sales fluctuations (see Figure 14.1).

■ **Promoting Products and Organisations**

Advertising is used to promote goods, services, ideas, images, issues, people, and indeed anything that the advertiser wants to publicise or foster. Depending on what is being promoted, advertising can be classified as institutional or product advertising. **Institutional advertising** promotes organisational images, ideas, or political issues. For example, some of Seagram's advertising promotes the idea that drinking and driving do not mix, in order to create and develop a socially responsible image. Hanson Trust and BOC have successfully used advertising to explain and promote their different subsidiaries and products: their corporate composition.

Product advertising promotes goods and services. Business, government, and private non-business organisations turn to it to promote the uses, features, images, and benefits of their products. When Monsanto introduced a new pesticide to help farmers clean up weeds in the post-harvest stubble, it used press advertising to tout the benefits of Sting CT, including a competition (a trip to Italy) and a coupon to send off for further technical details of the product.

■ **Stimulating Primary and Selective Demand**

When a specific firm is the first to introduce an innovation, it tries to stimulate *primary demand*—demand for a product category rather than a specific brand of the product—through pioneer advertising. **Pioneer advertising** informs people about a product: what it is, what it does, how it can be used, and where it can be purchased. Because pioneer advertising is used in the introductory stage of the product life cycle when there are no competitive brands, it neither emphasises the brand name nor compares brands. The first company to introduce the compact disc player, for instance, initially tried to stimulate primary demand by emphasising the benefits of compact disc players in general rather than the benefits of its brand. Product advertising is also used sometimes to stimulate primary demand for an established product. Occasionally, an industry trade group, rather than a single firm, sponsors advertisements to stimulate primary demand. For example, to stimulate demand for milk, the Milk Marketing Board sponsors advertisements that demonstrate how healthy and nice it is to drink (see Figure 14.2).

To build *selective demand,* or demand for a specific brand, an advertiser turns to competitive advertising. **Competitive advertising** points out a brand's uses, features, and advantages that benefit consumers but may not be available in competing brands. For example, Volvo heavily promotes the safety and crash-worthiness of Volvo cars in its advertising.

Another form of competitive advertising is **comparative advertising**, in which two or more brands are compared on the basis of one or more product attributes. Companies must not, however, misrepresent the qualities or characteristics of the comparison product.

■ **Offsetting Competitors' Advertising**

When marketers advertise to offset or lessen the effects of a competitor's promotional programme, they are using **defensive advertising**. Although defensive advertising does not necessarily increase a company's sales or market share, it may prevent a loss in these areas. For example, when McDonald's test-marketed pizza in

FIGURE 14.1
*Major uses of
advertising*

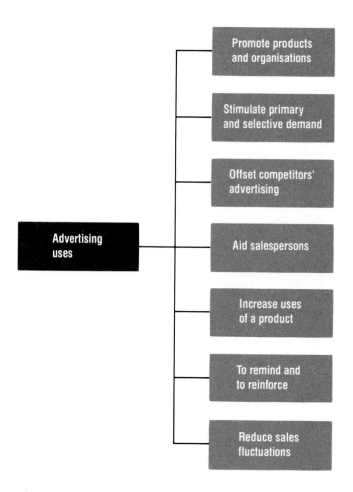

Advertising uses

- Promote products and organisations
- Stimulate primary and selective demand
- Offset competitors' advertising
- Aid salespersons
- Increase uses of a product
- To remind and to reinforce
- Reduce sales fluctuations

Evansville, Indiana, and Owensboro, Kentucky, Pizza Hut countered with defensive advertising to protect its market share and sales. Pizza Hut advertised both on television and in newspapers in the two test cities, emphasising that its product is made from scratch while McDonald's uses frozen dough.[3] Defensive advertising is used most often by firms in extremely competitive consumer product markets, such as the fast-food industry.

■ **Making
Salespersons
More Effective**

Business organisations that stress personal selling often use advertising to improve the effectiveness of sales personnel. Advertising created specifically to support personal selling activities tries to pre-sell a product to buyers by informing them about its uses, features, and benefits and by encouraging them to contact local dealers or sales representatives. This form of advertising helps salespeople find good sales prospects. Advertising is often designed to support personal selling efforts for industrial products, insurance, and consumer durables, such as cars and major household appliances. For example, advertising may bring a prospective buyer to a showroom, but usually a salesperson plays a key role in closing the sale.

3. Scott Hume, "Pizza Hut Is Frosted; New Ad Takes Slap at McDonald's Test Product," *Advertising Age,* 18 Sept. 1989, p. 4.

FIGURE 14.2
Stimulating primary demand.
By advertising its new Milk Can, the Milk Marketing Board is attempting to stimulate primary demand for its product.

SOURCE: Milk Can is a trademark of the Milk Marketing Board

■ **Increasing the Uses of a Product**

The absolute demand for any product is limited because people in a market will consume only so much of it. Given both this limit on demand and competitive conditions, marketers can increase sales of a specific product in a defined geographic market only to a certain point. To improve sales beyond this point, they must either enlarge the geographic market and sell to more people or develop and promote a larger number of uses for the product. If a firm's advertising convinces buyers to use its products in more ways, then the sales of the products go up. For example, Nabisco, the U.S. manufacturer of Shredded Wheat, used advertising to inform consumers that Shredded Wheat contains no added sugar and is high in natural fibre, essential to a healthy, balanced diet. The company is thus attempting to position Shredded Wheat as a part of a wholesome diet, as well as a popular children's cereal. When promoting new uses, an advertiser attempts to increase the demand for its own brand without driving up the demand for competing brands.

■ **Reminding and Reinforcing Customers**

Marketers sometimes employ **reminder advertising** to let consumers know that an established brand is still around and that it has certain uses, characteristics, and benefits. Procter & Gamble, for example, reminds consumers that its Crest toothpaste is still the best one for preventing cavities. **Reinforcement advertising**, on

FIGURE 14.3
General steps for
developing and im-
plementing an ad-
vertising campaign

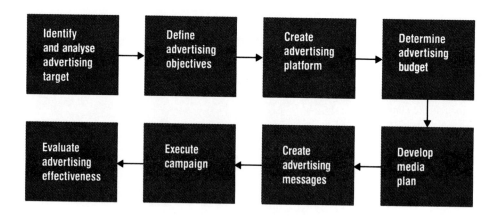

the other hand, tries to assure current users that they have made the right choice and tells them how to get the most satisfaction from the product. The aim of both reminder and reinforcement advertising is to prevent a loss in sales or market share.

■ **Reducing
Sales Fluctuations**

The demand for many products varies from month to month because of such factors as climate, holidays, seasons, and customs. A business, however, cannot operate at peak efficiency when sales fluctuate rapidly. Changes in sales volume translate into changes in the production or inventory, personnel, and financial resources required. To the extent that marketers can generate sales during slow periods, they can smooth out the fluctuations. When advertising reduces fluctuations, a manager can use the firm's resources more efficiently.

Advertising is often designed to stimulate sales during sales slumps. For example, advertisements promoting price reductions of lawn-care equipment or package holidays can increase sales during the winter months. On occasions, a business advertises that customers will get better service by coming in on certain days rather than others. During peak sales periods, a marketer may refrain from advertising to prevent over-stimulating sales to the point where the firm cannot handle all the demand. For example, coupons for the delivery of pizza are often valid only for Monday to Thursday, not Friday to Sunday, which are the peak delivery days.

A firm's use of advertising depends on the firm's objectives, resources, and environmental forces. The degree to which advertising accomplishes the marketer's goals depends in large part on the advertising campaign.

DEVELOPING AN ADVERTISING CAMPAIGN

An **advertising campaign** involves designing a series of advertisements and placing them in various advertising media to reach a particular target market. As Figure 14.3 indicates, the major steps in creating an advertising campaign are (1) identifying and analysing the advertising target, (2) defining the advertising objectives, (3) creating the advertising platform or property, (4) determining the advertising budget, (5) developing the media plan, (6) creating the advertising message, (7) executing the campaign, and (8) evaluating the effectiveness of the advertising. The number of steps and the exact order in which they are carried out may vary according to an organisation's resources, the nature of its product, the types of target markets or audiences to be reached, and the advertising agency selected.[4] These general guidelines for developing an advertising campaign are appropriate for all types of organisations.

■ Identifying and Analysing the Advertising Target

The **advertising target** is the group of people at which advertisements are aimed. For example, the target audience for Special K and All-Bran cereals is health-conscious adults. Identifying and analysing the advertising target are critical processes; the information they yield helps determine the other steps in developing the campaign. The advertising target often includes everyone in a firm's target market. Marketers may, however, seize some opportunities to slant a campaign at only a portion of the target market.

Advertisers analyse advertising targets to establish an information base for a campaign. Information commonly needed includes the location and geographic distribution of the target group; the distribution of age, income, ethnic origin, sex, and education; and consumer attitudes regarding the purchase and use of both the advertiser's products and competing products. The exact kinds of information that an organisation will find useful depend on the type of product being advertised, the characteristics of the advertising target, and the type and amount of competition. Generally, the more advertisers know about the advertising target, the more likely they are to develop an effective advertising campaign. When the advertising target is not precisely identified and properly analysed, the campaign may not succeed.

■ Defining the Advertising Objectives

The advertiser's next step is to consider what the firm hopes to accomplish with the campaign. Because advertising objectives guide campaign development, advertisers should define their objectives carefully to ensure that the campaign will achieve what they want. Advertising campaigns based on poorly defined objectives seldom succeed.

Advertising objectives should be stated clearly, precisely, and in measurable terms. Precision and measurability allow advertisers to evaluate advertising success: to judge, at the campaign's end, whether the objectives have been met, and if so, how well. To provide precision and measurability, advertising objectives should contain bench-marks—the current condition or position of the firm—and indicate how far and in what direction the advertiser wishes to move from these bench-marks. For example, the advertiser should state the current sales level (the bench-mark) and the amount of sales increase that is sought through advertising. An advertising objective also should specify a time frame, so that advertisers know exactly how long they have to accomplish the objective. Thus an advertiser with average monthly sales of £450,000 (the bench-mark) might set the following objective: "Our primary advertising objective is to increase average monthly sales from £450,000 to £540,000 within twelve months." This also tells the advertiser when evaluation of the campaign should begin.

If an advertiser defines objectives by sales, the objectives focus on raising absolute monetary sales, increasing sales by a certain percentage, or increasing the firm's market share. Alberto Culver decided to pump £12.5 million into advertising its

4. Torin Douglas, *The Complete Guide to Advertising* (London: Macmillan, 1985).

haircare brands in 1990, mainly to revitalise Alberto VO5 shampoo and conditioners. Spend on VO5 alone was to double to £5 million to relaunch the brand, which the company believed had lost its way.[5] However, even though an advertiser's long-run goal is to increase sales, not all campaigns are designed to produce immediate sales. Some campaigns are designed to increase product or brand awareness, make consumers' attitudes more favourable, or increase consumers' knowledge of a product's features. These objectives are stated in terms of communication. For example, when Apple Computers introduced home computers, its initial campaign did not focus on sales but on creating brand awareness and educating consumers about the features and uses of home computers. A specific communication objective might be to increase product feature awareness from 0 to 40 percent in the target market by the end of six months.

■ Creating the Advertising Platform

Before launching a political campaign, party leaders develop a political platform, which states the major issues that will be the basis of the campaign. Like a political platform, an **advertising platform** consists of the basic issues or selling points that an advertiser wishes to include in the advertising campaign. A single advertisement in an advertising campaign may contain one or several issues in the platform. Although the platform sets forth the basic issues, it does not indicate how they should be presented.

A marketer's advertising platform should consist of issues that are important to consumers. One of the best ways to determine what those issues are is to survey consumers about what they consider most important in the selection and use of the product involved. For example, Procter & Gamble is testing refill packages for some of its cleaning products. The refill packages provide a unique benefit by not adding to solid-waste disposal problems.[6] Environmentally conscious consumers will consider this a positive selling feature. The selling features of a product must not only be important to consumers; if possible, they should also be features that competitive products do not have.

Although research is the most effective method for determining the issues of an advertising platform, it is expensive. As a result, the advertising platform is most commonly based on the opinions of personnel within the firm and of individuals in the advertising agency, if an agency is used. This trial-and-error approach generally leads to some successes and some failures.

Because the advertising platform is a base on which to build the message, marketers should analyse this stage carefully. A campaign can be perfect as to the selection and analysis of its advertising target, the statement of its objectives, its media strategy, and the form of its message. But the campaign will still fail if the advertisements communicate information that consumers do not consider important when they select and use the product.

■ Determining the Advertising Budget

The **advertising budget** is the total amount of money that a marketer allocates for advertising for a specific time period. It is difficult to decide how much to spend on advertising for a specific period of time because there is no way to measure what the precise effects of spending a certain amount of money on advertising will be.

5. "Alberto Bounces Back," *Marketing*, 24 May 1990, p. 2.

6. Laurie Freeman, "P&G to Unveil Refill Package," *Advertising Age*, 6 Nov. 1989, pp. 1, 69.

Many factors affect a firm's decision about how much to spend for advertising. The geographic size of the market and the distribution of buyers within the market have a great bearing on this decision. Both the type of product being advertised and a firm's sales volume relative to competitors' sales volumes also play a part in determining what proportion of a firm's revenue is spent on advertising. Advertising budgets for industrial products are usually quite small relative to the sales of the products, whereas consumer convenience items, such as soft drinks, soaps, and cosmetics, generally have large budgets. The U.K. launch of Ragu pasta sauce had a budget of £2 million, for two weeks' advertising and below-the-line support. Marketing Update 14.1 describes one firm's success in negotiating a pan-European airtime advertising discount.

Of the many techniques used to determine the advertising budget, one of the most logical is the **objective and task approach**. Using this approach, marketers initially determine the objectives that a campaign is to achieve and then attempt to list the tasks required to accomplish them. The costs of the tasks are then calculated and added to arrive at the amount of the total budget. This approach has one main problem: marketers usually find it hard to estimate the level of effort needed to achieve certain objectives. A coffee marketer, for example, might find it extremely difficult to determine how much to increase national television advertising to raise a brand's market share from 8 to 12 percent. Because of this problem, advertisers do not widely use the objective and task approach.

In the more widely used **percentage of sales approach**, marketers simply multiply a firm's past sales, plus a factor for planned sales growth or declines, by a standard percentage that is based on both what the firm traditionally spends on advertising and what the industry averages. This approach has one major flaw: it is based on the incorrect assumption that sales create advertising, rather than the reverse. Consequently, a marketer using the approach at a time of declining sales will reduce the amount spent on advertising. But such a reduction may further diminish sales. Though illogical, this technique has gained wide acceptance because it is easy to use and less disruptive competitively; it stabilises a firm's market share within an industry. However, in times of declining sales, many firms do increase their contribution to advertising in the hope of reversing the decline.

Another way to determine the advertising budget is the **competition-matching approach**. Marketers who follow this approach try to match their major competitors' budgets in terms of pounds or to allocate the same percentage of sales for advertising as their competitors do. Although a wise marketer should be aware of what competitors spend on advertising, this technique should not be used by itself because a firm's competitors probably have different advertising objectives and different resources available for advertising. Many companies and advertising agencies engage in quarterly competitive spending reviews, comparing competitors' expenditures in print, radio, and television with their own spending levels. Competitive tracking of this nature occurs at both the national and regional levels.

At times, marketers use the **arbitrary approach**: a high-level executive in the firm states how much can be spent on advertising for a certain time period. The arbitrary approach often leads to under-spending or over-spending. Although hardly a scientific budgeting technique, it is expedient.

Establishing the advertising budget is critically important. If it is set too low, the campaign cannot achieve its full potential for stimulating demand. When too much money is appropriated for advertising, over-spending results, and financial resources are wasted.

PAN-EUROPEAN AIRTIME DISCOUNTING

Central and Anglia Television's airtime sales arm TSMS has negotiated with Italian media magnate Silvio Berlusconi a pan-European discount deal for television advertising with Gillette. The deal gives Gillette volume discounts across Berlusconi's Italian, French, German, and Spanish TV stations. The co-ordination of Gillette's overall TV-buying strategy is handled from London by Gillette's European advertising agency BBDO.

The pan-European deal gives Gillette an overall audience potential of 124 million, but it also demonstrates a belief that the practical difficulties of co-ordinating four advertising agencies, television stations, and Gillette marketing operations across Europe can be overcome. Other major European advertisers are expected to follow the lead of TSMS and Gillette.

In the U.K., BBDO, following its merger with Abbott Mead Vickers and the sharp down-turn in media spending during the early 1990s, had shed 50 staff in London. BBDO is particularly dependent on its multinational Pepsi, Gillette, Wrigley, and Alberto Culver business. In the U.K., Gillette's Sensor shaving range with BBDO's "best a man can get" theme is receiving a £6 million boost: hefty promotional support for a six-month campaign.

SOURCE: "Gillette's Sharp Deal in Europe," *Marketing,* 2 August 1990, p. 11; Mark Edwards, "Carat Group-Buying," *Campaign,* 2 November 1990, p. 2; Raymond Snoddy, "Europe-wide Advertising Deal Agreed," *Financial Times,* 1 August 1990, p. 8d; Susan Bidlake, "BBDO Sheds Staff in Merger," *Marketing,* 14 February 1991, p. 4; "Stop Press," *Marketing,* 14 February 1991, p. 5.

Developing the Media Plan

As Table 14.3 shows, advertisers spend tremendous amounts of money on advertising media. These amounts have grown rapidly during the past two decades. To derive the maximum results from media expenditures, a marketer must develop an effective media plan. A **media plan** sets forth the exact media vehicles to be used (specific magazines, television channels, newspapers, and so forth) and the dates and times that the advertisements will appear. The effectiveness of the plan determines how many people in the advertising target will be exposed to the message. It also determines, to some degree, the effects of the message on those individuals. Media planning is a complex task that requires thorough analysis of the advertising target as well as any legal restrictions that might apply (see Marketing Update 14.2).

To formulate a media plan, the planner selects the media for a campaign and draws up a time schedule for each medium. The media planner's primary goal is to reach the largest number of persons in the advertising target per pound spent on media. In addition, a secondary goal is to achieve the appropriate message reach and frequency for the target audience while staying within the budget. *Reach* refers to the percentage of consumers in the advertising target actually exposed to a particular advertisement in a stated time period. *Frequency* is the number of times these targeted consumers were exposed to the advertisement.

Media planners begin with rather broad decisions; eventually, however, they must make very specific choices. A planner must first decide which kinds of media to use: radio, television, newspapers, magazines, direct mail, outdoor displays, public transport, or a combination of two or more of these. After making the general media decision, the planner selects specific sub-classes within each medium. Estee Lauder, for example, might advertise its Clinique cosmetic line in women's magazines, as well as during day-time, prime-time, and late night television.

Media planners take many factors into account as they devise a media plan. They analyse the location and demographic characteristics of people in the advertising target because the various media appeal to particular demographic groups in particular locations. For example, there are radio stations directed mainly at teenagers, magazines for men in the 18 to 34 age group, and television programmes aimed at adults of both sexes. Media planners should also consider the size and type of audiences that specific media reach. Several data services collect and periodically publish information about the circulations and audiences of various media.

The cost of media is an important but troublesome consideration. Planners try to obtain the best coverage possible for each pound spent, yet there is no accurate way of comparing the cost and impact of a television commercial with the cost and impact of a newspaper advertisement.

The content of the message sometimes affects the choice of media. Print media can be used more effectively than broadcast media to present many issues or numerous details. The makers of Tartare Light Fromage Frais produce wordy magazine advertisements including recipes as well as product details to boost demand and educate consumers about the product's uses. The advertisements appear in most women's and food magazines. If an advertiser wants to promote beautiful colours, patterns, or textures, media that offer high-quality colour reproduction—magazines or television—should be used instead of newspapers. For example, cosmetics can be effectively promoted in a full-colour magazine advertisement, but the ad would be far less effective in black and white. Compare the black and white and colour versions of the advertisement in Figure 14.4.

TABLE 14.3 *Top advertisers in the U.K.*

TOP 10 SPENDING BRANDS 1989

Position 1989	Position 1988	Brand	Agency/Media Buyer	Press (£000s)	TV (£000s)	Total (£000s)
1	–	Water authorities	Collett Dickenson Pearce (CDP)	10,840	11,633	22,472
2	3	Woolworths	BSB Dorland/Zenith	11,635	9,486	21,121
3	–	Sky Television	Arc Advertising	12,990	5,080	18,020
4	–	Water and sewage	DMB&B	4,247	12,019	16,266
5	2	B&Q	BSB Dorland/Zenith	13,041	2,200	15,242
6	8	McDonald's	Leo Burnett	285	14,028	14,312
7	1	MFI/Hygena	Index Advertising/Geers	12,494	1,661	14,155
8	5	Currys	Saatchi and Saatchi/Zenith	13,706	344	14,050
9	9	B&H Special Kingsize	Collett Dickenson Pearce (CDP)	13,617	0	13,617
10	43	Tesco	Lowe Howard-Spink (LH-S)	10,193	3,105	13,298

TOP 10 SPENDERS 1989

Position 1988	Position 1989	Company	Billings (£000s) 1989	Billings (£000s) 1988	Change (%)	Number of brands 1989	Number of brands 1988
1	1	Unilever	81,356	68,435	18.9	24	25
2	2	Procter & Gamble	71,422	64,703	10.4	20	18
3	5	Kellogg	48,353	42,990	12.5	13	13
4	4	Kingfisher	47,974	44,241	8.4	3	3
5	3	Mars[1]	46,009	59,053	−22.1	14	17
6	–	Water authorities	38,738	(–)	(–)	2	–
7	–	News International	36,531	14,828	146.4	6	4
8	6	Nestlé[2]	31,405	37,524	−16.3	8	12
9	10	Rover Group	31,147	26,143	19.1	6	5
10	9	British Telecom	30,442	27,029	12.6	5	4
Total spend (top 10)			**463,377**	**429,663[3]**	**7.8**	**91**	**96[3]**

TOP 10 PRESS SPENDERS

Position[4]		Brands	Agency/Media Buyer	Press 1989 (£000s)	Press 1988 (£000s)	Change (%)
1	(3)	Currys	Saatchis/Zenith	13,706	13,137	4.33
2	(5)	B&H Special Kingsize	CDP	13,617	11,415	19.30
3	(4)	B&Q	BSB Dorland/Zenith	13,041	12,363	5.49
4	(–)	Sky	Arc Advertising	12,940		
5	(1)	MFI/Hygena	Index Advertising/Geers Gross	12,494	16,618	−24.82
6	(2)	Dixons	Saatchis/Zenith	11,718	13,585	−13.74
7	(6)	Woolworths	BSB Dorland/Zenith	11,635	11,076	5.04
8	(–)	Water share offer	CDP	10,840		
9	(8)	Texas Homecare	Hilton/MGr	10,517	7,960	32.13
10	(–)	Tesco	LH-S	10,193	5,162	97.45
Total				**120,701**	**108,755[5]**	**11.00**

TABLE 14.3 *continued*

TOP 10 TV SPENDERS 1989

Position[6]		Brand	Agency/Media Buyer	TV 1989 (£000s)	TV 1988 (£000s)	Change (%)
1	(1)	McDonald's	Leo Burnett	14,028	11,685	20.04
2	(–)	Water sewage businesses	DMB&B	12,019		
3	(–)	Water share offer	CDP	11,633		
4	(5)	BT call stimulation	JWT/IDK/CIA Billett	10,944	8,184	33.73
5	(–)	Woolworths	BSB Dorland/Zenith	9,486	5,171	83.46
6	(7)	Ariel Automatic Powder	Saatchis	8,978	8,030	11.80
7	(–)	Yellow Pages	Abbott Mead Vickers/IDK	8,909	5,078	75.45
8	(–)	Carlsberg Pilsner Lager	KHBB/Zenith	8,485	5,460	55.41
9	(8)	NDC/MMB Milk	BMP DDB Needham	8,063		
10	(–)	Maxwell House	DMB&B/Zenith	7,847	3,627	116.35
Total				**100,329**	**88,297**[7]	**13.70**

TOP SPENDING CATEGORIES 1989

Position 1988	Position 1989	Category	Press 1989 (£000s)	Change (%)	TV 1989 (£000s)	Change (%)	Total 1989 (£000s)	Change (%)
1	1	Financial	329,628	8.3	185,399	14.3	515,027	10.4
2	2	Food	77,401	2.0	374,138	2.6	451,539	2.5
4	3	Motors	298,936	25.4	134,984	12.5	433,921	21.1
3	4	Retail	282,230	0.6	139,635	1.8	421,866	1.0
5	5	Business to business	337,789	20.1	5,216	–13.5	343,006	19.4
6	6	Drink	61,214	12.2	180,102	12.0	241,316	12.1
8	7	Cosmetics and toiletries	56,144	19.4	134,083	19.1	190,228	19.2
7	8	Household stores	10,797	17.7	156,508	3.9	167,305	4.7
9	9	Travel	122,808	10.5	43,985	–1.8	166,794	7.0
11	10	Publishing and broadcasting	65,926	53.5	99,467	12.3	165,393	25.8

[1] Including Pedigree
[2] Including Rowntree
[3] Last year's top 10 spenders' billings and brands
[4] Figures in brackets show position in the 1988 top ten press brands.
[5] 1988 top ten press spend
[6] Figures in brackets show position in 1988 top ten TV brands.
[7] 1988 top ten TV spend

SOURCE: *Marketing,* 1 March 1990. Reproduced by permission of *Marketing.*

Table 14.4 provides data on the relative amounts of advertising expenditure in Europe by media. The data indicate that different countries give more priority to certain types of advertising media. The medium selected is determined by the characteristics, advantages, and disadvantages of the major media available (see Table 14.5).

Given the variety of vehicles within each medium, media planners must deal with a vast number of choices. The multitude of factors that affect media rates obviously adds to the complexity of media planning. A **cost comparison indicator** lets an

EC ADVERTISING LEGISLATION

Already Here

Existing European legislation

Cross-frontier broadcasting directive The broadcasting directive which was agreed in October 1988 is designed to liberalise the transmission of TV channels across national frontiers. TV also sets minimum controls on advertising. Originally, Germany and other member states pressed for highly restrictive rules on advertising "minutage" around programmes. But the directive enshrines a relatively liberal ITV-style system.

TV tobacco advertising is banned by the directive, which must be implemented within two years. It includes IBA-style controls on alcohol advertising and guidelines for advertising to children and sponsorship.

Misleading advertising directive Adopted in 1984, the directive provides procedures for the control of misleading advertising. It prohibits the use of misleading information about products or advertisers. It requires member states to have a supervisory body with legal powers to regulate misleading advertising, but allows for self-regulation.

On the Way

Proposed European legislation

Tobacco advertising directive Proposed in March, the directive puts forward a ban on "creative" ad campaigns. Press and poster ads would be restricted to pack shots on blank backgrounds, plus health warnings taking up to 20 percent of space. The European Parliament has taken a tougher stance by backing a total ban.

Food claims The commission is pushing for a formal directive on food claims in advertising, banning the use of nutritional claims which cannot be substantiated.

Pharmaceutical directive Details on the active ingredients and recommended use of branded over-the-counter drugs must be carried in ads.

Comparative advertising The commission is circulating a preliminary text to amend the existing directive on misleading advertising to encourage direct comparisons between competing products and services. Ads will be allowed to mention competitors and their products, as long as they are fair and stick to verifiable facts.

In the Future

Alcohol The Council of Europe, which operates separately from the EC, is considering proposals that would ban all TV alcohol ads carried by channels operating in its 23 member states. But there is little chance that they will come into effect.

Financial services There have been calls from MEPs to restrict advertising of financial services across all media. Loans and mortgages offered in non-domestic currencies are current targets of MEPs' attention.

Car advertising Discussions on road safety within the EC include car advertising. Failed proposals to ban references to maximum speeds and acceleration in car ads may be resurrected.

Environmental labelling The commission is considering a system of labelling products which are considered environmentally benign.

Portrayal of women Controversy over the portrayal of women in several member states could spill over into the EC as the European Parliament's women's rights committee presses for a review of sexism in the media.

Country by Country . . .

U.K. *Ad restrictions agreed by media owners and advertisers face stricter Euro-laws on tobacco and alcohol.*

Germany *Advertising to children has become "an issue." But strict limits on TV ad breaks will crumble under EC legislation.*

France *A total ban on tobacco ads is expected to become law this summer. TV alcohol ads are already banned.*

Italy *A ban on tobacco advertising already exists. Proposed new drink laws restrict alcohol ads, mainly for spirits.*

Spain *Already bans tobacco advertising. TV alcohol ad controls are also being tightened.*

Greece *A ban on toy advertising on television is already in place. Tobacco and ads for medicines are banned.*

Belgium *Bans on-TV tobacco advertising. But restrictions on ads for certain types of alcoholic drinks have been liberalised.*

Portugal *Tight controls on tobacco ads, with time restrictions on alcohol ads.*

Holland *TV tobacco ads are out, alcohol and sweets ads face time restrictions.*

Denmark *TV bans on tobacco advertising, medicines and all but the weakest alcohol products.*

Ireland *Broadcast ad controls largely mirror the U.K. But a ban on press ads for abortion advice clinics still causes some problems.*

Luxembourg *Hard liquor ads are allowed on TV, but sole state broadcaster RTL imposes its own ban on tobacco products.*

SOURCE: *Marketing*, 2 August 1990. Reprinted by permission of *Marketing*.

FIGURE 14.4 *Comparison of black and white and colour advertisements.*
This example highlights the importance of selecting the right media for a message. This advert ran in *Vogue* in full colour.
SOURCE: Visage Beauté Cosmetics, Inc. P.O. Box 10928, B.H., CA 90213

advertiser compare the costs of several vehicles within a specific medium (such as two newspapers) in relation to the number of persons reached by each vehicle. For example, the "milline rate" is the cost comparison indicator for newspapers; it shows the cost of exposing a million persons to a space equal to one agate line.[7]

■ **Creating the Advertising Message**

The basic content and form of an advertising message are a function of several factors. The product's features, uses, and benefits affect the content of the message. Characteristics of the people in the advertising target—their sex, age, education, ethnic origin, income, occupation, and other attributes—influence both the content and form. When Procter & Gamble promotes its Crest toothpaste to children, the company emphasises the importance of daily brushing and decay control. When Crest is marketed to adults, tartar and plaque are discussed. To communicate effectively, an advertiser must use words, symbols, and illustrations that are meaningful, familiar, and attractive to the people who constitute the advertising target.

7. An agate line is one column wide and the height of the smallest type normally used in classified newspaper advertisements. There are fourteen agate lines in one column inch.

TABLE 14.4 *Relative percentages of advertising expenditure in Europe, by media, 1990*

	France	Germany	Italy	Spain	U.K.	Belgium	Netherlands	Denmark	Norway	Finland	Sweden
TV	25	13	47	32.8	31	26	13.6	7.7	1.5	11	–
Press	51	78	44.2	57.4	62.8	57	73.6	87.1	94.3	85	95:7
Radio	11	5	3.6	8.4	2	1	1.8	1.7	0.8	2	–
Posters	12	3	4.8	3	3.8	14	10.7	2.8	2.3	2	3.7
Cinema	1	1	0.4	0.4	0.4	2	0.3	0.7	1.1	–	0.6

SOURCE: "The Campaign Report," *Campaign,* 30 November 1990, pp. 1–24.

The objectives and platform of an advertising campaign also affect the content and form of its messages. For example, if a firm's advertising objectives involve large sales increases, the message demands hard-hitting, high-impact language and symbols. When campaign objectives aim at increasing brand awareness, the message may use much repetition of the brand name and words and illustrations associated with it. Thus, the advertising platform is the foundation on which campaign messages are built.

The choice of media obviously influences the content and form of the message. Effective outdoor displays and short broadcast spot announcements require concise, simple messages. Magazine and newspaper advertisements can include more detail and long explanations. Because several different kinds of media offer geographic selectivity, a precise message content can be tailored to a particular geographic section of the advertising target. Some magazine publishers produce **regional issues**: for a particular issue, the advertisements and editorial content of copies appearing in one geographic area differ from those appearing in other areas. A clothing manufacturer might decide to use one message in London and another in the rest of the U.K. A company may also choose to advertise in only a few regions. Such geographic selectivity lets a firm use the same message in different regions at different times.

The basic components of a print advertising message are shown in Figure 14.5. The messages for most advertisements depend on the use of copy and artwork. Let us examine these two elements in more detail.

Copy.   **Copy** is the verbal portion of an advertisement. It includes headlines, sub-headlines, body copy, and the signature (see Figure 14.5). When preparing advertising copy, marketers attempt to move readers through a persuasive sequence called AIDA: attention, interest, desire, and action. Not all copy need be this extensive, however.

The headline is critical because often it is the only part of the copy that people read. It should attract readers' attention and create enough interest to make them want to read the body copy. The sub-headline, if there is one, links the headline to the body copy. Sometimes it helps explain the headline.

Body copy for most advertisements consists of an introductory statement or paragraph, several explanatory paragraphs, and a closing paragraph. Some copywriters

TABLE 14.5 *Characteristics, advantages, and disadvantages of major advertising media*

MEDIUM	TYPES	UNIT OF SALE	FACTORS AFFECTING RATES	COST COMPARISON INDICATOR	ADVANTAGES	DIS-ADVANTAGES
Newspaper	National Local Morning Evening Sunday Sunday supplement Weekly Special	Column inches Counted words Printed lines Agate lines	Volume and frequency discounts Number of colours Position charges for preferred and guaranteed positions Circulation level	Milline rate = cost per agate line × 1,000,000 divided by circulation Cost per column inch/cm	Almost everyone reads a newspaper; purchased to be read; selective for socio-economic groups; national geographic flexibility; short lead time; frequent publication; favourable for co-operative advertising; merchandising services	Short life; limited reproduction capabilities; large advertising volume limits exposure to any one advertisement
Magazine	Consumer Farm Business etc.	Pages Partial pages Column inches	Circulation level Cost of publishing Type of audience Volume discounts Frequency discounts Size of advertisement Position of advertisement (covers) Number of colours Regional issues	Cost per thousand (CPM) = cost per page × 1,000 divided by circulation	Socio-economic selectivity; good reproduction; long life; prestige; geographic selectivity when regional issues are available; read in leisurely manner	High absolute monetary cost; long lead time

Direct mail	Letters Catalogues Price lists Calendars Brochures Coupons Circulars Newsletters Postcards Booklets Samples	Not applicable	Cost of mailing lists Postage Production costs	Cost per contact	Little wasted circulation; highly selective; circulation controlled by advertiser; few distractions; personal; stimulates action; use of novelty; relatively easy to measure performance; hidden from competitors	Expensive; no editorial matter to attract readers; considered junk mail by many; criticised as invasion of privacy
Radio	AM FM	Programme types Spots: 5, 10, 20, 30, 60 seconds	Time of day Audience size Length of spot or programme Volume and frequency discounts	Cost per thousand (CPM) = cost per minute × 1,000 divided by audience size	Highly mobile; low-cost broadcast medium; message can be quickly changed; geographic selectivity; socio-economic selectivity	Little national radio advertising; provides only audio message; has lost prestige; short life of message; listeners' attention limited because of other activities while listening
Television	ITV Satellite Cable	Programme type Spots: 15, 20, 30, 60, etc. seconds	Time of day Length of spot Volume and frequency discounts Audience size	Cost per thousand (CPM) = cost per minute × 1,000 divided by audience size	Reaches large audience; low cost per exposure; uses both audio and video; highly visible; high prestige; geographic and socio-economic selectivity	High monetary costs; highly perishable message; size of audience not guaranteed; amount of prime time limited
Inside public transport	Buses Underground	Full, half, and quarter showings are sold on a monthly basis	Number of passengers Multiple-month discounts Production costs Position.	Cost per thousand passengers	Low cost; "captive" audience; geographic selectivity	Does not secure quick results

TABLE 14.5 *(continued)*

MEDIUM	TYPES	UNIT OF SALE	FACTORS AFFECTING RATES	COST COMPARISON INDICATOR	ADVANTAGES	DIS-ADVANTAGES
Outside public transport	Buses Taxis	Full, half, and quarter show-ings; space also rented on per-unit basis	Number of advert-isements Position Size	Cost per 100 exposures	Low cost; geographic selectivity; reaches broad, diverse audience	Lacks socio-economic selec-tivity; does not have high im-pact on readers
Outdoor	Papered posters Painted displays Spectaculars Poster vans	Papered post-ers: sold on monthly basis in multiples Painted displays and spectac-ulars: sold on per-unit basis	Length of time purchased Land rental Cost of produc-tion Intensity of traffic Frequency and continuity dis-counts Location	No standard indicator	Allows for repetition; low cost; message can be placed close to the point of sale; geographic selec-tivity; works 24 hours a day	Message must be short and sim-ple; no socio-economic selec-tivity; seldom attracts readers' full attention; criticised for be-ing traffic haz-ard and blight on countryside

SOURCE: Some of the information in this table is from S. Watson Dunn and Arnold M. Barban, *Advertising: Its Role in Modern Marketing,* 6th ed. (Hinsdale, Ill.: Dryden Press, 1986); and Anthony F. McGann and J. Thomas Russell, *Advertising Media* (Homewood, Ill.: Irwin, 1981).

FIGURE 14.5

Copy and artwork elements of printed advertisements.
This ad clearly differentiates the basic elements of print advertising.

Headline

Body Copy

Sub-headline
Signature

Illustration

SOURCE: Lufthansa German Airlines

have adopted a pattern or set of guidelines to develop body copy systematically: (1) identify a specific desire or problem of consumers, (2) suggest the good or service as the best way to satisfy that desire or solve that problem, (3) state the advantages and benefits of the product, (4) indicate why the advertised product is the best for the buyer's particular situation, (5) substantiate the claims and advantages, and (6) ask the buyer for action.[8]

The signature identifies the sponsor of the advertisement. It may contain several elements, including the firm's trade mark, logo, name, and address. The signature should be designed to be attractive, legible, distinctive, and easy to identify in a variety of sizes.

Because radio listeners often are not fully "tuned in" mentally, radio copy should be informal and conversational to attract their attention, resulting in greater impact. The radio message is highly perishable. Thus radio copy should consist of short, familiar terms. Its length should not require a delivery rate exceeding approximately two and one-half words per second.

In television copy, the audio material must not over-power the visual material and vice versa. However, a television message should make optimal use of its visual

8. James E. Littlefield and C. A. Kirkpatrick, *Advertising Mass Communication in Marketing* (Boston: Houghton Mifflin, 1970), p. 178.

COGENT

| VAUXHALL | 7812 | 12.6.90 |
| NETWORK Q 40' TV | PJ | FOURTH |

"THANK Q"

VISION	SOUND
A ball bounces out in front of a car in a wet, busy street. A child is about to follow but is stopped by his mother. The car screeches to a halt in time. The man at the wheel lifts his eyes in relief and mouths thank you.	SFX: Screech of brakes.
Cut to black screen with white title - THANK Q.	
A woman is parked at the kerb, where two policemen are checking over her car. As one checks the tyres, the other checks the lights.	Policeman1: Indicators Policeman2: O.K.
They give her the OK. She taps her steering wheel and mouths thank you to herself.	
Cut to black screen with white title - THANK Q.	
Inside a parked car a flashy young man is showing off his new car to his date.	Young Man: And it's got electric windows. Girl: Ooh, do they work?
She presses the button, the window comes down. Relieved, he mouths thank you to himself.	

VISION	SOUND
Cut to black screen with white title - THANK Q.	
A man and heavily pregnant woman rush out to their car in heavy snow. He wills it to start. It does, first time.	Woman: Hurry, hurry!
He closes his eyes and mouths thank you.	
Cut to black screen with white title - THANK Q.	
Cut to a red Vauxhall in Network Q showroom having a final check by two white overalled technicians.	MVO: When you buy a used car from Network Q, you'll be saying Thank Q. Because at Network Q, every used car gets 114 separate checks...
Quick cuts of different checks, close-ups of checks being ticked off.	... just like a new car.
Cut to salesman handing over the keys and documents to an obviously happy customer. Customer thanks him.	Customer: Thank Q.
Customer gets into red Vauxhall and drives off through the forecourt.	
Vauxhall Logo spins as car drives past.	MVO: Network Q. Used cars like new.
SUPER: NETWORK Q Used cars like new.	

FIGURE 14.6 *Example of a parallel script*

SOURCE: Vauxhall Motors U.K.

portion. As Figure 14.6 illustrates, copy for a television commercial is initially written in parallel script form. The video is described in the left column and the audio in the right column. When the parallel script is approved, the copywriter and the artist combine the copy with the visual material through use of a **storyboard** (see Figure 14.7), which depicts a series of miniature television screens to show the sequence of major scenes in the commercial. Technical personnel use the storyboard as a blueprint when they produce the commercial.

Artwork. **Artwork** consists of the illustration and layout of the advertisement (see Figure 14.5). Although **illustrations** are often photographs, they can also be drawings, graphs, charts, and tables. Illustrations are used to attract attention, to encourage the audience to read or listen to the copy, to communicate an idea quickly, or to communicate an idea that is difficult to put into words.[9] They are especially important because consumers tend to recall the visual portion of advertisements better than the verbal portions. Advertisers use a variety of illustration techniques, which are identified and described in Table 14.6.

9. S. Watson Dunn and Arnold M. Barban, *Advertising: Its Role in Modern Marketing*, 6th ed. (Hinsdale, Ill.: Dryden Press, 1986), p. 493.

FIGURE 14.7 *Final storyboard.* This is the final storyboard for the Vauxhall Network Q.

SOURCE: Vauxhall Motors U.K.

The **layout** of an advertisement is the physical arrangement of the illustration, headline, sub-headline, body copy, and signature. The arrangement of these parts in Figure 14.5 is only one possible layout. These same elements could be arranged in many ways. The final layout is the result of several stages of layout preparation. As it moves through these stages, the layout helps people involved in developing the advertising campaign exchange ideas. It also provides instructions for production personnel.

■ **Executing the Campaign**

The execution of an advertising campaign requires an extensive amount of planning and co-ordination. Regardless of whether or not an organisation uses an advertising agency, many people and organisations are involved in the execution of a campaign.[10] Production companies, research organisations, media firms, printers, photo-engravers, and commercial artists are just a few of the people and organisations that contribute to a campaign.

Implementation requires detailed schedules to ensure that various phases of the work are done on time. Advertising management personnel must evaluate the qual-

10. Patrick Quinn, *Low Budget Advertising* (London: Heinemann, 1988).

TABLE 14.6 *Illustration techniques for advertisements*

ILLUSTRATION TECHNIQUE	DESCRIPTION
Product alone	Simplest method; advantageous when appearance is important, when identification is important, when trying to keep a brand name or package in the public eye, or when selling through mail order
Emphasis on special features	Shows and emphasises special details or features as well as advantages; used when product is unique because of special features
Product in setting	Shows what can be done with product; people, surroundings, or environment hint at what product can do; often used in food advertisements
Product in use	Puts action into the advertisement; can remind readers of benefits gained from using product; must be careful not to make visual cliché; should not include anything in illustration that will divert attention from product; used to direct readers' eyes towards product
Product being tested	Uses test to dramatise product's uses and benefits versus competing products
Results of product's use	Emphasises satisfaction from using product; can liven up dull product; useful when nothing new can be said
Dramatising headline	Appeal of illustration dramatises headline; can emphasise appeal but dangerous to use illustrations that do not correlate with headlines
Dramatising situation	Presents problem situation or shows situation in which problem has been resolved
Comparison	Compares product with "something" established; the something must be positive and familiar to audience
Contrast	Shows difference between two products or two ideas or differences in effects between use and non-use; before-and-after format is a commonly used contrast technique
Diagrams, charts, and graphs	Used to communicate complex information quickly; may make presentations more interesting
Phantom effects	X-ray or internal view; can see inside product; helpful to explain concealed or internal mechanism
Symbolic	Symbols used to represent abstract ideas that are difficult to illustrate; effective if readers understand symbol; must be positive correlation between symbol and idea
Testimonials	Actually shows the testifier; should use famous person or someone to whom audience can relate

SOURCE: Dorothy Cohen, *Advertising* (New York: Wiley, 1972), pp. 458–464; and S. Watson Dunn and Arnold M. Barban, *Advertising: Its Role in Modern Marketing*, 6th ed. (Hinsdale, Ill.: Dryden Press, 1986), pp. 497–498.

ity of the work and take corrective action when necessary. In some instances, changes have to be made during the campaign so that it meets campaign objectives more effectively.

■ **Evaluating the Effectiveness of the Advertising**

There are a variety of ways to test the effectiveness of advertising. They include measuring achievement of advertising objectives; assessing the effectiveness of copy, illustrations, or layouts; and evaluating certain media.

Advertising can be evaluated before, during, and after the campaign. Evaluations performed before the campaign begins are called **pre-tests** and usually attempt to evaluate the effectiveness of one or more elements of the message. To pretest advertisements, marketers sometimes use a **consumer focus group,** a number of persons who are actual or potential buyers of the advertised product. Members are asked to judge one or several dimensions of two or more advertisements. Such tests are based on the belief that consumers are more likely than advertising experts to know what will influence them.

To measure advertising effectiveness during a campaign, marketers usually take advantage of "enquiries". In the initial stages of a campaign, an advertiser may use several advertisements simultaneously, each containing a coupon or a form requesting information. The advertiser records the number of coupons that are returned from each type of advertisement. If an advertiser receives 78,528 coupons from advertisement A, 37,072 coupons from advertisement B, and 47,932 coupons from advertisement C, advertisement A is judged superior to advertisements B and C.

Evaluation of advertising effectiveness after the campaign is called a **post-campaign test** (or **post-test**). Advertising objectives often indicate what kind of post-test will be appropriate. If an advertiser sets objectives in terms of communication—product awareness, brand awareness, or attitude change—then the post-test should measure changes in one or more of these dimensions. Advertisers sometimes use consumer surveys or experiments to evaluate a campaign based on communication objectives. These methods are costly, however.

For campaign objectives that are stated in terms of sales, advertisers should determine the change in sales or market share that can be attributed to the campaign. Unfortunately, such changes brought about by advertising cannot be measured precisely; many factors independent of advertisements affect a firm's sales and market share. Competitive actions, government actions, and changes in economic conditions, consumer preferences, and weather are only a few factors that might enhance or diminish a company's sales or market share. However, by using data about past and current sales and advertising expenditures, an advertiser can make gross estimates of the effects of a campaign on sales or market share.

Because consumer surveys and experiments are so expensive, and because it is so difficult to determine the direct effects of advertising on sales, many advertisers evaluate print advertisements according to the degree to which consumers can remember them. The post-test methods based on memory include recognition and recall tests. Such tests are usually performed by research organisations through consumer surveys. If a **recognition test** is used, individual respondents are shown the actual advertisement and asked whether they recognise it. If they do, the interviewer asks additional questions to determine how much of the advertisement each respondent read. When recall is evaluated, the respondents are not shown the actual advertisement but instead are asked about what they have seen or heard recently.

Recall can be measured through either unaided recall or aided recall methods. In an **unaided** (or **spontaneous**) **recall test**, subjects are asked to identify advertisements that they have seen recently but are not shown any clues to help them remember. A similar procedure is used with an **aided** (or **prompted**) **recall test**, except that subjects are shown a list of products, brands, company names, or trade marks to jog their memories. Several research organisations, such as Nielsen, Audience Selection, and Gallup, provide research services that test recognition and recall of advertisements (see Table 14.7).

The major justification for using recognition and recall methods is that people are more likely to buy a product if they can remember an advertisement about it than if they cannot. However, recalling an advertisement does not necessarily lead to buy-

TABLE 14.7 *Results of tested recall of advertisements*

PROMPTED RECALL

Q: *Which of the following advertisements and commercials do you remember seeing or hearing recently?*

		Account	Agency	%
1	(1)	Nescafé Gold Blend	McCanns	79
2	(2)	Coca-Cola	McCanns	69
3	(4)	Pepsi-Cola	BBDO	69
4	(–)	Pedigree Chum	BSB Dorland	66
5	(–)	Foster's Lager	BMP DDB Needham	65
6	(5)	British Gas	Y&R	61
7	(–)	Royal Mail	McCanns	61
8	(6)	Radion Powder and Liquid	O&M	61
9	(3)	Whiskas	DMB&B	59
10	(–)	Vauxhall	LH-S	53
11	(–)	Penguin Chocolate Biscuits	Publicis	50
12	(–)	NatWest—Card Plus Account	JWT	50
13	(–)	Tesco	LH-S	47
14	(–)	Powergen	Bartle Bogle Hegarty	46
15	(–)	St Ivel Shape Yoghurt	JWT	41
16	(–)	Shell Advanced Petrol	Bartle Bogle Hegarty	40
17	(–)	Lynx Body Spray	Y&R	39
18	(–)	Dairy Crest Clover	Y&R	37
19	(18)	Cream	DMB&B	35
20	(–)	Appletise	Edwards Martin Thornton	31

SPONTANEOUS RECALL

Q: *Thinking back over the past week, which advertisements and commercials can you remember seeing or hearing?*

	Account	Agency
1	Nescafé Gold Blend	McCanns
2	Hamlet Cigars	CDP
3	British Telecom/BT	JWT
4	Carling Black Label	WCRSMM
5	Coke/Coca-Cola	McCanns
6	Ariel/Ariel Automatic	Saatchis
7	Nescafé	McCanns
8	Tesco	LH-S
9	Heineken	LH-S
10	Guinness	O&M

Research for the Adwatch survey is conducted exclusively for *Marketing* by Audience Selection using Phonebus, the company's weekly telephone omnibus survey among a sample of more than 1,000 adults aged 15 and over. The commercials in the research are chosen by the Communications Trading Company. Analytical assistance from *The Planning Partnership*.

SOURCE: "Audience Selection," *Marketing*, 2 August 1990, p. 7. Reprinted by permission.

ing the product or brand advertised. Research shows that the more "likable" an advertisement is, the more persuasive it will be with consumers. People who enjoy an advertisement are twice as likely to be convinced that the advertised brand is best. Of about 16 percent of those who liked an advertisement, a significant number increased their preference for the brand. Only a small percentage of those who were neutral about the advertisement felt more favourable towards the brand as a result of the advertisement.[11] The type of programme in which the product is advertised can also affect consumers' feelings about the commercial and the product it promotes. Viewers judge commercials placed in happy programmes as more effective and recall them somewhat better.[12]

Researchers are also using a sophisticated technique called single-source data to help evaluate advertisements. With this technique, individuals' behaviour is

11. Ronald Alsop, "TV Ads That Are Likable Get Plus Ratings for Persuasiveness," *Wall Street Journal*, 20 Feb. 1986, p. 21.

12. Marvin E. Goldberg and Gerald J. Gorn, "Happy and Sad TV Programs: How They Affect Reactions to Commercials," *Journal of Consumer Research*, December 1987, pp. 387–403.

tracked from television sets to the check-out counter. Monitors are placed in pre-selected homes, and microcomputers record when the television set is on and which channel is being viewed. At the supermarket check-out, the individual in the sample household presents an identification card. The cashier records the purchases by scanner, and the data are sent to the research facility. This technique is bringing more insight into people's buying patterns than ever before.

Who Develops the Advertising Campaign?

An advertising campaign may be handled by (1) an individual or a few people within the firm, (2) an advertising department within the organisation, or (3) an advertising agency.

In very small firms, one or two individuals are responsible for advertising (and many other activities as well). Usually these individuals depend heavily on personnel at local newspapers and broadcasting stations for copywriting, artwork, and advice about scheduling media.

In certain types of large businesses—especially in larger retail organisations—advertising departments create and implement advertising campaigns. Depending on the size of the advertising programme, an advertising department may consist of a few multi-skilled persons or a sizeable number of specialists, such as copywriters, artists, media buyers, and technical production co-ordinators. An advertising department sometimes obtains the services of independent research organisations and also hires free-lance specialists when they are needed for a particular project.

When an organisation uses an advertising agency, such as Ogilvy & Mather or BBH, the firm and the agency usually develop the advertising campaign jointly. How much each party participates in the campaign's total development depends on the working relationship between the firm and the agency. Ordinarily, a firm relies on the agency for copywriting, artwork, technical production, and formulation of the media plan.

An advertising agency can assist a business in several ways. An agency, especially a larger one, supplies the firm with the services of highly skilled specialists—not only copywriters, artists, and production co-ordinators, but also media experts, researchers, and legal advisers. Agency personnel often have had broad experience in advertising and are usually more objective than a firm's employees about the organisation's products. Figure 14.8 outlines the composition of a typical advertising agency.

Because an agency traditionally receives most of its income from a 15 percent commission on media purchases, a firm can obtain some agency services at a low or moderate cost. For example, if an agency contracts for £400,000 of television time for a firm, it receives a commission of £60,000 from the television company. Although the traditional compensation method for agencies is changing and now includes other factors, the media commission still offsets some costs of using an agency. BMP DDB Needham is considering breaking the mould; the agency would be paid by results. Clients would pay a bonus to the agency for meeting targets or receive a pay-back (refund) if the advertising failed to deliver.[13]

Now that we have explored advertising as a potential promotional-mix ingredient, let us consider a related ingredient, publicity.

13. *Marketing*, 24 May 1990, p. 5.

FIGURE 14.8
*A typical advertising
agency structure*

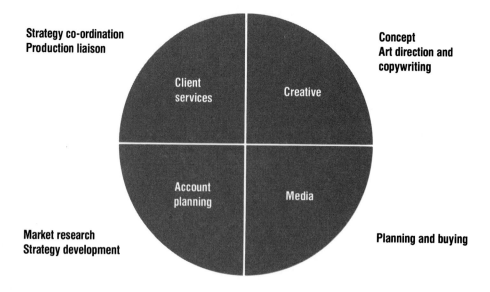

Strategy co-ordination
Production liaison

Concept
Art direction and
copywriting

Market research
Strategy development

Planning and buying

PUBLICITY AND PUBLIC RELATIONS

As indicated in Chapter 13, **publicity** is communication in news story form about an organisation, its products, or both that is transmitted through a mass medium at no charge (although the publicity activity will incur production/personnel costs). Publicity can be presented through a variety of vehicles, several of which we'll examine.

Within an organisation, publicity is sometimes viewed as part of public relations—a larger, more comprehensive communication function. **Public relations** is the planned and sustained effort to establish and maintain good will and mutual understanding between an organisation and its publics: customers, employees, shareholders, trade bodies, suppliers, government officials, and society in general.[14] Publicity is the result of various public relations efforts. For example, when Tesco decided to make a special effort to stock environmentally safe products and packaging, its public relations department sent out press releases to various newspapers, magazines, and television contacts, as well as to its suppliers. The result was publicity in the form of magazine articles, newspaper acknowledgements, and TV coverage. Marketing Update 14.3 describes the growth of public relations in the U.K.

■ Publicity
and Advertising
Compared

Although publicity and advertising both depend on mass media, they differ in several respects. Advertising messages tend to be informative or persuasive, whereas publicity is primarily informative. Advertisements are sometimes designed to have an immediate impact on sales; publicity messages are more subdued. Publicity releases do not identify sponsors; advertisements do. The sponsor pays for media time or space for advertising, but not for publicity, and there is therefore no guarantee of inclusion. Communications through publicity are usually included as part of a programme or a print story, but advertisements are normally separated from the broadcast programmes or editorial portions of print media so that the audience or

14. *Public Relations Practice—Its Role and Parameters* (London: The Institute of Public Relations, 1984).

THE GROWTH OF PUBLIC RELATIONS

In 1988 the U.K. advertising market—the largest in Europe—grew by 15 percent; in 1989 it grew by 13 percent to billings of over £8 billion (1.48 percent of the U.K.'s GNP). However, 1990 saw the bubble burst. Yellowhammer went into receivership, saved by D'Arcy Masius Benton & Bowles of America; Carlson saved FKB; share prices in the publicly quoted companies, Lowe Group and Saatchi & Saatchi, for example, plummeted. The downturn in British business and the slowdown in consumer spending led companies to cut costs, a situation in which the advertising budget is always a prime target.

In contrast to the depression in advertising, the public relations (PR) business is booming. The industry view is that business grew by 20 percent in 1989 and a similar figure was achieved in 1990. Unlike the saturated advertising sector, public relations is a relatively new and immature market. In 1989, the 170 members (85 percent of the industry) of the Public Relations Consultants Association generated fee income of £162 million, compared with £10 million in 1981.

Compared with advertising, PR is remarkably cheap. Average fees are around £50,000 p.a. Cutting out such costs will make little difference to most clients, so advertising tends to be the target. In addition, PR is needed in the good times and also when times are hard: prior to the 1987 stock-market crash companies used PR to help with takeovers; since the recession they have used PR to improve their image for the benefit of investors.

SOURCES: The Advertising Association, London, 1990; *The Independent,* 12 August 1990; Robin Cobb, "The Art of Gentle Persuasion," *Marketing,* 6 September 1990, pp. 25–26; and Bill Britt, "PR Leads from Front as Buy-Up Battles Rage," *Marketing,* 1 February 1990, p. 13.

FIGURE 14.9
Example of a press (news) release

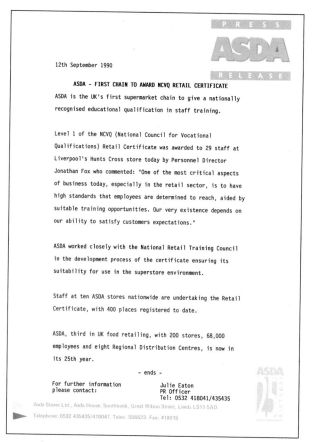

12th September 1990

ASDA - FIRST CHAIN TO AWARD NCVQ RETAIL CERTIFICATE

ASDA is the UK's first supermarket chain to give a nationally recognised educational qualification in staff training.

Level 1 of the NCVQ (National Council for Vocational Qualifications) Retail Certificate was awarded to 29 staff at Liverpool's Hunts Cross store today by Personnel Director Jonathan Fox who commented: "One of the most critical aspects of business today, especially in the retail sector, is to have high standards that employees are determined to reach, aided by suitable training opportunities. Our very existence depends on our ability to satisfy customers expectations."

ASDA worked closely with the National Retail Training Council in the development process of the certificate ensuring its suitability for use in the superstore environment.

Staff at ten ASDA stores nationwide are undertaking the Retail Certificate, with 400 places registered to date.

ASDA, third in UK food retailing, with 200 stores, 68,000 employees and eight Regional Distribution Centres, is now in its 25th year.

- ends -

For further information please contact:
Julie Eaton
PR Officer
Tel: 0532 418041/435435

Asda Stores Ltd., Asda House, Southbank, Great Wilson Street, Leeds LS11 5AD

Telephone: 0532 435435/418047, Telex: 556623, Fax: 418015

SOURCE: Countrywide Communications Ltd. Consultancy of the Year, 1989–1990

readers can easily recognise (or ignore) them. Publicity may have greater credibility than advertising among consumers because as a news story it may appear more objective. Finally, a firm can use advertising to repeat the same messages as many times as desired; publicity is generally not subject to repetition.

Kinds of Publicity

There are several types of publicity mechanism.[15] The most common is the **press (news) release**, which is usually a single page of typewritten copy containing fewer than three hundred words. A press release, sometimes called a news release, also gives the firm's or agency's name, its address and phone number, and the contact person. Car makers often use press releases to introduce new products. Figure 14.9 is an example of a press release. A **feature article** is a longer manuscript (up to three thousand words) that is usually prepared for a specific publication. A **captioned photograph** is a photograph with a brief description explaining the picture's content. Captioned photographs are especially effective for illustrating a new or improved product with highly visible features.

There are several other kinds of publicity. A **press conference** is a meeting called to announce major news events. Media personnel are invited and are usually supplied with written materials and photographs. In addition, letters to the editor and editorials are sometimes prepared and sent to newspapers and magazines.

15. David Wragg, *Public Relations for Sales and Marketing Management* (London: Kogan Page, 1987).

However, newspaper editors frequently allocate space on their editorial pages to local writers and national columnists. Finally, films and tapes may be distributed to broadcasting companies in the hope that they will be aired.

A marketer's choice of specific types of publicity depends on considerations that include the type of information being transmitted, the characteristics of the target audience, the receptivity of media personnel, the importance of the item to the public, and the amount of information that needs to be presented. Sometimes a marketer uses a single type of publicity in a promotional mix. In other cases, a marketer may use a variety of publicity mechanisms, with publicity being the primary ingredient in the promotional mix. **Third-party endorsement** increases the credibility of publicity and public relations; this is a recommendation (written, verbal, or visual) from an opinion leader.

■ Uses of Publicity

Publicity has a number of uses. It can make people aware of a firm's products, brands, or activities; help a company maintain a certain level of positive public visibility; and enhance a particular image, such as innovativeness or progressiveness. Companies also try to overcome negative images through publicity. Some firms seek publicity for a single purpose and others for several purposes. As Table 14.8 shows, publicity releases can tackle a multitude of specific issues.

■ Requirements of a Publicity Programme

For maximum benefit, a firm should create and maintain a systematic, continuous publicity programme.[16] A single individual or department—within the organisation or from its advertising agency or public relations firm—should be responsible for managing the programme. Relationships must be maintained with the media, particularly to facilitate crisis-management public relations.

It is important to establish and maintain good working relationships with media personnel. Often personal contact with editors, reporters, and other news personnel is essential; without their input a company may find it hard to design its publicity programme so as to facilitate the work of newspeople.

Media personnel reject a great deal of publicity material because it is poorly written or not newsworthy. To maintain an effective publicity programme, a firm must strive to avoid these flaws. Guidelines and checklists can aid it in this task. Material submitted must match the particular newspaper's style, for example, for length of article, punctuation, and layout.

Finally, a firm has to evaluate its publicity efforts. Usually, the effectiveness of publicity is measured by the number of releases actually published or broadcast. To monitor print media and determine which releases are published and how often, an organisation can hire a cuttings service—a firm that cuts out and sends published news releases to client companies. To measure the effectiveness of television publicity, a firm can enclose a card with its publicity releases and request that the company record its name and the dates when the news item is broadcast, but companies do not always comply. Though some television and radio tracking services do exist, they are extremely costly.

■ Dealing with Unfavourable Publicity

Up to this point we have discussed publicity as a planned promotional-mix ingredient. However, companies may have to deal with unfavourable publicity regarding an unsafe product, an accident, the actions of a dishonest employee, or some other negative event. For example, when a United Airlines plane crashed in Sioux City,

16. Frank Jefkins, *Public Relations Techniques* (London: Heinemann, 1988).

TABLE 14.8
Possible issues for publicity releases

Marketing developments	Reports on current developments
New products	Reports of experiments
New uses for old products	Reports on industry conditions
Research developments	Company progress reports
Changes of marketing personnel	Employment, production, and sales statistics
Large orders received	Reports on new discoveries
Successful bids	Tax reports
Awards of contracts	Speeches by principals
Special events	Analyses of economic conditions
Company policies	Employment gains
New guarantees	Financial statements
Changes in credit terms	Organisation appointments
Changes in distribution policies	Opening of new markets
Changes in service policies	Government trade awards
Changes in prices	**Personalities—names are news**
News of general interest	Visits by famous persons
Annual election of directors	Accomplishments of individuals
Meetings of the board of directors	Winners of company contests
Anniversaries of the organisation	Employees' and directors' advancements
Anniversaries of an invention	Interviews with company officials
Anniversaries of the senior directors	Company employees serving as judges for contests
Holidays that can be tied to the organisation's activities	Interviews with employees
Annual banquets	**Slogans, symbols, endorsements**
Conferences and special meetings	Company's slogan—its history and development
Open house to the community	A tie-in of company activities with slogan
Athletic events	Creation of a slogan
Awards of merit to employees	The company's trade mark
Laying of cornerstone	The company's name plate
Opening of an exhibition	Product endorsements

SOURCE: Albert Wesley Frey, ed., *Marketing Handbook,* 2nd ed. (New York: Ronald Press, 1965), pp. 19–35. Copyright © 1965. Reprinted by permission of John Wiley & Sons, Inc.

Iowa, killing half the passengers on board, the airline was faced with a negative situation. Such unfavourable publicity can be quick and dramatic. A single negative event that produces unfavourable publicity can wipe out a company's favourable image and destroy consumer attitudes that took years to build through promotional efforts. Moreover, the mass media today can disseminate information faster and to larger audiences than ever before, and bad news generally receives much attention in the media. Thus the negative publicity surrounding an unfavourable event now reaches more people.[17] By dealing effectively with a negative situation, an organisation can minimise the damage from unfavourable publicity.

17. Marc G. Weinberger and Jean B. Romeo, "The Impact of Negative Product News," *Business Horisons,* January-February 1989, p. 44.

To protect an organisation's image, it is important to avoid unfavourable publicity or at least to lessen its effects. First and foremost, the organisation can directly reduce negative incidents and events through safety programmes, inspections, and effective quality control procedures. However, because organisations obviously cannot eliminate all negative occurrences, they need to establish policies and procedures for the news coverage of such events. These policies and procedures should aim at reducing negative impact.

In most cases, organisations should expedite news coverage of negative events rather than try to discourage or block it. This approach not only tends to diminish the fallout from negative events, but also fosters a positive relationship with media personnel. Such a relationship is essential if news personnel are to co-operate with a company and broadcast favourable news stories about it. Facts are likely to be reported accurately, but if news coverage is discouraged, rumours and misinformation may be passed along. An unfavourable event can easily be blown up into a scandal or a tragedy. It can even cause public panic.

■ Limitations in Using Publicity

Free media publicity is a double-edged sword: the financial advantage comes with several drawbacks. If company messages are to be published or broadcast, media personnel must judge them newsworthy. Consequently, messages must be timely, interesting, and accurate. Many communications simply do not qualify. It may take time and effort to convince media personnel of the news value of publicity releases. Even a top public relations consultancy achieves a hit rate of only one out of every four press releases being published in the press.

Although marketers usually encourage media personnel to air a publicity release at a certain time, they control neither the content nor the timing of the communication. Media personnel alter the length and content of publicity releases to fit publishers' or broadcasters' requirements and may even delete the parts of the message that the firm deems most important. Furthermore, media personnel use publicity releases in time slots or positions that are most convenient for them; thus the messages often appear at times or in locations that may not reach the firm's target audiences. These limitations can be frustrating. Nevertheless, as you have seen in the earlier portions of this section, properly managed publicity offers an organisation substantial benefits.

SUMMARY

Advertising is a paid form of non-personal communication that is transmitted to consumers through mass media, such as television, radio, newspapers, magazines, direct mail, public transport, and outdoor displays. Both non-business and business organisations use advertising.

Marketers use advertising in many ways. Institutional advertising promotes organisations' images and ideas, as well as political issues and candidates. Product advertising focuses on the uses, features, images, and benefits of goods and services. To make people aware of a new or innovative product's existence, uses, and benefits, marketers rely on pioneer advertising in the introductory stage to stimulate primary demand for a general product category. Then they switch to competitive advertising to boost selective demand by promoting a particular brand's uses, features, and advantages.

Through advertising, a company can sometimes lessen the impact of a competitor's promotional programme or make its own sales force more effective. To increase market penetration, an advertiser sometimes focuses a campaign on promoting a greater number of uses for the product. Some advertisements for an established product remind consumers that the product is still around and that it has certain characteristics and uses. Marketers may try to assure users of a particular brand that they are selecting the best brand. Marketers also use advertising to smooth out fluctuations in sales.

Although marketers may vary in how they develop advertising campaigns, they should follow a general pattern. First, they must identify and analyse the advertising target. Second, they should establish what they want the campaign to accomplish by defining the advertising objectives. The third step is creating the advertising platform, which contains the basic issues to be presented in the campaign. Fourth, advertisers must decide how much money to spend on the campaign; they arrive at this decision through the objective and task approach, the percentage of sales approach, the competition-matching approach, or the arbitrary approach. Fifth, they must develop the media plan by selecting and scheduling the media to be used in the campaign. In the sixth stage, advertisers use copy and artwork to create the message. In the seventh stage, the execution of an advertising campaign requires extensive planning and co-ordination. Finally, advertisers must devise one or more methods for evaluating the effectiveness of the advertisements.

Advertising campaigns can be developed by personnel within the firm or in conjunction with advertising agencies. When a campaign is created by the firm's personnel, it may be developed by only a few people, or it may be the product of an advertising department within the firm. The use of an advertising agency may be advantageous to a firm because an agency can provide highly skilled, objective specialists with broad experience in the advertising field at low to moderate costs to the firm.

Publicity is communication in news story form, regarding an organisation, its products, or both, that is transmitted through a mass medium at no charge. Generally, publicity is part of the larger, more comprehensive communication function of public relations. Publicity is mainly informative and usually more subdued than advertising. There are many types of publicity, including news releases, feature articles, captioned photographs, press conferences, editorials, films, and tapes. Marketers can use one or more of these forms to achieve a variety of objectives. To have an effective publicity programme, someone—either in the organisation or in the firm's agency—must be responsible for creating and maintaining systematic and continuous publicity efforts.

An organisation should avoid negative publicity by reducing the number of negative events that result in unfavourable publicity. To diminish the impact of unfavourable publicity, an organisation should institute policies and procedures for dealing with news personnel when negative events do occur. Problems that organisations confront when seeking publicity include the reluctance of media personnel to print or broadcast releases and a lack of control over the timing and content of messages.

Important Terms

Advertising
Institutional advertising
Product advertising
Pioneer advertising
Competitive advertising
Comparative advertising
Defensive advertising
Reminder advertising
Reinforcement advertising
Advertising campaign
Advertising target
Advertising platform
Advertising budget
Objective and task approach
Percentage of sales approach
Competition-matching approach
Arbitrary approach
Media plan
Cost comparison indicator

Regional issues
Copy
Storyboard
Artwork
Illustrations
Layout
Pre-tests
Consumer focus group
Post-campaign test or post-test
Recognition test
Unaided (spontaneous) recall test
Aided (prompted) recall test
Publicity
Public relations
Press (news) release
Feature article
Captioned photograph
Press conference
Third-party endorsement

Discussion and Review Questions

1. What is the difference between institutional and product advertising?
2. When should advertising be used to stimulate primary demand? When should advertising be used to stimulate selective demand?
3. What are the major steps in creating an advertising campaign?
4. What is an advertising target? How does a marketer analyse the target audience after it has been identified?
5. Why is it necessary to define advertising objectives?
6. What is an advertising platform, and how is it used?
7. What factors affect the size of an advertising budget? What techniques are used to determine this budget?
8. Describe the steps required in developing a media plan.
9. What is the role of copy in an advertising message?
10. What role does an advertising agency play in developing an advertising campaign?
11. Discuss several ways to post-test the effectiveness of advertising.
12. What is publicity? How does it differ from advertising?
13. How do organisations use publicity? Give several examples of publicity releases that you have observed recently in local media.
14. How should an organisation handle negative publicity? Identify a recent example of a firm that received negative publicity. Did the firm deal with it effectively?
15. Explain the problems and limitations associated with using publicity. How can some of these limitations be minimised?

14.1   British Airways' Evolving Promotion

In the late 1970s British Airways (BA) had lost its way as the U.K.'s national airline. The merger of BOAC and BEA had not gone smoothly, financial performance was poor, and travel surveys showed customer satisfaction to be low. The 1979 election of a Conservative government gave new impetus to improve as the government wished to privatise the state-owned airline. Lord King was appointed chairman in 1983, and under him the airline quickly became operationally sound, although customers had not perceived the change.

The subsequent promotional strategy can be divided into three distinct phases. From 1983 to 1985 the global campaigns of Saatchi & Saatchi aimed "to make the airline feel proud again". Employees were to feel valued and part of a successful organisation, customers were to believe BA was superior to competitors, and financial institutions were to see the turnaround in BA as a prelude to privatisation. The now famous Manhattan Landing commercial made no attempt to demonstrate product benefits, or to create category need or purchase intention. The message was that BA was large and "The World's Favourite Airline". The campaign was hugely successful in the U.K. and U.S.A.—BA's main markets. Sales increased by 28 percent in the U.S.A. and 13 percent elsewhere; America voted the commercial the best of all airlines' promotion in 1984. Perceptions of BA changed.

By 1985, awareness of BA had grown. The objective now was to alter customer attitudes, particularly in the lucrative business-class sector. Advertisements stressed service and comfort, and were targeted at business travellers, particularly in America: the Superclub Seats, Supercare, and Putting People First commercials. The campaign was influenced by Colin Marshall, who had recently joined BA from Avis and believed in service as a means of differentiation. Training programmes improved service levels so that the reality of the product offer matched the message of BA's promotion.

Since 1987, BA's advertising has concentrated on its "pillar" brands. BA had promoted a recognisable corporate image but had only haphazardly promoted its various services such as Club Class and the Shuttles. Mike Batt joined from Mars and brought marketing techniques which focused on the product rather than on the company or corporate image. He introduced the concept of pillar brands, which are the key products supporting the global and corporate branding already in place. The corporate identity remained part of the promotion, but the focus was on selling specific products to particular market segments with distinctive brands—Club World, Saver Shuttle, Executive Shuttle, etc. The "Boardroom" commercial sold Club World to businesspeople—a long-haul service which gives comfort, convenience, and allows passengers to arrive fit for work. Following these branding and promotion exercises, business-class passengers increased by 31 percent worldwide and 12 percent in Europe.

SOURCES: Saatchi & Saatchi directors; *Sunday Times,* 27 May 1990; John Francis, "BA Promotions in the 1980s," University of Warwick MBA, 1990.

Questions for Discussion

1. How important is a strong corporate identity in the successful advertising of services?

2. Creating a successful platform is difficult. Keeping it fresh is more so. Discuss the problems of building on the powerful and innovative Manhattan Landing commercial.

14.2 Public Relations and Perrier's Crisis

On 10 February 1990 in North Carolina, bottles of Perrier were found to be contaminated with benzene. For the best-selling brand of mineral water in the world this meant a huge crisis. "Once a critical situation arises the most vital task is to do everything you can to reduce damage to the absolute minimum. We were fortunate that we had agreed procedures in advance and these procedures were followed absolutely," stated Perrier spokesperson Wenche Marshall Foster. "From the very beginning we were determined to keep everyone fully informed."

Perrier's crisis team in the U.K. moved quickly; senior executives of Perrier, its PR agency Infoplan and advertising agency Leo Burnett had been briefed before the contamination scare on the needs of crisis management. Within hours of the contamination announcement Perrier had set up tests with independent consultant Hydrotechnica so as to have accurate information to give out. The crisis team knew it had to be truthful throughout. Infoplan immediately set up a telephone information service, which dealt with 1700 calls each day from distributors, retailers, and consumers. Within three days of the crisis breaking, shelves worldwide had been cleared and all stocks returned to Perrier. The company achieved goodwill by moving so decisively. No press conferences were given. Instead, the five members of the crisis team individually met journalists for in-depth head-to-heads to give precise and clear information and to minimise poor publicity.

Perrier risked competitors moving to take advantage of the crisis, since retailers would not leave shelves empty. Perrier, though, was the clear brand leader with the only established image worldwide. Competitors would take time to develop such strength, and their stocks were not high. Evian and the like had nothing to gain from drawing further attention to Perrier's crisis, which was damaging the industry as a whole.

Perrier handled the crisis in PR textbook fashion. With 85 percent of the American and 60 percent of the U.K. market it had a great deal to lose. The company informed its publics of its problems, tackled the contamination problem, and relaunched the product with new packaging and bottle sizes—clearly to be seen as new stock—with a "Welcome Back" promotional campaign. Within months, Perrier's market share was climbing back and shelf space had been regained. The company did not hide anything, it identified the various audiences to brief, and tackled its production to ensure there were no repeat problems. Consumers, distributors, public health bodies, and the media were made to feel part of Perrier's solution through the effective use of PR.

SOURCES: *Marketing Week*, 2 March 1990; *Personally Speaking*, 27 March 1990; *Fortune*, 23 April 1990.

Questions for Discussion

1. How important is it to have an on-going commitment to public relations in the event of a crisis?
2. Could Perrier's competitors have taken more advantage of the crisis?
3. Did the same publicity message go out to all of Perrier's publics or target audiences?

15 PERSONAL SELLING AND SALES PROMOTION

Objectives

To understand the major purposes of personal selling

To learn the basic steps in the personal selling process

To identify the types of sales force personnel

To gain insight into sales management decisions and activities

To become aware of what sales promotion activities are and how they can be used

To become familiar with specific sales promotion methods used

*T*he RSPCA (Royal Society for the Prevention of Cruelty to Animals) has become the latest charity to add sales promotion techniques to its traditional fund-raising activities. In addition to flag-selling days—a derivative of personal selling—membership schemes, and fund-raising events, many charities are turning to ties with consumer goods companies for on-pack promotions. Save the Children with Weetabix, the Family Heart Association with Heinz Baked Beans, the National Children's Home with Dunlop, and Guide Dogs for the Blind with Andrex toilet tissues are recent examples. Charity promotions boost client companies' sales but also provide a source of funding for the charities and image-building for both parties.

In the U.K., with over 80 percent of young people caring most about animals, Golden Wonder crisps profited from an on-pack promotion endorsed by the RSPCA. Consumers were asked to collect proof of purchase coupons and return them in exchange for a set of RSPCA wildlife badges. Massive regional press coverage reinforced the Golden Wonder marketing campaign; and £100,000 was raised for the RSPCA. An on-pack promotion with Nescafé resulted in 50,000 responses and £33,000 for the RSPCA. Compton & Woodhouse, the luxury gift company, produced a porcelain figurine with a purchase linked donation for the charity, netting over £6,000. Much goodwill is generated for these, and other, collaborating companies. ◆

Based on information from "Promotion Boost for Charities," *Marketing*, 24 May 1990, p. 13; Louella Miles, "An Infinite Solution for Brand or Charity," *Marketing*, 10 January 1991, pp. 27–28; Clare Sambrook, "Charity Founds Green Coupon," *Marketing*, 27 September 1990, p. 16; Suzanne Bidlake and Karen Hogan, "Does Charity Begin or End with Marketing?" *Marketing*, 22 November 1990, pp. 2–3; "Some Companies Have Already Found Out," RSPCA, Horsham, 1990, pp. 13–14.

A s indicated in Chapter 13, personal selling and sales promotion are two possible ingredients in a promotional mix. Personal selling is the more widely used. Sometimes it is a company's sole promotional tool, although it is generally used in conjunction with other promotional-mix ingredients. Personal selling is becoming more professional and sophisticated, with sales personnel acting more as consultants and advisers. The use of laptop computers has better equipped the salesperson to satisfy customers. Laptop computers allow the salesperson to have easier access to inventory listings and prices, to spend more time interacting with customers, and to gain more credibility with clients. Sales promotion, too, is playing an increasingly important role in marketing strategies.[1]

This chapter focuses on personal selling and sales promotion. We consider the purposes of personal selling, its basic steps, the types of salespersons, and how they are selected. We also discuss the major sales management decisions and activities, including setting objectives for the sales force and determining its size; recruiting, selecting, training, compensating, and motivating salespeople; managing sales territories; and controlling sales personnel. Then we examine several characteristics of sales promotion, the reasons for using sales promotion, and the sales promotion methods available for use in a promotional mix.

THE NATURE OF PERSONAL SELLING

Personal selling is a process of informing customers and persuading them to purchase products through personal communication in an exchange situation. For example, a salesperson describing the benefits of a Braun shaver to a customer in a Boots store is using personal selling. Personal selling gives marketers the greatest freedom to adjust a message to satisfy customers' information needs. In comparison with other promotional methods, personal selling is the most precise, enabling marketers to focus on the most promising sales prospects. Other promotional mix ingredients are aimed at groups of people, some of whom may not be prospective customers. A major disadvantage of personal selling is its cost. Generally, it is the most expensive ingredient in the promotional mix (salaries, cars, expenses). Personal selling costs are increasing faster than advertising costs.

Businesses spend more money on personal selling than on any other promotional mix ingredient. Millions of people, including increasing numbers of women, earn their living through personal selling. In the U.K. it is estimated that 600,000 people are directly employed as salespeople.[2] A selling career offers high income, a great deal of freedom, a high level of training, and a high level of job satisfaction.[3] Unfortunately, consumers often view personal selling negatively. A study of how marketing students perceived personal selling showed that approximately 25 percent of the survey group thought directly of door-to-door selling. In addition, 59 percent of all students surveyed had a negative impression of personal selling. Major corpo-

1. *Marketing,* 28 June 1990, p. 13.

2. Julian Cummins, *Sales Promotion* (London: Kogan Page, 1989).

3. Myron Gable and B. J. Reed, "The Current Status of Women in Professional Selling," *Journal of Personal Selling and Sales Management,* May 1987, pp. 33–39.

rations, professional sales associations (such as the Sales Lead Body), and academic institutions are making an effort to change the negative stereotypes of salespeople.[4]

Personal selling goals vary from one firm to another. However, they usually involve finding prospects, convincing prospects to buy, and keeping customers satisfied. Identifying potential buyers who are interested in an organisation's products is critical. Because most potential buyers seek information before they make a purchase, salespersons must ascertain prospects' informational needs and then provide the relevant information. To do so, sales personnel must be well trained, both in regard to their products and in regard to the selling process in general.

Salespeople need to be aware of their competitors. They need to monitor new products being developed, and they should be aware of all competitors' sales activities in their sales territories. Salespeople must emphasise the advantages their products provide when their competitors' products do not offer that specific advantage.[5] Later in this chapter we discuss this issue in greater detail.

Few businesses survive solely on profits from one-sale customers. For long-run survival, most marketers depend on repeat sales. A company has to keep its customers satisfied to obtain repeat purchases. Besides, satisfied customers help attract new ones by telling potential customers about the organisation and its products. Even though the whole organisation is responsible for providing customer satisfaction, much of the burden falls on salespeople. The salesperson is almost always closer to customers than anyone else in the company and often provides buyers with information and service after the sale. Such contact not only gives salespeople an opportunity to generate additional sales, but also offers them a good vantage point for evaluating the strengths and weaknesses of the company's products and other marketing mix ingredients. Their observations are helpful in developing and maintaining a marketing mix that better satisfies both customers and the firm.

A salesperson may be involved with achieving one or more of the three general goals. In some organisations, there are persons whose sole job is to find prospects. This information is relayed to salespeople, who contact the prospects. After the sale, these same salespeople may do the follow-up work, or a third group of employees may have the job of maintaining customer satisfaction. In many smaller organisations, a single person handles all these functions. No matter how many groups are involved, several major sales tasks must be performed to achieve these general goals.

ELEMENTS OF THE PERSONAL SELLING PROCESS

The exact activities involved in the selling process vary among salespersons and differ for particular selling situations. No two salespersons use exactly the same selling methods. None the less, many salespersons—either consciously or unconsciously—move through a general selling process as they sell products. This process consists of seven elements, or steps: prospecting and evaluating, preparing, approaching the customer, making the presentation, overcoming objections, closing, and following up.

4. William A. Weeks and Darrel D. Muehing, "Students' Perceptions of Personal Selling," *Industrial Marketing Management*, May 1987, pp. 145–151.

5. "Getting Ahead and Staying Ahead as the Competition Heats Up," *Agency Sales Magazine*, June 1987, pp. 38–42.

Prospecting and Evaluating

Developing a list of potential customers is called **prospecting**. A salesperson seeks the names of prospects from the company's sales records, referrals, trade shows, newspaper announcements (of marriages, births, deaths, and so on), public records, telephone directories, trade association directories, telemarketing lists,[6] and many other sources. Sales personnel also use responses from advertisements that encourage interested persons to send in an information request form. Seminars and meetings may produce good leads. Seminars may be targeted at particular types of clients, such as solicitors, accountants, the over-55s, and specific business persons.

After developing the prospect list, a salesperson evaluates whether each prospect is able, willing, and authorised to buy the product. On the basis of this evaluation, some prospects may be deleted, and others are deemed acceptable and ranked according to their desirability or potential.

Preparing

Before contacting acceptable prospects, a salesperson should find and analyse information about each prospect's specific product needs, current use of brands, feelings about available brands, and personal characteristics. The most successful salespeople are thorough in their preparation. They prepare by identifying key decision-makers, reviewing account histories and reports, contacting other clients for information, assessing credit histories and problems, preparing sales presentations, identifying product needs, and obtaining all relevant literature.[7] A salesperson with a lot of information about a prospect is better equipped to develop a presentation that precisely communicates with the prospect.

For example, Xerox developed an automated sales process to help salespersons prepare for complex sales situations after discovering that half its salespersons' time was taken up by sales-inhibiting activities, such as looking for forms and gathering information. Preparing an order required five to thirteen forms, and one-third of all orders were rejected because of mistakes on the forms. To overcome the problem, Xerox developed computer work stations to assist salespersons in shaping proposals, prospecting, and preparing, and to link salespersons throughout the company without a piece of paper having to be touched.[8]

Approaching the Customer

The **approach**—the manner in which a salesperson contacts a potential customer—is a critical step in the sales process. In more than 80 percent of initial sales calls, the purpose is to gather information about the buyer's needs and objectives. Creating a favourable impression and building rapport with the prospective client are also important tasks in the approach because the prospect's first impression of the salesperson is usually a lasting one, with long-run consequences. During the initial visit, the salesperson strives to develop a relationship rather than just push a product. The salesperson may have to call on a prospect several times before the product is considered.[9]

One type of approach is based on referrals. The salesperson approaches the prospect and explains that an acquaintance, an associate, or a relative had suggested the call. The salesperson who uses the cold canvass method calls on potential

6. Chris de Winter, *Telephone Selling* (London: Heinemann, 1988).

7. Thomas W. Leigh and Patrick F. McGraw, "Mapping the Procedural Knowledge of Industrial Sales Personnel: A Script-Theoretic Investigation," *Journal of Marketing*, January 1989, pp. 16–34.

8. Thayer C. Taylor, "Xerox: Who Says You Can't Be Big and Fast?" *Sales & Marketing Management*, November 1987, pp. 62–65.

9. Leigh and McGraw, pp. 16–34.

FIGURE 15.1

Enhancing the sales presentation.
To stimulate interest and stir up desire for a product, the salesperson should have the prospect touch, hold, or actually use the product.

SOURCE: Gary Gladstone/The Image Bank

customers without their prior consent. Repeat contact is another common approach; when making the contact, the salesperson mentions a prior meeting. The exact type of approach depends on the salesperson's preferences, the product being sold, the firm's resources, and the characteristics of the prospect.

■ **Making the Presentation**

During the sales presentation, the salesperson must attract and hold the prospect's attention to stimulate interest and stir up a desire for the product. The salesperson should have the prospect touch, hold, or actually use the product (see Figure 15.1). If possible, the salesperson should demonstrate the product and get the prospect more involved with it to stimulate greater interest. Audio-visual materials may be used to enhance the presentation.

During the presentation, the salesperson must not only talk but also listen. The sales presentation gives the salesperson the greatest opportunity to determine the prospect's specific needs by listening to questions and comments and observing responses. Even though the salesperson has planned the presentation in advance, she or he must be able to adjust the message to meet the prospect's information needs.

■ **Overcoming Objections**

An effective salesperson usually seeks out a prospect's objections in order to address them. If they are not apparent, the salesperson cannot deal with them, and they may keep the prospect from buying. One of the best ways to overcome a prospect's objections is to anticipate and counter them before the prospect has an opportunity to raise them. However, this approach can be risky because the salesperson may mention some objections that the prospect would not have raised. If possible, the salesperson should handle objections when they arise. They also can be dealt with at the end of the presentation.

■ **Closing**

Closing is the element in the selling process whereby the salesperson asks the prospect to buy the product or products. During the presentation, the salesperson may use a "trial close" by asking questions that assume the prospect will buy the product. For example, the salesperson might ask the potential customer about financial terms, desired colours or sizes, delivery arrangements, or the quantity to be purchased. The reactions to such questions usually indicate how close the prospect is to buying. A trial close allows prospects to indicate indirectly that they will buy the product without having to say those sometimes difficult words, "I'll take it".

A salesperson should try to close at several points during the presentation because the prospect may be ready to buy. One closing strategy involves asking the potential customer to take a trial order. The sales representative should either guarantee a refund if the customer is not satisfied or make the order a free offer.[10] Often an attempt to close the sale will result in objections. Thus closing can be an important stimulus that uncovers hidden objections, which can then be addressed.

■ **Following Up**

After a successful closing, the salesperson must follow up the sale. In the follow-up stage, the salesperson should determine whether the order was delivered on time and installed properly, if installation was required. He or she should contact the customer to learn what problems or questions have arisen regarding the product. The follow-up stage can also be used to determine customers' future product needs.

TYPES OF SALESPERSONS

To develop a sales force, a marketing manager must decide what kind of salesperson will sell the firm's products most effectively. Most business organisations use several different kinds of sales personnel. Based on the functions they perform, salespersons can be classified into three groups: order getters, order takers, and support personnel. One salesperson can, and often does, perform all three functions.

■ **Order Getters**

To obtain orders, a salesperson must inform prospects and persuade them to buy the product. The **order getters**' job is to increase the firm's sales by selling to new customers and by increasing sales to present customers. This task is sometimes called creative selling. It requires salespeople to recognise potential buyers' needs and then give them the necessary information. Order-getting activities sometimes are divided into two categories: current customer sales and new-business sales.

Current Customer Sales. Sales personnel who concentrate on current customers call on people and organisations that have purchased products from the firm at least once. These salespeople seek more sales from existing customers by following up previous sales. Current customers can also be sources of leads for new prospects.

10. John Nemec, "Do You Have Grand Finales?" *American Salesman,* June 1987, pp. 3–6.

New-Business Sales. Business organisations depend on sales to new customers, at least to some degree. New-business sales personnel locate prospects and convert them to buyers. Salespersons in many industries help to generate new business, but industries that depend in large part on new-customer sales are insurance, heavy industrial machinery, fleet cars, and office stationery.

The time-share industry uses various sales promotion techniques (direct mail, competitions, free offers) to attract potential buyers to attend seminars or open days at the time-share site. Once they are there, however, the sales force has to explain the concept of time-share, show the site's facilities, and close the deal. It is unlikely that other promotional techniques alone would be sufficient to get new customers signed up.

■ **Order Takers**

Taking orders is a repetitive task that salespersons perform to perpetuate long-lasting, satisfying relationships with customers. **Order takers** seek repeat sales. One of their major objectives is to be absolutely certain that customers have sufficient product quantities where and when they are needed. Most order takers handle orders for standardised products that are purchased routinely and therefore do not require extensive sales efforts.[11] There are two groups of order takers: inside order takers and field order takers.

Inside Order Takers. In many businesses, inside order takers, who work in sales offices, receive orders by mail and telephone (telesales). Certain producers, whole-salers, and even retailers have sales personnel who sell from within the firm rather than in the field. That does not mean that inside order takers never communicate with customers face to face. For example, salespersons in retail stores are classified as inside order takers.

Field Order Takers. Salespersons who travel to customers are referred to as "outside", or "field", order takers: the field force. Often a customer and a field order taker develop an interdependent relationship. The buyer relies on the salesperson to take orders periodically (and sometimes to deliver them), and the salesperson counts on the buyer to purchase a certain quantity of products periodically. Use of laptop computers such as the one shown in Figure 15.2 can improve the field order taker's tracking of inventory and orders.

Field and inside order takers should not be thought of as passive functionaries who simply record orders in a machine-like manner. Order takers generate the bulk of many organisations' total sales.

■ **Support Personnel**

Support personnel facilitate the selling function but usually are not involved solely with making sales. They are engaged primarily in marketing industrial products. They locate prospects, educate customers, build goodwill, and provide service after the sale. Although there are many kinds of sales support personnel, the three most common are missionary, trade, and technical.

Missionary Salespersons. **Missionary salespersons**, who are usually employed by manufacturers, assist the producer's customers in selling to their own customers. A missionary salesperson may call on retailers to inform and persuade them to buy

11. William C. Moncrief, "Five Types of Industrial Sales Jobs," *Industrial Marketing Management,* 17 (1988), p. 164.

FIGURE 15.2
A tool for field order takers

SOURCE: Courtesy of GRiD Systems

the manufacturer's products. If the call is successful, the retailers purchase the products from wholesalers, who are the producer's customers. Manufacturers of medical supplies and pharmaceutical products often use missionary salespersons to promote their products to doctors, hospitals, and retail chemists.

Trade Salespersons.   **Trade salespersons** are not strictly support personnel because they usually perform the order-taking function as well. However, they direct much of their efforts towards helping customers, especially retail stores, promote the product. They are likely to re-stock shelves, obtain more shelf space, set up displays, provide in-store demonstrations, and distribute samples to store customers. Food producers and cosmetics companies commonly employ trade salespersons.

Technical Salespersons.   **Technical salespersons** give technical assistance to the organisation's current customers. They advise customers on product characteristics and applications, system designs, and installation procedures. Because this job is often highly technical, the salesperson usually needs to have formal training in one of the physical sciences or in engineering. Technical sales personnel often sell technical industrial products, such as computers, heavy equipment, and steel.

When hiring sales personnel, marketers seldom restrict themselves to a single category because most firms require different types. Several factors dictate how many of each type of salesperson a particular company should have. A product's uses, characteristics, complexity, price, and margin influence the kind of sales personnel used, as do the number of customers and their characteristics. The kinds of marketing channels and the intensity and type of advertising also have an impact on the selection of sales personnel.

MANAGEMENT OF THE SALES FORCE

The sales force is directly responsible for generating an organisation's primary input: sales revenue. Without adequate sales revenue, a business cannot survive long. A firm's reputation is often determined by the ethical conduct of the sales force. On the other hand, the morale, and ultimately the success, of a firm's sales force is determined in large part by adequate compensation, room for advancement, adequate training, and management support, all key areas of sales management. When these elements are not satisfying to salespersons, they may leave for more satisfying jobs elsewhere. This problem of sales force turnover is the subject of Marketing Update 15.1. It is important to evaluate the input of salespeople because effective sales-force management determines a firm's success.

In this section we explore eight general areas of sales management: (1) establishing sales-force objectives, (2) determining sales-force size, (3) recruiting and selecting salespeople, (4) training sales personnel, (5) compensating salespeople, (6) motivating salespeople, (7) managing sales territories, and (8) controlling and evaluating sales-force performance.

■ **Establishing Sales-Force Objectives**

To manage a sales force effectively, a sales manager must develop sales objectives. Sales objectives tell salespersons what they are expected to accomplish during a specified time period. They give the sales force direction and purpose and serve as performance standards for the evaluation and control of sales personnel. For example in Figure 15.3 the manufacturer of software, Intel, is encouraging salespeople to suggest an additional piece of software—just as McDonald's suggests fries and soft drinks. A sales-force objective for Intel would be to generate 5 percent additional units in sales through suggestion selling. As with all types of objectives, sales objectives should be stated in precise, measurable terms and should specify the time period and the geographic areas involved.

Sales objectives are usually developed for both the total sales force and each salesperson. Objectives for the entire force are normally stated in terms of sales volume, market share, or profit. Volume objectives refer to a quantity of pounds or sales units. For example, the objective for an electric drill manufacturer's sales force might be to sell £6 million worth of drills annually or 600,000 drills annually. When sales goals are stated in terms of market share, they usually call for an increase in the proportion of the company's sales relative to the total number of products sold by all businesses in that particular industry. When sales objectives are based on profit, they are generally stated in terms of monetary amounts or in terms of return on investment.

Sales objectives, or quotas, for individual salespersons are commonly stated in terms of monetary or unit sales volume. Other bases used for individual sales objectives include average order size, average number of calls per time period, and the ratio of orders to calls.

MANAGING SALES-FORCE TURNOVER

Sales-force turnover—the replacement of employees who leave a company—is an area of increasing concern for U.S. companies that rely on personal selling. Turnover across all sales positions more than tripled from 1983 to 1988, from an average of 7.6 percent to 27 percent. Turnover costs the average company nearly $250,000 a year in time spent in recruiting and training replacements and in the loss of potential business.

A survey of 500 sales representatives and managers in the United States and Canada found that the top three reasons salespeople cite for leaving their jobs are inadequate compensation, lack of advancement opportunities, and personality conflicts. A natural conflict often exists between salespeople, who are generally motivated by self-achievement, and managers, who are motivated by power and who often make less money than those they manage. About one-third of the survey respondents indicated better management support would improve their jobs. Although a majority of the respondents were highly satisfied with both the quality of the goods or services they sold and their companies' reputations, they were least satisfied with the things that management used to help salespeople prepare for and perform their jobs: sales tools, sales incentives, and sales training programmes.

Sales force managers can reduce turnover by promoting greater job satisfaction and stronger company loyalty. Conducting surveys to determine how salespeople feel about their jobs may indicate that different reward systems are needed. High performers tend to respond to pay satisfaction; low performers generally leave when they are no longer satisfied with their jobs.

Another suggestion for reducing turnover is using an open-door style of management, including weekly sessions with salespeople to spot potential problems. Other suggestions include keeping issues in perspective (e.g., compensation versus other work-related issues), conducting periodic audits to determine causes of job dissatisfaction, establishing recruiting standards for prospective employees, and re-evaluating training programmes so that salespeople have essential product knowledge and sales skills.

SOURCES: Lynn G. Coleman, "Sales Force Turnover Has Managers Wondering Why," *Marketing News,* 4 Dec. 1989, pp. 6, 21; George H. Lucas, Jr., A. Parasuraman, Robert A. Davis, and Ben M. Enis, "An Empirical Study of Salesforce Turnover," *Journal of Marketing,* July 1987, pp. 34–59; Lester L. Tobias, "Is Salesperson Turnover Bashing Your Bottom Line?" *Business Marketing,* June 1986, pp. 78–82; George H. Lucas, Jr., Emin Babakus, and Thomas N. Ingram, "An Empirical Test of the Job Satisfaction-Turnover Relationship: Assessing the Role of Job Performance for Retail Managers," *Journal of the Academy of Marketing Science,* 1990.

FIGURE 15.3
Establishing objectives. Intel promotes suggestion selling of software to assist salespeople in meeting their sales goals.

SOURCE: Courtesy of Intel Corporation

Determining Sales Force Size

Deciding how many salespersons to use is important because it influences the company's ability to generate sales and profits. Moreover, the size of the sales force affects the compensation methods used, salespersons' morale, and overall sales force management. Sales force size must be adjusted from time to time because a firm's marketing plans change, as do markets and forces in the marketing environment. One danger is to cut back the size of the sales force to increase profits by cutting costs. The sales organisation could lose its strength and resiliency, preventing it from rebounding when growth rebounds or better market conditions prevail. The organisation that loses capacity through cutbacks may not have the energy to accelerate.[12]

There are several analytical methods for determining the optimal size of the sales force; however, a detailed discussion of these methods is beyond the scope of this text. Although marketing managers may use one or several analytical methods, they normally temper their decisions with a good deal of subjective judgement.[13]

12. A. J. Magrath, "Are You Overdoing 'Lean and Mean'?" *Sales & Marketing Management,* January 1988, pp. 46–53.

13. Tony Adams, *Successful Sales Management* (London: Heinemann, 1988).

■ Recruiting and Selecting Salespeople

To create and maintain an effective sales force, a sales manager must recruit the right type of salespeople. **Recruiting** is a process by which the sales manager develops a list of applicants for sales positions. The cost of hiring, training, and retaining a salesperson is soaring; currently, costs can reach £60,000 or more.[14]

To ensure that the recruiting process results in a pool of qualified salespersons from which to choose, a sales manager should establish a set of required qualifications before beginning to recruit. Although for years marketers have attempted to identify a set of traits that characterise effective salespeople, there is currently no such set of generally accepted characteristics. Therefore a sales manager must develop a set tailored to the sales tasks in a particular company. Two activities can help establish this set of requirements. The sales manager should prepare a job description that lists the specific tasks salespersons are to perform. The manager also should analyse the characteristics of the firm's successful salespersons, as well as those of ineffective sales personnel. From the job description and the analysis of traits, the sales manager should be able to develop a set of specific requirements and be aware of potential weaknesses that could lead to failure.

A sales manager generally recruits applicants from several sources: departments within the firm, other firms, employment agencies, educational institutions, respondents to advertisements, and individuals recommended by current employees. The specific sources a sales manager uses depend on the type of salesperson required and the manager's experiences with particular sources.

The process of hiring a sales force varies tremendously from one company to another. One technique used to determine whether potential candidates will be good salespeople is an assessment centre. Assessment centres are intense training environments that place candidates in realistic problem settings in which they must give priorities to their activities, make decisions, and act on their decisions. Candidates are judged by experienced managers or trained observers. Assessment centres have proved to be valuable in selecting good salespeople.[15]

Sales management should design a selection procedure that satisfies the company's specific needs. The process should include enough steps to yield the information needed for making accurate selection decisions. However, because each step incurs a certain expense, there should be no more steps than necessary. The stages of the selection process should be sequenced so that the more expensive steps, such as physical examination, are near the end. Fewer people will then move through the higher-cost stages.

Recruitment should not be sporadic; it should be a continuous activity aimed at reaching the best applicants. The selection process should systematically and effectively match applicants' characteristics and needs with the requirements of specific selling tasks. Finally, the selection process should ensure that new sales personnel are available where and when they are needed.

Recruitment and selection of salespeople are not one-time decisions. The market and marketing environment change, as do an organisation's objectives, resources, and marketing strategies. Maintaining the proper mix of salespeople thus requires the firm's sales management's continued decision-making.

14. Coleman, pp. 6, 21.

15. Patrick C. Fleenor, "Selling and Sales Management in Action: Assessment Center Selection of Sales Representatives," *Journal of Personal Selling & Sales Management,* May 1987, pp. 57–59.

FIGURE 15.4
Toyota's sales training approach.
In the U.S., Toyota boasts that its sales force does not pressure potential customers and practises common courtesy.

THE **TOYOTA** TOUCH

THE ONLY PRESSURE
IN A SHOWROOM
SHOULD BE IN
THE TIRES.

Nobody wants to be pressured into anything. Especially anything as important as buying a car or truck. Toyota understands that a relaxed shopping environment leads to a productive shopping experience. And a productive shopping experience is what every car manufacturer should strive for. That's the thinking behind The Toyota Touch. A philosophy based on the simple notion of common courtesy. Our goal is to make the only pressure you feel in a Toyota showroom that of a good, firm handshake.

TOYOTA QUALITY
WHO COULD ASK FOR ANYTHING MORE!

SOURCE: Courtesy of Toyota Motor Sales U.S.A., Inc.

■ Training Sales Personnel

Many organisations have formal training programmes; others depend on informal on-the-job training. Some systematic training programmes are quite extensive; others are rather short and rudimentary. Regardless of whether the training programme is complex or simple, its developers must consider what to teach, who to train, and how to train them. In Figure 15.4, Toyota communicates that its sales force provides minimal pressure in dealing with potential customers.

A sales training programme can concentrate on the company, on products, or on selling methods. Training programmes often cover all three areas. Training for experienced company salespersons usually emphasises product information, although they must also be informed about new selling techniques and any changes in company plans, policies, and procedures.

Training programmes can be aimed at newly hired salespeople, at experienced salespersons, or both. Ordinarily, new sales personnel require comprehensive training, whereas experienced personnel need both refresher courses about established products and training that gives them new-product information. Training programmes can be directed at the entire sales force or at one segment of it.

Sales training may be done in the field, at educational institutions, in company facilities, or in several of these locations. Some firms train new employees before assigning them to a specific sales position. Other businesses, however, put them into the field immediately and provide formal training only after the new salespersons have gained a little experience. Training programmes for new personnel can be as short as several days or as long as three years; some are even longer. Sales training for experienced personnel is often scheduled during a period when sales activities are not too demanding. Because training of experienced salespeople is usually a recurring effort, a firm's sales management must determine the frequency, sequencing, and duration of these activities.

Sales managers, as well as other salespeople, often engage in sales training—whether daily on the job or periodically in sales meetings. Salespeople sometimes receive training from technical specialists within their own organisations. In addition, a number of individuals and organisations sell special sales training programmes. Appropriate materials for sales training programmes range from films, texts, manuals, and cases to programmed learning devices and audio and video cassettes. As for teaching methods, lectures, demonstrations, simulation exercises, and on-the-job training can all be effective. The choice of methods and materials for a particular sales training programme depends on the type and number of trainees, the programme's content and complexity, its length and location, the size of the training budget, the number of teachers, and the teachers' preferences.

■ Compensating Salespeople

To develop and maintain a highly productive sales force, a business must formulate and administer a compensation plan that attracts, motivates, and retains the most effective individuals. The plan should give sales management the desired level of control and provide sales personnel with an acceptable level of freedom, income, and incentive. It should also be flexible, equitable, easy to administer, and easy to understand. Good compensation programmes facilitate and encourage proper treatment of customers.

Even though these requirements appear to be logical and easily satisfied, it is actually quite difficult to incorporate them all into a simple programme. Some of them will be satisfied, and others will not. Studies evaluating the impact of financial incentives on sales performance indicate five general responses. For money-sensitive individuals, an increase in incentives will usually increase their sales efforts, and a decrease in financial rewards will diminish their efforts. Unresponsive salespeople will sell at the same level regardless of the incentive. Leisure-sensitive salespeople tend to work less when the incentive system is implemented. Income satisfiers normally adjust their performance to match their income goal. Understanding potential reactions and analysing the personalities of the sales force can help management evaluate whether an incentive programme might work.[16] Therefore, in formulating a compensation plan, sales management must strive for a proper balance of freedom, income, and incentives.

The developer of a compensation programme must determine the general level of compensation required and the most desirable method of calculating it. In analysing the required compensation level, sales management must ascertain a salesperson's value to the company on the basis of the tasks and responsibilities

16. Rene Y. Darmon, "The Impact of Incentive Compensation on the Salesperson's Work Habits: An Economic Model," *Journal of Personal Selling & Sales Management,* May 1987, pp. 21–32.

associated with the sales position. The sales manager may consider a number of factors, including salaries of other types of personnel in the firm, competitors' compensation plans, costs of sales-force turnover, and the size of non-salary selling expenses and perks.

Sales compensation programmes usually reimburse salespersons for their selling expenses, provide a certain number of fringe benefits, and deliver the required compensation level. To do that, a firm may use one or more of three basic compensation methods: straight salary, straight commission, or a combination of salary and commission. In a **straight salary compensation plan**, salespeople are paid a specified amount per time period. This sum remains the same until they receive a pay increase or decrease. In a **straight commission compensation plan**, salespeople's compensation is determined solely by the amount of their sales for a given time period. A commission may be based on a single percentage of sales or on a sliding scale involving several sales levels and percentage rates. In a **combination compensation plan**, salespeople are paid a fixed salary and a commission based on sales volume. Some combination programmes require a salesperson to exceed a certain sales level before earning a commission; others offer commissions for any level of sales.

Traditionally, department stores have paid salespeople straight salaries, but combination compensation plans are becoming popular. Concessionaires in Debenhams, for example, are offering commissions (averaging 6 to 8 percent) to a large segment of their sales force. The practice has made the salespeople more attentive to a customer's presence and needs; it has also attracted older, more experienced salespeople, who tend to be in short supply.[17] Car salespersons traditionally receive low basic salaries (£5,000 to £9,500 p.a.), with the remainder coming from commission.

Table 15.1 lists the major characteristics of each sales-force compensation method. Notice that the combination method is most popular. When selecting a compensation method, sales management weighs the advantages and disadvantages shown in Table 15.1.

Proper administration of the sales-force compensation programme is crucial for developing high morale and productivity among sales personnel. A good salesperson is very marketable in today's work place, and successful sales managers switch industries on a regular basis. Basic knowledge and skills related to sales management are in demand, and sometimes new insights can be gained from different work experiences. For example, one of British Steel's best sales managers was recruited from the grocery sector. To maintain an effective compensation programme and retain productive employees, sales management should periodically review and evaluate the plan and make necessary adjustments.

■ Motivating Salespeople

A sales manager should develop a systematic approach for motivating salespersons to be productive. Motivating should not be viewed as a sporadic activity reserved for periods of sales decline. Effective sales-force motivation is achieved through an organised set of activities performed continuously by the company's sales management. For example, scheduled sales meetings can motivate salespeople. Periodic sales meetings have four main functions: recognising and reinforcing the performance of salespeople, sharing sales techniques that are working, focusing employees'

17. Aimee Stern, "Commissions Catch on at Department Stores," *Adweek's Marketing Week,* 1 Feb. 1988, p. 5.

TABLE 15.1 *Characteristics of sales-force compensation methods*

COMPENSATION METHOD	FREQUENCY OF USE (%)[a]	WHEN ESPECIALLY USEFUL	ADVANTAGES	DISADVANTAGES
Straight salary	17.4	Compensating new salespersons; firm moves into new sales territories that require developmental work; salespersons need to perform many non-selling activities	Gives salesperson maximum amount of security; gives sales manager large amount of control over salespersons; easy to administer; yields more predictable selling expenses	Provides no incentive; necessitates closer supervision of salespersons' activities; during sales declines, selling expenses remain at same level
Straight commission	6.5	Highly aggressive selling is required; non-selling tasks are minimised; company cannot closely control sales-force activities	Provides maximum amount of incentive; by increasing commission rate, sales managers can encourage salespersons to sell certain items; selling expenses relate directly to sales resources	Salespersons have little financial security; sales manager has minimum control over sales force; may cause salespeople to give inadequate service to smaller accounts; selling costs less predictable
Combination	76.1	Sales territories have relatively similar sales potentials; firm wishes to provide incentive but still control sales-force activities	Provides certain level of financial security; provides some incentive; selling expenses fluctuate with sales revenue	Selling expenses less predictable; may be difficult to administer

[a]The figures are computed from "Alternative Sales Compensation and Incentive Plans," *Sales & Marketing Management,* 17 Feb. 1986, p. 57. *Note:* The percentage for Combination includes compensation methods that involved any combination of salary, commission, or bonus.

SOURCE: Based on the *Harvard Business Review* article "How to Pay Your Sales Force" by John P. Steinbrink (July/August 1978).

efforts on matching the corporate goals and evaluating their progress towards achieving these goals, and teaching the sales staff about new products and services.[18]

Although financial compensation is important, a motivational programme must also satisfy non-financial needs. Sales personnel, like other people, join organisations to satisfy personal needs and achieve personal goals. Sales managers must become aware of their sales personnel's motives and goals and then attempt to create an organisational climate that lets them satisfy their personal needs.

18. Terese Hudson, "Holding Meetings Sharpens Employees' Sales Skills," *Savings Institutions,* July 1987, pp. 109–111.

A sales manager can use a variety of positive motivational incentives as well as financial compensation (see Figure 15.5). For example, enjoyable working conditions, power and authority, job security, and an opportunity to excel can be effective motivators. Salespeople can also be motivated by their company's efforts to make their job more productive and efficient. For example, Honeywell Information Systems developed a computerised sales support system that has increased sales productivity by 31 percent and reduced sales-force turnover by 40 percent within a year. This system can track leads and provide customer profiles and competitor data.[19]

Sales contests and other incentive programmes can also be effective motivators. Sales contests can motivate salespersons to focus on increasing sales or new accounts, promote special items, achieve greater volume per sales call, cover territories better, and increase activity in new geographic areas.[20] Some companies have found such incentive programmes to be powerful motivating tools that marketing managers can use to achieve corporate goals. Properly designed, an incentive programme can pay for itself many times over. However, for an incentive system to succeed, the marketing objectives must be accepted by the participants and prove effective in the market-place. Some organisations also use negative motivational measures: financial penalties, demotions, even terminations of employment.

■ Managing Sales Territories

The effectiveness of a sales force that must travel to its customers is influenced, to some degree, by sales management's decisions regarding sales territories. Sales managers deciding on territories must consider size, shape, routing, and scheduling.

Creating Sales Territories.   Several factors enter into the design of the size and shape of sales territories. First, sales managers must construct the territories so that sales potentials can be measured. Thus sales territories often consist of several geographic units for which market data are obtainable, such as census tracts, cities, counties, or regions. Sales managers usually try to create territories that have similar sales potentials or that require about the same amount of work. If territories have equal sales potentials, they will almost always be unequal in geographic size. The salespersons who get the larger territories will have to work longer and harder to generate a certain sales volume. Conversely, if sales territories that require equal amounts of work are created, sales potentials for those territories will often vary. If sales personnel are partially or fully compensated through commissions, they will have unequal income potentials. Many sales managers try to balance territorial workloads and earning potentials by using differential commission rates. Although a sales manager seeks equity when developing and maintaining sales territories, some inequities will always prevail.

A territory's size and shape should also be designed to help the sales force provide the best possible customer coverage and to minimise selling costs. Territory size and shape should take into account the density and distribution of customers.

Routing and Scheduling Salespeople.   The geographic size and shape of a sales territory are the most important factors affecting routing and scheduling of sales

19. Dan Woog, "Taking Sales High Tech," *High Tech Marketing*, May 1987, pp. 17–22.

20. Sandra Hile Hart, William C. Moncrief, and A. Parasuraman, "An Empirical Investigation of Salespeople's Performance, Effort and Selling Method During a Sales Contest," *Journal of the Academy of Marketing Science*, Winter 1989, pp. 29–39.

calls. Next are the number and distribution of customers within the territory, followed by the frequency and duration of sales calls. The person in charge of routing and scheduling must consider the sequence in which customers are called on, the specific roads or transport schedules to be used, the number of calls to be made in a given period, and what time of day the calls will occur. In some firms, salespeople plan their own routes and schedules with little or no assistance from the sales manager; in other organisations, the sales manager draws up the routes and schedules. No matter who plans the routing and scheduling, the major goals should be to minimise salespersons' non-selling time (the time spent travelling and waiting) and maximise their selling time. The planners should try to achieve these goals in a way that holds a salesperson's travel and accommodation costs to a minimum. Many companies use agencies, such as SPA Ltd, to construct databases of actual and potential customers and associated sales territories. SPA has a database of car and lorry drive-times, even taking account of road works, which allows sales territories to be delineated. These territories can share out actual and potential customers and allocate the sales force in relation to the time taken to service them.

■ Controlling and Evaluating Sales-Force Performance

To control and evaluate sales-force activities properly, sales management needs information. A sales manager cannot observe the field sales force daily and so relies on call reports, customer feedback, and invoices. Call reports identify the customers called on and present detailed information about interaction with those clients. Travelling sales personnel must often file work schedules indicating where they plan to be during specific future time periods.

The dimensions used to measure a salesperson's performance are determined largely by sales objectives. These objectives are normally set by the sales manager. If an individual's sales objective is stated in terms of sales volume, then that person should be evaluated on the basis of sales volume generated. Even though a salesperson may be assigned a major objective, he or she is ordinarily expected to achieve several related objectives as well. Thus salespeople are often judged along several dimensions. Sales managers evaluate many performance indicators, including average number of calls per day, average sales per customer, actual sales relative to sales potential, number of new-customer orders, average cost per call, and average gross profit per customer.

To evaluate a salesperson, a sales manager may compare one or more of these dimensions with a predetermined performance standard. However, sales management commonly compares one salesperson's performance with the performance of other employees operating under similar selling conditions or compares current performance with past performance. Sometimes management judges factors that have less direct bearing on sales performance, such as personal appearance, knowledge of the product, and competitors.

After evaluating salespeople, sales managers must take any needed corrective action because it is their job to improve the performance of the sales force. They may have to adjust performance standards, provide additional sales training, or try other motivational methods. Corrective action may demand comprehensive changes in the sales force.

Many industries, especially technical ones, are monitoring their sales forces and increasing productivity through the use of laptop (portable) computers. In part, the increasing use of computers in technical sales is a response to customers' greater technical sophistication. Product information—especially information on price, specifications, and availability of products—helps salespeople to be more valuable. Some companies that have provided their sales forces with laptops expect a 15 to 20 percent increase in their sales.[21]

THE NATURE OF SALES PROMOTION

As defined earlier, **sales promotion** is an activity or material (or both) that acts as a direct inducement, offering added value or incentive to buy the product, to resellers, salespersons, or consumers.[22] The sale probably would have taken place without the sales promotion activity, but not for a while; the promotion has brought the sale forward. For example, a consumer loyal to Persil washing powder may purchase a

21. Robert Martinott, "The Traveling Salesman Goes High Tech," *Chemical Week,* 10 June 1987, pp. 22–24.

22. John F. Luick and William L. Ziegler, *Sales Promotion and Modern Merchandising* (New York: McGraw-Hill, 1968); and Don E. Schultz and William A. Robinson, *Sales Promotion Management* (Chicago: Crain Books, 1982).

FIGURE 15.6
Breakdown of spend on marketing services (1989)

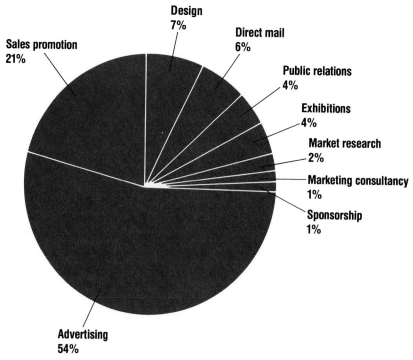

SOURCE: Data from Mintel, Marketing Research Special Report, 1990, *Marketing,* 1990. Reprinted by permission.

packet every four weeks. If, however, on the third week, Sainsbury or Tesco has Persil on offer or with an on-pack promotion, the consumer will probably buy a week early to take advantage of the deal. Sales promotion encompasses all promotional activities and materials other than personal selling, advertising, and publicity. In competitive markets, where products are very similar, sales promotion provides additional inducements that encourage purchases. Sales promotions are designed to generate short-term sales and good will towards the promoter.

Sales promotion has grown dramatically in the last ten years, largely because of the focus of business on short-term profits and value and the perceived need for promotional strategies that produce short-term sales boosts.[23] Current estimates in the U.K. suggest consumer sales promotion to be worth £2 billion annually. Include price discounting and the figure could be £4 billion higher; include trade sales promotion and the total reaches £8 billion.[24] The most significant change in promotion expenditures in recent years has been the transfer of funds usually earmarked for advertising to sales promotion. Companies now spend 54 percent of their combined marketing services budgets on advertising and 21 percent on sales promotion (see Figure 15.6).[25] Fundamental changes in marketing, which have led to a greater emphasis on sales promotion, mean that specialist sales promotion agencies have increased and major advertising agencies have developed sales promotion departments.

23. Thomas McCann, "Promotions Will Gain More Clout in the '90s," *Marketing News,* 6 Nov. 1989, pp. 4, 24.

24. Cummins, p. 14.

25. "Factfile," *Marketing,* 12 July 1990, p. 18.

FIGURE 15.7

The "ratchet effect."
Sales promotion (SP) brings forward sales but has an immediate effect. An advertising campaign (A) takes time to take off and to generate sales, but can switch other-brand users and non-users. The ratchet effect has been identified in most U.S. consumer and service markets.

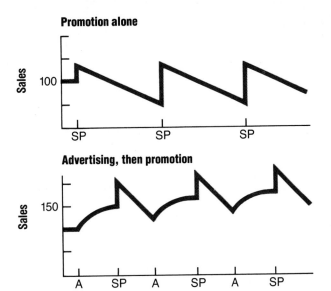

Promotion alone

Advertising, then promotion

SOURCE: W.T. Moran, "Insights from Pricing Research," in E.B. Bailey (ed.), *Pricing Practices and Strategies* (New York: The Conference Board, 1978), pp. 7–13. Used by permission.

An organisation often uses sales promotion activities in concert with other promotional efforts to facilitate personal selling, advertising, or both. Figure 15.7 depicts what is known as the **ratchet effect**—the impact of using sales promotion (short-term sales brought forward) and advertising (longer-term build-up to generate sales) together. Sales promotion efforts are not always secondary to other promotional mix ingredients. Companies sometimes use advertising and personal selling to support sales promotion activities. For example, marketers frequently use advertising to promote contests, free samples, and premiums. Manufacturers' sales personnel occasionally administer sales contests for wholesale or retail salespersons. The most effective sales promotion efforts are highly interrelated with other promotional activities. Decisions regarding sales promotion therefore often affect advertising and personal selling decisions, and vice versa.

SALES-PROMOTION OPPORTUNITIES AND LIMITATIONS

Sales promotion can increase sales by providing an extra incentive to purchase. There are many opportunities to motivate consumers, resellers, and salespeople to take a desired action. Some kinds of sales promotion are designed specifically to stimulate resellers' demand and effectiveness; some are directed at increasing consumer demand; and others focus on both resellers and consumers. Regardless of the purpose, marketers need to ensure that the sales promotion objectives are consistent with the organisation's overall objectives, as well as with its marketing and promotion objectives. As Marketing Update 15.2 reveals, even the mega-marketers sometimes get it wrong!

Although sales promotion can support a brand image, excessive price-reduction sales promotion, such as coupons, can affect it adversely. Firms therefore must decide between short-term sales increases and the long-run need for a desired

COKE'S SALES PROMOTION AWRY

Sales-promotion agencies in Europe must beware. As Coca-Cola's experiences in America show, not every programme is successful. The soft-drinks giant launched its biggest-ever summer sales-promotion campaign in 1990: a $100-million push behind Coca-Cola Classic, centred on "magicans".

Magicans appear to be and feel like normal cans and are sold similarly to Coca-Cola's other merchandise. When the tab is pulled, though, a mechanism in the can pops up coupons or rolled-up cash—$5 to $200. Unfortunately for Coca-Cola, the magicans did not all work properly, and these few failures were widely reported in the media. Either the mechanism was faulty or the seal holding the liquid that gave the can the feel of the real item had broken.

Coca-Cola delayed, temporarily, distribution of the 750,000 cans so each could be shaken to determine whether the seal had broken. A TV and press advertising campaign was hurriedly put together to explain the sales promotion and to warn people not to drink the liquid if the seal had broken. Pepsi Cola's promotion continued on schedule with, for a while, no promotional competition from Coca-Cola.

SOURCE: Bill Britt, "Coke's Magic Spells Trouble," *Marketing,* 31 May 1990, p. 1; "World News," *Marketing,* 7 June 1990, p. 4; "Coca-Cola Toys with Huge Mattel Promotion," *Marketing,* 15 November 1990, p. 16.

reputation and brand image.[26] As already noted, sales promotion has been catching up with advertising in total expenditure, but in the future brand advertising may become more important relative to sales promotion. Some firms that shifted from brand advertising to sales promotion have lost market share, particularly in consumer markets where advertising is essential to maintain awareness and brand recognition. Advertising does not necessarily work better than sales promotion. There are trade-offs between these two forms of promotion, and the marketing manager must determine the right balance to achieve maximum promotional effectiveness.

SALES PROMOTION METHODS

Most sales promotion methods can be grouped into the categories of consumer sales promotion and trade sales promotion. **Consumer sales promotion techniques** encourage or stimulate consumers to patronise a specific retail store or to try a particular product. **Trade sales promotion methods** stimulate wholesalers and retailers to carry a producer's products and to market these products aggressively.

Marketers consider a number of factors before deciding which sales promotion methods to use. They must take into account both product characteristics (size, weight, costs, durability, uses, features, and hazards) and target market characteristics (age, sex, income, location, density, usage rate, and shopping patterns). How the product is distributed and the number and types of resellers may determine the type of method used. The competitive and legal environment may also influence the choice.

In this section we look closely at several consumer and trade sales promotion methods to learn what they entail and what goals they can help marketers achieve.

Figure 15.8 shows how all members of a marketing channel can be engaged in sales promotion activities with different target audiences and techniques.

■ Consumer Sales Promotion Methods

In this section we discuss coupons, demonstrations, frequent-user incentives, point-of-sale displays, free samples, money refunds, premiums, price-off offers, and consumer contests and sweepstakes.

Coupons. **Coupons** are used to stimulate consumers to try a new or established product, to increase sales volume quickly, to attract repeat purchasers, or to introduce new package sizes or features. Coupons usually reduce the purchase price of an item. For example, Figure 15.9 illustrates how Schwarzkopf hoped to increase sales of its Neutral Line haircare products with a 50p-off coupon. The savings may be deducted from the purchase price or offered as cash. For best results, coupons should be easy to recognise and state the offer clearly. The nature of the product (seasonality, maturity, frequency of purchase, and the like) is the prime consideration in setting up a coupon promotion.

Several thousand manufacturers distribute coupons, which are used by approximately 80 percent of all households. One study found that pride and satisfaction from obtaining savings through the use of coupons and price consciousness were the

26. W. E. Phillips and Bill Robinson, "Continued Sales (Price) Promotion Destroys Brands: Yes; No," *Marketing News,* 16 Jan. 1989, pp. 4, 8.

FIGURE 15.8

*Uses of sales promotion
in the marketing channel*

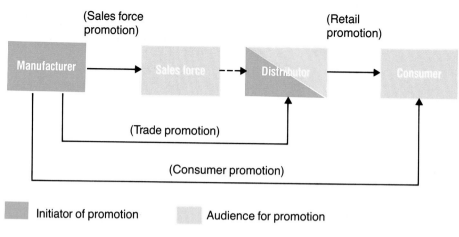

Initiator of promotion   Audience for promotion

Consumer: Coupons, free samples, demonstrations, competitions
Trade (at wholesalers, retailers, salespeople): Sales competitions, free merchandise,
   P.O.S. displays, plus trade shows and conferences

SOURCE: Figure from p. 310 in *Advertising and Promotion Management* by John Rossiter and Larry Percy.
Copyright © 1987 by McGraw-Hill, Inc. Reprinted by permission of McGraw-Hill, Inc.

most important determinants of coupon use.[27] Coupons are distributed through free-standing inserts (FSIs), print advertising, direct mail/leaflet drops, and in stores. Historically, FSIs have been the dominant vehicle for coupons.[28] When deciding on the proper vehicle for their coupons, marketers should consider strategies and objectives, redemption rates, availability, circulation, and exclusivity. The whole coupon distribution and redemption area has become very competitive. To draw customers to their stores, grocers may double and sometimes even triple the value of the coupons they bring in. But because the practice of doubling and tripling coupons is expensive, many of these retailers have asked manufacturers to reduce the face value of the coupons they offer.[29]

There are several advantages to using coupons. Print advertisements with coupons are often more effective than non-promotional advertising for generating brand awareness. Generally, the larger the coupon's cash offer, the better the recognition generated. Another advantage is that coupons are a good way to reward present users of the product, win back former users, and encourage purchases in larger quantities. Coupons also let manufacturers determine whether the coupons reached the intended target market because they get the coupons back.

Coupons also have drawbacks. Fraud and misredemption are possible, and the redemption period can be quite lengthy. Table 15.2 illustrates coupon redemption rates in the U.K. In addition, some experts believe that coupons are losing their value because so many manufacturers are offering them, and consumers have therefore learned not to buy without some incentive, whether it be a coupon, a rebate, or a refund. There has been a general decline in brand loyalty among heavy coupon

27. Emin Babakus, Peter Tat, and William Cunningham, "Coupon Redemption: A Motivational Perspective," *Journal of Consumer Marketing,* Spring 1988, p. 40.

28. Donna Campanella, "Sales Promotion: Couponmania," *Marketing and Media Decisions,* June 1987, pp. 118–122.

29. Alison Fahey, "Coupon War Fallout," *Advertising Age,* 4 Sept. 1989, p. 2.

THE PURCHASE OF ULTRA PURE NEUTRAL LINE PRODUCTS

TO THE CONSUMER – to obtain 50p off your purchase of Neutral Line Ultra Pure Hair Care hand this coupon to the retailer when you purchase the product. Only one coupon per product purchased.

TO THE MANAGER – this coupon will be redeemed by Schwarzkopf if it has been accepted by you in part payment for any single purchase of Neutral Line Ultra Pure Hair Care.

TO REDEEM YOUR COUPONS SEND TO:
Schwarzkopf Limited, Department 308, Corby, Northants, NN17 1NN.
Schwarzkopf reserve the right:- (a) to require proof of purchase. (b) to refuse redemption on any coupon they consider shall not have been validly redeemed.

Surname _____ First Name _____

Address _____

Postcode _____

Age _____ Telephone No. _____

If you *do not* wish to receive valuable information and special offers in the future please tick here. ☐

03901235

*n*eutral Line, from Schwarzkopf, is special. It is the most pure, the most delicate way, to cleanse and care for your hair.

Neutral Line is truly revolutionary. It contains *only* those ingredients which are really necessary – pure materials, with *no* added colouring or chemical preservatives. Neutral Line is *ultra* pure.

Sensitive to your hair and scalp, the range has been dermatologically tested to ensure there's no risk of allergy reaction.

Totally biodegradable, Neutral Line is sensitive to the environment too. Only water-soluble detergents are used and even the packaging is environmentally sound – it is all produced from recyclable materials. And, as you'd expect, the range is ozone friendly and involves no animal testing.

FIGURE 15.9 *Example of a coupon.*
Schwarzkopf used a 50p-off coupon to increase sales of its Neutral Line hair care products.

SOURCE: Courtesy of Schwarzkopf Ltd.

users. On the other hand, many consumers only redeem coupons for products they normally buy. Studies have shown that about 75 percent of coupons are redeemed by people who already use the brand on the coupon. So, as an incentive to try and to continue to use a new brand or product, coupons have questionable success. Another problem with coupons is that stores often do not have enough of the coupon item in stock. This situation can generate ill will towards both the store and the product.[30]

Although the use of coupons as a sales promotion technique is expected to grow in the next few years, a concern among marketers about their effectiveness could well diminish their appeal. However, coupons will probably remain a major sales promotion component for stimulating trial of new products. Coupons will also be used to increase the frequency of purchase for established products that show sluggish sales. On the other hand, successful established products may be reducing their profits if 75 percent of the coupons are redeemed by brand-loyal customers.[31]

30. Campanella, pp. 118–122.

31. Ibid.

TABLE 15.2
Coupon redemption rates in the U.K.

	1982	1984	1986
COMPARATIVE COUPON REDEMPTION RATES (%)			
Newspaper	1.0	1.5	1.9
Magazine	2.4	2.0	2.1
Door-to-door	9.8	8.3	10.2
In/on pack	30.2	24.5	21.8
Other	44.7	20.2	11.6
Overall	6.7	9.0	7.5
BREAKDOWN OF REDEMPTION BY METHOD OF DISTRIBUTION (%)			
Newspaper	8	5	8
Magazine	4	4	6
Door-to-door	32	24	34
In/on pack	36	49	38
Other	20	18	14
COUPON DISTRIBUTION METHODS (%)			
Newspaper	56	30	32
Magazine	11	18	21
Door-to-door	22	26	25
In/on pack	8	18	13
Other	3	8	9
NO. OF COUPONS DISTRIBUTED (MILLIONS)	4,758	3,045	4,592
NO. OF COUPONS REDEEMED (MILLIONS)	320	274	343

SOURCE: NCH Promotional Services. Reprinted by permission of Nielsen Marketing Services, Oxford, U.K.

Demonstrations.   **Demonstrations** are excellent attention-getters. Manufacturers often use them temporarily either to encourage trial use and purchase of the product or to show how the product actually works. Because labour costs can be extremely high, demonstrations are not used widely. They can, however, be highly effective for promoting certain types of products, such as appliances, cosmetics, and cars. Cosmetics marketers such as Clinique (owned by Estee Lauder), for example, sometimes offer potential customers "makeovers" to demonstrate their products' benefits and proper application.

Frequent-User Incentives.   Many firms develop incentive programmes to reward individual consumers who engage in repeat (frequent) purchases. For example, most major international airlines offer a frequent-flyer programme through which customers who have flown a specified number of miles are rewarded with free tickets for additional travel (see Figure 15.10). Thus frequent-user incentives help foster customer loyalty to a specific company or group of co-operating companies that provide extra incentives for patronage. Frequent-user incentives have also been used by service businesses, such as car rental agencies, hotels, and credit card companies, as well as by marketers of consumer goods.

FIGURE 15.10
Example of a user incentive.
TWA promotes its Frequent Flight Bonus Programme to encourage repeat business.

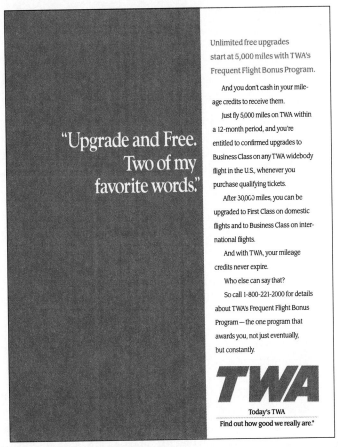

Unlimited free upgrades start at 5,000 miles with TWA's Frequent Flight Bonus Program.

And you don't cash in your mileage credits to receive them.

Just fly 5,000 miles on TWA within a 12-month period, and you're entitled to confirmed upgrades to Business Class on any TWA widebody flight in the U.S., whenever you purchase qualifying tickets.

After 30,000 miles, you can be upgraded to First Class on domestic flights and to Business Class on international flights.

And with TWA, your mileage credits never expire.

Who else can say that?

So call 1-800-221-2000 for details about TWA's Frequent Flight Bonus Program—the one program that awards you, not just eventually, but constantly.

"Upgrade and Free. Two of my favorite words."

TWA

Today's TWA
Find out how good we really are.®

SOURCE: Courtesy of Trans World Airlines

An older frequent-user incentive is trading stamps. **Trading stamps** are dispensed in proportion to the amount of a consumer's purchase and can be accumulated and redeemed for goods. Retailers use trading stamps to attract consumers to specific stores. Stamps are attractive to consumers as long as they do not drive up the price of goods. They are effective for many types of retailers. Trading stamps were very popular in the 1960s, but their use as a sales promotion method declined dramatically in the 1970s. However, Green Shield stamps have made a comeback and petrol retailers are offering in-house stamps redeemable for limited collections of goods.

Point-of-Sale Displays. **Point-of-sale (P-O-S) materials** include such items as outside signs, window displays, counter pieces, display racks, and self-service cartons. Innovations in P-O-S displays include sniff-teasers, which give off a product's aroma in the store as consumers walk within a radius of four feet, and computerised interactive displays, which ask a series of multiple-choice questions and then display information on a screen to help consumers make a product decision.[32] These items, which are often supplied by producers, attract attention, inform customers, and

32. Joe Agnew, "P-O-P [P-O-S] Displays Are Becoming a Matter of Consumer Convenience," *Marketing News,* 9 Oct. 1987, p. 14.

encourage retailers to carry particular products. A retailer is likely to use point-of-sale materials if they are attractive, informative, well constructed, and in harmony with the store. With two-thirds of all purchases resulting from in-store decisions, P-O-S materials can help sustain incremental sales if a brand's essential components—brand name, positioning, and visual image—are the basis of the P-O-S display.[33]

A survey of retail store managers indicated that almost 90 percent believed that P-O-S materials sell products. The retailers surveyed also said that P-O-S is essential for product introductions. Different forms of display material are carried by different types of retailers. Convenience stores, for example, favour window banners and "shelf talkers" (on-the-shelf displays or signs), whereas chain chemists prefer floor stands and devices that provide samples.[34]

Free Samples. Marketers use **free samples** for several reasons: to stimulate trial of a product, to increase sales volume in the early stages of a product's life cycle, or to obtain desirable distribution. The sampling programme should be planned as a total event, not merely a giveaway.[35] Sampling is the most expensive of all sales promotion methods because production and distribution through such channels as mail delivery, door-to-door delivery, in-store distribution, and on-package distribution entail very high costs. In designing a free sample, marketers should consider certain factors, such as the seasonality of the product, the characteristics of the market, and prior advertising. Free samples are not appropriate for mature products and slow turnover products.

Money Refunds. With **money refunds**, consumers submit proof of purchase and are mailed a specific amount of money. Usually, manufacturers demand multiple purchases of the product before a consumer can qualify for a refund. For example, Panasonic marketed a line of VHS tapes that featured a £1 rebate per tape, for up to twelve purchases. A customer had to send in a proof of purchase from inside each tape package and the sales receipt. This method, used primarily to promote trial use of a product, is relatively low in cost. Nevertheless, because money refunds sometimes generate a low response rate, they have limited impact on sales.

One of the problems with money refunds or rebates is that many people perceive the redemption process as too complicated. Consumers also have negative perceptions of manufacturers' reasons for offering rebates. They may believe that these are new, untested products or products that have not sold well. If these perceptions are not changed, rebate offers may degrade the image and desirability of the product being promoted. If the promotion objective in the rebate offer is to increase sales, then an effort should be made to simplify the redemption process and proof-of-purchase requirements.[36]

Premiums. **Premiums** are items offered free or at minimum cost as a bonus for purchasing a product. Vidal Sassoon offered a free on-pack 50-ml "travel size" container of shampoo with its 200-ml size of Salon Formula shampoo. Kellogg's

33. Ibid., p. 16.

34. Alison Fahey, "Study Shows Retailers Rely on P-O-P [P-O-S]," *Advertising Age,* 27 Nov. 1989, p. 83.

35. "Sampling Accelerates Adoption of New Products," *Marketing News,* 11 Sept. 1987, p. 21.

36. Peter Tat, William A. Cunningham, and Emin Babakus, "Consumer Perceptions of Rebates," *Journal of Advertising Research,* August-September 1988, p. 48.

offered easy art books with its Variety Packs. Premiums can attract competitors' customers, introduce different sizes of established products, add variety to other promotional efforts, and stimulate loyalty. Inventiveness is necessary, however; if an offer is to stand out and achieve a significant number of redemptions, the premium must be matched to both the target audience and the brand's image.[37] To be effective, premiums must be easily recognisable and desirable. Premiums usually are distributed through retail outlets or the mail, but they may also be placed on or in packages.

Price-off Offers. When a **price-off offer** is used, buyers receive a certain amount off the regular price shown on the label or package. Similar to coupons, this method can be a strong incentive for trying the product; it can stimulate product sales, yield short-lived sales increases, and promote products in off-seasons. It is an easy method to control and is used frequently for specific purposes. However, if used on an on-going basis, it reduces the price to customers who would buy at the regular price, and frequent use of price-off offers may cheapen a product's image. In addition, the method often requires special handling by retailers.

Consumer Contests and Sweepstakes. In **consumer contests**, individuals compete for prizes based on their analytical or creative skill. This method generates traffic at the retail level. Marriott and Hertz co-sponsored a scratch-card contest with a golf theme to boost sales during the slow winter travel season. Contestants received game cards when they checked in at a Marriott hotel or a Hertz rental counter and scratched off spots to see if they had won prizes such as cars, vacations, or golf clubs.[38] However, marketers should exercise care in setting up a contest. Problems or errors may anger consumers or result in lawsuits. Contestants are usually more involved in consumer contests than they are in sweepstakes, which we discuss next, even though the total participation may be lower. Contests may be used in conjunction with other sales promotion methods, such as coupons.

The entrants in a **consumer sweepstake** submit their names for inclusion in a drawing for prizes. Sweepstakes are used to stimulate sales and, as with contests, are sometimes teamed with other sales promotion methods. Sweepstakes are used more often than consumer contests, and they tend to attract a greater number of participants. The cost of a sweepstake is considerably less than the cost of a contest.[39] Successful sweepstakes can generate widespread interest and short-term increases in sales or market share.

■ **Trade Sales Promotion Methods**

Producers use sales promotion methods to encourage resellers, especially retailers, to carry their products and promote them effectively. The methods include buy-back allowances, buying allowances, counts and recounts, free merchandise, merchandise allowances, co-operative advertising, dealer listings, premium or push money, sales contests, and dealer loaders.

Buy-Back Allowances. A **buy-back allowance** is a certain sum of money given to a purchaser for each unit bought after an initial deal is over. This method is a secondary incentive in which the total amount of money that resellers can receive is

37. Gerrie Anthea, "Sales Promotion: Putting up the Premium," *Marketing*, 16 Apr. 1987.

38. Steven W. Colford, "Marriott Sets Largest Promo," *Advertising Age*, 2 Oct. 1989, p. 58.

39. Eileen Norris, "Everyone Will Grab at a Chance to Win," *Advertising Age*, 22 Aug. 1983, p. M10.

proportional to their purchases during an initial trade deal, such as a coupon offer. Buy-back allowances foster co-operation during an initial sales promotion effort and stimulate repurchase afterwards. The main drawback of this method is its expense.

Buying Allowances.　A **buying allowance** is a temporary price reduction to resellers for purchasing specified quantities of a product. A soap producer, for example, might give retailers £1 for each case of soap purchased. Such offers may be an incentive to handle a new product, achieve a temporary price reduction, or stimulate the purchase of an item in larger than normal quantities. The buying allowance, which takes the form of money, yields profits to resellers and is simple and straightforward to use. There are no restrictions on how resellers use the money, which increases the method's effectiveness.

Counts and Recounts.　The **count and recount** promotion method is based on the payment of a specific amount of money for each product unit moved from a reseller's warehouse in a given time period. Units of a product are counted at the start of the promotion and again at the end to determine how many have moved from the warehouse. This method can reduce retail stock-outs by moving inventory out of warehouses and can also clear distribution channels of obsolete products or packages and reduce warehouse inventories. The count and recount method might benefit a producer by decreasing resellers' inventories, making resellers more likely to place new orders. However, this method is often difficult to administer and may not appeal to resellers who have small warehouses.

Free Merchandise.　**Free merchandise** is sometimes offered to resellers who purchase a stated quantity of the same or different products. Occasionally, free merchandise is used as payment for allowances provided through other sales promotion methods. To avoid handling and bookkeeping problems, the giving of free merchandise usually is accomplished by reducing the invoice.

Merchandise Allowances.　A **merchandise allowance** is a manufacturer's agreement to pay resellers certain amounts of money for providing special promotional efforts, such as advertising or displays. This method is best suited to high-volume, high-profit, easily handled products. One major problem with using merchandise allowances is that some retailers perform their activities at a minimally acceptable level simply to obtain the allowances. Before paying retailers, manufacturers usually verify their performance. Manufacturers hope that the retailers' additional promotional efforts will yield substantial sales increases.

Co-operative Advertising.　**Co-operative advertising** is an arrangement whereby a manufacturer agrees to pay a certain amount of a retailer's media costs for advertising the manufacturer's products. The amount allowed is usually based on the quantities purchased. Before payment is made, a retailer must show proof that advertisements did appear. These payments give retailers additional funds for advertising. They can, however, put a severe burden on the producer's advertising budget. Some retailers exploit co-operative advertising programmes by crowding too many products into one advertisement. Some retailers cannot afford to advertise; others can afford it but do not want to advertise. Still others actually do advertising that qualifies for an allowance but are not willing to undertake the paperwork required for reimbursement from producers.[40]

Dealer Listings.   A **dealer listing** is an advertisement that promotes a product and identifies the names of participating retailers who sell the product. Dealer listings can influence retailers to carry the product, build traffic at the retail level, and encourage consumers to buy the product at participating dealers.

Premium or Push Money.   **Premium** or **push money** is used to push a line of goods by providing additional compensation to salespeople. This promotion method is appropriate when personal selling is an important part of the marketing effort; it is not effective for promoting products that are sold through self-service. Although this method often helps a manufacturer obtain commitment from the sales force, often it can be very expensive.

Sales Contests.   A **sales contest** is designed to motivate distributers, retailers, and sales personnel by recognising outstanding achievements. The Colt Car Co., importer of Japanese-made Mitsubishi cars into the United Kingdom, designed a sales contest that offered dealers an incentive trip for two to Barbados if they improved their sales figures by 10 to 12 percent. Approximately 50 percent of the dealers met this sales goal and won the trip.[41] To be effective, this method must be equitable for all salespersons involved. One advantage to the method is that it can achieve participation at all levels of distribution. However, the results are temporary, and prizes are usually expensive.

Dealer Loaders.   A **dealer loader** is a gift to a retailer who purchases a specified quantity of merchandise. Often dealer loaders are used to obtain special display efforts from retailers by offering essential display parts as premiums. For example, a manufacturer might design a display that includes a sterling silver tray as a major component and give the tray to the retailer. Marketers use dealer loaders to obtain new distributors and push larger quantities of goods.

SUMMARY

Personal selling is the process of informing customers and persuading them to purchase products through personal communication in an exchange situation. The three general purposes of personal selling are finding prospects, convincing them to buy, and keeping customers satisfied.

Many salespersons—either consciously or unconsciously—move through a general selling process as they sell products. In prospecting, the salesperson develops a list of potential customers. Before contacting acceptable prospects, the salesperson prepares by finding and analysing information about the prospects and their needs.

40. Ed Crimmins, "A Co-op Myth: It Is a Tragedy That Stores Don't Spend All Their Accruals," *Sales & Marketing Management*, 7 Feb. 1983, pp. 72–73.

41. Gillian Upton, "Sales Promotion: Getting Results Barbados Style," *Marketing*, 16 Apr. 1987, pp. 37–40.

The approach is the manner in which a salesperson contacts a potential customer. During the sales presentation, the salesperson must attract and hold the prospect's attention to stimulate interest and desire for the product. If possible, the salesperson should handle objections when they arise. Closing is the stage in the selling process when the salesperson asks the prospect to buy the product or products. After a successful closing, the salesperson must follow up the sale.

In developing a sales force, marketing managers must consider which types of salespersons will sell the firm's products most effectively. The three classifications of salespersons are order getters, order takers, and support personnel. Order getters inform both current customers and new prospects and persuade them to buy. Order takers seek repeat sales and fall into two categories: inside order takers and field order takers. Sales support personnel facilitate the selling function, but their duties usually extend beyond making sales. The three types of support personnel are missionary, trade, and technical salespersons.

The effectiveness of sales-force management is an important determinant of a firm's success because the sales force is directly responsible for generating an organisation's sales revenue. The major decision areas and activities on which sales managers must focus are establishing sales-force objectives, determining sales-force size, recruiting and selecting salespeople, training sales personnel, compensating salespeople, motivating salespeople, managing sales territories, and controlling and evaluating the sales force.

Sales objectives should be stated in precise, measurable terms and specify the time period and the geographic areas involved. The size of the sales force must be adjusted from time to time because a firm's marketing plans change, as do markets and forces in the marketing environment.

Recruiting and selecting salespeople involves attracting and choosing the right type of salesperson to maintain an effective sales force. When developing a training programme, managers must consider a variety of dimensions, such as who should be trained, what should be taught, and how the training should occur. Compensation of salespeople involves formulating and administrating a compensation plan that attracts, motivates, and holds the right types of salespeople for the firm. Motivation of salespeople should allow the firm to attain high productivity. Managing sales territories, another aspect of sales-force management, focuses on such factors as size, shape, routing, and scheduling. To control and evaluate sales-force performance, the sales manager must use information obtained through salespersons' call reports, customer feedback, and invoices.

Sales promotion is an activity or material (or both) that acts as a direct inducement, offering added value or incentive for the product, to resellers, salespersons, or consumers. Marketers use sales promotion to identify and attract new customers, to introduce a new product, and to increase reseller inventories. Sales promotion techniques fall into two general categories: consumer and trade. Consumer sales promotion methods encourage consumers to trade at specific stores or to try a specific product. These methods include coupons, demonstrations, frequent-user incentives, free samples, money refunds, premiums, price-off offers, and consumer sweepstakes and contests. Trade sales promotion techniques stimulate resellers to handle a manufacturer's products and market these products aggressively. These techniques include buy-back allowances, buying allowances, counts and recounts, free merchandise, merchandise allowances, co-operative advertising, dealer listings, premium or push money, sales contests, and dealer loaders.

Important Terms

Personal selling
Prospecting
Approach
Closing
Order getters
Order takers
Support personnel
Missionary salespersons
Trade salespersons
Technical salespersons
Recruiting
Straight salary compensation plan
Straight commission
   compensation plan
Combination compensation plan
Sales promotion
Ratchet effect
Consumer sales promotion
   techniques
Trade sales promotion
   methods

Coupons
Demonstrations
Trading stamps
Point-of-sale (P-O-S)
   materials
Free samples
Money refunds
Premiums
Price-off offers
Consumer contests
Consumer sweepstake
Buy-back allowance
Buying allowance
Count and recount
Free merchandise
Merchandise allowance
Co-operative advertising
Dealer listing
Premium or push money
Sales contest
Dealer loader

Discussion and Review Questions

1. What is personal selling? How does personal selling differ from other types of promotional activities?
2. What are the primary purposes of personal selling?
3. Identify the elements of the personal selling process. Must a salesperson include all these elements when selling a product to a customer? Why or why not?
4. How does a salesperson find and evaluate prospects? Do you consider any of these methods questionable ethically?
5. Are order getters more aggressive or creative than order takers? Why or why not?
6. Identify several characteristics of effective sales objectives.
7. How should a sales manager establish criteria for selecting sales personnel? What are the general characteristics of a good salesperson?
8. What major issues or questions should be considered when developing a training programme for the sales force?
9. Explain the major advantages and disadvantages of the three basic methods of compensating salespersons. In general, which method do you most prefer? Why?
10. What major factors should be taken into account when designing the size and shape of a sales territory?
11. How does a sales manager—who cannot be with each salesperson in the field on a daily basis—control the performance of sales personnel?
12. What is sales promotion? Why is it used?

13. Does sales promotion work well in isolation from the other promotional mix elements?
14. For each of the following, identify and describe three techniques and give several examples: (a) consumer sales promotion methods, (b) trade sales promotion methods, (c) retail sales promotion methods.
15. What types of sales promotion methods have you observed recently?

■ CASES

15.1 Turtles' Fast Food Link

The U.K.'s third-largest fast food chain, Burger King, launched in the summer of 1990 the first sales promotion between a retailer and the best-selling toy and cartoon, Teenage Mutant Hero Turtles. Burger King, now owned by Grand Metropolitan, hoped Turtlemania would boost membership of the Burger King Kids' Club. The club, launched a few months previously, hopes to shake McDonald's stranglehold over the children's fast food market. Kids' Club is positioned as a sub-brand to the Burger King name and is pitched at six- to eleven-year-olds, a slightly older group than in McDonald's case.

Children receive a membership pack, and a different free toy every week of the year when a children's meal is purchased. In a similar link with Teenage Mutant Ninja Turtles in the U.S.A., Burger King gave away 14 million turtle toys over a six-week period. The U.K. Turtle link-up was supported with a £250,000 television advertising campaign developed by Saatchi & Saatchi.

The children's market is growing, with forecasts of 5 million six- to eleven-year-olds in the U.K. by 1996. McDonald's has for several years successfully used its clown character Ronald McDonald pitched at children to create brand recognition and loyalty. It remains to be seen whether Burger King's Kids' Club and its "fad" promotions have the staying power of Ronald McDonald.

SOURCES: *The Independent,* 12 August 1990; "Turtles' Fast Food Link," *Marketing,* 2 August 1990, p. 3; *Kids' Club Adventures,* Issues 1, 2, Burger King, 1990.

Questions for Discussion

1. Discuss the role of sales promotion in creating brand loyalty.
2. How well do sales promotion activities work in conjunction with television advertising?
3. Can sales promotions be effectively sustained over a prolonged period?

15.2 Wilkinson Sword USA Develops Its Own Sales Force

In November 1984, Wilkinson Sword USA, the U.S. subsidiary of London-based Wilkinson Sword Ltd., consisted of only two persons: Norman Prolux, president, and Ronald Mineo, vice-president of sales. For the previous thirty years, the company had relied on the sales forces of other companies to sell its line of razors and blades. The company decided that it needed to develop its own sales force to gain better control over its selling activities. According to vice-president Mineo, with independent salespersons the company was not able to achieve the focus its product lines required to compete efficiently. All its competitors had their own sales forces. Once the decision had been made to establish an independent sales force, company president Prolux pointed out, "No longer will our products be sixteenth in line in the manufacturers' rep's bag." In less than two years, the firm grew to nearly a hundred employees, including thirty-four salespeople, through a careful recruitment and selection process.

Before recruiting and hiring the first new salesperson, Wilkinson developed a marketing and sales strategy. Next, the company analysed its existing and potential accounts. The account analysis identified twenty-five key accounts that would be assigned to two key account managers working out of Wilkinson's Atlanta headquarters. Another four hundred primary and secondary accounts would be divided among field salespeople and sales managers.

However, designing Wilkinson's sales force was easy compared with finding just the right people to fill the sales positions. The New York area was especially difficult to staff because the company had to find two truly exceptional salespeople who could be trusted with its multi-million-dollar territories in the area. The fact that Prolux and Mineo had to function as salespeople themselves to maintain the business while attempting to recruit and hire permanent salespersons further complicated the process. Furthermore, Wilkinson set high standards for its sales force: it wanted salespeople with five years of experience in the better health and beauty aids companies. Its new recruits included salespeople with experience at Procter & Gamble, Colgate, and Gillette.

Hiring experienced salespeople can be a costly proposition. Mineo estimates that the twenty-four salespeople hired during the first year cost the company $0.5 million in recruiting, training, salaries, bonuses, and related costs. In some cases, Wilkinson paid as much as $15,000 to an employment agency to lure one person. To ensure that it was offering competitive salaries, Wilkinson surveyed other firms in the field. Its strategy was to offer a compensation package at least as good as the competition and, in some cases, as much as 10 percent better.

In January 1985, Wilkinson began interviewing candidates for its new sales force. The first seven were hired by early February; and by the beginning of April, eight more had been hired. By mid-September, the company had hired twenty-four salespersons. Thus it took the firm nine months to find qualified and compatible salespersons. Plans were then approved to hire the last ten salespeople to complete the initial sales force.

The new Wilkinson sales force seemed to work out quite well from the beginning. Wilkinson Sword was acquired by Swedish Match in 1987, and the company's future looks positive. The company has begun hiring retail merchandisers to support its sales efforts by reducing out-of-stocks, building incremental facings and displays, and monitoring pricing.

SOURCES: Rayna Skolink, "The Birth of a Sales Force," *Sales & Marketing Management*, 10 March 1986, pp. 42–44; Jules Arbose, "Swedish Match Again Strikes Out in New Directions," *International Management*, Oct. 1987, pp. 87–90; Gay Jervey, "Gillette, Wilkinson Heat Up Disposable Duel," *Advertising Age*, 10 June 1985, p. 12.

Questions for Discussion

1. What can Wilkinson expect to gain from having its own sales force?
2. Evaluate Wilkinson's approach to developing a sales force.

PART V

PRICING DECISIONS

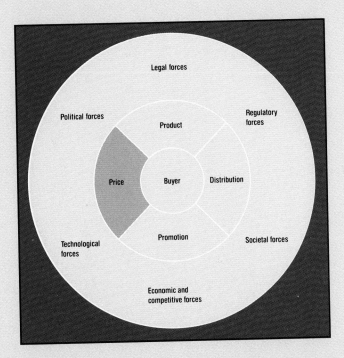

If an organisation is to provide a satisfying marketing mix, the price of its product must be acceptable to target market members. Pricing decisions can have numerous effects on other parts of the marketing mix. For example, a product's price can influence how customers perceive it, what types of marketing institutions are used in distributing it, and how the product is promoted. In Chapter 16, we discuss the importance of price and look at some of the characteristics of price and non-price competition. Then we examine the major factors that affect marketers' pricing decisions. Eight major stages used by marketers in establishing prices are discussed in Chapter 17. ◆

16 PRICING CONCEPTS

Objectives

To understand the nature and importance of price

To become aware of the characteristics of price and non-price competition

To examine various pricing objectives

To explore key factors that may influence marketers' pricing decisions

To consider issues affecting the pricing of products for industrial markets

Status symbols are expensive by nature—sleek European sports cars, eighteen-carat gold watches, and ostrich-skin briefcases are all very costly. Though smaller and less expensive, fancy fountain pens have become a common sight in the hands of influential businesspeople. Such pens have high price tags and are much more difficult to maintain than ballpoints, felt-tip pens, or roller-ball pens. However, recent sales figures indicate that the semi-obsolete fountain pen is making a comeback as the writing instrument of choice for status-minded individuals.

Of the premium-priced fountain pens, Montblanc pens are probably the most prestigious. Named after the highest mountain in Europe, these German-made fountain pens cost from about £100 to £5,000 (for a solid gold one). The most popular model costs about £300. Prestige pricing has worked well for Montblanc, placing the pen in the same category as Rolex watches, Porsche sunglasses, BMW cars, and Gucci luggage. Former U.S. president Ronald Reagan, ex-prime minister Margaret Thatcher, and fictional super-spy James Bond all use Montblanc pens.

Parker also makes high-priced "power" pens, bringing back its Duofold model, which was popular during the 1920s. The Duofold comes in a blue and maroon marbled finish and sells for about £175. Waterman and S.T. Dupont also sell fine fountain pens. The Waterman Le Man series comes in seven sizes and the pens are priced at around £160. Dupont pens have a distinctive Chinese lacquer finish and are priced from £200 to £300 (for the gold-flecked models). ◆

Based on information in Michelle Hill, "Writing in Rarefied Air," *Bridgewater Courier-News* (Bridgewater, N.J.), 25 June 1989, pp. G1, G2; Allen Norwood, "Pen Offers Status—At Only $295," *Charlotte Observer*, (Charlotte, N.C.), 20 Nov. 1988, pp. 1C, 3C; and Sharon Schlegel, "Fountain Pens Ink New Success as Status Symbols," *Chicago Sun-Times*, 26 Mar. 1989.

$\boxed{\text{T}}$hese companies are using price, along with other elements, to distinguish their pens from competitive brands and to give them an exclusive, up-market image. As in the case of these firms, pricing is a crucial element in most organisations' marketing mixes. In this chapter we focus first on the nature of price and its importance to marketers. Then we consider some of the characteristics of price and non-price competition. Next we explore the various types of pricing objectives that marketers may establish, and we examine in some detail the numerous factors that can influence pricing decisions. Finally, we discuss selected issues related to the pricing of products for industrial markets.

The Nature of Price

To a buyer, **price** is the value placed on what is exchanged. Something of value —usually buying power—is exchanged for satisfaction or utility. As described in Chapter 2, buying power depends on a buyer's income, credit, and wealth. It is a mistake to believe that price is always money paid or some other financial consideration. In fact, trading of products—**barter**—is the oldest form of exchange. Money may or may not be involved.

Buyers' interest in price stems from their expectations about the usefulness of a product or the satisfaction they may derive from it. Because buyers have limited resources, they must allocate their buying power so that they can obtain the most desired products. Buyers must decide whether the utility gained in an exchange is worth the buying power sacrificed. Almost anything of value—ideas, services, rights, and goods—can be assessed by a price because in many societies the financial price is the measurement of value commonly used in exchanges. Thus a painting by Picasso may be valued, or priced, at £1 million. Financial price, then, quantifies value. It is the basis of most market exchanges.

■ **Terms Used to Describe Price**

Price is expressed in different terms for different exchanges. For instance, motor insurance companies charge a *premium* for protection from the cost of injuries or repairs stemming from a car accident. A police officer who stops you for speeding writes a ticket that requires you to pay a *fine*. If a lawyer defends you, a *fee* is charged, and if you use a railway or taxi, a *fare* is charged. A *toll* is sometimes charged for the use of bridges. *Rent* is paid for the use of equipment or for a flat. An estate agent receives a *commission* on the sale of a property. A *deposit* is made to reserve merchandise. A *tip* helps pay waitresses or waiters for their services. *Interest* is charged for the loan that you take out, and *taxes* are paid for government services. The value of many products is called *price*. Although price may be expressed in a variety of ways, it is important to remember that the purpose of this concept is to quantify and express the value of the items in a market exchange.

■ **The Importance of Price to Marketers**

As pointed out in Chapter 8, developing a product may be a lengthy process. It takes time to plan promotion and to communicate benefits. Distribution usually requires a long-term commitment to dealers who will handle the product. Often price is the only thing a marketer can change quickly to respond to changes in demand or to the actions of competitors. Bear in mind, however, that under certain circumstances the price variable may be relatively inflexible.

Price is also a key element in the marketing mix because it relates directly to the generation of total revenue. The following equation is an important one for the entire organisation:

$$\text{Profits} = \text{Total Revenues} - \text{Total Costs}$$

or

$$\text{Profits} = (\text{Prices} \times \text{Quantities Sold}) - \text{Total Costs}$$

Prices affect an organisation's profits, which are its life-blood for long-term survival. Price affects the profit equation in several ways. It directly influences the equation because it is a major component. It has an indirect impact because it can be a major determinant of the quantities sold. Even more indirectly, price influences total costs through its impact on quantities sold.

Because price has a psychological impact on customers, marketers can use it symbolically. By raising a price, they can emphasise the quality of a product and try to increase the status associated with its ownership. By lowering a price, they can emphasise a bargain and attract customers who go out of their way—spending extra time and effort—to save a small amount. Price can have a strong effect on sales.

PRICE AND NON-PRICE COMPETITION

A product offering can compete on a price or non-price basis. The choice will affect not only pricing decisions and activities, but also those associated with other marketing mix decision variables.

■ **Price Competition**

When **price competition** is used, a marketer emphasises price as an issue and matches or beats the prices of competitors. As discussed in Marketing Update 16.1, Bic engages in price competition by pricing its perfume low and emphasising price in its advertisements. To compete effectively on a price basis, a firm should be the low-cost producer of the product. If all firms producing goods in an industry charge the same price, the firm with the lowest costs is the most profitable. Firms that stress low price as a key element in the marketing mix tend to produce standardised products. A seller using price competition may change prices frequently or at least must be willing and able to do so (see Figure 16.1). Whenever competitors change their prices, the seller must respond quickly and aggressively. In the U.S., the postal service and United Parcel Service engage in direct price competition in their pricing of overnight air express services. In the U.K., fast printing services adopt a similar approach.

Price competition gives a marketer flexibility. Prices can be altered to account for changes in the firm's costs or in demand for the product. If competitors try to gain market share by cutting prices, an organisation competing on a price basis can react quickly to such efforts. However, a major drawback of price competition is that competitors, too, have the flexibility to adjust their prices. Thus they can quickly match or beat an organisation's price cuts. A price war may result. In the U.K. in the 1970s both grocery and petrol retailers were engaged in highly visible price wars. Many grocery retailers—led by Fine Fare and Tesco—traded purely on price and their promotional material (newspaper advertisements and window posters) pushed the latest price reductions on major brands. The petrol companies and independent forecourt operators were engaged in a price war in which neighbouring competing

BIC PERFUME ENGAGES IN PRICE COMPETITION

The Milford, Connecticut–based Bic Corp., known for its disposable lighters, shavers, and pens, has entered the perfume business. By diversifying, Bic is attempting to subsidise its profitable core products. With more individuals becoming health-conscious and fewer and fewer people smoking, Bic executives realise that future sales of Bic lighters—Bic's largest and most profitable line—will probably drop sharply. Furthermore, Bic's shavers are facing increasing competition from companies such as Gillette and a host of foreign challengers; and, though Bic still controls 50 percent of the pen market, Gillette's Paper Mate, Write Brothers, and Flair pens are making gains. The growing popularity of Mitsubishi Pencil Co.'s metal-point roller pens, currently holding a 10 percent market share, has also weakened Bic's market position.

Bic's French parent company, Société Bic (which owns 61 percent of Bic), introduced a fragrance line in Europe in 1988, hoping to capitalise on the £2 billion retail perfume market. Later that year, Bic launched the perfumes in the United States. Though some analysts think that Bic will certainly fail in an industry where a glamorous image is so important, Bic hopes to attract consumers with low prices.

Imported from France, Bic's four fragrances—Parfum Bic Jour, Parfum Bic Nuit, Parfum Bic for men, and Parfum Bic Sport—sell at about £2.50 for a quarter-ounce bottle. Bic packages the perfumes in unbreakable glass spray bottles with a specially developed atomiser that delivers about a third less perfume than other pumps, providing about 300 sprays per bottle. Bic hopes the fragrances will attract men and women between the ages of 18 and 40 because of their portability and fun image, as well as their low prices. Société Bic, the actual manufacturer of the products, has focused on improving the production process while maintaining quality to increase sales volume and keep prices low.

Bic supported the introduction of its perfumes into the United States with a £15 million advertising and promotions budget that stressed the product's price. The fragrances have been popular in Europe, and Bic executives hope that the perfumes—sold at locations next to their lighters, shavers, and pens—will also become the first successful mass-marketed fragrances in the United States.

SOURCES: "Bic Begins Campaign for New Perfume Line," *New York Times,* 20 Mar. 1989, p. D9; "Bic Counts on a New Age for Spray Perfume," *New York Times,* 17 Oct. 1988, p. 28; "France's Bic Bets U.S. Customers Will Go for Perfume on the Cheap," *Wall Street Journal,* 12 Jan. 1989, p. B4; Resa W. King, "Will $4 Perfume Do the Trick for Bic?" *Business Week,* 20 June 1988, pp. 89, 92.

FIGURE 16.1 *Price competition.*
Retailers of appliance and electronics products often compete on the basis of price.

SOURCE: Janet Gill/Tony Stone Worldwide

garages might reduce pump prices several times in one day in tit-for-tat reactions. Furthermore, if a user of price competition is forced to raise prices, competing firms that are not under the same pressures may decide not to raise their prices.

■ **Non-price Competition**

Non-price competition occurs when a seller elects not to focus on price and instead emphasises distinctive product features, service, product quality, promotion, packaging, or other factors to distinguish its product from competing brands. Thus non-price competition is based on factors other than price. Non-price competition gives an organisation the opportunity to increase its brand's unit sales through means other than changing the brand's price. As shown in Figure 16.2, John Deere, for instance, does not compete on a price basis but instead offers a money-back trial period for its lawn-mowers. One major advantage of non-price competition is that a firm can build customer loyalty towards its brand. If customers prefer a brand because of non-price issues, they may not be easily lured away by competing firms and brands. Customers whose primary attraction to a store is based on non-price factors are less likely to leave their regular store for a lower competitive price. Price is not the most durable factor from the standpoint of maintaining customer loyalty.[1] But when price is the primary reason that customers buy a particular brand, the competition can attract such customers through price cuts.

1. Michael J. O'Connor, "What Is the Logic of a Price War?" Arthur Andersen & Company, *International Trends in Retailing*, Spring 1986.

FIGURE 16.2

Non-price competition.
For its lawn-mowers,
John Deere uses non-
price competition by pro-
moting issues other than
price.

SOURCE: Deere and Company

Non-price competition is workable under the right conditions. A company must be able to distinguish its brand through unique product features, higher quality, customer service, promotion, packaging, and the like. Buyers not only must be able to perceive these distinguishing characteristics but must also view them as desirable. The distinguishing features that set a particular brand apart from its competitors should be difficult, if not impossible, for competitors to imitate. Finally, the organisation must extensively promote the distinguishing characteristics of the brand to establish its superiority and to set it apart from competitors in the minds of buyers.

Many European and non-U.S. firms put less emphasis on price than do their American counterparts. They look for a competitive edge by concentrating on promotion, research and development, marketing research, and marketing channel considerations. In a study of pricing strategy, five such firms stated specifically that they emphasise research and development and technological superiority; competition based on price was seldom a major marketing consideration.[2]

A marketer attempting to compete on a non-price basis is still not able to simply ignore competitors' prices, however. The organisation must be aware of competitors'

2. Saeed Samier, "Pricing in Marketing Strategies of U.S. and Foreign-Based Companies," *Journal of Business Research*, 1987, pp. 15–23.

prices and will probably price its brand near or slightly above competing brands. As an example, Sony sells television sets in a highly competitive market and charges higher prices for its sets; but it is successful none the less. Sony's emphasis on high product quality both distinguishes it from its competitors and allows it to set higher prices. Therefore, price still remains a crucial marketing mix component in situations that call for non-price competition.

PRICING OBJECTIVES

Pricing objectives are overall goals that describe what the firm wants to achieve through its pricing efforts. Because pricing objectives influence decisions in most functional areas—including finance, accounting, and production—the objectives must be consistent with the organisation's overall mission and purpose. Banking is an area where pricing is a major concern. As competition has intensified, bank executives have realised that their products must be priced to meet not only short-term profit goals, but also long-term strategic objectives.[3] Because of the many areas involved, a marketer often uses multiple pricing objectives. In this section we look at a few of the typical pricing objectives that companies might set for themselves.

■ Survival

A fundamental pricing objective is survival. Most organisations will tolerate difficulties such as short-run losses and internal upheaval if they are necessary for survival. Because price is a flexible and convenient variable to adjust, it is sometimes used to increase sales volume to levels that match the organisation's expenses.

■ Profit

Although businesses may claim that their objective is to maximise profits for their owners, the objective of profit maximisation is rarely operational because its achievement is difficult to measure. Because of this difficulty, profit objectives tend to be set at levels that the owners and top-level decision-makers view as satisfactory. Specific profit objectives may be stated in terms of actual monetary amounts or in terms of percentage change relative to the profits of a previous period.

■ Return on Investment

Pricing to attain a specified rate of return on the company's investment is a profit-related pricing objective. Most pricing objectives based on return on investment (ROI) are achieved by trial and error because not all cost and revenue data needed to project the return on investment are available when prices are set. General Motors, for example, uses ROI pricing objectives.

The objective of return on investment may be used less as managers and marketers in diversified companies stress the creation of shareholder value. When shareholder value is used as a performance objective, strategies—including those involving price—are evaluated on the basis of the impact they will have on the value investors perceive in the firm.[4]

■ Market Share

Market share, which is a product's sales in relation to total industry sales, can be an appropriate pricing objective. Many firms establish pricing objectives to maintain or increase market share. For example, Volkswagen AG cut prices on its 1990 model

3. Robert P. Ford, "Pricing Operating Services," *Bankers Magazine,* May-June 1987.

4. George S. Day and Liam Fahey, "Valuing Market Strategies," *Journal of Marketing,* July 1988, pp. 45–57.

Jettas, Golfs, Cabriolets, and Carats by 5 to 14 percent, and introduced two new models—the Corrado and Passat—at lower than expected prices to boost its share of the car market.[5]

Maintaining or increasing market share need not depend on growth in industry sales. Remember that an organisation can increase its market share even though sales for the total industry are decreasing. On the other hand, an organisation's sales volume may, in fact, increase while its market share within the industry decreases, assuming that the overall market is growing.

■ **Cash Flow**

Some organisations set prices to recover cash as fast as possible. Financial managers are understandably interested in quickly recovering capital spent to develop products. This objective may have the support of the marketing manager who anticipates a short product life cycle.

Although it may be acceptable in some situations, the use of cash flow and recovery as an objective oversimplifies the value of price in contributing to profits. A disadvantage of this pricing objective could be high prices, which might allow competitors with lower prices to gain a large share of the market.

■ **Status Quo**

In some cases, an organisation may be in a favourable position and, desiring nothing more, may set an objective of status quo. Status quo objectives can focus on several dimensions—maintaining a certain market share, meeting (but not beating) competitors' prices, achieving price stability, or maintaining a favourable public image. A status quo pricing objective can reduce a firm's risks by helping stabilise demand for its products. The use of status quo pricing objectives sometimes minimises pricing as a competitive tool, leading to a climate of non-price competition in an industry.

■ **Product Quality**

A company might have the objective of product quality leadership in the industry. For example, AM International, an industrial marketer of graphics equipment and supplies, has said that one of its organisational objectives is to be ranked within two years as one of the top two firms in its industry in terms of product quality and customer satisfaction.[6] This goal normally dictates a high price to cover the high product quality and, in some instances, the high cost of research and development. Cross pens, shown in Figure 16.3, are premium-priced to cover high production costs and to help maintain their high-quality image.

FACTORS AFFECTING PRICING DECISIONS

Pricing decisions can be complex because of the number of details that must be considered. Frequently there is considerable uncertainty about the reactions to price on the part of buyers, channel members, competitors, and others. Price is also an important consideration in marketing planning, market analysis, and sales forecasting. It is a major issue when assessing a brand's position relative to competing brands. Most factors that affect pricing decisions can be grouped into one of the eight categories shown in Figure 16.4. In this section we explore how each of these eight groups of factors enters into price decision-making.

5. David Landis, "It's Cutting Prices to Win Lost Ground," *USA Today*, 4 Oct. 1989, pp. 1B, 2B.
6. *AM International 1989 Annual Report,* p. 5.

FIGURE 16.3
Product quality pricing objective.
Cross pens carry a high price to cover high production costs and to help maintain a high quality image.

In writing instruments, the world knows no higher form of precision and workmanship. Each is a masterpiece. That is why there is only one Cross.

FLAWLESS CLASSICS.

CROSS
SINCE 1846

Available from $13 to $1,000.
Unconditional lifetime mechanical guarantee.
All pen and pencil sets include our 0.9mm pencil. Our new 0.5mm pencil may be purchased separately.

SOURCE: Courtesy A.T. Cross Co.

■ Organisational and Marketing Objectives

Marketers should set prices that are consistent with the organisation's goals and mission. For example, a retailer trying to position itself as value for money may wish to set prices that are quite reasonable relative to product quality. In this case, a marketer would not want to set premium prices on products but would strive to price products in line with this overall organisational goal.

The firm's marketing objectives must also be considered. Decision-makers should make pricing decisions that are compatible with the organisation's marketing objectives. Say, for instance, that one of a producer's marketing objectives is a 12 percent increase in unit sales by the end of the next year. Assuming that buyers are price sensitive, increasing the price or setting a price above the average market price would not be in line with the firm's sales objective. For example, Polaroid chose to focus on price when developing the marketing strategy for its Impulse instant camera. The Impulse complements the Spectra camera, a much higher-priced product in the category. Although the Spectra has been quite successful, Polaroid executives believed that there was a need for new products at a low cost. Polaroid has chosen price as the key variable in its advertising campaign for the Impulse camera.[7]

7. "Polaroid to Introduce New Instant Camera," *Adweek's Marketing Week*, 11 Jan. 1988, p. 3.

FIGURE 16.4
Factors that affect pricing decisions

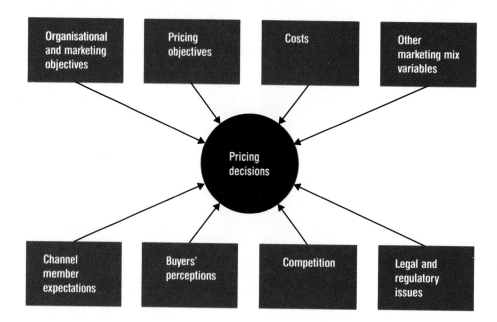

Types of Pricing Objectives

The type of pricing objectives a marketer uses obviously will have considerable bearing on the determination of prices.[8] An objective of a certain target return on investment requires that prices be set at a level that will generate a sales volume high enough to yield the specified target. A market share pricing objective usually causes a firm to price a product below competing brands of similar quality to attract competitors' customers to the company's brand. This type of pricing can lead to lower profits. A marketer sometimes uses temporary price reductions in the hope of gaining market share. A cash flow pricing objective may cause an organisation to set a relatively high price, which can place the product at a competitive disadvantage. On the other hand, a cash flow pricing objective sometimes results in a long, sustained low price. However, this type of objective is more likely to be addressed by using temporary price reductions, such as sales, refunds, and special discounts.

Costs

Obviously, costs must be an issue when establishing price. A firm may temporarily sell products below cost to match competition, to generate cash flow, or even to increase market share, but in the long run it cannot survive by selling its products below cost. Even when a firm has a high volume business, it cannot survive if each item is sold slightly below what it costs. A marketer should be careful to analyse all costs so that they can be included in the total cost associated with a product.

Besides considering the costs associated with a particular product, marketers must also take into account the costs that the product shares with others in the product line. Products often share some costs, particularly the costs of research and development, production, and distribution. Services are especially subject to cost sharing. For example, the costs of a bank building are spread over the costs of all services the bank offers.[9] Most marketers view a product's cost as a minimum, or

8. J. Winkler, "Pricing," in *The Marketing Book,* M. Baker, Ed. (London: The Institute of Marketing, 1987).

9. Joseph P. Guiltinan, "The Price-Bundling of Services: A Normative Framework," *Journal of Marketing,* April 1987, pp. 74–85.

floor, below which the product cannot be priced. We discuss cost analysis in more detail in the next chapter and in Chapter 19.

Other Marketing Mix Variables

All marketing mix variables are highly interrelated. Pricing decisions can influence decisions and activities associated with product, distribution, and promotion variables. A product's price frequently affects the demand for the item. A high price, for instance, may result in low unit sales, which in turn may lead to higher production costs per unit. Conversely, lower per unit production costs may result from a low price. For many products, buyers associate better product quality with a high price and poorer product quality with a low price. This perceived price-quality relationship influences customers' overall image of products or brands. The price sometimes determines the degree of status associated with ownership of the product.

Pricing decisions influence the number of competing brands in a product category. When a firm introduces a product, sets a relatively high price, and achieves high unit sales, competitors may be attracted to this product category. If a firm uses a low price, the low profit margin may be unattractive to potential competition.

The price of a product is linked to several dimensions of its distribution. Premium priced products often are marketed through selective or exclusive distribution; lower priced products in the same product category may be sold through intensive distribution. For example, Cross pens are distributed through selective distribution and Bic pens through intensive distribution. The manner in which a product is stored and transported may also be associated with its price. When a producer is developing the price of a product, the profit margins of marketing channel members such as wholesalers and retailers must be considered. Channel members must be adequately compensated for the functions they perform. Inadequately compensated channel members will withdraw from a marketing channel.

The way a product is promoted can be affected by its price. Bargain prices are often included in advertisements, whereas premium prices are less likely to appear in advertising messages. The issue of a premium price is sometimes included in advertisements for up-market items, such as luxury cars or fine jewellery. Higher priced products are more likely to require personal selling efforts than lower priced ones. A customer may purchase an inexpensive watch in a self-service environment but hesitate to buy an expensive watch in the same store, if it is available there.

The price structure can affect a salesperson's relationship with customers. A complex pricing structure takes longer to explain to customers, is more likely to confuse the buyer, and may cause misunderstandings that result in long term customer dissatisfaction. For example, the pricing structures of many airlines are complex and frequently confuse ticket sales agents and travellers alike.

Channel Member Expectations

When making price decisions, a producer must consider what distribution channel members (such as wholesalers and retailers) expect. A channel member certainly expects to receive a profit for the functions it performs. The amount of profit expected depends on what the intermediary could make if it were handling a competing product instead. Also, the amount of time and the resources required to carry the product influence intermediaries' expectations.

Channel members often expect producers to provide discounts for large orders and quick payment. (Discounts are discussed later in this chapter.) At times, resellers expect producers to provide several support activities, such as sales training, service training, repair advisory service, co-operative advertising, sales promotions, and perhaps a programme for returning unsold merchandise to the producer. These support activities clearly have costs associated with them, and a producer must consider these costs when determining prices. Failure to price the product so that the producer can provide some of these support activities may cause resellers to view the product less favourably.

■ Buyers' Perceptions

One important question that marketers should assess when making price decisions is "How important is the price to people in the target market?" The importance of price is not absolute; it can vary from market segment to market segment and from person to person. Members of one market segment may be more sensitive to price than members in a different target market. Moreover, the importance of price will vary across different product categories. Price may be a more important factor in the purchase of petrol than in the purchase of a pair of jeans because buyers may be more sensitive to the price of petrol than to the price of jeans.

For numerous products, buyers have a range of acceptable prices. This range can be fairly narrow in some product categories but wider in others. A marketer should become aware of the acceptable range of prices in the relevant product category. (This issue and related ones are discussed in more detail in Chapter 17.)

Consumers' perceptions of price may also be influenced by all the products in a firm's product line. The perception of price depends on a product's actual price, plus the consumer's reference price—that is, the consumer's expectation of price. Exposure to a range of prices in a product line affects the consumer's expectations and perceptions of acceptable prices.[10]

Buyers' perceptions of a product relative to competing products may allow or encourage a firm to set a price that differs significantly from the prices of competing products. If the product is deemed superior to most of the competition, a premium price may be feasible. Strong brand loyalty sometimes provides the opportunity to charge a premium price. Thus, it is able to charge premium prices for its products. On the other hand, if buyers view the product unfavourably (assuming that they are not extremely negative), a lower price may be required to generate sales. There is a considerable body of research on the relationship between price and consumers' perceptions of quality. Consumers use price as an indicator of quality when brands are unfamiliar, and the perceived risk of making unsatisfactory choices is high. They also rely on price if there is little information available and judging a product's attributes is difficult.[11]

■ Competition

A marketer needs to know competitors' prices so that the firm can adjust its own prices accordingly. This does not mean that a company will necessarily match competitors' prices; it may set its price above or below theirs. However, matching competitors' fares is an important strategy for survival in the airline industry.[12] Also, as indicated in Marketing Update 16.2, Amstrad's pricing strategy is putting pressure on competitors in the computer industry.

10. Susan M. Petroshius and Kent B. Monroe, "Effect of Product-Line Pricing Characteristics on Product Evaluations," *Journal of Consumer Research,* March 1988, pp. 511–519.

11. Valerie A. Zeithaml, "Consumer Perceptions of Price, Quality and Value: A Means-End Model and Synthesis of Evidence," *Journal of Marketing,* July 1988, pp. 2–22.

12. Andrew T. Chalk and John A. Steiber, "Managing the Airlines in the 1990's," *Journal of Business Strategy,* Winter 1987, pp. 87–91.

AMSTRAD PRICE PRESSURES MICROCOMPUTER BUSINESS

Amstrad Consumer Electronics, created by Alan Sugar, only entered the microcomputer business in 1984. Prior to that, it operated in the electronics business, manufacturing budget hi-fi equipment, television sets, car stereos, and other consumer goods. In the summer of 1984, Amstrad launched its first computer—the CPC 464—priced at just under £200 and clearly positioned at the home computer market. The strategy was to offer mass-produced products at extremely competitive prices. In this respect, the CPC 464 was typical of the offerings to follow, building on the breakthroughs of other companies, rather than offering technological novelty. The computer was sold in the U.K. through the large electrical retailers Dixons, Rumbelows, and Comet and through Boots and John Menzies. The distribution adopted is indicative of Amstrad's mass-marketing approach.

Through the 1980s Amstrad's sales went from strength to strength. During the second half of 1984 the company sold 200,000 computers, despite adverse press comment about its late entry into the home computer market. In the same year, 5,000 Amstrad computers were sold in France. By April 1986, Sinclair's major financial problems forced it to sell its name and product rights to Amstrad, making Amstrad one of the largest world suppliers of home computers, with 50 percent of the U.K. market.

Late in 1986, Amstrad launched its new PC-1512 series of computers. Designed as IBM compatibles, the eight models competed head-on with Big Brother and represented Amstrad's move towards the personal computer market. The basic PC-1512 was priced at under £500, straddling the price gap between home and personal computers (usually costing in excess of £800). The promotional message was "compatible with you know who, priced as only we know how". Sales soared and by the end of 1986 Amstrad was leader in the U.K. market for personal home computers.

SOURCES: M. Labrou, "Ten Marketing Cases," MBA Dissertation, University of Warwick, 1989; London: Keynote, "Home Computers/Software," 1987; *The Times,* 25 Aug. 1984, p. 24; *Marketing Week,* 11 April 1985, pp. 20, 25; and *Computer Weekly,* 7 Nov. 1985, pp. 42–43.

FIGURE 16.5

Competitive price changes.

Is it likely that the producer of the $35,000 Range Rover will change its price in America?

A Rover Within Your Range.

If you're contemplating the purchase of a 4x4 utility vehicle, consider your options. You could pay over $35,000 for a Range Rover and impress all your friends. Or you could spend substantially less for an Isuzu Trooper and impress someone far more important. Yourself.

Isuzu Trooper
$13,149*

Like the Range Rover, the Trooper offers high glass areas for excellent visibility and enough interior space to comfortably carry five adults!

Yet unlike the Range Rover, the Trooper offers you a choice of engines. You can get an economical, fuel-injected four-cylinder or opt for a beefier V6.

And while the Range Rover comes with only one type of transmission, the Trooper offers a choice between two: a rugged five-speed manual or an optional four-speed automatic transmission.

Of course, the Range Rover does offer an impressive 70 cubic feet of cargo space with its rear seat folded down. But, once again, the Trooper offers you even more.

The way we see it, there's only one thing keeping the Trooper from being the vehicle in vogue. It's affordable. And that's just not chic.

For free Isuzu brochures call (800) 245-4549.

ISUZU

*M.S.R.P., P.O.E. excluding tax, license and transportation fees as of 11/10/88. Optional equipment shown. †Rear seat optional.

The First Car Builders of Japan.

SOURCE: American Isuzu Motors, Inc.

When adjusting prices, a marketer must assess how competitors will respond. Will they change their prices (some, in fact, may not), and if so, will they raise or lower them? For example, is it likely that the maker of the $35,000 Range Rover will change its price in America based on the pricing of the Isuzu Trooper shown in Figure 16.5? In Chapter 2 we describe several types of competitive market structures. The structure that characterises the industry to which a firm belongs affects the flexibility of price setting.

When an organisation operates as a monopoly and is unregulated, it can set whatever prices the market will bear. However, the company may avoid pricing the product at the highest possible level for fear of inviting government regulation or because it wants to penetrate a market by using a lower price. If the monopoly is regulated, it normally has less pricing flexibility; the regulatory body lets it set prices that generate a reasonable, but not excessive, return. A government-owned monopoly may price products below cost to make them accessible to people who otherwise could not afford them. However, government-owned monopolies sometimes charge higher prices to control demand.

In an oligopoly there are only a few sellers and there are high barriers to competitive entry. The motor, mainframe computer, and steel industries exemplify oligopolies. A firm in such an industry can raise its price, hoping that its competitors will do the same. When an organisation cuts its price to gain a competitive edge, other firms are likely to follow suit. Thus very little is gained through price cuts in an oligopolistic market structure.

A market structure characterised by monopolistic competition means numerous sellers with differentiated product offerings. The products are differentiated by physical characteristics, features, quality, and brand images. The distinguishing characteristics of its product may allow a company to set a different price from its competitors. However, firms engaged in a monopolistic competitive market structure are likely to practice non-price competition, discussed earlier in this chapter.

Under conditions of perfect competition, there are many sellers. Buyers view all sellers' products as the same. All firms sell their products at the going market price, and buyers will not pay more than that. This type of market structure, then, gives a marketer no flexibility in setting prices.

■ Legal and Regulatory Issues

At times government action sways marketers' pricing decisions. To curb inflation, the government may invoke price controls, "freeze" prices at certain levels, or determine the rates at which prices can be increased. With the privatisation of once public utilities, the U.K. government has set up regulatory bodies which stress minimum and maximum charges (e.g., OFTEL for telecommunications).

Many regulations and laws affect pricing decisions and activities. Not only must marketers refrain from fixing prices; they must also develop independent pricing policies and set prices in ways that do not even suggest collusion. Over the years legislation has been established to safeguard the consumer and organisations from the sharp practices of other companies. In the U.K. the Monopolies and Mergers Commission prevents the creation of monopolistic situations. The consumer is protected by the Trade Descriptions Act, the Fair Trading Act, the Consumer Protection Act, and much more. The European Community legislates to protect consumers within the community.

PRICING FOR INDUSTRIAL MARKETS

As previously mentioned, industrial markets consist of individuals and organisations that purchase products for resale, for use in their own operations, or for producing other products. Establishing prices for this category of buyers is sometimes different from setting prices for consumers. Industrial marketers have experienced much change because of economic uncertainty, sporadic supply shortages, and an increasing interest in service. Differences in the size of purchases, geographic factors, and transport considerations require sellers to adjust prices. In this section, we discuss several issues unique to the pricing of industrial products, including discounts, geographic pricing, transfer pricing, and price discrimination.

■ Price Discounting

Producers commonly provide intermediaries with discounts off list prices. Although there are many types of discounts, they usually fall into one of five categories: trade, quantity, cash, seasonal discounts, and allowances.

Trade Discounts.   A reduction off the list price given by a producer to a middle-man for performing certain functions is called a **trade**, or **functional**, **discount**. A trade discount is usually stated in terms of a percentage or series of percentages off the list price. Middlemen are given trade discounts as compensation for performing various functions, such as selling, transporting, storing, final processing, and perhaps providing credit services. Although certain trade discounts are often a standard practice within an industry, discounts do vary considerably among industries.

Quantity Discounts.   Deductions from list price that reflect the economies of purchasing in large quantities are called **quantity discounts**. Price quantity discounts are used to pass cost savings, gained through economies of scale, to the buyer. Cost savings usually occur in four areas. First, fewer but larger orders reduce per unit selling costs. Second, fixed costs, such as invoicing and sales contracts, remain the same—or even go down. Third, there are lower costs for raw materials because quantity discounts are often available to the seller. Fourth, longer production runs mean no increases in holding costs.[13] Finally, a large purchase may shift some of the storage, finance, and risk taking functions to the buyer. Thus quantity discounts usually reflect legitimate reductions in costs.

Quantity discounts can be either cumulative or non-cumulative. **Cumulative discounts** are quantity discounts aggregated over a stated period of time. Purchases of £10,000 in a three month period, for example, might entitle the buyer to a 5 percent, or £500, rebate. Such discounts are supposed to reflect economies in selling and encourage the buyer to purchase from one seller. **Non-cumulative discounts** are one-time reductions in prices based on the number of units purchased, the monetary value of the order, or the product mix purchased. Like cumulative discounts, these discounts should reflect some economies in selling or trade functions.

Cash Discounts.   A **cash discount**, or price reduction, is given to a buyer for prompt payment or cash payment. Accounts receivable are an expense and a collection problem for many organisations. A policy to encourage prompt payment is a popular practice and sometimes a major concern in setting prices.

Discounts are based on cash payments or cash paid within a stated time. For example, "2/10 net 30" means that a 2 percent discount will be allowed if the account is paid within 10 days. However, if the buyer does not make payment within the 10-day period, the entire balance is due within 30 days without a discount. If the account is not paid within 30 days, interest may be charged.

Seasonal Discounts.   A price reduction to buyers who purchase goods or services out of season is a **seasonal discount**. These discounts let the seller maintain steadier production during the year. For example, car hire companies offer seasonal discounts in winter and early spring to encourage firms to use cars during the slow months for the car hire business.

Allowances.   Another type of reduction from the list price is an **allowance**—a concession in price to achieve a desired goal. Trade-in allowances, for example, are

13. James B. Wilcox, Roy D. Howell, Paul Kuzdrall, and Robert Britney, "Price Quantity Discounts: Some Implications for Buyers and Sellers," *Journal of Marketing*, July 1987, pp. 60–61.

price reductions granted for turning in a used item when purchasing a new one. Allowances help give the buyer the ability to make the new purchase. This type of discount is popular in the aircraft industry. Another example is promotional allowances, which are price reductions granted to dealers for participating in advertising and sales support programmes intended to increase sales of a particular item.

■ Geographic Pricing

Geographic pricing involves reductions for transport costs or other costs associated with the physical distance between the buyer and the seller. Prices may be quoted as being F.O.B. (free-on-board) factory or destination. An **F.O.B. factory** price indicates the price of the merchandise at the factory, before it is loaded onto the carrier vehicle, and thus excludes transport costs. The buyer must pay for shipping. An **F.O.B. destination** price means that the producer absorbs the costs of shipping the merchandise to the customer. This policy may be used to attract distant customers. Although F.O.B. pricing is an easy way to price products, it is sometimes difficult for marketers to administer, especially when a firm has a wide product mix or when customers are dispersed widely. Because customers will want to know about the most economical method of shipping, the seller must keep abreast of shipping rates.

To avoid the problems involved in charging different prices to each customer, **uniform geographic pricing**, sometimes called postage-stamp pricing, may be used. The same price is charged to all customers regardless of geographic location, and the price is based on average shipping costs for all customers. Petrol, paper products, and office equipment are often priced on a uniform basis.

Zone prices are regional prices that take advantage of a uniform pricing system; prices are adjusted for major geographic zones as the transport costs increase. For example, a Lille manufacturer's prices may be higher for buyers in the South of France than for buyers in Paris.

Base-point pricing is a geographic pricing policy that includes the price at the factory, plus freight charges from the base point nearest the buyer. This approach to pricing has virtually been abandoned because its legal status has been questioned. In America, this policy resulted in all buyers paying freight charges from one location regardless of where the product was manufactured.

When the seller absorbs all or part of the actual freight costs, **freight absorption pricing** is being used. The seller might choose this method because it wishes to do business with a particular customer or to get more business; more business will cause the average cost to fall and counterbalance the extra freight cost. This strategy is used to improve market penetration and to retain a hold in an increasingly competitive market.

■ Transfer Pricing

When one unit in a company sells a product to another unit, **transfer pricing** occurs. The price is determined by one of the following methods:

Actual full cost: calculated by dividing all fixed and variable expenses for a period into the number of units produced

Standard full cost: calculated on what it would cost to produce the goods at full plant capacity

Cost plus investment: calculated as full cost, plus the cost of a portion of the selling unit's assets used for internal needs

Market-based cost: calculated at the market price less a small discount to reflect the lack of sales effort and other expenses

The choice of a method of transfer pricing depends on the company's management strategy and the nature of the units' interaction. The company might initially choose to determine price by the actual full cost method. But later price changes could result in a market-based method or another method that the management of the company decides is best for its changed business situation.[14]

An organisation must also ensure that transfer pricing is fair to all units that must purchase its goods or services. For example, Bellcore, the centralised research organisation that supports the seven regional telephone companies formed from the break-up of AT&T in the U.S.A., found that the prices charged by its secretarial, word-processing, graphics, and technical publications divisions for the services they provided were too high. As a result, engineers and researchers had to take time away from their duties to type documents and prepare presentation materials in order to reduce their own costs. Upon investigation, Bellcore discovered that the four service divisions were themselves paying more than their fair share of overheads and rent expenses. Bellcore revised its methods of allocating overheads and rent. Lower overhead and rental charges, coupled with improved efficiency in the four service divisions, allowed them to reduce their costs by 31 percent, enabling them to charge more reasonable prices for their services provided to other divisions.[15]

■ **Price Discrimination**

A policy of **price discrimination** results in different prices being charged to give a group of buyers a competitive advantage. In some countries price discrimination is regarded as illegal in certain circumstances. For example, in America price differentials are only legal when they can be justified on the basis of cost savings, when they are used to meet competition in good faith, or when they do not damage competition. Thus, if customers are not in competition with each other, different prices may be charged legally. The EC is keen to stamp out price discrimination.

Price differentiation is a form of market segmentation that companies use to provide a marketing mix that satisfies different segments. Because different market segments perceive the value of a particular product differently, depending on the product's importance and value to the industrial buyer, marketers may charge different prices to different market segments. Price discrimination can also be used to modify demand patterns, support sales of other products, help move obsolete goods or excessive inventories, fill excess production capacity, and respond to competitors' activities in particular markets.[16] Table 16.1 shows the principal forms of price discrimination. For price discrimination to work, several conditions are necessary: (1) the market must be segmentable; (2) the cost of segmenting should not exceed the extra revenue from price discrimination; (3) the practice should not breed customer discontent; (4) competition should not be able to steal the segment that is charged the higher price; and (5) the practice should not violate any applicable laws.

14. Robert G. Eccles, "Control with Fairness in Transfer Pricing," *Harvard Business Review,* November-December 1983, pp. 149–161.

15. Edward J. Kovac and Henry P. Troy, "Getting Transfer Prices Right: What Bellcore Did," *Harvard Business Review,* September-October 1989, pp. 148–154.

16. Michael H. Morris, "Separate Prices as a Marketing Tool," *Industrial Marketing Management,* 16, 1987, pp. 79–86.

TABLE 16.1
Principal forms of price discrimination

BASES OF DISCRIMINATION	EXAMPLES
Buyers' incomes	Low priced admission to leisure and recreation facilities for the unemployed.
Buyers' age	Children's haircuts, lower admission charges for students and senior citizens
Buyers' location	Zone prices and season ticket reductions for bus and train travel
Buyers' status	Lower prices to new customers, quantity discounts to big buyers
Use of product	Eat-in and take-away prices for fast foods
Qualities of products	Relatively higher prices for de luxe models
Labels on products	Lower prices of unbranded products
Sizes of products	Relatively lower prices for larger sizes (the "giant economy" size)
Peak and off-peak services	Lower prices for off-peak services, excursion rates on public transport, off-season rates at resorts, holiday and evening telephone rates

SUMMARY

Price is the value placed on what is exchanged. The buyer exchanges buying power —which depends on the buyer's income, credit, and wealth—for satisfaction or utility. Price is not always money paid; barter, the trading of products, is the oldest form of exchange. Price is a key element in the marketing mix because it relates directly to the generation of total revenue. The profit factor can be determined mathematically by multiplying price by quantity sold to get total revenues, and then subtracting total costs. Price is the only variable in the marketing mix that can be adjusted quickly and easily to respond to changes in the external environment.

A product offering can compete on either a price or a non-price basis. Price competition emphasises price as the product differential. Prices fluctuate frequently, and price competition among sellers is aggressive. Non-price competition emphasises product differentiation through distinctive features, services, product quality, or other factors. Establishing brand loyalty by using non-price competition works best when the product can be physically differentiated and the customer can recognise these distinguishing characteristics.

Pricing objectives are overall goals that describe the role of price in a firm's long-range plans. The most fundamental pricing objective is the organisation's survival. Price can be easily adjusted to increase sales volume or to combat competition so that the organisation can stay alive. Profit objectives, which are usually stated in terms of monetary sales volume or percentage change, are normally set at a satisfactory level rather than at a level designed for profit maximisation. A sales growth objective focuses on increasing the profit base by increasing sales volume. Pricing for return on investment (ROI) has a specified profit as its objective. A pricing objective to maintain or increase market share implies that market position is linked to success. Other types of pricing objectives include cash flow and recovery, status quo, and product quality.

A group of eight factors enters into price decision-making: organisational and marketing objectives, pricing objectives, costs, other marketing mix variables, channel member expectations, buyers' perceptions, competition, and legal and regulatory issues. When setting prices, marketers should make decisions consistent with the organisation's goals and mission. Pricing objectives heavily influence price-setting decisions. Most marketers view a product's cost as the floor below which a product cannot be priced. Due to the interrelation of the marketing mix variables, price can affect product, promotion, and distribution decisions. The revenue that channel members expect for the functions they perform must also be considered when making price decisions.

Buyers' perceptions of price vary. Some consumer segments are sensitive to price, but others may not be; thus before determining price, a marketer needs to be aware of its importance to the target market. Knowledge of the prices charged for competing brands is essential for the firm so that it can adjust its prices relative to those of competitors. Government regulations and legislation can also influence pricing decisions through laws to enhance competition and by invoking price controls to curb inflation, for example.

Unlike consumers, industrial buyers purchase products to use in their own operations or for producing other products. When adjusting prices, industrial sellers take into consideration the size of the purchase, geographical factors, and transport requirements. Producers commonly provide discounts off list prices to intermediaries. The categories of discounts include trade, quantity, cash, and seasonal discounts, and allowances. A trade discount is a price reduction for performing such functions as storing, transporting, final processing, or providing credit services. If a middle-man purchases in large enough quantities, the producer gives a quantity discount, which can be either cumulative or non-cumulative. A cash discount is a price reduction for prompt payment or payment in cash. Buyers who purchase goods or services out of season may be granted a seasonal discount. A final type of reduction from the list price is an allowance, such as a trade-in allowance.

Geographic pricing involves reductions for transport costs or other costs associated with the physical distance between the buyer and the seller. A price quoted as F.O.B. factory means that the buyer pays for shipping from the factory; an F.O.B. destination price means that the producer pays for shipping. This is the easiest way to price products, but it can be difficult for marketers to administer. When the seller charges a fixed average cost for transport, the practice is known as uniform geographic pricing. Zone prices take advantage of a uniform pricing system adjusted for major geographical zones as the transport costs increase. Base-point pricing resembles zone pricing; prices are adjusted for shipping expenses incurred by the seller from the base point nearest the buyer. A seller who absorbs all or part of the freight costs is using freight absorption pricing.

When a price discrimination policy is adopted, different prices are charged to give a group of buyers a competitive advantage. In some countries, price differentials are legal only when they can be justified on the basis of cost savings, when they meet competition in good faith, or when they do not attempt to damage competition.

IMPORTANT TERMS

Price
Barter
Price competition
Non-price competition
Pricing objectives
Trade, or functional, discount
Quantity discounts
Cumulative discounts
Non-cumulative discounts
Cash discount
Seasonal discount

Allowance
Geographic pricing
F.O.B. factory
F.O.B. destination
Uniform geographic pricing
Zone prices
Base-point pricing
Freight absorption pricing
Transfer pricing
Price discrimination

DISCUSSION AND REVIEW QUESTIONS

1. Why are pricing decisions so important to an organisation?
2. Compare and contrast price and non-price competition. Describe the conditions under which each form works best.
3. How does a pricing objective of sales growth and expansion differ from an objective to increase market share?
4. Why is it crucial that marketing objectives and pricing objectives be considered when making pricing decisions?
5. In what ways do other marketing mix variables affect pricing decisions?
6. What types of expectations may channel members have about producers' prices, and how do these expectations affect pricing decisions?
7. How do legal and regulatory forces influence pricing decisions?
8. Compare and contrast a trade discount and a quantity discount.
9. What is the reason for using the term F.O.B.?
10. What is the difference between a price discount and price discrimination?

■ CASES

16.1   The BMW Z1

In September 1988 at the Paris Motor Show BMW unveiled its new sports car, the Z1. Described by critics as BMW's jaunty, expensive, two-seater 170-bhp roadster with slide-down electric doors and bounce-back bodywork, the Z1 was priced at DM83,000 in West Germany. The car had been intended as a limited-edition pilot project but its entire production was immediately sold out until the end of 1990. The Z1 is priced well above the BMW 325i (whose engine and transmission it uses and which has similar performance) but is considerably under the price of, for example, the Porsche 911 Carrera Cabrie.

   The planned production quota for the U.K. was twenty-five units in 1989, rising to only fifty units in 1990. Demand is significantly higher than supply and BMW

(GB) has been receiving orders—with a £5,000 deposit—since August 1988. The official U.K. price for the Z1 in August 1989 was £36,925. However, in the summer of 1989 sixteen Z1s were advertised in the press by owners or dealers, with an average price of £46,822. Gradually, these private "black-market" prices dropped from a peak of £50,000 to close to the official retail price.

SOURCES: M. Labrou, "Ten Marketing Cases," MBA Dissertation, University of Warwick, 1989; Douglas Hamilton, Reuters, 30 Sept. 1988 and 17 Oct. 1988; and *Autocar and Motor,* 19 July 1989.

Questions for Discussion

1. Could BMW have priced the car significantly higher (or lower)? What would have been the consequences?
2. Setting production levels in such a market is not straightforward. Could BMW have predicted demand for the Z1 more accurately?
3. BMW positions itself as a prestige car manufacturer. If it were producing cars for the mass market—like Ford or Volkswagen—would the company adopt a different pricing policy?

16.2 The Coke and Pepsi Price War

Particularly in the U.S., Coca-Cola Company and PepsiCo, Inc. have fought for soft-drink supremacy on supermarket shelves, in vending machines, in cafés, and in the media. In the $43 billion retail soft-drinks market, both firms want to be the clear market leader. A one percentage point shift in the $16 billion food store soft-drinks market amounts to $160 million in sales. In the scramble for consumers' cash, a price war broke out between the two companies as each slashed prices to attract consumers.

At a store in Tempe, Arizona, traffic jams developed in the car park and check-out queues stretched to the meat department as shoppers hauled away cases of Coke priced at 59 cents per six-pack. The store was selling Coca-Cola at the rate of 2,900 cases a day. At another Tempe store, six-packs of Pepsi priced at 79 cents were selling almost as quickly.

Though grocery prices recently have increased overall, soft-drink prices have declined sharply. In the past, the price war generally intensified around holidays and in the summer but now battles are fought daily. In food stores, where the price war is primarily centred, 90 percent of the soft drinks sold have been on sale. Sometimes, by featuring their own price specials to draw consumers, retailers play the two companies off against each other, pressuring them either to lower prices more, to offer lower prices for longer periods of time, or both.

The numbers change constantly, but current figures indicate that Coca-Cola leads the industry overall and Pepsi leads in the supermarket category. Pepsi has held the position as supermarket leader since the disastrous introduction of New Coke. Both companies are eager to become the choice of the average American—who drinks over 42 gallons of soft drinks a year. According to Pepsi's statistics, 50 percent of the individuals who consume soft drinks are not completely loyal to either Pepsi or Coke.

Pepsi's own internal bottling division accounts for 40 percent of the Pepsi sold in the United States. Coca-Cola owns 49 percent of its primary bottler, Coca-Cola Enterprises. Both companies sell soft-drink concentrate to their bottlers. It is the bottlers who actually combine the syrup with carbonated water and sell it to grocers. In the midst of the cola price war, Pepsi and Coca-Cola bottlers are on the front line. The cola war is especially heated (that is, the price-slashing is particularly heavy) in Los Angeles, Phoenix, and several Texas cities where respective company-owned bottlers compete directly with each other.

When the soft-drink giants wage price wars, the producers of brands such as Dr Pepper, Royal Crown Cola, and 7 Up suffer the most. Because 75 percent of the soft-drinks market belongs to Coca-Cola and Pepsi, smaller competitors must continuously try to underprice them. When Coca-Cola and Pepsi lower prices, earnings of the smaller firms decrease rapidly.

Some marketers think that the extended price war between Pepsi and Coke has damaged the brand image of both. The price war has also affected brand loyalty as consumers seek bargains rather than a particular soft drink. The price war may last indefinitely since it is unlikely that one company will raise prices if the other does not. Consumers, accustomed to paying low prices, might reject higher prices altogether and look to other brands to satisfy their thirsts.

SOURCES: Mike Duff, "Soft Drinks," *Supermarket Business,* Sept. 1989, pp. 217–222; Kevin Hanley, "Couponing for Customers," *Target Marketing,* Nov. 1986, pp. 13–14; Karen Hoggan, "Head to Head," *Marketing,* 22 June 1989, pp. 20–21; Warren Kornblum, "More Than the Price Has to Be Right," *Retail Control,* Oct. 1987, pp. 7–16; Betsy Morris, "Coke and Pepsi: Cola War Marches On," *Wall Street Journal,* 3 June 1987, p. 33; Stephen W. Quickel, "Coke vs. Pepsi: A 100 Years War," *Business Month,* Jan. 1989, pp. 10–11; Patricia Winters, "Coke's Game Plan," *Advertising Age,* 7 Nov. 1988, p. 4; and Patricia Winters, "Jackson, Houston Hard Acts to Follow," *Advertising Age,* 11 Sept. 1989, pp. S13, S14.

Questions for Discussion

1. What type of pricing objectives are Coca-Cola and Pepsi most likely to have? Explain.
2. Does a price war help to build brand loyalty? Why or why not? If brand loyalty were stronger among cola drinkers, would a price war be advisable? Explain.
3. What major factors are most likely to influence which company will win an extended price war?

17 SETTING PRICES

Objectives

To understand eight major stages of the process used to establish prices

To explore issues connected with selecting pricing objectives

To grasp the importance of identifying the target market's evaluation of price

To gain insight into demand curves and the price elasticity of demand

To examine the relationships among demand, costs, and profits

To learn about analysing competitive prices

To understand the different types of pricing policies

To scrutinise the major kinds of pricing methods

*B*usinesses are experiencing a general fax frenzy. Customers are faxing orders to restaurants, architects are faxing tentative plans to their offices, and freelance artists are faxing designs everywhere. In the U.K. more than 53,000 fax machines were sold in 1988, up from only around 25,000 in 1987. The market is led by Canon and NEC, each with a 20 percent share by volume. Worldwide industry leaders Sharp and Murata both achieve strength by producing relatively inexpensive machines that appeal to small- and medium-sized businesses.

The purchase of fax machines actually saves money for smaller companies by reducing the need for express mail service and messengers. Business analysts expect sales of fax machines to increase dramatically in the future as more and more individuals start working from home. These workers are most likely to be attracted to basic "low-end" machines, costing less than £1,000.

Xerox created the first commercial fax machine in 1970, but it was Sharp and Murata that produced the earliest no-frills models. With a continually growing list of competitors in the low-priced part of the market, both Sharp and Murata are investing heavily in research and development to solidify their positions as industry leaders. South Korean fax machine manufacturers, such as Samsung and Daewoo, might pose a challenge to established companies. Analysts expect these Korean firms to drive the price of fax machines down to about £200. ◆

Based on information in Jeffrey H. Epstein, "The Future in Fax," *Direct Marketing,* March 1989, pp. 28, 30; Sherli Evans, "Fax: Looking Fine in '89," *Industry Week,* 15 May 1989, pp. BC3–BC4, BC6–BC7; Frederick H. Katayama, "Who's Fueling the Fax Frenzy," *Fortune,* 23 Oct. 1989, pp. 151–152, 156; and HARVEST, *Trade Estimates/Market Assessment,* 1990, 42221438.

In the fax machine market, demand is strong and the number of producers is increasing. These conditions require that fax machine marketers give frequent consideration to setting and altering prices. Setting prices of products such as fax machines requires careful analysis of numerous issues. In this chapter we examine eight stages of a process that marketers can use when setting prices.

Figure 17.1 illustrates these eight stages. Stage 1 is the development of a pricing objective that is congruent with the organisation's overall objectives and its marketing objectives. In stage 2, both the target market's evaluation of price and its ability to buy must be assessed. Then, in stage 3, marketers should examine the nature and price elasticity of demand. Stage 4, which consists of analysing demand, cost, and profit relationships, is necessary for estimating the economic feasibility of alternative prices. Evaluation of competitors' prices, which constitutes stage 5, helps determine the role of price in the marketing strategy. Stage 6 is the selection of a pricing policy, or the guidelines for using price in the marketing mix. Stage 7 involves choosing a method for calculating the price charged to customers. Stage 8, the determining of the final price, depends on environmental forces and marketers' understanding and use of a systematic approach to establishing prices. These stages are not rigid steps that all marketers must follow but rather guidelines that provide a logical sequence for establishing prices. In some situations, additional stages may need to be included in the price setting process; in others, certain stages may not be necessary.

SELECTION OF PRICING OBJECTIVES

Chapter 16 considers the various types of pricing objectives. Selecting pricing objectives is an important task because they form the basis for decisions about other stages of pricing. Thus pricing objectives must be explicitly stated. The statement of pricing objectives should include the time period during which the objectives are to be accomplished.

FIGURE 17.1
Stages for establishing prices

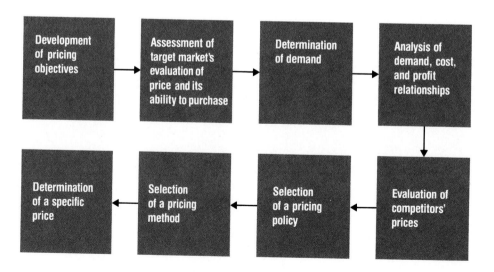

Marketers must be certain that the pricing objectives they set are consistent with the organisation's overall objectives and marketing objectives. Inconsistent objectives cause internal conflicts and confusion and can prevent the organisation from achieving its overall goals. Furthermore, pricing objectives inconsistent with organisational and marketing objectives may cause marketers to make poor decisions during the other stages in the price setting process.

Organisations normally have multiple pricing objectives, some short-term and others long-term. For example, the pricing objective of gaining market share is normally short-term because it often requires the firm to price its product quite low relative to competitors' prices. An organisation should have one or more pricing objectives for each product. For the same product aimed at different market segments, marketers sometimes choose different pricing objectives. A marketer typically alters pricing objectives over time.

ASSESSING THE TARGET MARKET'S EVALUATION OF PRICE AND ITS ABILITY TO BUY

Although we generally assume that price is a significant issue for buyers, the importance of price depends on the type of product, the type of target market, and the purchase situation. For example, in general, buyers are probably more sensitive to petrol prices than to luggage prices. With respect to the type of target market, the price of an airline ticket is much more important to a tourist than to a business traveller. The purchase situation also affects the buyer's view of price. Most cinemagoers would never pay, in other situations, the prices asked for soft drinks, popcorn, and confectionery in cinema foyers. By assessing the target market's evaluation of price, a marketer is in a better position to know how much emphasis to place on price. Information about the target market's price evaluation may also help a marketer determine how far above the competition a firm can set its prices.

As we point out in Chapter 3, the people who make up a market must have the ability to buy a product. Buyers must need a product, be willing to use their buying power, and have the authority (by law or social custom) to buy. Their ability to buy, like their evaluation of price, has direct consequences for marketers. The ability to purchase involves such resources as money, credit, wealth, and other products that could be traded in an exchange. Understanding customers' buying power and knowing how important a product is to them in comparison with other products helps marketers correctly assess the target market's evaluation of price.

DETERMINING DEMAND

Determining the demand for a product is the responsibility of marketing managers, who are aided in this task by marketing researchers and forecasters. Marketing research and forecasting techniques yield estimates of sales potential or the quantity of a product that could be sold during a specific period. (Chapter 3 describes such techniques as surveys, time series analyses, correlation methods, and market tests.) These estimates are helpful in establishing the relationship between a product's price and the quantity demanded.

FIGURE 17.2
Demand curve illustrating
the price-quantity rela-
tionship and an increase
in demand

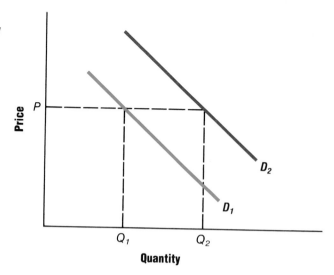

The Demand Curve

For most products, the quantity demanded goes up as the price goes down, and as the price goes up, the quantity demanded goes down. Thus there is an inverse relationship between price and quantity demanded. As long as the marketing environment and buyers' needs, ability (purchasing power), willingness, and authority to buy remain stable, this fundamental inverse relationship will continue.

Figure 17.2 illustrates the effect of one variable—price—on the quantity demanded. The classic **demand curve** (D1) is a graph of the quantity of products expected to be sold at various prices, if other factors remain constant.[1] It illustrates that as price falls the quantity demanded usually rises. Demand depends on other factors in the marketing mix, including product quality, promotion, and distribution. An improvement in any of these factors may cause a shift to, say, demand curve D2. In such a case, an increased quantity (Q2) will be sold at the same price (P).

There are many types of demand and not all conform to the classic demand curve shown in Figure 17.2. Prestige products, such as selected perfumes and jewellery, seem to sell better at high prices than at low ones. For example, the jewellery shown in Figure 17.3 is known to be expensive and thus has a prestigious image. These products are desirable partly because their cost makes buyers feel superior. If the price fell drastically and many people owned them, they would lose some of their appeal.

The demand curve in Figure 17.4 shows the relationship between price and quantity for prestige products. Demand is greater, not less, at higher prices. For a certain price range—from P1 to P2—the quantity demanded (Q1) goes up to Q2. After a point, however, raising the price backfires. If the price of a product goes too high, the quantity demanded goes down. The figure shows that if the price is raised from P2 to P3, quantity demanded goes back down from Q2 to Q1.

Demand Fluctuations

Changes in buyers' needs, variations in the effectiveness of other marketing mix variables, the presence of substitutes, and dynamic environmental factors can influence demand. Restaurants and utility companies experience large fluctuations in

1. Reprinted from *Dictionary of Marketing Terms,* Peter D. Bennett, Ed., 1988, p. 54, published by the American Marketing Association. Used by permission.

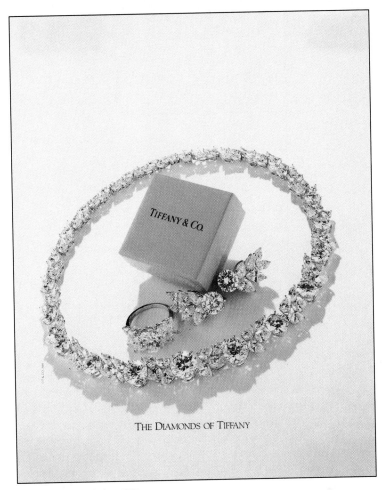

THE DIAMONDS OF TIFFANY

SOURCE: © Tiffany & Co., 1989

demand daily. Toy manufacturers, fireworks suppliers, and air-conditioning and heating contractors also face demand fluctuations because of the seasonal nature of these items. The demand for fax machines, single-serving low-calorie meals, and fur coats has changed significantly over the last few years. In some cases, demand fluctuations are predictable. It is no surprise to restaurants and public utilities that demand fluctuates. However, changes in demand for other products may be less predictable and this leads to problems for some companies. Marketing Update 17.1 discusses the impact of the Gulf crisis on fuel prices around the world. Although demand can fluctuate unpredictably, some firms have been able to anticipate changes in demand by correlating demand for a specific product with demand for the total industry or with some other economic variable. If a brand maintains a fairly constant market share, its sales can be estimated as a percentage of industry sales.

■ **Gauging Price Elasticity of Demand**

Up to this point, we have been discussing how marketers identify the target market's evaluation of price and its ability to purchase and how they examine demand to learn whether price is related inversely or directly to quantity. The next stage in the process is to gauge price elasticity of demand. **Price elasticity of demand** provides a measure of the sensitivity of demand to changes in price. It is formally defined as

FIGURE 17.4

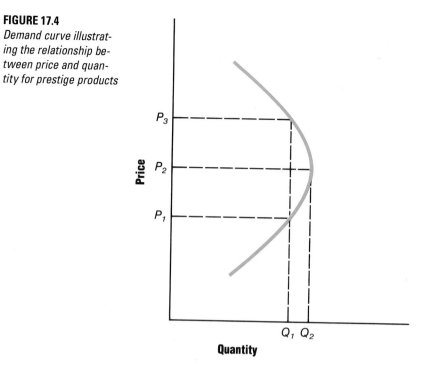

the percentage change in quantity demanded relative to a given percentage change in price[2] (see Figure 17.5). The percentage change in quantity demanded caused by a percentage change in price is much greater for elastic demand than for inelastic demand. For a product such as electricity, demand is relatively inelastic. When its price is increased, say from P1 to P2, quantity demanded goes down only a little, from Q1 to Q2. For products such as recreational vehicles, demand is relatively elastic. When price rises sharply, from P1 to P2, quantity demanded goes down a great deal, from Q1 to Q2.

If marketers can determine price elasticity of demand, then setting a price is much easier. By analysing total revenues as prices change, marketers can determine whether a product is price elastic. Total revenue is price times quantity; thus 10,000 rolls of wallpaper sold in one year at a price of £10 per roll equals £100,000 of total revenue. If demand is *elastic*, a change in price causes an opposite change in total revenue—an increase in price will decrease total revenue, and a decrease in price will increase total revenue. An *inelastic* demand results in a change in the same direction in total revenue—an increase in price will increase total revenue, and a decrease in price will decrease total revenue. The following formula determines the price elasticity of demand:

$$\text{Price Elasticity of Demand} = \frac{\% \text{ Change in Quantity Demanded}}{\% \text{ Change in Price}}$$

For example, if demand falls by 8 percent when a seller raises the price by 2 percent, the price elasticity of demand is −4 (the negative sign indicating the inverse relationship between price and demand). If demand falls by 2 percent when price is

2. Bennett, p. 150. Reprinted by permission.

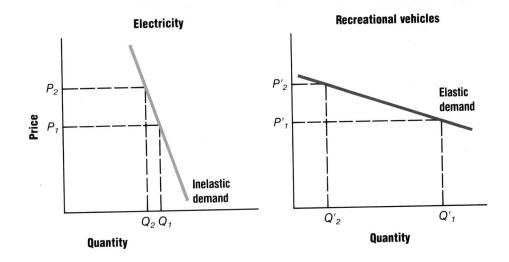

FIGURE 17.5
Elasticity of demand

increased by 4 percent, then elasticity is $-1/2$. The less elastic the demand, the more beneficial it is for the seller to raise the price. Products without readily available substitutes and for which consumers have strong needs (for example, electricity or petrol) usually have inelastic demand.

Marketers cannot base prices solely on elasticity considerations. They must also examine the costs associated with different volumes and see what happens to profits.

ANALYSIS OF DEMAND, COST, AND PROFIT RELATIONSHIPS

Having examined the role of demand in setting prices and the various costs and their relationships, we can now explore the relationships among demand, cost, and profit. To stay in business, a company has to set prices that cover all its costs. There are two approaches to understanding demand, cost, and profit relationships: marginal analysis and break-even analysis.

■ Marginal Analysis

Marginal analysis is the examination of what happens to a firm's costs and revenues when production (or sales volume) is changed by one unit. Both production costs and revenues must be evaluated. To determine the costs of production, it is necessary to distinguish among several types of costs. **Fixed costs** do not vary with changes in the number of units produced or sold. The cost of renting a factory does not change because production increases from one shift to two shifts a day or because twice as much wallpaper is sold. Rent may go up, but not because the factory has doubled production or revenue. **Average fixed cost** is the fixed cost per unit produced and is calculated by dividing fixed costs by the number of units produced.

Variable costs vary directly with changes in the number of units produced or sold. The wages for a second shift and the cost of twice as much paper are extra costs that occur when production is doubled. Variable costs are usually constant per unit; that is, twice as many workers and twice as much material produces twice as

GULF CRISIS HITS FUEL PRICES

Following Iraq's invasion of Kuwait in August 1990, oil and petrol prices soared as a result of panic buying on stock exchanges around the world. The price of British North Sea oil quickly rose to $30 a barrel. Oil companies Texaco, Esso, and Shell responded with retail petrol price increases of around 10.5 pence per gallon. The repercussions were significant. With the possibility of further rises looming, many airlines and tour operators were forced to act. While Pan Am increased the cost of all fares by 10 percent, tour companies tied into "no-surcharge" agreements looked on anxiously.

Meanwhile, U.K. marketers who were asked about the likely impact of the increasing prices expressed concern about the probable effects on profits.

1. **What direct impact, if any, do you think the rise in oil prices will have on your profits? See pie-chart.**

No impact at all 32%

Fairly negative 49%

Fairly positive 13%

Very positive 2%

Very negative 2%

Don't know 2%

2. Is the price of petrol or other oil-related products a significant element of your overall costs or not? Yes, 39%; no, 58%; don't know, 3%.

3. What indirect impact, if any, do you think the rise in oil prices will have on your profits? a) Very positive, 2%; b) fairly positive, 10%; c) no impact at all, 14%; d) fairly negative, 62%; e) very negative, 10%; f) don't know, 2%.

4. Do you anticipate having to raise prices above what you had previously planned because of the Gulf crisis or not? Yes, 16%; no, 67%; don't know, 17%.

5. What impact, if any, do you think the Gulf crisis will have on UK business? a) Very positive, 3%; b) fairly positive, 10%; c) no impact at all, 6%; d) fairly negative, 70%; e) very negative, 9%; f) don't know, 2%.

Marketing Forum is a weekly poll carried out for *Marketing* by research specialist Network. The poll was carried out...among a panel of marketing directors and managers drawn from the U.K.'s top 300 advertisers. Total response: 87.

SOURCES: "Marketing Forum," *Marketing,* 16 August 1990, p. 40; Mike Johnson and Robert Dweek, "Gulf Crisis Bites Hard," *Marketing,* 9 August 1990, p. 2 (Figure reproduced by permission); Clare Samorook, "Tour Firms Get Jitters," *Marketing,* 23 August 1990, p. 2; Steven Butler, "A Question of Market Psychology," *Financial Times,* 28 September 1990, p. 20c; Richard Gourlay, "No Goodwill from Slick Ads," *Financial Times,* 27 September 1990, p. 10c.

TABLE 17.1 *Costs and their relationships*

1 QUANTITY	2 FIXED COST	3 AVERAGE FIXED COST (2) ÷ (1)	4 AVERAGE VARIABLE COST	5 AVERAGE TOTAL COST (3) + (4)	6 TOTAL COST (5) × (1)	7 MARGINAL COST
1	£40	£40.00	£20.00	£60.00	£ 60	£10
2	40	20.00	15.00	35.00	70	5
3	40	13.33	11.67	25.00	75	15
4	40	10.00	12.50	22.50	90	20
5	40	8.00	14.00	22.00	110	30
6	40	6.67	16.67	23.33	140	40
7	40	5.71	20.00	25.71	180	

many rolls of wallpaper. **Average variable cost**, the variable cost per unit produced, is calculated by dividing the variable costs by the number of units produced.

Total cost is the sum of average fixed costs and average variable costs times the quantity produced. The **average total cost** is the sum of the average fixed cost and the average variable cost. **Marginal cost (MC)** is the extra cost a firm incurs when it produces one more unit of a product. Table 17.1 illustrates various costs and their relationships. Notice that the average fixed cost declines as the output increases. The average variable cost follows a U shape, as does the average total cost. Because the average total cost continues to fall after the average variable cost begins to rise, its lowest point is at a higher level of output than that of the average variable cost. The average total cost is lowest at 5 units at a cost of £22, whereas the average variable cost is lowest at 3 units at a cost of £11.67. As shown in Figure 17.6, marginal cost equals average total cost at the latter's lowest level, between 5 and 6 units of production. In Table 17.1 this occurs between 5 and 6 units of production. Average total cost decreases as long as the marginal cost is less than the average total cost, and it increases when marginal cost rises above average total cost.

Marginal revenue (MR) is the change in total revenue that occurs when a firm sells an additional unit of a product. Figure 17.7 depicts marginal revenue and a demand curve. Most firms in Europe face downward-sloping demand curves for their products. In other words, they must lower their prices to sell additional units. This situation means that each additional product sold provides the firm with less revenue than the previous unit sold. MR then becomes less than average revenue, as Figure 17.7 shows. Eventually, MR reaches zero and the sale of additional units merely hurts the firm.

However, before the firm can determine if a unit makes a profit, it must know its cost, as well as its revenue, because profit equals revenue minus cost. If MR is a unit's addition to revenue and MC is a unit's addition to cost, then MR minus MC tells us whether the unit is profitable or not. Table 17.2 illustrates the relationships between price, quantity sold, total revenue, marginal revenue, marginal cost, and total cost. It indicates where maximum profits are possible at various combinations of price and cost.

FIGURE 17.6

Typical marginal cost and average cost relationships

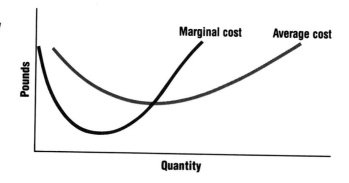

Profit is maximised where MC = MR (see Table 17.2). In this table MC = MR at four units. The best price is £33.75 and the profit is £45. Up to this point, the additional revenue generated from an extra unit of sale exceeds the additional total cost. Beyond this point, the additional cost of another unit sold exceeds the additional revenue generated, and profits decrease. If the price was based on minimum average total cost—£22 (Table 17.1)—it would result in less profit: only £40 (Table 17.2) for five units at a price of £30 versus £45 for four units at a price of £33.75.

Graphically combining Figures 17.6 and 17.7 into Figure 17.8 shows that any unit for which MR exceeds MC adds to a firm's profits, and any unit for which MC exceeds MR subtracts from a firm's profits. The firm should produce at the point where MR equals MC because this is the most profitable level of production.

This discussion of marginal analysis may give the false impression that pricing can be highly precise. If revenue (demand) and cost (supply) remained constant, then prices could be set for maximum profits. In practice, however, cost and revenue change frequently. The competitive tactics of other firms or government action can quickly undermine a company's expectations of revenue. Thus marginal analysis is only a model from which to work. It offers little help in pricing new products before costs and revenues are established. On the other hand, in setting prices of existing products, especially in competitive situations, most marketers can benefit by understanding the relationship between marginal cost and marginal revenue.

FIGURE 17.7

Typical marginal revenue and average revenue relationships

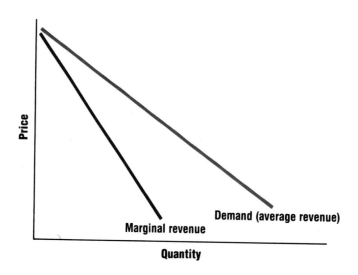

TABLE 17.2 *Marginal analysis: method of obtaining maximum profit-producing price*

1 PRICE	2 QUANTITY SOLD	3 TOTAL REVENUE (1) × (2)	4 MARGINAL REVENUE	5 MARGINAL COST	6 TOTAL COST	7 PROFIT (3) – (6)
£57.00	1	£ 57	£57	£—	£ 60	£ 3
55.00	2	110	53	10	70	40
40.00	3	120	10	5	75	45
33.75[a]	**4**	**135**	**15**	**15**	**90**	**45**
30.00	5	150	15	20	110	40
27.00	6	162	12	30	140	22
25.00	7	175	13	40	180	–5

[a]Boldface indicates best price-profit combination.

Break-even Analysis

The point at which the costs of producing a product equal the revenue made from selling the product is the **break-even point**. If a wallpaper manufacturer has total annual costs of £100,000 and in the same year it sells £100,000 worth of wallpaper, then the company has broken even.

Figure 17.9 illustrates the relationships of costs, revenue, profits, and losses involved in determining the break-even point. Knowing the number of units necessary to break even is important in setting the price. If a product priced at £100 per unit has an average variable cost of £60 per unit, then the contribution to fixed costs is £40. If total fixed costs are £120,000, here is the way to determine the break-even point in units:

$$\text{Break-even Point} = \frac{\text{Fixed Costs}}{\text{Per Unit Contribution to Fixed Costs}}$$

$$= \frac{\text{Fixed Costs}}{\text{Price} - \text{Variable Costs}}$$

$$= \frac{£120,000}{£40}$$

$$= 3,000 \text{ Units}$$

To calculate the break-even point in terms of cash sales volume, multiply the break-even point in units by the price per unit. In the preceding example, the break-even point in terms of cash sales volume is 3,000 (units) times £100, or £300,000.

To use break-even analysis effectively, a marketer should determine the break-even point for each of several alternative prices. This determination allows the marketer to compare the effects on total revenue, total costs, and the break-even point for each price under consideration. Although this comparative analysis may not tell the marketer exactly what price to charge, it will identify highly undesirable price alternatives that should definitely be avoided.

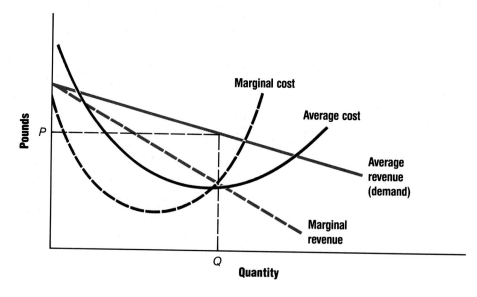

FIGURE 17.8
Combining the marginal cost and marginal revenue concepts for optimal profit

Break-even analysis is simple and straightforward. It does assume, however, that the quantity demanded is basically fixed (inelastic) and that the major task in setting prices is to recover costs. It focuses more on how to break even than on how to achieve a pricing objective, such as percentage of market share or return on investment. None the less, marketing managers can use this concept to determine whether a product will achieve at least a break-even volume. In other words, it is easier to answer the question "Will we sell at least the minimum volume necessary to break even?" than the question "What volume of sales will we expect to sell?"

EVALUATION OF COMPETITORS' PRICES

In most cases, marketers are in a better position to establish prices when they know the prices charged for competing brands. Learning competitors' prices may be a regular function of marketing research. Some grocery and department stores, for example, have full-time comparative shoppers who systematically collect data on prices. Companies may also purchase price lists, sometimes weekly, from syndicated marketing research agencies.

Finding out what prices competitors are charging is not always easy, especially in producer and reseller markets. Competitors' price lists are often closely guarded. Even if a marketer has access to price lists, they may not reflect the actual prices at which competitive products are sold because those prices may be established through negotiation.

Knowing the prices of competing brands can be very important for a marketer. Competitors' prices and the marketing mix variables that they emphasise partly determine how important price will be to customers. Marketers in an industry in which non-price competition prevails need competitive price information to ensure that their organisation's prices are the same as its competitors' prices. In some instances, an organisation's prices are designed to be slightly above competitors'

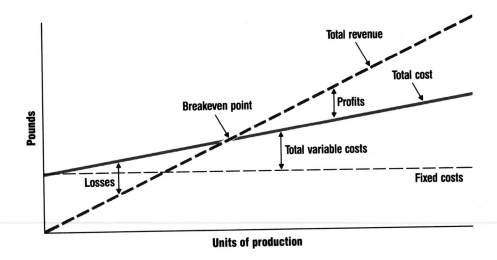

FIGURE 17.9
Determining the break-even point

(Figure labels: Pounds (vertical axis), Units of production (horizontal axis), Total revenue, Total cost, Breakeven point, Profits, Total variable costs, Fixed costs, Losses)

prices to give its products an exclusive image. Alternatively, another company may use price as a competitive tool and attempt to price its product below those of competitors. Toys "R" Us, for example, has acquired a large market share through aggressive competitive prices.

SELECTION OF A PRICING POLICY

A **pricing policy** is a guiding philosophy or course of action designed to influence and determine pricing decisions. Pricing policies set guidelines for achieving pricing objectives. They are an important component of an overall marketing strategy. Generally, pricing policies should answer this recurring question: How will price be used as a variable in the marketing mix? This question may relate to (1) introduction of new products, (2) competitive situations, (3) government pricing regulations, (4) economic conditions, or (5) implementation of pricing objectives. Pricing policies help marketers solve the practical problems of establishing prices. Let us examine the most common pricing policies.

■ **Pioneer Pricing Policies**

Pioneer pricing—setting the base price for a new product—is a necessary part of formulating a marketing strategy. The base price is easily adjusted (in the absence of government price controls), and its establishment is one of the most fundamental decisions in the marketing mix. The base price can be set high to recover development costs quickly or to provide a reference point for developing discount prices to different market segments.

When marketers set base prices, they also consider how quickly competitors will enter the market, whether they will mount a strong campaign on entry, and what effect their entry will have on the development of primary demand. If competitors will enter quickly, with considerable marketing force, and with limited effect on the primary demand, then a firm may adopt a base price that will discourage their entry.

Price Skimming. **Price skimming** is charging the highest possible price that buyers who most desire the product will pay. This pioneer approach provides the

FIGURE 17.10
Penetration pricing.
To gain market share Proton employs a penetration pricing policy for its cars.

SOURCE: Proton Cars U.K., Ltd.

most flexible introductory base price. Demand tends to be inelastic in the introductory stage of the product life cycle (for example, the CD player and the pocket calculator).

Price skimming can provide several benefits, especially when a product is in the introductory stage of its life cycle. A skimming policy can generate much-needed initial cash flows to help offset sizeable developmental costs. When introducing a new model of camera, Polaroid initially uses a skimming price to defray large research and development costs. Price skimming protects the marketer from problems that arise when the price is set too low to cover costs. When a firm introduces a product, its production capacity may be limited. A skimming price can help keep demand consistent with a firm's production capabilities. The use of a skimming price may attract competition into an industry because the high price makes that type of business appear to be quite lucrative.

Penetration Price.   A **penetration price** is a price below the prices of competing brands and is designed to penetrate a market and produce a larger unit sales volume. When introducing a product, a marketer sometimes uses a penetration price to gain a large market share quickly. As shown in Figure 17.10, Proton is using penetration pricing for its cars. This approach places the marketer in a less flexible position than price skimming because it is more difficult to raise a penetration price than to lower or discount a skimming price. It is not unusual for a firm to use a penetration price after having skimmed the market with a higher price.

Penetration pricing can be especially beneficial when marketers suspect that competitors could enter the market easily. First, if the penetration price lets one marketer gain a large market share quickly, competitors might be discouraged from entering the market. Second, entering the market may be less attractive to competitors when a penetration price is used because the lower per unit price results in lower per unit profit; this may cause competitors to view the market as not being especially lucrative. Mazda, for instance, used penetration pricing when it introduced the MX-5 to gain market share quickly and to discourage competitors from entering that market segment (see Marketing Update 17.2).

A penetration price is particularly appropriate when demand is highly elastic. Highly elastic demand means that target market members would purchase the product if it was priced at the penetration level but few would buy the item if it was priced higher. A marketer should consider using a penetration price when a lower price would result in longer production runs, increasing production significantly and reducing the firm's per unit production costs.

■ Psychological Pricing

Psychological pricing encourages purchases based on emotional rather than rational responses. It is used most often at the retail level. Psychological pricing has limited use for industrial products.

Odd-Even Pricing.   Through **odd-even pricing**—that is, ending the price with certain numbers—marketers try to influence buyers' perceptions of the price or the product. Odd pricing assumes that more of a product will be sold at £99.95 than at £100. Supposedly, customers will think, or at least tell friends, that the product is a bargain—not £100, mind you, but £99, plus a few insignificant pence. Also, customers are supposed to think that the store could have charged £100 but instead cut the price to the last penny, to £99.95. Some claim, too, that certain types of customer are more attracted by odd prices than by even ones. However, there are no substantial research findings to support the notion that odd prices produce greater sales. None the less, even prices are far more unusual today than odd prices.

Even prices are used to give a product an exclusive or up-market image. An even price supposedly will influence a customer to view the product as being a high-quality, premium brand. A shirt manufacturer, for example, may print on a premium shirt package a suggested retail price of £32 instead of £31.95; the even price of the shirt is used to enhance its up-market image.

Customary Pricing.   In **customary pricing**, certain goods are priced primarily on the basis of tradition. Recent economic uncertainties have made most prices fluctuate fairly widely, but the classic example of the customary, or traditional, price is the telephone call. Until the mid-1980s, U.K. public telephones were geared to the use of particular coins. For years the 2-pence and later the 10-pence slots were widely recognised. British Telecom's response to rising prices was, initially, to alter the cost of units so that less call time was allowed for the same money. Since then, demands for greater flexibility of use have seen public call-boxes altered to accept most British coins.

PRICING OF THE MAZDA MX-5

Mazda is anxious to overhaul its image: it no longer wants to be known as the lower-priced Japanese alternative to Honda and Toyota. As part of its image alteration, Mazda has introduced the Mazda MX-5. Mazda engineers designed the MX-5 along the lines of the classic British two-seater cars of the 1960s. Mazda's new model does resemble earlier Triumphs and Austin-Healeys, but it does not require as much maintenance. Car magazines such as *What Car?* in the U.K. and *Road & Track* in the United States have praised the MX-5. They tout the car as solid and fun to drive, but register amazement at the price. At a reasonable manufacturer-suggested retail price of £14,250, Mazda has made high-performance cars affordable.

A research and development specialist at Mazda concluded that there was a great demand for a "cheap" two-seater sports car. So, from the beginning, Mazda designers and engineers considered cost as important as performance and styling. According to Mazda's product programme manager, the MX-5 is a much simpler car than either the Mazda 323 or 626. For example, it uses a 120-horsepower, 1.6-litre four-cylinder engine instead of Mazda's expensive rotary engine.

To keep consumer costs down, the MX-5 lacks many of the sophisticated gadgets that sports cars today are noted for. Options on the car are limited and the MX-5 is available in only a few colours. Mazda limited production of the MX-5 to 20,000 the first year and 40,000 every year after that. The simple design and great performance of the MX-5 have caught the public's attention, but the low price has made the car an automotive sensation. In some places, people were actually paying *more* than the retail price to get one. The relative scarcity of the car has helped MX-5 sales. As one analyst stated, the scarcity "raises the mystique of the cars".

SOURCES: Larry Armstrong, "Mazda Rolls out a Poor Man's Maserati," *Business Week,* 26 June 1989, p. 66; Ken Gross, "Back to the Future," *Automotive Industries,* April 1989, pp. 92–94; Kathy Barks Hoffman, "Sporty Miata Zips to Fast Start," *USA Today,* 11 July 1989, p. B1; and "The New Seekers," *What Car?* June 1990, pp. 80–87.

FIGURE 17.11
Prestige pricing.
The Tank Watch by
Cartier is a high quality
product that is prestige
priced.

CARTIER – THE TANK WATCH

CREATED TO HONOUR THE
AMERICAN HEROES OF THE
FIRST WORLD WAR. A CASE
IN 18 CARAT GOLD
DESIGNED ON THE PURE,
GEOMETRIC LINES OF THE
POWERFUL VEHICLES WHOSE
NAME IT BEARS. ELEGANT,
REMARKABLY ACCURATE,
ADORNED WITH A SAPPHIRE
AND FEATURING THE
FAMOUS FOLDING BUCKLE,
THE TANK WATCH BY
CARTIER* IS A MASTER
CREATION. FOREVER
CONTEMPORARY, IT IS QUITE
SIMPLY "THE WATCH".

*Trade-Mark registered by the Cartier Group.

Cartier
L'ART D'ÊTRE UNIQUE

Available at *Cartier Ltd* 175/176 New Bond Street, London W1, The Fine Jewellery Room at Harrods,
and *les must de Cartier* Boutiques at Harvey Nichols, Harrods and 188 Sloane Street and from leading jewellers.

SOURCE: Courtesy of Cartier, Ltd.

Prestige Pricing.   In **prestige pricing**, prices are set at an artificially high level
to provide prestige or a quality image. In the United States, pharmacists report that
some consumers complain if a prescription does not cost enough. Apparently, some
consumers associate a drug's price with its potency. Consumers in the U.K. often
associate the quality of service provided by a hairdresser with price. In some cases,
this is demonstrated by a willingness to pay more than twice as much for a perm at
an establishment like Vidal Sassoon than at the local hairdresser, even though the
treatment given may be comparable.

Prestige pricing is used especially when buyers associate a higher price with
higher quality. Typical product categories in which selected products are prestige priced include perfumes, cars, alcoholic beverages, jewellery, and electrical
appliances (see Figure 17.11). If producers that use prestige pricing lowered their
prices dramatically, it would be inconsistent with the perceived images of such
products.

Price Lining.   When an organisation sets a limited number of prices for selected
groups or lines of merchandise, it is using **price lining**. A retailer may have various
styles and brands of similar quality men's shirts that sell for £10. Another line of

FIGURE 17.12
Price lining

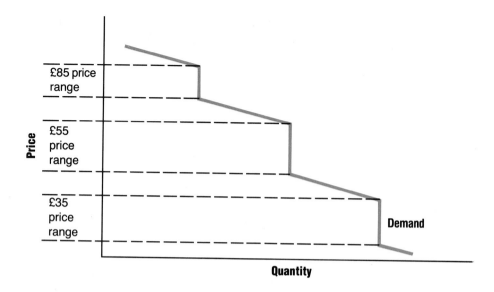

higher quality shirts may sell for £20. Price lining simplifies consumers' decision-making by holding constant one key variable in the final selection of style and brand within a line. In product line pricing, the company should look at the prices of the overall product line to ensure that the price of the new model lies within the range of existing prices for that line. Failure to consider the impact of the new model's price relative to the existing product line may change buyers' perceptions of all the models in the line.[3]

The basic assumption in price lining is that the demand is inelastic for various groups or sets of products. If the prices are attractive, customers will concentrate their purchases without responding to slight changes in price. Thus a women's dress shop that carries dresses priced at £85, £55, and £35 might not attract many more sales with a drop to, say, £83, £53, and £33. The "space" between the prices of £55 and £35, however, can stir changes in consumer response. With price lining, the demand curve looks like a series of steps, as shown in Figure 17.12.

■ **Professional Pricing**

Professional pricing is used by people who have great skill or experience in a particular field or activity. Some professionals who provide such products as medical services feel that their fees (prices) should not relate directly to the time and involvement in specific cases; rather, a standard fee is charged regardless of the problems involved in performing the job. Some estate agents' and solicitors' fees are prime examples: 2 percent of a house sale price, plus VAT, and £300 for house conveyancing. Other professionals set prices in other ways.

The concept of professional pricing carries with it the idea that professionals have an ethical responsibility not to overcharge unknowing customers. In some situations, a seller can charge customers a high price and continue to sell many units of the product. Medicine offers several examples. If a patient with high blood pressure requires four tablets a day to survive, the individual will pay for the prescription whether it costs £3 or £30 per month. In fact, the patient would purchase the pills

3. Kent B. Monroe, "Effect of Product Line Pricing Characteristics on Product Evaluation," *Journal of Consumer Research*, March 1987, p. 518.

even if the price went higher. In these situations sellers could charge exorbitant fees. Drug companies claim that despite their positions of strength in this regard, they charge "ethical" prices rather than what the market will bear. In 1989 Burroughs-Wellcome reduced the price of its AIDS-treatment drug AZT by 20 percent partly in response to pressure from AIDS patients and activists. However, some feel that the $6,400 annual price tag for AZT treatments in the U.S.A. is still far too high.[4]

■ Promotional Pricing

Price is an ingredient in the marketing mix, and it often is co-ordinated with promotion. The two variables sometimes are so interrelated that the pricing policy is promotion orientated. Examples of promotional pricing include price leaders, special-event pricing, and experience-curve pricing.

Price Leaders.   Sometimes a firm prices a few products below the usual mark-up, near cost, or below cost, which results in prices known as **price leaders**. This type of pricing is used most often in supermarkets and department stores to attract consumers by giving them special low prices on a few items. Management hopes that sales of regularly priced merchandise will more than offset the reduced revenue from the price leaders.

Special-Event Pricing.   To increase sales volume, many organisations co-ordinate price with advertising or sales promotion for seasonal or special situations. **Special-event pricing** involves advertised sales or price cutting that is linked to a holiday, season, or event. As shown in Figure 17.13, many retailers, such as Allied Maples, organise sales which are linked to bank holidays, for example. If the pricing objective is survival, then special sales events may be designed to generate the necessary operating capital. Special-event pricing also entails co-ordination of production, scheduling, storage, and physical distribution. Whenever there is a sales lag, special-event pricing is an alternative that marketers should consider.

■ Misleading Prices

The Consumer Protection Act (1987) contains a code of practice intended to give advice on **misleading prices**. The Act makes it illegal to mislead customers about the price at which products or services are offered for sale. However, the code—which is not legally binding—encourages companies to offer explanations whenever price comparisons or reductions are made. According to the *Which?* handbook of consumer law, "Unexplained reductions from a store's own prices should be used only if the goods have been on sale at the same store for 28 days in the preceding six months, and if the price quoted was the last price at which the goods were on sale."[5]

■ Experience-Curve Pricing

In **experience-curve pricing**, a company fixes a low price that high-cost competitors cannot match and thus expands its market share. This practice is possible when a firm gains cumulative production experience and is able to reduce its manufacturing costs at a predictable rate through improved methods, materials, skills, and machinery. Texas Instruments used this strategy in marketing its calculators. The

4. Marylin Chase, "Burroughs-Wellcome Cuts Price of AZT Under Pressure from AIDS Activists," *Wall Street Journal,* 19 Sept. 1989, p. A3.

5. National Federation of Consumer Groups, *A Handbook of Consumer Law, Which? Books* (London, 1989).

FIGURE 17.13

Special-event pricing. Allied Maples organises sales which are linked to bank holidays—one example of special-event pricing.

SOURCE: Courtesy of Allied Maples Group Limited

experience curve depicts the inverse relationship between production costs per unit and cumulative production quantity. To take advantage of the experience curve, a company must gain a dominant market share early in a product's life cycle. An early market share lead, with the greater cumulative production experience that it implies, will place a company further down the experience curve than its competitors.

DEVELOPMENT OF A PRICING METHOD

After selecting a pricing policy, a marketer must choose a **pricing method**, a mechanical procedure for setting prices on a regular basis. The pricing method structures the calculation of the actual price. The nature of a product, its sales volume, or the amount of product the organisation carries will determine how prices are calculated. For example, a procedure for pricing the thousands of products in a supermarket must be simpler and more direct than that for calculating the price of a new earth-moving machine manufactured by Caterpillar. In this section we examine three types of market-orientated pricing methods: cost-orientated, demand-orientated, and competition-orientated pricing.

■ Cost-Orientated Pricing

In **cost-orientated pricing**, a monetary amount or percentage is added to the cost of a product. The method thus involves calculations of desired margins or profit margins. Cost-orientated pricing methods do not necessarily take into account the economic aspects of supply and demand, nor do they necessarily relate to a specific pricing policy or ensure the attainment of pricing objectives. They are, however, simple and easy to implement. Two common cost-orientated pricing methods are cost-plus and mark-up pricing.

Cost-Plus Pricing. In **cost-plus pricing**, the seller's costs are determined (usually during a project or after a project is completed), and then a specified amount or percentage of the cost is added to the seller's cost to set the price. When production costs are difficult to predict or production takes a long time, cost-plus pricing is appropriate. Custom-made equipment and commercial construction projects are often priced by this method. The government frequently uses such cost-orientated pricing in granting defence contracts. One pitfall for the buyer is that the seller may increase costs to establish a larger profit base. Furthermore, some costs, such as overheads, may be difficult to determine.

In periods of rapid inflation, cost-plus pricing is popular, especially when the producer must use raw materials that are fluctuating in price. For industries in which cost-plus pricing is common and sellers have similar costs, price competition may not be especially intense.

Mark-up Pricing. A common pricing method among retailers is **mark-up pricing**. In mark-up pricing, a product's price is derived by adding a predetermined percentage of the cost, called *mark-up,* to the cost of the product. Although the percentage mark-up in a retail store varies from one category of goods to another (35 percent of cost for hardware items and 100 percent of cost for greeting cards, for example), the same percentage is often used to determine the price of items within a single product category, and the same or similar percentage mark-up may be standardised across an industry at the retail level. Using a rigid percentage mark-up for a specific product category reduces pricing to a routine task that can be performed quickly.

Mark-up can be stated as a percentage of the cost or as a percentage of the selling price. The following example illustrates how percentage mark-ups are determined and points out the differences in the two methods. Assume that a retailer purchases a tin of tuna at 45 pence, adds 15 pence to the cost, and then prices the tuna at 60 pence. Here are the figures:

$$\text{Mark-up as a Percentage of Cost} = \frac{\text{Mark-up}}{\text{Cost}}$$

$$\text{Mark-up as a Percentage of Selling Price} = \frac{\text{Mark-up}}{\text{Selling Price}}$$

$$= \frac{15}{60}$$

$$= 25.0\%$$

Obviously, when discussing a percentage mark-up, it is important to know whether the mark-up is based on cost or selling price.

Mark-ups normally reflect expectations about operating costs, risks, and stock turnovers. Wholesalers and manufacturers often suggest standard retail mark-ups that are considered profitable. An average percentage mark-up on cost may be as high as 100 percent or more for jewellery or as low as 20 percent for the textbook you are reading. To the extent that retailers use similar mark-ups for the same product category, price competition is reduced. In addition, using rigid mark-ups is a convenient method for retailers who face numerous pricing decisions.

■ Demand-Orientated Pricing

Rather than basing the price of a product on its cost, marketers sometimes use a pricing method based on the level of demand for the product: **demand-orientated pricing**. This method results in a high price when demand for the product is strong and a low price when demand is weak. Admission to night-clubs often operates on this basis, with higher prices when demand is highest, on Friday nights and at weekends. To use this method, a marketer must be able to estimate the amounts of a product that consumers will demand at different prices. The marketer then chooses the price that generates the highest total revenue. Obviously, the effectiveness of this method depends on the marketer's ability to estimate demand accurately.

A marketer may favour a demand-orientated pricing method called **price differentiation** when the firm wants to use more than one price in the marketing of a specific product. Price differentiation can be based on such considerations as type of customer, type of distribution channel used, or the time of the purchase. Here are several examples. A twelve-ounce can of soft drink costs less from a supermarket than from a vending machine. London hotel accommodation is more expensive in the summer than in the winter. Christmas tree ornaments and cards are usually cheaper on 27 December than on 16 December. Some hotels offer special "week-ender" prices (see Figure 17.14). Prices may start from only £37 per person, a significant reduction on mid-week rates. Holiday Inn hotels' "Weekender" customers are rewarded with "VIP Weekender Passports," which offer the chance of winning various prizes.

For price differentiation to work properly, the marketer must be able to segment a market on the basis of different strengths of demand and then keep the segments separate enough so that segment members who buy at lower prices cannot then sell to buyers in segments that are charged a higher price. This isolation could be accomplished, for example, by selling to geographically separated segments.

Price differentiation is often facilitated in international marketing by the geographic distance between markets. For example, Matsushita Electric Co. sells cordless Panasonic telephones in Japan at eight times what cordless telephones of slightly lower quality sell for in the United States. When a Japanese trading company reimported the U.S. cordless phones and sold them for $80 instead of the Japanese model, which cost $657, consumers lined up to buy the cheaper telephone. To combat the reimportation, Matsushita bought up all the unsold made-for-export Panasonic telephones it could find to eliminate the wide price differential. (The major difference between the telephones was that the U.S. telephone had a range of forty metres and the Japanese telephone had a range of fifty metres, which is surprising, because the average Japanese home is much smaller than the average U.S. home.) For years, U.S. manufacturers have accused the Japanese of subsidising foreign trade wars with high profits from their relatively closed home market.[6]

6. "Frantic Cheap Phone Buy-up Reveals a Lot About Japanese Marketing," *Ann Arbor News* (Ann Arbor, Mich.), 14 Feb. 1988, p. C9.

FIGURE 17.14
Price differentiation.
Many hotels offer special
reduced "weekender"
prices to stimulate de-
mand.

SOURCE: Schmid/Langsfield/The Image Bank

Price differentiation can also be based on employment in a public service position. For example, many bookshops offer a 15 percent discount to teachers.

Compared with cost-orientated pricing, demand-orientated pricing places a firm
in a better position to reach higher profit levels, assuming that buyers value the
product at levels sufficiently above the product's cost. To use demand-orientated
pricing, however, a marketer must be able to estimate demand at different price
levels, which is often difficult to do accurately.

■ **Competition-
Orientated Pricing**

In using **competition-orientated pricing**, an organisation considers costs and
revenue to be secondary to competitors' prices. The importance of this method
increases if competing products are almost homogeneous and the organisation is
serving markets in which price is the key variable of the marketing strategy. A firm
that uses competition-orientated pricing may choose to be below competitors'
prices, above competitors' prices, or at the same level. The price of this textbook
that the bookshop paid to the publishing company was determined using competition-orientated pricing. Competition-orientated pricing should help attain a pricing
objective to increase sales or market share. Competition-orientated pricing methods
may be combined with cost approaches to arrive at price levels necessary for a
profit.

Determining a Specific Price

Pricing policies and methods should direct and structure the selection of a final price. If they are to do so, it is important for marketers to establish pricing objectives, to know something about the target market, and to determine demand, price elasticity, costs, and competitive factors. In addition to those economic factors, the manner in which pricing is used in the marketing mix will affect the final price.

Although we suggest a systematic approach to pricing, in practice prices are often finalised after only limited planning, or they may be set without planning, just by trial and error. Then marketers determine whether revenue, minus costs, yields a profit. This approach to pricing is not recommended because it makes it difficult to discover pricing errors. If prices are based on both unrealistic pricing methods and unrealistic sales forecasts, a firm may resort to price gimmickry to sell its products. This approach should be avoided because it can become permanent. The car industry is a current example of how pricing incentives, such as discounts, cheap credit facilities, and trade-in deals, can become an essential and permanent part of pricing.

In the absence of government price controls, pricing remains a flexible and convenient way to adjust the marketing mix. In most situations, prices can be adjusted quickly—in a matter of minutes or over a few days. This flexibility and freedom do not characterise the other components of the marketing mix. Because so many complex issues are involved in establishing the right price, pricing is indeed as much an art as a science.

Summary

The eight stages in the process of establishing prices are these: (1) selecting pricing objectives; (2) assessing the target market's evaluation of price and its ability to purchase; (3) determining demand; (4) analysing demand, cost, and profit relationships; (5) analysing competitors' prices; (6) selecting a pricing policy; (7) developing a pricing method; and (8) determining a specific price.

The first stage, setting pricing objectives, is critical because pricing objectives form a foundation on which the decisions of subsequent stages are based. Organisations may use numerous pricing objectives: short-term and long-term ones, and different ones for different products and market segments.

The second stage in establishing prices is an assessment of the target market's evaluation of price and its ability to purchase. This stage tells a marketer how much emphasis to place on price and may help the marketer determine how far above the competition the firm can set its prices. Understanding customers' buying power and knowing how important a product is to the customers in comparison with other products helps marketers correctly assess the target market's evaluation of price.

In the third stage, the organisation must determine the demand for its product. The classic demand curve is a graph of the quantity of products expected to be sold at various prices, if other factors are held constant. It illustrates that, as price falls, the quantity demanded usually increases. However, for prestige products, there is a direct positive relationship between price and quantity demanded: demand increases as price increases. Next, price elasticity of demand—the percentage change in quantity demanded relative to a given percentage change in price—must be determined. If demand is elastic, a change in price causes an opposite change in total revenue. Inelastic demand results in parallel change in total revenue when a product's price is changed.

Analysis of demand, cost, and profit relationships—the fourth stage of the process—can be accomplished through marginal analysis or break-even analysis. Marginal analysis is the examination of what happens to a firm's costs and revenues when production (or sales volume) is changed by one unit. Marginal analysis combines the demand curve with a firm's costs to develop an optimum price for maximum profit. Fixed costs do not vary with changes in the number of units produced or sold; average fixed cost is the fixed cost per unit produced. Variable costs vary directly with changes in the number of units produced or sold. Average variable cost is the variable cost per unit produced. Average total cost is the sum of average fixed cost and average variable cost times the quantity produced. The optimum price is the point at which marginal cost (the cost associated with producing one more unit of the product) equals marginal revenue (the change in total revenue that occurs when one additional unit of the product is sold). Marginal analysis is only a model; it offers little help in pricing new products before costs and revenues are established.

Break-even analysis—determining the number of units necessary to break even—is important in setting the price. The point at which the costs of production equal the revenue made from selling the product is the break-even point. To use break-even analysis effectively, a marketer should determine the break-even point for each of several alternative prices. This determination makes it possible to compare the effects on total revenue, total costs, and the break-even point for each price under consideration. However, this approach assumes that the quantity demanded is basically fixed and that the major task is to set prices to recover costs.

A marketer needs to be aware of the prices charged for competing brands. This allows a firm to keep its prices the same as competitors' prices when non-price competition is used. If a company uses price as a competitive tool, it can price its brand below competing brands.

A pricing policy is a guiding philosophy or course of action designed to influence and determine pricing decisions. Pricing policies help marketers solve the practical problems of establishing prices. Two types of pioneer pricing policies are price skimming and penetration pricing. With price skimming, an organisation charges the highest price that buyers who most desire the product will pay. A penetration price is a lower price designed to penetrate the market and produce a larger unit sales volume. Psychological pricing, another pricing policy, encourages purchases that are based on emotional rather than rational responses. It includes odd-even pricing, customary pricing, prestige pricing, and price lining. A third pricing policy, professional pricing, is used by people who have great skill or experience in a particular field. Promotional pricing, in which price is co-ordinated with promotion, is another type of pricing policy. Price leaders and special-event pricing are examples of promotional pricing. Experience-curve pricing fixes a low price that high-cost competitors cannot match. Experience-curve pricing is possible when experience reduces manufacturing costs at a predictable rate.

A pricing method is a mechanical procedure for assigning prices to specific products on a regular basis. Three types of pricing methods are cost-orientated, demand-orientated, and competition-orientated pricing. In using cost-orientated pricing, a firm determines price by adding a monetary amount or percentage to the cost of the product. Two common cost-orientated pricing methods are cost-plus and mark-up pricing. Demand-orientated pricing is based on the level of demand for the product. To use this method, a marketer must be able to estimate the amounts of a product that buyers will demand at different prices. Demand-orientated pricing results in a high price when demand for a product is strong and a low price when demand is weak. In the case of competition-orientated pricing, costs and revenues are secondary to competitors' prices. Competition-orientated pricing and cost approaches may be combined to arrive at price levels necessary for a profit.

IMPORTANT TERMS

Demand curve	Customary pricing
Price elasticity of demand	Prestige pricing
Fixed costs	Price lining
Average fixed cost	Professional pricing
Variable costs	Price leaders
Average variable cost	Special-event pricing
Total cost	Misleading prices
Average total cost	Experience-curve pricing
Marginal cost (MC)	Pricing method
Marginal revenue (MR)	Cost-orientated pricing
Break-even point	Cost-plus pricing
Pricing policy	Mark-up pricing
Price skimming	Demand-orientated pricing
Penetration price	Price differentiation
Psychological pricing	Competition-orientated pricing
Odd-even pricing	

DISCUSSION AND REVIEW QUESTIONS

1. Identify the eight stages that make up the process of establishing prices.
2. Why do most demand curves demonstrate an inverse relationship between price and quantity?
3. List the characteristics of products that have inelastic demand. Give several examples of such products.
4. Explain why optimum profits should occur when marginal cost equals marginal revenue.
5. The Chambers Company has just gathered estimates for doing a break-even analysis for a new product. Variable costs are £7 a unit. The additional plant will cost £48,000. The new product will be charged £18,000 a year for its share of general overheads. Advertising expenditure will be £80,000, and £55,000 will be spent on distribution. If the product sells for £12, what is the break-even point in units? What is the break-even point in sales volume?
6. Why should a marketer be aware of competitors' prices?
7. For what type of products would a pioneer price-skimming policy be most appropriate? For what type of products would penetration pricing be more effective?
8. Why do consumers associate price with quality? When should prestige pricing be used?

9. Are price leaders a realistic approach to pricing?
10. What are the benefits of cost-orientated pricing?
11. Under what conditions is cost-plus pricing most appropriate?
12. If a retailer purchases a tin of soup for 24 pence and sells it for 36 pence, what is the percentage mark-up on selling price?

■ CASES

17.1 No-Frills Hotels

The U.K. hotel industry had for decades been dominated by two extremes—large hotel groups, increasingly competing on amenities and service, and small, independently owned private hotels. As the major groups, such as THF, Mount Charlotte, Holiday Inn, or Queen's Moat, competed for the lucrative business and conference market, they added similar facilities and amenities, offering familiar service levels. Price points inevitably rose, so that a mid-week one-night stay in a three- or four-star hotel would cost £60 to £90 per person.

In the late 1980s several companies identified a significant niche in the market. Between the low-cost private hotels and the bottom end of the major groups' offerings was a budget-conscious segment desiring modern amenities and well-appointed bedrooms at low cost, but without the luxury hotel features such as swimming pools, selection of bars or restaurants, and sports amenities.

Most of the major groups have entered this market, but with different concepts. THF's Travelodge—"little luxuries, little prices"—offers en suite bedroom, TV, and drinks facilities for under £30, irrespective of how many share the room. There are no catering facilities but customers can use on-site Little Chef or Happy Eater restaurants. Over eighty Travelodges are operating on major routes in the U.K.

Stakis (Country Court) and Holiday Inn (Garden Court) have entered the budget-conscious market but at a higher price point and amenity level. Most Holiday Inns offer de luxe four-star accommodation. The company's Garden Court hotels offer "competitively priced three-star hotels featuring all the benefits of luxury accommodation but without the extras like swimming pools and a choice of restaurants". They do have fitness centres, a bar and a bistro restaurant, in-house movies, and added bedroom extras such as trouser presses and hair-dryers. The room rate is £46 Monday to Thursday and £35 at weekends, irrespective of how many people occupy the room. Mondays to Thursdays give consistent business custom. Weekend business is leisure-orientated and is largely generated by the area and local attractions, ease of travel, and hotel pricing and availability.

SOURCES: Holiday Inn and Travelodge promotional literature; *Marketing*, 16 August 1990, p. 4; *Leamington Spa Business Times*, August 1990, p. 5.

Questions for Discussion

1. What opportunities is Garden Court aiming to exploit? How does this differ from the Travelodge concept?
2. Why do the companies have different weekend price points?
3. What pricing policy might a new entrant into the budget-price bracket adopt?

17.2 Toys "R" Us Competes Through Price

Toys "R" Us leads the U.S. toy market with its chain of over 400 warehouse-style toy supermarkets spread across the nation. The company is expanding rapidly in Europe and the Pacific Rim. It has long been an innovator, in both its pricing policies and its toy supermarket design. Toys "R" Us brings customers into the store by discounting such baby-care products as buggies and disposable nappies below cost. The strategy is that once parents are in the store, they will spend on toys the money they saved on the discounted baby goods.

Toys "R" Us stores are usually located along road arteries, well away from CBD shopping malls, to keep down costs and prevent customers from being distracted by other toy merchants. Isolation from shopping malls also means that customers will load up their shopping trolleys because they do not have to lug their purchases through crowded malls.

The first Toys "R" Us store was opened in 1957 as the Children's Supermarket (with the "r's" printed backwards to encourage name recognition) and offered name-brand toys and baby goods below normal retail prices. Today, it still offers name-brand toys at 20 to 50 percent below retail price. Each store has a full stock of thousands of different toys and baby goods tracked by a computer system that almost eliminates stock-outs. Managers don't place orders for toys, the toys just arrive on time, thus averting the Toys "R" Us definition of a major disaster—not having a certain toy on display and ready to sell.

Toys "R" Us sets its price for a particular item based on how much it projects customers will pay for it. The company then determines the price at which it is willing to purchase the toy from the manufacturer and negotiates fiercely with the manufacturer to get the toy at that price. The company has a definite advantage in negotiations because it buys in such large volume. Toy manufacturers also treat Toys "R" Us well because the company is often a testing ground for new toys. Price is so important to the Toys "R" Us strategy that even when demand for a toy is high and supplies are short, the company will not raise its price on the toy to make a quick profit.

Market share is the Toys "R" Us main pricing objective; and for now it is the number-one toy store in the United States. The company says it is willing to cut prices to retain its leading position. Other toy stores are scrambling to meet the competition from Toys "R" Us; those that do not change their strategies wind up out of the toy market altogether. Many stores, such as K mart, or Asda in the U.K., expand their toy lines only for the six-week Christmas season and bring customers in with sales. Although Toys "R" Us never holds sales, it maintains its huge selection and discount prices year-round. Customers who found good buys at Toys "R" Us at Christmas will also shop there for children's birthdays and other special days, when other retail stores have a limited selection. Even new parents who drop in to Toys "R" Us for discounted baby products tend to return to buy toys. The company also sells sporting-goods "toys", such as footballs and bicycles, suitable for older teens, young adults, and family members of almost any age.

Some competitors (in the U.K., Boots-owned Children's World) have adopted the Toys "R" Us supermarket approach and have tried to meet Toys "R" Us prices throughout the year. Other stores are trying non-price competition, by offering educational and baby-sitting services. However, Toys "R" Us intends to rely on its non-price attributes of convenience, selection, and inventory, as well as price competition, to hold its position.

Toys "R" Us has expanded internationally to Britain, Germany, Canada, Japan, and other parts of Asia with over 80 stores. The company has plans for many more stores overseas to take advantage of the world toy market, which is nearly double that of the United States. Additionally, it opened Kids "R" Us in the United States, a chain of children's clothing stores similar to the toy stores.

Toys "R" Us has customer loyalty behind it. Customers know that they can find *the* toy that a child wants, at the best price, at Toys "R" Us. And if the child does not like the toy, the purchaser may return it for a full refund with no questions asked.

SOURCES: Robert J. Cole, "Toys 'R' Us to Open Stores in Japan Within Two Years," *New York Times*, 27 Sept. 1989, pp. D1, D6; Dan Dorfman, "Toys 'R' Us: Mattel Play?" *USA Today*, 28 June 1987, p. 2B; Trish Hall, "Finding Gold in Overalls and Bibs," *New York Times*, 25 Dec. 1988, pp. F1, F10; Mark Maremont, Dori Jones Yang, and Amy Dunkin, "Toys 'R' Us Goes Overseas—and Finds that Toys 'R' Them, Too," *Business Week*, 26 Jan. 1987, pp. 71–72; David Owen, "Where Toys Come From," *Atlantic Monthly*, Oct. 1986, pp. 64–78; Jesus Sanchez, "Toymakers Make a Play for Market," *USA Today*, 10 Feb. 1987, pp. 1B–2B.

Questions for Discussion

1. What are the Toys "R" Us major pricing objectives?
2. Assess the Toys "R" Us practice of not raising the prices of products that are scarce and in high demand.
3. A major disadvantage of using price competition is that competitors can match prices. Evaluate this potential for Toys "R" Us.

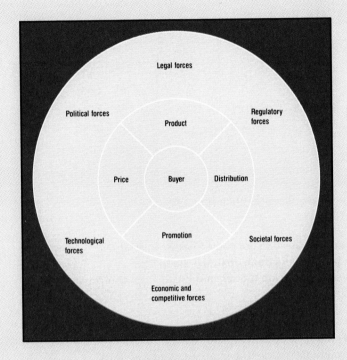

We have divided marketing into several sets of variables and have discussed the decisions and activities associated with each variable. By now, you should understand (1) how to analyse marketing opportunities, and (2) the components of the marketing mix. It is time to put all these components together in a discussion of marketing management issues. In Chapter 18 we discuss strategic market planning, focusing on the planning process, the setting of marketing objectives, the assessment of opportunities and resources, and specific product/market matching approaches to strategic market planning. Chapter 19 deals with other marketing management issues, including organisation, implementation, and control. It explores approaches to organising a marketing unit, issues regarding strategy implementation, and techniques for controlling marketing strategies. Chapter 20 deals with the role of ethics and social responsibility in marketing decisions and activities. ◆

18 STRATEGIC MARKET PLANNING

Objectives

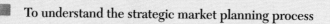

To understand the strategic market planning process

To explore and examine three major tools to assist in strategic market planning: product-portfolio analysis, the market attractiveness–business position model, and Profit Impact on Marketing Strategy (PIMS)

To evaluate strategic market planning and relate it to the development of functional marketing strategies and activities

To gain an overview of the marketing plan

S igma Marketing Concepts is a publisher of high-quality, creatively designed promotional calendars, which are sold directly to businesses for use as marketing tools. From 1985 to 1987, Sigma's sales volume grew rapidly. To ensure continued growth, Sigma reviewed its recent performance and organisational changes; from these findings, it developed long-range strategic market plans and made several changes in its marketing strategy.

Sigma's management first sold the printing and production portion of its business so that it could focus exclusively on marketing custom-designed desk-pad calendar products. Sigma and the buyer of the production plant entered into a long-term contract under which the buyer would handle all of Sigma's calendar production, using the same plant and staff that had handled production for the past twenty years. This transaction freed Sigma from the daily problems of production and plant management and allowed it to concentrate all its resources and efforts on creating and marketing new calendar products.

The company developed a revised marketing strategy that focused on a new target market and improved promotion and distribution of its product line. It also expanded the product line to include wall planners, pocket planners, and diaries. Each product was designed to allow Sigma to maintain its differential advantage of offering high advertising flexibility and creativity. The target market was revised to focus on large, service-customer contact companies. After choosing prospects, Sigma initially contacted key marketing executives by phone and then sent them direct-mail packages containing samples. This was followed by a call to answer questions and to encourage/close orders.

The new marketing strategy appears to be very successful. The company has added to its list of satisfied customers such prime accounts as Federal Express, Nabisco Brands, Fidelity Investments, and Jacob Suchard. Sigma Marketing Concepts continues to monitor and evaluate its internal and external environments. The company's founder, Don Sapit, believes that this practice contributes to Sigma's current level of success. ◆

Based on interviews with Donald Sapit, Renee Mudd, and Warren Eldridge, Sigma Marketing Concepts, 1987. Reprinted by permission.

his chapter looks closely at one portion of strategic marketing: planning. We start with an overview of the strategic market planning process, including the development of organisational goals and corporate strategy. We also examine organisational opportunities and resources as they relate to planning. We then look at some tools used in strategic market planning: the product-portfolio analysis, the market attractiveness–business position model, and Profit Impact on Marketing Strategy (PIMS). Next we examine competitive strategies for marketing and close with a look at marketing planning and the development of a marketing plan. Other aspects of the marketing management process—organising, implementing, and controlling—are covered in Chapter 19.

STRATEGIC MARKET PLANNING DEFINED

A **strategic market plan** is an outline of the methods and resources required to achieve an organisation's goals within a specific target market. It takes into account not only marketing, but also all functional aspects of a business unit that must be co-ordinated. These functional aspects include production, finance, and personnel. Environmental issues are an important consideration as well. The concept of the strategic business unit is used to define areas for consideration in a specific strategic market plan. Each **strategic business unit (SBU)** is a division, product line, or other profit centre within the parent company. For example, Sketchley's strategic business units include high street dry-cleaning, contract collect-and-deliver dry-cleaning, workwear rental, badging and labelling, and vending machines. Each sells a distinct set of products to an identifiable group of customers, and each competes with a well-defined set of competitors. Each SBU's revenues, costs, investments, and strategic plans can be separated and evaluated apart from those of the parent company. SBUs operate in a variety of markets, which have differing growth rates, opportunities, degrees of competition, and profit-making potential. The Coca-Cola Company, for example, includes the Coca-Cola European Community Group, a strategic business unit (see Figure 18.1). Strategic planners therefore must recognise the different performance capabilities of each SBU and carefully allocate resources.

The process of **strategic market planning** yields a marketing strategy that is the framework for a marketing plan. A **marketing plan** includes the framework and entire set of activities to be performed; it is the written document or blueprint for implementing and controlling an organisation's marketing activities. Thus a strategic market plan is *not* the same as a marketing plan; it is a plan of *all* aspects of an organisation's strategy in the market-place. A marketing plan, in contrast, deals primarily with implementing the market strategy as it relates to target markets and the marketing mix.[1]

Figure 18.2 shows the components of strategic market planning. The process is based on the establishment of an organisation's overall goals, and it must stay within the bounds of the organisation's opportunities and resources. When the firm has determined its overall goals and identified its resources, it can then assess its opportunities and develop a corporate strategy. Marketing objectives must be designed so

1. Derek F. Abell and John S. Hammond, *Strategic Market Planning* (Englewood Cliffs, N.J.: Prentice-Hall, 1979), p. 10.

FIGURE 18.1 *An SBU in operation.*
The Coca-Cola European Community Group is charged with addressing Europe's 12-country market, including Norway—Europe's largest per capita consumer of Coca-Cola.
SOURCE: © 1990 Arthur Meyerson

that their achievement will contribute to the corporate strategy and so that they can be accomplished through efficient use of the firm's resources.

To achieve its marketing objectives, an organisation must develop a marketing strategy, or a set of marketing strategies, as shown in Figure 18.2. The set of marketing strategies that are implemented and used at the same time is referred to as the organisation's **marketing programme**. Through the process of strategic market planning, an organisation can develop marketing strategies that, when properly implemented and controlled, will contribute to the achievement of its marketing objectives and its overall goals. As we have mentioned before, to formulate a marketing strategy, the marketer identifies and analyses the target market and develops a marketing mix to satisfy individuals in that market. Marketing Update 18.1 discusses the various ways Alton Towers is planning to maintain its market leadership by catering to the needs of its key market segments. Marketing strategy is best formulated when it reflects the overall direction of the organisation and is coordinated with all the firm's functional areas.

As indicated in Figure 18.2, the strategic market planning process is based on an analysis of the environment, by which it is very much affected. Environmental forces can place constraints on an organisation and possibly influence its overall goals; they also affect the amount and type of resources that a firm can acquire. However, these forces can create favourable opportunities as well—opportunities that can be translated into overall organisational goals and marketing objectives. For

FIGURE 18.2
*Components of strategic
market planning*

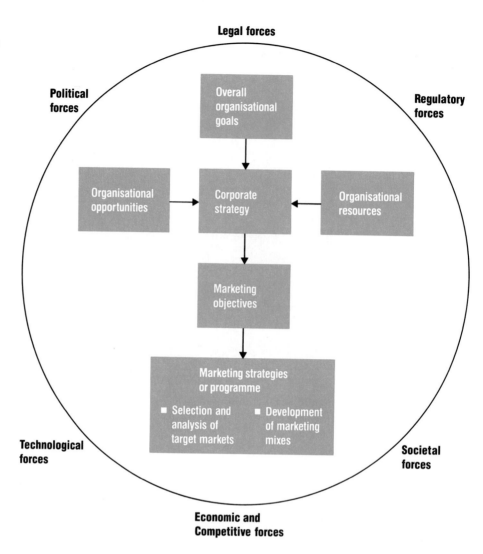

example, when oil prices declined during the second half of the 1980s, consumers viewed cars with high petrol consumption more favourably. This situation created an opportunity for manufacturers of large vehicles, such as Cadillac, BMW, and Volvo.

Marketers differ in their viewpoints concerning the effect of environmental variables on marketing planning and strategy. Some take a deterministic perspective, believing that firms must react to external conditions and tailor their strategies and organisational structures to deal with these conditions. According to others, however, companies can influence their environments by choosing what markets to compete in. Furthermore, they can change the structures of their industries, engaging in activities such as mergers and acquisitions, demand creation, or technological innovation.[2]

Regardless of which viewpoint is adopted, environmental variables play a part in the creation of a marketing strategy. When environmental variables affect an organi-

---

2. P. Rajan Varadarajan, Terry Clark, and William Pride, "Determining Your Company's Destiny," working paper, Texas A&M University, 1990.

PLANNING A DAY OUT—ALTON TOWERS

The theme park is a leisure park consisting of rides and attractions built around a central theme or themes. Walt Disney created the concept in America and the Disney Corporation has since taken the concept to Japan and now to France. The U.K. theme park industry really took off in the early 1980s. By 1985 there were 4.5 million visitors; and by 1989, 9.5 million spending £105 million. By 1994, current estimates are for 12.5 million visitors spending £182 million, although the opening of the Paris Disney World and of the Channel Tunnel may have some bearing. The top five theme parks in the U.K. are

Alton Towers	2.4 million visitors
Chessington World of Adventure	1.3
Thorpe Park	1.3
Frontierland	1.3
The American Adventure	0.7

Not only do theme parks compete with each other, though geographically many cater for purely local markets, they compete also with a whole variety of day-trip activities:

Museums and Galleries	33.0% of day trippers
Historic properties	22.5
Wildlife attractions	10.0
Theme parks	5.5
Gardens	4.0
Other (Seaside resorts, holiday centres, etc.)	25.0

Despite the 1990–1991 economic down-turn in the U.K. and the crisis in the Middle East, all economic indicators point to an increase in leisure time and in discretionary income. Alton Towers aims to maintain its market leadership. It continually invests in new rides and facilities and is planning a £20 million holiday village next to the park (for the leisure and business conference markets). The strategy is to attract new visitors in the U.K. and from continental Europe while encouraging repeat visits from current users. Key targets are young adults aged 15 to 24, families with children, school parties, and increasingly the corporate sector for sales incentive schemes and corporate events (AGMs, product launches, sales force parties, etc.). Each segment has its own marketing mix and strategy: separate price policies, promotional tactics, and even product offerings. From being a day-tripper park orientated towards the family, Alton Towers has monitored demographic changes and competitor activity and is planning to cater for its key segments' differing needs well into the 1990s.

SOURCES: British Tourist Authority, 1988; "Visits to Tourist Attractions," British Tourist Authority, 1987–1989; *Leisure Management,* Volume 9, April 1989 and Volume 10, July 1990; Alton Towers' promotional material, 1990; K. M. Bon, "The UK Leisure Industry," Warwick MBA Dissertation, University of Warwick, 1990.

sation's overall goals, resources, opportunities, or marketing objectives, they also affect its marketing strategies, which are based on these factors. Environmental forces more directly influence the development of a marketing strategy through their impact on consumers' needs and desires. In addition, these forces have a bearing on marketing mix decisions. For instance, competition strongly influences marketing mix decisions. The organisation must diagnose the marketing mix activities it performs, taking into account competitors' marketing mix decisions, and develop some competitive advantage to support a strategy. Thus as Honda and Toyota entered the luxury car market with the Acura and Lexus models, European car makers BMW, Mercedes, and Jaguar had to change their marketing strategies to maintain their market shares. They did so by lowering prices to compete with the new Japanese models.

In the next sections we discuss the major components of the strategic market planning process: organisational goals, organisational opportunities and resources, and corporate strategy, as well as the tools that aid in strategic market planning and some competitive marketing strategies.

Organisational Goals

A firm's organisational goals should be derived from its *mission*, the broad tasks that the organisation wants to accomplish. IBM, for example, has stated that its mission is helping businesspeople make decisions. A company's mission and overall organisational goals should guide all its planning efforts. Its goals should specify the ends or results that are sought. For example, a firm in serious financial trouble may be concerned solely with short-run results needed for staying in business. There usually is an airline or major retailer being forced by cash shortages to take drastic action to stay in business. Lowndes Queensway, once the U.K.'s largest retailer of carpets and furniture, had several times to renegotiate its financing with City institutions, alter payment and credit times and terms with its suppliers, and ultimately identify which of its 500 superstores should be closed to save costs. The company went into receivership, despite all its efforts. On the other hand, some companies have more optimistic goals. Often manufacturers such as General Motors have goals that relate to return on investment. A successful company, however, may want to sacrifice the current year's profits for the long run and at the same time pursue other goals, such as increasing market share.

Organisational Opportunities and Resources

There are three major considerations in assessing opportunities and resources: evaluating market opportunities, environmental scanning (discussed in Chapter 2), and understanding the firm's capabilities. An appreciation of these elements is essential if an organisation is to build up a sustainable differential or competitive advantage.

■ **Differential Advantage**

Achieving a **differential advantage** or competitive edge requires an organisation to make the most of its opportunities and resources while offering customers a mix of tangible and intangible benefits which satisfies them.[3] When striking a balance

3. David A. Aaker, *Strategic Market Management*, 2nd ed. (New York: Wiley, 1988), p. 35.

between customer requirements on the one hand and company resources on the other, competitor activity must also be monitored. For example, there is little sense in promoting speedy distribution to customers if several large competing organisations offer a faster service. There are many different sources of differential advantage which firms can pursue.

For some firms, such as 3M, innovativeness is the focus, while for others, like Vidal Sassoon hair salons, image plays an important part. Body Shop concentrates on environment-friendly cosmetics, while for Multiplex Cinemas the differential advantage is multiple-screen choice at one location. Some of these ways of gaining an edge are easier to sustain than others. For example, many U.K. companies which have traditionally focused on low price have found this difficult to maintain in the long term.[4] The airline industry is just one to be plagued by periodic price wars.

■ Market Opportunities

A **market opportunity** arises when the right combination of circumstances occurs at the right time to allow an organisation to take action towards reaching a target market. An opportunity provides a favourable chance or opening for the firm to generate sales from identifiable markets. For example, in reaction to the overwhelming growth in cereals and other foods containing oat bran (which some researchers believe helps lower cholesterol levels), the Quaker Oats Company developed an advertising campaign to remind consumers that Quaker porridge oats have always contained oat bran. The commercials told consumers that eating porridge is "the right thing to do", and helped boost sales of Quaker Oats dramatically.[5] Increasing concerns about cancer and heart disease gave Quaker a market opportunity to reach consumers who are especially health conscious by touting the health benefits of its oats. Kellogg also took advantage of the popularity of oat bran by creating its Common Sense™ Oat Bran cereal (see Figure 18.3). Interestingly, in 1990, a study published in a leading medical journal questioned the effect of oat bran on lowering cholesterol. The conclusion was that avoiding high-cholesterol animal products was what really lowered cholesterol. Therefore, some of the oat bran mystique vanished overnight. The term *strategic window* has been used to describe what are often temporary periods of optimum fit between the key requirements of a market and the particular capabilities of a firm competing in that market.[6]

The attractiveness of market opportunities is determined by market factors, such as size and growth rate, as well as competitive, financial, economic, technological, social, legal, and political factors.[7] Because each industry and product are somewhat different, the factors that determine attractiveness tend to vary.

Market requirements relate to customers' needs or desired benefits. Market requirements are satisfied by components of the marketing mix that provide buyers with these benefits. Of course, buyers' perceptions of what requirements fulfil their needs and provide the desired benefits determine the success of any marketing effort. Marketers must devise strategies to out-perform competitors by finding out what product attributes buyers use to select products. An attribute must be important and differentiating if it is to be useful in strategy development. When marketers

4. John Saunders, "Marketing and Competitive Success," in *The Marketing Book*, Michael J. Baker, Ed. (London: Heinemann, 1987), pp. 10–28.

5. Zachary Schiller, with Russell Mitchell, Wendy Zellner, Lois Therrien, Andrea Rothman, and Walecia Konrad, "The Great American Health Pitch," *Business Week*, 9 Oct. 1989, p. 116.

6. Derek F. Abell, "Strategic Windows," *Journal of Marketing*, July 1978, p. 21.

7. Abell and Hammond, p. 213.

FIGURE 18.3
Responding to marketing opportunities.
When research high-lighted the potential benefits of oat bran, Kellogg responded to this opportunity by creating its new Common Sense™ Oat Bran cereal.

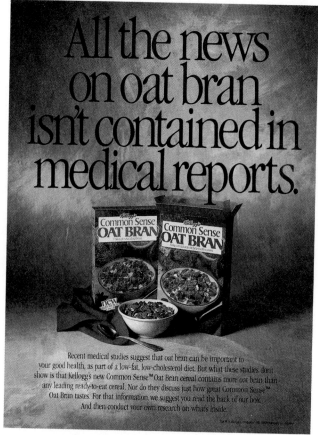

SOURCE: *Kellogg's*® and *Common Sense*™ are registered trade marks of Kellogg Company, all rights reserved. © 1989.

fail to understand buyers' perceptions and market requirements, the result may be failure. Freemans, prior to its takeover by Sears, launched its by-mail "Specialogue", aimed at yuppie men. The company failed to realise that such target customers wanted branded goods from prestigious specialty retail outlets; they did not perceive mail-order shopping to be suitable for them.

Environmental Scanning

In Chapter 2 we define environmental scanning as the process of collecting information about the marketing environment because such knowledge helps marketers identify opportunities and assists in planning. Some companies have derived substantial benefits from establishing an "environmental scanning (or monitoring) unit" within the strategic planning group or including line management in teams or committees to conduct environmental analysis. This approach engages management in the process of environmental forecasting and enhances the likelihood of successfully integrating forecasting efforts into strategic market planning.[8] Results of forecasting research show that even simple quantitative forecasting techniques out-

8. Liam Fahey, William K. King, and Vodake K. Naraganan, "Environmental Scanning and Forecasting in Strategic Planning—The State of the Art," *Long Range Planning*, February 1981, p. 38.

perform the unstructured intuitive assessments of experts.[9] Many builders and developers in the U.K. believe that the house-buying public is unwilling to pay the increased cost of energy-efficient new housing. However, research suggests that consumers *are* happy to pay extra, within reason, for the increased comfort levels and reduced fuel bills associated with such property.[10]

Environmental scanning to detect changes in the environment is extremely important if a firm is to avoid crisis management. An environmental change can suddenly alter a firm's opportunities or resources. Re-formulated, more effective strategies may then be needed to guide marketing efforts. For example, after the U.S. Congress passed legislation requiring that 10 percent of all cars sold in the United States in the late 1990s should run on "clean" fuels such as methanol and ethanol, American car makers had to re-formulate their strategies to provide for the development and marketing of cars that will cost more and will run on higher-priced fuels.[11] Because car manufacturers have engaged in environmental scanning and were aware that such legislation might indeed be enacted because of social and political concerns, most had already begun developing plans for cars powered by clean fuel. Ford Motor Company, for example, is already testing a car that can run on methanol, ethanol, petrol, or any combination of those fuels.[12] Similarly, in the U.K. increased concern about the cleanliness of the environment has left manufacturers looking for ways to pass on the costs of catalytic converters, which are necessary if some cars are to run on lead-free fuels, to the consumer. Environmental scanning should identify new developments and determine the nature and rate of change.

■ Capabilities and Resources

A firm's capabilities relate to distinctive competencies that it has developed to do something well and efficiently. A company is likely to enjoy a differential advantage in an area where its competencies out-do those of its potential competition.[13] Often a company may possess manufacturing or technical skills that are valuable in areas outside its traditional industry. For example, BASF, known for its manufacture and development of audio and video tapes, produced a new type of lightweight plastic that has uses in other industries.

Today marketing planners are especially concerned with resource constraints. Shortages in energy and other scarce economic resources often limit strategic planning options (see Figure 18.4). On the other hand, planning to avoid shortages can backfire. In many countries electricity suppliers decided to build nuclear power plants in the 1970s, to compensate for an expected shortfall of fossil fuels, only to find the political, social, and technological problems of nuclear power almost impossible to overcome. Moreover, an adequate supply of fossil fuels still exists to power traditional plants that generate electricity. But as the public grows more concerned about pollution and the so-called greenhouse effect—the increased warming of the earth caused by pollution—nuclear power plants may once again become a plausible alternative.

9. David M. Georgaff and Robert G. Mundick, "Managers' Guide to Forecasting," *Harvard Business Review,* January-February 1986, p. 120.

10. "Energy Efficient House Design," *House Builder Magazine,* September 1986.

11. "The Bumpy Road to 'Clean Fuels,'" *U.S. News & World Report,* 26 June 1989, pp. 10–11.

12. Ibid.

13. Philip Kotler, "Strategic Planning and the Marketing Process," *Business,* May-June 1980, pp. 6–7.

FIGURE 18.4

*Marketing planners must
be concerned with
resource constraints.*
As awareness of and
concern about the deple-
tion of natural resources
increases, marketing
planners must carefully
consider the options
available to them.

SOURCE: Helmut Eberhoffer/The Image Bank

CORPORATE STRATEGY

Corporate strategy determines the means for utilising resources in the areas of production, finance, research and development, personnel, and marketing to reach the organisation's goals. A corporate strategy determines not only the scope of the business but also its resource deployment, competitive advantages, and overall co-ordination of production, finance, marketing, and other functional areas. The term *corporate* in this context does not apply only to corporations; corporate strategy is used by all organisations, from the smallest sole proprietorship to the largest multi-national corporation.

Corporate strategy planners are concerned with issues such as diversification, competition, differentiation, interrelationships among business units, and environmental issues. Strategy planners attempt to match the resources of the organisation with the various opportunities and risks in the environment. Corporate strategy planners are also concerned with defining the scope and role of the strategic business units of the organisation so that they are co-ordinated to reach the ultimate goals desired.

TOOLS FOR STRATEGIC MARKET PLANNING

A number of tools have been proposed to aid marketing managers in their planning efforts. Based on ideas used in the management of financial portfolios, several models that classify an organisation's product portfolio have been proposed. These models allow strategic business units or products to be classified and visually displayed according to the attractiveness of various markets and the business's relative market share within those markets. Three of these tools—the Boston Consulting Group (BCG) product-portfolio analysis, the market attractiveness–business position model, and the Profit Impact on Marketing Strategy (PIMS)—are discussed next.

■ The Boston Consulting Group (BCG) Product-Portfolio Analysis

Just as financial investors have different investments with varying risks and rates of return, firms have a portfolio of products characterised by different market growth rates and relative market shares. **Product-portfolio analysis**, the Boston Consulting Group approach, is based on the philosophy that a product's market growth rate and its relative market share are important considerations in determining its marketing strategy. All the firm's products should be integrated into a single, overall matrix and evaluated to determine appropriate strategies for individual SBUs and the overall portfolio strategies. However, a balanced product-portfolio matrix is the end result of a number of actions—not just the result of the analysis alone. Portfolio models can be created on the basis of present and projected market growth rate and proposed market share strategies (build share, maintain share, harvest share, or divest business). Managers can use these models to determine and classify each product's expected future cash contributions and future cash requirements.

Generally, managers who use a portfolio model must examine the competitive position of a product (or product line) and the opportunities for improving that product's contribution to profitability and cash flow.[14] The BCG analytical approach is more of a diagnostic tool than a guide for making strategy prescriptions.

Figure 18.5, which is based on work by the BCG, enables the marketing manager to classify a firm's products into four basic types: stars, cash cows, dogs, and problem children.[15] **Stars** are products with a dominant share of the market and good prospects for growth. However, they use more cash than they generate to finance growth, add capacity, and increase market share. **Cash cows** have a dominant share of the market but low prospects for growth; typically, they generate more cash than is required to maintain market share. **Dogs** have a subordinate share of the market and low prospects for growth; these products are often found in mature markets. **Problem children,** sometimes called "question marks," have a small share of a growing market and generally require a large amount of cash to build share.

The growth-share matrix in Figure 18.5 can be expanded to show a firm's whole portfolio by providing for each product (1) its cash sales volume, illustrated by the size of a circle on the matrix; (2) its market share relative to competition, represented by the horizontal position of the product on the matrix, and (3) the growth rate of the market, indicated by the position of the product in the vertical direction. Figure 18.6 suggests marketing strategies appropriate for cash cows, stars, dogs, and problem children.

14. Joseph P. Guiltinan and Gordon W. Paul, *Marketing Management: Strategies and Programs* (New York: McGraw-Hill, 1982), p. 31.

15. George S. Day, "Diagnosing the Product Portfolio," *Journal of Marketing*, April 1977, pp. 30–31.

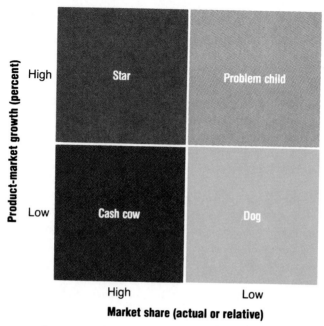

FIGURE 18.5
Illustrative growth-share matrix developed by the Boston Consulting Group

SOURCE: *Perspectives,* No. 66, "The Product Portfolio." Reprinted by permission from The Boston Consulting Group, Inc., Boston, MA. © copyright 1970.

The long-term health of an organisation depends on having some products that generate cash (and provide acceptable profits) and others that use cash to support growth. Among the indicators of overall health are the size and vulnerability of the cash cows, the prospects for the stars, if any, and the number of problem children and dogs. Particular attention must be paid to those products with large cash appetites. Unless the company has an abundant cash flow, it cannot afford to sponsor many such products at one time. If resources, including debt capacity, are spread too thinly, the company will end up with too many marginal products and will be unable to finance promising new product entries or acquisitions in the future.

■ **Market Attractiveness– Business Position Model**

The **market attractiveness–business position model**, illustrated in Figure 18.7, is another two-dimensional matrix. However, rather than using single measures to define the vertical and horizontal dimensions of the matrix, the model employs multiple measurements and observations. The vertical dimension, *market attractiveness,* includes all strengths and resources that relate to the market, such as seasonality, economies of scale, competitive intensity, industry sales, and the overall cost and feasibility of entering the market. The horizontal axis, *business position,* is a composite of factors such as sales, relative market share, research and development, price competitiveness, product quality, and market knowledge as they relate to the product in building market share. A slight variation of this matrix is called **General Electric's Strategic Business Planning Grid** because General Electric is credited with extending the product-portfolio planning tool to examine market attractiveness and business strength.

The best situation is for a firm to have a strong business position in an attractive market. The upper left area in Figure 18.7 represents the opportunity for an invest/ grow strategy, but the matrix does not indicate how to implement this strategy. The

FIGURE 18.6
*Characteristics and
strategies for the four
basic product types in
the growth-share matrix*

Product-market growth rate

High

Low

Relative market share

High

Low

Stars

Characteristics

- Market leaders
- Fast growing
- Substantial profits
- Require large investment
  to finance growth

Strategies

- Protect existing share
- Reinvest earnings in the
  form of price reductions,
  product improvements,
  providing better market
  coverage, production
  efficiency, etc.
- Obtain a large share of
  the new users

Problem children

Characteristics

- Rapid growth
- Poor profit margins
- Enormous demand for
  cash

Strategies

- Invest heavily to get a
  disproportionate share
  of new sales
- Buy existing market
  shares by acquiring
  competitors
- Divestment (see Dogs)
- Harvesting (see Dogs)
- Abandonment (see Dogs)
- Focus on a definable niche
  where dominance can be
  achieved

Cash cows

Characteristics

- Profitable products
- Generate more cash than
  needed to maintain market
  share

Strategies

- Maintain market dominance
- Invest in process improvements
  and technological leadership
- Maintain price leadership
- Use excess cash to support
  research and growth
  elsewhere in the company

Dogs

Characteristics

- Greatest number of products
  fall in this category
- Operate at a cost disadvantage
- Few opportunities for growth
  at a reasonable cost
- Markets are not growing;
  therefore, little new business

Strategies

- Focus on a specialised
  segment of the market that
  can be dominated and
  protected from competitive
  inroads
- Harvesting—cut back all support
  costs to a minimum level;
  supports cash flow over the
  product's remaining life
- Divestment—sale of a growing
  concern
- Abandonment—deletion from the
  product line

SOURCE: Concepts in this figure adapted from George S. Day, "Diagnosing the Product Portfolio," *Journal of Marketing,* April 1977, pp. 30–31. Reprinted by permission of the American Marketing Association.

FIGURE 18.7
Market attractiveness–business position matrix

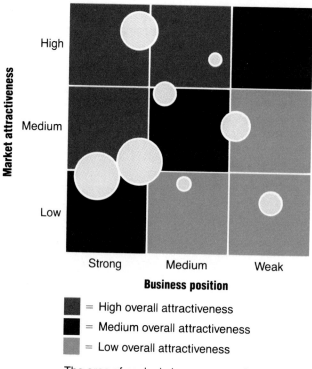

= High overall attractiveness

= Medium overall attractiveness

= Low overall attractiveness

The area of each circle represents the relative monetary sales on the matrix.

SOURCE: Adapted from Derek F. Abell and John S. Hammond, *Strategic Market Planning: Problems and Analytical Approaches,* © 1979, p. 213. Reprinted by permission of Prentice-Hall, Inc., Englewood Cliffs, N.J.

purpose of the model is to serve as a diagnostic tool to highlight SBUs that have an opportunity to grow or that should be divested or approached selectively. SBUs that occupy the invest/grow position can lose their position through faulty marketing strategies.

Decisions on allocating resources to SBUs of medium overall attractiveness should be arrived at on a basis relative to other SBUs that are either more or less attractive. The lower right area of the matrix is a low-growth harvest/divest area. Harvesting is a gradual withdrawal of marketing resources on the assumption that sales will decline at a slow rate but profits will still be significant at a lower sales volume. Harvesting and divesting may be appropriate strategies for SBUs characterised by low overall attractiveness.

■ **Profit Impact on Marketing Strategy (PIMS)**

The Strategic Planning Institute (SPI) developed a databank of information on three thousand strategic business units of two hundred different firms during the period 1970–1983 for the **Profit Impact on Marketing Strategy (PIMS)** research programme.[16] The sample is somewhat biased because it is composed primarily of large, profitable manufacturing firms marketing mature products, and service firms and distribution companies are under-represented. However, 19 percent of the sample is

16. Robert Jacobson, "Distinguishing Among Competing Theories of the Market Share Effect," *Journal of Marketing,* October 1988, pp. 68–80.

FIGURE 18.8

Sample page from PIMS data forms

103: "LIFE CYCLE" STAGE OF PRODUCT CATEGORY

How would you describe the stage of development of the types of products or services sold by this business during the last three years? *(Check one)*

... Introductory Stage: Primary demand for product just starting to grow; products or services still unfamiliar to many potential users ☐ 1

... Growth Stage: Demand growing at 10% or more annually in real terms; technology or competitive structure still changing ☐ 2

... Maturity Stage: Products or services familiar to vast majority of prospective users; technology and competitive structure reasonably stable ☐ 3

... Decline Stage: Products viewed as commodities; weaker competitors beginning to exit ☐ 4

104: What was this business's first year of commercial sales? *(Check one)*

Prior to 1930	1930-1949	1950-1954	1955-1959	1960-1964	1965-1969	1970-1974	1975-
☐ 0	☐ 1	☐ 2	☐ 3	☐ 4	☐ 5	☐ 6	☐ 7

105: At the time this business first entered the market, was it ... *(Check one)*

... One of the pioneers in first developing such products or services? ☐ 1

... An early follower of the pioneer(s) in a still growing, dynamic market? ☐ 2

... A later entrant into a more established market situation? ☐ 3

106-107: PATENTS AND TRADE SECRETS

Does this business benefit *to a significant degree* from patents, trade secrets, or other proprietary methods of production or operation ...

106: Pertaining to products or services? NO ☐ 0 YES ☐ 1

107: Pertaining to processes? NO ☐ 0 YES ☐ 1

108: STANDARDIZATION OF PRODUCTS OR SERVICES

Are the products or services of this business ... *(Check one)*

... More or less standardized for all customers? ☐ 0

... Designed or produced to order for individual customers? ☐ 1

109: FREQUENCY OF PRODUCT CHANGES

Is it typical practice for the business and its major competitors to change all or part of the line of products or services offered ... *(Check one)*

... Annually (for example, annual model changes)? ☐ 1

... Seasonally? ☐ 2

... Periodically, but at intervals longer than one year? ☐ 3

... No regular, periodic pattern of change? ☐ 4

110: TECHNOLOGICAL CHANGE

Have there been *major* technological changes in the products offered by the business or its major competitors, or in methods of production, during the last 8 years? *(If in doubt about whether a change was "major," answer NO.)* NO ☐ 0 YES ☐ 1

SOURCE: PIMS Data Form reproduced by permission of the Strategic Planning Institute [PIMS programme], Cambridge, Mass., 1979.

composed of international businesses.[17] The member organisations of the institute provide confidential information on successes, failures, and marginal products. Figure 18.8 shows a PIMS data form. The data are analysed to provide members with information about how similar organisations have performed under a given set of circumstances and about the factors that contribute to success or failure in given market conditions.

The unit of observation in PIMS is the SBU. Table 18.1 shows the types of information provided on each business in the PIMS database. The PIMS database includes both diagnostic and prescriptive information to assist in analysing marketing performance and formulating marketing strategies. The analysis focuses on options, problems, resources, and opportunities.

The PIMS project has identified more than thirty factors that affect the performance of firms. These factors can be grouped into three sets of variables: (1) those relating to the structure of the market-place in which the firm competes; (2) those

17. George S. Day, *Analysis for Strategic Market Decisions* (St. Paul, Minn.: West, 1986), pp. 117–118.

TABLE 18.1 *Types of information provided on each business in the PIMS database*

Characteristics of the business environment	Structure of the production process
Long-run growth rate of the market	Capital intensity (degree of automation, etc.)
Short-run growth rate of the market	Degree of vertical integration
Rate of inflation of selling price levels	Capacity utilisation
Number and size of customers	Productivity of capital equipment
Purchase frequency and magnitude	Productivity of people
	Inventory levels
Competitive position of the business	
Share of the served market	**Discretionary budget allocations**
Share relative to largest competitors	Research and development budgets
Product quality relative to competitors	Advertising and promotion budgets
Prices relative to competitors	Sales force expenditures
Pay scales relative to competitors	
Marketing efforts relative to competitors	**Strategic moves**
Pattern of market segmentation	Patterns of change in the controllable
Rate of new product introductions	elements above
	Operating results
	Profitability results
	Cash flow results
	Growth results

SOURCE: Reproduced by permission of the Strategic Planning Institute [PIMS programme], Cambridge, MA.

that describe the firm's competitive position within that market; and (3) those that relate to the strategy chosen by the firm.[18] These factors may interact, as well as directly affect performance and profitability. Some of the main findings of the PIMS project are discussed briefly below.

Strong Market Position.   Market position refers to the relative market share that a firm holds in relation to its competition. Firms that have a large share of a market tend to be the most profitable. However, it should be noted that market share does not necessarily create profitability. It is the result of business strategies such as the marketing of high quality products, or the provision of good service.

High Quality Products.   Organisations that offer higher quality products tend to be more profitable than their competitors. They are able to demand higher prices for those products. Moreover, high quality offerings instil customer loyalty, foster repeat purchases, insulate firms from price wars, and help build market share. In Figure 18.9, Coca-Cola promotes its on-going commitment to quality. It appears impossible for firms to overcome inferior offerings with high levels of marketing expenditures. Advertising is no substitute for product quality.

Lower Costs.   Firms achieve lower costs through economies of scale, ability to bargain with suppliers, or backward integration. Low costs heighten profitability levels.

18. Robert D. Buzzell and Bradley T. Gale, *The PIMS Principles: Linking Strategy to Performance* (New York: Free Press, 1987).

FIGURE 18.9
A commitment to quality.
Coca-Cola offers a high-quality product and remains the number-one-selling soft drink.

SOURCE: Coca-Cola, diet Coca-Cola, Sprite, and cherry Coca-Cola are registered trademarks of The Coca Cola Company. Permission for reproduction of materials granted by the Company.

Investment and Capital Intensity.   The higher the required investment to compete in an industry, the more pressure there is on a firm to fully use its production capacity. Moreover, these factors tend to have a negative impact on profitability.

■ **Significance of Strategic Market Planning Approaches**

The approaches presented here provide an overview of the most popular analytical methods used in strategic market planning. However, the Boston Consulting Group's portfolio analysis, the market attractiveness–business position model, and the Profit Impact on Marketing Strategy research programme are used not only to diagnose problem areas or to recognise opportunities, but also to facilitate the allocation of resources among business units. They are not intended to serve as formulae for success or prescriptive guides, which lay out cut-and-dried strategic action plans.[19] These approaches are supplements to, not substitutes for, the marketing manager's

19. Day, *Analysis for Strategic Market Decisions,* p. 10.

own judgement. The real test of each approach, or any integrated approach, is how well it helps management diagnose the firm's strengths and weaknesses and prescribe strategic actions for maintaining or improving performance. The emphasis should be on making sound decisions with the aid of these analytical tools.[20]

Another word of caution regarding the use of portfolio approaches is necessary. The classification of SBUs into a specific portfolio position hinges on four factors: (1) the operational definition of the matrix dimensions; (2) the rules used to divide a dimension into high and low categories; (3) the weighting of the variables used in composite dimensions, if composite dimensions are used; and (4) the specific model used.[21] In other words, changes in any of these four factors may well result in a different classification for a single SBU.

The key to understanding the tools for strategic market planning described in this chapter is recognition that strategic market planning takes into account all aspects of a firm's strategy in the market-place. Most of this book is about functional decisions and strategies of marketing as a part of business. This chapter focuses on the recognition that all functional strategies, including marketing, production, and finance, must be co-ordinated to reach organisational goals. Results of a survey of top industrial firms sponsored by the *Harvard Business Review* indicate that portfolio planning and other general planning techniques help managers strengthen their planning process and solve the problems of managing diversified industrial companies. However, the results also indicate that analytical techniques alone do not result in success. Management must blend these analyses with managerial judgement to deal with the reality of the existing situation.

There are other tools that aid strategic market planning besides those examined here. For example, for many years marketing planners have used the product life-cycle concept, discussed in Chapters 7 and 8. Many firms have their own approaches to planning that incorporate, to varying degrees, some of the approaches discussed here. All strategic planning approaches have some similarity in that several of the components of strategic market planning outlined in Figure 18.2 (especially market/product relationships) are related to a plan of action for reaching objectives.

Developing Competitive Strategies for Marketing

After analysing business operations and business performance, the next step in strategic market planning is to determine future business directions and develop marketing strategies. A business may choose one or more competitive strategies, including intense growth, diversified growth, and integrated growth. Figure 18.10 shows these competitive strategies on a product-market matrix. This matrix can help in determining growth that can be implemented through marketing strategies.

Intense Growth

Intense growth can take place when current products and current markets have the potential for increasing sales. There are three main strategies for intense growth: market penetration, market development, and product development.

20. David W. Cravens, "Strategic Marketing's New Challenge," *Business Horizons,* March-April 1983, p. 19.

21. Yoram Wind, Vijay Majahan, and Donald J. Swire, "An Empirical Comparison of Standardized Portfolio Models," *Journal of Marketing,* Spring 1983, pp. 89–99.

FIGURE 18.10
*Competitive
strategies*

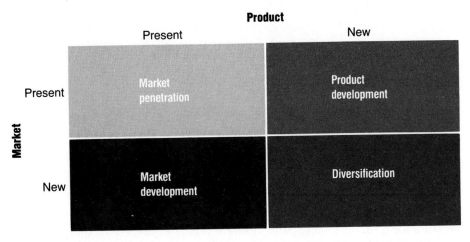

SOURCE: H.I. Ansoff, *The New Corporate Strategy.* (New York, N.Y.: John Wiley & Sons, 1988) p. 83, Figure 6.1. Reproduced by permission of the author.

Market penetration is a strategy of increasing sales in current markets with current products. For example, Coca-Cola and Pepsi try to achieve increased market share through aggressive advertising.

Market development is a strategy of increasing sales of current products in new markets. For example, a European aircraft manufacturer was able to enter the U.S. market by offering Eastern Airlines financing that Boeing could not match. Evian devised a new use for its mineral water by developing its "Brumisateur", an atomiser spray for the skin.

Product development is a strategy of increasing sales by improving present products or developing new products for current markets. Tandem Computers, for example, has marketed specialty computers for commercial use for several years but only recently developed its first mainframe computer—the NonStop Cyclone—to compete head-on with IBM in Tandem's market.[22]

■ **Diversified Growth**

Diversified growth occurs when new products are developed to be sold in new markets. Firms have become increasingly diversified since the 1960s. Diversification offers some advantages over single-business firms because it allows firms to spread their risk across a number of markets. More importantly, it allows firms to make better and wider use of their management, technical, and financial resources. For example, marketing expertise can be used across businesses, and they may also share advertising themes, distribution channels, warehouse facilities, or even sales forces.[23] The three forms of diversification are horizontal, concentric, and conglomerate.

Horizontal diversification results when new products that are not technologically related to current products are introduced to current markets. Sony, for example, has diversified from an electronics giant to a film-maker through its purchase of Columbia Pictures. The purchase gave Sony a library of 2,700 films, including

22. Jonathan B. Levine, "This Cyclone Is Out to Rain on IBM's Parade," *Business Week*, 23 Oct. 1989, p. 114.

23. Roger A. Kerin, Vijay Majahan, and P. Rajan Varadarajan, *Contemporary Perspectives on Strategic Marketing Planning* (Boston: Allyn & Bacon, 1990).

Ghostbusters 2 and *When Harry Met Sally,* as well as 23,000 television episodes, which it may use to help establish its new line of 8mm videos.[24]

In *concentric diversification,* the marketing and technology of new products are related to current products, but the new ones are introduced into new markets. For instance, Dow Chemical is diversifying into agricultural chemicals and pharmaceuticals through joint ventures with corporations in those industries.[25]

Conglomerate diversification occurs when new products are unrelated to current technology, products, or markets and are introduced to markets new to the firm. For example, Bass, the British brewers, acquired the American Holiday Inn hotel chain, and Laura Ashley, the U.K. clothing and furnishings company, has moved into the fragrance market, with Laura Ashley No. 1.

■ **Integrated Growth**

Integrated growth can occur in the same industry that the firm is in and in three possible directions: forwards, backwards, and horizontally. A company growing through forward integration takes ownership or increased control of its distribution system. For example, a shoe manufacturer might start selling its products through wholly owned retail outlets. In backward integration, a firm takes ownership or increased control of its supply systems. A newspaper company that buys a paper mill is integrating backwards. Horizontal integration occurs when a firm takes ownership or control of some of its competitors. For example, Polly Peck International, the British/Cypriot fruit grower and distributor, purchased Del Monte's fresh fruit division.[26]

MARKETING PLANNING

As we noted at the start, this chapter deals with the planning aspect of marketing management. In this section we describe how the strategic plan is implemented. **Marketing planning** is a systematic process that involves assessing marketing opportunities and resources, determining marketing objectives, and developing a plan for implementation and control. The objective of marketing planning is the creation of a marketing plan.

Figure 18.11 illustrates the **marketing planning cycle**. Note that marketing planning is a circular process. As the dotted feedback lines in the figure indicate, planning is not one way. Feedback is used to co-ordinate and synchronise all the stages of the planning cycle.

The duration of marketing plans varies. Plans that cover a period of one year or less are called **short-range plans**. **Medium-range plans** are usually for two to five years. Marketing plans that extend beyond five years are generally viewed as **long-range plans**. These plans can sometimes cover a period as long as twenty years. Marketing managers may have short-, medium-, and long-range plans all at the same time. Long-range plans are relatively rare. However, as the marketing environment continues to change and business decisions become more complex,

24. Ronald Grover, "When Columbia Met Sony . . . A Love Story," *Business Week,* 9 Oct. 1989, pp. 44–45.

25. David Woodruff, "Has Dow Chemical Found the Right Formula?" *Business Week,* 7 Aug. 1989, pp. 62, 64.

26. Mark Maremont, with Judith H. Dobrzynski, "Meet Asil Nadir, the Billion-Dollar Fruit King," *Business Week,* 18 Sept. 1989, p. 32.

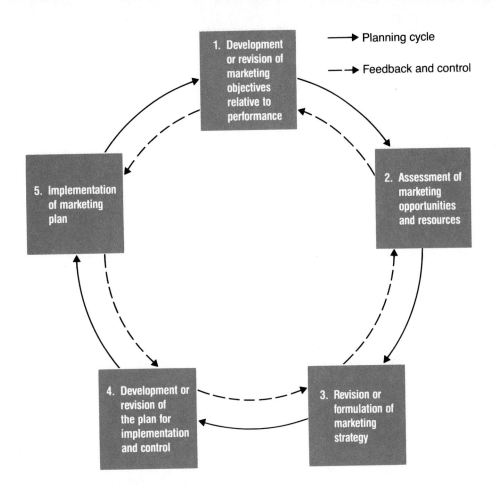

FIGURE 18.11
The marketing planning cycle

1. Development or revision of marketing objectives relative to performance

2. Assessment of marketing opportunities and resources

3. Revision or formulation of marketing strategy

4. Development or revision of the plan for implementation and control

5. Implementation of marketing plan

→ Planning cycle

⇢ Feedback and control

profitability and survival will depend more and more on the development of long-range plans.[27]

The extent to which marketing managers develop and use plans also varies. Although planning provides numerous benefits, some managers do not use formal marketing plans because they spend almost all their time dealing with daily problems, many of which would be eliminated by adequate planning. However, planning is becoming more important to marketing managers, who realise that planning is necessary to develop, co-ordinate, and control marketing activities effectively and efficiently. When formulating a marketing plan, a new enterprise or a firm with a new product does not have current performance to evaluate or an existing plan to revise. Therefore, its marketing planning centres on analysing available resources and options to assess opportunities. Managers can then develop marketing objectives and a strategy. In addition, many firms recognise the need to include information systems in their plans so that they can have continuous feedback and keep their marketing activities orientated towards objectives. (Information systems are discussed in Chapter 6.) One research study, which examined 207 different companies, found that those that have maintained or increased their planning departments

27. Ronald D. Michman, "Linking Futuristics with Marketing Planning, Forecasting, and Strategy," *Journal of Consumer Marketing*, Summer 1984, pp. 17, 23.

TABLE 18.2
*Planning for the intro-
duction of a national
newspaper:* USA Today

Objective: Achieve 1 million in circulation by reaching an up-scale market, primarily of males who hold professional and managerial positions and who made at least one trip of 200 miles or more within the last year.

Opportunity: Paper tends to be a second newspaper purchase for readers. *USA Today* is not in competition directly with local papers, and it is not positioned against other national newspapers/magazines.

Market: Circulation within a 200-mile radius of 15 major markets, representing 54% of the U.S. population, including such cities as Chicago, Houston, New York, Los Angeles, and Denver.

Product: Superior graphic quality; appeal to the TV generation through short news items, a colour weather map, and other contemporary features.

Price: Competitive.

Promotion: Pedestal-like vending machines with attention-grabbing design and a higher position than competitors to differentiate the paper and bring it closer to eye level. Outdoor advertising and some print advertising promotes the paper.

Distribution: News-stands, vending machines in busy locations, and direct mail.

Implementation and control: Personnel with experience in the newspaper business who can assist in developing a systematic approach for implementing the marketing strategy and design as well as an information system to monitor and control the results.

SOURCE: Kevin Higgins, *"USA Today* Nears Million Reader Mark," *Marketing News,* 15 Apr. 1983, pp. 1, 5. Reprinted by permission of the American Marketing Association.

during the past five years and increased their allocation of resources to planning activities out-performed those whose planning departments have become smaller.[28]

To illustrate the marketing planning process, consider the decisions that went into the planning in America of the national newspaper *USA Today*. Table 18.2 lists several of the more important marketing decisions. Of course, to reach the objective, a detailed course of action was communicated throughout the organisation. In short, specific marketing plans should do the following:

1. Specify expected results so that the organisation can anticipate what its situation will be at the end of the current planning period
2. Identify the resources needed to carry out the planned activities so that a budget can be developed
3. Describe in sufficient detail the activities that are to take place so that responsibilities for implementation can be assigned
4. Provide for the monitoring of activities and results so control can be exerted[29]

Obviously, the marketing plan needs to be carefully written to attain these objectives. In the final section of this chapter, we will take a closer look at the marketing plan itself.

28. Vasudevan Ramanujam and N. Venkatraman, "Planning and Performance: A New Look at an Old Question," *Business Horizons,* May-June 1987, pp. 19–25.

29. David J. Luck, O. C. Ferrell, and George Lucas, *Marketing Strategy and Plans,* 3rd ed. (Englewood Cliffs, N.J.: Prentice-Hall, 1989), p. 328.

THE MARKETING PLAN

As mentioned earlier, the marketing plan is the written document or blueprint governing all of a firm's marketing activities, including the implementation and control of those activities. A marketing plan serves a number of purposes:

1. It offers a "road map" for implementing the firm's strategies and achieving its objectives.
2. It assists in management control and monitoring of implementation of strategy.
3. It informs new participants in the plan of their role and function.
4. It specifies how resources are to be allocated.
5. It stimulates thinking and makes better use of resources.
6. It assigns responsibilities, tasks, and timing.
7. It makes participants aware of problems, opportunities, and threats.[30]

A firm should have a plan for each marketing strategy it develops. Because such plans must be changed as forces in the firm and in the environment change, marketing planning is a continuous process.

Organisations use many different formats when devising marketing plans. Plans may be written for strategic business units, product lines, individual products or brands, or specific markets. Most plans share some common ground, however, by including an executive summary, situation analysis, opportunity and threat analysis, a description of environmental forces, an inventory of company resources, a description of marketing objectives, an outline of the marketing strategy, financial projections and budgets, and bench-marks or controls for monitoring and evaluating the action taken (see Table 18.3). In the following sections we consider the major parts of a typical marketing plan, as well as the purpose that each part serves.

■ Executive Summary

The executive summary is a synopsis (often only one or two pages long) outlining the main thrust of the entire report. It includes an introduction, the major aspects of the marketing plan, and a statement about the costs of implementing the plan. Such a summary helps executives who need to know what information the plan contains but are not involved in approving or making decisions related to the plan and can pass over the details.

■ Situation Analysis

The situation analysis provides an appraisal of the difference between the firm's current performance and past stated objectives. It includes a summary of data that relate to the creation of the current marketing situation. This information is obtained from both the firm's external and internal environment, usually through its marketing information system. Depending on the situation, details on the composition of target market segments, marketing objectives, current marketing strategies, market trends, sales history, and profitability may be included.

■ Opportunity and Threat Analysis

In the analysis of opportunities and threats, a detailed examination of opportunities or threats present in the firm's operating environment is provided. It examines opportunities and threats with regard to specific target markets along with their size and growth potential. Possible market opportunities may be described in this sec-

30. William A. Cohen, *The Practice of Marketing Management; Analysis, Planning, and Implementation* (New York: Macmillan, 1988), pp. 44–46.

TABLE 18.3
A marketing plan

I. **Executive Summary**

II. **Situation Analysis**
   A. Description of markets, current marketing strategies
   B. Description of measures of performance

III. **Opportunities and Threats**
   A. Greatest challenges or threats to future marketing activities
   B. Opportunity analysis

IV. **Environment**
   A. Legal, political, and regulatory factors
   B. Social and cultural factors
   C. Economic factors
   D. Competitive factors
   E. Technological factors

V. **Company Resources**
   A. Financial resources
   B. Human resources
   C. Experience and expertise

VI. **Marketing Objectives**

VII. **Marketing Strategies**
   A. Target market
   B. Marketing mix

VIII. **Financial Projections and Budgets**
   A. Delineation of costs
   B. Estimates of sales and revenues
   C. Expected return on investment for implementing the marketing plan

IX. **Controls and Evaluation**
   A. Measures of performance
   B. Monitoring and evaluating performance

tion. It develops an ordering of priorities for action in light of the unit's internal capabilities for dealing with the circumstances.

Environmental Analysis

The environmental section of the marketing plan describes the current state of the marketing environment, including the legal, political, regulatory, technological, competitive, social, and economic forces, as well as ethical considerations. It also makes predictions about future directions of those forces.

For example, the retailer Safeway was among the first to respond to consumer concern about the use of artificial fertilisers and pesticides. It offered its customers a choice of regular fruit and vegetables or organically grown produce, at a higher price.

As mentioned earlier, environmental forces can hamper an organisation in achieving its objectives. The section also describes the possible impact of these forces on the implementation of the marketing plan. Most marketing plans include extensive analyses of competitive, legal, and regulatory forces, perhaps even creating separate sections for these influential forces of the marketing environment. It is important to note here that, because the forces of the marketing environment are dynamic, marketing plans should be reviewed and possibly modified periodically to adjust to change.

■ Company Resources

A firm's human and financial resources, as well as its experiences and expertise, are major considerations in developing a marketing plan. Thus the marketing plan should describe the human, financial, and physical resources available for implementing the plan, as well as describe resource constraints that may affect implementation. It should also describe any distinctive competencies that may give the firm an edge in the market-place. The plan should take into account strengths and weaknesses that may influence the firm's ability to implement a selected marketing strategy.

Instead of adopting the stages of situation, opportunity and threat, and environmental analysis and evaluation of company resources, many marketers conduct a **SWOT analysis**: Strengths, Weaknesses, Opportunities, Threats. The first half of this analysis—strengths and weaknesses—examines the company's position, or that of its product, vis-à-vis customers, competitor activity, environmental trends and company resources. The second half of the SWOT takes this review further to examine the opportunities and threats identified and make recommendations about marketing strategy and the marketing mix.

■ Marketing Objectives

This section describes the objectives underlying the plan. A **marketing objective** is a statement of what is to be accomplished through marketing activities. It specifies the results expected from marketing efforts. A marketing objective should be expressed in clear, simple terms so that all marketing personnel understand exactly what they are trying to achieve. It should be written in such a way that its accomplishment can be measured accurately. If a company has an objective of increasing its market share by 12 percent, the firm should be able to measure changes in its market share accurately. A marketing objective should also indicate the time frame for accomplishing the objective. For example, a firm that sets an objective of introducing three new products should state the time period in which this is to be done.

Objectives may be stated in terms of degree of product introduction or innovation, sales volume, profitability per unit, or gains in market share. They must also be consistent with the firm's overall organisational goals.

■ Marketing Strategies

This section provides a broad overview of the plan for achieving the marketing objectives and, ultimately, the organisational goals. Marketing strategy focuses on defining a target market and developing a marketing mix to gain long-run competitive and consumer advantages. There is a degree of overlap between corporate strategy and marketing strategy. Marketing strategy is unique in that it has the responsibility to assess buyer needs and the firm's potential for gaining competitive advantage, both of which ultimately must guide the corporate mission.[31] In other words, marketing strategy guides the firm's direction in relationships between customers and competitors. Marketing Update 18.2 describes the development of InterCity's marketing strategy to attract the business travel market. The bottom line is that a marketing strategy must be consistent with consumer needs, perceptions,

31. Yoram Wind and Thomas S. Robertson, "Marketing Strategy: New Directions for Theory and Research," *Journal of Marketing*, Spring 1983, p. 12.

INTERCITY CATERS FOR BUSINESS

British Rail employs over 100,000 staff, has a turnover close to £3 billion and a passenger volume of over 20 billion passenger miles. Divided into five business units, InterCity is the U.K. national passenger rail network competing for long distance passenger journeys. There are three clearly identifiable segments: business travel, leisure travel, obligatory travel (commuting).

Every business needs to regularly re-appraise its activities, and InterCity is no exception. Recognising the importance of the business market, InterCity consults customers to ascertain what they seek and whether their requirements are being met. Products may need relaunching, improving, or promoting to make customers aware of them. InterCity conducted a major programme of consumer research, comparing the advantages and disadvantages for customers of rail, car, and air travel. Consumers most often indicated these advantages:

Car   Privacy/Flexibility/Accessibility/Control/Speed

Plane   Standard of service/Thrill of flying/Arrive fresh

Intercity   Space to move around/Work while travelling/Centre to centre

The major finding from the research, however, was that business travellers cared greatly about the status accompanying their choice of transport. Because InterCity offered less privacy and appeared less exclusive, it did not satisfy status needs as much.

Knowing the problems, InterCity decided to alter its perceived position and to be seen as a more up-market product. To carry out this repositioning, InterCity designed a marketing package aimed at increasing the status of business travel by rail coupled with the existing advantages of lack of strain, space to move, and ability to work while travelling. Executive tickets, for example, include seat reservations, 24 hours' car parking, refreshment voucher and London Underground travel. Pullman luxury carriages have been added on more services and Pullman executive lounges have been built at various major stations.

Saatchi and Saatchi's advertising campaigns emphasised this repositioning and the benefits of InterCity. British Rail identified what its business travellers wanted, provided the required service and communicated with existing and potential customers about the improvements and changes.

SOURCES: "How InterCity Caters for Its Business Customers," Wetherby: Target, 1990; R. Mason, InterCity Marketing Director 1990, British Railways Board, London; "A Selection of Case Studies from Organisations That Have Demonstrated Excellence in Marketing and Recruitment," Target, Wetherby: Michael Benn and Associates, 1990; Fiona Plant, "Agencies Vie for BR's £4m," *Campaign,* 19 October 1990, p. 4; Nicholas Faith, "British Rail's Market Express," *Business,* July 1989, pp. 52–62; Roland Rudd, "Full Steam Ahead for the Big State Sell-Off," *The Independent on Sunday,* 13 January 1991, pp. 4–5.

John Cleese. Cardmember since 1971.

Membership Has Its Privileges.
Call 0800 700 777 to apply

FIGURE 18.12 *Developing strategies that meet consumers' perceptions.*
Celebrity endorsers enhance the American Express card's image as a privilege and an achievement of success.
SOURCE: Courtesy of American Express Europe Ltd.

and beliefs. American Express shows highly successful individuals as card members, fulfilling consumers' perceptions that to be a member is a privilege (see Figure 18.12). Thus this section should describe the firm's intended target market and how product, promotion, distribution, and price will be used to satisfy the needs of the members of the target market.

Michael Porter[32] describes three **generic strategies** which, he maintains, help firms to achieve industry success (see Figure 18.13). The first is *cost leadership,* where low-cost producers exploit experience-curve effects to achieve market penetration. The key is the development of a low cost structure which allows high returns even when competition is intense. Amstrad and Texas Instruments have both successfully operated as cost leaders. *Differentiation,* the second generic strategy, involves firms developing a product or service which is unique or superior in some way. Products which have this quality, whether in terms of features, image, or design, often have higher-than-average prices. Sony stereos and Raleigh bicycles are both examples of where a high price can be demanded. Indeed, the price of items like these is part of the products' character and ethos. The final generic strategy is

32. M. E. Porter, *Competitive Strategy: Techniques for Analysing Industries and Competitors* (New York: Free Press, 1980).

FIGURE 18.13
*Generic routes to
competitive advantage*

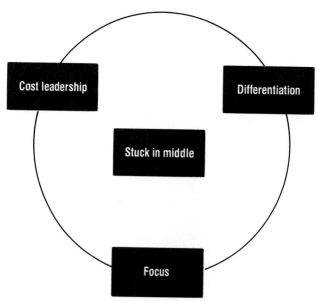

SOURCE: Based on M. E. Porter, *Competitive Strategy: Techniques for Analysing
Industries and Competitors* (New York: Free Press, 1980). From *Distance
Learning MBA Notes,* Warwick Business School, 1987.

focus. Here companies concentrate their efforts on particular segments of the market. In some instances this is because there are insufficient resources to compete on a larger scale. Focus allows companies like Rolex watches and Porsche in the car market to service particular sub-groups of customers. Although focusing has attractions in terms of gearing the marketing mix to a quite specific and narrow customer target, the associated risks are high. The danger is that, if attacked head-on, such highly specialised companies may find it difficult to develop alternative competences. Porter warns against firms becoming "stuck in the middle" between the three strategies. This, he argues, can lead to customers not having a good reason for purchasing a company's products or services.

■ **Financial
Projections
and Budgets**

The financial projections and budgets section outlines the returns expected through implementation of the plan. The costs incurred will be weighed against expected revenues. A budget must be prepared to allocate resources in order to accomplish marketing objectives. It should contain estimates of the costs of implementing the plan, including the costs of advertising, sales-force training and compensation, development of distribution channels, and marketing research.

■ **Controls
and Evaluation**

This section details how the results of the plan will be measured. For example, the results of an advertising campaign designed to increase market share may be measured in terms of increases in sales volume or improved brand recognition and acceptance by consumers. Next, a schedule for comparing the results achieved with the objectives set forth in the marketing plan is developed. Finally, guidelines may be offered outlining who is responsible for monitoring the programme and taking remedial action.

Summary

A strategic market plan is an outline of the methods and resources required to achieve the organisation's goals within a specific target market; it takes into account all the functional areas of a business unit that must be co-ordinated. A strategic business unit (SBU) is a division, product line, or other profit centre within the parent company and is used to define areas for consideration in a specific strategic market plan. The process of strategic market planning yields a marketing strategy that is the framework for a marketing plan. A marketing plan includes the framework and entire set of activities to be performed; it is the written document or blueprint for implementing and controlling an organisation's marketing activities.

Through the process of strategic market planning, an organisation can develop marketing strategies that, when properly implemented and controlled, will contribute to achieving the organisation's overall goals. The set of marketing strategies that are implemented and used at the same time is referred to as the organisation's marketing programme. Environmental forces are important in the strategic market planning process and very much affect it. These forces imply opportunities and threats that influence an organisation's overall goals.

A firm's organisational goals should be derived from its mission, the broad tasks the organisation wants to achieve. These goals should guide planning efforts.

There are three major considerations in assessing opportunities and resources: evaluation of market opportunities, monitoring of environmental forces, and understanding the firm's capabilities. A market opportunity, or strategic window, opens when the right combination of circumstances occurs at the right time, and an organisation can take action towards a target market. An opportunity offers a favourable chance for the company to generate sales from markets. Market requirements relate to the customers' needs or desired benefits. The market requirements are satisfied by components of the marketing mix that provide buyers with these benefits. Environmental scanning is a search for information about events and relationships in a company's outside environment; such information aids marketers in planning. A firm's capabilities relate to distinctive competencies that it has developed to do something well and efficiently. A firm is likely to enjoy a differential advantage in an area where its competencies out-do those of its potential competition.

Corporate strategy determines the means for utilising resources in the areas of production, finance, research and development, personnel, and marketing to reach the organisation's goals.

A number of tools have been developed to aid marketing managers in their planning efforts, including the Boston Consulting Group (BCG) product-portfolio analysis, the market attractiveness–business position model, and Profit Impact on Marketing Strategy (PIMS). The BCG approach is based on the philosophy that a product's market growth rate and its market share are key factors influencing marketing strategy. All the firm's products are integrated into a single, overall matrix and evaluated to determine appropriate strategies for individual SBUs and the overall portfolio strategies.

The market attractiveness–business position model is a two-dimensional matrix. The market-attractiveness dimension includes all the sources of strength and resources that relate to the market; competition, industry sales, and the cost of competing are among the sources. The business-position axis measures sales, relative market share, research and development, and other factors that relate to building a market share for a product.

The Profit Impact on Marketing Strategy (PIMS) research programme has developed a databank of confidential information on the successes, failures, and marginal products of more than three thousand strategic business units of the two hundred members of the Strategic Planning Institute. The unit of observation in PIMS is an SBU. The results of PIMS include diagnostic and prescriptive information to assist in analysing marketing performance and formulating marketing strategies. The analysis focuses on options, problems, resources, and opportunities.

These tools for strategic market planning are used only to diagnose problem areas or recognise opportunities. They are supplements to, not substitutes for, the marketing manager's own judgement. The real test of each approach, or any integrated approach, is how well it helps management diagnose the firm's strengths and weaknesses and prescribe strategic actions for maintaining or improving performance.

Competitive strategies that can be implemented through marketing include intense growth, diversified growth, and integrated growth. Intense growth includes market penetration, market development, or product development. Diversified growth includes horizontal, concentric, and conglomerate diversification. Integrated growth includes forward, backward, and horizontal integration.

Marketing planning is a systematic process that involves assessing opportunities and resources, determining marketing objectives, developing a marketing strategy, and developing plans for implementation and control. Short-range marketing plans cover one year or less; medium-range plans are usually for two to five years; plans that last for more than five years are long-range.

A marketing plan is the written document or blueprint for implementing and controlling an organisation's marketing activities. A well-written plan clearly specifies when, how, and who is to perform marketing activities. Typical marketing plans include an executive summary, situation analysis, opportunity and threat analysis, a description of the impact of the marketing environment forces, a summary of company resources, marketing objectives, marketing strategies, financial projections and budgets, and prescriptions for controlling and evaluating results.

IMPORTANT TERMS

Strategic market plan
Strategic business unit (SBU)
Strategic market planning
Marketing plan
Marketing programme
Differential advantage
Market opportunity
Market requirements
Corporate strategy
Product-portfolio analysis
"Stars"
"Cash cows"
"Dogs"
"Problem children"
Market attractiveness–business
   position model

General Electric's Strategic Business
   Planning Grid
Profit Impact on Marketing
   Strategy (PIMS)
Intense growth
Diversified growth
Integrated growth
Marketing planning
Marketing planning cycle
Short-range plans
Medium-range plans
Long-range plans
SWOT analysis
Marketing objective
Generic strategies

Discussion and Review Questions

1. Why should an organisation develop a marketing strategy? What is the difference between strategic market planning and the strategy itself?
2. Identify the major components of strategic market planning, and explain how they are interrelated.
3. In what ways do environmental forces affect strategic market planning? Give specific examples.
4. What are some of the issues that must be considered in analysing a firm's opportunities and resources? How do these issues affect marketing objectives and market strategy?
5. Why is market opportunity analysis necessary? What are the determinants of market opportunity?
6. In relation to resource constraints, how can environmental scanning affect a firm's long-term strategic market planning? Consider product costs and benefits affected by the environment.
7. What are the major considerations in developing the product-portfolio grid? Define and explain the four basic types of products suggested by the Boston Consulting Group.
8. When should marketers consider using PIMS for strategic market planning?
9. Why do you think more firms are diversifying? Give some examples of diversified firms.
10. What benefits do marketing managers gain from planning? Is planning necessary for long-run survival? Why or why not?
11. How should an organisation establish marketing objectives?

▪ Cases

18.1   Stepcan

In 1988, Metal Box (MB) developed a unique container to rival the tin can: the Stepcan. Made of flexible, transparent plastic with a metal ring-pull lid, which was resealable, the container gave consumers the opportunity of seeing its contents. Initial market research justified the company's faith as consumers preferred the non-breakable Stepcan with its clearly viewed contents. Indeed, consumers claimed they would happily pay a price premium. Marks & Spencer wanted exclusivity and Sainsbury, Waitrose, and Tesco were all interested. Research in Scandinavia and France revealed similar levels of interest. In Germany, however, the "green" movement was well advanced: recyclable glass was preferred to the plastic Stepcan.

The Stepcan was initially test-marketed containing fruit cocktail. A similar weight and quality cost 47p in a tin can but £1.29 in a Stepcan. Placed on supermarket shelves adjacent to each other, the higher-priced Stepcan out-sold its neighbouring tin cans. As more retailers adopted Stepcans for their own-label products, more and more lines were found to be suitable, from "tinned" fruits to soups. Although such a large price differential over similar products in tin cans was difficult to maintain, the Stepcan did keep a healthy premium price.

Management changes and a refocusing of its core businesses forced MB to drop the Stepcan, but other packaging manufacturers stepped in to produce similar containers. Through technical innovation and product attributes (transparency and flexibility) MB had gained a significant competitive advantage, as did those retailers that originally had faith in the concept of the Stepcan.

SOURCES: "M and S Adopts Clear Plastics Stepcan for Premium Fruit Pack Presentation," *Packaging News*, May 1988; "Stepcan: The Choice Is Clear," Metal Box Food Packaging promotional literature, 1988; "What's in a Can?" *Inside News*, Marks and Spencer plc. April/May, 1989; "Full Speed Ahead," *Metal Box News*, April 1988, p. 1.

Questions for Discussion

1. Why is a differential advantage difficult to sustain in the grocery industry?
2. Is it a reasonably straightforward process to create a differential advantage on the basis of packaging? Discuss, using various product examples.
3. How best should MB have researched the full potential of the Stepcan?

18.2   Paramount Pictures

Although the products marketed by Hollywood studios differ from those of other companies, like any other business, the studios are vulnerable to threats and open to opportunities. They must develop marketing strategies and implement them if they are to produce the blockbuster films and hit television shows that consumers want to see. Paramount Pictures Corporation is one studio that has developed successful marketing strategies.

Business is good for Paramount today, with blockbusters such as *Indiana Jones and the Last Crusade* and hit television shows, "Cheers", "Dear John", "The Arsenio Hall Show", and "Star Trek: The Next Generation". But things were not always so glamorous for the studio division of Paramount Communications (formerly Gulf & Western). In early 1986, Paramount had a dismal 1.5 percent share of the market, down from a 1984 high of 19.1 percent. In addition, the management team that had led the studio to glory with the films *Flashdance, An Officer and a Gentleman,* and *Raiders of the Lost Ark* had left for positions with 20th Century-Fox or the Walt Disney Company. With the exception of one huge hit, *Beverly Hills Cop,* Paramount was also the owner of a large collection of flops.

Then, Frank Mancuso, a twenty-seven-year Paramount veteran, assumed the post of chairman of the company. Mancuso hired the industry's best production and marketing executives and began a strategy of establishing long-term relationships between the studio and major film producers and stars. This strategy proved to be the answer to Paramount's film production woes.

Shortly after Mancuso assumed the chairmanship of Paramount, the company began turning out one hit after another—often from ideas turned down by other film studios. One such idea was a script about young naval air cadets, which Paramount produced at a cost of more than $17.5 million under the name *Top Gun*. *Top Gun* went on to become the top-grossing hit of 1986 with revenues of $270 million. *Crocodile Dundee* in 1986 and *Beverly Hills Cop II, Fatal Attraction,* and *The Untouchables* in 1987 were other Paramount success stories. By the end of 1987, Paramount had captured the number-one position in the market for two years in a row and a 20 percent share of the U.S. market.

The secret of Paramount's success lies partly in the capricious entertainment tastes of American consumers. However, a great deal of its success can be attributed to its strategy of nurturing successful long-term relationships and projects. Paramount has carefully milked one of its oldest TV cash cows, "Star Trek", with video releases of the original episodes, five feature films, and the current number one programme on U.S. television—"Star Trek: The Next Generation". Long-term relationships with other cash cows and stars, such as actor/comedian Eddie Murphy and major directors Steven Spielberg and George Lucas, have also contributed to the studio's current string of hits.

Nurturing such long-term relationships is the only means of securing success through the development of sequels and television spin-offs. The success of film "franchises" such as the *Indiana Jones* trilogy, the five *Star Trek* films, and seven Eddie Murphy pictures bears out the importance of securing these long-term contracts. Within the industry, Paramount's exclusive contract with Eddie Murphy is considered to be the best of them all. Murphy's seven films with Paramount have produced a combined income of more than $1 billion, not counting the additional revenue generated through television, video cassettes, and cable TV.

The success of these long-term relationships has allowed Paramount to be aggressive in marketing and media usage. Paramount's landmark deal with Pepsi, which placed a Pepsi promotional spot on the *Top Gun* video release, was the first of its kind. The joint Paramount/Pepsi promotion of the *Top Gun* video made the film the most heavily promoted title in history. The video sold an estimated 3 million units. As a result of this and other promotions, Paramount became known as the master of publicity and word-of-mouth promotion.

However, Paramount's product-line style of movie-making strategy is not without risks. Paramount runs the risk of staking its future on past successes, and even on a single superstar, Eddie Murphy. Some of its franchises are already mature, such as the *Star Trek* films because of the ageing of the principal actors. Other franchises have finished: *Indiana Jones and the Last Crusade* was the last of the highly successful trilogy featuring Harrison Ford.

Thus, despite its successful long-term relationships and successful franchises, Paramount must constantly look for new franchises and hot new stars. The company is currently exploring the possibility of doing a series of films based on its *Star Trek: The Next Generation* television series. In addition, Paramount is looking overseas for new ideas and stars. One project under development is a remake of the French film, *Trop Belle pour Toi (Too Beautiful for You)*. The firm's European production operation will produce two to four films annually, boosting the studio's film output to nineteen or twenty from its current average of fourteen.

Thus, Paramount Picture's strategy is to milk its cash cows, while constantly looking for and developing its stars. As one company executive said, "We won't just sit back and make *Beverly Hills Cop III, IV*, and V and call it a day."

SOURCES: Ronald Grover, "Fat Times for Studios, Fatter Times for Stars," *Business Week,* 24 July 1989, p. 48; Laura Landro, "It's a Record Race for Movie Makers," *Wall Street Journal,* 3 Nov. 1989, p. B2; Laura Landro, "Paramount Plans Movie Unit in London to Tap Growing International Market," *Wall Street Journal,* 12 Jan. 1990, p. B4; Laura Landro, "Paramount's Marketers Try for a 'New' Eddie Murphy," *Wall Street Journal,* 7 July 1988, p. E25; Laura Landro, "Sequels and Stars Help Top Movie Studios Avoid Major Risks," *Wall Street Journal,* 6 June 1989, pp. A1, A18; Marcy Magiera, "Paramount Axes DMB&B as Studios Watch Costs," *Advertising Age,* 15 Jan. 1990, p. 4; Joe Mandese, "Hollywood's Top Gun," *Marketing & Media Decisions,* Mar. 1988, pp. 109, 112, 114; Paramount Communications, Inc. (formerly Gulf & Western), *Annual Report,* 1988.

Questions for Discussion

1. What is the role of strategic market planning at Paramount Pictures?
2. Relate the product-portfolio matrix scheme to the analysis of products (films) at Paramount Pictures.

19

IMPLEMENTING STRATEGIES AND MEASURING PERFORMANCE

Objectives

To understand how the marketing unit fits into a firm's organisational structure

To become familiar with the ways of organising a marketing unit

To examine several issues relating to the implementation of marketing strategies

To understand the control processes used in managing marketing strategies

To learn how cost and sales analyses can be used to evaluate the performance of marketing strategies

To become aware of the major components of a marketing audit

The DIY market in the U.K. is worth £6.4 billion annually, with 6,000 stores; it is dominated by B&Q (250), Do-It-All/Payless (230), and Texas (220). Sainsbury-controlled Homebase trades from only 50 locations but leads the market in terms of customer service and staff retention. Most DIY retailers trade on low price and, typically, provide unhelpful customer service. Homebase aims to demystify the mechanics of DIY with an emphasis on customer service. Hands-on management carefully implements its market plan and controls operations. Homebase's organisation is based on expert buying, innovative merchandising, efficient inventory control, and well-motivated sales assistants.

To determine what products customers want, Homebase conducts extensive market research. The company's computerised stock control monitors which products are fast- or slow-moving and has increased the company's stock-turn. Sales assistants are given detailed product information and hands-on training in helping purchasers. There are information and customer service points, special-order facilities, and home delivery. There are management training programmes and regular courses for sales assistants, which emphasise operational issues but also the company's service- and quality-led culture. ◆

Based on information in "Trade Review 2," *EIU Retail Business Quarterly,* March 1990; *Marketing,* 7 June 1990, p. 1; "Homebase," *Harvest,* 1990; N. Tall, "Sainsbury Beats Forecasts at £421m, *Financial Times,* 16 May 1990, p. 29L; "Sainsbury Wins Appeal for Relief on Homebase Losses," *Financial Times,* 7 June 1990, p. 8f.

This chapter focuses first on the marketing unit's position in the organisation and the ways the unit itself can be organised. Then we examine several issues regarding the implementation of marketing strategies. Next we consider the basic components of the process of control and discuss the use of cost and sales analyses to evaluate the effectiveness of marketing strategies and measure the firm's performance. Finally, we describe a marketing audit.

ORGANISING MARKETING ACTIVITIES

The structure and relationships of a marketing unit, including lines of authority and responsibility that connect and co-ordinate individuals, strongly affect marketing activities. This section first looks at the place of marketing within an organisation and examines the major alternatives available for organising a marketing unit. Then it shows how marketing activities can be structured to fit into an organisation so as to contribute to the accomplishment of overall objectives.

■ **Centralisation Versus Decentralisation**

The organisational structure that a company uses to connect and co-ordinate various activities affects its success. Basic decisions relate to how various participants in the company will work together to make important decisions, as well as to co-ordinate, implement, and control activities. Top managers create corporate strategies and co-ordinate lower levels. A **centralised organisation** is one in which the top-level managers delegate very little authority to lower levels of the organisation. In a **decentralised organisation**, decision-making authority is delegated as far down the chain of command as possible. The decision to centralise or decentralise directly affects marketing in the organisation.

In a centralised organisation, major marketing decisions originate with top management and are transmitted to lower levels of management. A decentralised structure gives marketing managers more opportunity for making key strategic decisions. IBM has adopted a decentralised management structure so that its marketing managers have a chance to customise strategies for customers. On the other hand, Hewlett-Packard and 3M have become more centralised by consolidating functions or eliminating divisional managers.[1] Although decentralising may foster innovation and a greater responsiveness to customers, a decentralised company may be inefficient or appear to have a blurred marketing strategy when dealing with larger customers. A centralised organisation avoids confusion among the marketing staff, vagueness in marketing strategy, and autonomous decision-makers who are out of control. Of course, over-centralised companies often become dependent on top management and respond too slowly to be able to solve problems or seize new opportunities. Obviously, finding the right degree of centralisation for a particular company is a difficult balancing act.

1. Larry Reibstein, "IBM's Plan to Decentralize May Set a Trend—But Imitation Has a Price," *Wall Street Journal*, 19 Feb. 1988, p. 17.

FIGURE 19.1
Organising the marketing unit by types of customers.

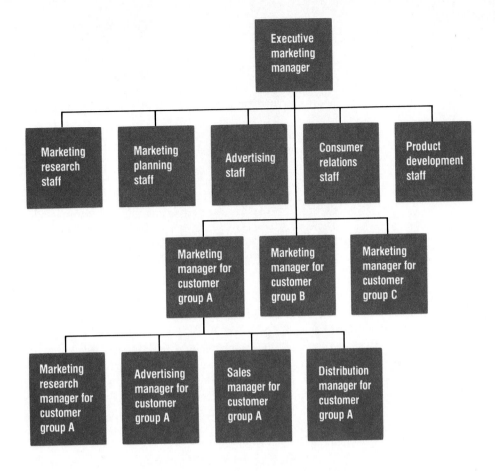

Because the marketing environment is so dynamic, the position of the marketing unit within the organisation has risen during the past twenty-five years. Firms that truly adopt the marketing concept develop a distinct organisational culture—a culture based on a shared set of beliefs that make the customer's needs the pivotal point of a firm's decisions about strategy and operations.[2] Instead of developing products in a vacuum and then trying to convince consumers to buy them, companies using the marketing concept begin with an orientation towards their customers' needs and desires. If the marketing concept serves as a guiding philosophy, the marketing unit will be closely co-ordinated with other functional areas, such as production, finance, and personnel. Figure 19.1 shows the organisation of a marketing unit by types of customers. This form of internal organisation works well for firms having several groups of customers whose needs differ significantly.

Marketing must interact with other functional departments in a number of key areas. It needs to work with manufacturing in determining the volume and variety of the company's products. Those in charge of production rely on marketers for accu-

2. Rohit Despande and Frederick E. Webster, Jr., "Organizational Culture and Marketing: Defining the Research Agenda," *Journal of Marketing*, January 1989, pp. 3–15.

FIGURE 19.2
Organisational chart of a marketing-orientated firm

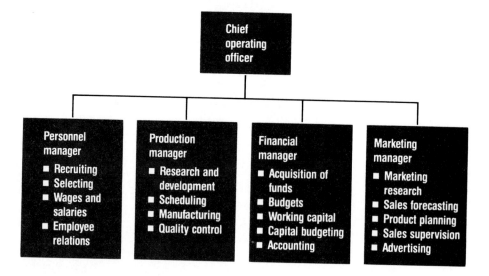

rate sales forecasts. Research and development departments depend heavily on information gathered by marketers about product features and benefits desired by consumers. Decisions made by the physical distribution department hinge on information about the urgency of delivery schedules and cost/service trade-offs.[3] For example, at Honda, all departments have worked together for a long time, whereas at Chrysler the manufacturing group was not even on the product-design committee until 1981. With rapid market segmentation forcing companies to design cars even faster than in the past, co-ordination among engineering, production, marketing, and finance is essential.[4]

A **marketing-orientated organisation** concentrates on discovering what buyers want and providing it in a way that lets the company achieve its objectives. Such a company has an organisational culture that effectively and efficiently produces a sustainable competitive advantage. It focuses on customer analysis, competitor analysis, and the integration of the firm's resources to provide customer value and satisfaction, as well as long-term profits.[5] As Figure 19.2 shows, the marketing manager's position is at the same level as those of the financial, production, and personnel managers. Thus the marketing manager takes part in top-level decision-making. Note, too, that the marketing manager is responsible for a variety of activities. Some of them—sales forecasting and supervision and product planning—would be under the jurisdiction of other functional managers in production- or sales-orientated firms.

Both the links between marketing and other functional areas (such as production, finance, and personnel) and the importance of marketing to management evolve from the firm's basic orientation. Marketing encompasses the greatest number of

3. Michael D. Hutt and Thomas W. Speth, "The Marketing Strategy Center: Diagnosing the Industrial Marketer's Interdisciplinary Role," *Journal of Marketing,* Fall 1984, pp. 16–53.

4. John Bussy, "Manufacturers Strive to Slice Time Needed to Develop Products," *Wall Street Journal,* 23 Feb. 1988, p. 18.

5. John C. Narver and Stanley F. Slater, "Creating a Market-Oriented Business," *The Channel of Communications,* Summer 1989, pp. 5–8.

business functions and occupies an important position when a firm is marketing orientated; it has a limited role when the firm views the role of marketing as simply selling products that the company makes. However, a marketing orientation is not achieved simply by redrawing the organisational chart; management must also adopt and use the marketing orientation as a management philosophy.

■ Major Alternatives for Organising the Marketing Unit

How effectively a firm's marketing management can plan and implement marketing strategies depends on how the marketing unit is organised. Effective organisational planning can give the firm a competitive advantage. The organisational structure of a marketing department establishes the authority relationships among marketing personnel and specifies who is responsible for making certain decisions and performing particular activities. This internal structure is the vehicle for directing marketing activities.

In organising a marketing unit, managers divide the work into specific activities and delegate responsibility and authority for those activities to persons in various positions within the unit. These positions include, for example, the sales manager, the research manager, and the advertising manager.

No single approach to organising a marketing unit works equally well in all businesses. A marketing unit can be organised according to (1) functions, (2) products, (3) regions, or (4) types of customer. The best approach or approaches depend on the number and diversity of the firm's products, the characteristics and needs of the people in the target market, and many other factors.

Firms often use some combination of organisation by functions, products, regions, or customer types. Product features may dictate that the marketing unit be structured by products, whereas customers' characteristics require that it be organised by geographical region or by type of customer. IBM has organised by product types (mainframe and mini computers, personal computers, and so on), but many financial institutions organise by customers because personal banking needs differ from commercial ones. By using more than one type of organisation, a flexible marketing unit can develop and implement marketing plans to match customers' needs precisely. To develop organisational plans that give a firm a competitive advantage, four issues should be considered:

1. Which jobs or levels of jobs need to be added, deleted, or modified? For example, if new products are important to the success of the firm, marketers with strong product-development skills should be added to the organisation.
2. How should reporting relationships be structured to create a competitive advantage? This question is discussed further in the following descriptions of organisational structure.
3. Who should be assigned the primary responsibility for accomplishing work? Identifying primary responsibility explicitly is critical for effective performance appraisal and reward systems.
4. Should any committees or task forces be organised?[6]

Organising by Functions.   Some marketing departments are organised by general marketing functions, such as marketing research, product development, distribution,

6. Dave Ulrich, "Strategic Human Resources Planning: Why and How?" *Human Resources Planning,* 10, No. 1, 1987, pp. 25–57.

sales, advertising, and customer relations. The personnel who direct these functions report directly to the top-level marketing executive. This structure is fairly common because it works well for some businesses with centralised marketing operations, such as Ford and General Motors. In more decentralised firms, such as grocery store chains, functional organisation can raise severe co-ordination problems. The functional approach may, however, suit a large centralised company whose products and customers are neither numerous nor diverse.

Organising by Products. An organisation that produces and markets diverse products may find the functional approach inadequate. The decisions and problems related to a single marketing function for one product may be quite different from those related to the same marketing function for another product. As a result, businesses that produce diverse products sometimes organise their marketing units according to product groups. Organising by product groups gives a firm the flexibility to develop special marketing mixes for different products.

The product management system, which was introduced by Procter & Gamble, operates in about 85 percent of firms in the consumer packaged goods industry. In this structure, the product manager oversees all activities related to his or her assigned product. He or she develops product plans, sees that they are implemented, monitors the results, and takes corrective action as necessary. The product manager is also responsible for acting as a liaison between the firm and its marketing environment, transmitting essential information about the environment to the firm.[7] The product manager may also draw on the resources of specialised staff in the company.

Organising by Regions. A large company that markets products nationally (or internationally) may organise its marketing activities by geographic regions. Managers of marketing functions for each region report to their regional marketing manager; all the regional marketing managers report directly to the executive marketing manager. In the U.S.A., at Frito-Lay (a subsidiary of PepsiCo), for example, four regional marketing vice-presidents who have responsibility for marketing efforts in their regions report to the senior vice-president for marketing at the company's Dallas headquarters. Frito-Lay adopted this regional structure to put more senior management personnel into the field, to get closer to customers, and to enable the company to respond more quickly and efficiently to regional competitors.[8] This form of organisation is especially effective for a firm whose customers' characteristics and needs vary greatly from one region to another.

A firm with marketing managers for each separate region has a complete marketing staff at its headquarters to provide assistance and guidance to regional marketing managers. The major U.K. brewers have national headquarters and marketing centres, often in London, but regional brands, each with a marketing department, in major provincial conurbations. The regional office controls the marketing and promotion of its brand within guidelines specified by head office. However, not all firms organised by regions maintain a full marketing staff at their head offices. Firms that try to penetrate the national market intensively sometimes divide regions into subregions.

7. Steven Lysonski, "A Boundary Theory Investigation of the Product Manager's Role," *Journal of Marketing*, Winter 1985, pp. 26–40.

8. Jennifer Lawrence, "Frito Reorganizes," *Advertising Age*, 26 June 1989, p. 4.

Organising by Type of Customer. Sometimes the marketing unit is organised according to type of customer. This form of internal organisation works well for a firm that has several groups of customers whose needs and problems differ significantly. For example, Bic may sell pens to large retail stores, wholesalers, and institutions. Retailers may want more rapid delivery of small shipments and more personal selling by the producer than do either wholesalers or institutional buyers. Because the marketing decisions and activities required for these two groups of customers differ considerably, the company may find it efficient to organise its marketing unit by type of customer.

In an organisation with a marketing department broken down by customer group, the marketing manager for each group reports to the top-level marketing executive and directs most marketing activities for that group. A marketing manager controls all activities needed to market products to a specific customer group.

IMPLEMENTING MARKETING ACTIVITIES

The planning and organising functions provide purpose, direction, and structure for marketing activities. However, until marketing managers implement the marketing plan, exchanges cannot occur. In fact, organisers of marketing activities can become overly concerned with planning strategy while neglecting implementation. Before John Harvey Jones joined ICI, some analysts believed that the management's preoccupation with procedures and plans caused the business to suffer. Obviously, implementation of plans is important to the success of any organisation.[9] Proper implementation of a marketing plan depends on internal marketing to employees, the motivation of personnel who perform marketing activities, effective communication within the marketing organisation, and the co-ordination of marketing activities. In Figure 19.3, Aerospatiale promotes its teamwork philosophy in business with other countries and internally.

■ **Internal Marketing**

Marketing activities cannot be effectively implemented without the co-operation of employees. Employees are the essential ingredient in increasing productivity, providing customer service, and beating the competition. Thus, in addition to marketing activities targeted at external customers, firms use internal marketing to attract, motivate, and retain qualified internal customers (employees) by designing internal products (jobs) that satisfy employees' wants and needs.[10] **Internal marketing** refers to the managerial actions necessary to make all members of the marketing organisation understand and accept their respective roles in implementing the marketing strategy. This means that everyone, from the chairman of the company down to the manual workers on the shop-floor, must understand the role they play in carrying out their jobs and implementing the marketing strategy. Everyone must do his or her part to ensure that customers are satisfied. All personnel within the firm, both marketers and those who perform other functions, must recognise the tenet of customer orientation and service that underlies the marketing concept. Customer

9. Richard Gibson and Robert Johnson, "Why Pillsbury's Chief from the 70's Is Again Taking Firm's Helm," *Wall Street Journal*, 1 Mar. 1988, p. 25.

10. James H. Donnelly, Jr., Leonard L. Berry, and Thomas O. Thompson, *Marketing Financial Services* (Homewood, Ill.: Dow Jones-Irwin, 1985), pp. 229–245.

FIGURE 19.3
*Implementing plans
involves co-operation.*
Aerospatiale's teamwork
message supports the
idea that co-operation is
needed to implement
marketing strategies.

SOURCE: Courtesy of Aerospatiale

orientation is fostered by training and education and by keeping the lines of communication open throughout the firm.

Like external marketing activities, internal marketing may involve market segmentation, product development, research, distribution, and even public relations and sales promotion.[11] For example, an organisation may sponsor sales contests to encourage sales personnel to boost their selling efforts. Some companies, such as IBM, encourage employees to work for their companies' industrial customers for a period of time, often while continuing to receive their regular salaries. This helps the employees (and ultimately the company) to understand better the customer's needs and problems, allows them to learn valuable new skills, and heightens their enthusiasm for their regular jobs. The ultimate result is more satisfied employees and improved customer relations.

■ **Motivating Marketing Personnel**

An important element in implementing the marketing plan, and in internal marketing, is motivating marketing personnel to perform effectively. People work to satisfy physical, psychological, and social needs. To motivate marketing personnel, manag-

11. Sybil F. Stershic, "Internal Marketing Campaign Reinforces Service Goals," *Marketing News,* 31 July 1989, p. 11.

ers must discover their employees' needs and then develop motivational methods that help them satisfy those needs. It is crucial that the plan for motivating employees be fair, ethical, and well understood by them. Additionally, rewards to employees must be tied to organisational goals. In general, to improve employee motivation, companies need to find out what workers think, how they feel, and what they want. Some of this information can be obtained from an employee attitude survey. A business organisation can motivate its workers by directly linking pay with performance, informing workers how their performance affects department and corporate results, following through with appropriate compensation, promoting or implementing a flexible benefits programme, and adopting a participative management approach.[12]

Consider the following example. Suppose a salesperson can sell product A or B to a particular customer, but not both products. Product A sells for £200,000 and contributes £20,000 to the company's profit margin. Product B sells for £60,000 and has a contribution margin of £40,000. If the salesperson receives a commission of 3 percent of sales, he or she would obviously prefer to sell product A, even though the sale of product B contributes more to the company's profits. If the salesperson's commission was based on contribution margin instead of sales and the firm's goal was to maximise profits, both the firm and the salesperson would benefit more from the sale of product B.[13] By tying rewards to organisational goals, the company encourages behaviour that meets organisational goals.

Besides tying rewards to organisational goals, managers must use different motivational tools to motivate individuals, based on an individual's value system. For example, some employees value recognition more than a slight pay increase. Managers can reward employees with money, plus additional fringe benefits, prestige or recognition, or even non-financial rewards such as job autonomy, skill variety, task significance, and increased feedback. A survey of Fortune 1000 companies found that "the majority of organisations feel that they get more for their money through non-cash awards, if given in addition to a basic compensation plan".[14]

■ Communicating Within the Marketing Unit

With good communication, marketing managers can motivate personnel and co-ordinate their efforts. Marketing managers must be able to communicate with the firm's high-level management to ensure that marketing activities are consistent with the company's overall goals. Communication with top-level executives keeps marketing managers aware of the company's overall plans and achievements. It also guides what the marketing unit is to do and how its activities are to be integrated with those of other departments—such as finance, production, or personnel—with whose management the marketing manager must also communicate to co-ordinate marketing efforts. For example, marketing personnel must work with the production staff to help design products that customers want. To direct marketing activities, marketing managers must communicate with marketing personnel at the operations level, such as sales and advertising personnel, researchers, wholesalers, retailers, and package designers.

12. David C. Jones, "Motivation the Catalyst in Profit Formula," *National Underwriter,* 13 July 1987, pp. 10, 13.

13. The example is adapted from Edward B. Deakin and Michael W. Maher, *Cost Accounting,* 2nd ed. (Homewood, Ill.: Irwin, 1987), pp. 838–839.

14. Jerry McAdams, "Rewarding Sales and Marketing Performance," *Management Review,* April 1987, p. 36.

FIGURE 19.4 *Ford's new Scorpio is promoted in many media.*
The Ford message is familiar because it is spread through the mass media in a co-ordinated way.

To facilitate communication, marketing managers should establish an information system within the marketing unit. The marketing information system (discussed in Chapter 6) should allow for easy communication among marketing managers, sales managers, and sales personnel. Marketers need an information system to support a variety of activities, such as planning, budgeting, sales analyses, performance evaluations, and the preparation of reports. An information system should also expedite communications with other departments in the organisation and minimise destructive competition among departments for organisational resources.

Co-ordinating Marketing Activities

Because of job specialisation and differences related to marketing activities, marketing managers must synchronise individuals' actions to achieve marketing objectives. In addition, they must work closely with managers in research and development, production, finance, accounting, and personnel to see that marketing activities mesh with other functions of the firm. Marketing managers must co-ordinate the activities of marketing staff within the firm and integrate those activities with the marketing efforts of external organisations—advertising agencies, resellers (wholesalers and retailers), researchers, and shippers, among others. In Figure 19.4, Ford promotes

...different ending.

The new Scorpio saloon.

FIGURE 19.4 *continued*

SOURCE: Ford Motor Company Ltd. Advertisement courtesy of Ogilvy & Mather

its new Scorpio in a magazine advert. Co-ordinated efforts make this message evident to customers in TV commercials and other media. Marketing managers can improve co-ordination by using internal marketing activities to make each employee aware of how his or her job relates to others and how his or her actions contribute to the achievement of marketing plans.

CONTROLLING MARKETING ACTIVITIES

To achieve marketing objectives as well as general organisational objectives, marketing managers must effectively control marketing efforts. The **marketing control process** consists of establishing performance standards, evaluating actual performance by comparing it with established standards, and reducing the differences between desired and actual performance. Dunkin' Donuts, for example, has developed a programme to ensure consistency throughout its franchises. Dunkin' Donuts controls the quality of operations in its franchised units by having franchisees attend Dunkin' Donuts University. Owners and managers of Dunkin' Donuts are required to take a six-week training course, covering everything from customer relations and marketing to production, including a test of making 140 dozen doughnuts in 8 hours. As part of the test, an instructor randomly selects 6 of the 1,680 doughnuts made to ascertain that they weigh around 350 grams and measure just under 20 centimetres when stacked. The Dunkin' Donuts University was opened to guarantee uniformity in all aspects of the business operations throughout the 1,700 franchise units.[15] The Coca-Cola Company's efforts to implement and control its marketing strategy are discussed in Marketing Update 19.1.

Although the control function is a fundamental management activity, it has received little attention in marketing. There are both formal and informal control systems in organisations. The formal marketing control process, as mentioned before, involves performance standards, evaluation of actual performance, and corrective action to remedy shortfalls (see Figure 19.5). The informal control process, however, involves self-control, social or group control, and cultural control through acceptance of a firm's value system. Which type of control system dominates depends on the environmental context of the firm.[16] We next discuss these steps in the control process and consider the major problems they involve.

◼ Establishing Performance Standards

Planning and controlling are closely linked because plans include statements about what is to be accomplished. For purposes of control, these statements function as performance standards. A **performance standard** is an expected level of performance against which actual performance can be compared. Examples of performance standards might be the reduction of customers' complaints by 20 percent, a monthly sales quota of £150,000, or a 10 percent increase per month in new customer accounts. Marketing Update 19.2 describes the Competitiveness Achievement Plans at Lucas, in which performance standards were set according to the actual performance of competitors. Performance standards are also given in the form of budget accounts; that is, marketers are expected to achieve a certain objective without spending more than a given amount of resources. As stated earlier, performance standards should be tied to organisational goals. Performance standards can relate to product quality.

◼ Evaluating Actual Performance

To compare actual performance with performance standards, marketing managers must know what marketers within the company are doing and have information about the activities of external organisations that provide the firm with marketing assistance. (We discuss specific methods for assessing actual performance later in this chapter.) Information is required about the activities of marketing personnel at the operations level and at various marketing management levels. Most businesses obtain marketing assistance from one or more external individuals or organisations, such as advertising agencies, middlemen, marketing research firms, and consultants. To maximise benefits from external sources, a firm's marketing control process must monitor their activities. Although it may be difficult to obtain the necessary information, it is impossible to measure actual performance without it.

Records of actual performance are compared with performance standards to determine whether and how much of a discrepancy exists. For example, a salesperson's actual sales are compared with her or his sales quota. If there is a significant negative discrepancy, the marketing manager takes corrective action.

15. "Higher Education in Doughnuts," *Ann Arbor News,* 9 Mar. 1988, p. B7.

16. Bernard J. Jaworski, "Toward a Theory of Marketing Control: Environmental Context, Control Types, and Consequences," *Journal of Marketing,* July 1988, pp. 23–39.

COCA-COLA MANAGES INTERNATIONAL BOTTLERS

Coca-Cola may seem as American as apple pie, but the Coca-Cola name is one of the most recognised brands in the world. The company sells roughly 47 percent of all the soft drinks consumed globally, more than twice as much as PepsiCo, its nearest rival. In 1989, 80 percent of Coke's operating earnings came from foreign markets, up from 50 percent in 1985. Amazing as it may seem, more Coca-Cola is sold in Japan each year than in the United States.

Coke's international success did not happen overnight. When most American companies were only thinking about global marketing strategies, Coke was implementing them. First, Coke carefully guided and set standards for its overseas bottling partners. To maintain control of its overseas bottlers, Coke generally invested in them, spending more than $1 billion in joint bottling ventures worldwide in the 1980s. If bottlers fail to perform as expected, Coke reviews their contracts and takes corrective action, sometimes resulting in ownership of its own bottling plants. When French bottler Pernod Richard S.A. disagreed with Coke over how to revive slow soft-drink sales in France, the company took control to solve the problem.

The second part of Coke's international strategy consists of aggressive advertising, packaging, and marketing to foreign consumers. Sometimes being "The Real Thing" isn't enough to ensure success. In many countries, such as Indonesia, Coke attempted to change consumer tastes by incorporating local tastes into the Coca-Cola formula. Thus, by buying strawberry, pineapple, and banana-flavoured soft drinks, Indonesians became accustomed to carbonated beverages.

By aggressively marketing to foreign consumers, Coke created markets with a high probability of success. It is this high probability of success that allows Coke to be firm but fair with its bottlers. At times, Coke's international bottlers may feel pressure to achieve the company's high standards. However, the dominance of the Coca-Cola brand in most foreign markets all but guarantees success for Coke and its bottlers. Until its competitors move to adopt global marketing strategies, Coca-Cola will remain not just "The Real Thing" but "The Only Thing" in many foreign markets.

SOURCES: "How Coke Markets to the World," *Journal of Business Strategy,* Sept.-Oct. 1988, pp. 4–7; Michael J. McCarthy, "The Real Thing: As a Global Marketer, Coke Excels by Being Tough and Consistent," *Wall Street Journal,* 19 Dec. 1989, pp. A1, A6; Robert McGough, "No More Mr. Nice Guy," *Financial World,* 25 July 1989, pp. 30–34.

FIGURE 19.5
The marketing control process

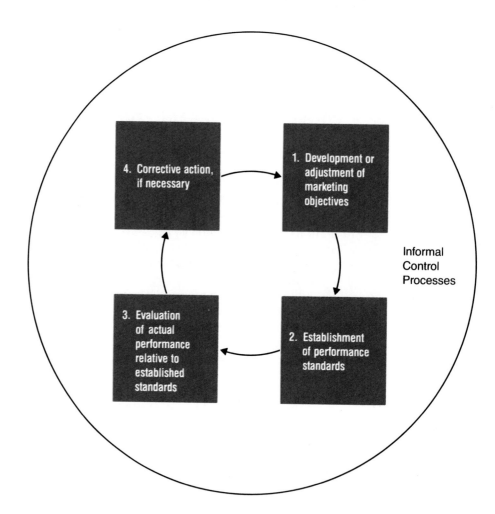

Informal
Control
Processes

■ **Taking**
Corrective Action

Marketing managers have several options for reducing a discrepancy between established performance standards and actual performance. They can take steps to improve actual performance, can reduce or totally change the performance standard, or do both. Changes in actual performance may require the marketing manager to use better methods of motivating marketing personnel or find more effective techniques for co-ordinating marketing efforts.

Sometimes performance standards are unrealistic when they are written. In other cases, changes in the marketing environment make them unrealistic. For example, a company's annual sales goal may become unrealistic if several aggressive competitors enter the firm's market. In fact, changes in the marketing environment may force managers to change their marketing strategy completely.

■ **Requirements**
for an Effective
Control Process

A marketing manager should consider several requirements in creating and maintaining effective control processes.[17] Effective control hinges on the quantity and quality of information available to the marketing manager and the speed at which it

17. See Theo Haimann, William G. Scott, and Patrick E. Connor, *Management,* 5th ed. (Boston: Houghton Mifflin, 1985), pp. 478–492.

LUCAS: COMPETITIVENESS ACHIEVEMENT PLANS

Lucas is a large, British-owned, engineering multinational. Its product range includes goods for the automotive and aerospace industries. Traditionally a cornerstone of British industry, the company was dogged through the 1960s and 1970s by a poor reputation and the collapse in 1980 of the U.K. automotive market. This was the background for management's introduction in 1984 of a system known as "Competitiveness Achievement Plans" or CAP for short. The philosophy was simple. Each business manager was required to identify and attempt to match the performance of his or her best U.K. or international rival. Failure would bring the threat of factory closure.

Lucas's brake factory at Cwmbran in Wales, built in 1947, is one of the main beneficiaries of the CAP system. The last four years have seen a change from mainly manual to automated assembly and from traditional production lines to "modules", where small groups of workers are responsible for the manufacture of a particular product. The benefits of this form of product ownership can be measured in higher worker morale and better standards of workmanship.

Change is on-going, being particularly focused on quality improvement, with the introduction of quality circles in 1987 and a "total-quality" programme in 1988. Generally, the new regime has been accepted well in the factory. Although some managers feel threatened by the shifting emphasis towards the shop-floor, many general and skilled workers are positive about working more closely with management. Long-term success, it seems, is linked to the ability of Lucas management to balance continuing change with keeping the work-force happy.

SOURCES: David Bowen, "How Lucas Learnt to Live with the Rest of the World," *Independent on Sunday,* 8 July 1990; "U.K.: Lucas Is Intent on Establishing Itself as a World-force in the Supply of Automotive Electronics," *ENG,* 26 Oct. 1989, p. 41; Lucas, *Annual Report,* 1989.

is received. The control process should be designed so that the flow of information is rapid enough to allow the marketing manager to quickly detect differences between actual and planned levels of performance. A single control procedure is not suitable for all types of marketing activities, and internal and environmental changes affect an organisation's activities. Therefore, control procedures should be flexible enough to adjust to both varied activities and changes in the organisation's situation. For the control process to be usable, its costs must be low relative to the costs that would arise if controls were lacking. Finally, the control process should be designed so that both managers and subordinates can understand it.

■ **Problems in Controlling Marketing Activities**

When marketing managers attempt to control marketing activities, they frequently run into several problems. Often the information required to control marketing activities is unavailable or is only available at a high cost. Even though marketing controls should be flexible enough to allow for environmental changes, the frequency, intensity, and unpredictability of such changes may hamper effective control. In addition, the time lag between marketing activities and their effects limits a marketing manager's ability to measure the effectiveness of marketing activities.

Consider the problems of demand fluctuation in the video games industry. By failing to control the number of video game products offered, Nintendo (which controls 70 percent of the U.S. market and is at the forefront in the U.K. market), Atari (16 percent of the U.S. market), and Sega (10 percent of the U.S. market) glutted the market with so many video game titles that consumers were confused and disappointed with the numerous look-alike products. Companies are avoiding past mistakes by carefully analysing the success of video games and deleting older games that are no longer profitable. For example, Nintendo withdrew eighteen of its thirty-six games to make room for new-product introductions. This careful analysis and control of product offerings has helped home video games make a comeback from being a spectacular but short-lived fad of the early 1980s.[18]

Because marketing and other business activities overlap, marketing managers cannot determine the precise cost of marketing activities. Without an accurate measure of marketing costs, it is difficult to know if the effects of marketing activities are worth their expense. Finally, marketing control may be difficult because it is very hard to develop exact performance standards for marketing personnel.

METHODS OF EVALUATING PERFORMANCE

There are specific methods for assessing and improving the effectiveness of a marketing strategy. A marketer should state in the marketing plan what a marketing strategy is supposed to accomplish. These statements should set forth performance standards, which usually are stated in terms of profits, sales, or costs. Actual performance must be measured in similar terms so that comparisons are possible. This section describes sales analysis and cost analysis, two general ways of evaluating the actual performance of marketing strategies.

■ **Sales Analysis**

Sales analysis uses sales figures to evaluate a firm's current performance. It is probably the most common method of evaluation because sales data partially reflect

18. Jeffrey A. Tannenbaum, "Video Games Revive—and Makers Hope This Time the Fad Will Last," *Wall Street Journal,* 8 Mar. 1988, p. 35.

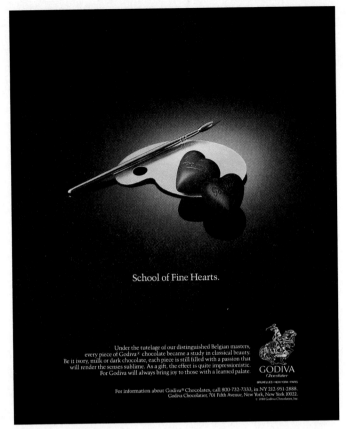

School of Fine Hearts.

Under the tutelage of our distinguished Belgian masters, every piece of Godiva® chocolate became a study in classical beauty. Be it ivory, milk or dark chocolate, each piece is still filled with a passion that will render the senses sublime. As a gift, the effect is quite impressionistic. For Godiva will always bring joy to those with a learned palate.

GODIVA
Chocolatier
BRUXELLES · NEW YORK · PARIS

For information about Godiva® Chocolates, call 800-732-7333, in NY 212-951-2888. Godiva Chocolatier, 701 Fifth Avenue, New York, New York 10022.
© 1998 Godiva Chocolatier, Inc.

SOURCE: Godiva Chocolatier

the target market's reactions to a marketing mix and often are readily available, at least in aggregate form.

Marketers use current sales data to monitor the impact of current marketing efforts. For example, Godiva (Figure 19.6) attempts to measure the sales of its chocolates during selected holiday seasons. However, that information alone is not enough. To provide useful analyses, current sales data must be compared with forecast sales, industry sales, specific competitors' sales, or the costs incurred to achieve the sales volume. For example, knowing that a department store attained a £600,000 sales volume this year does not tell management whether its marketing strategy has been successful. However, if managers know that expected sales were £550,000, then they are in a better position to determine the effectiveness of the firm's marketing efforts. In addition, if they know that the marketing costs needed to achieve the £600,000 volume were 12 percent less than budgeted, they are in an even better position to analyse their marketing strategy precisely.

Types of Sales Measurements. Although sales may be measured in several ways, the basic unit of measurement is the sales transaction. A sales transaction results in a customer order for a specified quantity of an organisation's product sold under specified terms by a particular salesperson or sales group on a certain date. Many organisations record these bits of information about their transactions. With such a record, a company can analyse sales in terms of cash volume or market share.

CHAPTER 19   Implementing Strategies and Measuring Performance   **599**

TABLE 19.1
Top ten U.K. beauty care brands, 1989[a]

POSITION	BRAND	OWNER	SALES (£m)
1	Estée Lauder	Estée Lauder	over 100
2	Yves St Laurent	Cerus	over 100
3	L'Oréal	L'Oréal	over 100
4	Elizabeth Arden	Eli Lilly	70–100
5	Chanel	Chanel	70–100
6	Clinique	Estée Lauder	70–100
7	Christian Dior	LVMH	70–100
8	Lancôme	L'Oréal	40–70
9	Aramis	Estée Lauder	40–70
10	Helena Rubinstein	L'Oréal	40–70

[a] Sector defined as: make-up, female and male fragrance, consultant skin care

SOURCE: NCH Promotional Services. Reprinted by permission of Nielsen Marketing Services, Oxford, U.K.

Firms frequently use cash volume sales analysis because the pound is a common denominator of sales, costs, and profits (see Table 19.1). However, price increases and decreases affect total sales figures. For example, if a company increased its prices by 10 percent this year and its sales volume is 10 percent greater than last year, it has not experienced any increase in unit sales. A marketing manager who uses cash volume analysis should factor out the effects of price changes.

A firm's market share is the firm's sales of a product stated as a percentage of industry sales of that product. For example, KP, Golden Wonder, Smiths, and Walkers account for around 70 percent of the U.K. savoury snacks market. In the carbonated-drinks sector, Coca-Cola has a leading 16 percent share by volume.[19] Market share analysis lets a company compare its marketing strategy with competitors' strategies. The primary reason for using market share analysis is to estimate whether sales changes have resulted from the firm's marketing strategy or from uncontrollable environmental forces. When a company's sales volume declines but its share of the market stays the same, the marketer can assume that industry sales declined (because of some uncontrollable factors) and that this decline was reflected in the firm's sales. However, if a company experiences a decline in both sales and market share, it should consider the possibility that its marketing strategy is not effective.

Even though market share analysis can be helpful in evaluating the performance of a marketing strategy, the user must interpret results cautiously. When attributing a sales decline to uncontrollable factors, a marketer must keep in mind that such factors do not affect all firms in the industry equally. Not all firms in an industry have the same objectives, and some change objectives from one year to the next. Changes in the objectives of one company can affect the market shares of one or all companies in that industry. For example, if a competitor significantly increases promotional efforts or drastically reduces prices to increase market share, then a company could lose market share despite a well-designed marketing strategy. Within an industry, the entrance of new firms or the demise of established ones also affects

19. "Carbonates and Concentrates," *Market Intelligence,* January 1990, pp. 2.10–2.17.

a specific firm's market share, and market share analysts should attempt to account for these effects. Kentucky Fried Chicken, for example, probably re-evaluated its marketing strategies when McDonald's introduced its own fried chicken product.

Bases for Sales Analysis.   Whether it is based on sales volume or market share, sales analysis can be performed on aggregate sales figures or on disaggregated data. Aggregate sales analysis provides an overview of current sales. Although helpful, aggregate sales analysis is often insufficient because it does not bring to light sales variations within the aggregate. It is not uncommon for a marketer to find that a large proportion of aggregate sales comes from a small number of products, geographic areas, or customers. (This is sometimes called the "iceberg principle" because only a small part of an iceberg is visible above the water.) To find such disparities, total sales figures usually are broken down by geographic unit, salesperson, product, customer type, or a combination of these categories.

In sales analysis by geographic unit, sales data can be classified by city, county, region, country, or any other geographic designation for which a marketer collects sales information. Actual sales in a geographic unit can be compared with sales in a similar geographic unit, with last year's sales, or with an estimated market potential for the area. For example, if a firm finds that 18 percent of its sales are coming from an area that represents only 8 percent of the potential sales for the product, then it can be assumed that the marketing strategy is successful in that geographic unit.

Because of the cost associated with hiring and maintaining a sales force, businesses commonly analyse sales by salesperson to determine the contribution each salesperson makes. Performance standards for each salesperson are often set in terms of sales quotas for a given time period. Evaluation of actual performance is accomplished by comparing a salesperson's current sales with a pre-established quota or some other standard, such as the previous period's sales. If actual sales meet or exceed the standard and the sales representative has not incurred costs above those budgeted, that person's efforts are acceptable.

Sales analysis is often performed according to product group or specific product item. Marketers break down their aggregate sales figures by product to determine the proportion that each contributed to total sales. Columbia Pictures, for example, might break down its total sales figures by box office figures for each film produced. A firm usually sets a sales volume objective—and sometimes a market share objective—for each product item or product group, and sales analysis by product is the only way to measure such objectives. A marketer can compare the breakdown of current sales by product with those of previous years. In addition, within industries for which sales data by product are available, a firm's sales by product type can be compared with industry averages. To gain an accurate picture of where sales of specific products are occurring, marketers sometimes combine sales analysis by product with sales analysis by geographic area or salesperson.

Analyses based on customers are usually broken down by type of customer. Customers can be classified by the way they use a firm's products, their distribution level (producer, wholesaler, retailer), their size, the size of orders, or other characteristics. Sales analysis by customer type lets a firm ascertain whether its marketing resources are allocated in a way that achieves the greatest productivity. For example, sales analysis by type of customer may reveal that 60 percent of the sales force is serving a group that makes only 15 percent of total sales.

A considerable amount of information is needed for sales analyses, especially if disaggregated analyses are desired. The marketer must develop an operational system for collecting sales information; obviously, the effectiveness of the system for collecting sales information largely determines a company's ability to develop useful sales analyses.

■ Marketing Cost Analysis

Although sales analysis is critical for evaluating the effectiveness of a marketing strategy, it gives only part of the picture. A marketing strategy that successfully generates sales may also be extremely costly. To get a complete picture, a firm must know the marketing costs associated with using a given strategy to achieve a certain sales level. **Marketing cost analysis** breaks down and classifies costs to determine which are associated with specific marketing activities. By comparing costs of previous marketing activities with results generated, a marketer can better allocate the firm's marketing resources in the future. Marketing cost analysis lets a company evaluate the effectiveness of an on-going or recent marketing strategy by comparing sales achieved and costs incurred. By pinpointing exactly where a company is experiencing high costs, this form of analysis can help isolate profitable or unprofitable customer segments, products, or geographic areas.

For example, the market share of Komatsu, a Japanese construction equipment manufacturer, was declining in the United States when prices increased because of the high yen value. Komatsu thus developed an equal joint venture with Dresser Industries, making it the second largest company in this industry. The joint venture with Dresser allowed Komatsu to shift a large amount of its final assembly to the United States, to Dresser plants that had been running at 50 percent capacity. By using Dresser's unused capacity and existing U.S. plants, Komatsu avoided the start-up costs of new construction and gained an immediate manufacturing presence in the United States.[20] This cost-control tactic should enable Komatsu to use price more effectively as a marketing variable to compete with number-one Caterpillar Tractor Co.

In some organisations, personnel in other functional areas—such as production or accounting—see marketers as primarily concerned with generating sales, regardless of the costs incurred. By conducting cost analyses, marketers can counter this criticism and put themselves in a better position to demonstrate how marketing activities contribute to generating profits. Even though hiring a sports figure such as John McEnroe (see Figure 19.7) is costly, in many sectors sales goals cannot be reached without large expenditures for promotion. Many advertisers believe that using celebrities helps to increase sales. Research shows that the public are good at identifying which personalities are linked to advertised brands (See Table 19.2). Ultimately, cost analysis should show if promotion costs are effective in increasing sales.

Determining Marketing Costs.

The task of determining marketing costs is often complex and difficult. Simply ascertaining the costs associated with marketing a product is rarely adequate. Marketers must usually determine the marketing costs of serving specific geographical areas, market segments, or even specific customers.

A first step in determining the costs is to examine accounting records. Most accounting systems classify costs into **natural accounts**—such as rent, salaries,

---

20. Kevin Kelly and Neil Gross, "A Weakened Komatsu Tries to Come Back Swinging," *Business Week*, 22 Feb. 1988, p. 48.

FIGURE 19.7 *Marketing costs generate sales.*
Hiring celebrities to promote a product is usually effective, though often costly.

SOURCE: Courtesy of Canon U.K. Limited/Monitor Advertising & Design Limited

office supplies, and utilities—which are based on how the money was actually spent. Unfortunately, many natural accounts do not help explain what marketing functions were performed through the expenditure of those funds. It does little good, for example, to know that £80,000 is spent for rent each year. The analyst has no way of knowing whether the money is spent for the rental of production, storage, or sales facilities. Therefore, marketing cost analysis usually requires that some of the costs in natural accounts be reclassified into **marketing function accounts**, which indicate the function performed through the expenditure of funds. Common marketing function accounts are transport, storage, order processing, selling, advertising, sales promotion, marketing research, and customer credit.

Natural accounts can be reclassified into marketing function accounts as shown in the simplified example in Table 19.3. Note that a few natural accounts, such as advertising, can be reclassified easily into functional accounts because they do not have to be split across several accounts. For most of the natural accounts, however, marketers must develop criteria for assigning them to the various functional accounts. For example, the number of square feet of floor space used was the criterion for dividing the rental costs in Table 19.3 into functional accounts. In some in-

TABLE 19.2
Results of a survey testing correct association of personalities with brands

PERSONALITY/ACCOUNT	AGENCY	PERCENTAGE CORRECT
1 Maureen Lipman—British Telecom	JWT	76
2 Daley Thompson—Lucozade	O&M	67
3 Paul Hogan—Foster's	BMPDDB Needham	63
4 Nannette Newman—Fairy Liquid	Grey	50
5 Dudley Moore—Tesco	LH-S	47
6 Billy Connolly—Kaliber	FCO	36
7 Nigel Havers/Jan Francis—Lloyds	LH-S	35
8 Richard Briers/Penelope Wilton — Nescafé	McCanns	32
9 Burt Lancaster—Foster's	BMPDDB Needham	31
10 John Barnes—Lucozade Sport	O&M	30
11 John Cleese—Schweppes	Saatchis	25
12 Warren Mitchell—British Gas	Y&R	22
13 Mel Smith/Griff Rhys Jones—Nationwide Anglia	Leagas Delaney	21
14 Twiggy—Silvikrin	O&M	20
15 Stephen Fry/Hugh Laurie—Alliance & Leicester	BMPDDB Needham	19

SOURCE: "Personalities Prove There Is Life After Death," *Marketing,* 8 February 1990, p. 7.

stances, a specific marketing cost is incurred to perform several functions. A packaging cost, for example, could be considered a production function, a distribution function, a promotional function, or all three. The marketing cost analyst must reclassify such costs across multiple functions.

Three broad categories are used in marketing cost analysis: direct costs, traceable common costs, and non-traceable common costs. **Direct costs** are directly attributable to the performance of marketing functions. For example, sales force salaries might be allocated to the cost of selling a specific product item, selling in a specific geographic area, or selling to a particular customer. **Traceable common costs** can be allocated indirectly, using one or several criteria, to the functions that they support. For example, if the firm spends £80,000 annually to rent space for production, storage, and selling, the rental costs of storage could be determined on the basis of cost per square foot used for storage. **Non-traceable common costs** cannot be assigned according to any logical criteria and thus are assignable only on an arbitrary basis. Interest, taxes, and the salaries of top management are non-traceable common costs.

The manner of dealing with these three categories of costs depends on whether the analyst uses a full-cost or a direct-cost approach. When a **full-cost approach** is used, cost analysis includes direct costs, traceable common costs, and non-traceable common costs. Proponents of this approach claim that if an accurate profit picture is desired, all costs must be included in the analysis. However, opponents point out that full costing does not yield actual costs because non-traceable common costs are determined by arbitrary criteria. With different criteria, the full-costing approach

TABLE 19.3 *Reclassification of natural accounts into functional accounts*

PROFIT AND LOSS STATEMENT

				FUNCTIONAL ACCOUNTS			
		ADVERTISING	PERSONAL SELLING	TRANSPORT	STORAGE	MARKETING RESEARCH	NON-MARKETING
Sales	£250,000						
Cost of goods sold	45,000						
Gross profit	205,000						
Expenses (natural accounts)							
Rent	£ 14,000		£ 7,000		£6,000		£ 1,000
Salaries	72,000	£12,000	32,000	£7,000		£1,000	20,000
Supplies	4,000	1,500	1,000			1,000	500
Advertising	16,000	16,000					
Freight	4,000			2,000			2,000
Taxes	2,000				200		1,800
Insurance	1,000				600		400
Interest	3,000						3,000
Bad debts	6,000						6,000
Total	£ 122,000	£ 29,500	£ 40,000	£9,000	£6,800	£2,000	£34,700
Net profit	£ 83,000						

yields different results. A cost-conscious operating unit can be discouraged if numerous costs are assigned to it arbitrarily. To eliminate such problems, the **direct-cost approach**, which includes direct costs and traceable common costs but not non-traceable common costs, is used. Opponents say that this approach is not accurate because it omits one cost category.

Methods of Marketing Cost Analysis.   Marketers can use several methods to analyse costs. The methods vary in their precision. This section examines three cost-analysis methods—analysis of natural accounts; analysis of functional accounts; and cost analysis by product, geographic area, or customer.

Marketers sometimes can determine marketing costs by performing an analysis of natural accounts. The precision of this method depends on how detailed the firm's accounts are. For example, if accounting records contain separate accounts for production wages, sales-force wages, and executive salaries, the analysis can be more precise than if all wages and salaries are lumped into a single account. An analysis of natural accounts is more meaningful, and thus more useful, when current cost data can be compared with those of previous periods or with average cost figures for the entire industry. Cost analysis of natural accounts frequently treats costs as percentages of sales. The periodic use of cost-to-sales ratios lets a marketer ascertain cost fluctuations quickly.

As indicated earlier, the analysis of natural accounts may not shed much light on the cost of marketing activities. In such cases, natural accounts must be reclassified into marketing function accounts for analysis. Whether certain natural accounts are reclassified into functional accounts and what criteria are used to reclassify them will depend to some degree on whether the analyst is using direct costing or full costing. After natural accounts have been reclassified into functional accounts, the cost of each function is determined by summing the costs in each functional account. Once the costs of these marketing functions have been determined, the analyst is ready to compare the resulting figures with budgeted costs, sales analysis data, cost data from earlier operating periods, or perhaps average industry cost figures, if these are available.

Although marketers ordinarily get a more detailed picture of marketing costs by analysing functional accounts than by analysing natural accounts, some firms need an even more precise cost analysis. The need is especially great if the firms sell several types of products, sell in multiple geographic areas, or sell to a wide variety of customers. Activities vary in marketing different products in specific geographic locations to certain customer groups. Therefore the costs of these activities also vary. By analysing the functional costs of specific product groups, geographic areas, or customer groups, a marketer can find out which of these marketing entities are the most cost effective to serve. In Table 19.4, the functional costs derived in Table 19.3 are allocated to specific product categories.

A similar type of analysis could be performed for geographic areas or for specific customer groups. The criteria used to allocate the functional accounts must be developed so as to yield results that are as accurate as possible. Use of faulty criteria is likely to yield inaccurate cost estimates that in turn lead to less effective control of marketing strategies. Marketers determine the marketing costs for various product categories, geographic areas, or customer groups and then compare them with sales. This analysis lets them evaluate the effectiveness of the firm's marketing strategy or strategies.

TABLE 19.4 *Functional accounts divided into product group costs*

FUNCTIONAL ACCOUNTS		PRODUCT GROUPS		
		A	B	C
Advertising	£29,500	£14,000	£ 8,000	£ 7,500
Personal selling	40,000	18,000	10,000	12,000
Transport	9,000	5,000	2,000	2,000
Storage	6,800	1,800	2,000	3,000
Marketing research	2,000		1,000	1,000
Total	**£87,300**	**£38,800**	**£23,000**	**£25,500**

THE MARKETING AUDIT

A **marketing audit** is a systematic examination of the marketing group's objectives, strategies, organisation, and performance. Its primary purpose is to identify weaknesses in on-going marketing operations and plan the necessary improvements to correct these weaknesses. The marketing audit does not concern itself with the firm's marketing position because that is the purpose of the firm's marketing plan. Rather, the marketing audit evaluates how effectively the marketing organisation performed its assigned functions.[21]

Like an accounting or financial audit, a marketing audit should be conducted regularly instead of just when performance control mechanisms show that the system is out of control. The marketing audit is not a control process to be used only during a crisis, although a business in trouble may use it to isolate problems and generate solutions.

A marketing audit may be specific and focus on one or a few marketing activities, or it may be comprehensive and encompass all of a company's marketing activities. Table 19.5 lists many possible dimensions of a marketing audit. An audit might deal with only a few of these areas, or it might include them all. Its scope depends on the costs involved, the target markets served, the structure of the marketing mix, and environmental conditions. The results of the audit can be used to reallocate marketing effort and to re-examine marketing opportunities. For example, after the rise in consumer interest in buying unleaded petrol during the 1980s, the oil companies realised that many customers were still using leaded fuel, because the engine performance of their cars was better. Launching the new "super" unleaded brands late in the 1980s helped to counter these problems.

The marketing audit should aid evaluation by doing the following:

1. Describing current activities and results related to sales, costs, prices, profits, and other performance feedback
2. Gathering information about customers, competition, and environmental developments that may affect the marketing strategy

21. William A. Band, "A Marketing Audit Provides an Opportunity for Improvement," *Sales & Marketing Management in Canada*, March 1984, pp. 24–26.

TABLE 19.5 *Dimensions of a marketing audit*

Part I. The Marketing Environment Audit

Macroenvironment

A. Economic-demographic

1. What does the company expect in the way of inflation, material shortages, unemployment, and credit availability in the short run, intermediate run, and long run?
2. What effect will forecast trends in the size, age distribution, and regional distribution of population have on the business?

B. Technological

1. What major changes are occurring in product technology? In process technology?
2. What are the major generic substitutes that might replace this product?

C. Political-legal

1. What laws are being proposed that may affect marketing strategy and tactics?
2. What national and local government actions should be watched? What is happening with pollution control, equal opportunity employment, product safety, advertising, price controls, etc., that is relevant to marketing planning?

D. Cultural

1. What attitude is the public taking towards business and the types of product produced by the company?
2. What changes in consumer lifestyles and values have a bearing on the company's target markets and marketing methods?

E. Ecological

1. Will the cost and availability of natural resources directly affect the company?
2. Are there public concerns about the company's role in pollution and conservation? If so, what is the company's reaction?

Task Environment

A. Markets

1. What is happening to market size, growth, geographical distribution, and profits?
2. What are the major market segments and their expected rates of growth? Which are high-opportunity and low-opportunity segments?

B. Customers

1. How do current customers and prospects judge the company and its competitors on reputation, product quality, service, sales force, and price?
2. How do different classes of customers make their buying decisions?
3. What evolving needs and satisfactions are the buyers in this market seeking?

C. Competitors

1. Who are the major competitors? What are the objectives and strategy of each major competitor? What are their strengths and weaknesses? What are the sizes and trends in market shares?
2. What trends can be foreseen in future competition and substitutes for this product?

D. Distribution and dealers

1. What are the main trade channels bringing products to customers?
2. What are the efficiency levels and growth potentials of the different trade channels?

E. Suppliers

1. What is the outlook for the availability of key resources used in production?
2. What trends are occurring among suppliers in their patterns of selling?

F. Facilitators and marketing firms

1. What is the outlook for the cost and availability of transport services?
2. What is the outlook for the cost and availability of warehousing facilities?
3. What is the outlook for the cost and availability of financial resources?
4. How effectively is the advertising agency performing? What trends are occurring in advertising agency services?

G. Publics

1. Where are the opportunity areas or problems for the company?
2. How effectively is the company dealing with publics?

Part II. Marketing Strategy Audit

A. Business mission

1. Is the business mission clearly focused with marketing terms and is it attainable?

TABLE 19.5 *Dimensions of a marketing audit (continued)*

B. Marketing objectives and goals

1. Are the corporate objectives clearly stated? Do they lead logically to the marketing objectives?
2. Are the marketing objectives stated clearly enough to guide marketing planning and subsequent performance measurement?
3. Are the marketing objectives appropriate, given the company's competitive position, resources, and opportunities? Is the appropriate strategic objective to build, hold, harvest, or terminate this business?

C. Strategy

1. What is the core marketing strategy for achieving the objectives? Is it sound?
2. Are the resources budgeted to accomplish the marketing objectives inadequate, adequate, or excessive?
3. Are the marketing resources allocated optimally to prime market segments, territories, and products?
4. Are the marketing resources allocated optimally to the major elements of the marketing mix, i.e., product quality, service, sales force, advertising, promotion, and distribution?

Part III. Marketing Organisation Audit

A. Formal structure

1. Is there a high-level marketing manager with adequate authority and responsibility over those company activities that affect customer satisfaction?
2. Are the marketing responsibilities optimally structured along functional, product, end user, and territorial lines?

B. Functional efficiency

1. Are there good communications and working relations between marketing and sales?
2. Is the product-management system working effectively? Are the product managers able to plan profits or only sales volume?
3. Are there any groups in marketing that need more training, motivation, supervision, or evaluation?

C. Interface efficiency

1. Are there any problems between marketing and manufacturing, R&D, purchasing, finance, accounting, and legal departments that need attention?

Part IV. Marketing Systems Audit

A. Marketing information system

1. Is the marketing intelligence system producing accurate, sufficient, and timely information about developments in the market-place?
2. Is marketing research being adequately used by company decision-makers?

B. Marketing-planning system

1. Is the marketing-planning system well conceived and effective?
2. Is sales forecasting and market-potential measurement soundly carried out?
3. Are sales quotas set on a proper basis?

C. Marketing control system

1. Are the control procedures (monthly, quarterly, etc.) adequate to ensure that the annual-plan objectives are being achieved?
2. Is provision made to analyse periodically the profitability of different products, markets, territories, and channels of distribution?
3. Is provision made to examine and validate periodically various marketing costs?

D. New product development system

1. Is the company well organised to gather, generate, and screen new product ideas?
2. Does the company do adequate concept research and business analysis before investing heavily in a new idea?
3. Does the company carry out adequate product and market testing before launching a new product?

Part V. Marketing-Productivity Audit

A. Profitability analysis

1. What is the profitability of the company's different products, served markets, territories, and channels of distribution?
2. Should the company enter, expand, contract, or withdraw from any business segments, and what would be the short- and long-run profit consequences?

B. Cost-effective analysis

1. Do any marketing activities seem to have excessive costs? Are these costs valid? Can cost-reducing steps be taken?

TABLE 19.5 *Dimensions of a marketing audit (continued)*

Part VI. Marketing Function Audits

A. Products

1. What are the product line objectives? Are these objectives sound? Is the current product line meeting these objectives?
2. Are there particular products that should be phased out?
3. Are there new products that are worth adding?
4. Are any products able to benefit from quality, feature, or style improvements?

B. Price

1. What are the pricing objectives, policies, strategies, and procedures? Are prices set on sound cost, demand, and competitive criteria?
2. Do the customers see the company's prices as being in or out of line with the perceived value of its products?
3. Does the company use price promotions effectively?

C. Distribution

1. What are the distribution objectives and strategies?
2. Is there adequate market coverage and service?
3. How effective are the following channel members: distributors, manufacturers' reps, brokers, agents, etc.?
4. Should the company consider changing its distribution channels?

D. Advertising, sales promotion, and publicity

1. What are the organisation's advertising objectives? Are they sound?

2. Is the right amount being spent on advertising? How is the budget determined?
3. Are the ad themes and copy effective? What do customers and the public think about the advertising?
4. Are the advertising media well chosen?
5. Is the internal advertising staff adequate?
6. Is the sales promotion budget adequate? Is there effective and sufficient use of sales promotion tools, such as samples, coupons, displays, and sales contests?
7. Is the publicity budget adequate? Is the public relations staff competent and creative?

E. Sales force

1. What are the organisation's sales-force objectives?
2. Is the sales force large enough to accomplish the company's objectives?
3. Is the sales force organised along the proper principle(s) of specialisation (territory, market, product)? Are there enough (or too many) sales managers to guide the field sales reps?
4. Does the sales compensation level and structure provide adequate incentive and reward?
5. Does the sales force show high morale, ability, and effort?
6. Are the procedures adequate for setting quotas and evaluating performance?
7. How does the company's sales force compare to the sales forces of competitors?

SOURCE: Philip Kotler, *Marketing Management: Analysis, Planning, and Control,* 6th ed. © 1988, pp. 748–751. Adapted by permission of Prentice-Hall, Inc., Englewood Cliffs, N.J.

3. Exploring opportunities and alternatives for improving the marketing strategy
4. Providing an overall database to be used in evaluating the attainment of organisational goals and marketing objectives

Marketing audits can be performed internally or externally. An internal auditor may be a top-level marketing executive, a company-wide auditing committee, or a manager from another office or of another function. Although it is more expensive, an audit by outside consultants is usually more effective because external auditors have more objectivity, more time for the audit, and greater experience.

There is no single set of procedures for all marketing audits. However, firms should adhere to several general guidelines. Audits are often based on a series of questionnaires that are administered to the firm's personnel. These questionnaires should be developed carefully to ensure that the audit focuses on the right issues. Auditors should develop and follow a step-by-step plan to guarantee that the audit is systematic. When interviewing company personnel, the auditors should strive to talk to a diverse group of people from many parts of the company. The auditor should become familiar with the product line, meet headquarters staff, visit field organisations, interview customers, interview competitors, and analyse information for a report on the marketing environment.[22]

To achieve adequate support, the auditors normally focus first on the firm's top management and then move down through the organisational hierarchy. The auditor looks for different points of view within various departments of the organisation or a mismatch between the customers' and the company's perception of the product as signs of trouble in an organisation.[23] The results of the audit should be reported in a comprehensive written document, which should include recommendations that will increase marketing productivity and determine the company's general direction.

The marketing audit lets an organisation change tactics or alter day-to-day activities as problems arise. For example, marketing auditors often wonder whether a change in budgeted sales activity is caused by general market conditions or is due to a change in the firm's market share.

Although the concept of auditing implies an official examination of marketing activities, many organisations audit their marketing activities informally. Any attempt to verify operating results and to compare them with standards can be considered an auditing activity. Many smaller firms probably would not use the word *audit,* but they do perform auditing activities.

Several problems may arise in an audit of marketing activities. Marketing audits can be expensive in time and money. Selecting the auditors may be difficult because objective, qualified personnel may not be available. Marketing audits can also be extremely disruptive because employees sometimes fear comprehensive evaluations, especially by outsiders.

SUMMARY

The organisation of marketing activities involves the development of an internal structure for the marketing unit. The internal structure is the key to directing marketing activities. A centralised organisation is one in which the top-level managers delegate very little authority to lower levels of the firm. In a decentralised organisation, decision-making authority is delegated as far down the chain of command as possible. In a marketing-orientated organisation, the focus is on finding out what buyers want and providing it in a way that lets the organisation achieve its objectives. The marketing unit can be organised by (1) functions, (2) products, (3) regions, or (4) type of customer. An organisation may use only one approach or a combination.

Implementation is an important part of the marketing management process. Proper implementation of a marketing plan depends on internal marketing to em-

22. Ely S. Lurin, "Audit Determines the Weak Link in Marketing Chain," *Marketing News,* 12 Sept. 1986, pp. 35–37.

23. Ibid.

ployees, the motivation of personnel who perform marketing activities, effective communication within the marketing organisation, and the co-ordination of marketing activities. Internal marketing refers to the managerial actions necessary to make all members of the marketing organisation understand and accept their respective roles in implementing the marketing strategy. To attract, motivate, and retain qualified internal customers (employees), firms employ internal marketing by designing internal products (jobs) that satisfy employees' wants and needs. Marketing managers must also motivate marketing personnel. A company's communication system must allow the marketing manager to communicate with high-level management, with managers of other functional areas in the firm, and with personnel involved in marketing activities both inside and outside the organisation. Finally, marketing managers must co-ordinate the activities of marketing personnel and integrate these activities with those in other areas of the company and with the marketing efforts of personnel in external organisations.

The marketing control process consists of establishing performance standards, evaluating actual performance by comparing it with established standards, and reducing the difference between desired and actual performance. Performance standards, which are established in the planning process, are expected levels of performance with which actual performance can be compared. In evaluating actual performance, marketing managers must know what marketers within the firm are doing and must have information about the activities of external organisations that provide the firm with marketing assistance. Then actual performance is compared with performance standards. Marketers must determine whether a discrepancy exists and, if so, whether it requires corrective action, such as changing the performance standards or improving actual performance.

To maintain effective marketing control, an organisation needs to develop a comprehensive control process that evaluates its marketing operations at a given time. The control of marketing activities is not a simple task. Problems encountered include environmental changes, time lags between marketing activities and their effects, and difficulty in determining the costs of marketing activities. In addition to these, it may be hard to develop performance standards.

Control of marketing strategy can be achieved through sales and cost analyses. For the purpose of analysis, sales are usually measured in terms of either cash volume or market share. For a sales analysis to be effective, it must compare current sales performance with forecast company sales, industry sales, specific competitors' sales, or the costs incurred to generate the current sales volume. A sales analysis can be performed on the firm's total sales, or the total sales can be disaggregated and analysed by product, geographic area, or customer group.

Marketing cost analysis involves an examination of accounting records and, frequently, a reclassification of natural accounts into marketing function accounts. Such an analysis is often difficult because there may be no logical, clear-cut way to allocate natural accounts into functional accounts. The analyst may choose either direct costing or full costing. Cost analysis can focus on (1) an aggregate cost analysis of natural accounts or functional accounts or (2) an analysis of functional accounts for products, geographic areas, or customer groups.

To control marketing strategies, it is sometimes necessary to audit marketing activities. A marketing audit is a systematic examination of the marketing group's objectives, strategies, organisation, and performance. A marketing audit attempts to identify what a marketing unit is doing, to evaluate the effectiveness of these activities, and to recommend future marketing activities.

IMPORTANT TERMS

Centralised organisation
Decentralised organisation
Marketing-orientated organisation
Internal marketing
Marketing control process
Performance standard
Sales analysis
Marketing cost analysis

Natural accounts
Marketing function accounts
Direct costs
Traceable common costs
Non-traceable common costs
Full-cost approach
Direct-cost approach
Marketing audit

DISCUSSION AND REVIEW QUESTIONS

1. What determines the place of marketing within an organisation? Which type of organisation is best suited to the marketing concept? Why?
2. What factors can be used to organise the internal aspects of a marketing unit? Discuss the benefits of each type of organisation.
3. Why might an organisation use multiple bases for organising its marketing unit?
4. What is internal marketing? Why is it important in implementing marketing strategies?
5. Why is motivation of marketing personnel important in implementing marketing plans?
6. How does communication help in implementing marketing plans?
7. What are the major steps of the marketing control process?
8. List and discuss the five requirements for an effective control process.
9. Discuss the major problems in controlling marketing activities.
10. What is a sales analysis? What makes it an effective control tool?
11. Identify and describe three cost analysis methods. Compare and contrast direct costing and full costing.
12. How is the marketing audit used to control marketing programme performance?

■ CASES

19.1   IBM Struggles to Maintain Leadership in the Computer Industry

International Business Machines, or "Big Blue," has been a leader in the computer industry since the 1960s. Several of its products, including the System/370 mainframe computers and the IBM PC line of personal computers, set standards followed by many computer makers. However, despite its reputation for providing high-quality computers and strong service to its customers, the company has experienced declining sales, profits, and market share in recent years.

Recognising that IBM's performance was not up to par, Chairman John Akers reorganised IBM early in 1988 to make it more responsive to customers' needs and more competitive in a stagnating computer market. The reorganisation effort was intended to boost sales, speed up new product development time, remove excessive corporate layers, and improve products and service to customers. It was also expected to improve co-ordination among the firm's various divisions and improve morale. IBM combined its personal computer and typewriter divisions because customers of those products have similar needs. It also merged its mainframe division with the less profitable mini computer division. The organisation was decentralised somewhat, giving decision-making responsibilities to six major product and marketing divisions to help reduce the bureaucracy that had slowed down new-product development and dissatisfied customers. To avoid laying off employees, IBM asked 15,000 employees, mostly in management, to retire early, and allowed another 25,000 positions to remain vacant. It retrained and moved thousands of other employees to new positions within the company. Although these efforts helped improve the company's performance somewhat, IBM faced two more years of slow growth, in part because of increasing competition in its mainframe and personal computer markets.

Analysts believe that IBM's problems stem from having too many employees, high overheads, and too great a reliance on its cash cow, mainframe computers. Mainframe computer sales contribute 50 percent to the company's revenues and 65 percent to its profits. The multi-million dollar mainframes also link the company to its largest, most profitable customers and influence all their computer and software purchases. But the IBM-dominated mainframe computer market is maturing; growth has been slowing and competition is fierce. Amdahl Corp. and Hitachi Data Systems, which market IBM-compatible machines, and Digital Equipment Corp. have been stealing market share with computers that are more powerful and less expensive than IBM's System/370 workhorse. Moreover, more powerful mini computers and personal computers can now tackle some jobs that only mainframes could handle before. As a result, sales of mainframes in general are flat, with growth slowing down to 3 or 4 percent a year.

IBM also faces problems in other segments of the computer market. Sales of mid-range computers, including the AS/400 mini computer, have been soft. As with mainframes, the slow sales of mid-range computers can be attributed to increasingly powerful personal computers and work-stations which can handle more complex applications that once required a mini computer or mainframe. IBM also lacks products in two growth segments of the computer industry. IBM has no products in the Japanese-dominated laptop-computer market, which is growing at 40 percent annually. In the work-station market, which is growing at 30 percent annually, IBM has few products and commands only a 2 percent share.

IBM is also suffering because of numerous product delays. For example, it delayed deliveries of its Model 3090–S central mainframe processors by a few months because of quality problems in the processors' logic microchips. And, in January 1990, it announced that it had indefinitely postponed the introduction of a long-awaited mainframe disc drive, which was to have been introduced late in 1989, because of technical problems.

Everything is not all bad for IBM, however. It continues to lease System/370 and AS/400 equipment at competitive rates that other firms find hard to match. Leasing, however, accounts for only 4 percent of IBM's revenues. Analysts also praise the company's recent investments in software companies, the use of faster chips in its PCs, and plans to introduce another mainframe disc drive in 1990. In the personal computer market, IBM is recovering somewhat from a slow period with the help of new products such as the PS/2 systems that run on OS/2 software. In 1989, these and other IBM PCs accounted for 30 percent of dealer sales, up slightly from the previous year.

To correct IBM's current poor performance several steps have been taken. IBM is discounting prices on many products by up to 40 percent. However, the price discounting has turned customers' focus to price instead of IBM's traditionally strong service. The price competition in the mainframe market is especially harmful to IBM because the profits from that division are used to subsidise low prices in other, more competitive markets and to help fund vital product development. In an industry in which equipment can become obsolete in a matter of a few years, continued product and technology development is critical to computer manufacturers' survival.

Moreover, IBM announced in January 1990 that it would mount yet another restructuring to cut costs. Company executives say they will make the company more competitive by slashing costs by $1 billion, and by eliminating 10,000 jobs, again through early retirements and attrition rather than layoffs. The company took a $2.3 billion pretax charge against earnings, fourth quarter 1989, to cover severance pay, consolidations, and other expenses associated with reorganising. After restructuring, Akers vows that IBM will show "modest growth" in revenues in 1990, for the first time since 1985.

Despite Akers' positive forecast, analysts continue to predict gloom for Big Blue. They point out that IBM has repeatedly forecasted turnarounds that have yet to materialise. Critics blame John Akers for IBM's dismal performance in the last few years, particularly for the manufacturing problems, product delays, and managerial decisions that have blemished IBM's reputation and its earnings. They urge IBM to cut costs even further and eliminate another 30,000 jobs to reach Akers' goal of operating margins of 18 percent. Many believe that IBM's long standing policy of no layoffs has been preserved at the expense of shareholder value and that IBM's board of directors is reluctant to criticize executives or enact tough cost-cutting measures. They also accuse IBM of clinging to its old line of mainframe computers at the expense of developing technologically sophisticated new products that could help boost the company's revenue and image. One analyst said, "Times have changed. But I'm not sure IBM adapted to those changes fast enough for themselves or their shareholders."

Thus, even after two restructurings and drastic cost-cutting measures, IBM managers must continue to monitor the marketing environment as well as the company's performance. Further changes in the company's corporate and marketing strategies may be necessary to make the company more profitable by developing and marketing products that satisfy consumers.

SOURCES: Paul B. Carroll, "Big Blues: Hurt by a Pricing War, IBM Plans a Writeoff and Cut of 10,000 Jobs," *Wall Street Journal*, 6 Dec. 1989, pp. A1, A8; John Hillkirk, "As IBM Falters, Shareholders and Critics Take Aim at Akers," *USA Today*, 6 Dec. 1989, p. 10B; Geoff Lewis, with Anne R. Field, John J. Keller, and John W. Verity, "Big Changes at Big Blue," *Business Week*, 15 Feb. 1988, pp. 92–98; Larry Reibstein, "IBM's Plan to Decentralize May Set a Trend—But Imitation Has a Price," *Wall Street Journal*, 19 Feb. 1988, p. 17; John W. Verity, "A Slimmer IBM May Still Be Overweight," *Business Week*, 18 Dec. 1989, pp. 107–108; and John W. Verity, "What's Ailing IBM? More Than This Year's Earnings," *Business Week*, 16 Oct. 1989, pp. 75–86.

Questions for Discussion

1. Why is IBM's performance so disappointing?
2. Are organisation or implementation important considerations in turning IBM around?

In the U.S. in 1957, Ford introduced the Edsel to fill a gap between its low-end and high-end car lines. Although Ford saw the move as a good positioning tactic, the consumer saw the Edsel as too much like other available cars. As a result, Ford lost $350 million on the Edsel and eventually stopped producing it.

Almost 30 years later in 1985, Ford introduced the Merkur (the Granada), a $28,000 luxury sedan built by Ford of Europe in West Germany. The Merkur, a top-selling model in Germany, was the company's first new car franchise in the United States since the Edsel. However, much to the dismay of Ford, the Merkur would fare no better than its predecessor. In a surprising repeat of history, Ford discontinued imports of the Merkur in 1989, only four years after the luxury car's debut.

The Merkur (pronounced mare-COOR) was originally intended to entice young, affluent buyers who did not like the Lincoln Town Car image to visit Lincoln-Mercury dealerships. The Town Car was a barge-like flagship of the Lincoln-Mercury division which had a strong appeal to older consumers. The first Merkur, the XR4Ti, did not sell well in part because American buyers did not like the car's unusual double-wing rear spoiler. In May 1987, Ford began importing the Scorpio sedan from West Germany to sell next to a redesigned XR4Ti in Lincoln-Mercury showrooms. Ford officials expected the two Merkurs to sell about 15,000 cars per year. In 1988, Ford reached that goal as Merkur sales climbed to 15,261 cars.

However, it was all downhill from there. Less than a year after the Merkur's 1985 launch, the West German mark rose sharply against the dollar, causing Merkur prices to rise. In addition, both the Scorpio and the XR4Ti suffered from poor quality. Ford promised Merkur owners that it would fix for free a variety of problems, including malfunctioning air conditioners, engine stalling, and general electrical problems. By the third quarter of 1988, Ford had most of the problems solved and Merkur satisfaction ratings were on the rise.

But the improvements came too late. In the autumn of 1988, Ford stopped importing the XR4Ti because of the slow sales. Sales of the Scorpio also plummeted. Total Merkur sales for the first nine months of 1989 dropped 46 percent from the previous year to only 6,320 cars. In September of 1989 alone, the 670 Merkur dealers nationwide managed to sell only 93 Scorpios. As a result, Ford cancelled plans to outfit the Scorpio with air bags; and in October of 1989, it stopped importing the Merkur altogether.

The Scorpio continues to be sold in Europe where company officials call it a "success." But European Scorpio sales have been slipping since it won the European Car of the Year title in 1986. In 1988, Ford had sold 86,185 Scorpios in Europe, down 6 percent from 1987. Moreover, as of October 1989, Ford had sold only 67,405 Scorpios in Europe.

Why did the Merkur fail in the U.S.? Although Ford and its advertising agency, Young and Rubicam, claimed not to know what went wrong, the most likely answer seems to be the lack of a sound marketing strategy. Like the Edsel, the Merkur was introduced to satisfy Ford's marketing needs rather than the needs of the consumer. As a result, the Merkur was brought into the U.S. market with few changes in marketing style.

For example, many felt that the Merkur suffered from an image problem because it was a European import selling side by side with domestic models. As a result, many dealers considered the Merkur an outsider that they did not feel obligated to support. Others believed that the name, XR4Ti, and the styling did not convey prestige. Still others cite the ineffectiveness of the $13 million advertising campaign Ford used to introduce the Merkur as a cause of its failure. Many import car buyers want taut suspension, quick steering, quick acceleration, and high quality in a neat roomy package. They were comparing the Merkur to BMWs, Volvos, and Audis.

Although Ford spent about $50 million to convert the Merkur to U.S. safety and emission standards, it overlooked other items in the design that were essential to U.S. consumers of luxury cars. As a result, many import buyers felt that the car was overpriced. In 1989, the Merkur Scorpio listed for nearly as much as a Lincoln Continental.

The death of the Merkur wasn't nearly as costly to Ford as was the demise of the Edsel because Merkur was a relatively low-budget project with limited sales goals. Still, Ford's "Edsel of the '80s" came at a time when the company's golden image was showing signs of strain.

SOURCES: "Detroit's New Goal: Putting Yuppies in the Driver's Seat," *Business Week, (Industrial/Technology Edition)*, 3 September 1984, pp. 46, 50; Rebecca Fannin, "Who Killed Merkur?" *Marketing and Media Decisions,* January 1989, pp. 66–69; William J. Hampton, "Detroit's Big Gamble," *Business Week (Industrial/Technology Edition),* 13 January 1986, pp. 30–31; Jesse Snyder, "U.S. Drawing More Foreign Car Entries," *Advertising Age,* 8 July 1985, pp. 3, 63; Joseph B. White, "Ford Ends Imports of Merkur in an '80s Echo of Edsel," *Wall Street Journal,* 20 October 1989, pp. B1, B6.

Questions for Discussion

1. Why did the Merkur fail in America?
2. Did Ford effectively implement the Merkur marketing strategy?

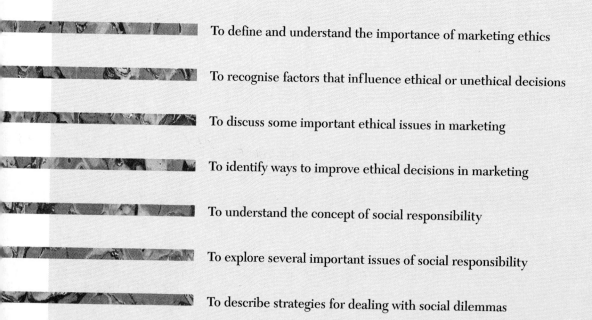

20

MARKETING ETHICS AND SOCIAL RESPONSIBILITY

Objectives

To define and understand the importance of marketing ethics

To recognise factors that influence ethical or unethical decisions

To discuss some important ethical issues in marketing

To identify ways to improve ethical decisions in marketing

To understand the concept of social responsibility

To explore several important issues of social responsibility

To describe strategies for dealing with social dilemmas

In the summer of 1990 Japanese film and camera company Fuji ran into a storm when its U.K. marketing team launched a revolutionary advertising campaign. As *Marketing* magazine's editorial read, opinions were mixed:

Fuji has used the issues of racism and hostility towards handicapped people to promote its film. Does this herald a new wave of social concern in advertising, and if so, what are the pitfalls? Is it exploitation or is it a step forward?

Some media watchers thought the advertisements—which depicted everyday scenes from the lives of handicapped workers and Asian families—to be callous or exploitative, while others described them as enlightened and brilliant. For Fuji and agency Henry Howell Chaldecott Lury, the aim was to achieve more than brand and product awareness and to provide educational value as well. Fuji was pinning its social conscience on its sleeve. Negative reaction to its campaign was not, therefore, expected. "Fuji produces the best film" was the key message; Fuji as a caring company—an opinion supported by consumer research—was the secondary message.

Fuji's advertisements were checked by the Independent Broadcasting Authority, and were measured against the guidelines set by the Race Relations Act and the Equal Opportunities Act. Mencap, the charity for the mentally handicapped, and the Commission for Racial Equality have both praised the sensitivity of the advertisements. While many companies' advertisements include disabled people and those representing ethnic minorities, none had previously so prominently featured situations which for many people are an every-day aspect of life. ◆

SOURCES: Suzanne Bidlake, "Shooting the Victims," *Marketing,* 19 July 1990, pp. 20–21; Phil Dourado, "Parity not Charity," *Marketing,* 16 August 1990, pp. 26–27; Liz Levy, "Bitter-Sweet Charity," *Marketing,* 15 March 1990, pp. 34–35; "The Old Year's Honours List," *Campaign,* 11 January 1991, pp. 25–31.

ost marketers avoid sensitive issues; a few abuse them. Fuji has taken a bold step and most consumers believe the company cared rather than exploited. The ethics of such a campaign were discussed at great length, by the companies concerned in developing the campaign, regulatory bodies, organisations representing the groups featured, and by the media. Ethics in marketing is an evolving issue and an area set to increase in prominence.

Issues such as the Fuji advertising controversy illustrate that all marketing activities can be judged as morally right or wrong by society, consumers, interest groups, competitors, and others. Although most marketers operate within the limits of the law, some do engage in activities that are not considered acceptable by other marketers, consumers, and society in general. A number of recently publicised incidents in marketing, such as deceptive or objectionable advertising, misleading packaging, questionable selling practices, manipulation, corruption, and pollution, have raised questions as to whether specific marketing practices are acceptable and beneficial to society. The issues of what is acceptable in marketing practices and what obligations marketers have to society are issues of marketing ethics and social responsibility.

This chapter gives an overview of the role of ethics and social responsibility in marketing decision-making. We first define marketing ethics and discuss the factors that influence ethical decision-making in marketing. We also outline some specific ethical issues in marketing and discuss ways to improve ethics in marketing decisions. Then we address the issue of social responsibility and consider the impact of marketing decisions on society. Some strategies for dealing with social responsibility dilemmas are also developed. We close the chapter by comparing and contrasting the concepts of marketing ethics and social responsibility.

The Nature of Marketing Ethics

Although it is a very important concern in marketing decisions, ethics may be one of the most misunderstood and controversial concepts in marketing. No one has yet discovered a universally accepted approach to dealing with marketing ethics. However, this concept and its application need to be examined in order to foster marketing decisions that are acceptable and beneficial to society. In this section we consider the meaning of marketing ethics.

■ **Marketing Ethics Defined**

Ethics relate to moral evaluations of decisions and actions as right or wrong on the basis of commonly accepted principles of behaviour. For our purposes, then, **marketing ethics** are moral principles that define right and wrong behaviour in marketing. The most basic ethical issues have been formalised through laws and regulations to provide conformity to the standards of society. At the very least, marketers are expected to conform to these laws and regulations. However, it is important to realise that marketing ethics go beyond legal issues; ethical marketing decisions foster mutual trust among individuals and in marketing relationships.

Ethics are individually defined and may vary from one person to another. Although individual marketers often act in their own self-interest, there must be standards of acceptable behaviour to guide all marketing decisions. Marketers need to operate in accordance with sound moral principles based on ideals such as fairness, justice, and trust.[1] Consumers generally regard unethical marketing activities—for instance, deceptive advertising, misleading selling tactics, price-fixing, and the deliberate marketing of harmful products—as unacceptable and often refuse to do business with marketers that engage in such practices. Thus when marketers deviate from accepted moral principles to further their own interests at the expense of others, continued marketing exchanges become difficult, if not impossible.[2]

■ **Marketing Ethics Are Controversial**

Few topics in marketing are more controversial than ethics. Most marketing decisions can be judged as right or wrong, ethical or unethical. But everyone has different ideas as to what is ethical or unethical depending on personal values, the nature of the organisation, and their experiences in life. Many marketers have such strong convictions about what is morally right or wrong that they deeply resent discussions of alternative ways to make ethical decisions.

Regardless of how a person or an organisation views the acceptability of a particular activity, if society judges that activity to be wrong or unethical, then this view directly affects the organisation's ability to achieve its goals. Although not all activities deemed unethical by society may be illegal, consumer protests against a particular activity may result in legislation that restricts or bans it. When an organisation engages in unethical marketing activities, it may not only lose sales as dissatisfied consumers refuse to deal with it, but it may also face lawsuits, fines, and even prison for its executives. Street Clothing of Leeds, for example, alleged breach of copyright by Next when that company opened its new flagship store "Department X." Since 1977, Street Clothing of Leeds has used the X name: it manufactures clothing under the brand name X and also has three stores in Leeds, Hull, and Sheffield called X. The legal battle specifically centres around the Department X logo.[3] Such an example illustrates the importance of understanding marketing ethics and recognizing ethical issues.

Because marketing ethics are so controversial, it is important to state that it is not the purpose of this chapter to question anyone's personal ethical beliefs and convictions. Nor is it the purpose of this chapter to examine the behaviour of consumers, although consumers, too, may be unethical (engaging, for instance, in coupon fraud, shoplifting, and other abuses). Instead, its goal is to underscore the importance of ethical issues and help you learn about ethical decision-making in marketing. Understanding the impact of ethical decisions in marketing can help you recognise and resolve ethical issues within an organisation.

UNDERSTANDING THE ETHICAL DECISION-MAKING PROCESS

To grasp the significance of ethics in marketing decision-making, one must first examine the factors that influence the ethical decision-making process. Personal moral philosophies, organisational relationships, and opportunity are three factors that interact to determine ethical decisions in marketing (see Figure 20.1).

1. Donald P. Robin and R. Eric Reidenbach, "Social Responsibility, Ethics in Marketing Strategy, Closing the Gap Between Concept and Application," *Journal of Marketing*, January 1987, pp. 44–58.

2. Vernon R. Loucks, Jr., "A CEO Looks at Ethics," *Business Horizons*, March-April 1987, p. 4.

3. *Marketing*, 1 Sept. 1988.

FIGURE 20.1

Factors that influence the ethical decision-making process

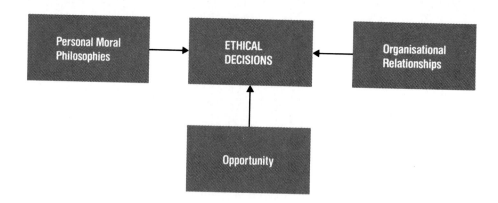

Personal Moral Philosophies → ETHICAL DECISIONS ← Organisational Relationships

Opportunity →

■ **Moral Philosophies**

Moral philosophies are principles or rules that individuals use to determine the right way to behave. They provide guidelines for resolving conflicts and ensuring mutual benefit for all members of society.[4] People learn these principles and rules through socialisation by family members, social groups, religion, and formal education. Each moral philosophy has its own concept of rightness or ethicalness and rules for behaviour. We discuss here two distinct moral philosophies: utilitarianism and ethical formalism.

Utilitarianism.   Utilitarian moral philosophies are concerned with maximising the greatest good for the greatest number of people. Utilitarians judge an action on the basis of the consequences for all the people affected by the action. In other words, in a situation with an ethical component, utilitarians compare all possible options and select the one that promises the best results. Under utilitarianism, then, it would be unethical to act in a way that leads to personal gain at the expense of society in general. Consider the following example of an organisation adopting a utilitarian philosophy. In 1990, the offices of Delta Airlines in Ireland received a telephone threat from terrorists that one of its transatlantic flights would be bombed. Delta decided to publicise the threat and announced that it would allow customers holding tickets on its transatlantic flights to transfer them to other airlines without penalty.[5] When Pan Am Airlines received a bomb threat in 1988, it did not notify the public; the loss of more than two hundred lives in the terrorist bombing of Pan Am Flight 103 over Lockerbie and the negative publicity directed at Pan Am damaged the firm. Thus, after weighing the possible loss of life and the negative publicity surrounding a terrorist bombing or crash against the loss of revenue and profits, Delta executives probably concluded that publicising the bomb threat and letting passengers decide whether to fly on Delta would be best.

Ethical Formalism.   Other moral philosophies focus on the intentions associated with a particular behaviour and on the rights of the individual. Ethical formalism develops specific rules for behaviour by determining whether an action can be taken consistently as a general rule without concern for alternative results.[6] Behaviour is judged on the basis of whether it infringes individual rights or universal rules. The Golden Rule—do unto others as you would have them do unto you—exemplifies

4. James R. Rest, *Moral Development Advances in Research and Theory* (New York: Praeger, 1986), p. 1.

5. "CNN Worldday," Cable News Network (TV), 5 Jan. 1990.

6. F. Neil Brady, *Ethical Managing: Rules and Results* (New York: Macmillan, 1990), pp. 4–6.

ethical formalism. So does Immanuel Kant's categorical imperative: that every action should be based on reasons that everyone could act on, at least in principle, and that action must be based on reasons that the decision-maker would be willing to have others use.[7] In marketing, ethical formalism is consistent with the idea of consumer choice. For example, consumers have a right to know about possible defects in a car or other products that involve safety.[8]

Applying Moral Philosophies to Marketing Decision-Making.   Traditionally, it has been assumed that personal moral philosophies remain constant in both work and non-work situations. However, research has shown that most businesspersons use one moral philosophy at work and a completely different one outside work.[9]

Another study found that although personal moral philosophies and values enter into ethical decisions in business, they are not the central component that guides the decisions, actions, and policies of an organisation.[10] This finding may explain why individuals switch moral philosophies between home and work and why personal values make up only one part of an organisation's total value system.

Some marketers use the logic that anything is fair which defeats the competition and increases profits. They have used warfare concepts such as "guerrilla warfare", "pre-emptive first strikes", and "counter attacks" to justify questionable and possibly unethical actions. A distinction should be made between competitors and enemies. Competitors are rivals that compete for customers and markets according to socially accepted rules, whereas central to the science of warfare is total conquest and elimination, in some cases, of the enemy. Therefore the marketing as warfare comparison raises ethical concerns, given the destructive nature of the history of warfare.[11]

Others view marketing as a game like football or boxing, in which ordinary rules and morality do not apply. For example, what if a boxer decided it was wrong to try to injure another person or a rugby player was afraid of hurting another player if he made contact? Sports have rules and referees to regulate the game to ensure safety and equality. However, because customers in marketing exchanges are not economically self-sufficient, they cannot choose to withdraw from the "game of marketing". Given this condition, marketing ethics must make clear what rules do and should apply in the "game of marketing". Even more important, the rules developed must be appropriate to the non-voluntary character of participation in the game. Most members of society hold that moral principles and standards of acceptable behaviour should guide decisions related to the welfare of customers.[12]

7. O.C. Ferrell and Larry G. Gresham, "A Contingency Framework for Understanding Ethical Decision Making in Marketing," *Journal of Marketing*, Summer 1985, p. 90.

8. Ibid.

9. John Fraedrich, "Philosophy Type Interaction in the Ethical Decision Making Process of Retailers" (Ph.D. diss., Texas A&M University, 1988).

10. William C. Frederick and James Weber, "The Value of Corporate Managers and Their Critics: An Empirical Description and Normative Implications," in *Research in Corporate Social Performance and Social Responsibility*, ed. William C. Frederick and Lee E. Preston (Greenwich, Conn.: JAI Press, 1987), pp. 149–150.

11. Charles L. Tomkovick, "Time for a Cease-Fire with Strategic Marketing Warfare," in *Advances in Marketing*, Peter J. Gordon and Bert J. Kellerman, eds. (Southwest Marketing Association, 1990), p. 212.

12. Eric H. Beversluis, "Is There 'No Such Thing as Business Ethics'?" *Journal of Business Ethics*, No. 6, 1987, pp. 81–88.

Ethical behaviour may be a function of two different dimensions of an organisation's value structure: the organisation's values and traditions, or corporate culture, and the personal moral philosophies of the organisation's individual members. An employee assumes some measure of moral responsibility by agreeing to abide by an organisation's rules and standard operating procedures. When a marketer decides to behave unethically or even illegally, it may be that competitive pressures and organisational rewards provided the incentive.

■ Organisational Relationships

People learn personal moral philosophies, and therefore ethical behaviour, not only from society in general, but also from members of their social groups and their organisational environment. Relationships with one's employees, co-workers, or superiors create ethical problems, such as maintaining confidentiality in personal relations; meeting obligations, responsibilities and mutual agreements; and avoiding undue pressure that may force others to behave unethically. Employees may have to deal with assignments that they perceive as creating ethical dilemmas. For example, a salesperson may be asked to lie to a customer over the phone. Likewise, an employee who sees another employee cheating a customer must decide whether to report the incident.

Marketing managers must carefully balance their duties to the owners or shareholders who hired them to carry out the organisation's objectives and to the employees who look to them for guidance and direction. In addition, managers must also comply with society's wishes and ethical evaluations. Striking an ethical balance among these areas, then, is a difficult task for today's marketing decision-makers.

The role of top management is extremely important in developing the culture of an organisation. Most experts agree that the chief executive officer or the director in charge of marketing sets the ethical tone for the entire marketing organisation. Lower-level managers take their cues from top management, yet they, too, impose some of their personal values on the company. This interaction between corporate culture and executive leadership helps determine the ethical value system of the firm.

Powerful superiors can affect employees' activities and directly influence behaviour by putting into practice the company's standards of ethics. Young marketers in particular indicate that they often go along with their superiors to demonstrate loyalty in matters related to judgements of morality. The status and power of significant others is directly related to the amount of pressure they can exert to get others to conform to their expectations. A manager in a position of authority can exert strong pressure to ensure compliance on ethically related issues. In organisations where ethical standards are vague and supervision by superiors is limited, peers may provide guidance in an ethical decision.

The role of peers (significant others) in the decision-making process depends on the person's ratio of exposure to unethical behaviour to exposure to ethical behaviour. The more a person is exposed to unethical activity in the organisational environment, the more likely it is that he or she will behave unethically.[13] Employees experience conflict between what is expected of them as workers and managers and what they expect of themselves based on their own personal ethical standards.

13. O.C. Ferrell, Larry G. Gresham, and John Fraedrich, "A Synthesis of Ethical Decision Models for Marketing," *Journal of Macromarketing*, Fall 1989, pp. 58–59.

Opportunity provides another pressure that may determine whether a person will behave ethically. Opportunity is a favourable set of conditions that limit barriers or provide rewards. Rewards may be internal or external. Internal rewards are the feelings of goodness and worth one experiences after an altruistic action. External rewards are what people expect to receive from others in terms of values generated and provided on an exchange basis. External rewards are often received from peers and top management in the form of praise, promotions, and pay rises.

If a marketer takes advantage of an opportunity to act unethically and is rewarded or suffers no penalty, he or she may repeat such acts as other opportunities arise. For example, a salesperson who receives a rise after using a deceptive sales presentation to increase sales is being rewarded for this behaviour and so will probably continue it. Indeed, opportunity to engage in unethical conduct is often a better predictor of unethical activities than personal values.[14]

Besides rewards and the absence of punishment, other elements in the business environment help to create opportunities. Professional codes of ethics and ethics-related corporate policy also influence opportunity by prescribing what behaviours are acceptable. The larger the rewards and the lesser the punishment for unethical behaviour, the greater is the probability that unethical behaviour will be practised.

ETHICAL ISSUES IN MARKETING

A person will not make an ethical decision unless he or she recognises that a particular issue or situation has an ethical or moral component. Thus developing awareness of ethical issues is important in understanding marketing ethics. An **ethical issue** is an identifiable problem, situation, or opportunity requiring an individual or organisation to choose from among several actions that must be evaluated as right or wrong, ethical or unethical. Any time an activity causes consumers to feel deceived, manipulated, or cheated, a marketing ethical issue exists, regardless of the legality of that activity.

Ethical issues typically arise because of conflicts among individuals' personal moral philosophies and the marketing strategies, policies, and organisational environment in which they work. Ethical issues may stem from conflicts between a marketer's attempts to achieve organisational objectives and customers' desires for safe and reliable products. For example, the Reliant Robin became highly controversial in the 1970s after consumer advocates ("That's Life" on BBC television) claimed that Reliant had saved money in the design of the car's steering system and that Reliants ran a greater risk of being involved in accidents. Similarly, organisational objectives that call for increased profits or market share may pressure marketers to steal competitors' secrets, knowingly put an unsafe product on the market, or engage in some other questionable activity. For example, in South Korea, Lucky Goldstar Group markets a detergent packaged in an orange box with a whirlpool design just like Procter & Gamble's Tide brand. The product is called Tie, and Procter & Gamble does not make it or license it to Goldstar.[15] Obviously, the attempt to develop a Tide look-alike without Procter & Gamble's permission creates an ethical issue.

14. Ferrell and Gresham, p. 92.
15. Damon Darlin, "Where Trademarks Are Up for Grabs," *Wall Street Journal*, 5 Dec. 1989, p. B1.

FIGURE 20.2
Product safety.
N.L. Chemicals communicates its concerns for environmental protection and consumer safety.

Making the world white, clean and bright.

From the coating on a golf ball to the ink and paper of this page, NL Chemicals' products are in many of the everyday items that surround you. Our titanium pigment products are used worldwide to provide whiteness, brightness and opacity to paint, paper, plastics and ceramics. In addition, our broad line of specialty chemicals is found in inks, coatings, adhesives, cosmetics and more.

Ranked among the FORTUNE 500, we have earned our success by producing innovative, quality products using state-of-the-art processes that are protective of our environment and the health and safety of our neighbors, employees and those who use our products. At NL Chemicals, we believe a clean world means a bright future.

NL
Chemicals, Inc.
P.O. Box 700
Hightstown, NJ 08520
(609) 443-2000

Circle 125 on Reader Service Card

SOURCE: Courtesy of Kronos, Inc.

Regardless of the reasons behind specific ethical issues, once the issues are identified, marketers and organisations must decide how to deal with them. Thus it is essential to become familiar with many of the ethical issues that may arise in marketing so that they can be identified and resolved when they occur. We cannot, of course, discuss every possible issue that could develop in the different marketing mix elements. But our examination of a few issues can provide some direction and lead to an understanding of the ethical problems that marketers must confront.

■ **Product Issues**

In general, product-related ethical issues arise when marketers fail to disclose risks associated with the product or information about its function, value, or use. Figure 20.2 illustrates that N.L. Chemicals provides chemicals used in printing, adhesives, and cosmetics that protect the health and safety of consumers and minimise environmental pollution. Competitive pressures can also create product-related ethical issues. As competition intensifies and profit margins diminish, pressures can build to substitute inferior materials or product components so as to reduce costs. An ethical issue arises when marketers fail to inform customers about changes in product quality; this failure is a form of dishonesty about the nature of the product. Consider the following example. Shell launched a new petrol—the first attempt to differentiate the petrol product—Formula Shell. Despite much publicity for Formula Shell, the additives (which improved performance) were not specified. Many engines suffered from the use of the new variant; consumers were caught unawares. At great cost, the product was withdrawn.

A similar ethical problem arose when the chairman of Chrysler Corporation, Lee Iacocca, learned that several Chrysler executives had driven new Chryslers with the odometers disconnected and then sold the cars as new, without disclosing that the cars had been driven. Some of the cars had been involved in accidents and repaired. In this case, however, Iacocca apologised for the company's unethical behaviour at a national press conference and developed a programme to compensate customers who had bought the pre-driven cars. Iacocca took out two-page advertisements in *USA Today*, *The Wall Street Journal*, and *The New York Times* to apologise for the unethical mistake and added that "the only thing we're recalling here is our integrity". Such messages send a signal to all employees in the organisation, as well as to customers, concerning a firm's ethical standards.[16]

■ Promotion Issues

The communication process provides a variety of situations that can create ethical issues: for instance, false and misleading advertising and manipulative or deceptive sales promotions, tactics, or publicity efforts. In this section we consider some ethical issues linked to advertising and personal selling. We also examine the use of bribery in personal selling situations.

Advertising. Unethical actions in advertising can destroy the trust customers have in an organisation. Sometimes adverts are questioned because they are unfair to a competitor. For example, after McDonald's introduced a chicken product in some regions of the U.S.A., Kentucky Fried Chicken used TV commercials featuring a clown named Mr R. McDonald being questioned by a congressional committee. In one ad, when asked what McDonald's has that Kentucky Fried Chicken does not, Mr McDonald replies, "Toys . . . Lots of toys." CBS refused to broadcast the ad, saying, "We felt the commercial was unfairly denigrating to the corporate image of McDonald's." Although both NBC and ABC showed the commercials, CBS considered the ads to be ethically questionable.[17]

Abuses in advertising can range from exaggerated claims and concealed facts to outright lying. Exaggerated claims cannot be substantiated; for example, commercial claims that a certain pain reliever or cough syrup is superior to any other on the market often cannot be verified by consumers or experts. Concealed facts are material facts deliberately omitted from a message. Perrier's packaging implies that the bubbles in its mineral water are natural and are bottled at source. Sainsbury refused to stock this brand leader because the labelling was misleading—the bubbles are added during the bottling process: the mineral water does not contain them naturally. When consumers learn that promotion messages are untrue, they may feel cheated and refuse to buy the product again; they may also complain to government or other regulatory agencies. Consequently, marketers should take care to provide all the important facts and avoid making claims that cannot be supported. Otherwise they risk alienating their customers.

16. Jacob Scheslinger, "Chrysler Finds a Way to Settle Odometer Issue," *Wall Street Journal*, 10 Dec. 1987, p. 7.

17. Scott Hume, "Squawk over KFC Ads—Company Challenges Y&R with New Strategy," *Advertising Age*, 15 Jan. 1990, p. 16.

Another form of advertising abuse involves ambiguous statements—statements using words so weak that the viewer, reader, or listener must infer advertisers' intended messages. These "weasel" words are inherently vague and enable the advertiser to deny any intent to deceive. For example, *help* is a common "weasel" word, as in "helps prevent, helps fight, or helps make you feel".[18] Such advertising practices are questionable if they deceive the consumer outright. Although some marketers view such statements as acceptable, others do not. Thus vague messages remain an ethical issue in advertising.

Personal Selling. A common problem in selling activities is judging what types of sales activities are acceptable. Consumers may perceive salespeople as unethical because of the common belief that sales personnel often pressure customers to purchase products they neither need nor want. Nevertheless, the sales forces of most firms, such as IBM and Procter & Gamble, are well educated, well trained, and professional, and they know that they must act ethically or risk losing valuable customers and sales. Although most salespersons are ethical, some do engage in questionable actions. For example, some salespersons have used very aggressive and manipulative tactics to sell almost worthless securities, gemstones, vacations, or other products over the phone. Marketing Update 20.1 details the questionable methods employed by some time-share operators. Even though these salespeople may be fined for their activities, their unethical and often illegal actions contribute to consumers' mistrust of telephone selling and of personal selling in general.

At one time or another, most salespeople face an ethical conflict in their jobs. For example, a salesperson may have to decide whether to tell a customer the truth and risk losing the customer's business, or somehow mislead the customer to appease him or her and ensure a sale. Failure to train salespeople adequately in how to deal with such situations leaves them unprepared to cope with ethical issues when they arise. Furthermore, sales personnel who are untrained and confused about what action to take when facing an ethical dilemma often experience high levels of job frustration, anxiety, and stress.

Frequently, the problem of ethics has a snowball effect. Once a salesperson has deceived a customer, it becomes increasingly difficult to tell the truth later. If the customer learns of the deception, the sales representative will lose all credibility in the eyes of the customer, as well as that customer's associates and friends. Thus the manner in which a salesperson deals with an ethical issue can have far reaching consequences for both the individual and the firm.

Bribery in Selling Situations. When payments, gifts, or special favours are granted to obtain a sale or for some other reason, there is always some question of bribery. A bribe is anything given to improperly influence the outcome of a decision. Even when a bribe is offered to benefit the organisation, it is usually considered unethical, and it hurts the organisation in the long run for it jeopardises trust and fairness. Table 20.1 lists some possible gifts that could be offered by a salesperson in an attempt to gain sales. As you can see, defining a bribe is often a matter of personal values and judgement. Such practices are pernicious, for they stifle fair competition among businesses and limit consumer choice.

18. Archie B. Carroll, *Business and Society: Ethics and Stakeholder Management* (Cincinnati: South-Western Publishing, 1989), pp. 228–230.

TABLE 20.1
Which of these gifts could be considered a bribe?

Pen and pencil set (with company logo)
Five-year supply of notepads (with company logo)
Dinner at a four-star French restaurant
Box of grapefruit shipped to your house each Christmas
Season tickets to sport of your choice
Weekend break
Three-day, all-expenses-paid golfing holiday
Trip to a ski resort
Lavish trip to an exotic foreign locale
£1,000 in cash
Free PC and software

SOURCE: Adapted from E.J. Muller, "Traffigraft: Is Accepting a Gift from a Vendor a Breach of Ethics? To Some People, It's Just a Perk. To Others, It's Poison." *Distribution,* January 1990, p. 38. © 1990 Distribution Magazine. Reprinted with permission.

■ **Pricing Issues**

Price-fixing, predatory pricing, and failure to disclose the full price associated with a purchase are typical ethical issues. The emotional and subjective nature of price creates many situations in which misunderstandings between the seller and buyer cause ethical problems. Marketers have the right to price their products so that they earn a reasonable profit, but ethical issues may crop up when a company seeks to earn high profits at the expense of its customers. For example, the U.S. Federal Communications Commission found that Nynex, which owns the New York and New England telephone companies, had been inflating the prices it charged its subsidiaries for goods and services in order to boost its own profits. There is some concern that the practice may have resulted in higher telephone rates for Nynex customers.[19]

■ **Distribution Issues**

Ethical issues in distribution involve relationships among producers and marketing middlemen. Marketing middlemen, or intermediaries (wholesalers and retailers), facilitate the flow of products from the producer to the ultimate consumer. Each intermediary performs a different role and accepts certain rights, responsibilities, and rewards associated with that role. For example, producers can expect retailers to honour payment agreements and keep them informed of inventory needs. Failure to make payments in a timely manner may be considered an ethical issue.

The numerous relationships among marketing intermediaries present many opportunities for conflicts and disputes, including judgements about right or wrong, ethical or unethical behaviour. Manipulating a product's availability for purposes of exploitation and using coercion to force intermediaries to behave in a specific manner are particularly serious ethical issues in the distribution sphere. For example, a powerful manufacturer can exert undue influence over an intermediary's choice of whether to handle a product or how to handle it.

Other ethical issues in distribution relate to some stores' refusal to deal with some types of middlemen. A number of conflicts are developing in the distribution of microcomputer software. Many software-only stores are by-passing wholesalers and

19. John R. Wilke and Mary Lu Carnevale, "Wrong Numbers: Nynex Overcharged Phone Units for Years, An FCC Audit Finds," *Wall Street Journal,* 9 Jan. 1990, pp. A1, A10.

TIME-SHARE—QUESTIONABLE TACTICS

During the 1980s there has been a growth in the European time-share business. Hotel apartments, villas, boats, and country club accommodation are all available: customers buy a flat or a boat for use during only a few weeks of the year. The same boat or flat is "owned" by other customers for the remainder of the year.

Various selling and promotional techniques have been used. Typically, direct mail informs people of open days near to their town and invites prospective buyers to a free champagne reception where there will be a seminar discussing a particular time-share property.

Unfortunately, this has been taken a step further by some unscrupulous operators. The direct mail does not overtly mention time-share or selling. Instead it implies the recipient has "definitely" won a Ford Fiesta or cash prize. The smaller print points out that collection of the prize can only be at a weekend residential time-share seminar, for example. In many cases the even smaller print states that a prize has not definitely been awarded; it is only possible to win it. Clearly, many people are taken in and do not read the small print. Nothing illegal has taken place—just misleading and not completely ethical marketing tactics. The U.K. government has announced that it intends tightening up on time-share companies and their sales techniques.

SOURCES: "Borrie Blasts Time-Share," *Marketing,* 5 July 1990; *Marketing,* 22 March 1990; Robert Dwek, "Time-share Body Out to Foil OFT," *Marketing,* 14 June 1990, p. 13; "Curbs on Holiday Share Gift Schemes," *Coventry Evening Telegraph,* 11 December 1990, p. 14.

establishing direct relationships with software producers. Some dishonest stores are "hacking", or making unauthorised copies of software, preventing the producers from getting their due compensation. These occurrences have spawned suspicion and general ethical conflict in the distribution of software.[20]

Much controversy also surrounds retailers such as Tesco or Marks & Spencer, which often insist on doing business only with a producer rather than going through an intermediary. Marks & Spencer has been accused of threatening to buy from other producers if firms refuse to sell directly to it. Similar buy-direct policies are in effect at B&Q, the largest U.K. retailer of do-it-yourself building supplies, and at Do-It-All, the home improvement chain. These retailers, which emphasise low prices, maintain that the no-middleman approach cuts costs and does not involve any ethical issues. However, some small companies cannot afford to maintain their own sales forces and must rely on intermediaries to sell their products to retailers. The refusal of Tesco or B&Q and others to deal with intermediaries effectively shuts these smaller companies out of the market because they cannot compete with companies that have their own sales forces.

IMPROVING ETHICAL DECISIONS IN MARKETING

Conflicts between personal moral philosophies and corporate values, organisational pressures, and opportunity interact to create situations that may cause unethical behaviour. It is possible to improve ethical behaviour in an organisation by eliminating unethical persons and improving the organisation's ethical standards.

One way to approach improvement of an organisation's ethical standards is by considering a "bad apple–bad barrel" analogy. Some people always do things in their own self-interest regardless of organisational goals or accepted moral standards; they are sometimes called "bad apples". To eliminate unethical behaviour, an organisation must rid itself of the bad apples, or unethical persons. It can attain this goal through screening techniques and through the enforcement of ethics codes.[21] However, organisations too sometimes become "bad barrels"—not because the individuals within them are bad, but because the pressures to survive and succeed create conditions that reward unethical behaviour. A way of resolving the problem of the bad barrel is to redesign the organisation's image and culture so that it conforms to industry and societal norms of ethical behaviour.[22]

By making marketers aware of ethical issues and potential areas of conflict, it is possible to eliminate or defuse some of the ethical pressures that occur in daily marketing activities. Awareness of and sensitivity towards ethical issues can eliminate the risk of making unethical decisions. Ethical values must be built into the organisational culture and marketing strategy.[23] This can be achieved by establishing codes of ethics and by controlling unethical behaviour when it occurs.

20. Lanny J. Ryan, Gay C. Dawson, and Thomas Galek, "New Distribution Channels for Microcomputer Software," *Business*, October-December 1985, pp. 21–22.

21. Linda K. Trevino and Stuart Youngblood, "Bad Apples in Bad Barrels: A Causal Analysis of Ethical Decision Making Behavior," *Journal of Applied Psychology*, 1990.

22. Ibid.

23. Robin and Reidenbach, pp. 44–58.

TABLE 20.2 *Code of Ethics, American Marketing Association**

Members of the American Marketing Association (AMA) are committed to ethical professional conduct. They have joined together in subscribing to this Code of Ethics embracing the following topics:

Responsibilities of the Marketer

Marketers must accept responsibility for the consequences of their activities and make every effort to ensure that their decisions, recommendations, and actions function to identify, serve, and satisfy all relevant publics: consumers, organizations and society. Marketers' professional conduct must be guided by:

1. The basic rule of professional ethics: not knowingly to do harm;
2. The adherence to all applicable laws and regulations;
3. The accurate representation of their education, training and experience; and
4. The active support, practice and promotion of this Code of Ethics.

Honesty and Fairness

Marketers shall uphold and advance the integrity, honor, and dignity of the marketing profession by:

1. Being honest in serving consumers, clients, employees, suppliers, distributors and the public;
2. Not knowingly participating in conflict of interest without prior notice to all parties involved; and

° A similar code has yet to be produced in the EC.

3. Establishing equitable fee schedules including the payment or receipt of usual, customary and/or legal compensation for marketing exchanges.

Rights and Duties of Parties

Participants in the marketing exchange process should be able to expect that:

1. Products and services offered are safe and fit for their intended uses;
2. Communications about offered products and services are not deceptive;
3. All parties intend to discharge their obligations, financial and otherwise, in good faith; and
4. Appropriate internal methods exist for equitable adjustment and/or redress of grievances concerning purchases.

It is understood that the above would include, *but is not limited to,* the following responsibilities of the marketer:

In the area of product development management:

Disclosure of all substantial risks associated with product or service usage

Identification of any product component substitution that might materially change the product or impact on the buyer's purchase decision

Identification of extra-cost added features

Codes of Ethics

It is difficult for employees to determine what is acceptable behaviour within an organisation if the organisation does not have uniform policies and standards. Without standards of behaviour, employees will generally make decisions based on their observations of how their peers and managers behave. **Codes of ethics** are formalised rules and standards that describe what the company expects of its employees. Codes of ethics encourage ethical behaviour by eliminating opportunities for unethical behaviour: the company's employees know both what is expected of them and what the punishment is for violating the rules. Codes of ethics also help marketers deal with ethical issues or dilemmas that develop in daily operations by prescribing or limiting certain activities. The codes of ethics do not have to be so detailed that they take into account every situation, but they should provide general guidelines for achieving organisational goals and objectives in a morally acceptable manner. Top management also should provide leadership and guidelines in implementing the codes.

Table 20.2 is the American Marketing Association Code of Ethics. The code does not cover every ethical issue, but it is a useful overview of what marketers believe

TABLE 20.2 *continued*

In the area of promotions:

Avoidance of false and misleading advertising

Rejection of high pressure manipulations, or misleading sales tactics

Avoidance of sales promotions that use deception or manipulation

In the area of distribution:

Not manipulating the availability of a product for purpose of exploitation

Not using coercion in the marketing channel

Not exerting undue influence over the resellers' choice to handle a product

In the area of pricing:

Not engaging in price fixing

Not practicing predatory pricing

Disclosing the full price associated with any purchase

In the area of marketing research:

Prohibiting selling or fund raising under the guise of conducting research

Maintaining research integrity by avoiding misrepresentation and omission of pertinent research data

Treating outside clients and suppliers fairly

Organizational Relationships

Marketers should be aware of how their behavior may influence or impact on the behavior of others in organizational relationships. They should not encourage or apply coercion to obtain unethical behavior in their relationships with others, such as employees, suppliers or customers.

1. Apply confidentiality and anonymity in professional relationships with regard to privileged information.
2. Meet their obligations and responsibilities in contracts and mutual agreements in a timely manner.
3. Avoid taking the work of others, in whole, or in part, and represent this work as their own or directly benefit from it without compensation or consent of the originator or owner.
4. Avoid manipulation to take advantage of situations to maximize personal welfare in a way that unfairly deprives or damages the organization or others.

Any AMA members found to be in violation of any provision of this Code of Ethics may have his or her Association membership suspended or revoked.

SOURCE: Reprinted by permission of the American Marketing Association.

are sound moral principles for guiding marketing activities. This code could be used to help structure an organisation's code of ethics.

■ **Controlling Unethical Behaviour**

Ethical behaviour in marketing must be based on a strong moral foundation, including personal moral development and an organisational structure that encourages and rewards desired ethical action. The pressures of competition must be understood and coped with to improve ethical behaviour. The idea that marketing ethics is learned at home, at school and in family relationships does not recognise the impact of opportunity and the organisation on ethical decision-makers.

If a company is to maintain ethical behaviour, its policies, rules, and standards must be worked into its control system. If the number of employees making ethical decisions on a regular basis is not satisfactory, then the company needs to determine why and take corrective action through enforcement. Enforcement of standards is what makes codes of ethics effective. If codes are mere window-dressing and do not relate to what is expected or what is rewarded in the corporate culture, then they serve no purpose except to give an illusion of concern about ethical behaviour.

THE NATURE OF SOCIAL RESPONSIBILITY

The concepts of ethics and social responsibility are often used interchangeably, although each has a distinct meaning. **Social responsibility** in marketing refers to an organisation's obligation to maximise its positive impact and minimise its negative impact on society. Whereas ethics relate to individual decisions, social responsibility concerns the impact of an organisation's decisions on society.

For example, years ago the U.S. brewer Anheuser-Busch test-marketed a new adult beverage called Chelsea. Because it contained less than one-half percent alcohol, consumer groups labelled the beverage "kiddie beer" and protested that the company was being socially irresponsible by making an alcoholic drink available to minors. Owing to the low alcohol content, Chelsea was not subject to alcohol retail controls and was thus available in many shops selling sweets and drinks to children. Anheuser-Busch's first reaction was defensive; it tried to claim that the beverage was not dangerous and would not lead children to stronger drink. However, the company later decided to withdraw the beverage from the market-place and re-formulate it so that it would be viewed as more acceptable by society.[24] Social responsibility, then, can be viewed as a contract with society, whereas ethics relate to carefully thought-out rules of moral values that guide individual and group decision-making.

■ **Impact of Social Responsibility on Marketing**

Marketing managers try to determine what accepted relationships, obligations, and duties exist between the marketing organisation and society. Recognition is growing that for a firm's survival and competitive advantage, the long-term value of conducting business in a socially responsible manner far outweighs short-term costs.[25] To preserve socially responsible behaviour while achieving organisational goals, organisations must monitor changes and trends in society's values. For example, food companies around the world are developing and marketing healthier products in response to increasing public concern about cancer and heart disease. Furthermore, marketers must develop control procedures to ensure that daily decisions do not damage their company's relations with the public. An organisation's top management must assume some responsibility for its employees' conduct by establishing and enforcing policies.

Being socially responsible may be a noble and necessary endeavour, but it is not a simple one. To be socially responsible, marketers must confront certain major issues. Robertson's had, for four decades, used its Golliwog brandmark on its market-leading jams. Racial tension and increasingly vocal ethnic groups persuaded the company to minimise this potentially offensive symbol. Marketers therefore must determine what society wants and then predict the long-term effects of their decisions, often by turning to experts such as lawyers, doctors, and scientists. However, experts do not necessarily agree with each other, and the fields in which they work can yield findings that undermine previously acceptable marketing decisions.

Forty years ago, for example, tobacco marketers promoted cigarettes as being good for one's health. Now, years after the discovery that cigarette smoking is linked to cancer and other medical problems, society's attitude towards smoking is changing, and marketers are confronted with new social responsibilities, such as providing

24. Carroll, *Business and Society*, p. 45.

25. Margaret A. Stroup, Ralph L. Newbert, and Jerry W. Anderson, Jr., "Doing Good, Doing Better: Two Views of Social Responsibility," *Business Horizons*, March-April 1987, p. 23.

FIGURE 20.3
Caring for the environment.
Esso promotes its support of U.K. 2000 by its efforts to help make the environment cleaner and safer.

If UK 2000 wasn't so important, we'd be happy to remain anonymous.

Is making Britain a better place a bit of a pipedream? Those of us who have become involved in UK 2000 don't think so.

The thrust of this new national venture is to 'green' our cities; restore our industrial heritage, the 19th century mills and warehouses; tackle litter and recycle waste; turn neglected woodlands, canals, ponds and footpaths from eyesores into amenities; and make our tourist sites more attractive.

UK 2000 will run to the year 2000 and provide local, community-run projects, involving volunteers and the unemployed.

Esso is helping projects and training by providing funds, experience and people. We have seconded skilled staff to contribute to the management of UK 2000, including the Director of UK 2000's Scottish operation. We already support the British Trust for Conservation Volunteers,

the Civic Trust, Community Service Volunteers and Groundwork, four of the many groups taking part.

Esso is also active with bodies like the RSPB, the Nature Conservancy Council and the Countryside Commission on other environmental projects. In this European Year of the Environment we hope our involvement in UK 2000 will be even more helpful.

UK 2000 is a partnership between industry, voluntary groups and government, but it also needs individual support.

Please can we urge you to find out more, by writing to UK 2000, 2–3 Horse and Dolphin Yard, Macclesfield Street, London W1V 7LG.

Or telephone 01-631 3826/5160.

UK 2000

(Esso)

Quality at work for Britain.

SOURCE: Reproduced with kind permission of Esso Petroleum U.K. Ltd.

a smoke-free atmosphere for customers. Most major hotel chains reserve at least some of their rooms for non-smokers, and most other businesses within the food, travel, and entertainment industries provide smoke-free environments or sections.

Because society is made up of many diverse groups, finding out what society as a whole wants is difficult, if not impossible. In trying to satisfy the desires of one group, marketers may dissatisfy others. For example, in the smoking debate, marketers must balance smokers' desire to continue to smoke cigarettes against non-smokers' desire for a smoke-free environment.

Moreover, there are costs associated with many of society's demands. For example, society wants a cleaner environment and the preservation of wildlife and habitats, but it also wants low-priced petrol and heating oil. Figure 20.3 illustrates how Esso acknowledges the need to care for the environment. Thus, companies that market petrol and oil must carefully balance the costs of providing low-priced products against the costs of manufacturing and packaging their products in an environmentally responsible manner. Such a balance is difficult to achieve to the satisfaction of all members of society. Marketers must also evaluate the extent to which members of society are willing to pay for what they want. For instance, consumers may want more information about a product yet be unwilling to pay the

TABLE 20.3
*Social responsibility
issues*

ISSUE	DESCRIPTION	MAJOR SOCIETAL CONCERNS
Consumer Movement	Activities undertaken by independent individuals, groups, and organisations to protect their rights as consumers	The right to safety The right to be informed The right to choose The right to be heard
Community Relations	Society anxious to have marketers contribute to its well-being, wishing to know what businesses do to help solve social problems Communities demanding that firms listen to their grievances and ideas	Equality issues Disadvantaged members of society Safety and health Education and general welfare
Green Products	Consumers insisting not only on the quality of life but also on a healthy environment so that they can maintain a high standard of living during their lifetimes	Conservation Water pollution Air pollution Land pollution

costs the firm incurs in providing the data. Thus marketers who want to make socially responsible decisions may find the task difficult.

■ **Social Responsibility Issues**

Although social responsibility may seem to be an abstract ideal, managers make decisions related to social responsibility on a daily basis. To be successful, a business must determine what customers, government inspectors, and competitors, as well as society in general, want or expect in terms of social responsibility. Table 20.3 summarises several major categories of social responsibility issues, which include the consumer movement, community relations, and green marketing.

Consumer Issues.   One of the most significant social responsibility issues in marketing is the consumer movement, which Chapter 2 defines as the efforts of independent individuals, groups, and organisations to protect the rights of consumers. A number of interest groups and individuals have taken actions such as lobbying government officials and agencies, letter-writing campaigns, placing advertisements, and boycotting companies they consider are irresponsible.

David Tench, one of the best known consumer activists, continues to crusade for consumer rights. Consumer activism on the part of Tench and others has resulted in legislation requiring various safety features in cars: seat-belts, padded dashboards, stronger door catches, headrests, shatter-proof windscreens, and collapsible steering columns. Activists' efforts have furthered the passage of several consumer protection laws, such as the Trade Descriptions Act 1968, the Consumer Protection Act 1987, the Fair Trading Act 1973, the Food Act 1984, and the Weights and Measures Act 1985.

Community Relations.   Social responsibility also extends to marketers' roles as community members. Individual communities expect marketers to contribute to the satisfaction and growth of their communities. Thus many marketers view social responsibility as including contributions of resources (money, products, time) to community causes such as education, the arts, recreation, disadvantaged members of the community, and others. Honeywell, Shell, Ogilvy & Mather, and Hewlett-Packard all have programmes that contribute funds, equipment, and personnel to educational reform. Similarly, IBM donates or reduces the price of computer equipment to educational institutions. All these efforts, of course, have a positive impact on local communities, but they also indirectly help the organisations in the form of good will, publicity, and exposure to potential future customers. Thus, although social responsibility is certainly a positive concept, most organisations do not embrace it without the expectation of some indirect long-term benefit.

Green Marketing.   **Green marketing** refers to the specific development, pricing, promotion, and distribution of products that do not harm the environment. An independent coalition of environmentalists, scientists, and marketers is one group involved in evaluating products to determine their environmental impact and marketers' commitment to the environment and producing *The Green Guide*. In Germany, several environmental groups have joined together to create a seal of approval, the Blue Angel, to distinguish products that are environmentally safe. Companies receiving this seal will be able to use it in advertising and public information campaigns and on packaging. Marketing Update 20.2 describes an environmentally responsible decision by Du Pont.

■ **Strategies for Dealing with Social Responsibility Issues**

There are four basic strategies for systematically dealing with social responsibility issues: reaction, defence, accommodation, and proaction.

Reaction Strategy.   A business adopting a **reaction strategy** allows a condition or potential problem to go unresolved until the public learns about it. The situation may be known to management (as were one car maker's problems with fuel tank combustibility) or it may be unknown (as was the sudden acceleration of the Audi without direct action from the driver). In either case, the business denies responsibility but tries to resolve the problem, deal with its consequences, and continue doing business as usual to minimise the negative impact.

Defence Strategy.   A business using a **defence strategy** tries to minimise or avoid additional obligations linked to a problem or problems. Commonly used defence tactics include legal manoeuvring and seeking the support of trade unions that embrace the company's way of doing business and support the industry. Businesses often lobby to avoid government action or regulation. For example, the U.S. direct-mail industry lobbied against an increase in bulk postal rates because it knew it would have to pass on these increases to its clients, advertisers, and advertising agencies. Sizeable increases in postal rates could put it at a competitive disadvantage in relation to print media, such as newspaper inserts, which do not use the mail. Thus the industry took a defensive position to protect its own and its clients' interests.

Accommodation Strategy.   A business using an **accommodation strategy** assumes responsibility for its actions. A business might adopt the accommodation strategy when special-interest groups are encouraging a particular action or when

DU PONT STOPS MAKING
ENVIRONMENTALLY HARMFUL PRODUCT

Scientists have long contended that chlorofluorocarbons (CFCs) are destroying the ozone layer in the upper atmosphere—the layer that shields the earth from the sun's harmful ultraviolet rays. Chlorofluorocarbons are inert substances used in refrigeration and foam packaging. Their use as propellants in aerosol containers was banned in the U.S. in the 1970s, when researchers first learned that CFCs were destroying the ozone. In March 1988, an international study reported that the ozone layer over the Northern Hemisphere was being rapidly and seriously depleted. Scientists had already discovered a hole in it over Antarctica the year before. Du Pont & Co., which holds 25 percent of the CFC market with its product Freon, realised that it had to act responsibly to protect the environment.

After the results of the international study were publicised, the company announced that it would phase out production of Freon, which contributes £450 million to Du Pont's sales, as soon as it had substitutes ready for the market. The company expects to reduce production by 95 percent by the year 2003. Du Pont has been spending £7 million a year trying to develop a substitute for CFCs and already has two in production.

Du Pont has also asked nations and companies that produce chlorofluorocarbons to abide by a 1987 treaty that calls for at least a 50 percent reduction in the production of CFCs by 1999. Scientists, however, say the treaty is too little and too late to stop the problem of the deteriorating ozone. They believe that the decay of the ozone layer will result in an increase in skin cancer, damaged crops, and harm to marine life.

Environmental groups praised Du Pont's decision to stop making the harmful chemical as an example of corporate social responsibility. These groups hope that the company's action will encourage other companies to stop producing chlorofluorocarbons. Although Du Pont stands to lose millions of pounds in sales by discontinuing the production of Freon, the company realised that it had an obligation to stop making the product because of the damage it has done, and is yet to do, to the environment.

SOURCES: Mary Lu Carnevale, "Du Pont Plans to Phase Out CFC Output," *Wall Street Journal,* 25 Mar. 1988, pp. 2, 4; "Ozone: Du Pont Does Good," *U.S. News & World Report,* 4 Apr. 1988, p. 13; Tim Smart, with Joseph Weber, "An Ozone Hole over Capitol Hill," *Business Week,* 4 Apr. 1988, p. 35.

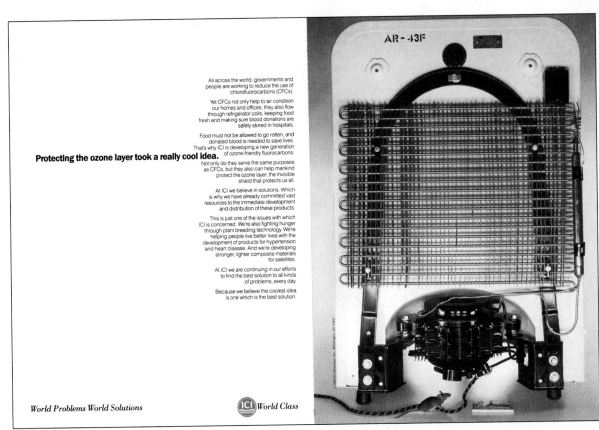

All across the world, governments and people are working to reduce the use of chlorofluorocarbons (CFCs).

Yet CFCs not only help to air condition our homes and offices, they also flow through refrigerator coils, keeping food fresh and making sure blood donations are safely stored in hospitals.

Food must not be allowed to go rotten, and donated blood is needed to save lives. That's why ICI is developing a new generation of ozone-friendly fluorocarbons.

Protecting the ozone layer took a really cool idea.

Not only do they serve the same purposes as CFCs, but they also can help mankind protect the ozone layer, the invisible shield that protects us all.

At ICI we believe in solutions. Which is why we have already committed vast resources to the immediate development and distribution of these products.

This is just one of the issues with which ICI is concerned. We're also fighting hunger through plant breeding technology. We're helping people live better lives with the development of products for hypertension and heart disease. And we're developing stronger, lighter composite materials for satellites.

At ICI we are continuing in our efforts to find the best solution to all kinds of problems, every day.

Because we believe the coolest idea is one which is the best solution.

World Problems World Solutions   (ICI) *World Class*

FIGURE 20.4   *Developing products that solve ecological problems.*
ICI shows its concern about protecting the ozone layer by developing products that do not contain chlorofluorocarbons.
SOURCE: Courtesy of ICI America Inc. Created by Saatchi and Saatchi

the business perceives that if it fails to react the government will pass a law to ensure compliance. Figure 20.4 illustrates how ICI is developing cooling systems that use ozone-friendly fluorocarbons.

For example, McDonald's developed a nutrition-orientated advertising campaign to appease dietitians and nutritionists who had urged that accurate nutritional information should be provided on all fast-food products. However, McDonald's campaign, instead of soothing the interest groups, antagonised them. The groups claim that McDonald's portrayal of its food as healthful was inaccurate. A McDLT, French fries, and milkshake contain 1,283 calories, approximately 60 percent of the entire recommended daily calorie intake for an adult woman. In addition, that meal contains 15 teaspoons of fat, 10 teaspoons of sugar, no fibre, and approximately 70 percent of the daily allowance of sodium. Dietitians and nutritionists petitioned the U.S. Food and Drug Administration in the hope that it would require product nutritional labelling to alert consumers to the high levels of fat, sodium, and sugar and low levels of starch and fibre.[26] McDonald's chose to take an accommodation strategy to curtail lobbying against nutritional information disclosure when it probably should have adopted a proactive strategy.

26. "McD Ads Draw Protests from Nutritional Experts," *Nation's Restaurant News*, 22 June 1987, p. 26.

Proactive Strategy.   A business that uses a **proactive strategy** assumes responsibility for its actions and responds to accusations made against it without outside pressure or the threat of government intervention. A proactive strategy requires management, of its own free will, to support an action or cause. For example, Toyota decided to recall its popular 1990 model Lexus car to repair several defects. Although none of the defects had caused any accidents or injuries, Toyota has a reputation for quality and excellence, which it promotes heavily in advertising. Consequently, its executives probably concluded that the most responsible action to take was to deal with the defects before any injuries or deaths occurred.[27] Even if the recall should temporarily harm the Lexus image, Toyota's prompt and responsible action will probably draw a positive response from consumers in the long run.

SOCIAL RESPONSIBILITY AND MARKETING ETHICS

Although the concepts of marketing ethics and social responsibility are often used interchangeably, it is important to remember that ethics relate to individual moral evaluations—judgements about what is right or wrong in a particular decision-making situation. Social responsibility is the obligation of an organisation to maximise its positive impact and minimise its negative impact on society. Thus social responsibility deals with the total effect of marketing decisions on society. These two concepts work together because a company that supports both socially acceptable moral philosophies and individuals who act ethically is likely to make decisions that have a positive impact on society.

One way to evaluate whether a specific behaviour is ethical and socially responsible is to ask other persons in an organisation if they approve of it. For social responsibility issues, contact with concerned consumer groups and industry or government regulatory groups may be helpful. Also a check to see if there is a specific company policy about the activity may resolve the issue. If other persons in the organisation approve of the activity and it is legal and customary within the industry, chances are the activity is acceptable from both an ethical and social responsibility perspective.

A rule of thumb for ethical and social responsibility issues is that if they can withstand open discussion and result in agreements or limited debate, then an acceptable solution may exist. Still, even after a final decision is reached, different viewpoints on the issue may remain. Openness is not the complete solution to the ethics problem; but it does create trust and facilitates learning relationships.[28]

SUMMARY

Marketing ethics are moral principles that define right and wrong behaviour in marketing. Most marketing decisions can be judged as ethical or unethical. Ethics are a very important concern in marketing decisions, yet they may be one of the most misunderstood and controversial concepts in marketing.

27. Gregory A. Patterson, "Lexus to Recall All Its LS 400 Luxury Models," *Wall Street Journal*, 5 Dec. 1989, pp. B1, B11.

28. Sir Adrian Cadbury, "Ethical Managers Make Their Own Rules," *Harvard Business Review,* September-October 1987, p. 33.

Personal moral philosophies, organisational factors, and opportunity are three important components of ethical decision-making. Moral philosophies are principles or rules that individuals use to determine the right way to behave. They provide guidelines for resolving conflicts and ensuring mutual benefit for all members of society. Utilitarian moral philosophies are concerned with maximising the greatest good for the greatest number of people. Ethical formalism philosophies, on the other hand, focus on general rules for guiding behaviour and on the rights of the individual. Organisational relationships with one's employees or superiors create ethical problems such as maintaining confidentiality in personal relations; meeting obligations, responsibilities, and mutual agreements; and avoiding undue pressure that may force others to behave unethically. Opportunity—a favourable set of conditions that limit barriers or provide internal or external rewards—to engage in unethical behaviour provides another pressure that may determine whether a person behaves ethically. If an individual uses an opportunity afforded him or her to act unethically and escapes punishment or even gains a reward, that person is more likely to repeat such acts when circumstances favour them.

An ethical issue is an identifiable problem, situation, or opportunity requiring an individual or organisation to choose from among alternatives that must be evaluated as right or wrong. Ethical issues typically arise because of conflicts among individuals' personal moral philosophies and the marketing strategies, policies, and organisational environment in which they work. Product-related ethical issues may develop when marketers fail to disclose risks associated with the product or information that relates to understanding the function, value, or use of the product. Competitive pressures can also create product-related ethical issues. The promotion process provides situations that can result in ethical issues, such as false and misleading advertising and deceptive sales tactics. Sales promotions and publicity that use deception or manipulation also create significant ethical issues. Bribery may be an ethical issue in some selling situations. The emotional and subjective nature of price creates conditions where misunderstandings between the seller and buyer lead to ethical problems. Ethical issues in distribution relate to relationships and conflicts among producers and marketing middlemen.

Codes of ethics, which formalise what an organisation expects of its employees, eliminate the opportunity for unethical behaviour because they provide rules to guide conduct and punishments for violating the rules. If the number of employees making ethical decisions on a regular basis is not satisfactory, the company needs to determine why and take corrective action through enforcement. Enforcement of standards is what makes codes of ethics effective.

Social responsibility in marketing refers to an organisation's obligation to maximise its positive impact and minimise its negative impact on society. Marketing managers try to determine what accepted relationships, obligations, and duties exist between the business organisation and society.

To be successful, a business must determine what customers, government officials, and competitors, as well as society in general, want or expect in terms of social responsibility. Major categories of social responsibility issues include the consumer movement, community relations, and green marketing. The consumer movement refers to the activities of independent individuals, groups, and organisations in trying to protect the rights of consumers. Communities expect marketers to contribute to the satisfaction and growth of their communities. Green marketing refers to the specific development, pricing, promotion, and distribution of products that do not harm the environment.

Four basic strategies for dealing with social responsibility issues are reaction, defence, accommodation, and proaction. A business adopting a reaction strategy allows a condition or potential problem to go unresolved until the public learns about it. A business using the defence strategy tries to minimise or avoid additional obligations associated with a problem or problems. In the accommodation strategy, a business assumes responsibility for its actions. A business that uses the proactive strategy assumes responsibility for its actions and responds to accusations made against it without outside pressure or the threat of government intervention.

The concepts of marketing ethics and social responsibility work together because a firm that has a corporate culture built on socially acceptable moral philosophies will generally make decisions that have a positive impact on society. If other persons in the firm approve of an activity and it is legal and customary within the industry, chances are the activity is ethical and socially responsible.

IMPORTANT TERMS

Marketing ethics	Green marketing
Moral philosophies	Reaction strategy
Ethical issue	Defence strategy
Codes of ethics	Accommodation strategy
Social responsibility	Proactive strategy

DISCUSSION AND REVIEW QUESTIONS

1. Why are ethics an important consideration in marketing decisions?
2. How do the factors that influence ethical or unethical decisions interact?
3. Are there ethical concerns in seeing marketing as warfare, with the view that competitors are the enemy?
4. What are some of the areas that result in major ethical issues in marketing?
5. How can ethical decisions in marketing be improved?
6. How can people with different personal values join together to make ethical decisions in an organisation?
7. What is the difference between ethics and social responsibility?
8. What are major social responsibility issues?
9. Describe strategies for dealing with social responsibility issues.
10. How do you determine when a gift or payment is a bribe in marketing?

■ CASES

20.1 The Growth of "Green" Companies

In April 1990 the environmental charity Landbank Trust announced the launch of its Green Alternative range of household products. Joining Ark and Ecover products on the supermarket shelves, the launch symbolised the rapid take-off for the environmentally conscious sector. Ecology charity Worldwatch 2000 decided to launch an index of the top 100 "Green" companies—"the environmental version of the FT index." The financial, general, and marketing press was eager to feature items relating to the Green movement. Such publicity, along with the materialisation on supermarket shelves of Green products, could not go unnoticed by the public. Few companies, therefore, could ignore the environmental issue and its effect on the marketing of their brands.

Until the autumn of 1989, the detergent giants had been content to leave the market for environment friendly detergents to the likes of Ark and Ecover—niche marketers in the extreme. Without warning, in October, Procter & Gamble launched Ariel Ultra, the first environmentally sound and concentrated soap powder to hit the U.K. Even Anglo-Dutch giant Unilever was caught out, with no comparable product to compete in the ever increasingly Green detergents environment. Procter & Gamble stole the lead in an extremely competitive market.

Questions for Discussion

1. What will be the likely impact on the market of Ariel Ultra?
2. By marketing a Green soap powder, is Procter & Gamble risking the credentials of the rest of its portfolio?
3. For what reasons did Unilever not, in such a dynamic market, launch a product orientated towards the Green consumer?

SOURCES: Liz Levy, "P & G Sets Off Green Powder Keg," *Marketing,* 12 October 1989, pp. 16–17; Clare Sambrook, "Advertisers Cut Green Excess," *Marketing,* 18 January 1990, p. 4; Liz Levy, "Angry Greens Attack 'Unscrupulous Sharks'," *Marketing,* 5 October 1989, p. 3; Clare Sambrook, "Ecover Demands Bill to Control Phosphates," *Marketing,* 12 July 1990, p. 1; Clare Sambrook, "Eco-charity Logs the Firm Top 100," *Marketing,* 28 September 1989, p. 3; Stephen Hounslow, "Green Charity Claims Brand Policy First," *Marketing,* 19 April 1990, p. 5; Nick Hall, "Green Goods Set for Closer Investigation," *Marketing Week,* 10 March 1989, p. 7; "Where There's a Green There's Brass," *Business,* August 1990, pp. 109–116.

20.2   The Wreck of the *Exxon Valdez*

In 1989, Exxon Corporation and Alyeska Pipeline Service Company—a consortium, owned by Exxon and seven other oil companies, that operates the Trans-Alaska pipeline and the shipping terminal in Valdez, Alaska—faced much criticism over their handling of a major oil spill from an Exxon tanker. The *Exxon Valdez* ran aground near Valdez, Alaska, spilling 240,000 barrels—11 million gallons—of crude oil that eventually covered 2,600 square miles of Prince William Sound and the Gulf of Alaska.

The *Exxon Valdez* ran aground atop Bligh Reef, rupturing its hull, soon after midnight on March 24, 1989, while the helmsman was attempting to manoeuvre the nearly 1,000-foot ship around some floating ice. Captain Joseph Hazelwood had left the ship's third mate, who was not licensed to pilot the vessel through the treacherous waters of Prince William Sound, at the helm while he slept below deck. The spill spread rapidly during the next few days, killing thousands of sea birds, sea otters, and other wildlife; covering the pristine coastline with oil; and curtailing the fishing season in the sound.

The events following the spill reveal that neither Exxon nor Alyeska was prepared to handle a spill the size of that leaked by the *Exxon Valdez,* despite repeated assurances to the contrary. To relieve public concern about the safety of the Alaskan environment, Alyeska Pipeline Service, its eight oil company owners, and federal officials promised in 1972 that the tanker fleet operating out of Valdez would incorporate safety features such as double hulls and protective ballast tanks to minimise the possibility of spills. By 1977, however, Alyeska had convinced the Coast Guard that the safety features were unnecessary, and few ships in the Valdez fleet incorporated them. The *Exxon Valdez* did not.

Alyeska had also filed a comprehensive contingency plan detailing how it would handle spills from the pipeline or the Valdez terminal. The contingency plan provided that in the event of an oil spill from a tanker, emergency crews would encircle the spill with containment booms within five hours. But it took them thirty-six hours to fully encircle the *Exxon Valdez*. Alyeska's contingency plan further specified that an emergency crew would be on hand at all times. For a time, Alyeska did have an emergency team on location to respond to a spill but disbanded most of it by 1981 to cut costs. Exxon's staff of oil spill experts had also been reduced because of personnel cutbacks. An Exxon spokesman said that he was not aware that the cutbacks affected Alyeska's initial readiness to combat a spill.

A state audit of the equipment Alyeska should have had on hand at the time of the spill demonstrated that the company was unprepared. The company had only two of the three tugboats and seven of the thirteen oil skimmers that were supposed to be available. The company also had only 14,000 feet of boom for containing spills; the contingency plan specified 21,000 feet. The barge that carried the booms and stored skimmed oil was also out of service because it had been damaged in a storm before the spill. In any case, the required equipment would not have been enough because a tanker such as the *Exxon Valdez* is almost 1,000 feet long and holds 1.2 million barrels of oil. The booms available barely encircled the giant ship, much less a sizable slick. Moreover, Alyeska was in violation of its own contingency plans when it failed to notify state officials that the barge was out of service. The damaged barge was pressed into service for clean-up operations anyway.

Furthermore, Alyeska and Exxon did not have enough chemical dispersants to fight the spill. They were not ready to test the effectiveness of the dispersants until eighteen hours after the spill, and then they conducted the test by tossing buckets of chemicals out of the door of a helicopter. The helicopter's rotor wash dispersed the chemicals, and they missed their target altogether. Exxon eventually applied tens of thousands of gallons of dispersants, but by then the oil had become too emulsified for dispersants to work properly. Moreover, the skimmer boats used to scoop oil out of the sea were so old that they kept breaking down and clogging. The skimmers filled rapidly and had to be emptied into nearby barges, requiring long periods of inactivity. Clean-up efforts were further hampered by communication breakdowns between co-ordinators on shore and crews at the scene because of technical problems and limited range. Despite pleas from fishermen, Exxon and Alyeska also failed to mobilise the fleet of private fishing boats standing by. Exxon admitted that the early efforts were chaotic, but no more so than the response to any major disaster.

Nine hours after the wreck, Captain Hazelwood was tested for alcohol. The test showed that his blood alcohol content exceeded that allowed by Coast Guard regulations for a person operating a ship. Four other crewmen, including the third mate, tested negative for alcohol. Exxon officials later admitted they knew that the captain had gone through an alcohol detoxification programme, yet they still gave him command of the *Exxon Valdez*, Exxon's largest tanker.

The public was outraged by the spill itself and highly critical of Exxon's and Alyeska's clean-up efforts. Exxon's chairman, Lawrence Rawl, apologised to the public and accepted liability for the spill and responsibility for its clean-up. By the summer, the company had 11,000 people, 1,400 vessels, 38 oil skimmers, and 72 aircraft working to clean up beaches and save wildlife. Still, many felt that Exxon and Alyeska's efforts were inadequate and slow. There were also disputes as to how much oil had actually been cleaned up. Several thousand Exxon credit card holders returned their cards; others boycotted Exxon service stations and products.

Exxon also came under fire for a number of public relations disasters during the crisis. Mr Rawl did not comment on the spill for nearly six days, and then he did so from New York. Crisis management experts believe that Rawl's delayed response and failure to appear on the scene angered consumers, despite Exxon's efforts to clean up the spill. Consumers also became angry over some of Exxon's public statements. For example, one Exxon executive told reporters that consumers would pay for the costs of the clean-up in higher petrol prices. Exxon's attempts to blame the clean-up delays on the Coast Guard and Alaskan officials were also damaging. Furthermore, Exxon insisted in a July memorandum that it would stop all clean-up operations on 15 September 1989, regardless of how much shoreline remained to be cleaned. However, when the memo was made public, it generated so much public and government protest that Exxon officials promised to resume the clean-up in the spring of 1990 if the Coast Guard determined a need for it.

Exxon's response to the crisis certainly hurt its reputation and credibility with the public. Exxon claims that it had saved $22 million by not building the *Exxon Valdez* with a second hull. But some experts believe that the cost of the clean-up effort may exceed $2 billion, of which insurance companies would pay only $400 million. In addition, more than 150 lawsuits had been filed against Exxon as a result of the spill; more are expected. On 15 August 1989, the state of Alaska also filed suit against Exxon, as well as subsidiaries of Amerada Hess, Atlantic Richfield, British Petroleum, Mobil, Phillips Petroleum, and Unocal—the largest owners of Alyeska Pipeline Services—for mismanaging the response to the oil spill. The suit demands both compensatory and punitive damages that may exceed $1 billion. However, although Captain Hazelwood was indicted for his actions in the incident, he was acquitted on all the charges except negligent discharge of oil. He was fined and sentenced to clean Alaskan beaches for 1,000 hours. Exxon may have to pay billions more to settle lawsuits and claims from fishermen and Alaskan businesses, as well as any civil and criminal penalties levied by the Alaskan and federal governments.

SOURCES: Stuart Elliot, "Public Angry at Slow Action on Oil Spill," *USA Today*, 21 Apr. 1989, pp. B1, B2; William Glasgall and Vicky Cahan, "Questions That Keep Surfacing After the Spill," *Business Week*, 17 Apr. 1989, p. 18; "In Ten Years You'll See 'Nothing,'" *Fortune*, 8 May 1989, pp. 50–54; Charles McCoy and Ken Wells, "Alaska, U.S. Knew of Flaws in Oil-Spill Response Plans," *Wall Street Journal*, 7 Apr. 1989, p. A3; Bill Nichols, "State Fears Exxon Will 'Walk Away,'" *USA Today*, 13 Sept. 1989, pp. 1A, 2A; Lawrence G. Rawl, Letter to Exxon Shareholders, 14 Apr. 1989; Richard B. Schmitt, "Exxon, Alyeska May Be Exposed on Damages," *Wall Street Journal*, 10 Apr. 1989, p. A8; Allanna Sullivan, "Alaska Sues Exxon Corp., 6 Other Firms," *Wall Street Journal*, 16 Aug. 1989, pp. A3, A4; Ken Wells, "Alaska Begins Criminal Inquiry of Valdez Spill," *Wall Street Journal*, 30 Mar. 1989, p. A4; and Ken Wells and Charles McCoy, "How Unpreparedness Turned the Alaska Spill into Ecological Debacle," *Wall Street Journal*, 3 Apr. 1989, pp. A1, A4; Cable News Network, 22 March 1990.

Questions for Discussion

1. Ethics relate to individual decisions. What were the ethical issues in this case?
2. What were the social responsibility issues in this case?
3. What effect did the wreck of the *Exxon Valdez* have on Exxon's marketing strategy for consumer products such as petrol?

PART VII SELECTED APPLICATIONS

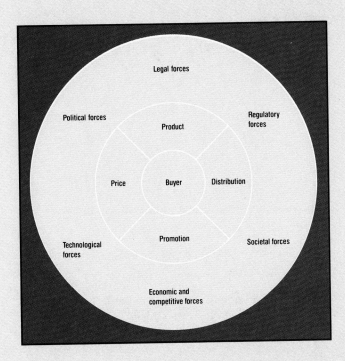

The remaining chapters in this book discuss and highlight strategic applications in industrial, services, and international marketing. We emphasise the features and issues that are unique to each of these selected areas of marketing. We also focus on aspects that impact on formulating and implementing marketing strategies. Chapter 21 analyses the development of industrial marketing strategy and discusses the decisions and activities that characterise industrial marketing. Chapter 22 explores selected aspects of services and non-business marketing strategies. Chapter 23 focuses on international marketing and on the development and implementation of marketing strategies for markets across national boundaries. ◆

21 INDUSTRIAL MARKETING

Objectives

To understand some unique characteristics of industrial marketing

To learn how to select and analyse industrial target markets

To find out how industrial marketing mix components differ from the components in consumer product marketing mixes olvo Trucks is a wholly-owned subsidiary of Volvo. In the U.K., it is the division which handles the importing, manufacturing, sales and marketing, and after-sales support for all Volvo heavy goods vehicles. Currently, Volvo has an approximately 18 percent market share of U.K. trucks over 15 tonnes, placing it second behind Leyland Daf, with a 22 percent market share.

Sales of all makes of trucks heavier than 3.5 tonnes were the highest of the decade in 1989, with sales of 69,234. However, in the summer and autumn of 1990, sales fell by nearly 40 percent. As the U.K. economic recession worsened, most hauliers cancelled or delayed orders for replacement vehicles. As a result, many suppliers, who had scheduled high levels of production based on 1989 sales, found themselves in a serious overstock position.

For most of the major players in the European truck market, there are two major trends which are dictating current marketing strategies. The decline in new vehicle sales is leading to an increased focus on the after-market. The market for replacement parts is more stable and offers some degree of cushioning against the more extreme fluctuations in demand for new vehicles. Similarly, tyres, fuels, and lubricants continue to sell steadily even when there is a down turn in truck sales. Most truck manufacturers are devoting more of their marketing effort to servicing, maintenance, and provision of parts.

The second trend has been a move by hauliers and large companies with their own transport fleets away from purchasing new vehicles outright. There has been a switch to leasing and contract hire, whereby the truck manufacturer ultimately retains ownership of the vehicle and has to off-load the vehicles when they are returned by the haulier. This has forced marketers to learn a variety of new financial skills. They have to set leasing and contract hire rates sufficiently high to make an operating profit, bearing in mind the increased competition in the market. They must also be prepared to take back and resell large numbers of used vehicles. For the industrial marketer working in the truck business, the task is no longer simply one of marketing and selling new vehicles—the provision of after-sales services and parts and the negotiating of complex leasing and contract hire agreements are becoming increasingly important. ◆

SOURCES: "Heavy Going," *Automotive Management,* 13 September 1990; John Griffiths, "Truck Sales Suffer Fall in September of Nearly 40%," *Financial Times,* 17 October 1990; Richard Longworth, "Glitter, Shadows and Lights at the Ends of Tunnels," *Transport Week,* 22 September 1990, pp. 40–41.

S ome of the problems that industrial marketers experience resemble those of consumer product marketers, and industrial marketers, too, rely on basic marketing concepts and decisions. However, they apply those concepts and decisions in different ways, which take into account the nature of industrial markets and products.

Industrial marketing is a set of activities directed towards facilitating and expediting exchanges involving industrial products and customers in industrial markets. As mentioned in Chapter 5, an industrial product differs from a consumer product in that it is purchased to be used directly or indirectly to produce other products or to be used in the operations of an organisation. Chapter 5 also classifies industrial products into seven categories: raw materials, major equipment, accessory equipment, component parts, process materials, consumable supplies, and industrial services. As Chapter 5 explains, an organisational or industrial market consists of individuals or groups who purchase a specific kind of product for one of three purposes: resale, direct use in producing other products, or use in general daily operations. Industrial markets consist of numerous types of customers, including commercial producers, governments, and institutions.

Aside from product and market differences, industrial marketing is unique for these reasons: (1) the buyer's decision-making process, (2) characteristics of the product market, and (3) the nature of environmental influences.[1] These differences influence the development and implementation of industrial marketing strategies.

This chapter focuses on dimensions unique to developing marketing strategies for industrial products. First, we examine the selection and analysis of industrial target markets. Then we discuss the distinctive features of industrial marketing mixes.

SELECTION AND ANALYSIS OF INDUSTRIAL TARGET MARKETS

Marketing research is becoming more important in industrial marketing, especially in selecting and analysing target markets. Most of the marketing research techniques that we discuss in Chapter 6 can be applied to industrial marketing. In this section we focus on important and unique approaches to selecting and analysing industrial target markets.

Industrial marketers have easy access to a considerable amount of information about potential customers, for much of this information appears in government and industry publications. However, comparable data about ultimate consumers are not available. Even though industrial marketers may use different procedures to isolate and analyse target markets, most follow a similar pattern: (1) determining who potential customers are and how many there are, (2) locating where they are, and (3) estimating their purchase potential.[2]

1. Edward F. Fern and James R. Brown, "The Industrial/Consumer Marketing Dichotomy: A Case of Insufficient Justification," *Journal of Marketing*, Spring 1984, pp. 168–177.

2. Robert W. Haas, *Industrial Marketing Management* (New York: Petrocelli Charter, 1976), pp. 37–48.

TABLE 21.1
SIC divisions

0	Agriculture, forestry, and fishing
1	Energy and water supply industries
2	Extraction of minerals and ores other than fuels; manufacture of metals, mineral products, and chemicals
3	Metal goods, engineering, and vehicles
4	Other manufacturing industries
5	Construction
6	Distribution, hotels, and catering; repairs
7	Transport and communication
8	Banking, finance, insurance, business services, and leasing
9	Other services

■ **Determining Who Potential Customers Are and How Many There Are**

Much information about industrial customers is based on the **Standard Industrial Classification (SIC) system**, which the government developed to classify selected economic characteristics of industrial, commercial, financial, and service organisations. This system is administered by the Central Statistical Office. Table 21.1 shows how the SIC system can be used to categorise products. In the most recent SIC Manual, there are ten broad divisions, each denoted by a single digit from 0 to 9. These are subdivided into classes (each denoted by the addition of a second digit); the classes are divided into groups (three digits); and the groups into activity headings (four more digits). There are 10 divisions, 60 classes, 222 groups, and 334 activity headings. For example, Division 4 (see Table 21.1), other manufacturing industries, has 8 classes, 50 groups, and 91 activity headings. The numbering system follows that of NACE (Nomenclature Générale des Activités Économiques dans les Communautés Européennes) as far as possible.[3] To categorise manufacturers in more detail, the *Census of Distribution* further subdivides manufacturers.

Data are available for each SIC category through various government publications and departments. Table 21.2 shows the types of information that can be obtained from government sources. Some data are available by town, county, and metropolitan area. Industrial market data also appear in such non-government sources as Dun & Bradstreet's *Market Identifiers*.

The SIC system is a ready-made tool that allows industrial marketers to divide industrial organisations into market segments based mainly on the type of product manufactured or handled. Although the SIC system is a vehicle for segmentation, it must be used in conjunction with other types of data to enable a specific industrial marketer to determine exactly which customers it can reach and how many of them there are to be reached.

Input-output analysis works well in conjunction with the SIC system. This type of analysis is based on the assumption that the output or sales of one industry are the input or purchases of other industries. **Input-output data** tell what types of industries purchase the products of a particular industry.

3. *Standard Industrial Classification Revision* (London: Central Statistical Office, 1979).

Value of industry shipments
Number of establishments
Number of employees
Exports as a percentage of shipments
Imports as a percentage of apparent consumption
Compound annual average rate of growth
Major producing areas

After learning which industries purchase the major portion of an industry's out-put, the next step is to find the SIC numbers for those industries. Because firms are grouped differently in the input-output tables and the SIC system, ascertaining SIC numbers can be difficult. However, the Central Statistical Office does provide some limited conversion tables with the input-output data. These tables can assist indus-trial marketers in assigning SIC numbers to the industry categories used in the input-output analysis. Having determined the SIC numbers of the industries that buy the firm's output, an industrial marketer is in a position to ascertain the number of firms that are potential buyers nationally, by town, and by county. Government publications report the number of establishments within SIC classifications, along with other types of data, such as those shown in Table 21.2.

■ Locating Industrial Customers

At this point, an industrial marketer knows what industries purchase the kind of products her or his firm produces, as well as the number of establishments in those industries and certain other information. However, that marketer still has to find out the names and addresses of potential customers. Du Pont, in Figure 21.1, utilises a reply ad to encourage potential customers to send directly for information about its Tysul brand chemicals, providing Du Pont with viable sales leads.

One approach to identifying and locating potential customers is to use industrial directories, such as *Kompass* and *Kelly's*. These sources contain such information about a firm as its name, SIC number, address, phone number, and annual sales. By referring to one or more of these sources, an industrial marketer can isolate indus-trial customers that have certain SIC numbers, determine their locations, and thus develop lists of potential customers by area.

A second approach, which is more expedient but also more expensive, is to use a market research agency. For example, Market Locations Ltd. is able to provide lists of organisations which fall into particular SIC groups. Information can include name, location, sales volume, number of employees, type of products handled, and names of chief executives.

Either approach can effectively identify and locate a group of potential industrial customers. However, an industrial marketer probably cannot pursue all firms on the list. Because some companies have a greater purchase potential than others, the marketer must determine which segment or segments to pursue.

In industrial marketing, situation-specific variables may be more relevant in seg-menting markets than general customer characteristics. Industrial customers con-centrate on benefits sought; therefore, understanding the end use of the product is

It's ironic. Most chemicals used to treat polluted water can themselves become pollutants.
TYSUL® is different. It's DuPont's brand of wastewater hydrogen peroxide, and it decomposes to water and oxygen. Nothing else.
So, unlike treatment chemicals containing chlorine or manganese, excess TYSUL actually *improves* wastewater streams, by increasing dissolved oxygen. It also supports—rather than poisons—bio-oxidation systems.
But make no mistake. TYSUL is a versatile oxidant/reducing agent that destroys a host of pollutants. Including cyanide, sulfides, sulfites, and thiosulfates. Hypochlorite, formaldehyde, amines, and phenols.

It even aids in the precipitation of many heavy metals.
And since it's highly selective, TYSUL is often less expensive to use than other chemicals, because less is needed. Capital cost is also small, usually just a storage tank, metering pump, and piping.
TYSUL is easy to handle, too. It's an extremely stable, relatively non-toxic liquid that isn't flammable or explosive.
Look to DuPont.
DuPont has the breadth of technical knowledge and experience with hydrogen peroxide to show you the most economical way to treat your waste stream.

As for reliable, on-time delivery, DuPont has more distribution terminals situated across North America than anyone else in the hydrogen peroxide business. Backed up by two manufacturing facilities.
Clip and return the coupon or call DuPont at 1-800-341-4004 to find out more about TYSUL.
Because water and oxygen are one environmental trend that's here to stay.

TYSUL WasteWater H₂O₂ **DU PONT**

Circle 305 on Reader Service Card

TELL ME MORE ABOUT TYSUL.
☐ Please send me detailed information about TYSUL, the environmentally superior choice in wastewater treatment.
☐ Please have a DuPont representative phone me about TYSUL.

Name
Company _____ Title
Company Address
City _____ State _____ Zip
Telephone ( )
MAIL TO: DuPont Company • TYSUL® Oxidant
Room G-51135 • Wilmington, DE 19898

FIGURE 21.1 *Locating industrial customers.*
Du Pont locates potential customers for its Tysul brand waste-water hydrogen peroxide by advertising its benefits and providing an information request form.

SOURCE: Du Pont Company

more important than the psychology of decisions or socio-economic characteristics. Segmenting by benefits rather than customer characteristics can provide insight into the structure of the market and opportunities for new customers.[4]

■ Estimating Purchase Potential

To estimate the purchase potential of industrial customers or groups of customers, an industrial marketer must find a relationship between the size of potential customers' purchases and a variable available in SIC data, such as the number of employees. For example, a paint manufacturer might attempt to determine the average number of gallons purchased by a specific type of potential industrial customer relative to the number of persons employed. If the industrial marketer has no previous experience in this market segment, it will probably be necessary to survey a random sample of potential customers to establish a relationship between purchase sizes and numbers of persons employed. Once this relationship has been established, it can be applied to potential customer segments to estimate their purchases. After deriving these estimates, the industrial marketer selects the customers to be included in the target market.

4. Peter Doyle and John Saunders, "Market Segmentation and Positioning in Specialized Industrial Markets," *Journal of Marketing*, Spring 1985, p. 25.

Characteristics of Industrial Marketing Mixes

After selecting and analysing a target market, an industrial marketer must create a marketing mix that will satisfy the customers in that target market. In many respects, the general concepts and methods involved in developing an industrial marketing mix are similar to those used in consumer product marketing. Here we focus on the features of industrial marketing mixes that differ from the marketing mixes for consumer products. We examine each of the four components in an industrial marketing mix: product, distribution, promotion, and price.

■ **Product**

After selecting a target market, the industrial marketer has to decide how to compete. Production orientated managers fail to understand the need to develop a distinct appeal for their product to give it a competitive advantage. Positioning the product (discussed in Chapter 8) is necessary to successfully serve a market, whether it is consumer or industrial.[5]

Compared with consumer marketing mixes, the product ingredients of industrial marketing mixes often include a greater emphasis on services, both before and after sales. Services, including on-time delivery, quality control, custom design, and a nation-wide parts distribution system, may be important components of the product. Coca-Cola USA focuses on its product offering and service for industrial markets (see Figure 21.2). Marketing Update 21.1 reveals the importance of a service "package" in the shipping and forwarding industry.

Before making a sale, industrial marketers provide potential customers with technical advice regarding product specifications, installation, and applications. Many industrial marketers depend heavily on long-term customer relationships that perpetuate sizeable repeat purchases. Therefore industrial marketers also make a considerable effort to provide services after the sale. Because industrial customers must have products available when needed, on-time delivery is another service included in the product component of many industrial marketing mixes. An industrial marketer unable to provide on-time delivery cannot expect the marketing mix to satisfy industrial customers. Availability of parts must also be included in the product mixes of many industrial marketers because a lack of parts can result in costly production delays. The industrial marketer who includes availability of parts within the product component has a competitive advantage over a marketer who fails to offer this service. Furthermore, customers whose average purchases are large often desire credit; thus some industrial marketers include credit services in their product mixes.

When planning and developing an industrial product mix, an industrial marketer of component parts and semi-finished products must realise that a customer may decide to make the items instead of buying them. In some cases, then, industrial marketers compete not only with each other, but with their own potential customers as well.

Frequently, industrial products must conform to standard technical specifications that industrial customers want. Thus industrial marketers often concentrate on functional product features rather than on marketing considerations. This fact has important implications for industrial salespeople. Rather than concentrating just on selling activities, they must assume the role of consultants, seeking to solve their

5. Doyle and Saunders, p. 25.

ADD-ON SERVICES COST P&O DEARLY

P&O Containers, a subsidiary of P&O plc, is a major container shipping line serving most of the world's trade routes. The U.K. Agency, part of P&O Containers, provides a full range of commercial and logistical services for U.K. importers and exporters shipping with P&O Containers. The agency has recently branched out into providing forwarding services for non-P&O Containers' customers.

The agency, which employs 900 people in 15 locations throughout the U.K., arranges bespoke packages which include combined sea-air freight services, cargo insurance, cargo consolidation, cargo management, full European distribution, EDI (Electronic Data Interchange) links, export finance, cross trade and relay links, and regulations/customs advisory service. No other container shipping company offers such a range of add-on services, which for P&O supplements the company's rail services and trailer park facilities.

Expensive to provide and resource hungry to arrange, many of these services are rarely used. Few customers want all; most take advantage of only a small selection. However, as competitors offer many of these services, but not all, customers have come to expect a major player to be able to offer all such services. Some may cost the agency to provide; others may barely break even. Nevertheless, it is necessary for P&O Containers to not only be seen as a key shipping force, but as also having the facilities and products to be able to provide customers—large or small—with the required range of services and assistance. Customer needs—real and perceived—must be catered for, and even in industrial marketing, service provision is a key determinant of success.

SOURCES: "P&O Containers—the U.K. Agency," *P&O Containers,* 1989; P&O Containers' promotional leaflets, 1988–1990; "Freight Forwarding in the 1990s," *Freight News Express,* 16 April 1990; "Freight Forwarding," London: *Keynote,* 1990; "Sea-air," *British Shipper and Forwarder,* March 1988.

FIGURE 21.2

Product in industrial marketing.
Coca-Cola USA promotes its product offerings and service to industrial customers. The number of brands, marketing, and operational support are key components of its marketing strategy.

SOURCE: Coca-Cola, diet Coca-Cola, Sprite, and cherry Coca-Cola are registered trademarks of The Coca Cola Company. Permission for reproduction of materials granted by the Company.

customers' problems and influencing the writing of specifications.[6] For example, salespersons for computer hardware often provide consultancy-type advice on software as well as the basic computer kit (see Marketing Update 21.2). Most customers now expect this level of service. In the U.K. many suppliers went out of business because of their inability to offer such a service.

Because industrial products are rarely sold through self-service, the major consideration in package design is protection. There is less emphasis on the package as a promotional device.

Research on industrial customer complaints indicates that industrial buyers usually complain when they encounter problems with product quality or delivery time. On the other hand, consumers' complaints refer to other problems, such as customer service and pricing. This type of buyer feedback allows industrial marketers to gauge marketing performance. It is important that industrial marketers respond to valid complaints because the success of most industrial products depends on

6. Erin Anderson and Anne T. Coughlan, "International Market Entry and Expansion via Independent or Integrated Channels of Distribution," *Journal of Marketing,* January 1987, pp. 71–82.

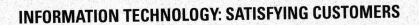

INFORMATION TECHNOLOGY: SATISFYING CUSTOMERS

During the early 1980s in the U.K. there was a rapid convergence of computing, communications, and word-processing technologies. The result was that manufacturers who traditionally had operated in only one of the areas began to seek out new market opportunities arising out of the convergence. Rivalry between domestic and overseas companies alike was intense. In addition, the relative power of customers increased as the number of products and suppliers exploded. Within this environment, industrial customers, whose investment in IT was often considerable, were particularly anxious to receive a complete service. Many horror stories circulated of inappropriate systems installed by fly-by-night operators, often with no software, which were of no practical use to the customers.

According to the managing director of a small, independent computer dealership, a willingness to provide a wide range of customer services—in addition to basic software and hardware—is an essential requirement for survival and growth. This customer adaptability often covered the provision of consultancy services, installation, training, maintenance contracts and even product modification.

SOURCES: Caroline S. Dibb, "The Role of Trading Companies in the International Marketing and Distribution of Information Technology—A Network Approach," unpublished MSc dissertation, UMIST, 1985; Peter Turnbull and S. Ellwood, "Internationalisation in the Information Technology Industry," UMIST Occasional Paper, 1984; F. A. Hug and Peter Turnbull, "Report on the Telecommunications Industry," Department of Management Sciences, UMIST, 1983.

repeat purchases. Because buyer complaints serve a useful purpose, many industrial firms facilitate this feedback by providing customer service departments.[7]

If an industrial marketer is in a mature market, growth can come from attracting market share from another industrial marketer, or a firm can look at new applications or uses for its products. Wescon Products of Wichita, Kansas, is a maker of hand-trucks and other handling devices, mainly for heavy industrial customers. In recent years, prospects for sales growth have been quite limited because heavy manufacturing has been on the decline in the United States. To compensate, the company developed the Gadabout, a stylish hand-truck that is useful in offices, and thereby made further growth in its hand-truck business possible.[8]

■ **Distribution**

The distribution ingredient in industrial marketing mixes differs from that for consumer products with respect to the types of channels used; the kinds of intermediaries available; and the transport, storage, and inventory policies. None the less, the primary objective of the physical distribution of industrial products is to ensure that the right products are available when and where needed.

As discussed in Chapter 9, distribution channels tend to be shorter for industrial products than for consumer products (refer back to Figure 9.2, which shows four commonly used industrial distribution channels). Although **direct distribution channels**, in which products are sold directly from producers to users, are not used frequently in the distribution of consumer products, they are the most widely used for industrial products. More than half of all industrial products are sold through direct channels. Industrial buyers like to communicate directly with producers, especially when expensive or technically complex products are involved. For this reason, industrial buyers prefer to purchase expensive and highly complex mainframe computers directly from IBM, Hewlett-Packard, and other mainframe producers. In these circumstances, an industrial customer wants the technical assistance and personal assurances that only a producer can provide.

A second industrial distribution channel involves an industrial distributor to facilitate exchanges between the producer and customer (channel F in Figure 9.2). An **industrial distributor** is an independent business organisation that takes title to products and carries inventories. Thus industrial distributors are merchant wholesalers; they assume possession and ownership of goods, as well as the risks associated with ownership. Figure 21.3 describes how Canon provides colour laser copying. Although an 0800 Freephone number is provided, service and sales are provided through a dealer network. Industrial distributors usually sell standardised items, such as maintenance supplies, production tools, and small operating equipment. Some industrial distributors carry a wide variety of product lines; others specialise in one or a small number of lines. Industrial distributors can be most effectively used when a product has broad market appeal, is easily stocked and serviced, is sold in small quantities, and is needed rapidly to avoid high losses (as is a part for an assembly-line machine).[9]

---

7. Hiram C. Barksdale, Jr., Terry E. Powell, and Ernestine Hargrove, "Complaint Voicing by Industrial Buyers," *Industrial Marketing Management*, May 1984, pp. 93–99.

8. "Consider: Industrial Marketers Entering the Consumer Zone," *Marketing News*, 30 Aug. 1985, p. 1.

9. James D. Hlavacek and Tommy J. McCuistion, "Industrial Distributors: When, Who, and How?" *Harvard Business Review*, March-April 1983, p. 97.

Imagine what a Canon Color Laser Copier could do with a pie chart.

One look at the high quality color and clarity of the new Canon Color Laser Copier 200 and its benefits for business become equally clear.

After all, it's the only true full-color copier for business with Canon's unique Digital Image Processing

System. A remarkable technology that uses a finely focused laser to reproduce graphics, photos, slides, or negatives at quality comparable with professional printing. An extraordinary 256 gradations per color and 400 dots per inch.

Digital creative functions allow presentation materials like charts, graphs and transparencies to be enlarged up to 400%, reduced up to 50% or edited instantly—and all with complete

confidentiality. For faster multi-page reports, the ACS function will automatically recognize and copy black-and-white text pages at a quick 20 per minute. Together with automatic document feeding and sorting capability, this very well may be the only copier an office needs.

If a Canon Color Laser Copier 200 can do all this for proposals and pie charts, imagine what it can do for your business.

To find out more call 1-800-OK-CANON or write to Canon USA Inc., P.O. Box 3900, Peoria, Illinois 61614.

Canon COLOR LASER COPIER 200
The Digital Difference.

FIGURE 21.3 *Industrial distribution.*
While Canon provides promotional support, colour copiers are purchased through dealers and retailers.

SOURCE: By permission of Canon USA, Inc.

Industrial distributors offer sellers several advantages. They can perform the needed selling activities in local markets at relatively low cost to a manufacturer. They can reduce a producer's financial burden by providing their customers with credit services. And because industrial distributors usually maintain close relationships with their customers, they are aware of local needs and can pass on market information to producers. By holding adequate inventories in their local markets, industrial distributors reduce the producers' capital requirements.

There are, though, several disadvantages to using industrial distributors. Industrial distributors may be difficult to control because they are independent firms. Because they often stock competing brands, an industrial seller cannot depend on them to sell a specific brand aggressively. Furthermore, industrial distributors maintain inventories, for which they incur numerous expenses; consequently, they are less likely to handle bulky items or items that are slow sellers relative to profit margin, need specialised facilities, or require extraordinary selling efforts. In some cases, industrial distributors lack the technical knowledge necessary to sell and service certain industrial items.

In the third industrial distribution channel (Channel G in Figure 9.2), a manufacturers' agent is employed. As described in Chapter 9, a manufacturers' agent or representative is an independent businessperson who sells complementary products of several producers in assigned territories and is compensated through commissions. Unlike an industrial distributor, a manufacturers' agent does not acquire title to the products and usually does not take possession. Acting as a salesperson on behalf of the producers, a manufacturers' agent has no latitude, or very little, in negotiating prices or sales terms.

Using manufacturers' agents can benefit an industrial marketer. These agents usually possess considerable technical and market information and have an established set of customers. For an industrial seller with highly seasonal demand, a manufacturers' agent can be an asset because the seller does not have to support a year-round sales force. That manufacturers' agents are paid on a commission basis may also be an economical alternative for a firm that has highly limited resources and cannot afford a full-time sales force.

Certainly, the use of manufacturers' agents is not problem-free. Even though straight commissions may be cheaper for an industrial seller, the seller may have little control over manufacturers' agents. Because of the compensation method, manufacturers' agents generally want to concentrate on their larger accounts. They are often reluctant to spend adequate time following up sales, to put forward special selling efforts, or to provide sellers with market information when such activities reduce the amount of productive selling time. Because they rarely maintain inventories, manufacturers' agents have a limited ability to provide customers quickly with parts or repair services.

The fourth industrial distribution channel (Channel H in Figure 9.2) has both a manufacturers' agent and an industrial distributor between the producer and the industrial customer. This channel may be appropriate when the industrial marketer wishes to cover a large geographical area but maintains no sales force because of highly seasonal demand or because the firm cannot afford a sales force. This type of channel can also be useful for an industrial marketer that wants to enter a new geographic market without expanding the firm's existing sales force.

So far, our discussion has implied that all channels are equally available and that an industrial producer can select the most desirable option. However, in a number of cases, only one or perhaps two channels are available for the distribution of certain types of products. An important issue in channel selection is the manner in which particular products are normally purchased. If customers ordinarily buy certain types of products directly from producers, it is unlikely that channels with intermediaries will be effective. Other dimensions that should be considered are the product's cost and physical characteristics, the costs of using various channels, the amount of technical assistance customers need, and the size of product and parts inventory needed in local markets.

Physical distribution decisions regarding transport, storage, and inventory control are especially important for industrial marketers. Some raw materials and other industrial products may require special handling; for example, toxic chemicals used in the manufacture of some products must be shipped, stored, and disposed of properly to ensure that they do not harm people or the environment. In addition, the continuity of most industrial buyer-seller relationships depends on the seller's having the right products available when and where the customer needs them. This requirement is so important that industrial marketers must sometimes make a considerable investment in order-processing systems, materials-handling equipment, warehousing facilities, and inventory control systems. In the U.S.A., Archer Daniels Midland Company processes agricultural commodities from their purchase to finished product (see Figure 21.4). In the U.K., British Tubes Stockholding, a subsid-

FIGURE 21.4
Archer Daniels Midland Company is an industrial distributor.
This company must carefully control its purchase of grains and production of vegetable oils, flours, sweeteners, and soy products for industrial markets.

OUR JOB BEGINS WHERE HIS LEAVES OFF.

At the Archer Daniels Midland Company, we buy, transport, process and sell the agricultural abundance of America. We are the bridge between the farmer and an increasingly hungry world.
  As such, we play a major role in bringing America's grain and oilseed crops to market in a virtually endless number of forms. We make vegetable oils, flours, sweeteners and soy proteins. We process corn, wheat, soybeans, peanuts, sunflowers, flax, barley, sugarcane and rice.
  Take the hard work of millions of farmers like this one. Add the hard work of thousands of ADM people. The sum is a single-minded, systematic approach to using America's abundance to help feed a hungry world.

ADM
ARCHER DANIELS MIDLAND COMPANY

SOURCE: Archer Daniels Midland Company

iary of British Steel, holds extensive stocks of steel tubes, pipes, and girders for distribution to a variety of industrial markets—ranging from North Sea oil to general construction to lawn-mower production.

Many industrial purchasers are moving away from traditional marketing exchange relationships, where the buyer buys primarily on price from multiple suppliers, to more tightly knit, relational exchanges, which are long-lasting agreements between manufacturers and suppliers that are less price driven.[10] Just-in-time inventory management systems are providing the rationale underlying these new types of relationships. In order to reduce inventory costs and to eliminate waste, buyers purchase new stock just before it is needed in the manufacturing process. In order for this system to be effective, they must share a great deal of information with their suppliers, since these relationships are collaborative.

■ **Promotion**

The combination of promotional efforts used in industrial marketing mixes generally differs greatly from those for consumer products, especially convenience goods. The differences are evident in the emphasis on various promotional mix ingredients and the activities performed in connection with each promotional mix ingredient.

10. Gary L. Frazier, Robert E. Spekman, and Charles R. O'Neal, "Just-In-Time Exchange Relationships in Industrial Markets," *Journal of Marketing*, October 1988, pp. 52–67.

For several reasons, most industrial marketers rely on personal selling to a much greater extent than do consumer product marketers (except, perhaps, marketers of consumer durables). Because an industrial seller often has fewer customers, personal contact with each customer is more feasible. Some industrial products have technical features that are too numerous or too complex to explain through nonpersonal forms of promotion. Moreover, industrial purchases are frequently high in value and must be suited to the job and available where and when needed; thus industrial buyers want reinforcement and personal assurances from industrial sales personnel. Because industrial marketers depend on repeat purchases, sales personnel must follow up sales to make certain that customers know how to use the purchased items effectively, as well as to ensure that the products work properly.

Salespeople need to perform the role of educators, showing buyers clearly how the product fits their needs. When purchase of a product is critical to the future profitability of the industrial buyer, buying decision-makers gather extensive amounts of information about all alternative products. To deal with such buyers successfully, the seller must have an extremely well trained sales force that is knowledgeable not only about its own company's products, but also about competitors' offerings. Besides, if sales representatives offer thorough and reliable information, they can reduce the industrial buyer's uncertainty, as well as differentiate their firm's product from the competition. Finally, the gathering of information lengthens the decision-making process. Thus it is important for salespeople to be patient; not to pressure their clients as they make important, new, and complex decisions; and to continue providing information to their prospects throughout the entire process.[11]

As Table 21.3 illustrates, the average cost of an industrial sales call varies from industry to industry. Selling costs are comprised of salaries, commissions, bonuses, and travel and entertainment expenses. In America, the average cost of an industrial call is $229.70.[12] Keep in mind, though, that some industrial sales are very large. A Boeing salesperson, for instance, closed a sale with Delta Airlines for commercial aircraft worth $3 billion.[13] But on the average, only 350 aircraft are sold each year, resulting in sales of $105 billion. Generally, aircraft salespeople work hardest in the three to five years before a sale is made.[14]

Because of the escalating costs of advertising and personal selling, telemarketing, the creative use of the telephone to enhance the salesperson's function, is on the increase. Some of the activities in telemarketing include Freephone 0800 phone lines and data-terminal-assisted personal sales work-stations that take orders, check stock and order status, and provide shipping and billing information.

Although not all industrial salespeople perform the same sales activities, they can generally be grouped into the following categories, as described in Chapter 15: technical, missionary, and trade or inside order takers. An inside order taker could effectively use telemarketing. Regardless of how sales personnel are classified, industrial selling activities differ from consumer sales efforts. Because industrial sellers are frequently asked for technical advice about product specifications and uses, they often need technical backgrounds and are more likely to have them than consumer sales personnel. Compared with typical buyer-seller relationships in con-

11. Daniel H. McQuiston, "Novelty, Complexity, and Importance as Causal Determinants of Industrial Buyer Behavior," *Journal of Marketing,* April 1989, pp. 66–79.

12. Laboratory of Advertising Performance (LAP) Report 8052.3. McGraw-Hill Research.

13. Steve Sulerno, "The Close of the New Salesmanship," *PSA,* April 1985, p. 63.

14. "Aircraft Industry Emerging from Engineering Dominance," *Marketing News,* 2 Aug. 1985, p. 7.

TABLE 21.3 *The average cost of an industrial sales call among selected industries in America[a]*

SIC NUMBER	INDUSTRY	NUMBER OF INDUSTRIAL COMPANIES REPORTING	AVERAGE DAILY NUMBER OF SALES CALLS PER SALESPERSON	AVERAGE COST OF INDUSTRIAL SALES CALL	AVERAGE DAILY SALES CALL COSTS[b] PER SALESPERSON
26	Paper and allied products	12	3.3	$263.70	$ 870.21
27	Printing and publishing	18	3.2	$148.60	$ 475.52
28	Chemicals and allied products	41	4.0	$155.20	$ 620.80
29	Petroleum and coal products	12	5.3	$ 99.10	$ 525.23
30	Rubber and miscellaneous plastics products	37	4.4	$129.30	$ 568.92
32	Stone, clay and glass products	18	4.3	$169.70	$ 729.71
33	Primary metal industries	15	3.9	$363.90	$1,419.21
34	Fabricated metal products	113	3.9	$186.10	$ 725.79
35	Machinery, except electrical	275	3.5	$257.30	$ 900.55
3573	Electronic computing equipment (computer hardware)	17	4.2	$452.60	$1,900.92
36	Electrical and electronic equipment	137	3.5	$238.40	$ 834.40
37	Transport equipment	41	2.9	$255.90	$ 742.11
38	Instruments and related products	73	3.9	$209.50	$ 817.05
39	Miscellaneous manufacturing industries	16	3.8	$130.90	$ 497.42
50	Wholesale trade– durable goods	29	5.1	$139.80	$ 712.98
73	Business services	30	2.8	$227.20	$ 636.16

[a] No comparable U.K./EC statistics available.
[b] This cost is determined by multiplying the average daily number of calls per salesperson by the average cost per sales call for each industry.

SOURCE: Laboratory of Advertising Performance (LAP), Report No. 8052.3, McGraw-Hill Research, 1221 Avenue of the Americas, New York, N.Y. 10020. Reprinted by permission of McGraw-Hill, Inc.

sumer product sales, the interdependence that develops between industrial buyers and sellers is likely to be stronger; sellers count on buyers to purchase their particular products and buyers rely on sellers to provide information, products, and related services when and where needed. Although industrial salespeople do market their products aggressively, they almost never use hard-sell tactics because of their role as technical consultants and the inter-dependence between buyers and sellers.

Advertising is emphasised less in industrial sales than in consumer transactions. Some of the reasons given earlier for the importance of personal selling in industrial promotional mixes explain why. However, advertising often supplements personal selling efforts. Because the cost of an industrial sales call is high and continues to rise, advertisements that allow sales personnel to perform more efficiently and effectively are worthwhile for industrial marketers. For instance, the advertisement in Figure 21.5 confirms the positive standing of CAST, supporting the personal selling process. Advertising can make industrial customers aware of new products and brands; inform buyers about general product features, representatives, and organisations; and isolate promising prospects by providing enquiry forms or the addresses and phone numbers of company representatives. To ensure that appropriate information is sent to a respondent, it is crucial that the enquiry be specific as to the type of information desired, the name of the company and respondent, the company's SIC number, and the size of the organisation.

Because the demand for most industrial products is derived demand, marketers can sometimes stimulate demand for their products by stimulating consumer demand. Thus an industrial marketer occasionally sponsors an advertisement promoting the products sold by the marketer's customers.

When selecting advertising media, industrial marketers primarily choose such print media as trade publications and direct mail; they seldom use broadcast media. Trade publications and direct mail reach precise groups of industrial customers and avoid wasted circulation. In addition, they are best suited for advertising messages that present numerous details and complex product information (which are frequently the types of messages that industrial advertisers wish to get across).

Compared with consumer product advertisements, industrial advertisements are usually less persuasive and more likely to contain a large amount of copy and numerous details. In contrast, marketers that advertise to reach ultimate consumers sometimes avoid extensive advertising copy because consumers are reluctant to read it. Industrial advertisers, however, believe that industrial purchasers with any interest in their products will search for information and read long messages.

Sales-promotion activities, too, can play a significant role in industrial promotional mixes. They encompass such efforts as catalogues, trade shows, and trade sales promotion methods that include merchandise allowances, buy-back allowances, displays, sales contests, and other methods discussed in Chapter 15. Industrial marketers go to great lengths and considerable expense to provide catalogues that describe their products to customers. Customers refer to various sellers' catalogues to determine specifications, terms of sale, delivery times, and other information about products. Catalogues thus help buyers decide which suppliers to contact.

Trade shows can be effective vehicles for making many customer contacts in a short time. One study found that firms allocate 25 percent of their annual promotional budgets to trade shows in order to communicate with their current and potential customers, promote their corporate image, introduce new products, meet key account executives, develop mailing lists, identify sales prospects, and find out what their competitors are doing. Although trade shows take second place to per-

FIGURE 21.5

A typical industrial ad. In industrial selling, advertising often supplements personal selling efforts.

Blue Chip.

The Blue Box
System of container shipping
is a trusted performer for many of
the world's major
corporations.

CAST

The Blue Box System of Container Shipping

SOURCE: CAST

sonal selling, they rank above print advertising in influencing industrial purchases, particularly at the need recognition and supplier evaluation stages of the industrial buying process.[15]

Many firms that participate in trade shows lack specific objectives for what they hope to accomplish by such participation. Firms with the most successful trade show programmes have written objectives for the tasks they wish to achieve, and they carefully select the type of show in which to take part so that those attending match the firm's target market.[16]

How industrial marketers use publicity in their promotional mixes may not be much different from the way that marketers of consumer products use it.

■ **Price**

Compared with consumer product marketers, industrial marketers face many more price constraints from legal and economic forces. With respect to economic forces, an individual industrial firm's demand is often highly elastic, requiring the firm to approximate competitors' prices. This condition often results in non-price competition and a considerable amount of price stability.

15. Roger A. Kerin and William L. Cron, "Assessing Trade Show Functions and Performance; An Exploratory Study," *Journal of Marketing,* July 1987, pp. 87–94.

16. Ibid.

Today's route to sustainable competitive advantage lies in offering customers something that the competition does not offer—something that helps them increase their productivity and profitability. Firms achieve high market share not by offering low prices, but by offering their customers superior value and product quality.[17] Customers are willing to pay higher prices for quality products.[18] Companies such as Caterpillar Tractor, Hewlett-Packard, and 3M have shown that a value-based strategy can win a commanding lead over competition. Such firms emphasise the highest quality products at slightly higher prices.

Although there are a variety of ways for determining prices of industrial products, the three most common are administered pricing, bid pricing, and negotiated pricing. With **administered pricing**, the seller determines the price (or series of prices) for a product, and the customer pays that specified price. Marketers who use this approach may employ a one price policy in which all buyers pay the same price, or they may set a series of prices that are determined by one or more discounts. In some cases, list prices are posted on a price sheet or in a catalogue. The list price is a beginning point from which trade, quantity, and cash discounts are deducted. Thus the actual (net) price an industrial customer pays is the list price less the discount(s). When a list price is used, an industrial marketer sometimes specifies the price in terms of list price times a multiplier. For example, the price of an item might be quoted as "list price × .78", which means the seller is discounting the item so that the buyer can purchase the product at 78 percent of the list price. Simply changing the multiplier lets the seller revise prices without having to issue new catalogues or price sheets.

With **bid pricing**, prices are determined through sealed or open bids. When a buyer uses sealed bids, selected sellers are notified that they are to submit their bids by a certain date. Normally, the lowest bidder is awarded the contract, providing the buyer believes the firm is able to supply the specified products when and where needed. In an open bidding approach, several but not all sellers are asked to submit bids. In contrast to sealed bidding, the amounts of the bids are made public. Finally, an industrial purchaser sometimes uses negotiated bids. Under this arrangement, the customer seeks bids from a number of sellers and screens the bids. Then the customer negotiates the price and terms of sale with the most favourable bidders, until a final transaction is consummated or until negotiations are terminated with all sellers.

Sometimes a buyer will be seeking either component parts to be used in production for several years or custom-built equipment to be purchased currently and through future contracts. In such instances, an industrial seller may submit an initial, less profitable bid to win "follow-on" (subsequent) contracts. The seller that wins the initial contract is often substantially favoured in the competition for follow-on contracts. In such a bidding situation, an industrial marketer must determine how low the initial bid should be, the probability of winning a follow-on contract, and the combination of bid prices on both the initial and the follow-on contract that will yield an acceptable profit.[19]

17. John C. Narver and Stanley F. Slater, "Creating a Market-Oriented Business," *The Channel of Communications,* Summer 1989, pp. 5–8.

18. Robert Jacobson and David A. Aaker, "The Strategic Role of Product Quality," *Journal of Marketing,* October 1987, pp. 31–44.

19. Douglas G. Brooks, "Bidding for the Sake of Follow-on Contracts," *Journal of Marketing,* January 1978, p. 35.

For certain types of industrial markets, a seller's pricing component may have to allow for **negotiated pricing**. That is, even when there are stated list prices and discount structures, negotiations may determine the actual price an industrial customer pays. Negotiated pricing can benefit seller and buyer because price negotiations frequently lead to discussions of product specifications, applications, and perhaps product substitutions. Such negotiations may give the seller an opportunity to provide the customer with technical assistance and perhaps sell a product that better fits the customer's requirements; the final product choice might also be more profitable for the seller. The buyer benefits by gaining more information about the array of products and terms of sale available and may acquire a more suitable product at a lower price.

Some industrial marketers sell in markets in which only one of these general pricing approaches prevails. Such marketers can simplify the price components of their marketing mixes. However, a number of industrial marketers sell to a wide variety of industrial customers and must maintain considerable flexibility in pricing.

SUMMARY

Industrial marketing is a set of activities directed at facilitating and expediting exchanges involving industrial products and customers in industrial markets.

Industrial marketers have a considerable amount of information available to them for use in planning their marketing strategies. Much of this information is based on the Standard Industrial Classification (SIC) system, which categorises businesses into major industry divisions, classes, groups, and activities. The SIC system provides industrial marketers with information needed to identify market segments. It can best be used for this purpose in conjunction with other information, such as input-output data. After identifying target industries, the marketer can locate potential customers by using industrial directories or by employing a market research agency. The marketer must then estimate the potential purchases of industrial customers by finding a relationship between a potential customer's purchases and a variable available in published sources.

Like marketers of consumer products, an industrial marketer must develop a marketing mix that satisfies the needs of customers in the industrial target market. The product component frequently emphasises services because they are often of primary interest to industrial customers. The marketer must also consider that the customer may elect to make the product rather than buy it. Industrial products must meet certain standard specifications that industrial users want.

The distribution of industrial products differs from that of consumer products in the types of channels used; the kinds of intermediaries available; and transport, storage, and inventory policies. A direct distribution channel is common in industrial marketing. Also used are channels containing manufacturers' agents, industrial distributors, or both agents and distributors. Channels are chosen on the basis of availability, the typical mode of purchase for a product, and several other variables.

Personal selling is a primary ingredient of the promotional component in industrial marketing mixes. Sales personnel often act as technical advisers both before and after a sale. Advertising sometimes is used to supplement personal selling efforts. Industrial marketers generally use print advertisements containing more information but less persuasive content than consumer advertisements. Other promotional activities include catalogues and trade shows.

The price component for industrial marketing mixes is influenced by legal and economic forces to a greater extent than it is for consumer marketing mixes. Pricing may be affected by competitors' prices, as well as by the type of customer who buys the product.

IMPORTANT TERMS

Industrial marketing
Standard Industrial Classification
   (SIC) system
Input-output data
Direct distribution channels

Industrial distributor
Administered pricing
Bid pricing
Negotiated pricing

DISCUSSION AND REVIEW QUESTIONS

1. How do industrial products differ from consumer products?
2. What function does the SIC system help industrial marketers perform?
3. List some sources that an industrial marketer can use to determine the names and addresses of potential customers.
4. How do industrial marketing mixes differ from those of consumer products?
5. What are the major advantages and disadvantages of using industrial distributors?
6. Why do industrial marketers rely on personal selling more than consumer products marketers?
7. Why would an industrial marketer spend resources on advertising aimed at stimulating consumer demand?
8. Compare three methods for determining the price of industrial products.

■ CASES

21.1   Hoskyns Group plc—Success in Computer Services

Computer services companies engage in activities which are basically divided into processing- and operating-related tasks and professional services. Hoskyns, operating in a highly competitive market, is one of the largest and oldest computer services companies. In 1965 the organisation was acquired by Martin Marietta, a large U.S. aerospace company. During 1986 Hoskyns went public, when Martin Marietta sold a 25 percent stake in the business. Further changes occurred in July 1988, when Plessey acquired Martin Marietta's remaining 68 percent share of Hoskyns.

Throughout this period, Hoskyns continued to operate autonomously. With around 3,000 employees and more than 2,000 customers during 1988, the company maintained its reputation for consistent growth in excess of the computer-services industry as a whole (see Tables 21.4 and 21.5).

TABLE 21.4
Hoskyns's turnover and profit 1983–1988

YEAR	TOTAL SALES (£m)	GROWTH OVER PREVIOUS YEAR (%)	PROFIT BEFORE TAX (£m)
1983	28.7	–	2.5
1984	40	41.3	2.8
1985	56	40	3.5
1986	67.7	20.8	4.4
1987	79	16.7	6.5
1988	110	39	9.5

TABLE 21.5
Top seven computer-services companies by 1988 revenue

RANK	COMPANY	U.K. REVENUE (£m)	TOTAL REVENUE (£m)
1	SD-Scion	100	260
2	Hoskyns	97	110
3	SEMA	95	280
4	Istel	83	85
5	EDS	75	2,823
6	Logica	70	132
7	Anderson Consultancy	67	597

Hoskyns's low level of exports, at only 12 percent of turnover, is potentially a disadvantage with the likely changes in environment associated with 1992. Companies in other countries, like SEMA, have already made strong in-roads into Europe. If Hoskyns is to be a successful European competitor, it must therefore capitalise on its particular strengths, which include:

- Expertise on IBM, ICL, DEC, and Hewlett-Packard hardware.

- Modular Application Systems (MAS) software, which allows customers to use software matching their own requirements without having to order "bespoke" software.

- Considerable breadth of services, markets, and customer base and ability to offer practical computer-based solutions.

- Offering creative and innovative services. For example, the launching of "Re-engineering" in 1988—a novel approach to systems developments where the underlying structure of software is retained when hardware is replaced.

- "People" culture in its working environment with a happy and satisfied work force.

In addition, Hoskyns has undertaken a number of useful acquisitions. During October 1987, the company acquired Thomas and Co. Ltd (TCL), a financial services specialist. This was quickly followed by the acquisition of Computer Based Training (CBT), which specialised in both distance learning and classroom-based courses. In May 1988, a further three companies were acquired. Insight Database Systems, Insight Software (Export) and Vector Software were expert in IBM mid-range computers and were bought in anticipation of the new IBM AS/400 mainframe launch. During 1988, Hoskyns moved one step closer to Europe by winning a facilities management contract with BP. This led to the opening of a new facilities management centre in Holland.

SOURCES: Michael Labrou, "Ten Marketing Case Studies," MBA Dissertation, University of Warwick, 1989; Extel Cards for Hoskyns; Dataline, 22 Feb. 1989, p. 36; Hoskyns Annual Reports, 1987, 1988; *Computing*, 29 Oct. 1987, p. 19; *Computer Weekly*, 17 July 1988, p. 124; *Electronic Times*, 28 July 1988, p. 2.

Questions for Discussion

1. Why is Hoskyns successful?
2. How might Hoskyns capitalise on its qualities to improve its chances of success in the Europe of 1992?

21.2 JCB, A Brand into the Language

The worldwide market for construction, agricultural, and materials-handling equipment is estimated to be worth $50 billion. Worldwide, JCB is the tenth largest company, but actually has only a 1.5 percent market share. However, the JCB digger has a 21 percent market share, behind only the U.S. company Case, and in the telescopic-handler market JCB has a 31 percent market share and is the world's number one. Despite significant competition from Caterpillar, Case, and Japan's Komatsu, JCB dominates the U.K. market and many markets within Europe. In 1989, the company had a turnover of U.S.$739 million.

The JCB company, named after Joseph Cyril Bamford, commenced operations in 1945, originally from a £1 a week lock-up garage in Uttoxeter. At first, the company manufactured farm trucks (using steel from air-raid shelters) and converted wartime jeeps to shooting brakes. In the 1950s, JCB launched Europe's first hydraulic loader, selling 2,000 units. In 1953 the Mark I JCB loader was the turning-point, leading to the development of an extensive worldwide network of distributors. By 1961 exports were a third of JCB's business, and, following the 1968 purchase of Chaseside Engineering, exports were 50 percent of the company's business by 1969. In 1975 Anthony Bamford took over from his father, and in 1979 was named Young Businessman of the Year. In the market segments where the company is active, JCB now has market dominance in over 50 countries; only North America has not been conquered.

The company mission is that JCB's "business is the design, manufacture, sale and product support of machines and attachments for construction, agriculture and materials handling. The mission is to improve continuously JCB's products and services to meet customers' needs, allowing JCB to prosper as a business." The JCB brand is built on the attributes of its quality, the company's commitment to its market, specialisation, innovation, and a thorough knowledge of its marketing environment.

JCB, as with other companies within this market, is particularly prone to changes in its operating and marketing environment. The company has predicted that U.K. GDP growth will rise very slightly in the near future. Interest rate cuts encourage house-building growth. Currently housing starts are static, but as interest rates fall prior to the next general election, there may be a pick-up in the house-building market. However, despite the contraction of this market, which is particularly important to JCB, the government has announced a significant increase in the building of trunk roads, British Rail is to invest £5 billion in the next few years in improving its infrastructure, and the newly privatised water industry is to invest £3 billion per annum over the next three years—mainly for sea defences—which will create a significant demand for JCB equipment.

SOURCES: JCB Company Reports; JCB personnel; presentation to undergraduate students, University of Warwick, 8 November 1990; "JCB Company History," JCB Video, 1989; Matthew Lynn, "Digging for Victory," *Business*, October 1990, pp. 112–115.

Questions for Discussion

1. How can JCB best use the familiarity of its brand and products to fend off new entrants, particularly those from Japan?
2. How important is the marketing environment to a company such as JCB?
3. How can JCB research the environmental trends which have direct impact on its business?

22

SERVICES MARKETING

Objectives

- To understand the nature and characteristics of services

- To classify services

- To understand the development of strategies for services

- To explore the concept of marketing services in non-business situations

- To understand the development of service strategies in non-business organisations

- To describe methods for controlling non-business service activities

In consumer or industrial marketing there is a product—be it a BMW car, a Sony hi-fi or a JCB digger—for customers to approve or dislike. In services marketing the actual product is not as discernible to the customer. Sketchley is the largest dry cleaner in the U.K., with nearly 500 branches. Is Sketchley's product the quality and reliability of its cleaning and thereby the way the returned garment is perceived? Or, in addition, do consumers' impressions of the shop atmosphere and ambience, of staff ability and friendliness, and of the shop image become part of the perceived product?

Research has shown that consumers desire a fast and reliable dry-cleaning service with well-presented, informal branches and competent, friendly sales assistants. The shop, the transaction and, above all, the impression given to the customer by the sales staff all become core elements of the dry-cleaning "product". Sketchley has a training college at which all personnel are taught to be informative, technically knowledgeable, friendly, and efficient. Store design is constantly updated to reflect customers' expectations. These activities cost hundreds of thousands of pounds each year but the company's management knows how important such intangibles are in a dry-cleaning business, as they are in any service organisation. ◆

Based on information in "Sketchley, the Care Experts," Sketchley promotional literature 1989; "Sketchley Executive: The Modern Approach to Clothes Care," Sketchley press release, 1989.

This chapter presents concepts that apply specifically to the marketing of services. Services marketing involves marketing in non-profit organisations such as education, health care, charities, and government, as well as for-profit areas such as finance, personal services, and professional services.

The chapter first focuses on the growing importance of service industries in our economy. Second, it addresses the unique characteristics of services and the problems they present to marketers. Third, it presents various classification schemes that can help service marketers develop marketing strategies. In addition, we discuss a variety of marketing-mix considerations. Finally, we define non-business marketing and examine the development of non-business marketing strategies and the control of non-business marketing activities.

THE NATURE AND CHARACTERISTICS OF SERVICES

As we mention in Chapter 7, all products—goods, services, or ideas—possess a certain amount of intangibility. A service is an intangible product involving a deed, a performance, or an effort that cannot be physically possessed.[1] We should note that few products can be classified as a pure good or a pure service. Consider, for example, a car. When consumers purchase a car, they take ownership of a physical item that provides transport, but the warranty associated with the purchase is a service. When consumers rent a car, they purchase a transport service that is provided through temporary use of a car. Most products, such as cars and car hire, contain both tangible and intangible components. One component, however, will dominate, and it is this dominant component that leads to the classification of goods, services, and ideas.

Figure 22.1 illustrates the tangibility concept by placing a variety of products on a continuum of tangibility and intangibility. Tangible-dominant products are typically classified as goods, and intangible-dominant products are typically considered services. Thus, as defined in Chapter 7, services are intangible-dominant products that involve the application of human and mechanical efforts to people or objects.

■ **Growth and Importance of Services**

The increasing importance of services in the U.S. economy has led many people to call the United States the world's first service economy. The service industries—encompassing trade, communications, transport, food and lodging, financial and medical services, education, government, and technical services—account for about 60 percent of the national income and three-quarters of the non-farm jobs in the United States. In the U.K. and in Europe, the service sector is just as important (see Figures 22.2 and 22.3).

One major catalyst of the growth in consumer services has been general economic prosperity, which has led to an increase in financial services, travel, entertainment, and personal care. Lifestyle changes have similarly encouraged expansion of the service sector. In the past forty years, the number of women in the workforce has more than doubled. Consumers want to avoid tasks such as meal preparation, house cleaning, home maintenance, and preparation of tax returns. Furthermore, Europeans have become more fitness and recreation orientated, and so the demand for

---

1. Leonard L. Berry, "Services Marketing Is Different," *Business Horizons,* May-June 1980, pp. 24–29.

Goods (tangible) — Bananas · Jewellery · Compact disc player · Cars/maintenance · Fast food restaurants · Airlines · Financial services · Beauty parlours · Telephone services · Education — **Services (intangible)**

FIGURE 22.1 *A continuum of product tangibility and intangibility*

fitness and recreational facilities has escalated. In terms of demographics, the population is growing older, and this change has promoted tremendous expansion of health-care services. Finally, the number and complexity of goods needing servicing have spurred demand for repair services.

Not only have consumer services grown in the economy; business services have prospered as well. Business or industrial services include repairs and maintenance, consulting, installation, equipment leasing, market research, advertising, temporary office personnel, and caretaking services. Expenditures for business and industrial services have risen even faster than expenditures for consumer services. This growth has been attributed to the increasingly complex, specialised, and competitive business environment. Large retailers, such as Burton Group or Marks & Spencer, are successfully incorporating additional services into their retail stores. Providing additional services at one location is an excellent way to satisfy and keep customers who need and want more and more services. Burton Group operates its traditional department stores but in addition offers optical services, financial services, and so on. If customers enter a store for one service, they are more likely to shop at the store again or try another service that the retailer provides.[2]

■ Characteristics of Services

The problems of service marketing are not the same as those of goods marketing.[3] To understand these unique problems, it is first necessary to understand the distinguishing characteristics of services. Services have four basic characteristics: (1) intangibility, (2) inseparability of production and consumption, (3) perishability, and (4) heterogeneity.[4] Table 22.1 summarises these characteristics and the marketing problems they entail.

Intangibility stems from the fact that services are performances. They cannot be seen, touched, tasted, or smelled, nor can they be possessed. Intangibility also relates to the difficulty that consumers may have in understanding service offerings.[5] Services have a few tangible attributes, called **search qualities**, that can be viewed prior to purchase. When consumers cannot view a product in advance and examine its properties, they may not understand exactly what is being offered. Even when consumers do gain sufficient knowledge about service offerings, they may not be able to evaluate the possible choices. On the other hand, services are rich in experi-

2. David Pottruck, "Building Company Loyalty and Retention Through Direct Marketing," *Journal of Services Marketing,* Autumn 1987, p. 56.

3. Donald Cowell, *The Marketing of Services* (London: Heinemann, 1984).

4. Valarie A. Zeithaml, A. Parasuraman, and Leonard L. Berry, "Problems and Strategies in Services Marketing," *Journal of Marketing,* Spring 1985, pp. 33–46.

5. John E. G. Bateson, "Why We Need Service Marketing," in *Conceptual and Theoretical Developments in Marketing,* ed. O. C. Ferrell, S. W. Brown, and C. W. Lamb, Jr. (Chicago: American Marketing Association, 1979), pp. 131–146.

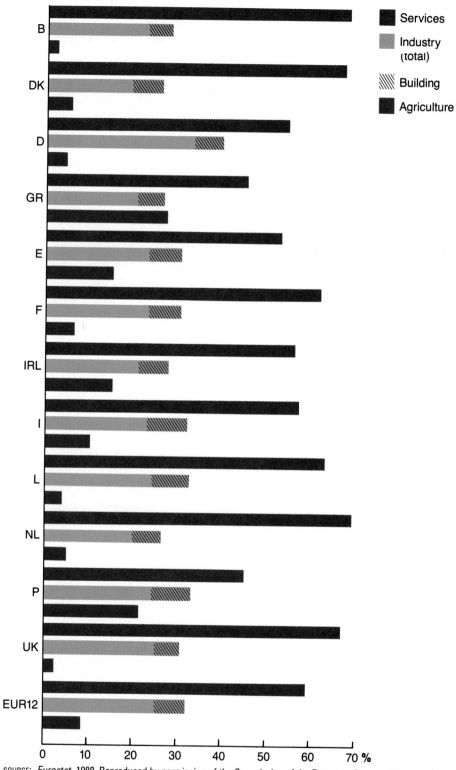

FIGURE 22.2
European Community total employment by economic activity

Legend:
- Services
- Industry (total)
- Building
- Agriculture

B
DK
D
GR
E
F
IRL
I
L
NL
P
UK
EUR12

0   10   20   30   40   50   60   70 %

SOURCE: *Eurostat*, 1988. Reproduced by permission of the Commission of the European Communities.

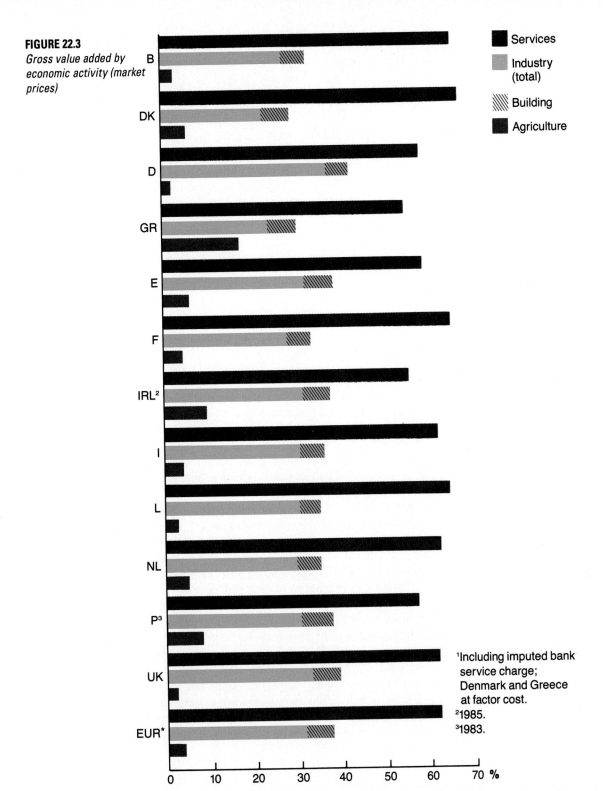

FIGURE 22.3
Gross value added by economic activity (market prices)

Services

Industry (total)

Building

Agriculture

B

DK

D

GR

E

F

IRL[2]

I

L

NL

P[3]

UK

EUR*

[1]Including imputed bank service charge; Denmark and Greece at factor cost.
[2]1985.
[3]1983.

0 10 20 30 40 50 60 70 %

SOURCE: *Eurostat*, 1988. Reproduced by permission of the Commission of the European Communities.

TABLE 22.1
Service character-istics and marketing problems

UNIQUE SERVICE FEATURES	RESULTING MARKETING PROBLEMS
Intangibility	Cannot be stored
	Cannot be protected through patents
	Cannot be readily displayed or communicated
	Prices are difficult to set
Inseparability	Consumer is involved in production
	Other consumers are involved in production
	Centralised mass production is difficult
Perishability	Services cannot be inventoried
Heterogeneity	Standardisation and quality are difficult to control

SOURCE: Valarie A. Zeithaml, A. Parasuraman, Leonard L. Berry, "Problems and Strategies in Services Marketing," *Journal of Marketing,* Spring 1985, pp. 33–46. Used by permission of the American Marketing Association.

ence and credence qualities. **Experience qualities** are those qualities that can be assessed only after purchase and consumption (satisfaction, courtesy, and the like). **Credence qualities** are those qualities that cannot be assessed even after purchase and consumption.[6] An appendix operation is an example of a service high in credence qualities. How many consumers are knowledgeable enough to assess the quality of an appendectomy, even after it has been performed? In summary, it is difficult to go into a store, examine a service, purchase it, and take it home with you.

Related to intangibility is **inseparability** of production and consumption. Services are normally produced at the same time they are consumed. A medical examination is an example of simultaneous production and consumption. In fact, the doctor cannot possibly perform the service without the patient's presence, and the consumer is actually involved in the production process. Dining out in a restaurant is a similar example. With other services, such as air travel, many consumers are simultaneously involved in production. Because of high consumer involvement in most services, standardisation and control are difficult to maintain.

Because production and consumption are simultaneous, services are also characterised by **perishability**. In other words, unused capacity in one time period cannot be stockpiled or inventoried for future time periods. Consider the airlines' seating-capacity dilemma. Each carrier maintains a sophisticated reservations system to juggle ticket prices and ensure maximum revenues for every flight. This attempt to maximise profit on each flight has led to overbooking, which means that airlines may sell tickets for more seats than are available so as to compensate for "no-shows"—people who have made reservations but do not actually take that particular flight. The airlines' dilemma illustrates how service perishability presents problems very different from the supply and demand problems encountered in the marketing of goods.[7] Unoccupied seats on an airline flight cannot be stored for use on another

6. Valarie A. Zeithaml, "How Consumer Evaluation Processes Differ Between Goods and Services," in *Marketing of Services,* ed. James H. Donnelly and William R. George (Chicago: American Marketing Association, 1981), pp. 186–190.

7. Leonard L. Berry, Valarie A. Zeithaml, and A. Parasuraman, "Responding to Demand Fluctuations: Key Challenge for Service Businesses," in *AMA Educators' Proceedings,* ed. Russell Belk et al. (Chicago: American Marketing Association, 1984), pp. 231–234.

flight that is booked to capacity. Hotel operators offer bargain breaks—discount deals—to fill underutilised capacity in slack periods.

Finally, because most services are labour-intensive, they are susceptible to **heterogeneity**. People typically perform services, and people do not always perform consistently. There may be variation from one service to another within the same organisation or variation in the service that a single individual provides from day to day and from customer to customer. A good branch manager is crucial for a company such as Sketchley. Poor customer reaction and branch performance can often be traced back to a poor branch manager.[8] Queuing times in McDonald's can vary greatly, often due to teamwork, speed and efficiency variations between branches. Thus standardisation and quality are extremely difficult to control. But this fact may also lead to customising services to meet consumers' specific needs. Because of these factors, service marketers often face a dilemma: how does one provide efficient, standardised service at some acceptable level of quality while simultaneously treating each customer as a unique person? Giving "good service" is a major concern of all service organisations, and it is often translated into more personalised service.

CLASSIFICATION OF SERVICES

Services are a very diverse group of products, and an organisation may provide more than one kind. Examples of services include car rental, repairs, health care, hairdressers, health centres, child care, domestic services, legal advice, banking, insurance, air travel, education, entertainment, catering, business consulting, dry-cleaning, and accounting. Nevertheless, services can be meaningfully analysed by using a five-category classification scheme: (1) type of market, (2) degree of labour-intensiveness, (3) degree of customer contact, (4) skill of service provider, and (5) goal of the service provider. Table 22.2 summarises this scheme.

Services can be viewed in terms of the market or type of customer they serve—consumer or industrial. The implications of this distinction are very similar to those for all products and therefore are not discussed here. In Figure 22.4, the Leeds markets its savings related share option to companies rather than to individual domestic consumers.

A second way to classify services is by degree of labour-intensiveness. Many services, such as repairs, education, and hair care, rely heavily on human labour. Other services, such as telecommunications, health farms/fitness centres, and public transport, are more equipment-intensive.

Labour- (people-) based services are more susceptible to heterogeneity than are most equipment-based services. Marketers of people-based services must recognise that service providers are often viewed as the service itself. Therefore, strategies relating to selecting, training, motivating, and controlling employees are very important.

The third way services can be classified is by customer contact. High-contact services include health care, hotels, estate agencies, and restaurants; low-contact services include repairs, theatres, dry-cleaning, and spectator sports.[9] Note that high-contact services generally involve actions that are directed towards individuals.

8. Brian Moores, *Are They Being Served?* (Oxford: Philip Allan, 1986).

9. Christopher H. Lovelock, "Classifying Services to Gain Strategic Marketing Insights," *Journal of Marketing,* Summer 1983, p. 15.

TABLE 22.2
Classification of services

CATEGORY	EXAMPLES
TYPE OF MARKET	
Consumer	Repairs, child care, legal advice
Industrial	Consulting, caretaking services, installation
DEGREE OF LABOUR-INTENSIVENESS	
Labour-based	Repairs, education, haircuts
Equipment-based	Telecommunications, health farms, public transport
DEGREE OF CUSTOMER CONTACT	
High	Health care, hotels, air travel
Low	Repairs, home deliveries, postal service
SKILL OF THE SERVICE PROVIDER	
Professional	Legal advice, health care, accountancy
Non-professional	Domestic services, dry-cleaning, public transport
GOAL OF THE SERVICE PROVIDER	
Profit	Financial services, insurance, health care
Non-profit	Health care, education, government

Because these services are directed at people, the consumer must be present during production. Although it is sometimes possible for the service provider to go to the consumer, high-contact services typically require that the consumer goes to the production facility. Thus the physical appearance of the facility may be a major component of the consumer's overall evaluation of the service. Because the consumer must be present during production of a high-contact service, the process of production may be just as important as its final outcome.

Low-contact service, in contrast, commonly involves actions directed at things. Consequently, the consumer is usually not required to be present during service delivery. The consumer's presence, however, may be required to initiate or terminate the service. The Post Office maintains a network of branches, sorting offices, and vehicles. The process of sending a parcel from Cardiff to London or Lille is lengthy. Although they must be present to initiate the provision of the service, consumers need not be present during the process. The appearance of the production facilities and the interpersonal skills of actual service providers are thus not as critical in low-contact services as they are in high-contact services.[10]

Skill of the service provider is a fourth way to classify services. Professional services tend to be more complex and more highly regulated than non-professional services. In the case of legal advice, for example, consumers often do not know what the actual service will involve or how much it will cost until the service is completed because the final product is very situation-specific. Additionally, solicitors are regulated both by law and by professional associations.

10. Christopher H. Lovelock, *Services Marketing* (Englewood Cliffs, N.J.: Prentice-Hall, 1984), pp. 49–64.

FIGURE 22.4
*Promoting services to in-
dustrial consumers.*
The Leeds markets its
savings related share
option to companies
rather than to individual
consumers.

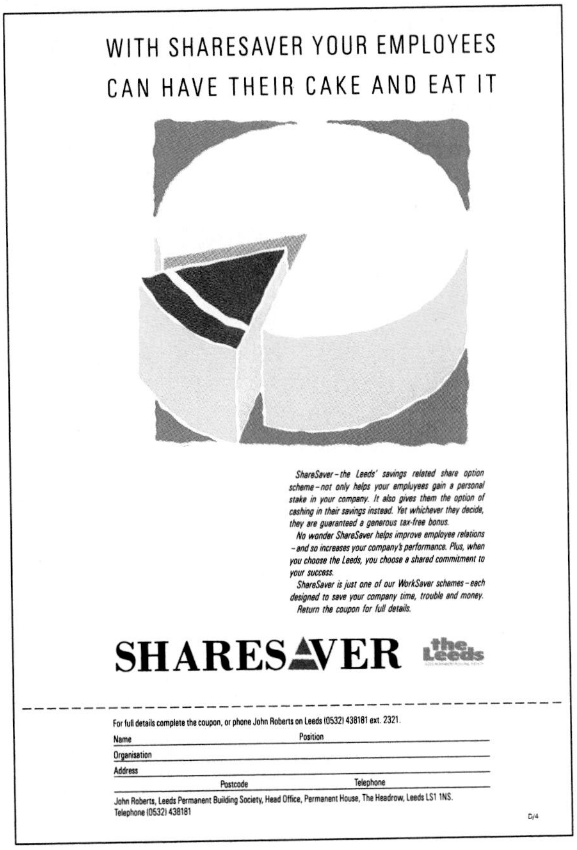

WITH SHARESAVER YOUR EMPLOYEES
CAN HAVE THEIR CAKE AND EAT IT

*ShareSaver – the Leeds' savings related share option
scheme – not only helps your employees gain a personal
stake in your company. It also gives them the option of
cashing in their savings instead. Yet whichever they decide,
they are guaranteed a generous tax-free bonus.*
*No wonder ShareSaver helps improve employee relations
– and so increases your company's performance. Plus, when
you choose the Leeds, you choose a shared commitment to
your success.*
*ShareSaver is just one of our WorkSaver schemes – each
designed to save your company time, trouble and money.
Return the coupon for full details.*

SHARES▲VER the Leeds

For full details complete the coupon, or phone John Roberts on Leeds (0532) 438181 ext. 2321.

Name _____ Position _____
Organisation _____
Address _____
_____ Postcode _____ Telephone _____

John Roberts, Leeds Permanent Building Society, Head Office, Permanent House, The Headrow, Leeds LS1 1NS.
Telephone (0532) 438181

SOURCE: Leeds Permanent Building Society

Finally, services can be classified according to the goal of the service provider—
profit or non-profit. The second half of this chapter examines non-business marketing. Most non-business organisations provide services rather than goods.

DEVELOPING MARKETING STRATEGIES FOR SERVICES

Before we discuss the development of a marketing mix for service firms, we need to
reiterate a major point: the marketing concept is equally applicable to goods, services, and ideas. The marketing of services, like the marketing of goods, requires the
identification of a viable target market segment, the development of a service concept that addresses the consumer's needs within that segment, the creation and
implementation of an operating strategy that will adequately support the service
concept, and the design of a service delivery system that will support the chosen
operating strategy.[11]

Table 22.3 illustrates the approaches that marketers of services can take to
achieve consumer satisfaction. A basic requirement of any marketing strategy, however, is a development phase, which includes defining target markets and finalising a

11. Heskett, pp. 118–126.

TABLE 22.3 *Examples of approaches to consumer satisfaction for marketers of services*

SERVICE INDUSTRY	OUTCOME SOUGHT BY BUYER	TECHNICAL POSSIBILITIES	STRATEGIC POSSIBILITIES
Higher education	Educational attainment	Help lecturers to be effective teachers; offer tutoring	Admit better prepared students (or, for a fee, give them better preparation before entry)
Hospitals	Health	Instruct patients in how to manage their current problems and prevent others	Market preventive medicine services (weight loss, stress reduction, etc.)
Banks	Prosperity	Offer money management courses; provide management assistance to small businesses	Market financial expertise, probably by industry specialisation
Plumbing repairs	Free-flowing pipes	Provide consumers with instructions and supplies to prevent further blockages	Diversify (e.g., point-of-use water-purification systems)

SOURCE: Adapted from Betsy D. Gelb, "How Marketers of Intangibles Can Raise the Odds for Consumer Satisfaction," *Journal of Services Marketing,* Summer 1987, p. 15. Reprinted by permission of the publisher.

marketing mix. The following seven preconditions need to be considered when developing a service marketing strategy:

1. Make sure that marketing occurs at all levels, from the marketing department to the point where the service is provided.
2. Allow flexibility in providing the service—when there is direct interaction with the customers, customise the service to their wants and needs.
3. Hire and maintain high-quality personnel and market your organisation or service to them; often it is the people in a service organisation who differentiate one organisation from another.
4. Consider marketing to existing customers to increase their use of the service or create loyalty to the service provider.
5. Quickly resolve any problems in providing the service, to avoid damaging your firm's reputation for quality.
6. Think high technology to provide improved services at a lower cost. Continually evaluate how to customise the service to each consumer's unique needs.
7. Brand your service to distinguish it from that of the competition. For example, instead of simply seeking a pest controller, a customer would seek assistance from Rentokil because of Rentokil's name recognition.[12]

In the following sections we discuss the marketing-mix requirements for finalising a services marketing strategy.

12. Leonard L. Berry, "Big Ideas in Services Marketing," *Journal of Services Marketing,* Fall 1987, pp. 5–9.

■ Product

Goods can be defined in terms of their physical attributes, but services cannot because they are intangible. As we point out earlier in the chapter, it is often difficult for consumers to understand service offerings and to evaluate possible service alternatives. The utilities advertise in the press and on television to explain their services. British Gas, for example, has schemes to spread bill payments and to assist those financially disadvantaged, plus several methods of making payments. These are explained in advertisements.

There may also be tangibles (such as facilities, employees, or communications) associated with a service. These tangible elements help form a part of the product and are often the only aspects of a service that can be viewed prior to purchase. Consequently, marketers must pay close attention to associated tangibles and make sure that they are consistent with the selected image of the service product.[13] For example, consumers perceive public transport at night as plagued by crime and therefore hesitate to use it. Improving the physical appearance of tube stations and reducing the time between trains are tangible cues that consumers can use to judge public transport services. Figure 22.5 relates AT&T's speed of service directly to the speed of a Porsche 911 luxury sports car.

The service product is often equated with the service provider; for example, the bank clerk or the stylist becomes the service a bank or a beauty salon provides. Because consumers tend to view services in terms of the service personnel and because personnel are inconsistent in their behaviour, it is imperative that marketers effectively select, train, motivate, and control contact people. Service marketers are selling long-term relationships as well as performance.

After testing many variables, the Strategic Planning Institute (SPI) in America developed an extensive database on the impact of various business strategies on profits. The institute found that "relative perceived product quality" is the single most important factor in determining long-term profitability. In fact, because there are generally no objective measures to evaluate the quality of professional services (medical care, legal services, and so forth), the customer is actually purchasing confidence in the service provider.[14] The strength or weakness of the service provided often affects consumers' perceptions of product quality. Of the companies in the SPI database, businesses that rate low on service lose market share at the rate of 2 percent a year and average a 1 percent return on sales. Companies that score high on service gain market share at the rate of 6 percent a year, average a 12 percent return on sales, and charge a significantly higher price.[15] These data indicate that firms having service-dominant products must score high on service quality.

Because services are performances rather than tangible goods, the concept of service quality is difficult to grasp. However, price, quality, and value are important considerations of consumer choice and buying behaviour for both goods and services.[16] It should be noted that it is not objective quality that matters, but the consumer's subjective perceptions. Instead of quality meaning conformity to a set of specifications—which frequently determine levels of product quality—service qual-

---

13. G. Lynn Shostack, "Breaking Free from Product Marketing," *Journal of Marketing*, April 1977, pp. 73–80.

14. Sak Onkvisit and John J. Shaw, "Service Marketing: Image, Branding, and Competition," *Business Horizons*, January-February 1989, p. 16.

15. Tom Peters, "More Expensive, But Worth It," *U.S. News & World Report*, 3 Feb. 1986, p. 54.

16. Valarie A. Zeithaml, "Consumer Perceptions of Price, Quality, and Value: A Means-End Model and Synthesis of Evidence," *Journal of Marketing*, July 1988, pp. 2–22.

FIGURE 22.5

Providing speed of service.

To reinforce in consumers' minds and provide a tangible cue about the speed of service, AT&T in America equates its ability to connect long-distance calls with the time it takes a Porsche 911 to go from 0 to 60 mph.

Both come with a service guarantee. One won't get stuck in traffic.

A Porsche 911 Carrera can do 0 to 60 in 6.1 seconds. But not during rush hour.

The AT&T Worldwide Intelligent Network can connect most long distance calls in under 6 seconds, twenty-four hours a day, 365 days a year. AT&T has a special signaling system that actually scouts ahead for clear message paths before each call is routed. Only AT&T gives you the most reliable service available, and a service guarantee.

That means, no matter where you call from, you're assured of AT&T's low prices, uncompromising sound quality, immediate credit for misdialed calls, efficient operators, and the ability to call anywhere in the world.

When you're on the road, you want a service guarantee, so make sure you hear "Thank you for using AT&T." Then your calls won't get stuck in traffic.

We're here to help. For assistance, call 1 800 222-0300.

AT&T
The right choice.

© 1989 AT&T

SOURCE: © 1989 AT&T

ity is defined by customers.[17] Moreover, quality is frequently determined in a comparison context. In the case of services, quality is determined by contrasting what the consumer expected a service to be with her or his actual service experience.[18] Marketing Update 22.1 describes how AT&T dealt with a quality problem in its long-distance telephone service.

Service providers and service consumers may have quite different views of what constitutes service quality. Consumers frequently enter service exchanges with a set of predetermined expectations. Whether a consumer's actual experiences exceed, match, or fall below these expectations will have a great effect on future relationships between the consumer and the service provider. To improve service quality, a service provider must adjust its own behaviour to be consistent with consumers' expectations or re-educate consumers so that their expectations will parallel the service levels that can be achieved.[19] Marketing Update 22.2 describes Beefeater's consumer-orientated marketing strategy.

17. Leonard L. Berry, "8 Keys to Top Service at Financial Institutions," *American Banker*, August 1987.

18. A. Parasuraman, Valarie A. Zeithaml, and Leonard L. Berry, "SERVQUAL: A Multiple-Item Scale for Measuring Consumer Perceptions of Service Quality," *Journal of Retailing*, Spring 1988, pp. 12–40.

19. Stephen W. Brown and Teresa A. Swartz, "A Gap Analysis of Professional Service Quality," *Journal of Marketing*, April 1989, pp. 92–98.

AT&T FACES DISRUPTION OF ITS
LONG-DISTANCE TELEPHONE SERVICE

On 15 January 1990, American Telephone and Telegraph (AT&T), the largest long-distance telephone service provider in the United States, faced a crisis as millions of Americans across the nation inexplicably got busy signals when dialling outside their local area. The nine-hour disruption of service, the first ever to affect AT&T's entire nation-wide network, was frustrating to both customers and AT&T, which has long promoted its reputation for quality and reliable service.

Especially frustrating to AT&T executives was the fact that experts could not quickly pinpoint the cause of the service disruption; they could only stand by helplessly while AT&T customers complained and threatened to take their business elsewhere. Engineers eventually traced the shutdown to a defective switch that sent out trouble messages to other switches across the country. When the switch recovered, it sent out a burst of backed-up calls, overwhelming another switch. This started a chain reaction that caused other AT&T switches to block calls. It was nearly midnight before engineers identified the problem and sent software to the switches that would stop the problem and break the cycle.

Fortunately, the incident occurred on Martin Luther King Day, a national holiday honoured by many businesses. The volume of calls on that day was therefore less than the eighty million calls AT&T handles on a regular weekday. None the less, the shutdown affected normal long-distance calls and Freephone 0800 lines. Among the companies hurt by it were telemarketers and airline reservation systems.

AT&T not only lost revenue from the disruption, but it also lost credibility with customers who believed in its promoted reputation for quality, reliability, and high technology. AT&T's largest competitors, MCI and Sprint, quickly took advantage of the situation. They launched an avalanche of advertising, promoting the reliability of their own services, and made sales calls on regular AT&T long-distance customers, hoping to get new business after the disaster. To make amends to its customers, AT&T offered one day of free long-distance calls to consumers who were inconvenienced by the disruption of service.

SOURCES: Peter Coy, with Mark Lewyn, "The Day That Every Phone Seemed Off the Hook," *Business Week,* 29 Jan. 1990, pp. 39–40; Andrea Gabor, "A Busy Signal Heard Round the World," *U.S. News & World Report,* 29 Jan. 1990, p. 46; John J. Keller, Mary Lu Carnevale, and Julie Amparano Lopez, "Glitch Imperils AT&T's Marketing Edge," *Wall Street Journal,* 17 Jan. 1990, pp. B1, B2; and John J. Keller, "Software Bug Closes AT&T's Network, Cutting Phone Service for Millions in U.S.," *Wall Street Journal,* 16 Jan. 1990, p. A3.

BEEFEATER—STEAK HOUSES BITE

In the U.K., as in Europe, there has been tremendous growth, as living standards have risen, in the restaurant sector. Between 1985 and 1989, in real terms, expenditure on eating out in the U.K. rose by 51 percent. Traditional restaurants have 60 percent of the market, dominated by the likes of Beefeater, Berni, Harvester, and Porterhouse. Despite the presence of such large national chains, most of which are brewery owned, overall the majority of U.K. restaurants are independently owner-run establishments with a large proportion concentrating on ethnic cuisine. Within the middle, mass market, the brewery operated grill-pubs and steak houses dominate.

RESTAURANTS: PERCENT SHARE BY TYPE

Pubs (bars), clubs, winebars	40
Hotels	17
Up-market restaurants	6
Mid-market chains	19
Owner-run	15
Roadside	3

Of the mid-market chains, Beefeater leads with 240 outlets, followed by Berni (190), Toby (120), Porterhouse (90), and Harvester (70). Whitbread's Beefeater began in 1974. By 1981 there were 50 outlets. Now the company has coverage throughout the U.K. and is operating in Germany.

Beefeater's success in the past was attributed mainly to its ability to target specific groups of customers and to change its products/trading concept from time to time. The company knows that such success is not guaranteed and has placed an emphasis on staff training and customer care—the Beefeater Care programme—with the aim of establishing a caring culture in the company. Management believes this "software for success" will be difficult for competitors to copy or match, and with the customer becoming increasingly discerning and sophisticated, it is an essential ingredient for continued growth and success.

SOURCES: *Harvest,* 1990; Beefeater promotional literature, 1990; *Restaurateur,* April and June 1990; *Mintel Leisure Intelligence,* Volume 2 (London: Mintel, 1990); "European Consumer Catering," *Euromonitor,* 1990; "Eating Out Report," *Harvest,* 1989; K. M. Bon, "The U.K. Leisure Industry," Warwick MBA Dissertation, University of Warwick, 1990.

FIGURE 22.6

Complexity/variability grid for medical services

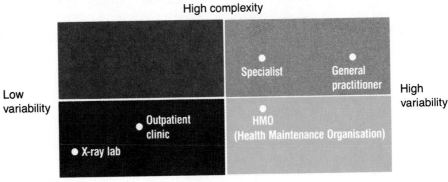

SOURCE: Adapted from Lynn Shostack, 1985 American Marketing Association Faculty Consortium on Services Marketing, Texas A&M University, July 7–11. Reprinted by permission of the American Marketing Association.

A study of doctor-patient relationships proposed that when professional service exceeds client expectations, a true person-to-person bonding relationship develops. However, the research also revealed that what doctors viewed as being quality service was not necessarily what patients perceived as quality service. Although interaction with the doctor was the primary determinant of the overall service evaluation, patients made judgements about the entire service experience, including factors such as the appearance and behaviour of receptionists, nurses, and technicians; the decor; and even the appearance of the building.[20]

Other product concepts discussed in Chapters 7 and 8 are also relevant here. Management must make decisions regarding the product mix, positioning, branding, and new-product development of services. It can make better decisions if it analyses the organisation's service products as to complexity and variability. Complexity is determined by the number of steps required to perform the service. Variability reflects the amount of diversity allowed in each step of service provision. In a highly variable service, every step in performing the service may be unique, whereas in cases of low variability, every performance of the service is standardised.[21] For example, services provided by doctors are both complex and variable. Patient treatment may involve many steps, and the doctor has considerable discretion in shaping the treatment for each individual patient.

An examination of the complete service delivery process, including the number of steps and the number of decisions, enables marketers to plot their service products on a complexity/variability grid, such as the one in Figure 22.6. The position of a service on the grid has implications for its positioning in the market. Furthermore, any alterations in the service delivery process that shift the position of the service on the complexity/variability grid have an impact on the positioning of the service in the market-place. Table 22.4 details the effects of such changes. When structuring the service delivery system, marketers should explicitly consider the firm's marketing goals and target market.

20. Ibid.

21. G. Lynn Shostack, "Service Positioning Through Structural Change," *Journal of Marketing*, January 1987, pp. 34–43.

TABLE 22.4
Effects of shifting positions on the complexity/ variability grid

DOWNSHIFTING COMPLEXITY/VARIABILITY	UPSHIFTING COMPLEXITY/ VARIABILITY
Standardises the service	Increases costs
Requires strict operating controls	Indicates higher-margin/lower-volume strategy
Generally widens potential market	Personalises the service
Lowers costs	Generally narrows potential market
Indicates lower-margin/higher-volume strategy	Makes quality more difficult to control
Can alienate existing markets	

SOURCE: Adapted from G. Lynn Shostack, 1985 American Marketing Association Faculty Consortium on Services Marketing, Texas A&M University, July 7–11, 1985. Reprinted by permission of American Marketing Association.

■ Promotion

As intangible-dominant products, services are not easily promoted. The intangible is difficult to depict in advertising, whether the medium is print, television, or radio. Service advertising should thus emphasise tangible cues that will help consumers understand and evaluate the service. The cues may be the physical facilities in which the service is performed or some relevant tangible object that symbolises the service itself.[22] For example, restaurants may stress their physical facilities—clean, elegant, casual, and so on—to provide cues as to the quality or nature of the service. Insurance firms, such as Legal and General, use objects as symbols to help consumers understand their services. Legal and General's umbrella symbol reflects an image of paternalistic protection. Midland Bank's slogan "The Listening Bank" gave the impression of understanding, helpfulness, and service. Service providers may also focus their advertising on the characteristics they believe customers want from their services. National Westminster Bank's promotion stresses its ability to offer unbiased, independent advice about pensions. Commercial Union Assurance—"We don't make a drama out of a crisis"—emphasises speed of service in dealing with insurance claims and the provision of assistance in sorting out the problem.

In order to be successful, firms must not only maximise the difference between the value of the service to the customer and the cost of providing it; they must also design the service with employees in mind. Contact personnel are critical to the perception of quality service. They must be provided with sufficient tools and knowledge to furnish the type of service that the customer desires. Because service industries are information-driven, they can substitute knowledgeable, highly trained personnel for the capital assets used in more product-orientated businesses.[23]

Thus employees in a service organisation are an important secondary audience for service advertising. We have seen that variability in service quality, which arises from the labour-intensive nature of many services, is a problem for service marketers and that consumers often associate the service with the service provider. Advertising can have a positive effect on customer contact personnel. It can shape em-

22. William R. George and Leonard L. Berry, "Guidelines for the Advertising of Services," *Business Horizons*, July-August 1981, pp. 52–56.

23. Heskett, pp. 118–125.

ployees' perceptions of the company, their jobs, and how management expects them to perform. It can be a tool for motivating, educating, and communicating with employees.[24]

Personal selling is potentially powerful in services because this form of promotion lets consumers and salespeople interact. When consumers enter into a service transaction, they must, as a general rule, interact with service firm employees. Customer contact personnel can be trained to use this opportunity to reduce customer uncertainty, give reassurance, reduce dissonance, and promote the reputation of the organisation.[25] Once again, this emphasises the importance of properly managing contact personnel.

Although consumer-service firms have the opportunity to interact with actual customers and those potential customers who contact them, they have little opportunity to go out into the field and solicit business from all potential consumers. The very large number of potential customers and the high cost per sales call rule out such efforts. On the other hand, marketers of industrial services, like the marketers of industrial goods, are dealing with a much more limited target market and may find personal selling the most effective way of reaching customers.

Sales promotions, such as contests, are feasible for service firms, but other types of promotions are more difficult to implement. How do you display a service? How do you give a free sample without giving away the whole service? A complementary visit to a health club or a free skiing lesson could possibly be considered a free sample to entice a consumer into purchasing a membership or taking lessons. Although the role of publicity and the implementation of a publicity campaign do not differ significantly in the goods and service sectors, service marketers appear to rely on publicity much more than goods marketers do.[26]

Consumers tend to value word-of-mouth communications more than company-sponsored communications. This preference is probably true for all products but especially for services because they are experiential in nature. For this reason, service firms should attempt to stimulate word-of-mouth communications.[27] They can do so by encouraging consumers to tell their friends about satisfactory performance. Many firms, for instance, prominently display signs urging customers to tell their friends if they like the service and to tell the firm if they do not. Some service providers, such as hairdressers, give their regular customers discounts or free services for encouraging friends to come in for a haircut. Word of mouth can be simulated through communications messages that feature a testimonial—for example, television advertisements showing consumers who vouch for the benefits of a service a particular firm offers.

One final note should be made in regard to service promotion. The promotional activities of most professional service providers, such as doctors, lawyers, and accountants, are severely limited. Until recently, all these professionals were prohibited by law from advertising. Although these restrictions have now been lifted, there are still many obstacles to be overcome. Not being used to seeing professionals advertise, consumers may reject advertisements for those who do. Furthermore, professionals are not familiar with advertising and consequently do not always develop advertise-

---

24. George and Berry, pp. 55–70.

25. William R. George and J. Patrick Kelly, "The Promotion and Selling of Services," *Business,* July-September 1983, pp. 14–20.

26. John M. Rathmell, *Marketing in the Services Sector* (Cambridge, Mass.: Winthrop, 1974), p. 100.

27. George and Kelly, pp. 14–20; George and Berry, pp. 55–70.

ments appropriate for their services. In the U.S., lawyers are being forced to consider advertising because many potential clients do not know that they need legal services, and there is an oversupply of lawyers. Consumers want more information about legal services, and lawyers have a very poor public image.[28] On the other hand, doctors and dentists are more sceptical about the impact of advertising on their image and business. Despite the trend towards professional services advertising, the professions themselves exert pressure on their members to advertise or promote only within limited parameters because such activities are still viewed as somewhat risqué.

■ Price

Price plays both an economic and a psychological role in the service sector, just as it does with physical goods. However, the psychological role of price in respect to services is magnified somewhat because consumers must rely on price as the sole indicator of service quality when other quality indicators are absent. In its economic role, price determines revenue and influences profits. Knowing the real costs of each service provided is vital to sound pricing decisions.[29]

Services may also be bundled together and then sold for a single price. Service bundling is a practical strategy because in many types of service there is a high ratio of fixed to variable costs and high cost sharing among service offerings. Moreover, the demand for certain services is often interdependent. For example, banks offer packages of banking services—current and savings accounts and credit lines that become active when customers overdraw their other accounts. Price bundling may help service marketers cross-sell to their current customers, or acquire new customers. The policy of price leaders also may be used by discounting the price of one service product when the customer purchases another service at full price.[30]

As noted in Table 22.1, service intangibility may complicate the setting of prices. When pricing physical goods, management can look to the cost of production (direct and indirect materials, direct and indirect labour, and overheads) as an indicator of price. It is often difficult, however, to determine the cost of service provision and thus identify a minimum price. Price competition is severe in many service areas characterised by standardisation. Usually price is not a key variable when marketing is first implemented in an organisation. Once market segmentation and specialised services are directed to specific markets, specialised prices are set. Next comes comparative pricing as the service becomes fairly standardised. Price competition is quite common in the hotel and leisure sectors, banking, and insurance.

Many services, especially professional services, are situation-specific. Thus neither the service firm nor the consumer knows the extent of the service prior to production and consumption. Once again, because cost is not known beforehand, price is difficult to set. Despite the difficulties in determining cost, many service firms use cost-plus pricing. Others set prices according to the competition or market demand.

Pricing of services can also help smooth out fluctuations in demand. Given the perishability of service products, this is an important function. A higher price may be used to deter or off-set demand during peak periods, and a lower price may be

---

28. Doris C. Van Doren and Louise W. Smith, "Marketing in the Restructured Professional Services Field," *Journal of Services Marketing*, Summer 1987, pp. 69–70.

29. James B. Ayers, "Lessons from Industry for Healthcare," *Administrative Radiology*, July 1987, p. 53.

30. Joseph P. Guiltinan, "The Price Bundling of Services: A Normative Framework," *Journal of Marketing*, April 1987, p. 74.

FIGURE 22.7

Distributing services. British Telecom promotes its Voice Messaging service—a method of distributing telephoned information more efficiently.

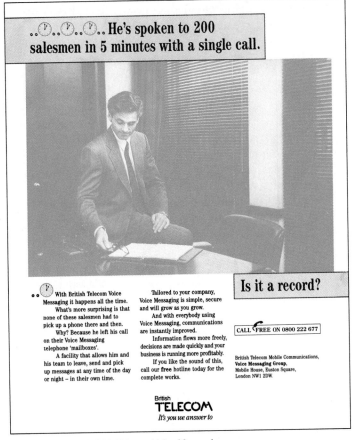

SOURCE: Copyright British Telecom Voice Messaging

used to stimulate demand during slack periods. British Rail's cheap day returns and Savers minimise sales declines in slack periods. Airlines rely heavily on price to help smooth out their demand, as do many other operations, such as pubs and entertainment clubs, cinemas, resorts, and hotels.

■ **Distribution**

In the service context, distribution is making services available to prospective users. Marketing intermediaries are the entities between the actual service provider and the consumer that make the service more available and more convenient to use.[31] In Figure 22.7, British Telecom promotes its Voice Messaging service. This communications tool allows telephoned information to flow more easily and efficiently throughout a company. The distribution of services is very closely related to product development. Indirect distribution of services may be made possible by a tangible representation or a facilitating good, for example, a bank credit card.[32]

Almost by definition, service industries are limited to direct channels of distribution. Many services are produced and consumed simultaneously; in high-contact

31. James H. Donnelly, Jr., "Marketing Intermediaries in Channels of Distribution for Services," *Journal of Marketing,* January 1976, pp. 55–70.

32. Ibid.

services in particular, service providers and consumers cannot be separated. In low-contact services, however, service providers may be separated from customers by intermediaries. Dry cleaners, for example, generally maintain strategically located retail stores as drop-off centres, and these stores may be independent or company owned. Consumers go to the branch to initiate and terminate service, but the actual service may be performed at a different location. The separation is possible because the service is directed towards the consumer's physical possessions, and the consumer is not required to be present during delivery.

Other service industries are developing unique ways to distribute their services. To make it more convenient for consumers to obtain their services, airlines, car hire companies, and hotels have long been using intermediaries: travel agencies. In financial services marketing, the two most important strategic concerns are the application of technology and the use of electronic product delivery channels—such as automatic cash dispensers and electronic funds transfer systems—to provide customers with financial services in a more widespread and convenient manner.[33] Consumers no longer have to go to their bank for routine transactions; they can now receive service from the nearest cash dispenser. Bank credit cards have enabled banks to extend their credit services to consumers over widely dispersed geographic areas through a nation-wide network of intermediaries, namely, the retail merchants who assist consumers in applying for and using the cards.

■ Strategic Considerations

In developing marketing strategies, the marketer must first understand what benefits the customer wants, how the marketer is perceived relative to the competition, and what services consumers buy.[34] In other words, the marketer must develop the right service for the right people at the right price and at the right place. The marketer must remember to communicate with consumers so that they are aware of the need-satisfying services available to them.

One of the unique challenges service marketers face is matching supply and demand. We have seen that price can be used to help smooth out demand for a service. There are other ways, too, that marketers can alter the marketing mix to deal with the problem of fluctuating demand. Through price incentives, advertising, and other promotional efforts, marketers can remind consumers of busy times and encourage them to come for service during slack periods. Additionally, the product itself can be altered to cope with fluctuating demand. Restaurants, for example, may change their menus, vary their lighting and decor, open or close the bar, and add or delete entertainment. A ski resort may install an alpine slide to attract customers during the summer. Finally, distribution can be modified to reflect changes in demand. Theatres have traditionally offered matinées during the weekend, when demand is greater, and some libraries have mobile units that travel to different locations during slack periods.[35]

Before understanding such strategies, service marketers must first grasp the pattern and determinants of demand. Does the level of demand follow a cycle? What

33. Nigel A. L. Brooks, "Strategic Issues for Financial Services Marketing," *Journal of Services Marketing,* Summer 1987, p. 65.

34. Yoram Wind, "Financial Services: Increasing Your Marketing Productivity and Profitability," *Journal of Services Marketing,* Fall 1987, p. 8.

35. Lovelock, *Services Marketing,* pp. 279–289.

TABLE 22.5

Strategies for coping with fluctuations in demand for services

MARKETING STRATEGIES	NON-MARKETING STRATEGIES
Use different pricing	Hire extra staff/lay off employees
Alter product	Work employees overtime/part-time
Change distribution	Cross-train employees
Use promotional efforts	Use employees to perform non-vital tasks during slack times
	Subcontract work/seek subcontract work
	Slow the pace of work
	Turn away business

are the causes of this cycle? Are the changes random?[36] The need to answer such questions is best illustrated through an example. An attempt to use price decreases to shift demand for public transport to off-peak periods would most likely fail because of the cause of the cyclical demand for public transport: employment hours. Employees have little control over working hours and are therefore unable to take advantage of pricing incentives.

Table 22.5 summarises ways service firms may deal with the problem of fluctuating demand. Note that the strategies fall into two categories: marketing and non-marketing strategies. Non-marketing strategies essentially involve internal, employee-related actions.[37] They may be the only available choices when fluctuations in demand are random. For example, a strike or natural disaster may cause fluctuations in consumer demand for public transport.

Non-business Marketing

Remember that earlier we broadly defined marketing as a set of individual and organisational activities aimed at facilitating and expediting satisfying exchanges in a dynamic environment through the creation, distribution, promotion, and pricing of goods, services, and ideas. Most of the previously discussed concepts and approaches to managing marketing activities also apply to non-business situations. Of special relevance is the material offered in the first half of this chapter because many non-business organisations provide services.

Non-business marketing includes marketing activities conducted by individuals and organisations to achieve some goal other than ordinary business goals of profit, market share, or return on investment. Non-business marketing can be divided into two categories: non-profit-organisation marketing and social marketing. Non-profit-organisation marketing is the application of marketing concepts and techniques to organisations such as hospitals and colleges. Social marketing is the development of programmes designed to influence the acceptability of social ideas, such as contrib-

36. Ibid.
37. Berry, Zeithaml, and Parasuraman, pp. 231–234.

FIGURE 22.8

Non-business marketing.
Art Against AIDS represents social marketing designed to raise money for AIDS research through this public art project.

Views of Hotel Well III, 1984–85

DAVID HOCKNEY
for Art Against AIDS • On The Road

The Werner Erhard Foundation is a sponsor of this public art

project of The American Foundation For AIDS Research (AmFAR)

Support Art Against AIDS by sending your contribution to AmFAR, Box AIDS, New York, NY 10016

SOURCE: American Foundation for AIDS Research/Livet Richard Co.

uting to a foundation for AIDS research or getting people to recycle more newspapers, plastics, and aluminium.[38] Art Against Aids is a fund-raising association to support AIDS research (see Figure 22.8).

As discussed in Chapter 1, an exchange situation exists when individuals, groups, or organisations possess something that they are willing to give up in an exchange. In non-business marketing, the objects of the exchange may not be specified in financial terms. Usually, such exchanges are facilitated through **negotiation** (mutual discussion or communication of terms and methods) and **persuasion** (convincing and prevailing upon by argument). Often negotiation and persuasion are conducted without reference to or awareness of the role that marketing plays in transactions. We are concerned with non-business performance of marketing activities, whether the exchange is consummated or not.

In the rest of this chapter, we first examine the concept of non-business marketing to determine how it differs from marketing activities in business organisations.

38. J. Whyte, "Organization, Person and Idea Marketing as Exchange," *Quarterly Review of Marketing,* January 1985, pp. 25–30.

Next we explore the overall objectives of non-business organisations, their marketing objectives, and the development of their marketing strategies. We close the discussion by illustrating how an audit of marketing activities can promote marketing awareness in a non-business organisation.

■ Why Is Non-business Marketing Different?

Traditionally and mistakenly, people have not thought of non-business exchange activities as marketing. But consider the following example. Warwick Business School used to promote its degree courses solely through the University of Warwick's prospectuses. In recent years, its main programmes received small advertising budgets. As courses were improved, the wider use of advertising increased awareness of the school and its programmes. A new corporate identity was developed by Coley Porter Bell of London and each programme, led by the MBA, developed its own full marketing mix and more extensive promotional strategy, all in line with the school's new mission statement. Many university departments and state-maintained schools are now engaging in marketing strategy.

Many non-business organisations strive for effective marketing activities. Charitable organisations and supporters of social causes are major non-business marketers. Political parties, unions, religious groups, and student organisations also perform marketing activities, yet they are not considered businesses. Whereas the chief beneficiary of a business enterprise is whoever owns or holds shares in it, in theory the only beneficiaries of a non-business organisation are its clients, its members, or the public at large.

Non-businesses have a greater opportunity for creativity than most business organisations, but trustees or board members of non-businesses are likely to have trouble judging performance when services can be provided only by trained professionals. It is harder for administrators to evaluate the performance of doctors, lecturers, or social workers than it is for sales managers to evaluate the performance of salespersons in a for-profit organisation.

Another way in which non-business marketing differs from for-profit marketing is that non-business is sometimes quite controversial. Non-business organisations such as Greenpeace, CND, and Shelter spend lavishly on lobbying efforts to persuade government and even the courts to support their interests, in part because acceptance of their aims by all of society is not always guaranteed. However, marketing as a field of study does not attempt to state what an organisation's goals should be or to debate the issue of non-business versus business goals. Marketing only attempts to provide a body of knowledge and concepts to help further an organisation's goals. Individuals must decide whether they approve of a particular organisation's goal orientation. Most marketers would agree that profit and consumer satisfaction are appropriate goals for business enterprises, but there probably would be considerable disagreement about the goals of a controversial non-business organisation.

■ Non-business Marketing Objectives

The basic aim of non-business organisations is to obtain a desired response from a target market. The response could be a change in values, a financial contribution, the donation of services, or some other type of exchange. Non-business marketing objectives are shaped by the nature of the exchange and the goals of the organisation. BBC-sponsored "Children in Need" and "Comic Relief" telethons have raised millions of pounds. Telethons have three specific marketing objectives: (1) to raise funds to support programmes, (2) to plead a case on behalf of disadvantaged groups, and (3) to inform the public about the organisation's programmes and services.

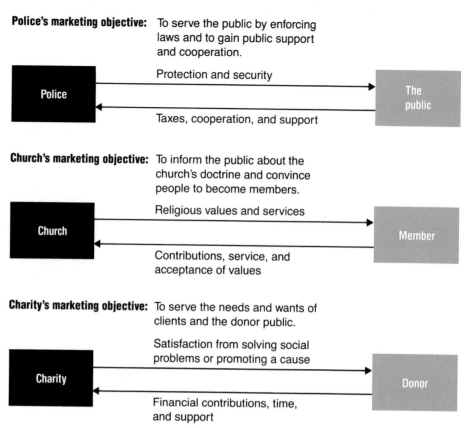

Police's marketing objective: To serve the public by enforcing laws and to gain public support and cooperation.

Police → Protection and security → The public

The public → Taxes, cooperation, and support → Police

Church's marketing objective: To inform the public about the church's doctrine and convince people to become members.

Church → Religious values and services → Member

Member → Contributions, service, and acceptance of values → Church

Charity's marketing objective: To serve the needs and wants of clients and the donor public.

Charity → Satisfaction from solving social problems or promoting a cause → Donor

Donor → Financial contributions, time, and support → Charity

SOURCE: Philip Kotler, *Marketing for Nonprofit Organizations,* 2nd ed., © 1982, p. 38. Adapted by permission of Prentice-Hall, Inc., Englewood Cliffs, N.J.

Tactically, telethons have received support by choosing good causes; generating extensive grassroots support; portraying disabled people in a positive and dignified way; developing national, regional, and local support; and providing quality entertainment.[39] Figure 22.9 illustrates how the exchanges and the purpose of the organisation can influence marketing objectives. (These objectives are used as examples and may or may not apply to specific organisations.)

Non-business marketing objectives should state the rationale for an organisation's existence. An organisation that defines its marketing objective as providing a product can be left without a purpose if the product becomes obsolete. However, serving and adapting to the perceived needs and wants of a target public, or market, enhances an organisation's chance to survive and achieve its goals.

■ **Developing Non-business Marketing Strategies**

Non-business organisations must also develop marketing strategies by defining and analysing a target market and creating and maintaining a marketing mix that appeals to that market.

Target Markets. We must revise the concept of target markets slightly to apply it to non-business organisations. Whereas a business is supposed to have target groups

39. John Garrison, "Telethons—The Positive Story," *Fund Raising Management,* November 1987, pp. 48–52.

FIGURE 22.10
Non-business markets.
The University of Warwick serves many groups: students, the community at large through employment and student development, and philanthropists who may be looking for worthwhile organisations to support.

Warwick is rated as one of Europe's most innovative and outstanding business schools; research led and outward-looking, maintaining close links with international, national and local businesses.

■ Management Development Programmes ■ Research and Consultancy
■ MBA: full- and part-time,

WAYS AHEAD

WARWICK
BUSINESS SCHOOL

distance-learning and in consortium with leading-edge companies
■ Masters' Programmes in Operational Research, Industrial Relations, Business Management Systems

Warwick has pioneered industry-university collaboration and is working with many of Britain's major companies, providing executive development courses in marketing, finance, the management of change, operations management information systems, retailing and strategic management.
If you are interested in

■ management training ■ research or ■consultancy,
contact Warwick Business School
University of Warwick, Coventry CV4 7AL, U.K.
Telephone: 0203 523523 ext. 2834
Fax: 0203 523719 Telex: 31406

WARWICK BUSINESS SCHOOL

SOURCE: Courtesy Warwick Business School, University of Warwick

that are potential purchasers of its product, a non-business organisation may attempt to serve many diverse groups. In Figure 22.10, the University of Warwick is promoting excellence to potential and current students, financial supporters, and the general public. For our purposes, a **target public** is broadly defined as a collective of individuals who have an interest in or concern about an organisation, a product, or a social cause. The terms *target market* and *target public* are difficult to distinguish for many non-business organisations. The target public of the Partnership for a Drug Free America is parents, adults, and concerned teenagers. However, the target market for the organisation's advertisements is potential and current drug users. When an organisation is concerned about changing values or obtaining a response from the public, it views the public as a market.[40]

In non-business organisations, direct consumers of the product are called **client publics** and indirect consumers are called **general publics**.[41] For example, the client public for a university is its student body, and its general public includes parents, graduates, and University Senate. The client public usually receives most of the attention when an organisation develops a marketing strategy. The techniques and approaches to segmenting and defining target markets discussed in Chapter 3 apply also to non-business target markets.

Developing a Marketing Mix. A marketing-mix strategy limits choices and directs marketing activities towards achieving organisational goals. The strategy should outline or develop a blueprint for making decisions about product, distribution, promotion, and price. These decision variables should be blended to serve the target market.

40. Philip Kotler, *Marketing for Nonprofit Organizations* (Englewood Cliffs, N.J.: Prentice-Hall, 1982), p. 37.
41. Ibid.

In tackling the product variable, non-business organisations deal more often with ideas and services than with goods. Problems may evolve when an organisation fails to define what is being provided. What products do the Women's Institute, the Scout movement, or the Chamber of Commerce provide? They offer a forum for social gatherings, courses, outings, and a sense of co-operation. Their products are more difficult to define than the average business product. As indicated in the first part of this chapter, services are intangible and therefore need special marketing efforts. The marketing of ideas and concepts is likewise more abstract than the marketing of tangibles, and it requires considerable effort to present benefits.

Because most non-business products are ideas and services, distribution decisions relate to how these ideas and services will be made available to clients. If the product is an idea, selecting the right media (the promotional strategy) to communicate the idea will facilitate distribution. The availability of services is closely related to product decisions. By nature, services consist of assistance, convenience, and availability. Availability is part of the total service. For example, making a product such as health services available calls for knowledge of such retailing concepts as site location analysis.

Developing a channel of distribution to co-ordinate and facilitate the flow of non-business products to clients is a necessary task, but in a non-business setting the traditional concept of the marketing channel may need to be reviewed. The independent wholesalers available to a business enterprise do not exist in most non-business situations. Instead, a very short channel—non-business organisation to client—is prevalent because production and consumption of ideas and services are often simultaneous.

Making promotional decisions may be the first sign that non-business organisations are performing marketing activities. Non-business organisations use advertising and publicity to communicate with clients and the public. Direct mail remains the primary means of fund-raising for social services such as those provided by the Red Cross or Oxfam. In addition to direct mail, Oxfam uses press advertising and public relations. Personal selling is also used by many non-business organisations, although it may be called something else. Churches and charities rely on personal selling when they send volunteers to recruit new members or request donations. The armed forces use personal selling when recruiting officers attempt to convince men and women to enlist. Special events to obtain funds, communicate ideas, or provide services are sales-promotion activities. Contests, entertainment, and prizes offered to attract donations resemble the sales-promotion activities of business enterprises. Amnesty International, for example, has held worldwide concert tours, featuring artists such as Sting and Phil Collins, to raise funds and increase public awareness of political prisoners around the world.

The number of advertising agencies that are donating their time for public service announcements (PSAs) or public information films is increasing, and the quality of print PSAs is improving noticeably. Non-profit groups are becoming increasingly interested in the impact of advertising on their organisations, and they realise that second-rate PSAs can cause a credibility loss.[42]

Although product and promotion techniques might require only slight modification when applied to non-business organisations, pricing is generally quite different and the decision-making more complex. The different pricing concepts that the

---

42. Meryl Davids, "Doing Well by Doing Good," *Public Relations Journal*, July 1987, pp. 17–21.

non-business organisation faces include pricing in user and donor markets. There are two types of monetary pricing: *fixed* and *variable.* Membership fees, such as the amount paid to become a friend of a zoo, represent a fixed approach to pricing, whereas zoo fund-raising activities that lead to donations represent a variable pricing structure.[43]

The broadest definition of price (valuation) must be used to develop non-business marketing strategies. Financial price, an exact monetary value, may or may not be charged for a non-business product. Economists recognise the giving up of alternatives as a cost. **Opportunity cost** is the value of the benefit that is given up by selecting one alternative rather than another. This traditional economic view of price means that if a non-business organisation can persuade someone to donate time to a cause or to change his or her behaviour, then the alternatives given up are a cost to (or a price paid by) the individual. Volunteers who answer phones for a university counselling service or suicide hotline, for example, give up the time they could have spent studying or doing other things, and the income they might have earned from working in a business organisation.

For other non-business organisations, financial price is an important part of the marketing mix. Non-business organisations today are raising money by increasing the prices of their services or starting to charge for services if they have not done so before. They are using marketing research to determine what kinds of products people will pay for.[44] Pricing strategies of non-business organisations often stress public and client welfare over equalisation of costs and revenues. If additional funds are needed to cover costs, then donations, contributions, or grants may be solicited.

■ Controlling Non-business Marketing Activities

To control marketing activities in non-business organisations, managers use information obtained in the marketing audit to make sure that goals are achieved. Table 22.6 lists several helpful summary statistics. It should be obvious that the data in Table 22.6 are useful for both planning and control. Control is designed to identify what activities have occurred in conformity with the marketing strategy and to take corrective action where any deviations are found. The purpose of control is not only to point out errors and mistakes but to revise organisational goals and marketing objectives as necessary. One way to measure the impact of the advertisement is to audit the number of requests for information or membership applications, such as those received by BUPA health care (see Figure 22.11).

Many potential contributors decide which charities to support based on the amount of money actually used for charitable purposes. Charities are more aggressively examining their own performance and effectiveness. For example, the Salvation Army contributes to the needy most of every pound it receives; its employees are basically volunteers who work for almost nothing. Charities are making internal changes to increase their effectiveness, and many are hiring professional managers to help with strategic planning in developing short-term and long-range goals, marketing strategies, and promotional plans.

To control non-business marketing activities, managers must make a proper inventory of activities performed and prepare to adjust or correct deviations from standards. Knowing where and how to look for deviations and knowing what types

43. Leyland F. Pitt and Russell Abratt, "Pricing in Non-Profit Organizations—A Framework and Conceptual Overview," *Quarterly Review of Marketing,* Spring-Summer 1987, pp. 13–15.

44. Kelly Walker, "Not-for-Profit Profits," *Forbes,* 10 September 1984, p. 165.

TABLE 22.6

Examples of data useful in controlling non-business marketing activities

1. **Product mix offerings**
   A. Types of product or services
   B. Number of organisations offering the product or service

2. **Financial resources**
   A. Types of funding used
      1. Local government grants
      2. Government grants
      3. Foundations
      4. Public appeals
      5. Fees charged
   B. Number using each type of funding
   C. Number using combinations of funding sources

3. **Size**
   A. Budget (cash flows)

   B. Number of employees
      1. By organisation
      2. Total industry-wide
   C. Number of volunteers
      1. By organisation
      2. Total industry-wide
   D. Number of customers serviced
      1. By type of service
      2. By organisation
      3. Total industry-wide

4. **Facilities**
   A. Number and type
      1. By organisation
      2. Total industry-wide
   B. Location
      1. By address
      2. By postal code

SOURCE: Adapted from Philip D. Cooper and George E. McIlvain, "Factors Influencing Marketing's Ability to Assist Non-Profit Organizations," *Evolving Marketing Thought for 1980, Proceedings of the Southern Marketing Association,* John H. Summey and Ronald D. Taylor, eds. (Nov. 19–22, 1980), p. 315. Used by permission.

of deviations to expect are especially important in non-business situations. Because non-business marketing activities may not be perceived as marketing, managers must clearly define what activity is being examined and how it should function.

It may be difficult to control non-business marketing activities because it is often hard to determine whether goals are being achieved. A homeless support group that wants to inform community members of its services may not be able to find out whether it is communicating with persons who need assistance. Surveying to discover the percentage of the population that is aware of a programme to help the homeless can show whether the awareness objective has been achieved, but it fails to indicate what percentage of people without housing has been assisted. The detection and correction of deviations from standards are certainly major purposes of control, but standards must support the organisation's overall goals. Managers can refine goals by examining the results that are being achieved and analysing the ramifications of those results.

Techniques for controlling overall marketing performance must be compatible with the nature of an organisation's operations. Obviously, it is necessary to control the marketing budget in most non-business organisations, but budgetary control is not tied to profit and loss standards; responsible management of funds is the objective. Central control responsibility can facilitate orderly, efficient administration and planning. For example, in America, Illinois Wesleyan University evaluates graduating students' progress to control and improve the quality of the educational product. The audit phase relies on questionnaires sent to students and their employers after graduation. The employer completes a questionnaire to indicate the student's progress; the student completes a questionnaire to indicate what additional concepts or

FIGURE 22.11
Measuring the impact of advertising.
BUPA can measure the impact of its advertising by keeping a count of the number of requests for information.

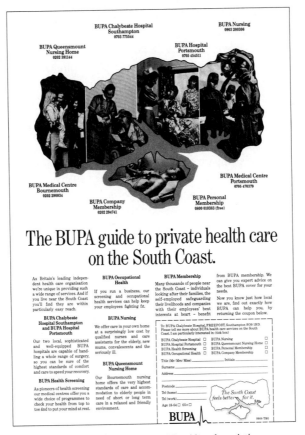

SOURCE: Courtesy of the British United Provident Association

skills were needed to perform duties. In addition, a number of faculty members interview certain employers and students to obtain information for control purposes. Results of the audit are used to develop corrective action if university standards have not been met. Corrective action might include an evaluation of the deficiency and a revision of the curriculum.

SUMMARY

Services are intangible-dominant products that cannot be physically possessed—the result of applying human or mechanical efforts to people or objects. They are a growing part of the economy. Services have four distinguishing characteristics: intangibility, inseparability of production and consumption, perishability, and heterogeneity. Because services include a diverse group of industries, classification schemes are used to help marketers analyse their products and develop the most appropriate marketing mix. Services can be viewed as to type of market, degree of labour-intensiveness, degree of customer contact, skill of the service provider, and goal of the service provider.

When developing a marketing mix for services, several aspects deserve special consideration. Regarding product, service offerings are often difficult for consumers to understand and evaluate. The tangibles associated with a service may be the only visible aspect of the service, and marketers must manage these scarce tangibles with care. Because services are often viewed in terms of the providers, service firms must carefully select, train, motivate, and control employees. Service marketers are selling long-term relationships as well as performance.

Promoting services is problematic because of their intangibility. Advertising should stress the tangibles associated with the service or use some relevant tangible object. Customer contact personnel should be considered an important secondary audience for advertising. Personal selling is very powerful in service firms because customers must interact with personnel; some forms of sales promotion, however, such as displays and free samples, are difficult to implement. The final component of the promotion mix, publicity, is vital to many service firms. Because customers value word-of-mouth communications, messages should attempt to stimulate or simulate word of mouth. Many professional service providers, however, are severely restricted in their use of promotional activities.

Price plays three major roles in service firms. It plays a psychological role by indicating quality and an economic role by determining revenues. Price is also a way to help smooth out fluctuations in demand.

Service distribution channels are typically direct because of simultaneous production and consumption. However, innovative approaches such as drop-off points, intermediaries, and electronic distribution are being developed.

Fluctuating demand is a major problem for most service firms. Marketing strategies (product, price, promotion, and distribution), as well as non-marketing strategies (primarily internal, employee-based actions), can be used to deal with the problem. Before attempting to undertake any such strategies, however, service marketers must understand the patterns and determinants of demand.

Non-business marketing includes marketing activities conducted by individuals and organisations to achieve goals other than normal business goals. Non-business marketing uses most of the concepts and approaches applied to business situations.

The chief beneficiary of a business enterprise is whoever owns or holds shares in the business, but the beneficiary of a non-business enterprise should be its clients, its members, or its public at large. The goals of a non-business organisation reflect its unique philosophy or mission. Some non-business organisations have very controversial goals, but many organisations exist to further generally accepted social causes.

The marketing objective of non-business organisations is to obtain a desired response from a target market. Developing a non-business marketing strategy consists of defining and analysing a target market and creating and maintaining a marketing mix. In non-business marketing, the product is usually an idea or service. Distribution is involved not so much with the movement of goods as with the communication of ideas and the delivery of services, which results in a very short marketing channel. Promotion is very important in non-business marketing; personal selling, sales promotion, advertising, and publicity are all used to communicate ideas and inform people about services. Price is more difficult to define in non-business marketing because of opportunity costs and the difficulty of quantifying the values exchanged.

It is important to control non-business marketing strategies. Control is designed to identify what activities have occurred in conformity with marketing strategy and to take corrective action where deviations are found. The standards against which performance is measured must support the non-business organisation's overall goals.

IMPORTANT TERMS

Intangibility
Search qualities
Experience qualities
Credence qualities
Inseparability
Perishability
Heterogeneity

Non-business marketing
Negotiation
Persuasion
Target public
Client publics
General publics
Opportunity cost

DISCUSSION AND REVIEW QUESTIONS

1. Identify and discuss the distinguishing characteristics of services. What problems do these characteristics present to marketers?
2. What is the significance of "tangibles" in service industries?
3. Analyse a house-cleaning service in terms of the five classification schemes, and discuss the implications for marketing-mix development.
4. How do search, experience, and credence qualities affect the way consumers view and evaluate services?
5. Discuss the role of promotion in services marketing.
6. Analyse the demand for dry-cleaning, and discuss ways to cope with fluctuating demand.
7. Compare and contrast the controversial aspects of non-business versus business marketing.
8. Relate the concepts of product, distribution, promotion, and price to a marketing strategy aimed at preventing drug abuse.
9. What are the differences between clients, publics, and consumers? What is the difference between a target public and a target market?
10. What is the function of control in a non-business marketing strategy?
11. Discuss the development of a marketing strategy for a university. What marketing decisions should be made in developing this strategy?

■ CASES

22.1 THF Hotels—Branding and Service

Trusthouse Forte (THF) is one of the largest hotel operators and caterers in the world and the dominant player in the U.K. The company has grown through acquisition—Kennedy Brooks, the Strand Palace, and more recently Crest. Around 250 hotels are branded THF in the U.K., be they the purposely created Post Houses, budget-orientated Travelodges, well-positioned Crests, or the remaining bulk of the portfolio, which includes de luxe country hotels, international London hotels, and resort-based establishments.

Certain hotels are internationally focused for overseas tourists or business travellers; others are leisure or vacation orientated, while many—particularly in the large conurbations—cater for U.K. businesspeople and conferences. Standards, though, are not uniform. In London it is possible to stay at the two-star Regent Palace Hotel at £50 per night without en suite bathroom or at the five-star Grosvenor House at £200. Both hotels are clearly branded as THF but their facilities, service levels, image, and impressions on the consumer vary greatly.

THF must re-brand, grouping hotels with similar target customers and facilities under sub-brands (e.g. Exclusive hotels or Forte hotels) and guarantee within each group or category uniformly high standards, amenities, service levels, and price points. The company invests heavily in maintaining standards—refurbishing hotels and restaurants, training personnel, installing IT applications—and is, with the help of McKinsey, establishing sub-brands of groups of similarly pitched hotels.

The problem remains, however, that each hotel is clearly identified as being part of the Trusthouse Forte company. A poor meal, delayed check in or out, slow room service, or a dilapidated room may be the exception to the rule but does not only tarnish a particular customer's perception of the one THF hotel or restaurant. The customer is likely to associate such a poor experience with the THF name and thereby with the company's other hotels, even though he or she would have been unlikely to have suffered such problems in a different THF hotel. The product is intangible and inseparable from the place of consumption; it is perishable and highly susceptible to heterogeneity. Personnel are the key.

SOURCES: Ellen Freilich, "Salomon Sees Opportunity in European Hotel Chains," Reuters, 1990; Gareth David, "The Hotel Market Strategies of John Jarvis and Peter Tyne," *Sunday Times,* 22 July 1990; "Investment in Hotel Industry Increases, But Prices Are Still Too High," *Economist,* 5 May 1990, p. 44; "Room at The Inn—The Outlook for Britain's Hotel Industry over the Next Years," *Management Today,* December 1989, pp. 99–108; "THF to Rename?" *Caterer and Hotelkeeper,* 10–16 January 1991, p. 12.

Questions for Discussion

1. How can a service business such as THF maintain uniformity of product quality?
2. How best can THF promote its product?
3. Is branding important in all services?

22.2   Multiplex Cinemas

After a long period of decline the U.K. cinema industry has recovered slightly.

YEAR	ADMISSIONS (M)	GROSS BOX OFFICE INCOME (£m)
1985	72	138
1986	75	144
1987	78	156
1988	84	190
1989	89	207
1990°	90	201

° Forecast

SOURCE: Key Note/Leisure Consultants

Industry watchers believe the recovery is due to recent "blockbuster" releases, the fall in youth unemployment and, most importantly, the launch of multiplex cinemas.

United Cinemas International (UCI) is the leader in the development of multiplex cinemas. Each multiplex cinema has 8 to 10 screens offering a wide choice of movies for all social and age groups: in addition to the mainstream releases there are children's clubs, late-night adult clubs, and showings of critically acclaimed "art" films. The auditoria are luxuriously appointed, with extra leg room, comfortable seating, and Dolby stereo Surroundsound. All multiplexes offer extensive refreshment facilities with some, such as the complex in Milton Keynes, housing a restaurant, nightclub, and amusement area.

By offering comfort, catering, extensive film selection, convenience (in terms of near-town-centre locations with ample parking), and various "club" packages, the multiplex cinemas have breathed new life into the U.K. cinema industry. Forecasts estimate admissions will be 97 million (worth £279 million) by 1994.

SOURCES: *Screen Digest,* August 1990; Key Note, *The Cinema Industry,* 1989; K. Bon, "The U.K. Leisure Industry," Warwick MBA Dissertation, University of Warwick, 1990.

Questions for Discussion

1. What social trends does the multiplex concept suit?
2. Will satellite television and cable television have an impact on the growth of multiplex cinema networks? Why?
3. In Derby, Warner and UCI are competing head-on in providing multiplex cinemas for the first time. How can the various companies operating multiplex cinemas differentiate themselves?

23 INTERNATIONAL MARKETING

Objectives

To define the nature of international marketing

To understand the importance of international marketing intelligence

To recognise the impact of environmental forces on international marketing efforts

To become aware of regional trade alliances and markets

To examine the potential of marketing mix standardisation among nations

To describe adaptation of the international marketing mix when standardisation is impossible

To look at ways of becoming involved in international marketing activities

The chocolate confectionery business of Swiss-based Jacob Suchard represents 58 percent of its Sw. fr. 6 billion turnover. The company has been gearing up for global markets since the late 1960s, by developing global brands, such as Milka and Toblerone, and undertaking a number of strategically important acquisitions. In taking over other European confectionery companies, such as Du Lac (Italian) and Pavlides (Greek), Suchard has sought established distribution and retail channels in areas where it was not traditionally strong. This has helped the company to develop its own global brands alongside smaller, local products. The acquisition of the West German cocoa trader Van Houten in 1987 has given Suchard closer control over its raw materials.

It seems likely that, at the European level, global brands will be assisted by the single market in 1992, which will allow the unrestricted flow of goods between EC countries. Companies like Suchard, with pan-European brands, will benefit from the advertising opportunities offered by European satellites, which are less likely to be exploited by national brands. It is probable that after 1992 European preferences and eating habits will gradually converge as communication of this type increases. ◆

SOURCES: *Le Journal de Genève*, 29 Apr. 1989, p. 9; *24 Ore* (Italian), 15 April 1987, p. 15; *Marketing Week*, 8 July 1988, p. 19; Michael Labrou, "Ten Marketing Cases," MBA Dissertation, University of Warwick, 1989.

International marketing is marketing activities performed across national boundaries.[1] In many cases, serving a foreign target market requires more than minor adjustments of marketing strategies.

This chapter looks closely at the unique features of international marketing and at the marketing-mix adjustments businesses make when they cross national boundaries. We begin by examining companies' level of commitment to and degree of involvement in international marketing. Then we consider the importance of international marketing intelligence when a firm is moving beyond its domestic market. Next we focus on the need to understand various environmental forces in international markets and discuss several regional alliances and markets. We also analyse marketing-mix standardisation and adaptation. At the close of the chapter, we describe a number of ways of getting involved in international marketing.

INVOLVEMENT IN INTERNATIONAL MARKETING

Before international marketing could achieve its current level of importance, enterprises with the necessary resources had to develop an interest in expanding their businesses beyond national boundaries. Once interested, marketers engage in international marketing activities at several levels of involvement. Regardless of the level of involvement, however, they must choose either to customise their marketing strategies for different regions of the world or to standardise their marketing strategies for the entire world.

■ **Multinational Involvement**

The level of involvement in international marketing covers a wide spectrum, as shown in Figure 23.1. Casual or accidental exporting is the lowest level of commitment. For example, the products of a small medical-supplies manufacturer might occasionally be purchased by hospitals or clinics in nearby countries; its products might also be purchased by other countries through an export agent. Active exporting concentrates on selling activities to gain foreign market acceptance of existing products. Full-scale international marketing involvement means that top management recognises the importance of developing international marketing strategies to achieve the firm's goals. Globalisation of markets requires total commitment to international marketing; it embodies the view that the world is a single market.

■ **Globalisation Versus Customisation of Marketing Strategies**

Only full-scale international marketing involvement and globalisation of markets represent a full integration of international marketing into strategic market planning. Traditional full-scale international marketing involvement is based on products customised according to cultural, regional, and national differences. In full-scale international marketing, marketing strategies are developed to serve specific target markets. From a practical standpoint, this means that to standardise the marketing mix, the strategy needs to group countries by social, cultural, technological, political, and economic similarities.

In contrast, **globalisation** involves developing marketing strategies as though the entire world (or regions of it) were a single entity; a globalised firm markets

1. Vern Terpstra, *International Marketing*, 4th ed. (Hinsdale, Ill.: Dryden Press, 1987), p. 4.

Casual or accidental exporting	Active exporting	Full-scale international marketing involvement	Globalization of markets
Occasional, unsolicited foreign orders are received. There is no real commitment to international marketing.	This is an attempt to create sales without significant changes in the firm's products and overall operations. An active effort to find foreign markets for existing products is most typical.	Markets across national boundaries are a consideration in the marketing strategy. International marketing activities are seen as a part of overall planning.	Companies try to operate as if the world were one large market, ignoring regional and national differences.

National or domestic orientation ←——————————————————————→ Global orientation

FIGURE 23.1 *Levels of involvement in international marketing*

SOURCE: Excerpt from *International Marketing,* 4th ed., by Vern Terpstra. Copyright © 1987 by The Dryden Press, a division of Holt, Rinehart and Winston, Inc. Reprinted by permission of the publisher.

standardised products in the same way everywhere.[2] For many years, organisations have attempted to globalise the marketing mix as much as possible by employing standardised products, promotion campaigns, prices, and distribution channels for all markets. The economic and competitive pay-offs for globalised marketing strategies are certainly great. Brand name, product characteristics, packaging, and labelling are among the easiest marketing-mix variables to standardise; media allocation, retail outlets, and price may be more difficult. In the end, the degree of similarity among the various environmental and market conditions determines the feasibility of globalisation.

Some companies have moved from customising or standardising products for a particular region of the world to offering globally standardised products that are advanced, functional, reliable, and low priced.[3] Nike, for example, provides a standardised product worldwide (see Figure 23.2). As we stated earlier, a firm committed to globalisation develops marketing strategies as if the entire world (or major regions of it) were a single entity. Examples of globalised products are electrical equipment, videos, films, soft drinks, rock music, cosmetics, and toothpaste. Sony televisions, Levi jeans, and U.K. confectionery brands seem to make year-by-year gains in the world market. Even McDonald's, Pizza Hut, and Kentucky Fried Chicken restaurants seem to be widely accepted in markets throughout the world. Attempts are now being made to globalise industrial products, such as computers, robots, and carbon filters, and professional engineering products, such as earth-moving equipment and communications equipment. But the question remains whether promotion, pricing, and distribution of these products can also be standardised.

Debate about the feasibility of globalised marketing strategies has continued since the birth of the idea in the 1960s. Surprisingly, questions about standardised advertising policies are the leading concern. However, it should be remembered

2. Theodore Levitt, "The Globalization of Markets," *Harvard Business Review,* May-June 1983, p. 92.

3. Ibid.

FIGURE 23.2 *Example of globalisation.*
Nike offers globally standardised products.

SOURCE: Pete Stone, Photographer; Weiden and Kennedy, Ad agency

that there are degrees of both customisation and globalisation. Neither strategy is implemented in its pure form.[4] The debate will doubtless continue about which products, if any, can be fully globalised. Some firms, such as Black & Decker and Coca-Cola, have adopted globalised marketing strategies. For some products—such as soft drinks—a global marketing strategy, including advertising, seems to work well, but for others—such as beer—strategies must accommodate local, regional, and national differences.[5]

INTERNATIONAL MARKETING INTELLIGENCE

Despite the debate over globalisation of markets, most firms perceive international markets as differing in some ways from domestic markets. Analyses of international markets and possible marketing efforts can be based on many dimensions. Table 23.1 lists the types of information that international marketers need.

4. Subhash C. Jain, "Standardization of International Marketing Strategy: Some Research Hypotheses," *Journal of Marketing,* January 1989, pp. 70–79.

5. "Global Brands Need Local Ad Flavor," *Advertising Age,* 3 Sept. 1984, p. 26.

TABLE 23.1 *Information needed for international marketing analyses*

PRELIMINARY SCREENING

Demographic/Physical Environment
Population size, growth, density
Urban and rural distribution
Climate and weather variations
Shipping distance
Product-significant demographics
Physical distribution and communications network
Natural resources

Political Environment
System of government
Political stability and continuity
Ideological orientation
Government involvement in business
Government involvement in communications
Attitudes towards foreign business (trade restrictions, tariffs, non-tariff barriers, bilateral trade agreements)
National economic and developmental priorities

Economic Environment
Overall level of development
Economic growth: GNP, industrial sector
Role of foreign trade in the economy
Currency, inflation rate, availability, controls, stability of exchange rate
Balance of payments
Per capita income and distribution
Disposable income and expenditure patterns

Social/Cultural Environment
Literacy rate, educational level
Existence of middle class
Similarities and differences in relation to home market
Language and other cultural considerations

ANALYSIS OF INDUSTRY MARKET POTENTIAL

Market Access
Limitations on trade: tariff levels, quotas
Documentation and import regulations
Local standards, practices, and other non-tariff barriers
Patents and trade marks
Preferential treaties
Legal considerations: investment, taxation, repatriation, employment, code of laws

Product Potential
Customer needs and desires
Local production, imports, consumption
Exposure to and acceptance of product
Availability of linking products
Industry-specific key indicators of demand
Attitudes towards products of foreign origin
Competitive offerings
Availability of intermediaries
Regional and local transport facilities
Availability of manpower
Conditions for local manufacture

ANALYSIS OF COMPANY SALES POTENTIAL

Sales Volume Forecasting
Size and concentration of customer segments
Projected consumption statistics
Competitive pressures
Expectations of local distributors/agents

Landed Cost
Costing method for exports
Domestic distribution costs
International freight insurance
Cost of product modification

Cost of Internal Distribution
Tariffs and duties
Value-added tax
Local packaging and assembly
Margins/commission allowed for the trade
Local distribution and inventory costs
Promotional expenditures

Other Determinants of Profitability
Going price levels
Competitive strengths and weaknesses
Credit practices
Current and projected exchange rates

SOURCE: Adapted from S. Tamer Cavusgil, "Guidelines for Export Market Research," *Business Horizons,* November-December 1985, pp. 30–31. Used by permission.

TABLE 23.2 *Sources of secondary information for international marketing*

TYPE OF INFORMATION	SOURCES	OTHER SOURCES
Foreign market information	Foreign economic trends Overseas business reports International economic indicators Foreign governments (e.g., U.S. Department of Commerce) DTI EC (Eurostat, etc.)	*Financial Times* surveys Business International Dun & Bradstreet International Chase World Information Corp. International Trade Reporter Accounting and stock market firms Foreign trade organisations Economic Intelligence Unit
Export market research	Country market sectoral surveys Global market surveys International market research	Market research firms Advertising agencies Publishing companies Trade associations
International statistics	Export statistics profile Customer service statistics	Predicasts Foreign brokerage houses United Nations International Monetary Fund OECD, EC, GATT
Overseas representatives	Customised export mailing list World traders data reports Agent/distributor service	Banks International Chambers of Commerce Consulting firms Direct telephone contact
Sales leads	Trade opportunities programme Strategic and industrial product sales group Major export projects programme Export information reference room	Banks International Chambers of Commerce Consulting firms State development agencies
Reference data on foreign markets	World traders data reports	Banks International Chambers of Commerce Consulting firms State development agencies Corporate information databases

SOURCES: S. Tamer Cavusgil, "Guidelines for Export Market Research," *Business Horizons*, November-December 1985, p. 32; and Leonard M. Fuld, "How to Gather Foreign Intelligence Without Leaving Home," *Market News*, 4 Jan. 1988, pp. 24, 47. Data used by permission.

Gathering secondary data (see Table 23.2) should be the first step in analysing a foreign market. Sources of information include government publications, financial services firms, international organisations such as the United Nations, foreign governments, and international trade organisations. Firms seeking to market their products in the Soviet Union, for example, can obtain information about Soviet markets and regulations from the U.K. Department of Trade and Industry (DTI), the USSR Chamber of Commerce and Industry, the Soviet trade organisation Amtorg, and numerous other organisations. Depending on the source, however, secondary data can be misleading. The reliability, validity, and comparability of data from some countries are often problematic.

To overcome these shortcomings, marketers may need primary data to understand consumers' buying behaviour in the country under investigation. Marketers may have to adjust their techniques of collecting primary data for foreign markets. Attitudes towards privacy, unwillingness to be interviewed, language differences, and low literacy rates can be serious research obstacles. In a bicultural country such as Canada, a national questionnaire that uses identical questions is impossible because of the cultural and language differences. In many areas of Africa, where the literacy rate is low, self-administered questionnaires would never work.

Primary research should uncover significant cultural characteristics before a product is launched so that the marketing strategy is appropriate for the target market. It may be necessary to investigate basic patterns of social behaviour, values, and attitudes to plan a final marketing strategy. Overall, the cost of obtaining such information may be higher than the cost of domestic research; the reasons include the large number of foreign markets to be investigated, the distance between the marketer and the foreign market, unfamiliar cultural and marketing practices, language differences, and the scarcity or unreliability of published statistics.[6]

After analysing secondary and primary data, marketers should plan a marketing strategy. Finally, after market entry, review and control will result in decisions to withdraw from the foreign market, to continue to expand operations, or to consider additional foreign markets.

ENVIRONMENTAL FORCES IN INTERNATIONAL MARKETS

A detailed analysis of the environment is essential before a company enters a foreign market. If a marketing strategy is to be effective across national borders, the complexities of all the environments involved must be understood. In this section we see how the cultural, social, economic, political and legal, and technological forces of the marketing environment in different countries vary.

■ **Cultural Forces**
In Chapter 3 we define culture as the concepts, values, and tangible items, such as tools, buildings, and foods, that make up a particular society. Culture is passed on from one generation to another; in a way, it is the blueprint for acceptable behaviour in a given society. When products are introduced into one nation from another, acceptance is far more likely if there are similarities between the two cultures.

The connotations associated with body motions, greetings, colours, numbers, shapes, sizes, and symbols vary considerably across cultures (Table 23.3 gives a few examples). For multinational marketers, these cultural differences have implications for product development, personal selling, advertising, packaging, and pricing. For example, the illustration of feet is regarded as despicable in Thailand. An international marketer must also know a country's customs regarding male-female social interaction. In Italy it is unacceptable for a salesman to call on a woman if her husband is not at home. In Thailand certain Listerine television commercials that portrayed boy-girl romantic relationships were unacceptable.

6. Vern Terpstra, "Critical Mass and International Marketing Strategy," *Journal of the Academy of Marketing Science*, Summer 1983, pp. 269–282.

TABLE 23.3 *Sampling of cultural variations*

COUNTRY/ REGION	BODY MOTIONS	GREETINGS	COLOURS	NUMBERS	SHAPES, SIZES, SYMBOLS
Japan	Pointing to one's own chest with a forefinger indicates one wants a bath. A forefinger to the nose indicates "me".	Bowing is the traditional form of greeting.	Positive colours are in muted shades. Combinations of black, dark grey, and white have negative overtones.	Positive numbers are 1, 3, 5, 8. Negative numbers are 4, 9.	Pine, bamboo, or plum patterns are positive. Cultural shapes such as Buddha-shaped jars should be avoided.
India	Kissing is considered offensive and not seen on television, in films, or in public places.	The palms of the hands touch and the head is nodded for greeting. It is considered rude to touch or shake hands with a woman.	Positive colours are bold colours such as green, red, yellow, or orange. Negative colours are black and white if they appear in relation to weddings.	To create brand awareness, numbers are often used as a brand name.	Animals such as parrots, elephants, tigers, or cheetahs are often used as brand names or on packaging. Sexually explicit symbols are avoided.
Europe	When counting on one's fingers, "one" is often indicated by thumb, "two" by thumb and forefinger.	It is acceptable to send flowers in thanks for a dinner invitation, but not roses (for sweethearts) or chrysanthemums (for funerals).	Generally, white and blue are considered positive. Black often has negative overtones.	The numbers 3 or 7 are usually positive. 13 is a negative number.	Circles are symbols of perfection. Hearts are considered favourably at Christmas time.
Latin America	General arm gestures are used for emphasis.	The traditional greeting is a hearty embrace and a friendly slap on the back.	Popular colours are generally bright or bold yellow, red, blue, or green.	Generally, 7 is a positive number. Negative numbers are 13, 14.	Religious symbols should be respected. Avoid national symbols such as flag colours. Round or square shapes are acceptable.
Middle East	The raised eyebrow facial expression indicates "yes".	The word "no" must be mentioned three times before it is accepted.	Positive colours are brown, black, dark blues, and reds. Pink, violets, and yellows are not favoured.	Positive numbers are 3, 5, 7, 9; 13, 15 are negative.	Symbols of six-pointed star, raised thumb, or Koranic sayings are avoided.

SOURCE: James C. Simmons, "A Matter of Interpretation," *American Way,* April 1983, pp. 106–111; and "Adapting Export Packaging to Cultural Differences," *Business America,* 3 Dec. 1979, pp. 3–7.

Product adoption and use are also influenced by consumers' perceptions of other countries. When consumers are generally unfamiliar with products from another country, their perceptions of the country itself affect their attitude towards and adoption of the products. If a country has a reputation for producing quality products, and therefore has a positive image in consumers' minds, marketers from that country will want to make the country of origin well known. Conversely, marketers may want to disassociate themselves from a particular country. Because American cars have not been viewed by the world as being quality products, Chrysler, for example, may want to advertise in Japan that Colt is "not another American compact".[7]

Culture may also affect marketing negotiations and decision-making behaviour on the part of marketers, industrial buyers, and other executives. Research has shown that when marketers use a problem-solving approach—that is, gain information about a particular client's needs and tailor products or services to meet those needs—it leads to increased customer satisfaction in marketing negotiations in France, Germany, the United Kingdom, and the United States. However, the attractiveness of the salesperson and his or her similarity to the customer increase the levels of satisfaction only for Americans. Furthermore, marketing negotiations proceed differently in the various cultures, and the role and status of the seller are more important in both the United Kingdom and France.[8]

■ Social Forces

Marketing activities are primarily social in purpose; therefore they are structured by the institutions of family, religion, education, health, and recreation. For example, in the U.K., where listening to music on hi-fi systems is a common form of relaxation, Japanese products have a large target market (see Figure 23.3). In every nation, these social institutions can be identified. By finding major deviations in institutions among countries, marketers can gain insights into the adaptation of a marketing strategy. Although American football is a popular sport in the United States and a major opportunity for many television advertisers, soccer is the most popular television sport in Europe. Yet football hooliganism has caused major advertisers in the United Kingdom to have second thoughts about supporting such events with millions of pounds of advertising.[9] The role of children in the family and a society's overall view of children also influence marketing activities. For example, the use of cute, cereal-loving children in advertising for Kellogg's is illegal in France. In the Netherlands, children are banned from confectionery advertisements, and sweet manufacturers are required to place a little toothbrush symbol at the end of each confectionery spot.[10]

■ Economic Forces

Economic differences dictate many of the adjustments that must be made in marketing abroad. The most prominent adjustments are caused by differences in standards of living, availability of credit, discretionary buying power, income distribution, national resources, and conditions that affect transport.

7. C. Min Han, "Country Image: Halo or Summary Construct?" *Journal of Marketing Research,* May 1989, pp. 222–229.

8. Nigel G. G. Campbell, John L. Graham, Alain Jolibert, and Hans Gunther Meissner, "Marketing Negotiations in France, Germany, the United Kingdom, and the United States," *Journal of Marketing,* April 1988, pp. 49–62.

9. Brian Oliver, "U.K. Soccer Advertising in Trouble," *Advertising Age,* July 8, 1985, p. 36.

10. Laurel Wentz, "Local Laws Keep International Marketers Hopping," *Advertising Age,* 11 July 1985, p. 20.

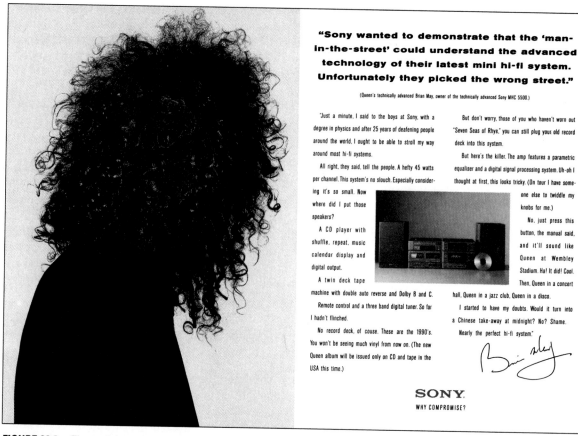

FIGURE 23.3 *The social aspects of international marketing.*
Widespread societal acceptance of relaxing to music makes a Japanese product marketable in the U.K.
SOURCE: Courtesy of SONY (U.K.) Ltd.

Gross domestic product (GDP) is the total value of all goods and services produced by a country domestically in one year. GDP therefore offers a measure of a country's income. A comparison of GDP for Europe, America, and Japan (see Table 23.4) shows that the United States has the largest gross domestic product in the world. However, in order to attain a measure of standard of living, it is necessary to divide this figure by the size of the population. In this way it is possible to gain insight into the level of discretionary income or "buyer power" of individual consumers. This kind of knowledge about aggregate GDP, credit, and the distribution of income provides general insights into market potential.

Opportunities for international marketers are certainly not limited to countries with the highest incomes. Some nations are progressing at a markedly faster rate than they were even a few years ago; and these countries—especially in Latin America, Africa, Eastern Europe, and the Middle East—have great market potential for specific products. However, marketers must first understand the political and legal environment before they can convert buying power into actual demand for specific products.

TABLE 23.4
Comparison of European, U.S., and Japanese gross domestic product by economic activity (1985 market prices; Mrd ECU)

ECONOMIC ACTIVITY	EUROPE	USA	JAPAN
All activities	3,361.2	5,224.3	1,817.1
Agriculture, hunting, forestry, and fishing	111.6	110.9	55.1
Industry	1,179.8	1,616.1	715.3
Manufacturing industry	789.3	1,052.8	522.0
Building and civil engineering	183.4	214.5	128.1
Services	1,942.4	3,497.2	1,046.7

SOURCE: *Eurostat,* 1988. Reproduced by permission of the Commission of the European Communities.

■ Political and Legal Forces

A country's political system, national laws, regulatory bodies, national pressure groups, and courts all have great impact on international marketing. A government's policies towards public and private enterprise, consumers, and foreign firms influence marketing across national boundaries. For example, the Japanese have established many barriers to imports into their country. Even though they are reducing the tariffs on thousands of items, many non-tariff barriers still make it difficult for other companies to export their products to Japan.[11] Just a few years ago, companies exporting electronic equipment to Japan had to wait for the Japanese government to inspect each item. A government's attitude towards co-operation with importers has a direct impact on the economic feasibility of exporting to that country.

Differences in political and government ethical standards are enormous. The use of pay-offs and bribes is deeply entrenched in many governments, while in others direct involvement in pay-offs and bribes is prohibited. European companies that do not engage in such practices may have a hard time competing with foreign firms that do. Some businesses that refuse to make pay-offs are forced to hire local consultants, public relations firms, or advertising agencies—which results in indirect pay-offs. The ultimate decision about whether to give small tips or gifts where they are customary must be based on a company's code of ethics.

■ Technological Forces

Much of the marketing technology used in Europe and other industrialised regions of the world may be ill suited for developing countries. For example, advertising on television or through direct-mail campaigns may be difficult in countries that lack up-to-date broadcasting and postal services. None the less, many countries—particularly China, South Korea, Mexico, and the Soviet Union—want to engage in international trade, often through partnerships with American, European, and Japanese firms, so that they can gain valuable industrial and agricultural technology. However, in certain cases companies need permission to export goods. For example, in the U.K. and other EC countries government approval is needed before defence equipment can be exported.

11. Lee Smith, "Japan Wants to Make Friends," *Fortune*, 2 Sept. 1985, p. 84.

Although some firms are beginning to view the world as one huge market-place, various regional trade alliances and specific markets may create difficulties or opportunities for companies engaging in international marketing. This section examines several regional trade alliances and changing markets, including the 1992 unification of Europe, the Pacific Rim markets, changing conditions in eastern Europe and the Soviet Union, and the United States and Canada trade pact.

■ Europe 1992

The unification of Europe in 1992 will permit virtually free trade among the twelve member nations of the European Community (EC). Although Germany, France, Italy, the United Kingdom, Spain, the Netherlands, Belgium, Denmark, Greece, Portugal, Ireland, and Luxembourg currently exist as separate markets, in 1992 they will merge into the largest single market in the world, with more than 320 million consumers. The unification will allow marketers to develop one standardised product for all twelve nations instead of customising products to satisfy the regulations and restrictions of each country.[12] Before completely free trade can be established, a large number of barriers still need to be overcome. Some businesspeople and economists believe that because of inconsistencies between the administrations of member states—for example, VAT levels, tax systems, and laws—1992 serves only as a symbolic date. In reality, there is likely to be continued discussion between member states over outstanding issues of this type.[13]

Although the twelve nations of the EC will essentially function as one large market and consumers in the EC are likely to become more homogeneous in their needs and wants, marketers must be aware that cultural and social differences among the twelve member nations may require modifications in the marketing mix for consumers in each nation. Some researchers believe that after 1992 it will be possible to segment the European Community into six markets on the basis of cultural, geographic, demographic, and economic variables. The six markets would be (1) the United Kingdom and Ireland; (2) central and northern France, southern Belgium, central Germany, and Luxembourg; (3) Spain and Portugal; (4) southern Germany, northern Italy, and southeastern France; (5) Greece and southern Italy; and (6) Denmark, northern Germany, the Netherlands, and northern Belgium.[14] Differences in taste and preferences among these markets are significant for international marketers. For example, the British prefer front-loading washing machines while the French prefer top-loading ones. Consumers in Spain eat far more poultry products than Germans do.[15] Preference differences may exist even within the same country, depending on the geographic region. Thus international marketing intelligence efforts are likely to remain very important in determining European consum-

12. John Hillkirk, "It Could Be Trade Boom or Bust," *USA Today,* 12 Jan. 1989, p. 4B.

13. Nicholas Colchester, "1992 = 1990 + 2 or Thereabouts," in *The World in 1990* (London: Economist Publications, 1990), pp. 49–50; and Stephen Young, James Hamill, Colin Wheeler, and J. Richard Davies, *International Market Entry and Development* (London: Harvester Wheatsheaf, 1989), pp. 280–282.

14. Sandra Vandermerwe and Marc-André L'Huillier, "Euro-Consumers in 1992," *Business Horizons,* January-February 1989, pp. 34–40.

15. Eric G. Friberg, "1992: Moves Europeans Are Making," *Harvard Business Review,* May-June 1989, p. 89.

ers' needs and in developing marketing mixes that will satisfy those needs. It is also clear that EC organizations will have to face up to considerable changes in the way they operate. In sectors where there is little within-EC trade and many manufacturers, restructuring will be the most radical. For pharmaceutical companies, the prospects include harmonisation of prices and formulations and likely job losses. In this, as in other sectors, much collaborative activity through mergers and acquisitions is likely to occur.

■ **Pacific Rim Nations**

Companies of the Pacific Rim nations—Japan, China, South Korea, Taiwan, Singapore, Hong Kong, the Philippines, Malaysia, Indonesia, Australia, and Indochina—have become increasingly competitive and sophisticated in their marketing efforts in the last three decades. The Japanese in particular have made tremendous inroads into world consumer markets for cars, motorcycles, watches, cameras, and audio and video equipment. Products from Sony, Sanyo, Toyota, Mitsubishi, Canon, Suzuki, and others are sold all over the world and have set standards of quality by which other products are often judged. Managers from other nations study and imitate Japan's highly efficient management and manufacturing techniques. However, Japan's marketing muscle has not escaped criticism. Europe and the United States rely on Japan's informal trade restraints on its exports of cars, textiles, steel, and audio and video consumer products. There has also been considerable international criticism of Japan's reluctance to accept imports from other nations.

South Korea has become very successful in world markets with familiar brands such as Samsung, Daewoo, and Hyundai. But even before those companies became household names, their products achieved strong success under company labels such as RCA and J. C. Penney, for example, in America. Korean companies are now taking market share away from Japanese companies in the world markets for video recorders, colour televisions, and computers, despite the fact that the Korean market for these products is limited. In Canada, the Hyundai Excel overtook Japan's Honda in just eighteen months.[16] Faced with EC quotas, Hyundai is taking on Japanese and American manufacturers for a piece of the U.S. market.

Because of its drive towards modernisation, the People's Republic of China was thought to have great market potential and opportunities for joint venture projects. However, limited consumer demand and political instability dimmed those prospects. In particular, a 1989 student pro-democracy uprising in Beijing reversed several years of business progress in China. Given the political instability, many foreign companies reduced their presence in China or left altogether; other firms became more cautious in their relations with China.[17]

Less-visible Pacific Rim regions, such as Singapore, Taiwan, and Hong Kong, are major manufacturing and financial centres. Singapore also has large world markets for pharmaceutical and rubber goods. Hong Kong, however, faces an uncertain future after it moves from British control to control by the People's Republic of China in 1997. Taiwan may have the most promising future of all the Pacific Rim nations. It has a strong local economy and has lowered many import barriers, sending imports up by 42 percent, to nearly £35 billion in 1988. Taiwan is beginning

---

16. Leslie Helm, with Laxmi Nakarmi, Jang Jung Soo, William J. Holstein, and Edith Terry, "The Koreans Are Coming," *Business Week,* 25 Dec. 1985, pp. 46–52.

17. Dori Jones Yang and Dinah Lee, with William J. Holstein and Maria Shao, "China: The Great Backward Leap," *Business Week,* 19 June 1989, pp. 28–32.

to privatise state-run banks and is also opening its markets to foreign firms. Some analysts believe that it may replace Hong Kong as a regional financial power centre when Hong Kong reverts to Chinese control.[18] Firms from Thailand and Malaysia are also blossoming, carving out niches in the world markets for a variety of products, from toys to car parts.[19]

The Soviet Union and other Eastern European nations (Poland, Hungary, East Germany, Yugoslavia, Czechoslovakia, Romania, and Bulgaria), following a policy of *perestroika*, are experiencing great political and economic changes. The Communist Party's centrally planned economies are being replaced by democratic institutions in most of these countries. In fact, changes in the Eastern Bloc countries have been the fastest-breaking developments in international marketing. As a result, they are becoming increasingly market-orientated. These seven countries are very different in terms of technology, infrastructure, foreign investment laws, and speed of change.[20]

The Soviet leader Mikhail Gorbachev has implemented widespread measures to improve the economic environment of the Soviet Union, measures aimed primarily at making his nation more responsive to the forces of supply and demand. For instance, government-owned businesses have been granted more autonomy to make marketing decisions.[21] Other economic reform plans include replacing the Soviet Union's system of state-owned enterprises and farms with independent businesses leased or owned by workers, shareholders, co-operatives, and joint ventures; overhauling the system of centrally determined prices; and setting free-market prices for many products. For the first time, businesses from the West have begun to advertise and sell their products. *The Economist* was the first English billboard advertisement in May 1989.

The reformers of the Soviet, Polish, and Hungarian economies want to reduce trade restrictions on imports and offer incentives to encourage exports to and investment in their countries.[22] One such move involves seven U.K. companies which have formed a consortium to look at opportunities in the personal care and food and drink areas of the Soviet market. So far, the initiative has led to a number of developments, including joint venture agreements between Tambrands and the Ukrainian ministry of public health to sell tampons to a market of 70 million women and between Allied Lyons and the Russian ministry of trade to market eight million gallons of ice-cream a year under the Baskin-Robbins label.[23] Because of these economic and political reforms, productivity in Eastern Europe and the Soviet Union is expected to increase as workers are given more incentives and control, raising the possibility that Eastern Europe will become an economic powerhouse rivalling the United States and Japan. There is also speculation that some of the Eastern European nations will ultimately join the European Community, allowing

18. Dori Jones Yang, with Dirk Bennett and Bill Javerski, "The Other China Is Starting to Soar," *Business Week*, 6 Nov. 1989, pp. 60–62.

19. Louis Kraar, "Asia's Rising Export Powers," *Fortune*, Special Pacific Rim 1989 issue, pp. 43–50.

20. "East Bloc Business," *USA Today*, 19 March 1990, p. 6B.

21. Richard L. Kirkland, "Russia: Where Gorbanomics Is Leading," *Fortune*, 28 Sept. 1987, pp. 82–84; and Misha G. Knight, "The Russian Bear Turns Bullish on Trade," *Business Marketing*, April 1987, pp. 83–84.

22. Peter Gumbel, "Soviet Reformers Urge Bold Push to Liberalize Faltering Economy," *Wall Street Journal*, 27 Oct. 1989, p. A9.

23. Paul Meller, "Back to the USSR," *Marketing*, 9 Aug. 1990, pp. 22–23.

freer trade across all European borders.[24] In free elections, East Germany voted to reunify with West Germany. As Germany becomes one unified country, its impact on the European Community will be great.

Because of the changing economic conditions in Eastern bloc and the Soviet Union, there are many marketing opportunities in these countries for Western European, American, and Asian firms. Siemens, Federal Express, Procter & Gamble, and Occidental Petroleum are among the many companies considering doing business in Eastern Europe. The countries of Eastern Europe are building new hotels and improving telephone, airline, and land transport services to facilitate international trade, as well as for the benefit of their citizens.[25] Marketing Update 23.1 highlights the actions taken by some firms in response to the fall of the Berlin Wall in 1989. However, because of the swift and uncontrolled nature of the changes taking place in Eastern Europe and the Soviet Union, firms considering marketing their products in these countries must carefully monitor events and proceed cautiously.

■ United States and Canada Trade Pact

In 1989 the United States and Canada signed the Free Trade Agreement (FTA), which essentially merged the American and Canadian markets and formed the largest free-trade zone in the world. The agreement calls for the elimination of most tariffs and other trade restrictions over a ten-year period so that goods and services can flow more easily each way across the U.S.–Canadian border. Trade between the United States and Canada already totals more than £100 billion annually, and the FTA will make trade and investment across the border even "more profitable, less cumbersome, and more secure".[26] In Figure 23.4, CNGT promotes its efficient transport system for goods between Canada and the United States.

Although passage of the trade pact was controversial and required lengthy negotiations, most experts believe that it will enable firms in both countries to compete more successfully against Asian and European rivals. When all the provisions are in effect in the year 2000, the treaty will enlarge Canada's markets ten times, and the United States will have unrestricted access to a market the size of California. Canadians are expected to ship more minerals, livestock, and forest products to the United States; American investments in Canada and sales of paper goods are likely to increase. Some experts estimate that the gross national products of the two countries could rise by 1 to 5 percent, as keener competition spurs companies on both sides to greater efficiency and productivity.[27] The tariff reductions mandated by the FTA will especially benefit smaller American and Canadian firms because it will allow them to create more efficient economies of scale for the unified market and to earn higher profit margins.[28]

---

24. John Templeman, Thane Peterson, Gail E. Schares, and Jonathan Kapstein, "The Shape of Europe to Come," *Business Week,* 27 Nov. 1989, pp. 60–64.

25. Kevin Maney, "Eager East's Welcome Mat Is a Bit Shabby," *USA Today,* 23 Oct. 1989, pp. 1B, 2B; and Peter Gumbel, "Corporate America Flocking to Moscow," *Wall Street Journal,* 24 Oct. 1989, p. A18.

26. Albert G. Holzinger, "A New Era in Trade," *Nation's Business,* September 1989, p. 67.

27. Gordon Bock, "Big Hug from Uncle Sam," *Time,* 19 Oct. 1987, p. 50; Madelaine Drohan, "A Critical Concern," *Maclean's,* 4 Jan. 1988, pp. 42–43; Mushtaq Luqmani and Zahir A. Quraeshi, "The U.S.–Canada Free Trade Pact: Issues and Perspectives," *Developments in Marketing Science,* Vol. XII, Academy of Marketing Science Proceedings, 1989, pp. 113–115; Edith Terry, Bill Javerski, Steven Dryden, and John Pearson, "A Free-Trade Milestone," *Business Week,* 19 Oct. 1987, pp. 52–53; "The Trade Pact Benefits Both Sides," *Business Week,* 19 Oct. 1987, p. 154.

28. Holzinger, pp. 67–69.

AS THE BERLIN WALL CRUMBLES, MARKETING OPPORTUNITIES EMERGE

For nearly thirty years, the concrete Berlin Wall loomed as both a physical barrier and a symbol of the political, social, and economic differences between democratic West Germany and communist East Germany. It had been erected in August 1961 to stop a massive westward flow of refugees. With the over-throw of Communist regimes throughout Eastern Europe in 1989, the wall became just a physical barrier between East and West Germans. While residents and souvenir seekers chiselled away at the wall itself, the symbolic implications of the fall of the wall resulted in new marketing opportunities.

Less than a month after the dramatic decision was made to open the wall, PepsiCo, AT&T, and Quintessence, which makes Jovan fragrances, filmed commercials at the site. The three companies designed their commercials first to make an emotional appeal and second to stimulate product sales. The Quintessence commercial depicts the reunion of a family split by the wall. An East German grandfather, laden with gifts, drops a teddy bear while crossing through a newly opened gate in the wall. It is returned by a guard, and a "peace on earth" message flashes on the screen followed by a list of Quintessence products. Pepsi's advertisement shows a child giving a border guard a rose with Handel's "Hallelujah" Chorus playing in the background. The AT&T advertisements focus on communication between family and friends previously separated by the wall.

The rapidly changing political climate in Europe has opened more than just the Berlin Wall for entrepreneurs willing to invest in ventures. Although such investments can be risky and the obstacles to trade are many, some companies are overcoming the obstacles and reaching trade agreements. For example, U.K. newspaper tycoon Robert Maxwell is to buy a share in Berliner Verlag GmbH. The company—which publishes two daily newspapers and a number of magazines—is owned by the political party PDS, the new name for the SED party which formerly held power in East Germany. A trade newsletter publisher is exploring the feasibility of publishing a newsletter about trade with Eastern Europeans. One entrepreneur compared the opportunities in Eastern Europe to the Gold Rush days of America. Although there is a chance to strike it rich, many companies may find only fool's gold.

SOURCES: "A Batch of Really Off-the-Wall Ads," *U.S. News & World Report,* 18 Dec. 1989, pp. 11–12; "Colas Toast Crumbling of Berlin Wall," *Adweek,* 11 Dec. 1989, p. 61; Marc Fisher, "East Germany to Tear Down Berlin Wall," *Commercial Appeal,* 3 Jan. 1990, pp. A1, A10; Thomas R. King, "Berlin Wall Lands Role in 3 U.S. Spots," *Wall Street Journal,* 5 Dec. 1989, p. B6; and "World News," *Marketing,* 24 May 1990, p. 4.

FIGURE 23.4 *The Canada–U.S. partnership.*
CNGT acknowledges the importance of free trade between Canada and the United States.

SOURCE: Courtesy of Canadian National/Grand Trunk Western Railways

STRATEGIC ADAPTATION OF MARKETING MIXES

Once a U.K. firm determines overseas market potential and understands the foreign environment, it develops and adapts its marketing mix. Creating and maintaining the marketing mix is the final step in developing the international marketing strategy. Only if foreign marketing opportunities justify the risk will a company go to the expense of adapting the marketing mix. Of course, in some situations new products are developed for a specific country. In these cases, there is no existing marketing mix and no extra expense to consider in serving the foreign target market.

■ **Product and Promotion**

As Figure 23.5 shows, there are five possible strategies for adapting product and promotion across national boundaries: (1) keep product and promotion the same worldwide, (2) adapt promotion only, (3) adapt product only, (4) adapt both product and promotion, and (5) invent new products.[29]

29. Warren J. Keegan, *Global Marketing Management*, 4th ed. (Englewood Cliffs, N.J.: Prentice-Hall, 1989), pp. 378–382.

FIGURE 23.5

International product and promotion strategies

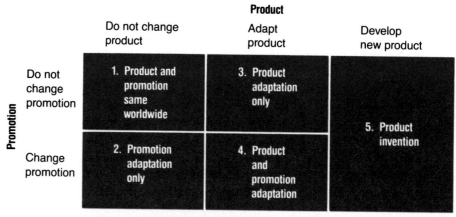

SOURCE: Adapted from Warren J. Keegan, *Global Marketing Management,* 4th ed., Englewood Cliffs, N.J.: Prentice-Hall, 1989, pp. 378–382. Used by permission.

Keep Product and Promotion the Same Worldwide.   This strategy attempts to use in the foreign country the product and promotion developed for the home market, an approach that seems desirable wherever possible because it eliminates the expenses of marketing research and product re-development. American companies PepsiCo and Coca-Cola use this approach in marketing their soft drinks. Although both translate promotional messages into the language of a particular country, they market the same product and promotion messages around the world. Despite certain inherent risks that stem from cultural differences in interpretation, exporting advertising copy does provide the efficiency of international standardisation, or globalisation. Global advertising embraces the same concept as global marketing, discussed earlier in this chapter. An advertiser can save hundreds of thousands of pounds by running the same advertisement world-wide.

Adapt Promotion Only.   This strategy leaves the product basically unchanged but modifies its promotion. For example, Coca-Cola provides similar products throughout the world but may modify the media for its advertising messages (see Figure 23.6). This approach may be necessary because of language, legal, or cultural differences associated with the advertising copy. When Polaroid introduced its SX-70 camera in Europe, for example, it used the same television commercials and print advertisements, featuring "well-known" celebrities, that it used in the United States. However, because the celebrities were not well known in Europe, the commercials were not effective, and sales of the SX-70 were low initially. Only when Polaroid adapted its promotion to appeal to regional needs and tastes did the SX-70 begin to achieve success.[30] Promotional adaptation is a low-cost modification compared with the costs of redeveloping engineering and production and physically changing products.

Generally, the strategy of adapting only promotion infuses advertising with the culture of people who will be exposed to it. Often promotion combines thinking globally and acting locally. At company headquarters, a basic global marketing strategy is developed, but promotion is modified to fit each market's needs.

30. Kamran Kashani, "Beware the Pitfalls of Global Marketing," *Harvard Business Review,* September-October 1989, pp. 93–94.

FIGURE 23.6
Adapting promotion across national boundaries.
Coca-Cola adapts the promotion of its product.

SOURCE: Ira Block/The Image Bank

Adapt Product Only.   The basic assumption in modifying a product without changing its promotion is that the product will serve the same function under different conditions of use. Soap and washing powder manufacturers have adapted their products to local water conditions and washing equipment without changing their promotions. Household appliances also have been altered to use different types of electricity.

A product may have to be adjusted for legal reasons. Japan, for example, has some of the most stringent car emission requirements in the world. European cars that fail emission standards cannot be marketed in Japan. Sometimes, products must be adjusted to overcome social and cultural obstacles. Jell-O introduced a powdered jelly mix that failed in England because people were used to buying jelly in cube form. Resistance to a product is frequently based on attitudes and ignorance about the nature of new technology. It is often easier to change the product than to overcome technological biases.

Adapt Both Product and Promotion.   When a product serves a new function or is used differently in a foreign market, then both the product and its promotion need to be altered. For example, when Procter & Gamble marketed its Cheer washing powder in Japan, it promoted the product as being effective in all temperatures. Most Japanese, however, wash clothes in cold water and therefore do not care about

FIGURE 23.7
Strategies for international distribution and pricing

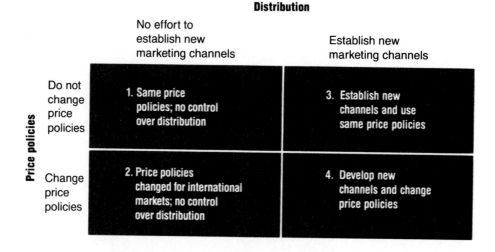

Distribution

	No effort to establish new marketing channels	Establish new marketing channels
Do not change price policies	1. Same price policies; no control over distribution	3. Establish new channels and use same price policies
Change price policies	2. Price policies changed for international markets; no control over distribution	4. Develop new channels and change price policies

*(left axis: **Price policies**)*

all-temperature washing. Moreover, the Japanese often add a lot of fabric softener to the wash, and Cheer did not produce many suds under those conditions. Procter & Gamble thus reformulated Cheer so that it would not be affected by the addition of fabric softeners and changed the promotion to emphasise "superior" cleaning in cold water. Cheer then became one of Procter & Gamble's most successful products in Japan.[31] Adaptation of both product and promotion is the most expensive strategy discussed thus far, but it should be considered if the foreign market appears large enough.

Invent New Products. This strategy is selected when existing products cannot meet the needs of a foreign market. General Motors developed an all-purpose, jeep-like motor vehicle that can be assembled in underdeveloped nations by mechanics with no special training. The vehicle is designed to operate under varied conditions; it has standardised parts and is inexpensive. Colgate-Palmolive developed an inexpensive, all-plastic, hand-powered washing machine that has the tumbling action of a modern automatic machine. The product, marketed in underdeveloped countries, was invented for households that have no electricity. Strategies that involve the invention of products are often the most costly, but the pay-off can be great.

■ **Distribution and Pricing**

Decisions about the distribution system and pricing policies are important in developing an international marketing mix. Figure 23.7 illustrates different approaches to these decisions.

Distribution. A firm can sell its product to an intermediary that is willing to buy from existing market channels, or it can develop new international marketing channels. Obviously, a service company, such as Citicorp, needs to develop its own distribution systems to market its products (see Figure 23.8). However, many products, such as toothpaste, are distributed through intermediaries and brokers. The firm must consider distribution both between countries and within the foreign country.

31. Allecia Swasy, "After Early Stumbles, P&G Is Making Inroads Overseas," *Wall Street Journal,* 6 Feb. 1989, p. B1.

FIGURE 23.8 *International distribution.*
A services-orientated company, such as Citicorp, must develop its own distribution channels to ensure adequate control of its marketing processes.

SOURCE: Citibank, N.A., a subsidiary of Citicorp

In determining distribution alternatives, the existence of retailers and wholesalers that can perform marketing functions between and within nations is one major factor. If a country has a segmented retail structure consisting primarily of one-person shops or street sellers, it may be difficult to develop new marketing channels for products such as packaged goods and prepared foods. Quite often in Third World countries, certain channels of distribution are characterised by ethnodomination. *Ethnodomination* occurs when an ethnic group occupies a majority position within a marketing channel. Indians, for example, own approximately 90 percent of the cotton gins in Uganda; the Hausa tribe in Nigeria dominates the trade in kola nuts, cattle, and housing; and Chinese merchants dominate the rice economy in Thailand. Marketers must be sensitive to ethnodomination and recognise that the ethnic groups operate in sub-cultures with a unique social and economic organisation.[32]

If the product being sold across national boundaries requires service and information, then control of the distribution process is desirable. Caterpillar, for example,

32. Douglass G. Norvell and Robert Morey, "Ethnodomination in the Channels of Distribution of Third World Nations," *Journal of the Academy of Marketing Science,* Summer 1983, pp. 204–235.

sells more than half its construction and earth-moving equipment abroad. Because it must provide services and replacement parts, Caterpillar has established its own dealers in foreign markets. Regional sales offices and technical experts are also available to support local dealers. A manufacturer of paintbrushes, on the other hand, would be more concerned about agents, wholesalers, or other manufacturers that would facilitate the product's exposure in a foreign market. Control over the distribution process would not be so important for that product because services and replacement parts are not needed.

Research suggests that international firms use independently owned marketing channels when they market in countries perceived to be highly dissimilar to their home markets. However, when they market complex products, they develop vertically integrated marketing channels to gain control of distribution. To manage the distribution process from manufacturer to customer contact requires an expert sales force that must be trained specifically to sell the firm's products. Moreover, when products are unique or highly differentiated from those of current competitors, international firms also tend to design and establish vertically integrated channels.[33]

It is crucial to realise that a nation's political instability can jeopardise the distribution of goods. For example, when the United States invaded Panama in late 1989, the Panama Canal was closed for several days, delaying shipments of goods through the canal. Similarly, during the political unrest in China, military activity and fighting made it difficult to move goods into and out of certain areas. Instability centring on Iraq and the Persian Gulf was having a similar effect. Thus we want to stress again the importance of monitoring the environment when engaging in international marketing. Companies that market products in unstable nations may need to develop alternate plans to allow for sudden unrest or hostility and ensure that the distribution of their products is not jeopardised.

Pricing.   The domestic and non-domestic prices of products are usually different. For example, the prices charged for Walt Disney videos in the U.K., Germany, and Spain will all vary, as well as being different from U.S. prices. The increased costs of transport, supplies, taxes, tariffs, and other expenses necessary to adjust a firm's operations to international marketing can raise prices. A key decision is whether the basic pricing policy will change (as discussed in Chapter 17). If it is a firm's policy not to allocate fixed costs to non-domestic sales, then lower foreign prices could result.

It is common practice for EC countries to sell off foodstuffs and pharmaceuticals at knock-down prices to Eastern bloc and African states respectively. This kind of sale of products in non-domestic markets—or vice versa—at lower prices (when all the costs have not been allocated or when surplus products are sold) is called **dumping**. Dumping is illegal in some countries if it damages domestic firms and workers.

A cost-plus approach to international pricing is probably the most common method used because of the compounding number of costs necessary to move products from their country of origin. Of course, as the discussion of pricing policies in Chapter 17 points out, understanding consumer demand and the competitive environment is a necessary step in selecting a price.

33. Erin Anderson and Anne T. Coughlan, "International Market Entry and Expansion via Independent or Integrated Channels of Distribution," *Journal of Marketing*, January 1987, pp. 71–82.

The price charged in other countries is also a function of foreign currency exchange rates. Fluctuations in the international monetary market can change the prices charged across national boundaries on a daily basis. There has been a trend toward greater fluctuation (or float) in world money markets. For example, a sudden variation in the exchange rate, which occurs when a nation devalues its currency, can have wide-ranging effects on consumer prices.

DEVELOPING ORGANISATIONAL STRUCTURES FOR INTERNATIONAL MARKETING

The level of commitment to international marketing is a major variable in deciding what kind of involvement is appropriate. A firm's options range from occasional exporting to expanding overall operations (production and marketing) into other countries. In this section we examine exporting, licensing, joint ventures, trading companies, direct ownership, and other approaches to international involvement.

■ **Exporting**

Exporting is the lowest level of commitment to international marketing and the most flexible approach. A firm may find an exporting intermediary that can perform most marketing functions associated with selling to other countries. This approach entails minimum effort and cost. Modifications in packaging, labelling, style, or colour may be the major expenses in adapting a product. There is limited risk in using export agents and merchants because there is no direct investment in the foreign country.

Export agents bring together buyers and sellers from different countries; they collect a commission for arranging sales. Export houses and export merchants purchase products from different companies and then sell them to foreign countries. They are specialists at understanding customers' needs in foreign countries.

Foreign buyers from companies and governments provide a direct method of exporting and eliminate the need for an intermediary. Foreign buyers encourage international exchange by contacting domestic firms about their needs and the opportunities available in exporting. Domestic firms that want to export with a minimum of effort and investment seek out foreign importers and buyers.

■ **Licensing**

When potential markets are found across national boundaries—and when production, technical assistance, or marketing know-how is required—**licensing** is an alternative to direct investment. The licensee (the owner of the foreign operation) pays commissions or royalties on sales or supplies used in manufacturing. An initial down payment or fee may be charged when the licensing agreement is signed. Exchanges of management techniques or technical assistance are primary reasons for licensing agreements. Yoplait yogurt is a French yogurt that is licensed for production in the United States; the Yoplait brand tries to maintain a French image.

Licensing is an attractive alternative to direct investment when the political stability of a foreign country is in doubt or when resources are unavailable for direct investment. Licensing is especially advantageous for small manufacturers wanting to launch a well-known brand internationally. For example, all Spalding sporting products are licensed worldwide. The Questor Corporation owns the Spalding name but produces no goods itself. Pierre Cardin has issued five hundred licences and Yves St Laurent two hundred to make their products.[34] Lowenbrau has used licensing agreements to increase sales worldwide without committing capital to build breweries.

■ Joint Ventures

In international marketing, a **joint venture** is a partnership between a domestic firm and a foreign firm or government. Joint ventures are especially popular in industries that call for large investments, such as natural resources extraction or car manufacturing. Control of the joint venture can be split equally, or one party may control decision-making. Joint ventures are often a political necessity because of nationalism and governmental restrictions on foreign ownership. They also provide legitimacy in the eyes of the host country's people. Local partners have first-hand knowledge of the economic and socio-political environment, access to distribution networks, or privileged access to local resources (raw material, labour management, contacts, and so on). Moreover, entrepreneurs in many less-developed countries actively seek associations with an overseas partner as a ready means of implementing their own corporate strategy.[35]

Joint ventures are assuming greater global importance because of cost advantages and the number of inexperienced firms entering foreign markets. They may be the result of a trade-off between a firm's desire for completely unambiguous control of an enterprise and its quest for additional resources. They may occur when internal development or acquisition is not feasible or unavailable or when the risks and constraints leave no other alternative. As project sizes increase in the face of global competition and firms attempt to spread the huge costs of technological innovation, there is increased impetus to form joint ventures.[36] Several European truck makers are considering mergers and joint ventures with other European firms to consolidate their power after the unification of Europe in 1992 and the deregulation of the European haulage industry in 1993. Volvo and Renault have developed a partnership, and Britain's Leyland and the Netherlands' DAF have already joined forces.[37]

Increasingly, once a joint venture succeeds, nationalism spurs a trend towards expropriating or purchasing foreign shares of the enterprise. On the other hand, a joint venture may be the only available means for entering a foreign market. For example, European construction firms bidding for business in Saudi Arabia have found that joint ventures with Arab construction companies gain local support among the handful of people who make the contracting decisions.

Strategic alliances, the newest form of international business structure, are partnerships formed to create competitive advantage on a worldwide basis. They are very similar to joint ventures. Strategic alliances have been defined as "cooperation between two or more industrial corporations, belonging to different countries, whereby each partner seeks to add to its competencies by combining its

---

34. John A. Quelch, "How to Build a Product Licensing Program," *Harvard Business Review*, May-June 1985, pp. 186–187.

35. Andrew Kupfer, "How to Be a Global Manager," *Fortune*, 14 Mar. 1988, pp. 52–58.

36. Kathryn Rudie Harrigan, "Joint Ventures and Competitive Advantage," *Strategic Management Journal*, May 1988, pp. 141–158.

37. A. Dunlap Smith, "Europe's Truckmakers Face Survival of the Biggest," *Business Week*, 6 Nov. 1989, p. 68.

TABLE 23.5

Examples of international strategic alliances

PARTNERS	PRODUCTS
General Motors; Toyota	Cars
Rover; Honda	Cars
American Motors; Renault	Cars
Chrysler; Mitsubishi	Cars
Ford; Toyo Kogyo	Cars
Alfa Romeo; Nissan; Fiat	Cars
ATT; Olivetti	Office equipment; computers
Amdahl; Fujitsu	Computers
ICL; Fujitsu	Computers
ATT; Philips	Telecommunications equipment
Honeywell; L.M. Ericsson	PBX system
General Motors; Fanuc	Robotics
AEG Telefunken; JVC; Thorn-EMI; Thomson	Video recorders
General Electric; Matsushita	Electrical appliances
Corning Glass; Siemens	Optical cables
Hercules; Montedison	Polypropylene resin
United Technologies; Rolls-Royce	Aircraft engines

SOURCE: S. Young, J. Hamill, C. Wheeler, R. Davies, *International Market Entry and Development,* First Edition, London: Harvester Wheatsheaf, 1989, p. 273. Reprinted by permission of the publisher.

resources with those of its partner."[38] The number of strategic alliances is growing at an estimated rate of about 20 percent per year.[39] In fact, in some industries, such as cars and high-tech, strategic alliances are becoming the predominant means of competing. International competition is so fierce and the costs of competing on a global basis so high that few firms have the individual resources to go it alone. Thus individual firms that lack all the internal resources essential for international success may seek to collaborate with other companies.[40]

The partners forming international strategic alliances often retain their distinct identities, and each brings a distinctive competence to the union. However, the firms share common long-term goals. What distinguishes international strategic alliances from other business structures is that member firms in the alliance may have been traditional rivals competing for market share in the same product class.[41] Table 23.5 shows some examples of strategic alliances.[42] Marketing Update 23.2 describes a typical marketing alliance.

38. S. C. Jain, "Perspectives on International Strategic Alliances," in *Advances in International Marketing* (New York: JAI Press, 1987), pp. 103–120

39. "More Companies Prefer Liaisons to Marriage," *Wall Street Journal,* 12 Apr. 1988, p. 35.

40. Thomas Gross and John Neuman, "Strategic Alliances Vital in Global Marketing," *Marketing News,* June 1989, pp. 1–2.

41. Margaret H. Cunningham, "Marketing's New Frontier: International Strategic Alliances," working paper, Queens University (Ontario), 1990.

42. Stephen Young, James Hamill, Colin Wheeler, and J. Richard Davies, *International Market Entry and Development. Strategies and Management* (Englewood Cliffs, N.J.: Prentice-Hall, 1989).

STRATEGIC ALLIANCES

Cathay Pacific Airways and Japan Air Lines will begin operating a direct service between Hong Kong and Sapporo on Japan's northern island of Hokkaido in their first joint venture. Cathay Pacific's manager in Sapporo, Mark Nakayasu, said the two airlines had been negotiating a joint service since May 1990 in a bid to attract more Hong Kong tourists to Hokkaido's wealthy ski resorts.

Hokkaido, considered Japan's last frontier, has a population of 5.7 million people, but accounts for one-fifth of Japan's land mass. Most famous for its winter skiing and the Snow Festival in February, the island has become especially attractive to Japanese tourists and students all year round as favourable summer temperatures range between 20° and 28°C. The two airlines hope that direct flights will promote Hokkaido not only for a winter get-away resort, but also as a year-round destination for golf, boating, sightseeing and the Japanese *onsen,* or hot bath.

It is the first joint-venture operation between Cathay Pacific and Japan's national flag-carrier. Cathay will operate a Lockheed TriStar, which can carry 281 passengers, with one JAL crew member.

Mr Nakayasu said 16 Cathay staff and more than 100 JAL staff will be involved with ground operations in Sapporo. "We need JAL to help us at Chitose Airport, but we will use Cathay's style for passenger handling and catering," he said. "No one from Cathay has been in Sapporo for 10 years, so we had to get help from JAL to avoid the risks. We decided on a joint venture at the beginning to test the waters. If we feel confident then later on we may separate."

Strategic alliances enable companies to expand, often into new territories, with reduced capital outlay and risk. Citroën is entering the car market in China through a joint venture with Second Automobile Works. The jointly controlled company Aeolus Citroën Automobile Company will produce 150,000 Citroën ZXs per year. A £50 million joint venture between Coca-Cola and Nestlé will manufacture and market a fresh range of ready-made beverages under the Nescafé and Nestea brand names. Nescafé will gain a distribution system of unparalleled reach and Coca-Cola will benefit by linking with internationally recognized brand names.

SOURCES: Sondra Dunn, "Cathay and JAL Link Up," *South China Morning Post,* 10 September 1990; "Citroën Gears Up for China," *Marketing,* 24 January 1991; Karen Hoggan, "Coca-Cola/Nestlé Venture Revives Iced Tea and Coffee," *Marketing,* 6 December 1990, p. 7.

FIGURE 23.9

Example of a multi-national enterprise. Opel is the product of General Motors's direct ownership of a foreign subsidiary in Germany.

OPEL KADETT GT.
ESTE DEPORTIVO LE SERA MUY FAMILIAR.

El Opel Kadett sigue en la línea de su vida. Ahora Opel le ofrece el Kadett GT. Deportivo de espíritu.

Familiar de concepto.

Su línea más estilizada con una nueva parrilla y un spoiler trasero le dan una mayor aerodinámica.

Su nuevo motor de 1.8 inyección mejora sus prestaciones. Potencia de 112 CV, velocidad punta de 195 Km/h. y una aceleración de 0 a 100 en tan sólo 9,3 seg. Y con la comodidad y capacidad más alta de su categoría: 550 L.

Hasta ahora, nadie había podido ofrecerle esto: un coche con ingeniería alemana, de tres volúmenes y además, deportivo. Y por eso, le resultará muy familiar.

OPEL

INGENIERIA ALEMANA A SU ALCANCE.

SOURCE: Reprinted with permission of General Motors Corporation

■ **Trading Companies**

A **trading company** provides a link between buyers and sellers in different countries. A trading company, as its name implies, is not involved in manufacturing or owning assets related to manufacturing. It buys in one country at the lowest price consistent with quality and sells to buyers in another country. An important function of trading companies is taking title to products and undertaking all the activities necessary to move the products from the domestic country to a foreign country. For example, large grain-trading companies control a major portion of the world's trade in basic food commodities. These trading companies sell agricultural commodities that are homogeneous and can be stored and moved rapidly in response to market conditions.

Trading companies reduce risk for companies interested in getting involved in international marketing. A trading company will assist producers with information about products that meet quality and price expectations in domestic or international markets. Additional services a trading company may provide include consulting, marketing research, advertising, insurance, research and development, legal assistance, warehousing, and foreign exchange.

RANK	COMPANY	SALES
1	NV Kon. Nederlandse Petroleum Maatschappij	69,443
2	The British Petroleum Co. plc	41,684
3	Daimler-Benz AG	37,042
4	Fiat SPA	36,540
5	Volkswagen Aktiengesellschaft (Konzern)	31,689
6	B A T Industries plc	30,426
7	Unilever plc	30,264
8	Siemens Aktiengesellschaft (Konzern)	29,640
9	Unilever NV	28,542
10	Renault (Regie Nationale des Usines)	25,197
11	NV Philips' Gloeilampenfabrieken	26,640
12	Veba Aktiengesellschaft	23,860
13	Nestlé SA	23,340
14	BASF Aktiengesellschaft (Konzern)	23,089
15	Hoechst Aktiengesellschaft (Konzern)	22,255
16	Phibro-Salomon Ltd.	22,172
17	Bayer Aktiengesellschaft (Konzern)	20,995
18	Electricité (Compagnie Générale d')	20,778
19	Electricité de France	20,147
20	Marc Rich & Co. Holding AG	20,079
21	Peugeot SA	19,992
22	RWE Aktiengesellschaft	19,334
23	Agip Petroli SPA	18,664
24	Imperial Chemical Industries plc	18,522
25	Elf Aquitaine (Ste Natl)	18,208
26	British Telecommunications plc	17,318
27	Metro International AG	17,311

■ Direct Ownership

Once a company makes a long-term commitment to marketing in a foreign nation that has a promising political and economic environment, **direct ownership** of a foreign subsidiary or division is a possibility. Although most discussions of foreign investment concern only manufacturing equipment or personnel, the expenses of developing a separate foreign distribution system can be tremendous. The opening of retail stores in Europe, Canada, or Mexico can require a large financial investment in facilities, research, and management.

The term **multinational enterprise** refers to firms that have operations or subsidiaries located in many countries. Often the parent firm is based in one country, and it cultivates production, management, and marketing activities in other countries. The firm's subsidiaries may be quite autonomous in order to respond to the needs of individual international markets. Firms such as ICI, Unilever, and General Motors are multinational companies with worldwide operations (see Figure

TABLE 23.6
continued

RANK	COMPANY	SALES
28	Marc Rich & Co. AG	17,211
29	Metro Vermoegensverwaltung GmbH & Co. Kommanditgesellschaft	17,209
30	Thyssen Aktiengesellschaft	16,607
31	ABB Asea Brown Boveri Ltd.	16,368
32	BBC Brown Boveri AG	14,911
33	Fiat Auto SPA	14,184
34	France Telecom	13,732
35	Petrofina SA	13,633
36	Robert Bosch GmbH (Konzern)	13,419
37	Grand Metropolitan plc	13,075
38	Austrian Industries Aktiengesellschaft	12,953
39	Bayerische Motorenwerke AG (Konzern)	12,857
40	Pechiney	12,775
41	Peugeot (Automobiles)	12,650
42	Central Electricity Generating Board	12,565
43	Alcatel NV	12,521
44	Eaux (Compagnie Générale)	12,304
45	Stet Società Finanziaria Telefonica SPA	12,065
46	Total Cie Française des Petroles	12,027
47	Ferruzzi Finanziaria SPA	11,564
48	Usinor Sacilor	11,391
49	British Gas plc	11,228
50	Enel Ente Nazionale per l'Energia Elettrica	11,119

SOURCE: From *Duns Europa*, 1991. Reprinted by permission of Dun & Bradstreet Limited, Dun's Marketing Services.

23.9). Table 23.6 lists the top fifty European companies, ranked by sales (turnover) in ECUs, the EC monetary unit.

A wholly owned foreign subsidiary may be allowed to operate independently of the parent company so that its management can have more freedom to adjust to the local environment. Co-operative arrangements are developed to assist in marketing efforts, production, and management. A wholly owned foreign subsidiary may export products to the home nation. Some car manufacturers, such as Ford and General Motors, for example, import cars built by their foreign subsidiaries. A foreign subsidiary offers important tax, tariff, and other operating advantages. One of the greatest advantages is the cross-cultural approach. A subsidiary usually operates under foreign management, so that it can develop a local identity. The greatest danger in such an arrangement comes from political uncertainty: a firm may lose its foreign investment.

SUMMARY

Marketing activities performed across national boundaries are usually significantly different from domestic marketing activities. International marketers must have a profound awareness of the foreign environment. The marketing strategy ordinarily is adjusted to meet the needs and desires of markets across national boundaries.

The level of involvement in international marketing can range from casual exporting to globalisation of markets. Although most firms adjust their marketing mixes for differences in target markets, some firms are able to standardise their marketing efforts worldwide. Traditional full-scale international marketing involvement is based on products customised according to cultural, regional, and national differences. Globalisation, however, involves developing marketing strategies as if the entire world (or regions of it) were a single entity; a globalised firm markets standardised products in the same way everywhere.

Marketers must rely on international marketing intelligence to understand the complexities of the international marketing environment before they can formulate a marketing mix. Therefore, they collect and analyse secondary data and primary data about international markets.

Environmental aspects of special importance include cultural, social, economic, political, and legal forces. Cultural aspects of the environment that are most important to international marketers include customs, concepts, values, attitudes, morals, and knowledge. Marketing activities are primarily social in purpose; therefore they are structured by the institutions of family, religion, education, health, and recreation. The most prominent economic forces that affect international marketing are those that can be measured by income and resources. Credit, buying power, and income distribution are aggregate measures of market potential. Political and legal forces include the political system, national laws, regulatory bodies, national pressure groups, and courts. The foreign policies of all nations involved in trade determine how marketing can be conducted. The level of technology helps define economic development within a nation and indicates the existence of methods to facilitate marketing.

Various regional trade alliances and specific markets are creating difficulties and opportunities for firms, including the unification of Europe in 1992, the Pacific Rim markets, changing conditions in Eastern Europe and the Soviet Union, and the United States and Canada trade pact.

After a country's environment has been analysed, marketers must develop a marketing mix and decide whether to adapt product or promotion. There are five possible strategies for adapting product and promotion across national boundaries: (1) keep product and promotion the same worldwide, (2) adapt promotion only, (3) adapt product only, (4) adapt both product and promotion, and (5) invent new products. Foreign distribution channels are nearly always different from domestic ones. The allocation of costs, transport considerations, or the costs of doing business in foreign nations will affect pricing.

There are several ways of getting involved in international marketing. Exporting is the easiest and most flexible method. Licensing is an alternative to direct investment; it may be necessitated by political and economic conditions. Joint ventures and strategic alliances are often appropriate when outside resources are needed, when there are governmental restrictions on foreign ownership, or when changes in global markets encourage competitive consolidation. Trading companies are experts at buying products in the domestic market and selling to foreign markets, thereby taking most of the risk in international involvement. Direct ownership of foreign divisions or subsidiaries is the strongest commitment to international marketing and involves the greatest risk. When a company has operations or subsidiaries located in many countries, it is termed a multinational enterprise.

Important Terms

International marketing
Globalisation
Gross domestic product (GDP)
Dumping
Licensing

Joint venture
Strategic alliances
Trading company
Direct ownership
Multinational enterprise

Discussion and Review Questions

1. How does international marketing differ from domestic marketing?
2. What must marketers consider before deciding whether to become involved in international marketing?
3. Are the largest industrial companies in Europe committed to international marketing? Why or why not?
4. Why is so much of this chapter devoted to an analysis of the international marketing environment?
5. A manufacturer recently exported peanut butter with a green label to a nation in the Far East. The product failed because it was associated with jungle sickness. How could this mistake have been avoided?
6. Relate the concept of reference groups (Chapter 4) to international marketing.
7. How do religious systems influence marketing activities in foreign countries?
8. Which is more important to international marketers, a country's aggregate GDP or its GDP per capita? Why?
9. If you were asked to provide a small tip (or bribe) to have a document approved in a foreign nation where this practice was customary, what would you do?
10. In marketing dog food to Latin America, what aspects of the marketing mix need to be altered?
11. What should marketers consider as they decide whether to license or to enter into a joint venture in a foreign nation?
12. Discuss the impact of strategic alliances on marketing strategies.

23.1 Porsche AG

Founded in 1930 by Dr Ferdinand Porsche, the company known today as Porsche AG began as a research and development firm. The original company accepted contracts from individuals and firms to design new cars, airplanes, and ships. The company built prototypes of each design and thoroughly tested them. If the firm that commissioned the work approved the design, the product was then produced by one of the large manufacturing companies in Germany. After World War II, the Porsche family experienced a period of hardship, disappointment, and personal tragedy. Porsche's son, Dr Ferry Porsche, began a company to manufacture family-designed sports cars in 1948. Despite depressed economic conditions, the company persevered and prospered. By 1973, Porsche AG had built and sold some 200,000 Porsches, gaining world recognition for its cars and their promise of "driving in its purest form".

Porsche today is organised into three divisions located in three suburbs of Stuttgart: the factory, in Zuffenhausen; testing, engineering, and design, in Weissach; and marketing, in Ludwigsburg. The Porsche Research and Development Centre has produced the 959 race car, an aircraft engine, the TAG motor, and designs for ambulances, mobile surgery units, gliders, fire engines, and fork-lift trucks. The company holds more than two thousand patents, and innovations developed by Porsche are in several manufacturers' car models.

The popularity of Porsche cars stems from their reputation for outstanding performance. Not only are the cars produced in a painstaking fashion, but Porsche AG also takes maintenance and repair very seriously. Porsche mechanics receive five days of instruction each year at the Porsche marketing centre in Ludwigsburg, more training than any other car company provides. In its advertising, the company encourages customers to rely only on Porsche experts for repair and maintenance of their cars to prevent the customers from having unsatisfactory experiences with unqualified mechanics. This action further differentiates Porsche cars from the competition.

Despite Porsche's reputation for excellence, the company has fallen on hard times. It was forced to raise prices on cars sold in the U.S. because of changes in the dollar-market exchange rate. Because of the price increases, a weakening U.S. dollar, and lower-priced Japanese imitations, sales in the United States dropped significantly in 1988. Roughly 60 percent of all Porsches are sold in the United States. Production in 1988 dropped from the record levels in 1986–1987 (more than fifty thousand cars). This over-dependence on the U.S. market caused the firm to implement an austerity programme. The programme includes lowering production output, reducing costs (lower dividends and fewer employees), revamping all three model lines, and pulling out of the lower end of the luxury car market. The company is also trying to enter new markets, including Spain and Japan, to boost sales and increase profits.

Porsche is successful in markets where the social climate favours people who want to demonstrate their success and the economic climate is conducive to the entrepreneur. Porsche management believes that its customers have high personal goals and a drive to achieve, do not like to compromise, and give their best efforts every time. Although not averse to risk, they prepare thoroughly for new ventures.

Porsche customers are goers and doers, but not show-offs. To succeed, Porsche AG must exhibit some of its customers' traits. Customers must be able to identify with the firm, to see in the company the same characteristics they see in themselves.

SOURCES: Joseph M. Callahan and Lance A. Ealey, "Porsche's Schutz Reveals U.S. Marketing Plans," *Industries,* March 1985, p. 50; Gred V. Guterl, John Dornberg, and Kevin Sullivan, "Three to Get Ready," *Business Month,* March 1988, pp. 42–50; "It Shortens the Path," *Christophorous,* August 1984; Maria Kielmas, "Stalled Porsche: But Is There a U-Turn in Its Future?" *Barron's,* 27 June 1988, pp. 14–15, 37; Ron Lewald, "Porsche's U.S. Backfire," *International Management,* April 1988, pp. 42–45; Richard Morais, "What Price Excellence?" *Forbes,* 17 Nov. 1986, p. 234; *Plan Your Success,* 2nd ed. (Stuttgart: Dr. Ing. h.c. Ferry Porsche, 1985), pp. 1, 3; Dr. Ing. h.c. Ferry Porsche and John Bentley, *We at Porsche* (Garden City, N.Y.: Doubleday, 1976), p. 263; "Porsche," *Ward's Auto World,* January 1985, pp. 52–53; *Porsche Brochure for Distribution,* Stuttgart: Dr. Ing. h.c. F. Porsche AG, 1984; John A. Russell, "Porsche Puts High Value on Its People, Schutz Says," *Automotive News,* 4 Aug. 1986, p. 64; Gail Schares and Mark Maremont, "Jaguar and Porsche Try to Pull out of the Slow Lane," *Business Week,* 12 Dec. 1988, pp. 84–85; Peter Schutz and Jack Cook, "Porsche and Nichemanship," *Harvard Business Review,* March-April 1986, pp. 98–106; and Jesse Snyder, "Porsche Looks for New Brand to Sell in U.S.," *Automotive News,* 15 Dec. 1986, p. 1.

Questions for Discussion

1. Evaluate international marketing opportunities for Porsche AG. What are the company's strengths and weaknesses?
2. What obstacles must Porsche overcome to be successful selling its cars in the United States?
3. What is the role of diversification in the Porsche AG corporate strategy?

23.2   Body Shop's Overseas Expansion

The first Body Shop, based on a whim of Anita Roddick's, opened in tiny premises in Brighton with only a handful of products. Now the company has 140 U.K. branches and 320 overseas, with plans during 1990–91 to add 25 U.K. branches and 120 overseas. The company is trading in 37 countries with retail turnover of £175 million in 1990–91. A recent deal with Jusco of Japan gives Jusco the head franchise rights for Japan, and a branch is due to open in Tokyo in 1990. Franchising has been the key to the company's expansion since the first franchise was sold in 1978.

Anita Roddick continues to maintain her original principles and beliefs: cosmetics sold worldwide with the minimum of hype, little packaging, promoting health rather than glamour, using natural, close-to-source ingredients, with no tests on animals. By maintaining a uniform concept and set of standards Body Shop has crossed most borders and is a truly successful retailer on an international scale. Tight control of franchises has prevented dilution of the company's ethos and the well-proven formula has brought rewards to franchise holders worldwide.

SOURCES: *Body Shop Annual Report,* 1989 and 1990; Keith Monk, *Go International* (London: McGraw-Hill, 1989); "Overseas Growth Lifts Body Shop," *Financial Times,* 14 November 1990, p. 25; "Body Shop First," *Times,* 25 October 1990.

Questions for Discussion

1. Is it typical for a uniform marketing concept to be applied in so many countries? What are the likely problems associated with adhering to a single concept?
2. How can franchisees be managed to maintain operating standards?
3. What are the cultural differences likely to have caused Body Shop the most problems?

A CAREERS IN
MARKETING

Some General Issues

As we note in Chapter 1, between one-fourth and one-third of the civilian work forces in the United States and Europe are employed in marketing-related jobs. Although there obviously are a multitude of diverse career opportunities in the field, the number of positions in its different areas varies. For example, millions of workers are employed in many facets of sales, but relatively few people work in public relations and marketing research.

Many non-business organisations now recognise that they do, in fact, perform marketing activities. For that reason, marketing positions are increasing in government agencies, hospitals, charitable and religious groups, educational institutions, and similar organisations.

Even though financial reward is not the sole criterion for selecting a career, it is only practical to consider how much you might earn in a marketing job. Table A.1 illustrates top ten salary positions for American middle managers in marketing. Note that all these careers relate directly to marketing. A national sales manager may earn $60,000 to $100,000 or an even higher salary. Brand managers make $35,000 to $60,000. A media manager could earn $30,000 to $55,000. Generally, entry-level marketing personnel earn more than their counterparts in economics and social studies but not as much as people who enter accounting, chemistry, or engineering positions. Starting salaries for marketing graduates averaged $20,844, according to the 1988 College Placement Council Salary Survey. Marketers who advance to higher-level positions often earn high salaries, and a significant proportion of corporate executives held marketing jobs before attaining top-level positions.

As *Marketing* magazine's annual U.K. salary review indicates, there is a great range of marketing job positions and associated remuneration and perks. A marketing assistant earns on average £12,400 with no perks; a marketing manager, £26,700, with a car, pension, and health cover; a marketing director, £42,600 with a full package of perks (see Table A.2). Figure A.1 shows current statistics for the proportion of men and women in each job category.

POSITION	SALARY RANGE
National sales manager	$60,000– $100,000
Corporate strategic market planner	55,000– 75,000
International sales	50,000– 75,000
Advertising account supervisor	40,000– 70,000
Distribution manager	40,000– 60,000
Sales promotion manager	40,000– 55,000
Product/brand manager	35,000– 60,000
Purchasing manager	35,000– 55,000
Media manager	30,000– 55,000
Retail manager	25,000– 45,000

Another important issue is whether you can enjoy the work associated with a particular career. Because you will spend almost 40 percent of your waking hours on the job, you should not allow such factors as economic conditions or status to override your personal goals as you select a lifelong career. Too often, people do not weigh these factors realistically. You should give considerable thought to your choice of a career, and you should adopt a well-planned, systematic approach to finding a position that meets your personal and career objectives.

After determining your objectives, you should identify the organisations that are likely to offer desirable opportunities. Learn as much as possible about these organisations before setting up employment interviews; job recruiters are impressed with applicants who have done their homework.

When making initial contact with potential employers by mail, enclose a brief, clearly written letter of introduction. After an initial interview, you should send a brief letter of thanks to the interviewer. The job of getting the right job is important, and you owe it to yourself to take this process seriously.

THE RÉSUMÉ OR CURRICULUM VITAE

The résumé or curriculum vitae (CV) is one of the keys to being considered for a good job. Because it states your qualifications, experiences, education, and career goals, the résumé is a chance for a potential employer to assess your compatibility with the job requirements. For the employer's and individual's benefit, the résumé should be accurate and current.

To be effective, the résumé can be targeted towards a specific position, as Figure A.2 shows. This document is only one example of an acceptable résumé. The job target section is specific and leads directly to the applicant's qualifications for the job. Capabilities show what the applicant can do and that the person has an understanding of the job's requirements. Skills and strengths should be highlighted as to how they relate to the specific job. The achievement section indicates success at accomplishing tasks or goals within the job market and at school. The work experience section includes educational background, which adds credibility to the résumé

TABLE A.2 *A career in U.K. marketing: Career profiles and expectations*

	SEX	AGE	EDUCATION	WORK EXPERIENCE	PERKS
MARKETING ASSISTANT (£12,400)	F	25.7	degree	less than 2 years	none
MARKETING EXECUTIVE (£15,600)	F	28	degree	3–5 years	contributory pension
PRODUCT BRAND MANAGER (£18,650)	F	28.6	degree	3–5 years	company car, medical insurance, contributory pension scheme
GROUP PRODUCT MANAGER (£24,800)	M	32.8	degree	6–10 years	company car, car running costs, medical insurance, contributory pension
MARKETING MANAGER (£26,700)	M	35	degree	6–15 years	company car, car running costs, medical insurance, contributory pension
MARKETING DIRECTOR (£42,600)	M	30	degree	11+ years	company car, car running costs, medical insurance, contributory pension
PROPRIETOR (£36,300)	M	44.7	degree	21+ years	company car, car running costs
MANAGING DIRECTOR/ DEPUTY MANAGING DIRECTOR (£47,550)	M	43	degree	21+ years	company car, car running costs, car telephone, medical insurance, contributory pension
CHAIRMAN/CHIEF EXECUTIVE (£49,300)	M	43.5	degree	21+ years	company car, car running costs, medical insurance, contributory pension

SOURCE: "The *Marketing* Salary Survey," *Marketing,* 17 January 1991, pp. 19–22.

but is not the major area of focus; the applicant's ability to function successfully in a specific job is the major emphasis.

Common suggestions for improving résumés include deleting useless information, improving organisation, using professional printing and typing, listing duties (not accomplishments), maintaining grammatical perfection, and avoiding an overly elaborate or fancy format.[1] One of the biggest problems in résumés, according to a survey of personnel experts, is distortions and lies; 36 percent of the experts thought that this was a major problem.[2] People lie most often about previous salaries and tasks performed in former jobs.

1. T. Jackson, "Writing the Targeted Resume," *Business Week's Guide to Careers,* Spring 1983, pp. 26–27.

2. Burke Marketing Research for Robert Hall Inc. Reported in *USA Today,* Oct. 2, 1987, p. B–1

FIGURE A.1
Proportion of men and women in each job category

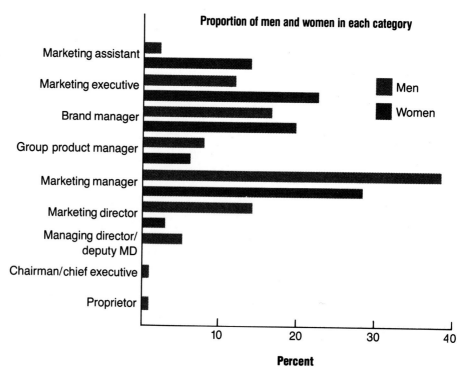

Proportion of men and women in each category

Marketing assistant

Marketing executive

Brand manager

Group product manager

Marketing manager

Marketing director

Managing director/ deputy MD

Chairman/chief executive

Proprietor

■ Men
■ Women

10   20   30   40

Percent

SOURCE: "The *Marketing* Salary Survey," *Marketing,* 17 January 1991, p. 20.

TYPES OF MARKETING CAREERS

In considering marketing as a career, the first step is to evaluate broad categories of career opportunities in the areas of marketing research, sales, public relations, industrial buying, distribution management, product management, advertising, retail management, and direct marketing. Keep in mind that the categories described here are not all-inclusive and that each encompasses hundreds of marketing jobs.

■ **Marketing Research**

Clearly, marketing research and information systems are vital aspects of marketing decision-making. The information about buyers and environmental forces that research and information systems provide improves a marketer's ability to understand the dynamics of the market-place and make effective decisions.

Marketing researchers gather and analyse data relating to specific problems. Marketing research firms are usually employed by a client organisation, which could be a provider of goods or services, a non-business organisation, the government, a research consulting firm, or an advertising agency. The activities performed include concept testing, product testing, package testing, advertising testing, test-market research, and new-product research.

A researcher may be involved in one or several stages of research, depending on the size of the project, the organisation of the research unit, and the researcher's experience. Marketing research trainees in large organisations usually perform a considerable amount of clerical work, such as compiling secondary data from a firm's accounting and sales records and periodicals, government publications, syndi-

FIGURE A.2
A résumé targeted
toward a specific
position

```
                         LORRAINE WHEELER
                         35 EAST PARK ROAD
                         REEDLEY
                         LEEDS, L517 9NP
                         (0532) 482111

        EDUCATION: B.Sc. Honours, The Best University   1984  Marketing

        DATE OF BIRTH: 2/8/59

        POSITION DESIRED: PRODUCT MANAGER WITH AN INTERNATIONAL FIRM
                          PROVIDING FUTURE CAREER DEVELOPMENT AT THE
                          EXECUTIVE LEVEL.

        QUALIFICATIONS:

          * communicates well with individuals to achieve a common goal

          * handles tasks efficiently and in a timely manner

          * knowledge of advertising, sales, management, marketing
            research, packaging, pricing, distribution, and warehousing

          * co-ordinates many activities at one time

          * receives and carries out assigned tasks or directives

          * writes complete status or research reports

        EXPERIENCE:

          * Assistant Editor on student newspaper

          * Treasurer of the hockey club

          * Student researcher with Dr. Steven Who, Lecturer of
            Marketing, The Best University

          * Achieved 2.1 degree

        WORK RECORD:

        1984 - Present      Wiggins & Co.
                            * Junior Advertising Account Executive

        1981 - 1983         The Place
                            * Retail sales and consumer relations

        1979 - 1981         Do All Builders
                            * Labourer (part time/holidays)
```

cated data services, and unpublished sources. A junior analyst may edit and code questionnaires or tabulate survey results. Trainees also may participate in primary data-gathering by learning to conduct mail and telephone surveys, conducting personal interviews, and using observational methods of primary data collection. As a marketing researcher gains experience, the researcher may become involved in defining problems and developing hypotheses; designing research procedures; and analysing, interpreting, and reporting findings. Exceptional personnel may assume responsibility for entire research projects.

Although most employers consider an honours degree sufficient qualification for a marketing research trainee, many specialised positions require a graduate degree in business administration, statistics, or other related fields. Today, trainees are more likely to have a marketing or statistics degree than a social science degree. Also, trainees who are capable of immediate productivity and more complex tasks are more desirable.[3] Courses in statistics, data processing, psychology, sociology, com-

3. Marcia Fleschner, "Evolution of Research Takes the Profession to New Heights," *Collegiate Edition Marketing News*, March 1986, p. 1.

munications, economics, and English composition are valuable preparations for a career in marketing research.

Marketing research provides abundant employment opportunity, especially for applicants with graduate training in marketing research, statistics, economics, and the social sciences. Generally, the value of information gathered by marketing information and research systems will become more important as competition increases, thus expanding the opportunities for prospective marketing research personnel.

The three major career paths in marketing research are with independent marketing research agencies/data suppliers, advertising agency marketing research departments, and marketing research departments in businesses. In a company in which marketing research plays a key role, the researcher is often a member of the marketing strategy team. Surveying or interviewing consumers is the heart of the marketing research firm's activities. A statistician selects the sample to be surveyed, analysts design the questionnaire and synthesise the gathered data into a final report, data processors tabulate the data, and the research director controls and co-ordinates all these activities so that each project is computed to the client's satisfaction (i.e., consumer and industrial product manufacturers).[4] In marketing research agencies, a researcher deals with many clients, products, and problems. Advertising agencies use research as an ingredient in developing and refining campaigns for existing or potentially new clients.[5]

Salaries in marketing research depend on the type, size, and location of the firm as well as the nature of the positions. Generally, starting salaries are somewhat higher and promotions somewhat slower than in other occupations requiring similar training. In addition, the role of marketing in overall corporate planning is becoming more important as companies seek marketing information for strategic planning purposes. Marketing research directors are reporting to higher levels of management than ever before, and the number of corporate directors who receive marketing research as regular input in decision-making has doubled in recent years.

■ **Sales**

Millions of people earn a living through personal selling. Chapter 15 defines personal selling as a process of informing customers and persuading them to purchase products through personal communication in an exchange situation. Although this definition describes the general nature of many sales positions, individual selling jobs vary enormously with respect to the type of businesses and products involved, the educational background and skills required, and the specific activities sales personnel perform. Because the work is so varied, sales occupations offer numerous career opportunities for people with a wide range of qualifications, interests, and goals. A sales career offers the greatest potential compensation. The following two sections describe what is involved in wholesale and manufacturer sales.

Wholesale Sales.   Wholesalers perform activities to expedite transactions in which purchases are intended for resale or to be used to make other products. Wholesalers thus provide services to both retailers and producers. They can help match producers' products to retailers' needs and can provide accumulation and allocation services that save producers time, money, and resources. Some activities associated with wholesaling include planning and negotiating transactions; assisting

4. Judith George, "Market Researcher," *Business Week Careers*, October 1987, p. 10.

5. "What It's Like to Work in Marketing Research Depends on Where You Work—Supplier, Ad Agency, Manufacturer," *Collegiate Edition Marketing News*, December 1985, pp. 1 and 3.

customers with sales, advertising, sales promotion, and publicity; handling transport and storage activities; providing customers with inventory control and data processing assistance; establishing prices; and giving customers technical, management, and merchandising assistance.

The background wholesale personnel need depends on the nature of the product handled. A pharmaceuticals wholesaler, for example, needs extensive technical training and product knowledge and may have a degree in chemistry, biology, or pharmacy. A wholesaler of standard office supplies, on the other hand, may find it more important to be familiar with various brands, suppliers, and prices than to have technical knowledge about the products. A new wholesale representative may begin a career as a sales trainee or hold a non-selling job that provides experience with inventory, prices, discounts, and the firm's customers.

The number of wholesale sales positions is expected to grow about as fast as the average for all occupations. Earnings for wholesale personnel vary widely because commissions often make up a large proportion of their incomes.

Manufacturer Sales.   Manufacturer sales personnel sell a firm's products to wholesalers, retailers, and industrial buyers; they thus perform many of the same activities wholesale salespersons handle. As is the case with wholesaling, the educational requirements for manufacturer sales depend largely on the type and complexity of the products and markets. Manufacturers of non-technical products usually hire graduates who have a social studies or business degree and give them training and information about the firm's products, prices, and customers. Manufacturers of highly technical products generally prefer applicants who have degrees in fields associated with the particular industry and market involved.

More and more sophisticated marketing skills are being utilised in industrial sales. Industrial marketing originally followed the commodity approach to complete a sale, whereby the right product is in the right place at the right time and for the right price. Today industrial sales use the same marketing concepts and strategies as do marketers selling to consumers.

Employment opportunities in manufacturer sales are expected to experience average growth. Manufacturer sales personnel are well compensated and earn above-average salaries. Most are paid a combination of salaries and commissions. Commissions vary according to the salesperson's efforts, abilities, and sales territory and the type of products sold.

■ **Public Relations**   Public relations encompasses a broad set of communication activities designed to create and maintain favourable relations between the organisation and its publics—customers, employees, shareholders, government officials, and society in general. Public relations specialists help clients both create the image, issue, or message they wish to present and communicate it to the appropriate audience. According to the Public Relations Society of America, 120,000 persons work in public relations in the United States. Half the billings found in the 4,000 public relations agencies and firms come from Chicago and New York. The highest starting salaries can also be found there. Expect the average starting salary to be $15,000 or less, but salaries can increase rapidly.[6] In the U.K., the concentration is in London, although the agency of the year, Countrywide, is in a market town—Banbury. Starting salaries range from £6,500 to £9,500. Of all persons working in this field, 55 percent earn over £20,000

6. Jan Greenberg, "Inside Public Relations," *Business Week Careers*, February 1988, pp. 46–48.

per year, with a package of perks.[7] Communication is basic to all public relations programmes. To communicate effectively, public relations practitioners first must gather data about the firm's client publics to assess their needs, identify problems, formulate recommendations, implement new plans, and evaluate current activities.

Public relations personnel disseminate large amounts of information to the organisation's client publics. Written communication is the most versatile tool of public relations, and good writing ability is essential. Public relations practitioners must be adept at writing for a variety of media and audiences. It is not unusual for a person in public relations to prepare reports, news releases, speeches, broadcast scripts, technical manuals, employee publications, shareholder reports, and other communications aimed at both organisational personnel and external groups. In addition, a public relations practitioner needs a thorough knowledge of the production techniques used in preparing various communications.

Public relations personnel also establish distribution channels for the organisation's publicity. They must have a thorough understanding of the various media, their areas of specialisation, the characteristics of their target audiences, and their policies regarding publicity. Anyone who hopes to succeed in public relations must develop close working relationships with numerous media personnel to enlist their interest in disseminating an organisation's communications.

Further education combined with writing or media-related experience is the best preparation for a career in public relations. Some beginners have a degree in journalism, communications, or public relations, but some employers prefer a business background. Courses in journalism, business administration, marketing, creative writing, psychology, sociology, political science, economics, advertising, English, and public speaking are recommended. Some employers require applicants to present a portfolio of published articles, television or radio programmes, slide presentations, and other work samples. Other agencies are requiring written tests that include activities such as writing sample press releases. Manufacturing firms, public utilities, transport and insurance companies, and trade and professional associations are the largest employers of public relations personnel. In addition, sizeable numbers of public relations personnel work for health-related organisations, government agencies, educational institutions, museums, and religious and service groups.

Although some larger companies provide extensive formal training for new personnel, most new public relations employees learn on the job. Beginners usually perform routine tasks such as maintaining files about company activities and searching secondary data sources for information that can be used in publicity materials. More experienced employees write press releases, speeches, and articles and help plan public relations campaigns.

Employment opportunities in public relations are expected to increase faster than the average for all occupations through the 1990s. One caveat is in order, however: Competition for first jobs is keen. The prospects are best for applicants who have solid academic preparation and some media experience. Areas that are projected to offer the most opportunity are in public relations agencies in the areas of product publicity, mergers and acquisitions, and financial and investor relations.[8] Abilities that differentiate candidates such as a basic understanding of computers are becoming increasingly important.

7. The Institute of Public Relations, 15 Northburgh Street, London.

8. Jan Greenberg, "Inside Public Relations," *Business Week Careers,* February 1988, p. 47.

■ Industrial Buying

Industrial buyers, or purchasing agents, are responsible for maintaining an adequate supply of the goods and services that an organisation needs for operations. In general, industrial buyers purchase all items needed for direct use in producing other products and for use in the day-to-day operations. Industrial buyers in large firms often specialise in purchasing a single, specific class of products, for example, all petroleum-based lubricants. In smaller organisations, buyers may be responsible for purchasing many different categories of items, including such goods as raw materials, component parts, office supplies, and operating services.

An industrial buyer's main job is selecting suppliers who offer the best quality, service, and price. When the products to be purchased are standardised, buyers may compare suppliers by examining catalogues and trade journals, making purchases by description. Buyers who purchase highly homogeneous products often meet with salespeople to examine samples and observe demonstrations. Sometimes, buyers must inspect the actual product before purchasing; in other cases, they invite suppliers to bid on large orders. Buyers who purchase specialised equipment often deal directly with manufacturers to obtain specially designed items made to specifications. After choosing a supplier and placing an order, an industrial buyer usually must trace the shipment to ensure on-time delivery. Finally, the buyer sometimes is responsible for receiving and inspecting an order and authorising payment to the shipper.

Training requirements for a career in industrial buying relate to the needs of the firm and the types of products purchased. A manufacturer of heavy machinery may prefer an applicant who has a background in engineering; a service company, on the other hand, may recruit social studies graduates. Although it is not generally required, a college degree is becoming increasingly important for buyers who wish to advance to management positions.

Employment prospects for industrial buyers are expected to increase faster than average through the 1990s. Opportunities will be excellent for individuals with a master's degree in business administration or an honours degree in engineering, science, or business administration. In addition, companies that manufacture heavy equipment, computer equipment, and communications equipment will need buyers with technical backgrounds.

■ Distribution Management

A distribution (or traffic) manager arranges for the transport of goods within firms and through marketing channels. Transport is an essential distribution activity that permits a firm to create time and place utility for its products. It is the distribution manager's job to analyse various transport modes and select the combination that minimises cost and transit time while providing acceptable levels of reliability, capability, accessibility, and security.

To accomplish this task, a distribution manager performs many activities. First, the individual must choose one or a combination of transport modes from the five major modes available: railways, motor vehicles, inland waterways, pipelines, and airways. Then the distribution manager must select the specific routes the goods will travel and the particular carriers to be used, weighing such factors as freight classifications and regulations, freight charges, time schedules, shipment sizes, and loss and damage ratios. In addition, this person may be responsible for preparing shipping documents, tracing shipments, handling loss and damage claims, keeping records of freight rates, and monitoring changes in government regulations and transport technology.

Distribution management employs relatively few people and is expected to grow about as fast as the average for all occupations in the near future. Manufacturing firms are the largest employers of distribution managers, although some traffic managers work for wholesalers, retail stores, and consulting firms. Salaries of experienced distribution managers vary but generally are much higher than the average for all non-supervisory personnel.

Starting jobs are diverse, varying from inventory/stock control, traffic scheduling, operations management, or distribution management. Inventory management is an area of great opportunity because many firms see inventory costs as high relative to foreign competition, especially that from the Japanese. Just-in-time inventory systems are designed by inventory control specialists to work with the bare minimum of inventory.[9]

Most employers prefer graduates of technical programmes or seek people who have completed courses in transport, logistics, distribution management, economics, statistics, computer science, management, marketing, and commercial law. A successful distribution manager must be adept at handling technical data and be able to interpret and communicate highly technical information.

■ Product
Management

The product manager occupies a staff position and is responsible for the success or failure of a product line. Product managers co-ordinate most of the marketing activities required to market a product; however, because they hold a staff position, they have relatively little actual authority over marketing personnel. Even so, they take on a large amount of responsibility and typically are paid quite well relative to other marketing employees. Being a product manager can be rewarding both financially and psychologically, but it can also be frustrating because of the disparity between responsibility and authority.

A product manager should have a general knowledge of advertising, transport modes, inventory control, selling and sales management, sales promotion, marketing research, packaging, pricing, and warehousing. The individual must be knowledgeable enough to communicate effectively with personnel in these functional areas and to make suggestions and help assess alternatives when major decisions are being made.

Product managers usually need university training in an area of business administration. A master's degree is helpful, although a person usually does not become a product manager directly out of university or polytechnic. Frequently, several years of selling and sales management are prerequisites for a product management position, which often is a major step in the career path of top-level marketing executives.

■ Advertising

Advertising pervades our daily lives. As we detail in Chapter 14, business and non-business organisations use advertising in many ways and for many reasons. Advertising clearly needs individuals with diverse skills to fill a variety of jobs. Creative imagination, artistic talent, and expertise in expression and persuasion are important for copywriters, artists, and account executives. Sales and managerial ability are vital to the success of advertising managers, media buyers, and production managers. Research directors must have a solid understanding of research techniques and human behaviour.

9. Nicholas Basta, "Inventory and Distribution," *Business Week's Guide to Careers,* Spring–Summer 1985, p. 23.

Advertising professionals disagree on the most beneficial educational background for a career in advertising. Most employers prefer university graduates. Some employers seek individuals with degrees in advertising, journalism, or business; most prefer graduates with broad classics and social studies backgrounds. Still other employers rank relevant work experience above educational background.

"Advertisers look for generalists," says Kate Preston, a staff executive of the American Association of Advertising Agencies, "thus there are just as many economics or general liberal arts majors as M.B.A.s." Starting salaries in these positions are often quite low; but to gain experience in the advertising industry, employees must work their way up in the system. The entry-level salaries of media assistants and account coordinators are often £12,000 or less.[10]

A variety of organisations employ advertising personnel. Although advertising agencies are perhaps the most visible and glamorous of employers, many manufacturing firms, retail stores, banks, utility companies, and professional and trade associations maintain advertising departments. Advertising jobs also can be found with television and radio stations, newspapers, and magazines. Other businesses that employ advertising personnel include printers, art studios, letter shops, and package-design firms. Specific advertising jobs include advertising manager, account executive, research director, copywriter, media specialist, and production manager.[11]

Employment opportunities for advertising personnel are expected to decrease in the early nineties as agency acquisitions and mergers continue. General economic conditions, however, strongly influence the size of advertising budgets and, hence, employment opportunities.

■ Retail Management

Several million people in the U.K. and in each EC country work in the retail industry. Although a career in retailing may begin in sales, there is more to retailing than simply selling. Many retail personnel occupy management positions. Besides managing the sales force, they focus on selecting and ordering merchandise, promotional activities, inventory control, customer credit operations, accounting, personnel, and store security.

How retail stores are organised varies. In many large department stores, retail management personnel rarely get involved with actually selling to customers; these duties are performed by retail sales assistants. However, other types of retail organisations may require management personnel to perform selling activities from time to time.

Large retail groups offer a variety of management positions besides those at the very top, including assistant buyers, buyers, department managers, section managers, store managers, division managers, regional managers, and directors of merchandising. The following list describes the general duties of four of these positions; the precise nature of these duties varies from one retail organisation to another.

A section or department manager coordinates inventory and promotions and interacts with buyers, salespeople, and ultimate consumers. The manager performs merchandising, labour relations, and managerial activities and can rarely expect to get away with as little as a forty-hour work week.

10. Vincent Daddiego, "Making It in Advertising," *Business Week Careers*, February 1988, p. 42.

11. The Institute of Practitioners in Advertising, 44 Belgrave Square, London, and the Advertising Association, 15 Wilton Road, London.

The buyer's task is more focused. In this fast-paced occupation, there is much travel, pressure, and need to be open-minded with respect to new and potentially successful items.

The regional manager co-ordinates the activities of several stores within a given area. Sales, promotions, and procedures in general are monitored and supported.

The director of merchandising has a broad scope of managerial responsibility and reports to the managing director at the top of the organisation.

Traditionally, retail managers began their careers as sales assistants. Today, many large retailers hire university- or polytechnic-educated people, put them through management training programmes, and then place them directly into management positions. They frequently hire people with backgrounds in social studies or business administration. Sales and retailing are the greatest employment opportunities for marketing students.

Retail management positions can be exciting and challenging. Competent, ambitious individuals often assume a great deal of responsibility very quickly and advance rapidly. However, pay for entry-level positions (management trainees) has historically been below average. This situation is changing with major specialty, department, and discount stores offering entry salaries in the £12,000 to £15,000 range. In addition, a retail manager's job is physically demanding and sometimes entails long working hours. None the less, positions in retail management often provide numerous opportunities to excel and advance.

■ Direct Marketing

One of the most dynamic areas in marketing is direct marketing, in which the seller uses one or more direct media (telephone, mail, print, or television) to solicit a response. The telephone is a major vehicle for selling many consumer products and services. Telemarketing is direct selling to customers using a variety of technological improvements in telephone services. Much of the industry's sales come from business-to-business marketing, not from selling to consumers at home. In addition, the telemarketing industry has been growing an average of 30 percent per year.

The use of direct mail catalogues appeals to market segments such as working women or people who find going to retail stores difficult or inconvenient. Newspapers and magazines offer great opportunity, especially in special market segments. *Golf Digest*, for example, is obviously a good medium for selling golfing equipment. Cable television provides many new opportunities for selling directly to consumers. Interactive cable will offer a new method to expand direct marketing by developing timely exchange opportunities for consumers.

The most important asset in direct marketing is experience. Employers often look to other industries to locate experienced professionals. In a choice between an M.B.A. or an individual with a direct marketing background, the experienced individual would be hired.[12] This preference means that if you can get an entry-level position in direct marketing, you will have a real advantage in developing a career.

Jobs in direct marketing include buyers, such as department store buyers, who select goods for catalogue, telephone, or direct mail sales. Catalogue managers develop marketing strategies for each new catalogue that goes into the mail. Research/mail-list management involves developing lists of products that will sell in direct marketing and lists of names that will respond to a direct mail effort. Order

---

12. Kevin Higgins, "Economic Recovery Puts Marketers in Catbird Seat," *Marketing News,* Oct. 14, 1983, pp. 1, 8.

fulfillment managers direct the shipment of products once they are sold. Nearly all not-for-profit organisations have fund-raising managers who use direct marketing to obtain financial support.[13]

The executive vice president of the advertising agency Young & Rubicam, Inc. in New York stated that direct marketing will have to be used "not as a tactic, but as a strategic tool."[14] Direct marketing's effectiveness is enhanced by periodic analysis of advertising and communications at all phases of contact with the consumer. Direct marketing involves all aspects of the marketing decision. It is becoming a more professional career area that provides great opportunity.

13. Nicholas Basta, "Direct Marketing," *Business Week Careers,* March 1986, p. 52.

14. "Wonderman Urges: Replace Marketing War Muskets with the Authentic Weapon—Direct Marketing," *Marketing News*, July 8, 1983, pp. 1, 12.

APPENDIX B **FINANCIAL ANALYSIS IN MARKETING**

Our discussion in this book focused more on fundamental concepts and decisions in marketing than on financial details. However, marketers must understand the basic components of selected financial analyses if they are to explain and defend their decisions. In fact, they must be familiar with certain financial analyses if they are to reach good decisions in the first place. We therefore examine three areas of financial analyses: cost-profit aspects of the income statement, selected performance ratios, and price calculations.[1] To control and evaluate marketing activities, marketers must understand the income statement and what it says about the operations of their organization. They also need to be acquainted with performance ratios, which compare current operating results with past results and with results in the industry at large. In the last part of the appendix, we discuss price calculations as the basis of price adjustments. Marketers are likely to use all these areas of financial analysis at various times to support their decisions and to make necessary adjustments in their operations.

THE INCOME STATEMENT

The income, or operating, statement presents the financial results of an organisation's operations over a period of time. The statement summarises revenues earned and expenses incurred by a profit centre, whether it is a department, brand, product line, division, or entire firm. The income statement presents the firm's net profit or net loss for a month, quarter, or year.

Table B.1 is a simplified income statement for a retail store. The owners of the store, Rose Costa and Nick Schultz, see that net sales of $250,000 are decreased by the cost of goods sold and by other business expenses to yield a net income of $83,000. Of course, these figures are only highlights of the complete income statement, which appears in Table B.2.

---

1. We gratefully acknowledge the assistance of Jim L. Grimm, Professor of Marketing, Illinois State University, in writing this appendix.

STONEHAM AUTO SUPPLIES INCOME STATEMENT FOR THE YEAR ENDED DECEMBER 31, 1990

Net Sales	$250,000
Cost of Goods Sold	45,000
Gross Margin	$205,000
Expenses	122,000
Net Income	$ 83,000

The income statement can be used in several ways to improve the management of a business. First, it enables an owner or manager to compare actual results with budgets for various parts of the statement. For example, Rose and Nick see that the total amount of merchandise sold (gross sales) is $260,000. Customers returned merchandise or received allowances (price reductions) totaling $10,000. Suppose the budgeted amount was only $9,000. By checking the ticket for sales returns and allowances, the owners can determine why these events occurred and whether the $10,000 figure could be lowered by adjusting the marketing mix.

After subtracting returns and allowances from gross sales, Rose and Nick can determine net sales from the statement. They are pleased with this figure because it is higher than their sales target of $240,000. Net sales is the amount the firm has available to pay its expenses.

A major expense for most companies that sell goods (as opposed to services) is the cost of goods sold. For Stoneham Auto Supplies, it amounts to 18 percent of net sales. Other expenses are treated in various ways by different companies. In our example, they are broken down into standard categories of selling expenses, administrative expenses, and general expenses.

The income statement shows that the cost of goods Stoneham Auto Supplies sold during financial year 1990 was $45,000. This figure was derived in the following way. First, the statement shows that merchandise in the amount of $51,000 was purchased during the year. In paying the invoices associated with these inventory additions, purchase (cash) discounts of $4,000 were earned, resulting in net purchases of $47,000. Special requests for selected merchandise throughout the year resulted in $2,000 of freight charges, which increased the net cost of delivered purchases to $49,000. Adding this amount to the beginning inventory of $48,000, the cost of goods available for sale during 1990 was $97,000. However, the records indicate that the value of inventory at the end of the year was $52,000. Because this amount was not sold, the cost of goods that were sold during the year was $45,000.

Rose and Nick observe that the total value of their inventory increased by 8.3 percent during the year:

$$\frac{\$52,000 - \$48,000}{\$48,000} = \frac{\$4,000}{\$48,000} = \frac{1}{12} = .0825 \text{ or } 8.3\%$$

Further analysis is needed to determine whether this increase is desirable or undesirable. (Note that the income statement provides no details concerning the composition of the inventory held on December 31; other records supply this information.)

STONEHAM AUTO SUPPLIES INCOME STATEMENT FOR THE YEAR ENDED DECEMBER 31, 1990

Gross Sales			$260,000
Less: Sales returns and allowances			10,000
Net Sales			$250,000
Cost of Goods Sold			
Stock/Inventory, January 1, 1990 (at cost)		$48,000	
Purchases	$51,000		
Less: Purchase discounts	4,000		
Net purchases	$47,000		
Plus: Freight-in	2,000		
Net cost of delivered purchases		$49,000	
Cost of goods available for sale		$97,000	
Less: Stock/Inventory, December 31, 1990 (at cost)		52,000	
Cost of goods sold			$ 45,000
Gross Margin			$205,000
Expenses			
Selling expenses			
Sales salaries and commissions	$32,000		
Advertising	16,000		
Sales promotions	3,000		
Delivery	2,000		
Total selling expenses		$53,000	
Administrative expenses			
Administrative salaries	$20,000		
Office salaries	20,000		
Office supplies	2,000		
Miscellaneous	1,000		
Total administrative expenses		$43,000	
General expenses			
Rent	$14,000		
Utilities	7,000		
Bad debts	1,000		
Miscellaneous (local taxes, insurance, interest, depreciation)	4,000		
Total general expenses		$26,000	
Total expenses			$122,000
Net Income			**$ 83,000**

If Nick and Rose determine that inventory on December 31 is excessive, they can implement appropriate marketing action.

Gross margin is the difference between net sales and cost of goods sold. Gross margin reflects the markup on products and is the amount available to pay all other expenses and provide a return to the owners. Stoneham Auto Supplies had a gross margin of $205,000:

Net Sales	$250,000
Cost of Goods Sold	− 45,000
Gross Margin	$205,000

Stoneham's expenses (other than cost of goods sold) during 1990 totaled $122,000. Observe that $53,000, or slightly more than 43 percent of the total, constituted direct selling expenses:

$$\frac{\$53,000 \text{ selling expenses}}{\$122,000 \text{ total expenses}} = .434 \text{ or } 43\%$$

The business employs three salespersons (one full-time) and pays competitive wages for the area. All selling expenses are similar to dollar amounts for fiscal year 1989, but Nick and Rose wonder whether more advertising is necessary because inventory increased by more than 8 percent during the year.

The administrative and general expenses are also essential for operating the business. A comparison of these expenses with trade statistics for similar businesses indicates that the figures are in line with industry amounts.

Net income, or net profit, is the amount of gross margin remaining after deducting expenses. Stoneham Auto Supplies earned a net profit of $83,000 for the fiscal year ending December 31, 1990. Note that net income on this statement is figured before payment of state and federal income taxes.

Income statements for intermediaries and for businesses that provide services follow the same general format as that shown for Stoneham Auto Supplies in Table B.2. The income statement for a manufacturer, however, is somewhat different in that the "purchases" portion is replaced by "cost of goods manufactured." Table B.3 shows the entire Cost of Goods Sold section for a manufacturer, including cost of goods manufactured. In other respects, income statements for retailers and manufacturers are similar.

■ Selected
Performance Ratios

Rose and Nick's assessment of how well their business did during fiscal year 1990 can be improved through selective use of analytical ratios. These ratios enable a manager to compare the results for the current year with data from previous years and industry statistics. Unfortunately, comparisons of the current income statement with income statements and industry statistics from other years are not very meaningful because factors such as inflation are not accounted for when comparing dollar amounts. More meaningful comparisons can be made by converting these figures to a percentage of net sales, as this section shows.

The first analytical ratios we discuss, the operating ratios, are based on the net sales figure from the income statement.

■ Operating
Ratios

Operating ratios express items on the income, or operating, statement as percentages of net sales. The first step is to convert the income statement into percentages of net sales, as illustrated in Table B.4.

STONEHAM AUTO SUPPLIES INCOME STATEMENT FOR THE YEAR ENDED DECEMBER 31, 1990

Cost of Goods Sold

Finished goods inventory, January 1, 1990				$ 50,000
Cost of goods manufactured				
Work-in-process inventory, January 1, 1990			$ 20,000	
Raw materials inventory, January 1, 1990	$ 40,000			
Net cost of delivered purchases	240,000			
Cost of goods available for use	$280,000			
Less: Raw materials inventory December 31, 1990	42,000			
Cost of goods placed in production		$238,000		
Direct labor		$ 32,000		
Manufacturing overhead				
Indirect labor	$ 12,000			
Supervisory salaries	10,000			
Operating supplies	6,000			
Depreciation	12,000			
Utilities	10,000			
Total manufacturing overhead		$ 50,000		
Total manufacturing costs		$320,000		
Total work-in-process		$340,000		
Less: Work-in process inventory, December 31, 1990		22,000		

Cost of goods manufactured $318,000

$368,000

Cost of goods available for sale

Less: Finished goods inventory, December 31, 1990	48,000

Cost of Goods Sold **$320,000**

TABLE B.4

Income statement components as percentages of net sales

STONEHAM AUTO SUPPLIES INCOME STATEMENT AS A PERCENTAGE OF NET SALES FOR THE YEAR ENDED DECEMBER 31, 1990

		Percentage of net sales
Gross Sales		103.8%
Less: Sales returns and allowances		3.8
Net Sales		100.0%
Cost of Goods Sold		
Inventory, January 1, 1990 (at cost)		19.2%
Purchases	20.4%	
Less: Purchase discounts	1.6	
Net purchases	18.8%	
Plus: Freight-in	.8	
Net cost of delivered purchases		19.6
Cost of goods available for sale		38.8%
Less: Inventory, December 31, 1990 (at cost)		20.8
Cost of goods sold		18.0
Gross Margin		82.0%
Expenses		
Selling expenses		
Sales salaries and commissions	12.8%	
Advertising	6.4	
Sales promotions	1.2	
Delivery	0.8	
Total selling expenses		21.2%
Administrative expenses		
Administrative salaries	8.0%	
Office salaries	8.0	
Office supplies	0.8	
Miscellaneous	0.4	
Total administrative expenses		17.2%
General expenses		
Rent	5.6%	
Utilities	2.8	
Bad debts	0.4	
Miscellaneous	1.6	
Total general expenses		10.4%
Total expenses		48.8
Net Income		33.2%

After making this conversion, the manager looks at several key operating ratios: two profitability ratios (the gross margin ratio and the net income ratio) and the operating expense ratio.

For Stoneham Auto Supplies, these ratios are determined as follows (see Tables B.2 and B.4 for supporting data):

$$\text{Gross margin ratio} = \frac{\text{gross margin}}{\text{net sales}} = \frac{\$205,000}{\$250,000} = 82\%$$

$$\text{Net income ratio} = \frac{\text{net income}}{\text{net sales}} = \frac{\$83,000}{\$250,000} = 33.2\%$$

$$\text{Operating expense ratio} = \frac{\text{total expense}}{\text{net sales}} = \frac{\$122,000}{\$250,000} = 48.8\%$$

The gross margin ratio indicates the percentage of each sales dollar available to cover operating expenses and achieve profit objectives. The net income ratio indicates the percentage of each sales dollar that is classified as earnings (profit) before payment of income taxes. The operating expense ratio indicates the percentage of each dollar needed to cover operating expenses.

If Nick and Rose feel that the operating expense ratio is higher than historical data and industry standards, they can analyze each operating expense ratio in Table B.4 to determine which expenses are too high and can then take corrective action.

After reviewing several key operating ratios, in fact, managers will probably want to analyze all the items on the income statement. For instance, by doing so, Nick and Rose can determine whether the 8 percent increase in inventory was necessary.

■ **Inventory Turnover**

The inventory turnover rate, or stockturn rate, is an analytical ratio that can be used to answer the question, "Is the inventory level appropriate for this business?" The inventory turnover rate indicates the number of times that an inventory is sold (turns over) during one year. To be useful, this figure is then compared with historical turnover rates and industry rates.

The inventory turnover rate can be computed on cost as follows:

$$\text{Inventory turnover} = \frac{\text{cost of goods sold}}{\text{average inventory at cost}}$$

Rose and Nick would calculate the turnover rate from Table B.2 as follows:

$$\frac{\text{Cost of goods sold}}{\text{Average inventory at cost}} = \frac{\$45,000}{\$50,000} = 0.9 \text{ time}$$

They find that inventory turnover is less than once per year (0.9 time). Industry averages for competitive firms are 2.8 times. This figure convinces Rose and Nick that their investment in inventory is too large and that they need to reduce their inventory.

■ **Return on Investment**

Return on investment (ROI) is a ratio that indicates management's efficiency in generating sales and profits from the total amount invested in the firm. For example, for Stoneham Auto Supplies the ROI is 41.5 percent, which compares well with competing businesses.

We use figures from two different financial statements to arrive at ROI. The income statement (profit and loss sheet), already discussed, gives us net income.

The balance sheet, which states the firm's assets and liabilities at a given point in time, provides the figure for total assets (or investment) in the firm.

The basic formula for ROI is

$$\text{ROI} = \frac{\text{net income}}{\text{total investment}}$$

For Stoneham Auto Supplies, net income for fiscal year 1990 is $83,000 (see Table B.2). If total investment (taken from the balance sheet for December 31, 1990) is $200,000, then

$$\text{ROI} = \frac{\$83,000}{\$200,000} = 0.415 \text{ or } 41.5\%$$

The ROI formula can be expanded to isolate the impact of capital turnover and the operating income ratio separately. Capital turnover is a measure of net sales per dollar of investment; the ratio is figured by dividing net sales by total investment. For Stoneham Auto Supplies,

$$\text{Capital turnover} = \frac{\text{net sales}}{\text{total investment}}$$

$$= \frac{\$250,000}{\$200,000} = 1.25$$

ROI is equal to capital turnover times the net income ratio. The expanded formula for Stoneham Auto Supplies is

$$\text{ROI} = (\text{capital turnover}) \times (\text{net income ratio})$$

or

$$\text{ROI} = \frac{\text{net sales}}{\text{total investment}} \times \frac{\text{net income}}{\text{net sales}}$$

$$= \frac{\$250,000}{\$200,000} \times \frac{\$83,000}{\$250,000}$$

$$= (1.25)\,(33.2\%) = 41.5\%$$

PRICE CALCULATIONS

An important step in setting prices is selecting a pricing method, as indicated in Chapter 17. The systematic use of markups, markdowns, and various conversion formulae helps in calculating the selling price and evaluating the effects of various prices. The following sections will provide more detailed information about price calculations.

■ Markups

As indicated in the text, markup is the difference between the selling price and the cost of the item. That is, selling price equals cost plus markup. The markup must cover cost and contribute to profit; thus markup is similar to gross margin on the income statement.

Markup can be calculated on either cost or selling price as follows:

$$\text{Markup as percentage of cost} = \frac{\text{amount added to cost}}{\text{cost}} = \frac{\text{dollar markup}}{\text{cost}}$$

$$\text{Markup as percentage of selling price} = \frac{\text{amount added to cost}}{\text{selling price}} = \frac{\text{dollar markup}}{\text{selling price}}$$

Retailers tend to calculate the markup percentage on selling price.

■ Examples of Markup

To review the use of these markup formulae, assume that an item costs $10 and the markup is $5.

$$\text{Selling price} = \text{cost} + \text{markup}$$

$$\$15 = \$10 + \$5$$

Thus

$$\text{Markup percentage on cost} = \frac{\$5}{\$10} = 50\%$$

$$\text{Markup percentage on selling price} = \frac{\$5}{\$15} = 33\ 1/3\%$$

It is necessary to know the base (cost or selling price) to use markup pricing effectively. Markup percentage on cost will always exceed markup percentage on price, given the same dollar markup, so long as selling price exceeds cost.

On occasion, we may need to convert markup on cost to markup on selling price, or vice versa. The conversion formulae are

$$\text{Markup percentage on selling price} = \frac{\text{markup percentage on cost}}{100\% + \text{markup percentage on cost}}$$

$$\text{Markup percentage on cost} = \frac{\text{markup percentage on selling price}}{100\% - \text{markup percentage on selling price}}$$

For example, if the markup percentage on cost is 33 1/3 percent, then the markup percentage on selling price is

$$\frac{33\ 1/3\%}{100\% + 33\ 1/3\%} = \frac{33\ 1/3\%}{133\ 1/3\%} = 25\%$$

If the markup percentage on selling price is 40 percent, then the corresponding percentage on cost would be as follows:

$$\frac{40\%}{100\% - 40\%} = \frac{40\%}{60\%} = 66\ 2/3\%$$

Finally, we can show how to determine selling price if we know the cost of the item and the markup percentage on selling price. Assume that an item costs $36 and the usual markup percentage on selling price is 40 percent. Remember that selling price equals markup plus cost. Thus if

$$100\% = 40\% \text{ of selling price} + \text{cost}$$

then

$$60\% \text{ of selling price} = \text{cost}$$

In our example, cost equals $36. Then

$$0.6X = \$36$$

$$X = \frac{\$36}{0.6}$$

$$\text{Selling price} = \$60$$

Alternatively, the markup percentage could be converted to a cost basis as follows:

$$\frac{40\%}{100\% - 40\%} = 66 \; 2/3\%$$

Then the computed selling price would be as follows:

$$\text{Selling price} = 66 \; 2/3\% \; (\text{cost}) + \text{cost}$$

$$= 66 \; 2/3\% \; (\$36) + \$36$$

$$= \$24 + \$36$$

$$= \$60$$

By remembering the basic formula—selling price equals cost plus markup—you will find these calculations straightforward.

■ Markdowns

Markdowns are price reductions a retailer makes on merchandise. Markdowns may be useful on items that are damaged, priced too high, or selected for a special sales event. The income statement does not express markdowns directly because the change in price is made before the sale takes place. Therefore separate records of markdowns would be needed to evaluate the performance of various buyers and departments.

The markdown ratio (percentage) is calculated as follows:

$$\text{Markdown percentage} = \frac{\text{dollar markdowns}}{\text{net sales in dollars}}$$

In analyzing their inventory, Nick and Rose discover three special automobile jacks that have gone unsold for several months. They decide to reduce the price of each item from $25 to $20. Subsequently, these items are sold. The markdown percentage for these three items is

$$\text{Markdown percentage} = \frac{3 \; (\$5)}{3 \; (\$20)} = \frac{\$15}{\$60} = 25\%$$

Net sales, however, include all units of this product sold during the period, not just those marked down. If ten of these items have already been sold at $25 each, in addition to the three items sold at $20, then the overall markdown percentage would be

$$\text{Markdown percentage} = \frac{3 \; (\$5)}{10 \; (\$25) + 3 \; (\$20)}$$

$$= \frac{\$15}{\$250 + \$60} = \frac{\$15}{\$310} = 4.8\%$$

Sales allowances also are a reduction in price. Thus the markdown percentages should also include any sales allowances. It would be computed as follows:

$$\text{Markdown percentage} = \frac{\text{dollar markdowns} + \text{dollar allowances}}{\text{net sales in dollars}}$$

DISCUSSION AND REVIEW QUESTIONS

1. How does a manufacturer's income statement differ from a retailer's income statement?

2. Use the following information to answer questions a through c:

Company TEA
Financial year ended June 30, 1991

Net Sales	$500,000
Cost of Goods Sold	300,000
Net Income	50,000
Average Inventory/Stock at Cost	100,000
Total Assets (total investment)	200,000

   a. What is the inventory/stock turnover rate for TEA Company? From what sources will the marketing manager determine the significance of the inventory/stock turnover rate?

   b. What is the capital turnover ratio for financial year 1991? What is the net income ratio? What is the return on investment (ROI)?

   c. How many dollars of sales did each dollar of investment produce for TEA Company in fiscal year 1991?

3. Product A has a markup percentage on cost of 40 percent. What is the markup percentage on selling price?

4. Product B has a markup percentage on selling price of 30 percent. What is the markup percentage on cost?

5. Product C has a cost of $60 and a usual markup percentage of 25 percent on selling price. What price should be placed on this item?

6. Apex Appliance Company sells twenty units of product Q for $100 each and ten units for $80 each. What is the markdown percentage for product Q?

Glossary

A

Accessory equipment Equipment used in production or office activities; does not become a part of the final physical product.

Accumulation A process through which an inventory of homogeneous products that have similar production or demand requirements is developed.

ACORN (A Classification of Residential Neighbourhoods) A market segmentation/analysis system which allows consumers to be classified according to the type of residential area in which they live. Developed by CACI.

Administered pricing A process in which the seller sets a price for a product, and the customer pays that specified price.

Advertising A paid form of non-personal communication about an organisation and/or its products that is transmitted to a target audience through a mass medium.

Advertising budget (Advertising appropriation) The amount of money set aside to cover all the expenses and cost of a particular campaign.

Advertising platform The basic issues or selling points that an advertiser wishes to include in the advertising campaign.

Advertising Standards Authority (ASA) An independent body which handles the public's and companies' complaints relating to dishonest or misleading, shocking or unethical advertising.

Advertising target The group of people at whom advertisements are aimed.

Agent A marketing intermediary who receives a commission or fee for expediting exchanges; represents either buyers or sellers on a permanent basis.

Aided (prompted) recall test A post-test method of evaluating the effectiveness of advertising in which subjects are asked to identify advertisements they have seen recently; they are shown a list of products, brands, company names, or trade marks to jog their memory.

Allocation The breaking down of large homogeneous inventories into smaller lots.

Allowance Concession in price to achieve a desired goal; for example, industrial equipment manufacturers give trade-in allowances on used industrial equipment to enable customers to purchase new equipment.

Approach The manner in which a salesperson contacts a potential customer.

Arbitrary approach A method for determining the advertising appropriation in which a high-level executive in the firm states how much can be spent on advertising for a certain time period.

Area sampling A variation of stratified sampling, with the geographic areas serving as the segments, or primary units, used in random sampling.

Artwork The illustration in an advertisement and the layout of the components of an advertisement.

Assessment centre An intense training centre at which sales candidates are put into realistic, problematic settings where they must prioritise activities, make decisions, and act on their decisions to determine whether each candidate will make a good salesperson.

Assorting Combining products into collections, or assortments, that buyers want to have available at one place.

Assortment A combination of similar or complementary products put together to provide benefits to a specific market.

Atmospherics The conscious designing of a store's space to create emotional effects that enhance the probability that consumers will buy.

Attitude The knowledge and positive or negative feelings about an object.

Attitude scale A measurement instrument that usually consists of a series of adjectives, phrases, or sentences about an object; subjects are asked to indicate the intensity of their feelings towards the object by reacting to the statements in a certain way. It can be used to measure consumer attitudes.

Automatic vending Non-store, non-personal retailing; includes coin-operated, self-service machines.

Average cost Total costs divided by the quantity produced.

Average fixed cost The fixed cost per unit produced; it is calculated by dividing the fixed costs by the number of units produced.

Average revenue Total revenue divided by the quantity produced.

Average total cost The sum of the average fixed cost and the average variable cost.

Average variable cost The variable cost per unit produced; it is calculated by dividing the variable cost by the number of units produced.

B

Barter The trading of products.

Base-point pricing A geographic pricing policy that includes the price at the factory, plus transport charges from the base point nearest the buyer.

Base variable *See* Segmentation variable.

Benefit segmentation The division of a market according to the various benefits that customers want from the product.

Bid pricing A determination of prices through sealed bids or open bids.

Bonded storage A storage service provided by many public warehouses, whereby the goods are not released until customs duties, taxes, or other fees are paid.

Brand A name, term, symbol, design, or combination of these that identifies a seller's products and differentiates them from competitors' products.

Brand attitude The buyer's overall evaluation of the brand with respect to its perceived ability to meet a relevant motivation. This evaluation generally takes account of competing brands' ability to meet the need. The third communication effect.

Brand awareness The buyer's ability to identify (recognise or recall) the brand within the category in sufficient detail to make a purchase. The second communication effect.

Brand-extension branding A type of branding in which a firm uses one of its existing brand names as part of a brand for an improved or new product that is usually in the same product category as the existing brand.

Brand manager A person who holds a staff position in a multi-product company and is responsible for a product, a product line, or several distinct products that are considered an interrelated group.

Brand mark The element of a brand, such as a symbol or design, that cannot be spoken.

Brand name The part of a brand that can be spoken—including letters, words, and numbers.

Brand purchase intention The buyer's "self-instruction" to purchase the brand: a conscious decision to buy. The fourth communication effect.

Break-down approach A general approach for measuring company sales potential based on a general economic forecast—or other aggregate data—and the market sales potential derived from it; company sales potential is based on the general economic forecast and the estimated market sales potential.

Break-even point The point at which the costs of producing a product equal the revenue made from selling the product.

Broker A functional middleman who performs fewer functions than other intermediaries; the primary function is to bring buyers and sellers together for a fee.

Build-up approach A general approach to measuring company sales potential in which the analyst initially estimates how much the average purchaser of a product will buy in a specified time period and then multiplies that amount by the number of potential buyers; estimates are generally calculated by individual geographic areas.

Business analysis An analysis providing a tentative sketch of a product's compatibility in the market-place, including its probable profitability.

Buy-back allowance A certain sum of money given to a purchaser for each unit bought after an initial deal is over.

Buying allowance A temporary price reduction to resellers for purchasing specified quantities of a product.

Buying behaviour The decision processes and acts of people involved in buying and using products.

Buying centre The group of people within an organisation who are involved in making organisational purchase decisions; these people take part in the purchase decision process as users, influencers, buyers, deciders, technologists, and gatekeepers.

Buying power Resources such as money, goods, and services that can be traded in an exchange situation.

Buying power index A weighted index consisting of population, effective buying income, and retail sales data. The higher the index number, the greater the buying power. Common usage in the U.S.A.

C

Captioned photograph A photograph with a brief description that explains the picture's content.

Cash-and-carry wholesaler A limited service wholesaler that sells to customers who will pay cash and furnish transport or pay extra to have products delivered.

Cash discount A price reduction to the buyer for prompt payment or cash payment.

Catalogue retailing A type of mail-order retailing in which selling may be handled by telephone or in-store visits and products are delivered by post or picked up by the customers.

Catalogue showrooms A form of warehouse showroom in which consumers shop from a mailed catalogue and buy at a warehouse where all products are stored out of buyers' reach. Products are provided in the manufacturer's packaging.

Category need The buyer's perception of requiring a product or service to remove or satisfy a perceived discrepancy between current motivational state and the desired motivational state. The first communication effect.

Causal study Research planned to prove or disprove that *x* causes *y* or that *x* does not cause *y*.

Central Business District (CBD) The traditional city centre or downtown hub containing most retail, financial, legal and office functions in the city, plus many transport foci and public transport stations.

Centralised organisation An organisation in which the top-level managers delegate very little authority to lower levels of the organisation.

Channel capacity The limit on the volume of information that a communication channel can handle effectively.

Channel conflict Friction between marketing channel members, often resulting from role deviance or malfunction; absence of an expected mode of conduct that contributes to the channel as a system.

Channel cooperation A helping relationship among channel members that enhances the welfare and survival of all necessary channel members.

Channel leadership The guidance that a channel member with one or more sources of power gives to other channel members to help achieve channel objectives.

Channel of distribution *See* Marketing channel.

Channel power The ability of one channel member to influence another channel member's goal achievement.

Client public The direct consumers of the product of a non-business organisation; for example, the client public of a university is its student body.

Closing The element in the selling process in which the salesperson asks the prospect to buy the product.

Code of ethics Formalised statement of what a company expects of its employees with regard to ethical behaviour.

Coding process The process by which a meaning is placed into a series of signs that represent ideas; also called encoding.

Cognitive dissonance Dissatisfaction that may occur shortly after the purchase of a product, when the buyer questions whether he or she should have purchased the product at all or would have been better off purchasing another brand that was evaluated very favourably.

Combination compensation plan A plan by which salespeople are paid a fixed salary and a commission based on sales volume.

Commercialisation A phase of new-product development in which plans for full-scale manufacturing and marketing must be refined and settled and budgets for the product must be prepared.

Commission merchant An agent often used in agricultural marketing who usually exercises physical control over products, negotiates sales, and is given broad powers regarding prices and terms of sale.

Communication A sharing of meaning through the transmission of information.

Company sales forecast The amount of a product that a firm actually expects to sell during a specific period at a specified level of company marketing activities.

Comparative advertising Advertising that compares two or more identified brands in the same general product class; the comparison is made in terms of one or more specific product characteristics.

Competition Generally viewed by a business as those firms that market products similar to, or substitutable for, its products in the same target market.

Competition-matching approach A method of ascertaining the advertising appropriation in which an advertiser tries to match a major competitor's appropriations in terms of absolute budget or in terms of using the same percentage of sales for advertising.

Competition-orientated pricing A pricing method in which an organisation considers costs and revenue secondary to competitors' prices.

Competitive advertising Advertising that points out a brand's uses, features, and advantages that benefit consumers but may not be available in competing brands.

Competitive structure The model used to describe the number of firms that control the supply of a product and how it affects the strength of competition; factors include number of competitors, ease of entry into the market, the nature of the product, and knowledge of the market.

Component part A finished item ready for assembly or a product that needs little processing before assembly and that becomes a part of the physical product.

Comprehensive spending patterns The percentages of family income allotted to annual expenditures for general classes of goods and services.

Concentration strategy A market segmentation strategy in which an organisation directs its marketing efforts towards a single market segment through one marketing mix.

Conflict of interest Results from marketers' taking advantage of situations for their own selfish interests rather than for the long-run interest of the business.

Consumable supplies Items that facilitate an organisation's production and operations, but do not become part of the finished product.

Consumer buying behaviour The buying behaviour of ultimate consumers—people who purchase products for personal or household use and not for business purposes.

Consumer buying decision process The five-stage decision process consumers use in making purchases.

Consumer contest A sales promotion device for established products based on the analytical or creative skill of contestants.

Consumer jury A panel used to pretest advertisements; it consists of a number of persons who are actual or potential buyers of the product to be advertised.

Consumer market Purchasers and/or individuals in their households who intend to consume or benefit from the purchased products and who do not buy products for the main purpose of making a profit.

Consumer movement A social movement through which people attempt to defend and exercise their rights as buyers.

Consumer movement forces The major forces in the consumer movement are consumer organisations, consumer laws, consumer education, and independent consumer advocates. The three major areas stressed are product safety, disclosure of information, and protection of the environment.

Consumer panels In market research, consumer panels consist of volunteers—usually paid—who either offer jury style instantaneous opinions or who keep records of their general household, personal, leisure, and occasionally business purchases. The information is collected by market research agencies which sell on the findings to marketers.

Consumer product Product purchased for ultimate satisfaction of personal and family needs.

Consumer protection legislation Laws enacted to protect consumers' safety, to enhance the amount of information available, and to warn of deceptive marketing techniques.

Consumer sales promotion method A sales promotion method that encourages or stimulates customers to patronise a specific retail store or to try and/or purchase a particular product.

Consumer spending patterns Information indicating the relative proportions of annual family expenditures or the actual amount of money that is spent on certain types of goods or services.

Consumer sweepstakes A sales promotion device for established products in which entrants submit their names for inclusion in a drawing for prizes.

Containerisation The practice of consolidating many items into one container that is sealed at the point of origin and opened at the destination.

Convenience products Relatively inexpensive, frequently purchased items for which buyers want to exert only minimal effort.

Co-operative advertising An arrangement in which a manufacturer agrees to pay a certain amount of a retailer's media costs for advertising the manufacturer's products.

Copy The verbal portion of advertisements; includes headlines, subheadlines, body copy, and signature.

Corporate strategy The strategy that determines the means for utilising resources in the areas of production, finance, research and development, personnel, and marketing to reach the organisation's goals.

Correlation methods Methods used to develop sales forecasts as the forecasters attempt to find a relationship between past sales and one or more variables, such as population, per capita income, or gross domestic product.

Cost comparison indicator Allows an advertiser to compare the costs of several vehicles within a specific medium relative to the number of persons reached by each vehicle.

Cost-orientated pricing A pricing policy in which a firm determines price by adding a monetary amount or percentage to the cost of a product.

Cost-plus pricing A form of cost-orientated pricing in which first the seller's costs are determined and then a specified monetary amount or percentage of the cost is added to the seller's cost to set the price.

Count and recount A sales promotion method based on the payment of a specific amount of money for each product unit moved from a reseller's warehouse in a given period of time.

Coupon A new-product sales promotion technique used to stimulate trial of a new or improved product, to increase sales volume quickly, to attract repeat purchasers, or to introduce new package sizes or features.

Credence qualities Qualities of services that cannot be assessed even after purchase and consumption; for example, few consumers are knowledgeable enough to assess the quality of an appendix operation, even after it has been performed.

Culture Everything in our surroundings that is made by human beings, consisting of tangible items as well as intangible concepts and values.

Cumulative discount Quantity discount that is aggregated over a stated period of time.

Customary pricing A type of psychological pricing in which certain goods are priced primarily on the basis of tradition.

Customer forecasting survey The technique of asking customers what types and quantities of products they intend to buy during a specific period so as to predict the sales level for that period.

Customer orientation An approach to marketing in which a marketer tries to provide a marketing mix that satisfies the needs of buyers in the target market.

Cycle analysis A method of predicting sales by analysing sales figures for a period of three to five years to ascertain whether sales fluctuate in a consistent, periodic manner.

D

Dealer listing An advertisement that promotes a product and identifies the names of participating retailers that sell the product.

Dealer loader A gift, often part of a display, that is given to a retailer for the purchase of a specified quantity of merchandise.

Decentralised organisation An organisation in which decision-making authority is delegated as far down the chain of command as possible.

Decline stage The stage in a product's life cycle in which sales fall rapidly and profits decrease.

Decoding process The stage in the communication process in which signs are converted into concepts and ideas.

Defensive advertising Advertising used to offset or lessen the effects of a competitor's promotional programme.

Demand curve A line showing the relationship between price and quantity demanded.

Demand-orientated pricing A pricing policy based on the level of demand for the product—resulting in a higher price when demand for the product is strong and a lower price when demand is weak.

Demand schedule The relationship, usually inverse, between price and quantity demanded; classically, a line sloping downward to the right, showing that as price falls, quantity demanded will increase.

Demographic factors Personal characteristics such as age, sex, race, nationality, income, family, life-cycle stage, and occupation; also called socio-economic factors.

Demonstration A sales promotion method manufacturers use temporarily to encourage trial use and purchase of the product or to show how the product works.

Department for Trade and Industry (DTI) The U.K.'s central government department controlling all aspects of trade and industry.

Department store A type of retail store having a wide product mix; organised into separate departments to facilitate marketing efforts and international management.

Dependent variable A variable contingent on, or restricted to, one or a set of values assumed by the independent variable.

Depression A stage of the business cycle during which unemployment is extremely high, wages are very low, total disposable income is at a minimum, and consumers lack confidence in the economy.

Depth (of product mix) The average number of different products offered to buyers in a firm's product line.

Depth interview Personal interview within an open, informal atmosphere; this interview may take several hours. It is used to study motives.

Derived demand A characteristic of industrial demand that arises because industrial demand derives from the consumer demand.

Descriptive study A type of study undertaken when marketers see that knowledge of the characteristics of certain phenomena is needed to solve a problem; may require statistical analysis and predictive tools.

Descriptor variables The characteristics used to describe individuals, groups, or organisations that have been grouped into segments.

Direct cost approach An approach to determining marketing costs in which cost analysis includes direct costs and traceable common costs but does not include non-traceable common costs.

Direct costs Costs directly attributable to the performance of marketing functions.

Direct distribution channels Distribution channels in which products are sold directly from producer to ultimate users.

Direct marketing The use of non-personal media to introduce products by mail or telephone.

Director General of Fair Trading Reporting to the Secretary of State for Trade and Industry, the Director General of Fair Trading can investigate any business practice which restricts, distorts or prevents competition and hinders fair trading.

Direct ownership A long-run commitment to marketing in a foreign nation in which a subsidiary or division is owned by a foreign country through purchase.

Discretionary income Disposable income that is available for spending and saving after an individual has purchased the basic necessities of food, clothing, and shelter.

Disposable income After-tax income.

Distribution The activities that make products available to customers when and where they want to purchase them.

Distribution centre A large, centralised warehouse that receives goods from factories and suppliers, regroups the goods into orders, and ships the orders to customers quickly, with the focus on active movement of goods rather than passive storage.

Distribution variable The marketing mix variable in which marketing management attempts to make products available in the quantities desired, with adequate service, to a target market and to keep the total inventory, transport, communication, storage, and materials handling costs as low as possible.

Diversified growth A type of growth that occurs in three forms, depending on the technology of the new products and the nature of the new markets the firm enters; the three forms are horizontal, concentric, and conglomerate.

Drop shipper A limited service wholesaler that takes title to products and negotiates sales but never physically handles products.

Dual distribution A channel practice whereby a producer distributes the same product through two or more different channels.

Dumping The sale of products in foreign markets at lower prices than those charged in the domestic market (when all costs are not allocated or when surplus products are sold).

E

Early adopters Individuals who choose new products carefully and are viewed by persons in the early majority, late majority, and laggard categories as being "the people to check with."

Early majority Individuals who adopt a new product just prior to the average person; they are deliberate and cautious in trying new products.

Economic forces Forces that determine the strength of a firm's competitive atmosphere and affect the impact of marketing activities because they determine the size and strength of demand for products.

Economic institutions An environmental force in international markets made up of producers, wholesalers, retailers, buyers, and other organisations that produce, distribute, and purchase products.

Economic order quantity (EOQ) The order size that minimises the total cost of ordering and carrying inventory.

Edge of town In retail terms, recent expansion of superstores and discount warehouses away from the traditional city centre to the edge of conurbations close to ring roads and residential suburbs.

Effective buying income Similar to disposable income; it includes salaries, wages, dividends, interest, profits, and rents, less taxes.

Electronic Funds Transfer at Point of Sale (EFTPOS) The use of scanning equipment for both product sale data capture and cash transfer from consumer to retailer (typically via the debit or credit card).

Electronic Point of Sale (EPOS) Data capture, typically with scanning equipment reading product bar codes in retail stores.

Encoding *See* Coding process.

Environmental monitoring The process of seeking information about events and relationships in a company's environment to assist marketers in identifying opportunities and in planning.

Environmental scanning The collecting of information about the forces in the marketing environment.

Equalised workload method A method of determining sales-force size in which the number of customers multiplied by the number of sales calls per year required to serve these customers effectively is divided by the average number of calls each salesperson makes annually.

Ethical pricing A form of professional pricing in which the demand for the product is inelastic and the seller is a professional who has a responsibility not to overcharge the client.

European Community (EC) Twelve member countries in Europe promoting common agricultural, trade, economic, and legislative policies.

Exchange Participation by two or more individuals, groups, or organisations, with each party possessing something of value that the other party desires. Each must be willing to give up its "something of value" to get "something of value" held by the other, and all parties must be willing to communicate with each other.

Exclusive dealing A situation in which a manufacturer forbids an intermediary to carry products of competing manufacturers.

Exclusive distribution A type of market coverage in which only one outlet is used in a geographic area.

Executive judgement A sales forecasting method based on the intuition of one or more executives.

Exhibition hall *See* Trade market.

Experience curve pricing A pricing approach in which a company fixes a low price that high-cost competitors cannot match and thus expands its market share; this approach is possible when a firm gains cumulative production experience and is able to reduce its manufacturing costs to a predictable rate through improved methods, materials, skills, and machinery.

Experience qualities Qualities of services that can be assessed only after purchase and consumption (taste, satisfaction, courtesy, and the like).

Experimentation Research in which the factors that are related to or may affect the variables under investigation are maintained as constants so that the effects of the experimental variables may be measured.

Expert forecasting survey Preparation of the sales forecast by experts, such as economists, management consultants, advertising executives, academics, or other persons outside the firm.

Exploratory studies A type of research conducted when more information is needed about a problem and the tentative hypothesis needs to be made more specific; it permits marketers to conduct mini-studies with a very restricted database.

Extensive decision-making The considerable time and effort a buyer spends seeking alternative products, searching for information about them, and then evaluating them to determine which one will be most satisfying.

External search The process of seeking information from sources other than one's memory.

F

Facilitating agency An organisation that performs activities helpful in performing channel functions but does not buy, sell, or transfer title to the product; it can be a transport company, an insurance company, an advertising agency, a marketing research agency, or a financial institution.

Family packaging A policy in an organisation that all packages are to be similar or are to include one major element of the design.

Feature article A form of publicity that is up to three

thousand words long and is usually prepared for a specific publication.

Federal Trade Commission A U.S. governmental group established to prevent the free enterprise system from being stifled or fettered by monopoly or anticompetitive practices; it provides direct protection to consumers from unfair or deceptive trade practices.

Feedback The receiver's response to a decoded message.

Field public warehouse A warehouse established by a public warehouse at the owner's inventory location; the warehouser becomes the custodian of the products and issues a receipt that can be used as collateral for a loan.

Financial Services Act 1986 Supervised by the Director General of Fair Trading, legislation in the U.K. for the protection of investors.

Fixed cost The cost that does not vary with changes in the number of units produced or sold.

F.O.B. (free-on-board) destination Part of a price quotation, used to indicate who must pay shipping charges. F.O.B. destination price means that the producer absorbs the costs of shipping the merchandise to the customer.

F.O.B. (free-on-board) factory Part of a price quotation; used to indicate who must pay shipping charges. F.O.B. factory price indicates the price of the merchandise at the factory, before it is loaded onto the carrier vehicle; the buyer must pay for shipping.

Focus group Between six and eight people, usually single sex, who—for a small fee or product sample—take part in, typically, discussions for two hours or three hours. These discussions commence in a general manner examining a particular market or product field before narrowing to focus on a specific brand or product.

Food broker An intermediary that sells food and other grocery products to retailer-owned and merchant wholesalers, grocery chains, industrial buyers, and food processors. Both buyers and sellers use food brokers to cope with fluctuating market conditions.

Franchising An arrangement in which a supplier (franchisor) grants a dealer (franchisee) the right to sell products in exchange for some type of consideration.

Free merchandise A sales promotion method aimed at retailers whereby free merchandise is offered to resellers that purchase a stated quantity of product.

Free samples A new-product sales promotion technique that marketers use to stimulate trial of a product, to increase sales volume in early stages of the product's life cycle, or to obtain desirable distribution.

Freight absorption pricing Pricing for a particular customer or geographical area whereby the seller absorbs all or part of the actual freight costs.

Freight forwarders Businesses that consolidate shipments from several organisations into efficient lot sizes, which increases transit time and sometimes lowers shipping costs.

Full-cost approach An approach to determining marketing costs in which cost analysis includes direct costs, traceable common costs, and non-traceable common costs.

Full-service wholesaler A marketing intermediary that provides most services that can be performed by wholesalers.

Functional discount *See* Trade discount.

Functional middleman A marketing intermediary that does not take title to products but usually receives a fee for expediting exchanges.

Functional modification A change that affects a product's versatility, effectiveness, convenience, or safety, usually requiring the redesigning of one or more parts of the product.

Functional wholesaler A marketing intermediary that expedites exchanges among producers and resellers and is compensated by fees or commission.

G

General merchandise wholesaler Full-service merchant wholesaler that carries a very wide product mix.

General public The indirect consumers of the product of a non-business organisation; for instance, the general public of a university includes alumni, trustees, parents of students, and other groups.

Generic brand A brand that indicates only the product category (such as *aluminium foil*), not the company name and other identifying terms.

Geographic pricing A form of pricing that involves reductions for transport costs or other costs associated with the physical distance between the buyer and the seller.

Globalisation of markets The development of marketing strategies as if the entire world (or regions of it) were a single entity; products are marketed the same way everywhere.

Good A tangible item.

Government markets Markets made up of national and local government, spending millions of pounds annually for goods and services to support their internal operations and to provide such products as defence, energy, and education.

Gross Domestic Product (GDP) Total output of goods and services by the national economy in a full year.

Gross National Product (GNP) An overall measure of a nation's economic standing in terms of the value of all products produced by that nation for a given period of time.

Growth state The product life-cycle stage in which sales rise rapidly; profits reach a peak and then start to decline.

Guarantee Document that specifies what the producer will do if the product malfunctions.

H

Heterogeneity A condition resulting from the fact that people typically perform services; there may be variation from one service provider to another or variation in the service provided by a single individual from day to day and from customer to customer.

Heterogeneous market A market made up of individuals with diverse product needs for products in a specific product class.

Horizontal channel integration The combining of institutions at the same level of operation under one management.

Hypothesis A guess or assumption about a certain problem or set of circumstances; reasonable supposition that may be right or wrong.

I

Idea A concept, image, or issue.

Idea generation The search by businesses and other organisations for product ideas that help them achieve their objectives.

Illustrations Photographs, drawings, graphs, charts, and tables, used to encourage an audience to read or watch an advertisement.

Implicit bargaining A method of employee motivation that recognises the various needs of different employees and is based on the theory that there is no one best way to motivate individuals.

Impulse buying An unplanned buying behaviour that involves a powerful, persistent urge to buy something immediately.

Income The amount of money received through wages, rents, investments, pensions, and benefit payments for a given period.

Incremental productivity method A plan by which a marketer should continue to increase the sales force as long as the additional sales increases are greater than the additional selling costs that arise from employing more salespeople.

Independent Broadcasting Authority (IBA) Responsible for control and monitoring of non-BBC broadcasting companies in the U.K. Replaced by the Independent Television Commission.

Independent Television (ITV) The regional television stations in the U.K. which compete with the national networks.

Independent Television Commission See Independent Broadcasting Authority.

Independent variable A variable free from the influence of, or not dependent on, other variables.

Individual branding A branding policy in which each product is named differently.

Industrial buying behaviour See Organisational buying behaviour.

Industrial distributor An independent business organisation that takes title to industrial products and carries inventories.

Industrial market A market consisting of individuals, groups, or organisations that purchase specific kinds of products for resale, for direct use in producing other products, or for use in day-to-day operations; also called organisational market.

Industrial marketing A set of activities directed towards facilitating and expediting exchanges involving industrial markets and industrial products.

Industrial product A product purchased to be used directly or indirectly to produce other products or to be used in the operations of an organisation.

Industrial service An intangible product that an organisation uses in its operations, such as a financial product or a legal service.

Inelastic demand A type of demand in which a price increase or decrease will not significantly affect the quantity demanded.

Inflation A condition in which price levels increase faster than incomes, causing a decline in buying power.

Information inputs The sensations we receive through our sense organs.

In-home retailing A type of non-store retailing that involves personal selling in consumers' homes.

Innovators The first consumers to adopt a new product; they enjoy trying new products and tend to be venturesome, rash, and daring.

Input-output data A type of information, sometimes used in conjunction with the SIC system, that is based on the assumption that the output or sales of one industry are the input or purchases of other industries.

Inseparability A condition in which the consumer frequently is directly involved in the production process because services normally are produced at the same time that they are consumed.

Institutional advertising A form of advertising promoting organisational images, ideas, and political issues.

Institutional market A market that consists of organisations seeking to achieve goals other than such normal business goals as profit, market share, or return on investment.

Intangibility A characteristic of services: because services are performances, they cannot be seen, touched, tasted, or smelled, nor can they be possessed.

Integrated growth The type of growth that a firm can have within its industry; three possible growth directions include forward, backward, and horizontal.

Intense growth The type of growth that can occur when current products and current markets have the potential for increasing sales.

Intensive distribution A form of market coverage in which all available outlets are used for distributing a product.

Intermodal transport Combining and coordinating two or more modes of transport.

Internal search An aspect of an information search where buyers first search their memory for information about products that might solve their problem.

International marketing Marketing activities which are performed across national boundaries.

Introduction stage The stage in a product's life cycle beginning at a product's first appearance in the marketplace, when sales are zero and profits are negative.

J

Job enrichment A method of employee motivation that gives employees a sense of autonomy and control over their work, with employees being encouraged to set their own goals.

Joint demand A characteristic of industrial demand that occurs when two or more items are used in combination to produce a product.

Joint venture A partnership between a domestic firm and foreign firms and/or governments.

K

Kinesic communication Commonly known as body language, this type of interpersonal communication occurs in face-to-face selling situations when the salesperson and customers move their heads, eyes, arms, hands, legs, and torsos.

L

Labelling An important dimension of packaging for promotional, informational, and legal reasons; regulated by numerous national and EC laws.

Laggards The last consumers to adopt a new product; they are orientated towards the past and suspicious of new products.

Late majority People who are quite sceptical of new products; they eventually adopt new products because of economic necessity or social pressure.

Layout The physical arrangement of the illustration, headline, subheadline, body copy, and signature of an advertisement.

Learning A change in an individual's behaviour that arises from prior behaviour in similar situations.

Legal forces Forces that arise from the legislation and interpretation of laws; these laws, enacted by government units, restrain and control marketing decisions and activities.

Level of involvement The intensity of interest that one has for a certain product in a particular buying decision.

Licensing (international) An arrangement in international marketing in which the licensee pays commissions or royalties on sales or supplies used in manufacturing.

Limited decision-making Consumer decision-making used for products that are purchased occasionally. Also used when a buyer needs to acquire information about an unfamiliar brand in a familiar product category.

Limited-line wholesaler Full-service merchant wholesaler that carries only a few product lines.

Limited service wholesaler A marketing intermediary that provides only some marketing services and specialises in a few functions.

Line family branding A branding policy in which an organisation uses family branding only for products within a line, not for all its products.

Location For retailers, a key factor. Location is the general locality. Site is the specific terrain on which the store stands.

Long-range plan A plan that covers more than five years.

M

Mail-order retailing A type of non-personal, non-store retailing that uses direct mail advertising and catalogues and is typified by selling by description. The buyer usually does not see the actual product until it is delivered.

Mail-order wholesaler A firm that sells through direct mail by sending catalogues to retail, industrial, and institutional customers.

Mail surveys Questionnaires sent to respondents, who are encouraged to complete and return them.

Major equipment A category of industrial products that includes large tools and machines used for production purposes.

Manufacturer brand A brand initiated by a producer; makes it possible for a producer to be identified with its product at the point of purchase.

Manufacturers' agent An independent businessperson who sells complementary products of several producers in assigned territories and is compensated through commission.

Marginal cost The cost associated with producing one more unit of a product.

Marginal revenue (MR) The change in total revenue that occurs after an additional unit of a product is sold.

Market An aggregate of people who, as individuals or as organisations, have needs for products in a product class and who have the ability, willingness, and authority to purchase such products.

Market attractiveness/business position model A two-dimensional matrix designed to serve as a diagnostic tool to highlight SBUs that have an opportunity to grow or that should be divested.

Market density The number of potential customers within a unit of land area, such as a square mile.

Marketing Individual and organisational activities that facilitate and expedite satisfying exchange relationships in a dynamic environment through the creation, distribution, promotion, and pricing of goods, services, and ideas.

Marketing audit A systematic examination of the objectives, strategies, organisation, and performance of a firm's marketing unit.

Marketing audit report A written summary produced after the marketing audit has been conducted; it includes recommendations that will increase marketing productivity and develops a recommendation as to the business's general direction.

Marketing channel A group of interrelated intermediaries who direct products to customers; also called channel of distribution.

Marketing concept A managerial philosophy that an organisation should try to satisfy customers' needs through a coordinated set of activities that at the same time allows the organisation to achieve its goals.

Marketing control process A process that consists of establishing performance standards, evaluating actual performance by comparing it with established standards, and reducing the differences between desired and actual performance.

Marketing cost analysis A method for helping to control marketing strategies whereby various costs are broken down and classified to determine which costs are associated with specific marketing activities.

Marketing databank A file of data collected through both the marketing information system and marketing research projects.

Marketing environment The environment that surrounds both the buyer and the marketing mix; it consists of political, legal, regulatory, societal, consumer movement, economic, and technological forces. Environmental variables affect a marketer's ability to facilitate and expedite exchanges.

Marketing ethics Moral evaluation of decisions based on accepted principles of behaviour that result in an action being judged right or wrong.

Marketing experimentation A set of rules and procedures under which the task of data gathering is organised to expedite analysis and interpretation.

Marketing function account Classification of costs that indicates which function was performed through the expenditure of funds.

Marketing information system (MIS) A system that establishes a framework for the day-to-day managing and structuring of information gathered regularly from sources both inside and outside an organisation.

Marketing intelligence All the data gathered as a basis for marketing decisions.

Marketing intermediary A member of a marketing channel, usually a merchant or an agent, acting to direct products to buyers.

Marketing management A process of planning, organising, implementing, and controlling marketing activities to facilitate and expedite exchanges effectively and efficiently.

Marketing mix Consists of four major variables: product, price, distribution, and promotion.

Marketing objective A statement of what is to be accomplished through marketing activities.

Marketing-orientated organisation An organisation that attempts to determine what target market members want and then tries to produce it.

Marketing plan The written document or blueprint for implementing and controlling an organisation's marketing activities related to a particular marketing strategy.

Marketing planning A systematic process that involves assessing marketing opportunities and resources, determining market objectives, and developing a plan for implementation and control.

Marketing programme A set of marketing strategies that are implemented and used at the same time.

Marketing research The part of marketing intelligence that involves specific inquiries into problems and marketing activities to discover new information so as to guide marketing decisions.

Marketing strategy A plan for selecting and analysing a target market and creating and maintaining a marketing mix.

Market manager A person responsible for the marketing activities that are necessary to serve a particular group or class of customers.

Market opportunity An opportunity that arises when the right combination of circumstances occurs at the right time to allow an organisation to take action towards generating sales from a target market.

Market planning cycle The five-step cycle that involves developing or revising marketing objectives relative to performance, assessing marketing opportunities and resources, formulating marketing strategy, developing the plan for implementation and control, and implementing the marketing plan.

Market requirement Related to customers' needs or desired benefits, the market requirement is satisfied by components of the marketing mix that provide benefits to buyers.

Market sales potential The amount of a product that

specific customer groups would purchase within a specified period at a specific level of industry-wide marketing activity.

Market segment A group of individuals, groups, or organisations sharing one or more similar characteristics that make them have relatively similar product needs.

Market segmentation The process of dividing a total market into groups of people with relatively similar product needs, for the purpose of designing a marketing mix (or mixes) that more precisely matches the needs of individuals in a selected segment (or segments).

Market share A firm's sales in relation to total industry sales, expressed as a decimal or percentage.

Market test A stage of new-product development that involves making a product available to buyers in one or more test areas and measuring purchases and consumer responses to promotion, price, and distribution efforts.

Mark-up A percentage of the cost or price of a product added to the cost.

Mark-up pricing A pricing method in which the price is derived by adding a predetermined percentage of the cost to the cost of the product.

Materials handling Physical handling of products.

Maturity stage A stage in the product life cycle in which the sales curve peaks and starts to decline as profits continue to decline.

Mechanical observation devices Cameras, recorders, counting machines, and equipment to record movement, behaviour, or physiological changes in individuals.

Media plan A plan that sets forth the exact media vehicles to be used for advertisements and the dates and times that the advertisements are to appear.

Medium of transmission That which carries the coded message from the source to the receiver or audience; examples include ink on paper and vibrations of air waves produced by vocal cords.

Medium-range plans Plans that usually encompass two to five years.

Megacarrier A freight transport company that provides many methods of shipment, such as rail, truck, and air service.

Merchandise allowance A sales promotion method aimed at retailers; it consists of a manufacturer's agreement to pay resellers certain amounts of money for providing special promotional efforts, such as setting up and maintaining a display.

Merchant A marketing intermediary who takes title to merchandise and resells it for a profit.

Merchant wholesaler A marketing intermediary who takes title to products, assumes risk, and is generally involved in buying and reselling products.

Missionary salesperson A support salesperson, usually employed by a manufacturer, who assists the producer's customers in selling to their own customers.

Moderator The market researcher who controls, runs, and prompts a focus group discussion.

Modified-rebuy purchase A type of industrial purchase in which a new-task purchase is changed the second or third time, or the requirements associated with a straight-rebuy purchase are modified.

Money-off offer A sales promotion device for established products whereby buyers receive a certain amount off the regular price shown on the label or package.

Money refund A new-product sales promotion technique in which the producer mails a consumer a specific amount of money when proof of purchase is established.

Monopolies and Mergers Commission In the U.K. where at least a quarter of a particular good or service is supplied by a single person or a group of connected companies, restricting and distorting competition, the Department for Trade and Industry and the Director General of Fair Trading seek an investigation by the Monopolies and Mergers Commission.

Monopolistic competition A market structure in which a firm has many potential competitors; to compete, the firm tries to develop a differential marketing strategy to establish its own market share.

Monopoly A market structure existing when a firm produces a product that has no close substitutes and/or when a single seller may erect barriers to potential competitors.

Motive An internal energising force that directs a person's behaviour towards his or her goals.

MRO items An alternative term for supplies: supplies can be divided into maintenance, repair, and operating (or overhaul) items.

Multinational enterprise A firm that has operations or subsidiaries in several countries.

Multi-segment strategy A market segmentation strategy in which an organisation directs its marketing efforts at two or more segments by developing a marketing mix for each selected segment.

Multi-variable segmentation Market division achieved by using more than one characteristic to divide the total market; this approach provides more information about the individuals in each segment than does single-variable segmentation.

N

Natural account Classification of costs based on what the money is actually spent for; typically a part of a regular accounting system.

Negotiated pricing A determination of price through

bargaining even when there are stated list prices and discount structures.

Negotiation Mutual discussion or communication of the terms and methods of an exchange.

New product Any product that a given firm has not marketed previously.

New-product development A process consisting of six phases: idea generation, screening, business analysis, product development, test-marketing, and commercialisation.

New-task purchase A type of industrial purchase in which an organisation is making an initial purchase of an item to be used to perform a new job or to solve a new problem.

Noise A condition in the communication process existing when the decoded message is different from what was coded.

Non-business marketing Marketing activities conducted by individuals and organisations to achieve some goal other than ordinary business goals such as profit, market share, or return on investment.

Non-cumulative discount A once-only price reduction based on the number of units purchased, the size of the order, or the product combination purchased.

Non-price competition A policy in which a seller elects not to focus on price and instead emphasises distinctive product features, service, product quality, promotion, packaging, or other factors to distinguish its product from competing brands.

Non-profit organisation marketing The application of marketing concepts and techniques to such non-profit groups as hospitals and colleges.

Non-store retailing A type of retailing where consumers purchase products without visiting a store.

Non-traceable common costs Costs that cannot be assigned to any specific function according to any logical criteria and thus are assignable only on an arbitrary basis.

O

Objective and task approach An approach to determining the advertising budget: marketers first determine the objectives that a campaign is to achieve, and then ascertain the tasks required to accomplish those objectives; the costs of all tasks are added to ascertain the total budget.

Observation method A research method in which researchers record the overt behaviour of subjects, noting physical conditions and events. Direct contact with subjects is avoided; instead, their actions are examined and noted systematically.

Odd-even pricing A type of psychological pricing that assumes that more of a product will be sold at £99.99

than at £100.00, indicating that an odd price is more appealing than an even price to customers.

Oligopoly A competitive structure existing when a few sellers control the supply of a large proportion of a product; each seller must consider the actions of other sellers to make changes in marketing activities.

Omnibus survey Continuous survey used to examine a number of topics together. Client companies "buy in" to the survey having a limited number of questions included in the survey on their behalf. Market research agencies sell on the findings to a wide audience.

Open bids Prices submitted by several, but not all, sellers; the amounts of these bids are not made public.

Opportunity cost The value of the benefit that is given up by selecting one alternative rather than another.

Order getter A type of salesperson who increases the firm's sales by selling to new customers and by increasing sales to present customers.

Order processing The receipt and transmission of sales order information in the physical distribution process.

Order taker A type of salesperson who primarily seeks repeat sales.

Organisational buying behaviour The purchase behaviour of producers, government units, institutions, and resellers; also called industrial buying behaviour.

Organisational market Individuals or groups who purchase a specific kind of product for one of three purposes: resale, direct use in producing other products, or use in general daily operations; also called industrial market.

Overall family branding A policy of branding all of a firm's products with the same name or at least a part of the name.

Own label (private label) Many large retail groups have in stock, in addition to manufacturers' brands, their own retail brand. This can simply be the name of the retailer or a name especially created for a retailer's use to allow competition with the manufacturers' brands. The brand name is owned and controlled by the retailer.

P

Patronage motives Motives that influence where a person purchases products on a regular basis.

Penetration price A lower price designed to penetrate the market and thus quickly produce a larger unit sales volume.

Percent of sales approach A method for establishing the advertising budget whereby marketers simply multiply a firm's past sales, forecasted sales, or a combination of the two by a standard percentage based on both what the firm traditionally has spent on advertising and what the industry averages.

Perception The process by which an individual selects, organises, and interprets information inputs to create a meaningful picture of the world.

Perceptual mapping A variety of mathematical approaches designed to place or describe consumers' perceptions of brands or products on one or a series of "spatial maps." A means of visually depicting consumers' perceptions.

Perfect competition Ideal competitive structure that would entail a large number of sellers, none of which could significantly influence price or supply.

Performance standard An expected level of performance against which actual performance can be compared.

Perishability A condition where, because of simultaneous production and consumption, unused capacity to produce services in one time period cannot be stockpiled or inventoried for future time periods.

Personal factors Factors influencing the consumer buying decision process that are unique to particular individuals.

Personal interview survey A face-to-face interview that allows more in-depth interviewing, probing, follow-up questions, or psychological tests.

Personality An internal structure in which experience and behaviour are related in an orderly way.

Personal selling A process of informing customers and persuading them to purchase products through personal communication in an exchange situation.

Persuasion The activity of convincing or prevailing upon an individual or organisation to bring about an exchange.

Physical distribution An integrated set of activities that deal with managing the movement of products within firms and through marketing channels.

PIMS (Profit Impact on Marketing Strategy) A Strategic Planning Institute (SPI) research programme which provides reports on the products of SPI member firms; these reports assist the member firms in analysing marketing performance and formulating marketing strategies.

Pioneer advertising A type of advertising that informs persons about what a product is, what it does, how it can be used, and where it can be purchased.

Point-of-purchase materials A sales promotion method that uses such items as outside signs, window displays, and display racks to attract attention, to inform customers, and to encourage retailers to carry particular products.

Political and legal institutions Public agencies, laws, courts, legislatures, and government bureaux.

Political forces Forces that strongly influence the economic and political stability of a country, not only through decisions that affect domestic matters but through their authority to negotiate trade agreements and to determine foreign policy.

Population All elements, units, or individuals that are of interest to researchers for a specific study.

Positioning *See* Product positioning.

Post-test An evaluation of advertising effectiveness after the campaign.

Premiums Items that are offered free or at a minimum cost as a bonus for purchasing.

Press conference A meeting used to announce major news events.

Press release A form of publicity that is usually a single page of typewritten copy containing fewer than three hundred words. A news release.

Prestige pricing Setting prices at a high level to facilitate a prestige or quality image.

Pre-test Evaluation of an advertisement before it is actually used.

Price The value placed on what is exchanged.

Price competition A policy whereby a marketer emphasises price as an issue and matches or beats the prices of competitors also emphasising low prices.

Price differentiation A demand-orientated pricing method whereby a firm uses more than one price in the marketing of a specific product; differentiation of prices can be based on several dimensions, such as type of customers, type of distribution used, or the time of the purchase.

Price discrimination A policy of charging some buyers lower prices than other buyers, which gives those paying less a competitive advantage.

Price elasticity of demand A measure of the sensitivity of demand to changes in price.

Price leaders Products sold at less than cost to increase sales of regular merchandise.

Price lining A form of psychological pricing in which an organisation sets a limited number of prices for selected lines of products.

Price skimming A pricing policy whereby an organisation charges the highest possible price that buyers who most desire the product will pay.

Price variable A critical marketing mix variable in which marketing management is concerned with establishing a value for what is exchanged.

Pricing method A mechanical procedure for setting prices on a regular basis.

Pricing objectives Overall goals that describe the role of price in an organisation's long-range plans.

Pricing policy A guiding philosophy or course of action designed to influence and determine pricing decisions.

Primary data Information observed and recorded or collected directly from subjects.

Private brand *See* Private distributor brand.

Private distributor brand A brand that is initiated and

owned by a reseller; also called private brand and own label. *See* Own label.

Private warehouse A storage facility operated by an organisation for the purpose of distributing its own products.

Problem definition The first step in the research process toward finding a solution or launching a research study; the researcher thinks about the best ways to discover the nature and boundaries of a problem or opportunity.

Process materials Materials used directly in the production of other products; unlike component parts, they are not readily identifiable.

Pro-competitive legislation Laws enacted to preserve competition.

Producer market A market consisting of individuals and business organisations that purchase products for the purpose of making a profit by using them to produce other products or by using them in their operations.

Product Everything (both favourable and unfavourable) that one receives in an exchange; it is a complexity of tangible and intangible attributes, including functional, social, and psychological utilities or benefits. A product may be a good, a service, or an idea.

Product adoption process The five-stage process of buyer acceptance of a product: awareness, interest, evaluation, trial, and adoption.

Product advertising Advertising that promotes goods and services.

Product assortment A collection of a variety of different products.

Product deletion The elimination of some products that no longer satisfy target market customers or contribute to achievement of an organisation's overall goals.

Product development A stage in creating new products that moves the product from concept to test phase and also involves the development of the other elements of the marketing mix (promotion, distribution, and price).

Product differentiation The use of promotional efforts to differentiate a company's products from its competitors' products, with the hope of establishing the superiority and preferability of its products relative to competing brands.

Production-orientated organisation A firm that concentrates on either improving production efficiency or producing high-quality, technically improved products; it has little regard for customers' desires.

Production orientation The viewpoint that increasing the efficiency of production is the primary means of increasing an organisation's profits.

Product item A specific version of a product that can be designated as a unique offering among an organisation's products.

Product life cycle The course of product development, consisting of several stages: introduction, growth, maturity, and decline. As a product moves through these stages, the strategies relating to competition, pricing, promotion, distribution, and market information must be evaluated and possibly changed.

Product line A group of closely related products that are considered a unit because of marketing, technical, or end-use considerations.

Product mix The composite of products that an organisation makes available to consumers.

Product mix depth *See* Depth (of product mix).

Product mix width *See* Width (of product mix).

Product modification The changing of one or more of a product's characteristics.

Product-portfolio analysis (BCG approach) A strategic planning approach based on the philosophy that a product's market growth rate and its relative market share are important considerations in determining its marketing strategy.

Product-portfolio approach An approach to managing the product mix that attempts to create specific marketing strategies to achieve a balanced mix of products that will produce maximum long-run profits.

Product positioning The decisions and activities that are directed towards trying to create and maintain the firm's intended product concept in customers' minds. The creation of a product's perceived image.

Product-specific spending patterns The monetary amounts families spend for specific products within a general product class.

Product variable That aspect of the marketing mix dealing with researching consumers' product wants and planning the product to achieve the desired product characteristics.

Professional pricing Pricing used by persons who have great skill or experience in a particular field or activity, indicating that a price should not relate directly to the time and involvement in a specific case; rather, a standard fee is charged regardless of the problems involved in performing the job.

Professional services Complex and frequently regulated services that usually require the provider to be highly skilled; for example, accounting or legal services.

Projective technique A test in which subjects are asked to perform specific tasks for particular purposes while in fact they are being evaluated for other purposes; assumes that subjects will unconsciously "project" their motives as they perform the tasks.

Promotion The communication with individuals, groups, or organisations to directly or indirectly facilitate exchanges by influencing audience members to accept an organisation's products.

Promotion mix The specific combination of promotional methods that an organisation uses for a particular product.

Promotion variable A major marketing mix component used to facilitate exchanges by informing an individual or one or more groups of people about an organisation and its products.

Prospecting Developing a list of potential customers for personal selling purposes.

Prosperity A stage of the business cycle characterised by a combination of low unemployment and relatively high aggregate income, which causes buying power to be high (assuming a low inflation rate).

Proxemic communication A subtle form of interpersonal communication used in face-to-face interactions when either party varies the physical distance that separates them.

Psychological factors Factors that operate within individuals to partially determine their general behaviour and thus influence their behaviour as buyers.

Psychological pricing A pricing method designed to encourage purchases that are based on emotional reactions rather than rational responses.

Publicity Non-personal communication in news story form, regarding an organisation and/or its products, that is transmitted through a mass medium at no charge.

Public relations A broad set of communication activities used to create and maintain favourable relations between the organisation and its publics, such as customers, employees, stockholders, government officials, and society in general.

Public warehouses Business organisations that provide rented storage facilities and related physical distribution facilities.

Pull policy Promotion of a product directly to consumers with the intention of developing strong consumer demand.

Purchase facilitation The final communication effect. The product or brand has to be suitably accessible for the buyer to make the purchase: the elements of the marketing mix must facilitate the purchase.

Purchasing power A buyer's income, credit, and wealth available for purchasing products.

Push money An incentive programme designed to push a line of goods by providing salespeople with additional compensation.

Push policy The promotion of a product only to the next institution down the marketing channel.

Q

Quality modification A change that relates to a product's dependability and durability and is generally executed by alterations in the materials or production process used.

Quality of life The enjoyment of daily living, enhanced by leisure time, clean air and water, an unlittered earth, conservation of wildlife and natural resources, and security from radiation and poisonous substances.

Quantity discounts Deductions from list price that reflect the economies of purchasing in large quantities.

Quota sampling Non-probability sampling in which the final choice of respondents is left to the interviewers.

R

Rack jobbers Middlemen (also called service merchandisers) similar to truck wholesalers but providing the extra service of cleaning and filling a display rack.

Random factor analysis A method of predicting sales whereby an attempt is made to attribute erratic sales variations to random, non-recurrent events, such as a regional power failure or a natural disaster.

Random sampling A type of sampling in which all the units in a population have an equal chance of appearing in the sample; probability sampling.

Raw materials Basic materials that become part of a physical product; obtained from mines, farms, forests, oceans, and recycled solid wastes.

Real-estate brokers Brokers who, for a fee or commission, bring buyers and sellers together to exchange real estate.

Receiver The individual, group, or organisation that decodes a coded message.

Recession A stage in the business cycle during which unemployment rises and total buying power declines, stifling both consumers' and businesspeople's propensity to spend.

Reciprocity A practice unique to industrial sales in which two organisations agree to buy from each other.

Recognition test A post-test method of evaluating the effectiveness of advertising; individual respondents are shown the actual advertisement and asked whether they recognise it.

Recovery A stage of the business cycle during which the economy moves from recession towards prosperity.

Recruiting A process by which the sales manager develops a list of applicants for sales positions.

Reference group A group with which an individual identifies so much that he or she takes on many of the values, attitudes, or behaviours of group members.

Regional issues Versions of a magazine that differ across geographic regions so that a publisher can vary the advertisements and editorial content.

Regulatory forces Forces arising from regulatory units at all levels of government; these units create and enforce numerous regulations that affect marketing decisions.

Reinforcement advertising An advertisement attempting to assure current users that they have made the right choice and telling them how to get the most satisfaction from the product.

Reliability A condition existing when a sample is representative of the population; it also exists when repeated use of an instrument produces almost identical results.

Reminder advertising Advertising used to remind consumers that an established brand is still around and that it has certain uses, characteristics, and benefits.

Reorder point The inventory level that signals that more inventory should be ordered.

Reseller market A market consisting of intermediaries, such as wholesalers and retailers, that buy finished goods and resell them for the purpose of making a profit.

Restrictive Trade Practices Act, 1976 The Restrictive Practices Court in the U.K., following on recommendations from the Director General of Fair Trading, examines trading agreements which limit freedom of choice in terms of trade and price setting which may be against the public interest.

Retailer An intermediary that purchases products for the purpose of reselling them to ultimate consumers.

Retailer coupon A sales promotion method used by retailers when price is a primary motivation for consumers' purchasing behaviour; usually takes the form of a "money-off" coupon that is distributed through advertisements and is redeemable only at a specific store.

Retailing Activities required for exchanges in which ultimate consumers are the buyers.

Retail park In the 1970s most superstores were free-standing, isolated stores. Throughout Europe, as planning regulations were relaxed, developers found sites either formerly used by heavy industry or adjacent to suburbs on the edge of towns to accommodate several neighbouring superstores. Recently full-scale covered shopping malls have appeared on such retail parks, along with the superstores.

Role A set of actions and activities that a person in a particular position is supposed to perform, based on the expectations of both the individual and the persons around the individual.

Routine response behaviour The type of decision-making used by a consumer when buying frequently purchased, low-cost items that require very little search and decision effort.

S

Safety stock The inventory needed to prevent running out of stock.

Sales analysis A process for controlling marketing strategies whereby sales figures are used to evaluate performance.

Sales branches Similar to merchant wholesalers in their operations; may offer credit, delivery, give promotional assistance, and furnish other services.

Sales contest A sales promotion method used to motivate distributors, retailers, and sales personnel through the recognition of outstanding achievements.

Sales-force forecasting survey Estimation by members of a firm's sales force of the anticipated sales in their territories for a specified period.

Sales forecast The amount of a product that a company expects to sell during a specific period at a specified level of marketing activities.

Sales office Provides service normally associated with agents; owned and controlled by the producer.

Sales-orientated organisation An organisation acting on its belief that personal selling and advertising are the primary tools used to generate profits and that most products—regardless of consumers' needs—can be sold if the right quantity and quality of personal selling and advertising are used.

Sales orientation A focus on increasing an organisation's sales as the major way to increase profits.

Sales potential The maximum percentage of market potential that an individual firm within an industry can expect to obtain for a specific product.

Sales promotion An activity and/or material that acts as a direct inducement to resellers, salespersons, or consumers; it offers added value or incentive to buy or sell the product.

Sample A limited number of units that are believed to be representative of the total population under study for marketing research purposes.

Sampling Selecting representative units from a total population.

Scientific decision-making An approach that involves systematically seeking facts and then applying decision-making methods other than trial and error or generalisation from experience.

Scrambled merchandising The addition of unrelated products and product lines to an existing product mix, particularly fast-moving items that can be sold in large volume.

Screening ideas A stage in the product development process in which the ideas that do not match organisational objectives are rejected and those with the greatest potential are selected for further development.

Sealed bids Prices submitted to a buyer, to be opened and made public at a specified time.

Search qualities Tangible attributes of services that can be viewed prior to purchase.

Seasonal analysis A method of predicting sales whereby an analyst studies daily, weekly, or monthly sales figures to evaluate the degree to which seasonal factors, such as climate and holiday activities, influence a firm's sales.

Seasonal discounts A price reduction that sellers give to buyers who purchase goods or services out of season; these discounts allow the seller to maintain steadier production during the year.

Secondary data Information compiled inside or outside the organisation for some purpose other than the current investigations.

Segmentation variable A dimension or characteristic of individuals, groups, or organisations that is used to divide a total market into segments.

Selective distortion The changing or twisting of currently received information that occurs when a person receives information inconsistent with his or her feelings or beliefs.

Selective distribution A form of market coverage in which only some available outlets in an area are chosen to distribute a product.

Selective exposure Selection of some inputs to be exposed to our awareness while many others are ignored because of the inability to be conscious of all inputs at one time.

Selective retention The phenomenon of remembering information inputs that support personal feelings and beliefs and forgetting inputs that do not.

Self-concept One's own perception of oneself.

Selling agents Intermediaries who market all of a specified product line or the entire output of a manufacturer; they have control over the manufacturer's marketing effort and may be used in place of a marketing department.

Service An intangible that results from applying human and mechanical efforts to people or objects.

Service heterogeneity *See* Heterogeneity.

Service inseparability *See* Inseparability.

Service intangibility *See* Intangibility.

Service perishability *See* Perishability.

Shopping product An item for which buyers are willing to put forth considerable effort in planning and making the purchase.

Shop-within-a-shop Concessions operated in most department stores operated by retail companies independent of the host department store company.

Short-range plans Plans that cover a period of one year or less.

Single-variable segmentation The simplest form of segmentation, achieved by using only one characteristic to divide—or segment—the market.

Situational factors The set of circumstances or conditions that exist when a consumer is making a purchase decision.

Social class An open aggregate of people with similar social ranking.

Social factors The forces that other people exert on one's buying behaviour.

Social institutions An environmental force in international markets, including the family, education, religion, health, and recreational systems.

Social marketing Marketing that involves the development of programmes designed to influence the acceptability of social ideas or causes.

Social responsibility An approach to marketing decisions that takes into account how these decisions may affect society as a whole and various groups and individuals within society.

Societal forces Forces that pressure marketers to provide high living standards and enjoyable lifestyles through socially responsible decisions and activities; the structure and dynamics of individuals and groups and the issues of concern to them.

Socio-economic factors *See* Demographic factors.

Sorting activities The way channel members divide roles and separate tasks, including the roles of sorting out, accumulating, allocating, and assorting products.

Sorting out The first step in developing an assortment; involves breaking down conglomerates of heterogeneous supplies into relatively homogeneous groups.

Source A person, group, or organisation that has a meaning that it intends and attempts to share with a receiver or an audience.

Special-event pricing Advertised sales or price cutting to increase revenue or lower costs.

Specialty-line wholesaler A merchant wholesaler that carries a very limited variety of products designed to meet customers' specialised requirements.

Specialty product An item that possesses one or more unique characteristics that motivates a significant group of buyers to obtain it.

Specialty retail A type of store that carries a narrow product mix with deep product lines.

Standard Industrial Classification (SIC) System A system developed by the government for classifying industrial organisations, based on what the firm primarily produces; also classifies selected economic characteristics of commercial, financial, and service organisations; uses code numbers to classify firms in different industries.

Statistical interpretation An analysis that focuses on what is typical or what deviates from the average; indicates how widely respondents vary and how they are distributed in relation to the variable being measured.

Stockout A condition that exists when a firm runs out of a product.

Storyboard A blueprint used by technical personnel to produce a television commercial; combines the copy with the visual material to show the sequence of major scenes in the commercial.

Straight commission compensation plan A plan according to which a salesperson's compensation is determined solely by the amount of his or her sales for a given time period.

Straight-rebuy purchase A type of industrial purchase in which a buyer purchases the same products routinely under approximately the same terms of sale.

Straight salary compensation plan A plan according to which salespeople are paid a specified amount per time period.

Strategic business unit (SBU) A division, product line, or other profit centre within a parent company that sells a distinct set of products and/or services to an identifiable group of customers and competes against a well-defined set of competitors.

Strategic marketing planning A process through which an organisation can develop marketing strategies that, when properly implemented and controlled, will contribute to achieving the organisation's overall goals.

Strategic market plan A comprehensive plan that takes into account not only marketing but all other functional areas of a business unit that must be coordinated, such as production, finance, and personnel, as well as concern about the environment.

Strategy The key decision or plan of action required to reach an objective or set of objectives.

Stratified sampling A type of sampling in which units in a population are divided into groups according to a common characteristic or attribute; then a probability sample is conducted within each group.

Style modification Modification directed at changing the sensory appeal of a product by altering its taste, texture, sound, smell, or visual characteristics.

Sub-culture A division of a culture based on geographic regions or human characteristics, such as age or ethnic background.

Suburban centre Many cities and towns have large shopping centres in their suburbs, not just the one CBD retail centre. Typically near or on major road intersections.

Superficial discounting A deceptive mark-down sometimes called "was-is pricing" (the firm never intended to sell at the higher price); fictitious comparative pricing.

Supermarket A large, self-service store that carries broad and complete lines of food products, and perhaps some non-food products.

Superstore A giant store that carries all food and non-food products found in supermarkets, as well as most products purchased on a routine basis; sales are much greater than at discount stores or supermarkets.

Supplies See Consumable supplies.

Support personnel Members of the sales staff who facilitate the selling function but usually are not involved only with making sales.

Survey methods Interviews conducted by mail, telephone, or in person to obtain factual information from or about those being interviewed, or to find out their opinions and values.

Symbolic pricing A type of psychological pricing in which prices are set at an artificially high level to provide prestige or a quality image.

Syndicated data services External sources of information that a marketer uses to study a marketing problem. Examples are provided by AGB, Selling Areas Marketing, Inc. (SAMI), and A.C. Nielson Company. They collect general information that is sold to subscribing clients.

T

Tactile communication Interpersonal communication through touching.

Targeting Deciding which segment or segments at which to aim marketing effort.

Target market A group of people for whom a firm creates and maintains a marketing mix.

Target public A group of people who have an interest in or a concern about an organisation, a product, or a social cause.

Technical salesperson A support salesperson who directs efforts towards the organisation's current customers by providing technical assistance in system design, product application, product characteristics, or installation.

Technological forces Forces that influence marketing decisions and activities because they affect people's lifestyles and standards of living, influence their desire for products and their reaction to marketing mixes, and have a direct impact on maintaining a marketing mix by influencing all its variables.

Technology The knowledge of how to accomplish tasks and goals.

Technology assessment A procedure by means of which managers try to foresee the effects of new products and processes on the firm's operation, on other business organisations, and on society in general.

Telemarketing A form of personal selling where highly trained account executives do everything over the telephone that face-to-face salespeople do.

Telephone retailing A type of non-store retailing based on a cold canvass of the telephone directory or a screening of prospective clients before calling.

Telephone surveys The soliciting of respondents' answers to a questionnaire over the telephone, with the answers being written down by the interviewer.

Telesales See Telemarketing.

Test marketing A limited introduction of a product in areas chosen to represent the intended market to determine probable buyers' reactions to various parts of a marketing mix.

Third-party endorsement In public relations, apparently independent recommendation by a person or organisation separate from the brand owner (the manufacturer or supplier) gives the product credibility, particularly if the recommendation is from an influential body or well-known personality.

Time series analysis A technique in which the forecaster, using the firm's historical sales data, tries to discover patterns in the firm's sales volume over time.

Total costs The sum of fixed costs and variable costs.

Total market approach An approach in which an organisation designs a single marketing mix and directs it at an entire market for a specific product category; also called undifferentiated approach.

Total revenue The price times quantity.

Traceable common costs Costs that can be allocated indirectly, using one or several criteria, to the functions that they support.

Trade (or functional) discount A reduction off the list price a producer gives to a middleman for performing certain functions.

Trade mark A legal designation indicating that the owner has exclusive use of a brand or part of a brand and that others are prohibited by law from using it.

Trade market A relatively permanent facility that firms can rent to exhibit products year-round.

Trade name The legal name of an organisation, rather than the name of a specific product.

Trade salesperson A type of salesperson not strictly classified as support personnel because he or she performs the order-taking function as well.

Trade sales promotion method A category of sales promotion techniques that stimulate wholesalers and retailers to carry a producer's products and to market these products aggressively.

Trade show A show whose purpose is to let manufacturers or wholesalers exhibit products to potential buyers; therefore assists in the selling and buying functions; commonly held annually at a specified location.

Trading company A company that provides a link between buyers and sellers in different countries; it takes title to products and provides all the activities necessary to move the product from the domestic country to a market in a foreign country.

Trading stamps A sales promotion method used by retailers to attract consumers to specific stores and to increase sales of specific items by giving extra stamps to purchasers of those items.

Transfer pricing The type of pricing used when one unit in a company sells a product to another unit; the price is determined by one of the following methods: actual full cost, standard full cost, cost plus investment, or market-based cost.

Transit time The total time that a carrier has possession of the goods.

Transport Moving a product from where it is made to where it is purchased and used, and thus adding time and place utility to the product.

Transport modes Railways, motor vehicles, waterways, pipelines, and airways used to move goods from one location to another.

Trend analysis An analysis that focuses on aggregate sales data, such as company's annual sales figures, over a period of many years to determine whether annual sales are generally rising, falling, or staying about the same.

Tying contract An agreement in which a supplier agrees to sell certain products to a dealer if the dealer consents to buy other products the supplier sells.

U

Unaided (spontaneous) recall test A post-test method of evaluating the effectiveness of advertising; subjects are asked to identify advertisements that they have seen or heard recently but are not shown any clues to stimulate their memories.

Undifferentiated approach An approach in which an organisation designs a single marketing mix and directs it at an entire market for a specific product category; same as total market approach.

Uniform geographic pricing A type of pricing, sometimes called "postage-stamp price," that results in fixed average transport; used to avoid the problems involved in charging different prices to each customer.

Unit loading Grouping one or more boxes on a pallet or skid.

Unsought products Products purchased because of a sudden need that must be solved (e.g., emergency automobile repairs) or when aggressive selling is used to obtain a sale that otherwise would not take place (e.g., encyclopaedias).

V

Validity A condition that exists when an instrument does measure what it is supposed to measure.

Variable cost A cost that varies directly with changes in the number of units produced or sold.

Vending See Automatic vending.

Venture team An organisational unit established to create entirely new products that may be aimed at new markets.

Vertical channel integration The combining of two or more stages of a marketing channel under one management.

Vertical marketing system A marketing channel in which channel activities are co-ordinated or managed by a single channel member to achieve efficient, low-cost distribution aimed at satisfying target market customers.

Warehouse showroom A type of retail store with high volume and low overhead; lower costs are effected by shifting some marketing functions to consumers, who must transport, finance, and perhaps even store merchandise.

Warehousing Designing and operating facilities for storing and moving goods.

Wealth The accumulation of past income, natural resources, and financial resources.

Wheel of retailing A hypothesis that holds that new types of retailers usually enter the market as low-status, low-margin, low-price operators but eventually evolve into high-cost, high-price merchants.

Wholesaler An intermediary that buys from a producer or another intermediary and sells to another reseller; performs such marketing activities as transport, storage, and information gathering necessary to expedite exchanges.

Wholesaling All marketing transactions in which purchases are intended for resale or are used in making other products.

Width (of product mix) The number of product lines a company offers.

Willingness to spend A disposition towards expected satisfaction from a product; influenced by the ability to buy, as well as numerous psychological and social forces.

Zone prices Regional prices that vary for major geographic zones, as the transport costs differ.

Name Index

Subject Index